Miniatures
Dictionary and Guide

Daphne Foskett

Antique Collectors' Club

This book combines *A Dictionary of British Miniature
Painters* (Volume I) first published by Faber & Faber
in 1972, and *Collecting Miniatures,* first published by
the Antique Collectors' Club Ltd. in 1979. Some
revisions have been made to the Dictionary.

British Library CIP Data
  Foskett, Daphne
  Miniatures: dictionary and guide
  1. Portrait miniatures, British—Collectors
  and collecting
  I. Title
  757'.7'0941   ND1337.G7

Published for the Antique Collectors' Club
by the Antique Collectors' Club Ltd.

Frontispiece: By **Peter Cross(e),** *an unknown lady in classical dress in a landscape background,
holding a horn in her right hand, her left elbow resting on a book on a rock, vellum, 10ins. Signed in
monogram: 'PLC'. This is the only known example by Cross(e) on this scale and is superbly painted.*
Private Collection.

Printed in England by the Antique Collectors' Club Ltd.,
5 Church Street, Woodbridge, Suffolk

The Antique Collectors' Club

The Antique Collectors' Club was formed in 1966 and now has a five figure membership spread throughout the world. It publishes the only independently run monthly antiques magazine *Antique Collecting* which caters for those collectors who are interested in widening their knowledge of antiques, both by greater awareness of quality and by discussion of the factors which influence the price that is likely to be asked. The Antique Collectors' Club pioneered the provision of information on prices for collectors and the magazine still leads in the provision of detailed articles on a variety of subjects.

It was in response to the enormous demand for information on ''what to pay'' that the price guide series was introduced in 1968 with the first edition of *The Price Guide to Antique Furniture* (completely revised, 1978), a book which broke new ground by illustrating the more common types of antique furniture, the sort that collectors could buy in shops and at auctions rather than the rare museum pieces which had previously been used (and still to a large extent are used) to make up the limited amount of illustrations in books published by commercial publishers. Many other price guides have followed, all copiously illustrated, and greatly appreciated by collectors for the valuable information they contain, quite apart from prices. The Antique Collectors' Club also publishes other books on antiques, including horology and art reference works, and a full book list is available.

Club membership, which is open to all collectors, costs £17.50 per annum. Members receive free of charge *Antique Collecting,* the Club's magazine (published every month except August), which contains well-illustrated articles dealing with the practical aspects of collecting not normally dealt with by magazines. Prices, features of value, investment potential, fakes and forgeries are all given prominence in the magazine.

Among other facilities available to members are private buying and selling facilities, the longest list of ''For Sales'' of any antiques magazine, an annual ceramics conference and the opportunity to meet other collectors at their local antique collectors' clubs. There are over eighty in Britain and more than a dozen overseas. Members may also buy the Club's publications at special pre-publication prices.

As its motto implies, the Club is an amateur organisation designed to help collectors get the most out of their hobby: it is informal and friendly and gives enormous enjoyment to all concerned.

For Collectors — By Collectors — About Collecting

The Antique Collectors' Club, 5 Church Street, Woodbridge, Suffolk

To
A.J.B. Kiddell
(d. February 1980)
affectionately known as 'Jim'
with love and gratitude for never-failing
help and advice, without which many of
my books could never have been written

Contents

Colour Plates

Preface

I was delighted when I was told that The Antique Collectors' Club were reprinting *Collecting Miniatures* published in 1979 and are including with it the text of *A Dictionary of British Miniature Painters* published in 1972. They have kindly allowed me to insert a limited number of hitherto unrecorded artists into the text, and some vital fresh information relating to such artists as Holbein, Hornebolte and Teerlinc, whose works were exhibited and reappraised in the Victoria and Albert Museum in 1983 at *Artists of The Tudor Court*. The catalogue for this exhibition is a valuable work of reference for the period and is supplemented by Roy Strong's *The English Renaissance Miniature, 1983*.

Previously unrecorded artists have been included in the Dictionary section alphabetically so this new work will be a valuable addition for collectors and students alike.

I am grateful to Diana and John Steel and their staff for the immense amount of thought that they have put into this project and delighted that its publication will fill a much needed gap in the bookshops.

I have been fortunate in having been allowed access to a number of both private and public collections from which very many illustrations, both black and white and colour, have been taken.

The black and white illustrations in the book are referred to either as Figures or Plates. In the case of the former, these are used to indicate a specific point of miniature painting; for example a particular style or use of materials, or an interesting signature or reverse.

In the case of Plates, these quite simply illustrate the artists' works, in most instances several miniatures going to make up one plate. When the miniatures making up one plate are not together on a page, we have kept the individual plate number with each miniature to indicate groups of works of one artist, or contemporary artists where comparisons are interesting.

In order to accommodate the greatest number possible of as many artists' works as space provides, it has not always been possible to illustrate each miniature in its actual size, nor, in some cases, to maintain the proportions between miniatures. However, the captions provide the exact measurements for reference purposes, the height of the miniature being given.

Daphne Foskett
1987

Acknowledgements

In particular I wish to record my gratitude to the following people and institutions without whose help neither *Collecting Miniatures* nor *A Dictionary of British Miniature Painters* would have been possible:

Her Majesty the Queen; Her Majesty Queen Juliana of the Netherlands; Sir Windham Carmichael Anstruther, Bt.; Mr Kingsley Adams; Mr. Richard Allen; Dr. Mildred Archer; The Ashmolean Museum, Oxford; Asprey p.l.c.; The Duke of Atholl; Mrs. P. Bainbridge; The Misses Baumgartner; Mr. Robert Bayne Powell; The late Earl Beauchamp; The late Duke of Beaufort; The Trustees of Berkeley Castle; Dr. and Mrs. A.M. Blain; Mrs. T.R.C. Blofeld; Bonhams; the late Denys Eyre Bower; Mrs. H. Bowlby; Mrs. Simon Brett; The Trustees of the British Museum; Dr. A.K. Brown, F.R.C.P.; The late Duke of Buccleuch and Queensberry, K.T.; J. Byan Shaw; the late Mr. B.W. Cave-Browne-Cave; Mr. Robert Cecil; Mrs. Chalmers Davidson and Miss B. Constable Maxwell; Mrs. E. Chew; Mr. R.A. Chew; Messrs. Christie, Manson & Woods; The City Art Gallery, Bristol; the late Mr. A.S. Clay; The Cleveland Museum of Art, Ohio (Edward B. Greene Collection); the late Lord Clifford of Chudleigh, O.B.E.; Messrs A.C. Cooper Ltd.; T. Cottrell-Dormer; Messrs. Coutts & Co.; Lt. Col. Reeder-Crosse-Upcott; Miss P. Cummings; Mrs. Darroch; Mrs. J.A.M. Dawes; Major R.M.O. de la Hey; Mrs. C. de Lancy Gibbs; Miss L. de Montfort; The Derby Art Gallery; The Earl of Derby; Dr. A.B. de Vries, The Hague; the late Mrs. D. Dickson; Mrs. P. Sholto Douglas; Miss M. Edmond; Mrs. F.H.A. Engleheart; The late Marquess of Exeter, K.C.M.G.; Faber and Faber Ltd.; Mr. Philip Falk; Mrs. J. Field; The Fine Art Society; The Fitzwilliam Museum, Cambridge; Mr. C. Fliechmann, U.S.A.; Miss C.M. Forbes; the late Mr. Charles Gibbs-Smith; Miss E. Gibson; the late Mrs. K. Gifford-Scott; Mrs. R. Goodman; the late Mr. F. Gordon Roe; Mr. Arthur Grave; Miss P. Grigg; Mr. K.M. Guichard; The Guildhall Art Gallery, London; The late Earl of Haddington, K.T.; B. Hall; Mrs. E.M. Hamilton; Mr. A.H. Harford; the late Mr. E. Hawtin; Mrs. F. Herrmann; Capt. and Mrs. A.F.L. Hills; The Holburne of Menstrie Museum, Bath; The Huntington Art Gallery, San Marino, California; The Huntington Library, California; Mr. Robin Hutchison; Mr. Sidney Hutchison; Brand Inglis Ltd.; the late Sir Bruce Ingram, O.B.E., The Institut Neerlandaise; Mr. Richard Jeffree; Mr. F. Joachim; Mrs. H. Kahn; Kenneth Kendall, Los Angeles; the late Mr. A.J.B. Kiddell; M. Kimber; Miss D.M. Kleinfeldt; Lt. Col and Mrs. F.S.P.H. Lang; Dr. F. Lappin; Mr. D.S. Lavender; Miss M. Lawson-Tancred; The City of Liverpool Museums; Mrs. T.O. Lloyd; the late W. Lowenhaupt; Mrs. D. McKay; the late Mrs. S.L. Marks; The Mauritshuis, The Hague; Mr. and Mrs. F, Mellish, Cape Town; the late Lord Methuen, R.A.; The Metropolitan Museum, New York; Mr.

and Mrs. M.D. Middleton; Mrs. J. Morris; Mr. J. Morton Morris; Mr. John Murdoch; Mr. V.J. Murrell; The National Gallery of Ireland, Dublin; The National Gallery of Scotland, Edinburgh; The National Museum, Stockholm; The National Portrait Gallery, London; The Nelson Gallery and Atkins Museum (Starr Collection), Kansas City, U.S.A.; Mr. D. Nicholas; The Duke of Northumberland, K.G.; Mr. E. Grosvenor Paine, New York; Paul Mellon Foundation for British Art.; Mr. E. Pelinck, The Hague; Phillips Son & Neale; Sir David Piper; Mr. and Mrs. M. Platt; the late Ivy, Duchess of Portland; The late Duke of Portland, K.G.; The Earl of Powis; Miss B. Priss; J.M.A. Ramsay; Mr. and Mrs. W. Rappolt; Mr. Graham Reynolds; The Rijksmuseum, Amsterdam; Mr. J.B. Robertson; Mrs. H. Rogers; Rosenborg Castle, Copenhagen; The Royal Ontario Museum, Toronto, Canada; The Royal Pavilion, Bernard Falk Collection, Brighton; A. Rubens; K.W. Sanderson; Mrs. S.P. Sewell; the late Mrs. L. Schott-Holzscheiter, Meilen; Mrs. W. Scott; Miss. A. Scott-Elliot; The Scottish National Portrait Gallery; Miss. C. Sharp; Miss V. Slowe; The Smithsonian Institution, National Collection of Fine Arts, Washington; Sotheby Parke Bernet & Co.; The late Earl Spencer; Mr. and Mrs. J.W. Starr; N. Stelman; Sir Roy Strong; the late Madame H. Stuart Stevenson; Miss S. Tatham; Lt. Col. and Mrs. C.H.F. Thompson; Lord Thomson of Fleet; Mrs. R.J. Tirard; the late A.G. Tite; The Tullie House Museum, Carlisle; The Ulster Museum; Mr.P.J.J. van Thiel, Amsterdam; Mr. A.J.W. Vaughan; The Victoria and Albert Museum, London; Brigadier and Mrs. C.G.T. Viner; The Walker Art Gallery, Liverpool; The Wallace Collection, London; The Walters Art Gallery, Baltimore; the late Col. G. Warland; Miss Alison Warner; Miss H. Waterfield; Sir Francis Watson; The Rev. R.M.L. Westropp; the late Lord Wharton; Mr. Donald C. Whitton, California; the late Capt. E.B. Woollett; Mr. S. Young.

Abbreviations

A.E.R.A.	Associate Engraver Royal Academy
A.N.A.	Associate National Academician (America)
A.R.A.	Associate Royal Academy
A.R.C.A.	Associate Royal College of Art
	Associate Royal Cambrian Academy
A.R.E.	Associate Royal Society of Painter Etchers
A.R.H.A.	Associate Royal Hibernian Academy
A.R.I.B.A.	Associate Royal Institute of British Architects
A.R.M.S.	Associate Royal Society of Miniature Painters
A.R.P.E.	Associate Royal Society of Painter Etchers
A.R.S.A.	Associate Royal Scottish Academy
A.R.W.A.	Associate Royal West of England Academy
A.R.W.S.	Associate Royal Society of Painters in Water Colours
Attributed	Reasonably supposed to be by the author quoted
b.	born
bapt.	baptised
Bénézit	Emmanuel Bénézit, *Dictionnaire des Peintres, Sculpteurs, Dessinateurs et Graveurs,* new edition 1976
B.F.A.C.	Burlington Fine Arts Club
B.F.A.C. Cat. 1889	Burlington Fine Arts Club, *Illustrated Catalogue of the Exhibition of Portrait Miniatures,* 1889
B.I.	British Institution
B.M.	British Museum
Bolton	Theodore Bolton, *Early American Portrait Painters in Miniature,* 1921
B.P.M.	Daphne Foskett, *British Portrait Miniatures,* 1963.
Bryan	Michael Bryan, *Dictionary of Painters and Engravers,* edited by Dr. G.C. Williamson, 1903-1905
Brydall	Robert Brydall, *History of Art in Scotland,* 1889
c.	circa
called	Doubt as to the identity of the sitter
Christie's	Christie Manson and Woods Ltd.
Clouzot	Henri Clouzot, *Dictionnaire des Miniaturistes sur Émail,* 1924
C.M.	Royal Academy Council Minutes
d.	died
d.aft.	died after
D.N.B.	*Dictionary of National Biography*
E.I.	East India
E.I.C.S.	East India Company's Service
E.I.R.	East India Register
Farington	Joseph Farington, R.A., *The Farington Diary,* 1922-1928
F.A.S.	Fellow Antiquarian Society
F.B.A.	Fellow British Academy
F.G.S.	Fellow Geographical Society
F.H.S.	Fellow Historical Society
Fielding	Mantle Fielding, *Dictionary of American Painters, Sculptors and Engravers,* 2nd edition, 1965
fl.	flourished or worked
Foster	J.J. Foster, *Dictionary of Painters of Miniatures,* 1926

Foster (*M.P.B.F.*)	J.J. Foster, *Miniature Painters British and Foreign,* 1903
F.R.S.	Fellow Royal Society
F.R.S.A.	Fellow Royal Society of Arts
F.S.A.	Fellow Royal Society of Artists (before 1791)
	Fellow Society of Antiquaries
Goulding	R.W. Goulding, *The Welbeck Abbey Miniatures, The Walpole Society,* Vol. IV
Graves	Algernon Graves, *A Dictionary of Artists 1760-1893,* 1901
Graves (*B.I.*)	Algernon Graves, *The British Institution 1806-1867,* 1908
Graves (*R.A.*)	Algernon Graves, *The Royal Academy of Arts, 1769-1904, 1905-6,* reprinted 1970
Graves (*S.A.*)	Algernon Graves, *The Society of Artists of Great Britain 1760-1791; the Free Society of Artists 1761-1783,* 1907
Groce & Wallace	G.C. Groce and D.H. Wallace, *Dictionary of Artists in America,* 2nd edition, 1964
Hand	Sidney Hand, *Signed Miniatures,* 1925
H.R.C.A.	Honorary Member Royal Cambrian Academy
H.R.H.A.	Honorary Member Royal Hibernian Academy
H.R.S.A.	Honorary Member Royal Scottish Academy
K.C.H.	Knight Commander of Hanover
K.C.M.G.	Knight Commander of St. Michael and St. George
K.S.L.	Knight of St. Luke's Academy, Rome
K.T.	Knight of the Order of the Thistle
L.A.	Liverpool Academy
Long	Basil S. Long, *British Miniaturists,* 1929 Annotations taken by the author from Long's own copy.
M.F.H.	Master of Foxhounds
N.G.	National Gallery
N.P.G.	National Portrait Gallery
N.W.C.S.	New Water Colour Society (now Royal Institute of Painters in Water Colours)
O'Brien	The Hon. D. O'Brien, *Miniatures in the 18th and 19th Centuries,* 1951
O.W.C.S.	Old Water Colour Society or Society of Painters in Water Colours, later Royal Society of Painters in Water Colours
P.R.A.	President Royal Academy
P.R.C.A.	President Royal Cambrian Academy
P.R.H.A.	President Royal Hibernian Academy
P.R.I.	President Royal Institute of Painters in Water Colours
P.R.M.S.	President Royal Miniature Society
Propert	J.L. Propert, *A History of Miniature Art,* 1887
P.R.S.	President Royal Society
P.R.S.A.	President Royal Scottish Academy
R.A.	Royal Academy; Royal Academician
R.A. Cats.	Royal Academy Catalogues (author's set ex Duveen)
R.B.A.	Royal Society of British Artists
R.C.A.	Member Royal Cambrian Academy
R.E.	Fellow Royal Society of Painter Etchers
Redgrave	Samuel Redgrave, *A Dictionary of Artists of the English School,* 1878
Reynolds	Graham Reynolds, *English Portrait Miniatures,* 1952

R.H.A.	Royal Hibernian Academy; Royal Hibernian Academician	Sotheby's	Sotheby Parke Bernet and Co.
R.I.	Royal Institute of Painters in Water Colours	Strickland	W.G. Strickland, *Dictionary of Irish Artists,* 1913
R.I.B.A.	Royal Institute of British Architects	Th.B.	Dr. Ulrich Thieme and Dr. Felix Becker,
R.M.S.	Royal Society of Miniature Painters, Sculptors and Gravers		*Allegemeines Lexicon der bildenden Kunstler,* 1907
R.S.A.	Royal Scottish Academy, Royal Scottish Academician	V.& A.M.	Victoria and Albert Museum
	Royal Society of Arts	Van Der Doort	*Abraham Van Der Doort's Catalogue of the Collection of Charles I,* edited by Oliver Miller, The Walpole Society, Vol. XXXVII, 1958-60
R.S.B.A.	Royal Society of British Artists		
R.W.A.	Royal West of England Academy	V.P.R.I.	Vice-President Royal Institute of Painters in Water Colours
R.W.S.	Royal Society of Painters in Water Colours	V.P.R.M.S.	Vice President Royal Society of Miniature Painters, Sculptors and Gravers
S.A.	Society of Artists (incorporated 1765)		
S.B.A.	Society of British Artists (Royal Society of British Artists)	Walpole	Horace Walpole, *Anecdotes of Painting in England,* 1762-1771 and subsequent editions
Schidlof	Leo. R. Schidlof, *The Miniature in Europe,* 1964	*The Walpole Society*	*The Walpole Society,* Volumes I-XLV
S.M.	Society of Miniaturists	Wehle	Harry B. Wehle, *American Miniaturists,* 1927
S.N.P.G.	Scottish National Portrait Gallery	Williamson	Dr. G.C. Williamson, *The History of Portrait Miniatures,* 1904. For details of works by Dr. Williamson on particular artists, and on private collections, *see* Bibliography.
Soc. of Arts	Society for the Encouragement of Arts, Manufactures and Commerce (Royal Society of Arts)		

An asterisk (*) before an artist's name denotes that the painter is NOT included in Basil Long's *British Miniaturists.*

/ A fresh line when used in an inscription.

Chapter I

Forming a Miniature Collection

ONE OF THE most frustrating things for any new collector is lack of fundamental information on his subject. There may be dozens of books on collecting, but if he has chosen miniatures as his field then the scope is limited and information either out of date or in many areas unobtainable. The purpose of this book is to provide the reader with as many facts as possible to assist him in the formation of a collection which will bear the stamp of his or her own personality regarding choice of both period and subject, but will be built up with care and ever increasing knowledge. I hope that readers will forgive me if what I am about to say appears rather elementary and basic, but I know from experience that people are shy to ask what may appear to be a simple question. For anyone embarking on a new collection there are many pitfalls, and forewarned is forearmed.

Miniature painting has for many years been a specialist subject and one that has been sadly neglected as far as published works are concerned. Although in recent years these small portraits have commanded a higher price in the sale rooms and attracted the attention of the national press, a vast number of people still do not know what a miniature is. The majority of the most important collections are still in private hands and have been formed by people like myself, who have been attracted to these portraits and purchased them either with care and a discerning eye, or under the guidance of a dealer or friend. Others, such as the collections belonging to H.M. The Queen, the Duke of Portland, the Duke of Buccleuch and Queensberry, the Earl Beauchamp and the Duke of Rutland, to mention a few, have been passed down and added to by succeeding generations. It has been through the generosity of some of these collectors that many of our museums such as the Victoria and Albert Museum, London, the Ashmolean Museum, Oxford, and the Fitzwilliam Museum, Cambridge, as well as the Wallace Collection, London, and many others in the provinces, have obtained examples of this art which are now enjoyed by the public.

It is to these collections that one must turn for rare or interesting examples of different artists' work, and for inspiration to attempt such a book as this.

Figure 1. N. Hilliard (1547-1619), an unknown lady, c.1600, vellum, 1½ins. diameter. A fine example of an early portrait miniature showing Hilliard's perfect draughtsmanship and details of the lace ruff. The way the sitter's hair is dressed is typical of the period. Courtesy Sotheby's.

What is a miniature?

Since people are frequently confused about the terms used for miniature painting it may be as well to try and clear the matter up at the outset. Put simply, a miniature is a portrait or scene, painted on a small scale and based on the technique handed down from the illuminators of the fifteenth and sixteenth centuries. Originally these paintings were called *limnings* or

Figure 2. **I. Oliver,** *Edward Herbert, 1st Baron Herbert of Cherbury (1583-1648), vellum, 7⅛ins., c.1605-10. This large cabinet miniature is of great interest from the point of view of costume and armour. The landscape setting is one frequently used on this type of miniature.* Courtesy The Earl of Powis.

paintings in little, and this term survived into the seventeenth century when the word *miniature* came into use. This word does not, as many people think, imply a small portrait, the derivation coming from the Latin word *minium,* meaning red lead or vermilion, the pigment used by the illuminators on manuscripts. The word has now altered its meaning and in modern usage refers to such things as small silver objects, bottles and even miniature furniture and pieces of porcelain.

For the purpose of this book the term implies a small painting which may be executed in any medium, and on any base. It is impossible to lay down a hard and fast rule about the size which is acceptable as a miniature. Although the majority are anything from one inch to six or eight inches in height, larger ones of all periods do exist, and for many years it has been agreed that these paintings cannot be larger than can conveniently be held in the hand.

Broadly speaking miniatures may be divided into two classes, *portrait miniatures* and *cabinet miniatures.* The former were portraits or small scenes, usually circular or oval, which were commissioned as personal mementoes of loved ones, intended to be worn on the person, or carried about when travelling (Figure 1). The latter class are larger and encased in oval or rectangular frames to be hung on the wall or placed on a table (Figure 2). Throughout the sixteenth and seventeenth centuries these large limnings were frequently copies of works by old masters, or depicted mythological or religious subjects, although a number of original works of this type also exist. The practice of copying large portraits or scenes has continued throughout the centuries and was particularly popular with those miniaturists who painted in enamel.

Colour Plate 1 (right).
A top left. **Hans Holbein,** *Anne of Cleves (1515-57), fourth Queen of Henry VIII, vellum, 1²³/₃₂ins., c.1539. The miniature is contained in its original ivory box.*
B top right. **Nicholas Hilliard,** *Richard Hilliard, father of the artist (1518/19-1594), aged fifty-eight, vellum, 1⅝ins. diameter. Inscribed: 'Ætatis Suæ 58: Anno Dnī 1577.' The companion piece to Hilliard's self-portrait painted the same year.*
C centre. **Nicholas Hilliard,** *an unknown youth, vellum, 2ins., c.1585. Contained in an ivory box. A replica of this miniature is in the collection of the Duke of Rutland. From the collection of the Earl of Radnor.*
D bottom left. **Nicholas Hilliard,** *an unknown lady, vellum, 2¾ins. Inscribed and dated on either side of the oval: 'Videtur et Vere est [It seems and truly it is] Anō Dnī 1602.' This attractive miniature is interesting for costume.*
E bottom right. **Isaac Oliver,** *an unknown lady in masque costume, vellum, 2½ins., c.1610. Signed in monogram: 'IO' surrounded by four dots. This is a brilliant example of this type of miniature.*

Courtesy Victoria and Albert Museum

Figure 3. **Hans Holbein the Younger** *(1497/8 - 1543), thought to be a self-portrait, vellum, 1⁷/₁₆ins. Inscribed: 'HH / A^ON 1543 ETATIS SVE 45'. Four versions of this portrait exist. They all bear the same inscription, but the largest, in the Clowes Collection, Indianapolis, is dated 1542, the year before the artist's death. The attribution to Holbein is still in dispute.* Courtesy The Duke of Buccleuch and Queensberry, K.T.

Figure 4. Attributed to **L. Horenbout,** *an unknown young lady, vellum, 1⁷/₈ins. diameter. Inscribed: 'A^ON xviii'. The sitter is wearing a Tudor hood and low cut dress, which was popular in the mid-sixteenth century.* Courtesy Sotheby's.

With the economic situation as it is many people feel that their wealth is best put into tangible objects, and one could almost say that 'collecting mania' has spread like measles. It is hardly surprising, at a time when such articles as buttons, thimbles, cigarette cards and ancient Rolls Royce cars are all collectors' pieces, that miniatures should be desirable. Not only are they things of beauty in themselves, but also interesting links with the past as well as conveniently small enough to be housed in frames or small cabinets which fit happily into modern homes.

Whether they prove an investment depends upon the taste, knowledge and luck of the purchaser. As with all antiques, values fluctuate, and at present prices have risen according to the demand. It is hard to realise that a small miniature formerly in my collection which cost £5 twenty-five years ago is now being offered in London for £475!

This is not quoted to frighten off the would-be collector, but to give an idea of how values can rise. It is still possible to purchase good eighteenth and nineteenth century miniatures at reasonable prices if one is patient and is prepared to attend some of the auction rooms and seek out dealers who include them in their stock. Seventeenth century examples are scarce and consequently expensive. They may well be beyond the purse of the new collector who will want to obtain more examples at lesser prices until such time as his or her knowledge grows, or examples of earlier periods become desirable. Historically, the early miniatures are fascinating and in many cases the only known likeness of the sitter, but aesthetically many people understand and prefer the attractive examples of the eighteenth century and later.

Having decided to form a collection of miniatures there are certain facts which it is essential to know in order to understand something of the more technical aspect of the art and how it developed. Unless one is lucky enough to have a *flair* or built-in instinct enabling one to spot good or interesting miniatures which can be purchased and enjoyed with the hope of discovering information at a later date, it is necessary to have some knowledge of the paints used, what miniatures were painted on, and how they were framed, not to mention the most important aspect of how to preserve a collection so that it does not deteriorate.

Bearing all this in mind I hope that the following information will be of use.

When did miniature painting start?

The earliest known miniatures were painted in the sixteenth century. **Hans Holbein** (1497/8-1543) (Figure 3) has always been considered the founder of the art, but it is now known that **Lucas Horenbout,** or Hornebolte (d.1544) (Figure 4), who is reputed to have instructed Holbein, was in all probability responsible for some of the earliest miniatures including some of Henry VIII. At the time of writing fresh research is going on regarding the authenticity of these early miniatures, and in course of time more accurate information regarding their attributions may be forthcoming. For the present we still accept a small number of portraits attributed to Horenbout and about a dozen attributed to Holbein. Undoubtedly the art of miniature painting was born and nurtured in Britain.

Methods of forming a collection

There are two methods open to the would-be collector, and the choice may well be determined by the sum of money he can afford to spend on his hobby. The first, and in my opinion by far the most interesting way is to buy any miniatures which appeal to him and which may be found in antique shops up and down the country or in auction rooms. In this way he will assemble a collection which will not necessarily be of equal merit, but from which he can learn something about the art, and gradually become discriminating and better able to select good examples, and at a later date weed out the lesser lights to improve the quality of the collection.

This method presupposes that the collector will have taken the trouble to read up something on the subject and, if possible, gone to see the collections in museums such as those on display in the Victoria and Albert Museum, and possibly visited one or other of the auction rooms where miniatures are sold. Information acquired in this way is rewarding and gives a great deal of pleasure as well as increasing knowledge and training the eye to judge what to look for when purchasing a miniature.

The second method is for the collector who has ample means and either does not wish to purchase unaided, or wishes to possess a miniature collection of specific artists' works chosen from the more important names. This collector, unless he has a friend who is knowledgeable on the subject, will have to rely on a reputable dealer for advice. If money is no object then a collection can easily be assembled which will in all probability contain examples of many of the well-known artists' works and will possibly be smaller in number, but more selective than that formed by the first method. If this latter course is taken it is still essential for the person forming the collection to have his own ideas regarding the selection; it is not the same to purchase items purely through the eye of the expert or adviser as this leaves nothing of the owner's personality behind and is merely a collection amassed with the aid of a cheque book.

Techniques and pigments

It is impossible to discuss in great detail the complex question of what techniques and pigments the various miniaturists used, and a brief survey of the main points will have to suffice.

The technique and pigments used by the sixteenth and seventeenth century miniaturists were closely allied to those used by the illuminators. This is borne out by the fact that Lucas Horenbout, who has already been mentioned, came of a family of illuminators. The colours were bought in their raw state and ground down to a fine powder by the artists before being stored in small ivory containers. Each artist would, no doubt, have had his own formula for mixing his paints, some of which had to be separated by washing because grinding would have destroyed their hue, but all the colours would have been mixed with a 'binder'. The most usual one appears to have been gum arabic, or gum senegal, which is the cleanest and most easily soluble of the acacia gums. It has been suggested that some form of sugar or honey was also added, and the mixture dissolved in water before test patches could be made for correct colouring. These were applied to the 'support' or 'tablet' (usually vellum), i.e. the base, on which the miniature was to be painted, the details of which will be dealt with later.

The preparation of artists' pigments is a complex subject, and was a tedious business, the finer details of which were no doubt jealously guarded by each artist. The mixture used produced opaque colours, generally termed *gouache,* which gives the impression of a fine watercolour technique, although as Mr. V.J. Murrell has pointed out it was "not a watercolour technique as we know it today, neither was it true gouache". In his article on pigments in *Samuel Cooper and His Contemporaries,* p.XIX, Mr. Murrell gives a clear definition of the term watercolour. He says "in modern terms a watercolour is a transparent painting carried out in a water-soluble medium, whereas a gouache is a painting carried out in a water-soluble medium which is completely opaque, those colours which are not naturally opaque being rendered so by the addition of white".

This method of painting was used by Holbein and his followers including the great Elizabethan artist **Nicholas Hilliard** (1547-1619), and later in the seventeenth century by **Samuel Cooper** (1609-1672), although the latter worked over the transparent areas with more opaque colour, thus giving a more solid gouache effect.

Miniaturists continued this method of painting until the turn of the eighteenth century when the Italian artist **Rosalba Carriera** (1675-1757) discovered that pieces of bone or ivory made a good base on which to paint and enabled the artist to use thin washes of colour where the flesh was visible, thus producing a certain amount of luminosity in the painting. The dress and backgrounds were still painted in opaque colours, and it was not until the second half of the century that artists discovered how to paint with thinner washes of watercolour allowing larger areas of ivory to show through.

Miniaturists have always had to be careful in their choice of pigments, as not all of them are durable; lakes (reddish pigments) are particularly fugitive when exposed to light, as may be seen by an examination of many of the Elizabethan miniatures where the flesh tints have gone completely, and it is also true of some of the eighteenth and nineteenth century miniatures. To give an example, many miniatures by **Richard Crosse** (1742-1810) have lost their flesh tints, whereas I know of no example of the work of **John Smart** (1742/3-1811) where the flesh colours have deteriorated at all.

Other problems that the early miniaturists had to guard against were disastrous chemical reactions from certain colours, particularly verdigris and artificial copper, blues and greens.

In keeping with their close connection with jewellery, the Elizabethan miniaturists took great delight in the use of gold powder, ground from pure gold leaf, for elaborate inscriptions and metallic pigments which they burnished to a high polish to highlight armour, jewellery, gilt buttons and embroidery on the sitter's costume. On rare occasions, such as in the miniature by Cooper of a gentleman *called* Sir R. Henley (Figure 5), in the Victoria and Albert Museum, powdered gold was used to highlight the sheen of satin on the doublet. Amongst the more impermanent colours used by early miniaturists were sap green, pink and the lakes. Lead white was used extensively in the seventeenth century but it has a serious disadvantage in that, in the presence of atmospheric hydrogen sulphide, it turns black, thus spoiling the appearance of the miniature. Many early miniatures have suffered from this and fortunately, thanks to modern research, it is now

Figure 5. **S. Cooper,** *a gentleman* called *Sir Robert Henley, vellum,* 2²⁷/₃₂ *ins. Signed in monogram 'SC' and dated: '1659'. This shows Cooper's method of using gold to emphasise the folds of the costume. (See Colour Plate 7A).* Courtesy Victoria and Albert Museum.

possible for those who know enough about conservation to remove much of the damage and reseal the miniature in its frame.

The early artists put on their colours with brushes, or 'pencils' as they were called, many of these being made by the artists themselves although it was possible to purchase them in London. A pencil was not, as has been frequently stated, a brush with one hair, as this would not in fact have been sufficient to carry the colour, while if the brush is too fine it leaves a scratchy appearance. Brushes were in all probability made from hair taken from the tip of a squirrel's tail, and bound together in small bunches with the hairs curving in to form a suitable tip with which to paint; these were then set into goose quills which were mounted on sticks in much the same way as a modern paint brush. Good brushes are now very expensive and the best and longest lived are made of sable hair, while others made of squirrel hair are cheaper but not as satisfactory for an expert as they are not as pliant nor do they last as long. They may be bought in various sizes to suit the requirements of the artist.

From the second half of the eighteenth century miniaturists painted with much the same pigments as those used today and, although some still mixed their own colours, the majority probably bought them ready-made and used them according to their own choice of palette.

In England it was customary to paint the flesh parts on a pale ground rather than directly on the vellum. The artist would load his brush with a liquid colour, usually basically white, to which small amounts of red, yellow or brown and even blue were added, according to the complexion of the sitter. This tone was kept very light in order that it could serve as the highlight of the modelling. The flesh ground was called the 'carnation' by the early limners, and the method continued in England from the time of Holbein until the eighteenth century when the use of ivory became popular. Once the 'carnation' was painted the artist proceeded to sketch in lightly the outline of the features and to build up gradually the colours and modelling of the face.

Support, tablet or base on which watercolour miniatures were painted

One of the most important facts which a collector must learn is the base on which miniatures were painted at different periods, as this information helps considerably to date the miniature. Following the tradition of the illuminators, the early limners painted on vellum made from the finest skin of a sheep or calf. This was stuck down with starch paste on to a card, the most suitable being old playing cards. It is not unusual to find the pips of the suit of cards still showing on the reverse of the painting when it is taken out of the frame. The best vellum was supposed to be the skin of an abortive, and Hilliard in his treatise *The Arte of Limning* (edited by P. Norman in The Walpole Society, Vol. 1, p.34), gives this advice: "Knowe also that parchment is the only good and best thinge to limme one, but it must be virgine parchment, such as neuer bore haire, but younge things found in the dames bellye; some calle it vellym, some abertiue (deriued from the word abhortiue for vntimly birthe). It must be most finly drest, as smothe as any sattine, and pasted with starch well strained one pastbourd well burnished that it maye be pure without speckes or staynes, very smothe and white." Having decided on the shape of the miniature, which could be circular, oval or square according to the desire of the sitter, the artist would cut the card and prepare it by rubbing it on the white side until it was as smooth as possible before pasting the vellum on to the shape to be used. It is interesting to know that vellum could be bought at this time (sixteenth century) in Paternoster Row among other places. **Edward Norgate** (c.1581-1650) in his Treatise *Miniatura,* c.1650, gives clear and detailed instructions for the preparation of the supports used by the early limners and suggests that after the vellum has been pasted on to the playing card the back should be varnished to make it smooth. Another method adopted in the seventeenth century, when the size of the miniature had been enlarged to about three inches, was to coat the back of the support with a thin layer of gesso. This was a mixture of glue size and chalk, and the advantage of using it lay in the fact that it acted as a stiffener so that the sheet of parchment did not pull and cause the card to warp. Many of Samuel Cooper's miniatures were prepared in this way.

Miniatures in watercolour continued to be painted in this manner until the eighteenth century when it was discovered, as has already been mentioned, that ivory was a good base on which to paint. This a very important point to remember, as all too often the collector is offered miniatures painted on ivory reputed to have been executed in the sixteenth or seventeenth century. Some of these started as genuine copies and others are blatant fakes. These will be dealt with in a later chapter.

One of the first British artists to use ivory as a base was **Bernard Lens** (1682-1740), and although a number of his miniatures were still painted on vellum, the majority were on the newly discovered material. Due no doubt to the difficulty in cutting ivory without damage, the bases used were rather thick, and it was not until later in the century that thinner and more translucent slips of ivory were in use. Lens painted in the old way, in that he used opaque watercolour on the dress, draperies and backgrounds, and only painted the flesh parts in transparent watercolour. This in itself was a great innovation and when, by the middle of the eighteenth century, artists such as **Richard Cosway** (1742-1821) had discovered its full potential and how watercolour could be floated on to prepared sheets of ivory in much the same way as painting on paper, it totally revolutionised the technique of miniature painting. This method has stayed popular up to the present day. Because of the rising costs it is now difficult if not impossible for modern miniaturists to buy ivory and a form of ivorine is used as a substitute.

By the time vellum was no longer used, paper was available for the artists who did not wish to use ivory, and this was of course much cheaper. Card was another suitable alternative. When photography was invented in the middle of the nineteenth century a few artists used a thin photographic base on the ivory and painted over it. For those who could not easily catch a likeness this was a cheap way of producing a portrait, but it is not a truly acceptable method and the experienced eye can usually detect miniatures painted in this way. They are not fakes, but lack the finesse of the artist's skill in producing a likeness from life.

Eye miniatures
During the latter part of the eighteenth century and slightly later small miniatures representing a single eye and a small portion of the face were in

fashion set in lockets, brooches, rings and small boxes (Figures 6 and 7). Traditionally these became popular because the Prince of Wales had Mrs. Fitzherbert's eye painted by **George Engleheart** (1750-1829), but they were also painted by other artists including Richard Cosway, **William Wood** (1769-1810) and **Charles Hayter** (1761-1835).

Figure 6. **G. Engleheart,** *an eye miniature, ivory, 1¼ins. Set into an eighteenth century locket.* Courtesy Sotheby's.

Figure 7. **W. Wood,** *an eye miniature, ivory, ⅞in. deep (the box 3¾ins. long), set into an ivory patch box. This is a good example of this type of miniature.* Private Collection.

Miniatures painted in enamel

Although enamel miniatures have never enjoyed the same popularity as those painted in watercolour, the medium has much to commend it. It is impervious to light, so does not fade, and can only be damaged by dropping or carelessness which will cause the surface to chip. The art of enamelling is lost in antiquity and is one that has been practised for centuries in simple forms in China, Egypt, Assyria, Greece and Rome. The two main methods of enamelling were *cloisonné* and *champlevé*, the term 'painted enamel' being a later one. The earliest known portrait miniature in enamel is the self-portrait of **Jean Fouquet** (1420-1480) which is in the Louvre, Paris. It is painted in gold upon a black background and signed with the sitter's name. It is an isolated and exceptional work executed more in the style of that produced by the flourishing school of enamellers at Limoges, who at that time concentrated largely on painting religious subjects and only used a limited palette.

Enamels are painted on a metal base and have to be fired in much the same way as porcelain. The substance used for enamelling is a combination of a flux which contains proportions of silica, nitrate of potash and powdered glass, to which are added different metallic oxides which, when mixed together, produce a variety of colours. This compound has to be placed on a metal surface of copper, gold, or silver and fired at a given temperature. *Champlevé*, a word derived from two French words *champ* — a field, and *levé,* — raised, described a form of enamelling in which the artists first traced the design on to the metal base, then hollowed out the centres in order to leave space for the enamel preparation, thin ridges of metal being left to form the outline and separate the colours. *Cloisonné* was executed in much the same way, except that after scratching the design on the metal, thin strips of metal were soldered on to form *cloisons* or cells which were then filled with the enamel as in *champlevé*; in both cases the object was fired in a kiln.

25

Enamelling is not a simple process and is one which requires great skill. The colours change in firing and any slight error in temperature may result in the whole painting being ruined. Occasionally miniatures may be seen where the metal has warped, or bubbles appeared in firing. It was not until about 1632 that a French goldsmith named **Jean Toutin** (1578-1644) discovered that a variety of colours could be laid upon a thin ground of previously fired white enamel and the portrait refired without any damage to the tints. This method allowed opaque colours to be laid upon the white enamel ground in the same way that watercolour could be painted upon ivory or vellum. The process was a tedious one as the portrait had to be fired several times. Under the tuition of Jean Toutin and his son **Henri Toutin** (1614-1683), a school of enamellers grew up, much of their time being devoted to the embellishment of elaborate watch cases, which were in great demand during the reign of Louis XIII (Figure 8).

The art of this more sophisticated form of enamelling was brought over to Britain by two Swiss artists, **Jean Petitot** (1607-1691) and a goldsmith **Jacques Bordier** (1616-1684), who became great friends and are reputed to have been at one time pupils of Jean and Henri Toutin in Paris c.1633. From Paris, Petitot came to England in about 1637 and was given employment by Charles I. Signed and dated miniatures by him cover the years between 1638-c.1643 and many of them represent most of the people of importance at Court; a number of the portraits were taken from large pictures by Van Dyck and other Court painters. Five fine examples are in the collection of the Duke of Portland and a large enamel of the Countess of Southampton is in the collection of the Duke of Devonshire. One of Mary, Duchess of Richmond and Lennox, signed and dated 1643, after Van Dyck, formerly in the Pierpont Morgan Collection, is in the Nationalmuseum, Stockholm, and is a superb example of the artist's work. He is known to have executed a few miniatures in watercolour. There is not at present any evidence as to the date Petitot returned to France, but he probably left during the unrest in England and was certainly back in France by 1650.

*Figure 8. **Henri Toutin**, a miniature on enamel of Charles I (1600-1649), in a contemporary enamel locket, 2½ins. This is an early specimen of a miniature in this medium.* Courtesy The Mauritshuis, The Hague.

After his departure enamel miniatures seem to have lost their appeal and it was not until the end of the seventeenth century that the art was re-established by an artist from Sweden, **Charles Boit** (1662-1727), who came over to Britain in 1687 and was working in London by c.1690. Boit was responsible for popularising enamel miniatures again and his influence was far-reaching. Through his pupils, who included **Christian Friedrich Zincke** (1683/4-1767), a native of Dresden, who in turn taught **Jeremiah Meyer, R.A.** (1735-1789), the art followed through to the eighteenth and nineteenth centuries (Figure 9). Towards the end of the eighteenth century interest in enamel miniatures began to flag again, but fresh impetus was given to it by a family of artists named Bone. **Henry Bone, R.A.** (1755-1834), whose family were prolific artists, began his career by painting on china at Plymouth and, later, at Bristol. Details of the family will be given in a later chapter; many of their miniatures are large and are copies of the works of well-known portrait painters. The majority of them are fully inscribed on the reverse so leave no doubt as to their authenticity.

I have deliberately left out details of the eighteenth century artists who painted enamel miniatures since these will be dealt with later, as will other nineteenth century miniaturists. By c.1900 enamel miniatures had again lost their appeal and only a few artists attempted to paint any after that date.

Miniatures painted on porcelain

Miniatures painted on porcelain have for many years been ignored, but as they are so closely related to those painted in enamel I propose to deal with them here.

Miniatures on porcelain must not be confused with the porcelain plaques made on the Continent which are usually either imaginary scenes, or copies from well-known paintings. Some are set in frames and smaller ones in brooches, but these were turned out by the dozen and bear no resemblance to miniatures painted from life, or executed by artists from portraits, the majority of which were isolated examples.

Few porcelain miniatures are signed, so attribution is difficult, but it seems reasonable to suppose that the artists were all in some way connected with one or other of the porcelain factories and did a few miniatures for pleasure or as commissions. **John Simpson** (1811-after 1871) was connected with the Minton Porcelain Works and for some years painted miniatures in enamel and on porcelain. **James Rouse** (1802-1888), whose self-portrait is in the Derby Art Gallery, was an apprentice at the Derby China Factory and also painted portraits in oil. **John Haslem** (1818-1884), also of the Derby China Factory (now the Royal Crown Derby Porcelain Company), painted miniatures on porcelain and in enamel as well as executing paintings in watercolour. Some of his miniatures were from life, others copies of the works of old masters.

There is a miniature on porcelain of a young man, reputed to be one of the Davenport family; it is unsigned, but of such a high quality that one would expect it to have been from life. The reverse bears the impressed mark used at Davenport from c.1850-1870 (Figure 10). There is no doubt that some of the miniatures on porcelain are of a high quality and compare favourably with those executed in enamel.

Figure 9. **C.F. Zincke,** *Lady Mary Wortley Montagu (1689-1762), enamel, 2ins. Inscribed with the sitter's name on the reverse and signed: 'C.F. Zincke / pinxt 1738'. This is one of several attractive miniatures by Zincke in the Portland Collection, and shows the contemporary hair style, pearls and low cut dress.* Courtesy Ivy, Duchess of Portland.

Figure 10. A member of the Davenport family, porcelain, 5¾ins. The plaque bears the impressed china mark of c.1850-1870 on the reverse. The sitter's costume suggests a date of c.1850. The texture of the painting is such that it might easily be mistaken for an enamel miniature on metal. Private Collection.

Oil miniatures

The study of miniatures painted in oil is a frustrating one, as only a handful appear to bear any signature at all, thus making identification almost impossible. Miniatures in this medium appear to have been painted from the sixteenth century and probably the greater number of them were painted on the Continent (Plate 1A). Many of the early ones are circular, set into ivory or wooden boxes, some of which have a lid with the sitter's coat of arms painted on the inside. Others are to be found placed in the lid of a painted or enamel snuff box. By the seventeenth century artists had adopted the oval format and the miniatures were usually placed in wooden or metal frames, some of the metal ones being quite elaborately designed. Aesthetically oil miniatures have not in the past had the same appeal to collectors as those painted in watercolour or enamel, but recently they have become more sought after.

Lack of interest in oil miniatures is probably due to two things; firstly, oil paintings reduced to such a small scale appear rather dull and are frequently dark through lack of space available for backgrounds; secondly, they were produced in large numbers on the Continent depicting numerous copies of Court noblemen, many even bearing ficticious names of artists. There was a time when dealers and connoisseurs thought it important to try and attribute all miniatures and one frequently comes across oil miniatures attributed to such artists as Reynolds, Gainsborough, etc., when the paintings bear no resemblance to the artists' styles. Attributions of this kind merely add to the confusion and oil miniatures should be bought only on their merit as works of art.

One of the few artists who did occasionally sign his miniatures was **Cornelius Johnson** (1593-1661/2). He produced some fine oil miniatures as well as larger portraits and his work, although scarce, is much sought after. A miniature of Sir Dudley Carleton, later Viscount Dorchester (1573-1632) by Johnson was sold for £2,600 at Sotheby's on 28th March, 1977. Only a few artists painted oil miniatures in Britain and they will be dealt with in later chapters. They were painted on a great variety of bases, copper being the most usual, but vellum, gold, silver, tin, brass, tortoiseshell, glass, ivory, semi-precious stones and various woods were all used, and in modern times hardboard. I have also seen them painted on the reverse of silver coins which have been rubbed smooth, and occasionally encased in a screw top box made of two coins. One of a man c.1650 is painted on a piece of rock amethyst (Figure 11).

Figure 11. A portrait in oil of an unknown man c.1650, painted on rock amethyst, 2¾ins. This miniature by an **unknown artist** *is contained in a modern copy of a seventeenth century locket with spiral cresting. This is a rare example of a miniature painted on a semi-precious stone.* Private Collection.

Plumbago miniatures

It has been the custom for centuries for artists to make sketches or fine drawings of their sitters before painting finished portraits. These were executed in a number of different techniques and one only has to look at the catalogue of the famous drawings by Holbein owned by H.M. The Queen to see the variety of ways in which they were executed. Silver point, chalk and pen and ink were all used and not infrequently the portraits were heightened with a coloured wash. Plumbago miniatures were, however, a type which became popular between c.1660-1720. They were drawn with pure graphite or plumbago, a term derived from the Latin *plumbum* (lead), sharpened to a point and used in the same way as a pencil is used today. In the early part of the sixteenth century a mine which produced graphite or plumbago of the finest quality was discovered at Seathwaite in Borrowdale, Cumberland, and it was from there that the artists obtained it. Such drawings, which were finished works in themselves, were executed on vellum or paper, which was not, as in the case of watercolour miniatures, stuck on to card.

Many of these drawings are of superb quality and very desirable. The majority are executed only in plumbago with the occasional addition of small areas of watercolour. Some fifteen years ago these drawings could be purchased for £50-£100, but today a really fine one of a known sitter might sell for around £700-£800.

Amongst the most important artists who executed plumbago miniatures in Britain were **David Loggan** (1635-1692), **Robert White** (1645-1703) and **Thomas Forster** (b.c.1677). All these artists drew portraits of exquisite quality and the dexterity with which they drew draperies and lace was such that every stitch can be discerned. Whilst a few foreign artists also executed works in plumbago, the majority of these miniatures were in watercolour. Those working in Britain seem to have confined themselves to plumbago with the occasional soft wash of colour on the flesh parts. At a later date a few artists drew miniatures in black lead, and as a boy Sir Thomas Lawrence amused himself by drawing portraits in pencil of patrons at his father's inns at Bristol and Devizes. I have seen three examples of these drawings, all signed in a childish copperplate hand and executed when he was between the age of eight and ten years old (Figures 12 and 13).

STELLA ×PIDVCE INCRVCE SALVS

Plate 1.
A. *A miniature of Baron Sohier De Warmerhuysen, oil on copper, 3ins. Seventeenth century Dutch School, set within a superb enamelled locket.*
B. *Interior of the lid of locket in Plate 1A, bearing the sitter's coat of arms, enamel, 3ins.*
C. *Reverse of locket in Plate 1A, bearing the sitter's cypher and ducal coronet, enamel, 3ins.*
D. *Seventeenth century enamelled locket decorated with red flower heads within a lace border, 1³/8ins.*
E. *Reverse of a locket (a pair to Plate 1A) containing another version of the same sitter. Note the slight variation on the cypher, 3ins.*
F. *Seventeenth century locket enamelled in the rare technique of resille sur verre, on a green ground, 1¹/8ins.*
G. *Seventeenth century enamelled locket with a black and gold diaper design, 1³/8ins.*
H. *Reverse of a fine seventeenth century locket, decorated with flowers and a raised crown and sceptre in diamonds. The interior of the lid bearing a crowned monogram: 'F.W.C.', 1³/8ins.*
I. *A seventeenth century green enamel locket with white acanthus leaf border, 1³/8ins.*

Courtesy Sotheby's

Figure 12. **Sir Thomas Lawrence,** *pencil sketch of Mrs. Grier (pair to Figure 13), pencil on paper, 2½ins. Signed on the front: 'T. Lawrence', and inscribed on the reverse of the frame: 'These pictures of Mr & Mrs Grier were done by Sir Thos Lawrence, when scarcely ten years of age having never received any instruction.'* Private Collection.

Figure 13. **Sir Thomas Lawrence,** *Mr. Grier (pair to Figure 12), pencil on paper, 2½ins. Signed on the front: 'T. Lawrence, fecit'. These two drawings are interesting examples of a budding artist's work.* Private Collection.

Frames for miniatures

The type, shape and material used to frame miniatures has varied throughout the centuries and as far as I know, with the exception of certain books on jewellery, no research has ever been undertaken regarding the names and training of those who fashioned the settings into which these precious portraits were placed. Unfortunately, with changes of fashion, many of the miniatures have been taken out of their original settings and rehoused in different ones that were popular at the time, and all too often the original frames have been lost or destroyed. In spite of this there are still many miniatures which have remained in family collections for centuries which still have their original frames and from which we can learn what materials were used.

The early limnings of the Holbein period appear to have been placed in simple frames of wood, silver or ivory, some of which had lids to protect the painting. A good example of this is the portrait by Holbein of Anne of Cleves, which is in the Victoria and Albert Museum, still housed in its circular ivory box with the lid carved in the shape of a rose (Colour Plate 1A). The wooden frames were almost certainly hand-carved and some of the bone ones stained to darken them. The art of miniature painting was so closely allied to that of the goldsmith — and indeed artists such as Nicholas Hilliard were apprenticed as goldsmiths — that it is not surprising that from the

Figure 14. **L. Hilliard,** *an unknown man, vellum, 2¼ins. Inscribed and dated: 'Ano Dni. 1621 Ætatis Suae 74', enclosed within a contemporary gold and green enamel locket, from which is suspended a drop pearl. This is a good example of the flowery inscriptions popularised by N. Hilliard.* Private Collection.

Elizabethan period onwards many of the portraits were set into elaborately engraved or bejewelled frames adorned with precious or semi-precious stones. These frames were made in gold and silver and frequently the backs were made of either translucent enamel fired over a design or plain enamel decorated with flowers or monograms. Occasionally the lockets, which were made with a loop at the top from which they could be suspended, also had the addition of drop pearls at the base (Figure 14). In Elizabethan times miniatures were treasured symbols of loyalty and love and were encased in lockets suspended over the heart of loved ones, or worn boldly by courtiers, hanging from a jewelled chain as in the case of the famous 'Lyte jewel' of c.1610, of James I, in the British Museum. This jewel is said to have been given to Mr. Thomas Lyte by James I on 12th July, 1610, so that the miniature would have been painted slightly earlier. It is a thing of great beauty and importance. The case is made of gold and decorated with enamel and diamonds, the lid which covers the portrait being executed in filigree work so that the painting is partly visible. A large portrait by an unknown artist of Lyte wearing the jewel is in the Somerset County Museum. A miniature of Anne of Denmark, c.1610, is in the Fitzwilliam Museum, Cambridge. It is enamelled in tawny red and set with diamonds, the reverse of the locket decorated in white with a monogram AA, crowned, and the S device, which the Queen also wore as a brooch (see Figure 15). Similar initials are set in diamonds on the lid with the addition of two linked CCs. According to Joan Evans, *A History of Jewellery,* p.138, a number of engraved designs for miniature cases were produced about 1610 by engravers such as Daniel Mignot, who published designs at Augsburg between 1590-1616, Nicholas Rouillart, an engraver, and Etienne Carteron, 1615.

Two other miniature cases of great importance are the Armada Jewel and the Drake Pendant. The Armada Jewel, c.1588, in the Victoria and Albert Museum (Figures 16, 16a and 16b), contains a rather damaged miniature of Elizabeth I by Hilliard. The jewel is of enamelled gold, set with diamonds and rubies, and was probably designed if not executed by Hilliard. On the front of the lid which covers the miniature is a golden profile portrait bust of the Queen set against a blue enamel background encircled with an inscription ELIZABETHA D.G. ANG. ERA. ET. HIB. REGINA. The opposite side of the

Figure 15. **I. Oliver,** *Queen Anne of Denmark (1574-1619), vellum, 2¾ins. The Queen is depicted wearing two of her favourite jewels, a crowned S and a sea horse. It is one of a number of presentation miniatures of her.* **Ex-de la Hey Collection.**

*Figures 16, 16a and 16b. Attributed to **N. Hilliard**, the Armada Jewel, c.1588. This fine jewel contains a rather damaged miniature of Queen Elizabeth I. Hilliard is thought to have designed, if not executed, the pendant which is made of enamelled gold set with diamonds and rubies. For further information see page 32. Courtesy Victoria and Albert Museum.*

locket is enamelled and shows the Ark floating on a troubled sea with rain falling in torrents from heaven, the border is inscribed with a Latin motto: 'Calm through the savage waves', and the inside of the lid enamelled with a Tudor rose encircled with its foliage and another Latin motto: 'Alas that virtue endued with so much beauty should not unscathed enjoy perpetual life.' By tradition this jewel was given to Sir Thomas Heneage by the Queen on the defeat of the Spanish Armada. It was Lot 99 in the sale of the Pierpont Morgan Collection, 24th June, 1935, when it was bought by Lord Wakefield and presented to the Victoria and Albert Museum.

The Drake Pendant is another fine example of this type of miniature locket; it is made of gold set with a cameo cut in Oriental sardonyx and embellished with enamelling, rubies and pearls. Hanging from the bottom of the locket is a bunch of pearls looking like grapes and one large drop pearl. Behind the cameo is a miniature of Queen Elizabeth by Hilliard, inscribed: 'Ano Dni 157(5?) Regni 20' (the twentieth year of the Queen's reign). The pendant was presented to Sir Francis Drake by the Queen in 1579 and he is seen wearing it in the portrait at the National Maritime Museum, Greenwich. The portrait is dated 1591, so the miniature may have been painted in 1578.

Many of the elaborately decorated enamel lockets, such as those on Plate 1, were in all probability made on the Continent and when they occasionally find their way into the sale rooms as in the case of the double-sided marriage miniature of an unknown man and woman by Alexander Cooper, c.1645, they are a delight to the eye (Plate 20). This miniature case is thought to be Dutch enamel on gold and is beautifully decorated with flowers and a monogram. Further details regarding these miniatures will be found in Chapter IV.

As time went on the more elaborate frames went out of fashion and simpler shapes made of silver, gold and wood were used. On 11th October,

*Figure 17. **S. Cooper**, Sir Thomas Hanmer (1612-1678). vellum, 2⁷/8ins., c.1660-65. Sir Thomas was a noted man of taste and an authority on horticulture. The miniature is a fine example of a portrait by Cooper and, until recently, has always been in the Warner family. It is set in a contemporary gold locket with spiral cresting. It was sold for £7,500 on 15th June, 1976. Courtesy Christie's.*

33

A

B

C

D

E

F

G

H

Figure 18. **N. Hilliard** *(1547-1619), self-portrait in his thirteenth year, vellum, 1in. diameter, 1560. Signed in monogram: 'NH / 1550' (the second 5 having been altered from a 6 at a later date). The miniature is inscribed:* 'OPERA QVEDAM IPSIVS NICHOLAIS HELIARD IN ÆTATIS SUÆ 13'. *The frame is typical of those made by Lens for the Portland miniatures.* Courtesy Ivy, Duchess of Portland.

1955, 'The Sotheby Heirlooms' as they were called were sold at Sotheby's. This collection although small was one of the most important ever formed containing miniatures of the sixteenth and seventeenth centuries. James Sotheby (1655-1720) was a London merchant who, according to an inscription on his monument, was imprisoned by James II, in favour with King William and "skilled in polite literature in most branches of which he left a very valuable collection". Records of his purchases date from 1691 and include some of the prices paid for frames. Thirteen of these were in all probability made by James Seamer, a goldsmith, who is known to have made the frame for Lot 48, 'Venus and Cupid', by Peter Oliver, dated 1645. This miniature was bought by James Sotheby on 30th November, 1703, for £10 and, according to another entry in the notebooks dated 21st January, 1705, Sotheby "Pd. Mr. James Seamer, Goldsmith for ye Case, Cristal & co. of the Venus by Oliver. £9.5.3." These frames were gilded metal, engraved with the monogram of James Sotheby, and chased with leaves or laurel garlands (Plate 2G). The 'Cristal' referred to would of course be the crystal glass placed over the miniature to protect it, in the same way as convex glass is used in

Plate 2. Examples of Eighteenth Century Miniature Frames.
A. *The reverse of a gold eighteenth century locket engraved round the outer edge, and containing the sitter's hair and monogram, 2³⁄8ins.*
B. *The reverse of a gold eighteenth century memorial locket containing a miniature by J. Downman. The locket has a surround of blue glass and a centre-piece of the sitter's hair and an urn, embellished with diamonds and a monogram: 'LL', 2¼ins.*
C. *The reverse of an eighteenth century gold locket, containing a design made from the sitter's hair entwined with gold and pearls set over opalescent glass, 3ins.*
D. *An eye miniature set in a ring as a memorial and inscribed: 'Mrs Eliz. Toovey. OB: 20. Nov: 1782 AE 60'. It is unusual to be able to identify the sitter on this type of miniature. Eighteenth century, 1in.*
E. *Early nineteenth century gold frame set with hair and a monogram over opalescent glass, containing a miniature of a young girl by J. Smart, dated 1809, 3¾ins.*
F. *The reverse of an eighteenth century gold frame with a design made from the sitter's hair with a blue glass and pearl centre-piece, and the monogram: 'MB' (Miss Mary Brisbane), 3ins.*
G. *An early eighteenth century gold frame, made and engraved by James Seamer, c.1703, bearing the monogram of James Sotheby for whom it was made to contain a miniature, by P. Oliver, of the Head of St. John, 3¹⁄8ins.*
H. *An eighteenth century gold frame inset with Bristol glass and a design of the sitter's hair over opalescent glass with tin-foil behind to look like enamel, 3ins.*

Private Collection

modern frames. The term 'crystal' in this context does not necessarily imply that it was 'rock crystal', a valuable mineral (although this may have been used occasionally) but an artificial raw material, of such especial transparency that it could justly be described as 'clear as crystal'. Even today 'crystal' glass is preferable to cover miniatures, but it is difficult to obtain and expensive.

Lot 67 in the same sale was a very important cabinet miniature of Sir Thomas More and his family based on a painting by Holbein and painted by **Rowland Lockey**. The miniature is now in the Victoria and Albert Museum and is still in a superb wooden frame with closing doors. According to James Sotheby's notebooks he had the frame made to house the miniature: "1716, Janu. 22nd. Pd. Mr. Tho. Bridgwater for wallnut Tree case for Sr. Tho. More's Picture & in full of all Accts. £3.10.0." (Colour Plate 4).

Samuel Cooper and his followers appear to have housed their miniatures in simple gold or silver lockets with a scroll of metal on the top and a ring from which the portrait could be suspended (Figure 17), others were placed in simple turned ebony frames without any ornamentation and with the occasional carved lid to protect the painting. Lids, some of which concealed a miniature, were also used for a few cases made of silver or gold (Plate 3) and later small leather cases, often made of shagreen, were popular. Miniatures kept in these closed frames have retained their brilliance as they have not been exposed to the light.

Figure 19 (left). **S. Shelley,** *a miniature of an officer, ivory, 1¾ins. Set in a gold flexible bracelet of the period.* **Courtesy Christie's.**

Figure 19a (below). **S.J. Rochard,** *a miniature of an unknown lady, ivory, 2ins. Set in a nineteenth century gold clasp frame with a plaited hair bracelet.* **Private collection.**

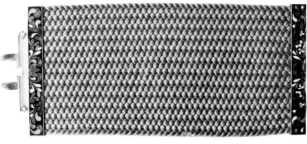

Colour Plate 2.
A. **John Hoskins,** *an unknown lady, vellum, 2⅜ins., c.1600. Signed: 'IH' in monogram. This is a particularly colourful and attractive miniature.*
B. **Isaac Oliver,** *an unknown youth, vellum, 2¾ins. Based on a miniature by N. Hilliard of which there is an original at Belvoir Castle.*
C. **An unknown artist,** *an Elizabethan Maundy, vellum, 2¾ins. This is an unusual and interesting miniature.*
D. **Nicholas Hilliard,** *an unknown man, vellum, 2¼ins. Inscribed: 'Anõ Dnī 1582 Ætatis Suæ 28.' This miniature was once attributed to I. Oliver.*

Courtesy The Earl Beauchamp

A

B

C

D

A

C

B

D

E

F

Little change took place in framing during the Restoration and those used in the early part of the eighteenth century were still plain. Bernard Lens, who was employed for some time by Edward Harley, 2nd Earl of Oxford, seems to have popularised a form of rectangular pearwood frame in which a number of miniatures in the Portland Collection are housed. These frames were stained black and many of the bills for them are in the Portland archives. They are still referred to as 'Lens type frames', some of which cost '12 shillings' and others '10/6d' (Figure 18). By the middle of the eighteenth century, the size of miniatures had diminished and the frames were again usually silver, gold or pinchbeck, a form of imitation gold containing an alloy of copper and zinc. This was invented by a Fleet Street watchmaker called Christopher Pinchbeck (d.1732); a similar alloy was also used in Holland and other parts of the Continent. Many of the small miniatures painted between c.1760-1780 were set in lockets which had a clasp and holes so that they could be stitched on to a ribbon to be worn round the neck or on the wrist as a bracelet; some of them had straps woven in human hair (Figures 19 and 19a). Besides the traditional lockets which hung from a chain, some miniatures were worn as brooches (Figure 20), which by c.1770 onwards were frequently encircled with diamonds, garnets or pearls and the more elaborate ones were set with rubies, emeralds or other precious stones. The reverse of the lockets were sometimes left plain, but the majority were engraved with some motif or monogram. Many of them had some of the sitter's hair set under the glass and either a monogram or decoration in seed pearls added. Some of the lockets were backed with coloured glass placed over silver foil indented with a pattern to look like enamel and are very attractive. This type of locket and brooch continued to be made into the nineteenth and twentieth centuries (Plate 2). Sentiment played an important part in the details used in nineteenth century jewellery and memorial lockets and rings were very popular. The reverse of these miniature lockets frequently has an urn and a figure obviously denoting death as the centrepiece, and memorial rings often have the person's dates and a motto engraved on them. Many miniatures are set into beautiful boxes, made of ivory, tortoiseshell or gold, embellished with designs in gold or enamel (Plate 3).

After the advent of photography miniatures were put into larger frames, which were made of wood, metal or leather, and many were placed behind thick brass mounts which helped to keep the larger pieces of ivory in position. For those who could afford it miniatures were still sometimes set in

Figure 20. **Sir W.C. Ross, R.A.,** *a miniature of Queen Victoria (1819-1901), ivory, 1¾ins. Inscribed on the reverse by the artist: 'London 1840 / Painted by / W.C. Ross, A.R.A. / Miniature Painter / To / The Queen'. The portrait is set within a gold period frame.* **Private Collection.**

Plate 3.

A. A miniature of Martha North by **G. Spencer,** *signed on the reverse and dated 1749, 2ins. Set in an attractive eighteenth century circular gold and tortoiseshell snuff box.*

B. An interesting ivory oblong snuff box, eighteenth century, 3¹³/₁₆ins. Containing a miniature of an unknown gentleman by **J. Nixon,** *signed: 'N', 2¼ins.*

Courtesy Bernard Falk Collection, The Royal Pavilion, Brighton

C. A unique gold box of the late seventeenth century, the lid and base both inset with an oval bloodstone, and the base having a removable panel which slides out to reveal a miniature of an unknown man in armour by **N. Dixon.** *Vellum, 3¹/₈ins.*

D. The sliding base to the gold box in Plate 3C, engraved with a floral design into which is incorporated squirrels and rabbits. The box is thought to be one of a small corpus of seventeenth century English boxes, but possibly made by one of the many Dutch émigré goldsmiths working in England. 3¹/₈ins.

Courtesy Brand Inglis

E. A gold mounted tortoiseshell snuff box inset with an enamel miniature of Mary (d.1764), wife of the 4th Duke of Leeds, by **C.F. Zincke,** *c.1750, 1⁷/₈ins. diameter. Size of the box 2¹⁵/₁₆ins. This is a fine example both of this type of box and of an enamel miniature.*

F. A nineteenth century papier mâché frame with the usual acorn metal motif, containing a miniature of Sir Mark Wood, 1st Bart., by **J. Comerford,** *dated 1802, 2¾ins.*

Courtesy Sotheby's

pearl or diamond lockets. With the decline in the demand for miniatures, the frames remained plain metal or even papier mâché, a type which had been in vogue from the mid-eighteenth century and which is mainly associated with silhouettes (Plate 3F). This latter type may still be obtained, as well as oval and rectangular metal ones, in various sizes. One of the firms which specialised in producing miniature frames was Hatfield and Sons of 86 and 88 Charlotte Street, London. When in the latter part of Queen Victoria's reign it was decided to reframe almost the entire Royal miniature collection at Windsor, Hatfield obtained the commission. The result was a disaster; not only were the original frames removed, but those which replaced them are of heavily designed bright gilt, quite out of keeping with the majority of the miniatures. This type of heavy gilt frame is met with in other collections and, one suspects, came from the same source. There are still a few jewellers who make copies of seventeenth century frames for special orders and although as hand-made objects they are expensive, if the miniature is of sufficient merit they are well worth obtaining.

Inscriptions and signatures

Although these points will be dealt with to some extent in later chapters, a brief account of the differences will, I hope, be helpful here. First of all it is important to remember that not every artist signed his works, in fact by far the greater number omitted to do so. It probably never occurred to them that it would matter to future generations. This being so, attributions have to be made with knowledge of style and technique and this only comes with many years' experience. An essential piece of equipment for a collector is a good magnifying glass, strong enough to suit his eyesight, and if he is a serious collector this glass should always be with him and ready for action!

Signatures are not easy to find and, in many cases, not easy to read. It is often necessary to turn the miniature this way and that to let the light fall on one small spot that may reveal the identity of the miniaturist. Early sixteenth and seventeenth century miniatures were not often signed, those painted by Holbein and Horenbout were occasionally inscribed with the sitter's age and a date in block capitals in gold or black, the inscription usually being in Latin. Hilliard introduced more flowery cursive inscriptions and, apart from the sitter's age or the date of the portrait, added a motto or symbol bearing some significance to the sitter's position or family. Followers of Hilliard and later artists had their own way of signing and these need to be studied carefully. It must also be remembered that false signatures were all too often added to miniatures in the hope of increasing their value, and these are not always easy to detect.

From the late seventeenth century onwards inscriptions are often to be found on the reverse of the backing inside the frame and, although I do not advise the inexperienced person to attempt to open up a valuable frame, I do suggest that miniatures should be examined by an expert who can open the case and see if there is any information regarding either the sitter or artist inside. The collector may in time feel able to do this himself, but it is important to remember that the miniature should be handled with great care, as once out of its frame it is very vulnerable. Those painted in watercolour should only be held with the tips of the fingers at the edge and not breathed on, as moisture can drop on to the portrait and destroy it completely.

Artists' signatures were not always consistent and initials may vary from block capitals to cursive initials or monograms where the letters are entwined. Some miniaturists signed in full on the front with both Christian name and surname and possibly even a date, others invariably inscribed the miniature on the reverse of the backing paper and in many cases added the address from which they were working. All this is important information, as it helps to document where artists were at different dates. Even scraps of paper placed within the case should be looked at with care, as there may be a note written on one which will be of value, or even the sitter's name. A great number of nineteenth century enamels have very full inscriptions on the reverse giving details of both the sitter and the artist as well as information as to whether or not the miniature is a copy of a large portrait. No information discovered in a miniature case should be destroyed; all too often I have come across instances where miniatures representing important known sitters have passed through the sale rooms to collectors, who within a few years have forgotten who the miniatures were of and the sitters have become 'an unknown man' or 'an unknown lady'. In my own collection I have two which had lost their identity when I bought them and only by chance was I able to discover that some fifty years ago they were illustrated in a collection and the sitters' names known!

John Smart occasionally put inscriptions on the reverse of his drawings with instructions as to how they should be hung to best advantage and Dr. G.C. Williamson quotes an amusing story relating to a miniature of a Mrs. Whittington by Cosway. Apparently the artist and the sitter did not get on, and the portrait was returned unfinished with a hidden inscription in the frame. The present whereabouts of the miniature was unknown until I saw it quite by chance in a sale at Phillips, Son & Neale on the 27th September, 1977. The inscription, now uncovered, reads: 'Impatient to advice. Excessive Pride upon a false foundation. A Specious Exterior — An Unfeeling Heart, Inconstant, Ungrateful, and the writer of this may justly add, as he has woefully experienced it, Cruel & mercenary' (Figures 21 and 21a)!

Many inscriptions placed on the frames or cases of miniatures are not contemporary and unfortunately not always accurate either. Families are notoriously bad at keeping documents of their possessions and information tends to be passed down by word of mouth from one generation to another. This can become very confused and, in an effort to leave the details for posterity, these bits of information are written up in all good faith. Later research on dates and costume of the supposed sitter often prove such information to be incorrect and the portrait of someone of a different generation.

When collectors purchase miniatures where inscriptions are written on the reverse of the backing it is important that care should be taken when these are opened that the inscription is not damaged, or, even worse, destroyed. Where information is discovered it should all be documented by the collector who should keep a list of his purchases with details of artists, sitters, signatures, inscriptions, dates of purchase and prices paid, together with any biographical information that he can find out about the sitter. This is important not only for his own interest but for valuation and insurance purposes. Many collectors also keep photographs of their collection for identification and number the collection on the reverse as it is purchased. My

Figure 21. **R. Cosway, R.A.,** *an unfinished miniature of Mrs. Whittington, ivory, 3¼ins. Bearing a full inscription on the reverse.* Courtesy Phillips, Son & Neale.

Figure 21a. Inscription on the reverse of Figure 21, said to be written by R. Cosway. paper, 3¼ins. Courtesy Phillips, Son & Neale.

own method is never to reissue a number as this can cause confusion.

Restoration

The question as to whether or not miniatures, when damaged, should be restored is a difficult one to answer, as each one has to be taken on its merit. I do not recommend the purchase of any miniature that is badly damaged unless it is a great rarity; those painted on ivory that are badly cracked should be avoided as, although they can be laid flat, the crack usually shows and the value of the miniature is reduced. Sixteenth and seventeenth century miniatures, because of their rarity, may be worth careful restoration. The Victoria and Albert Museum have published various notes on the care of art objects and *The Care of Portrait Miniatures,* 1970, is well worth studying. Miniatures painted in oil can be restored without too much difficulty; those executed in enamel should only be restored by a trustworthy jeweller. Those painted in gouache or watercolour present the greatest problem and, to quote the Victoria and Albert Museum pamphlet: "The restorative treatment of miniatures by the unskilled is to be strongly discouraged. The majority of miniatures are sealed in lockets which, in themselves, are a specialist problem. An amateur attempt to open such a locket can, and frequently does, result in the ruin of the locket, the convex glass and, in many cases, the miniature itself. When a miniature is out of its frame it is one of the most vulnerable of all art objects and it should be handled with great respect. It must be touched with the hands as little as possible, never on the painted surface and only by the tips of the fingers on the outside edge. If it is an ivory miniature the slightest pressure needed to hold it should be on the end grain of the ivory, that is at the top and bottom of the miniature. Pressure at the sides can cause bending, paint loss or even cracking. If a miniature is held in the palm of the hand it may instantly react to the warmth and moisture and begin to warp, causing paint loss."

From this it will be realised that the restoration of a miniature is not without risk and expert advice should be sought before anything is done, as there are very few artists qualified to deal with the restoration of these delicate objects.

Examination under X-ray

Until comparatively recently it has not been possible to detect accurately what retouching, if any, had been done on miniatures. Now, with the help of X-ray, ultra-violet and infra-red viewers, much can be discovered. The X-ray reveals the use and pattern of lead white on the miniature, the infra-red distinguishes between lapis lazuli and copper blues and occasionally helps to decipher indistinct inscriptions. The ultra-violet shows up any retouching and reveals the use of zinc white. These methods are all used by Mr. V.J. Murrell in the Conservation Department at the Victoria and Albert Museum, and it is due to his research that this aspect of preservation and conservation has developed.

Storing and exhibiting a miniature collection

Having dealt briefly with most, if not all, of the most important points to know when forming a collection of miniatures, it now only remains for me to suggest some of the ways in which such a collection can be displayed and stored so that the least possible damage is caused. When the collector is deciding on the method he will adopt to house his collection several things must be borne in mind. Firstly as has already been mentioned miniatures painted in watercolour soon fade if exposed to too much daylight, and as many of them are painted with the addition of fairly large quantities of gum this in itself is a hazard as it tends to attract a form of fungoid growth when kept in conditions of high humidity. Those painted on ivory have a tendency to flake if exposed to changes of temperature and the ivory also tends to cockle or split. Ideally miniatures in this medium should be kept in an even temperature of about 65 degrees F, the light falling on them being as little as possible, and cases should be kept covered except when the contents are being examined. Ideal conditions are seldom possible in an ordinary home, so the following points may be useful. If central heating is in use, it is advisable to have humidifiers in the rooms as this prevents the atmosphere getting too dry. Extreme changes of temperature are dangerous and tend to produce sweating under the convex glass which drops on to the miniature and causes damage. When hung on the wall they should be on an inside partition rather than an outside wall, which is always more susceptible to damp. They should have a small gap between the frame and the wall to permit the air to circulate — this may be done with small pieces of cork being cut and stuck to the corners of the frame. They should not be hung near a fireplace or radiator, or where there are draughts. If they are placed in cabinets or cases, then a piece of cambric or brocade placed over the case will prevent light from falling on the paintings. If the miniatures are painted in oil or enamel, these cannot fade and do not normally produce any great problems, unless a form of verdigris appears on the copper. This usually comes round the edges of the enamel and should be dealt with at once by an expert.

There are a variety of ways in which miniatures can be displayed. Cases can be bought, or made by a good joiner, to hang on the wall. The case should be suitably deep to allow the miniatures to be hung easily and the front covered with either glass or wooden doors. Display cases on legs are attractive, and both antique and modern ones may be purchased. Fan cases can sometimes be found at auctions and are an attractive method of displaying choice examples; flat cases to sit on a table can also be used. I have obtained attractive old frames of a suitable size to hold up to twelve miniatures and had a false back made to give sufficient depth for the miniatures to be hung. The backgrounds can be covered with material or suitable wallpaper.

If miniatures have to be stored away or wrapped up for any reason the best protection is to wrap them in the best quality white tissue paper, never with cotton wool or any material which can hold damp. They should be loosely wrapped to allow air to circulate freely round them. This latter method is valuable when miniatures, for security reasons, have to be kept in a bank. It is a sad reflection on the state of the world that a number of collectors use a bank almost entirely for housing their collections. Although they may be safe from thieves, kept in this way they can give no pleasure to their owners nor be enjoyed by their friends without considerable trouble. Such miniatures tend to become purely an investment and not treasures to be enjoyed and lived with, reminders of a bygone age and symbols of love and fidelity.

Chapter II

The Early Masters

Plate 4A. Attributed to **L. Horenbout,** *Mary I (1516-1558), daughter of Henry VIII, vellum, 1½ins. diameter. Although this miniature has had slight restoration it is an interesting portrayal of Mary as a young girl. She is wearing an unusual brooch on which are the words 'The Emperor'. Her Tudor hood is edged with pearls.* Private Collection.

Plate 4B. Attributed to **L. Horenbout,** *Lady Jane Seymour (1509?-1537), 3rd wife of Henry VIII. Inscribed: 'A°N XXV'. Painted c.1534, vellum, 1½ins. diameter. Note the slightly more elaborate hood.* Courtesy Christie's.

THE DOMINATING FIGURE of Henry VIII is known throughout the world, and the mention of his name immediately conjures up a picture of a man who, even to his contemporaries, appeared a Colossus. His power was absolute — his Court one of magnificence and grandeur which attracted many men of genius such as Sir Thomas More, and Hans Holbein the younger (1497/8-1543). Indeed it is Holbein's portrayal of the King that has come down to us through the centuries and has been illustrated and copied time without number. Henry VIII became a serious patron of the arts, and encouraged numerous men of talent to come over from the Continent and work at the English Court, including a family of Flemish illuminators called **Horenbout** or Hornebolte. **Gerard** (d.c.1540), **Lucas** (d.1544), and **Susanna** (1503-1545), were best known for their work as illuminators, but are all thought to have painted a few miniatures. Gerard was a native of Ghent, whose family had been noted artists for some generations, and was the son of Willem Hornebolte. Gerard is best known for his Books of Hours and other illuminated manuscripts, but also painted altarpieces and portraits and executed designs for stained glass windows, vestments and tapestries. He was admitted to full membership of the Guild of St. Luke at Ghent in 1487. By his wife, Margarethe de Vandere (or Swanders), died 1529, he had two children, Susanna and Lucas. The family came to England in c.1522, and were employed by the King. Gerard's name appears in the Royal household accounts in 1528-1531, after which time it is thought he returned to Ghent. Lucas was employed by Henry VIII from 1525 until his death, his name being recorded in the Royal accounts in the same year as that of his father. Susanna was taught art by her father and is reputed to have painted miniatures. According to tradition she met Albrecht Dürer in 1521, when she and her father were in Antwerp, and Dürer is said to have purchased a miniature she had painted, which he considered a remarkable achievement for a girl of eighteen.

Unfortunately no signed miniatures by any of the family have so far come to light, but it is generally accepted that a small number can with safety be ascribed to Lucas. These include three, and possibly four, miniatures of Henry VIII, one of Lady Jane Seymour, third wife of Henry, painted in her twenty-fifth year (Plate 4B), and one of Mary I (Plate 4A). Two of the versions of Henry are in the collection of H.M. The Queen, both painted in his thirty-fifth year, one with a beard (Plate 4D), and one without. The Fitzwilliam Museum have another similar one without a beard. A fourth version also showing the King shaven is in the collection of the Duke of Buccleuch and may possibly be by Horenbout. A circular miniature of

Catherine of Aragon, ascribed to Lucas (Plate 4C), is in the National Portrait Gallery, London, and other limnings have tentatively been given to him.

It is only recently that these early miniatures have been examined under X-ray and the paints analysed, and it may be some time before any conclusions can be arrived at which will clarify some of these attributions.

For the present **Hans Holbein** is still considered the 'father of the art of miniature painting', and according to tradition he was taught by Horenbout. Holbein was born in Augsburg and was the son of Hans Holbein the Elder, by whom he was taught art. Holbein is recorded as being in Basle in December 1515, where, according to tradition he and his brother, Ambrosius, became pupils of Hans Herbster (1468-1550). Holbein excelled in designing title pages and book illustrations, besides producing woodcuts, engravings, designs for glass-painting and frescoes. As early as 1516 he was commissioned to paint Jacob Mayer zum Hasen, the Mayor of Basle, and his second wife, Dorothea Kannengiesser. These portraits are in the Kunstmuseum, Basle, and are painted in tempera on wood.

Soon after these portraits were painted, Holbein joined his father in Lucerne, and is said to have visited Italy. Returning later to Basle he was, on 25th September, 1519, admitted to the painters' guild there, and in 1520 became a citizen, for which privilege he did not have to pay! The reason for this was that he had in the meantime married a citizen of Basle, Elsbeth Binzenstock, the widow of a tanner, Ulrich Schmid. Interesting information about Holbein's life is given by Hans Reinhardt in *Apollo*, December 1976.

Armed with letters of introduction from Erasmus to Sir Thomas More, Holbein left Basle for England in 1526, and was entertained by More at his house in Chelsea. He became known to the King and, after returning to Basle in 1528 for about three years, finally settled in England in 1531 and obtained Royal patronage, which he retained right up to his untimely death

Plate 4C. Attributed to **L. Horenbout,** *Catherine of Aragon (1485-1536), 1st Queen of Henry VIII, and mother of Mary I. Inscribed: 'REGINA KATHERINA EIVS VXOR'. Vellum, 1³/₈ins. diameter. This miniature has suffered damage, but is of great interest historically, and is now at the National Portrait Gallery.* Courtesy Sotheby's.

Plate 4D. **L. Horenbout,** *Henry VIII (1491-1547). Vellum, 1³/₄ins. diameter. Inscribed: 'H.R. VIII:· AN̊. ETATIS . XXXV̊:·' Three versions of this miniature exist, one with the King wearing a beard, and two without, c.1525. It is clear from the miniature that Holbein based his style on that of Horenbout.* Gracious permission of H.M. The Queen.

Plate 4E. **H. Holbein**, *Lady Audley, vellum, 2³/16 ins. diameter. Based on a drawing by Holbein in the Royal Collection. The sitter has not yet been identified with certainty. The portrait is a good guide to costume and shows the Tudor hood, and square-cut neckline to the dress, as well as period jewellery. Gracious permission of H.M. The Queen.*

Plate 4F. **H. Holbein**, *Charles Brandon, later Duke of Suffolk (1538-1551), vellum, 2¼ins. diameter. Inscribed on the paper in the boy's hand: 'AÑN / 1541 / ETATIS SVÆ 3 / 10 MARCI'. He and his brother were both painted by Holbein. Both succeeded to the Dukedom, but both died young. Note the flat cap popular at this time. Gracious permission of H.M. The Queen.*

during the plague in 1543. In 1536 he was appointed painter to Henry VIII, who commissioned him to paint numerous portraits, including some on the Continent in 1538. This mission gave him the opportunity to revisit Basle and see his family. The citizens were much impressed with his fine clothes and prosperity, and he received pressing invitations to remain and work there. In spite of this Holbein only stayed a few weeks and left on 16th October, 1538, together with his eldest son, Philip, whom he placed for six years as an apprentice to Jacob David, a Basle goldsmith working in Paris.

Back in England Holbein appears to have had many commissions, and was held in great esteem as an outstanding artist. As no signed and dated miniatures by him have so far come to light that can be accepted without doubt, we cannot be sure when he began to paint miniatures. In 1539 Holbein was sent to paint Anne of Cleves, who had been suggested as a possible wife for the King after the death of Jane Seymour. Two portraits exist, the three-quarter one painted in oil now in The Louvre, and the superb miniature showing only the head and shoulders, housed in its original ivory box, in the Victoria and Albert Museum (Colour Plate 1A). In the same museum is the miniature of Mrs. Pemberton, also attributed to Holbein; it portrays a young woman of twenty-three years of age, simply dressed, without embroidery or elaborate jewellery, sitting calmly with her hands clasped, and a serene expression on her face. It is probably the simplicity of the modelling and economy of line in Holbein's work that marks him out as a great artist.

It is the excellence of Holbein's large portraits and drawings representing Henry VIII and his Court which reveals so clearly the sitter's character and the features and stature of an all-powerful monarch. Had it not been for Henry's admiration of Holbein, miniature painting might never have been born in Britain. In view of the fact that limnings by Horenbout are now accepted, it is impossible to be sure what stage the art had reached by the time Holbein came to England. Because of his immense popularity a vast number of portraits of uneven quality and even impossible dates have at one time or another been assigned to his hand. A number of Holbein's works have no doubt perished, and others may still be hidden away in private houses where they are unrecognised. The following limnings have up to the present been accepted as genuine works by Holbein:

Mrs. Pemberton Anne of Cleves	(Victoria and Albert Museum)
Lady Audley Henry Brandon Charles Brandon	(Collection of H.M. The Queen)
Thomas Wriothesley, 1st Earl of Southampton	(The Metropolitan Museum, New York)
A Youth	(Collection of H.M. Queen Juliana of the Netherlands)
A Man, aged twenty-four in 1543	(The Stadt Museum, Danzig)
A Lady, called Catherine Howard	(Buccleuch Collection)

Other portraits have been suggested as possibly authentic, and recently those of Margaret Roper and her husband William Roper, both in the Metropolitan Museum of Art, New York, have been added to the list. One of a man in the Fritz Lugt Collection, Paris, was discussed and illustrated by Graham Reynolds in *Apollo,* October 1976, who claimed that it was an undoubted work by Holbein. In addition there are certain alleged self-portraits, including one in the collection of the Duke of Buccleuch, and another in the Wallace Collection. These have never been accepted with confidence, and there is the possibility that they are by other hands. A self-portrait, which is undoubtedly by Holbein, was drawn when the artist was forty-five; this is in the Uffizi, Florence, and must have been executed the year he died. This is typical of all his portraits, finely drawn, serene, and unsmiling. He seems to have been able to penetrate his sitters' characters without any attempt to flatter them, but with great attention to detail, especially costume and accessories, which is what one might expect from someone who, apart from his other attributes, also designed jewellery.

The majority of Holbein's miniatures have blue backgrounds, and are painted in watercolour on thin parchment stuck on to card. There is not at present any reason to suppose that he ever painted directly on to card. The colours used were opaque no doubt mixed with gum. The sitters are placed well within the circle, some of which are jagged at the edges, and the painting of the background is relieved only by the occasional inscription of the sitter's age in block lettering painted in pure gold. This would be consistent with the style adopted in small oil portraits executed on the Continent, some of which Holbein is thought to have painted before coming to England.

Little is known about Holbein's private life, or whether he ever intended to return to his family in Basle. The portrait of his wife and two eldest children painted in 1528 is in the Kuntsmuseum, Basle. By this time the artist was sufficiently wealthy to purchase a house in the St. Johann district of the city. In 1511 his father drew a portrait of Hans and his elder brother, Ambrosius, which is in the Print Room, Berlin. This, when compared with Holbein's self-portrait, shows how little his features had changed from childhood to maturity. Both portraits reveal certain characteristics: clear, penetrating eyes, a firm mouth and determined chin. He made his will on 7th October, 1543, and according to Hans Rienhardt he "left most of his property to his wife, his court robes, costly silverware and many drawings". He was buried on 29th November of the same year at St. Andrew Undershaft, London. (Plates 4E and F.)

Holbein does not seem to have left behind any school of miniature painters, and few contemporary artists are even reputed to have painted them. Of these **John Shute** (fl.1550-1570?), **Gwillim Stretes** (fl.1546-1556), **John Bettes** (b.c.1530), **Thomas Bettes** (sixteenth century), have all had miniatures attributed to them, but none are authenticated with any certainty. **A. van Brounckhurst** (fl.1565-1598), who was associated with Nicholas Hilliard, painted some small portraits, and one in miniature of James I and VI, after a larger oil portrait by van Brounckhurst, is in The Mauritshuis, The Hague.

Another family of Flemish illuminators working in England were the Bennincks. **Simon Benninck** (1483?-1561), whose self-portrait is in the Victoria and Albert Museum, was reputed to be one of the leading illuminators in Europe. Stylistically this is as one would expect, more akin to that of an illuminator, but it is a portrait and, as such, shows the link between that art and early limnings. Benninck's second daughter, Levina, is known to have painted miniatures, and although several have been assigned to her over the years, positive attribution is still a matter of conjecture. She married George Teerlinc of Blankenberg, and settled in London in 1545. **Levina Teerlinc** (d.1576) held the position of Court Painter for a salary of £40 or £44 a year, and it is frustrating that up to the present no authentic miniatures by her have come to light. One can only hope that eventually some positive conclusions about her work can be reached.

The name of **Nicholas Hilliard** (1547-1619) is known to most people, even if they know nothing about miniature painting. To those who study the art, his life and work are of the utmost importance, as it was under his guidance that the British School was established. Nicholas was born in Exeter in 1547, son of Richard Hilliard and his wife Laurence, née Wall, both families being well-known goldsmiths. The family included four boys, Nicholas, John, Jeremy and Ezechiel. The latter brother became a clergyman, and the other three followed their father's profession as goldsmiths. Richard Hilliard took an active part in the life of the community, serving both as Bailiff and High Sheriff of Exeter, and was known to be a zealous Protestant. The local community was led at that time by John Bodley, a rich merchant, whose son, Thomas, became the founder of the Bodleian Library, Oxford. Under the reign of Mary Tudor and the wave of heretic-burnings, England was not a very healthy spot for a person who held such views. Bodley evidently decided to take refuge on the Continent and early in 1557 he fled to Germany. He managed somehow to arrange the escape of his family which included his wife, three sons, Thomas, John and Lawrence, one daughter, two servants, a maid, his brother Nicholas, and 'Nicholas Hilliarde'. As no other boy of this name can be traced, this must be the miniaturist Nicholas Hilliard, who was then a boy of ten years of age. The custom of educating one's son in a household of higher rank was quite usual for those who could afford it, and as the families must have been well known to each other, the Bodleys' departure for the Continent would be an opportunity to send Nicholas with them. The family settled in Geneva, and his knowledge of the French language was to stand him in good stead in later life. This information about Hilliard's stay abroad was published by Dr. Leslie Hotson in *The Sunday Times Magazine,* March 1970, too late to be included in my *Dictionary,* which was already in the press. The date when the young Hilliard returned to England is not known, but it must have been sometime in or before 1562, as on Friday, 13th November of that year his apprenticeship to Robert Brandon is recorded in the Minutes of the Goldsmiths' Company, by which time he must have been fifteen. This poses an interesting question as three miniatures exist all painted when he was thirteen: two self-portraits (Figure 18), and one of Edward Seymour, Duke of Somerset, dated 1560, and painted from an earlier portrait (Plate 5A). It has always been assumed that these were painted in England, but they may well have been experimental works done on the Continent.

Having served the usual seven years' apprenticeship to Robert Brandon (d.1591), a leading goldsmith and jeweller to Elizabeth I, in 1569 he set up a business with his brother, John, and became a Freeman of the Goldsmiths' Company on 29th July, 1569 He had a number of apprentices including his son, **Laurence Hilliard** (1581/2-1647/8), **Isaac Oliver** (d.1617), and **Rowland Lockey** (fl.1581-c.1616). The fact that Hilliard worked under the Queen's leading goldsmith would immediately have given him the entrée into Court circles, and although we do not know the date that he entered the Queen's service it was probably by c.1569. His earliest known dated portrait of her is that of 1572, in the National Portrait Gallery. In 1573 the Queen granted him the reversion of a lease of the Rectory and Church of Clyve in Somerset for his "good true and loyal service".

Hilliard fell in love with Alice (b.c.1557), the beautiful daughter of Robert Brandon, and the couple were married on 15th July, 1576, at St. Vedast, Foster Lane, London. His self-portrait, 1577, and portrait of Alice, 1578, are in the Victoria and Albert Museum; both are signed. The self-portrait painted when the artist was thirty is a companion piece to the one of Richard Hilliard, his father (Colour Plate 1B). According to tradition both these portraits once had a border bearing full inscriptions regarding the sitters, and are probably those described in 1706 in the translation of De Pile's *Art of Painting.* The miniature of Alice which is rightly considered one of his most lovely works was painted in France and is fully inscribed: 'Ano Dni. 1578. Æs S.22.' and signed twice in monogram. The outer border was evidently added after Alice's death and is inscribed as follows: 'ALICIA. BRANDON. NICOLAI HILLYARDI. QVI PROPRIA MANV DEPINXIT

Plate 5A. N. Hilliard, *Edward Seymour, Duke of Somerset (1506-1552), vellum, 1¼ins. diameter. Based on an earlier portrait. Signed 'NH' (monogram) and inscribed: 'EDWARDE, DVKE OF SOMERSET. ANNO DOMINI. 1560'. This is one of the few signed miniatures by Hilliard, and an example of his early work when only thirteen years of age.* Courtesy, The Duke of Buccleuch and Queensberry, K.T.

Plate 5B. N. Hilliard, Mrs. Nicholas Hilliard, née Alice Brandon (b.1557/8), vellum, 2³/₈ins. diameter. This scintillating miniature of Hilliard's first wife is signed and dated with a double monogram : 'NH', and inscribed: 'Ano Dni. 1578. Æs S.22'. A further inscription was added round the outer edge after her death: 'ALICIA. BRANDON. NICOLAI HILLYARDI. QVI PROPRIA MANV DEPINXIT VXOR PRIMA' (He who with his own hand has painted his first wife). The details of the costume and lace ruff are superb. Courtesy Victoria and Albert Museum.

VXOR PRIMA' (the translation of which reads: He who with his own hand has painted his first wife). On the left are the arms of Hilliard, and on the right those of Brandon (Plate 5B). Alice's date of death is not known, nor do we know anything about Hilliard's second wife, who presumably pre-deceased him as she is not mentioned in his will. Alice, who was still alive in 1591 when her father died, bore him at least eight children of whom Laurence (1581/2-1647/8) followed his father's profession.

Nicholas Hilliard's life seems to have been marred by his reckless extravagance and failure to cope with money matters. He was constantly in debt, and lost his father-in-law's confidence to such an extent that neither Nicholas nor the children were mentioned in his will, and Alice was given a quarterly allowance, made through the Goldsmiths' Company. For thirty-five years he occupied and worked from a house and shop in Gutter Lane, the premises being owned by the Goldsmiths' Company and on a lease. He had difficulty in renewing the lease, and in paying the rent. In 1613 the house was leased to his son, Laurence, Nicholas having moved to an unknown address in the parish of St. Martin-in-the-Fields. In 1617 he was imprisoned in Ludgate for standing surety for one William Pereman, a debt he refused to pay. In his will made on 24th December, 1618, he does not mention any substantial bequests and, apart from minor gifts, he left the residue to his son, Laurence. He died early in 1619, and was buried on 7th January of that year in the church of St. Martin-in-the-Fields.

Fortunately for the student there is no need for speculation about the way in which Hilliard painted his miniatures, for he left detailed information in his *Treatise Concerning the Arte of Limning* (published with notes in Vol. I, The Walpole Society, 1912). This treatise is of such importance that every student of miniature painting should try and obtain a copy from a library and read it with care. Throughout the treatise Hilliard insists that the art is one to be practised by gentlemen. In it he says: "Now therfor I wish it weare so that none should medle with limning but gentlemen alone, for that it is a kind of gentill painting of lesse subiection than any other; for one may leaue when hee will, his coullers nor his work taketh any harme by it". He goes on to describe it as a secret art, sweet and clean to use, and a thing apart from all other painting or drawing, " and tendeth not to comon mens vsse . . ." He considered that it excelled all other painting in giving true lustre to pearls and precious stones set into gold or silver, and that such creations were "euen the worke of God and not of man, benning fittest for the decking of princes bookes or to put in jeuuells of gould . . ." Hilliard acknowledges his debt to Holbein: "Yet had the King in wages for limning diurs others; but Holbeans maner of limning I haue euer imitated and howld it for the best . . ."

Although Hilliard based his early work on that of Holbein, his training as a jeweller and the influences which must have come his way in Geneva where he was surrounded by so much art soon introduced him to a different style of portraiture. Among the refugees who had flocked to the city were no less than forty-three goldsmiths, chiefly from Rouen and Paris, who must have set up in shops and workrooms to which the young boy undoubtedly had access.

The fashions of the time with embroidered dresses and men's clothes, exquisitely made lace collars and ruffs, all gave him great scope (Plate 5D), and he made full use of his gifts and painted them with all the artistry of a genius. Every thread of the lace can be picked out, the jewels and head-dresses or simple caps are all drawn to perfection. Hilliard truly believed that the people of England were endowed with more beauty than any other race. "I saye not for the face only, but euery part, for euen the hand and foott excelleth all pictures that yet I euer sawe. This moued a certaine Pope [Gregory I] to say that England was rightly called Anglia of Angely, as the country of Angels, God grant it." He was also convinced that the face was the mirror of the soul, and that the artist had to catch the different expressions quickly, ". . . catch thesse louely graces, wittye smilings, and thesse stolne glances which sudainely like lighting passe and another countenance taketh place . . ."

Hilliard set down certain rules which he felt were of the utmost importance for anyone embarking on a limning. Silk clothes should be worn rather than those of inferior quality which might produce specks of dust to spoil the picture, the work should not be touched with the fingers, no dandruff or spit should fall upon it to destroy or spoil the colours. The artist should choose a room where a clear easterly light can shine through the window and where there are no reflections, only the sky. Discreet talk or reading and even quiet mirth is permitted or soft music, but questioners and "busi fingers" should be shut out!

Hilliard's art was influenced by several contacts: his training as a goldsmith under his father as a child, and later Robert Brandon, his time in Geneva, and his admiration and imitation of Hans Holbein. Besides all this, soon after his marriage in 1576, he and Alice spent at least two years in Paris mixing with the artistic circle gathered round the Court of Henry III. Part of his stay was at the French Embassy, where he painted a portrait of young Francis Bacon, and for a time he was employed by Francis, Duke of Anjou, Queen Elizabeth's suitor. During this time he would have absorbed much of the French style of painting and sculpture, and the type of French Court portraiture so superbly expressed by François Clouet, many of whose portraits must have come to England in connection with various marriage negotiations. These chalk drawings are inspired works of art, spontaneous and intimate. Last but not least he accepted the very pronounced views of Elizabeth I, that no shadow should fall on the portrait. She had noticed that the Italians avoided shadows and, as miniatures were so small that they were things to be held close to the eye to be enjoyed, and could be spoiled by too much shading, the Queen chose to "sit for that purpose in the open ally of a goodly garden, where no tree was neere, nor any shadowe at all . . ."

I am indebted to Mr. V.J. Murrell of the Conservation Department at the Victoria and Albert Museum for furnishing me with some of his latest research regarding Hilliard's method of painting. It has become apparent that the special techniques used for painting jewels — the burnished silver ground under diamonds, the polished round silver highlights on pearls, and the use of coloured resin over silver ground to represent rubies, etc. — were all Hilliard's invention, and do not seem to have been used prior to c.1580. Another peculiarity seems to be his invention of using the normal floating technique for red curtain backgrounds up to c.1600, after which time he lifted out the lights with a dry brush, giving a much sharper effect.

A fascinating miniature of Queen Elizabeth c.1575-1580 is at Berkeley

Plate 5C. **N. Hilliard,** *portrait of a young girl, vellum, 2³/₁₆ins. Signed and dated: 'Ano Dni 1609. NH' (monogram) and inscribed: 'AEtatis Suæ 10'. This delightful miniature is an enchanting example of Hilliard's work. It is in brilliant condition and is important as it is one of the rare occasions, particularly at this late period in Hilliard's career, when he added his signature.* Courtesy Victoria and Albert Museum.

Plate 5D (left). **N. Hilliard,** *An unknown lady (once* called *Queen Elizabeth, when Princess, but the costume makes this impossible). Vellum, 2⁵/₈ins., c.1585-90, in a contemporary turned ivory case (lid missing). It is a good example of costume, with the wide full lace ruff, tight waisted bodice, full skirt and ornaments in the hair.* Courtesy The Duke of Buccleuch and Queensbury, K.T.

Plate 5E. **N. Hilliard,** *a gentleman thought to be Henry Carey, 2nd Earl of Monmouth (1596-1661), vellum, 2½ins. Inscribed: 'Encores Vn* Luit pour moy', with a further inscription on the outer mount, dated 1616. It is of great importance as an example of Hilliard's work at the age of seventy.* Courtesy Ivy, Duchess of Portland.

Castle. It is of great importance as one of the earliest miniatures by Hilliard of the Queen and because of the whole treatment of the painting. The Queen is seated on a throne, playing a lute, this rests on a balustrade and is drawn in great detail. The throne is embellished with architectural devices such as pillars and balls, and the feeling of the whole scene is that of an interior executed more in the manner of an illumination (Plate 6B).

To appreciate Hilliard's miniatures to the full they should be viewed separately and with great care and understanding for they are precious and intimate paintings, executed for his patrons as tokens of love and fidelity. Many of them bear symbols and mottoes, and have hands clasped to the bosom in token of devotion or, as in the case of the splendid miniature of George Clifford, 3rd Earl of Cumberland (1558-1605), at Greenwich (painted c.1590), depict an important person – the Queen's Champion, also described as "a typical Elizabethan sailor – courtier, gambler and buccaneer"! He wears the Queen's glove set with diamonds in his hat, a splendidly embroidered surcoat, clasping his long lance in his right hand, his helmet and gloves scattered in the landscape, his personal device fastened to a tree behind him, depicting the world between the sun and the moon. The portrait of Sir Anthony Mildmay (d.1617) in the Cleveland Museum, Ohio (painted c.1595), is another outstanding example of these large, full-length limnings by Hilliard, all of which have to be looked at in depth before they can be fully appreciated.

Hilliard's artistic career lasted for some fifty-six years, during which time there was, as one would expect, development, change, and some variation in his style. By the time he was twenty-five, he had reached maturity, and from then until c.1600 he produced what has accurately been described as a "dazzling series of exquisitely studied and characterized portraits." During the years that Shakespeare was composing his sonnets and plays, Hilliard was leaving his own mark on history by painting portraits which mirrored one important aspect of the Elizabethan age — its admiration of the male virtues. Almost everyone knows the painting of the 'Unknown Young Man Among Roses', c.1590, in the Victoria and Albert Museum. The subject is one of his most famous paintings and symbolises unrequited love. The young man stands clasping his hand to his heart, he is entwined by eglantine roses, symbols of chastity, whilst a motto surrounds the upper edge alluding to the suffering caused by loyalty!

By the turn of the century, and after the death of the artist's beloved patron, Elizabeth I, in 1603, he seems to have lost a little of his impetus. He was ageing, suffering from ill health, financially embarrassed, and by this time losing many of his patrons to his pupil, **Isaac Oliver** (d.1617). He painted numerous portraits of James I, most of them for presentation purposes, and good though they are they lack the sparkle of his earlier works. However, he never really lost his mastery, and he executed some beautiful portraits when he was over sixty: attractive paintings of pretty ladies with their hair hanging loosely over their shoulders, as in the miniature of Lady Elizabeth Stanley, painted c.1605-1610, in the Bearstead Collection, and the exquisite painting of Mrs. Mole, c.1605, whose husband, John Mole, also painted by Hilliard c.1595, was treasurer to the English army in Brittany. After crossing the Alps with Lord Roos, Mr. Mole was imprisoned as a Protestant for a period, it is said, of "thirty years or for life". The miniature of his wife was believed to have been with him in prison. The pair were formerly in the collection of Lady Clinton. In 1602 Hilliard executed a superb portrait of an unknown lady wearing a hat, and bearing an inscription which translated means: "It seems and truly it is" (Colour Plate 1D). This miniature was sold at Sotheby's on 29th March, 1965, for £5,000, and it is now in the Victoria and Albert Museum. Quite apart from its beauty as a miniature it is of great importance regarding costume. The sitter's hair is

Plate 5F. **N. Hilliard,** *James I and VI (1566-1625), vellum, 1¾ins., c.1610. Several versions of this presentation portrait of the King exist, the colour of the doublet varying. Those painted up to c.1608 show him wearing a hat, and later ones do not. This version shows James wearing a pale blue doublet, the Garter ribbon lying under the lace to show up the detail of the design. It has a red curtain background and is in perfect condition.* Private Collection.

Plate 5G. **N. Hilliard,** *an 'Elizabethan Gallant', vellum, 1¹⁵/₁₆ ins. Inscribed 'Anõ Dnĩ 1576. Ætatis Suae 39.' This outstanding miniature depicts a dashing young man in period costume and wearing the jaunty type of hat decorated with a plume, so popular at that time. Courtesy Cleveland Museum of Art, Ohio, E.B. Greene Collection.*

dressed high and smooth beneath a fine lace coif, under a tall black hat; her exquisitely painted lace ruff is slightly open at the front with a single forget-me-not tucked between the pleats on the right side. The sitter is wearing a white dress, ruched bodice to the waist, black sleeves padded at the shoulders. Black lacework edges the upper part of the bodice, sprays of pink flowers are placed at the armpits, and a single yellow flower at the breast, from which hangs a small locket set in a gold border.

Hilliard left us a vivid impression of people and costume of the period, and pictorially one can trace the changes in fashion from his miniatures right up to the end of his life. Because of their size and intimacy miniatures are on the whole a much better guide to costume than the traditional set portraits which were stylised and posed, and I have tried to bear this in mind when selecting illustrations for this book. A portrait of an 'Unknown Youth', formerly in the collection of the Earl of Radnor, and now at the Victoria and Albert Museum, is a superb example of Hilliard's ability to portray youth simply and elegantly. The boy is dressed in a yellow ruched doublet, finely painted lace ruff, and black feathered bonnet. The portrait, c.1585-1590, is in a turned ivory box (Colour Plate 1). Three years before his death Hilliard painted a miniature thought to be of Henry Carey, 2nd Earl of Monmouth (1596-1661) which is in the Portland Collection (Plate 5E). The sitter is wearing a simple black doublet, white stiff standing collar, with white strings attached which he holds with his carefully drawn left hand, the veins delicately painted. Round the wrist is a triple black cord to which is attached a gold ring, below a white cuff. It is inscribed: 'Encores Vn Luit pour moy' (Still one Star shines for me) and on a separate oval card on which the miniature is mounted: 'Quadragessimo Anõ Dnĩ 1616 Vera Effigigies Ætatis Suæ 20.' A most attractive miniature of a young girl came to light comparatively recently and is on loan to the Victoria and Albert Museum. It is unusual both for its brilliant condition and the fact that it is one of the rare occasions when the artist signed his work. The young girl has upswept hair dressed with ribbons, and is wearing a low-cut dress with a high lace collar and jewels round her neck, her bodice is also edged with lace. It is inscribed on either side of the sitter: 'Anõ Dni 1609 NH' (monogram) 'Ætatis Suæ 10' (Plate 5C).

Only a small number of signed miniatures by Hilliard are known. Seven were listed by the late Basil Long and to these can be added the one of a young girl already mentioned, dated 1609, and one of an unknown man signed in monogram and dated 1572. It was Lot 124 in the Heckett Collection which was sold at Sotheby's on 11th July, 1977, when it reached the record price of £64,000, before the addition of the 10 per cent premium!

Hilliard varied the shapes of his miniatures, the majority of them are oval, but rectangular, elliptical, and the occasional circular or heart shape format is seen (Colour Plate 3C). He is known to have painted large-scale portraits, but only two can so far be attributed to him with certainty: the 'Pelican' portrait of Elizabeth I in the Walker Art Gallery, Liverpool, and the 'Phoenix' portrait in the National Portrait Gallery, London. Hilliard's design for the Queen's second Great Seal, and various medallions are different subjects and can be looked up in books recommended in the bibliography. Drawings or pen and ink sketches by him there almost certainly were, and many may lie unrecognised. One of a lady in Court costume is in the Victoria and Albert Museum, and the design for the obverse of Elizabeth I's Great Seal of Ireland, drawn c.1585 (which was not however used) is in the British Museum (Plate 6A).

Hilliard outlived his pupil and latterly his rival, Isaac Oliver, by two years, and as late as 1617 James I granted him a twelve year monopoly of Royal portraiture. In the same year we find him imprisoned, for standing security for a yeoman usher. Whether or not he painted any miniatures towards the end of his life we do not know. He was evidently a sick man when he made his will and as a token of his gratitude left "goods to the value of 10 1. to my Trustie Servannte Elizabeth Deacon my Attendant in this my sickness."

There are a few references to the prices that Hilliard was paid for his work, and indications that he sometimes made the frames. Included among the expenses of James I is a mention of "1 tablet of gold graven and enamelled blue with the picture of the princes Highness and crystal . . . £12," for a small picture sent to Mr. Heriot, the King's jeweller, he was paid £4, but for another work "of His Majesty's picture garnished with diamonds" he received £35.

I like to think of Hilliard in the words of Henry Peacham in his book *The Gentleman's Exercise,* 1612: ". . . nor must I be ingratefully unmindfull of mine owne Countriemen, who have been, and are able to equall the best, if occasion served, as old Mr. Hiliard, Mr. Isaac Oliver inferior to none in Christendome for the countenance in small . . ."

Of all Hilliard's pupils none excelled in the art of limning more than **Isaac Oliver** (d.1617) — so much was he in demand that he became a serious rival of the older man. Up to the present little is known about his early life and even the date on which he was born is in dispute. His parents were Huguenots who came from Rouen, and his father Pierre Ollivier, a goldsmith and pewterer. Dr. Hotson, in his article on Hilliard, 1970, published interesting information which may well have some bearing on the family. Professor P.F. Geisendorf, in his *Livre des Habitants de Genève,* 1957, mentions two interesting names of goldsmiths "received for inhabitants": "10 June 1555. Robert Olivier, goldsmith, native of Rouen in Normandy", and over two years later "15 October 1557. Pierre Olivyer, goldsmith, native of Rouen". It seems reasonable to suppose that Pierre Olivyer was Isaac Oliver's father. If this is so the family arrived in Geneva only a few months after Robert Bodley, his family and young Hilliard. In all probability the families met and when at a later date Pierre's son, who was already in London, decided to serve his apprenticeship, what could be more natural than that he should be placed under the care of someone as well established as Hilliard?

Isaac's year of birth is still in doubt. Certainly it was before 1568, in which year his parents fled to England from Rouen due to the religious persecutions. George Vertue gives the year of his birth as 1556, but other authorities place it at 1565/7. In any event he was presumably only a youth when the family arrived in England. His mother's name is said to have been Typhan or Tyffen, and according to the late Basil Long, a return for 1576 gives his father's name as Isaack Peter. The family lived at first at a "Mr. Harrison's house" in Fleet Street.

Unfortunately no indenture seems to have survived to give the date on

Colour Plate 3 (left).
A. **Laurence Hilliard**, *an unknown man, vellum, 2ins., c.1620.*
B. **Isaac Oliver**, *an unknown man, vellum, 2ins., c.1615.*
C. **Nicholas Hilliard**, *an unknown man painted within an inverted heart, vellum, 1⅞ins.*
D. **Peter Oliver**, *Lord Vere of Tilbury (1565-1635), vellum, 2¼ins.*
E. **Matthew Snelling**, *an unknown lady, vellum, 2½ins. Signed and dated on the reverse: 'M.S. fe / Aprill / 1655.' Miniatures by Snelling are scarce.*
Courtesy R. Bayne Powell

Plate 6A. **N. Hilliard**, *a design of the obverse of Elizabeth I's Great Seal of Ireland, pen and ink, strengthened with wash over black lead, vellum, 5ins. diameter. Inscribed: 'ELIZABET D.G. ANGLIE FRAN. ET HIBERNIE REGINA', c.1585. The design was never carried out and, although it has been suggested that it may have been a pattern for the third Great Seal of England (also never completed), the drawing includes a harp and three crowns, two essentially Irish emblems.* Courtesy The Trustees of The British Museum.

Plate 6B. **N. Hilliard**, *Queen Elizabeth I (1533-1603), playing a lute, vellum, 2ins., c.1575-80. This miniature is of great importance as one of the earliest known portraits by Hilliard of the Queen. The manner in which it is painted and the interior details and embellishments are all close in style to the work of early illuminators.* Courtesy The Trustees of Berkeley Castle.

Plate 7A. I. Oliver (d.1617). supposed self-portrait, vellum, 2¹/₈ins. This miniature does not bear a facial resemblance to the two known self-portraits of the artist. It is however a good example of the style of hat and ruff of c.1590. Gracious permission of H.M. Queen Juliana of the Netherlands.

Plate 7B. I. Oliver, an unknown lady called Arabella Stuart, vellum, 2¾ins. Signed in monogram: 'IO.' This is one of several portraits of a similar lady. This attractive miniature shows the change in hair style and low-cut embroidered dress. Courtesy The Mauritshuis, The Hague.

which Isaac Oliver became Hilliard's apprentice, and neither does his name nor that of his father appear in the minutes of the Goldsmiths' Company. In all probability he was in his early teens, and would have served about the usual seven years under his master.

Oliver appears to have had three wives, his first, said to have been called Elizabeth, died in 1599, aged twenty-eight. She bore him a son, Peter, who followed his father's profession and whose work will be discussed later. In February, 1602, Isaac married as his second wife Sarah Gheeraerts, daughter of Marcus Gheeraerts the elder, a painter who came with his son, Marcus, to England in 1568, and whose wife was Susanna de Critz. Isaac and Sarah were married at the Dutch Church of Austin Friars. The date of her death is not so far known, but another Elizabeth, by whom he had a son, Jacques, baptised 9th January, 1609, was his executrix and survived him (Plate 7C).

There was by this time a large circle of foreign artists working in London, and Oliver appears to have had a close contact, if not kinship, with some of the most influential ones such as John de Critz the Elder, the Gheeraerts, Robert Peake and Cornelius Johnson. Throughout his life Oliver remained proud of his French nationality, and only became an English subject in 1606.

With no concrete evidence to go on it is fruitless to try and speculate on the date that Oliver emerged in his own right as a mature artist. The earliest portrait at present known is of a young girl in the collection of the Duke of Buccleuch. It is signed and inscribed: 'Anno Domini 1587 Ætatis Suæ 20.' In the following year he painted a fine miniature of a man identified by Mr. E. Pelinck, Director of the Koninklijk Huisarchief, as Diederik Sonoy, a Dutch merchant who visited England in that year. The miniature, which is in the collection of H.M. Queen Juliana of the Netherlands, is signed, dated and inscribed: 'Sonder erch Verhouve. Æ Suæ 59. Aº Dmj. 1588. Isacs Olivers f.' (Plate 7D). Prior to the sitter's identification it had been thought that Oliver had gone to Holland in that year, but this now seems unlikely. From an inscription on the reverse of a miniature of Sir Arundell Talbot, in the Victoria and Albert Museum, we know that he was in Venice in 1596, and the portrait is signed and dated May 13th, the inscription, being translated, reading: "made by Isaac Oliver the Frenchman in Venice."

Oliver does not appear to have been employed by Queen Elizabeth, or if he was, no payments are recorded. An unfinished portrait of the Queen, c.1600, is in the Victoria and Albert Museum and is a realistic representation of her without any attempt to conceal the marks of her age, and even as an unfinished sketch, it represents the countenance of an ageing woman.

In spite of the fact that Nicholas Hilliard retained his position as Court limner, Isaac Oliver as an up and coming young artist made his mark, and his work was in great demand. He was in the prime of life whilst his master was past middle age and, due to his improvidence, harassed with debts which he never succeeded in paying. Payments to Oliver from the Court started during the reign of James I, and in 1604 he was appointed limner to Queen Anne of Denmark for a fee of £40. He later became a member of the household of Henry Frederick, Prince of Wales, whose portrait he painted many times. One of Oliver's outstanding limnings is of Prince Henry, in the collection of H.M. The Queen. Van Der Doort described it as "The biggest lim'd Picture that was made by Prince-Henry, being lim'd in a sett laced Roofe in a- gilded

Armo^r and Landskip by wherin some Souldiers and Tents are made, in a square frame with a shuting Glass over it."

So great was the demand for presentation portraits of the King and Queen, as well as Prince Henry and Prince Charles, that Oliver was kept busily employed producing one after another, and towards the end of his life had the assistance of his son, Peter, in completing these commissions.

His visit to Italy had fired Oliver with enthusiasm for painting historical subjects as well as miniatures of people. He copied the drawings of Parmigianino and executed a number of large limnings of historical and religious subjects. Many of these have been lost, but two accessible to the public are in the British Museum; they are the preliminary full-size drawing of 'The Burial of Christ', c.1616, containing twenty-six figures (the finished version, now lost, was in the collection of Charles I, and was completed by Peter after his father's death), and 'The Adoration of the Magi', which is signed: 'Is: Olliuier.' A few unfinished sketches and studies by Oliver also exist. An important cabinet miniature, described as 'An Elizabethan Hunting Party' or 'A Love Theme', was painted by Oliver, c.1590 (Plate 8A). It contains groups of figures set in a landscape executed in the Flemish manner, and yet is so detailed that any of the people portrayed could have been taken from his portrait miniatures of the period. These illustrate the transition between the small limnings of people and the more ambitious types of historical drawings in the manner of large oil paintings. Oliver is thought to have painted a few large oil portraits, and one of Henry, Prince of Wales, c.1610, in a private collection, is attributed to him (No. 180 in *The Elizabethan Image*, 1970).

His usual fee for a miniature appears to have been about £5 10s. to £10 according to size (Colour Plate 3C), and the late Erna Auerbach, *Nicholas Hilliard*, p.234, records that Oliver was paid £34 for "one greate Picture", which is presumed to refer to a large oil rather than a miniature.

Plate 7C. **I. Oliver,** *Mrs. Oliver, vellum, 2ins. As Oliver married three times, it is not clear which wife this represents. Her exquisitely embroidered dress is worthy of attention.* Courtesy Ivy, Duchess of Portland.

Plate 7D. **I. Oliver,** *Diederik Sonoy (b.c.1529), vellum, 2⅝ins. Signed: 'Isac^s Oliver^s f.' and inscribed: 'Sonder erch Verhouve. Æ Suae 59 A° D m̃j 1588'. Sonoy was a Dutch merchant who came over to England in the year this was painted. Note the hat and small ruff worn in Holland.* Gracious permission of H.M. Queen Juliana of the Netherlands.

Plate 7E. **I. Oliver**, *a lady in masque costume as 'Flora', vellum, 2¹/8ins. The dress is in the style of those designed by Inigo Jones for Masques held at the Court of James I.* Courtesy The Mauritshuis The Hague.

Isaac Oliver's work can be divided into three phases, the first up to 1596, when he went to Venice, was based on the work of Hilliard combined with Flemish influence. The works were executed in crisp, precise brush strokes, and the sitters painted against blue backgrounds. The second period from c.1596 shows the Italian influence, and his adaptation to the use of softer tones and more varied colours such as pinks and browns in the shading and background. He also used dark greys and black for shading (a method condemned by his master) and unlike Hilliard did not emphasise lines as opposed to tone, except when drawing hair — and even this is executed with a finer and sharper stroke. His last phase after his return to England was marked by a freer and more dramatic style in which he incorporated landscapes and interiors of rooms. Examples of this type of painting include the miniature of Richard Sackville, 3rd Earl of Dorset, in the Victoria and Albert Musuem (Plate 9), the superb rectangular miniature of Edward Herbert,

Plate 7F. **I. Oliver**, *an unknown lady, called Frances Walsingham, Countess of Essex, vellum, 2¹/8ins., c.1600. The features of the lady do not resemble those of the portrait of the Countess exhibited at the National Portrait Gallery in 1866.* Courtesy The Duke of Buccleuch and Queensberry, K.T.

Plate 7G. **I. Oliver**, *self-portrait, vellum, 2½ins. This miniature was in Horace Walpole's Collection, and he said of it: "This picture alone would justify all I have said of him. The art of the master and the imitation of nature are so great in it that the largest magnifying-glass only calls out new beauties." The miniature went into the Earl of Derby's Collection from which it was purchased by the National Portrait Gallery in 1971.* Courtesy The National Portrait Gallery.

1st Baron Herbert of Cherbury, in the collection of the Earl of Powis (Figure 2), and the ambitious painting in the Burghley House Collection of 'The Three Brothers Browne' (Plate 8B), standing in a panelled room. This latter miniature is signed in monogram and inscribed on the panelling with the age of each of the subjects. The fact that Oliver's early miniatures are painted so much in the manner of Hilliard has in the past caused a lot of confusion, and made accurate attributions difficult. Oliver's miniatures are not dated and inscribed as frequently as those of Hilliard, and those that are inscribed lack the finesse of Hilliard's flowing style. Unlike Hilliard, Oliver

Colour Plate 4.
Rowland Lockey, *Sir Thomas More, his father, his household and his descendants, vellum, 9¹¹/₁₆ins., c.1595-1600. Encased in a "walnut tree frame" with double doors. Based on a painting by H. Holbein, of which there is an oil painting by Lockey of c.1593 in the National Portrait Gallery. Other versions exist, and a pen and ink drawing by Holbein is in the Kunstmuseum, Basel. The versions have slight differences in composition. See* The King's Good Servant, *NPG Catalogue, 1977. This miniature is of outstanding merit, and in a good state of preservation.* Courtesy Victoria and Albert Museum.

frequently signed his work, the most usual signature being 'IO' in monogram surrounded by four dots. He occasionally signed in full and added a Latin or French inscription, but did not often follow his master's practice of including poetical backgrounds, symbols or emblems. A number of his miniatures show one of the sitter's hands placed in front of the bosom in a slightly theatrical manner, but drawn with better modelling than those executed by Hilliard.

Oliver painted a series of attractive miniatures of young ladies, but none is more beautiful than the large circular miniature said to represent Frances Howard, Countess of Essex and Somerset, formerly in the Derby Collection, and now in the Victoria and Albert Museum. The small but important collection belonging to the Earl of Derby was sold at Christie's on 8th June, 1971, when the one called Frances Howard realised 62,100 guineas. Three other important miniatures in this sale were bought by the National Portrait Gallery, namely, Sir Francis Drake, by Hilliard, for 33,600 guineas, Isaac Oliver's self-portrait for 39,900 guineas, and the self-portrait of Peter Oliver and that of his wife for 3,800 guineas. This is some indication of the heights to which miniature prices can rise if the portraits are of sufficient importance.

The Elizabethan love of elaborate costume and jewellery was exploited to the full by both Hilliard and Oliver, and their miniatures are a very good

Plate 8A. **I. Oliver,** *'An Elizabethan Hunting Party' or 'A Love Theme', vellum, 4³/₈ins., c.1590. This most important and ambitious miniature is executed in great detail, and gives an excellent idea of the various costumes of the period.* Present whereabouts unknown.

Plate 8B. **I. Oliver,** *'The Three Brothers Browne and their Servant', vellum, 9ins. x 10ins. Signed in monogram: 'IO'*
on the background, and inscribed with the ages of all the sitters, The Hon. John Browne, Anthony Maria Browne, 2nd
Viscount Montacute and the Hon. William Browne. The centre panel bears an inscription: 'FIGURÆ CONFORMIS
AFFECTVS. Ano Dom 1598'. This miniature is one of the most important in existence. Courtesy The Marquess of Exeter,
Burghley House Collection.

guide to change in fashion (Plate 7E). This can be studied in greater depth in
standard works of reference on costume such as *Handbook of English
Costume in the Sixteenth Century* and *Handbook of English Costume in the
Seventeenth Century,* both by C.W. and P. Cunnington. The various changes
in ladies' hair styles gave ample opportunity for artists to paint their sitters
with jewels and flowers adorning their caps and lace ruffs. When, towards the
end of the sixteenth century, higher coiffures became popular, Oliver
painted some superb miniatures with the ladies' hair decked with jewels in a
wide variety of themes, with the addition of necklaces which show to
perfection against the open neck dresses and higher open ruffs. Some of his
portraits show the sitters with flowing hair, a falling ruff, and a simple cord
of gold thread to which was probably attached a 'picture box', or locket of

cut agate or onyx. A number of miniatures representing a young woman have been *called* Lady Arabella Stuart, but are not thought to represent the lady (Pl. 7B). To study fashions in hair style through the ages one should consult *Women's Headdress and Hairstyle,* G. de Courtais, 1973.

Isaac Oliver left us a superb array of miniatures by which his work can be judged and compared with that of Hilliard. It is sad that no letters or documents have survived to tell us more about his art or personal life. In his will, proved on 30th October, 1617, he left all his drawings "already finished and unfinished and limned pictures, be they histories, stories, or anything of limning whatsoever, of my own hand work as yet unfinished . . . to my eldest son Peter, if he shall live and exercise that art or science which he and I now do".

We know that Peter did survive, and that he carried out his father's last wishes. An interesting gold portrait medallion of Queen Elizabeth I was Lot 210 in the Heckett Collection, sold at Sotheby's on 25th March, 1977. It was made and engraved by Simon de Passe (c.1595-1647) in c.1615, after the full length drawing by Isaac Oliver at Windsor Castle. The Queen is wearing the dress traditionally thought to be the one she wore to attend the Thanksgiving Service at St. Paul's after the defeat of the Armada. The medal is signed: 'Si.Pas.fe,' and engraved on the reverse with an inscription and the Arms of France and England. This medal was Lot 197 in the Pierpont Morgan sale at Christie's, 24th June, 1935 (Figures 22 and 22a).

Figure 22. Gold portrait medallion of Queen Elizabeth I by **Simon de Passe,** *after a full length drawing of the Queen at Windsor Castle by* **I. Oliver.** *This is a unique example of a medallion of this period taken from the work of a miniaturist. 3ins. Courtesy Brand Inglis.*

Figure 22a. Reverse of Figure 22, bearing the Arms of France and England. Fully inscribed and signed: 'Si. Pas. fe'. The motto beneath the coat of arms is said to have been the impromptu production of a Westminster scholar, the free translation of which reads: 'May Judah's Lion and the rod of Jesse Protect thy Lions and thy Flowers our own Sweet Bess'. 3ins. Courtesy Brand Inglis.

Plate 9. **I. Oliver,** *Richard Sackville, 3rd Earl of Dorset (1589-1624), vellum, 9¼ins. Signed: 'Isaac. Olliuierus . fecit . 1616.'*
This miniature is a superb example of a combination of an interior of a room, curtain draperies and a typical seventeenth century gallant. Note the armour, costume, embroidered stockings and fancy shoes. Courtesy Victoria and Albert Museum.

Rowland Lockey (fl.c.1581-c.1616) was probably born c.1566/9, if as is assumed he was about twelve or fifteen years of age when he became apprenticed to Nicholas Hilliard in 1581. He was the son of Leonard Lockey, a crossbow maker, who had a house in Fleet Street, in the parish of St. Bride's, London. Rowland is described as a painter, miniaturist and copyist and although he must have executed numerous works of different kinds, only a handful can be attributed to him with any degree of certainty. Once again we are faced with the problem of scanty information regarding his life and family and only a small amount of documentary evidence about his patrons and training. According to an entry in the *Apprentice Books of the Goldsmiths' Company* "I Rowland Lockey son of Lenard Lockey of thi paresh of St. Brids in Flitstrete crasbomaker haue put myself prentice to Nicholas Hilliard for the terme of 8 yiers biginning at the fest of St. Meghel in anno dni 1581

by me Rouland Lockey".

Lockey presumably ended his apprenticeship in 1589, and was probably made a freeman of the Goldsmiths' Company soon after. He was certainly a freeman by 1600, in which year the *Apprentice Book of the Goldsmiths' Company* contains a memorandum that his younger brother, Nicholas, became his apprentice for a term of eight years, beginning "Midsummer 1600". Rowland Lockey appears to have kept up his contact with Hilliard, and both their names appear in the account book of Elizabeth, Countess of Shrewsbury, for the years 1591-1597. It was no doubt through Hilliard that Lockey was introduced to Bess of Hardwick, and this connection was evidently continued as an account book of Sir William Cavendish, second husband of Bess, records a number of payments to Lockey from 1608-1613. From these payments it would appear that the artist was employed to paint most of the family. A large painting of Mary, Queen of Scots, is listed as being presented to "... my lord privy seale". This was probably either a copy of another portrait or an adaptation of one.

Apart from painting miniatures, portraits in oil and 'perspectives', he was an active goldsmith of the Goldsmiths' Company. On 23rd September, 1611, he and "five of the yeomanrie" were appointed by the Wardens "to attend with others in gownes at the Guildhall on the Lord Maiors daye for the serving up of the Dynner, to be of them in all 24".

Lockey had several apprentices, but none of them are mentioned as miniaturists nor, as far as we know, was his brother Nicholas. If he had any family they must have predeceased him, as, in his will, made on 15th February, 1615/1616, he left his wife, Martha, his executrix and, apart from certain legacies, she received all he possessed. He left his brother "all my Italian Printes and all my plasters ...", as well as the lease of his father's house in Fleet Street. The will was made when he was resident in the parish of St. Dunstan's in the West. He died during the early part of the summer of 1616.

Few miniatures can at present be ascribed to Lockey and even his large oil paintings are rare. A portrait of Margaret Beaufort, Countess of Richmond and Derby, is in St. John's College, Cambridge. It is fully signed and inscribed on the reverse and painted in 1598. Two oil paintings after Holbein of Sir Thomas More and his family exist, one painted c.1593 is in the collection of the Lord St. Oswald and signed: 'Rowlandus Locky/fecit A.D./1530' (an impossible date added later). The other painting is in the National Portrait Gallery; it is inscribed with the details of the More family and their dates. The painting is dated 1593. For full details of this painting see Dr. Roy Strong, *Tudor and Jacobean Portraits*, Vol. I, pp.345-351.

Finally Lockey painted a miniature of this group which is of great importance as far as his work on this scale is concerned. Its history is unknown until the early eighteenth century when it was purchased on 15th May, 1705, by James Sotheby for the sum of £10 15s. It is partly based on the oil painting in the National Portrait Gallery, but with variations. The Sotheby Heirlooms were sold at Sotheby's on 11th October, 1955, when this miniature, then tentatively attributed to Lockey, was sold to the Rev. and Mrs. Strickland for £2,000. It is now in the Victoria and Albert Museum. This miniature is described by George Vertue in 1741 in his *Notebooks*, V, p.10 (The Walpole Society, 1937/1938). Vertue says "... I think this limning was done at the expence of M[r]. — Thomas More after that large one

Plate 10. **P. Oliver,** *'Venus and Adonis,' after Titian, vellum, 7½ins. Signed and dated: '1631 / P. Oliuier / Fe' and inscribed on the left side: 'Titianus / Inuin'. This miniature was probably once in the collection of Charles I, as on the reverse are the initials 'CR' surmounted by a crown. It is a splendid example of this type of cabinet miniature.* **Courtesy the Marquess of Exeter, Burghley House Collection.**

done Ano 1593. — but with some variations . . . I guess the painter who painted the large one in oyl". This large cabinet miniature is in superb condition, the colours are fresh, and the painting is superior to the oil painting also by Lockey in the National Portrait Gallery. The miniature is still preserved in its early eighteenth century walnut frame which, as had already been mentioned, was made for it in 1716. One of the attractive features not in the oil painting is the inclusion of a view of Sir Thomas More's garden at his house in Chelsea (Colour Plate 4).

Amongst the few portrait miniatures which are tentatively attributed to Lockey is an attractive one of an unknown lady with a dog, painted in circular format, with a curtain and landscape background. It is in the National Gallery of Victoria, Melbourne. This miniature was No. 645 at the Loan Exhibition of Miniatures held at the South Kensington Museum (now the Victoria and Albert Museum) in 1865. It was in the collection of Mr. Hollingworth Magniac, when it was unattributed, and incorrectly identified as Mary, Queen of Scots. A set of photographs of this Exhibition taken by C. Thurston Thompson (d.1867) has recently come into my possession, and a photograph of this miniature was included. This was one of the first occasions when paintings were photographed.

The absence of signed and dated works by which others can be attributed is frustrating and, as in the case of Levina Teerlinc, it is to be hoped that some fresh information will come to light that will make it possible to identify some of the works which for the present must remain anonymous.

The reign of James I brought many changes in the art world. The romantic melancholy which pervaded the latter part of the sixteenth century, when love-lorn men were painted reclining under trees, as in the case of Lord Herbert of Cherbury, or sitting in deep contemplation with sad and gloomy expressions, reflected what was supposed to be "high intellectual abilities in the field of scholarship, philosophy and poetry", to quote Dr. Roy Strong, *The English Icon,* p.35. By c.1590, sitters began to want to see themselves more in terms of human emotions and feelings and in less symbolic attitudes. Much of the change in attitude was probably due to the advent of the great Stuart Masques, written by Ben Jonson, and staged under the direction of Inigo Jones. The first of these, *The Masque of Blackness,* was produced in 1605, and for this perspective stage scenery was used for the first time. Inigo Jones defined the masque as "nothing else but pictures with light and motion". Five years after, Henry, Prince of Wales, was given a separate household with its own offices and set about collecting pictures from Venice to adorn a gallery as well as books for a library. His patronage extended to sumptuous buildings which housed fine Italian paintings and expensive Renaissance bronzes. His sudden death in 1612 brought an end to what might have been one of the great periods in the art world. As it was, with the death of James I in 1625, it was Charles I who inherited the great love of art and gathered together one of the finest collections in the world.

Chapter III

Miniature Painting under the Early Stuarts

THE SIXTEENTH CENTURY was drawing to a close when in c.1597 **Laurence Hilliard** (1581/2-1647/8) began his apprenticeship under his father. Laurence was the fourth of eight children born to Nicholas and Alice Hilliard. He was baptised at St. Vedast, Foster Lane, London, on 5th March, 1582 and, allowing the usual term of eight years' apprenticeship, his training was completed by 7th June, 1605, when he was declared freeman of the Goldsmiths' Company. He was the only one of the family to follow his father's profession, and from letters written to Sir Robert Cecil, we know that Nicholas was proud of his son's education and anxious that he should be provided for. Writing to Sir Robert on 28th July, 1601, Hilliard says "I hope you (in remembrance of your loving kindness promised) will take my son into your service, to place him with one of your secretaries or otherwise. He has the Spanish tongue, and an entrance into well writing and drawing . . ." Hilliard is obviously distressed that due to financial reasons he cannot keep Laurence working with him. In a letter of 1606, Hilliard writes of Laurence "doing His Majesty good service both in limned pictures and in medals of gold". On 13th October, 1608, a patent was drawn up appointing Laurence 'his Majesty's limner' in reversion after the death of his father, an office which carried with it an annuity of £40.

Plate 11A. L. Hilliard, an unknown man aged thirty-seven in 1636, vellum, 1¾ins. Signed: 'LH' and inscribed: 'Ano Dñi 1636 Ætatis Suae, 37'. This is one of the few signed miniatures by Laurence. It is painted in his father's manner, but lacks his attention to detail on the costume. Courtesy The Earl Beauchamp.

Laurence took an active part in the proceedings of the Goldsmiths' Company, and in 1611 was one of the 'batchelors' asked to wear suitable apparel for the Lord Mayor's show and to serve. On 28th October of the same year he was listed as one of the 'Budg Batchelors', which meant that he was wearing fur. He leased a tenement in Gutter Lane from c.1612, and this lease was renewed in 1613 for a further twenty-one years. By this time he appears to have been occupying a house in Fleet Street, to which he was returning on the evening of 18th June, 1622, when he was attacked by "four turbulent people", and his right hand was so badly damaged that he lost the use of one of his fingers. This seriously affected his painting, and the case went to court.

Unlike his father Laurence seems to have been careful with money, and owned property. He became a "perfect and sole tenant of the Manor of Tythehurst [Ticehurst], Sussex", and property near "Witingham", in the County of Lancaster, which was granted to him by Sir Richard Hogton, for the payment of £500.

The date of Laurence Hilliard's marriage is not known, but he and his wife, Jane, who survived him, had four children, Brandon, Thomas, Charles, and a daughter, Laurence, to whom he was especially attached.

Plate 11B (far left). **L. Hilliard,** *portrait of an unknown woman, vellum, 2³/16ins. Signed: 'HL' (monogram). This is a splendid example of the wide-brimmed hat of the period, and stiff ruff. Courtesy Victoria and Albert Museum.*

Plate 11C (left). **P. Oliver,** *Sir Robert Harley, K.B. (1580-1656), vellum, 2³/8ins. Signed in monogram: 'PO' surrounded by four dots, and inscribed with a motto: 'ter & amplius'. This fine portrait shows to perfection the falling ruff, edged with point lace, the doublet embroidered with black flowers, and round his neck the red ribbon of the Order of the Bath. It is set in a gold locket with a bloodstone back. Courtesy Ivy, Duchess of Portland.*

Plate 11D. **P. Oliver,** *Charles I, when Prince of Wales (1600-1649), vellum, 2¹/8ins. Signed with the monogram: 'PO', surrounded by four dots and dated '1621'. This portrait is close in style to that of Sir Robert Harley, and shows Peter Oliver's development of a freer and more relaxed representation of his sitters.* Gracious permission of H.M. The Queen.

James I seems to have made regular payments to Laurence Hilliard, and in 1624 he paid him £40 for five pictures, which were presumably miniatures at £8 apiece. He was also employed by William Cecil, 2nd Earl of Salisbury, but these commissions seem to have been decorative work of a heraldic nature, rather than miniatures. Of his sons, Brandon became a member of the Goldsmiths' Company, Charles also worked as a goldsmith (in his will proved in 1675 he bequeathed large sums of money to the Goldsmiths' Company), and Thomas was a painter-stainer, who had a house in St. Brides, having married on 20th January, 1623/4 Anne Baker, at St. Andrew in the Wardrobe. Erna Auerbach in *Nicholas Hilliard,* 1961, gives many interesting details regarding the family.

Laurence Hilliard signed his will on 21st February, 1640, appointing his wife, Jane, his executrix. When he died she did not wish to exercise the right, and the will was proved and probate granted to his son, Thomas, on 8th March, 1647/8.

It is impossible to judge how many miniatures the young Hilliard painted. He is known to have helped his father in his studio, and to have been responsible for many of the stock replicas of presentation miniatures representing James I and Queen Anne, but none of them is at present identifiable. Only a few signed miniatures by him have survived, and these bear a Roman monogram: 'LH' or 'HL'. Other portraits are attributed to him on the basis of style. Those that are known show only the bust of the sitter, three-quarter view, the men's portraits turned to the left, and those of the women to the right. He used a variety of blue and cerise curtain backgrounds, and some of his miniatures are painted in the manner of his father on blue with a gold flowing inscription. The general appearance of his miniatures is close in style to that of Nicholas, but he does not appear to have attempted any ambitious compositions, and the productions lack the brilliance so apparent in the older man's work (Colour Plates 3A and 6B).

The best known signed miniature by Laurence is the portrait of a lady wearing a broad-brimmed hat, in the Victoria and Albert Museum. The miniature, which has a gold background, is signed in monogram 'H', and was painted c.1615-1630 (Plate 11B). Two fine miniatures, both painted against a blue background, are in the collection of the Earl Beauchamp, one of an unknown man, signed 'LH' and inscribed: 'Ano Dñi 1636. Ætatis Suæ 37' (Plate 11A), and the other signed 'LH' and inscribed: 'Año Dñi 1638. Ætatis Svæ 31.' A miniature of an unknown man aged sixty-five is in the Fitzwilliam Museum, Cambridge, and is signed 'LH' and inscribed: 'Ano Dni. 1640 Ætatis Suæ 65.' Amongst the other miniatures attributed to Laurence is one of an unknown Countess, with a ladybird painted on her ruff. This was formerly in the Buckingham Collection at Stowe. Another one of interest shows an unknown man wearing an embroidered black doublet with a lace ruff, painted against a brilliant blue background. It is inscribed in cursive writing: 'Año Dñi. 1621. Ætatis suæ 74.' The miniature is in the Hilliard tradition and set into a period locket of green translucent enamel, with a diamond and a drop pearl suspended from the base (Figure 14).

Although according to his father the young Hilliard executed gold medals for the King, I am not aware of any having been positively identified as his work.

In spite of the fact that the art of Laurence Hilliard cannot be compared with that of his father or of the Olivers, as a follower and pupil of Nicholas Hilliard he is an important link in the history of miniature painting at a time when only a handful of artists were keeping it alive.

Plate 11E (far left). **P. Oliver,** *Frederick V, Elector Palatine and King of Bohemia (1596-1648), vellum, 2ins. Signed in monogram: 'PO' within four dots, c.1620. This miniature is similar in style to Plates 11C and D. Frederick wears a black figured doublet with slashed sleeves and a falling lace collar. The blue Garter ribbon is about his neck. The portrait is set in an eighteenth century gold and diamond frame.* Private Collection.

Plate 11F (left). **P. Oliver,** *Elizabeth of Bohemia (1596-1662), daughter of James I and wife of Frederick V, vellum, 2ins. Signed in monogram: 'PO', c.1620. The Queen is wearing a broad upstanding collar and a jewelled low cut robe decorated with pink ribbon rosettes. It is a pair to Plate 11E and set in a similar frame.* Private Collection.

Colour Plate 5.

A. **John Hoskins** *after Van Dyck, Lady Mary Villiers, Duchess of Richmond and Lennox (1622-85), vellum, 4⅝ins. This miniature was at one time attributed to Samuel Cooper, but is almost certainly by J. Hoskins. Other versions of this portrait exist including the large enamel by J. Petitot in the Nationalmuseum, Stockholm (Plate 33D). The original is in the Collection of H.M. The Queen.*

B. **Lawrence Cross(e)**, *Lady Elizabeth Cavendish, Duchess of Albemarle and Duchess of Montagu (1655-1734), vellum, 3⁷/₁₆ins. Signed: 'LC' (monogram).*

C. **Lawrence Cross(e)**, *John Holles, Duke of Newcastle, K.G. (1662-1711), vellum, 3⁵/₁₆ins. Signed: 'LC' (monogram), and inscribed on the reverse: 'John Duke of New Castle, L.Cross F :.'*

Courtesy Ivy, Duchess of Portland.

Plate 11G. **P. Oliver,** *Edmund Waller, the poet (1606-1687), vellum, 2⁵/₁₆ins. Signed in monogram: 'PO' surrounded by four dots. Note the difference in hair style on this miniature: it is flat on the crown and falls in curls over the sitter's left shoulder. The black doublet is slashed with white, with a falling collar edged with point lace. The sitter is painted against a blue background within a gold border.* Courtesy Ivy, Duchess of Portland.

Peter Oliver (c.1594-1647) was the eldest son of Isaac Oliver by his first wife, Elizabeth (d.1599). He studied under his father and assisted him in his studio. Peter presumably started his apprenticeship as a youth of about fifteen years of age and does not appear to have ever set up on his own during his father's lifetime. Isaac Oliver was kept busily employed producing miniatures of King James I and other members of the Royal family, and no doubt many of the stock replicas were either finished off by Peter, or even painted by him as he became more accomplished. The fact that father and son worked so closely together, and that neither always signed his work has made accurate identification difficult, particularly after Peter finished his apprenticeship in c.1610 and up to his father's death in 1617. In his will made on 4th June, 1617, Isaac Oliver had every confidence in Peter being able to carry on the work and left him his paintings as follows: ". . . except all my drawings allready finished and unfinished and lymning pictures be they historyes, or any thing of lymning whatsoever of my owne hande worke as yet unfinished; all which I give and bequeathe to my eldest sonne Peter, yf he shall live and exercise that arte or science which he and I nowe doe . . ."

Little is known about Peter's private life, nor do we know if he married more than once. One Pierre Ollivier, of London, married Catherinne de la Haye, also born in London, 26th December, 1626, and/or the same Pierre Olivier, born in London married in London, 26th December, 1638, a widow named Rosse du Moulin, born at Valenciennes. He did not, as far as we know, have any family, and the name of the wife who survived him was Anne. In his will made on 12th December, 1647 and proved 15th December 1648, he appointed Anne sole heir and executrix to his estate and house at Isleworth. Peter was evidently a sick man when his will was made and it was signed only with his mark. Only ten days later, on 22nd December, 1647, Peter Oliver was buried at St. Anne's, Blackfriars, two years before his patron Charles I went to the scaffold.

Peter's early works are close in style to those of his father's later paintings with a broader and freer modelling. Like his contemporaries he painted on vellum stuck on to card, the shapes of his miniatures varying from oval to

Plate 12. **P. Oliver,** *after Raphael, The Madonna and Child with the infant St. John, vellum, 9½ins., brush and grey ink. Inscribed: 'Raf Vrbino / Imitator' and signed: 'P. Oliuier.fe / 1631'. This is a good example of one of the large subject pictures for which P. Oliver was noted, and was formerly in the John Evelyn Collection.* Courtesy Christie's.

74

heart shape and, in the case of his large pieces, rectangular. The greater number of his original portraits were painted in the 1620s. Basil Long in *British Miniaturists,* p.321, lists two dated 1619, and signed cabinet miniatures after the works of Titian, Correggio, Raphael, etc., date from c.1628 until c.1639. In the catalogue of this latter year compiled by Abraham Van Der Doort, no less than fourteen "limnd peeces" by Peter Oliver were in the King's Collection. Details of these paintings are to be found in *Abraham Van Der Doort's Catalogue of the Collection of Charles I,* The Walpole Society, Vol. XXXVII, edited by Sir Oliver Millar, 1960.

Peter Oliver was a good draughtsman and some of his work is considered to be of a finer quality than that of his father, to be more life-like, and to show more character in the sitters' faces. He used a variety of colours on his backgrounds, blue, grey, violet and brown being predominant; occasionally he introduced a reddish curtain to the rear of the sitter. His usual signature is a monogram 'PO', the P cuts the O, and the monogram is often surrounded by four dots, following the type of monogram used by his father (Plate 11C). He also signed some of his works in full, as in the case of two large limnings in the Victoria and Albert Museum: 'Tarquin and Lucretia', signed: 'P. Oliuier / Fe:', and 'The Flight into Egypt', signed and dated: '1628 / Pe: Oliuier/Fec-.' An interesting drawing by Oliver from the John Evelyn Collection was Lot 152 at Christie's on June 14th, 1977. It is after Raphael, of the Madonna and Child with St. John as an infant, and is signed and inscribed: 'Raf: Vrbino / Imitator' on the left and signed on a rock on the right: 'P.Oliuier. fe. / 1631' (Plate 12). George Vertue mentions having seen the drawing in 1741, and the fact that it had been copied from the original in Charles I's collection. Its provenance goes back to Peter Oliver's widow, from whom it was bought by Jerome Laniere, who in turn sold it to John Evelyn for £20.

We know that in at least one instance Peter carried out his father's wishes to complete his works. The historical piece of 'The Burial of Christ' was finished by Peter from his father's drawing, which is in the British Museum. The finished limning which was listed by Van Der Doort in Charles I's collection is now lost. Van Der Doort records it in detail, and notes that it was 11½ins. by 1ft. 3½ins., "Which peece was begun by the old Oliver and since by yor Ma^{ts} appointm^t finished by his sonn Peter Oliver".

The fact that Charles I not only continued the Royal patronage after the death of James I in 1625, but commissioned Oliver to copy many famous oil paintings in 'little', must have kept him busy. These large limnings would have taken a long time to produce, and consequently Peter would have had little time to devote to original portraiture. The large copies were made for Charles I from paintings in his collection, and the limnings went into the Royal Collection on completion. It is said that Charles I liked to carry the small copies with him on his travels. After his death, when the Royal Collection was plundered and dispersed, many of these limnings were lost, and only a proportion of them was ever recovered. Interesting though these copies of historical pieces are, they do not have the same appeal as original works or portraits from life.

Peter Oliver's self-portrait, and that of his wife, drawn in black lead on vellum, formerly in the Derby Collection, is now in the National Portrait Gallery. It is signed 'PO' in monogram, and inscribed: 'se ipse fe.' Another self-portrait of Oliver is in the collection of H.M. The Queen.

As with other artists in Britain, Oliver came under the influence of Titian, whose works he copied, and the Venetian style of painting made a great impression on his work. He was prepared to experiment with colours, and according to Edward Norgate in his *Miniatura*, c.1648, he tried some of Sir Nathaniel Bacon's pink, which he thought so good that he "... used none other to his dying day".

As is to be expected, Oliver executed numerous replicas of Charles I, Elizabeth of Bohemia, her husband, Frederick V, Elector Palatine (Plates 11E and F), and an attractive girl called variously 'Lady Arabella Stuart', or probably more correctly 'Lady Venetia Digby'. Amongst his most important copies of portraiture is the diptych at Sherborne Castle of Sir Kenelm and Lady Digby, after Van Dyck. Small miniatures by Oliver of Sir Kenelm Digby, also based on Van Dyck, have appeared in the sale rooms from time to time.

Little is known about the latter part of Peter Oliver's life, and he does not appear to have any dated works after the large drawing of 1640, now at Windsor, representing the Holy Family and St. John after Raphael. After the Restoration, Charles II was anxious to recover as much as possible of his father's art collection and, hearing that Peter Oliver's widow was alive and had many of his miniatures including some copies of paintings he had executed for Charles I, the King decided to visit Mrs. Oliver. He chose a number of miniatures for which he granted her a pension of £300 a year. When, later, she heard that he had given some of them to his mistresses, she was unwise enough to remark that had she known that they would have been given to "such whores, bastards or strumpets, the King should never have had them". This remark got back to the King, and apparently her pension ceased!

Examples of Peter Oliver's work are in the Victoria and Albert Museum, the National Portrait Gallery, the British Museum, the Ashmolean Museum, Oxford, the Rijksmuseum, Amsterdam, and a number of private collections including those of H.M. The Queen, the Duke of Portland and the Earl Beauchamp. (Colour Plate 3D.)

Edward Norgate (bapt.1581, d.1650) was the second son of Dr. Robert Norgate, Master of Corpus Christi College, Cambridge, where he was born.

Colour Plate 6.
A. **Bernard Lens,** *called Mary Queen of Scots, vellum, 2¾ins. Signed in monogram and inscribed: 'Maria Regina Scotorum BL', and on the reverse: 'Bernard Lens Juni* Fecit et Londini 1720.' *Several versions and copies of this portrait exist.*
B. **Laurence Hilliard,** *an unknown countess, wearing a ladybird on her ruff, vellum, 2⁵/₁₆ins.*
C. **George Perfect Harding, F.S.A.,** *called The Countess of Pembroke, watercolour on card, 2ins. Signed in monogram: 'GPH' surrounded by dots. This is the only known miniature on this scale bearing this monogram, and as such is documentary.*
D. **Bernard Lens,** *Miss Elizabeth Whitmore (1710-35), daughter of William and Elizabeth Whitmore, ivory, 3ins. It was one of a series of fifteen miniatures of the family sold in 1971. Elizabeth and her mother were buried on the same day at Lower Slaughter, Gloucestershire. Signed in monogram: 'BL.' and inscribed with the sitter's name and age on the reverse.*
E. **Andrew Benjamin Lens,** *an unknown young girl, ivory, 2ins., c.1750-60.*
F. **David des Grange,** *James Stuart, 4th Duke of Lennox (1612-55), son of Esme, 3rd Duke of Lennox, vellum, 3¹/₈ins. This miniature was once in the collection of the late H.J. Pfungst, when it was first identified by experts as the Duke when on loan to the Victoria and Albert Museum in 1914.*
G. *Attributed to* **Peter Cross,** *an unknown lady wearing an attractive lace cap tied with black ribbon under her chin, vellum, 2¹/₈ins.*
Private Collection

Plate 13A. **E. Norgate,** *Mrs. Edward Norgate, née Judith Lanier (c.1592-c.1617), vellum, 2⁵/₃₂ins. This miniature is a replica of another one by Norgate which is at the Victoria and Albert Museum and is signed and dated by the artist on the reverse: '1617'. The costume is attractive and the lace cap, collar and bodice are exquisitely painted.* Courtesy Miss Lawson-Tancred.

Plate 13B. **E. Norgate,** *John Harrison, Junior (1598-1650), vellum, 2¼ins., c.1620. Note the costume, tied falling collar and beard. This miniature bears the sitter's coat of arms in miniature on the reverse, dated: '1622'.* Courtesy Miss Lawson-Tancred.

Norgate is chiefly associated with the art of illuminating, but was also a miniaturist, and as such deserves a place in the story of those who contributed to the art of limning in the seventeenth century. His treatise, *Miniatura or the Art of Limning,* which was edited by Martin Hardie and published in 1919 from the MS in the Bodleian Library, Oxford, is of great importance and contains much valuable information. Norgate became well-known in London, and included amongst his friends many of the leading painters of the day including Van Dyck and Sir Balthasar Gerbier. He held various positions at the Courts of James I and Charles I, including that of tuner and "Keeper of his Majesties virginals, organs and other instruments" (1611). He was a versatile man, and described as "A Civil servant, calligrapher, miniaturist, art expert and musician, as well as herald". Edward was brought up by his stepfather, Nicholas Felton, Master of Pembroke College, Cambridge, and Bishop of Ely. He studied limning and heraldry in London, possibly in the household of Lord Arundel, whose sons were his pupils. He became Blue Mantle Pursuivant in 1616, Windsor Herald, 1633, and Clerk of the Signet, 1638, and was employed to take letters to the Continent and Ireland from 1612 onwards, and received payment for writing and limning letters to foreign sovereigns. In 1639 he accompanied Charles I to Scotland and in the same year was commissioned to purchase pictures for Queen Henrietta Maria and went to the Low Countries. In 1646 he went to Holland with Lord Stanhope. Only a very small number of authentic miniatures by Norgate are at present known. The first to be identified was a portrait of his first wife, Judith, née Lanier, whom he married in 1613 and who died c.1617. This miniature is in the Victoria and Albert Museum, and a replica is in a private collection. The miniature in the Victoria and Albert Museum is inscribed and signed on the reverse: 'Juditha Norgate. 1617. æt 25. Non obijt sed abijt Pudicitæ, Pietatis, et Venustatis rarissimum decus. Suaussimæ Conjugi Ed: Norgate.' the translation of which reads: '. . . She has not died: she has departed. Rarest ornament of Modesty, Affection and Beauty. To his most sweet wife, Ed: Norgate". He married as his second wife Ursula Brighouse of Coleby, Lincolnshire, on 15th October, 1619, at St. Margaret's, Westminster; they had three sons and two daughters.

Among the few authentic miniatures by Norgate there exists a replica of the one of his wife already mentioned which is in a fine state of preservation (Plate 13A); one of a man thought to represent John Harrison, Junior (painted c.1620) (Plate 13B); one of his coat of arms, and one of his wife, Mary, née Buceuham (painted c.1630) (Plate 13E). These last four belong to the Lawson-Tancred family, who also possess an oil portrait of Mary Harrison dated 1630. John Harrison was interested in heraldry, and may have been friendly with, or related to, Norgate. There may even have been a link with the Olivers, as it was at a "Mr. Harrison's house" in Fleet Street that the Oliver family lived when they came to London in 1568.

Norgate's miniatures are executed meticulously and are in the Hilliard/Oliver tradition. The sitters' hair is painted in fairly thick strands, and the details of the costume finely portrayed. It is to be hoped that more of his works can be traced. One of an unknown gentleman, c.1605, was sold at Sotheby's, Lot 74, 29th March, 1965, when it was tentatively attributed to Norgate and realised £1,000.

Sir Balthasar Gerbier (1592-1667) was born in Middelburg, 23rd February, 1592. He was the son of Anthony Gerbier, by his wife, Radigonde Blavet, who were Protestant refugees. He may have been a pupil of Hendrik Golzius (1558-1616), and a number of Gerbier's small portraits in pen and ink are in the manner of Golzius. Gerbier was a man of parts, described as an adventurer, painter, courtier, architect, musician, author, lecturer and diplomatist! Besides all these accomplishments, he was a good linguist. His wife's name does not appear to have been recorded, but she bore him at least eight children, three sons and five daughters. Gerbier went to Rome where he made copies in crayon of paintings by Raphael. His knowledge of architecture, fortifications and armaments brought him to the notice of Prince Maurice of Orange, in whose service he was in 1615. A miniature by him of the Prince is in the collection of H.M. Queen Juliana of the Netherlands. By 1616 Gerbier was in England, where he entered the service of the Duke of Buckingham, and became known at Court. His varied interests and accomplishments brought him into contact with many people of importance both in the art world and politics. He knew Rubens, with whom he corresponded, and who stayed with him in London, and was connected with Edward Norgate in business relating to diplomacy and the

Plate 13C. **Sir Balthasar Gerbier,** *George Villiers, 1st Duke of Buckingham, K.G. (1592-1628), vellum, 5ins. Signed and dated: 'BGerbier / 1618', and inscribed: 'Fidei Coticula Crux'. This splendid equestrian portrait is one of Gerbier's finest works.* Courtesy The Duke of Northumberland.

Royal Collection. He travelled widely, and most of his life was taken up with politics. In 1628 he entered the service of Charles I, and was knighted in the same year. In 1631 he was sent by the King as envoy to Brussels, where he betrayed his position of trust by giving information to the Infanta Isabella regarding secret negotiations between Charles I and the revolutionary nobles of the Spanish Netherlands. He left Brussels in 1641, so heavily in debt that he had difficulty in financing the return of his family. In 1652 he opened an Academy in his house in Bethnal Green, London, where he gave lectures and published pamphlets. After various visits to Holland and Surinam, he set off with his family on a mining project in Guiana. A mutiny broke out when they reached Cayenne, and his followers killed his daughter, Katherine. He was saved by the arrival of the Governor. After the Restoration he failed to regain his position at Court, and turned his attention to architecture. He died whilst supervising the building of Lord Craven's house at Hampstead Marshall in 1667, and was buried in the chancel of the church there.

Works by Gerbier are scarce; they include miniatures drawn in pen and ink and crayons as well as miniatures on vellum. One of his finest miniatures is in the collection of the Duke of Northumberland. It is of George Villiers, 1st Duke of Buckingham, K.G. (1592-1628), portrayed mounted on a prancing horse and holding a lance. It is signed and dated: 'BGerbier / 1618' and inscribed: 'Fidei Coticula Crux' (the cross is the touchstone of faith). The miniature is superbly painted and the horse trappings almost gem-like

Plate 13D. **Sir Balthasar Gerbier,** *an unknown man aged twenty-two in 1616, pencil on vellum, 3²⁷/₃₂ins. Signed: 'BGerbier fecit / 1616', and inscribed: 'Ætatis XXII'. The outer edge of the miniature has a further inscription, the free translation of which would seem to be: 'I spread my wings to the sky advancing towards the Cross.'* Courtesy Victoria and Albert Museum, Alan Evans Collection.

Plate 13E. **E. Norgate,** *Mrs. John Harrison, née Mary Buceuham (b. c.1610), wife of John Harrison Junior, vellum, 2¼ins., c.1630. This charming miniature is yet another guide to costume, the wide-brimmed hat and deep white collar edged with lace set off the design on the dress.* Courtesy Miss Lawson-Tancred.

(Plate 13C). A triple portrait, by W. Dobson, of Dobson, Sir C. Cotterell and a man said to be Gerbier is in the Northumberland Collection. Examples of his work are in the British Museum, and the Pepys Library, Cambridge. A fine miniature of an unknown man aged twenty-two in 1616 is in the Alan Evans Collection in the Victoria and Albert Museum. It is signed: 'B GERBIER Fecit / 1616' (the first two letters in monogram), and inscribed round the outer edge: 'au Ciel je tends les aislos cheminant sur la Croix' (I spread my wings to the sky advancing towards the cross) (Plate 13D).

Sir James Palmer (1584-1657) was the third son of Sir Thomas Palmer of Wingham, Kent and his wife, née Margaret Pooley. Palmer is best known as a connoisseur of art and as adviser to Charles I, with whom he became friendly. A miniature copy of Titian's 'Tarquin and Lucretia' by Palmer was listed by Van Der Doort. This was given to the King by the artist and is now lost. Although he was known to have been a limner, no miniatures by him had been authenticated until Graham Reynolds wrote an article in the *Burlington Magazine,* Vol. 91. In this he supplied fresh evidence of Palmer's work as a limner, and details about a series of miniatures signed in monogram 'JP', much in the manner of Isaac Oliver's monogram. This led to the identification of his work by a comparison with family portraits of Sir James's wife, father, and mother-in-law still in the possession of his descendants. Only a few miniatures by him are at present known, and these have an affinity with the works of Hilliard and Oliver. He appears to have had a mannerism which is useful to remember, in that he wrote the date of

Plate 14A. Attributed to **C. Johnson the Elder,** *an unknown man, oils on copper, 2³/₈ins., c.1639. In a Bernard Lens 'pear tree' frame.* **Courtesy Ivy, Duchess of Portland.**

Plate 14B. **C. Johnson the Elder,** *an unknown man, oils on copper, 2¹/₈ins. Signed and dated on the reverse: 'C. Johnson Fecit 1639'. Framed by B. Lens in May, 1719. This miniature is rich in tone, and perfectly drawn with great expression. It is close in style to Plate 14A.* **Courtesy Ivy, Duchess of Portland.**

Plate 14C. **Sir James Palmer,** called *Henry Wriothesley, 3rd Earl of Southampton, vellum, 1⅞ins. Signed and dated: '1623 IP' (monogram). The monogram is very similar to that used by P. Oliver. It is one of the rare examples of this artist's work.* Courtesy Sotheby's.

the miniature horizontally across the background, and used a rather scratchy stroke for shading under the sitter's chin. For further details see *A Dictionary of British Miniature Painters,* 1972, p.434-435. Palmer's son, Roger, was the husband of the notorious Countess of Castlemaine. He died in 1657. (Plate 14C).

Wenceslaus Hollar (1607-1677) did not play a major part in the history of miniature painting, and is best known for his etchings and engravings which include landscapes and portraits. He was born at Prague on 13th July, 1607, the son of a Court official, and left the city during the political troubles in 1619. Hollar went to Frankfurt where he became a pupil of M. Merian, a topographical engraver. His work as a miniaturist is known only by an example in the collection of H.M. The Queen, at Windsor. The portrait represents Margaret Roper, daughter of Sir Thomas More, and was probably copied from a portrait by Holbein. Among Hollar's best known works are his illustrations for Thoroton's *Antiquities of Nottinghamshire,* 1677.

Hollar became known to Thomas Howard, 2nd Earl of Arundel, with whom he came to London in 1636. He was captured by the Parliamentarians at the siege of Basing House in 1645, but later escaped, and by 1644 was living at Antwerp. Travelling appealed to him and he returned to London where he died on 25th March, 1677.

Cornelius Johnson, the Elder (1593-1661/2) was baptised in London, 14th October, 1593. His name has been spelt in various ways including Jonson and Jansenns, but the modern usage is Johnson. His family came from Cologne, but later settled in Antwerp, and from there fled to London where Cornelius was born. Nothing appears to be known about his artistic training or early education. He is best known for his large oil portraits, but painted a small number of oil miniatures which are of great importance, and is reputed to have executed some in watercolour. No signed examples in this latter medium have so far been discovered, and it may well be that some of the miniatures which are unattributed are by him.

Among his acquaintances was John Hoskins (d.1665), a contemporary miniaturist, and it is interesting to note that there is a slight similarity in the way the two artists worked, and interpreted the character of their sitters with a shy reticence, rather than the more grandiose manner of earlier artists.

Johnson married on 16th July, 1622 a lady called Elizabeth Beck, or Beke, and the couple made their home in Blackfriars, London. He had been brought up within the group of closely connected families of French or Flemish origin who had sought refuge in England during the religious persecutions. These included the Olivers, the Gheeraerts and the De Critzes, who all congregated in the area of the Dutch Reformed Church of Austin Friars. Johnson's early work is generally considered to be based on a combination of the Anglo-Netherlandish style and the more English approach reflected in the later works of Hilliard.

From c.1630-1640 Johnson spent much of his time at Bridge in Kent, where he obtained a number of commissions for large portraits from well-known families. After Van Dyck became established in England, Johnson's work was not in such demand. This, combined with the outbreak of the Civil War, led his wife to persuade him to leave the country, and in 1643 the family left for Holland. They went first to Middleburg, where Cornelius became a member of the Painters' Guild, and from there went to

Plate 14D. **C. Johnson the Elder,** *Mrs. Peter Vanderput, née Jane Hoste, oils on copper, 3⁷/8ins. A fine example of Johnson's work, showing a pillar and landscape background. Note the deep lace-edged collar and drop pearl earrings.* Courtesy Lord Thomson of Fleet.

Plate 14E. **C. Johnson the Elder,** *Peter Vanderput, son of Giles Vanderput, a merchant of London whose family originated in Antwerp, oils on copper, 3⁷/8ins. A trace of a signature is visible. Husband of Plate 14D. Both are superb examples of miniatures in this medium.* Courtesy Lord Thomson of Fleet.

Amsterdam, where he continued to paint until his death in Utrecht or Amsterdam in c.1661/2. He is said to have married a second time and to have been ruined by his wife's extravagance. His son, Cornelius Johnson the Younger (b. after 1622) followed his father's profession in Holland.

Examples of Johnson's work in miniature are scarce. The Duke of Portland has two, one of an unknown man is signed on the reverse: 'C. Johnson Fecit 1639.' It is oils on copper and the sitter is wearing a black doublet slashed with white, and a falling ruff. The dark background is typical of his work (Plate 14B). Another miniature of an unknown man is in the collection of the Duke of Devonshire, and a superb pair of miniatures of Mr. and Mrs. Peter Vanderput are in the collection of Lord Thomson of Fleet. There is a trace of a signature on both portraits, which were Nos. 222 and 223 in the Samuel Cooper Exhibition at the National Portrait Gallery in 1974. The sitters were of London: Peter was a merchant, and his wife, Jane, née Hoste, the daughter of a merchant. Both portraits have an attractive landscape background (Plates 14D and E). Johnson signed his work 'CJ' in monogram as well as in full and with his initials. His price for a head was said to be "five broad pieces". Many of his works in miniature were copies of large paintings. A set of three small full-length portraits by Johnson have just been purchased by the National Portrait Gallery. They represent three of Charles I's children — Charles II, James II and Princess Mary — and were painted for Charles I in c.1640. At the time of the King's death they were in the hands of Jan van Belcamp, when their total value was put at £6! The portraits only measure 11½ inches in depth and are painted very much in the style of a miniaturist. Each sitter is placed against a curtain and landscape background with scenes of troops, huntsmen and, in the case of Princess Mary, a garden. The portrait of Prince Charles is signed: 'CJ' (Plate 15). A large supposed self-portrait, signed 'CJ' and dated 1636 (No. 1887 in the National Portrait Gallery), is not now thought to represent the artist.

Plate 15. **C. Johnson the Elder,** *Charles II (1630-1685) when Prince of Wales, oils on panel, 11½ins. This portrait was painted for Charles I, c.1640, together with one of Princess Mary and another of James II when Duke of York. Traces of a signature 'CJ' can be seen on this painting. The three portraits are now at the National Portrait Gallery. They are meticulously painted and show the influence of miniature painting.* Courtesy John Morton Morris.

Plate 16A. J. Hoskins, *Robert Carr or Ker, Earl of Somerset* (d. 1645), vellum, 1⅝ins. Signed in monogram: 'IH' on the curtain background, c.1620-30. This is an early work by Hoskins. Courtesy Mr. and Mrs. John Starr, Kansas City.

Plate 16B (left). J. Hoskins, *Elizabeth Rogers, Viscountess Mansfield, afterwards Duchess of Richmond* (d. 1661), vellum, 2⅜ins. Signed: '1655 / iH.' This attractive miniature shows the change in dress and coiffure. The sitter's hair is swept back flat over her head into a bun, and falls in curls over her shoulders. A simple string of pearls was fashionable, as was a low-cut dress. Hers is lilac colour, with a blue scarf over one arm, and a green curtain background to set the portrait off. Courtesy Ivy, Duchess of Portland.

A typical example of how Johnson was influenced by Van Dyck is his large group of Arthur, 1st Baron Capel, and his family, c.1640. This is in the collection of the Earl of Wilton, and is based on the painting by Van Dyck of the King and Queen with their two eldest children, painted in 1632. Some of Johnson's portraits have great charm, whilst others are unambitious.

John Hoskins (d.1664/5) was one of the great miniaturists of the early part of the seventeenth century. In spite of much research, details about his birth and early life have so far proved elusive. Judging from the fact that his earliest miniatures dated from c.1620, he was probably born before the end of the sixteenth century. The approximate date of c.1595 has been suggested, allowing time for his apprenticeship. It is generally accepted that his miniatures were the finest painted in England between the death of Nicholas Hilliard and the rise to fame of Hoskin's nephew, Samuel Cooper, who will be dealt with in the next chapter. Information of vital importance to the Hoskins and Cooper families has been discovered by Miss Mary Edmond, who has kindly allowed me to publish her findings. In the registers in the Guildhall Library relating to St. Nicholas Cole Abbey (first reg. Guildhall MS 5685) she discovered an entry for 1st September, 1607, for the marriage of 'Richard Cowper of the parish and Barbara Hoskens.' The marriage took place by Faculty Office licence, and the bride's father, John (i.e. John Hoskins' father) was "in yᵉ Fleett" [Prison] at the time. For what reason we do not know! Miss Edmond also discovered the marriage of Roger Johnsonne and Mary Hoskins, both of the parish of St. Nicholas Cole Abbey, on 30th April, 1609. Mary was presumably John Hoskins' sister. Thus the exact relationship between John Hoskins and his nephews, Samuel and Alexander Cooper, is explained at last. They were the sons of Richard and Barbara Cooper, and Alexander was baptised at St. Nicholas Church on 11th December, 1609.

In his will made in 1662, Hoskins gives his wife's name as Sarah and leaves bequests to a son, John. This son is supposed to have painted miniatures, or at any rate assisted his father in his studio. In the past efforts have been made to distinguish between the two men's work, but this has proved impossible, and for the present all works attributed to 'Hoskins' are taken to refer to the elder man. One exception is a miniature in the collection of the Duke of Buccleuch which may represent John Junior. It is signed and dated: '1656 / iH / IPSE.' The features of the sitter are not inconsistent with those of a man drawn by Samuel Cooper which is thought to be of John Hoskins Junior.

The fact that Hoskins' father's name was also John is slightly confusing, but as there is no reason to suppose that he was an artist, the term 'Senior' is still applicable to the John Hoskins who died 1664/5.

We do not know by whom John Hoskins was taught to paint, but according to De Piles' *The Art of Painting,* 1706, Hoskins was "a very eminent limner in the reign of King Charles I, whom he drew with his Queen and most of his court. He was bred a face-painter in oil, but afterwards taking to miniature he far exceeded what he did before. He died in Covent Garden about 40 years ago". Up to the present no oil paintings by Hoskins have been discovered, but he left behind a large number of superbly painted miniatures so that we are left in no doubt about his ability as an artist. W. Sanderson in his treatise *Graphice,* 1658, says "For Miniature or Limning, in water-colours, Hoskins and his son, the next modern since the Hilliards, father and son; these Pieces of the father (if my judgment faile not) incomparable". The earliest miniatures datable by costume signed 'I.H.' fall between the years 1620-24. The Duke of Portland has at Welbeck an invoice stating that on 16th July, 1626 John Holles, 1st Earl of Clare, paid £14 "to Hoskins ye picture drawer for 2 pictures in little". (Colour Plate 5.) Hoskins was known to Constantine Huygens, the Dutch poet and statesman who visited England sporadically between 1618-1624, and was a friend of Cornelius Johnson, to whom he gave a miniature of George Villiers, Duke of Buckingham. The miniature was sold at Sotheby's from the Weardale

Plate 16C. **J. Hoskins,** *Queen Henrietta Maria (1609-1669), vellum, 2¹/₈ins. Signed: 'iH.' This miniature was for many years thought to represent Elizabeth of Bohemia, but has recently been identified as being of Queen Henrietta. It is a good example of costume at the early part of the seventeenth century, with a beautiful wide lace collar and bejewelled costume, necklace and coronet.* **Courtesy The Mauritshuis, The Hague.**

Plate 16E. **J. Hoskins,** *William, 2nd Duke of Hamilton (1616-1651), vellum, 2¾ins. Signed and dated: 'iH / 1647.' This superb yet simple portrait shows the change in men's fashions. The straight long hair, plain linen collar and dark cloak are set off by the cloud and landscape background. It is contained within its original blue enamel locket.* Courtesy The Earl of Haddington, K.T.

Plate 16D. Queen Henrietta Maria, attributed to **J. Hoskins,** *but bearing* **S. Cooper's** *signature: 'SC' on the reverse, vellum, 3½ins. The identity of the artist has for many years been in dispute, and the painting closely resembles the work of Cooper. The Queen is shown wearing an elaborate dress with the bodice edged with lace. On her head is a jewelled diadem from which falls a white plume, the whole concept being more in the manner of a masque costume.* Gracious permission of H.M. The Queen.

Collection in 1925, and was inscribed on the reverse: 'Hoskins drawne by himself & by him given to Old Johnson, Yᵉ painter of whose son I bought it at Utrecht. 1700 F.St.J.' John Aubrey in *Brief Lives* gives an amusing piece of gossip in which Hoskins is mentioned. It relates to the wife of Dr. Overall, Dean of St. Paul's, London. Aubrey says of her she was "the greatest Beautie of her time in England. That she was so, I have it attested from the famous Limmer Mr. Hoskins, and other old Painters, besides old Courtiers. She was not more beautifull than she was obligeing and kind, and was so tender-hearted that (truly) she could scarce denie any one. She had (they told me) the loveliest Eies that were ever seen, but wondrous wanton. When she came to Court or to the Play-house, the Gallants would so flock about her".

She had in all probability been painted by Hoskins, although we have no proof of this, but he must have known her to testify about her beauty! Aubrey goes on to say that "he must have had a hard heart that did not admire her", and quotes some words written by Bishop Hall (1574-1656) in his *Meditations:* "there is none so old that a beautifull person loves not: nor so young whom a lovely feature moves not". Among Mrs. Overall's admirers

*Plate 16F. **J. Hoskins**, Sir Thomas Bendish, 2nd Bt. (d. 1672), vellum, 3ins. Signed and dated: 'IH / 1647', against a sea-scape background. The sitter's costume differs from Plate 16E, as he is wearing an open necked shirt and a cloak tied on one shoulder.* Courtesy Sotheby's.

was Sir John Selby of Yorkshire, and Aubrey was told of a song written about them, part of which is as follows:

> The Deane of Paule's did search for his wife,
> and where d'ee thinke he found her?
> Even upon Sir John Selbye's bed,
> As flatte as any Flounder.

The reason for Samuel and Alexander Cooper being brought up by their uncle John Hoskins is still not known, but presumably one or both of their parents had died and Hoskins took them under his care. Both boys must have received their training in art from their uncle, and followed his profession. Alexander left England for the Continent in c.1631, but Samuel was still working with Hoskins in 1634/5 when Sir Theodore Turquet de Mayerne (1573-1655), a notable physician at the English Court, visited Hoskins in his studio and met Samuel Cooper. The doctor's interest in chemistry led him to note how Hoskins used his paints. These were put into small turned ivory dishes, so that they did not dry up too quickly. Hoskins used a turned ivory palette about four inches in diameter and slightly hollow in the middle. The colours were placed in small quantities one beside the other at the end of the palette, and mixed with gum and water. When the artist wanted to use them he moistened his brush in clear water before applying the colour he required. Whites and blues were kept in separate little ivory pots. Like his predecessors, Hoskins painted on vellum stuck on to card and used mainly the oval upright format, the exception to this being his large cabinet miniatures which were rectangular. They include the copy of 'Mercury, Venus and Cupid' after Correggio, at Burghley House; the superb portrait of Charles I, in the collection of Earl Beauchamp, signed and dated 1632 (Plate 17). This latter portrait is in my opinion one of the most moving and sensitive portrayals of the King, and is thought to have been taken from life as opposed to some of his other large 'limnings' which were based on paintings by Van Dyck. One of Henrietta Maria in the collection of the Duke of Devonshire at Chatsworth is based on Van Dyck's portrait of the Queen, but Hoskins varied it by introducing a charming small landscape of London. Of these large limnings the one most accessible to the public is at Ham House, Richmond. It represents Catherine Bruce, Countess of Dysart, and is thought to be from life although it shows the influence of Van Dyck. An attractive miniature, once thought to be Elizabeth of Bohemia, but now identified as Queen Henrietta Maria, is in The Mauritshuis, The Hague; it is typical of Hoskins' work in the Hilliard-Oliver tradition, and is signed on the curtain background: 'iH' (Plate 16C). A rectangular miniature of Queen Henrietta Maria, painted c.1632, is said to be the one recorded by Van Der Doort as "Don by the life by Haskins". There are however various reasons for doubting both the attribution and the identification of the portrait and the matter is still one of dispute. Van Der Doort describes one such limning in detail: ". . . the Queenes Picture in limning with a white feather and in a white laced dressing about her brest in a- blewish purple habitt and Carnacon sleeves - and part of goulden Tissue Curteine in a goulden square enamoled wrought Case wth theis white enamoled Letters MR A Christall the Rock over it." (The Walpole Society, Vol. XXXVII, p.106.) If indeed this is the miniature referred to it has been reframed, as the present frame is of silver. In this ravishing portrait of the Queen she is wearing a blue dress with stars embroidered upon it, a white bodice edged with lace, and her sleeves are not carnation in colour. No reference is made by Van Der Doort to the alcove background, nor does he mention her jewelled head-dress. To add to the confusion the portrait is signed on the reverse in monogram 'SC' in pencil on the prepared gesso base. The miniature was for many years in the de la Hey Collection. It was Lot 51 when the collection was sold on 27th May, 1968 (not 1960, as stated by Oliver Millar in *The Queen's Pictures,* p.218). It fetched what was then a record price of £7,500, and passed into the Royal Collection. For the present it is attributed to John Hoskins, rather than Cooper. The Queen's dress was thought to be one designed by Inigo Jones for the masque *Tempe Restor'd,* but no sketch for such a dress has been discovered. The one thing that has never been disputed is its quality or beauty (Plate 16D).

Plate 16G. **J. Hoskins,** *George Villiers, 1st Duke of Bucking-ham, vellum, 2¹/₁₆ins. Signed: 'IH' (monogram). This is a fine example of Hoskins' work and is a sensitive portrayal of the sitter. The absence of the florid inscrip-tions, so popular in the Hilliard-Oliver period, gives opportunity for more natural backgrounds and seascapes. Courtesy Ivy, Duchess of Portland.*

Although in his early works Hoskins painted in the Hilliard-Oliver tradition, he succeeded in adapting his style of miniature painting to conform to the new ideas introduced into England by Van Dyck. He painted his sitters' eyes in the manner of Hilliard, showing the pupils clear with light reflected in them, but used a more subdued colouring when painting costume and backgrounds. His miniatures painted before c.1632 were usually on a blue or brown background, with the introduction of an occasional red curtain or landscape (Plate 16A). The whole effect of his portraits is to portray his sitters in a simple and dignified manner. After he came under the influence of Van Dyck he ceased to use the soft yellowish colours which merged so perfectly with the others used in his early work.

From c.1644 onwards, Hoskins painted with a freer and more vigorous brush stroke, and occasionally introduced a *pointilliste* dotting of a greenish colour, more frequently used on the Continent. A fine example of Hoskins'

Plate 17. **J. Hoskins,**
Charles I, vellum,
8½ins. Signed and
dated beneath the
c r o w n e d cipher:
'CR / 1632 / IH f'. If
proof were needed of
Hoskins' ability as a
miniaturist, this por-
trait provides it. It is a
human interpretation
of the Monarch, wear-
ing the ribbon and
Order of the Garter
against a doublet em-
broidered with gold,
onto which falls a deep
lace collar. Courtesy
The Earl Beauchamp.

copies after Van Dyck is in the collection of the Duke of Northumberland. It is of Charles I and Queen Henrietta Maria and is inscribed between the two figures with the initials 'CMR' (in monogram), surmounted by a crown and dated on the background 1636. The miniature was originally in the collection of Charles I, and bears on the reverse the cypher 'CR' surmounted by a crown. It is listed in Van Der Doort's catalogue of the King's Collection (The Walpole Society, Vol. XXXVII, p.106). The original large painting by Van Dyck is in the Archbishop's Palace, Kremsier, and a similar painting by Daniel Mytens is in the collection of H.M. The Queen (Catalogue no. 119, *Tudor, Stuart, and Early Georgian Pictures,* by Oliver Millar).

Charles I appointed Hoskins his limner on 20th April, 1640, and granted him a life annuity of £200 "providing that he work not for any other without his Majesty's licence". The appointment was a doubtful honour, as Royal patrons were not always good payers, and Hoskins only received one payment of £50 and twenty years later had to petition for a sum of £4,150 which was in arrears.

Hoskins used various signatures, the earliest as has already been mentioned was 'i.H' or 'IH' in monogram, the crossbar of the H being traversed by an I (Colour Plate 2A). The next is an H with a dot above the first vertical line, and a further form of signature is for the first stroke of the H to be elongated into a J. The punctuation varies, a semi-colon often being placed after initials. Many of Hoskins' signatures are followed by a date. A large number of his miniatures are signed in gold, others in brown or red.

The fact that Hoskins' nephew, Samuel Cooper, became so popular caused some jealousy, and according to De Piles this led Hoskins to take Samuel into partnership but "finding that the court was better pleas'd with his nephew's performances than with his," he must have decided to remain on his own and "was pleas'd to dismiss the partnership". No date is known, but it must have been sometime before 1642 when Cooper was living in Henrietta Street, Covent Garden, in which year he began to sign and date his own miniatures.

Hoskins appears to have been painting up to the end of his life in spite of failing health when he made his will in 1662. An interesting miniature said to represent the artist is in the collection of the Duke of Buccleuch; it is a profile portrait of a man in an open necked white shirt. On the reverse of the miniature is a sketch of what is taken to be a family group composed of Hoskins, his wife and four children, two of whom may represent Samuel and Alexander Cooper. It is inscribed in a later hand: 'J. Hoskins / by himself.'

The problem of attributions regarding Hoskins' miniatures is discussed at length by John Murdoch in *The Burlington,* May, 1978, pp.248-290.

On 15th February, 1664 a memorandum was appended to Hoskins' will in which he confirmed the appointment of his wife, Sarah, as his sole executrix and the disposition of his property and goods and chattels to her. One interesting detail in the memorandum is the fact that he refers to himself as "the elder Lymner", which rather emphasises that there was another Hoskins who painted miniatures. A week later, on 22nd February, Hoskins died at his house in Bedford Street, Covent Garden, and was buried in St. Paul's Church.

Hoskins lived through an interesting period of British history. He grew up and started his career during the reign of James I, was patronised by Charles I, and appears to have continued his profession undisturbed throughout the Civil Wars and was still an important figure in the art world when in 1660 Charles II was restored to the throne. By this time Samuel Cooper was at the height of his power and had a world-wide reputation. It was, therefore, to him that the King sat for his portrait when he returned to these shores, not to the elder limner who was by this time in declining health. Hoskins was a great artist, and had the distinction of training one who was to become one of the greatest miniaturists who ever worked in Britain.

Chapter IV

Roundhead and Royalist Patronage

Plate 18A. S. Cooper, Algernon Percy, 10th Earl of Northumberland (1602-68), vellum, 1²⁷/₃₂ins. Signed: 'SC:'. This portrait is almost certainly based on the portrait by Van Dyck at Petworth House, and is thought to be one of Cooper's early works. Courtesy Victoria and Albert Museum.

AS WE HAVE already seen, the art of miniature painting received Royal patronage right from its birth during the reign of Henry VIII. This patronage was to flourish under Queen Elizabeth I, whose limner Nicholas Hilliard left such an astonishingly large series of brilliant court portraits. The Queen was painted time and time again, and miniatures became so popular that they were not only distributed as symbols of love and affection, but were sent as presents to foreign·courts. They were in fact given to any person who by his service or diplomacy found favour with the Sovereign.

James I had numerous miniatures painted of himself, his Queen and their children; almost all were for presentation purposes. Prince Henry and Prince Charles would have been accustomed to seeing works of art of all kinds around them, and they in turn developed their own artistic taste and love of collecting.

The untimely death of Prince Henry in 1612 of typhoid fever left Prince Charles heir to the throne which he ascended in 1625 on the death of James I. Prince Charles inherited his brother's art collection, and this, together with his own which was already of some importance, was to be the beginning of one of the most famous in the world. Details of great interest regarding the acquisitions made by Charles I during his reign are recorded by Oliver Millar in *The Queen's Pictures,* in which the Royal Collection is traced from Tudor times up to the present day. Charles I received many paintings as gifts from friends, courtiers and collectors, and ambassadors and special envoys were sent all over the world to find suitable works of art. Miniatures were both commissioned and purchased by Charles I who took a delight in his 'limnings'. They were catalogued in great detail together with his other works of art, by Abraham Van Der Doort. This inventory is thought to be the finest of its kind ever compiled in England, and is extremely important as a source of information regarding the growth, arrangement and quality of its contents, most of which were sold and dispersed during the Commonwealth. Those who embark on research relating to art in the seventeenth century are indebted to The Walpole Society for commissioning a reprint edited by Oliver Millar in 1960, Vol. XXXVII.

In 1625 Van Der Doort was appointed Surveyor of the King's Pictures. This was a life appointment and carried with it an annual salary of £40. In spite of his lack of fluency in the English language, the catalogue is very detailed and comprehensive. The collection contained seventy-seven "limnd peeces" many of which can be identified and some of which have been recovered for the present Royal Collection. Van Der Doort did not live to see his task completed, as in 1640 he committed suicide, having apparently

Plate 18B (left). **S. Cooper,** *Barbara Villiers, Duchess of Cleveland (1641-1709), vellum, 3½ins. Signed in monogram: 'SC' and dated '166-(?)'. Note the coiffure and jewellery of this period.* Courtesy the late Earl Spencer.

Plate 18C. Attributed to **S. Cooper,** *John Leslie, 6th Earl of Rothes (1600-41), vellum, 2¹/₁₆ins., c.1635-40. This portrait is attributed to Cooper on basis of style.* Courtesy The Earl of Haddington, K.T.

been driven to despair at the loss of a miniature entrusted to him by the King or through fear that Charles might ask someone else to keep his pictures. On his death, Jan van Belcamp took charge of the King's pictures and Daniel Soreau the Queen's.

Among the miniatures in Charles's possession were thirteen by Hilliard, thirteen by Isaac Oliver, fourteen by Peter Oliver, four by Holbein, and eight by Hoskins.

In spite of political unrest and Civil War, artists continued to receive patronage and in a curious way a large proportion of their works came through unscathed. With the execution of Charles I in 1649 one might have expected that such a very personal art as miniature painting might have suffered a decline under the rule of Oliver Cromwell and his followers. The fact that it survived speaks well for the diplomacy of the artists working at that time, who must have kept out of political intrigue and been respected for their artistry and personal integrity.

One of those who succeeded in pleasing both Royalists and Roundheads alike was **Samuel Cooper** (1609-1672). For many years scholars and students of art have speculated about Cooper's birth and parentage, and been frustrated at the almost total lack of biographical information. At last, thanks to the diligent research of Miss Mary Edmond, we know that he was the son of Richard Cowper (or Cooper), and his wife, Barbara Hoskins, the sister of John Hoskins, Senior. The couple were married, as has already been mentioned in the previous chapter, in the parish of St. Nicholas Cole Abbey, and the marriage took place by Faculty Office licence. Samuel was presumably born in the same parish, although the details of his baptism have not so far been found. His brother, Alexander, who has always been said to be the elder son, was baptised on 11th December, 1609. Miss Edmond puts forward a theory that we may be incorrect in assuming that Alexander was

Plate 18D. **S. Cooper,** *Amelia Ann Sophia Stanley, Marchioness of Atholl, vellum, 2¾ins. Signed and dated: 'SC / 1667'. This brilliant miniature is a good example of costume and hair style.* Courtesy The Duke of Atholl, Blair Castle.

the elder brother, and that the words 'Aetatis Suae 63' on Samuel's tombstone might mean aged 63 rather than 'in his 63rd year', in which case Samuel could have been born in 1608. Be that as it may, we are a step nearer the truth, and Samuel's date of birth may yet be found.

One of the earliest accounts of Cooper's life is given by Richard Graham, pp.338, 339 of the appendix to *The Art of Painting by C.A. Du Fresnoy, translated into English by Mr. Dryden, 1695.* Graham was the person who stated that Alexander was the elder brother and as he gave no evidence for this he may well have taken the date from the inscription on Cooper's tombstone. He says that Cooper was: "Bred up (together with his elder brother Alexander) under the Care and Discipline of Mr. Hoskins his Uncle: but derived the most considerable advantages, from the *Observations* which he made on the Works of *Van Dyck* . . . his *Talent* was so extraordinary, that for the *Honour* of our *Nation*, it may without Vanity be affirmed he was (at least) equal to the most famous *Italians;* and that hardly any of his *Predecessors* has ever been able to show so much *Perfection* in so *narrow* a *Compass.* Answerable to his *Abilities* in this *Art* was his *skill* in *Music*: and he was reckon'd one of the best *Lutenists*, as well as the most excellent *Limner* in his time. He spent several years of his Life *abroad*, was personally acquainted with the greatest Men of *France, Holland,* and his *own Country,* and by his *works* more universally known in all parts of *Christendom.* He died *Anno* 1672, and lies bury'd in Pancras Church in the Fields."

Plate 18E. **S. Cooper,** *Margaret Lemon, vellum, 4¾ins., c.1635. Signed in monogram: 'S.C.' and inscribed with the sitter's name: 'MARGARET' and 'LEMON'. Margaret Lemon, who was Van Dyck's mistress, is dressed as a young cavalier. The portrait is of great importance as the earliest known signed work by Cooper. Courtesy The Fondation Custodia (Collection F. Lugt), Institut Néerlandais, Paris.*

Plate 18F. **S. Cooper,** *Thomas Clifford, Lord Clifford of Chudleigh (1630-73), vellum, 3¼ins. Signed in monogram: 'SC' and inscribed on the reverse: 'Sʳ Thomas Clifford 1672. Æta: 42. Sam: Cooper fecit'. This magnificent portrait was painted in the year of Cooper's death and shows that his skill was as great as ever. Courtesy Lord Clifford of Chudleigh.*

In view of the fact that this was published only twenty-three years after the artist's death it is sad that biographical details of Cooper's life were not recorded in greater detail. It is presumed that one or both of his parents died when he was young, and Hoskins and his wife brought him and his brother up. The boys would have had the opportunity of seeing an artist at work from an early age, and become accustomed to seeing important sitters come to and from Hoskins' studio. No documentary evidence has so far come to light to establish the dates of Samuel's apprenticeship, or indeed the year in which he left his uncle and set up on his own. The first positive information regarding his time with Hoskins is provided in the de Mayerne *MS. Sloane 2052*, in the British Museum. Sir Theodore Turquet de Mayerne (1573-1655) was an eminent physician, who attended James I, and was also appointed physician to Charles I and his Queen. He had a life-long interest in chemistry, and was universally respected for his knowledge and upright character. In 1634 he visited John Hoskins in his studio, where he met Samuel Cooper, and, being interested in the technical aspect of painting, got him to write down for him a recipe for preparing lead white. This recipe is in Cooper's own hand, and is, apart from signatures or inscriptions on his miniatures, the only known manuscript of his in existence.

It was in 1634 that Hoskins became the first occupant of 29 Bedford Street, Covent Garden, for which he held a thirty-one-year lease, and where he lived until his death. No information is available about any previous house, and it was probably to Bedford Street that de Mayerne went and noted that Cooper was working with his uncle. Where and how Cooper was educated remains a mystery but Hoskins must have seen to it that he was well tutored as he was clearly a man of culture with varied gifts, was a good linguist, a keen traveller and an accomplished musician. He appears to have had a wide circle of friends both in Britain and on the Continent, and was undoubtedly a man of some standing, who had the *entrée* into both artistic and literary circles. Samuel Pepys in his diary on 6th July, 1668 went to Cooper's house whilst he was painting Mrs. Pepys' miniature and says: ". . . he is a most admirable workman — and good company". We get a glimpse of Cooper's character from a handful of close friends such as John Aubrey, Samuel Butler, Thomas Hobbes and Sir William Petty, and an illuminating description of him is given by Cosimo III of Tuscany. Cosimo de Medici came to England in 1669, and among those who came to pay their respects to him in London was Samuel Cooper. Cosimo had already heard of Cooper's ability and been told that "no person of quality visits that city without endeavouring to obtain some of his performance to take out of the Kingdom".

The Prince accordingly arranged for his portrait to be painted and described Cooper as: "a tiny man all wit and courtesy as well housed as Lely, with his table covered with velvet".

The dates and extent of Cooper's travels abroad are not known, but the most likely period would seem to be between 1634 and 1642, when the least number of his miniatures are traceable. According to *The Survey of London,* XXXVI, Cooper was paying rates in King Street, Covent Garden in 1643, and in Henrietta Street from c.1650-1672.

No evidence has yet been found of the date or place of Cooper's marriage to Christiana (or Christina) Turner (1623-1693), a daughter of William

Turner of York whose family owned land in Yorkshire., Christiana was one of the seventeen children, of whom Edith was the mother of Alexander Pope, the poet. According to Dr. G.C. Williamson, *The Miniature Collector*, p.65, Mrs. Cooper is reputed to have given over to her sister many sketch books belonging to her husband together with his colour boxes, colours, and some "cups of precious agate". Williamson did not give the source of his information and went on to say that the items were deposited in a bank. If this were the case they may still be hidden away waiting to be claimed.

There is no evidence that the Coopers had any children, and if they did they must have died before he made his last will in which he appointed his "deare and loving wife Christiana Cooper my sole executrix". Cooper's will and that of his wife are published in full in *Samuel Cooper*, by D. Foskett, Appendix I, pp.94-99. Cooper left bequests to both the Hoskins and des Granges families to whom he was related, and to another cousin, John Hayles, Hayls or Hales, the portrait painter. Apart from bequests he left all his estate to his wife, and this included a considerable amount of property near Coventry.

Christiana was fourteen years younger than her husband, and survived him by twenty-one years. It seems strange that only one portrait of her is known; this is the superb unfinished miniature in the collection of the Duke of Portland. It was purchased by Edward, Lord Harley, for £26 at the sale of the collection of Lawrence Cross(e), on 5th December, 1722, and mentioned in Vertue's notes of the sale as "Cooper's wife not finisht, very good" (Plate 18G).

The tercentenary of Cooper's death was on 5th May, 1972, and at the time the event passed unnoticed, but in 1974 a major exhibition of his work and that of some of his contemporaries was mounted at the National Portrait Gallery. The problem of assembling a representative collection of miniatures by or ascribed to Samuel Cooper was not an easy one, but in spite of many

Plate 18G (right). **S. Cooper,** *Mrs. Samuel Cooper, née Christiana Turner (1623?-93), unfinished, vellum, 3½ins. Christiana's family came from York, and her sister, Edith Pope, was the mother of Alexander Pope, the poet.* Courtesy Ivy, Duchess of Portland.

Colour Plate 7 (left).

A. **Samuel Cooper,** *possibly Sir R. Henley, vellum, 2¾ins. Signed with monogram and dated: 'SC / 1659.' This is a superb example of Cooper's work and shows the use of gold shading on the doublet.*

B. **Samuel Cooper,** *called a self-portrait, but the identification is now in doubt, as the sitter seems too young to be Cooper, vellum, 2¾ins. Signed with a monogram and dated: 'SC / 1657.'*

C. **Samuel Cooper,** *James II, when Duke of York (1633-1701), vellum, 3¼ins. Signed with a monogram and dated: 'SC / [16]61.' Formerly in the collection of James Sotheby, by whom it was bought on 6th March, 1711 for £21 10s. Purchased by the Victoria and Albert Museum, 11th October, 1955.*

D. **Samuel Cooper,** *Henrietta, Duchess of Orleans (1644-70), vellum, 2²⁷/32ins. Signed with a monogram: 'SC.' This attractive miniature is a good example of costume and hair style c.1660, with corkscrew curls massed on each side of the sitter's face.*

Courtesy Victoria and Albert Museum

difficulties as many as 230 miniatures were on view of which 141 were by, or attributed to, Cooper. The inclusion of large oil portraits by such artists as Sir Godfrey Kneller, John Hayls, Sir Peter Lely, Mary Beale and Sir Anthony Van Dyck made it possible to make interesting comparisons between the works executed by these painters and miniatures by Cooper and his followers. Cooper's reputation as a great artist was acknowledged even during his lifetime and, to those who study and love the art of miniature painting, he has always been considered one of the most important, if not the most important artist of the seventeenth century, and this irrespective of scale or medium. Charles Beale in his diary recorded that on "Sunday May 5, 1672 Mr. Samuel Cooper, the most famous limner of the world for a face died". Others eulogised him as "the Vandyck in little". In recent years he has been rather overshadowed by the renewed interest in many of the important artists who painted on a large scale. Dr. Roy Strong described him as a "diminished figure, a name which never springs to mind alongside that of Holbein and Hilliard, Hogarth and Gainsborough or Reynolds and Romney". In his Appreciation of *Samuel Cooper,* 1974, Dr. Strong reasserts the belief that "Cooper is one of our great artists, consistently more evocative and more perceptive than the slick interpreters of his age, wooden Robert Walker or languorous Peter Lely". He reminds us that Cooper painted in Covent Garden for three decades, his sitters including the great and the ordinary people who made up the population of Caroline, Cromwellian and Restoration London. The reason that Cooper's art has been neglected is due in part to the hazards of fashion and the fact that much more interest has been shown in the Tudor and Victorian ages. The majority of art historians only make brief references to miniaturists and not only Cooper but the art itself gets sadly neglected. Those who visited the Cooper exhibition all agreed that the contemporary assessment of Cooper's ability was fully justified. One reviewer remarked that: "Even if they were life-sized, the portraits by Samuel Cooper could not be more engrossing . . ." He came away "tired eyed, but spiritually enriched by the sight of the artistic genius of the 'prince of limners, the greate (tho' little) limner, the famous Mr. Cooper'."

Cooper's early works are difficult to attribute with certainty as although he must have executed some miniatures before he left his uncle's studio, no signed and dated work occurs before 1642, when the charming miniature of Elizabeth Cecil, Countess of Devonshire was painted. It is signed and dated: 'Sa: Cooper / pinx A° 1642', and belongs to the Marquess of Exeter. The composition and breadth of handling show the influence of Van Dyck used on a small scale, whilst the competent modelling of the features and use of colours are all indicative of Cooper's mastery of the art of 'limning' even at this stage of his career. His earliest signed miniature is of Margaret Lemon, Van Dyck's mistress. The sitter is dressed as a young cavalier, and the miniature signed in monogram: 'S.C.' and inscribed with the sitter's name: 'MARGARET' and 'LEMON'. The miniature is in the F. Lugt Collection in the Fondation Custodia, Institut Néerlandais, Paris (Plate 18E). A handful of other miniatures have been attributed to Cooper on the basis of style, and these include one of an unknown man in the collection of H.M. The Queen, painted c.1630/5, John Leslie, 6th Earl of Rothes (Plate 18C), and Sir John Hamilton, both in the collection of the Earl of Haddington, and painted c.1635-40. From 1642 onwards we are on sure ground, as signed and dated

Plate 19A. **S. Cooper,** *Charles II, vellum, 3⅝ins. An unfinished sketch from life, of which other finished versions exist.* Courtesy the late Denys Eyre Bower.

miniatures exist right up to the time of his death when he was still painting.

Cooper was in great demand throughout the whole of his career, yet he never seems to have succumbed to the temptation of repeating himself, or executing 'stock' portraits. He seems to have had the ability to approach each sitter with fresh eyes and painted them as individuals with their own personalities clearly shown. He gives them the reality of living people without being idealistic, and by the pose and positioning of the sitter's head, the draughtsmanship of the lips, the look in the eyes, one often feels that the sitter is about to speak. Although Cooper was trained in the early tradition which went back to the time of Holbein, he broke away from this and raised the art to new heights by creating a sense of solid reality and atmospheric space. Horace Walpole made some perceptive comments on Cooper's ability and says that he "may be called an original genius, as he was the first who gave the strength and freedom of oil to miniatures". Comparing Cooper's work with that of Oliver he says: "Oliver's works are touched and retouched with such careful fidelity that you cannot help perceiving they are nature in abstract; Cooper's pictures are so bold that they seem perfect nature only of a less standard; magnify the former, they are still diminutively conceived: if a glass could expand Cooper's pictures to the size of Vandyck's they would appear to have been painted for that proportion."

Cooper's miniatures were enriched by the use of strong contrasts of light and tone, his colours were more subdued than those used by earlier limners, and his general effect more in accord with the realism introduced into British painting during the age of Van Dyck. His miniatures were painted in watercolour on thin sheets of fine vellum attached to a support of card. The question of pigments has already been discussed, and Cooper would have followed his predecessors in preparing his own materials and judging the quality of the pigments to be used. The fact that such a large number of Cooper's miniatures have remained in such fine condition is a reflection on the scrupulous care with which he selected his paints. I think that it is fair to say that only those which have suffered from careless treatment have needed restoration. Many of Cooper's miniatures were painted on formats which measured from three inches upwards, and in order to strengthen the back of the card a coating of gesso was applied, the purpose of which was to counter the pull of the parchment which might otherwise have caused the card to warp. The substance used was a mixture of glue size and chalk. As Mr. V.J. Murrell has pointed out, Cooper's method of painting can best be described as a mixed gouache and watercolour technique based on that used in previous periods, but with the difference that he worked over the transparent areas again with opaque colours, the result of which was to give the finished paintings a more solid gouache effect. He used a fairly limited palette, avoiding the impermanent colours such as sap green, pink and the lakes. For representing armour and metallic objects Cooper tended to use ordinary pigments. Gold was occasionally used for buttons and signatures, and on rare occasions he used powdered gold for rendering the highlights in satin. The use of white lead was unavoidable during Cooper's time as there were few acceptable substitutes. That he used it extensively is evident from the number of miniatures where this colour has turned black due to the presence of hydrogen sulphide. Fortunately, with modern methods under expert hands, this can be removed. His flesh tint (commonly called

Plate 19B. S. Cooper, Oliver Cromwell (1599-1658), vellum, 3¹/₈ins. This famous unfinished sketch of the Protector was probably painted c.1650, from which year Cooper was working for the Cromwell family. Courtesy The Duke of Buccleuch and Queensberry, K.T.

'carnation' by the early limners) was usually rendered by the use of a warm reddish brown rather than the 'pink over white' method used by earlier artists. This innovation must have seemed strange to his contemporaries, and Samuel Pepys remarked when he visited Cooper's house for the first time and saw his work, which he thought excellent, that the colouring of the flesh was "a little forced". Viewed today, even supposing that the colours have faded slightly, Cooper's miniatures appear to be modelled to perfection with colours which blend in complete harmony. The majority of his limnings are painted with a plain background, but occasionally he introduced a cloudy sky, a curtain, landscape, or even, as in the case of his miniature of James II, as Duke of York, a seascape (National Portrait Gallery Cat. No. 105). The tradition, based on a statement by John Evelyn, that Cooper painted by candlelight is now treated with reserve. It may well have referred only to the occasion when he was sketching Charles II's head for the new coinage. Although it is possible to paint by candlelight, it would be difficult to choose colours with any correct judgement, and as Pepys noted many details in connection with Cooper during the eight or nine sittings which his wife had for her portrait, it would be surprising if he had not noted that her sittings were by candlelight!

The miniature of Mrs. Pepys was finished in August 1668, and although Pepys had reservations about the likeness and was not entirely satisfied with the "blue garment", he acknowledged that it "is most certainly a most rare work, as to the painting", and paid Cooper £30 for the portrait and a further £8 3s. 4d. for the crystal and gold case. The present whereabout of this miniature is unknown and it was last heard of in 1850, when the details of the owner were not given.

A large number of Cooper's miniatures are unfinished, due probably to the fact that they were to be kept as a prototype in cases where replicas might be needed. His signatures vary from 'S.C.' to 'SC' (monogram) the two letters being entwined in cursive lettering, sometimes followed by a date which is usually on a lower line. Occasionally he signed in full, either: 'Sa: Cooper pinx', followed by a date, or: 'S: Cooper fe: 1645', as in the case of the miniature of an unknown man in the collection of H.M. The Queen. This miniature was once thought to represent Robert Walker, and is of particular significance as an outstanding example of the dramatic change of style and lighting which was to remain a characteristic and hallmark of Cooper's work throughout the rest of his career. In addition, this portrait bears an incised inscription by Cooper on the reverse of the gesso back: 'Samuel Cooper fecit feberuaris 1644 ould stile.'

Colour Plate 8.
A. **Thomas Flatman,** *an unknown man, vellum, 2¾ins., c.1665-70. Signed in monogram: 'TF.'*
B. **Franciszek Smiadecki,** *an unknown man, watercolour on vellum, 2¼ins.*
C. **Richard Gibson,** *Lady Dorothy Franklin, probably Dorothy (1657-1707) the 2nd wife of Sir John Franklin of Bolhurst, Bedfordshire, vellum, 2¾ins. Inscribed on the reverse: 'My Lady Franklin.'*
D. **Benjamin Arlaud,** *an unknown man, vellum, 2¾ins., c.1700.*
E. **Peter Cross,** *Sir James Ogilvy, 4th Earl of Findlater and 1st Earl of Seafield (1664-1730), vellum, 3¼ins. Signed in monogram on the front: 'PLC' or 'PC', and inscribed by the artist on the reverse: 'Sʳ James Ogilby / Secretery of Statte / for ye Kingdom of Scotland / Ætatis Sua 35 / Peeter Cross fesitt / i698.'*

Private Collection

A   B

C

D   E

Plate 19C. **S. Cooper,** *James Scott, Duke of Monmouth and Buccleuch, K.G. (1649-85), vellum, 4⁷/₈ins., c.1664. The sitter was the natural son of Charles II by Lucy Walter. It is one of the five important unfinished sketches by Cooper in the Royal Collection.* Gracious permission of H.M. The Queen.

Portrait miniatures are a valuable guide to fashion, which was largely the prerogative of those in Court circles and the aristocracy although, in Cooper's case, he also depicted sitters from a wide variety of backgrounds. The fact that so many of his miniatures are dated is helpful in tracing the change in dress and hair style for both men and women. Women's hair styles did not change dramatically throughout Cooper's career and that of his followers, but were for the most part a variation of that adopted in the late 1620s when the hair was parted on either side and the centre portion drawn back and arranged with the rest of the back hair into a high flat bun. On either side of the face the hair was either frizzed, or worn in ringlets with a straight fringe on the forehead. By c.1640 the back hair was either brushed up and braided into a circular bun, or parted and taken to either side of the head to increase the number of curls. These tended to be longer and occasionally a long ringlet was allowed to fall over the sitter's shoulder. Often the bun was ornamented with a string of pearls or ribbon entwined in knots or bows. Pearls were fashionable throughout the whole of Cooper's time, and were worn as necklaces with matching drop earrings. Sometimes they were used as ornaments for a dress as in the case of Plate 18B. By the middle of the seventeenth century only slight variations had taken place, curls replaced the straight fringe on the forehead, and by c.1660 more elaborate ringlets or corkscrew curls were in vogue, and the hair wired to stand away from the head (Plate 18D). Locks of artificial hair were used and sometimes the hair was dyed. Throughout almost the whole of Cooper's time the ladies wore simple low-cut dresses, which by the 1660s were almost 'off the shoulder'. This *décolleté* fashion was even worn by Cromwell's family. Men's hair fashion was to some extent dictated by natural growth. The Royalists wore their hair shoulder length, whilst the Puritans kept it shorter.

Cooper's miniature of Cromwell (Plate 19B) shows him with his hair down to his neck. After the Restoration men wore their hair as long as possible and eventually the periwig was introduced and worn by Charles II. This fashion continued in ecclesiastical circles up to the middle of the nineteenth century and is still worn by judges today.

Men's collars underwent several changes during the seventeenth century. In the early 1630s they were made of wide lace, which was adapted to a linen collar edged with lace (Plate 18C). During the Civil War a plain linen collar was more practical and the men's doublets were made of plain materials rather than silks. After the Restoration the cravat or *rabat* of expensive *gros-point de venise* lace became popular (Plate 18F). This was later replaced by a shorter knotted scarf tied in front with a bow of coloured ribbon. Various forms of cravats continued to be worn throughout the eighteenth century.

Five of Cooper's finest works are the unfinished miniatures in the collection of H.M. The Queen. They represent the Duke of Monmouth as a boy, General Monck, Queen Catherine of Braganza, the Duchess of Richmond, and the Duchess of Cleveland. Although these portraits are traditionally said to have been acquired by Charles II, the first certain reference to them as being in the Royal Collection was in 1728, when Queen Caroline received for display at Richmond "five heads in Black frames unfinish'd by Cowper" (Plate 19C).

Two supposed self-portraits of Cooper exist, and both are in the Victoria and Albert Museum. One is in pastel and generally considered to be of Cooper, but not necessarily by him; the other is a miniature signed and dated 1657. Both portraits were bequeathed to the Victoria and Albert Museum by the Rev. Alexander Dyce on his death in 1867. The miniature is identified as of Cooper only by an eighteenth century inscription on the reverse. The sitter seems to be too young to represent Cooper at that period, and the features are quite unlike those of the sitter in the chalk drawing, which seems a much more convincing portrait of a "small man", as Cooper was described by those who knew him (Colour Plate 7B). According to Vertue, the crayon was probably executed by Jackson, a relative of Cooper's. Copies of it exist, including two by Bernard Lens, one in the Portland Collection, and the other in the collection of the Marquess of Bristol.

Although Cooper undoubtedly worked for the Court, he did not, as far as we know, ever paint Charles I, who sat several times to his uncle, John Hoskins. It is impossible to say precisely when Cooper began to paint Oliver Cromwell and his family, but it was certainly in or before 1650. Evidence for this is to be found in the *Calendar of State Papers, 1650,* 1876, p.420, when a letter was sent to Lord Conway asking him to excuse the artist "one month longer, as he has some work to finish for Lord General Cromwell and his family".

Cromwell must have approved of Cooper and his work and gave him numerous commissions, not only to paint his family but to make presentation portraits of himself to be sent abroad, including one to Queen Christina of Sweden. Of all the portraits Cooper painted, the one which has aroused the greatest feeling and interest is unquestionably the unfinished sketch of Oliver Cromwell in the collection of the Duke of Buccleuch (Pl. 19B). It was probably painted c.1650-53, and kept as a prototype by the artist from which he could execute finished versions as and when required.

Plate 19D. **S. Cooper,** *'Portrait of a dead child,' black chalk heightened with white and greyish blue, on tinted paper, 7ins. This moving drawing bears on the reverse a sketch thought to represent J. Hoskins Junior, and an inscription: 'Dead Child', and in another hand: 'Mr S:C: child done by him', and: 'N.B. ye son of: Old Mr Hoskins' son'. The inference being that the drawing represents the son of J. Hoskins Junior.* Private Collection.

None dated before 1656 have so far come to light. David Piper in *The English Face,* pp.115-126, discusses the portrait and says: "It is to Cooper's portrait that I return again and again, it is an image in the light of which all accounts of Cromwell should be read ... It cancels the grudgingness in Clarendon's great assessment, and exposes Evelyn's description as peevish partisanship ... It is for me one of the most moving, one of the greatest of British portraits".

With the death of Oliver Cromwell, on 3rd September, 1658, political events moved swiftly: Richard Cromwell's Protectorate was short-lived, and on 29th May, 1660, King Charles returned to claim his throne. After the turbulence of civil war and the danger and unrest that pervaded England during the Commonwealth, the Restoration must have come as a relief to many. It was to be a period of Royal patronage and Cooper, who was already fully established as one of the leading limners of the age, was hard pressed to keep pace with his commissions. New coinage was required, and the King lost no time in arranging for Cooper to sketch his head in profile for this purpose. Two sketches exist, and both are at Windsor. Cooper painted numerous portraits of the King, as well as members of the Court and Charles's mistresses. In 1665, Cooper painted two magnificent portraits of the King in Garter robes. One is a large rectangular one which is at Goodwood, and the other, an oval version, is in The Mauritshuis, The Hague. It is impossible to be sure which one was painted first as they are almost identical. The rectangular one shows the sitter's right hand and more of the robes, which suggests the possibility that the oval version was taken from it, on a slightly reduced scale.

Apart from the two sketches of Charles II for the coinage, five other superb drawings by Cooper are known. Two represent his aunt, Mrs. Hoskins, one is thought to represent John Hoskins, Junior, another is of Thomas Alcock, who was tutor to the children of the 2nd Earl of

Westmorland, and the last is a most moving drawing of a dead child (Plate 19D). The portrait of Thomas Alcock is in the Ashmolean Museum, Oxford, and is identifiable by an inscription by the sitter on the reverse and was drawn when he was eighteen years of age.

It is impossible to mention more than a few of Cooper's works here, and more detailed information may be found in the publications cited in the bibliography. The nature of Cooper's sudden illness is not known, and he was working up to the last few days of his life. In his will, made four days before his death, he described himself as "sick and weake in body but of a sound & perfect mind". Samuel Cooper's gifts can best be summed up in the words written by Dr. Strong: "His success in the highly artificial age in which he lived is a testimony to a talent which was so amazing that it could rise above and ignore the idiosyncrasies of transient contemporary fashionable attitudes. In this lay his true genius as one of our greatest portrait painters." He was buried as he requested in St. Pancras Church, London, where a monument commemorating Cooper and his wife may still be seen.

Alexander Cooper (1609-1660) was born in London, and, as has already been mentioned, was baptised on 11th December, 1609. Whether he was older or younger than his brother Samuel is still uncertain, but both boys were brought up under the care of their uncle and aunt, John and Sarah Hoskins. Alexander is thought to have had some instruction from Peter Oliver, and there are certain characteristics in style, such as the mauvish backgrounds, which show Oliver's influence, rather than that of John Hoskins. Little is known about Alexander's life, nor do we know where he was educated. It is presumed that he worked in his uncle's studio and had some of his artistic training under him, at least during the early part of his career. Unlike so many artists of the time who flocked to England to work, Alexander seems to have preferred the Continent. He is known to have been in Holland in c.1631, by which time he was twenty-two years of age and already an accomplished artist. In this year he painted miniatures of the King and Queen of Bohemia and of William, Lord Craven, who fought in their cause. These are all illustrated in *British Miniaturists* by Basil Long. Two are signed: 'A.C.', that of Elizabeth of Bohemia, and the one of Lord Craven which is an exceptionally good example of Cooper's work. Each has the date 1631 engraved on the reverse of the frame. In 1632 and 1633 Alexander painted an important series of miniatures representing the King and Queen of Bohemia and seven of their children. These portraits, framed together in a chain, are now in the Kaiser Friedrich Museum, Berlin. An unsigned miniature of Elizabeth of Bohemia by Cooper was Lot 150 in the Heckett sale at Sotheby's, 11th July, 1977, when it realised £650; had it not had slight restoration on the background the price would probably have been higher.

Alexander Cooper was working in The Hague from 1644 to 1646, and in Sweden from 1647 to 1657. Queen Christina appointed him Official Court Painter, which office he also held under Charles X, who succeeded to the throne on her abdication in 1654. In about 1655 he was working for the King of Denmark, probably in Copenhagen, and his name occurs in Danish and Swedish documents. Six charming miniatures of the Danish Royal family are in the Rosenborg Castle, Copenhagen, all of them painted against

Plate 20A (right). **A. Cooper,** *an unknown nobleman, vellum, 1½ins., c.1645. The pair to Plate 20C, and part of a fine double-sided marriage portrait set into a contemporary Dutch gold and enamelled locket. The bridegroom is painted against a pale green background. The pair realised £4,800 in 1976.* Courtesy Sotheby's.

Plate 20B (centre). Gold and enamelled locket, containing the double-sided marriage portraits of c.1645 by A. Cooper — see Plates 20A and C. The locket bears a mirror cypher 'LA' in green and black beneath a coronet, and is surrounded by a circlet of flowers. Courtesy Sotheby's.

Plate 20C (far right). **A. Cooper,** *an unknown lady, pair to Plate 20A, vellum, 1½ins., c.1645. Painted against an azure blue background. The sitter is wearing a pearl necklace, and a pink décolleté dress onto which is pinned a pearl pendant. A pair of seventeenth century miniatures of such charm and quality are great rarities.* Courtesy Sotheby's.

A

B

C

blue backgrounds and set in rich enamel lockets, on the reverse of which are monograms, and the date 1656. They represent King Frederik III (Plate 20G), Queen Sophie Amalie, and their children. Two of these were exhibited at the National Portrait Gallery in 1974, one of Princess Anna Sophie (Plate 20 I) and the other of Princess Frederikke Amalie.

Cooper's salary as Court Painter seems to have failed to mature, and in 1652 he was obliged to petition for eighteen months' arrears of salary as at this time he was ill and bedridden. This petition evidently fell on deaf ears, for in 1654 he was obliged to approach Prince Charles Gustavus for two years' arrears of pension, and money due to him for six and a half years' work.

No information is at present available regarding the latter part of the artist's life, but he is said to have died in Stockholm in 1660.

Only a small number of his miniatures have been authenticated by his initials 'AC' (Plates 20E and F); others are attributed to him on the basis of style and technique. It is at present impossible to follow his career in any detail as no records are available regarding his personal life or his sitters. There must be a number of his works still waiting to be discovered. Proof of this was when a superb double-sided marriage portrait miniature was taken to Sotheby's for identification in 1976 and was found to be by Alexander Cooper. The portraits were housed in a contemporary gold and enamel locket of Dutch origin, and are thought to be a marriage token. Each side is enamelled with a mirror cypher 'LA' in green and black beneath a coronet; the rest of the area is decorated with brightly coloured flowers on a white ground. It was sold at Sotheby's on 5th July, 1976 for £4,800 (Plates 20A, B and C). The style of painting on these miniatures is close to the fine and more precise style seen in the works of Isaac Oliver, and similar to the portraits in the Rosenborg Castle. It shows nothing of the broader and freer treatment which symbolises the works of his brother Samuel. The fact

E

D

F

G

H

I

Plate 20.

D. **A. Cooper,** *Charles Louis, Count Palatine (1617-80), vellum, 2ins. Although unsigned, this conforms in style to other miniatures by Cooper and is a fine portrait. The sitter's hair and costume are well painted.* Courtesy The Duke of Buccleuch and Queensberry, K.T.

E. **A. Cooper,** *portrait of an unknown lady, vellum, 2¼ins. Signed in monogram: 'AC'. This is one of the few signed works by Cooper at present known. Note the costume with the fine lace-edged lawn cap and the high, plain, lawn ruff over a deep V-shaped collar also edged with lace. Typical of that worn on the Continent in c.1640.* Gracious permission of H.M. Queen Juliana of the Netherlands.

F. **A. Cooper,** *portrait of an unknown lady, vellum, 1⁷/₈ins. Signed: 'AC'. This miniature shows to perfection the full ruff, lace cap and embroidered bodice of c.1625.* Gracious permission of H.M. Queen Juliana of the Netherlands.

G. **A. Cooper,** *King Frederik III of Denmark, vellum, 2ins. This and those of other members of the Royal family, were painted as a set and all encased in gold and enamelled lockets, dated 1656 on the reverse. Note the tied cravat instead of a ruff.* Courtesy Rosenborg Castle, Copenhagen.

H. *Attributed to* **A. Cooper,** *Lady Katherine Manners, Duchess of Buckingham (d.1649), vellum, 2¹/₁₆ins., c.1620-25. Note the straight fringe over the forehead, and matching jewellery.* Courtesy Ivy, Duchess of Portland.

I. **A. Cooper,** *Princess Anna Sophie of Denmark (1647-1717), vellum, 2ins., c.1656. This and other miniatures of the family, including Plate 20G of this sitter's father, Frederik III, are all encased in gold and enamelled lockets with the date 1656 on the reverse.* Courtesy Rosenborg Castle, Copenhagen.

Plate 21A. Attributed to **Mary Beale**, an unknown lady, vellum, 2⅝ ins., c.1670-80. Note the hair is worn in ringlets touching the face and parted in the centre. Ex. de la Hey Collection.

Plate 21B. T. **Flatman**, Sir Thomas Langton (1632-1701), vellum, 2⅛ins. Signed with a gold monogram: 'TF'. Painted against a curtain and sky background. The sitter's hair falling over his cloak. Courtesy the late Lord Methuen, R.A.

that this hitherto unknown miniature turned up unexpectedly is encouraging to the collector, as it proves that 'finds' may yet be possible!

Alexander Cooper is said to have executed miniature copies of oil portraits and landscapes as well as miniatures from life. All his known miniatures are painted on a small scale, I am not aware of any over 2½ inches high. Examples of his work are in the Victoria and Albert Museum and the collections of H.M. The Queen, H.M. Queen Juliana of the Netherlands, and the Duke of Buccleuch and Queensberry. Eight of his works are illustrated in the National Portrait Gallery catalogue, 1974.

There is no documentary evidence that **Thomas Flatman** (1635-1688) was actually taught by Samuel Cooper, but his work comes closer in style to that of the master than any other of his followers, and even if he never worked in Cooper's studio he certainly succeeded in assimilating much of Cooper's manner and technique. This is particularly apparent in his earlier miniatures where he appears to have copied the characteristics of the duller type of Cooper's portraits.

Flatman was born in London and was the son of a clerk in Chancery. He was educated at Winchester and New College, Oxford, where he was elected a Fellow in 1656. He seems to have been a versatile man, and after being admitted to the Inner Temple 31st May, 1655, and called to the Bar in 1662, he was admitted M.A. of Cambridge in 1666. In the meantime he had taken up art and his earliest known miniatures date from 1661, in which year he painted a miniature of the Rev. Samuel Woodford. This is now in the Fitzwilliam Museum, Cambridge, and is signed and dated. Flatman became a distinguished miniaturist, and justly deserved the reputation that he was "equal to Hoskins, senior or junior, and next in imitation of Samuel Cooper". Besides painting miniatures he executed oil portraits and published a volume of poems and songs. He had an artistic temperament and appears to have suffered from alternating periods of elation and depression which led him at one point almost to the brink of considering suicide. He was earnestly religious and was related to Sancroft, Dean of St. Paul's and later Archbishop of Canterbury, to whom he dedicated a poem. He had a wide circle of friends including the artists Charles and Mary Beale, whose son, Charles Junior, studied limning under Flatman in 1677. As a young man Flatman had shared rooms with Samuel Woodford, and he and the Beale family together with Dean Sancroft were his closest friends. Among his other friends were Izaac Walton, William Faithorne, and the musicians Henry Purcell, John Blow and Pelham Humfrey. It was a circle of young intellectuals, all gifted in their way but possessing the unstable temperament so frequently met with among this type of person. In spite of the fact that he wrote a *Bachelor's Song against Marriage* at the age of thirty-seven, he was, in the words of Anthony Wood, "smitten with a fair virgin; and more with her fortune"! The name of the lady is not recorded but they were married on 26th November, 1672. The son of this marriage died before his father. How successful this marriage was we do not know; Flatman had an estate in Tishton, near Diss in Norfolk, but appears to have resided for the most part in Three-Leg Alley, St. Bride's, London. He died there 8th December, 1688, and Anthony Wood's description that "at length he gave way to fate", is taken to imply that he committed suicide. Both he and his son were buried in St. Bride's. (Colour Plates 8A and 9F.)

His style of painting may be divided into two phases. His early miniatures based on works by Cooper and painted c.1661 are for the most part dull interpretations of the master's work, and lack the sure touch and inspiration of Cooper's portraits. The flesh colours are an unpleasant brown and the general effect of the portraits of this period is rather uninteresting. These include the one of Samuel Woodford, and two in the Victoria and Albert Museum, one of an unknown man signed and dated 1662, and the other of Charles Beale, Senior, 1664. He favoured the use of a sky background, and this can easily be distinguished from portraits by Cooper as he used a harsh blue not found in any of Cooper's works. Richard Goulding, in *The Welbeck Abbey Miniatures,* lists signed and dated miniatures spanning the years between 1661 and 1683. It is difficult to place his miniatures chronologically except by costume, and many of them are unsigned and those that are signed with his initials 'TF' are not always dated. His brilliantly painted self-portrait signed and dated 1673, and formerly in the Buccleuch Collection, is in the Victoria and Albert Museum. It was presented to the Museum in memory of the late Basil Long.

An interesting miniature was sold at Christie's, 6th July, 1965, bearing a false signature: 'SC / 1662' (Plate 21C). It is undoubtedly by Flatman, and bears out the often repeated statement that mature works by Flatman are of sufficiently good quality to pass as portraits by Samuel Cooper. The portrait was catalogued as 'An unknown Man', but it has been suggested by Graham Reynolds that it may represent Flatman himself, painted at an earlier age than the known self-portrait in the Victoria and Albert Museum. The

Plate 21C. **T. Flatman,** *portrait of a man, vellum 2¾ins., 1662. It has been suggested that this may be a self-portrait. It is an interesting example of a miniature which had a false Cooper signature added. The monogram: 'SC' has been removed by the present owner. Courtesy E. Hawtin, Esq.*

Plate 21D. **Mary Beale** *(1632/3-1699), self-portrait, vellum, 3½ins., c.1678-80. The attribution to Mary Beale seems reasonable and the portrait undoubtedly represents her. There is an inscription on the reverse: 'Mrs Mary Beale a famous woman for painting ye head in the Pall Mall. Died at ye age of . . . years in the year 1698. Painted in 1679.' This miniature was for many years in the collection of the Earl of Derby. Courtesy Christie's.*

Plate 21E. **T. Flatman,** *John Lee Warner, vellum, 3¹/₈ins., c.1660-70. Signed in monogram: 'TF'. This superb portrait shows Flatman at his best. The brown robe is shaded with pure gold, and the slashed sleeves and lace cravat are tied with green ribbons.* Courtesy The Walters Art Gallery, Baltimore.

Plate 21F. Attributed to **C. Beale, Junior,** *an unknown man, vellum, 2¼ins. The sitter is wearing a deep lace cravat and brown cloak. Ex. de la Hey Collection.*

addition of false signatures is met with in almost every period and one suspects that the motive was to enhance the value of the goods! There have always been collectors who demand miniatures that are signed, and there will always be those who will be willing to oblige by adding the necessary monogram or signature! I well recall an instance of an eighteenth century miniature which was sold in London some years ago unsigned, and which reappeared some months later, in another sale room, fully signed and dated!

To understand the difference in technique between miniatures by Flatman and those by Cooper, it is necessary to examine them under a strong glass. By so doing, one can see the difference in texture. Whereas Cooper's miniatures are painted with a broad brush stroke and the flesh colours blended together with a smooth finish. Flatman paints the features in a coarser style, with brownish lines for shading. Twenty-one of Flatman's miniatures were exhibited at the National Portrait Gallery together with those of Cooper, and this provided a good opportunity for students to make comparisons. He seems to have painted fewer portraits of women than men, two exceptionally good ones are the 'Portrait of an unknown Lady', formerly said to be the artist's wife, signed: 'TF' and dated 1661 in the Victoria and Albert Museum, and one of Lady Langley, signed: 'TF', in a private collection. Of his male portraits one of outstanding quality is in The Walters Art Gallery, Baltimore. It represents John Lee Warner, wearing a full bottom wig and brown robes with the slashed sleeves which came into fashion c.1660; the robe or 'doublet' is shaded with pure gold and is trimmed with green ribbons; the cravat is tied with green ribbon at the neck. The sitter is painted against the usual sky background (Plate 21E).

That he studied and copied the works of old masters is evident from the fine miniature copy of 'David and Goliath', taken from the original in the Royal Collection by Domenico Feti. Flatman's copy is dated 1667. Examples of his works are to be found in most of the great collections, including those of H.M. The Queen, the Dukes of Buccleuch and Portland, and the Earl Beauchamp. Those accessible to the public are in the Victoria and Albert Museum, the National Portrait Gallery (which has a large half-length portrait of him and attributed to him), the Wallace Collection, London, the Fitzwilliam Museum, Cambridge, and the Ashmolean Museum, Oxford.

In view of the fact that the Beale family were so closely connected with Flatman, it seems logical to deal with their contribution to miniature painting at this point. In 1975 an exhibition of works by the Beale family and others was mounted at the Geffrye Museum, London. The catalogue produced for the exhibition contained much new information about the family and their lives. The catalogue of the exhibition entitled *The Excellent Mrs. Mary Beale,* is well illustrated, and serves as an excellent guide to her portraiture and that of her son, Charles Beale Junior (1660-1714).

Mary Beale, née Craddock (1633-1699), was the eldest child of the Rev. John Craddock (c.1595-1651/2) and his wife, Dorothy. Her father was the Rector of Barrow in Suffolk, where Mary was baptised in the adjoining church of All Saints on 26th March, 1633. The Craddock family came from Staffordshire, where they had prospered through the boom in the wool trade in the late sixteenth century. Her grandfather, Richard Craddock (1562-1630), was ordained on 6th July, 1593, and is thought to have been a curate at Newark-on-Trent. By his wife, Mary, he had a son, John (Mary's father), and three daughters, of whom Priscilla married Richard Thach, whose son, Nathaniel, became a miniaturist and will be discussed later in the

chapter. John Craddock was ordained priest in 1628, and succeeded his father as Rector of Barrow on his death in 1630. The Craddock family had many connections in Suffolk, some of whom were related to the Beale family, and it was no doubt through these friends that Mary met her future husband, **Charles Beale** (1631-1705). Charles was the son of Bartholomew Beale, from whom he inherited the Manor of Walton-on-Thames, where Charles was baptised on 9th June, 1631. His marriage to Mary Craddock took place at Barrow on 8th March, 1651/2, only a few days before the death of Mary's father. Their first son, Bartholomew, died at Walton on 18th October, 1654, and shortly afterwards the family moved to London. Their second son, also named Bartholomew, was baptised at St. Paul's, Covent Garden, on 14th February, 1655/6. Charles Beale, besides being an officer of the Board of Green Cloth, was an amateur painter and maker of artists' colours. The move to Covent Garden would have given them the opportunity to mix with many of the important professional painters of the day. Mary is supposed to have had some instruction from Robert Walker, who painted her husband and herself at about this time, and whose painting seems to have influenced her style. Although she knew and copied the works of Sir Peter Lely, and those of Van Dyck, there is no evidence that she was ever a pupil of Lely — as was suggested by George Vertue — but rather that the close relationship was a social one formed as one might expect through their mutual interests.

In c.1660 Charles Beale took over his father's profession as Deputy Clerk of the Patents Office, which provided the family with a house of some size in Hind Court, Fleet Street. Reference to Beale acting in this capacity is made by Samuel Pepys in his diary on 13th July, 1660, when he was obtaining letters patent. Having obtained a receipt from the Chancellor, Pepys says: "And so carried it to Mr. Beale for a Dockett; but he was very angry, and unwilling to do it, because he said it was ill-writ (because I had got it writ by another hand and not by him); but by much importunity I got Mr. Spong to go to his office and make an end of my patent, and in the meantime Mr. Beale to be preparing my Dockett; which being done, I did give him two pieces, after which it was strange how civil and tractable he was to me". Pepys returned later to collect his patent, and paid Beale £9.

The Beales' younger son, Charles, was born at Hind Court on 16th June, 1660, and baptised on 23rd June, at St. Dunstan's-in-the-West, Fleet Street. The size of the house enabled them to set aside a "Paynting roome" for Mary, and Charles was able to increase and display his collection of books,

Colour Plate 9.

A top left. **Peter Paul Lens,** *an unknown young lady, ivory, 1²³/₃₂ins., c.1730-40. Signed in monogram: 'PL.' This is an attractive miniature by P. Lens, and not unlike Colour Plate 9B by his brother.*

B top right. **Andrew Benjamin Lens,** *Margaret (Peg) Woffington (1714?-60), ivory, 1¾ins. Signed in monogram and dated: 'ABL / 1744.'*

C centre. **Lawrence Cross(e),** *Lady Katherine Tufton, vellum, 3¹¹/₃₂ins. Signed in monogram on the front: 'LC' and on the reverse: 'Lady Katherein Tufton / LC [monogram] cross fe. / 1707.' This is one of the problem signatures that could be read as 'PLC.'*

D lower left. **Bernard Lens,** *an unknown girl, ivory, 1⅞ins., c.1730. Signed in monogram: 'BL.' It is interesting to compare the miniatures in Colour Plates 9A, B and D, all by the Lens family.*

E lower right. **Christian Richter,** *Eleanor Brownlow Viscountess Tyrconnel, vellum, 1⅞ins., c.1709.*

F bottom. **Thomas Flatman,** *Abraham Cowley (1618-67) poet, vellum, 2¾ins. Signed in monogram: 'TF.'*

Courtesy Victoria and Albert Museum, Alan Evans Collection

paintings and drawings which included works by Rubens, Van Dyck, Adriaen Hanneman and Lely, together with portraits of the Beales themselves by both Walker and Lely. The originals of both these latter portraits appear to have been lost.

Their wide circle of friends included men who were to rise to positions of importance in their professions such as the church, the sciences and the Civil Service. Many of them were painted by Mary, including two future Archbishops of Canterbury, Thomas Tenison and John Tillotson, whose portrait in oil is at Canterbury, and a miniature copy by Charles Beale, Junior in the collection of H.M. The Queen.

One of their most frequent visitors was Thomas Flatman, who was studying law at the Inner Temple. He does not appear ever to have practised law, but turned his attention to painting and writing verse, relying for subsistence on a meagre allowance from his family. In his letters to Charles Beale he addresses him as "Master", and calls Mary both his "Valentine" and his "Scholar". Whether or not he actually gave her any lessons in limning we do not know, but the few miniatures by or attributed to her show his influence.

Due to changes among the hierarchy in the Civil Service Charles felt his position to be insecure, and this, coupled with the danger caused by the Great Plague, made the family decide to leave London. They found a house in Albrook, at Otterbourne in Hampshire, and left London on 26th June, 1665 and remained there until 1670, when Charles obtained the lease of a house "next to the Golden Ball" in Pall Mall for £42 per annum. This return to a fashionable part of London was a golden opportunity for Mary to establish herself as a professional painter. Charles' role seems to have been that of housekeeper rather than that of breadwinner. He attended to the running of the studio, making careful notes of all sittings, and kept the accounts. His contribution to art was his knowledge of artists' colours, and his ability to prime canvases for his wife. He occasionally supplied colours to other painters, and his notebooks, which he kept up to 1681, provide valuable information regarding his wife's sitters. In spite of the fact that his "Dearest and most indefatigible Heart" often worked from dawn to dusk to earn sufficient money to support the family, Charles was inclined to be a spendthrift, and the family got into financial straits. Mary, as far as we know, did not paint many miniatures, or if she did they pass unrecognised. One of the finest is her self-portrait which was formerly in the collection of the Earl of Derby. This was sold at Christie's, 8th June, 1971, for 1,800 guineas, and had been purchased by the 13th Earl of Derby at Horace Walpole's sale at Strawberry Hill, 14th May, 1842. Although the attribution to Mary as the artist has been questioned it is generally believed that it is an authentic work by her (Plate 21D). A miniature said to represent Henry Somerset, 1st Duke of Beaufort, is in the collection of the Earl Beauchamp, and is signed: 'MB' (monogram) and dated 1674. A miniature of Catherine Sedley, Countess of Dorchester, signed: 'MB', was No. 49 in the Beale Exhibition, 1975, when it was attributed to Mary. It was not in my opinion by the same hand as the others and lacked the draughtsmanship of her work; it may have been a miniature by Margaret Bingham, later Countess of Lucan. Other miniatures have been attributed to Mrs. Beale on the basis of style, including one of Charles II and another of William III, which are painted in the same manner as that of Henry Somerset. It is not known for certain what Mary Beale charged for miniatures, but her fee for a three-quarter length portrait was £10, and for 'head and shoulders' she charged £5. If she used expensive pigments such as ultramarine an extra ten per cent was charged. Oil paintings "in little", which were probably oil portraits on a small scale rather than miniatures, were charged at the same rates as her big portraits. With the exception of important commissions, or copies after other artists, she seems to have completed her works in three sittings. Many of her best portraits are of children, although I know of no miniatures by her of a child. A characteristic of her miniatures of men seems to be the way she painted the hair in a mass with the curls looking rather like sausages! She used both a brownish and a blue shading on the flesh, and tended to paint the sitters against a brown background. Some of her large portraits were in crayon. Between 1681 and c.1691, Mary had students working with her; they included a girl called Keaty Trioche, Mr. More, and Sarah Curtis (1676-1743) from Yorkshire, a girl who married the Rev. Benjamin Hoadley in 1701. Her husband became, in turn, Bishop of Bangor, Hereford, Salisbury and Winchester. Mary Beale's most prolific period seems to have been from c.1670-1680, during which time she painted over thirty portraits for the Lowther family. Her sons, Charles and Bartholomew, both assisted her in her studio; Charles had a love and aptitude for art, but Bartholomew lost interest and took up medicine. From c.1681 onwards Mary's patronage diminished; Lely had died in 1680, and fashions changed. She continued to paint for at least another ten years, but rising costs caused her to use cheaper paints and coarser backings. She died in their house in Pall Mall in 1699, and was buried in St. James's Church, Piccadilly on 8th October. Her husband retired to live with his son, Bartholomew, in Coventry until his death. He was buried in St. Michael's Church, Coventry on 27th November, 1705. Bartholomew was buried in the same church on 17th May, 1709, and his widow on 25th January, 1726.

Charles Beale, Junior (1660-1714?) is best known for his large and very important collection of drawings executed in red chalk or black lead and, in some cases, a combination of the two. Having grown up in an artistic family, and seen his parents at work, he would have already had some knowledge of painting before he was sent to Thomas Flatman to be taught 'limning' on 5th March, 1677. His father provided him with the necessary equipment and a desk, but, according to Vertue, he only painted in miniature for about five years, when he had to give it up due to bad eyesight, and for the rest of his career he confined his art to drawing. Only a few authentic miniatures by him are known, of which four are in the Victoria and Albert Museum. These include a copy of a self-portrait by Lely, Antoine Trieste, after Van Dyck, Richard Maitland, 4th Earl of Lauderdale based on a double oil painting by Mary Beale, and one of Anne, Countess of Lauderdale, after the same portrait. Other examples of his works in miniature are in private collections. (Plate 21F.) Three sketch books of his drawings exist covering the period 1679-81. One is in the Pierpont Morgan Library, New York; further sketches are in a private collection, and some 175 drawings are in the British Museum.

One of his characteristics is the manner in which he modelled his portraits with long lines and cross hatching. This technique can be seen in a lesser degree on his miniatures, and is a useful pointer for identification. He did

Plate 22A (left). **M. Snelling,** *an unknown nobleman, vellum, 2¹³/₁₆ins. Signed on the reverse: 'M:S: Fecitt / 1663', painted against a castle background in a landscape. This is an exceptionally fine example of Snelling's work.* Courtesy Victoria and Albert Museum, Alan Evans Collection.

Plate 22B (right). **N. Thach,** *after a painting by Honthorst, Princess Sophia of the Palatine (1630-1714), Electress of Hanover, mother of George I, and wife of Ernest Augustus, Elector of Hanover, vellum, 2½ins. Signed: 'NThach 1651'.* Courtesy Sotheby's.

not always sign his works; those known are either signed 'B' or 'CB' in monogram.

As has already been mentioned, **Nathaniel Thach** (bapt. 4th July, 1617) was another miniaturist who was related to the Beale family. He was Mary Beale's cousin, his mother being Priscilla Craddock, daughter of the Rev. Richard Craddock, Rector of Barrow in Suffolk, where Nathaniel was baptised. His father was Richard Thach, chandler, of St. Martin-in-the-Fields, London. Nothing is known about Nathaniel's education or training in art but he became a miniaturist of above average merit and deserves more attention than has been accorded to him in the past. When, after the death of his wife in c.1643, John Craddock remade his will, he appointed a distant cousin, Walter Craddock, guardian to his two children, Mary and John, and divided most of his estate between them. His painting materials he left to his nephew, Nathaniel. In the will he bequeathed his "empastered rounds as wee call them" to "Nathaniell Thach late of London Picture Drawer". As in the case of Alexander Cooper, Thach appears to have gone to work on the Continent, and it is generally supposed from known examples of his work that he worked at The Hague. Only a small number of miniatures by Thach have so far been discovered, and these date between 1649-1651, but there must be others awaiting identification.

His first recorded work was that of a lady thought to represent Anne of Gonzaga, Princess Palatine, signed and dated: 'NThach / 1649' (Plate 22C). The sitter is wearing a feathered head-dress, which suggests that she was in a masque costume. The miniature is supposed to have been among a group taken by James II to St. Germain, passing later to Louis XIV, kept in the Jewel Office in Paris during the Revolution, and acquired from there by the 2nd Earl Spencer. The miniature was sold to the de la Hey Collection in 1928, and was Lot 53 in the de la Hey sale at Sotheby's on 27th May, 1968, when it realised £1,750, and was acquired by the Victoria and Albert Museum. The miniature may be after a painting by Honthorst: the identification was suggested after comparison with an engraving of Anne of

Gonzaga, but the matter is still in dispute. The sitter is undoubtedly someone of importance. A miniature of Prince Maurice, Count Palatine, after an unknown artist is in the collection of H.M. The Queen, and is signed: 'N. Thach'. A very interesting miniature of Princess Louise Hollandine, after a self-portrait, was No. 58 at the Mary Beale Exhibition in 1975. The Princess was an accomplished amateur artist who had instruction from Honthorst. The original which had for some reason been cut down, was formerly in the collection of the Earls of Craven. The miniature, although not signed, is attributed with some confidence on the basis of style. It is in the Musée Carnavalet, Paris. A portrait of Charles II as a young man signed: 'N.Thach / F / 165—', the last numeral being indecipherable, is in The Mauritshuis, The Hague. This latter miniature, which is a fine example of Thach's work, has blue shading on the face, slightly reminiscent of the work of P. Cross. A miniature of Princess Sophia of the Palatine, Electress of Hanover, and mother of George I, after a portrait by Honthorst, was sold at Sotheby's, 29th March. 1965, Lot 41; it was signed and dated: 'NThach / 1651' (Plate 22B). The sitter was then unidentified.

It is interesting to note that Thach and Alexander Cooper were probably in The Hague at the same time, and, as the art circle was a close one, they would no doubt have met, especially as both artists appear to have worked for the Bohemian Royal family.

Another artist working at this period was **Matthew Snelling** (1621-1678). It had always been supposed that Snelling was possibly of Flemish origin, but Mr. Richard Jeffree has kindly supplied me with exact information regarding his dates of birth and death, parentage and marriage. This information was obtained a few years ago from a descendant, Mrs. J. Hammond Snelling.

Plate 22C. N. Thach, portrait of a lady called Anne of Gonzaga, vellum, 2⅜ins. Signed and dated: 'NThach / 1649'. An interesting miniature by this little-known artist. Ex. de la Hey Collection, now in the Victoria and Albert Museum.

Plate 22D. M. Snelling, Queen Henrietta Maria, as St. Catherine, possibly after Van Dyck, vellum, 7ins. Signed and dated: 'M:S: / :fe: / 1649'. This is the largest known miniature by Snelling and as such is of great importance. Courtesy The Duke of Northumberland, K.G.

Plate 22E. **M. Snelling**, *Sir Thomas Hervey (d.1694), vellum, 3ins., c.1650. This and Plate 22F, are part of a small group of miniatures by Snelling painted for the Hervey family.* Courtesy The Earl of Bristol, Ickworth Park.

Plate 22F. **M. Snelling**, *Isabella, Lady Hervey, wife of Sir Thomas, vellum, 2¾ins., c.1650.* Courtesy The Earl of Bristol, Ickworth Park.

It now appears that the Snelling family came from King's Lynn in Norfolk, where Matthew was baptised on 14th October, 1621 He was the son of Thomas Snelling (later Mayor of the Town) and his wife, Margaret, daughter of Matthew Clark, who served twice as Mayor of King's Lynn. Matthew's father died in 1623, and was buried in the Chapel of St. Nicholas, on 24th April. His mother remarried on 21st July, 1625 at Garboldisham, Ambrose Blagge, a widower of Little Horringer, by whom she had a daughter, Margaret (aunt of John Evelyn's friend of the same name). Horringer is adjacent to Ickworth, the home of the Bristol family, where there is still an important group of miniatures by Matthew Snelling. They represent Sir Thomas Hervey, Isabella, Lady Hervey (Plate 22F), and Judith, Lady May. The portrait of Lord Hervey is painted against a landscape with the turrets of a castle in the background (Plate 22E). A fine miniature of an unknown man in armour against a similar background is in the Alan Evans Collection at the Victoria and Albert Museum, and there is a close facial resemblance with the one of Lord Hervey, making it tempting to consider a possible relationship (Plate 22A). Horringer is also near to Barrow, where Mary Beale's father, the Rev. John Craddock, was Rector, and the close connection between the families is now understandable, as Mary and Matthew would have known each other from childhood, although Matthew was twelve years her senior.

Like the Blagges, Matthew was a Royalist, from whom he probably obtained most of his commissions. He married at the Church of St. Dunstan-in-the-West, on 3rd December, 1663, Elizabeth, daughter of Peter

Maplesden. Snelling is known to have been working in London from c.1647, and possibly earlier, as he was known to Samuel Cooper, who executed his portrait in chalk in 1644. He was living in the parish of St. Martin-in-the-Fields, but was not apparently buried there. His wife must have predeceased him, as on his death in 1678, letters of administration were granted to his half-sister, Margaret Blagge, as his children, Peter and Isabella, were minors.

Snelling supplied the Beale family with colours on at least two occasions. These are recorded by Vertue in his notebooks, The Walpole Society, Vol. XXIV, p.168, taken from Charles Beale's notebook of '167½': "4th March 167½ Mr Matthew Snelling ⟨one Snelling a Limner Qu.⟩ offered me for my Venus & Cupid of Rottenhamer— 30 guineas. (at 18 pence above value) I refused it. and woud have 40 guineas. I reckon it worth 50¹¹. a parcell of Pink made by Mr Snelling of the weed before it flowerd. & sent my wife 7 July 1658. a small parcell sent by Mr Snelling. 13 Sept. 1654."

According to Vertue, Snelling was "a gentleman and seldom painted unless for Ladies with whom he was a mighty favorite & a gallant". This statement is not in fact true, as a number of miniatures of men are known to exist, including those already mentioned and one of Richard Sackville, 5th Earl of Dorset, signed and dated on the reverse: 'MS / fec / June / 1655'. This, and the companion miniature of Frances Cranfield, Countess of Dorset, signed and dated on the reverse: 'MS / August / 1654', are in the collection of The Earl Beauchamp.

Snelling's works vary both in quality and technique; some are after the works of other artists such as Van Dyck. One interesting one of Queen Henrietta Maria as St. Catherine, possibly after Van Dyck, is in the collection of the Duke of Northumberland, and is signed and dated: 'M:S: / :fe: / 1649' (Plate 22D). It is seven inches high, and one of his most important works. A miniature of Charles I, by Snelling, drawn with a fine brush stroke on prepared paper, is at Chiddingstone Castle. It is after Van Dyck, and signed: 'MS / fe / 1647'.

From this fresh information regarding Matthew Snelling, we now know that the Beale, Snelling and Thach families were closely connected, and formed a small group of artists who all came from the Norfolk-Suffolk area. (Colour Plate 3E.)

It is impossible to guess by whom Snelling was taught to paint, or whether he developed a natural gift. He is known to have executed at least one large oil portrait, representing Baldwin Harvey, which is owned by the Royal College of Physicians.

One of the seventeenth century artists who has received more recognition in recent years is **David des Granges** (1611/13-c.1675). He was the son of Samson des Granges of Guernsey and his wife, Marie Bouvier. David was baptised as a Huguenot in London, 24th May, 1611 or 20th January, 1613. Later in life he became a Roman Catholic, and was associated for a time with French Dominicans. Although he began his career as an engraver, and in 1628 engraved the painting of 'St. George and the Dragon' after Raphael, the majority of his works seem to have been miniatures. At least one large painting in oil is attributed to him, that of 'The Saltonstall Family', formerly in the collection of Sir Kenneth Clark, and now in the Tate Gallery. It was painted c.1675, and represents the family of Sir Richard Saltonstall

Plate 23A. **D. des Granges,** *Sir James Hamilton, 2nd son of the 1st Earl of Haddington, vellum, 2ins. Signed: 'D^DG'. Courtesy The Earl of Haddington, K.T.*

Plate 23B. **D. des Granges,** *an unknown man, vellum, 2½ins., c.1650. Signed: 'D^DG', and set in an attractive contemporary gold and enamelled locket. This miniature is in fine condition and well executed. Courtesy Christie's.*

(d.1650). Sir Richard is holding the hand of one of his two elder children and standing at the bedside of his wife, Elizabeth, who has just been delivered of a child which is in the arms of a lady seated by the bed. It is not of outstanding quality in that the figures are rather stiffly drawn, but is a charming example of a homely domestic scene of the period.

Des Granges was employed by both Charles I and Charles II, and accompanied the latter to Scotland in 1651, when he was appointed "His Majesty's limner in Scotland". He knew Inigo Jones, and painted two portraits of him which are in private collections. Whilst in Scotland he apparently executed at least thirteen miniatures of Charles II, painted c.1651, presumably for presentation purposes. Twenty years later, having still received no payment for these works, des Granges who, by this time, was old and infirm, had lost his sight and was no longer able to support his family; he was obliged to petition the King for £72 still owing to him. Record of this petition is in the Treasury Papers and the matter was put to the Lords of the Treasury in November 1671. Whether he ever received any payment is not recorded. His condition was pitiable, and he had to rely on charity in his declining years. He died c.1675.

His earliest known miniature is of an unknown lady in the Victoria and Albert Museum. The costume is c.1630, and the miniature signed but not dated. One at Windsor Castle said to represent Catherine Manners, Duchess of Buckingham, is signed in his usual way: 'D^DG' in a triangle, and dated 1639. Des Granges is known to have copied works by Hoskins, and a typical example of this is one illustrated in *A Dictionary of British Miniature Painters,* colour plate VII, No. 25. This miniature was sold at Sotheby's, 28th March, 1977, Lot 4, in the Holzscheiter Collection, when it realised £1,400. It is signed in monogram, and was painted c.1630-40. The sitter, wearing a black figured doublet and falling white lace-edged ruff, is painted against a blue background. Besides copying Hoskins, des Granges executed works after other artists such as Titian, etc. His miniatures of Charles II as a young man are interesting representations of the young Prince, before the stiffer and more stylised paintings of him as an older man, with the coarser features shown on many of his large portraits.

It has been said that his signature was 'DG', or 'DDG', but I think that this is incorrect and that all miniatures signed 'DG' are the works of D. Gibson. Long mentioned a miniature signed 'DG', of the 2nd Earl of Carnarvon, which was then attributed to des Granges. This miniature has since come on the market, and is by D. Gibson and will be discussed later in the chapter.

As one might expect from an artist who painted many of his works after other artists, des Granges' work varies a great deal. Some is rather dull and lacking in draughtsmanship, whilst other portraits are well painted and show some originality in colour tones. Many of the backgrounds are either brown or dark grey which harmonise well with the colours of his sitters' costumes.

In my *Dictionary* I mentioned a miniature of Catherine of Braganza, Queen of Charles II, which was exhibited at South Kensington in 1865, when she was said to be "dressed as a pilgrim holding a staff and wearing a wide hat". The identity of des Granges was not then known, and I have now been able to identify the miniature with one sold at Sotheby's on 11th July, 1977, Lot 155 (Plate 23D). The miniature is based on a painting of the Queen depicted as a shepherdess. It is after the full-length picture by Jacob

Huysmans (in the Royal Collection) where the Queen is seated in a landscape with a sheep by her knee and a cherub standing by. Des Granges' miniature is painted in brighter colours, no doubt to make it more attractive on a small scale, and is signed with his usual monogram: 'D^DG'. The Queen is wearing a large pink hat trimmed with blue ribbons and feathers, and is painted against a brown curtain background with a crook at her side. Examples of des Granges' work are in the Victoria and Albert Museum, Ham House, the National Portrait Gallery, and many private collections.

Almost total lack of biographical information regarding the lives of seventeenth century artists frustrates the scholar at every turn, and this is certainly so with the Gibson family. **Richard Gibson** (1615-1690), or 'Gibson the Dwarf' as he is so often called, was the most important member of the family. He is thought to have been born in Cumberland, and to have started his career as a page to a lady in Mortlake. Having shown an aptitude for art he became a pupil of Francis Cleyn, then director of the tapestry works at Mortlake. He was influenced by Lely, whose works he studied. By some means or other he became noticed at Court, and attracted the attention of Queen Henrietta Maria. The fact that he was a dwarf no doubt intrigued the courtiers, and a bride was found for him of the same height — three feet, ten inches! His wife's name was Ann or Anna Shepherd, by whom he had nine children, of whom five lived and grew to a normal size. I am indebted to Mr. Robert Bayne Powell for obtaining for me a photostat of Richard Gibson's will, from which valuable information can be gleaned.

The marriage of this tiny pair inspired the poet Edmund Waller to write a poem commemorating the event, one verse of which reads:

> Design or Chance make others wive,
> But Nature did this match contrive:
> Eve might as well have Adam fled,
> As she deny'd her little bed
> To him, for whom Heav'n seem'd to frame,
> And measure out this only dame . . .

The exact date of the marriage is not at present known, but the poem was first published in 1640. It was in the same year that Van Der Doort hanged himself because, it is said, he could not find a miniature by Gibson, 'The

Plate 23C. **R. Gibson,** *a young boy, vellum, 2½ins. Miniatures of boys of this period are scarce and this is a well painted and attractive example.* Courtesy Victoria and Albert Museum, Alan Evans Collection.

Plate 23D (left). **D. des Granges,** *Catherine of Braganza (1638-1705), Queen of Charles II, after a portrait by J. Huysmans, vellum, 3¹/8ins. Signed: 'D^DG'. The Queen is depicted as a shepherdess, with her shepherd's crook at her side.* Private Collection.
Plate 23E (right). **D. des Granges,** *Inigo Jones (1573-1652), vellum, 2³/8ins., c.1641. Inscribed and signed: 'Age / 68 / D^DG'. This splendid miniature was framed for Edward Harley by B. Lens in 1726 at a cost of "10s 6d." The sitter is wearing a grey doublet and black cloak against a blue background. Another version is in the Devonshire Collection, where the doublet is mauve.* Courtesy Ivy, Duchess of Portland.

Parable of the Lost Sheep', which had been entrusted to his care. If this was indeed the cause of his death it is sad, because the miniature was later found in his estate and returned to the King.

The names of the Gibsons' surviving children were Susan Penelope (later Mrs. Rosse), Rose Anna, or Anna (later the wife of Marinus van Vrijbergen), and Elizabeth — all mentioned in his will. The names of the two sons were John, or Johan, an officer in the Netherland Army, and Dirck, a master sculptor in The Hague. From the will we now know that Edward Gibson, also a miniaturist, was not as has previously been suggested Richard's son but his brother.

At least two oil portraits of Richard and Anne Gibson were painted by Lely, one c.1650 and the other dated 1658. An oil portrait of 'A Sleeping Dwarf', by Lely, and now identified as of Richard Gibson was No. 16 in the Lely Exhibition at the National Portrait Gallery, 1978. It was probably painted c.1640, and No. 18 in the same exhibition was the one of Gibson and his wife of c.1650. A self-portrait in chalk by Gibson is in the British Museum, together with a portrait drawing of a child signed in monogram: 'RG' and dated 1669, and a third of an unknown little girl, holding a doll and a pack of playing cards. Details of these, two of which are illustrated, are in *British Drawings,* by E. Croft-Murray and P. Hulton, 1960. Lack of signed works by Richard Gibson makes identification difficult, one said to represent Louise de Keroualle, Duchess of Portsmouth, signed on the reverse: 'R. Gibson Fecit / 1673', is in the Uffizi, Florence, who also have a miniature attributed to Gibson of Barbara Villers, Countess of Castlemaine. A miniature copy of Titian's 'Marquis del Guasto with his Mistress' is in the Portland Collection. On the reverse is an inscription by the 2nd Earl of Oxford: 'This Limning is by Gibson 1640' (Plate 24E). Three other miniatures attributed to Gibson are in the Portland Collection, including one of Mary of Modena, based on a portrait by Lely, and one of Lady Charlotte Fitzroy, Countess of Litchfield, which bears a label on the reverse: 'Lady Litchfield by Gibson the Dwarf'. Other miniatures attributed to Gibson are in private collections; four were exhibited at the National Portrait Gallery in 1974, Nos. 184-187. One, which is particularly attractive, is inscribed on the reverse: 'My Lady Franklin', and is now thought to represent Dorothy (1657-1707), second wife of Sir John Franklin of Bolnhurst, Beds. The sitter is wearing a pale yellow dress edged with white and a grey wrap, painted against a greenish-brown background. The draughtsmanship is good, and the miniature has a charm closely allied to the works of Cooper. The flesh is shaded with slight blue strokes (Colour Plate 8C).

Gibson is reputed to have painted several portraits of Cromwell, but none of them has so far been discovered. He became drawing master to the daughters of James II; both Mary and Anne subsequently became Queens of England. When Mary went to Holland in 1677 to marry William of Orange, Gibson accompanied her and lived at The Hague on and off for about ten years; in 1679 he rented a house there. He is thought to have returned to England in 1688 on the accession of William and Mary, and remained in London until his death on 23rd July, 1690. His chief patron was the Earl of Pembroke. An interesting unfinished portrait of his wife executed in plumbago and grey wash was sold at Sotheby's, 6th March, 1967, for £250. In his will dated 11th November, 1677, he describes himself as "of the Parish of St Martin's in the Fields". He left his two houses in Petty France to his wife, Ann, for life, and, after her death, to his three daughters. In the event of none of them surviving, the houses were left to the children of his brother, Edward, by his wife, Margaret. He forgives Edward all the debts owing to him, "Arrears of Rents Reckonings claims and demands". He further requests his wife to acknowledge satisfaction of all or any "Judgements" in any Court entered in his name against Edward. To his friend, William Towers, he left his "Little Birding Gun". He meant to leave some money to the poor of the Parish of St. Martin-in-the-Fields, but forgot to mention the amount! He appointed his wife sole executrix, and left her all the rest of his estate for life with the power to dispose of it between her three daughters "or any of them wch shee shall finde most Dutifull and to whome shee shall thinke most meet to bequeath the same". One of the witnesses to his will was William Gibson (c.1644-1702/3), presumably his nephew, also a miniaturist. Appended to the will was a memorandum dated July 20th, 1690, stating that "Mr Richd Gibson died ab^t 10 a clock or ab^t ii½: We whose names are underwritten found this

Mich^l Rosse
Sus Pen Rosse
Anne Vrybergen
W. Gibson
Edward Gibson".

No mention is made of his sons with whom he may have fallen out. He left his wife all the arrears of his annuity due to him from the Earl of Pembroke. The date of Mrs. Gibson's death is not known. The daughter, Anna, had become involved in matrimonial difficulties in Holland, where she became intimate with the younger son of a statesman, Marinus van Vrijbergen, by whom she had a daughter in 1681 in London, whom she called Elizabeth. Although in 1679 Marinus had "plighted his troth" to Anna in front of a Roman priest, when she went to England he went off with another girl and refused to marry her. Eventually matters were resolved and the couple were married in London: Graham Reynolds gives the date as 1702, but Anna was using his name on the above document in 1690.

Plate 23G. **R. Gibson**, *Barbara Villiers, Duchess of Cleveland (1641-1709), vellum, 3⅜ins., c.1660. This miniature is by family descent from Robert, 2nd Earl of Sunderland. It is a good example of how the hair was dressed with pearls. Courtesy the late Earl Spencer.*

Plate 24A. **D. Gibson**, *The Hon. Peregrine Bertie (d.1700), vellum, 2¾ins. By family descent. A miniature of the sitter's sister, Lady Catherine Dormer, also by Gibson is in the Victoria and Albert Museum. Private Collection.*

Plate 23F. **R. Gibson** *'The Dwarf', Elizabeth Dormer, Countess of Carnarvon, née Capel, vellum, 3¼ins. Signed on the reverse: 'La Camaruan: a Capel / by Mr. Richard Gibson'. This miniature is of particular interest as few signed works by R. Gibson are known. Courtesy Christie's.*

Plate 24B. **D. Gibson,** *portrait of an unknown man, vellum, 2½ins., c.1648. Signed in monogram 'DG'.* Courtesy Sotheby's.

Plate 24C. **D. Gibson,** *Elizabeth, Countess of Essex (d.1717), daughter of Algernon Percy, 10th Earl of Northumberland, and wife of Arthur, 1st Earl of Essex, vellum, 2¼ins. A smaller version of this miniature is at Castle Howard.* Private Collection.

The problem of sorting out miniatures and making accurate identification to either Richard or **D. Gibson** (fl.1656-1658) is not an easy one as their style of painting is very close. There is not so far any clue as to D. Gibson's identity unless he is Richard's son, Dirck, who is recorded as a sculptor in The Hague, c.1690-1712, but in view of the long gap in dates it seems unlikely. D. Gibson's works are dated from 1656-1658. One fully signed one is in the Victoria and Albert Museum. It represents Lady Catherine Dormer and is inscribed on the reverse: 'my Lady K. Dormer / picter done by mr / Gibsone'. A miniature of her brother, the Hon. Peregrine Bertie, was also painted by Gibson (Plate 24A), and two miniatures in the Beaufort Collection of Elizabeth Capel, Countess of Carnarvon, and her husband, Charles, 2nd Earl of Carnarvon, both signed: 'DG' in monogram are key pieces of his work (Plates 24D and F). The Dormer family were also painted by Samuel Cooper.

Seven miniatures by or attributed to D. Gibson were exhibited at the National Portrait Gallery in 1974, and since then a second version of Charles, 2nd Earl of Carnarvon, signed and dated: '1656 / DG' (monogram) was sold at Sotheby's, Lot 60, 29th November, 1976, when it realised £1,150. It was identical in pose and costume to the one in the Beaufort Collection. D. Gibson appears to have used the same dark brown or greenish backgrounds as Richard on his miniatures, but on those I have seen he has used rather more white in the flesh colours and the general effect seems to be slightly more forceful. A fine miniature of an unknown man in armour, in a seventeenth century gilt frame, is a good example of D. Gibson's style, and shows a marked affinity to the works of Samuel Cooper, to whom it was at one time attributed (Plate 25D).

Apart from the crayon self-portrait, signed and dated 1690, no authentic works by **Edward Gibson** (1668-1701) have been identified. He is known to have painted in oil and drawn in crayon, and may have painted miniatures. As has already been mentioned, he was Richard Gibson's brother and not his son, and was one of those who signed the memorandum to Richard's will. The wording of the will, in which Richard forgives him all his debts, suggests that he may have been improvident! The member of the Gibson family about whom we know rather more is **Susan Penelope Gibson (Mrs. Rosse)** (c.1652-1700), daughter of Richard Gibson. Susan followed her father's profession and was his pupil. Whether or not she actually had any tuition from Samuel Cooper is not known, but she certainly studied and frequently copied his miniatures, a number of which copies have for many years been attributed to Cooper. Some of her miniatures were taken from life and many of them are painted on a very small scale, an inch or less in height, as in the case of one of the Duchess of Portsmouth which is only ¹⁵/₁₆in. by ¾in. Susan married a jeweller named Michael Rosse (1650-aft.1735), from whom Vertue obtained much valuable information about her work, and who showed him portraits of the Gibson family. In 1723 Michael Rosse sold a large collection of miniatures and drawings at his house in Cecil Street, London. Extracts from this catalogue were published in *Samuel Cooper*, 1974. The sale contained a large number of miniatures by Richard Gibson, Susan Rosse, Samuel Cooper and others, and included works by Holbein and Isaac Oliver, and the catalogue is useful for identification purposes. Only a few of Mrs. Rosse's miniatures are signed, and those that are must have been

Plate 24D. **D. Gibson,** *Elizabeth Capel, Countess of Carnarvon, wife of Charles, 2nd Earl of Carnarvon, vellum, 3¼ins. Signed in monogram: 'DG'. This is another example of the sitter's hair being dressed with pearls. She wears a string of pearls round her neck, and jewels on her low-cut dress. Courtesy The Duke of Beaufort, K.G.*

Plate 24E. **R. Gibson** *after Titian, 'The Marquise del Guasto', vellum, 5¼ins. Dated '1640'. The Marquess is bidding farewell to his wife on his departure to war. She holds in her lap a globe of glass, symbolising fragile happiness. On the reverse of the Lens frame is an inscription by the 2nd Earl of Oxford: 'The Marquis del Guasto and his mistress. The original is by Titian. This Limning is by Gibson 1640.' Courtesy Ivy, Duchess of Portland.*

Plate 24F. **D. Gibson,** *Charles, 2nd Earl of Carnarvon (1632-1709), vellum, 3¼ins., c.1650-60. Signed in monogram: 'DG.' A pair to Plate 24D. A smaller version of this portrait, also by Gibson, signed and dated: '1656', was sold at Sotheby's in 1976. See page 124. Courtesy The Duke of Beaufort, K.G.*

painted after her marriage as she signed either: 'SR' or 'SPR'; occasionally the lettering is sloping. I know of none that is dated. She died in Covent Garden in 1700 at the age of forty-eight, and was buried in the church there. She adopted Cooper's method of painting a thin layer of white on the vellum before commencing the portrait, and a characteristic seems to be the way she gives her sitters a slightly pouting lower lip, on which the highlight is often dark. One of the most notable of her works is her full scale copy of Cooper's sketch of the Duke of Monmouth as a boy, the original of which is in the collection of H.M. The Queen. The draughtsmanship although good has not got the quality of the master's hand, and lacks Cooper's effortless modelling (Plate 26E). Eleven of her miniatures were at the National Portrait Gallery in 1974; these included her copies of Cooper's miniatures of James II, as Duke of York, in the Victoria and Albert Museum, and one of Frances Teresa Stuart, Duchess of Richmond, after the unfinished miniature in the Royal Collection. Both these miniatures had always been catalogued as by Cooper, but placed next to his works her copies appear much harsher and the painting lacks Cooper's fluency (Plate 25E and G).

Further proof of the difficulty faced in distinguishing between the two artists' work is the contents of the so-called 'Cooper's Pocket Book'. This is in the Victoria and Albert Museum, and was bought in 1892 by the Museum. It is an ornately decorated wallet containing fourteen seventeenth century miniatures, which at the time of purchase were attributed to Samuel Cooper. Further investigation led Dr. G.C. Williamson to point out that many of the wigs belong to a period of c.1690, long after Cooper's death, and that an inscription reading: 'My Father Rosse' pointed to S.P. Rosse as the artist.

A

B

C

D

E

F

G

This view was accepted by both Basil Long and Carl Winter. The miniatures were framed together in a single mount, and attributed to S.P. Rosse. In 1975 Graham Reynolds published a pamphlet, *Samuel Cooper's Pocket Book,* in which he went into the whole matter afresh and put forward new theories regarding these works. To follow Reynolds' thoughts in any depth it is necessary to read the pamphlet thoroughly, but, put briefly, he considers that on the basis of style, Nos. 1-4 in the sketch book may well be by Cooper. No. 1 is a sketch of the head of Barbara Villiers, Duchess of Cleveland, which appears to be the study for the finished miniature of her in the collection of Lord Spencer. Of the other three unfinished sketches which Reynolds considers to be by Cooper, two are of unknown ladies, and one of an unknown man. Among the remaining ten miniatures are two supposed self-portraits of Susan, one of her sister, Anna Vrijbergen (Plate 25B), one of: 'My Father Rosse' which is thought to represent her father-in-law, painted c.1685, and the remainder identifiable by inscriptions on the reverse of the drawings. One of them is a sketch of Anne, Countess of Sussex, née Anne Palmer, the first daughter of Barbara, Duchess of Cleveland, by Charles II. She was married at the age of twelve.

One of the few signed miniatures to be offered for sale in recent years was Lot 131 at Christie's, 20th February, 1973, and said to represent Nell Gwyn; it is an attractive small miniature and is signed: 'S.R.' (Plate 25A). Examples of her work are in the Victoria and Albert Museum, the Fitzwilliam Museum, Cambridge, and private collections including that of H.M. The Queen.

The identity of the artist who signed his miniatures: '**D.M.**' (fl.1659-1676) has not yet been discovered; it has been suggested that he may be **David Myers** (seventeenth century) about whom we also know nothing other than the fact that an inscription on an old box gives this name, and Long noted a miniature inscribed: 'To Earl Clarendon', signed 'DM' (monogram) in gold, and inscribed in old ink: 'Purchased 3 Sept 1803. Edw Hyde Ld Clarendon 1608 d 1674. Painted by David Myers.' This miniature of Clarendon is now in a private collection. Works signed: 'D.M.' date from 1659-1676. His work is unpretentious and has a naïve charm without succeeding in reaching any great heights. His draughtsmanship tends to be weak, and, when he attempts large miniatures, such as the one of a man said to be Henry Fitzroy, Duke of

Plate 25.
A. **S.P. Rosse,** called *Eleanor (Nell) Gwyn (1650-1687), vellum, 1⅝ins. Signed: 'S.R'. She was probably the most popular of Charles II's mistresses and was described by Pepys as "pretty witty Nell". Signed miniatures by S.P. Rosse are rare.* Courtesy Charles Fleischmann Esq., Cincinnati, Ohio.
B. **S.P. Rosse,** *Mrs. Marinus van Vrijbergen, née Anna Gibson, sister of the artist, vellum, 2¾ins. c.1690. Inscribed on the reverse in a later hand: 'Mrs Vryberge'. One of a series of portraits by the artist once in a 'Pocket Book', traditionally believed to contain sketches by S. Cooper. Whilst some are still in dispute, a number are identified as by Mrs. Rosse.* Courtesy Victoria and Albert Museum.
C. **S.P. Rosse,** *Mrs. Phillips, vellum, 3ins. Inscribed in a late seventeenth century hand: 'Mrs Pru Fillips'. The hair style suggests a date of c.1690. This is another of the portraits from the 'Cooper Pocket Book'.* Courtesy Victoria and Albert Museum.
D. **D. Gibson,** *an unknown man in armour, vellum, 3½ins., painted c.1655-60. Enclosed in a seventeenth century pierced silver gilt frame, decorated with fruit and flowers.* Private Collection.
E. *Attributed to* **S.P. Rosse,** *James II, when Duke of York (1633-1701), after S. Cooper, and copied from the original in the Victoria and Albert Museum, vellum, 3½ins. Inscribed on the reverse: 'The Duke of York, drawn 1660 / after the decease of Car 2 / Jac 2'. This miniature was for many years attributed to Cooper, but the treatment is too harsh when compared with the original. See Colour Plate 7C.* Courtesy The Duke of Beaufort, K.G.
F. **S.P. Rosse,** *called Elizabeth Percy, née Howard (d.1704/5), 2nd wife of the 10th Earl of Northumberland, vellum, 2½ins. Inscribed on the reverse of the gesso base: 'Elizabeth / Countess of / Northumberland / No 1006 / 5'.* Private Collection.
G. *Attributed to* **S.P. Rosse** *after S. Cooper, Frances Teresa Stuart, Duchess of Richmond, vellum, 3½ins. The original portrait (also unfinished), painted c.1663, is in the collection of H.M. The Queen. This miniature is inscribed on the reverse: 'Miss Stewart the favourite Mistress / of Car 2. Married the Duke of Richmond & Lennox'.* Courtesy The Duke of Beaufort, K.G.

Plate 26A. **Mrs. Carli(s)le,** *portrait of a lady* called *the Duchess of Cleveland, oils on copper, 4½ins., c.1640. This is a fine example of a miniature in this medium.* Courtesy Christie's.

Plate 26B. **F. Smiadecki,** *Sir Anthony Cope, 4th Bt. of Hanwell, oils on card, 2½ins. This is a typical example of Smiadecki's way of painting.* Courtesy Christie's.

Plate 26C. **F. Smiadecki,** *an unknown man in a landscape, vellum, 2½ins., mid-seventeenth century.* Ex. de la Hey Collection.

Grafton, seated with his arm round a spaniel, the result is almost comical! A miniature of an unknown man in armour, signed and dated: 'DM / 1663', was Lot 148 in the Heckett sale at Sotheby's, on 11th July, 1977, when it realised £950, a record price for this artist (Plate 26D).

The artist who signed his works: 'F.S.' is said to be **Franciszek Smiadecki** (seventeenth century). Little is known about him except that he is thought to have been either Polish or Russian, and is traditionally supposed to have been taught by either Samuel or Alexander Cooper, and it is for this reason that I have included him in this chapter. His miniatures are of outstanding quality and are painted in both oil and watercolour, although those in watercolour are rare. I have not so far seen one by him of a woman and those of men are not of known sitters, although all of them look to be distinguished people. Four miniatures by him were exhibited at the National Portrait Gallery in 1974, and created a lot of interest by their quality. Stylistically they are closer to Samuel Cooper than his brother; the features are well modelled, and the lace on the sitter's collar, as in the case of a miniature in the Buccleuch Collection of an unknown man, superbly painted. Many of his oil portraits are on rather dark backgrounds; occasionally he introduced a sky and landscape background, and, when these are painted in watercolour, the colour of the sky is a bright blue more like that used by Flatman than Cooper. His miniatures have become more sought after recently, and are well worth acquiring (Plates 26B and C, Colour Plate 8B).

Another miniaturist who painted oil portraits in the seventeenth century was **Mrs. Joan (or Anne) Carlisle or Carlile (1606?-1679).** She worked during the reigns of Charles I and Charles II, and was patronised by the former who is supposed to have made her a valuable gift of ultramarine. Many of her miniatures are said to have been copied in the manner of Peter Oliver, and she also copied the works of old masters. An oil miniature of Sir Thomas and Lady Browne ascribed to her is in the National Portrait Gallery. Sir Thomas was a noted physician. She was referred to as Anne Carlisle in the

Plate 26D. **D.M.,** *portrait of a nobleman, vellum, 2¹/₁₆ins. Signed and dated: 'DM / 1663'. This is a good example of the work of this little known artist, and typical of the rather fuzzy way he painted hair.* Courtesy Sotheby's.

Plate 26E (right). **S.P. Rosse,** *James Scott, Duke of Monmouth and Buccleuch, K.G., after the unfinished version by S. Cooper in the collection of H.M. The Queen, vellum, 8½ins. This portrait, although good, lacks the panache of the master's hand. Compare it with Plate 19C.* Courtesy The Duke of Buccleuch and Queensberry, K.T.

seventeenth century, but this is now thought to have been an error and her correct name Joan. Only a small number of works by her are at present known. One of particularly fine quality of a lady 'called' the Duchess of Cleveland was sold at Christie's, Lot 21 on 8th June, 1971, when it realised 850 guineas (Plate 26A). A miniature of Charles I, said to be from life, is in a private collection and attributed to her.

Although artists such as Nicholas Dixon obtained the patronage of Charles II, his miniatures and those of the artists who followed him in the latter part of the seventeenth century were not based on the paintings of Samuel Cooper and his followers. In many cases they absorbed the style and technique of artists working on the Continent. This influence was to become more marked as time went on.

Historically miniatures painted in the sixteenth and seventeenth centuries are fascinating as often they are the only likeness in existence of the sitters. New collectors should not be put off looking for examples of these periods if they appeal to them, as I know from my own experience that with luck and sufficient knowledge and enthusiasm it is still possible to have 'a find'.

Plate 26F. **D.M.,** *portrait of an unknown man aged forty, vellum, 2¼ins. Signed and dated: 'ÆE 40 / 1664 / DM' (monogram). Note the rather harsh line dividing the background from the landscape.* Courtesy Sotheby's.

129

Chapter V

17th century Miniaturists and Continental Influence

AFTER THE RESTORATION and throughout the latter part of the seventeenth century there was no loss of patronage for either miniaturists or those who executed large paintings. Cooper and his followers could not keep pace with the demands made upon them, and the great artists such as Van Dyck, Lely, De Critz and others were kept fully employed, providing their patrons with works which graced the walls of stately homes.

With the return of Charles II great efforts were made to reassemble his father's collection, much of which had been hidden away, dispersed, or sold abroad. A committee was set up to consider how best these works of art could be restored to the King. The royal houses – Whitehall, Somerset House and St. James's – all needed refurbishing with suitable goods and paintings. An order was issued that anyone having in his possession any of the "King's Goods" should deliver them to the committee within a week.

Plate 27A. **N. Dixon,** called *George Monk, 1st Duke of Albemarle, K.G., vellum, 1⅞ins. Signed in monogram: 'ND'. The short scarf tied with ribbon suggests a date of c.1663, by which time Monk would have been forty-five. This sitter appears to be younger.* Courtesy Victoria and Albert Museum, Alan Evans Collection.

The problem of tracing these items and recovering them was not simple, and the whole matter took several years to accomplish. An inventory was drawn up in the late 1660s, by which time over 450 pictures and limnings had been put up at Whitehall and a considerable number were in store. Approximately 1,000 pictures had been recovered and included "twenty eight King's and Queen's In Small". Among the large paintings hung at Hampton Court was Jacob Huysmans' portrait of Queen Catherine of Braganza, on which the miniature by des Granges, mentioned in the previous chapter, was based.

In c.1660, the miniaturist **Nicholas Dixon** (fl.1660-1708) came into prominence. His Christian name has sometimes erroneously been given as Nathaniel. Little is known about his life or education, but from the manner of his early work it has been suggested that he might have had some instruction from John Hoskins. Amongst the limnings which have the closest affinity to Hoskins's work is one of Sir Henry Blount, c.1660, in the collection of The Earl Beauchamp (Plate 27F). One of an unknown man, formerly in the H.J. Pfungst Collection, shows the sitter wearing a deep white collar and a black silk mantle. It is painted against a cloudy sky background, with a dark area of paint behind the sitter's head. It is signed and dated: 'ND 1668,' and is close in style to Hoskins' portraits. Although Dixon's career began at about the same time as that of Thomas Flatman and when Cooper's was at its height, there is no similarity at all between his works and those of Cooper, and the two artists' miniatures should never be confused. A miniature said to represent Abigail, Lady Harley, painted c.1660-67, is in the Portland Collection. It is another example of Dixon's work that leans to Hoskins. The hair style is typical of that of the 1660s,

Plate 27B. **N. Dixon,** called *Barbara Villiers, Countess of Castlemaine and later Duchess of Cleveland (1641-1709), vellum, 3⁷/8ins. This hair style was popular c.1680.* Courtesy The Earl Beauchamp.

Plate 27C. **N. Dixon,** *Sir Thomas Osborne (1631-1712), vellum, 2½ins. Signed in monogram: 'ND'. The sitter was successively 1st Earl of Danby, Marquess of Carmarthen and Duke of Leeds.* Courtesy The Earl Beauchamp.

with curls over the forehead, a bun at the back, and ringlets to the shoulders. The sitter is wearing the usual string of pearls, and drop earrings, and a low-cut dress. The majority of Dixon's miniatures of women seem to date slightly later, from c.1680, when the hair was parted in the centre, with masses of curls at either side, and the back hair falling over the shoulders. This may in some cases have been false hair (Plate 27B).

Dixon modelled the face in a soft and undramatic manner, one of his characteristics being the way he shaded with a rather scratchy line, and used a reddish-brown flesh colour.

When comparing Dixon's miniatures with those of Cooper, one should study the eyes. His approach is totally different from Cooper's method of modelling the eye by painting a subtly graduated shadow, which cast a reflection on the eyeball and emphasised the individual features of the sitter. Dixon drew a shadow of uniform thickness under the upper lid, which made the eye appear slightly almond-shaped and languorous. These mannerisms became more pronounced in Dixon's later works, and although he made an important contribution to the art of miniature painting during this period, his draughtsmanship became less careful and lost much of its impact. He is one of the artists who made a number of miniatures after oil paintings. Thirty of these large miniature copies after old masters are at Welbeck; one is signed. They are part of a much greater number which are known to have existed. Two very important large limnings by Dixon are 'The Wise Men Offering Their Gifts', at Burghley House, measuring over sixteen inches in height (Plate 28), and a superb limning of Anne, Countess of Exeter, her brother, William, later 1st Duke of Devonshire, and a black page boy. This is also at Burghley, and is signed and dated: 'ND' (monogram) '1668'. This latter miniature is again very close in style to the larger miniatures by

Plate 27D (left). **N. Dixon,** *Barbara Villiers, Duchess of Cleveland with her child, vellum, 3¼ins. Signed in monogram: 'ND'. This miniature is by family descent through Robert Spencer, 2nd Earl of Sunderland. It closely resembles the painting by Henri Gascars in the collection of Viscount Dillon.* Courtesy the late Earl Spencer.

Plate 27E (right). **N. Dixon,** *James Scott, Duke of Monmouth and Buccleuch, K.G., vellum, 3ins. Signed in monogram: 'ND'. The sitter is wearing a tied scarf of lawn and fine lace and the sash of the Order of the Garter.* Courtesy The Duke of Buccleuch and Queensberry, K.T.

Hoskins, and is one of Dixon's finest works. His usual signature is 'ND' in monogram, the right-hand stroke of the N forming the left-hand stroke of the D. He seems to have had a distinguished clientele, and in 1673 succeeded Samuel Cooper as King's limner. In the *Callendar of Treasury Books,* 1672-5, p.395, 16th September, it is recorded that Dixon was to receive £200 per annum, "to be paid quarterly in lieu of diet or board wages".

In 1684/5 we know from documents found in Florence that Dixon held a lottery "of excellent miniature paintings". In 1698 he started another one called the 'Hopeful Adventure'; a total sum of £40,000 was involved which was to be divided up into prizes ranging from £3,000-£20, together with a collection of pictures and limnings which were to be seen at his house. The venture must have been a fiasco, and by 1700 he was obliged to mortgage seventy miniatures. These were transferred to John Holles, Duke of Newcastle, for £450 on 14th February, 1707/8, and a deed of sale signed by

Plate 27F (left). **N. Dixon,** *Sir Henry Blount (1602-1682), vellum. 2½ins. Signed in monogram: 'ND'. Sir Henry was a noted traveller who sided with the Royalists in the Civil War. This miniature is a good character study.* Courtesy The Earl Beauchamp.

Plate 27G (right). **N. Dixon,** *Mary of Modena (1658-1718), Queen of James II, vellum, 3³/16ins. This miniature has been said to represent Nell Gwyn, but the sitter's features are close to those of Queen Mary with whom it has now been identified. She was the second wife of James II, when Duke of York, and was the mother of Prince James Francis Edward, with whom she escaped to France.* Private Collection.

Dixon is at Welbeck. Only thirty of these limnings are still in the Portland Collection. They include copies of mythological and religious paintings as well as portraits. Interesting details regarding this transaction and some lists of Dixon's works are published in *The Welbeck Abbey Miniatures,* by R.W. Goulding. No references to Dixon occur after the date on which he signed the deed of sale, and one must presume that he never recovered from his financial embarrassment. The exact date of his death has not so far been found, but Vertue records that he died in King's Bench Walk, where he was avoiding prosecution.

Plate 28. **N. Dixon,** *'The Wise Men Offering Their Gifts', vellum, 16³/₈ins. This splendid 'cabinet miniature', is one of the finest of the period, and in brilliant condition. It is one of the treasures of the Burghley House Collection.* Courtesy The Marquess of Exeter, K.C.M.G.

Examples of his miniatures may be seen in the Victoria and Albert Museum, and others of importance are in private collections, including that of the Duke of Buccleuch where signed works are to be found; a particularly good one represents James Scott, Duke of Monmouth, signed: 'ND' (monogram) (Plate 27E), and another unsigned one, *called* Lucy Walter. Another interesting miniature is thought to·represent Mary of Modena. It is in a private collection (Plate 27G).

Plumbago miniatures were introduced during the latter part of the seventeenth century, and were in vogue from c.1660-1720. These miniatures were not sketches for miniatures in watercolour, but were finished portraits in their own right. They were drawn with sharp pieces of graphite, or black lead, the term being derived from the Latin, *plumbum*. It is not known who first discovered that graphite could be sharpened and used for drawing. Prior to this period portraits had been drawn in chalk, silver point and pen and ink, and some artists continued to use these media. The portraits were executed on vellum and on paper, and were not usually stuck on to a support, as in the case of miniatures painted in watercolour. The majority of these miniatures were in monochrome, but occasionally slight washes of grey or sepia were introduced, or a pale carmine on the flesh.

One of the most important artists who drew miniatures in plumbago was **David Loggan** (1635-1692), who although he was born in Danzig was of Scottish descent. He studied under the engraver W. Hondius, and later became a pupil of Crispin van der Pass, in Amsterdam, where he lived for seven years before coming to London. Loggan was influenced by Wenceslaus Hollar, an engraver who travelled to London in 1636 with the 2nd Earl of Arundel. In 1662 Loggan was employed by the King's printers to engrave the

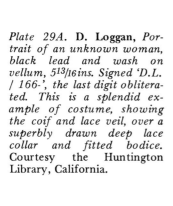

Plate 29A. **D. Loggan,** *Portrait of an unknown woman, black lead and wash on vellum, 5¹³/₁₆ins. Signed 'D.L. / 166-', the last digit obliterated. This is a splendid example of costume, showing the coif and lace veil, over a superbly drawn deep lace collar and fitted bodice.* Courtesy the Huntington Library, California.

Plate 29B. **R. White,** *self-portrait, black lead on vellum, within a feigned oval, 4⁹/₁₆ins. Inscribed: 'Ætat 16 / March 1 / 1661 / RW'. This is an interesting example of White's early work.* Courtesy the Huntington Library, California.

Plate 29C. **R. White,** *John Williams, Archbishop of York (1582-1650), black lead on vellum, 5½ins. Probably based on a portrait by C. Johnson as a preliminary drawing for White's engraving of Williams.* Courtesy the Huntington Library, California.

Plate 29D. **J. Faber,** *John Churchill, 1st Duke of Marlborough (1650-1722), pen and ink on vellum, 5¼ins. Possibly based on a portrait by Kneller. Inscribed round the outer edge: 'His Excell: IOHN Duke of Marlborough, Marquis of Blanford &c. Captain. Genl of all Her Majties Forces and Knight of the Garter'. Signed: 'J: Faber / A° 1705 / June 12'. This drawing shows clearly the minute details of an engraver.* Courtesy the Huntington Library, California.

Plate 29E. **J. Faber,** *Queen Anne (1665-1714), pen and ink, highly finished on vellum 4¾ins. Inscribed round the outer edge: 'ANNA . D.G. Angl. Scot. Fran. & Hiber. Regina. A° 1705', and signed 'J. Faber penna fecit 1705'. The drawing is thought to have been adapted from a portrait by Kneller. It is of a very high quality.* Courtesy the Huntington Library, California.

title of the *Book of Common Prayer,* published in that year. Apart from a short visit to Paris, Loggan lived in London where, on 15th June, 1663, he married Anna Jordan of Kencote, Oxfordshire, at the Church of St. Sepulchre. They left London to avoid the plague, and in 1665 were living at Nuffield, near Oxford. In 1669 Loggan moved into Oxford and was appointed Public Sculptor to the university, with a stipend of twenty shillings per annum!

In 1690 he was made engraver to Cambridge University, and is best known for his engraved works *Oxonia Illustrata,* 1675, and *Cantabrigia Illustrata,* c.1676-1690. Apart from his engravings and drawings he is said to have drawn a portrait on satin. Loggan had several pupils, including Edward Le Davis, Robert Shepherd, Michael Vandergucht and Robert White. This latter artist became equal to if not more proficient than his master. Loggan became known to a wide circle of people and numbered among his friends Sir Thomas Isham, 3rd Bart. He became a naturalised Englishman in 1675, and by the following year had an address in London. He died at his house in Leicester Fields in 1692 and was buried in St. Martin-in-the-Fields on 1st August.

Loggan's plumbago portraits are superbly drawn and expressive. One characteristic is the not infrequent use of a buff or yellowish tinge on the face. He signed his works in various ways: 'DL', 'DL del' (followed by a date), either in cursive or Roman initials. Occasionally he signed: 'D. Loggan' in full. Examples of his portraits are in the Victoria and Albert Museum, the British Museum, the National Portrait Gallery, the Ashmolean Museum, Oxford, etc. This latter has one of his finest works, representing Dr. Thomas Willis; and the Huntington Library, California, possesses some outstanding examples including a wonderful drawing of an unknown woman wearing a veiled hood over a wide lace collar and slashed sleeve dress. The drawing is so fine that every stitch can be seen (Plate 29A). In the same museum is a good miniature by Loggan of Charles, 6th Duke of Somerset. Other examples of his work are in numerous private collections (Plate 31F).

William Faithorne (c.1616-1691) was a native of London who studied painting and engraving under Robert Peake, James I's Serjeant-Painter, and under an engraver, John Payne. During the Civil War Faithorne joined the Royalists and he and Robert Peake's son, Sir Robert Peake, and W. Hollar were all taken prisoner at the siege of Basing House, 1645. Faithorne was imprisoned at Aldersgate, where he executed engravings. His draughtsmanship was above average, and whenever possible he drew his subjects from life. Having been banished to France, he is said to have had some tuition from Philippe de Champaigne and Nanteuil. On returning to London in

Colour Plate 10.
A. **Richard Collins,** *an unknown child, possibly Elizabeth Moore, ivory, 1³/8ins.*
B. **Charles Frederick Zincke,** *an unknown man, enamel, 1⁵/8ins. Signed: 'CF Zincke fecit / 1716.'*
C. **Joseph Lee,** *an unknown girl, probably after a portrait of c.1760, enamel, 1⁷/8ins. This is a most attractive miniature in fresh colours.*
D. **A. or N. Seaman,** *George II (1683-1760), possibly based on a large portrait, enamel, 2¹/8ins.*
E. **Nathaniel Hone,** *Mrs. Wilkes, enamel, 1¾ins. Inscribed on the reverse: 'Mrs (?) Wilkes / St.John's Square / Clerkenwell. London / 1753 / N.Hone Pinxt.'*
F. **James Scouler,** *an unknown man, ivory, 1½ins. Signed: 'Scouler 1771.'*
G. **Charles Frederick Zincke,** *Thomas, 4th Duke of Leeds (1713-89), enamel, 1⁷/8ins.*

Private Collection

A

B

C

D

E

F

G

Plate 30A. **W. Faithorne,** *John Aubrey (1626-97), vellum, 7¾ins. Inscribed with the sitter's name and dated: '1666', when Aubrey was forty years of age. This sensitive portrayal of Aubrey is one of the finest drawings of the period and shows the fashion for long hair and the* rabat *or* cravat, *of* point de venise *lace.* **Courtesy the Ashmolean Museum.**

Plate 30B. **G. Vertue,** *possibly after an original by Lely, Richard Gibson, 'The Dwarf', pencil and pen and wash on paper, 6½ins. Inscribed: 'Gibson / Little Mr. Richard Gibson painted / P. Lilly. pinx. Ob 16g Æat 7.5. G.V'. This is one of the few portraits of Gibson in existence.* **Courtesy the Huntington Library, California.**

c.1650 he shared a house with Hollar for a time and sold prints in a shop near Temple Bar. Samuel Pepys mentions him several times in his *Diary,* and bought a number of prints from him. On 7th November, 1666, Pepys says: ". . . took a coach and called at Faythornes to buy some prints for my wife to draw by this winter; and here did see my Lady Castlemaynes picture done by him from Lilly's, in red chalke and other colours, by which he hath cut it in copper to be printed. The picture in chalke is the finest thing I ever saw in my life I think, and I did desire to buy it; but he says he must keep it awhile to correct his Copper plate by, and when it is done he will sell it to me." On 1st December of that year Pepys visited Faithorne again and bought three prints of the picture which had only been done that day.

Faithorne was a friend and contemporary of Thomas Flatman, who composed some verses in his praise. He married Mary, daughter of Captain Grand, or Cround, by whom he had two sons and a daughter. Mrs. Faithorne predeceased him, and William died in Printing House Square, London, in May, 1691, and was buried in St. Anne's Church, Blackfriars. He numbered amongst his pupils John Fillian and Thomas Hill. Original works by him are scarce; examples may be seen at the British Museum, the Bodleian Library, Oxford, and the Ashmolean Museum, Oxford, which owns the superb portrait of John Aubrey. This latter miniature is drawn in black lead and Indian ink on vellum and dated 1666 (Plate 30A). A supposed self-portrait of Faithorne is in the Huntington Library, California, which also possesses interesting drawings by George Vertue, whose work will be discussed in Chapter VI (Plates 30B and C).

Plate 30C. **G. Vertue,** *Mrs. Gibson, wife of Richard Gibson, black and red pencil on tinted paper, 7¾ins. Inscribed 'G.V.', and on the reverse: 'Mrs Gibson' (twice). Lely is known to have painted a double portrait of Gibson and his wife, but this drawing is not thought to be based on Lely's version.* Courtesy the Huntington Library, California.

Another artist who confined himself to executing drawings and engravings was **John Faber** (c.1650/60-1721). His exact date of birth is unknown, but he was born in The Hague and settled in London in c.1687, living at Fountains Court, Strand. Little is known about him, but his works, which are scarce, are of a very high quality. His portraits were drawn in plumbago, Indian ink and wash, and pen and ink. He is best known for his engravings, and his drawings are so meticulous that, on more than one occasion, they have been mistaken for engravings. The Victoria and Albert Museum have a fine miniature by him of Admiral Sir George Rooke, signed and dated: 'J. Faber Delineavit — in / A° 1705 Chatham / 18th August', illustrated in *British Portrait Miniatures,* Plate 175. He had a son, John Faber, Junior, who was also an engraver. A miniature of Sir John Rolleston by Faber was Lot 45 at Sotheby's, 29th November, 1976, when it realised £500. It was signed and dated: 'J: faber 1699 fecit / Lond:'. Faber varied his signatures, sometimes adding details of the sitter, and, if it was a picture, the name of the artist. Examples of his work are in the British Museum, the Rotterdam Museum, the National Gallery, Dublin, and the Huntington Library, California (Plates 29D and E).

Thomas Forster (b.1677?) left us no biographical information at all; his date of birth is arrived at from an entry by George Vertue which reads: "the

Plate 30D. **J. Thopas,** *portrait of an unknown man, plumbago on vellum, 6 ⅝ ins., c.1660-65. Signed: 'J: Tho pas. fecit'. The costume suggests that the sitter came from the Continent.* Present whereabouts unknown.

head of Mr. Foster done by himself on vellum aeta 31 1708, ditto his sister, sold to Mr Glynn". That he was an outstanding artist is unquestionable; his works are among the latest of the 'plumbago artists', and date from c.1690-1713. Forster was probably one of the greatest, if not the greatest, eighteenth century artist who worked in this medium. His portraits are very highly finished, full of character and elegant. They are also good guides to fashion, as the costume of his sitters is an indication of how fashions were changing. The ladies wore their hair dressed higher towards the front of the head, often with two peaks on either side of the parting, with the familiar ringlet falling over one shoulder. The dresses were less *décolleté*, and were called 'gowns'. These had a close fitting bodice joined to a full gathered skirt; the bodice was usually edged with a frilly border, and brought forward over the shoulders to form a V at the waist (Plate 31D). Men were wearing large French wigs falling over the shoulders, and their coats were closer fitting with a slight waist. The cravat, or neckcloth, was fashionable well into the eighteenth century and was, by c.1700, worn longer and tucked into the opening of the coat. Sometimes a cloak was worn slung over the shoulders.

One of the characteristics of Forster's work is the way he indicates the sheen of the material and delicate folds of the ladies' dresses. He signed: 'T. Forster', 'Thos Forster delin', 'T. Forster del' and 'Tho fforster', sometimes followed by a date. Drawings by him are in the Victoria and Albert Museum, the British Museum, the City of Liverpool Museum, and the Holburne Museum, Bath. Six fine drawings are in the Huntington Library, California, and others are in important private collections, such as the Portland Collection, which contains a fine miniature of William III.

Robert White (1645-1703), was born in London, and, apart from the fact that he is known to have studied under Loggan, little is known about his life.

He became an engraver and drew some fine miniatures in plumbago. He is reputed to have engraved at least 400 portraits, of which 275 are recorded by Vertue; some were after his own drawings and others title pages for books and landscapes. White travelled extensively and drew buildings for Loggan. He is said to have been quite wealthy, but evidently spent it before his death. He lived for many years in Bloomsbury Market, where he died in November, 1703. The majority of his drawings are based on the works of other artists, but some are from life. He copied Loggan's method of adding touches of wash to his drawings. Ten of his miniatures are in the Huntington Library, California, and include an interesting self-portrait drawn in black lead inscribed: 'Ætat 16 / March 1 / 1661 / RW' and lower down: 'R White, Drawn while an Apprentice LW' (Plate 29B). Three of what are probably his finest works are in the Portland Collection. These include another self-portrait signed on the front: 'R.W.f.' and on the reverse: 'Robert White, Engraver, Aetat : 33, 1679', one of James Scott, Duke of Monmouth, signed: 'R. White delin', and one of Charles II, signed: 'R. White / fecit / 1684' (see also Plate 31E). All his works are meticulous and the sitters' characters well portrayed. He drew with slightly more strength than Loggan, and the hair is executed strand by strand and not in masses.

Miniatures by White are in the Victoria and Albert Museum, the British Museum, the Ashmolean Museum, Oxford, as well as in private collections. His son **George White** (1671 or 1684-1732) followed his father's profession. He drew portraits in plumbago and crayon and also painted some in oil. Some of his works were after Lely and Kneller.

Although little is known about him, mention must be made of **Johannes or Johan Thopas** (c.1630-c.1700). He is thought to have been born in Assendelften, and for at least the last thirty-two years of his life he lived at Haarlem, where he died in c.1700. He may have visited England as at least two miniatures of English sitters exist; one of Charles II, signed and dated 1660,

Plate 31A. **T. Forster,** *the Rev. Thomas Crusoe, plumbago on vellum, 3¾ins. Signed and dated: 'T. Forster / Delin 94' (1694).* Courtesy Christie's.

Plate 31B. **A. Marshal,** *a child aged twenty-nine weeks, possibly the son of John, 2nd Earl of Thanet, plumbago on vellum. 3¼ins. Inscribed and signed: 'Ætatis. 29. / weekes / Alex: Marshal. Fecit / 1653'. This rather pathetic drawing of a child is one of the few known examples of Marshal's work.* Private Collection.

Plate 31C. **T. Forster**, *Mrs. Thomas Crusoe, plumbago on vellum, 3¾ins. Signed in monogram: 'F'. It is interesting to compare Forster's monogram with his full signature as shown in Plate 31A.* Courtesy Christie's.

Plate 31D. **T. Forster**, *Lucy Talbot, plumbago on vellum, 4¼ins. Signed and dated: 'TForster / Delin / 1701'. Lucy was the wife of William Talbot, Bishop of Durham in 1721. This is a good example of ladies' costume of the period, the dress open down to a V, worn with a shawl.* Courtesy Sotheby's.

Plate 31E. **R. White**, *Charles II, plumbago on vellum, 5ins. Signed and dated: 'R.White / fecit / 78' (1678). This drawing is very close in detail to a later one by White in the Portland Collection dated 1684. In this portrait the King is wearing a fuller curled wig, and a wider lace* rabat. Courtesy Sotheby's.

Plate 31F. **D. Loggan**, *portrait of an unknown man, plumbago on vellum, 5ins. Signed and dated: 'DL' (monogram) '1674'. It is interesting to see how close Loggan's technique is to that of R. White.* Private Collection.

and another of the Rev. John Kinderley were Lot 29, sold at Sotheby's, 18th February, 1963. His portraits are drawn in plumbago and Indian ink, and are sometimes heightened with white. Examples of his work were in the Wellesley Collection, sold at Sotheby's in June, 1920. On 26th April, 1971, Sotheby's sold a fine pair of miniatures of an unknown man and his wife, both signed in full and dated 1648. These are now in the Institut Néerlandais, Paris. (Plate 30D.)

Alexander Marshal (fl.1660-1690) is a shadowy figure, who is known to have painted portraits after Van Dyck and others, miniatures and flowers on parchment. I know of only one example of his work which is in a private collection. It is of a child aged twenty-nine weeks, possibly the son of John, 2nd Earl of Thanet (1608-1664). The portrait is drawn in plumbago and signed on the left: 'Alex: Marshal. Fecit / 1653' and above the child's head 'Ætatis. 29. / weekes' (Plate 31B).

Plate 32A. Monogrammist **CHPW,** *an unknown lady* called *Princess Mary, oils on copper, 2¾ins. Signed and dated: 'C$_W^{HP}$ / 1646'. It is thought that the sitter may be Spanish.* Courtesy Victoria and Albert Museum, Ham House.

Only four miniatures have so far been discovered by an artist with the monogram **CHPW** who signed his works variously: '$_W^{HP}$ fec / 1645', '$_W^{HP}$ / 164 (3)' or (5), and 'C $_W^{HP}$ / 1646', the C encircling the HP. The only dates so far discovered are 1645 and 1646. I have seen three of these portraits, all of which are painted in oils and show a Continental influence. It has been suggested that he may have been H. Pooley Wright, a relative of John Michael Wright, the portrait painter, but this is not conclusive. An oil portrait of a lady called Princess Mary is at Ham House (Plate 32A) and is one of those signed in monogram: 'C$_W^{HP}$ / 1646'. One of an unknown man in a private collection is signed with a similar monogram and dated in the same year. The sitter may be Dutch, and the mauvish curtain background is slightly reminiscent of the work of Alexander Cooper who was on the Continent at that time (Plate 32D).

Plate 32B. **C. Netscher,** *William III (1650-1702), oils on copper, 3ins. In a B. Lens frame.* Courtesy Ivy, Duchess of Portland.

Plate 32C. **C. Netscher,** *Mary II (1662-1694), wife of William III, oils on copper, 3⁵/16ins. Few miniatures by Netscher are known but this and Plate 32B have always been accepted with confidence.* Courtesy Ivy, Duchess of Portland.

Plate 32D (left). Monogrammist **CHPW**, *portrait of an unknown man, oils on copper, 2ins. diameter. Signed and dated: 'CHP / 1646'. Wearing a deep lace-edged collar, and the lesser order of St. John of Jerusalem, suspended from a black ribbon. Painted against a mauve curtain and landscape background.* Private Collection.

Plate 32E (right). **P. Prieur** *after Karl van Mander, Frederik III of Denmark (1609-1670), enamel on copper, 9¹¹/₁₆ins. Signed on the reverse: 'Paulus Prieur Fecit / Anno 1663'. Contained in an enamelled locket, the inscription encircled with a wreath of leaves.* Courtesy Rosenborg Castle, Copenhagen.

Plate 32F. **C. Boit,** *Victor Amadeus II, Duke of Savoy and 1st King of Sardinia (1666-1732), enamel, 2¾ins. Signed on the reverse by the artist.* Courtesy the late Lord Methuen, R.A.

Although it is known that a number of artists painted miniatures in oil on a metal base, these are a frustrating group to identify as they are rarely signed. One of those said to have painted oil miniatures in England with great success was **Caspar or Gaspard Netscher** (1639-1684), who was born in Heidelberg. He came over to England during the reign of Charles II, and obtained patronage of James, Duke of York. A miniature of William III and one of Queen Mary, attributed to Netscher, are in the Portland Collection (Plates 32B and C), and others are given to him on the basis of style. A signed miniature of an unknown girl is in the Institut Néerlandais, Paris. Although he did not as far as we know ever come to England, his son, **Constantijn Netscher** (1669-1722) painted members of the Portland family, and Henrietta Churchill, later Duchess of Marlborough.

The art of painting enamel miniatures came directly from the Continent where, as has already been mentioned in Chapter I, Jean Toutin discovered a method of laying a variety of colours upon a white enamel base. The portrait could then be fired in a kiln without any damage to tints. This new development was brought over to England in c.1637 by a Swiss enameller, **Jean Petitot, Senior** (1607-1691), and his friend, **Jacques Bordier** (1616-1684). Petitot was born in Geneva, 12th July, 1607, and was the fourth son of a French sculptor. In 1626 he was apprenticed to his uncle, Jean Royaume, a jeweller. In c.1633 Petitot left Geneva for Paris. Petitot was a pupil of Pierre Bordier, whose cousin, Jacques Bordier, became his lifelong friend and collaborator. Petitot may also have had some instruction from Jean and Henri Toutin, of Blois, before leaving the Continent. Sometime between 1633 and 1637 Petitot and Bordier came to England and both artists were patronised by Charles I, and had the encouragement of Van Dyck and Sir Theodore Turquet de Mayerne. The King gave Petitot an apartment in Whitehall, and according to some authorities knighted him. He had so many commissions that Bordier is supposed to have painted the hair and even the backgrounds and clothes, whilst Petitot painted the face. He may well have had assistants of whom we have no knowledge. The fact that these two artists worked so closely together makes identification difficult. By the time Petitot and Bordier reached England, a flourishing school of miniature painters was already established, and the introduction of this new medium soon became popular. Charles I employed Petitot to make rings and jewellery, and to paint enamel portraits of most of the important people at Court. Many of these were after Van Dyck and other well-known portrait painters. Miniatures painted by Petitot are usually signed, and date from c.1636 to c.1643. Most of his miniatures are small, an exception being the superb large enamel of Mary, Duchess of Richmond and Lennox, after Van Dyck, signed and dated on the reverse: 'J. Petitot. fec. 1643'. This is in the Nationalmuseum, Stockholm, and was lent to the Arts Council Exhibition in Edinburgh in 1965 (Plate 33D). The best of Petitot's works are beautifully painted in harmonious colours, the features being expressively drawn. Viewed under a lens, a slight stippling touch can be distinguished. He is known to have painted a small number of miniatures in watercolour, which were probably sketches for portraits on enamel. A large number of his works are in the Portland Collection where there is one of a man on vellum signed: 'P.72' (1672), and a self-portrait on enamel signed with a monogram: 'JP' on the reverse. Typical signatures are 'J.P. f 1639', 'J. Petitot. / 1640', 'J. Petitot fe / 1640', etc. (Plates 33B, C and E). Petitot and Bordier returned to France in c.1645-46, and in 1651 Petitot married, at Charendon, Marguerite Cuper, whose sister, Madeleine, married Bordier. Petitot received the patronage of Louis XIV and the French Court and was given a pension and a residence at The Louvre. In 1686 he became a zealous Protestant and was imprisoned for heresy. This impaired his health, and eventually he recanted and after his release fled to Switzerland, and settled in Geneva, where he practised his art. He was later received back into the Huguenot Communion. He is said to have had seventeen children, of whom his eldest son, Jean (1653-1702) followed his father's profession. Copies of Petitot Senior's works by later artists are numerous, and even contemporary miniatures painted by his assistants and followers are so alike that accurate identification is often difficult. Examples of his work are in the Victoria and Albert Museum, the National Portrait Gallery, as well as in museums abroad

Plate 32G. **P. Prieur**, *Peder Schumacher, Count of Griffenfeld (1635-1699), enamel, 3½ins. Signed on the reverse: 'Prieur 1673'. This is a fine example of the artist's work and is not as harsh as some of his paintings.* Courtesy Rosenborg Castle, Copenhagen.

Plate 33A. **C. Boit**, perhaps *Jane Martha Temple, Countess of Portland (1672-1751), enamel, 2⅞ins. Encased in a pale blue enamel locket.* Courtesy Ivy, Duchess of Portland.

Plate 33B. **J. Petitot**, *Lady Katherine Manners, Duchess of Buckingham (d.1649), enamel, 2ins. Signed on the reverse: 'J.Petitot / 1640'.* Courtesy Ivy, Duchess of Portland.

145

Plate 33C. **J. Petitot** *after G. Honthorst, George Villiers, 1st Duke of Buckingham K.G. (1592-1628), enamel, 2ins. Signed on the reverse: 'J.Petitot fe / 1640'.* Courtesy Ivy, Duchess of Portland.

Plate 33D. **J. Petitot**, *Mary, Duchess of Richmond and Lennox (1622-1685), enamel, 4¾ins. Signed and dated on the reverse: 'J.Petitot. fec. 1643'. After the portrait in the Royal Collection by Van Dyck. Other versions of this portrait exist.* Courtesy the Nationalmuseum, Stockholm.

Plate 33E. **J. Petitot**, *Charles I, when Prince of Wales, enamel, 2ins. Signed on the reverse: 'J.Petitot .fec. 1638'. After Van Dyck. Encased in a pale blue enamel locket.* Courtesy Ivy, Duchess of Portland.

such as The Louvre, Paris, the Rijksmuseum, Amsterdam, the Nationalmuseum, Munich, the Nationalmuseum, Stockholm, and a number of private collections. For further information see *The Connoisseur,* June 1968, pp.82-91.

Jean Petitot the Younger (1653-1702), was born in Blois, 2nd January, 1653. He was sent over to England at some point to have instruction from Samuel Cooper, but did not like the method of instruction and returned to France. He returned to England in 1677, and had some tuition under a miniaturist in London whose name is not known. He worked for Charles II until 1682, but was in Paris by 1683 when he married his cousin, Madeleine Bordier (1658-1736). Petitot returned to England again in c.1696, but evidently went back to France, and died in Paris 25th October, 1702, and was buried in his own garden, having refused to become a Catholic. According to Vertue, he painted in watercolour and enamel, but no examples in watercolour are at present known. He worked in the manner of his father, but did not succeed in attaining such a high standard. His flesh colours are rather pink, and the hair of his sitters painted with a fine brush stroke. Two self-portraits exist and both are signed in full on the reverse; one is dated 1674 and the other 1676. This latter miniature was sold in Vienna in 1930. It showed him wearing a yellow costume embroidered with flowers and signed on the reverse: 'Jean Petitot fait par lui-même l'an 1676 décembre âgé 23 ans.' The other self-portrait, dated 1674 and also signed and inscribed on the reverse is in the Institut Néerlandais, Paris. Miniatures attributed to him are in a number of private collections, and two are in the National Collection of Fine Arts, Smithsonian Institution, Washington (Plate 33F).

Another artist who executed enamel miniatures was **Paul Prieur** (c.1620-aft. 1683). He was born in Geneva and was the son of a Parisian

146

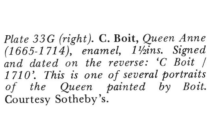

Plate 33F (left). Attributed to **J. Petitot the Younger,** *Louis De Bourbon, Prince De Condé (1621-1686),* enamel, 1⁹/₁₆ins. Set within a gold and enamelled pierced frame, decorated with leaves and flowers. Courtesy the National Collection of Fine Arts, Smithsonian Institution, Washington.

Plate 33G (right). **C. Boit,** *Queen Anne (1665-1714),* enamel, 1½ins. Signed and dated on the reverse: 'C Boit / 1710'. This is one of several portraits of the Queen painted by Boit. Courtesy Sotheby's.

jeweller. His father died when he was young, and from 1632-1638 he lived with his mother in Geneva, where in 1635 he was apprenticed to J. Plachant, a jeweller. He travelled extensively, going to Paris c.1640, later working in Spain, Denmark and England. From 1660-1681 Prieur worked as painter on enamel to the Court of Denmark, where he painted many miniatures for Frederick III and Christian V, and other members of the Royal families. Between 1671 and 1680 Royal orders amounted to 25,000 crowns. He was in London in 1682 and 1683. His miniatures are frequently signed and dated on the reverse. His work varied a great deal; some of it is rather harsh. He emphasised the outlines of the nose, eyes and mouth, and painted the faces with a very pronounced stippling which is quite unmistakable when once examined closely. A miniature formerly on loan to the Victoria and Albert Museum is signed on the reverse: 'Prieur a / Londres / 1682' (or 3). A large collection of his miniatures is at Rosenborg Castle, Copenhagen, including one of Frederick III after van Mander, inscribed on the reverse: 'Paulus Prieur Fecit / Anno 1663' (Plate 32E), and fourteen small replicas. A large circular miniature of Christian V as a child with his brothers and sisters (after an earlier painting) is also at Rosenborg and is signed: 'Prieur 1671', while another one represents the Count of Griffenfeld (Plate 32G).

One of the most important enamellists of the latter part of the seventeenth century was **Charles Boit** (1662-1727), a native of Sweden. He was born in Stockholm and was the son of Charles Boit, a French salt manufacturer and silk merchant, and his wife, Marie Creveleur of Calais. Boit was baptised in Stockholm in 1662, and from 1677-1682 was apprenticed to a goldsmith in the city. It is not known who taught him the art of enamelling. Signac, the Court enameller to Queen Christina, died in 1684, and the only two enamellers left in Sweden were Elias Brenner and Andreas Von Behn, either of whom may have taught Boit. In 1682 Boit went to Paris for three months, and then to Gothenburg. He married as his first wife a girl by the name of Flitzberg. Nothing is known about his married life, but he is supposed to have married three times, the last wife's name being Anne Marguerite Williart, whose portrait was painted by the Italian artist, Rosalba

147

Plate 34A. **P. Cross,** *Mr. William Gore, vellum, 2⁷⁄₁₆ins. Inscribed and signed on the reverse: 'Mr. Willm Gore Picto (r) / P: Cross fecit. 1670', and on the front: 'PC' (monogram). This was the first miniature to be identified as by P. Cross.* Courtesy Victoria and Albert Museum.

Plate 34B. **P. Cross,** *called John Maitland, 1st Duke of Lauderdale (1616-1682), vellum, 3ins. Signed: 'P.C.'* Courtesy the Ashmolean Museum.

Carriera, in August 1720, in Paris. Boit returned to Stockholm in 1685. In 1687, two years after James II had come to the throne, Boit was introduced into England by an Exeter merchant who had contacts in Sweden and had been instrumental in bringing Michael Dahl over to Britain five years earlier. In 1688 James II fled to France, and the reign of William of Orange and Mary II began.

After Petitot left England miniatures in enamel became less popular, and the art did not come into prominence again until the arrival of Boit. His success was no doubt due in part to his willingness to copy large paintings on a small scale, as well as make portraits from life. Boit is said to have been imprisoned for two years as a result of becoming engaged to a country gentleman's daughter!

In 1696 William III appointed him Court Enamellist, an appointment which had not hitherto been made. In 1699 Boit set off on a tour of the Continent; he was in Holland first and in 1700 obtained commissions at the Elector's Court in Düsseldorf, visiting Vienna in the same year where he painted a large group of the Emperor's family, which measured 15 by 18 inches. This was an ambitious project to undertake in this medium, as firing such a large painting would present great problems.

William III survived Queen Mary by eight years and died in 1702, so that on Boit's return to England in 1703 Queen Anne was on the throne. Her consort, Prince George of Denmark, was one of those who encouraged Boit to embark on a very pretentious enamel which was to measure approximately 22 by 18 inches, or 24 by 16 inches, various accounts as to size being given. It was to be copied from an allegorical design by Louis Laguerre commemorating the battle of Blenheim, representing the Duke of Marlborough being led to Queen Anne and her Court by Victory. This project required a special furnace, and Prince George advanced £1,000 for the purpose. In spite of the help of Boit's assistants, this proved too great an undertaking and ten years later it had still no hope of completion. On the death of Queen Anne the project was no longer even popular, and the Treasury demanded repayment of their expenditure! Boit had been living extravagantly, and would have been quite unable to pay the money required. He therefore fled to France, and never returned. He obtained employment at the French Court, as well as from Peter the Great of Russia, and died in Paris in the Rue du Petit Bourbon on 5th or 6th February, 1727, leaving a widow and five children heavily in debt.

Boit was a good artist and showed great ability of draughtsmanship, and used pleasant colours. Many of his paintings are dominated by pink and yellow colouring. Most of his works are smooth in appearance, and he did not use a form of dotting which is noticeable in the works of his pupil, C.F. Zincke, whose career will be dealt with in the next chapter. His pupils included C.F. Zincke, Martin van der Meytens, John Milward, Frederic Peterson, and Humphry Wanley, the Earl of Oxford's Librarian. A number of his miniatures were copied by a later artist, Joseph Lee. Many of Boit's enamels are after paintings by Dahl and Kneller. His earliest known miniature was Lot 97 at Sotheby's, 3rd July, 1961. It is of an unknown lady, signed and dated in full on the reverse: 'C. Boit p i.. / Coiventry / 1693'. The lady may be Sarah Middleton, 2nd wife of Robert Harley, 1st Earl of Oxford, whom she married in 1694. The same sale contained as Lot

100 an enamel by Boit of Sidney, 1st Earl of Godolphin, signed: 'C. Boit Pinxt'. The miniature was after Kneller. One of Boit's finest large miniatures is in the collection of H.M. The Queen, and represents Queen Anne and Prince George of Denmark. It is signed on the reverse: 'Anna D:G Angel : scot Franc: & Hiber: Regina &c / & his Royal Highness George Prince of Denmark / C. Boit Pinx: Anno 1706'. This was exhibited in Edinburgh in 1965. His signature varied, often he signed: 'CB' (monogram) or: 'C. Boit ft'. The Portland Collection contains a fine miniature by him of Henrietta, Countess of Oxford, signed: 'C. Boit ft', the receipt for which is still at Welbeck. (Plates 32F and 33A and G.)

Examples of his work are in the Victoria and Albert Museum, the National Portrait Gallery, the Ashmolean Museum, Oxford, The Louvre, Paris, the Rijksmuseum, Amsterdam, the Royal Museum, Stockholm, and many private collections. (Colour Plate 11E.)

It seemed sensible to discuss the work of those miniaturists who executed miniatures on enamel and in plumbago during the seventeenth century as a group, and having done so I shall now return to some of those who painted miniatures in watercolour and were influenced by techniques used on the Continent.

One of the problems facing those of us who study miniature painting is that of trying to disentangle the work of two, if not three, artists of this period whose names were Cross or Crosse.

The existence of **Lawrence Cross(e)** (d.1724) was recorded by George Vertue and others, but no mention was thought to have been made of **P. Cross** (fl.1661-1716) in any early books on painting, but recent research by John Murdoch of the Victoria and Albert Museum on this problem has revealed that Vertue did in fact mention a P. le Croix or Cross, miniaturist,

Plate 34C. **P. Cross,** *Robert Kerr, 4th Earl and 1st Marquess of Lothian (1636-1701), vellum, 3ins. inscribed in full on the reverse: 'ye Lord Kerr / 1667 / Peeter Cros / fecitt'. This fine miniature is one of the few fully signed examples by Cross. It realised £5,000 in 1977. Courtesy Sotheby's.*

Plate 34D. **P. Cross,** *Elizabeth, Countess of Chesterfield (d.1677), thought to be the third wife of Philip, 2nd Earl of Chesterfield, and daughter of the 2nd Earl of Carnarvon, vellum, 3¼ins. Signed and dated: 'PC' (monogram) '1667'. Set within a black mount of a later date, decorated with flowers, scrolls, a coronet and a coat of arms. The texture of the painting is smooth without stippling, and the miniature most attractive. The monogram differs from the others by Cross and is in rounder lettering. Courtesy Christie's.*

Plate 34E. **L. Cross(e),** *Colonel James Griffin aged 15, vellum, 3½ins. Signed and dated: 'LC' (monogram) '1682'. This is an interesting miniature of such a young officer, his long hair falling over his armour, and wearing a fine quality deep cravat or* rabat. *Courtesy Christie's.*

but this has been overlooked as the name was not in the index of the Vertue Notebooks. It was only a passing reference, and noted that he had been born in this country. Miniatures signed 'P.C.' had been variously distributed between Paolo Carandini and Penelope Cleyn. Carandini was always a doubtful contestant and there is no evidence that he ever accompanied Mary of Modena to England as was suggested. In fact according to a contemporary author he was dead by 1662. Penelope Cleyn was one of six children of Franz Cleyn, all of whom were described as miniaturists, but whose works are not at present identified.

In 1935 a miniature of Mr. William Gore came into the sale room and was found to be signed on the front 'PC' (monogram), and inscribed on the reverse: 'Mr. Willm Gore Picto (r) / P: Cross fecit. 1670' (Plate 34A). This miniature was purchased by the Victoria and Albert Museum, and the whole matter discussed by Graham Reynolds in *English Portrait Miniatures*, pp.90-92. At that time about seventeen miniatures by 'P.C.' dating between 1661-1691 were known, and since then numerous others have come to light. Miniatures by P. Cross like those by L. Cross(e) show Continental influence, such as the greenish flesh tint visible on the miniature of an unknown man in the Victoria and Albert Museum dated 1661. The miniature of William Gore is well painted, the cravat finely drawn and the features shaded with a thin brush stroke which develops into a dot-like stippling not usually found on English miniatures of the period. The style of painting is so close to that used by Lawrence Cross(e) that everything points to there having been some family connection. It has been suggested that the two artists might have been related to Michael Cross who worked for Charles I, and who in 1660 petitioned Charles II for the continuance of an annual sum of £200, granted by Charles I, whom he claimed to have served for twenty-eight years copying the works of famous painters in Spain and Italy.

Lawrence Cross(e) was a collector as well as a miniaturist and his cabinet contained miniatures by Hoskins, Cooper and others. His own works, judging from costume, date from c.1675 up to his death in October 1724, when he was said to be over seventy years of age. On 5th December, 1722, Crosse sold his collection at his house 'The Blue Anchor', Henrietta Street, Covent Garden. Vertue records seeing no less than twelve miniatures by Cooper, several of which were bought by Edward, Lord Harley and are still at Welbeck. They include the famous unfinished portrait of Cooper's wife.

Lawrence seems to have had a distinguished clientele, and was responsible for restoring a miniature of Mary, Queen of Scots, for the Duke of Hamilton. Having been told to make it beautiful and not knowing what the miniature originally looked like he painted the shape of the lady's face round, a feature it was subsequently discovered she did not possess! When it became fashionable to have portraits of Mary this so-called portrait of her was copied by Bernard Lens and other artists, and some of these copies appear from time to time in the London sale rooms.

Lawrence Crosse did not often date his miniatures and used a cursive monogram 'LC', the C attached to the stalk of the L. Other signatures are 'LC fecit' and 'L: Cross F:' on the reverse, sometimes followed by an inscription regarding the sitter, and a date. The miniatures are slightly sombre in colour, the backgrounds being plain brown or grey-brown, dull blue, reddish brown, and the occasional curtain or sky painted on one side.

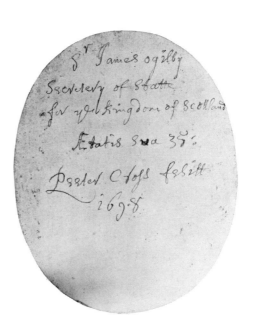

Plate 34F. **P. Cross,** *James Ogilvy, 4th Earl of Findlater and 1st Earl of Seafield (1664-1730), vellum, 3¼ins. Signed on the front in monogram: 'PLC' or 'PC' and in full on the reverse and dated 1698. See Figure 23 and Colour Plate 8E. This was the first fully signed miniature by P. Cross to come to light, though others have been discovered since. It is in mint condition and of great historic importance.* Private Collection.

Figure 23. The reverse of Plate 34F giving the full inscription and signature of **P. Cross:** *'Sr James ogilby / Secretery of Statte / for ye Kingdom of Scottland / Ætatis sua 35 / Peeter Cross fesitt / i698'.* Private Collection.

He modelled the face with varying shades of red, blue and green, similar to the method adopted by P. Cross, and used a form of *pointillisme* or dotting, which was practised on a much wider scale in the following century. Eight fine miniatures by L. Crosse are at Welbeck, all of which are signed and some inscribed on the reverse as in the case of one of James, Duke of Monmouth and Buccleuch. This is signed 'LC' (monogram) on the front, and on the reverse: 'his grace duck of monmoth : drawn by LC' (monogram) 'Cro[ss] Ye 30th of Aug̃. 1683.' (Plates 34E and G.)

When I was doing research for my *Dictionary of British Miniature Painters,* I suggested, on the basis of a note left by the late Carl Winter, that P. Cross's Christian name was Peter. I was unable to verify this until two years ago when a miniature of Sir James Ogilvy, 1st Earl of Seafield, came to my attention. This miniature, which is of superb quality, has presented a serious problem. It is signed on the front with what we have always taken to be Lawrence Crosse's cursive monogram LC, but is inscribed on the reverse: 'Sr James ogilby / Secretery of Statte / for ye Kingdom of Scottland / Ætatis sua 35 / ℟eeter Cross fesitt / i698' (Figure 23). It is undoubtedly one of the finest miniatures of the period.

The Earl is wearing a long French wig, the curls painted in great detail, his cravat falls down to a bright blue cloak over his right shoulder, and the background to the rear of the sitter's head is almost black. On the right side, as it is viewed, is a patch of blue and grey sky. The features are perfectly modelled, and shaded with short strokes of greys, red and green. There are distinct green lines shading the right eyelid and touches of opaque white in the hair (Colour Plate 8E and Plate 34F). A miniature of Elizabeth, Countess of Chesterfield, signed with a cursive monogram: 'PC' and dated 1667, was Lot 113 at Christie's, 15th June, 1976. The miniature came from the de Malahide Collection (Plate 34D). It is painted in the same soft style as the miniature of the Earl of Ogilvy. Both miniatures are of a far finer quality than some of those signed 'P.C.' in gold capitals, where the sitter's hair is more fuzzy and there is more *pointilliste* dotting on the face.

Plate 34G. **L. Cross(e)**, called, *Anne Countess of Winchester, vellum, 3¼ins. Signed in monogram: 'LC'. The hair style suggests a date of c.1700.* Private Collection.

To add to the confusion, a large cabinet miniature came on to the market in 1975, signed in monogram: 'LC' or 'PLC.' It is unique, as no such portrait limning on this scale (10 by 12½ inches) is known after the death of Hoskins and the Olivers. This is at present tentatively attributed to Lawrence Cross(e).

It represents a lady in classical dress, wearing a white robe falling off her right shoulder and exposing her bosom. She is draped with a long bright blue cloak pinned over her left shoulder. The lady is lying on the grass leaning on a rock, her left elbow on a book, a horn in her right hand. In her hair is a wreath of laurels. The background is of trees and a landscape with a river and hills in the distance and a Roman temple and waterfall. The overall tone of the painting is blue, with the sun coming from behind a cloud. The monogram is painted in black on a rock in the foreground. The whole composition of the painting is superb and the background almost certainly based on some unknown painting. All attempts to identify the sitter have so far failed, and there is no provenance known. The miniature is so expertly painted that it cannot possibly have been the only work executed by the artist on this scale. The assumption is that the sitter is either the wife or mistress of some well-known person, depicted as a Muse (see frontispiece).

All the Cross(e) miniatures are painted on vellum stuck on to card, following the earlier tradition. They are oval in shape, with the exception of the large rectangular one already discussed, and one seen by the late Basil Long, which he noted was rectangular and possibly a copy of a picture by Lely.

It is impossible at present to make any final pronouncement on the problem of the Cross family, or to disentangle them with any degree of certainty. Having examined a large number of works by both 'LC' and 'PC', one is left wondering if we have three artists — one who signed 'PLC' in cursive monogram, the top of the C forming the P on the stalk of the L, and who may have been either Peter Lawrence (or Le) Cross, or Lawrence Peter Cross, and who painted the miniatures typified by the Earl of Ogilvy; a second who signed 'PC' in gold block capitals and may be Peter Cross, who painted the miniature Lot 140 in the Heckett Collection, sold at Sotheby's 11th July, 1977, representing the 4th Earl and 1st Marquess of Lothian (Plate 34C), fully inscribed on the reverse: 'ye Lord Kerr / 1667 / Peeter Cros / fecitt'; and a third artist, who worked in the same manner as 'P.C.' and signed 'LC' (monogram), was possibly the Lawrence Crosse who died in 1724. I have not so far been able to trace any wills for the family, and until such time as fresh information comes to light the problem must remain unresolved.

Examples of these artists' work are in the Victoria and Albert Museum, the National Portrait Gallery, London, the Ashmolean Museum, Oxford, and private collections. Two signed ones by 'P.' or 'P.L.' Cross are in the Warren Lowenhaupt Collection, Wadsworth Athenaeum, Hertford, Connecticut. They are of Mr. and Mrs. Bradhill, and are dated 1711 and 1712.

Among the numerous artists who came to England from Geneva were two by the name of Arlaud. **Jacques Antoine Arlaud** (1668-1746) was a native of Geneva, where he was born on 18th May, 1668. His father was a watchmaker whose family came from Auvergne. Jacques is reputed to have given up a brilliant career in classical studies to devote his time to miniature painting. He studied in Geneva for two or three years and then in 1688 went to Paris, where he soon became well known. He obtained commissions from the Prince Regent, who granted him lodgings in his château at St. Cloud. Arlaud painted religious and mythological subjects in oils as well as portraits in miniature. In 1721 he came to London and brought with him a copy of a 'Leda' after Michelangelo, or Correggio, which he is said to have sold for £600. He arrived in England with a letter of introduction to Caroline, Princess of Wales, and is said to have had great success over here and been "loaded with presents". He was well known at Court, and met Sir Isaac Newton. In 1729 he returned to Geneva, where he remained until his death in June, 1746. He painted several miniatures of Prince James Francis Edward Stuart (1688-1766), one of which was exhibited in Edinburgh in 1965. It was lent by the family to whom it was given by the Prince, and is inscribed and dated on the reverse: 'Jacobus / Antonius / Arlaud / Pincabat ad Vivum / Mensis Octobris / ANNO. 1702 / Jacobus Rex.' This portrait shows the Prince when he was only fourteen years of age (Plate 35B). Another miniature of him when he was older is in the Wallace Collection, London. In spite of the fact that he seems to have had many patrons when in London, miniatures by Jacques Arlaud are very scarce. Those that I have seen have all been painted on vellum backed with card, the draughtsmanship is very good and the portraits painted with restrained colours. An interesting miniature of his sister-in-law is in the collection of H.M. Queen Juliana of the Netherlands, and is engraved in full on the reverse of the frame and dated 1721. Other examples of his work are in the Victoria and Albert Museum, The Louvre, the Nationalmuseum, Stockholm, and private collections such as that of H.M. The Queen. (Plate 35C.)

Plate 35A. **B. Arlaud**, *Elizabeth Knight, vellum, 2¾ins. Although unsigned, this is a typical example of Arlaud's work.* Courtesy Sotheby's.

Benjamin Arlaud (fl.1701-1721) was a brother of J.A. Arlaud, and also born in Geneva. Little is known about his life, but his miniatures are of a very high quality. He studied art in Geneva and like his brother took up miniature painting with great success. As with J.A. Arlaud, his works are scarce, and the majority of those known to me are in private collections. The miniature of his wife, Jeanne Marie Arlaud, née Walker, painted by his brother, bears an inscription on the frame which gives the information that the miniature was painted in London in September, 1721, when the sitter was a widow. He may possibly have been identical with a Benoît Arlaud, recorded by Bénézit as having died in London in 1719 and about whom practically nothing is known. Benjamin Arlaud executed some very fine miniatures. Characteristics of his work are the way he often delineated the eyebrows, upper eyelids and the corners of the eyes with red, and shaded the face with a greenish grey colour; the contours of the face are also sometimes delineated with a thin red line. Some of his miniatures are painted against a dull blue background. I know of none signed on the front; his usual signature on the reverse is: 'Benjamin Arlaud Pinxit', sometimes followed by a date. Five miniatures by him are in the Portland Collection, three of which are signed and dated. One of Count Patkul (1660-1707) is signed on the reverse: 'Benjamin Arlaud Pinxit 1714', and two miniatures, both signed and dated 1709 on the reverse, represent Henry Bentinck, 1st Duke of Portland, and his wife, Lady Elizabeth Noel, Duchess of Portland. One of John Churchill, 1st Duke of Marlborough, also in the Portland Collection, is identified by a label on the reverse. Examples of his miniatures are in the Rijksmuseum, Amsterdam, the National Museum, Munich, the Wallace Collection, London,

Plate 35B. **J.A. Arlaud**, *Prince James Francis Edward Stuart (1688-1766), vellum, 3ins. Inscribed and dated on the reverse: 'Jacobus / Antonius / Arlaud / Pincabat ad Vivum / Mensis Octobris / ANNO. 1702 / Jacobus Rex'. This miniature, painted when the Prince was only fourteen years of age, is by family descent.* Courtesy Madam H. Stuart Stevenson.

Plate 35C (left). **J.A. Arlaud,**
an unknown man in armour,
vellum, 3¹/8ins. c.1700. Cour-
tesy Christie's.

Plate 35D (right). **C. Richter,**
an unknown lady, vellum,
4¾ins. Signed in monogram:
'CR' on the front. This is a
large and particularly attract-
ive miniature by this artist.
The lady is holding a mask in
her hand and is painted
against a cloud and sky
background. Courtesy
Sotheby's.

Plate 35E. **B. Arlaud,** *portrait*
of an unknown lady, vellum,
4ins. This is a pretty minia-
ture, with the unusual ad-
dition of a landscape back-
ground. Most of B. Arlaud's
works have a plain back-
ground. Courtesy Sotheby's.

and private collections including those of H.M. The Queen, and the Duke of Buccleuch. (Colour Plate 8D and Plates 35A and E.)

Another Continental miniaturist who was contemporary with the Arlauds was **Christian Richter** (1678-1732). He was the son of Hans Davidson Richter, and his wife, Brita B. Snelling. Christian was born in Stockholm, where his father was assessor to the Goldsmiths' Corporation, and was apprenticed as a goldsmith from 1695-1698. He studied medal engraving under Arvid Karlsteen, and after visiting Berlin and Dresden came to London in 1702 where he knew the Swedish painters Hysing and Dahl, as well as the enamellist C. Boit. Augustus II sat for him for a wax portrait. He is best known for his miniatures in watercolour, but he also painted in oils, and is reputed to have executed some works on enamel. His brother, David, and his cousin, David, were both miniaturists, but neither of them as far as we know, ever came to England. The majority of Christian Richter's miniatures are copies of paintings by Lely, Kneller, Dahl and Cooper. The reason given for his being a copyist was that he had suffered from an unpleasant illness which had disfigured his face. In spite of the fact that many of his works are copies, he had his own style, and the end products are not, as is so often the case, dull repetitions of other men's work, but accurate and delightful miniatures in their own right. A perfect example of this is the attractive miniature of Lady Margaret Cavendish Harley, afterwards Duchess of Portland, which is in the Portland Collection, and was copied from the portrait by Michael Dahl, also in the Welbeck Collection of pictures. The miniature has a label on the reverse inscribed by the 2nd Earl of Oxford: 'Lady Margaret Cavendishe Harley by Mr Rector, from the Original painted by Mr Dalh' [sic].

Four miniatures by Richter are in the Portland Collection, one identified by Vertue, and two signed and dated. One is of Edward, Lord Harley, later 2nd Earl of Oxford, signed on the reverse: 'C. Richter 1720', and the other of Lady Henrietta Cavendish Harley, wife of the 2nd Duke of Portland, signed on the reverse: 'C. Richter 1721'. Both these miniatures are after portraits by Dahl.

Points to remember when trying to identify Richter's work are the way the face is painted with a minute stippling touch combined with a large number of small brush strokes which are often nearly perpendicular; these can be seen with a lens even on the eyeballs. He favoured a reddish brown shading, alternating with grey and touches of blue. The eyelids are usually strongly delineated, and often the sockets of the eyes are drawn in dark red lines. A copy of Cooper's miniature of Oliver Cromwell by him is in the Wallace Collection, and other almost identical copies are known; they are all well painted. Compared with miniatures painted by the Cross(e) family, Richter's miniatures appear harsher and the hair has a less woolly appearance, more like Cooper's manner of painting. Not all his miniatures are signed; those that are usually have a cursive monogram 'CR' in pencil with a date below. Long mentions seeing one written in ink. Richter sometimes signed in full, as on the Portland miniatures, and one of Lady M. Bagot, in the Victoria and Albert Museum, is signed on the front: '1710 / CR' (monogram). Also at the Victoria and Albert Museum is a large copy by Richter of Dr. John Radcliffe, after a portrait by Kneller, the miniature being dated 1719. Four miniatures of the family of Sir Richard Steele, attributed to Richter, are in the National Portrait Gallery, but these are not now considered to be by him. A miniature after Van Dyck is in the Rijksmuseum, Amsterdam, signed on the reverse: 'C. Richter, pinxit 1711'. Other examples are in private collections including those of H.M. The Queen, the Duke of Buccleuch, and the Earl Beauchamp. Richter died in Brewer Street, Golden Square, London, and was buried on 18th November, 1732, in St. James's, Piccadilly. Examples of Richter's miniatures were exhibited in Edinburgh, in 1965.

A superb example of Richter's work is in the Bernard Falk Collection, Brighton. It represents Henry Portman, and is signed and dated: 'C. Richter / 1714'. The sitter is wearing armour, a long knotted cravat, and a tricorn hat over a full bottom wig or long hair (Plate 35F). One of an unknown man of c.1710, signed in monogram is in the collection of Mrs. E.M. Hamilton (Plate 35G).

Plate 35F. C. Richter, Henry Portman, vellum, 3¹/8ins. Signed and dated : '1714' on the reverse. Apart from the fine quality of the miniature it is of great interest regarding costume. It is unusual to find a miniature of this period with the sitter wearing a hat. Courtesy the Bernard Falk Collection, The Royal Pavilion, Brighton.

Plate 35G. C. Richter, portrait of an unknown man, vellum, 2¾ins. c.1710. Signed in monogram: 'CR'. This miniature is very close in style to the works of P. and L. Cross(e). Courtesy Mrs. E.M. Hamilton.

Chapter VI

Early Georgian Miniaturists

THE EARLY PART of the eighteenth century could not boast of any large number of miniature painters working in England. The glorious period of Samuel Cooper and his followers had passed, and those who kept the art alive and who have been discussed in the previous chapter were either artists who came from the Continent to work in England, or who were influenced by Continental ways of painting. This influence was to continue into the Georgian era.

In view of the fact that the actual dates of birth and death of miniaturists are not always known, and that their span of life varied so much, it is not easy to discuss their work in relation to exact dates. I have tried to place them in the periods in which they worked for the greater part of their lives, but there will inevitably be borderline cases where they worked over into the next period. The majority of the miniaturists covered in this chapter were well-established by or before c.1760-1765, and worked during the reign of both George I and George II.

George I (1660-1727), Elector of Hanover, succeeded to the English throne on the death of Queen Anne in 1714, bringing to the end the House of Stuart, and replacing it with the House of Hanover which was to carry us on until the death of Queen Victoria in 1901. George I's rival to the throne was Prince James Francis Edward Stuart (the Old Pretender), who had made an unsuccessful invasion of England to try and reclaim the throne. This having failed, he returned to France and finally settled in Rome. Many portraits and miniatures were painted of 'the Old Pretender' and of his son, Prince Charles Edward, 'the Young Pretender'. They have always remained romantic figures in history, and portraits and miniatures of either of them tend to fetch big prices.

Plate 36A. P.P. Lens, an unknown girl, ivory, 1¾ins., c.1730-40. Signed in monogram: 'PL.' The type of small cap worn by the sitter became popular from c.1730. Private Collection.

Colour Plate 11.
A. Nathaniel Hone, R.A., an unknown lady, enamel, 1⅛ins., c.1760-65.
B. A.H. Groth, Walter Edwards Freeman, enamel, 1¾ins., c.1753.
C. Lucius Barber, an unknown girl, enamel, 1¾ins., c.1730.
D. William Prewett, an unknown man, enamel, 1⅝ins., c.1730-35. Signed on the reverse: 'W.Prewitt / Pinxit.'
E. Charles Boit, unknown lady, enamel, 2ins., c.1700. Signed on the reverse: 'C.Boit Pinx.'
F. Gervase Spencer, an unknown lady, enamel, 1⅞ins., c.1750-60.
G. Noah Seaman, an unknown man, enamel, 1½ins. Signed on the reverse: 'Noah Seaman / Pinx: 1729.' Signed works by N. Seaman are rare.

Courtesy R. Bayne Powell

*Plate 36B. **R. Carriera**, Marco Ricci (1679-1729), a Venetian artist, on bone, 2¾ins. Inscribed by the artist on the reverse. This is a good example of Rosalba's work in miniature. Courtesy Brigadier and Mrs. G. Viner.*

*Plate 36C. **B. Lens**, after an original painting by Charles d'Agar in the Welbeck Collection, Lady Margaret Cavendish Harley, later Duchess of Portland (1715-85), ivory, 3⅜ins., c.1717. Signed in monogram: 'BL.' Courtesy Ivy, Duchess of Portland.*

George I married his cousin, Princess Sophia Dorothea of Celle, in 1682, but she never became Queen as he divorced her in 1693 and imprisoned her for life. She was banished to the castle at Ahlden, where she remained. She had fallen in love with an attractive soldier, Count Philip von Konigsmark, with whom she had an affair. He disappeared under circumstances which were never explained, and was thought to have been murdered. Sophia was never allowed to leave the castle grounds, nor to receive visitors, nor to see her two children, George (later George II), and Sophia Dorothea, who married Frederick William II, King of Prussia.

George I never remarried but had numerous mistresses. Although he spoke several languages he never really mastered English, and this must have been a severe handicap to any normal communications. Unlike the Stuarts he did not have a deep appreciation of art, and is supposed to have said on one occasion, "I hate all boets and bainters"!

When the King arrived in England he found the German artist, Sir Godfrey Kneller, already fully established as the leading portrait painter at Court. Kneller had come to England in 1676 and had worked for Charles II, William and Mary, and Queen Anne, and many of his portraits were copied by contemporary miniaturists such as Charles Boit, who executed several enamels of Peter the Great after the full length portrait by Kneller painted in 1698.

Kneller had the patronage of George I and his Court and was responsible for the official state portrait of the King, of which there are many copies and variations. Kneller was knighted by William III in 1692, and made a baron in 1715 by George I. As far as miniatures are concerned I think that it is fair to say that most — if not all — of those representing the King are based on large portraits.

The most important miniature painter in the early part of the eighteenth century was **Bernard Lens (III)** (1682-1740). He was born in London, and came of a family who had been connected with art for four generations. His father, Bernard Lens (II), was a mezzotint engraver and drawing master, who with John Sturt was responsible for opening a drawing school in St. Paul's Church Yard, London. It was, no doubt, in this studio that the younger Lens began his training. Lens later studied at the Academy of Painting, in Great Queen Street, Westminster, which was founded in 1711. He soon became one of the principal miniaturists of the day, and was appointed miniature painter (unpaid) to George I and George II, obtaining the patronage of most of the influential people in the country. He taught drawing to the Duke of Cumberland and the Princesses Mary and Louisa, the Duchess of Portland, Horace Walpole, and Edward Harley, later 2nd Earl of Oxford. Lens also taught at Eton. It was fortunate that, at a time when great changes were taking place and fresh ideas and new experiments being tried in artistic circles, we had a miniaturist who was willing and able to absorb these new ideas and put them into practice. The arts were well patronised, and artists had no difficulty in obtaining work. For the wealthy the 'Grand Tour' had become an accepted part of one's education, and this broadened people's outlook. New vistas were opened up and many valuable possessions changed hands.

In 1717 Horace Walpole was born, and grew up to be one of the greatest connoisseurs of art in this country. He edited the material collected by

George Vertue published under the title *Anecdotes of Painting in England*, which was first published in 1762 and has remained one of the standard works of reference ever since. In the preface he says: "At this epoch of common sense one may reasonably expect to see the arts flourish to as proud a height as they attained at Athens, Rome or Florence". This prophecy was to a great extent fulfilled, as in every aspect of art, music, the theatre, science and literature, men of great ability came to the fore. They included Samuel Johnson, David Garrick, James Boswell, Sir Joshua Reynolds and many more.

Bernard Lens probably began his career soon after 1700, and was working in London and Bristol in 1714, and Bath in 1727. He travelled round the country, staying with important patrons amongst whom was Robert Harley, later Earl of Oxford. In a letter preserved at Welbeck, written 7th June, 1707, by George Tollet to Robert Harley, he says: "You was pleased to desire me to speak to a person that coud teach your son Mr. Edwd, to draw. I have sent for Mr. Lens, a very able and the best master we have in London — a sober, diligent man, and very carefull. His rate for teaching is a guinea entrance, and half-a-crown a time (for an hour's staying), his coming may be twice or thrice a week as you please."

Plate 36D. **A.B. Lens,** *a young girl, ivory, 1¾ins. Signed in monogram: 'ABL.' This is a particularly attractive example of the artist's work; the sitter is wearing a pink dress and tightly fitted bodice with a deep lace collar and blue bows of ribbon as decoration.* Private Collection.

Plate 36E. **B. Lens,** *portrait of an unknown lady, ivory, 5¾ins. Signed in monogram: 'BL.' This is a good example of eighteenth century costume and coiffure. The sitter holds in her lap the type of straw hat which became popular from c.1740.* Courtesy Christie's.

The Portland Collection of miniatures is one of the most important in Britain and is particularly rich in sixteenth, seventeenth and early eighteenth century works.

Edward Harley, 2nd Earl of Oxford, married Henrietta Cavendish Holles, and their daughter, Margaret, married William Bentinck, 2nd Duke of Portland, thus uniting the family treasures. Margaret inherited her family's love of art and in her turn added her own collection. Edward Harley kept a careful note of his purchases, including those relating to frames made for him by Lens. The majority of his notes are preserved in the British Museum and are described as the *Harleian Manuscripts.*

Plate 36F. Attributed to **N. Salway,** *called Francis, 2nd Earl of Godolphin (1678-1766), ivory, 2¼ins. Signed: 'N.S. / Pi.' Unless this is taken from an earlier portrait, the sitter is too young to represent Godolphin, as the costume is c.1720 by which time he would have been forty-two. The miniature is attractive with fresh colours. Courtesy Christie's.*

Sixteen signed and two unsigned miniatures by Lens are at Welbeck, dating from 1710-1723. His charge seems to have been about three guineas a portrait. Whilst working at Welbeck he was responsible for making a number of a particular kind of rectangular frame of pear wood stained black. Several bills for these frames are still at Welbeck, and this type of frame is frequently referred to as a 'Lens type frame.'

Lens married Catherine Woods on 30th November, 1706, at Gray's Inn Chapel. They had three sons; Benjamin became a clerk in the exchequer office, and A.B. Lens and P.P. Lens both followed their father's profession as miniaturists.

Lens painted several self-portraits: one is in the Portland Collection, signed and dated: 'BL' (monogram) '1718'; another is in the Ashmolean Museum, Oxford, signed and dated: '26th November, 1724'; and a third is in the National Portrait Gallery, signed and dated: '1721'. He painted a miniature of his wife in 1733, which was exhibited in Edinburgh in 1965. It is signed and dated: 'BL' (monogram) '1733', and inscribed on the reverse: 'Catherine Lens aged 52 / Bernard Lens fecit 1733 / July 2th.' This large

Plate 36G. **B. Lens,** *Mrs. Bernard Lens, née Catherine Woods (b.c. 1681), vellum, 3¼ins. diam. Wife of the artist. Signed and dated: 'BL' (monogram) / '1733', on the front, and inscribed on the reverse: 'Catherine Lens aged 52 / Bernard Lens fecit 1733 / July 2th.' This is a fine example of period costume. Courtesy the late Warren Lowenhaupt.*

Plate 36H. **J. Goupy,** *an unknown man, vellum, 2²³/₃₂ins., c.1730. Signed and dated: 'J. Goupy delt.' Courtesy Victoria and Albert Museum, Alan Evans Collection.*

Colour Plate 12.
A top centre. **Andrew Plimer,** *an unknown lady, ivory, 1½ins. This is an early work painted c.1786.*
B top left. **Nathaniel Hone, R.A.,** *an unknown man, ivory, 1¼ins. Signed and dated: 'NH / 176-', the last digit being cut off.*
C top right. **Thomas Redmond,** *an unknown man, ivory, 1³/₁₆ins. Signed and dated: 'TR / 1760.'*
D centre. **James Scouler,** *an unknown man, ivory, 1½ins. Signed and dated: 'J.Scouler / 1764.' This is a good example of Scouler's early work, and is close in style to that of John Smart.*
E bottom left. **Richard Collins,** *a young boy, ivory, 1½ins.*
F bottom centre. **Samuel Finney,** *an unknown girl, ivory, 1¾ins.*
G bottom right. **John Bogle,** *an unknown man, ivory, 1¼ins. Signed and dated: 'IB / 1776.'*

Private Collection

Plate 36 I. **B. Lens,** *Montague Garrard Drake of Shardiloes, Buckinghamshire (d.1728), ivory, 3¾ins. Signed and dated on the reverse: 'April 22nd 1708.'* Courtesy Sotheby's.

circular miniature shows clearly the type of stippling or dotting, which is characteristic of Lens and his followers. The sitter is portrayed against a blue background, and the treatment of the dress, lace and brocade trimmings are painted to perfection. It is a good example of costume and the wide-brimmed hats worn at that time (Plate 36G). Although many of Lens' miniatures were painted on vellum his great contribution to the art of miniature painting was the fact that he introduced into England the method of using ivory as a base on which to paint. This method had been used as early as 1696 by an Italian artist, Rosalba Carriera (1675-1757), who as far as we know never came to England. As we have no reason for thinking that Lens ever went abroad one can only suppose that examples of her work were brought back by someone who had been to Venice, and that Lens was so impressed with the idea that he followed her lead (Plate 36B).

This innovation was to have far-reaching results, and by the end of the eighteenth century the use of vellum had been supplanted by ivory. At first the slices of ivory were rather thick, and Lens painted in the old way, using gouache for the costume and background and only using a transparent watercolour on the flesh parts. This needs to be studied under magnification when the difference can be seen clearly, as it is only on these parts that the ivory is visible. The advantage that ivory has over vellum is its luminosity, and, for this to be apparent, the colours must be transparent so that the ivory can glow through. This fact was not fully appreciated until later in the century.

The exact date when Lens began to use ivory is uncertain but examples of his work on this base are to be found from c.1708 onwards, although he still reverted to vellum on occasions.

Lens' earliest dated works were seen by Vertue, who recorded drawings by him dated 1703 and 1704. The earliest known miniature by him is of the Rev. Dr. Harris of Rochester, inscribed: 'B. Lens ad vivum pinxt 1707.'

Besides painting miniatures Lens executed archaeological drawings and sketches. He published *The Granadier's Exercise, 1735,* and the *New and Complete Drawing Book* (published posthumously).

Lens was one of the last miniaturists to make copies of classical, mythological and religious oil paintings, some of which were quite large. He painted miniatures from life, but also copied the works of Hilliard, Rubens, Van Dyck, Raphael, J. Petitot, Kneller, etc. In 1723 he copied Samuel Cooper's unfinished portrait of Oliver Cromwell, now in the Buccleuch Collection. Lens' copy in its rectangular pear wood frame is still at Welbeck.

Many of his works show the influence of Kneller, particularly in the way he drew his sitters' faces in a rather unfortunate oval shape which is suggestive of mumps (Plate 37). He used a greenish-brown flesh colour which was not suited to ivory, rather than the fresher carnations used by earlier artists (Colour Plates 6A and D and 9D).

The costume of his sitters is usually well painted and meticulous, but not all his work was uniformly good, and some of his large portraits appear a little stiff. He used a variety of shapes for his miniatures, oval, rectangular and circular all being popular. The sizes vary from quite small portraits up to large rectangular ones measuring as much as fourteen inches high.

Among his pupils was **Catharina da Costa** (fl.1712-1730), the daughter of a Jewish doctor from Portugal. Lens made several copies of the so-called miniature of Mary, Queen of Scots, which had been repaired by L. Cross(e). This was also copied by Catharina da Costa, after Lens (Plate 38A). Often her copies are of an oval format, the oval on its side, the height narrower than the width.

The little-known miniaturist Louis Goupy (d.1747) was said to have been a nephew and pupil of Lens. His nephew, Joseph Goupy (1680?-1768?) was also a miniaturist (Plate 36H).

Lens usually signed his miniatures 'BL' (monogram), often in gold, and followed by a date. Occasionally he signed in full and dated his work on the reverse and, if the miniature was a copy of another painter, added the name of the original artist as in the case of one at Welbeck of Sir Theodore Turquet de Mayerne, which is inscribed on the reverse: 'Sr Theodore Myron a Famous Physhion in King Charles ye I Time after ye Originall of Petito, Inamill of ye same size, In ye hands of Doctor Sloan. Bernard Lens Fecit Londini Sep: 23: 1710.'

Lens' work served as a link during the transitional period between the early tradition based on the medieval illuminators and the birth of the more flattering and elusive charm achieved by the artists who followed him in the later part of the century. These later eighteenth century artists realised the full potential and advantage of using ivory, and gradually developed this method of painting which has been in vogue ever since.

Lens died at Knightsbridge on 30th December, 1740, and was survived by his three sons; his wife's date of death is unknown.

Examples of his work are in numerous private collections, as well as in the Victoria and Albert Museum, the British Museum, the National Portrait Gallery, and the Ashmolean Museum, Oxford. Miniatures of Princess Louisa, daughter of George II, and several others are in the collection of H.M. The Queen. (Plates 36C, E, G and I.)

Andrew Benjamin Lens (c.1713-d. aft. 1779) was the second son of Bernard Lens III. His date of birth is uncertain, but a miniature of him by his father in the Victoria and Albert Museum, painted in 1723, shows him as a youth of about ten years of age. A self-portrait formerly in the collection of

Plate 37. **B. Lens,** *after Kneller, George I (1660-1727), vellum, 9½ins. Signed and dated: 'B. Lens Fecit.1719.' This is a fine example of a Lens copy of a large portrait.* Private Collection.

Dr. G.C. Williamson was executed in 1742 when he was said to have been aged twenty-nine. This would accord with the suggested date of birth as 1713.

Nothing is known about his education, but it is presumed that he had at least some training in art from his father. He exhibited at the Free Society, and Society of Arts, 1764-1779. Andrew painted portraits, miniatures, mythological subjects, and executed engravings. He must not be confused with Andries Lens (1739-1822), who was a Director of the Antwerp Academy. A.B. Lens painted in much the same manner as his father, and their works are sometimes confused. The majority of his miniatures appear to have been painted on ivory, using his father's technique of painting the backgrounds and costume in gouache, and only leaving the flesh parts to be painted in transparent watercolour. Most of the backgrounds are greyish blue or a plain dark colour; the features are shaded with blue strokes or stippling and the backgrounds have dots and short strokes all over the area behind the sitter, these being painted in a darker colour than the actual background. Many of his works are attractive, and I have seen several where he has used a deep pink for the dress and painted the bodice in grey with a lace edging (Plate 36D). At best his miniatures are better than those painted by his brother, Peter Paul Lens. Not all his works are signed; those that are usually bear a cursive monogram: 'ABL'. Occasionally he signed in full on the reverse.

It is sometimes difficult to identify unsigned miniatures of this period, and as miniatures became more popular, and more artists found employment, several painted in the same style as the Lens family. One whose work is very close to that of A.B. Lens is Samuel Finney (1718/19-1798), who used the same stippling on the backgrounds. Lens is known to have copied some of his father's miniatures. One of his mother, probably after the one by B. Lens, is in the Ward Usher Museum, Lincoln, and is signed in monogram: 'ABL'. (Colour Plates 6E and 9B.)

Little is known about his life, but he appears to have worked with his father. A collection of miniatures by himself and his father was sold in 1777.

Plate 38A (left). **Catharina da Costa**, after B. Lens, called Mary Queen of Scots, ivory, 2½ins. This is a clever copy of the Lens version of this portrait which does not, in fact, represent the Queen. Private Collection.

Plate 38B (right). **Sarah Stanley**, an unknown girl with a hay rake, ivory, 3ins. Signed and dated in gold: 'S.S. / 1716.' This miniature is painted in fresh colours in the manner of the Lens School. Private Collection.

The announcement read: "To be SOLD by AUCTION, By Mess. LANGFORD, at their House in the Great Piazza, Covent Garden, on Wednesday the 16th instant, at twelve o'clock. THE COLLECTION of MINIATURES and other PICTURES of MR ANDREW BENJAMIN LENS. The chief of which are the works of that ingenious artist and his father." A profile miniature of Alexander Pope, after a painting by Kneller, is in the collection of the Duke of Buccleuch. It is signed: 'ABL' (monogram). A miniature by A.B. Lens is in the Victoria and Albert Museum, and three drawings by him after other artists are in the British Museum.

The exact dates of **Peter Paul Lens (1714?-1750?)** are not known, and these tentative ones are arrived at by inscriptions on two miniatures. One miniature of his mother, after a painting by B. Lens, listed by Basil Long, was inscribed on the reverse giving his age as fifteen in 1729, and one at Belvoir Castle is signed and dated: 'Peter Lens pinxit 1750.'

Long also mentions seeing a miniature which was sold at Sotheby's, Lot 77, 30th November, 1921, of a lady wearing the costume of c.1765-1770, signed: 'PL'. This was encased in a tortoiseshell snuff box, and may have been by Peter Lens.

Plate 38C (left). **T. Worlidge,** *an unknown man, vellum, 3³⁄₈ins. Signed and dated: 'T. Worlidge / fecit 1756.' This is a good example of the artist's draughtsmanship and shows the change in men's costume.* Courtesy Sotheby's.

Plate 38D (right). **W. Green,** *portrait of an unknown girl, vellum, 4ins. Signed: 'Gul. Green Junʳ / Delin. / 1752.' This is the only known example of this artist's work and is meticulously drawn.* Private Collection.

Lens was apprenticed to his father on 23rd July, 1729, when he would have been about fifteen years of age. He painted portraits and miniatures; some of his paintings were in oils. The majority of his miniatures are oval, some being quite small in size. A characteristic of his miniatures is the way in which he almost invariably painted his sitters full-face, the head occupying the greater part of the ivory. The backgrounds, which are usually a plain colour, have the same sort of stippling as that used by his brother. He often signed: 'PL' (monogram), 'P. Lens', usually in gold, or 'P.P. Lens pinxt', on the reverse. Sometimes these signatures were followed by a date. Many of his miniatures have a blue-grey shading on the face, and a large amount of opaque white used in the hair. He seems to have been a more prolific artist than his brother, and miniatures by him are not difficult to come by and do not command very high prices. P.P. Lens was in Dublin in 1737 and 1738 where he became a member of a hell-fire club, called the 'Blasters', and

Plate 38E. **RK,** *Miss Voss, Kneller's illegitimate daughter, vellum, 4½ins. Signed: 'RK' (monogram) 'After S^r G:Kneller / 1702.' It is thought that the artist may have been one of the Kneller family.* Courtesy Sotheby's.

professed himself to be a votary of the devil. According to a report sent to the Irish House of Lords, he had "several times uttered the most daring and execrable blasphemies." As a result of his activities he was forced to flee the country to avoid arrest, and returned to England where he continued to paint miniatures. Whether or not he also continued his wild and irresponsible behaviour is not recorded! (Colour Plate 9A and Plate 36A.)

It has been said that both the Lens brothers tended to leave an area of stippled background to the right of the sitter's head to emphasise a lighter shading, but the more miniatures I have examined, the less I find this to be true. He seems to have been good at drawing children, and his miniature in the Victoria and Albert Museum of the 'Ragged Little Boy' is particularly appealing. Two miniatures by him are in the Portland Collection: both are signed and dated, 1740. Four miniatures, of which three are signed, are in the collection of the Duke of Northumberland. One is of Hugh, 1st Duke of Northumberland, as a young man, and another of Elizabeth, 1st Duchess of Northumberland, as a child.

B. Lens and his two sons developed the use of ivory as a base on which to paint, but none of them was adventurous enough to try painting with transparent watercolour over the whole area. This was a gradual development; from their time, and from c.1740 onwards, more and more of the ivory was allowed to show through the paint, and opaque colours were reserved for men's coats and costumes, ladies' dresses, and decorations.

In view of his great contribution to our knowledge of artists, it would be impossible to omit a brief reference to **George Vertue** (1684-1756), who was responsible for collecting copious notes relating to artists and paintings. These were published in The Walpole Society, in seven volumes, and are indispensable for research. Most of his drawings are portraits, usually based on prints, and these are of immense value for identification where the

Plate 38F. **Robert French,** *self-portrait, on card, 2¾ins. Signed on the reverse: 'Rob^{tus} French / ipse pinxit / AD 1737/8.' The few works I have seen by this artist are all rather naïve and lacking in draughtsmanship.* Private Collection.

Plate 38G. **G. Vertue** *after Holbein, Sir Thomas Boleyn, Earl of Wiltshire and Ormond (1477-1539), vellum, 4ins. For other drawings by Vertue see Plates 30B and C.* Courtesy Sotheby's.

originals are now missing. Manuscripts by him are in the British Museum, and at Welbeck Abbey. Miniatures by him are rare; two are in the Portland Collection, one is a self-portrait, signed: 'GV' (monogram) '1729'. A large number of his drawings are in the Huntington Library, California, and are illustrated by Robert R. Wark in *Early British Drawings in the Huntington Collection, 1600-1750*. They include a drawing of R. Gibson, the Dwarf, and one of his wife, John Milton and Peter Oliver, etc. (Plates 30B and C, and 38G).

An interesting miniature signed: 'N.S. / Pi' of Francis, 2nd Earl of Godolphin (1678-1766) was Lot 50 at Christie's on 30th March, 1976. This miniature (Plate 36F) is mentioned by Basil Long in *British Miniaturists,* and has always been attributed to a practically unknown artist, **N. Salway** (fl. 1720-1760). The miniature represents the Earl as a young man, so was presumably taken from an earlier portrait. It is well painted and the artist followed the lead of Bernard Lens in using ivory as the base. It realised £440. Another interesting miniature signed: 'RK' (monogram) 'After S^r G: Kneller / 1702', was Lot 72 at Sotheby's, on 26th November, 1973. It represented Miss Voss, Kneller's illegitimate daughter, and was possibly painted by a member of the Kneller family who is unrecorded (Plate 38E). The original painting by Kneller was engraved by J. Smith in 1705. The painting is good, and the style close to that of B. Lens and C. Richter.

Another minor artist who was working c.1720-1740 was **R. French.** I have seen several miniatures by this artist, none of which was spectacular, but they are of interest to collectors like myself who wish to preserve examples of all periods and styles. I have a self-portrait of the artist signed on the reverse: 'Rob^{tus} French / ipse pinxit / AD 1737/8'. The miniature is painted in the Lens School style, on card. The face is shaded with blue and red stippling and the background, which is dark brown particularly to the rear of the sitter's head, is also stippled. The draughtsmanship is not very good (Plate 38F).

Plate 39A. **C.F. Zincke,** *Hannah Sophia, Countess of Exeter (d.1765), wife of the 8th Earl of Exeter, enamel, 1½ins. diam. The miniature is set within a gold and enamelled frame.* Courtesy The Marquess of Exeter, K.C.M.G.

Plate 39B. **C.F. Zincke,** *Lady Margaret Cavendish Bentinck (1739-56), enamel, 2ins. Inscribed with the sitter's name on the reverse and signed: 'C.F. Zincke ad vivum pinxt 1744.' This enchanting miniature of her as a child is set in a blue enamel locket.* Courtesy Ivy, Duchess of Portland.

Plate 39C. **C.F. Zincke,** *Lady Henrietta Cavendish Bentinck, afterwards Countess of Stafford (1737-1827), enamel, 2ins. Inscribed with the sitter's name on the reverse and signed: 'C.F. Zincke ad vivum pinxt 1741.' Set in a blue enamel locket similar to Plate 39B.* Courtesy Ivy, Duchess of Portland.

One of the most important enamellists of the early eighteenth century was **Christian Friedrich Zincke** (1683/4-1767), who was born in Dresden. His father was a goldsmith, into which trade he was apprenticed. As with miniaturists of previous centuries, the goldsmith's art led him on to an appreciation of painting, and he became a pupil of another Dresden artist, H.C. Fehling. He came to England in c.1704/6 at the invitation of C. Boit, who needed assistance in his unfruitful project of the large enamel miniature to commemorate the victory of Blenheim. Zincke became a pupil of Boit, and eventually became the leading enamellist in England. Although he painted a large number of miniatures from life he also copied the works of Kneller, Lely, etc. He obtained the patronage of the Royal family and served during three reigns, those of Queen Anne, George I and George II. The latter monarch gave him many commissions to paint him, and ordered numerous replicas of his portrait and of members of the Royal family. Vertue records an amusing story in 1732 about his paintings of the King and Queen, *The Walpole Society,* Vol. XXII, p.58: "Mr Zinke often at Court drawing the pictures of the Royal Family — having drawn the prince of Wales & the 3 Royal princes. — the young children — the Queen & King hav sat to him — the Queen advis'd him to be sure to make the Kings picture young. not above 25. — & the King commended his works & admonishd him not to make the Queens picture above 28 — these courtesies to each other. must be a mistery to posterity who sees them thus depicted without knowing partly the reason — ". (The King and Queen were forty-four on their accession in 1727!)

Vertue also says that: "His general employment is from the life, of people of Quality; so fully employ'd that for some years [1726] he has had more

Plate 39D. C.F. Zincke, *Lady Margaret Cavendish Harley (1715-85) and her father, Edward Harley, 2nd Earl of Oxford and Earl Mortimer (1689-1741), enamel, 2⅜ins. This small box is inscribed in full on the reverse with the names of the sitters and signed and dated: 'CF Zincke. Fecit / 1727' (as shown in Figure 24). Margaret was called by Prior "My noble lovely little Peggy". This miniature is one of Zincke's finest works, and is set within an enamelled and gold box.* Courtesy Ivy, Duchess of Portland.

Figure 24. *Reverse of box in Plate 39D by C.F. Zincke, depicting Edward Harley, 2nd Earl of Oxford, and his daughter Lady Margaret Harley.*

persons of distinction daily sitting to him than any Painter living. [1728] the Queen sate to him for her picture which was presented to the Lady of S[r] Robert Walpole richly sett with Diamonds & . . ."

Zincke was the first occupant of No. 13 Tavistock Row, Covent Garden, where he lived from 1715-1748. This was a very popular part of London and a number of well-known people and artists lived there. Zincke is said to have moved later to South Lambeth, where he died on 24th March, 1767, and was survived by his second wife, Elizabeth, who died in 1772. By his first wife, whose name is not recorded, he had a son, Christopher, and a daughter, and by Elizabeth he had three or four children. A mezzotint of Zincke and his wife after H. Hysing, was engraved by J. Faber, Junior (c.1684-1756). This is illustrated in *British Miniature Painters,* J.J. Foster, Plate XXVIII.

Frederick, Prince of Wales, took a great interest in art, and not only bought old masters but patronised many contemporary artists including Zincke, who was appointed his 'Cabinet Painter' in 1732. Vertue records a lot of information regarding Zincke's work and life, and is the main source of our knowledge.

Plate 39E. A. Seaman, *portrait of an unknown man, enamel, 2¼ins. Signed and dated on the reverse: '1725.' Signed miniatures by Seaman are rare, and this is a good example of his work.* Courtesy Christie's.

As early as 1725 he had begun to have trouble with his eyesight, and this gradually deteriorated, so that he found it necessary to cut down the number of commissions in order to preserve it as much as possible. In his early days he charged about £6 9s. for a miniature, but increased it to 15 guineas, and later to 20 guineas and even 30 guineas, in the hopes of reducing the number of portraits he had to paint in order to save what eyesight he could. By 1746 he was forced to give up painting except for his own amusement, and the only interesting detail we know is that in 1757 and 1758 he taught Jeremiah Meyer, then a young man of twenty-two, who in turn was to become one of the leading miniaturists of the latter part of the century. The art of painting miniatures on enamel had come from the Continent, and this influence took us through from the time of C. Boit in the seventeenth century up to the eighteenth century and beyond. (Colour Plates 10G and 13E.)

Zincke is known to have had a number of assistants and pupils, including Gambel (fl.1773), W. Prewett (fl.1735-1750?) and possibly A. or J. Rouquet (1701-1758). The question of accurate attribution of miniatures to Zincke is a difficult one in view of the vast output of portraits all in his style. Many of them may in fact have been the work of his assistants, and some are distinctly inferior in quality. It is possible that Zincke painted the faces and, as was the case with large portraits, someone else was responsible for the draperies. There is a great similarity in the looks of his female portraits, and even the correct identification of sitters is not always easy.

Not all his enamels are painted with the same smoothness as those of Boit, although the quality of his best works is superb. He used a red stippling on the face, the dots of which are sometimes blended together. One of the most important differences between works by Boit and those of Zincke is that the backs of miniatures painted by Zincke are almost always smooth, whereas those of Boit are more often than not rough. The uneven quality of Zincke's work was no doubt due to his eyesight. One of his most attractive enamels is that of Lady Margaret Cavendish Harley and her father, Edward Harley, 2nd Earl of Oxford (Plate 39D). This miniature, which is oblong, is painted in superbly fresh colours, and is signed on the reverse: 'CF' (monogram) 'Zincke. Fecit / 1727,' and inscribed with the names of the sitters (Figure 24). In a letter written to Edward Harley at this time he mentions his eyesight, and says: "... I have begun it ten times before any Lines pleased me, and really My Lord I find my Eyes scarce Capable of seeing them fine stroaks, wich I am obliged to use to bring it to any Perfection ..."

Not all his miniatures are signed; known signatures are: 'CFZ' (monogram), 'CF' (monogram), 'Zincke fecit', 'C.F. Zincke fecit', and other variations. With the exception of a few miniatures all known examples appear to have been signed on the reverse. One exception is a portrait of Catherine, Duchess of Buckingham, in the Ward Usher Museum, Lincoln.

Plate 39F. A.H. Groth, *Elizabeth Riveley*, enamel, 1⅞ins. Signed and dated on the reverse: 'Eliz.ᵗʰ Riveley / 1753. / A Groth Painter / to the King. Pinx.' So little is known about this artist that this miniature is of great documentary importance. The information regarding his appointment held under George II is interesting, as the King was not noted for his patronage of art. Private Collection.

Plate 39G. A. Rouquet, *Henry Pelham-Clinton, 2nd Duke of Newcastle*, enamel, 1¾ins. Signed: 'R.' The sitter was probably Henry Fiennes Clinton, 9th Earl of Lincoln and 2nd Duke of Newcastle-under-Lyme (1720-94). This is a fine miniature with a particularly clear signature. Courtesy Christie's.

Figure 25. Reverse of the miniature in Plate 39F by A.H. Groth of Elizabeth Riveley.

A

B

C

D

E

F

G

Plate 39H. **W. Prewett,** *portrait of an unknown man, enamel, 2ins. Set in a contemporary gold frame decorated with scrolls and flowers.* Private Collection.

Plate 39 I. **A. Rouquet,** *portrait of an unknown lady, enamel, 2⅛ins. Signed: 'R. Mid-eighteenth century.* Courtesy The Duke of Buccleuch and Queensbury, K.T.

This is signed on the front: 'FC' or 'CF' (monogram) 'Zincke' [or Zinke] fecit / 1724'. The Portland Collection is rich in works by Zincke and of these sixteen are signed and nine unsigned. Full details are given by R.W. Goulding in *The Welbeck Abbey Miniatures,* The Walpole Society, Vol. IV. Of these two appear to be signed: 'CFZ' on the front.

The number of miniatures by or attributed to Zincke, as well as those painted by his pupils and followers, makes it impossible to give precise details as to their whereabouts. Examples of his work are in the Victoria and Albert Museum, the British Museum, the Ashmolean Museum, Oxford, and many private collections. (Plates 39A, B and C.)

The artist whose work is closest to that of Zincke is **André or Jean Rouquet (1701-1758),** a native of Geneva. He was the son of French Protestants who fled to Switzerland. Rouquet came to London in c.1723, if one accepts his own statement that he had spent thirty years in England when he left for France in 1753. Another tradition is that he only came to England in the reign of George II, but his own statement seems more likely.

Vertue first mentions Rouquet in 1739, when he records that he was the best of Zincke's imitators, and that his charge for a portrait was 10 guineas a

Colour Plate 13.
A. **Jeremiah Meyer, R.A.,** *a member of the Deane family, ivory, 2¼ins. Sketch for Colour Plate 13F.*
B. **A.H. Groth,** *William Henry, Duke of Gloucester and Edinburgh, K.G. (1743-1805), enamel, 1⅝ins. Signed: 'G.' Few signed miniatures by Groth exist, and these tend to be signed on the reverse.*
C. **Charles Boit,** *Peter The Great, Tsar of Russia (1672-1725), based on the portrait by Kneller, painted in 1698, enamel, 1½ins. Signed on the reverse: 'CBoit pinx.' Given by Peter The Great to Mr. Styles, his interpreter. A note with these details was once with the miniature.*
D. **Henry Pierce Bone,** *Lady Dorothy Sidney, Countess of Sunderland (1617-84) after the portrait by Van Dyck at Althorp, enamel, 4ins. Inscribed and signed in full on the reverse and dated: '1842.'*
E. **Christian Friedrich Zincke,** *an unknown man, enamel, 1⅝ins., c.1700-10.*
F. **Jeremiah Meyer, R.A.,** *a member of the Deane family, enamel, 2¼ins. Finished portrait from the sketch shown in Colour Plate 13A.*
G. **A. Rouquet,** *Charlotte, Baroness de Ferrers and Compton (d.1770), wife of George, 4th Viscount and 1st Marquis Townshend, whom she married in 1751, enamel, 1¾ins. Signed: 'R.'*

Private Collection

head. Rouquet is said to have been friendly with Hogarth, David Garrick, and numerous wits of the day. He exhibited at the Paris Salon, 1753-1757, and published *L'Etat des Arts en Angleterre,* in 1755. In it he describes how a portrait painter could become for a time the rage of the town, by whom everyone must be painted! He also describes the fashionable habit of calling to see a painter's studio under the guidance of a lackey.

Rouquet painted the portraits of Louis XV and Mme. de Pompadour, and was given a studio in The Louvre. He joined the Académie Royale in 1753. Towards the end of his life he went mad, and died at Charenton on 28th December, 1758.

Rouquet's enamels are among the most attractive of the period, but are scarce and, because he did not always sign, may possibly pass unrecognised and be attributed to 'School of Zincke'. Although he copied the work of Zincke to a degree, his miniatures have much more charm and are painted with more delicacy of touch. The red stippling on the face is not so apparent and, in fact, in some cases is not used at all. A typical example of the grace and prettiness which marks out Rouquet's miniatures is to be found on one of Charlotte, Baroness de Ferrers and Compton, wife of George, 4th Viscount Townshend. This is signed with a cursive 'R' on the background, which is pale grey, and the colour of the sitter's dress is off-white, with a blue cloak over her shoulders. She is wearing no jewels, but has a bunch of blue and white flowers fastened in her hair (Colour Plate 13G). Points to look for on Rouquet's miniatures are the way he painted his sitters with small, slightly protruding eyes, and showed moisture on the lower lip. Only a small number of authentic works by him are known, and these are signed with a cursive: 'R' or 'JR' (monogram). The signature is not easy to see except under high magnification. Miniatures by Rouquet are in the collections of the Earl Beauchamp, the Duke of Buccleuch, and the Marquess of Exeter. A miniature of an unknown man c.1750, signed: 'R', is in the National Gallery, Dublin, and a typical signed example representing William

Pitt, Earl of Chatham, is in the Victoria and Albert Museum. (Plates 39G and I.)

Another artist from Geneva with French Protestant connections was **Jean Etienne Liotard** (1702-1789). He was the son of Antoine Liotard, a jeweller in Montélimar, and the twin brother of Michel Liotard, the engraver. Jean studied in Geneva under Daniel Gardelle, and from 1725 under J.B. Masse in Paris.

Liotard seems to have travelled extensively, visiting Italy in 1736 with the Marquis de Puysieux, and in the same year worked in Rome and Naples. He met Sir William Ponsonby (afterwards Lord Bessborough) whilst in Florence, and travelled with him to Constantinople where he remained for five years, living in Turkish fashion. Between 1743 and 1747 Liotard visited Vienna, Venice, Darmstadt, Lyons and Geneva. From 1748-1753 he worked in Paris where he became painter to the King and a member of the Academy of St. Luc, where he exhibited 1751-1753. Between 1753 and 1774 he came to England several times. Although he painted miniatures on ivory and enamel these are scarce, and he is probably best known for his excellent crayon drawings and oil portraits. One of the best sets of his crayons is in the collection of H.M. The Queen, representing Augusta, Princess of Wales and all her family. These are documented and illustrated by Oliver Millar in *Tudor, Stuart and Early Georgian Pictures,* Plates 215-225.

In 1753, Liotard married Mlle. Fragues at The Hague. She was the daughter of a French merchant who was living in Amsterdam. After visiting Paris in 1757, he settled in Geneva in 1758, where he died on 12th June, 1789.

The majority of his works are on the Continent, or in private collections. A miniature of Liotard's niece, Mlle. Lavergne from Lyons, was Lot 78 at Sotheby's in the Holzscheiter sale on 28th March, 1977, when it realised the then record price of £3,200 (Plate 40D). The Musée d'Art et d'Histoire, Geneva, has a whole room devoted to his work. A chalk drawing by him is in the Victoria and Albert Museum.

Although **Thomas Frye** (1710-1762) was Irish by birth he left Dublin at an early age and came to England, where he remained, and for this reason I have included him in this chapter. Frye was born in or near Dublin, and presumably had some training in art in Ireland. He came to England with Herbert Stoppelaer, where he was best noted for executing portraits in oil, black lead and crayons, and also painted a small number of miniatures in watercolour and enamel. He later became well known as a mezzotint engraver. Frye studied under John Brooks of the Battersea enamel factory. Portraits by him date from 1735 and in 1736 he was commissioned to paint a full-length portrait of Frederick, Prince of Wales, for the Saddlers' Company. The original was destroyed in 1940, but a half-length version of it by Frye is in the collection of H.M. The Queen, and was probably painted at

Colour Plate 14.
Joseph Lee, *Lady Georgina Agar Ellis, enamel, 5¾ins. Fully inscribed on the reverse: 'Lady Georgina Agar Ellis / from the Original by / John Jackson Esqr R.A. / Painted by Joseph Lee / 1826.' This is a particularly fine copy by Lee.* Courtesy Asprey's.

the same period. He had an introduction to Sir Joshua Reynolds with whom he became friendly. Possibly as a result of working at Battersea, Frye became interested in the manufacture of ceramics, and invented a form of porcelain for which he and Edward Heylyn took out a patent in 1744, from which year he was manager of the Bow china factory up to 1759. He took out his own patent in 1749, but must have lost interest and resumed work as a painter. Frye died of consumption on 2nd April, 1762 and was survived by his wife and three children, two daughters and a son, who "turned out an idle drunken fellow"!

Frye's miniatures are good and softly painted; the technique, as of many of the minor artists of this period, is difficult to describe; he signed: 'Frye / 1761' and 'T. Frye / 1761', the former signature is in gold, and the latter in yellow, the first two letters being in monogram. The background is stippled behind the sitter's head, and shaded with hatching in short strokes on the opposite side. The face is shaded with red and blue stippling and strokes. A mezzotint self-portrait is illustrated in Strickland's *Dictionary of Irish Artists,* Plate XXV. I have never seen an example of Frye's work on enamel, but this may be because they pass unrecognised. (Plate 40B.)

One of C.F. Zincke's outstanding pupils was **William Prewett or Prewitt** (fl. 1735-1750?). He is thought to have been born in Suffolk, and was one of the best enamellists of the British School. Nothing is known about his life or education and unfortunately works by him are scarce. (Colour Plate 11D.) Two of the best are in the Victoria and Albert Museum; one is of Mr. and Mrs. John Knight and Mr. Newsham, after Vanderbank, signed and dated on the front: 'W. Prewett / pinx 1735'. The other is of Mr. Newsham, signed and dated on the reverse: 'W. Prewett pinx 1736'. A miniature of an unknown man, signed in full on the reverse: 'W / Prewett / Pinxt' was Lot 52 at Sotheby's in the Holzscheiter sale, 28th March, 1977, when it realised £550. A good miniature, said to represent Horace Walpole, is in the collection of the Duke of Buccleuch, and is signed and dated: 'W. Prewett pinx 1735'. A miniature of an unknown man signed on the reverse: 'W. Prewett', is in the National Gallery, Dublin. This latter miniature is softly painted in water-colour. His miniatures on enamel are well painted and attractive; the face is stippled rather in the manner of Zincke and, viewed under a lens, is not as smoothly painted on the flesh parts as the miniatures by Rouquet. The stippling is executed in blue, yellow and pink dots, and the eyebrows strongly delineated. (Plate 39H.)

Another enamellist of this period about whom we know practically nothing is **Andreas Henry Groth** (fl. c.1730-1755). For many years all miniatures signed: 'G' were attributed either to an artist named Gambel, or another called Gardelle. The whole matter was resolved when, quite unexpectedly, three enamel miniatures were taken to Sotheby's in 1966. They were all of one family. One of Thomas Edwards Freeman is signed on the reverse: 'A. Groth pinxt. 1753'; another, possibly of his sister, is signed on the front: 'G', and the third of Walter Edwards Freeman is unsigned. Other miniatures signed 'G' are known, and are attributed to Groth. All these miniatures are well painted and meticulously executed especially in the details of the sitters' costume. Characteristics appear to be strong delineation of the eyebrows, shadows down the nose, and a thinly drawn mouth with the upper lip emphasised. The face is shaded with a greenish-yellow stippling,

Plate 41A. **G. Spencer,** *Lady Caroline Fox, enamel, 1⅞ins. Signed on the reverse and dated: '1747.' This is an attractive miniature showing the sitter wearing a tight-fitting bodice decorated with a rose at the bosom, a cloak over one arm and a shawl tied over her head.* Courtesy Christie's.

and touches of opaque white are fairly thickly painted on lace work. The general feeling of these miniatures is that the colouring is bright and fresh. One in a private collection, of William Henry, Duke of Gloucester, is very attractive and painted in brilliant colours. It is signed with a cursive: 'G' (Colour Plate 13B).

On 21st March, 1978, a very important miniature by Groth was sold at Christie's. It represented Elizabeth Riveley, and is signed and dated on the reverse: 'Elizth Riveley / 1753. / A. Groth Painter / to the King. Pinx'. This portrait was amongst family miniatures sold by the present Lord Redesdale. As a direct result of the discovery of this miniature, further enquiries were made on my behalf by Mr. Walter Rappolt, and the Christian names of the artist found in an entry in the Public Record Office. Under Appointments 1734-1756, is the following entry: "There are & c. Mr. Andreas Henry Groth into the Place and Quality of Painter in Enamel in Ordinary to his M.y in the room·of Mr. Bernard Lens dec'd / To have hold exercise and enjoy the said Place together with all rights, Profits, Privileges and Advantages thereunto belonging in as full and ample manner as the said Bernard Lens formerly held or of right ought to have held and enjoyed same. And & c. Given & c. this 18th Day of March 1741/2 in the Fifteenth Year of His M,y's reign. To the Gent, Ushers & c. [signed] Grafton."

From this it would appear that Groth held a more important position than had hitherto been supposed, and it is surprising that his work is still so little known. John, 1st Baron Redesdale inherited the estates of Thomas Edward(s)-Freeman, of Batsford Park, Gloucestershire, and assumed the additional name of Freeman. It was his daughter Frances Elizabeth (d. 7th November, 1806) who was painted by Groth (Plate 39F and Figure 25).

Plate 41B. **G. Spencer**, *Sir James Macdonald, enamel, 1¼ins. Signed and dated on the front: 'GS / 1759.' The sitter is wearing a Van Dyck costume with his hair en queue. It seems to have been popular to be painted in costume at this period.* Courtesy Christie's.

Plate 41C. **N. Hone R.A.**, *Thomas Stephens aged thirty-six, ivory, 1⅝ins. Signed and dated: 'NH (monogram) / 1753.' Wearing a crimson coat, white vest and cravat, and his hair en queue. This is a good example of men's costume of the mid-eighteenth century.* Courtesy Sotheby's.

Plate 41D. G. Spencer, Hester, Countess of Denbigh (d. 1725/6), wife of Basil, 4th Earl of Denbigh, vellum, 5ins. Signed: 'GS.' This is the largest work known by this artist and is of exceptionally high quality. It was probably copied from an earlier portrait as the hair style and costume suggest a date of c.1700. Courtesy Sotheby's.

Plate 41E. N. Hone R.A., portrait of an unknown child, enamel, 1¾ins. Signed and dated: 'NH (monogram) / 1750'. Wearing a pink dress with a white lace collar and white cuffs. Courtesy Sotheby's.

For some time now enamel miniatures painted in a certain style not unlike Zincke, have been attributed to either **Abraham Seaman or Seeman** (fl. 1724-1731), or **Noah Seaman** (fl. 1724-1741). Little is known about either of these artists, who may have been related to Enoch Seaman or Seeman (1694-1744), of Danzig, who is thought to have painted some portraits in Britain in c.1743. He is supposed to have painted miniatures. His brother, Isaac Seaman or Seeman (d.1751), also of Danzig, came to work in London, and Basil Long saw a miniature copy on vellum by him of Alexander Pope, after Kneller. He was working from Air Street, Piccadilly in 1745. There is a certain amount of confusion about the correct identification of works by Noah and Abraham Seaman, as a miniature in the collection of H.M. Queen Juliana of the Netherlands is signed on the front with a cursive: 'NS' and on the reverse: 'Abraham Seaman'. It is possible that the sitter was Abraham. Miniatures signed either: 'NS' or: 'A:S:' (cursive) are known, and the initials are sometimes followed by a date. (Colour Plate 10D.) One of an unknown man is signed on the reverse: 'A. Seaman 1731', and one signed: 'A:S: 1725', was sold in 1933. Abraham's works have strong delineation round the nose and eyebrows, and are slightly coarser than miniatures painted by Zincke and his followers.

Miniatures by Noah Seaman seem to be better drawn, and more stippling is apparent. A miniature of an unknown man signed on the reverse: 'Noah Seaman / Pinx: 1728' is in the Victoria and Albert Museum (see also Colour Plate 11G). A miniature of an unknown man, attributed to A. Seaman, was Lot 56 at Sotheby's in the Holzscheiter sale, 28th March, 1977, when it sold for £140. It was unframed. (Plate 39E.)

Another enamellist who came to work in London was **Lucius Barber or Barbor** (d.1767). Barber is thought to have been a Swede, but nothing is known about his life or education. He exhibited at the Society of Artists, 1763-1766, from addresses in Golden Square, London. Two exhibits were on enamel, and one in watercolour. His name was spelt 'Barbor' by Graves in *The Society of Artists and the Free Society,* but this may have been a

misprint. A miniature of Lord Edward Bentinck, signed on the reverse: 'L. Barber ad Vivum pinx^t 1749', is in the Portland Collection. He is identified with the artist whose death is recorded in *Lloyd's Evening Post,* 2nd November, 1767: "Mr Barber, painter Haymarket. Died 31 Oct. 1767." His widow is said to have been left in distressed circumstances.

One of the great difficulties in attributing enamels with any degree of certainty is that, unless they are signed, there is a sameness about them. The fact that so many of the portraits bear no signature only adds to the confusion, and exact descriptions of the different techniques are not easy to give. Barber's work is rather smoother than that of Zincke, and more in the manner of Rouquet. He used a greenish tone in shading the background, and signed with cursive initials: 'LB' (monogram) and: 'B'. He also occasionally signed in full. (Colour Plate 11C.) There may have been some confusion between the work of L. Barber and the Irish miniaturist, R. Barber. A miniature signed: 'B' on the front is in the National Gallery, Dublin, and is an attractive portrait of an unknown lady.

Miniature painting in the early years of the eighteenth century was to a large extent dominated by the Lens family who based their portraits on the work of earlier artists such as Richter, B. Arlaud, etc. The great innovation was Lens' adaptation to the use of ivory as a base on which to paint. Zincke followed with his great contribution to the art of enamelling, and by the middle of the century the artists working in Britain had become what Graham Reynolds aptly described as "The Modest School of Miniaturists". The size of the formats shrank to a small scale, anything from 1 to 2 inches in height being a popular size.

Due to the demand for miniature portraits, brought about by increased wealth, the number of artists working from c.1740 onwards was quite large. They were in many cases modest in their approach, and their painting slightly tentative. Many of them did not sign their work, or, if they did, it is only with one initial, or a monogram. Some of these artists are still unidentified. This makes attributions very difficult, and in a book such as

181

this it would be impossible to do more than mention a few, and give brief biographical sketches. I have been fortunate in obtaining a large number of illustrations of the works of minor artists whose portraits can still be bought at reasonable prices by new collectors, and I hope that this will be of help both for students of the art and collectors alike. For those who wish to know more details about the recorded artists I recommend the books cited in the bibliography.

From c.1720 onwards there were considerable changes in fashions, and these are noticeable on miniatures which are a good guide to styles of hair, and the upper part of the sitters' costume. Ladies tended to prefer a simpler form of hair style, the hair being loosely drawn back from the forehead, with a bun on top arranged slightly towards the back of the head. Curls were still used by some people, and were arranged about the face or a stray one allowed to fall over the temples. From c.1730, there were various changes: a false 'head' of close curls was popular, and 'top-knots', bunches of ribbons looped in various colours, artificial flowers, jewels, and pearls set on ribbons or pins were all worn as decorations. Necklaces were less fashionable, although ribbons or frills tied round the neck were worn. The use of grey or coloured hair powder was popular with many women, but usually for special occasions; it only came into more general favour from c.1760. Ladies' dresses had low-cut necklines, tight fitted bodices often trimmed with ribbon or lace, and sleeves to the elbow. Men wore shorter wigs tied *en queue* or had their hair powdered. Cravats were still in fashion, and fitted coats, often richly embroidered, were worn over waistcoats of different colours. Ladies wore caps of varying styles, and occasionally flattish hats for outdoor occasions. These were to be replaced by much more extravagant styles in the latter part of the eighteenth century.

Plate 42A. **P. Carwardine,** *portrait of an unknown child wearing an Oriental head-dress, pencil and red chalk on paper, 5½ins. One of a series of pencil sketches by this artist which have just come to light. A particularly attractive and well drawn example.* Private Collection.

Those who wish to include small drawings in black-lead in their miniature collection will be wise to be on the look-out for any executed by **Thomas Worlidge** (1700-1766). He was born in Peterborough of Roman Catholic parents, and having an interest in art became a pupil of Alessandro Maria Grimaldi (1659-1732), 6th Marquess, an artist from Genoa, related to the Princes of Monaco. Worlidge married Arabella Grimaldi, Alessandro's daughter. She died sometime before 1749, and he married twice more. The name of his second wife, whose dates are not known, was Mary, and in 1763 he married as his third wife, Elizabeth Wicksteed, the daughter of the proprietor of a shop in Bath where he had an address in 1754. He is said to have had thirty-two children, and was described as hot-tempered, gluttonous and extravagant! His wife, Elizabeth, was also an artist, and was reputed to have been very beautiful. Worlidge painted miniatures, and executed portraits in oils as well as small finished likenesses in black-lead, and etchings. He is said to have reintroduced painting on glass whilst in Birmingham. He worked in Bath, but moved to London in c.1740, and lived in The Piazza, Covent Garden, staying in Bath from time to time. After his last marriage he moved to a house in Great Queen Street which had been occupied by Kneller and Reynolds. He also owned a house near Hammersmith, where he died on 23rd September, 1766. He was buried in Hammersmith Church. (Plate 38C.)

His plumbago miniatures are well drawn, some in profile, and many are after the works of other artists including I. Oliver. He exhibited at the Free Society of Artists, 1761-1766, and is said to have had some training from F. Boitard. His portraits in oils are bolder in effect than his drawings; one of Garrick by him is in the Victoria and Albert Museum. Drawings by him are in the collection of H.M. The Queen, the British Museum has a drawing of

Plate 42B. **P. Carwardine,** *portrait of an unknown lady holding a looking-glass, pencil and red chalk on paper, 6ins., c.1780 judging by the hair style of curls and loose ringlets over the shoulder. The higher and more elaborate ornamentations worn earlier were becoming gradually discarded.* Courtesy Dr. A.K. Brown.

Plate 42C. **P. Hawk,** *portrait of an unknown scholar, pencil on vellum, 6¼ins. Signed and dated: 'P. Hawk / delint. / Oxon / 1775'. This is at present the only known work by Hawk and is reminiscent of drawings by J. Taylor. For comparison see Plates 76C and D.* Courtesy E. Grosvenor Paine, U.S.A.

George II, and the Huntington Library, California, has two examples of his drawings. A self-portrait signed: 'TW' and dated 176-? (the last figure being indistinct) is in *A Dictionary of British Miniature Painters,* Plate 394.

Gervase Spencer (d.1763) is one of the artists of this period who painted some most attractive miniatures both on enamel and ivory, and his work is typical of the unpretentious but interesting miniatures painted by the numerous artists who kept the art of miniature painting alive in Britain until the great masters of the late eighteenth and early nineteenth century reached their prime. Spencer's date of birth is not known, but c.1715 has been tentatively suggested. He started life as a gentleman's servant but, discovering that he could copy a miniature successfully, took up art and became a fashionable miniaturist. He was one of the last miniaturists to be recorded by Vertue, who noted that he had been a footman to a 'Dr. W.', and that he was self-taught. In view of the fact that a large proportion of his output was enamels, it seems unlikely that he could have taught himself that craft without some tuition. Without evidence it is fruitless to conjecture who his teacher might have been, but Rouquet's name has been put forward as a possibility.

It would be tempting to consider the possibility that the mysterious 'Dr. W.' was none other than Dr. John Wall (1708-1776), a physician and author of medical works and the son of a one-time Mayor of Worcester, where he was educated before going up to Oxford. He practised and lived in Worcester all his life, and was one of the original shareholders in the Worcester Porcelain Factory which was established in 1751. The period from 1752-1783 is known to collectors as 'Dr. Wall period'. He is said to have had "an unremitting attachment to the art of painting" which "engaged almost every moment of his leisure hours from his infancy to his death" (*Medical Tracts,* 1780). He and George Vertue could have met in Oxford, and Vertue obviously thought a passing reference to 'Dr. W.' was explanation enough!

Signed works by Spencer occur from c.1740, and he seems to have been able to alternate quite happily between painting in watercolour and on enamel. This latter medium, having been so successful under Zincke and his followers, was slowly losing its popularity. The pendulum swung back to a preference for miniatures painted in watercolour. Spencer seemed able to vary his style to suit either medium. He exhibited at the Society of Artists, 1761-1762, when his address was 28 Suffolk Street. Besides painting miniatures Spencer drew a self-portrait in Indian ink (now in the British Museum), and executed some etchings. A miniature self-portrait in watercolour was in the de la Hey Collection. One of his pupils was Henry Spicer. Although Spencer's work varied, and he is said to have been at his best when painting ladies, all his miniatures are clearly defined and meticulous. His enamel miniatures are particularly attractive. He was evidently an artist who needed to have a rapport with his sitters, and was not at his best when painting elderly men! One of his largest, and probably most ambitious, miniatures was Lot 126 at Sotheby's, 10th November, 1969. It was of Hester, Countess of Denbigh, signed: 'GS', and measured 5 inches high. The sitter is painted against a landscape background (Plate 41D).

His signatures vary, the most usual one being: 'G.S', in either red, black or gold (the punctuation varies). He also signed: 'G.S.f.' and: 'G. Spencer'. Some miniatures are signed on the reverse and dated. His style varies a great deal and is not easy to describe. (Colour Plate 11F and Plates 41A and B.)

Spencer died in Great Marlborough Street, London on 30th October, 1763, and was survived by a daughter, who married a Mr. Lloyd, after whose death all Spencer's remaining works and painting materials were sold in London in December, 1797. Spencer was painted by Reynolds, but the whereabouts of the painting is unknown.

One of the many artists who painted excellent miniatures, but who did not often sign his works was **Samuel Finney** (1718/19-1798). He was the son of Samuel Finney of Fulshaw, and his wife, Esther, née Davenport. The couple were married at St. Lawrence, Denton, Lancashire, on April 29th, 1718. Samuel is said to have been born nine months later, and seven more children were born to them. Details regarding the family, which are rather complicated, are in the Chester Record Office, and I am indebted to a descendant, Mr. M.S. Morgan, for helpful information regarding Samuel. His father, having got into some financial difficulties, sailed for the American Colonies in 1738/1739, leaving behind his wife and young family. Samuel was by this time articled to Mr. Samuel Worthington of Manchester to study law. After about three years he made his way to London, where he continued his tuition and existed on a mere pittance. Writing to his father in August, 1750 he says: "I have left off the practice of the Law not Having money to carry on the Business in a creditable manner and now follow another Imployment more agreeable to my Inclination and Genius wch. is painting portraits in water colours in miniatures. I have made a pretty good proficiency in it, and all my Friends are much pleased with my performances and flatter me wth. the hopes of being in a little time eminent in the profession."

It is frustrating that Finney gives no indication as to who taught him art, but he does say, in his notes, that he began by drawing portraits in Indian ink, and then painted miniatures in watercolour and lastly executed enamels. He kept a notebook of his paintings, but it does not go beyond 1767. He appears to have had a distinguished clientele, and exhibited at the Free Society of Artists (of which he was a member) from 1761-1766. In an extract from *The Cheshire and Lancashire Historical Collector,* 1853, there is a long article about Finney in which the author says that he was apprehensive of some rival painter starting up who might take his clients, and so decided to learn enamelling. Finney mentions Spencer as being self-taught, and says that he "had the Resolution to attempt this difficult Art too without a master". Although he succeeded in his attempt he apparently found this medium difficult, and the results uncertain. He charged from 12 to 50 guineas for these portraits, and was financially very successful. (Colour Plate 12F.)

George III came to the throne in 1760, and in the following year was married to Princess Charlotte of Mecklenburg-Strelitz, who appointed Finney her Enamel and Miniature Painter on 31st December, 1763. Finney had become known to the Queen in a curious way, according to his notes. Before the marriage a Colonel David Graeme, who was living abroad, was sent to England with a painting of Princess Charlotte for the King's approval. Finney at Colonel Graeme's request painted a miniature from the portrait, which enhanced her beauty somewhat, and this was also shown to the King before his bride's arrival! After the coronation Finney was invited to St. James's Palace, and the Queen sat to him for a miniature. Although she commissioned many portraits from him no work by Finney remains in the Royal Collection. Finney painted an enamel miniature of the Queen set in diamonds for Colonel Graeme to wear on his bonnet at a ball held in Edinburgh in January, 1762.

Finney married as his first wife, Martha Foster of Hereford, who died at Fulshaw in 1779. On June 4th, 1793, Samuel married Ann Barlow, of Fulshaw. The marriage was by licence and he gave his age as about forty-five,

Plate 42D. **J. Toomer,** *portrait of an unknown lady, pencil on paper, 5¼ins. Signed in full and dated: 'Joseph Toomer / Decr 18th / 1780.' Although slightly naïve in approach this is an interesting drawing showing the tall mob cap edged with lace and the tight-fitting bodice and full skirt. The bodice is edged with lace and a scarf is fastened at the bosom. The sleeves are trimmed with ribbons and have a lace cuff.* Courtesy E. Grosvenor Paine, U.S.A.

whereas he was seventy-four! Her age was given as thirty years. Samuel was buried at Wilmslow on 9th October, 1798, and was survived by Ann to whom he left the first choice of his drawings, pictures and plasters, etc.

Finney painted somewhat in the manner of the Lens School, using stippling on the background, but with a slightly lighter touch. There is a close affinity to the work of A.B. Lens. The stippling is painted in quite thick dots — almost like a minor snowstorm — getting darker at the outer edges of the oval. The only signed work I know of is an enamel sold by Christie's in Geneva on 26th April, 1977. It was signed on the reverse, and was of an unknown man. There is a distinct style about Finney's miniatures which is recognisable, and they are well worth acquiring. (Plates 40E and F.)

This is equally true of a number of miniatures painted by comparatively minor hands of this period; their work should be a fruitful field for the new collector as their prices are not as high as the more notable artists' and yet, aesthetically, they can form a very good collection.

Among the numerous minor artists who painted quite attractive miniatures at this time was C(harles?) Dixon (fl. 1748-1798). The identity of this little known artist who signed: 'C.D.' was discovered in 1955, by Charles Coleman Sellers, an American scholar. Nothing is known about the artist, but a number of his miniatures come into the sale rooms and are worth including in a collection. Like his contemporaries he painted on a small scale, and a number of his miniatures are mounted into attractive frames set with semi-precious stones. He painted with a soft technique, and sometimes used a lot of opaque white in the hair. His self-portrait is in the Victoria and Albert Museum and is signed: 'C.D. / Se ipse / P / 1748' (Plate 44A). I have not so far seen one dated later than 1798.

Although both Nathaniel Hone, R.A. (1718-1784) and Luke Sullivan (1705-1771) were Irish by birth, I am including them in this chapter as almost the whole of their working lives were spent in England. Hone was born in Dublin on 24th April, 1718, and was the third son of Nathaniel Hone, of Wood Quay, and his wife, Rebeckah, née Brindley. Nathaniel came to England as a young man and worked as an itinerant portrait painter. He did not, as far as is known, ever return to work in Ireland. He married in February, 1742 at York Minster; his bride's name was Mary Earl (d.1769). There appears to have been some mystery about her past, and she received an annuity from an unknown member of the nobility, upon whom she had some claim. One version of the story is that she was "some Lord's cast-off mistress", whom Hone married for a sum of £200 a year. Hone settled in London, and in 1750 went to Italy, where he studied for a time in Rome. In 1752 he became a member of the Academy in Florence, where he is thought to have met Sir Joshua Reynolds. Some sort of feud sprang up between the two men which later culminated in an unfortunate dispute between Hone and the Royal Academy. By 1752 Hone was back in London and living in Henrietta Street, Covent Garden. He visited Dublin in 1752 and Paris in 1753, by which time he had moved to Frith Street, London. He exhibited at the Society of Artists, 1760-1768, and was one of its earliest members. In 1769 Hone became one of the founder members of the Royal Academy, which opened that year. He put in five exhibits, one of which was a portrait in enamel. He exhibited at the Royal Academy from 1769-1784. In 1775 he sent a picture called 'The Conjurer' to the Royal Academy; this was taken to

Plate 43A. W. Singleton, Thomas Gibson (1749-1810), of Bradston Brook, ivory, 1½ins. Signed and dated: 'S / 75'. Works by Singleton are scarce. Courtesy Victoria and Albert Museum.

Plate 43B. ? Foy, portrait of an unknown man, ivory, 1½ins. Signed on the front: 'Foy / 1760'. This artist is hitherto unrecorded. It is an example of the work of a minor hand of this period and modest in its approach. Courtesy R. Bayne Powell.

be a satirical attack on Reynolds, who is depicted as an old man, holding a wand and performing incantations whilst various prints and designs float round in the air. The Royal Academy refused the picture on the grounds that one of the sketches closely resembled Angelica Kauffmann, with whom Reynolds' name had been linked for some time! Hone later held his own exhibition, in which the controversial painting had pride of place.

Hone is described by J.T. Smith, in his *Life of Nollekens,* as a "tall upright large man, with a broad brimmed hat, and a lapelled coat buttoned up to his stock". He is said to have been extravagant, and fond of pleasure and personal adornment. He married a second time, but the lady's name is not known. He had ten children, five boys and five girls, and was survived by his second wife, who died in 1791. Two of his sons, Horace, and John Camillus, became miniaturists.

Hone died on 14th August, 1784, at 44 Rathbone Place, London, and was buried in Hendon Churchyard. A large collection of his prints and drawings was sold by auction in February, 1785. Hone painted oil portraits as well as miniatures on ivory and enamel, and executed some etchings and mezzotints. His earliest known miniature is signed in full: 'N.Hone', and dated 1747. Almost all his miniatures are small, and many of them are set into bracelets or boxes.

His usual signature is: 'NH' (monogram), in which the last stroke of the N forms the first stroke of the H. No dated works are at present known after 1770. Hone seems to have been a prolific artist, and examples often come into the sale rooms. Those painted on enamel are more frequently seen than those in watercolour. He used a lot of opaque white when painting lace and shaded the faces of his male sitters with soft diagonal hatching. His portraits of ladies are usually attractive and have great charm. Two self-portraits are in the British Museum and a third, painted in oils, is in the National Gallery, Dublin. Examples of his work may be seen at the Victoria and Albert Museum, the Fitzwilliam Museum, Cambridge, and the Ashmolean Museum, Oxford, as well as in many private collections. (Colour Plates 10E, 11A and 12B and Plates 41C, E and F.)

Plate 43C. **J. Jennings,** *portrait of an unknown man, ivory, 1¹⁄₁₆ins., c.1760-65. Signed: 'JJ'. The miniature is set into a gold brooch. The style and signature are close to the early works by John Smart of the same period.* Private Collection.

Plate 43D. **Mrs. Barou,** *Samuel Horsley, Bishop of St. Asaph (1733-1806), ivory, 4¹⁄₈ins. Signed on the reverse: 'Mrs. Barou / St. Albans St. Pall Mall'. Works by this artist are scarce.* Courtesy R. Bayne Powell.

Luke Sullivan (1705-1771) was born in Co. Louth, but brought to England as a child by his father, who became groom to the Duke of Beaufort. The Duke must have taken an interest in the boy and realised that he had talent. He assisted him in obtaining instruction from Le Bas, an engraver.

The date of his birth as recorded by W.G. Strickland, in his *Dictionary of Irish Artists,* has been questioned. Graham Reynolds suggests that he may have been born later than was supposed on the basis of the fact that his earliest known works are engravings including a 'View of the Battle of Culloden', executed in 1746, and no miniatures have so far come to light dated before 1750. A charming miniature of a young girl (formerly in the de la Hey Collection, and sold 4th November, 1968, Lot 246, when no date was recorded) is, in fact, signed with the monogram: 'LS' and dated 1785. The miniature appears to be the work of Sullivan, but the signature and date must have been added later by someone who did not realise his date of death. In any case, the costume is c.1760-65.

Sullivan is known to have assisted Hogarth, and engraved his 'March to Finchley'. He exhibited at the Society of Artists, of which he was a member, from 1764-1770, from different London addresses. He seems to have been versatile and, besides executing miniatures and etchings, painted watercolour landscapes and architectural views.

Women had a fascination for Sullivan, and his chief practice is said to have been among the "girls of the town". He resided almost entirely at taverns and brothels and, according to J.T. Smith, in his *Life of Nollekens,* "he was a handsome lively fellow". He goes on to say that he lodged at the 'White Bear', Piccadilly and the 'Feathers', Leicester Fields; was much attached to the good things of this world and died in a miserable state of disease and poverty in the 'White Bear Tavern' in April, 1771. His miniatures are delicately painted and show great charm and prettiness; they are close in style to the French school of Pierre Adolphe Hall and Jean Honoré Fragonard. His signature is a monogram: 'LS', the S clinging to the stalk of the L. He is another artist of this period whose works are well worth collecting. (Plates 40C and H.)

Two artists whose works have caused understandable confusion are **James Jennings, F.S.A.** (fl. 1763-1793), and **John Jukes** (1772-1851). The fact that their working dates differ ought to have sorted them out, but both artists signed: 'J.J.' and did not always add a date. Their style of painting is, in fact, quite different. Jennings was a native of London, and exhibited at the Society of Artists, 1763-1783, being elected F.S.A. in 1771, and a Director in 1780. He exhibited at the Royal Academy in 1793. He painted in soft colours, often against a pale blue or grey background, and his style is slightly reminiscent of the early work of John Smart. His signatures are very difficult to detect, and frequently one has to turn the miniature this way and that before one can catch the initials: 'J.J.', sometimes followed by a date. They are very like Smart's initials, and I have seen some miniatures that might easily pass for an early Smart of the 1760s (Plate 43C).

Were it not for the confusion over signatures, John Jukes could have come in a later chapter, but it seemed important to discuss them together. Jukes was born on 6th January, 1772, and is thought either to have been related to, or the son of, Andrew Jukes of the Bombay Medical Service, an amateur

Plate 43E. **Mrs. Code,** *née Mary Benwell, self-portrait, ivory, 1⅞ins., c.1799. There is another version of this miniature in the Uffizi, Florence.* Courtesy R. Bayne Powell.

Plate 43F. **B. Diemar,** *Mrs. Maria Williamson, wife of the Rev. Edmund Williamson, Rector of Millbrook, Bedfordshire, ivory, 1¾ins. Signed and dated: 'BD (monogram — the D encircling the B) / 70.' This is an interesting work by a little known artist of 'the modest school'.* Courtesy R. Bayne Powell.

Plate 43G. **J. Jukes,** *portrait of an unknown man, ivory, 3ins. Signed: 'JJ.' Compare this miniature with Plate 43C by J. Jennings; there is no similarity of style in their painting.* Private Collection.

Plate 44A. **C(harles) Dixon,** *self-portrait, ivory, 1⅝ins. Signed and dated in gold: 'C.D. / Se ipse / P / 1748.'* Courtesy Victoria and Albert Museum.

landscape painter. According to tradition he was apprenticed to Sir Joshua Reynolds. Jukes entered the Royal Academy Schools on 14th October, 1791, when his age was recorded as nineteen. He exhibited at the Royal Academy, 1791-1799, from various London addresses. In August, 1812, Jukes sailed for India on the *Caroline,* which reached Bombay on 10th April, 1813. He remained in India until 1824, when according to a notice in the *Bombay Courier,* there was to be a sale of his effects preparatory to his departure for England. Details about Jukes' stay in India are given by Sir William Foster, in The Walpole Society, Vol. XIX. As recently as 1932, his family were in possession of a large number of his miniatures painted in oils and watercolour. Jukes died on 21st October, 1851. His style of painting differs so much from that of Jennings that the two artists' works need not be confused. Jukes was in any case working much later than Jennings, and painted on a larger format. His miniatures are painted in a bolder style, and in thicker paint more like oil paintings; those signed on the front usually have the 'J.J.' painted in fairly thick block letters rather than the cursive ones used by Jennings. Jukes' painting tends to be coarser and he used a scraper to indicate the strands in the hair. Some of his miniatures are painted against a dark curtain background. The treatment of the hair is rather wiry, and the general effect less pleasing than the work of Jennings (Plate 43G).

In spite of the fact that Graham Reynolds in his work, *English Portrait Miniatures,* 1952, discussed in great detail the problem of attribution for miniatures signed: 'P.C.', there are those who still refer to earlier books where two artists are cited. Prior to Reynolds' book, all miniatures signed: 'P.C.' were attributed to either **Penelope Carwardine** (c.1730-c.1801) or Penelope Cotes, the supposed sister of Francis and Samuel Cotes. There is no evidence to support the theory that P. Cotes ever existed: her name does not occur in any list of contemporary exhibitors, nor in any documents. Penelope Carwardine, on the other hand, was born c.1730, and was the eldest daughter of John Carwardine of Thingills Court, Withington, Herefordshire, and his wife, Anne Bullock. Her father having been recklessly extravagant, had ruined the family, and Penelope took up miniature painting to earn a living. For the present all miniatures signed: 'P.C.' are attributed to her. This identification is supported by family miniatures by her which closely resemble all the other miniatures signed in this way. Her miniatures are attractive, and painted on a small scale like most of those of this period. Her style of painting has been said to be slightly reminiscent of the School of Lens, but she shows greater character, and a more modern approach. In c.1772 she married a Mr. Butler, who was the organist at Ranleagh, St. Margaret's and St. Anne's, Westminster. She died childless c.1801, her husband having predeceased her. Miniatures by her often come into the sale rooms, and are usually attractive. In October, 1977, the Fry Gallery, Jermyn Street, St. James's, London, held an exhibition which included upwards of twenty-four drawings from an album of preparatory studies by Penelope Carwardine. They had been purchased unattributed, but Mr. Fry discovered notes with them which recorded that they were by 'Carwardine'. Most of them are executed in black and red chalk, or black chalk alone. The majority are obviously studies for miniatures, and are most attractive; others are after Van Dyck and Rubens and some may be after Ozias Humphry, or even Reynolds, with whom she was friendly. One very charming sketch is of a young girl wearing an Oriental head-dress (Plate 42A). This was one of several executed in the style of a miniaturist, which included one of a girl holding a book and another of a young woman viewing herself in a looking-glass (Plate 42B). One of the most outstanding full scale portraits is of an unknown man c.1780-90, executed in black chalk. The draughtsmanship is superb, and the whole drawing vigorous and of a very high quality. It is shaded with long lines and the contours of the face strongly delineated. This collection places the artist on a higher scale than had hitherto been supposed.

A miniature of Maria Gunning, afterwards Countess of Coventry, signed and dated: 'P.C. / 1757' is in the Wallace Collection, London.

Miniatures painted by a little known artist whose monogram is either: 'HV' or 'HN', in cursive lettering, sometimes followed by a date, are usually attributed to **Henry George Vigne** (1765-1787), but this is impossible as I know of one miniature signed with cursive initials: 'HV' or 'HN / 1761', and Lot 63 at Sotheby's on 20th January, 1975, is similarly signed and dated: '1767'. Both miniatures are naïve in their approach and are clearly by a minor hand, although they are meticulously painted regarding dress and not unattractive (Plate 45G). It has been suggested that the artist is possibly François Xavier Vispre (c.1730-d. aft. 1794), but examples I have seen by this artist are not, in my opinion, by the same hand as the monogrammist: 'HN' or 'HV', whose identity must for the present remain anonymous. Since writing my *Dictionary*, fresh information about the miniaturist Henry George Vigne has been given to me by one of his descendants, Randolph Vigne. H.G. Vigne was the first child of James Vigne (b.1734), watchmaker, of 2 The Strand, London, and his wife, Mary, née Keir. Both parents lived in the Parish of St. Martin-in-the-Fields. They were married by licence on 18th October, 1764, and the first child arrived only three months later. He was baptised at St. Martin-in-the-Fields, on 15th January, 1765.

Plate 44B. **Sophia H.M. Howell,** *portrait of an unknown man, ivory, 2¼ins. Signed and dated on the reverse: 'Soph Howell / 1786', and on the front: 'SH / 1786.' The miniature is well painted and expressive. Note the cravat and striped lapel to the jacket. Courtesy E. Grosvenor Paine, U.S.A.*

Plate 44C (left). **W. Dudman,** *miniature of an unknown officer, ivory, 3ins. Signed and inscribed on the reverse: 'W. Dudman pinxit / Ex Academia Regali. Arliam. Londini / 1801.' This is an interesting example of a work by a hitherto unrecorded artist. Courtesy E. Grosvenor Paine, U.S.A.*

Plate 44D (right). **P.E. Falconet,** *Mrs. Burke, pencil on paper, 4½ins. Signed and inscribed on the reverse: 'Mrs. Burke', and lower down: 'P.E. Falconet / Mrs Burke / (E.2755).' Private Collection.*

Plate 44E (left). **J. Alefounder,** *an Indian lady in national costume, ivory, 3ins. Signed on the reverse: 'Alefounder del / Bengal / 90'(1790). Signed miniatures by this artist are scarce and this is especially interesting as a portrait of an Indian sitter.* Courtesy E. Grosvenor Paine, U.S.A.

Plate 44F (right). **C. Dixon,** *George III, or Edward, Duke of York, when young, ivory, 1⅞ins.* Gracious permission of H.M. The Queen.

Plate 44G. **Mrs. Barou,** *Mr. Campbell, ivory, 3ins. Signed on the reverse: 'by Mrs Barou / St Albans St / Pall Mall / No 33.' This is a good example of the artist's work and it is interesting to compare it with Plate 43D which has the same loose brushwork.* Courtesy F. Joachim.

The family were Huguenot refugees, Henry's grandfather being Louis Ferdinand Vigne, also a watchmaker of some repute. The family had numerous artistic connections as silk designers, watchmakers and silversmiths. H.G. Vigne entered the Royal Academy Schools on 8th November, 1782, at the age of seventeen, and died at the age of twenty-two years at his father's house in The Strand, London. He exhibited at the Royal Academy in 1785 and 1787. The descendants of Jacques Vigne (b.1701), brother of Louis Ferdinand Vigne, emigrated to Dublin, where they practised as jewellers and watchmakers; Jacques' son, also named James (b.1745), had a daughter, Marianne, who married the miniaturist George Chinnery (c.1774-1853) in 1799. In view of the fact that H.G. Vigne died so young and would only have painted for about seven years his works are scarce and, unless a signed one turns up, will probably continue to pass unrecognised.

I have seen a few miniatures signed: **J. Tomlinson** (fl. c.1760-70). One, of an unknown man, signed in full on the reverse, was Lot 115 at Sotheby's, on 16th December, 1974. The sitter's costume looks like that of c.1760-70. As the only Tomlinson at present recorded worked from 1824-1853, it would appear that there were either two artists of this name, or that the miniature referred to was painted from an earlier portrait (Plate 45C). It is executed very much in the manner of Gustavus Hamilton, an Irish artist (1739-1775) whose work will be discussed in Chapter VII.

William Singleton (d.1793) was one of a family of artists, all of whom painted miniatures, and all of whom appear to have lived and worked in London. William was a pupil of Ozias Humphry, and a miniature of Thomas Gibson (1749-1810) in the Victoria and Albert Museum, signed and dated: 'S / 75' (1775), shows Humphry's influence (Plate 43A). He exhibited at the Society of Artists, 1770-1790, and at the Royal Academy, 1779-1790. Singleton is said to have painted portraits, sketches and 'fancy heads', as well as miniatures in watercolour and enamel.

I know of only one example in plumbago of the work of an artist named **William Green, Junior** (fl. 1752). It is of an unknown girl, wearing a cap and low-cut dress, with a cloak pinned at her shoulder. The miniature, which is superbly drawn, is signed: 'Gul. Green Junr / Delin. / 1752'. The sitter may well have been Dutch. The portrait, quite apart from its quality, is interesting from the point of view of costume (Plate 38D).

A fine miniature of an unknown scholar executed in plumbago on vellum by a hitherto unrecorded artist, **P. Hawk**, is in the collection of E.G. Paine, U.S.A. It is signed on the front: 'P. Hawk / delint. / Oxon / 1775' (Plate 42C), and is very reminiscent of the work of John Taylor, whose work will be discussed in Chapter IX. It is a pleasing portrait and well drawn.

Little is known about **Joseph Toomer** (fl.1780-81), who as far as I know only painted miniatures on paper. One of an unknown lady signed: 'Joseph Toomer / Decr 18th / 1780', is in the collection of E.G. Paine, U.S.A., (Plate 42D). This is the one mentioned in *A Dictionary of British Miniaturists*.

Sophia H.M. Howell (fl. 1781-1788) is not very well known and her works are scarce. Opinions vary as to her ability. The only example I have seen is the one illustrated. It is of an unknown man, painted against a cloud and sky background and is reminiscent of the work of H. Hone (Plate 44B).

A miniature painted by **W. Dudman** (fl. 1801), a hitherto unrecorded artist, is in the collection of E.G. Paine, U.S.A. The artist may be identical with, or related to, R. Dudman, recorded as exhibiting a portrait at the Royal Academy in 1797 from 41 Strand, London. The miniature is of an officer wearing a scarlet coat, with blue collar and revers, and white epaulettes. It is painted against a cloud and sky background. The portrait is loosely painted without any aim at great detail, but the general effect is pleasing. It is signed on the reverse: 'W. Dudman Pinxit / Ex Academia Regali Arliam. Londini / 1801' (Plate 44C).

John-Alefounder (1757?-1794) was born in London and was probably the son of a goldsmith and frame maker. He exhibited at the Royal Academy, 1777-1793, and won awards at the Royal Academy Schools in 1781 and 1784. He executed drawings, designs for buildings, portraits in chalk, oil portraits, groups and miniatures. In 1785 he went to India, and worked in Calcutta and Bengal. Due to worries in connection with his profession he went mad for a time, but by 1786 had recovered and took up painting again. He had to advertise for some of his paints and materials which had been sold during his illness. He died in Calcutta on 20th December, 1794, having committed suicide as a result of a fresh fit of insanity. Works by him are scarce, and consequently attribution is difficult. A miniature of an Indian

Plate 45A. **P.B.**, *portrait of an unknown man, ivory, 1½ins. The identity of the artist is unknown. Signed: 'PB / 1764.'* Courtesy F. Joachim.

Plate 45B. **J. Ballard**, *miniature of an unknown man, ivory, 1½ins. Signed on the front: 'Ballard / 1766.'* Courtesy R. Bayne Powell.

Plate 45C (left). **J. Tomlinson**, *portrait of an unknown man, ivory, 1½ins., c.1760-70. Signed in full on the reverse. The only artist of this name previously recorded was working c.1824-53.* Courtesy Sotheby's.

Plate 45D (right). Attributed to **R. Saunders**, *Mrs. David Carter, ivory, 2⅝ins., c.1820. Note the cropped hair tied with a bandeau decorated with pearls.* Courtesy R. Bayne Powell.

Plate 45E. **C. Maucourt or Mancourt,** *portrait of an unknown man, ivory, 1½ins., c.1760. Signed on the front: 'Maucourt Pinxt.' There seems to be a doubt about the spelling of this artist's name.* Courtesy R. Bayne Powell.

woman by him is in the collection of E.G. Paine, U.S.A., and is signed on the reverse: 'Alefounder del / Bengal / 90' (1790). It is well painted and the details are good (Plate 44E).

Two miniatures by unrecorded artists are worth mentioning. One is of a young woman of c.1756-60, signed: 'ES.' It is well painted and reminiscent of the work of P. Carwardine and others of the period. The details of the sitter's dress and features are well drawn and attractive. It is in the Alan Evans Collection at the Victoria and Albert Museum (Plate 45F). The other is signed: 'P.B. / 1764' and has for some time been thought to be by P. Carwardine, painted after her marriage, but as this did not take place before 1772 it is impossible, and the artist is unknown. The miniature of an unknown man is very much in her style, but I have been unable to trace an artist who could have painted it (Plate 45A).

The works of **Pierre Etienne Falconet** (1741-1791) fall more happily into this chapter than a later one, as many of them were executed from 1766 onwards. He was born in Paris on 8th October, 1741, and was the son of a sculptor, E.M. Falconet. Pierre came to London in 1766 to study under Reynolds. After winning a premium at the Society of Arts in 1766 and also 1768, he entered the Royal Academy Schools on 14th February, 1769. From 1767-1772, he exhibited portraits in black-lead at the Society of Artists, and was elected F.S.A. in 1771. He exhibited at the Royal Academy in 1773. On 30th January, 1777 he married M.A. Collot, a sculptress, from whom he appears to have been separated by 1778, when he returned to Paris. He worked for a time in St. Petersburg, painting oil portraits for the Empress Catherine. He died in Paris on 25th June, 1791. Although he was not a miniaturist in the strict sense of the word, he executed a number of small pencil portraits of artists and others, some of which were slightly tinted. A small portrait drawing on paper is inscribed on the reverse: 'Mrs Burke' (in ink at the top) and at the bottom: 'P.E. Falconet / Mrs Burke (E.2755)' (in pencil). The draughtsmanship is good and well modelled; the whole background to the sitter is shaded with a dark pencilling (Plate 44D).

Plate 45F. **ES.,** *portrait of an unknown young lady, ivory, 13¹/₃₂ins., c.1756-60. The identity of this artist is unknown and this is the only example of a miniature signed with these initials. It is attractive, and interesting for costume and hair style.* Courtesy Victoria and Albert Museum, Alan Evans. Collection.

Some engravings after Falconet and two of his portrait drawings are in the British Museum.

Miniatures painted by **Mrs. Sarah Stanley** (c.1697-1764) are among the many not always recognised. She was the elder daughter of Sir Hans and Lady Elizabeth Sloane. Nothing is known about her training in art, but she painted rather in the manner of Lens. She married in 1719, George Stanley, who committed suicide on 31st January, 1733/4; they had a son, Hans Stanley (1720-1780), and a daughter, Elizabeth, who died in 1738 aged eighteen years. Her mother erected a monument in her memory which was designed by J.M. Rysbrack, in the Chancel of Holy Rood Church, Southampton. An attractive miniature of a young girl with a hay rake is painted against a landscape background and signed: 'S.S. / 1716' in gold lettering. It is painted on ivory, and has clear, fresh colours; the dress and most of the background are in opaque pigments, whereas the flesh parts are painted in transparent watercolour. The laced bodice is picked out in gold. The shading on the flesh is executed in small blue stippling, and a large amount of opaque white is used on the costume (Plate 38B). Her signatures vary: 'S.S.', 'S. Stanley', 'Sarah Stanley' or 'Stanley Fecit', followed by a date. Six copies of the works of old masters by her are in the Victoria and Albert Museum, and are dated between 1732 and 1738.

The miniaturists included in this chapter worked for the most part during the reigns of George I and George II, but some overlapped well into the early years of George III, by which time a number of artists who were to become famous were painting their early works. Many received Royal patronage, and this was to be fostered by the young Prince of Wales, later George IV. Although the miniaturists who were working in the first half of the eighteenth century were not perhaps as outstanding as their forebears, or those who followed, they kept the art alive and for this alone we are greatly in their debt. Many of the portraits they produced had a simple charm, and when a number of them are placed together they form an interesting study.

Plate 45G. **HV**, *miniature of an unknown lady, ivory, 1⅞ins. Signed and dated: 'HV / 1767', though the signature could be: 'HN.' This rather naive and stiff little portrait is typical of the work produced by the minor artists of this period.* Courtesy Sotheby's.

Plate 45H. **HV**, *miniature of a young man in Tudor costume, ivory, 1⁷⁄16ins. Signed and dated: 'HV / 1760.' This is a good example showing a clear signature of this unidentified artist.* Courtesy Dr. F. Lappin.

Chapter VII

Scottish and Irish Miniaturists

PRIOR TO THE middle of the eighteenth century London was the main centre for British art and, regardless of their place of origin, portrait painters and miniaturists all made their way there. They knew that it was in London that the wealthy congregated and where patronage was more assured. By the early part of the century the 'Grand Tour' had become firmly established as a 'finishing school' for young gentlemen whose parents were wealthy enough to send them abroad, for a term of anything up to three or four years. The youth would be accompanied by a tutor or 'bear-leader' as they were called, whose duties included the supervision of his charge's morals and religious beliefs, as well as his knowledge of languages and cultural education. The young were expected to return from their travels with a good command of foreign languages, a broadened mind and a highly developed appreciation of things of architectural and artistic beauty. It was also hoped that they would have acquired greater poise and self-reliance and that their taste and grace of manners would have improved! How many of these attributes were attained depended to a large extent on the tutors, not all of whom were as desirable as they might have been. Nor were all the young men anxious to learn, and many of them returned thoroughly dissipated, having spent lavishly, and not always wisely. The general effect on those who took advantage of this opportunity to travel and see other cultures was to stimulate in them the desire to collect objects of beauty and interest, and to patronise artists who could produce such things in England.

After the death of Samuel Cooper and his followers we had been very dependent on 'limners', from the Continent whose work influenced those working in Britain. By about the 1730s, when patrons became plentiful, a more truly British school of miniaturists began to emerge again. Judged by

Colour Plate 15.
A top. **Samuel Cotes**, *an unknown man, ivory, 1¾ins. Signed on the front: 'S.C. / 1780.'*
B top left. **James Nixon, A.R.A.**, *an unknown man, ivory, 1¾ins. Signed on the front: 'N.'*
C top right. **J. Lacon**, *an unknown infantry officer, ivory, 1⅝ins., c.1787. Signed on the front: 'Lacon.'*
D centre. **Patrick John McMor(e)land**, *Miss Pringle, ivory, 1¾ins. Signed on the front: 'PM.' This is an attractive miniature by McMorland.*
E bottom left. **John Stordy**, *an unknown man, ivory, 1½ins. Signed on the front: 'Stordy / 1777.' Miniatures by this little-known artist are scarce.*
F bottom. **Solomon Polack**, *an unknown man, ivory, 1¾ins. Signed on the front: 'S.P. / 1789.'*
G bottom right. **Thomas Preston**, *J. Bowman, Esq., ivory, 1⅝ins. Signed on the front : 'Preston', and in full on the reverse, and dated: '1769.' This is a good example of work by a minor artist.*
Courtesy Victoria and Albert Museum, Alan Evans Collection

197

Plate 46A. **J. Ferguson,** *portrait of an unknown young lady, pen and ink on vellum, 2½ins., c.1750-60. This is a good example of Ferguson's work.* Courtesy Victoria and Albert Museum, Alan Evans Collection.

today's standards, one has to admit that many of them were comparatively minor hands, some of whom still remain anonymous. Nevertheless, they kept the art alive and cradled in their midst artists who, by the latter part of the century, were to become famous and raise the standard of miniature painting to heights that have never been equalled since.

By the 1750s this improvement in taste and elegance had reached the provinces, and more people could afford to spend their money in purchasing works of art. Miniatures, which had always been symbols of personal regard and affection, were in great demand, and a large number of artists with varying degrees of ability accepted commissions.

There had always been artists who had been prepared to travel to country houses and paint individual families, but this increased patronage made it worthwhile for artists to journey from place to place, staying for a short time in suitable centres where possible patrons congregated. Many of these miniaturists advertised in local papers that they would be available at certain times and places and indicated their fee for a miniature, which varied according to size and the type of frame required.

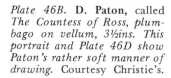

Plate 46B. **D. Paton,** called *The Countess of Ross, plumbago on vellum, 3½ins. This portrait and Plate 46D show Paton's rather soft manner of drawing.* Courtesy Christie's.

Plate 46C. **J. Ferguson,** *Prince Charles Edward Stuart (1720-1788), the 'Young Pretender', pen and ink on vellum, 2ins.* Courtesy Sotheby's.

Whilst it was still true that the most important miniaturists had their main studios in London where they hoped for distinguished, if not Royal, patrons, some spent a short time elsewhere. In Ireland, Dublin and later Belfast began to assume some importance, and in Scotland, Edinburgh and, to a lesser degree, Glasgow attracted a few artists whose main work lay in the north. Scotland was never a great centre for miniature painting; indeed before the middle of the eighteenth century a good artist would have been hard to find. Even later the majority of artists went south for the greater part of their careers.

It would be foolish to attempt to distinguish with any degree of certainty individual 'Schools', although there is sometimes a certain mannerism which suggests the influence of artists who worked in Scotland and Ireland. The main purpose of these chapters is to indicate to the collector some of the areas in which miniaturists worked, as sometimes this can be of help in

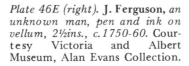

Plate 46D (left). **D. Paton,** *Sir Isaac Newton (1642-1727), plumbago, 3¾ins. Inscribed in full on the reverse: 'This original Drawing of Sir Isaac Newton belonged formerly to Professor Gregory of Oxford, by whom it was bequeathed to his youngest son Isaac (Sir Isaac's godson) who was the late Secretary of Sion College & by him left by will to the Rev^d Mr Mence who had the goodness to give it to Dr. Douglas, March 8th 1780.'* Private Collection.

Plate 46E (right). **J. Ferguson,** *an unknown man, pen and ink on vellum, 2½ins., c.1750-60.* Courtesy Victoria and Albert Museum, Alan Evans Collection.

attributing a miniature. Inscriptions on the reverse sometimes give the name of a town, and a knowledge of which artists worked there may be useful.

It is not always appreciated that many artists began to discover their talents when they were only eleven or twelve years of age and, unless they were lucky enough to become apprenticed to an artist, it was difficult for them to learn the basic techniques of drawing and painting. The need was felt for more drawing schools where the young, who could not afford private tuition, could obtain expert training in various aspects of art before setting out on their career.

In Ireland, the Dublin Society was founded in 1731, and in c.1740 a Drawing School was opened by Robert West, an accomplished artist. In 1758 the Society took over the school, and 'The Art Schools of the Dublin Society' were formed. These schools provided training for most of the Irish artists for over a hundred years and held regular exhibitions. Other societies were started, including the Society of Artists in Ireland, which held its first exhibition in February, 1765. This Society continued until 1773, when a dispute took place and the members split up, to be reunited in 1777 as the Society of Artists, which had to close in 1780, due to financial difficulties.

In 1814, the Hibernian Society of Artists (late the Royal Hibernian Academy) held its first exhibition in Dublin at which many important artists exhibited. In Scotland the Trustee's Academy was formed in Edinburgh in the early part of the nineteenth century. Instruction was free, but attendance was limited to four years and the number of pupils to twenty. The training given was fairly elementary, and most of the pupils who showed any promise went to London or, if they could afford it, to Italy, to improve their knowledge. In 1808, the Society of Incorporated Artists was opened and held very successful exhibitions. This was followed by the foundation of the Institute for the Encouragement of the Fine Arts in Scotland, modelled on the lines of the British Institution in London, which flourished from 1806-1867. In 1826, the Scottish Academy (later the Royal Scottish Academy) was founded and did much to encourage art in Scotland.

In England, the Society of Artists of Great Britain existed from 1761-1791, and the Free Society 1761-1783. In 1754, the Society of Arts or, to give it its full title, the Royal Society for the Encouragement of Arts, Manufactures and Commerce, had been founded under the leadership of William Shipley and has provided valuable stimulus to people working in a wide sphere ever since. The Royal Academy held its first exhibition in London in 1769, the Academy Schools having opened in the previous year. Besides these important societies, other smaller ones and drawing schools existed, and exhibitions were held in various parts of the country where artists could make themselves known to the public. This method of advertisement remains as popular as ever today.

It would be impossible to do more than mention a selection of miniaturists who worked in particular places out of London; many more will be included in the illustrations where collectors can see the style of work produced and get some sort of idea as to the quality of their art.

Although the number of miniaturists who worked for any length of time in Scotland was comparatively small, some of them were of great importance to the history of miniature painting. **David Paton** (fl. 1660-1695) was one of the best known artists of the seventeenth century. Little is known about his life, but he is thought to have practised only in Scotland. He is best known for his highly finished miniatures in plumbago, some of which were copies of larger pictures. According to Robert Brydall in his *History of Art in Scotland*, Paton painted several portraits in oils, but I have not so far discovered one that could be attributed to him. He is known to have accompanied the Hon. William Tollemache, youngest son of the Duchess of Lauderdale, on the Grand Tour, and MSS relating to this tour are at Ham House. A number of his portraits were engraved, including one of Sir James Dalrymple, which was engraved by Robert White, one of David Loggan's pupils. Characteristics of his work are the way in which he drew the sitter's hair in fairly thick strands, which appear less natural than those drawn by Loggan and White. A good example of his style is illustrated (Plate 46D). Not all his works are signed; his usual signature is: 'DP. Fec' or 'DP. fecit.' Occasionally, as in the case of a portrait of Charles II in the Buccleuch Collection after the miniature by Samuel Cooper at Goodwood, he inscribed in full: 'D. Paton fecit 1669 ∼/ S. Couper invenit 1665.' A miniature in plumbago said to be of Richard Maitland, 4th Earl of Lauderdale, is in the Victoria and Albert Museum. It is signed on the reverse: 'D. Paton fe. Romæ / 1674.' A number of examples of his work are in private collections. (Plate 46B.)

James Ferguson (1710-1776) was born in Banffshire on 25th April, 1710. His parents were poor, and he does not appear to have had any education apart from being taught to read. He began his career as a farm hand, then discovered he had an aptitude for mathematics, and studied the stars whilst looking after the sheep, which later earned him the name of 'Ferguson the astronomer'. Having shown a talent for drawing, with the assistance of some friends he was sent to study in Edinburgh. All his works were, as far as I know, executed in Indian ink. In 1752 he advertised that he drew pictures in 'China ink' for 12s. 6d. and 15s. He must in fact have moved to London some years before this, as in 1746 he put a notice in the *Daily Advertiser* to the effect that he had moved from Compton Street to 'The White Perriwig',

Plate 46F. **J. Ferguson,** *portrait of an unknown lady, pen and ink on vellum, 2½ins., c.1750-60.* Courtesy Sotheby's.

Plate 47A (left). **J.** Bogle, *portrait of an unknown man, ivory, 1⁷/8ins. Signed and dated: 'IB / 1780.'* Courtesy Sotheby's.

Plate 47B (right). **J.** Bogle, *portrait of an unknown lady, ivory, 2ins. Signed and dated: 'IB / 1795.' This is a good example of costume, showing the sitter's tall straw hat tied at the back over her cap.* Courtesy Sotheby's.

next to the 'Golden Ball' in Great Pultney Street, London, where he "draws pictures as usual for nine shillings, or goes abroad to do them for ½ guinea". His miniatures are usually small, and executed with a rather precise and neat brush stroke. The sitter's upper eyelids and eyebrows are usually strongly delineated. They are not, as far as I know, ever signed, but have a style of their own which an experienced eye can recognise. The majority of his works are in private collections, but examples are in the Victoria and Albert Museum (Plate 46E). One by Ferguson of Prince Charles Edward Stuart was Lot 29 at Sotheby's, 30th October, 1972 (Plate 46C).

Among the few miniaturists working in Scotland during the first half of the eighteenth century was **John Donaldson, F.S.A. (1737-1801).** Like Ferguson he came of poor parentage. He was born in Edinburgh, and was the son of a glovemaker. His love of drawing which showed itself when he was only a child was encouraged by his father and at the age of twelve he is said to have earned money by his pen-and-ink drawings, mostly copies from engravings. In 1757 and 1758 Donaldson was awarded premiums by the Edinburgh Society of Arts, and soon after this went to London where he exhibited at the Free Society of Artists, 1761-1774, becoming a member of the Society of Artists in 1764. The Society of Arts awarded him premiums in 1764 and 1768. In 1775 and 1791 Donaldson exhibited at the Royal Academy. He painted miniatures on ivory, enamel and Worcester porcelain, and drew in black lead as well as painting some large portraits and historical subjects and executing some etchings. In 1768 he was living in Newcastle, and was awarded three premiums for paintings on enamel. According to Robert Brydall, Donaldson was patronised and befriended by the Earl of Buchan, who purchased several of his works. He seems to have had an unstable disposition and to have been full of totally impractical ideas. He became interested in chemistry, and invented a method of preserving vegetables and meat during long voyages, but due to lack of any worldly knowledge he did not gain financially from this project. He published an *Essay on the Elements of Beauty* and some poems. The last twenty years of his life were spent in partial blindness and misery. Through the kindness of some friends he was lodged and cared for somewhere in Islington, where he died on 11th October, 1801.

Plate 47C. **J.** Bogle, *miniature of an unknown lady, ivory, 2¹/8ins. Signed and dated: 'I. Bogle.P. / 1787.' This shows a rather more elaborate costume and curled hair style with ringlets over the shoulders.* Courtesy Christie's.

Unfortunately few works by Donaldson are signed, and attribution is rather difficult. A nice miniature of a lady by him, signed on the front with a cursive: 'JD' and dated 1787, is in the National Gallery of Scotland. Characteristics appear to be the use of a rather pink and white flesh colour, the face is shaded with a bluish-grey, especially round the eyes, and a deeper bluish-grey is apparent on the hair which is drawn in lines, made partly by the use of a scraper and partly with opaque white. The red on the lips is usually still bright and the general effect pleasing. Superficially his miniatures resemble the work of Downman. (Colour Plate 16D.)

One of the most important Scottish artists of the eighteenth century was **John Bogle** (1746?-1803). He was the son of an excise officer whose wife, Mary, née Graham, was sister to the 'Beggar Earl of Menteith'. The Earldom became dormant on the death of the 8th Earl in 1694 and the right of succession was obscure. Mary, who died in May, 1787, had three children, John (the artist) and two daughters. John was considered the heir presumptive to the title but never made any claim, though his sister, Mary (d.1821) styled herself Lady Mary Bogle. The Earldom is now extinct. Bogle studied art in Glasgow at the Drawing School which had been formed in 1753 by the brothers Robert and Andrew Foulis. On 6th August, 1769, Bogle married Marion Wilson, daughter of James Wilson, a merchant, whose family came from Spango, Uppermost Nithsdale. She was described as the beautiful 'May or Mennie' Wilson.

Bogle was practising miniature painting in Edinburgh by 1767, and from 1769-1770 exhibited at the Society of Artists, giving his address as Edinburgh. He then went to London and exhibited at the Royal Academy, 1772-1794, from 1 Panton Square. In May, 1790, he accompanied Fanny Burney to Warren Hastings' trial in the Great Hall of Westminster, and in the following year returned to Edinburgh, where he remained until his death in c.1803. In his will, made on 9th December, 1786, he describes himself as "formerly of Panton, Middlesex, but late of the City of Edinburgh". He left to his "dear wife Mary" (his sole executrix) the whole of his estate. He exhibited a self-portrait at the Royal Academy in 1772, the whereabouts of which is unknown. Allan Cunningham, in *The Lives of British Painters,* describes him as "a little lame man, very poor, very proud and very singular".

Plate 47D. **J. Nixon A.R.A.,** *miniature of an unknown man, ivory, 1⅝ins., c.1760. Signed:* 'N.' *Courtesy Sotheby's.*

Colour Plate 16.
A top. **A. or J. Daniel,** *an unknown child, ivory, 2ins.*
B top left. **Ozias Humphry, R.A.,** *an unknown man, ivory, 1½ins., c.1770-75. Signed in monogram:* 'IO.'
C top right. **Philip Jean,** *an unknown lady, ivory, 1¼ins., c.1795.*
D centre. **John Downman, A.R.A.,** *an unknown lady, ivory, 2ins. A memorial urn on the reverse set with diamonds and enamel.*
E bottom left. **Gustavus Hamilton,** *an unknown man, ivory, 1½ins. Signed and dated:* 'GH^P 1759', *set within a gold and garnet frame, a pair to Colour Plate 16G.*
F bottom. **John Donaldson, F.S.A.,** *an unknown lady, ivory, 2¼ins. Courtesy Dr. A.K. Brown.*
G bottom right. **I.R.,** *an unknown lady, ivory, 1½ins. Signed and dated:* 'IR / 1760', *pair to Colour Plate 16E. Set in a gold and garnet frame.*

Private Collection with the exception of Colour Plate 16F

Plate 47E. **J. Bogle,** *'Fanny Burney' (Madam D'Arblay), novelist, ivory, 4ins. Signed and dated: 'Bogle P. / 1783.' This is a good example of a large miniature by Bogle, set in an interior of a room and showing to perfection the sitter's costume.* Courtesy Sotheby's.

Plate 47F. **J. Bogle,** *Mr. William Cross, ivory, 2⅛ins. Signed and dated: 'I.B. / 1794.' Note the tied scarf and wide lapels on the sitter's jacket.* Courtesy Sotheby's.

The majority of his miniatures are small and possibly because of this he has not always had the appreciation he deserves. His larger miniatures are extremely good, as in the case of one of Commodore Johnstone which is in the collection of E. Grosvenor Paine, U.S.A., signed: 'I. Bogle / Pinxt.' His usual signatures are: 'Bogle', 'I. Bogle', 'I.B.' (neatly written) or 'I.B.' in Roman capitals, often followed by a date. His technique is not easy to describe; he painted with a soft colouring and shaded with a minute stippling which, particularly in the treatment of the hair, often produces a curiously woolly effect when viewed under a lens. His draughtsmanship was good, and the sitters' costumes well painted. He often painted a small area of dark shading over the sitter's head. A fine miniature of Fanny Burney, signed and dated: 'Bogle P. / 1783', was sold in London in 1970: it measured 4 by 3 inches, and showed the sitter by a window with a curtain and bookcase in the background (Plate 47E). Examples of his work are in the Victoria and Albert Museum and the National Galleries of Scotland as well as in many private collections. (Plates 47A, B, C, E and F and Colour Plate 12G.)

The miniaturist **James Nixon, A.R.A.** (c.1741-1812) is described as "of London and Edinburgh". Nothing is known about his early life or education. He entered the Royal Academy Schools, 17th March, 1769. He became a member of the Society of Artists, and exhibited with them from 1765-1771, and at the Royal Academy and British Institute, 1772-1807. He was elected A.R.A. in 1778. Nixon painted portraits in oil and watercolour, historical subjects and book illustrations. His chief interest lay in miniature painting and, according to an undated MS in my possession, he was greatly influenced by Sir Joshua Reynolds. He had a great admiration for the Royal Academy, and repeatedly said that it was to the Royal Academy that he owed all his success in life. Many of his miniatures were of actresses in character, and his distinguished clientele included the Duchess of Rutland, the Duchess of Devonshire, and Joseph Farington. One of his pupils was Augustus Toussaint, a miniaturist and framemaker. Nixon was appointed limner to the Prince Regent and, in 1792, miniature painter to the Duchess of York. He was living in Edinburgh in 1797, at 9 St. Andew's Square, but later moved to Devonshire where he appears to have spent most of his latter years. He died in Tiverton on 9th May, 1812. Nixon's miniatures are not always easy to identify and many of them are unsigned. He painted with strong bright colours, and used a lot of gum with his paints. Many of his portraits have a dark background or thick foliage. His miniatures of ladies often depict them holding a bird; the faces of his sitters are usually shaded with irregular soft cross-strokes, the hair being painted in broad sweeping strokes without much detail.

Many of Nixon's works are of a very high quality, and he deserves more recognition than has hitherto been the case. He sometimes signed with a small 'N', partly concealed in the background and not always easy to detect. Those signed with a larger cursive 'N' are easier to attribute. His miniatures are reminiscent of Reynolds. Examples of his work may be found in the Victoria and Albert Museum, and the City of Liverpool Museum; the British Museum has engraved portraits after Nixon. (Plates 47D and H.)

One of Scotland's most famous portrait painters, **Sir Henry Raeburn, R.A.** (1756-1823) is known to have painted miniatures early'in his career, but probably ceased to do so after c.1780. I know of only two examples that can

Plate 47G. **C. Shirreff,** *an unknown officer, ivory, 2⅞ins. Signed and dated on the reverse: '1806.'* Courtesy Sotheby's.

Plate 47H. **J. Nixon A.R.A.,** *portrait of a young boy, ivory, 2¾ins. Signed: 'N.' This is an attractive and colourful miniature by Nixon.* Private Collection.

Plate 47 I. **C. Shirreff,** *an unknown man, ivory, 2⅞ins. Signed and dated on the reverse: '1798.' Compare the treatment of the eyes and eyebrows with Plate 47G.* Courtesy Sotheby's.

be said to be by him. One of these is of David Deuchar, the seal engraver, which is in the Scottish National Portrait Gallery; it is fully inscribed on the reverse (probably by the sitter's son): 'David Deuchar, Esq; of Morningside, by Sir Henry Raeburn, being the second portrait done by him during the time he was apprentice with Mr. Gilland, Jeweller, Parliament Square, Edinburgh' and in another hand: 'Painted about 1773'. The second miniature is in the collection of Earl Spencer, and is authenticated by family letters at Althorp. It represents George John, 2nd Earl Spencer (1758-1834), painted in Rome, after a portrait by Gavin Hamilton. There must be other miniatures which are unidentified, and it is to be hoped that some of them will come to light as they would be of great interest.

Thanks to information supplied to me by the descendants of the miniaturist **John Brown** (1749-1787), I have been able to add details regarding his family and his correct date of birth. He was born in Edinburgh, and was the son of Samuel Brown and his wife, Agnes Scoular (1716-1787), whose brother, James, was the father of another well known miniaturist, James Scouler or Scoular. Brown's father was a watchmaker and jeweller, and John is reputed to have had a good education and studied painting under Alexander Runciman and at the Trustee's Academy. From 1771-1781, he toured Italy and Sicily in the company of David Erskine, Mr. Townley and Sir W. Young. He painted miniatures, highly finished pencil portraits, drawings in pen and ink and made a few etchings. He also wrote some music. Brown had the patronage of Lord Buchan who, as founder of the Society of Antiquaries of Scotland, commissioned Brown to draw its members between 1780 and 1781. A series of thirty-one heads is still in the Society's possession. These are deposited at the Scottish National Portrait Gallery. They include a portrait of Lord Buchan, and are of great interest in providing likenesses of so many people of the period.

Although Brown is thought to have had a potential as a history-painter, he preferred to confine his work to drawings.

He married on 2nd February, 1786, Miss Mary Esplin(e); both of them were resident in New Kirk Parish, Edinburgh. Mary's father was a merchant. In 1786 the Browns went to London and in the same year he exhibited at the Royal Academy. He died at Leith on 5th September, 1787, after returning from London by ship, and was survived by his wife. Three examples of his work are in the Scottish National Portrait Gallery, one represents David Deuchar (1743-1808), a seal engraver, and the other Alexander Runciman, drawn from life in 1785.

Prior to this there had been no reason to connect Brown and Scouler: their ancestry is rather complicated in that they were second cousins, their grandmothers being half-sisters, and first cousins, their parents being brother and sister! Three miniatures by John Brown still remain in the family.

One of the best examples of Brown's work which I have seen is his pencil drawing of George Paton (1721-1807) which is in the Scottish National Portrait Gallery. It is slightly reminiscent of the work of John Taylor, a contemporary artist. The draughtsmanship is good, and the costume shaded with thin pencil lines.

Peter Paillou, Senior (fl.1744-1780/84) is best known for his paintings of birds, many of which were executed for Thomas Pennant (1726-1798) of Flintshire, who published *British Zoology,* for which Paillou painted the

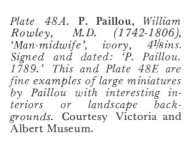

Plate 48A. **P. Paillou**, *William Rowley, M.D. (1742-1806), 'Man-midwife', ivory, 4⅛ins. Signed and dated: 'P. Paillou. 1789.' This and Plate 48E are fine examples of large miniatures by Paillou with interesting interiors or landscape backgrounds.* **Courtesy Victoria and Albert Museum.**

illustrations. It has always been said that he painted miniatures, but this is now in doubt, and it is probable that all miniatures signed: 'Paillou' are by his son, **Peter Paillou, Junior** (c.1757-d. aft. 1831). Both artists seem to have worked in London and Scotland, but Paillou Junior is always considered to be of the Scottish school. He entered the Royal Academy Schools, 27th February, 1784, when his age was given as twenty-seven — "27, I Decr". Peter exhibited at the Royal Academy, 1786-1800, from various London addresses. In 1820, he was working in Glasgow, when his address was given as 2 Queen Street. It is always useful to know miniaturists' addresses in different years, as this often helps to date the portraits. Clues like this should always be recorded by collectors where information is given on the reverse of the miniatures.

A characteristic of Paillou's work is the way he frequently painted his sitters against what can only be described as a 'sunset background'. A few miniatures tentatively attributed to his father are painted with a greenish colouring, and are unlike the usual style. Paillou's miniatures are well modelled, and are well worth acquiring. The flesh colours are usually smoothly painted, and not stippled. Some of his larger works have a bookcase or foliage background, as in the case of one of particularly fine quality, sold at Sotheby's on 5th July, 1976. It represented George Whatley (1708-1791), and was signed and dated: 'P. Paillou / 1789'. It measured 6¾ inches in height (Plate 48E). It is comparable with the one of William Rowley, M.D. in the Victoria and Albert Museum (Plate 48A). Nothing is known about Peter Paillou's life, nor is the date of his death known. The latest dated miniature I know of is signed and dated 1831. (Plates 48D and F.)

Archibald Skirving (1749-1819) was born at Athelstaneford, near Haddington, Scotland, and was the son of Adam Skirving, a song-writer and farmer. He is said to have started his career as an excise officer, but turned to miniature painting. He exhibited at the Royal Academy from a London address in 1778. He went to Rome c.1786-1794, and on his return journey was captured by the French and imprisoned for a year. He was back in

Plate 48B. **W.J. Thomson R.S.A.**, *portrait of an unknown lady, ivory, 3ins. Signed and dated on the reverse: '1813.' Note the rather plain turban and style of dress.* **Courtesy Christie's.**

Plate 48C. **J. Nixon A.R.A.,** *portrait of an unknown young lady, ivory, 2⅜ins. Signed: 'N.' Set within a contemporary locket with a pearl border.* Courtesy Sotheby's.

Edinburgh in 1796. His imprisonment caused him to suffer from a serious eye condition called unocular elipopia, which necessitated his giving up miniature painting. He took up large scale portraiture in pastel and oils and taught painting privately. According to Redgrave, *A Dictionary of Artists of the English School,* "his miniatures are excellent for their drawing, colour, and admirable expression. He possesses great taste, was ingenious, eccentric, and aspired to wit". An interesting sidelight on Skirving's character is given by Jessy Harden in her journal, *John Harden of Brathay Hall,* p.37. Writing to her sister, Agnes, in India in October, 1809, she describes their life staying in Edinburgh, and mentions the various people who dined with them, including Alexander Nasmyth, and Archibald Skirving. Jessy describes him as "an odd Fish & not in my opinion over agreeable".

Lack of any signed works has for many years made identification difficult, but recently a small number of signed miniatures have been seen. One of an officer signed with cursive initials: 'AS' was sold at Christie's in May, 1973 (Plate 49B), and one of an unknown lady by him signed on the front: 'Skirving / 1780' is in the Alan Evans Collection at the Victoria and Albert Museum (Colour Plate 20E). This has certain characteristics in colouring, pose and costume, by which other miniatures can with safety be attributed. He seems to have liked to paint his female sitters with feathers or large bows in their hair, wearing elaborately trimmed dresses, against a cloud and sky background (Plate 49E). He used a pinkish white flesh colour, and painted his sitters' hair in soft waves rather than in detailed strands.

He died at Inveresk in 1819, and was buried at Athelstaneford. Examples of his work are in the National Gallery, Edinburgh, the Scottish National Portrait Gallery, Edinburgh (who have a pastel self-portrait of him), and the Victoria and Albert Museum. (Colour Plate 27A.)

Charles Shirreff (b. c.1750) is thought to have been born in Edinburgh, and was certainly of Scottish blood. His father was Alexander Shirreff, who was reputed to have been a wealthy businessman. The name seems to have been spelt variously Shirreff or Sheriff, Shirreff being the one usually taken to be correct. Charles was deaf and dumb from the age of about four and

Plate 48D (right). **P. Paillou,** *miniature of an unknown man, ivory, 2¾ins. This miniature and Plate 48F are typical examples of Paillou painting his sitters against a sunset background.* Courtesy Christie's.

Plate 48E (far right). **P. Paillou,** *George Whatley (1708-1791), ivory, 6¾ins. The sitter was Governor, Vice President and Treasurer of the Foundling Hospital, London, and this miniature is especially interesting as the Foundling Hospital can be seen in the background. The portrait is a fine character study.* Courtesy Sotheby's.

Plate 48F. **P. Paillou,** *portrait of an unknown young man, ivory, 2⅞ins., c.1800. Painted against a sunset background.* Courtesy Sotheby's.

was obliged to make himself understood by signs. He was educated by a Thomas Branwood, who succeeded in teaching him to write and even to articulate slightly, but there is no record of who taught him art. John Bogle was in Edinburgh at the time and would have been the obvious choice but we have no evidence to support this theory. After the failure of Fordyce's Bank in 1772, in which his family must have lost money, Charles had to help to support them. In 1768 he was in London, and entered the Royal Academy Schools on 9th August, 1769, when his age was not recorded. He won a Silver Medal in 1772, and was exhibiting at the Free Society of Artists, 1770-1773, and at the Royal Academy, Society of British Artists, and British Institute, 1771-1831.

As early as 1778 Shirreff petitioned the East India Company to be allowed to go to India, and, in view of his infirmity, asked that his father and sister, Mary, should be allowed to accompany him. This request was granted, but for some reason the project was abandoned and he did not renew his application until 1795, when he sailed on the *Lord Hawkesbury,* which reached Madras on 9th January, 1797. He appears to have remained in Madras for some years, and worked in Calcutta in 1804. In 1807 he announced his intention of returning to England, and stated that his 'Finger Alphabet' was nearly completed. He left India on 25th January, 1809, and landed at Gravesend on 16th July. He had addresses in London for some time and is said to have retired to Bath, where he died, but no date of death has so far been found.

Shirreff took a keen interest in the stage, and many of his sitters were actors and actresses, including Mrs. Siddons. He is known to have worked in Bath from 1791-1795, and is said to have worked for a time in Brighton, Deptford and Cambridge.

The majority of his works were miniatures, but he also painted in oils and executed some portraits in crayon. Only a small number of his miniatures are signed and attribution is difficult. Characteristics of his work are the use of a criss-cross hatching to model the face and shade the background. His

Plate 49A. **A. Skirving,** *an unknown officer, ivory, 3ins., c.1790-95.* Courtesy Sotheby's.

portraits are well executed, but not flattering; they are drawn with a neat precise stroke. His signature is usually: 'C. Shirreff pinxt', followed by a date, and often the address is on the reverse. Many of the portraits have the eyebrows thickly delineated, and the contours of the face clearly defined (Colour Plate 18E). Examples of his miniatures are in the Victoria and Albert Museum, and the British Museum have some engravings after his portraits. (Plates 47G and I.)

Among the minor miniaturists who almost certainly worked in Scotland was an artist who signed: W.A. Smith (fl. 1792-93). He was probably identical with the **William Smith** (b.1754) who entered the Royal Academy Schools on 30th November, 1772, and exhibited at the Royal Academy in 1774. W.A. Smith painted portraits of Alexander, 4th Duke of Gordon, and three of the Countess of Westmorland. I know of three miniatures by him in a private collection in Scotland, representing members of the family. They are all signed differently; one is signed: 'WS. / 1780', one: 'W.A. Smith 1791', and the third: 'W / A. Smith / 1791'. They are interesting miniatures, but not of any great artistic merit. According to family papers the artist also executed oil portraits. (Plate 49F.)

Anthony Stewart (1773-1846) was born in Crieff, Perthshire. Nothing is known about his early life but, having decided to take up art, he became a pupil of Alexander Nasmyth in Edinburgh where he painted landscapes and executed sketches of Scottish scenery. He later devoted himself to miniature painting and obtained a fashionable clientele, including members of the

Colour Plate 17.
A. **William Grimaldi,** *an unknown lady, ivory, 3ins. Signed and dated: 'Grimaldi 1796.'*
B. **Charles Robertson,** *Baron Mount Sandford, ivory 2½ins. This is a good miniature by Robertson.*
C. **Samuel Shelley,** *an unknown lady, ivory, 3ins., c.1795. Signed in full on the reverse: '6 George Street.'*
D. **Andrew Robertson, M.A.,** *an unknown man, ivory, 2⅞ins. Signed with initials: 'AR.'*
E. **William Naish,** *an unknown staff officer, ivory, 2¾ins.*

Courtesy Brigadier and Mrs. G. Viner

Plate 49B (right). **A. Skirving,** *an unknown officer, ivory, 2¾ins., c.1790-95. Signed:* '*AS*' *(cursive monogram).* Courtesy Christie's.

Plate 49C (far right). **A. Gallaway,** *a member of the Henderson family, ivory, 3ins. Signed and dated:* '*A.G. / 96*' *[1796].* Private Collection.

Plate 49D. **Alexander Gallaway** *(fl.c.1794-1812?), self-portrait, ivory, 1¼ins., c.1790. By family descent.* Courtesy Christie's.

Royal family. He was particularly good at painting children, and was commissioned to paint portraits of Princess Charlotte and Princess Victoria (afterwards Queen Victoria). He practised first in Scotland, where he married on 5th July, 1793, Janet Weir, of Tron Parish, Edinburgh, the daughter of Alexander Weir, the painter. Stewart also practised in London, and exhibited at the Royal Academy, 1807-1820. In 1807 he is recorded as 'A. Stewart Jun.' of 26 Prince's Square, St. George's East, from which address he continued to exhibit. The majority of his miniatures show the sitters full-face; those of children are more attractive than those of adults. He used light clear colours, and many of the backgrounds have a lot of stippling. His two daughters, Grace Campbell Stewart and Margaret Stewart, were both miniaturists, and were pupils of their father. Stewart died in Stockwell, London, in December, 1846. Examples of his work are in the collection of H.M. The Queen, and also in the Victoria and Albert Museum, and the National Gallery, Scotland. (Plate 49 I.)

Plate 49E (right). **A. Skirving,** *portrait of an unknown lady, ivory, 3½ins., c.1790-1800. The sitter is wearing a white dress with blue trimmings and feathers in her hair. The recent discovery of a fully signed miniature by Skirving has made identification easier.* Private Collection.

Plate 49F (far right). **W.A. Smith,** *a member of the Gordon family of Letterfourie, ivory, 2½ins. Signed:* '*WS. / 1780.*' *This is one of a small collection of family miniatures by this minor artist.* Courtesy J.B. Robertson.

Amongst the more outstanding Scottish miniaturists were three brothers named Robertson: Archibald, Alexander and Andrew. They were the sons of William Robertson, an architect, and his wife, Jean, née Ross. The family was not well off, and William did delicate woodwork as a hobby and to supplement his income. **Archibald Robertson** (1765-1835) was born at Monymusk, near Aberdeen. He became friendly with Raeburn in Edinburgh where he first worked. He left Scotland for London in 1786, and became a pupil of Charles Shirreff, who it will be remembered had moved there some seventeen years earlier. Robertson also had some training under an artist named Peacock. In 1791, he went to New York where he eventually settled. He established the Columbian Academy in collaboration with his brother, Alexander, who joined him in 1792. Archibald painted miniatures in oil and watercolour, drew in crayon, and executed "devices in hair work for lockets". He also wrote a treatise on miniature painting. He married Eliza Abramse of New York, by whom he had a large family. His self-portrait and that of his wife

Plate 49G. **A. Gallaway,** *Mary Gallaway, later Mrs. Wallan Brown, daughter of the artist, ivory, 3¼ins., c.1810-1820. By family descent.* Courtesy Christie's.

Plate 49H (left). **A. Gallaway,** *Catherine Gallaway, later Mrs. Hadway, daughter of the artist, ivory, 3¾ins., c.1820. By family descent.* Courtesy Christie's.

Plate 49 I (right). **A. Stewart,** *a young child, ivory, 3¼ins. Stewart excelled at painting children and this portrait is typical of his work.* Courtesy Christie's.

213

Plate 50A. **R. Thorburn, A.R.A., H.R.S.A.,** *the Earl of Craven, pencil sketch on paper, 6ins. Signed: 'T R' (monogram) the T adjoining the R, and inscribed: 'The Earl of Craven / by / Thorburn.' Thorburn exhibited a portrait of The Earl of Craven at the R.A. in 1838. This is presumed to represent William, 2nd Earl of Craven (1809-66).* Private Collection.

are illustrated by H.B. Wehle in *American Miniatures,* Plates IV and XII. He signed his works: 'AR', in monogram. Works by him are rarely seen; the majority of them are probably in America. His paint box is in the Rosenbach Museum, Philadelphia. Examples of his work are in the Smithsonian Institution, Washington, the Metropolitan Museum of Art, New York, and the Philadelphia Museum of Art. A miniature of an unknown officer, signed: 'AR (monogram) / P', belonging to the Robertson family was exhibited at Edinburgh in 1965 (Plate 52E). An oil portrait of George Washington by Robertson is at Sulgrave Manor, Northampton.

Alexander Robertson (1772-1841) was also born in Aberdeen. Nothing appears to be known about his early education, but having studied under Samuel Shelley in London, he joined his brother, Archibald, in New York, where he remained until his death, assisting him with his drawing school and exhibiting at the American Academy from 1817. He was its secretary from 1817-1825, and Keeper 1820-1835. His wife's name was Mary, daughter of Bishop Provoost. He died in New York in 1841. Attributions to both Alexander and Archibald Robertson are difficult, as miniatures by them are scarce, and it is doubtful if all are signed.

Andrew Robertson, M.A. (1777-1845) is the most important of these brothers as far as British miniatures are concerned. He was born in Aberdeen on 14th October, 1777, and began his career as a miniaturist at the age of fourteen. He studied under both Nasmyth and Raeburn, presumably in Edinburgh. He also had an aptitude for music, and at the age of sixteen was Director of concerts in Aberdeen. He taught drawing, miniature painting and portraiture, etc. He took his M.A. in Aberdeen in 1794. In 1801 Andrew went to London, where his work was noticed by Benjamin West, whose portrait in miniature by him was exhibited in Edinburgh in 1965. On October 23rd, 1801, he entered the Royal Academy Schools, and exhibited at the Royal Academy, British Institution, Old Water Colour Society, etc.

Plate 50B (left). **Andrew Robertson,** *Princess Amelia (1783-1810), ivory, 3³⁄₈ins. Signed and dated 'AR (monogram) 1811',* presumably *taken from an identical miniature dated 1810.* Gracious permission H.M. The Queen.

Plate 50C (right). **Andrew Robertson,** *Miss Dobson, ivory, 4½ins. Signed and dated on the reverse: 'No 3 / Portrait of Miss Dobson / by A.Robertson / 34 Gerrard St / 1828.'* Courtesy Christie's.

from 1802-1842. He was in Aberdeen in 1803 and 1808, but remained for most of his life in London. He married twice; by his first wife (Jenny?) he had two sons, Charles, and Edward (who followed his father's profession). By his second wife, thought to have been the daughter of Samuel Boxhill of Barbados, he had a son, Samuel, and a daughter, Emily, who edited *Letters and Papers of Andrew Robertson,* in which was included Archibald Robertson's treatise, written in the form of a letter to Andrew. In 1803, during the threat of Napoleonic invasion, Robertson was among those who formed an Artists' Volunteer Corps. According to his letters home he seems to have lived for several years in great poverty, and had difficulty in helping his family who were also in need.

In 1805 he was appointed miniature painter to the Duke of Sussex, and by this time had built up a distinguished clientele. Frederick Cruickshank, a fellow Aberdonian, was for a time his pupil and assistant. Robertson was a member of the Associated Artists in Water-Colours, where in 1808 he exhibited the portraits of five princesses! Andrew Robertson is considered to be one of the best miniaturists of the nineteenth century. His works are elegant and well drawn. They are often reminiscent of the works of Raeburn. He sketched his sitters' features in brown monochrome placing his painting table so that the light slanted over his left shoulder, his sitter's head being posed in front of him, slightly to the right. A point to look for is the way he often shaded the nose and under the eyebrows with a darkish wash (Colour Plate 17D). He painted several miniatures of Princess Amelia, one of which is in the collection of H.M. The Queen, signed and dated: 'AR (monogram) / 1811' (Plate 50B). The size and shape of his miniatures varied, some are quite large as in the case of the portrait of the 6th Duke of Roxburghe, signed and dated: 'AR (monogram) / 1837'. This miniature is rectangular, and measures 7 by 5¼ inches. This and the companion miniature (now missing) of the Duchess were exhibited at the Royal Academy in the year they were painted. A number of miniatures by Robertson are still in the family, and I am indebted to his descendant, J.B. Robertson, for information regarding the family history. Examples of his work are in the Victoria and Albert Museum, National Portrait Gallery, London, and the Ashmolean Museum, Oxford, as well as many private collections. (Plate 50C.)

Plate 50D. **R. Thorburn, A.R.A.,** *Miss Fitzgibbon, ivory, 20ins. Inscribed in full on the reverse. Thorburn exhibited a miniature of a Miss Fitzgibbon at the R.A. in 1848. This is a good example of his large cabinet miniatures and painted in bright fresh colours. There are signs of the ivory cracking.* Courtesy Sotheby's.

Edward Robertson (b.1809) was the son of Andrew Robertson by his first wife. He is presumed to have had instruction in painting from his father, before entering the Royal Academy Schools on 6th December, 1827. He exhibited at the Royal Academy, 1830-1837. Edward was in Dublin c.1831-1832, where he exhibited at the Royal Hibernian Academy in 1826. Although the existence of an Edward Robertson was known to Basil Long, his relationship to Andrew was only discovered when Mr. J.B. Robertson lent a miniature by Edward, of his brother, Charles, to the Edinburgh Exhibition in 1965. This is inscribed and dated on the reverse: 'Portrait of / Captain Chas Robertson / Painted by / Mr. Edward Robertson / Glasgow / 1837.' Whether the artist was working in Glasgow at that time or visiting his relations is not known. His address in 1832 was 34 Gerrard Street, Soho, London. According to the Robertson family, he died in Dublin, but the date is unknown. His self-portrait was sold at Sotheby's, Lot 30, 24th June, 1974. It was signed and dated 1831, on the reverse, and painted in Dublin. His work is close in style to that of his father, and his draughtsmanship is good. (Plates 51A and 52A and B.)

William John Thomson, R.S.A. (1771/3-1845) was born in Savannah, Georgia, U.S.A., but was brought to England by his father, a Government official who lost his job during the rebellion. His father retired on a small pension and the family made their home in Edinburgh. William had to earn a living at an early age, and began his career by painting portraits and miniatures in London. He exhibited at the Royal Academy, British Institution, Associated Artists, Old Water Colour Society, and Society of British Artists, 1796-1843. Up to 1812 he gave various London addresses, after which he lived in Edinburgh until his death on 24th March, 1845, at 47 Northumberland Street. His marriage is recorded as taking place in the "Tron Parish", Edinburgh on "12.5.1797", his bride being Miss Helen Colhoun, daughter; of Captain James Colhoun.

Thomson exhibited at the Edinburgh Association of Artists, 1810-1813, the Edinburgh Exhibition Society, 1814-1815, the Institute for the Encouragement of the Fine Arts in Scotland, 1821-1830, and the Royal Scottish Academy, 1830-1843. He was elected R.S.A. in 1829. He seems to have been a versatile artist and painted portraits, miniatures, landscapes and genre subjects. His miniatures are well painted and slightly reminiscent of the work of Samuel John Stump. He tended to use a greenish tint for his shading, or occasionally a deep brown-red. A fair amount of cross-hatching is evident in the shading of the sitters' clothes and backgrounds. He painted a number of notable Scottish families including the Hunter Blairs, who still have examples of his work. A portrait of Catherine, Lady Blantyre, signed and dated on the reverse: 'Painted by W.J. Thomson / Decr 1812 / Edinburgh', is in the Victoria and Albert Museum, who also have other miniatures by him. (Plate 48B.)

Plate 51A. E. Robertson, Mrs. Margaret Gordon, ivory, 1¼ins. Signed in full on the reverse: 'Painted in Glasgow / by / Edward Robertson / 1843.' This miniature is close in style to the work of the artist's brother Andrew. Courtesy E. Grosvenor Paine, U.S.A.

A Scottish artist about whom little is known is **Alexander Gallaway** (fl. c.1794-1812?). As far as we know he only worked in Scotland. He appears to have run a Drawing Academy in Glasgow in collaboration with a Mr. Williams. The *Glasgow Courier*, 31st May and June 3rd, 1794, carried an advertisement announcing the removal of their 'Drawing Academy' to Horn's Court, Argyll Street, to be opened on 2nd June. The advertisement continued as follows:

"Miniature Painting
By Mr. Gallaway, and
Views of Any Particular Place,
Taken from Nature,
By Mr. Williams.
Specimens to be seen at the Academy."

Gallaway was living at Smith's Land, Trongate, Glasgow, and from 1811-1812 he was at 6 St. James's Square, Edinburgh. He exhibited at the Society of Artists, Edinburgh, in 1808.

On 18th March, 1975, six documentary family miniatures were sold at Christie's, which provided the name of his wife, Ann, née Rowland, and those of two daughters, Catherine, later Mrs. Hadway (1803-67) (Plate 49H), and Mary, later Mrs. Wallan Brown (Plate 49G). The other miniatures represented the artist's sister, Jean, and Colonel John Campbell, a cousin of Ann Rowland, and a self-portrait of the artist (Plate 49D). The self-portrait does not resemble the one sold as a possible self-portrait at Christie's on 10th July, 1972. This latter portrait was by Gallaway, but may represent another artist as he is holding a paint brush and seated by an easel. Gallaway's work is competent, without being spectacular. His miniatures are modelled with a minute soft stippling. A number of them are signed on the front in either block letters: 'AG' or a cursive 'AG', followed by a date. One characteristic

Plate 51B. **John Faed, R.S.A.,** *Thomas Allan, ivory, 3¼ins., c.1865-70. Encased in a gold period locket. The sitter was probably related to John Harden of Brathay Hall, an amateur artist whose brother-in-law Thomas Allan had a son, also Thomas (d.1873) whom this may represent.* Courtesy Christie's.

of his work is his fondness for drawing a pillar or a draped curtain in the background, as in the case of the miniature of his daughter, Mary (Plate 49G). The sitter's features such as the nose, eyebrows and eyelids are all clearly defined. Examples of his work are in the Victoria and Albert Museum (Colour Plate 22E).

Frederick Cruickshank (1800-1868) was a native of Aberdeen. Little seems to be known about his education, except that he became a pupil of Andrew Robertson, and many of his miniatures show Robertson's influence. Cruickshank lived for a time with relatives in Manchester, but is said to have spent most of his life in Scotland, working in Scottish country houses. His pupils included the miniaturists Mrs. F. Dixon, née Cowell (fl. 1851-1875) and Miss Margaret Gillies (1803-1887). He married a Miss Catherine Baly, by whom he had six children, of whom Dorothea Blanche was still living in 1933, aged eighty-four, in East Dulwich. Cruickshank painted miniatures and portraits in watercolour. Not all his miniatures are signed; those that are usually bear the initials 'FC', often followed by a date. Of his daughters, both Catherine Gertrude and Grace became miniaturists. A portrait of F. Cruickshank by Octavius Oakley is in the Victoria and Albert Museum. Cruickshank was a good artist whose miniatures show character. The features are painted in detail, but the costume is often washed in with a full brush of paint, only lightly indicating the folds of the material (Plate 53A). A good example of his work is that of an unknown lady in a private collection (Plate 53B).

Among the lesser known Scottish miniaturists was **William Douglas** (1780-1832). He was born in Fife on 14th April, 1780, and was descended from the Douglas family of Glenbervie. He was educated in Edinburgh, and was a pupil of Robert Scott, the engraver. Douglas exhibited in Edinburgh in 1808 and 1809, and at the Royal Academy, 1818-1826. He executed miniatures (including some of animals) and engravings, and held an appointment as miniature painter in Scotland to H.R.H. Prince Leopold of Saxe-Coburg. Douglas died at Hart Street, Edinburgh, on 30th January,

Plate 51C. **J. Heughan,** *portrait of an unknown man, ivory, 2½ins., bearing a scratched signature on the front: 'Heughan / at York / ..00' [1800]. Miniatures by this little-known artist are scarce.* Courtesy F. Joachim.

1832, leaving a widow, two sons and a daughter, Miss Archibald Ramsay Douglas (1807-1889), who practised as a miniaturist in Edinburgh. I know of no miniatures signed on the front, his usual signature being in full on the reverse: 'W. Douglas / Edinburgh / Pinxit 1816'. An example of his work is in the National Gallery of Scotland, and engravings after his work are in the British Museum.

Kenneth Macleay, R.S.A. (1802-1878) was the son of a physician, Dr. Kenneth Macleay of Glasgow and Oban, where he was born on 4th July, 1802. According to the *Dictionary of National Biography*, he spent his early years in Crieff. Macleay went to Edinburgh when he was eighteen years of age, and entered the Trustees' Academy on 26th February, 1822. His ability as a good miniaturist was soon recognised and he had no difficulty in obtaining sitters. He was one of the founder members of the Royal Scottish Academy in 1826; he resigned, but was re-elected an Associate and R.S.A. in 1829. Little is known about his early years; his mother was a member of the Macdonald family of Keppoch, Inverness-shire, and his wife a daughter of Sir A. Campbell of Aldenglass. Macleay executed miniatures, landscapes and portraits in oil and watercolour. Some of his most successful works are said to be his small portraits in watercolour in which the head and shoulders are broadly modelled and the figure and accessories lightly drawn in pencil and tinted. He exhibited at the Institute for the Encouragement of Fine Arts in Scotland 1822-1829, and at the Scottish Academy 1828-1879, his last exhibit being posthumous. In 1865 he exhibited three miniatures at the Royal Academy from 26 Hamilton Place, Edinburgh; they represented: Lord George Campbell, son of the Duke of Argyll, T.R.H. the Princes Arthur and Leopold, and H.R.H. Prince Alfred. These last two exhibits were painted "by command for her Majesty" [Queen Victoria]. He painted with a soft touch, rather in the manner of Robert Thorburn (1818-1885). All the miniatures I have seen by him are well painted. He used a sepia shading on the face, and often delineated the features with a reddish colour. Occasionally he shaded the face with a bluish tint. He painted the hair in a mass rather than in

Plate 51D. **James Faed**, *portrait of a man, possibly the artist's brother Thomas Faed, (1826-1900), ivory, 4½ins. Part of a letter addressed to J. Faed, Esq., is pasted on the reverse of the frame. The painting is close in style to Plate 51G.* Courtesy Christie's.

Plate 51E (left). **K. Macleay, R.S.A.**, *a pair of unknown children, ivory, 3¾ins. Signed on the reverse: 'Painted by / Kenneth Macleay / Edinburgh / March 1824.' Although superficially attractive, the pose is rather stiff and the draughtsmanship of the arms not good.* Courtesy F. Joachim.

Plate 51F (right). **S. Denny**, *an unknown Scotsman, ivory, 1¾ins. Wearing a scarlet coat and sash, green bonnet and white epaulettes. Signed on the reverse: 'Stephen Denny / pinxit / 1814 / No 11 Alfred Place / Newington Bis.' (Edinburgh). No other miniatures by this artist are known.* Courtesy E. Grosvenor Paine, U.S.A.

Plate 51G. **James Faed,** *Miss Mary Duncan, ivory, 3⅜ins. Signed on the reverse: 'N.2 portrait of Miss Mary [Duncan] / James Faed Senr / 7 Barnton Terrace / Edinburgh.' The sitter was the daughter of Thomas Duncan, A.R.A., R.S.A. Miniatures by this artist are scarce.* Private Collection.

strands, and the sitter's costume in broad washes of paint rather than in detail. Many of his miniatures are signed in full and dated on the reverse, as in one in my collection: 'Painted by / Kenneth Macleay / Edinb^r Feb^r 1829'. Some of his paintings were on paper. He was said to have been a "fine-looking man with the air of a Highland chieftain". He died in Edinburgh on 3rd November, 1878. Examples of his work are in the National Portrait Gallery, London, and the National Gallery, Edinburgh. (Plate 51E.)

One of the last of the really important Scottish miniaturists was **Robert Thorburn, A.R.A., H.R.S.A. (1818-1885).** He was the son of a tradesman, and was born in Dumfries on 10th March, 1818. He was educated at the High School in Dumfries, and at an early age showed an aptitude for drawing. At the age of fifteen he studied under Sir William Allan at the Royal Institution of Scotland, Edinburgh, where he won two first prizes. In 1836 he went to London, and studied at the Royal Academy Schools. In order to support himself and his family he took up miniature painting and obtained early recognition. He exhibited at the Royal Academy, etc.,

Colour Plate 18.
A. **John Comerford,** *Colonel Armstrong, ivory, 2½ins. This is a good example of Comerford's method of shading the features.*
B. **Horace Hone, A.R.A.,** *Hugh O'Connor, ivory, 2¾ins. Signed and dated in monogram: 'HH / 1793.'*
C. **Thomas Richmond,** *an unknown officer, ivory, 2½ins. The monogram 'AJC' is on the reverse of the frame.*
D. **Thomas H. Hull,** *Sir Charles Blicke (1745-1815), surgeon at St. Bartholomew's Hospital, 1787, ivory, 3ins. Signed: 'Hull.' This is a fine example of a miniature by Hull whose work is scarce.*
E. **Charles Shirreff,** *Richard Colley, Marquess Wellesley (1760-1842), Governor General of India, ivory, 3ins. A replica of this miniature was signed and dated: 'Calcutta 1804', and at least a third version exists.*

Private Collection

A

B

C

D

E

1837-1884, from various London addresses, and at the Royal Scottish Academy, 1835-1856. Thorburn was elected A.R.A. in 1848, and became an honorary member of the Royal Scottish Academy in 1857. In 1855 he was awarded a Gold Medal in Paris. He worked both in Edinburgh and London, and lived latterly in Kelso. He was living in Tunbridge Wells in 1884, and is believed to have died there in the following year.

His works include miniatures, crayon drawings, oil portraits and landscapes. He had a distinguished clientele which included the Queen, the Prince Consort, and members of the Royal family. The advent of photography had an adverse effect on miniature painting, and Thorburn was among those who turned to painting portraits in oil. In order to vie with photography which could produce portraits of a larger size than those normally painted by miniaturists, Thorburn was amongst those who experimented with very large pieces of ivory, which could be obtained by taking a thin slice of ivory from the circumference of the tusk with a lathe. This had to be made flat by means of heat and great pressure. It was then laid down on a thick slab of india-rubber, which was often stuck on to a mahogany panel. Sometimes more than one piece of ivory was used to make one base. The drawback to this method is that, since ivory is apt to warp or crack in changes of temperature, all too often these large miniatures are cracked and cannot be mended satisfactorily.

Many of Thorburn's miniatures are attractive and well painted, but their size detracts slightly from their merit. A large number of miniatures by him are at Windsor Castle. A particularly fine example of his work was sold at Sotheby's Belgravia on 3rd March, 1977. It represented Miss Fitzgibbon, and is fully inscribed on the reverse. This miniature was lent, by the artist's son Archibald (well known for his paintings of birds), to an Exhibition at Messrs. Dickensons, London, in 1894. It shows to perfection Thorburn's ability to

Plate 52A. **E. Robertson,** *portrait of an unknown man, ivory, 3ins., c.1837. Signed with initials: 'ER.' Until recently only one signed miniature by Edward Robertson was known.* Courtesy Christie's.

Plate 52B. **Edward Robertson** *(b.1809), self-portrait of the artist, ivory, 3½ins. Signed and dated on the reverse: 'Dublin 1831.' This is of historic interest as the only known miniature of the artist.* Courtesy Sotheby's.

222

Plate 52C. **Andrew Robertson,** *Mrs. W.J. Cotman, ivory, 4¹/8ins. Signed on the reverse and dated: '1818 / No 5 34 Gerrard Street / Portrait of Mrs. W.J. Cotman.'* Private Collection.

paint costume, and place his sitter in an attractive pose, to cover an area of 20 inches in height on the large ivory base. A characteristic also visible in this miniature is his way of enlarging the pupil of the eye to an almost perfect round (Plate 50D). That he was a good draughtsman is shown in a sketch of the Earl of Craven, which was presumably done prior to painting a large portrait (Plate 50A).

Although the brothers John and James Faed are best known for their landscapes and figure subjects, both of them painted miniatures early in their careers. **John Faed, R.S.A.** (1819/20-1902) was born at Burley Mill, Kirkcudbrightshire, and was the son of a millwright, farmer and engineer. Three of his sons became artists, John, Thomas Faed, R.A., and James. John took up miniature painting when quite young, and wandered about from place to place executing miniatures, figure subjects and landscapes. In 1841 he went to Edinburgh and lived for a time at 5 York Place. He exhibited at the Royal Scottish Academy 1841-1895, becoming A.R.S.A. in 1847, and R.S.A. in 1851. In 1862 he went to London, and exhibited at the Royal Academy, etc., 1855-1893. Faed returned to Scotland in 1880, and settled at Gatehouse of Fleet. He much preferred painting figure subjects and outdoor scenes to miniatures, and consequently examples by him are very scarce. A portrait group of the children of Dr. Archibald Bennie, painted on ivory, 13 by 9½ inches, is in the National Gallery of Scotland, and is called 'The Evening Hour'. The few examples of his miniatures which I have seen place him high among the ranks of those who practised this art in the nineteenth century. His work is reminiscent of that of Sir William Charles Ross, who will be discussed in a later chapter. He painted with fresh colours and depicted drapery to perfection (Colour Plate 35A). Faed had a number of children of whom four became artists. He died at Ardmore, Gatehouse of Fleet, on 22nd October, 1902. (Plate 51B.)

James Faed (1821-1911) was a younger brother of John Faed. He was born at Burley Mill, Kirkcudbrightshire, on 4th April, 1821. He is best known for his landscapes in oils, and genre subjects, but also painted a few

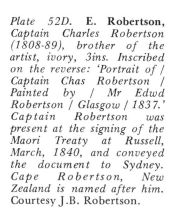

Plate 52D. **E. Robertson,** *Captain Charles Robertson (1808-89), brother of the artist, ivory, 3ins. Inscribed on the reverse: 'Portrait of / Captain Chas Robertson / Painted by / Mr Edwd Robertson / Glasgow / 1837.' Captain Robertson was present at the signing of the Maori Treaty at Russell, March, 1840, and conveyed the document to Sydney. Cape Robertson, New Zealand is named after him.* Courtesy J.B. Robertson.

Plate 52E. **Archibald Robertson,** *portrait of an unknown officer, ivory, 3¼ins. Signed with a cursive monogram: 'AR / P.' Miniatures by Archibald are scarce and the majority probably in America.* Courtesy J.B. Robertson.

miniatures and executed some engravings. He seems to have divided his time between Edinburgh and London. He exhibited at the Royal Academy 1855-1904. In 1855 he exhibited a portrait of his brother Thomas Faed, R.A. (1826-1900), also a painter. This may be the miniature sold at Christie's, on 18th April, 1972, Lot 56 (Plate 51D). The last of James Faed's exhibits at the Royal Academy was a miniature of a 'Mrs. M.'. His son, James Faed, Junior (fl. 1880-1900) was also an artist. Miniatures by him are scarce; one of Miss Mary Duncan, daughter of Thomas Duncan, A.R.A., R.S.A., is fully inscribed on the reverse: 'N.2 portrait of Miss Mary [Duncan] / James Faed Sen[r] / 7 Barnton Terrace / Edinburgh.' It is painted in fresh colours, against a bright blue background (Plate 51G). It is not of quite such a high quality as the miniatures painted by his brother, John Faed. James Faed died on 24th September, 1911.

A hitherto unrecorded artist is **Stephen Denny.** A miniature of an unknown Scotsman in uniform, wearing a scarlet coat, sash, green bonnet and white epaulettes, is signed on the reverse: 'Stephen Denny / pinxit / 1814 / No 11 Alfred Place / Newington Bis.' The miniature is in the collection of E.G. Paine, U.S.A. The colouring is good and the work slightly reminiscent of that of Luke Sullivan (Plate 51F).

Plate 53.

A. **F. Cruickshank,** *an unknown man, ivory, 3¼ins. Signed: 'FC / 1825.' This is a good example of Cruickshank's method of painting with a full brush and leaving areas unfinished.* Courtesy F. Joachim.

B. **F. Cruickshank,** *portrait of an unknown lady, ivory, 4½ins., c.1845. This is a particularly good example of the artist's work.* Private Collection.

C. **Andrew Robertson,** *Queen Adelaide, Queen of William IV, when Duchess of Clarence (1792-1849), ivory 3⅝ins. Signed and dated: 'AR (monogram) / 1820.'* Courtesy Christie's.

D. **F. Cruickshank,** *William Ebenezer Pattisson (1801-32), ivory, 6¼ins. This is another example of how Cruickshank often left his portraits unfinished and loosely painted.* Courtesy Victoria and Albert Museum.

E. **Artist unknown,** *Scottish School, Mrs. Elizabeth Baillie, ivory, 4¾ins., c.1826. Note the wide-brimmed hat trimmed with flowers and streamers falling over her bodice.* Courtesy F. Joachim.

A

B

C

D

E

Plate 54A. S. Digby, Bishop of Elphin, *John Hough (1651-1743), Bishop of Worcester, vellum, 3½ins. A number of miniatures by Digby are in Ireland, and in the Digby family. He was one of the earliest miniaturists in Ireland.* Courtesy the National Portrait Gallery.

Plate 54B. G. Hamilton, *portrait of an unknown lady, ivory, 1⅝ins. Signed and dated: 'Ham / 1772.'* Courtesy Sotheby's.

Plate 54C. G. Hamilton, *portrait of an unknown officer, ivory, 1¼ins. Signed: 'Ham^n.' Set within a clasp frame for a bracelet. This is a good example of the artist's work.* Courtesy F. Joachim.

In this brief survey of miniaturists who worked in Scotland I have tried to bring to the notice of collectors, artists whose works they may possibly see or purchase. There are of necessity many omissions due to space, and some artists, because of their importance, will be dealt with in other chapters. There were many artists who were of Scottish birth but who spent all their working life in England or elsewhere and it is difficult in some cases to decide where to place them. The same problem arises in dealing with Irish miniaturists, and indeed those who worked in the provinces, and I have not attempted to make many comparisons in this chapter as these are, in some cases, made in other parts of the book, or can be made by the reader from the illustrations.

When the Exhibition of Irish Portraits 1660-1860 was held in Dublin, London and Belfast in 1969-70, it attracted a lot of interest. The preface to the introduction of the catalogue was a quotation from William Carey, *Some Memoirs of the Fine Arts in England and Ireland*: "...Ireland had some native born artists, and was occasionally visited by straggling adventurers of the brush from London"! This very apt description of the 'Irish School of Painting' is what makes it so difficult to select the artists to be included in this chapter. Claims can be made for others to be called 'Irish School', but I have tried to select those whose work lay in Ireland for a reasonable space of time.

Much of our knowledge of Irish artists is gained from W.G. Strickland's *Dictionary of Irish Artists,* 1913, which is still a reliable guide to the subject, and contains a large number of illustrations, including some by miniaturists.

The origins of miniature painting in Ireland can be traced back to **Simon Digby, Bishop of Elphin** (d.1720). He was the son of Essex Digby, of Dromore, Ireland, and was educated at Trinity College, Dublin. He became successively Rector of Dunshaughlin, Chaplin to the Earl of Ossory in 1668, Bishop of Limerick in 1678, and Bishop of Elphin in 1691. Nothing is known about his artistic training, if any, but he was an accomplished miniaturist and painted many of the leading men of the day. These included Bishop Tillotson, Lord Capel and Henry, Lord Sidney. A miniature representing the artist and his family is in *A Dictionary of British Miniature Painters,* Plate 227. The present whereabouts of this miniature is unknown. A characteristic of his work is the way he paints the eyes of his sitters in a rather staring manner; his draughtsmanship is good, and the general effect bold. He used a bluish shading on the face, and touches of red to delineate the eyes, nose and mouth. A number of his miniatures are in the family of his descendants, the Wingfield Digbys of Sherborne Castle, and one of John Hough, Bishop of Worcester, is in the National Portrait Gallery (Plate 54A). Other examples are in the National Gallery, Dublin, and private collections. Digby died at Lacken, County Roscommon, on 7th April, 1720, and was buried on the 20th "in the church of Tosara (Mount Talbot), in the said county. together with his Lady who died a few days after him".

After the death of Digby, there were no specifically Irish miniaturists until the middle of the eighteenth century, by which time the art was becoming more popular, and a much greater number of patrons was available. Several English artists had visited Ireland, and this probably stimulated the development of the art in both Dublin and Belfast. Thomas Frye (1710-1762) has already been mentioned in a previous chapter as, although he was born in or

Plate 54D. **J. Reily,** *miniature of an unknown lady, ivory, 1¹¹/₃₂ins. Signed and dated: 'Reily / 1758.' This is typical of the rather naïve and stiff way that Reily painted.* Courtesy Victoria and Albert Museum, Alan Evans Collection.

Plate 54E. **Elish la Mont,** *Laetitia (aged seventeen), and Dorothea (aged seven) daughters of John and Mary Roberts, ivory, 4¼ins. Signed and dated: '1838.'* Private Collection.

Plate 54F. **G. Hamilton,** *portrait of an unknown man, ivory, 1¼ins. Signed: 'Hamⁿ / 1765.' Set within a clasp frame for a bracelet.* Courtesy Sotheby's.

Plate 54G. **C. Robertson,** *portrait of an unknown man, ivory, 2½ins. This is a good example of Robertson's work, which is not always easy to attribute as he seldom, if ever, signed his miniatures.* Courtesy Sotheby's.

near Dublin, he spent most of his working life in England. Other artists such as P.P. Lens went to Ireland for a short time, but were not really of the Irish School.

Rupert Barber (fl. 1736-1772) was the son of a Dublin woollen-draper, whose wife was Mary Barber, the poetess, friend and protégée of Swift. Both Ireland and Bath can claim his allegiance: in 1736 he went to study in Bath, where he remained until 1743, when he returned to Dublin where he set up as an enamellist. He appears to have divided his time between Dublin, Bath and London. Barber was befriended by Mrs. Delany, and was given a house at the end of the Delanys' garden at Delville, near Dublin. He is known to have painted several portraits of her on enamel. Besides painting miniatures on enamel, he painted portraits in oils and experimented in glass-making. In 1753 he was awarded a premium by the Dublin Society for making phials and green glass. Barber married in March, 1742, a Miss Wilson, who, according to Mrs. Delany, was "a very pretty and prudent woman", by whom he had two children, a son (who studied in the Dublin Society Schools and later became an officer in the Artillery) and a daughter, who was described by Mrs. Delany in 1746 as "a comical little girl of three years old, not pretty, but a smart girl, and he proposes to make her a mistress of his art as soon as she is capable of learning". In 1772 he became involved in a project with a distillery, through which he incurred a heavy debt.

One of his best known works is an enamel of a Dublin beggar, sold at Sotheby's on 11th December, 1958, in the Dyson Perrins Collection. It is inscribed on the reverse: 'Gulielms Thompson Mendicans Dublini Ann. 1744. Aetat 114. R. Barber Pinxt.' A sketch in black chalk for this miniature was sold at Sotheby's, on 4th May, 1921. His works are scarce, and there may be some confusion between his works and those of Lucius Barber (d.1767), who, as has already been mentioned, worked in London. Rupert Barber was living in Dublin up to 1772, but the date of his death is not known. Few examples of his work are known, and consequently attribution is difficult.

An enamel portrait of Mrs. Anne Donnellan by Barber is in the Ulster Museum, and is inscribed on the reverse: 'Mrs Anne Donnellan / R.B. pinxit 1752' (Plate 54H). A miniature of an unknown man by Barber is in the Victoria and Albert Museum and is signed on the reverse: 'R.B: f.'

William Bate (d. c.1845) came of a family who for several generations had been watchmakers and jewellers in Dublin. Little is known about his life, but he evidently had a good practice in London and Dublin, and was in Leeds in 1802. He exhibited at the Royal Academy 1799-1807, and in Dublin in 1819. He held the appointment as Painter in enamel to the Princess Elizabeth and the Duke of York. Bate painted miniatures in watercolour and enamel; the latter are more frequently seen (Plate 59D). He exhibited from various London addresses, and is said to have been at Tivoli in 1829. He died in or before 1845, in which year, on 10th June, his effects, including some pictures and his enamels, were auctioned in Dublin. A miniature of an unknown lady is signed on the reverse: 'W. Bate Pinxit / of 163 Strand London / Leeds Oct^r — / 1802.' It is painted on ivory and although the draughtsmanship is good it is not of outstanding merit (Plate 59A). He appears to have used a lot of gum with his paints and executed the draperies with fairly thick brush strokes.

Gustavus Hamilton (c.1739-1775) was the son of the Rev. Gustavus Hamilton, Vicar of Errigal in the Diocese of Clogher, and Rector of Gallen in Co. Meath, and his wife, Jan Cathcart, whom he married when serving as a curate in Enniskillen, 1721-2. The artist was one of the youngest of a large family, whose parents claimed descent from the Hamiltons of Prestfield, Midlothian.

Hamilton became a pupil of R. West at the Drawing School in George's Lane, and was an apprentice of Samuel Dixon in Dublin, where with J. Reilly and D. O'Keefe, he was employed to colour prints of birds and flowers produced by Dixon. Hamilton apparently turned his attention to miniature painting and obtained a fashionable clientele. He exhibited in Dublin from 1765-1773, from various addresses: Parliament Street, 1 Dame Street, and Cork Hill. A self-portrait in crayon is illustrated in Strickland's *Dictionary of Irish Artists,* Plate XXIX. He died young on 16th December, 1775, aged thirty-six, and was buried at St. Werburgh's, Dublin.

Hamilton's miniatures are usually small in size, and many of them were painted for lockets or bracelets; they are signed variously: 'Ham.', 'G. Ham.', 'G. Ham^{tn}', 'Gus Hamilton', etc., often followed by a date. His miniatures vary in quality; some of them appear a little stiff. Often the contours of the face, upper eyelids and eyebrows are delineated in brown and the face shaded with blue, particularly under the eyes. He frequently used a reddish flesh tint. A good example of his work is a miniature of an unknown man in a short wig, wearing a blue jacket and waistcoat, painted against a brownish background. It is signed: 'GHP / 1759', and encased in a frame for a bracelet, set with garnets (Colour Plate 16E). There is a companion miniature of a lady set in a similar frame, signed: 'I.R. / 1760', which may suggest that it was painted by J. Reilly, with whom Hamilton worked (Colour Plate 16G). The identity of the monogrammist 'I.R.' has never yet been established, and this may be a clue.

A miniature of an unknown lady by Hamilton, signed: 'Ham^n / 1764', is in the National Gallery, Dublin. (Plates 54B, C and F.)

Plate 54H. **R. Barber,** *Mrs. Anne Donnellan, enamel, 1⅞ins. Inscribed on the reverse: 'Mrs Anne Donnellan / R.B. pinxit 1752.' According to Mrs. Delany, this miniature was painted at Bath.* Courtesy the Ulster Museum.

Plate 54 I. Attributed to **W. Robertson,** *portrait of an unknown man, ivory, 2ins. This is a fine miniature with good fresh colours. The attribution is based on careful comparison with other works known to have been executed by him. His work is very close to that of his brother Charles.* Private Collection.

James Reilly or Reily (d.1780) was educated at the Blue-coat School, Oxmantown. He and G. Hamilton became apprentices to Samuel Dixon, and were employed by him to colour prints of birds and flowers. When Reilly finished his apprenticeship he set up as a miniaturist. He was very poor and was for a time a pupil at Robert West's Drawing School. After becoming a successful miniaturist he moved to a house in Grafton Street, where he lived until his death in 1780.

He married Jane Blackney, of Co. Meath, in 1760, when he was styled "a celebrated portrait painter". He attempted without success to paint historical pictures. A miniature of Robert Berry, signed: 'J. Reily / 1763', is in the Victoria and Albert Museum. Miniatures signed: 'I.R.' (fl. 1751-1774) have been variously attributed to J. Reilly and a little known artist, Jean Reubert. Attributions to this latter artist have been based on information given by Basil Long, who saw a miniature signed and dated: 'J. Reubert 1761'. As several miniatures I have seen during the past few years have had Irish connections (including one of Bishop Palliser, Archbishop of Cashel, signed: 'I.R. / 1759', and two others of his family), I am inclined to the view that these are probably painted by Reilly, especially with the connection between the pair of miniatures mentioned under G. Hamilton (Colour Plates 16E and G). A miniature signed and dated: 'Reily / 1758' is in the Alan Evans Collection at the Victoria and Albert Museum, and is very close in style to those signed: 'I.R.' (Plate 54D).

Plate 55A. H. Hone, A.R.A., called *Edward Gibbon (1737-94), ivory, 3ins. Signed and dated: 'HH (monogram) / 1785.' This miniature is thought to represent Gibbon, the notable historian. It is a good example of Hone's draughtsmanship, and bears a typical signature.* Courtesy J.B. Robertson.

Plate 55B. H. Pelham, *the Countess of Effingham, ivory, 3¹⁄₈ins. diameter. Signed and dated: 'HP 1779.' This enchanting miniature of the sitter in a riding habit, her horse beside her, is one of the few signed works by this artist. It probably represents Catherine (d.1791), wife of Thomas, 3rd Earl of Effingham, 9th Baron Howard.* Courtesy D.S. Lavender.

Plate 55C. C. Robertson, *portrait of an unknown lady, ivory, 2½ins., c.1800-10.* Courtesy Sotheby's.

Henry Pelham (1749-1806) was born on 14th February, 1749, in Boston, U.S.A., and was the son of Peter Pelham, a mezzotint engraver, and his second wife, Mary, widow of Richard Copley, of Irish descent. John Singleton Copley, R.A. (1737/8-1815) was her son by Richard Copley, and it is thought that Pelham may have studied art under him. He started his career as a civil engineer, but forsook this for art and left America in 1777 for England. Copley was already in London, and Pelham exhibited at the Royal Academy, 1777-1778, from 'Mr. Copley's Leicester Fields'. In 1778

Plate 55D. **H. Hone, A.R.A.**, *an unknown young man, ivory, 2⅞ins. Signed and dated: 'HH (monogram) / 1789.' This sensitive portrait of the sitter shows Hone's soft manner of painting with the eyes drawn round and clear. Courtesy Sotheby's.*

or 1779 Pelham went to Ireland, and became agent to Lord Lansdowne, but he evidently continued to paint and exhibited at the Society of Arts, Dublin, in 1780. He married a Miss Butler, daughter of William Butler of Castlecrine: the couple had no issue. Pelham was a portrait and miniature painter, engraver and map maker. He drew illustrations for J.H. Grose's *Antiquities of Ireland*.

He died on 20th September, 1806 as a result of a boating accident on the Kenmare River. He was a good artist and an accurate draughtsman. Many of the backgrounds of his miniatures are painted with a close oblique brush stroke, and the hair of his sitters is sometimes stippled. One of the most attractive miniatures I have seen by Pelham was then owned by D.S. Lavender, of South Molton Street, London, and represented the Countess of Effingham in riding habit; the head of her horse is beside her right shoulder. It is signed: 'HP 1779' (Plate 55B).

Horace Hone, A.R.A. (1754/6-1825) was born in Frith Street, London, and was the second son of N. Hone, by whom he was taught to paint. Horace entered the Royal Academy Schools, 19th October, 1770, when his date of birth was noted as "17 Feb 11th next", making his year of birth 1754, not 1756 as was supposed.

He exhibited at the Royal Academy, 1722-1822, and was elected A.R.A. in 1779. Hone went to Ireland in 1782, at the invitation of the Countess Temple, and soon had a successful practice in Dublin, living for some years in Dorset Street. In 1795 he became miniature painter to the Prince of Wales. After the Union of England and Ireland in 1800, Hone found his practice declining as many of his fashionable sitters moved to London; he decided to follow the trend, and settle in London in 1804. He took a house in Dover Street where he continued to practise with great success. He was friendly with Joseph Farington, who mentions him in his Diary. Hone had a distinguished clientele: a large number of his portraits are listed by Strickland. He was married and had a daughter, Mary Sophia Matilda, who died unmarried. He visited Bath in 1804. His sitters included Mrs. Siddons, of whom he painted two identical miniatures, both signed and dated:

Plate 55E. **H. Hone, A.R.A.**, *portrait of a lady, possibly Frances, wife of Arthur, 8th Earl of Fingall, ivory, 3½ins. Signed and dated: 'HH (monogram) / 1786.' This miniature shows the hair style dressed with pearls. Pearls also decorate the dress. Courtesy Sotheby's.*

Plate 55F. **H. Hone, A.R.A.,** *a fine miniature of Mrs. Ann Greenwood, enamel, 4ins. Signed and dated 'HH (monogram) 1807', and inscribed on the reverse: 'Ann. Mother of / Charles Greenwood Esq / Horace Hone A.R.A. Pinx / London 1807.' This portrait may have been taken from an earlier painting, as the upswept hair style and frilled cap tied under the chin were more popular in the latter part of the eighteenth century.* Courtesy Sotheby's.

'HH / 1784.' One of these is in the National Gallery, Dublin. Of these portraits one was engraved by Bartolozzi and published by H. Hone in Dublin in 1785. Hone's health deteriorated as early as 1807 and he became depressed. He died at his house in Dover Street on 24th May, 1825, and was buried in the grounds of St. George's Chapel, Bayswater Road.

He painted miniatures in watercolour and enamel, and copied some of the works of H. Douglas Hamilton (c.1739-1808). He also executed some engravings. His style of painting varies a great deal; it is usually elegant and his miniatures of ladies are attractive and well posed. He used the rich colouring and force of oil painting, and painted the eyelashes distinctly. The use of stippling can often be discerned in his modelling of features, and the sitter's eyes are frequently painted in dark colours. A fine enamel of Mrs. Prentice, wife of Thomas Prentice of Dublin, is fully inscribed on the reverse: 'Elizabeth / Wife of Thos. Prentice Esq / of Dublin / Horace Hone A.R.A. / Pinxt in London / 1807.' It is also signed on the front: 'HH 1807' (Plate 55G). His usual signature is a sloping 'HH', three sloping lines crossed by a horizontal one, often followed by a date. A self-portrait is in the National Portrait Gallery, and another in the National Gallery, Dublin. (Colour Plate 18B, Plates 55A, D, E and F.)

The brothers Adam and Frederick Buck are two well-known Irish miniaturists. **Adam Buck** (1759-1833) was the elder son of Jonathan Buck, a silversmith of Castle Street, Cork, where Adam was born. He took up art and practised for some years in Cork, painting miniatures and small portraits in watercolour. He is said to have worked in Dublin for a time. In 1795 he went to London and exhibited at the Royal Academy, British Institution, and Society of British Artists, 1795-1833, and at the Royal Hibernian Academy 1802. He was a versatile artist and taught portraiture and drawing. A number of his drawings of fancy figure subjects have been engraved, and a series of coloured aquatints were used to illustrate Sterne's *Sentimental Journey.*

Plate 55G. **H. Hone, A.R.A.,** *Mrs. Elizabeth Prentice, enamel, 4³/₈ins. Signed and dated: 'HH (monogram) 1807', on the front and inscribed on the reverse: 'Elizabeth / Wife of Thos. Prentice Esq / of Dublin / Horace Hone A.R.A. / Pinxt in London / 1807.' It is rare to find such a large enamel by Hone, and this is of exceptionally fine quality. Note the shorter hair swept into a bunch at the back, and the low-cut dress, popular at the time.* Present whereabouts unknown.

Buck wrote a work on *Paintings on Greek Vases,* published in 1811. He died at 15 Upper Seymour Street, London, in 1833, and was survived by his wife and two sons, Alfred and Sidney. The latter followed his father's profession as a miniaturist. Adam's technique varies a great deal, and not all of his works are of equal merit, although he was a far better artist than his brother. He tended to use a rather pink flesh colour, and some of his shading was executed with short and long strokes, with the occasional use of a scraper on the background and in the hair. One of the finest miniatures I have seen by him is of an Officer of the 50th Foot, which was Lot 188 in the Heckett Collection, sold at Sotheby's, 11th July, 1977. It is signed and dated: 'A Buck / 1802,' and is a much stronger and more vigorous painting than his usual style. Proof of its quality was the fact that it sold for the record price of £1,000, an unheard-of sum to be paid for a miniature by this artist (Plate 56C). He executed a number of full-length portraits in watercolour or wax crayons, usually on paper, and occasionally did decorative work on furniture. His signature varies; sometimes he signed: 'A. Buck' in cursive letters, sometimes in Roman lettering, and many works are signed and dated on the reverse. An attractive full-length watercolour of an unknown boy with a hoop painted against a landscape background is signed on the front: 'Adam Buck 1826.' It is painted in fresh colours, very much in the manner of a miniaturist in spite of its size -- 12½ inches (Colour Plate 19. See also Plate 56D).

Frederick Buck (1771-c.1839/40) was a son of Jonathan Buck, and younger brother of A. Buck. He was a pupil at the Dublin Society Schools in 1783, but later returned to Cork, where he practised for many years. He was a prolific artist, but the quality of his miniatures is rather indifferent. They are characterised by the use of a rather hot flesh colouring and the features tend to be sketchily drawn, and harsh. During the Peninsular War Cork was a busy port of embarkation, and Frederick was kept busy executing portraits for clients who wanted them done in a hurry. In order to keep pace with this demand he kept a supply of painted ivories, to which he added the heads and Regimental facings as required! The haste in which he so often painted is reflected in the miniatures which are frequently met with in the sale rooms. He sometimes painted cloudy sky backgrounds on the reverse of the ivory which he left white on the front. Examples of his work are in the Victoria and Albert Museum. (Plates 56A and F.)

It is impossible in one chapter to do more than mention a few artists of the Irish School, and I have tried to select some whose works may be found by the new collector. Further details can be found in books cited in the bibliography. As with English miniaturists, many of those who worked in Ireland were shadowy figures about whom we know very little. The following artists must be mentioned briefly before going on to other more important ones.

Plate 56A. **F. Buck,** *portrait of a young cadet, ivory, 2⅛ins., c.1800.* Private Collection.

Plate 56B. **J. Keenan,** *portrait of an unknown man, ivory, 2½ins. Signed on the reverse: 'Keenan delt / Reading.' Signed miniatures by this little-known artist are scarce.* Courtesy R. Bayne Powell.

Colour Plate 19.
Adam Buck, *an unknown boy standing in a landscape and holding a hoop and stick, watercolour on paper, 12½ins. Signed and dated: 'Adam Buck 1826.' This is a fine example of Buck's painting on a slightly larger scale.* Private Collection.

Plate 56C. **A. Buck,** *portrait of an unknown officer of the 50th Foot, ivory, 2¾ins. Signed in full and dated: 'ABuck / 1802.' This miniature must be one of the finest ever executed by Buck and realised the record price, for this artist, of £1,000 in 1977. Whereas his brother F. Buck dashed off his miniatures in a sketchy and amateurish manner, Adam drew with skill and imagination.* Private Collection.

Hugh Douglas Hamilton (c.1739-1808) was a well-known portrait painter of Dublin. He was not a miniaturist in the strict sense of the word, but a number of his portraits were executed on a small scale, and claims could be made for him to be included; however, he has always been classed with those who painted larger portraits.

Among the lesser known Irish artists is **Charles Byrne** (1757-1810) who was born in Dublin and became pupil, assistant and interpreter to S.T. Roche, who was deaf and dumb. Byrne had his own practice in Dublin, and worked for a short time in London. He became insane, and died in Dublin, c.1810. His self-portrait is in the National Gallery, Dublin.

Richard Bull (fl.1777-1809) is thought to have been born in Dublin. He painted miniatures and executed portraits in hair: some of his miniatures are quite attractive. He went to London in c.1790, and exhibited at the Royal Academy, 1794-1809. His miniatures are usually signed either: 'R. Bull,' followed by a date, or just: 'Bull.' A miniature of an officer signed on the front: 'R. Bull / 1786', was Lot 59 at Sotheby's on 10th November, 1969 (Plate 59C).

John Cooke (c.1778-1805) was another Dublin artist about whom very little is known. Having studied at the Dublin Society Schools, he had a practice in Dublin from c.1796, and exhibited with the Dublin Society of Artists, 1800-1803. Miniatures by him are scarce. He usually signed: 'J. Cooke,' or 'Cooke', followed by a date. Examples of his work are in the National Gallery, Dublin, and the Victoria and Albert Museum (Plate 59B).

Miss Elish Lamont or La Monte (c.1800-1870) was self-taught, and worked in Belfast where she was born. Little is known about her, and she seems to have obtained the patronage of many people of importance. She exhibited at the Royal Hibernian Academy, 1842-1857, and was working in Dublin from 1857-1859. She settled in England during the latter part of her life, and became friendly with Dickens and Ruskin. She and her sister, Frances, wrote and illustrated *Christmas Rhymes*, 1846. She died in Rochester, Kent, in 1870. Miniatures which I have seen by her show average

Plate 56D (left). **A. Buck,** *portrait of an unknown man, ivory, 2¾ins. Signed in full and dated: 'ABuck / 1802.' The draughtsmanship is good, and the character well expressed.* Courtesy Christie's.

Plate 56E (right). **S.T. Roch(e),** *miniature of an unknown Major General, ivory, 2¾ins. Signed and dated: 'Roch / 1801.' Note Plate 56G for comparison of shading the contours of the face.* Courtesy Sotheby's.

234

talent without being outstanding. A miniature of Laetitia and Dorothea Roberts, signed: 'Elish la Mont 1838', is in a private collection and is quite attractive (Plate 54E).

John Stordy (d.1799) was born in Ireland, and was the brother of Charles Stordy, a landscape painter. He worked as a watchmaker in Capel Street, Dublin and was awarded £4 11s. by the Dublin Society for making enamelled plates for watches. He exhibited at William Street, Dublin, 1769-1770, from Grafton Street, where he was a watchmaker and miniaturist. He came to London in c.1771 and exhibited at the Royal Academy, 1786-1788. His work did not receive much success, and he died in poverty in some obscure lodgings in Kensington Gravel Pits, in 1799. A miniature by him is in the Alan Evans Collection at the Victoria and Albert Museum (Colour Plate 15E).

Thomas Clement Thompson, R.H.A. (1778/80-1857) was another artist born in Belfast. He entered the Dublin Society Schools, in 1796 and practised as a miniature painter in Belfast and Dublin. He exhibited in Dublin 1801-1854, and was one of the original members of the Royal Hibernian Academy, from which he resigned in 1856, and was made an honorary member. He went to London in 1817, and also worked in Cheltenham, where he settled. He exhibited at the Royal Academy and British Institution, etc. from 1816-1857. Some of his works are reminiscent of the work of John Comerford. He gave up miniature painting sometime before 1809 and painted portraits in oils. Long records seeing a miniature by him signed: 'TT', followed by a date, and I have seen one signed: 'TT' which is attributable to him. A miniature of a man signed on the background: 'T. Thompson / 1802' is in the Victoria and Albert Museum. (Plate 57C.)

Two minor miniaturists, both of whom were in Dublin, are **John Newton** (fl.1824) and **George Lawrence** (c.1758-1802). Little is known about John Newton, who was working at 82 Dame Street, Dublin, in 1824. He may have been identical with, or related to, John Orr Newton (fl.1835-1843), a painter of subject pictures and domestic scenes. George Lawrence was one of three

B

A

C

D

E

F

G

brothers, all of whom were artists. The others were John (fl.1771-1793) and Robert (fl.1794-1820) who, like George, worked in Dublin and painted miniatures. George is the best known of the three. He became a pupil at the Dublin Society Schools in 1771, and worked under F.R. West and J. Mannin. He exhibited in Dublin from 1774 up to his death. Lawrence executed drawings and portraits in crayon as well as portraits in oils and miniatures. According to printed labels found on the reverse of his portraits, his charges for miniatures and crayons were from one guinea to two guineas. His works are usually signed: 'G. Lawrence' followed by a date, or: 'G.L.' followed by a date.

John Keenan (fl.1780-1819) is best known as a portrait painter, but also painted miniatures and groups of children. He was pupil and assistant to Robert Home, the portrait painter. Although he came from Dublin, he left for London in c.1790, and worked in various parts of the provinces, including Bath and Exeter. He had the patronage of the Royal family, and was appointed portrait painter to Queen Charlotte in 1809. In c.1817 Keenan returned to Ireland; nothing is known about him after 1819. He and his wife both taught drawing. He exhibited a miniature of Robert Southey in Ireland in 1817. Engraved portraits after Keenan are in the British Museum and in private collections. (Plate 56B.)

Andrew Dunn (fl.1800-1820) began his career as a pupil of F. West in the Dublin Society's Schools. He practised as a miniaturist for a time in Waterford and Kilkenny, and then went to London. In 1808 he returned to Ireland, evidently hoping to set up a practice there. He held an exhibition of his miniatures, which included portraits of many important sitters, at the Royal Dublin Society's House. He was evidently unsuccessful in establishing himself in Dublin, and went back to London, where he exhibited at the Royal Academy, 1809-1818, and at the Society of Artists, Dublin, 1809-1819. He painted portraits as well as miniatures. Works by Dunn are scarce; those I have seen are well painted and the draughtsmanship good. His signature is either: 'A. Dunn', followed by a date in cursive writing, or: 'A. Dunn', in capital letters.

Edward Hayes, R.H.A. (1797-1864) was an Irish artist born in Co. Tipperary. He studied at the Dublin Society's Schools under J.S. Alpenny.

Plate 57.
A. **H.B. Kirchhoffer, R.H.A.,** *Lieut. John Kent of the 50th Foot, ivory, 3ins. Signed and dated on the reverse: 'Cork 1806.' Miniatures by this artist are not easy to identify as his style changed, and he did not always sign his work. Courtesy Sotheby's.*
B. **J. Comerford,** *Colonel Bradshaw, ivory, 3½ins., painted c.1800-10. Courtesy Sotheby's.*
C. **T.C. Thompson, R.H.A.,** *Lieut. Fullerton, ivory, 3¼ins. Signed in full and dated: 'Painted by / T.Thompson / 1806.' Courtesy Sotheby's.*
D. **D.B. Murphy,** *after J. Comerford, John Harden (1772-1847) of Brathay Hall, Ambleside, enamel, 3½ins., 1804. Murphy and Harden were friends and toured the Lake District together. Harden is noted for his sketches of family life and furnishings. Courtesy A.S. Clay.*
E. **S.T. Roch(e),** *Hester Lynch Piozzi (Mrs. Thrale), née Salusbury (1741-1821), ivory, 5¼ins. Signed and dated: 'S.Roche / 1817.' This is one of the occasions when the artist signed his name with an 'e'. The sitter was a close friend of Dr. Johnson. Courtesy Miss D.M. Kleinfeldt.*
F. **J. Comerford,** *portrait of an unknown young man, ivory, 2⅝ins. Signed in full and dated: 'J Comerford / 1799.' Note the long lines in the shading on the face and background. Signed miniatures by Comerford are rare. Courtesy Sotheby's.*
G. **J. Comerford,** *portrait of an elderly lady, ivory, 4ins., c.1790. The sitter is wearing a lawn cap tied with ribbons. Comerford's way of shading the features with short lines can clearly be seen on this portrait which is a fine character study. Private Collection.*

Plate 58A. **Clementina Robertson (Mrs. John Siree),** *Miss Cynthia Harcourt, ivory, 5ins., c.1830. The sitter is wearing an elaborately trimmed large hat of the period with long floating ribbons attached.* Courtesy Dr. A.K. Brown.

Hayes painted miniatures, portraits, still-lifes and landscapes in oils, besides executing portraits in pencil and watercolour. He worked at Clonmel, Waterford and Kilkenny as well as in Dublin. His technique is difficult to discuss as works by him are scarce. A miniature on ivory of an unknown officer, in a private collection, is signed on the reverse: 'Painted by / Edw[d] Hayes / Dublin 1840.' The sitter is painted against a sunset background, wearing scarlet uniform trimmed with blue, and gold epaulettes. The hair is painted in soft brush strokes, and the face modelled with soft pinkish shading with faint touches of blue. There is a little stippling on the background (Plate 58D). He exhibited at the Royal Hibernian Academy from 1830 and became a member in 1861. Examples of his work are in the National Gallery, Dublin.

Denis Brownell Murphy (fl.1763-1842) was born in Dublin, where he became a pupil in the Dublin Society Schools, and was awarded a prize there in 1763. He painted miniatures and watercolours and exhibited at the Dublin Society of Artists in 1765 and 1768. Murphy went to London for a time and in 1792 advertised his return to Dublin. He failed to obtain a successful practice there and, in 1798, took his family to England working for a time in the North. Whilst in Dublin he evidently knew a young amateur artist called John Harden (1772-1847), who mentions staying with him in Lancaster in September, 1798. Details regarding this visit and a tour made round the Lake District by Harden and Murphy are given in *John Harden of Brathay Hall,* which includes as the frontispiece a reproduction of an enamel miniature of Harden by Murphy, after a miniature of John Comerford (Plate 57D). Harden recalls that when they returned to Lancaster they found that Mrs. Murphy and her two children, Anna and Camilla, had been obliged to move as a fire had destroyed all their belongings in their rooms. Murphy settled in London in 1803, and exhibited at the Royal Academy and British Institution, 1800-1827. Some of his miniatures were copies of large portraits which he executed on enamel. He was appointed Painter in Ordinary to

Princess Charlotte, and was commanded to copy Lely's 'Windsor Beauties'. A miniature on ivory of the poet William Wordsworth is in the National Gallery, Dublin. It is inscribed on the reverse in a later hand: 'W. Wordsworth / by / Murphy.'

Plate 58B (left). **Samuel Lover, R.H.A.** *(1797-1868), self-portrait of the artist, pencil on card, 6ins. This drawing was once in the Francis Wellesley Collection. A self-portrait as a younger man is in the National Gallery of Ireland.* Courtesy Christie's.
Plate 58C (right). **S. Lover,** *portrait of an unknown man in uniform, ivory, 6¼ins. Signed: 'S.Lover.' The sitter is wearing the ribbon and Order of the K.C.M.G., and was possibly a member of the Diplomatic Service or a Lord Lieutenant.* Private Collection.

James Heath Millington (1799-1872) was a native of Cork. He spent his early years in England, returning to Ireland in 1821, where he started a practice in Cork, but moved to Dublin in the same year where he exhibited an oil portrait. Millington entered the Royal Academy Schools on 1st April, 1826, where he won several prizes. He exhibited at the Royal Academy, British Institution and Society of British Artists, 1831-1870, and was for a short time Curator of the school of painting at the Royal Academy. He died at 3 Chepstow Place, Bayswater, on 11th August, 1872. Miniatures by him are scarce; he may have been influenced by W. Etty and A.E. Chalon. One of his most attractive miniatures, representing Lady Anne Hudson (d.1826), daughter of the 1st Marquess Townshend, and signed: 'J.H. Millington 1818', was sold at Christie's on 18th February, 1969. (Colour Plate 22D.)

Henry B. Kirchhoffer, R.H.A. (c.1781-1860) is thought to have been born in Dublin. He was the son of Francis Kirchhoffer and his wife, Sarah, née Brooke. The family were descended from a Swiss surgeon. Henry entered the Dublin Society Schools in 1797, and exhibited in Dublin in 1801. He lived for a time in Cork, but returned to Dublin in 1816. He was an original associate and, from 1826-1835, a member of the Royal Hibernian Academy. He painted miniatures, landscapes and figure subjects. He was one of the many Irish artists who went to London, where he exhibited at the Royal Academy from 1837-1843. He remained in London until his death on 20th March, 1860, at 71 St. John's Wood Terrace. He signed his work variously: 'H. Kirkhoffer', 'H. Kirchoffer', 'H. Kirchhoffer' and 'HK' (monogram). An example of his work is in the National Gallery, Dublin. (Plate 57A).

The miniaturist **George Place** (d.1805) is usually considered of the Irish School, as he was the son of a Dublin linen draper, and served his apprenticeship in art at the Dublin Society Schools in 1775. He practised for

a time in Dublin, but by 1791 was working in London and exhibited at the Royal Academy, from various London addresses. He worked for a time in York, and later obtained permission to go to India. He was allowed to take his wife with him, and established himself in Lucknow. He painted subject pictures in oils as well as miniatures. Few of his miniatures are signed, and this makes identification difficult. Characteristics are the way in which he tended to shade the faces of his sitters with a number of blue and grey strokes, particularly under the eyes. The features are modelled with long pinkish red brush strokes, and the sitter is often placed against a sky background which has long strokes in the shading. Examples of his work are in the Victoria and Albert Museum and private collections, including the Bernard Falk Collection, Brighton. (Plates 59E, F and G.)

Samuel Lover, R.H.A. (1797-1868) was another native of Dublin, whose father, S. Lover, was a lottery-office keeper and a money-changer. Samuel worked in his father's office from the age of thirteen to seventeen years, when he left, after a dispute with his father, and took up art. He had an aptitude for music and art, but his father disapproved of any pursuit which was not money-making. From 1814 he supported himself by teaching drawing, whilst studying at the same time. His early works were landscapes and marine subjects, but he was encouraged by John Comerford to take up miniature painting. He exhibited in Dublin between 1817 and 1823 and at the Royal Hibernian Academy, 1826-1835, becoming an Associate in 1828, and a Member in 1829. He resigned in 1836, and was made an Honorary Member. Lover took up residence in London in 1834, and exhibited at the Royal Academy, 1832-1862. From 1846-1848 he was in America, where he entertained audiences with his 'Irish Evenings'; these included his songs, recitations, and stories. He can justly be described as a painter, composer, author, and book illustrator. He married twice, firstly in 1827 a daughter of John Berrel, a Dublin architect. She died in 1847, and in 1852 he married a

Miss Wandby. He spent the last four years of his life in retirement in Jersey, where he died on 6th July, 1868; he was buried in Kensal Green Cemetery. Miniatures by Lover are scarce; those I have seen have varied in technique. He tended to use bright colours, some of the flesh tints being rather pink, and used a lot of gum with his paints. Some of his miniatures are reminiscent of the work of Sir W.C. Ross and S.J. Rochard. A well drawn self-portrait was sold at Christie's on 2nd April, 1968 (Plate 58B). The National Gallery, Dublin have another self-portrait signed on the reverse: 'Sam. Lover / R.H.A.' A miniature of an unknown man in uniform seated in a panelled room is in a private collection; it is signed on the front: 'S. Lover', in cursive lettering (Plate 58C).

Sampson Towgood Roch(e) (1759-1847) was born at Youghal, and was the son of Luke Roch, and grandson of James Roch of Glyn Castle, near Carrick-on-Suir. He was born deaf and dumb, but fortunately showed an aptitude for art and was sent to Dublin to study. He was not given any special training, but studied the work of artists who were practising in Dublin at that time. He is known to have been painting miniatures in Capel Street, Dublin, in 1784, but is supposed to have been in England before this time. Charles Byrne was, as has already been mentioned, pupil, assistant and interpreter to S.T. Roch(e). He may have been the Sampson Roche of the City of Cork who married, at Youghal, Miss Roch, only daughter of James Roch of Odel Lodge, Co. Waterford, on 7th June, 1788. He was living in Grafton Street, Dublin, from 1789-1792, and in the latter year he moved to Bath, where he had a flourishing practice, and was patronised by the Royal family. He exhibited at the Royal Academy in 1817 from Bath. He eventually retired and went to live with his relations at Woodbine Hill, Co. Waterford, where he died in February 1847. He was buried in the family burial ground at Ardmore. He seems to have been a prolific artist, and painted some good miniatures. A characteristic is the incipient smile or smirk which he often gave to his sitters. His work is precise and neat, and the contours of the face clearly delineated. He frequently painted the dress with opaque colours. His signature varied and he spelt Roch with and without an 'e'. His usual signature is: 'Roch', or 'Roche', with or without initials and followed by a date. Examples of his work are in the Victoria and Albert Museum, the Holbourne Museum, Bath and the National Gallery, Dublin. (Plates 56E and G and 57E.)

Charles Robertson (c.1760-1821) was the son of a Dublin jeweller, perhaps the Alexander Robertson who died at Ormond Quay in 1768. Charles began his artistic career by executing designs in hair, and when only about nine years of age he exhibited some of his work at the Dublin Society of Artists. His address was Essex Street, where he lived with his elder brother, Walter Robertson. Charles exhibited miniatures for the first time in 1775. He worked for most of his life in Dublin, but was in London from 1785-1792 and again in 1806. He exhibited at the Royal Academy, 1790-1810, and in Dublin until 1821. Besides painting miniatures, he executed small portraits in watercolour, and flower pieces. His wife was Christine, daughter of Thomas Jaffray. They had at least five children, Charles, Thomas, Christiana, Maria and Clementina. A miniature by Robertson of Charles, Thomas and Christiana was formerly in the de la Hey Collection. The fact that he does not seem ever to have signed his miniatures

Plate 59A. **W. Bate,** an unknown lady, ivory, 2¾ins. Signed and dated: 'W. Bate Pinxit / of 163 Strand London / Leeds Oct^r– / 1802.' Signed miniatures by Bate are scarce. **Private Collection.**

Plate 59B. **J. Cooke,** *an unknown officer, ivory, 2½ins. Signed in full and dated: 'J.Cooke / 180-' the last numeral being obliterated.* Courtesy Victoria and Albert Museum.

Plate 59C. **R. Bull,** *portrait of an unknown officer, ivory, 2⅛ins. Signed and dated: 'R. Bull / 1786.' Signed examples by this artist are scarce.* Courtesy Sotheby's.

has made identification difficult, and for many years his works were unattributed. More recently, his style has become recognised, and miniatures are more accurately attributed to him. His miniatures are of a very high quality; they are delicately painted with soft modelling, the face frequently being shaded with grey or blue. The hair is often painted in wiry strands rather than in masses. There is a great similarity between his miniatures and those of his brother, Walter. Examples of his work are in the Victoria and Albert Museum and the Fitzwilliam Museum, Cambridge, as well as in the National Gallery, Dublin, who have one by him of his brother, Walter. He died in Dublin on 10th November, 1821. (Colour Plate 17B and Plate 54G.)

Walter Robertson (d.1801) is thought to have been born in Dublin, the brother of Charles Robertson. Walter entered the Dublin Society Schools on 21st November, 1765. He soon established himself as a miniaturist in Dublin, where he had various addresses. Like his brother he also executed likenesses in hair as well as painting miniatures. He exhibited in Dublin from 1769-1777. He married twice: first in September, 1771, Margaret Bentley, of Stephen Street, Dublin, and secondly, in 1781, Eleanor Robertson, who survived him. In c.1784 he went to London where he practised for a few years. On returning to Dublin in 1792 he became bankrupt and his property which consisted of a number of houses was sold by auction. He had met Gilbert Stuart whilst in London, and in 1793 accompanied him to America, where he stayed for two years. He was known as 'Irish Robertson', to distinguish him from Archibald and Alexander Robertson, the two Scottish miniaturists working in America. Walter painted a portrait of George Washington which was engraved; the original miniature was lost in the great fire at Baltimore in 1904. He copied some of Gilbert Stuart's portraits, and painted Mrs. Washington and other distinguished people. In 1795 he left America for India, where he worked until his death at Futtehpore in 1801. His miniatures are all well drawn, and the heads skilfully modelled; characteristics of his work are the way he painted the backgrounds with fine cross-hatching, and modelled the contours of the face with long fine brush strokes, shaded with blue, particularly in the sockets of the eyes. His miniatures are elegant, and such items as starched frills, powdered hair and backgrounds are all painted with care. Many of his miniatures have a cloud and sky background, with fairly large areas at the base of the miniature shaded with a rusty brown. This colour is occasionally seen on miniatures by Charles Robertson, and accurate identification between the work of the two brothers is difficult. A miniature of him by his brother, Charles, is in the National Gallery, Dublin. (Colour Plate 26A and Plate 54 I.)

Clementina Robertson (Mrs. John Siree) (1795-c.1853/8) was born in Dublin, and was the daughter and pupil of Charles Robertson. She must not be confused with Mrs. James Robertson, née Christina Sanders, nor with her sister Christina, who is not known as an artist. Clementina exhibited in Dublin under her maiden name from 1812-1830, and up to 1832 as Mrs. Siree. She married John Siree, a medical student, in 1830. He never qualified, and died of fever five years after their marriage. She was evidently versatile, and besides painting miniatures taught music, languages and drawing. The exact date of her death has not been discovered. She painted portraits both on ivory and on paper. Those on paper are slightly reminiscent of the work of her father, but those on ivory are painted with much thicker paints mixed with gum, and although attractive, the draughtsmanship is not as good. Her flesh colours are rather pink, and the sitters are sometimes painted against a dark red curtain background (Plate 58A). The National Gallery, Dublin, has examples of her work.

The artist **John Comerford** (c.1770-1832) is usually considered to be one of the best Irish miniature painters. He was born in Kilkenny, and was the son of a flax-dresser. Nothing is known about his education, and he is said to have been self-taught and to have acquired his knowledge of art by copying pictures in Kilkenny Castle, Waterford and Carrick-on-Suir, etc. He began his career by painting portraits in oils in Kilkenny and other nearby places. He evidently visited Dublin sometime before 1793 and exhibited there in 1800, when his work was admired. He continued to exhibit in Dublin until 1813, and at the Royal Academy, 1804 and 1809. From 1802-c.1817 he lived at 27 Dame Street, after which he moved to 2 Leinster Street, where he remained for most of his life. His early work is thought to have been influenced by Gilbert Stuart (1755-1828), who was in Dublin for a short

Plate 59D. **W. Bate,** *after Beechey, George III (1738-1820), enamel, 3¾ins. This portrait of the King was copied by other artists. It is a good example of Bate's work on enamel.* Courtesy Sotheby's.

Plate 59E. **G. Place,** *portrait of an unknown man, ivory, 3½ins. c.1790-1800. Signed on the front: 'PLACE.'* Courtesy Christie's.

Plate 59F (left). **G. Place,** *miniature of an unknown girl, ivory, 2¾ins. This is an attractive miniature by Place painted in soft colours against a cloud and sky background.* Courtesy Sotheby's.

Plate 59G (right). **G. Place,** *miniature of an unknown man, ivory, 3ins., c.1790. Signed and inscribed on the reverse with instructions for framing: 'Mrs Selby / Blue Bowl & 2 Hair on / opal', with an indistinct signature: 'G / Pl . . ce / P . nt.' Compare the treatment of the wide open eyes with Plates 59D, E and F. The backgrounds are shaded with long strokes.* Private Collection.

time from 1789. Comerford met George Chinnery, who realised his talents and was probably responsible for encouraging him to enter paintings in the various exhibitions which he was promoting in Dublin. At about this time Comerford gave up painting portraits in oils and confined himself entirely to painting miniatures and executing small portraits in chalk or pencil. He was a member and Vice President of the Dublin Society of Artists in 1811. He strongly opposed the formation of an Academy as he thought all artists should learn from nature, as he had done. He must have had a flourishing practice, and was a prudent man who amassed a small fortune of at least £16,000. He is said to have been very popular among his friends. Little seems to be known about his private life except that he had an only daughter, to whom he left about £500 per annum. His pupils included John Doyle (1797-1868) and T.C. Thompson. He was a prolific artist, and a long list of his works, some of which were engraved, was published by Strickland in his *Dictionary of Irish Artists.* Some of his miniatures are reminiscent of oil paintings, as in the case of one of an elderly woman wearing a cap, which is a perfect character study; the features are drawn in great detail, with the parallel red and grey hatching which he so often used to model the face (Plate 57G). Some of his miniatures are painted with red brush strokes on the face and the dress is executed in loose brushwork almost as if it had been painted in haste (Colour Plate 18A). Not all his miniatures are signed, and some are painted in a much bolder style with a cloud and sky background. He sometimes signed in full on the front in cursive writing or on the reverse. Shortly before his death he moved to 28 Blessington Street, where he died of apoplexy on 25th January, 1832. A miniature of an unknown man was Lot 87 at Sotheby's on 10th November, 1969. It was signed on the front: 'J Comerford / 1799' in cursive writing (Plate 57F). Examples of his work are in the Victoria and Albert Museum and the National Gallery, Dublin.

The artist George Chinnery (1774-1852) has usually been included in the Irish School of painters, but he was in fact born in London and, because of his great ability, I am including him in a later chapter, together with the most notable miniaturists of the eighteenth century.

Chapter VIII

Miniature Painting in the Provinces

THE SOCIAL CHANGES brought about in the British way of life by a more affluent society which evolved during the eighteenth and early nineteenth centuries, has already been discussed in the previous chapter. We have seen how the Scottish and Irish schools of painting arose and the birth of numerous drawing schools and academies, including one of the most important, the Royal Academy, London.

This increase in wealth meant that families, who in the past had lived in comparatively modest accommodation, suddenly discovered that they could afford to purchase or build larger mansions. Such houses had to be furnished adequately and, as a result, their owners turned their attention to articles of artistic merit and set about obtaining them. It was a period of 'keeping up with the Jones's', and each one vied with another in an attempt to produce something bigger and better to show off to their friends!

Large portraits and paintings were needed to grace the walls and, in addition, such decorative items as porcelain figures and china of every shape and form were purchased by those who could afford them. Photography had not yet been invented so what could be more natural than that miniatures, which in the past had been mainly commissioned by the nobility, now became within the reach of the growing middle classes?

The demand for these delightful small portraits was just what was needed to give fresh impetus to the art, and miniaturists had to work hard to keep pace with the demand. As was to be expected their ability varied considerably and although many of them were excellent, others were not so skilled.

These artists moved freely about the country, working for short spells in cities or small country towns where they found patrons. Many miniaturists spent the greater part of their lives moving from place to place, whilst others settled in certain towns. They all made their contribution to the history of miniature painting and for this reason good and bad alike all merit our attention. It would be impossible to mention all the towns in which they worked, and I have selected some of the more important centres for discussion in this chapter. Due, no doubt, to the fact that so many people went there to 'take the waters' Bath became one of the most popular places in England for miniaturists to stay. Many wealthy families spent a season there and had time on their hands which could pleasantly be taken up by sitting for their portraits. 'Beau Nash,' or, to give him his correct name, Richard Nash (1674-1762) was the great leader of fashion at Bath, and a miniature of him, painted by Nathaniel Hone in 1750, is in the Holburne of Menstrie Museum, Bath. There is no evidence that Hone ever went to Bath and it is generally

Plate 60A. **C. Jagger,** an unknown officer, ivory, 2¾ins. Signed: 'Jagger'. This is a good miniature by this artist and unlike most of his works does not have the usual dotted and 'honeycomb' shading in the background. Courtesy Sotheby's.

Plate 60B (left). **C. Jagger**, *Mrs. Hand, ivory, 2¾ins., c.1800. Signed: 'Jagger'. The sitter was the wife of the Rev. Hand in Plate 60C.* Courtesy Sotheby's.

Plate 60C (right). **C. Jagger**, *the Rev. Hand, ivory, 2¾ins. Signed: 'Jagger'. Both this miniature and Plate 60B have the dotted and 'honeycomb' shading on the background that is so often seen on Jagger's work.* Courtesy Sotheby's.

believed that the portrait was probably painted in London.

There was never a distinct School of Bath miniaturists, but a number of them worked there for at least some part, if not all, of their careers. Many of these artists are represented in the Holburne of Menstrie Museum, which has a large and comprehensive collection of miniatures, many of them representing people of local importance such as Sir Thomas William Holburne (1793-1874), who formed the collection. This was left unconditionally to his sister, Miss Mary Anne Barbara Holburne, who founded the Museum as a "nucleus for the establishment of a Museum of Fine Art for the Inhabitants of Bath". The Museum opened in 1916, and is one of the most charming provincial museums in Britain.

The miniature of Sir Thomas Holburne was painted by an artist called **Charles Jagger** (c.1770-1827) who worked almost exclusively in Bath. The miniature was painted when the sitter was thirty-four years of age, and in the last year of the artist's life. According to a note on the reverse it cost thirty guineas. Little is known about Jagger who, it is thought, may have been a pupil of Thomas Hargreaves in Liverpool, but there is no similarity in the artists' styles. Jagger had addresses in Green Street and Milsom Street, Bath. He was a good artist who drew with accuracy. The faces of his sitters are usually finely modelled. He used both hatching and stippling in the backgrounds which sometimes gave the effect of a honeycomb technique. Many of his miniatures have a cloud and sky background. He signed with a scratched or written signature, which was often placed along the edge of the miniature, e.g.: 'Jagger pinxt', or: 'Jagger'. Examples of his work often appear in the sale rooms and are well worth acquiring. Some engravings after Jagger are in the British Museum and the Holburne Museum has at least three miniatures by him. (Plates 60A, B, C and D.)

Among the more important miniaturists who worked in Bath were the brothers **Abraham and Joseph Daniel**, both of whom were the sons of Nochaniah Daniel of Bridgwater, Somerset. Another brother, Phineas, was a watchmaker and silversmith. All three brothers are reputed to have received

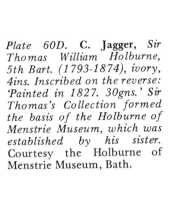

Plate 60D. **C. Jagger,** *Sir Thomas William Holburne, 5th Bart. (1793-1874), ivory, 4ins. Inscribed on the reverse: 'Painted in 1827. 30gns.' Sir Thomas's Collection formed the basis of the Holburne of Menstrie Museum, which was established by his sister. Courtesy the Holburne of Menstrie Museum, Bath.*

instruction from their mother, who was said to have been "a very ingenious woman". In spite of continued research it is still difficult to distinguish between the two artists' work with any degree of certainty. For many years they were all catalogued as 'Daniel of Bath', and in many ways this is still probably the safest description. Recently more specific attributions have been made and miniatures ascribed to either Abraham or Joseph, but I do not personally feel sufficiently confident over these attributions. To complicate matters further Abraham and Joseph seem to have set up in opposition, and both advertised in local papers as "Mr. Daniel of Bath". Miniatures attributed to 'Daniel of Bath' have many unmistakable characteristics which are easily recognised once a number of them have been studied. There is an overall similarity in style, but very different changes in technique. These are not easy to describe, and the whole question is most confusing. The problem was ventilated in the *Jewish Historical Society of England,* Vol. XVIII, 1958, when a signed drawing of Rabbi Moses Ephraim of Plymouth, from the collection of Dr. Cecil Roth, was illustrated. It was inscribed: 'A Daniel Delt.', and below: 'The very Learned Rabbi & Philosopher / Moses Ephraim.' A miniature of an unknown man in the collection of Mr. E. Hawtin is signed on the reverse: 'Daniel / Plymouth' (Plate 61A), which we assume refers to Abraham. A miniature of an unknown man (Plate 61F), presumably by Abraham, signed on the reverse: 'Daniel fec^t / may 27 / Plymouth 1794', was sold at Sotheby's in 1971. The inscription was only discovered later when the miniature was opened up (Figure 26). Whilst I was writing this chapter I was shown the first signed miniature by Joseph Daniel that is known. It is a half-length portrait against a sea-scape background, and reputed to represent William Pitt the Younger. The miniature is painted in brownish tones and is signed 'JD' (Plate 61D).

Broadly speaking, miniatures painted by 'Daniel' are in many cases painted with predominantly sepia tones and the sitters' features are given an almost

Plate 60E. **T. Peat,** *portrait of an unknown officer, ivory, 2⅝ins., c.1790-1800. Signed: 'Peat'. This is a typical example of works by this minor miniaturist. Courtesy Sotheby's.*

247

wax-like appearance. Little attention is given to the background, which is frequently greyish-buff in colour. The highlights and shadows on the sitters' faces are emphasised with unusual breadth. The eyes are large, and wide open, with a distinct dot of thick opaque white on the pupil. The eyebrows, nostrils and lips are all clearly delineated and there are distinct lines drawn over the upper eyelid. The hair is painted in soft masses rather than in distinct lines, and the lips picked out in a bright red. The upper lip is often slightly bowed.

Many of these miniatures give the impression of oil paintings due to the large amount of gum mixed with the paint. Occasionally one sees miniatures with all these characteristics, but painted against a cloud and sky background and in a much more cheerful blend of tones, as in the case of Plate 61C.

A point that has been overlooked is that Samuel Hart (fl.c.1785-1820) was apprenticed to Abraham Daniel to study miniature painting, and it may be that some of our so-called 'Daniel' miniatures are the work of his hand. It is to be hoped that in time this problem will be resolved, but I feel that as things stand more evidence is required before a final decision can be made on the question of which miniatures should (with the exception of signed ones) be attributed to either Abraham or Joseph. (Colour Plates 16A and 20B.)

Abraham Daniel (d.1806) was, as has already been mentioned, one of three brothers, whose family came from Bridgwater, Somerset. They are said to have "received instruction from their mother". Whether this was a basic education, or one that included painting, is not clear. Abraham seems to have divided his time between Bath and Plymouth, where his two sisters lived. He is thought to have had a larger practice in Plymouth, where he died on 11th March, 1806. In his will, which was taken down on his death-bed by Samuel Hart, he left legacies to his mistress and two illegitimate sons, as well as £20 to the charity of the Plymouth Synagogue. The residue of the estate which was valued at £1,500 went to his two sisters, Rachel Nathan and Rebecca Almon.

Abraham worked as an engraver, jeweller and miniaturist, but nothing is known about his engraving or jewellery. It is interesting that so often the art of miniature painter was allied to that of the jeweller, and in this case all

Plate 60F. **W.A. Hobday,** *miniature of an unknown officer, ivory, 2⅞ins., c.1800-10.* Courtesy Sotheby's.

Plate 60G. **W.A. Hobday,** *portrait of an unknown man, ivory, 2¾ins., c.1800. Miniatures by Hobday are not always identifiable and few are signed. This shows his characteristic way of painting the hair in sweeping strokes and emphasising the eyes.* Courtesy Sotheby's.

three brothers were jewellers, which was possibly an inherited talent.

We have no means of knowing which of the brothers was responsible for the advertisement in *The Bath Chronicle* for 11th January, 1787:

> "Miniature painting No 3 Abbey Green. Mr. Daniel begs leave to inform the Nobility and Gentry, that he is return'd to Bath for the season. Those who may not be acquainted with his terms etc. are respectfully informed that he will by no means accept payment for a Picture which is not esteemed a striking likeness, and an approved Painting."

This advertisement appeared again on 12th April of the same year. In September 1799 two advertisements were published, from which it would appear that both brothers were working in Bath at the same time. On 5th September: "Mr. Daniel Miniature Painter Begs to inform his Friends and the Public that he is returned to No 8 Alfred Street, Bath", and on 26th September, 1799: "Mr. Daniel Miniature Painter Begs leave to inform his Friends and the Public, that he is returned to No. 33 Milsom- street, Bath".

Joseph Daniel (c.1760-1803) was said to be aged forty-three when he died on 29th August, 1803, so must have been born c.1760. Apart from the fact that all three brothers are supposed to have been taught by their mother we know nothing of his education. Joseph is known to have worked in Bristol, Bath and London and was a jeweller, engraver and miniaturist, besides working in crayons and oils and executing pictures in hair. He was practising in Bristol from 1777 onwards, but made Bath his centre from c.1786, where his name can be traced through the Rate Books and Directories. In 1783 he exhibited a miniature of a 'Jew Rabbi', at the Society of Artists, from Clare Street, Bristol, and was "at Mr. Baker's, Clare Street" in 1785. In 1799 he exhibited five miniature portraits at the Royal Academy, from 17 New Bond Street, London.

From c.1796 Joseph seems to have suffered from ill-health, and on 11th April of that year there was an announcement in *The Bath Chronicle*, to the effect that he had recovered from "a most dangerous illness". Hopes were expressed that "his usual close application to painting will not again impair his health. . . . His renovated health will, it is hoped, add new charm to his admirable pictures".

Although he evidently continued to paint, his health was not good, and in 1802 he was obliged to put an announcement in the paper informing the public that he was still working in spite of rumours to the contrary. How long he was able to continue is not clear but he died on 29th August, 1803, leaving a widow and one son, John Daniel, who were living in Exeter in 1806. He also left a number of illegitimate children at Bristol. According to his obituary in *Felix Farley's Bristol Journal*, 3rd September, 1803, "he died after a painful and lingering illness, which he bore with the utmost fortitude for upwards of 13 months . . ."

Sir Thomas Lawrence, whose family settled in Bath in 1780, is known to have acquired his early knowledge of art in Bristol and Bath, where the budding painter was able to obtain introductions to the many influential members of London society who stayed there. The late Basil Long believed that Lawrence was a pupil of, or at least influenced by the work of, Joseph Daniel, and in 1935 wrote to the Director of the Bath Art Gallery on the subject. When Long published *British Miniaturists* in 1929 he was unaware

Plate 61A. **A. Daniel,** *an unknown man, ivory, 1⅜ins. Signed on the reverse: 'Daniel / Plymouth.' This can be attributed to Abraham with confidence, as he was the brother known to have worked in Plymouth. Courtesy E. Hawtin.*

Plate 61B. **A. or J. Daniel,** *portrait of an unknown woman, ivory, 2½ins. Courtesy Sotheby's.*

Plate 61C. **A. or J. Daniel,** *miniature of a young girl, ivory, 3ins. Painted against a deep blue and grey cloud and sky background. The whole painting is in brighter colours than usual. The flesh colours are very pink, the lips red, and she wears a deep blue sash to her dress.* Private Collection.

that Joseph and Abraham had any connection. We, at least, know some of the biographical details, but up to the present cannot feel on sure ground regarding attributions. The miniature reputed to be of William Pitt the Younger bears an inscription on the reverse, written by G. Blakie Morgan, who traced the miniature back to his father's death in 1877 when it was given to his mother; it had always been known in the family as 'Pitt the Statesman', and was sold by Sotheby's in Zurich on 15th November, 1977, for £1,200 (Plate 61D).

Works attributed to 'Daniel' are in the Victoria and Albert Museum, the Holburne Museum, Bath, and the Victoria Art Gallery, Bath, as well as in many private collections. They are of a very high quality, and much sought after by collectors. (Plates 61A-F and 62.)

Samuel Collins (1735?-1768) was born in Bristol and was the son of a clergyman. Nothing is known about his early education but he was later trained as an attorney, and forsook this profession for art. By the middle of the eighteenth century he had succeeded in establishing himself in a flourishing practice in Bath. He painted miniatures in watercolour and enamel and, according to Joseph Nollekens, was "a very indifferent miniature painter and what was worse, a man of gay and expensive habits". This assessment is not entirely fair as his miniatures, which are usually painted on a small scale, are quite well painted and typical of the minor artists who were his contemporaries.

Plate 61D. **J. Daniel,** *William Pitt the Younger (1759-1806), ivory, 5⅛ins., c.1800. Signed with initials: 'JD' on the front. This is a very important miniature both historically and artistically. It is the only signed work by J. Daniel at present known, painted in sepia tones which had hitherto been associated with works by Abraham. It is still not possible to make accurate attributions to the two brothers.* Courtesy Sotheby's.

Plate 61E. Attributed to **A. Daniel,** *portrait of a young woman called Grace Franklyn, ivory, 2¾ins.* Courtesy Sotheby's.

His extravagance got him into debt, and in 1762 he fled to Ireland to avoid his creditors and set up a good practice in Dublin. Ozias Humphry was his pupil, and after his master's departure succeeded to his practice in Bath.

There has always been some difficulty in attributing miniatures to Collins with any degree of certainty, as he shared the same initials as Samuel Cotes. Some of Collins' miniatures are signed in full and dated, the signature being written in neat separate letters. When he signed: 'S.C.' the letters are smooth unlike those of Cotes whose initials: 'S.C.' are made up of several short strokes, and this characteristic is now usually recognised by collectors.

Collins remained in Ireland, and died at his house in Summer Hill, Dublin, in October, 1768. A good example of his work signed: 'Collins / 1764' is in the collection of Brigadier and Mrs. G. Viner. The miniature, which is well painted, is of an unknown man; it is softly painted against a buff background (Plate 63D).

Although Ozias Humphry began his artistic career in the provinces his work is of such importance that it will be dealt with in a later chapter.

J. Lacon (fl.1740-1760) is a minor artist about whom there is very little information. As far as I know he only worked in Bath, where he owned a puppet show which was very popular. He is recorded as having copied one of Rembrandt's self-portraits in 1753. Miniatures by Lacon are scarce and, unless they are signed, may well pass unrecognised. Two examples are in the Victoria and Albert Museum. One of Miss Sarah Verney, painted on ivory, is signed and dated: 'J. Lacon / 1756.' His work is slightly reminiscent of the Lens School. (Colour Plate 15C.)

Lady Sarah Malden, Countess of Essex (c.1761-1838) was an amateur artist who worked in Bath for a short time from c.1788. She was the daughter of Henry Bazett of St. Helena. She married as her first husband Edward Stephenson and, secondly, on 6th June, 1786, Viscount Malden, who was created 5th Earl of Essex in 1799. She painted miniatures, many of which were copies of pictures, and executed enamels. An example of her work after Paul Veronese is in a private collection (Plate 63A), and one of Frances, Countess of Somerset, after an earlier portrait, was sold at Sotheby's on 29th November, 1976 (Plate 63E). Her works are signed: 'SM', 'S. Ex' and 'S. Essex.' She died on 16th January, 1838, at Hill Street, Berkeley Square, London, after a long separation from her husband. Some of her miniatures are very amateurish. Two examples of her work are in the National Gallery, Dublin.

J. Hewett (fl.1795) was apparently a miniature painter and drawing master of Cock Lane, Bath. From 17th December, 1795, his address is given as Bridge Street, Bath. I have not been able to trace any further information regarding his work.

Plate 61F (left). **A. Daniel,** *portrait of an unknown man, ivory, 2½ins. Signed and dated on the reverse: 'Daniel fec^t / may 27 / Plymouth 1794' (see Figure 26). As Abraham was the brother who is known to have worked in Plymouth, this can be attributed with certainty to him, and is of great importance. Present whereabouts unknown.*

Figure 26. Daniel's signature on the reverse of Plate 61F.

Plate 61G. Attributed to A. Daniel, a miniature of an unknown lady, ivory, 2¾ins. The treatment of the eyes and eyebrows is very similar to the style used in Plate 61F. Courtesy Victoria and Albert Museum.

W. Hay (fl.1776-1797) painted portraits, landscapes and miniatures. Nothing is known about his education and he was evidently one of the many painters who moved about from place to place as he is known to have worked in London, Plymouth (1787) and Bath (1790). He exhibited at the Royal Academy, 1776-1797, from various addresses, the majority of which were in London. Long records seeing a miniature of an officer c.1792, signed in cursive script: 'W. Hay' on the sky background. He noted that although the uniform was not very well painted the head and general effect was good. The face and hair were softly painted and there were definite touches of deeper colour at the nostrils and between the lips. The flesh colour on the face was rather brick-red. Two engravings of portraits after W. Hay are in the British Museum.

Another miniaturist who worked at Bath, and about whom there is only rather confused information, is **T. (Thomas?) Langdon** (fl.1785-1822). T. Langdon exhibited miniatures at the Royal Academy from 1785-1802, from various London addresses, and may have been the same person as the Thomas Langdon, an engraver, who entered the Royal Academy Schools on 10th March, 1783, aged fourteen years "last Feby". T. Langdon the miniaturist had addresses in Bath from 1809-1822, including 37 Milsom Street where another artist, Isaac Langdon, is recorded as living in 1830. The wife of T. Langdon of Bath taught painting on glass, velvet, etc. Four miniatures of the Burgoyne family by T. Langdon were sold at Christie's on 9th July, 1968; they included two delightful miniatures of the Misses Burgoyne as children (Plates 64A, B and C). An identical miniature of one of the girls painted by Andrew Plimer was sold in London a few years ago.

Thomas Redmond (c.1745-1785) was the son of a clergyman at Brecon. The exact year of his birth is uncertain. He was apprenticed to a house painter at Bristol but forsook this trade for art and went to London where he studied at the St. Martin's Lane Academy. He exhibited at the Society of Artists and the Free Society of Artists, 1762-1771, and at the Royal Academy, 1775-1783, from various addresses including London, Brecknock, South Wales and, from 1769 onwards, Bath, where he seems to have settled. The name of his wife is unknown, but when he died in Bath, 1785, he was survived by three sons. Redmond painted pictures, miniatures and small crayon portraits. He signed his miniatures: 'T R', or in full: 'T. Redmond', followed by a date on a lower line. The signatures sometimes look more like a JR, and this has caused confusion. Some of his miniatures are reminiscent of the early works of N. Hone. Others are more naïve, and the features drawn with long brush strokes. He often used a yellowish brown shading on the face, and signed his initials in a light colour on a dark spot of the

Colour Plate 20.
A top left. **William Barclay, Junior,** *an unknown lady, ivory, 2½ins. Signed on the front: 'Barclay.' This is a good example of a little-known artist.*
B top right. **A. or J. Daniel,** *an unknown man, ivory, 3ins.*
C centre. **Charles Hayter,** *Queen Adelaide (1792-1849), Queen of William IV, ivory, 3ins. Signed on the front: 'C.Hayter.' Portraits of Queen Adelaide are scarce.*
D bottom left. **Charles Robertson,** *an unknown infantry officer, ivory, 2½ins., c.1798.*
E bottom right. **Archibald Skirving,** *an unknown lady, ivory, 3ins. Signed: 'Skirving / 1780.' This is an important miniature as it is the first fully signed example by Skirving to be discovered.*
Courtesy Victoria and Albert Museum, Alan Evans Collection

background. Most of his backgrounds are shaded with short strokes, but occasionally he used stippling. A good miniature of an unknown naval officer is in the collection of R. Bayne Powell, and is signed 'T. Redmond / 1761' (Plate 64D). Examples of his work are in the Victoria and Albert Museum, and the Holburne Museum, Bath (Plate 64F).

Thomas Peat (fl.1791-1831) is thought to have started his artistic career in London, where he exhibited at the Royal Academy from 1791-1805. Nothing is known about his early life or education, nor do we know anything about his family. He was working in Bath (1819-1822), Leamington (1828), and Bristol (1830-1831), after which nothing more is known about him. He painted miniatures in watercolour and enamel and is said to have painted portraits in oils and to have imitated Reynolds. He seems to have had a distinguished clientele, and even inspired someone to write a poem about his skill, part of which reads:

> In striking likenesses, those talents rare,
> With the ingenious Peat few can compare;
> Whose finish'd portraits, and whose rising fame,
> Thy country's gratitude may justly claim.

His work can best be described as 'good average', but hardly merits the eloquence expressed by the poet! Those which I have seen are neatly painted but uninspiring. One of an officer signed: 'Peat' was Lot 83 at Sotheby's on 29th March, 1976. The painting was smooth, rather in the manner of an enamellist (Plate 60E). The British Museum has an engraving after Peat, and examples of his work are in the Victoria and Albert Museum, the Holburne Museum, Bath, The Louvre, and the Cognacq-Jay Museum, Paris. (Colour Plate 22B).

Albin Roberts Burt (1783-1842) was the son of Harry Burt and his wife, Mary, née Roberts. His brother, Henry F. Burt (d.1807) was Secretary to Lord Nelson and their mother was intimate with Emma Hamilton. Albin is thought to have been born in Wales. He began his career as an engraver and was a pupil of Robert Threw and Benjamin Smith. He exhibited at the Royal Academy in 1807 and 1830. Burt executed shell and stone cameos, portraits, miniatures and engraved and stippled a portrait after George Chinnery. In 1810 he married Sarah Jones, by whom he had eight children. He was one of the artists who moved about the country, working in Bath and Worcester (1812), Birmingham and Warwick (1814), Oxford (1817), London at intervals (from 1805-1830), Chester (c.1810-1830), Reading (1832) and Southampton (1834). He died in Reading on 1st March, 1842.

The majority of his miniatures seem to have been in profile, and indeed he advertised that he had invented a "New machine by which the most accurate likenesses can be taken . . ." He charged half a guinea for coloured profiles, and more finished ones cost one guinea. His fee for miniatures was three guineas upwards, and from five to ten guineas for full length portraits. His profile miniatures are not unlike those by T. Hamlet, who also worked in Bath. Burt usually signed his work: 'AR Burt', followed by a date, the two initial letters being conjoined. Most of them are framed in the popular black papier mâché frames which were suspended from an acorn and ring. Instead of an acorn, Burt had his name embossed on the metal (Plate 63 I).

T. Hamlet (fl.1779-1815) is best known as a silhouettist but also executed miniatures on ivory. A miniature, of no great merit, of a Mrs. Smith, bearing Hamlet's trade label on the reverse, was sold at Sotheby's on 11th November, 1968. The Holburne Museum, Bath, has a fine silhouette on glass by Hamlet of Captain Francis Holburne (1788-1814), the elder brother of Sir Thomas William Holburne. Examples of his work are in various private collections and in the Victoria and Albert Museum.

Miss Charlotte Jones (1768-1847) was the daughter of Thomas Jones of Cley, Norfolk. She studied under Richard Cosway, and although she probably spent the greater part of her time in London she moved about the country and was in Manchester in 1788, and Bath (6th December, 1792) when she was living in Grove Street. She exhibited at the Royal Academy, 1801-1823. In c.1808 she became miniature painter to H.R.H. Princess Charlotte of Wales. Miss Jones executed profile portraits in crayon as well as miniatures on ivory and enamel. Her works lack assurance and are not of outstanding merit, although some are quite attractive. Her self-portrait, which is signed in full and dated 1805 on the reverse (Plate 66B), is in the Holburne Museum, Bath, and a fine miniature — probably one of her best — of Dorothy Laurence, signed: 'CJ', is in the Smithsonian Institution, Washington (Plate 63H). In 1838 she received a bequest from Mrs. Cosway. Towards the end of her life she became partially blind, and died in Upper Gloucester Place, London, on 21st September, 1847. Examples of her work are at Windsor Castle.

James Scovell or Scovill (fl.1815-1840) was the son of an umbrella manufacturer of Wade's Passage, Bath. He is said to have had a natural aptitude for painting and to have been self-taught. It is traditionally supposed that he succeeded to C. Jagger's practice on his death in 1827. In c.1839 he was living at Paragon Buildings, Bath. Works by him are scarce and

Plate 63B. **J. Lacon**, *portrait of a young girl, ivory, 1¾ins. Signed and dated: 'JL / 1754.'* Courtesy Sotheby's.

Plate 63C. **Miss S. Smith**, *Mrs. Mellows, ivory, 1¼ins. Signed and dated: 'SS / 1767.' This is typical of works by minor artists of this period.* Courtesy Christie's.

Plate 63D. **S. Collins**, *portrait of an unknown man, ivory, 1⅜ins. Signed in full and dated: 'Collins / 1764.'* Courtesy of Brigadier and Mrs. G. Viner.

Plate 63E. **Lady Sarah Malden, Countess of Essex**, *Frances, Countess of Somerset, in court dress, after an earlier portrait in the collection of the Duke of Bedford, enamel, 3¼ins. Signed on the reverse: 'S. Essex / pinxt / 1813.'* Courtesy Sotheby's.

the first examples I saw were a pair of miniatures of Lieutenant Colonel and Mrs. Booth, which were Lot 58 at Christie's on 3rd February, 1970. Both miniatures were inscribed on the reverse and dated 1822. The Colonel is wearing the uniform of the Royal Engineers. The two miniatures were both well painted and the background on Colonel Booth's portrait is reminiscent of the cross hatching used by Jagger. The features were well modelled and show character (Plates 66D and E). Scovell is undoubtedly one of the many artists whose work is unrecognised because it is scarce and possibly not always signed.

Miss Sophia Smith (fl.1760-1767) is an artist about whom there has been a certain amount of confusion, having been erroneously identified with another Miss Smith, daughter of J.R. Smith. Sophia Smith is believed to have worked only in Bath. She exhibited at the Society of Artists in 1766 and 1767 (as an honorary exhibitor). She painted miniatures, flowers and insects. Miniatures attributed to her and signed: 'SS' are recorded between 1760-1767. A pair of miniatures of Mr. and Mrs. Mellows, signed and dated: 'SS / 1767', were sold at Christie's on 3rd February, 1970. They were quite well painted without being of outstanding merit (Plate 63C).

Plate 63F. **S. Collins,** *an attractive miniature of a child aged six, ivory, 1¾ins. Signed 'S.C. / 1757.' With the digit 6 inscribed over the child's shoulder. This miniature realised £250 in 1971. Courtesy Sotheby's.*

Colour Plate 21.
A. **Adam Buck,** *an unknown man, ivory, 2¾ins. Signed and dated: 'ABuck / 1799.'*
B. **John Wright,** *Louisa Ann Wright aged eleven, ivory, 2½ins. Signed and dated on the reverse: '1780.'*
C. **W.K. Burton,** *Lieut. Frederick Charles White, 16th Regiment of Foot, ivory, 2ins. Signed: 'WK.'*
D. **Joseph Lee,** *an unknown officer of the 5th Regiment of Foot, ivory, 2½ins. Signed on the reverse, with the address: '135 Upper Street / Islington.'*
E. **William Armfield Hobday,** *an unknown man, ivory, 2¾ins. Signed in full on the reverse with the address: 'Charles Street.' Signed miniatures by Hobday are rare.*

Courtesy Brigadier and Mrs. G. Viner

*Plate 63G. **T. Hamlet**, Mrs. Smith, watercolour on paper, 2¾ins. The artist's trade label is on the reverse. This is typical of a miniature painted by an artist whose main work was executing silhouettes. Courtesy Sotheby's.*

A miniature painted by a hitherto unrecorded artist, **R. (Robert?) Hancock** (fl. 1831), was sold at Sotheby's on 24th March, 1969. It was signed and inscribed on the reverse and dated: '1831. Bristol'. He may have been the Robert Hancock who exhibited portraits at the Royal Academy in 1805, from Pall Mall. The miniature was well painted and expressive; there was a lot of stippling on the background and in a lesser degree, on the face (Plate 66A). A miniature by Robert Hancock was illustrated by the Hon. D. O'Brien, *Miniatures in the XVIIIth & XIXth Centuries*, Plate 47, Figure 3; this is very much in the same style as that of the man already discussed. According to O'Brien, Hancock was living in Bristol in 1830-31 and was probably the son of Robert Hancock (1730-1817), an engraver of Bristol, who also drew small crayon portraits.

Charles Ford (1801-1870) was a native of Bath, and one of its leading miniaturists. Nothing is known about his parentage but he is supposed to have been related to Charles Ford, an ironmonger of Bath. Ford is said to have been a pupil and friend of Sir Thomas Lawrence. His friends considered that he would have obtained greater recognition had he moved to London, but he was apparently of a shy disposition and preferred to remain in the provinces. He was a very good artist and his portraits are well drawn and expressive. A fine miniature of Sir William Herschel, Bart., by Ford, after a painting by L. Abbot, is in the Holburne Museum, Bath. It is on paper and dated: '1860' (Plate 65A). Many of his miniatures are rectangular, but occasionally he painted quite large ones on an oval format, as in the case of one of a lady, signed and dated on the reverse: '1837', which was sold at Christie's on 18th April, 1972. It measured 5½ inches in height and was painted against a landscape background, which is unusual for this artist. Ford tended to paint the eyes of his sitters wide open, and frequently delineated the lower eyelashes rather distinctly. His flesh colours on portraits of ladies tend to be rather pinkish-white (Plate 64 I).

Plate 63H. **Charlotte Jones,** *Dorothy Laurence (Mrs. Spooner), ivory, 3⅛ins., c.1790-1800. Signed: 'CJ'. This is a good example of the artist's* **work.** Courtesy the National Collection of Fine Arts, Smithsonian Institution, Washington.

William Armfield Hobday (1771-1831) was born in Birmingham where his father was a wealthy manufacturer. Having shown an aptitude for drawing, he was sent to London when still a boy, and articled to an engraver named Barney with whom he is said to have remained for six years. He was at the same time a pupil at the Royal Academy Schools, which he entered in November, 1790, aged eighteen years. He exhibited at the Royal Academy, and British Institution, from 1794-1830. He worked in London, Bath and Bristol where he settled in c.1802 or 1804. Hobday painted miniatures and portraits in watercolour, as well as large portrait groups in oils and some subject pictures. He succeeded in securing a fashionable clientele and, on leaving the Royal Academy Schools, took accommodation in Charles Street near the Middlesex Hospital. In 1800 he married, but his wife's name is unknown. After his marriage he moved to Holles Street, Cavendish Square, where (according to the *Dictionary of National Biography*) "supported largely by his father he lived for a short time in a recklessly expensive style". He then moved to Bristol where he was in demand, painting the portraits of officers embarking for the seat of war in the Peninsular. He continued to be hopelessly extravagant and got into financial difficulties. When the war ended in 1817 he returned penniless to London where he took a large house, hoping to renew his earlier connections, but in this he was disappointed. Whilst in Bristol in c.1796 he met George Chinnery, with whom he became friendly, and Chinnery's influence can be seen in some of Hobday's miniatures. After his return to London he was patronised by Baron Rothschild, for whom he painted a family group for a thousand guineas. In 1821 he moved to 54 Pall Mall, which had large galleries attached to it. After a disastrous speculation in a panoramic exhibition he opened Hobday's Gallery of Modern Art, and sold pictures on commission. Although this was supported by other artists and his friends, it proved a complete failure and in 1829 Hobday became bankrupt. He died on 17th February, 1831, having lost his wife two years previously. Miniatures by him are scarce and not always easy to attribute. A well painted one of an officer by him was Lot 76 at Sotheby's on 10th May, 1971 (Plate 60F). A good miniature of an

Plate 63 I. **A.R. Burt,** *an unknown lady, watercolour on paper, 2¼ins. Signed and dated: 'Burt / 1817.'* Private Collection.

Plate 64A. **T. Langdon**, *Montagu Burgoyne (1750-1836), ivory, 2¼ins. The sitter was father of the Misses Burgoyne in Plates 64B and C.* Courtesy R. Bayne Powell.

Plate 64B. **T. Langdon**, *Miss Burgoyne, daughter of Montagu Burgoyne and his wife Elizabeth, née Harvey, ivory, 2¼ins., c.1795-1800. This is an enchanting miniature of a child wearing a large straw hat trimmed with pink ribbons, with a bunch of flowers in her lap.* Courtesy Sotheby's.

unknown man signed in full on the reverse with the Charles Street address is in the collection of Brigadier and Mrs. Viner. It is painted against a cloud and sky background, and is of particular interest in view of the address as it must have been painted during the early part of his career (Colour Plate 21E). Some of his portraits were engraved. A miniature self-portrait on paper, signed: 'W. Hobday pinxt', is in the Victoria and Albert Museum, which also have a miniature of an unknown lady which is signed on the reverse and illustrated in *Dictionary of British Miniature Painters,* Plate 164, No. 418.

Another artist who moved about the country and had connections with Bath was **Thomas Le Hardy** (fl.1794-1802). Information regarding his life, and what connection he had with two other artists named Hardy, is still confused. There were in all probability three artists: Thomas Le Hardy, the miniaturist, who exhibited at the Royal Academy, 1794-1802, from 24 Bedford Street, Covent Garden, Weymouth (1797), and Bath (1799); F. Le Hardy (fl.1793) of London; and Thomas Hardy, a portrait painter. Unfortunately miniatures by Thomas Le Hardy are scarce and this, as is so often the case, makes identification difficult. A miniature of an unknown man by him signed and dated: 'Le Hardy / 1798' is in the Victoria and Albert Museum. A good miniature of an unknown officer was Lot 30 at Sotheby's on 17th November, 1975. It is signed on the front: 'T Le Hardy / 1794.' It is well painted with soft brush work; the face is modelled with strong shadows (Plate 64H).

Charles Foot Tayler (fl.1818-1853) is an artist whose work deserves far greater attention than has hitherto been the case. Nothing appears to be known about his background or training. The first record of his existence is in 1818, when he was awarded a silver Isis medal by the Society of Arts for an original miniature. He exhibited at the Royal Academy from 1820-1853. From 1820-1821 he was living in the Isle of Wight, moving to Bath in 1822 where he remained for the rest of his life. He had several addresses in Bath, which included 4 Barton Buildings, 3 Oxford Row, 23 Gay Street, and from 1845-1853, 7 Oxford Row. He had a distinguished clientele and painted a number of the theatrical profession, including Fanny Kemble whose miniature as Portia he exhibited at the Royal Academy in 1831. He was a good miniaturist and his portraits are usually well drawn and expressive. He frequently painted his sitters against a stylised landscape background. His flesh colours are usually pale pink shaded with a slightly greenish tinge. A miniature of a Miss Poynter, in a private collection, is inscribed on the

Plate 64C. **T. Langdon**, *portrait of Miss Burgoyne, sister to Miss Burgoyne in Plate 64B, ivory, 2¼ins. The sitter is wearing a mob cap trimmed with blue ribbon. These family miniatures were first sold in 1968.* Courtesy Christie's.

reverse: 'By Chas Foot Tayler / 7 Oxford Row Bath From a picture painted by him in 1849.' The lady is seated against a landscape and foliage background (Plate 67C). He has a habit of picking out the eyelashes rather distinctly, and modelling the features with strong shading. Four of the finest miniatures that I have seen by Tayler were sold at Christie's on 2nd April, 1968. They represented the four eldest sons of Henry Allen Johnson, 2nd Baronet of Bath, and his wife, Charlotte Elizabeth Philipse of Philipseburg, New York. Of their nine sons all but one served in the army. The miniature of Sir Henry Franks Frederick Johnson, 3rd Baronet, was signed and dated 1837 on the reverse, when the artist gave his address as Oxford Row. They were presumably all painted at the same time. The other three miniatures represented: William Victor Johnson of the 90th Foot; George Vanderheyden Johnson, wearing the uniform of the Royal Artillery (Plate 67A); and Sir Edwin Beaumont Johnson, G.C.B., C.I.E., wearing the uniform of a Second Lieutenant of the Bengal Artillery. Sir Edwin served in a number of campaigns including the Indian Mutiny, becoming a General in 1878. He was a member for the Council of India from 1875-76, and Director of Military Education (Plate 67B). Engravings after Tayler's work are in the British Museum.

F. Read (d. aft. 1852) is an artist about whom we know very little. He worked in London, Bath (1829) and Cheltenham (1832-1843). He exhibited at the Royal Academy and Society of British Artists from 1817-1852, from a number of different addresses in London including 2 Alfred Place (from which address F. Read, Junior exhibited from 1855-1857). His work is slightly reminiscent of the work of Sir W.C. Ross. He used a minute stippling on the face of his sitters, and usually signed his work: 'F. Read. f^t' (scratched) or inscribed the miniature in full on the reverse. He painted a set of ten miniatures after Holbein, and others representing Henry VIII, his six wives, Elizabeth I, Mary, Queen of Scots, and Edward VI. These were sold at Sotheby's on 12th April, 1960. Of these, the miniatures of Henry VIII and

Plate 64D. **T. Redmond**, *an unknown naval officer, ivory, 1¾ins. Signed and dated: 'T. Redmond / 1761.'* Courtesy R. Bayne Powell.

Plate 64E (far left). **E. Shiercliffe**, *an unknown lady, enamel, 2⅝ins. Signed and dated on the reverse: 'Edward Shiercliffe. Bristol. 1765.' This is one of the few signed miniatures by this artist and is painted with bright fresh colours.* Courtesy Victoria and Albert Museum.

Plate 64F (left). **T. Redmond**, *an unknown man wearing 'Windsor Uniform', ivory, 1½ins., c.1770. Signed: 'TR'.* Courtesy the Holburne of Menstrie Museum, Bath.

Plate 64G. **Charlotte Jones,** *Lady Caroline Lamb (1785-1828), novelist, ivory, 2⅝ins., c.1820, wearing a man's cravat.* Courtesy Sotheby's.

his wives, signed: 'F. Read' on the reverse, were sold at Christie's, Lot 43, on 11th October, 1977, when they realised £1,100. Examples of his work are in the Victoria Art Gallery, Bath, and the Victoria and Albert Museum.

The artist S.T. Roch(e) (1759-1847) who worked for a time in Bath has already been discussed in Chapter VII. He worked in Bath from c.1792-1817, when he returned to Ireland. Examples of his work are in the Holbourne Museum, Bath.

Lewis Vaslet (d.1808) is often called 'Vaslet of Bath'. Little is known about him, and nothing about his parentage. It has been suggested that he might have been of French or Huguenot descent and related to Lewis Vaslet, master of Fulham School. Vaslet exhibited at the Royal Academy, 1770 and 1771, from London, and in 1775 and 1782 from Bath where he worked at intervals until 1808. For the rest of his career he moved about the country, working in York, c.1770, 1771 and 1778, Oxford, 1780, 1790 and 1796, Ramsgate (?) in 1792, and Norwich, 1793. He executed portraits in crayons and oils, miniatures, landscapes in oils, and painted pictures of game, fruit, flowers and animals. He is said to have married a lady of means. In 1787 he was living at 43 Walcot Street, Bath, but had several other addresses in the city during his life. He died at Bath in November, 1808. Miniatures by him are scarce, and it is impossible to give any indication as to his style. Merton College, Oxford own some pastels by him, and several engraved portraits after his work are in the British Museum.

Plate 64H (left). **T. Le Hardy,** *an unknown officer, ivory, 2½ins. Signed and dated: 'T Le Hardy / 1794.' Unless signed, Hardy's work is not easy to recognise.* Courtesy Sotheby's.

Plate 64 I (right). **C. Ford,** *Mary Dickenson (Mrs. Price), ivory, 2½ins. Signed and dated on the reverse: 'C. Ford pinxt / Bath 1838,' and inscribed in a later hand: 'Mary Dickenson afterwards Mary Price / Painted August 17th / 1838.' This is a good example of Ford's work and painted in fresh colours.* Private Collection.

Edward Shiercliffe (fl.c.1765-1786) was probably the son of Edward Shiercliffe, a bookseller who lived at the same address, 11 St. Augustine's Back, Bristol, in 1775. Shiercliffe worked in Bristol and Bath, c.1765-1786. He painted enamel miniatures, and his work is slightly reminiscent of Gervase Spencer. Unfortunately examples are scarce, and the best known one is an enamel of an unknown lady, signed on the reverse: 'Edward Shiercliffe. Bristol. 1765.' The colouring is attractive and the general effect elegant, showing a good example of costume with the sitter in a wide brimmed hat, pearls at her throat, and a posy of flowers at the bosom tucked into the fold of her collar. She is painted against a landscape background. This miniature was one of those exhibited in Edinburgh in 1965 (Plate 64E).

Plate 65A. **C. Ford,** *after an oil portrait by L.F. Abbott painted in 1785, Sir William Herschel Bart. (1738-1822), astronomer, watercolour on paper, 5⅝ins. Dated: '1860.'* Courtesy of the Holburne of Menstrie Museum, Bath.

Three brothers name Theweneti all seem to have worked and lived in Bath for the greater part of their lives. **Edward Theweneti** (1806-1889), **Lorenzo Theweneti** (c.1797-1878) and **Michael Theweneti** (19th century) all shared various houses in Bath, and a studio at 14 Bond Street, London.

Edward painted portraits, landscapes and miniatures, and was described in 1850 as "a fortification and drawing master". From 1860 onwards he and his brothers became photographers. Edward's wife was described in the *Bath Directory* in c.1868 as "a professor of pianoforte and engraving". Lorenzo is thought to have been born in Italy c.1797. When the family came to England is not known. Lorenzo exhibited at the Royal Academy, 1824-1831. All three brothers were described as drawing masters, portrait painters and miniaturists. Edward and Lorenzo were described latterly as 'Gentlemen'. Lorenzo was working in Cheltenham (1824), London (1826-1827) and Bath from 1829 onwards. He lived in Charles Street, Milsom Street, and in 1837 all three brothers lived at 7 Macaulay Buildings, moving later to Henrietta Street. Lorenzo died at 29 Henrietta Street in 1878. His obituary in the *Bath Chronicle* gives his age as eighty-nine, and says that he probably painted more portraits than any other artist in the neighbourhood! If this is true there must be a large number unrecognised or still in the possession of the families for whom they were painted, as his works are scarce. Two miniatures of unknown ladies are good examples of his work. One is in the collection of Robert Bayne Powell and is signed in full: 'L. Theweneti', in cursive writing on the front. It is c.1820-1825, well painted and with good colouring; the face is well modelled (Plate 67E). The other is in the collection of Mrs. Hamilton (Plate 65D). It is signed on the front in cursive initials: 'L.T.' The sitter, posed against a curtain background with pillars, is seated with her left

Plate 65B. **M. Theweneti**, *Mrs. Theweneti, the artist's mother, ivory, 3⁷/₁₆ins. Signed on the front in full: 'M. Theweneti', and inscribed on the reverse: 'Theweneti: Henrietta / St.' (Bath). All three brothers lived in Henrietta Street for many years.* Courtesy Victoria and Albert Museum.

arm resting on the chair which is draped with a shawl. She holds a rose in her right hand. The general effect is attractive and the miniature well painted. Examples of Lorenzo's work are in the Victoria and Albert Museum and the National Portrait Gallery.

Michael Theweneti shared the same addresses as his brothers from time to time and is said to have been a drawing master, portrait painter, miniaturist and landscape painter. From 1860 he took up photography, although he still continued to paint. A portrait of the artist by his brother, Lorenzo, was exhibited at Bath in 1903. A miniature of his mother, signed: 'M. Theweneti', is in the Victoria and Albert Museum (Plate 65B).

It will be readily realised that it would be impossible to include more than a fraction of the artists who worked in the area. Amongst those who appear to have hitherto had little recognition are the Sharples family, who really made quite a contribution to art in various ways.

James Sharples, Senior (1750/2-1811) was born in Lancashire, and he and his third wife, née Ellen Wallace, and their daughter, Rolinda, all had connections with Bath. James exhibited at the Royal Academy, 1779-1785. He painted miniatures and executed some in pastel. He has been identified as "Mr. Sharples of Duke Street, Liverpool", who exhibited there in 1774.

Colour Plate 22.
A top left. **N. Freese**, possibly *the 5th Duke of Manchester (1771-1843), ivory, 2¾ins.*
B top right. **Thomas Peat**, *Mrs. Savery, ivory, 2¾ins. Signed on the front: 'Peat.' This is a good example of a comparatively minor artist.*
C centre. **Henry Edridge, A.R.A.**, *an unknown officer, wearing the uniform of the Fencibles or Yeoman Cavalry, ivory, 3¾ins., c.1797. Signed on the front: 'HE.'*
D bottom left. **James Heath Millington**, *an unknown girl, ivory, 3ins., c.1835-40. Signed on the front: 'J.H.M.' A particularly attractive miniature by a little known artist.*
E bottom right. **Alexander Gallaway**, *an officer of the 37th or Northamptonshire Regiment of Foot, ivory, 2¾ins. Signed on the front: 'AG 1807.'*

Courtesy Victoria and Albert Museum, Alan Evans Collection

Plate 65C. **Mrs. James Sharples or Sharpless, née Ellen Wallace** *(1769-1849), self-portrait of the artist, ivory, 4½ins., c.1835.* Courtesy the City Art Gallery, Bristol.

Plate 65D. **L. Theweneti,** *portrait of an unknown lady, ivory, 4¾ins., c.1835. Signed on a pillar: 'L.T.' This is a good example of the artist's work which is scarce, and an attractive guide to costume and hair style.* Courtesy Mrs. E.M. Hamilton.

Nothing is known about his earlier marriages except that he had two sons, George and Felix, by one of them. The family went to America in c.1794/6. James and Ellen returned to Bath in c.1801 to look after some property there, but went back to America in 1809, accompanied by Rolinda. James died in New York on 26th February, 1811. Examples of his work are in the Metropolitan Museum, New York, the Independence Hall, Philadelphia and the Bristol Art Gallery.

Mrs. James Sharples or Sharpless (Ellen) (1769-1849) was born in either Birmingham or Bath. She was a pupil of James Sharples in Bath. Most of her work was confined to miniature copies of old masters and numerous copies (chiefly pastels) of portraits by her husband. She was an expert needlewoman. When the family went to America in c.1794/6, they were captured en route and imprisoned by the French. Mrs. Sharples exhibited at the Royal Academy in 1807, from Hatton Garden, London. After the death of her husband in America Ellen Sharples returned to Britain with her son, James, and her daughter, Rolinda, and took up residence in Clifton, Bristol, where she lived until her death on 14th March, 1849, having survived her children. She left £3,465 for founding the Bristol Fine Art Academy, now the Royal West of England Academy, to which she had already given £2,000.

Her self-portrait in miniature is in the City Art Gallery, Bristol, and shows her to have been a most attractive young woman, and a competent artist (Plate 65C). The National Portrait Gallery has examples of her work and occasionally miniatures by her come into the sale rooms, but she is not yet well known and deserves more attention.

Miss Rolinda Sharples (1793/4-1838) was presumably taught art by her parents. She was a good artist and painted miniatures, portraits in oils, and genre subjects. From 1820-1836, she exhibited at the Royal Academy and Society of British Artists, becoming a member of the latter. After her father's death she lived with her mother in Clifton, Bristol, where she died of cancer on 10th February, 1838. A self-portrait and other works, including a portrait by her of her mother, are in the Bristol Art Gallery where there is a large oil painting by her depicting 'The Trial of Col. Brereton, after the Bristol Riots 1831.' An article on the family was published in *Country Life*, 4th January, 1968.

In this part of the chapter I have discussed a cross-section of the numerous artists who worked in the Bath and Bristol area for all or part of their lives. Many more could have been added, but space does not permit, and collectors may like to pursue the subject for themselves and discover more about those who came into this part of the provinces.

Interesting information regarding the formation of Academies of Art in Liverpool are given by Joseph Mayer, *Early Art in Liverpool,* 1876. From as early as 1525 Liverpool had been sufficiently interested in art to support "a band of music for the entertainment of the citizens". By the middle of the eighteenth century, as we have already seen, many towns up and down the country became both larger and richer. Liverpool was no exception and the establishment of the Royal Academy in London, which held its first exhibition in 1769, produced an almost immediate reaction on Merseyside. Certain people of influence decided to attempt the formation of a similar Academy in Liverpool. They formed a society, and took an 'Academy Room' at 30 St. John Street; this consisted of twenty-one members, mostly drawing masters and others who had interests in art. This first association did not survive for long, and in 1773 another attempt was made, and arrangements planned for lectures on different topics. In 1774 the Society of Artists in Liverpool held an exhibition at their rooms, 30 St. John Street. Due to loss of commerce during the wars in America and France, Liverpool went through a difficult period and the Society only lasted a short time. When peace returned artistic projects were again considered. By 1783 William Roscoe (1753-1831), an historian, attorney and prominent businessman, had become one of the leaders of Liverpool's culture and commerce. The Society for Promoting the Arts in Liverpool was formed, with Roscoe as its Vice President. Exhibitions were held in 1784 and 1787, and Liverpool has always remained interested in the arts throughout the years. The Walker Art Gallery, the Liverpool City Museums, and the Sudley Art Gallery are proof of the importance which Liverpool has placed on art.

Patrick John McMor(e)land (1741-d. aft. 1809) was, as his name suggests, of Scottish extraction. Nothing is known about his education or training in

art, nor do we know how long he remained in Scotland where he presumably started his career. He was in Manchester, 1774-1777, London, 1777, and was working in Liverpool from c.1781 until c.1793, when he returned to Manchester. He exhibited at the Royal Academy, 1776-1782, and in Liverpool, 1784-1787. McMor(e)land painted miniatures on ivory and enamel (these latter being mainly for rings), executed 'stained' portrait sketches, tinted drawings of landscapes, Italian views and seascapes. According to Joseph Mayer, he executed mezzotints in collaboration with Paul Sandby, R.A. and "other frequenters of the Bootle Coffee House — a favourite resort of London artists spending their holiday in the North". McMor(e)land lectured on art in Liverpool and Manchester, where he also taught art in 1809. His work varies a good deal; at best it is of a high quality, but occasionally his miniatures are sketchily drawn. I have never seen any examples of his larger paintings. His miniatures are usually signed: 'P.M.' or 'P.M.^{C}.' The signature is not always easy to distinguish. Many of his miniatures are in private collections. Examples of his work are in the Victoria and Albert Museum and the Scottish National Portrait Gallery, Edinburgh. (Colour Plate 15D; Plates 68B, C, D and F.)

Thomas Hazlehurst (c.1740-c.1821) was one of the earliest of what we now called the 'Liverpool School of Miniaturists'. Since writing my *Dictionary* I have been kindly supplied with information regarding the family by the artist's great granddaughter, Miss M. Peal (b.1890). The Hazlehurst family came from Cheshire, where Thomas owned property called 'Broomhedge'. His date and place of birth are still unknown, nor do we know his father's Christian name, but his mother was Grace (Leigh?), the adopted daughter of John, or James, Hardman of Allerton Hall estate, Liverpool, which she should have inherited. Due to her marrying Hazlehurst against Hardman's wishes she was disinherited, and the property left in Chancery for ninety years!

Hazlehurst practised miniature painting from 1760 until at least 1818. According to the family he was a pupil of Sir Joshua Reynolds, and is noted as such when he exhibited at the Society for Promoting Painting and Design in Liverpool, in 1787, from 32 Hurst Street. It is interesting to record that Reynolds, Paul Sandby, Thomas Gainsborough and many other artists of importance exhibited in Liverpool in that year.

He married at some unknown date Martha Bentley (c.1760-1840), by whom he had thirteen children, of whom his eldest son, Joseph B. Hazlehurst, followed his father's profession as a miniaturist. Joseph died young, and is thought to have been murdered when en route to paint some patron's portrait. His parents lived in Liverpool all their married lives.

Colour Plate 23.
A top left. **Alfred Edward Chalon, R.A.,** *Miss Julia Anne Cockburn, ivory, 2¾ins. Signed and dated on the reverse: '1830.'*
B top right. **George Chinnery,** *Capt. Patrick Duff, R.H.A., ivory, 2⅝ins. Signed with initials on the reverse: 'G.C.' Miniatures by Chinnery are scarce and seldom signed.*
C centre. **William Grimaldi,** *Lord Grey de Wilton, ivory, 3ins. Signed on the front: 'W.Grimaldi 1827.'*
D bottom left. **George Engleheart,** *Lieut. Col. Robertson, A.D.C., ivory, 3¼ins. Signed on the front: 'E', and on the reverse signed and dated: '1800', in which year the sitter is recorded in Engleheart's fee book.*
E bottom right. **Joseph Pastorini,** *an unknown officer, ivory, 2½ins. Signed by the artist on the reverse. This is a fine example of his work.*

Courtesy Victoria and Albert Museum, Alan Evans Collection

A

B

C

D

E

Although Hazlehurst made over £20,000 from his paintings he lost nearly all of it through bad investments, and when he died his family was left in poverty. His last known address was in 1821, at Sidney Place, Edge Hill, Liverpool, and it is presumed that this is where he died, as by 1823 his widow was living at a different address. His self-portrait in miniature and one of his wife are still in the family (Plates 69B and C). He exhibited at the Liverpool Academy from 1810-1812.

His work had at least three phases: his early miniatures are slightly reminiscent of C. Robertson, later his style is more like that of J. Barry, and his mature style is developed from Barry but is painted in a tight and rather hard method. The hair is executed in curves combined with parallel straight lines, and the face shaded with blue, particularly round the eyes and contours. Many of his miniatures are painted against a cloud and sky background. He signed his work: 'T.H.' in neat Roman letters, usually on the front. Occasionally he omitted to sign at all. Miniatures by him are frequently seen in the sale rooms and are usually well painted. The Local History Department of the City of Liverpool Libraries contains a collection of 387 paintings of Lancashire flora by Thomas Hazlehurst. A number of his miniatures are in private collections, and examples are in the Victoria and Albert Museum. (Plates 68E, G, H and I.) According to Long he died c.1821.

Sylvester Harding (1751-1809) was born in Newcastle-under-Lyme on 5th August, 1751. He entered the Royal Academy Schools in November, 1776. He had been sent to London as a youth to learn a trade, which he disliked, and was living with an uncle. He ran away when he was fourteen and joined some strolling players with whom he toured until 1775, when he returned to London. He then took up miniature painting and exhibited at the Free Society of Artists in 1776 and 1782, at the Royal Academy 1777-1802, and at the Society for Promoting Painting and Design in Liverpool in 1787, when his address was given as 132, Fleet Street, London. One of the exhibits was a 'tinted drawing'. He painted miniatures, figure subjects, copied old family portraits in miniature, executed some engravings, and published among other works the *Biographical Mirror,* in which he was assisted by his brother, later Librarian at Windsor. Examples of his works are in the British Museum and the National Gallery, Dublin.

Three important artists who worked in Liverpool were Thomas, George and Francis Hargreaves. **Thomas Hargreaves** (1774-1846/7) was born in Liverpool on 16th March, 1774. His father was a woollen draper in the City. Thomas took up painting at an early age and on 29th March, 1790, entered

Plate 66
A. **R. Hancock,** *portrait of an unknown man, ivory, 4½ins. Signed on the reverse and dated: '1831. Bristol'. Note the distinct stippling on the background.* Courtesy Sotheby's.
B. **Miss Charlotte Jones** (1768-1847), *self-portrait of the artist, ivory, 3⁹/16ins. Inscribed on the reverse: 'Charlotte Jones 1805 Miss Charlotte Jones preceptress in miniature painting to the Princess Charlotte of Wales.'* Courtesy the Holburne of Menstrie Museum, Bath.
C. **C. Ford,** *portrait of an unknown lady, ivory, 5½ins. Signed on the reverse and dated: '1837'. Note the hair style and band round the forehead.* Courtesy Christie's.
D. **J. Scovell,** *Colonel Booth, ivory, 5¼ins. Inscribed on the reverse and dated: 'November 1822'. The sitter is wearing the scarlet uniform of the Royal Engineers.* Courtesy Christie's.
E. **J. Scovell,** *Mrs. Booth, wife of Colonel Booth, ivory, 5¼ins. This is also inscribed on the reverse and dated: 'November 1822.'* Courtesy Christie's.

A

B

C

D

E

the Royal Academy Schools. From March, 1793, he was an articled assistant to Sir Thomas Lawrence, by whom he was employed for some years, during which time he worked in oils. Ill health prevented his remaining in London, and he returned to Liverpool c.1795. From this time onwards he worked chiefly in Liverpool but also exhibited from London. He exhibited intermittently at the Royal Academy, Society of British Artists and Liverpool Academy, 1798-1835, was a member of the Liverpool Academy from 1810-1835, and in 1824 was one of the founder members of the Society of British Artists. He married a lady by the name of Quaile, by whom he had several sons, including Francis and George Hargreaves who were both miniaturists. James Hargreaves, T. Hargreaves (fl.1829-1843) and W. Hargreaves, who exhibited a miniature at the Royal Academy from Liverpool in 1813, are also thought to have been his sons. Thomas Hargreaves was one of the best miniaturists of the Liverpool School. He painted in both oils and watercolour, and used ivory and paper as bases. Many of his miniatures are rectangular, but he also used an oval format. Much of his work shows the influence of Lawrence, and many of his miniatures are reminiscent of oil paintings. He used a warm pink flesh colouring which is attractive, and painted his miniatures with a fine brush stroke. Like many other artists he made preliminary sketches for his portraits; of these some 785 are in the Local History Department of the City of Liverpool Library. Many of these drawings are excellent; the draughtsmanship is strong, and the sitters' characters admirably portrayed. He signed his works: 'T. Hargreaves', 'Thos Hargreaves pt' (on the reverse), followed by a date, and occasionally: 'T.H.' in cursive lettering on the front. His self-portrait is in the Walker Art Gallery, Liverpool, and miniatures by him are in the Victoria and Albert Museum. Some engravings after his portraits are in the British Museum. (Plates 69D and G.)

Plate 68A. T. Hazlehurst, portrait of an unknown man, ivory, 3ins., c.1785-90. Signed: 'T.H.' Courtesy Sotheby's.

George Hargreaves (1797-1870) was one of the sons of Thomas Hargreaves, and was presumably instructed by his father. He exhibited at the Royal Academy, 1818 and 1820, from London addresses, and at the Society of British Artists, 1824-1834; he became an Associate in 1822 and a Member of the Liverpool Academy, 1823-1831. In 1828, his address was Bold Place, Liverpool. He did not produce miniatures of anything like the same quality as his father's; they are painted slightly in the same manner but are lacking in draughtsmanship and are more amateurish. He used a pinkish-orange flesh colour; his painting is smooth without any stippling, and the sitter's hair is usually painted in distinct curls. Sometimes the backgrounds are greyish brown. He died in Liverpool in 1870. Two engravings after Hargreaves are in the British Museum. (Plate 69E.)

Plate 68B. P. McMor(e)land, Miss Evans, ivory, 1¼ins. One of a set of three family miniatures sold in 1974. Courtesy Sotheby's.

Plate 67
A. **C.F. Tayler**, *George Vanderheyden Johnson, 3rd son of Henry Allen Johnson, 2nd Bart., and his wife Charlotte Elizabeth, ivory, 4¾ins., c.1842. The sitter is wearing the uniform of a Second Lieutenant of the Royal Artillery. This was one of four miniatures of the Johnson brothers sold in 1968. They are all splendid examples of the artist's work.* Courtesy Christie's.
B. **C.F. Tayler**, *Sir Edwin Beaumont Johnson, G.C.B., C.I.E., 4th son of the 2nd Bart., ivory, 4¼ins., c.1842. The sitter is wearing the blue uniform of a Second Lieutenant of the Bengal Artillery. Sir Edwin served in the Punjab and in the Indian Mutiny, and was a member for the Council of India, 1875-76, and Director of Military Education.* Courtesy Christie's.
C. **C.F. Tayler**, *Miss Poynter, ivory, 3⅞ins. Inscribed on the reverse: 'By Chas Foot Tayler / 7 Oxford Row Bath From a picture painted by him in 1849.' It is not clear if this is from a miniature or from a large portrait.* Private Collection.
D. **C.F. Tayler**, *portrait of an unknown man, ivory, 4½ins., c.1840-50.* Courtesy Sotheby's.
E. **L. Theweneti**, *portrait of an unknown lady, ivory, 4⅛ins., c.1820-25. Signed in full: 'L. Theweneti.' Note the turban and low-cut dress with a shawl.* Courtesy R. Bayne Powell.

Francis Hargreaves (fl.1810-1854) was another son of Thomas Hargreaves, by whom he was taught to paint. Little information is available about him, and his works are scarce. Two examples are in Liverpool. One is of Henry Threlfall Wilson, inscribed on the reverse: 'Francis Hargreaves pinxit / 1846 / Liverpool'; this portrait is slightly hesitant and, although well modelled, lacks the panache of his father's work. The other example is in the Walker Art Gallery and is a portrait of John Gibson, R.A., after a portrait by Penry Williams. It is executed in watercolour on paper and is rectangular, 9 by 7¼ inches. An inscription on the reverse of the frame identifies it as a 'Copy by Francis Hargreaves, 1845, Liverpool.' There is a certain amount of confusion about the signatures of Thomas and Francis Hargreaves, the T.H. and F.H. both being in cursive writing. After comparing several signed miniatures by both artists I suggest that Thomas wrote a cursive T, followed by his surname, and Francis signed with a French F (the cross stroke can be seen under magnification). The latter has a flourish on the tail of the F, whereas Thomas wrote his with a straight down-stroke.

John Turmeau (II) (1777-1846) was the son of John Turmeau, Senior, of Huguenot descent, a jeweller who also painted a few miniatures and exhibited pictures in human hair. John Turmeau (II) is thought to have been born in London, and to have been educated at a school in Putney. He exhibited at the Royal Academy, 1793-1796, from various London addresses, but moved to Liverpool by 1799. He married in 1807 Sarah Wheeler, by whom he had seven or nine children. He settled in Liverpool, and was one of the founders of the Liverpool Academy in 1810, holding office as its President, 1812-1814, and Treasurer until 1833. He exhibited at the Liverpool Academy up to 1842, kept a print shop in Liverpool, and was very popular socially. He painted miniatures on ivory and paper, and large portraits in watercolour and oils. Some of his work is said to be reminiscent of Hazlehurst but it is, in my opinion, closer to Hargreaves, although he used

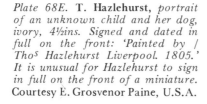

a brighter palette. He used a warm flesh tint, shaded with blue, and modelled the features with short strokes. His backgrounds are usually a plain greyish blue, or brown. His self-portrait is in the Walker Art Gallery. It is inscribed on the reverse in a later hand: 'John Turmeau / painted by himself / presented to the / Liverpool Walker Art Gallery / by the Misses E. & M. Turmeau / after their death.' An attractive miniature of an unknown lady wearing a mauve low-cut dress with lace edging, her upswept hair falling in deep curls on either side of her head, painted against a grey background and signed: 'IT', is in a private collection. Turmeau died on 10th September, 1846, in Castle Street, Liverpool, and was buried at Edge Hill. A striking miniature of a Negro youth signed: 'IT' is in the collection of E.G. Paine, New York, who lent it to the Edinburgh Exhibition in 1965 (Plate 69A.) Examples of his work are in the Ward Usher Museum, Lincoln, and the Walker Art Gallery, Liverpool, where there is a set of watercolour profiles of the Roach family. One of these is stamped: 'Turmeau' under his signature. His eldest son, John Caspar Turmeau, was an architect. (Plates 69F and 70F.)

Miss Eliza Knipe (fl.1784-1787) is an artist about whom practically nothing is known. She exhibited in Liverpool in 1784, when she was noted as "An artist and drawing mistress in Liverpool". Her exhibits were a miniature, and flowers in watercolour. In 1787 she entered four exhibits and her name was given as Eliza, and her address as John Street, Liverpool. One of her exhibits was a tinted sketch of a girl with flowers, one a portrait of a lady, and another a frame with five miniatures.

Peter Holland (b.1757, fl.-1812) is another artist whose early life and parentage are obscure. He entered the Royal Academy Schools on 8th October, 1779, aged twenty-two years. He may possibly have been a pupil of Samuel Finney, from whose address — 56 Frith Street, Soho — he exhibited at the Royal Academy in 1781 and 1782. In 1793 he exhibited views of Cumberland from Liverpool, having moved there in 1787, in which year his address was Tarleton Street. He became the first Vice President of the Liverpool Academy in 1810, and exhibited there in 1812, in which year he ceased to be a member. I know of only one signed miniature by him: it is of an unknown lady, signed on the front: 'P. Holland', and is in the Alan Evans Collection at the Victoria and Albert Museum (Plate 70A). It is a very distinctive style, with wide dark eyes, the eyelashes distinctly drawn, and the figure lightly sketched in; it is not easy to describe, but I have been able to attribute three miniatures since examining this one.

James Pelham, Senior (d.c.1850) and **James Pelham, Junior** (1800-1874) were both artists who worked in Liverpool. James Pelham, Senior, is recorded by H.C. Marillier in the *Liverpool School of Painters* as "a miniaturist of some skill whose work is now seldom seen". His son, James Pelham, Junior, is better known, and considered to be a better artist. No works by J. Pelham, Senior are at present known.

James Pelham, Junior (1800-1874) was born in London and was the son of J. Pelham, Senior, with whom he has often been confused. He began his career in London as a portrait painter, but later took to painting miniatures, portraits in oils and watercolour and, towards the latter part of his career, subject pictures. He moved about the country, working in Edinburgh, Norwich, Lincoln, Newcastle, York, Carlisle, Cheltenham, Bath and Bristol.

Plate 68F. **P. McMor(e)land,** *miniature of an unknown young lady, ivory, 1⅝ins., c.1785-90. Signed: 'P.Mᶜ.' Set within a clasp frame for a wrist strap.* Courtesy Christie's.

Plate 68G. **T. Hazlehurst,** *the Rt. Hon. J.A. Plantaganet Stewart, ivory, 3³³⁄₃₂ins. Signed: 'T.H.'* Courtesy Victoria and Albert Museum, Alan Evans Collection.

Plate 68H (left). **T. Hazlehurst,** *portrait of an unknown man, ivory, 3⅜ins., c.1800. Signed: 'T.H.'* Courtesy Christie's.

Plate 68 I (right). **T. Hazlehurst,** *Mrs. John Chorley of Prescot, ivory, 3ins., c.1790. Signed: 'T.H.' All these miniatures by Hazlehurst are typical of his work and signature.* Private Collection.

Plate 69A. **J. Turmeau,** *portrait of a negro youth, ivory, 2½ins. Signed: 'IT.' This is an interesting study by Turmeau.* Courtesy E. Grosvenor Paine, U.S.A.

He exhibited at the Royal Academy from 1832-1837 and at the Society of British Artists, Liverpool Academy, etc., up to 1868. He married in 1838 and is thought to have moved to Liverpool at about this time. In 1848 he became an Associate of the Liverpool Academy, and was elected a Member soon after. He was Secretary of the Liverpool Academy 1854-1860/7 and took a prominent part in directing the Liverpool Academy Schools. Pelham had nine children of whom all but one survived. His son, also James Pelham (1840-1906), and a daughter, Emily, became artists, and James succeeded his father as Secretary of the Liverpool Academy in 1867. With the advent of photography miniature painting was less in demand, and Pelham was obliged to turn to other forms of art. He died in Liverpool on 17th April, 1874 and was survived by his widow and children. Miniatures by Pelham are scarce and it may well be that some pass unrecognised. Those I have seen are well painted and the draughtsmanship is good. He used a pinkish flesh colour, and shaded with blues and greens. He sometimes used a scraper in the hair. The upper eyelids are clearly drawn, and the eyebrows often slightly arched. One of the best miniatures I have seen by him is a large one, painted on ivory, of two unknown young women. It is reminiscent of the Scottish School, and not unlike the work of Thorburn. The girls are seated, one holding opera-glasses, the other a fan. The miniature is attractive, and the sitters' faces expressive. The highlights on the hair are strongly picked out. The miniature is signed on the front: 'J. Pelham 1840', and was sold at Sotheby's in 1970 (Plate 71D). Examples of his work are in the Walker Art Gallery, Liverpool.

Aaron Edwin Penley (1807-1870) is thought to have been born in the north. Nothing is known about his early education, or what training, if any, he had in art. He was practising as a miniaturist in Manchester and Cheltenham from 1834-1835, and exhibited at the Royal Academy, British Institution, Society of British Artists, New Water Colour Society, etc., from 1838-1856. He was an associate of this latter society from 1859. He held an appointment as 'Water-Colour Painter in Ordinary' to William IV. He is best

Plate 69B (left). **Thomas Hazlehurst** *(c.1740-c.1821) self-portrait of the artist, ivory, 4ins. Signed: 'T.H.' This and the miniature of his wife, Plate 69C, are by family descent.* Private Collection.

Plate 69C (right). **T. Hazlehurst,** *Mrs. Thomas Hazlehurst, née Martha Bentley (c.1760-1840), wife of the artist, Plate 69B, ivory, 4ins., c.1800-20.* Private Collection.

known as a drawing master and landscape painter. He taught drawing at Addiscombe Military College and at Woolwich, and wrote works on watercolour painting. He died on 15th January, 1870, at 5 Eliot Hill, Lewisham. A miniature of Mrs. Fanshawe by him is in the collection of Mrs. Hamilton. The miniature is signed, and, judging by the hairstyle and costume, was probably painted c.1830-40 (Plate 70D).

Moses Haughton, Junior (1772/4-1848) was born in Wednesbury, Staffordshire, and was the nephew of Moses Haughton, Senior (1734-1804), also a miniaturist who came from Wednesbury. Haughton went to London and studied under George Stubbs, R.A., a native of Liverpool. He entered the Royal Academy Schools on 12th October, 1795, when he was twenty-one, and exhibited at the Royal Academy and British Institution, 1808-1848. Haughton was a successful miniaturist, and also painted scriptural and rural subjects in oils and executed some engravings. Haughton was friendly with Henri Fuseli (1741-1825), the famous painter and author, and lived for a time in his house in Berners Street, London, for which he paid him 100 guineas a year. Haughton charged from five to eight guineas for a portrait. It is not known if he ever worked in Liverpool, but he certainly became great friends with William Roscoe who had such a great influence on Liverpool art. Haughton painted at least two miniatures of Roscoe, and one of Mrs. Thomas Roscoe, wife of the fifth son of William Roscoe (Plate 71B). These miniatures are in the Walker Art Gallery, Liverpool. One of Roscoe is inscribed on the reverse and dated 1790, indicating that Houghton must have known Roscoe early in his career. The other, which is very well drawn and expressive, was painted in 1811 (Plate 71C). Examples of his work are in the British Museum.

Miss Sarah Biffin or Beffin (Mrs. Wright) (1784-1850) was born at East Quantoxhead, near Bridgwater, on 25th October, 1784, and was the daughter of Henry and Sarah Biffin. Her father was a farm labourer. Sarah had the misfortune to be born without hands, arms or feet. She proved to be a most remarkable woman of great courage. For a full account of her life see *A Dictionary of British Miniature Painters,* pp.165-166. She apparently showed an early aptitude for painting, and taught herself by holding a brush in her mouth. She painted miniatures and executed sketches. She had some

Plate 69D. **T. Hargreaves,** *Mrs. D. Penny, ivory, 3¼ins. The sitter is wearing a lace trimmed white dress and a crimson stole.* Courtesy Christie's.

Plate 69E. **G. Hargreaves,** *portrait of an unknown lady, ivory, 3ins. Signed and dated on the reverse: 'G. Hargreaves 1827.' This is a good miniature and close in style to the work of T. Hargreaves.* Private Collection.

Plate 69F. **J. Turmeau,** *portrait of an unknown man, ivory, 2⅞ins., c.1790-1800. Signed: 'IT.' It is interesting to compare the works of Turmeau with those of Hazlehurst and Hargreaves. Turmeau painted in a softer manner and used less gum.* Courtesy Sotheby's.

Plate 69G. **T. Hargreaves,** *Mrs. Samuel Henry Thompson, ivory 3⅜ins., painted 1837, the year of her marriage, and probably in her wedding dress.* Courtesy Mrs. C.H.F. Thompson.

Plate 70A. **P. Holland,** *an unknown lady, ivory, 2¾ins., c.1790-95. Signed in full: 'P. Holland.' The sitter's long hair is swathed with a bandeau. Note the distinct dotting for the eyelashes. Signed miniatures by this artist are rare, and his work often unrecognised.* Courtesy Victoria and Albert Museum, Alan Evans Collection.

instruction from a Mr. Dukes, who persuaded her parents to allow her to be bound to him by a written agreement to remain in his house for a term of years, to tour the country where she was exhibited as a freak and genius combined. For this she was paid £5 per year and her keep. The public paid 1s. or 6d. to see her and she painted miniatures at three guineas each, although she did not receive any extra money for this. The Earl of Morton saw her work at Bartholomew Fair, and was so impressed that he commissioned her to paint his portrait, and — according to tradition — took the portrait away between each sitting to prove that there was no deceit! He was so delighted with the result that he showed it to George III, who was so distressed to hear she was being exploited that he commanded an artist called W.M. Craig (fl.1787-1827) to tutor her. As a result her painting improved considerably and in 1821 she was awarded a silver medal by the Society of Arts for an historical miniature. The Earl of Morton offered her financial assistance in order that she might leave Mr. Dukes, but she declined, and lived with the family for some sixteen years. She exhibited at the Royal Academy from 1821-1850, and worked in Birmingham, Brighton and Brussels (1821). In 1824 she married a Mr. Wright; the marriage was not a success and he left her, taking with him what money she had, and made no attempt to provide for her. She had the patronage of members of the Royal family, including George III, George IV, William IV, Queen Victoria and Prince Albert, and for many years managed to support herself. After the death of the Earl of Morton she found it difficult to obtain orders, and by

1846 her health had deteriorated and she was in very reduced circumstances. A number of influential people raised a subscription list which enabled her to live in some degree of comfort for her remaining years. She was of a pleasant disposition and was popular with all who knew her and admired her courage. She died in her lodgings in Duke Street, Liverpool on 2nd October, 1850, and was buried in St. James's Cemetery. Her painting, although a little stiff, is remarkable when one considers her condition. Two examples are in a private collection: one is a self-portrait, painted c.1830, inscribed on the reverse: 'Painted by / Mrs Wright — / Born without hands or feet. —' A label with the miniature states that it was exhibited at a woman's exhibition, London, 1900. The miniature is well painted, and shows her with a kindly expression; she is wearing a turban type hat, and a fur draped over her shoulder. The shading on the face is predominantly blue, with red lines to delineate the eyelids (Plate 70G). The other miniature is rectangular, and represents

279

Plate 70F (left). **J. Turmeau,** *portrait of an unknown man, ivory, 3ins., c.1790-1800. Signed in monogram: 'T.' This is a rare signature.* Courtesy Christie's.

Plate 70G (right). **Sarah Biffin (Mrs. Wright),** *(1784-1850), self-portrait of the artist, ivory, 4½ins., c.1830. Signed on the reverse: 'Painted by / Mrs. Wright— / Born without hands or feet.—' This miniature is of great historic interest and a remarkable achievement for someone with her disabilities.* Private Collection.

Peregrine Edward Townley (1762-1846), a well known figure in Lancashire. It is signed and dated 1847, and was probably taken from an earlier portrait. The painting is much stiffer than in her self-portrait, but it is a competent miniature (Plate 70E). Examples of her work are in the Hornby Art Library, Liverpool, and in the Victoria and Albert Museum.

George Stubbs, A.R.A. (1724-1806) was born in Liverpool, and was the son of a currier and leather dresser. He is best known as a painter of animals and portraits and can hardly be classed as a miniaturist, but is of interest in this connection because Richard Cosway advised him to experiment in enamel painting, which he did in 1771. He studied chemistry, founded new colours, and painted some of the largest enamels ever executed. A self-portrait of Stubbs painted on a Wedgwood plaque, 26½ by 20½ inches, signed: 'Geo Stubbs / pinxit 1781', was sold at Sotheby's on 12th July, 1967 for £8,000 (Plate 71A). He died on 10th July, 1806, and was buried in Marylebone Church.

James Sillett or Sillet (1764-1840) is a little known miniaturist who was born in Norwich, where he spent the greater part of his life. He was the son of James Sillett of Eye, Suffolk. After starting his career in Norwich as a heraldic painter, he went to London, and became a good miniaturist. He also painted fruit, flowers and game, both in oils and watercolour, and theatrical scenery at Drury Lane and Covent Garden. He exhibited at the Royal Academy, etc., 1796-1837. In c.1804 he went to King's Lynn, and executed the illustrations for the *History of Lynn,* published in 1812. He returned to Norwich in 1810, and remained there for the rest of his life. He married in 1801 Miss Ann Banyard of East Dereham, through whom he inherited some property. They had a daughter, Emma, who was a well known flower-painter. Sillett became President of the Norwich Society of Artists in 1815, and in 1826 published *A Grammar of Flower Painting.* This was followed in 1828 by a set of fifty-nine views of public edifices in Norwich. He died in Norwich on 6th May, 1840. A pair of miniatures by him of Mr. and Mrs. Alexander Henderson, both signed: 'J. Sillet', are in a private

Plate 71A (left). **George Stubbs, A.R.A.** *(1724-1806), self-portrait painted in enamel on a Wedgwood plaque, 26½ins. Signed and dated: 'Geo Stubbs / pinxit 1781.' This is an interesting example of Stubbs experimenting in this medium.* Courtesy Sotheby's.

Plate 71C (above). **Moses Haughton, Junior,** *William Roscoe (1753-1831), ivory, 9³/16ins., 1811. This fine miniature is a good character study of a man who did so much for the welfare of Liverpool.* Courtesy the Walker Art Gallery, Liverpool.

Plate 71B (left). Attributed to **Moses Haughton, Junior,** *Mrs. Thomas Roscoe, ivory, 7¼ins., c.1828. This is a colourful miniature, with the sitter's eyes painted in a brilliant blue.* Courtesy the Walker Art Gallery, Liverpool.

281

Plate 71D. **J. Pelham,** *two young ladies, ivory, 8ins. Signed and dated: 'J. Pelham 1840.' Miniatures by Pelham are scarce, and this is a good specimen of a large example of the period.* Courtesy Sotheby's.

collection. They are softly painted and well drawn; the expressions on the sitters' faces are pleasing. He used a soft, small stippling to model the face, and on the backgrounds. The costume is painted in fairly thick opaque colours (Plates 70B and C).

Thomas Heathfield Carrick (1802-1874, not 1875 as previously thought), was born at Upperby, near Carlisle, on 7th April, 1802. His father was reputed to be a glass and china merchant. Carrick was educated at Carlisle Grammar School and, after a quarrel with his family, left home and worked for a chemist in Carlisle. He later started his own business, and taught himself painting in his spare time. He was one of the earliest artists to develop the method of painting miniatures on marble. Carrick worked in Carlisle, Newcastle, Scarborough and London. He exhibited at the Royal Academy, 1841-1866. In 1845 he received a medal from the Prince Consort for his invention of painting on marble. Some of his miniatures were painted after photographs, or had a light photographic base. He had a photographic business in Regent Circus, London. He seems to have had a wide circle of friends which included Charles Dickens, William Wordsworth, Sir John Russell, the Earl of Carlisle and Longfellow. Carrick gave up miniature painting in 1868, and retired to Newcastle on a Turner Annuity. He died in Newcastle in August, 1874. He was a good artist and an accurate draughtsman, who seems to have been able to express the character of his sitters. It was said that "the animation of his portraits was due to his own lively conversation during sittings." He is said to have made Thomas Carlyle laugh so much that his wife "was sure the portrait would not be characteristic"!

His works are not always signed, and often are unattributed. The fact that they are painted on marble confuses new collectors, and they do not attract the attention they deserve. He painted boldy, with crossed brush strokes; the flesh colours are sometimes a soft pink or orange. He used a blue shading to model the features, and often placed his sitters against a plain grey or brownish background. Examples of his work are in the Tullie House Museum, Carlisle, which has his self-portrait, which is a fine example of his style (Plate 72C). He painted a good miniature of William Wordsworth, which is inscribed on the reverse: 'No I. William Wordsworth / T. Carrick / 43 Upper Seymour Street / Portman Sq.' Miniatures by him are in the Victoria and Albert Museum, and engraved portraits after him are in the British Museum. (Plate 72A.)

Thomas Harper (fl.1817-1843) is one of the many artists about whom no biographical information is available. He exhibited at the Royal Academy, 1817-1843, from various London addresses; some of his miniatures were of actors and actresses in character. He exhibited a miniature of Mrs. Harper in 1840. He was working in Brighton in 1821 when he painted the portraits of two very interesting local people — Mr. and Mrs. Sake Deen Mahomed. This pair of miniatures is in a private collection; both are signed. Mrs. Mahomed is signed: 'T. Harper / pinx^t 1821', and inscribed with the sitter's name in block letters; the portrait of Mahomed is inscribed and signed: 'MAHOMED / Shampooing Surgeon / BRIGHTON / Thomas Harper pinx^t 137 North Street. Brighton 1821'.

Sake Deen Mahomed was born in Patna, in Hindustan, in either 1749 or 1759. According to the inscription on his tombstone he was 101 when he died in 1851, but other sources put his date of birth as 1759. He trained as a medical student in Calcutta, joined the army as a surgeon, and took part in various engagements under Captain Baker, an officer in the East India Company's service. In 1784 he resigned his commission and accompanied

Plate 72A. **T.H. Carrick,** *Randle W. Saunders, ivory, 5ins. Signed: 'T. Carrick 1841.' This is a good portrait by Carrick whose work is scarce.* Courtesy F. Joachim.

Plate 72B. **J. Steel(e),** *General Sir Gregor Macgregor (fl. c.1811-1839), ivory, 6^{1}/8ins. The sitter is described as a 'South American adventurer'. He became a General in the Venezuelan army in 1839 and settled at Caracas.* Private Collection.

Captain Baker to Cork where he perfected his knowledge of English. Whilst in Cork he met a beautiful Irish girl, with whom he eloped and married. He and his wife, Jane, settled in Brighton in 1786 just at the moment when the town was opening up as a centre of great prosperity. The Prince of Wales came for the season and the whole place was filled with wealthy members of society. Mahomed opened a 'Shampooing and Vapour bath' business which, after a slow start, became a great success and attracted many of the most important members of Brighton Society, including the Prince himself.

Plate 72C. **Thomas Heathfield Carrick** *(1802-1874), self-portrait, watercolour on marble, 4⅞ins. Carrick was one of those who used marble as a base for miniatures.* Courtesy Tullie House Museum, Carlisle.

Patients came from far and wide, and his treatment became so popular that he opened premises in Ryder Street, London. His sons entered the business which flourished, and many people derived benefit from his system of massage in conjunction with scented vapour baths which seemed to be successful with rheumatic disease. He was a highly respected member of the community and very kind hearted. He retired from business in 1843, and died on 24th February, 1851, his wife having predeceased him only two months earlier at the age of seventy.

Colour Plate 24.
A top left. **George Place,** *an unknown man, ivory, 2⅞ins. Signed on the reverse.*
B top right. **Horace Hone, A.R.A.,** *an unknown lady, ivory, 2¹³/₁₆ins. Signed and dated on the front: 'HH / 1789.' This is a typical example of Hone's work.*
C centre. **Samuel Shelley,** *Mrs. Dorothea or Dorothy Jordan (1762-1816), née Bland, actress, assumed the name of Mrs. Jordan, mistress of the Duke of Clarence, ivory, 3¼ins. This is typical of Shelley's work.*
D bottom left. **Samuel Shelley,** *an unknown officer, ivory, 2⅞ins., c.1790-1800.*
E bottom right. **William Wood,** *an unknown officer, ivory, 3³/₁₆ins., c.1795-1800. This is a superb example of Wood's work.*
Courtesy Bernard Falk Collection, Royal Pavilion, Brighton

Harper's portraits of the pair are an interesting link with a bygone age; they are not of outstanding merit artistically, but warrant him a place amongst those who worked in the provinces (Plates 72D and E). An example of his work is in the Victoria and Albert Museum.

Jeremiah Steel(e) (c.1780-d. aft. 1826) worked in Nottingham, Bath, Liverpool and London. He is said to have been a pupil of A. Robertson. He exhibited at the Royal Academy and British Institution, 1801-1826. He was an artist of only average ability. A miniature by him of General Gregor Macgregor is in a private collection and is a good example of his work at its best (Plate 72B)

Space does not permit me to do more than mention a small number of the artists who worked in certain parts of the provinces whose miniatures might be discovered by the new collector. For those who want to know more I suggest that they look through the long list compiled by Basil Long in *British Miniaturists,* and names listed in my *Dictionary of British Miniature Painters.* The fact that there were so many artists who, even if they worked in the provinces, went to London for at least part of their career, makes the selection of those to be discussed in this chapter difficult. The importance of Academies outside London is obvious, and this is a point which many people do not realise. The fact that patrons and others were enthusiastic enough to encourage artists in different areas helped to keep the art alive and flourishing, and centres such as Bath and Liverpool were of great importance in the history of miniature painting.

Plate 72D. **T. Harper,** *Mrs. Mahomed, watercolour on paper, 7½ins. Signed: 'T. Harper / pinxᵗ 1821.' Inscribed: 'Mʳˢ MAHOMED / wife of Mʳ. Mahomed Shampooing Surgeon / BRIGHTON.'* Private Collection.

Plate 72E. **T. Harper,** *Mr. Mahomed, Shampooing Surgeon of Brighton, watercolour on paper, 7⁷/₈ins. Signed and inscribed: 'MAHOMED / Shampooing Surgeon / BRIGHTON / Thomas Harper pinxt 137 North Street. Brighton 1821.' These two miniatures are historically interesting, see pages 283-284.*

Chapter IX

Later Georgian Miniaturists

Plate 73A. **James Scouler** *(1740-1812), self-portrait of the artist, ivory, 4½ins., wearing a grey/blue waistcoat and jacket over a white shirt with pleated cuffs. He has a paint brush in his hand.* Courtesy Sotheby's.

THE PERIOD FROM the accession of George III in 1760 to the death of George IV in 1830 was one of the most important and prolific in the history of miniature painting. The encouragement given by the formation of drawing schools and academies, which has already been discussed, did much to increase the number of potential artists in every field. Premiums were awarded to those who showed outstanding ability, and the exhibitions held at the Society of Artists and the Royal Academy brought the names of budding artists to the notice of the public.

In order to be able to make comparisons more easily, I have selected a small number of the most important miniaturists such as Richard Cosway, George Engleheart, John Smart and others to be dealt with in the next chapter. Because of the large number of miniaturists working at this time it is impossible to do more than mention a cross-section of those whose work may interest new collectors. Many more will be illustrated, and a brief list of some lesser known ones included in an Appendix at the end of this chapter.

It is not always realised that between 1700 and 1800 the population of Britain had risen from about 5½ million to 9 million. This, together with increased wealth in many quarters led to a greater appreciation and demand for art. Besides employing craftsmen to build houses and furniture and to assist in choosing suitable décor, the 'new rich' were prepared to commission those artists whose work appealed to them to paint portraits, landscapes and miniatures to be displayed and enjoyed. One has only to attend sale rooms or art exhibitions to realise how many attractive paintings date from this period.

Plate 73B. **S. Cotes,** *an attractive miniature of an unknown lady, ivory, 2⅛ins. Signed in full and dated: 'S.Cotes pinxt / 1766.' The sitter's upswept hair is entwined with pearls, and she is wearing a low-cut blue dress.* Courtesy Sotheby's.

Artists such as Turner, Constable, de Wint, Paul Sandby and Sir Thomas Lawrence, to mention a few, were amongst the large number of artists who were coming to the fore. Their attractive country scenes, domestic groups and portraits are now highly valued. It is interesting to note how lesser known artists' work has suddenly become better appreciated and, because examples of their paintings are not at present so expensive, they are well worth acquiring. This is also true in the miniature field. Few new collectors can, or should, start with the most expensive portraits by the most important artists. Although it is wise to have at least one first rate example in every collection as a yardstick by which to judge the rest, it is more rewarding to build up knowledge gradually and be prepared to look for good examples of miniatures by lesser known artists. Although a few miniaturists included in this chapter were born well before 1760 they did not start their careers before then, and for this reason I have included them here.

Samuel Cotes (1734-1818) was born in London and was the younger son

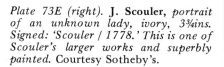

Plate 73C (left). **S. Cotes,** *portrait of an unknown lady, ivory, 2¼ins. Signed and dated: 'SC / 1778.' Wearing a blue dress with a yellow scarf over one shoulder. Set within a pearl bordered frame.* Courtesy Sotheby's.

Plate 73E (right). **J. Scouler,** *portrait of an unknown lady, ivory, 3¾ins. Signed: 'Scouler / 1778.' This is one of Scouler's larger works and superbly painted.* Courtesy Sotheby's.

Plate 73D. **S. Cotes,** *miniature of an elderly lady, ivory, 1¾ins. Signed and dated: 'SC / 1761.' Note the bonnet and black lace shawl.* Courtesy Sotheby's.

of an ex-Mayor of Galway who had become an apothecary in Cork Street, London. He was trained as an apothecary but preferred art, and was taught by his brother, Francis Cotes, R.A. (1725?-1770), a noted portrait painter.

Samuel painted miniatures on ivory and enamel, and executed pastel portraits. He exhibited at the Society of Artists, 1760-1768, and at the Royal Academy, 1769-1789. From 1769-1789 he was living at 25 Percy Street, Rathbone Place, London, but is said to have worked in Bath at some point. Cotes married twice; his only child died in infancy. His second wife, Sarah Shepherd or Sheppard (d.1814), was an amateur painter. Cotes apparently ceased to paint sometime before 1807. He died in Paradise Row, Chelsea, on 7th March, 1818. The fact that a mysterious Sarah Coote (fl.1777-1784), about whom nothing is known, shared the same initials, as did Samuel Collins, has caused some confusion regarding attributions. It is now generally accepted that all miniatures bearing the initials 'SC' and dated after 1768 are attributed to Cotes, and some dated as early as 1757 have also been tentatively assigned to him. Many of his signatures are made up of separate strokes, rather than the smooth 'S.C.' used by Collins (Colour Plate 15A).

Miniatures painted by Cotes are usually attractive, and graceful. He used opaque colours on the hair and on parts of the costume, such as lace edging and cravats. His work graduated from the smaller sizes used in the early part of the eighteenth century to larger formats, where he seems to have achieved a bolder effect. Occasionally he signed his miniatures in full. Examples of his work are in the Victoria and Albert Museum. (Plate 73B.) One of a lady, sold at Sotheby's on 10th November, 1969, signed and dated 1778, is a good example of the change in hair styles of the day, swept up high on to the head with a curl at the neck (Plate 73C).

William (Hopkins?) Craft or Croft (c.1730/5?-1811) was an enamellist whose exact date of birth and parentage is still uncertain. The whole matter, which is rather complicated, is set out in *A Dictionary of British Miniature Painters*, p.223. W.H. Craft was working for Wedgwood, in partnership with David Rhodes, for a few years from c.1768, and before that had worked in

Paris. W. Craft exhibited at the Royal Academy, 1774-1781 and 1794-1795. His initials are only given as W, and all examples painted before 1782 are signed: 'W. Craft'. Exceptions to this are a pair of large enamel plaques of George III and Queen Charlotte, signed: 'W.H. Craft. 1773', which are in the British Museum. There is the possibility that there were two artists who were related, but no conclusive evidence is so far forthcoming. For the present all works are attributed to W.H. Craft. Many of his works are rather large and include decorative compositions such as 'The Judgement of Paris', 'The Goddess of the Arts', and large plaques depicting rustic scenes in the manner of F. Boucher (one of these is in the British Museum). A large and ambitious work of c.1798 commemorates the naval heroes of the period; measuring 13 by 11¼ inches, it is illustrated in *A Dictionary of British Miniature Painters*, Plate 65, no. 184. An enamel of Francis Bacon after P. Van Somer by W.H.

Plate 73F. **J. Scouler,** *portrait of an unknown man, ivory, 1½ins. Signed and dated: 'Scouler / 176-' (the last digit being indecipherable). This is a typical example of Scouler's early work. Courtesy Dr. A.K. Brown.*

Plate 73G. **S. Cotes,** *Mr. John Whitelocke, ivory, 2⅛ins. Signed and dated: 'SC / 1772.' Part of a double-sided miniature set in a reversible brooch. Courtesy Sotheby's.*

Plate 73H. **J. Scouler,** *Henry Oswald Haughton, ivory, 4⅜ins. Signed and dated with a scratched signature: 'Scouler 1796.' Courtesy Christie's.*

Plate 73 I. **S. Cotes,** *Mrs. John Whitelocke, née Lutkins, ivory, 2⅛ins. Signed and dated: 'SC / 1772.' Part of the same reversible brooch in Plate 73G. Courtesy Sotheby's.*

Craft is in the National Gallery, Dublin. One of 'Capability' Brown, after Dance, signed and dated 1789, was sold at Sotheby's on 14th July, 1969 (Plate 74A), and a large one of Sir William Hamilton, inscribed on the reverse: 'The Rt Honble / Sr Wm Hamilton. / W.H. Craft fect: / 1802,' was sold at Sotheby's, 1st March, 1965 (Plate 74D and Figure 27).

Besides painting portraits and subject pieces Craft executed clock faces and landscapes. His work, although good, tends at times to be a little hesitant and often the colouring is rather harsh. Some of his miniatures are after Reynolds.

Thomas Day (c.1732?-1807?) is another artist about whom there has been a great deal of confusion. He is said to have been born in Devonshire, and to have had private means. He has been confused not only with Alexander Day

Plate 74A. **W.H. Craft** *after a portrait by N. Dance, Lancelot 'Capability' Brown (1715-83), enamel, 6⅝ins. Inscribed and dated: 'Lancelot Brown / ARM: OB: 6 feb: 1783 / AE 67 / W.H.Craft fecit: 1789.'* Courtesy Sotheby's.

(eighteenth century) who worked for some years in Rome and knew Ozias Humphry, but also with a little known artist nicknamed 'MacGilp Day' who was, in fact, one John Day, who prepared vehicles for varnishes. T. Day exhibited at the Royal Academy, 1773-1788, from various London addresses and from Brentwood, Essex. He painted landscapes, views, miniatures, and executed crayon drawings. His miniatures are not easy to recognise as only a few signed ones are known. A miniature of an unknown lady, signed and dated: 'TD / 1783', was formerly in the collection of Major R.M.O. de la Hey, and was exhibited in Edinburgh in 1965. Examples of his work are in the Victoria and Albert Museum.

John Singleton Copley, R.A., F.S.A. (1737/8-1815) was born in Boston, U.S.A., and was the son of Richard and Mary Copley, of Irish descent. His father died before John was ten years old, and his mother married, in May, 1748, Peter Pelham, a mezzotint engraver, portrait painter and schoolmaster.

Plate 74B (right). **W. Sherlock, F.S.A.,** *portrait of an unknown girl, ivory, 3¾ins. Signed in full and dated: 'Sherlock / 1806.' Signed miniatures by this artist are scarce.* Courtesy Christie's.

Plate 74C (far right). **W. Sherlock, F.S.A.,** *Sir John Andrew Stevenson (1761-1833), composer, ivory, 3⅛ins. Signed and dated: 'Sherlock / 1805.'* Courtesy Victoria and Albert Museum.

When his stepfather died three years later in 1751, the young man was left with Pelham's studio and equipment. He is best known for his portraits in oils and pastels, and historical and other subjects, but did execute some miniatures, most of which were probably painted between c.1760 and c.1770. He exhibited at the Society of Artists, 1768-1772, from Boston, and at the Royal Academy, British Institution, etc., 1776-1812. He was elected R.A. in 1779. Some of his miniature frames were made in gold and silver by Paul Revere and Nathaniel Hurd. He married, on 16th November, 1769, Susanna Farnham Clarke, daughter of Richard Clarke, agent of the East India Company and a wealthy merchant. They had five children, of whom one died young. He left America in June, 1774, and sailed for England, never to return. He later visited Italy and Paris, settling in London in 1775. His earliest known miniature is of Deborah Scollay, painted c.1762; this, and a pair representing Mr. and Mrs. Samuel Cary, painted in 1769, were reproduced in the catalogue of the Copley Exhibition held in 1965. The miniature of Mrs. Cary is signed in monogram: 'JSC', the C encircling the JS. These latter miniatures are attractive examples of his work on this scale, and there must be many more yet to be discovered.

William Sherlock, F.S.A. (c.1738-d. aft. 1806) was born in Dublin, the son of a fencing master who was said to have been identified with "Sherlock, the prize fighter". Nothing is known about his early life, but by 1759 he was in London, studying at the St. Martin's Lane Academy; he was awarded premiums for drawing and engraving in 1759 and 1760 from the Society of Arts. He was in Paris for a time and studied under Le Bas, the engraver. Sherlock exhibited at the Society of Artists from 1764-1780. He became a Director of the Society in 1773. He exhibited at the Royal Academy, 1796-1806. His works included portraits in oils and watercolour, small full-length portraits, miniatures and a series of engraved portraits for

Smollett's *History of England*. He also was a picture dealer and copyist. His signature varied: 'Shirlock', 'W Sh', and 'W S pinxt' have all been seen and his self-portrait in the collection of K. Guichard, Esq. is inscribed on the reverse: 'Portrait of / Wm. Sherlock. Sen. / 180(5) / by Wm Sherlock Sen. / 43 Broad St / Golden Square.' He and his son, W.P. Sherlock (b.1775?) both exhibited from this address in 1806. His style of painting varies, some of it showing a Continental influence. He shaded the background with a cross-hatching. His miniatures are softly painted, the hair being in soft waves rather than in strands. One of an unknown young girl sold at Christie's was signed on the front: 'Sherlock / 1806' (Plate 74B). Examples of his work are in the Victoria and Albert Museum (Plate 74C).

John Taylor (1739-1838) was born in Bishopsgate Street, London, and was the son of a customs officer. He was called 'Old Taylor'. He studied at the St. Martin's Lane Academy, and was a pupil of F. Hayman. He exhibited at the Society of Artists and the Free Society, 1764-1777, and at the Royal Academy, British Institution, etc., 1780-1838; he was elected F.S.A. in 1772 and Director in 1775. His works included miniatures (some of which were said to be on enamel) and minutely finished portraits in plumbago, oil portraits, and chalk drawings. He was in Oxford 1767-c.1771, Bristol, June 1775, and Manchester 1777. Taylor then took up teaching. He invested his earnings in annuities which expired in 1840 and died in Cirencester Place on 21st November, 1838, in his ninety-ninth year! His plumbago portraits are among the finest of the period. They are drawn with a soft touch and are artistically posed, often against a landscape or tree background. A point to note is the way in which he drew the leaves in a uniformly ovoid form. He may well have taught Henry Edridge, whose drawings often have the same style but are drawn with a harder pencil. A particularly fine example of Taylor's work is a drawing of a scholar and his pupil in a garden, signed on the back of a seat: 'John Taylor 1772'. The treatment of the leaves is noticeable in this drawing (Plate 76D). One of an unknown lady, signed and dated on a seat: 'John Taylor / 1775', is another good example of his work (Plate 76C).

James Scouler (1740-1812) was not, as has been supposed, born in London, but in Edinburgh. Proof of this has kindly been supplied to me by his descendant, Miss J. Brebner. His baptism is recorded in the Edinburgh Baptism Register: "1740 Jan 13 to James Scouller Turner and Grizel Fyfe a son James. Witnesses John Fyfe taylor and John Scouller Turner in Edinburgh born 10th inst." It is assumed that the witnesses were both grandfathers. Turnery was an unusual craft, and both James's father and grandfather were Turners, or 'Cop (Cup) Turner' as the grandfather was

Plate 75.
A. **J. Plott**, *portrait of an unknown man, pencil on paper, 5ins. Signed and dated: 'Drawn by M.ʳ Plott / Nov.11 1791.' This is one of the few known signed works by Plott; miniatures by him are scarce.* Courtesy Sotheby's.
B. **Joseph Slater, Junior**, *Carissima Matilda Slater (1810-47), niece of the artist. Pencil on paper, 7½ins. The sitter was the daughter of John and Elizabeth Slater, and the drawing comes from an album of portraits by different members of the Slater family kept by one of their descendants. The influence of Lawrence can be detected in this drawing.* Private Collection.
C. **H.J. Burch**, *portrait of an unknown lady, watercolour on paper, 5½ins. Signed: 'H Burch.'* Private Collection.
D. **T. Arrowsmith**, *John Nash (b.c.1718), watercolour on paper, 5ins. Inscribed on the reverse: 'John Nash. Sept 29th 1797, aged 79 years.' This is a good portrait by a little-known artist.* Courtesy F. Joachim.

A

B

C

D

293

Plate 76A. **J. Downman, A.R.A.**, *a fine portrait of George Poyntz Ricketts (d.1800), Governor of Barbados in 1798, watercolour on paper, 7¾ins. Probably painted in 1793, in which year Downman painted Mrs. Poyntz Ricketts.* Private Collection.

Plate 76B. **E.W. Thomson**, *an unknown lady, watercolour on paper, 6ins. Signed: 'E.W.Thomson pinxt 68 Rue du fg St.Honore.' Painted in 1824, in which year Thomson also painted the sitter's husband.* Private Collection.

Plate 76C. **J. Taylor**, *portrait of an unknown lady, pencil on paper, 6⅜ins. Signed and dated: 'John Taylor / 1775.' Taylor was an excellent draughtsman, and his works are well worth including in a collection.* Private Collection.

Plate 76D. **J. Taylor**, *a scholar and his tutor, pencil on paper, 7½ins. Signed and dated: 'John Taylor 1772.' These two portraits are fine examples of the artist's work.* Private Collection.

called. The son, James, started his career as a turner, but got into debt and became a musical instrument maker. Whether or not he also made organs is uncertain. He married Grizel Fife (bapt. 5th July, 1713), on 8th June, 1735. James was the youngest of four (or five) children born to them: John, the elder son (who must have died before his father), and two sisters, Mary and Agnes. James was heir to his father's estate. The fact that James Scouler and John Brown (also a miniaturist) were cousins has already been discussed in Chapter VII. Although his name is not recorded by the family, it would appear that James had another brother, Robert, as a miniature signed and dated: 'J. Scouler / 1768', and inscribed on the reverse: 'Robert Scouler / Ensign in India / Brother to James Scouler / Portrait Painter / 1768.', is in the collection of Lord Thomson and was exhibited in Edinburgh in 1965.

Plate 77A. **H. Spicer,** *Mrs. Martyr, enamel, 2⅞ins. Dated '1788.' This is an attractive portrait and interesting for costume.* Courtesy Sotheby's.

Scouler studied at the Duke of Richmond's Gallery and in the St. Martin's Lane Academy. He was awarded a premium for drawing in 1755 by the Society of Arts. He exhibited at the Society of Artists, 1761-1768, and at the Free Society in 1767. From 1780-1787 he exhibited at the Royal Academy. He lived in Great Newport Street up to c.1776 and 47 Great Russell Street from c.1780 until his death. Scouler painted miniatures and crayon portraits and is said to have painted on enamel. He may have visited India between 1776 and 1780, and he certainly had money invested in the East India Company. He died in London on 22nd February, 1812, leaving an estate of about £7,500. Most of Scouler's miniatures are small, but there are exceptions such as the miniature in the Victoria and Albert Museum of David Garrick and his wife, signed and dated: 'J. Scouler / 1768'. This miniature is 5⅜ inches high. Some of his early miniatures show a marked resemblance to the early works of John Smart, and the fact that they shared the same initials may have led to confusion in attributions. A number of these miniatures have a bluish shading on the face and a stippled background. He used a lot of gum with his paints, giving his miniatures the impression of oil paintings. His later works are often signed: 'Scouler' parallel to the edge of the miniature, or: 'J. Scouler Pinxt', followed by a date (Plates 73E, F and H). Sometimes the signature is scratched in the paint. Examples of his work are in the Glasgow Art Gallery and the Victoria and Albert Museum, as well as numerous private collections. His self-portrait (Plate 73A) was sold at Sotheby's, Lot 48 on 5th June, 1972. (Colour Plate 12D.)

Henry Spicer, F.S.A. (1743-1804) was born at Reepham, Norfolk. His parentage is unknown, nor do we know where he was educated. He studied under G. Spencer in London, and from 1765-1783 exhibited at the Society of Artists, acting as its secretary in 1773. Spicer exhibited at the Royal Academy, 1774-1804, and was elected F.S.A. in 1770. He exhibited from various London addresses including, from c.1784-1802, Great Newport Street. In 1804 he exhibited from 39 Lower Thornhaugh Street, but is said to have died on 8th June of the same year at 7 Great Newport Street. He went to Dublin, c.1776, where he was well received and painted portraits of prominent people. By 1782 he was back in London and was appointed Painter in Enamel to H.R.H. the Prince of Wales, whose portrait he painted. The Royal Warrant is still in the possession of his descendants, together with an unsigned painting of him attributed to Sir Joshua Reynolds. Spicer exhibited a posthumous enamel portrait of Reynolds at the Royal Academy in 1792. He had a distinguished clientele, which included the Duke of

Plate 77B. **H. Spicer,** *portrait of an unknown officer, enamel, 2¼ins., c.1780-90. The sitter is wearing a scarlet uniform with a blue collar and epaulettes.* Courtesy Sotheby's.

Plate 77C. **H. Spicer,** *an unknown officer, ivory, 1⁹⁄₁₆ins. Signed: 'HS.' The sitter is wearing a dicorn hat. This is an early work by Spicer and an interesting example of his work on ivory.* Courtesy Victoria and Albert Museum, Alan Evans Collection.

Plate 77D. **H. Spicer,** *portrait of Dr. Samuel Arnold (1740-1802), composer to Covent Garden, enamel, 3ins.* Courtesy Sotheby's.

Plate 77E. **E. Vaughan,** *Catharin Smyth, wife of Thomas Smyth, watercolour on paper, 6¼ins. Signed: 'E Vaughan / 1781.'* Courtesy A.J.W. Vaughan.

Northumberland, Earl Moira, Lord Nelson, and Charlotte Augusta, Princess of Wales. The portrait of the latter was amongst several by him that were engraved. He numbered among his friends George Stubbs, J.H. Mortimer, and Ozias Humphry. His wife's name is not known, but two of his daughters, Miss J. Spicer and Miss M.A. Spicer, were both miniaturists. Spicer was ill for some time before his death, by which time he was a poor man. Ozias Humphry lodged, until his death in 1810, with Spicer's widow, who lived at 39 Lower Thornhaugh Street, which was the last address from which Spicer exhibited. Spicer's miniatures are painted with fairly bright colours; his painting is smooth and the brush strokes on the face well blended. Many of his miniatures are unsigned; those that are, are often signed on the front with a cursive 'S', or 'HS', followed by a date, and occasionally he signed in full: 'H. Spicer pinxt', followed by a date. Some of his miniatures are after Reynolds. His miniatures on ivory are rare; one of an unknown officer in a dicorn hat, signed: 'HS', is in the Alan Evans Collection at the Victoria and Albert Museum (Plate 77C). Several miniatures by Spicer were sold at Sotheby's on 25th November, 1974, including one of Dr. Samuel Arnold (1740-1802), the composer (Plate 77D), and one of Mrs. Martyr, dated 1788 (Plate 77A and B).

Edward Vaughan, Junior (1746-1814) is an artist about whom little was known, but through the kindness of his descendant, Anthony J.W. Vaughan, I am now able to publish more exact details of his life and family. Edward was christened at St. Michael's Cornhill on 6th April, 1746, and was the younger of two surviving sons of Edward Vaughan (1705-1766), a citizen and fanmaker, and his wife, Amy Anne, née Gilbert, also a fanmaker. Edward, Senior, was a fanmaker of some repute as the inventor of the 'Necromatic Trick Fan'. He was made a Freeman and Member of the Fanmakers' Company in 1736. From 1736-1759 the family lived in a house at the Golden Fan, next to the Royal Exchange. This was destroyed in 1759 in a disastrous fire which swept Cornhill in November of that year. The family then moved to St. Michael's Alley, Cornhill, a house which they occupied for the next sixty years. Mrs. Vaughan continued the fanmaking business after her husband's death until her own death in 1799 at the great age of ninety-five. She was a woman of parts and served as sextoness and organ blower at St. Michael's Church, Cornhill, when already well in her eighties until the time of her death!

Edward Vaughan, Junior, was undoubtedly trained by his father as a fan painter, and from this turned to miniature painting. He married, on 29th May, 1773, Sarah King (b.1748), of Christchurch, Spitalfields. The marriage, which was by licence, took place at St. Michael's, Cornhill, when Edward was described as "Edward Vaughan of the Parish of St. Michael, Cornhill London Miniature Painter". He was one of ten children, six of whom died in infancy. Both Edward and his elder brother, Thomas, attended St. Paul's School; Edward was admitted on 15th September, 1755. He exhibited at the Society of Artists and the Free Society, 1772-1783, and at the Royal Academy, 1778-1814. He had four children, of whom the eldest, Thomas (1776-1856), was a portrait painter, and a pupil of Nasmyth in Edinburgh. He also studied at the Royal Academy Schools in 1800, and was later appointed full-time clerk to the Royal Academy. Edward Vaughan's grandson, H.W.M. Vaughan, was a furniture designer and cabinet maker, whose son was the founder of W.H. Vaughan & Co., who were well known London cabinet makers for over a hundred years. Edward Vaughan painted miniatures and small profile portraits in watercolour. His early works were slightly tentative but he later became more assured. He signed in full: 'E Vaughan / 1781', 'E.V.', and 'E.V.' followed by a date or: 'E.V.' (cursive) 'Delin.' Many of his profile portraits have dark backgrounds. A number of his works are in the collection of his descendant, A.J.W. Vaughan (Plates 77E, F and G).

Plate 77F. **E. Vaughan,** *an unknown Captain of the 53rd Foot, ivory, 2½ins. Signed and dated: 'E.V. / 1783.' This is a particularly good example of Vaughan's work, which is scarce.* Courtesy Victoria and Albert Museum, Alan Evans Collection.

Plate 77G. **E. Vaughan,** *Mr. Thomas Smyth, watercolour on paper, 6¼ins. Signed: 'EV Delt / 1781.' This and Plate 77E are interesting examples of portraits by this little-known artist.* Courtesy A.J.W. Vaughan.

Plate 78A. **J. Downman,** A.R.A., *portrait of an unknown lady, ivory, 3ins. This is a good example of Downman's work in miniature, of which no signed ones are known. It is almost certainly the same sitter as the one in Colour Plate 16D. Ex de la Hey Collection.*

John Downman, A.R.A. (1750-1824) was the son of Francis Downman, an attorney, and his wife, Charlotte, née Goodsend, eldest daughter of Francis Goodsend, private secretary to George I. His place of birth is uncertain: the family lived for some time at St. Neot's, Huntingdonshire, but later settled in Wales. Downman was educated at Ruabon, where he may well have been born. He was the youngest of five sons and was sent to Chester, and later to Liverpool, to learn drawing, but insisted on coming to London where, in March, 1769, he entered the Royal Academy Schools. He studied under B. West, for whom he had a great admiration. Downman exhibited at the Free Society in 1768 and at the Royal Academy, 1770-1819. He is best known for his delightful small portraits in watercolour, oil portraits, and historical subjects, but he also executed a few landscape drawings of Italy and the Lake District as well as miniatures. These latter works are very scarce and, as they are not signed, sometimes pass unrecognised. They are, in fact, very close in style to his larger portraits, and are amongst the most attractive miniatures of the period. One of Miss Farren, in a private collection, is inscribed on the reverse: 'Miss Farren / The Incomparable Actress / 1787' (Colour Plate 29E). A charming miniature in profile of an unknown lady, c.1785, was Lot 55 at Sotheby's on 30th May, 1977 (Plate 78E). A good example of his larger watercolours is the one of George Poyntz Ricketts (d.1800), Governor of Barbados (Plate 76A). It was probably painted in 1793, in which year he painted a portrait of Mrs. Poyntz Ricketts. A large number of his works are illustrated in *John Downman,* by Dr. G.C. Williamson. Downman was elected A.R.A. in 1795. He worked in London, Plymouth, Exeter, Cambridge, Chester and elsewhere, and in November, 1771, went to Italy with Joseph Wright of Derby, returning to England in 1775. He moved about a lot: he was in East Malling, Kent, from 1804-1806, and, after a stay in Plymouth and Exeter, returned to London in 1809. He toured the Lake District in 1817 and finally settled in Chester, moving later to Wrexham, where he died on 24th December, 1824. His works on any scale are elegant and well posed; his sketches are charming, and executed with great economy of line. He had a distinguished clientele which included Georgiana, Duchess of Devonshire, the Princess Royal, daughter of George III, and Mrs. Siddons. Many of his works have been engraved. A number of his drawings are in the British Museum, and other examples in the Victoria and Albert Museum. (Colour Plate 16D and Plate 78A.)

William Grimaldi (1751-1830) was born in Shoreditch on 26th August, 1751, and was the son of Alexander Grimaldi, 7th Marquess, and his second wife, Esther Barton (d.1774). He was descended from the family of Grimaldi of Genoa, the Merovingian Kings of France and the Princes of Monaco. He studied art under T. Worlidge, who may have been his uncle and who married Arabella Grimaldi. Grimaldi exhibited at the Free Society, 1768-1770, the Society of Artists in 1772, and at the Royal Academy, 1786-1830. He worked in London and the provinces, and was in Chester in 1774. In 1783 he married at Maidstone, Kent, Frances, daughter of Robert Willis, Esq. She was co-heiress with her sister Mary (wife of Sir John Stirling) to her father's estate. The Grimaldis had four children: William, Henry, Louisa Frances and Stacey, 9th Marquess. Neither he nor his father, the 8th Marquess, ever used the title as far as I know. Grimaldi was appointed miniature painter to the Duke and Duchess of York in 1791, also to George

Plate 78B. **W. Grimaldi,** *a charming miniature of a young girl, ivory, 2½ins. Signed and dated: 'Grimaldi 1795.' The child has long auburn hair and is wearing a white dress with a green sash, painted against a cloud and sky background. The miniature is mounted in a locket set with rose cut diamonds.* Courtesy Sotheby's.

III, and in 1824 to George IV. He painted miniatures in watercolour and enamel, and copied the works of Reynolds, Hoppner, Beechey, and others. He appears to have lived for most of his life in London, and latterly at 16 Upper Ebury Street, Chelsea, where he died on 27th May, 1830. His work shows Continental influence and is a little uneven in quality; at best it is excellent. A very unusual example is of Miss Sarah Anne Knupp standing in a landscape background. It is signed on the front: 'W.G. / 1826', and in full on the reverse (Plate 78D). A charming miniature of a young girl with auburn hair painted against a cloud and sky background, set in a frame of rose diamonds, was Lot 396, in the Heckett sale at Sotheby Parke Bernet, New York, on 5th October, 1977. It is signed and dated along the edge: 'Grimaldi 1795' (Plate 78B).

Characteristics of his work are the way he painted the features. He tended to pick out the eyelids, nostrils, lips, and contours of the face in a reddish colour, and shaded the face with short blue lines. Opaque white is sometimes used in the hair, and the eyes are sometimes rather staring. He used some stippling in the background and usually signed along the lower edge of the miniature either: 'Grimaldi', followed by a date, or: 'W. Grimaldi A.R.' in italics. (The A.R. is supposed to indicate Académie Royale, of which he was not in fact a member!) Occasionally he inscribed his miniatures on the reverse with his name and address and appointments to the Royal family. Some of his works were engraved. Examples of his miniatures are in the London Museum, the Wallace Collection, and the Victoria and Albert Museum. (Colour Plate 23C.)

Edward Miles (1752-1828) was born at Yarmouth, Norfolk, on 14th October, 1752. Nothing is known about his parentage or early education, but he became an errand boy to a surgeon who encouraged him to draw. He went to London in 1771, and entered the Royal Academy Schools on 20th January, 1772. He exhibited at the Royal Academy, 1775-1797, and copied pictures by Reynolds. His portrait was painted by Beechey. He was working in Norwich in 1779 and 1782, Russia, 1797-c.1806, and Philadelphia,

Plate 78C. **E. Miles,** *portrait of an unknown lady, ivory, 3ins. c.1780. Wearing a white dress with a yellow sash.* Courtesy Sotheby's.

Plate 78D. **W. Grimaldi,** *Sarah Anne Knupp, daughter of Thomas George Knupp, ivory, 5½ins. Signed: 'W.G. / 1826' on the front and fully signed and dated on the reverse. This is an unusual miniature for Grimaldi, and, although attractive, is a little hesitant in draughtsmanship.* Private Collection.

Plate 78E. **J. Downman, A.R.A.,** *an attractive miniature of an unknown lady, ivory, 3ins., c.1785. This is a good example of costume and hair style, and typical of Downman's larger portraits.* Courtesy Sotheby's.

1807-1828. In 1792 he was appointed miniature painter to the Duchess of York, and later to Queen Charlotte. Whilst in St. Petersburg he became Court Painter to the Czar. He settled in Philadelphia where he remained until his death on 7th March, 1828. He was friendly with Sir Thomas Lawrence. James Reid Lambdin, an American miniaturist, was his pupil. Due to the fact that most of his works are not signed attributions are difficult and some of his miniatures have been attributed to Cosway and others. They do, however, have a distinct style, and a characteristic is that they are frequently pale and have a yellowish colouring. The eyes, mouth and nose are clearly defined. Most of his miniatures are softly painted, as in the case of one of Princess Charlotte Augusta Matilda, sold at Christie's, on 15th June, 1976 (Plate 78F). One of an unknown officer by Miles in the Victoria and Albert Museum is painted in much stronger colours. Many of his miniatures are in America. He painted portraits and taught drawing. During the latter part of his life he practically abandoned portraiture and confined himself to teaching drawing at the Academy in Philadelphia, of which he was a founder member. Examples of his work are at Windsor Castle and the Victoria and Albert Museum, as well as in numerous private collections. (Plate 78C.)

Samuel Shelley (1750/56?-1808) was a native of London and was born in Whitechapel. He was said to be largely self-taught. On 21st March, 1774, he entered the Royal Academy Schools, when his age was recorded as "17 last March", making his date of birth 1756. He was awarded a premium at the Society of Arts in 1770, and exhibited at the Society of Artists, 1773 and 1775, and at the Royal Academy, 1774-1804. He also exhibited at the British Institution and Old Water Colour Society, of which he was a founder member. From c.1800-1804 he was a member of a sketching club whose other members included J. Ward and W.H. Pyne. Shelley was a versatile artist who, besides painting miniatures, executed figure subjects in watercolour, oil

Plate 78F (left). **E. Miles,** *Princess Charlotte Augusta Matilda (1766-1828), Princess Royal. eldest daughter of George III, married Frederick, Prince of Würtemberg in 1797. Ivory, 2¾ins. Other versions of this miniature exist, of which one is at Windsor Castle.* Courtesy Christie's.

Plate 78G (right). **W. Grimaldi,** *portrait of an unknown man, ivory, 2¾ins., c.1795. This is a typical example of Grimaldi's work.* Courtesy Sotheby's.

paintings, drew book illustrations, and engraved some of his own works; others were engraved by Bartolozzi, J.R. Smith, etc. Alexander Robertson and E. Nash were among his pupils. He had various London addresses including Henrietta Street, Covent Garden, and finally No. 6 George Street, Hanover Square. Long lists most of his addresses in *British Miniaturists*, p.397. Shelley was an artist of above average ability; his draughtsmanship was good and his miniatures of ladies and children charming. Miniatures by him are easily distinguishable once his style and technique have been closely examined. Characteristics to look for are a yellowish green flesh tint (this is sometimes apparent on the background as well), a slightly enlarged pupil of the eye, and the use of rather more gum, which gives the miniatures the appearance of oil paintings. He was one of the miniaturists who was fond of painting portrait groups, and for this purpose used larger and longer ivories than many of his contemporaries. Occasionally he placed the oval on its side to accommodate the group more artistically. His signatures vary: sometimes he signed: 'S.S.' on the front, but usually the signatures, if any, are in full on the reverse, followed by his address which is useful for dating purposes. He was a prolific artist and consequently not all his works are of equal merit. He sometimes copied works by Reynolds. He died at his house in Hanover Square on 22nd November, 1808, and on 22nd March, 1809, his effects were sold, including a collection of 'old masters', and a number of his miniatures and ivories, etc. A catalogue of the sale is in the Victoria and Albert Museum, who have examples of his work. A number of fine miniatures by Shelley are in the Bernard Falk Collection, on loan to the Royal Pavilion, Brighton. Other examples are in the Fitzwilliam Museum, Cambridge, the Ward Usher Museum, Lincoln, the City of Liverpool Museum, and the Victoria and Albert Museum. A few drawings by him and some engravings after him are in the British Museum, and the Victoria and Albert Museum also possess some sketch books and two watercolour paintings by him. (Colour Plates 24C and D, Plates 80A, B, D and E.)

Plate 79A. **H. Bone, R.A.,** *after Reynolds, William Cavendish, 5th Duke of Devonshire (1748-1811), enamel, 6ins. Bearing a brief inscription by Bone on the reverse: '13.6.B.'* Courtesy Christie's.

Plate 79B. **H. Bone, R.A.,** *after a portrait by H.P. Bone, Miss Isabell Cowell, enamel, 4¼ins. Signed and dated on the reverse: 'Miss Isabell Cowell / London 1826– / Painted by Henry Bone R.A. Enamel / Painter to his Majesty and the Duke of York after a Miniature by (H. Pierce) Bone.'* Courtesy Sotheby's.

Daniel Gardner (1750-1805) is one of the most noted pastellists and is not usually thought of as a miniaturist although he is supposed to have executed a few early in his career. One of Francis Powell, Esq., signed: 'D.G.', and attributed to him was sold at Sotheby's in the Hand Collection on 25th November, 1952. A small sketch of miniature size of an unrecorded self-portrait by Gardner is in a private collection, and was exhibited at Abbot Hall Art Gallery, Kendal (Plate 82D).

William Russell Birch (1755-1834) was born in Warwick on 9th April, 1755. Nothing is known about his early life or education. He was a pupil of Henry Spicer, from whose house he exhibited two mythological subjects on enamel at the Society of Artists in 1775. He exhibited at the Royal Academy, 1781-1794, and was awarded a silver palette by the Society of Arts in 1784. He was one of the many miniaturists who copied works by Reynolds in miniature. Besides executing enamel miniatures and engravings, he invented a new colour for the use of enamellists. In 1791, he published a book of engravings called *Délices de la Grande Bretagne.* His exhibits included portraits of Sir Joshua Reynolds, Mrs. Siddons and Lord Rockingham. Armed with a recommendation from Benjamin West, Birch went to America in 1793 or 1794, and settled in Philadelphia, where he died on 7th August, 1834. Birch painted copies on enamel of Washington, after Gilbert Stuart, and many other enamel miniatures. He also published views of Philadelphia and of American country houses, and wrote an autobiography.

Birch was a good enamellist, and his draughtsmanship was excellent; he signed: 'W. Birch', 'Wm. Birch', etc., often followed by a date. Works by him are scarce and many of them may be in America. Examples are in the Ashmolean Museum, Oxford, and the Victoria and Albert Museum. His son, Thomas Birch (1779 or 1787-1851), went with his father to Philadelphia and they worked together as William Birch and Son, designing and engraving views of Philadelphia, which they published.

Henry Bone, R.A. (1755-1834) was born in Truro on 6th February, 1755, and was the son of a wood-carver and cabinet maker. Whether or not he worked in his father's business is unknown, but he was evidently attracted to painting and decorated china for Cookworthy at Plymouth and, on 23rd January, 1772, was apprenticed to R. Champion in Bristol. The factory failed in 1778, and by c.1779 Bone had settled in London. He married, on 21st January, 1779, Elizabeth van der Meulen, by whom he had a number of children, some of whom became miniaturists; their work will be discussed in a later chapter. They included H.P. Bone, P.J. Bone, R.T. Bone, W. Bone, Senior, T.M. Bone, S.V. Bone, and one further child, probably a daughter. Henry painted designs for lockets, watches and jewellery as well as miniatures on ivory and enamel. His first enamel miniatures are said to have been painted in 1780. He exhibited chiefly at the Royal Academy, 1781-1834, but also at the British Institution and Society of British Artists, and at the Free Society in 1783. Although he spent most of his life in London he was an itinerant painter and toured the country, especially in the West. He was in Truro in 1796. During the season Bone had exhibitions of

Plate 79C. **H. Bone, R.A.,** *after Reynolds, Henry Gawler and John Bellenden Ker, enamel, 5¾ins. Inscribed in full on the reverse: 'Henry Gawler & John Bellenden / Ker, surviving Children of / John & Caroline Gawler — / London / Oct. 1820 / Painted by Henry Bone R.A. / Enamel Painter to His Majesty / after the Original picture by / the late Sᴿ Joshua Reynolds P.R.A.' This is a fine example of an enamel by Bone. Courtesy Sotheby's.*

his work at his house in Berners Street, London. He had many distinguished patrons, including George III, George IV, and William IV, but the majority of his miniatures were copies of the works of other artists. Those painted on ivory are mostly originals.

He and his sons gave fresh impetus to the interest in enamel miniatures, which had rather lost their popularity, and at the present time examples of their work are fetching high prices in the sale rooms. Some of them are rather large. His miniatures on ivory, which are scarce, are usually signed: 'HB' in Roman capitals which are conjoined; he occasionally adopted the same method on enamels but these are more frequently inscribed in full on the reverse, giving full details of the sitter and the artist from whom the miniature was copied. He became A.R.A. in 1801 and R.A. in 1811, and he is said to have received a pension from the Royal Academy after his sight failed in 1832.

A portrait of his wife by him is in the Victoria and Albert Museum, and one of two known portraits of himself after John Opie, R.A., is in the National Gallery, Dublin, and dated 1830; another version fully inscribed and dated 1828 was sold at Christie's on 27th February, 1968. His portrait by Opie is in the National Portrait Gallery, London. He died of paralysis at 6 Clarendon Street, Somers Town, London, on 17th December, 1834. Bone had many friends, and was described as a "worthy, kind liberal and affectionate man". In spite of the fact that so many of his portraits were copies he was a good artist, who drew well and used fresh natural colours. Eighty-five enamels by him, of illustrious characters in the reign of Queen Elizabeth, were exhibited at the Society of British Artists in 1834.

Examples of his miniatures are in many private collections and in a number of museums, including the Fitzwilliam Museum, Cambridge, the

Plate 79D (right). **H. Bone, R.A.,** *after Russell, Miss Elizabeth Georgina Morgan, later Mrs. John Sandford (1786-1857), enamel, 6½ins. Inscribed on the reverse: 'Miss Morgan London Dec* 1819 *painted by Henry Bone, R.A. Enamel painter to His Royal Highness the Prince Regent, after a crayon Picture by — Russell R.A.' Both the miniature and the original portrait are at Corsham Court.* Courtesy the late Lord Methuen, R.A.

Colour Plate 25.
A. **Louis Ami Arlaud,** *Mr. Bryan, ivory, 2¾ins. Signed: 'Arlaud.'*
B. **Thomas Hazelhurst,** *an unknown officer, ivory, 29/16ins., c.1790. Signed: 'TH.'*
C. **John Smart,** *an unknown young girl, ivory, 3½ins. Signed and dated: 'JS / 1807.' This is a fine example of a miniature painted towards the end of his life.*
D. **John Comerford,** *Capt. Samuel Lamb, ivory, 3⅛ins., c.1800.*
E. **George Engleheart,** *Lady Burrell Blunt, ivory, 3¼ins., 1792. Engleheart painted several portraits of the Blunt family, and at least one more of this sitter.*

Private Collection

Bristol Art Gallery (who have portraits on enamel of him and his wife), The Louvre, the National Gallery, Dublin, the National Portrait Gallery and the Victoria and Albert Museum. A good rectangular enamel of William, 5th Duke of Devonshire, after Reynolds, was sold at Christie's on 21st June, 1966 (Plate 79A), and one of Miss Isabell Cowell, after his son, H.P. Bone, signed and dated 1826, was Lot 51 at Sotheby's on 19th October, 1970 (Plate 79B). An attractive enamel of Miss Elizabeth Georgina Morgan, after a portrait by John Russell, was lent by the late Lord Methuen to the exhibition in Edinburgh in 1965. It is signed and inscribed in full on the reverse: 'Miss Morgan London Decr 1819 painted by Henry Bone, R.A. Enamel-painter to His Royal Highness the Prince Regent, after a crayon Picture by – Russell, R.A.' (Plate 79D).

Plate 80A (left). **S. Shelley**, *a family group, ivory, 3³⁄₈ins. Signed: 'SS.' This is an early work by Shelley, probably painted c.1775.* Courtesy Sotheby's.

Plate 80B (right). **S. Shelley**, *an attractive miniature of a young boy, ivory, 2½ins. Signed in full on the reverse.* Courtesy Sotheby's.

Richard Collins (1755-1831) was born at Gosport on 30th January, 1755. Of his parentage and early education we know nothing except that he was apprenticed to a mercer. He entered the Royal Academy Schools on 4th October, 1776, when he was twenty-one. He exhibited at the Royal Academy, 1777-1818, and was a pupil of J. Plott, O. Humphry and J. Meyer. In 1780 Collins lodged for a year with Humphry, who recorded in a manuscript some details about his friend's career and declared that he was "a miniature painter of great merit". Collins copied pictures at Petworth in 1798. He married a Miss Scale, who died in 1788 leaving him with one daughter. He was so distressed at the loss of his wife that, according to Humphry, George III took pity on him and appointed him principal portrait painter in enamel in 1789, in spite of the fact that R. Crosse and R. Bowyer had already been appointed to the same office. Miniatures by Collins are scarce, and as he seldom signed his portraits attribution is difficult. His miniatures are well painted and attractive, and are executed on ivory and enamel. He painted with such fine brush strokes that they are blended together in a manner which makes them indistinguishable. One of the finest miniatures I have seen by Collins is of an unknown lady, in the Rijksmuseum, Amsterdam. It is signed on the reverse: 'R. Collins' (Plate 80G). A miniature of a young man by him was Lot 94 at Christie's, 3rd October, 1972 (Plate 80C). Examples of his work are in the British Museum,

Victoria and Albert Museum, and private collections including that of H.M. The Queen. (Colour Plates 10A and 12E.)

Philip Jean (1755-1802) was born at St. Ouen, Jersey. He served in the navy as a youth under Rodney, and later devoted himself to painting. He married twice; his first wife was Anne Noel (d.1787), by whom he had a son, Roger Jean (c.1783-1828), who followed his father's profession, and secondly, Marie de Ste. Croix, by whom he had three daughters. Philip Jean painted miniatures and portraits in oils. He exhibited at the Royal Academy, 1787-1802. He obtained the patronage of the Royal family and painted full length oil portraits of George III and Queen Charlotte, as well as miniatures of the Duke and Duchess of Gloucester and their family. His style varies a great deal and is not easy to describe: he appears to have imitated a number of miniaturists, including Cosway, Shelley and Meyer, and occasionally there is an affinity to the work of Engleheart.

His draughtsmanship is meticulous, and shows character. Not all of his works are signed and so he has not always had the appreciation he deserves. More recently his style has become recognised, and his miniatures have attracted more attention. One of his most ambitious works is the miniature of Dominic Serres (1722-1793), seated at an easel, painting a landscape. This is in the National Portrait Gallery.

A miniature of the artist's second wife with her three children and her step-son, Roger, is owned by the Société Jersiaise. A miniature by him of his wife, Anne, was sold at Sotheby's on 9th June, 1969, and another miniature of her, also by her husband, signed and dated 1782, was sold at Christie's, Lot 72, 28th October, 1970 (Plate 81B). A number of his miniatures are in private collections. He died on 12th September, 1802, leaving a widow and his four children. His usual signatures are: 'P. Jean' and 'P. Jean pinxit', followed by a date. Occasionally he signed with cursive initials: 'PJ'. Two

Plate 80C. Attributed to **R. Collins,** *portrait of a young man, ivory, 2⅛ins. Courtesy Christie's.*

Plate 80D (left). **S. Shelley,** *a lady called Mrs. Delaney, ivory, 5⅜ins. Inscribed on the reverse: '1784. Painted by Samuel Shelley, Henrietta Street, Covent Garden, 6700, London, K.K., and exhibited at the Royal Academy Mrs. Delaney.' The sitter is wearing a white dress with a yellow sash and stole, her hair dressed with blue ribbon. This miniature was once in the J. Pierpont Morgan Collection. Courtesy Christie's.*

Plate 80E (right). **S. Shelley,** *portrait of an unknown officer, ivory, 3ins., wearing a scarlet jacket with a yellow collar and white cross-belt. Courtesy Sotheby's.*

Plate 80F. **R. Collins,** *'The Three Norns', ivory, 3¾ins. Initialled 'RC' on the reverse and signed in pencil: 'R.Collins inv^t & pinxt.' In Scandinavian mythology the Norns are the equivalent of the Greek Fates.* Private Collection.

Plate 80G. **R. Collins,** *an excellent portrait of an unknown lady, ivory, 3½ins., c.1790. Signed on the reverse: 'R.Collins.'* Courtesy the Rijksmuseum, Amsterdam.

attractive miniatures representing Master and Miss Tyers are in the collection of Mr. and Mrs. J. Starr of Kansas City. Examples of his work are in the Victoria and Albert Museum, and the British Museum has engravings after him. (Colour Plate 16C and Plates 81A-E.)

Roger Jean (c.1783-1828) was born at St. Helier, Jersey, the son of Philip Jean and his first wife, Anne. He exhibited at the Royal Academy, 1801-1803, from London addresses, but in 1813 moved to Norwich, where he lived until his death on 9th December, 1828. Miniatures by him are scarce, and unless they are signed probably pass unrecognised. One of Thomas Love Peacock, by him, is in the National Portrait Gallery, and is signed: 'R.Jean'; it is painted against a dark background, and with a much stronger style than that used by his father: the features are all clearly delineated (Plate 82E).

Nathaniel Plimer (1757-1822) was born in Wellington, Shropshire, and was the elder son of Nathaniel and Eliza Plimer, and brother of Andrew Plimer. The family owned a clockmaking business in the town, to which trade he was apprenticed, but neither he nor his brother liked the work and they are reputed to have run away and joined some gipsies with whom they wandered about the country for over two years. During this time they adapted themselves to the life, assisted in decorating caravans and making scenery, and learnt to make their own brushes. They arrived in London in 1781 and Nathaniel obtained a position as a servant or assistant to H. Bone, and subsequently became a pupil of Richard Cosway. He exhibited at the Royal Academy, 1787-1815, and at the Society of Artists, 1790-1791, from 31 Maddox Street. Little is known about his life, or the name of his wife by whom he had four children, Georgina, Mary, Louisa and Adela. This last daughter married in 1827 the well-known portrait painter, Andrew Geddes, a native of Edinburgh. A portrait by Geddes of Andrew Plimer is in the National Gallery, Edinburgh. According to Dr. G.C. Williamson, Nathaniel possessed a violent and ungovernable temper. He is thought to have lived in London all his working life, and died there in 1822. Apart from the Geddes family, who remained in Scotland, his other children are said to have gone to the Colonies. As far as I know, only his miniatures painted before c.1789 are signed and dated: 'N.P.', in small Roman capitals. He does not seem to have

Plate 81.
A. **P. Jean,** *portrait of an unknown man, ivory, 2½ins., c.1780-90.* Courtesy Christie's.
B. **P. Jean,** *Mrs. Philip Jean, née Anne Noel (d. 1787), first wife of the artist, ivory, 3ins. Signed and dated: 'P.Jean / 1782.' A smaller version of this miniature exists.* Courtesy Christie's.
C. **P. Jean,** *miniature of an unknown lady, ivory, 3¼ins., c.1780. Although attractive, this has a crack in the ivory which can be seen in the illustration.* Courtesy Christie's.
D. **P. Jean,** *Mr. Joseph Saunders, ivory, 2⅛ins. Signed and dated: 'P.Jean 1787.' This and Plate 81E are good examples of miniatures by Jean.* Courtesy Sotheby's.
E. **P. Jean,** *Mrs. Joseph Saunders, wife of the sitter in Plate 81E, ivory, 2⅛ins. Signed and dated: 'P.Jean 1787.' This is interesting for costume, showing the pleated cap trimmed with ribbon and a lace shawl.* Courtesy Sotheby's.

Plate 82A. **T. Arrowsmith,** *an unknown lady, ivory, 2⅞ins. Signed and dated on the reverse: '1794.' One of a pair by this little-known artist.* Private Collection.

Plate 82B. **W.S. Lethbridge,** *Mrs. James Octavius Norman, ivory, 2¾ins., c.1820. Signed in full on the reverse. This is a good example of the elaborate hair styles worn, dressed with ornaments and fea,hers; the sitter is wearing an empire line dress.* Courtesy Sotheby's.

Plate 82C (left). **W.S. Lethbridge,** *James Octavius Norman in officer's uniform, husband of Mrs. Norman (Plate 82B), ivory, 2¾ins. The scarlet jacket has white facings and gold epaulettes.* Courtesy Sotheby's.

Plate 82D (right). **Daniel Gardner** *(1750-1805), sketch for a self-portrait, watercolour on paper, 2½ins. Gardner painted a small number of miniatures and these are scarce.* Private Collection.

succeeded in obtaining the influential patronage enjoyed by his brother, and his miniatures, though excellent, do not have the same panache and brilliance as those executed by Andrew. Nevertheless Nathaniel painted a number of very good portraits, and many of them are executed in a softer and more realistic manner. He used more stippling in the shading, and the eyelashes are often to be found dotted in on the lower lid. The overall effect is slightly more woolly than portraits painted by his brother. Examples of his work are in many private collections, and in the Fitzwilliam Museum, Cambridge, the Cleveland Museum of Art, Ohio (E.B. Green Collection), and the Victoria and Albert Museum. (Colour Plates 29D and 30B and Plates 84A, B, D and E.)

Robert Bowyer (c.1758-1834) was self-taught, and is said to have begun by painting his own portrait for his sweetheart, Mary Shoveller, whom he eventually married. He was a pupil of John Smart, with whom he must have become close friends, and for whom he acted as attorney when Smart went to India. Bowyer also undertook the guardianship of Smart's two illegitimate children, Sarah and John Smart, Junior. Bowyer exhibited at the Free Society in 1782, and at the Royal Academy, 1783-1828. He had a distinguished clientele, and is reputed to have "made an extraordinary miniature" of George III, with a flat diamond over it half an inch square! He succeeded J. Meyer as miniature painter to the King and Queen and the Royal family in 1789. He published works on watercolour drawing, and was partly responsible for an illustrated *History of England*. He was a keen Baptist and a supporter of the anti-slavery movement. Signed miniatures by Bowyer are scarce, and attribution is confused at times due to the fact that he copied portraits by John Smart which, although good imitations, do not have the finesse of the master's hand. Superficially these miniatures could, and possibly do, pass as the work of Smart. Bowyer occasionally signed: 'RB / 1786', as in the case of one of an unknown man (Plate 82F). He had a daughter, Mary Ann Bowyer, who married John Crofts at St. Mary-le-Bone, on 8th June, 1797. Bowyer and his wife were both painted by Opie. He died at Byfleet on 4th June, 1834.

Plate 82E (left). **R. Jean,** *Thomas Love Peacock, ivory, 2⁷/₈ins. Signed: 'R. Jean.' Only a small number of miniatures by Jean are known. They lack the delicacy of his father's manner.* Courtesy the National Portrait Gallery.

Plate 82F (right). **R. Bowyer,** *miniature of an unknown man, ivory, 2¹/₁₆ins. Signed and dated: 'RB / 1786.' Painted in the manner of John Smart whose work he often copied.* Private Collection.

Sir Thomas Lawrence, P.R.A. (1769-1830) was one of the greatest portrait painters of this period. He is known to have painted a few miniatures, but only a handful of those attributed to him are at present accepted as authentic. He drew small portraits as a young boy when his father kept the 'White Lion' at Bristol, and later the 'Black Bear' at Devizes. His self-portrait in miniature is at Croft Castle, and one of Mary, Viscountess Templetown, was attributed to him when it was sold at Christie's on 16th November, 1976 (Plate 84C). For further information see *Sir Thomas Lawrence,* by Kenneth Garlick, and The Walpole Society, Vol. XXXIX, 1964.

Thomas Richmond (1771-1837) was born at Kew on 28th March, 1771; he was the younger son of a Yorkshireman, Thomas Richmond (1740-1794), who came from Bawtry, and his wife, Ann Bone, a cousin of George Engleheart. His father was groom of the stables to the Duke of Gloucester and later became proprietor of the 'Coach and Horses' at Kew. Thomas had tuition from George Engleheart and also studied at the St. Martin's Lane Academy. He worked in London and Portsmouth, and exhibited at the Royal Academy, 1795-1829. He married Anne Oram (d.1859), sometime before 1802; their sons, Thomas Richmond, Junior, and George Richmond, both followed their father's profession as miniaturists. Richmond was employed by the Royal family to copy miniatures by Cosway and Engleheart, and he also copied portraits by Reynolds. His works include miniatures on ivory and paper, and large oval portraits in watercolour. Some of his portraits on paper are in profile, and executed with the heads in colour and the rest in pencil. Not all his works are signed; some have a cursive 'R' followed by a date, and he occasionally inscribed them on the reverse with his address. His works show the influence of Engleheart, but few are comparable. He drew well and his miniatures have a feeling of strength and vitality, but there is a harshness about some of them and, frequently, his sitters' eyes are rather staring. One by him of Henry Tufton, signed and dated 1817, was Lot 28 at Christie's on 3rd March, 1971 (Plate 85D). He died in London on 15th November, 1837, and was buried in Paddington Churchyard. (Colour Plate 18C and Plates 85A, B, D and E.)

Thomas Richmond, Junior (1802-1874) was the elder son of Thomas

Plate 82G. **W.S. Lethbridge,** *portrait of an unknown young lady, ivory, 2⁷/₈ins., c.1820. Signed in full on the reverse with the address: 'No. 96 Strand.' Note the small cap trimmed with flowers and feathers.* Courtesy Sotheby's.

A

B

C

D

E

F

G

Richmond, and was born 16th September, 1802. He entered the Royal Academy Schools on 25th November, 1820, exhibited at the Royal Academy and Society of British Artists, 1822-1860, and was awarded a silver Isis medal by the Society of Arts in 1823. He worked in Sheffield and London, and visited Rome in 1840, when he met Ruskin. He painted miniatures and portraits in oils and watercolour. Miniatures by him are scarce. One of an unknown man was sold at Sotheby's in 1972. It was signed in full on the reverse: 'Thoˢ Richmond Jnr / 42 Half Moon St / Piccadilly / London / 1825' (Plate 85F and Figure 28). It is reminiscent of works by his father, and has a lot of stippling on the background. The draughtsmanship is good. He bought an estate in Windermere called Droomer, where he lived until his death at Park Range, Windermere, on 13th November, 1874. He was buried in Brompton, London. (Plate 85C.)

Plate 84A. **N. Plimer**, *portrait of an unknown lady, ivory, 2⁷/8ins., c.1780-85. Courtesy Sotheby's.*

Henry Edridge, A.R.A. (1768-1821) was a native of London, born in Paddington on 12th October, 1768. His father was a Westminster tradesman. Henry was apprenticed to W. Pether, an engraver, and entered the Royal Academy Schools on 7th January, 1784 "aged 15, 12 Oct. last". He was awarded a silver medal in 1786 and exhibited at the Royal Academy, 1786-1821. He copied some of Reynolds' pictures in miniature. In 1817 and 1819 he visited France, and in 1820 was elected A.R.A. He had a wide circle of friends including Sir George Beaumont, and the artists T. Hearne and J. Farington. He was a versatile artist who painted landscapes, portraits in watercolour, oil portraits and miniatures on ivory and paper. His early miniatures are chiefly on ivory, but he later took to executing his portraits in black lead or Indian ink on paper. This method was later abandoned and he drew the figure in lightly, finishing the face, and sometimes the costume, in watercolour. Many of his portraits in watercolour are painted against a landscape background and are amongst the most charming drawings of the period. A particularly fine one representing Lady Elizabeth and Lady Charlotte Bingham against a landscape background, signed and dated: 'H. Edridge 1803', is in a private collection. It is executed in pencil and watercolour, and was exhibited at the Royal Academy in 1803 (Plate 86).

Edridge's manner of drawing foliage• is reminiscent of the work of John

Plate 83.

A. **H.J. Burch**, *portrait of an unknown boy, ivory, 2¼ins. Signed: 'H. Burch.' This is a good example of this artist's work which is not easy to recognise. Courtesy Victoria and Albert Museum, Alan Evans Collection.*

B. **J. Wright**, *an attractive miniature of an unknown lady, ivory, 3ins. Signed and dated on the reverse: 'John Wright / Pinxt / Burlington Gardens corner of Old Bond / Sᵗ London / 1815.' The sitter is wearing a white dress with a deep pink bodice. Private Collection.*

C. **J. Wright** *after Lawrence, Lady Raglan, Harriet, 2nd daughter of the Earl of Mornington and wife of the 1st Lord Raglan, ivory, 2³/8ins. Courtesy Christie's.*

D. **S.J. Stump**, *Mrs. Dorothea Jordan (1782-1816), ivory, 6ins. Signed on the reverse with the address: '7 Cork St.' Dorothea was a noted actress and mistress of the Duke of Clarence. Courtesy Sotheby's.*

E. **R. Saunders**, *an unknown Guards officer, ivory, 2½ins. Signed and dated on the reverse: 'Saunders / Pinxt / 1819.' Note the soft way that Saunders painted. Courtesy Victoria and Albert Museum, Alan Evans Collection.*

F. **S.J. Stump**, *portrait of William Dobell, ivory, 2⁷/8ins. This is a well drawn and strong portrait by Stump. Courtesy Sotheby's.*

G. **S.J. Stump**, *portrait of an unknown man, ivory, 2⁵/8ins. Signed and dated: 'Stump / 1803.' This is a good example of the artist's signature, and the miniature is painted in a different style to that of Plate 83F. Courtesy Christie's.*

Plate 84B (left). **N. Plimer,** *miniature of an unknown man, ivory, 2¾ins.* Courtesy Sotheby's.

Plate 84D (right). **N. Plimer,** *miniature of an unknown man, ivory, 2½ins., c.1790-1800. This is a good example of Nathaniel's work which is painted in a softer manner than that of his brother Andrew.* Courtesy Sotheby's.

Plate 84C. Attributed to **Sir Thomas Lawrence, P.R.A.,** *Mary, Viscountess Templetown (d. 1824), ivory, 3½ins. Only a handful of miniatures by Lawrence have been accepted as authentic. This miniature is close in style to the large portrait, also by Lawrence, of the sitter in the same pose, with her son Henry, which is in the D.C. Mellon Collection, Washington.* Courtesy Christie's.

Taylor, and it is possible that he may have had some tuition from him. Very few of his miniatures are signed; those that are bear the initials: 'H.E.', either cursive or in monogram, and sometimes followed by a date. Occasionally he signed and inscribed in full on the reverse. A miniature of a young boy signed in monogram: 'HE' is in a private collection (Plate 87A). A few of his miniatures are painted somewhat in the manner of Shelley. His style is not easy to describe. He sometimes painted a blue shading under the eye and on the upper lip, with a sharp shadow under the nose; the eyebrows are usually strongly delineated, and the hair painted in soft masses. His pencil drawings are much more meticulous and executed in greater detail. He died on 23rd April, 1821, in Margaret Street, Cavendish Square, London. Examples of his work are in the British Museum, National Portrait Gallery and the Victoria and Albert Museum, etc. (Colour Plate 22C and Plates 87B, C and D.)

Mrs. Joseph Mee, née Anne Foldsone (c.1770/5-1851) was the daughter of the artist, John Foldsone, a picture copyist who, in 1770, was living in Little Castle Street, Oxford Market, London. Her father died young, and Anne was educated at a French ladies' school in London. She possessed several artistic gifts as a musician, poetess and painter, and was a protégée and pupil of Romney. The family were evidently left badly off due to her father's death, and she is said to have supported her mother and eight brothers and sisters at an early age.

Anne obtained the patronage of the Prince of Wales (later George IV) and was working at Windsor Castle in 1790 and 1791, where there are still numerous miniatures by her. She had the patronage of a distinguished clientele and was said to be so much in demand that it was inadvisable to pay for a miniature in advance! By 1804, she was able to charge 40 guineas for a portrait. In this latter year she married Joseph Mee of Mount Anna, County Armagh, by whom she had six children by the time she was thirty-three. Her husband, who was a barrister, is supposed to have been jealous and did not allow men to sit to her. According to family tradition he was proud of his wife's hair, and after a violent quarrel she cut it close to her head just to spite him! She exhibited at the Royal Academy and British Institution, 1804-1837, at least one exhibit being sent from Brighton. Her work was influenced by Cosway, but much of it is uneven in quality and not always well drawn. She tended to enlarge the sitters' eyes, outlining the lids in red, which frequently gives the impression that they have been crying. The face is usually painted with a mixture of stippling and hatching. Some of her miniatures are quite large. A miniature, said to be a self-portrait, was sold at Sotheby's, Lot 146, on 13th October, 1975. A particularly fine example of her work was Lot 367 in the Sotheby Parke Bernet sale of the Heckett Collection in New York on 5th October, 1977. It was of an army officer, wearing a tall busby, scarlet uniform and gold epaulettes. The sitter was reputed to be the Hon. Susan Carew, wearing the uniform of an officer in the Grenadier company of the 1st Foot Guards. The portrait was painted c.1796, and was once in the E.M. Hodgkins Collection (Plate 87E). Mrs. Mee

Plate 84E. **N. Plimer,** *portrait of an unknown lady, ivory, 3½ins., c.1790. Note the long falling curls and the bandeau in the hair.* Present whereabouts unknown.

Plate 85A (left). **T. Richmond,** *portrait of an unknown lady, ivory, 3ins. Signed and dated in full on the reverse: 'T. Richmond / pinxt 1810 / 42 Half Moon St. Mayfair.'* Courtesy Sotheby's.

Plate 85B (right). **T. Richmond,** *miniature of an unknown man, ivory, 3ins. One of a pair. Note the rather staring eyes, which is a characteristic of Richmond's work and quite unlike that of G. Engleheart.* Courtesy Sotheby's.

Plate 85C. **T. Richmond, Junior,** *portrait of an unknown man, ivory, 2½ins. Signed: 'Richmond 182–' (2?) on the front, and on the reverse: 'T. Richmond Jun / pinxt / 42 Half Moon St / Piccadilly.'* Courtesy E. Grosvenor Paine, U.S.A.

Plate 85D. **T. Richmond,** *Henry Tufton, ivory, 3¼ins. Signed and dated on the reverse: '1817' with Richmond's address in Half Moon Street.* Courtesy Christie's.

Plate 85E. **T. Richmond,** *portrait of an unknown lady, ivory, 3¼ins., c.1820.* Private Collection.

died on 28th May, 1851, at the advanced age of eighty-one. Some of her work was engraved. A self-portrait and three other family miniatures are in the Victoria and Albert Museum.

E.W. Thomson (1770-1847) worked in Paris and London for most of his life, but also worked in Scotland and was in Glasgow in 1806. He began his career as an engraver and then took up miniature painting. He exhibited at the Royal Academy, 1832-1839, and is thought to have been working in Paris from c.1824-1830. Some of his miniatures show the influence of Isabey and of A.E. Chalon. Most of his miniatures are painted with a yellowish flesh colouring and greyish brown shadows; the eyelids, nostrils and mouth are delineated in deep pink, and the hair painted in loose masses. Many of the backgrounds have a pinkish hue. A number of his miniatures are signed in pencil in full with his address in Paris: 'E.W. Thomson pinx^t / rue du fg St Honoré.' Some of his works are dated. He was a good artist and drew well, and most of his works are attractive. Those I have seen have all been executed on paper. One by him of the Princess de Lieven in the Holzscheiter Collection was sold at Sotheby's on 28th March, 1977 for £1,200. It was signed in full and dated 1827, and is illustrated in *A Dictionary of British Miniature Painters,* Vol. II, Plate 367. He died at Lincoln on 27th December, 1847. (Plate 76B.)

John Thomas Barber Beaumont, F.S.A., F.G.S. (1774-1841) was born in Marylebone, London, on 21st December, 1774. He was born John Barber, but was connected with the Beaumont family, and took the additional name of Beaumont c.1820. He entered the Royal Academy Schools on 14th October, 1791, under the name of J. Barber. He won awards from the Society of Arts in 1791, 1793, 1794 and 1795, and three medals at the Royal Academy

Plate 85F (left). **T. Richmond, Junior,** *portrait of an unknown man, ivory, 2¾ins. Signed and dated in full on the reverse: '1825', with his address. See Figure 28.* Courtesy Sotheby's.

Figure 28 (right). *Reverse of Plate 85F showing the signature of* **T. Richmond, Junior.** *Miniatures by him are scarce.* Courtesy Sotheby's.

Schools. These awards were for historical subjects, figure drawings and a drawing from a cast. He did not take up miniature painting until c.1784. He exhibited at the Royal Academy, 1794-1806, under the name of John Thomas Barber. His exhibit in 1794 was his self-portrait; this, and several other miniatures by him, are illustrated by Aubrey Noakes in his article, 'John Thomas Barber Beaumont Miniaturist and Art Tutor of Henry Alken', *The Connoisseur,* July 1977, pp.188-194. Beaumont had a fashionable clientele, which included members of the Royal family. He was appointed miniature painter to the Duke of Kent and the Duke of York and, in 1799, to Prince Edward whose miniature he exhibited in that year. Many of his sitters were members of the acting profession, including Mrs. Dorothy Jordan. In 1803 he published and illustrated *A Tour Through South Wales.* Beaumont was a man of parts, and seems to have been successful in all his various undertakings. During the threat of Napoleonic invasion he wrote tracts and letters to the press, setting out sound military preparations to foil any such attack. He organised and commanded a rifle corps called 'The Duke of Cumberland's Sharp Shooters', which was the first independent corps to take the field in this country. This corps has continued through various phases, becoming part of the Greenjacket Brigade, and since 1937 has had the additional title of 7th Battalion, The King's Royal Rifle Corps. By c.1806 Beaumont seems to have abandoned painting and, to put it in his own words, "drifted into the insurance world". He was the founder of the Provident Life Office and the County Fire Office, where both his son and grandson succeeded him as Managing Directors. The offices still possess fifteen miniatures by Beaumont. In a pamphlet he published in 1816 on *Provident or Parish Banks* he makes candid admission of his mistakes, but takes the view that "a man who never makes a mistake will never make anything". Beaumont became a rich man, and acquired property in Stepney where a Square is named after him. He also endowed the Beaumont Institute at the cost of about £20,000. This still exists under the name of Queen Mary College.

Plate 87.
A. **H. Edridge, A.R.A.,** *a miniature of a young boy, ivory, 1½ins. Signed: 'HE' (monogram). Set in a brooch.* Private Collection.
B. **H. Edridge, A.R.A.,** *Sir Stafford Henry Northcote, 7th Bart. (1762-1851), ivory, 2½ins., c.1790.* Courtesy Sotheby's.
C. **H. Edridge, A.R.A.,** *Anna Maria Blunt, daughter of Sir Thomas Gatehouse, and wife of Walter Blunt, ivory, 3¹/8ins. This miniature together with one of her husband, also by Edridge, was sold in 1975.* Courtesy Sotheby's.
D. **H. Edridge, A.R.A.,** *miniature of a young girl, ivory, 2⁷/8ins. The sitter is wearing a white dress with a blue sash and flowers in her lap. This is an exceptionally attractive miniature by Edridge.* Courtesy Christie's.
E. **Mrs. Mee,** *miniature of an officer, reputed to be the Hon. Susan Carew, wearing the uniform of the 1st Foot Guards, ivory, 2⁷/8ins., c.1796. This should be compared with Plate 87F.* Courtesy Sotheby's.
F. **Mrs. Mee,** *Captain the Hon. William Carew, wearing the uniform of the Dragoon Guards, ivory, 1⁷/8ins. This should be compared with Plate 87E, said to represent Susan Carew in officer's uniform. The miniatures must represent either the same sitter or twins. Set in a diamond pendant frame.* Courtesy Sotheby's.
G. **H. Edridge, A.R.A.,** *Jack Bannister (1760-1836), actor and comedian, ivory, 2½ins. Inscribed on the reverse and set within a gold frame with a paste border.* Courtesy Christie's.

A

B

C

D

E

F

G

Plate 88A. **J.T. Barber Beaumont,** *miniature of an officer, ivory, 2½ins. Signed with initials: 'ITB' and signed and dated in full on the reverse. Courtesy Sotheby's.*

Plate 88B. **J.T. Barber Beaumont,** *portrait of an unknown man, ivory, 2¾ins. Signed with initials: 'ITB.' Beaumont had so many different styles that unless the miniatures are signed, attribution is difficult. Courtesy Christie's.*

Beaumont must have been a prolific artist, but the great problem is one of accurate identification. His style varied so much that it is almost impossible to describe. Some miniatures are well drawn and colourful, whilst others are rather dull and have no definite characteristics. He signed: 'ITB' on the front, and occasionally, as in the case of a miniature of an officer sold at Sotheby's on 10th March, 1975, he signed in full with a date on the reverse (Plate 88A). He died at his official residence in Regent Street, London, on 15th May, 1841, and was buried at Stepney in a coffin he had ordered to be prepared long before with 'Kyan's process', for preventing dry-rot. He left an estate of just under £60,000. One of his most important pupils was Henry T. Alken (1785-1851), noted for his paintings of fox hunting and prints. Examples of his work are in the Victoria and Albert Museum. (Plates 88B, C and F.)

James Leakey (1775-1865) was born in Exeter on 20th September, 1775, and was the son of a wool-stapler of Bradford-on-Avon, Wiltshire. The family were said to be of Irish descent. Leakey worked in London and Exeter and painted oil portraits, landscapes, subject pictures and miniatures. No information is available about his training, but he exhibited at the Royal Academy, from 1821-1846. In 1815 he married Miss Eliza Hubbard Woolmer, by whom he had eleven or twelve children. Whilst in London he knew Constable, Lawrence, Wilkie, etc., and Lawrence once introduced him as "the English Wouvermans". He painted a portrait of Joseph Farington in oils in 1810. He was so successful that when, in 1809, he was commissioned to paint two "fancy pictures" for Sir Thomas Baring at 500 guineas each, he was too busy to accept. He did, however, paint portraits of the Baring family. Farington in his Diary for 11th November, 1810, notes that Leakey had practised in Exeter for some years, that he was having to support a large family of relatives who were all very poor, and that he made about £800 a year. On 13th November, Farington visited Leakey and saw his paintings; he says: "I found him a modest and ingenious young man". He had dinner with him on November 16th, and noted that Leakey had purchased a house for £1,200. Leakey's portrait of Farington was painted in three sittings. Leakey had so many commissions that he abandoned his project of emigrating to Canada. In 1811 he was living next to John Raphael Smith in Newman

Colour Plate 26.
A top left. **Walter Robertson,** *an unknown young lady, ivory, 2⁷/₁₆ins., c.1790-95.*
B top right. **Louisa Baine,** *Sir George Berkeley, possibly Sir George Henry Berkeley, K.C.M. (1785-1857), Colonel of the 35th Regiment, of whom there is no portrait at Berkeley Castle, ivory, 3ins. The sitter's and artist's names are engraved on the locket.*
C centre. **Richard Cosway, R.A.,** *an unknown lady, ivory, 3³/₈ins. Signed in full on the reverse: 'Rdus Cosway / R.A. / Primarius Pictor / Serenissimi Walliae / Principis / Pinxit / 1794.'*
D bottom left. **John Wright,** *an unknown man, ivory, 2¾ins., c.1790-1800.*
E bottom right. **John Barry,** *Inigo Thomas, Esq. of Ratton, Sussex, ivory, 2¾ins.*

Private Collection

Plate 88C. **J.T. Barber Beaumont,** *miniature of an unknown man, ivory, 2¾ins. Signed with initials: 'ITB.'* Courtesy the Bernard Falk Collection, The Royal Pavilion, Brighton.

Street, London, when, according to Mrs. Frankau in *John Raphael Smith,* 1902, Smith was known as "old Vice" and Leakey as "Young Virtue"! He is said to have retired from painting many years before his death, and, according to Mrs. Frankau, he "gave up the brush for the pulpit". He died at Exeter on 16th February, 1865, aged ninety, with the reputation of being a citizen whose character had "earned him general esteem and respect".

His miniatures, which all have the appearance of being in oils, are well painted; the flesh colours tend to be a deepish pink, and the backgrounds grey or greyish brown. They are all in opaque colours, and are well modelled. It has been suggested recently that he used a thick form of watercolour and gum, rather than oil paints, on at least some of his miniatures. An artist named Passmore, also noted by Farington, painted oil miniatures in the manner of Leakey but no examples of his work are known. All the miniatures I have seen by Leakey have been painted on ivory. He did not, as far as I know, ever sign his work. An oil portrait of S. Cousins by him is in the National Portrait Gallery, and examples of his work are in the Victoria and Albert Museum. An engraving after one of his works is in the British Museum. (Plate 88E.)

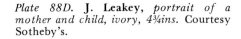

Plate 88D. **J. Leakey,** *portrait of a mother and child, ivory, 4¾ins.* Courtesy Sotheby's.

Plate 88E. **J. Leakey,** *an unknown child, ivory, 3⅛ins. This and Plate 88D are typical examples of works by Leakey which give the appearance of oil paintings.* Private Collection.

Details of the family of miniaturists named Slater have in the past been rather confusing, but in September, 1976, an exhibition was held at the Gerald Norman Gallery, London, which contained a number of drawings and watercolours by them, some of which were signed. These had been preserved in an album by the Slaters and notes on the different members written up in some detail. The facts are as follows: **Joseph Slater, Senior** (1750-1805) was the son of John Slater of Bromley, Middlesex. He entered the Royal Academy Schools on 18th December, 1771, and became a miniaturist. He exhibited at the Royal Academy from various addresses from 1773-1787, and may have been in Dublin in 1770. He married on 4th June, 1776, at St. James's, Westminster, Anne, daughter of Isaac Wane, by whom he had four sons and either two, or three, daughters. The family moved to The Cottage, Hounslow, where Joseph died in 1805. He executed crayon portraits,

Plate 88F (left). **J.T. Barber Beaumont**, *miniature of a sportsman, ivory, 3¹/8ins. Signed and dated on the reverse: '1798.' The sitter has a horn powder flask slung over one shoulder and a double-barrelled sporting gun in his right hand.* **Courtesy Sotheby's.**

Plate 88G (right). **Sophia Howell**, *after A. Plimer, Mrs. Hannay, ivory 3½ins. Signed in monogram: 'SH.' The original portrait by Plimer was in the J. Pierpont Morgan Collection.* **Courtesy Sotheby's.**

sketches and miniatures, and his work is very similar to that of the rest of the family, several of whom became miniaturists. His children included Joseph Slater, Junior (1779-1837), Anne (1777-1852), Susanah (d.1830, later Mrs. Bean), Isaac Wane Slater (c.1785-1836), Capt. Michael Atwell Slater, R.N. (1793-1842), and John Slater (1786-1835). Of these, three of the sons and one grandson of Joseph Senior became miniaturists.

Joseph Slater, Junior (1779-1837) was the eldest son. He exhibited at the Royal Academy intermittently from 1805-1833, from various London addresses. He married Catherine, daughter of the Rev. James Bean, Librarian of the British Museum, and his sister, Susanah, married a relative, the Rev. John Philipps Bean, of St. Paul's School. Joseph and Catherine had a son, also named Joseph (1809-1854), who is thought to have been an artist. Joseph Junior painted large oil portraits and sketches in watercolour, some of which were miniature size. A sketch for a self-portrait (head only) in pencil heightened with watercolour is in a private collection as is an attractive pencil sketch of the head of his niece, Carissima Matilda Slater (1810-1847). (Plate 75B.) He was a good draughtsman, and his watercolours are softly painted. He is said to have painted on stone. He died on 25th February, 1837, and was buried at Hove. (Plate 89E.)

Isaac Wane Slater (c.1785-1836) was the second son of Joseph Slater, Senior, and brother of Joseph and John. It is presumed that all the brothers had their initial training in art from their father. He exhibited at the Royal Academy, 1806-1836; the entries are confused as the initials J.W. are given in some, and both Joseph Slaters are catalogued as Josiah. I.W. Slater married Anne Holdsworth, and they seem to have spent all their life in London. I.W. Slater appears to have confined his work to miniatures on ivory rather than sketches on paper. Many of his works are very good, and show the influence of Cosway; his modelling is excellent and the sitters' characters well portrayed. One, of Mrs. Tayler, signed and dated 1822, was sold at Sotheby's on 28th July, 1975 (Plate 89B); it is a good example of his work and is interesting for costume. An attractive miniature

Plate 89A. **I.W. Slater,** *a miniature of an unknown lady, ivory, 3ins. Signed on the reverse: 'I.W. Slater 1808 / 21 Gt Russell St. Bloomb'y.'* Private Collection.

Plate 89B. **I.W. Slater,** *Mrs. Tayler, ivory, 3³⁄₈ins. Signed and dated on the reverse: 'Mrs Tayler / I.W. Slater pinxt / 70 Newman St / 1822. London.' Note the frilled mob cap.* Courtesy Sotheby's.

Plate 89C. **I.W. Slater,** *Master Watson, ivory, 3¹⁄₈ins. Signed on the reverse: 'Master Watson / I.W. Slater / pinxt / 1823 / June and July.'* Private Collection.

Plate 89D. **I.W. Slater,** *the Misses Elizabeth and (?) Bertie Mathews, ivory, 5¼ins. Signed and dated in full on the reverse: '1824.' This is a particularly attractive miniature by Slater. The children may have been related to Bertie Bertie Matthews who was painted in miniature by J.W. Child in 1844. This latter miniature is in the Victoria and Albert Museum.* Courtesy Sotheby's.

Plate 89E. **Joseph Slater, Junior,** *Thomas Henry Robinson, aged fourteen (d. 1819), pencil and wash on paper, 6½ins. Signed 'J. Slater / 1806.' There is an inscription on the reverse of the frame giving details of the sitter who died of apoplexy aged twenty-seven.* Private Collection.

Plate 90A. **J. Saunders,** *an unknown lady, ivory, 2ins. Signed: 'IS.' This is one of the few signed works by this artist.* Courtesy the City of Liverpool Museums.

of the Misses Elizabeth and (?)Bertie Mathews, signed and dated 1824, was Lot 50 at Sotheby's, 2nd June, 1975 (Plate 89D). Slater died in London on 17th April, 1836, and was buried in Kensal Green Cemetery. Some of his works are signed: 'I.W. Slater' along the edge, in cursive script or in capitals. Examples of his work are in the Victoria and Albert Museum.

John Slater (1786-1835) was the third son of Joseph Slater, Senior. He painted miniatures, portraits, flowers and studies of heads. He exhibited at the Royal Academy, 1808-1811, and probably 1818. In 1808 he married a cousin, Elizabeth Slater, by whom he had two sons and six daughters. Those I have traced are Adela Elizabeth (1809-1867), Carissima Matilda (1810-1847), Lavinia (1812-1854), who married the Rev. Alfred Fennell, Henrietta Vane Slater (1815-1866) and Lt. Col. Mortimer John Slater (1824-1863), who married Julia Bull (d.1863). I have not, so far, traced any works by John Slater.

Plate 90B (far left). **T.H. Hull,** *miniature of an unknown man, ivory, 2½ins. Signed: 'Hull.' Set within the attractive hinged case shown in Figure 29.* Courtesy Sotheby's.

Figure 29 (left). Reverse of the locket containing the miniature of T.H. Hull, Plate 90B. Courtesy Sotheby's.

Plate 90C. **N. Freese,** *Sir John Moore, ivory, 3ins. Signed: 'Freese / pinxt.' An important miniature as it is one of the few signed by this artist.* Courtesy Sotheby's.

Thomas H. Hull (fl.1775-1827) worked in London and Leeds. Nothing is known about his early life or education. He exhibited at the Royal Academy, 1775-1827, and was in Leeds in June, 1796. He may have been the Thomas Hull who married Frideswide Wells at St. Mary-le-Bone on 8th June, 1795. Miniatures by him are scarce. He was a good miniaturist, and one whose works are well worth acquiring. He sometimes used a blue shading around the chin of his male sitters, and drew the hair in separate strands, as in the case of the miniature of an unknown man which was Lot 92 at Sotheby's, on 2nd June, 1975. It is signed: 'Hull' on the front, and framed in a most attractive closed locket (Plate 90B and Figure 29). A fine miniature of Sir Charles Blicke, signed: 'Hull', is in a private collection (Colour Plate 18D). Examples of his work are in the Victoria and Albert Museum, and the British Museum has some engravings after his portraits.

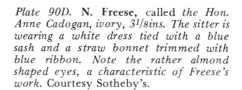

Plate 90D. **N. Freese,** called *the Hon. Anne Cadogan, ivory, 3¹/8ins. The sitter is wearing a white dress tied with a blue sash and a straw bonnet trimmed with blue ribbon. Note the rather almond shaped eyes, a characteristic of Freese's work.* Courtesy Sotheby's.

Plate 90E. **J. Barry,** *an unknown lady, ivory, 2ins. The sitter's hair is tied with a yellow bandeau.* Courtesy Sotheby's.

Joseph Saunders (fl.1772-1811) worked in London. Nothing is known about his early life, but he exhibited at the Free Society and the Society of Artists, 1772-1776, at the Royal Academy, 1778-1807, and the British Institution in 1808. His son Robert Saunders (1774-c.1828), was also a miniaturist. Miniatures by this artist are scarce, and not easy to identify. He signed: 'J. Saunders', or 'IS', and occasionally: 'Joseph Saunders'. An attractive miniature of an unknown lady, signed on the front: 'IS', is in the City of Liverpool Museum. It is reminiscent of the work of Cosway and Plimer. The hair is loosely painted in separate strands and the flesh colours are a fresh pink. There is a fair amount of gum mixed with the paint (Plate 90A). The artist is not, as is suggested in the *Dictionary of National Biography*, identical with John Sanders, Senior, who painted portraits, figures and views.

John Barry (fl.1784-1827) worked in London, and exhibited at the Royal Academy, 1784-1827. Nothing is known about his early life or education, and his works, which are excellent, have not always had the attention they deserve. He painted miniatures and domestic subjects. He may have been the John Barry who married Elizabeth Screech on 4th October, 1792, at St.

Plate 90F (left). **J. Barry,** *portrait of an unknown Guards officer, ivory, 2½ins.* Courtesy Victoria and Albert Museum, Alan Evans Collection.

Plate 90G (right). **J. Barry,** *portrait of Cadwallader Blairey, R.N., ivory, 2¾ins. This is a good example of the artist's way of shading the face and drawing the eyebrows.* Courtesy Sotheby's.

Mary-le-Bone. As he seldom signed his work identification is difficult; some of his miniatures are reminiscent of the work of T. Hazlehurst. He appears to have had two distinctly different styles. Characteristics to look for are the angular painting of the eyebrows, and almost vertical brush strokes on the face. He painted the hair in soft masses and shaded the features very distinctly. A good miniature of a Guards officer is in the Alan Evans Collection at the Victoria and Albert Museum (Plate 90F). Many of his miniatures have a brownish shading, whilst others are painted in bright fresh colours. (Plates 90E and G.)

N. Freese (fl.1794-1814) is another artist about whom we know very little. He worked in London and exhibited at the Royal Academy, 1794-1814. He is thought to have joined an Artists' Volunteer Corps in 1803. He exhibited a portrait of Lieut. G.F. Freese, who fell at the storming of Salamanca. The majority of his miniatures are not signed and, for this reason, identification is difficult. He sometimes used a small label on the reverse of the miniature which reads: 'Freese / Miniature Painter / No 411 Strand / London.' One of the few signed examples was Lot 39 at Sotheby's on 9th June, 1969. It was said to represent Sir John Moore, and was signed: 'Freese / pinxt' (Plate 90C). A fine miniature of an officer in the Light Dragoons, attributed to Freese, was sold at Christie's on 2nd November, 1971. The miniature was an example of good draughtsmanship and strong colours (Plate 90H). A characteristic of his work seems to be the way he paints the eyes in a slightly almond shape, and the mouth is drawn slightly bowed. (Plate 90D and Colour Plate 22A.)

Plate 90H. **N. Freese,** *a young officer in the Light Dragoons, ivory, 3ins., 1796-1800. The sitter is wearing a blue jacket trimmed with silver, a yellow collar, black stock and tall plumed bonnet.* Courtesy Christie's.

A few artists of this period went out to India to work and were successful in obtaining commissions. Of these **Miss Diana Hill, née Dietz, later Mrs. Harriott** (d.1844) was a miniaturist of outstanding merit. For many years her work was neither recognised nor appreciated as not all of her miniatures are signed, and confusion had arisen due to her change of names. She worked in London and for some time in India. She won an award at the Society of Arts in 1775, and exhibited at the Society of Artists in the same

A

B

C

D

E

year. From 1777-1780 she exhibited at the Royal Academy under her maiden name, and in 1785 as Mrs. Hill (Hon. Exhib.). The date of her marriage is not known, but her husband must have died young as, in 1785, she obtained permission to go to India as a portrait painter, and settled in Calcutta. On 15th November, 1786, Ozias Humphry described her as a "Pretty widow with two children". Her great popularity alarmed him and he said that he would "rather have all the male painters in England landed in Bengal than this single woman"! On 15th November, 1788, she married as her second husband Lieut. Thomas Harriott, of the 1st Native Infantry, by whom she had two sons, William Henry (d.1839), an artist, and Thomas George (d.1857), of the Royal Staffs Corps. Her husband retired from the Service in 1806, when the family returned to England. He died at West Hall, Mortlake, on 19th April, 1817, aged sixty-four, and Diana died at Twickenham on 10th February, 1844. She was an accomplished miniaturist, and deserves more attention than has hitherto been the case. Her style varies slightly: some of her miniatures have rather pink flesh tints, whilst others have a yellower tinge. One of the most attractive examples is in the Victoria and Albert Museum; the sitter is a half-caste girl, wearing a large white mob cap which dramatically sets off her face and long flowing hair (Plate 91C). A good miniature of an officer, signed and dated: 'Hill / 1787' (Plate 91B), was sold at Sotheby's in 1970, and one of Sir Charles Cockerell, Bart., signed and dated: 'Hill / 1786', was sold at Christie's (Plate 91A). This miniature is a good example of her draughtsmanship and is painted in her more yellowish style against a cloud and sky background. A miniature of Miss Mary Steuart, later Mrs. Timothy Powell, in the Victoria and Albert Museum has the pink flesh tints and the hair painted in masses.

Samuel Andrews (1767?-1807) is said to have been an Irishman by birth. No information is available about his early life. In 1791 he applied to the East India Company for permission to go to Bengal; this was refused, but Andrews must have found some other way and arrived in Madras in the same year. He may be the Samuel Andrews who married, in July 1795, Janetta Christina Elbracht. It was in this year that he moved into the house that John Smart had occupied in Madras, and advertised that he would attend to all orders for miniatures. He later moved to Calcutta and was there in 1798. He is best known for his portraits *en grisaille*: these are mainly profile portraits, painted in the manner of cameos against a dark brown background.

Plate 92A. J. Smart, Junior, portrait of an unknown officer, ivory, 2¾ins. Signed and dated: 'J.S.J. / 1809 / I.' Courtesy Sotheby's.

Plate 91.
A. **Diana Hill, née Dietz**, *Sir Charles Cockerel, Bart., ivory, 3⁵/8ins. Signed and dated: 'Hill / 1786.'* Courtesy Christie's.
B. **Diana Hill, née Dietz**, *portrait of an unknown officer, ivory, 3ins. Signed and dated: 'Hill / 1787.'* Courtesy Sotheby's.
C. **Diana Hill, née Dietz**, *portrait of an unknown girl, ivory, 3⁵/8ins., c.1780. This is a most dramatic and attractive portrait.* Courtesy Victoria and Albert Museum.
D. **Diana Hill, née Dietz**, *miniature of an unknown officer, ivory, 3½ins. Signed and dated: 'Hill / 1788.' The three portraits, Plates 91A, B and D, are all fine examples of Mrs. Hill's painting and differ in style from Plate 91C of the unknown girl.* Courtesy Christie's.
E. **A.M. Dietz**, *portrait of an unknown lady, ivory, 3½ins. Signed and dated on the reverse: 'Amelia Maria Dietz / 1796.' This is the only known miniature by this artist. It is interesting to compare it with those painted by Diana Hill (née Dietz) to whom she was related.* Courtesy R. Bayne Powell.

Plate 92B (left). **S. Andrews,** *Mrs. Murray, ivory, 2½ins. Signed and dated: 'SA / 1796.' This is a good example of work by Andrews painted in the manner of J. Smart, Senior.* Courtesy Christie's.

Plate 92C (right). **S. Andrews,** *Abdel Gooffar Cawn Bahauder, ivory, 3ins. The gold frame bears an inscription: 'Presented by Abdel Gooffar Cawn Bahauder to Hugh Gordon as a mark of his esteem. Madras. 12 March 1804.' This is an interesting and impressive miniature.* Courtesy Christie's.

His miniatures in watercolour vary in quality, many of them are excellent, but the fact that he imitated and often copied miniatures by Smart causes some confusion. Not all his miniatures are signed; his signature is either: 'S. Andrews Calcutta', followed by a date (this is usually found on the portraits *en grisaille*), or: 'S.A.' on the front in cursive lettering, followed by a date, or his signature in full on the reverse. For many years he and Sarah Addington (fl.1778) were confused, but as no miniatures are at present known to be by her, all those signed 'S.A.' are attributed to Andrews. A good example by Andrews showing the influence of Smart was Lot 42 at Christie's on 17th February, 1970; it was of Mrs. Murray, and signed and dated 1796 (Plate 92B). He died at Patna on 21st September, 1807, aged forty. Examples of his work are in private collections and in the Victoria and Albert Museum. (Plate 92C.)

Plate 92D. **J. Smart, Junior,** *Robert Woolf, Junior (1786/7-1825) of the 6th Madras Cavalry, cousin of the artist, watercolour on paper, 5⅛ins. Signed and dated: 'J.S.J. / 1805.'* Courtesy E. Grosvenor Paine, U.S.A.

John Smart, Junior (1776-1809) was the natural son of John Smart, Senior, and Sarah Midgeley; he was not, as has so often been stated, the offspring of his father's first marriage, that John having died in infancy. A full account of John Smart and John Junior is given in *John Smart the Man and His Miniatures,* 1964. He was taught art by his father, as is evidenced in a letter from his father to the Court of Directors of the East India Company in 1808, when John Junior was asking permission to go to India. In the letter Smart says: "Having been pleased formerly to allow me to go to India to follow my profession of a miniature painter, I respectfully solicit the same indulgence for my son John Smart who has been taught by me and has obtained a proficiency in the same line that will do honour to me and a credit to himself". It has been suggested that John Junior may also have had some tuition from Cosway during his father's absence in India. Permission was granted, and John arrived in Madras on 11th February, 1809. Although his permission was to go to India as a miniaturist, his name was at the head of a list of nine Cadets who had travelled on the *Asia,* and there is a profile miniature of him, in a private collection, signed and dated: 'J.S.J. / 1808', in which he is wearing cadet uniform. Before leaving England John made his will, in which he left all his property to his sister, Sarah, who was his sole executrix. His time in Madras was of short duration for he died on either the 1st or 2nd June, 1809.

Although not all his *œuvre* was of equal merit, he worked very closely in the manner of his father and copied several of his miniatures. Many of his portraits are painted on paper or card, although he also used ivory. He signed in lettering very like that of his father: 'J.S.J.' (i.e. Junior), 'J. Smart Jun', or 'J. Smart Junior', sometimes followed by a date. He copied the works of early masters, including Holbein, taken after the well-known portraits at Windsor and executed in 1798. A good miniature by him of George Rundle, signed on the front: 'J.S. Junᴿ / 1800', is in the Smithsonian Institution, Washington (Plate 92G), and one of an unknown officer, signed: 'J.S.J. / 1809 / I', was Lot 130 at Sotheby's, 13th October, 1975 (Plate 92A).

Plate 93. **J.B. Isabey,** *Prince Napoleon Louis (1804-1831) aged five, second son of Louis Bonaparte and Queen Hortense, ivory, 8½ins. Signed and dated: 'Isabey / 1810.' The prince is standing in the doorway of the Galerie Francois I of the Château de Fontainebleau. This splendid miniature realised the record price of £24,000 in 1977.* **Courtesy Sotheby's.**

Examples of his work are in the Victoria and Albert Museum and private collections. (Plate 92D.)

Paul Frederick de Caselli (fl.1803-1817) is identical with the De Cavelli listed in the *Dictionary of British Miniature Painters,* p.239, his signature on the only miniature known at that time having been misread. He was born at Basle, and went to India arriving at Madras in December, 1803. *The Calcutta Monthly Journal,* January, 1804, reports the arrival in Madras of "the *General Steuart* (Captain Mortimer) from England with five Swiss officers and thirty-eight Swiss soldiers on board", including a "Casselli". De Caselli became a Lieutenant in H.M. Regiment de Meuron, but resigned in July 1804. In 1805 he married, at Mysore, Petronille, daughter of Major H.D. de Meuron-Motiers. In the *East India Register* for 1806-1813 he is listed as "De Caselle, portrait painter", and "De Casaille, Paul F., portrait painter". He moved to Pondicherry in 1812, where he lived until his death on 23rd May, 1817, and was buried in the English cemetery. J. Wathen in *Journal of a voyage in 1811 and 1812 to Madras and China* mentions that he charged forty guineas for his miniatures and that he had plenty of work. The miniatures by him which I have seen all show Continental influence; the features are painted with a smoothness reminiscent of enamelling. A miniature of an unknown officer signed: 'De Caselli' is in the collection of Dr. A.K. Brown (Plate 92F).

Plate 94A. **Johns,** *an unknown man, ivory, 2½ins. Signed:* 'Johns.' Courtesy Sotheby's.

A number of other miniaturists from the Continent were working in England at this period and also some from America. Of these I have selected a small number.

H. de Janvry (fl.1793-1800) was a Frenchman who worked in England c.1793-1800, from various London addresses, and who may have worked in America. He painted miniatures *en grisaille* on a dark background (many in profile), miniatures in watercolour and enamel, and engraved stones. His signature varies; sometimes it is: 'H.J.' (monogram, the J passing through the

Plate 94B. **André Leon Larue,** called *Lady Charlotte Harley, later Lady Charlotte Bacon, aged twenty-one, ivory, 2½ins. Signed: 'Mansion.'* Lord Byron dedicated **Childe Harold** *to Lady Charlotte.* Private Collection.

Plate 94C (left). **H. de Janvry,** *portrait of an unknown boy, ivory, 2¹⁵/₁₆ins. Signed on the reverse.* Courtesy the Bernard Falk Collection, The Royal Pavilion, Brighton.

Plate 94D (right). **Johns,** *'The Flower Girl', ivory, 4ins. Signed: 'Johns.' This is one of the largest and most attractive miniatures known by Johns. The costume of the sitter suggests that she came from the Continent.* Private Collection.

Plate 94E. **J.H. Hurter,** *after Reynolds, William, 5th Duke of Devonshire, K.G. (1748-1811), enamel, 2¼ins. Signed and dated on the reverse: 'J. Hurter Pinx 1782.'* Courtesy The Earl Beauchamp.

cross bar of the H), or 'H.J.', and sometimes: 'H. de Janvry.' Some of his miniatures are dated. An attractive one of a young boy, signed in monogram, is in the Bernard Falk Collection at The Royal Pavilion, Brighton (Plate 94C). Examples of his work are in the National Portrait Gallery and the Victoria and Albert Museum.

Johann Heinrich Hurter (1734-1799) was born in Schaffhausen, Switzerland, on 9th September, 1734. He was working in Berne from 1768-1770, was advised to go to Versailles but did not meet with much success, and from there went to The Hague where, in 1772, he became a member of the Painters' Guild. By c.1777 he had settled in London, having obtained the patronage of Lord Dartrey, whose family have a number of miniatures by him. He exhibited at the Royal Academy, 1779-1781, and was appointed a court painter. Between 1785 and 1787 he travelled on the Continent, but returned to London and founded a factory for mathematical and other instruments. He divided his time between London and Germany, and in 1787 received a large commission for the Empress Catherine of Russia. He painted miniatures on enamel, many of which were copies of paintings by old masters, and executed some pastel portraits. Hurter was given the rank of 'Freiherr'. He died in Düsseldorf on 2nd September, 1799. He was a good artist and his colouring is pleasing. His work is often soft in effect and well modelled. Many of his enamel copies are very fine. A good circular enamel of Hélène Fourment, after Rubens, signed and dated 1777, was Lot 9 at Sotheby's on 13th December, 1976 (Plate 94F). A fine pair of William, 5th Duke of Devonshire, and Georgiana Spencer, Duchess of Devonshire, after Reynolds, is in the collection of the Earl Beauchamp (Plates 94E and G).

Jean Baptiste Isabey (1767-1855) was one of the greatest miniaturists of the French School and is only included here because he was apparently working in London from c.1815-1820. He was born at Nancy on 11th April, 1767, and was the son of a merchant. He had a distinguished clientele, and became very popular at the French Court, holding important appointments

Plate 94F. **J.H. Hurter,** *after Rubens, Hélène Fourment, enamel, 3½ins. diam. Signed and dated on the reverse: '1777.' The sitter was Rubens' second wife. The original portrait is in the Alte Pinakothek, Munich.* Courtesy Sotheby's.

under Charles X and Louis XVIII and controlling the ceremonies at Napoleon's coronation. He was given apartments at Versailles, and granted a pension by Napoleon III. He was a good draughtsman and one of the most important miniaturists of the eighteenth century. A miniature by him of Prince Napoleon Louis (1804-1831), second son of Louis Bonaparte and Queen Hortense, was sold at Sotheby's in the Holzscheiter Collection on 28th March, 1977, for £24,000. It was signed and dated: 'Isabey / 1810' (Plate 93).

André Leon Larue, called Mansion (1785-c.1834) was another well-known French miniaturist who worked in England for a short time. He was born at Nancy on 29th November, 1785, and was the son of Jacques Larue, called Mansion, a painter and miniaturist, who is said to have taught Isabey and the young Mansion was a pupil both of his father and of Isabey — he was much influenced by the latter but did not attain such excellence. He worked in Paris, and exhibited at the Paris Salon in 1808, 1819, 1822 and 1834, and at the Royal Academy in 1829 and 1831; but although he visited London several times he spent most of his life in France. He painted miniatures on ivory and card as well as enamel, and executed some pictures in oils and on porcelain as well as drawing portraits of British officers, which were engraved. He was the author of *Lettres sur la Miniature,* 1822.

A miniature by Mansion of Lady Charlotte Harley, later Lady Charlotte Bacon, by Mansion, is in a private collection and is signed: 'Mansion' (Plate 94B). Examples of his work are in the Wallace Collection, London, and the Nottingham Art Museum, as well as in The Louvre.

Johns (fl.1791-1816) is an artist about whom little is known. It has been suggested that he was Dutch, but this is still uncertain. He worked in England towards the end of the eighteenth century and in the early part of the nineteenth century and seems to have moved about a lot, working in London, Leeds, Halifax, Scarborough, York and, before 1795, in Brussels. Since his style seems to vary a great deal, it is not easy to describe, and because examples of his work are scarce, accurate identification is difficult.

Plate 94G. **J.H. Hurter,** *after Reynolds, Georgiana Spencer, Duchess of Devonshire (1757-1806), enamel, 2¼ins. Signed and dated on the reverse: 'J. Hurter P: 1781.'* Courtesy The Earl Beauchamp.

335

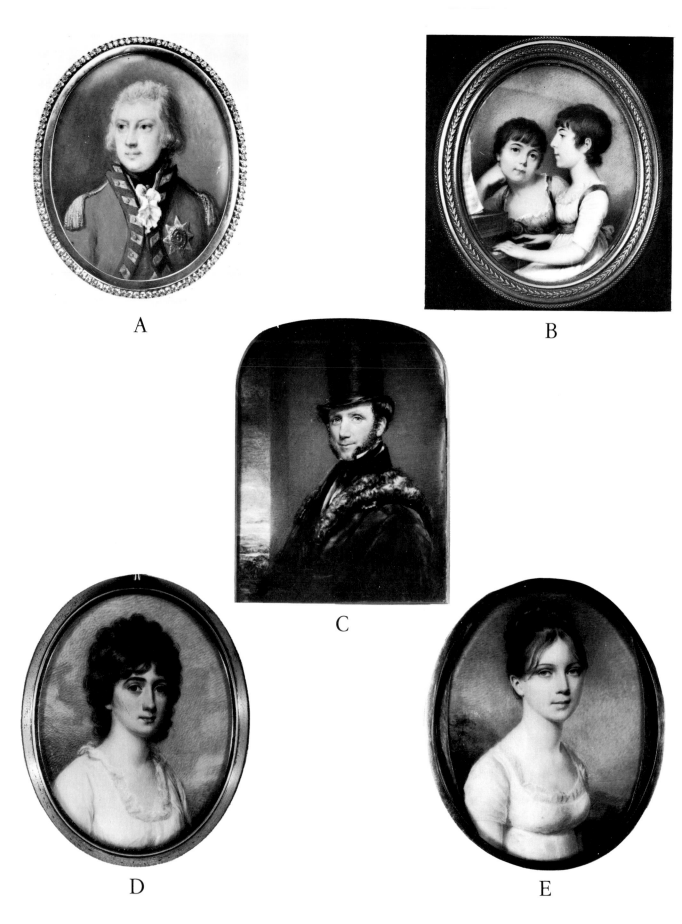

A

B

C

D

E

His normal signature is 'Johns.' One of his most attractive miniatures is called 'The Flower Girl' which is signed on the front: 'Johns'; formerly in the de la Hey Collection, sold at Sotheby's, 27th May, 1968 (Plate 94D). It is painted in bright, fresh colours against a dark background. Examples of his work are in the National Gallery, Washington, the Kaiser Friedrich Museum, Berlin, and the Victoria and Albert Museum. (Plate 94A.)

Louis Ami Arlaud (-Jurine) (1751-1829) was born in Geneva on 13th October, 1751, and was the grand-nephew of J.A. Arlaud. He was a pupil of J.E. Liotard in Geneva, and studied in Paris under Vivien, the historical painter. He painted miniatures on ivory and enamel, executed portraits in watercolour, and retouched pictures. Arlaud came to London in 1792 and soon became popular; he is said to have been a prolific artist although signed works by him are scarce and attribution difficult. He is thought to have been the Arlaud who exhibited at the Royal Academy from 1792-1800 from different London addresses, but no christian names are given for these exhibits. Arlaud was fond of fencing, riding and playing the violin. His pupils included A.E. Chalon, Mlle. Liotard, Mlle. Jurine, and Mme. Mayor. He returned to Geneva in 1802 and is reputed to have painted 645 more portraits. After his time in Britain his works show the influence of the English School. He often signed: 'Arlaud' on the front of the miniature, and occasionally: 'L. Arlaud.' An attractive oblong miniature on vellum of George Percy, later 5th Duke of Northumberland, and his sister, Charlotte Percy, signed and dated: 'L. Arlaud / 179-' (the last numeral being indecipherable) is in the collection of the Duke of Northumberland. It is beautifully painted and shows the sitters as children. One of Catherine and Frances Park seated at a piano, painted in 1800 and signed on the piano: 'Arlaud', is in the Bernard Falk Collection at The Royal Pavilion, Brighton (Plate 95B). Arlaud died at Pré-l'Evêque on 8th August, 1829.

François Ferrière (1752-1839) was another native of Geneva, where he was born on 11th July, 1752. After studying art in Paris in 1770 he returned to Geneva, where he married. Ferrière came to England in 1793, and exhibited at the Royal Academy and British Institution, 1793-1804 and 1817-1822. His work met with great success, and he was a prolific painter who was patronised by the Royal family. In 1804 he went to St. Petersburg, and to Moscow (c.1810) where he lost his fortune in the French invasion. He returned to St. Petersburg where he was made a member of the Academy in 1813. By c.1817 he was back in London, but returned to Geneva in 1822 where he worked until 1835; he then retired to Morges where he lived until his death on 25th December, 1839.

Plate 95.
A. *F. Ferrière, Frederick Augustus, Duke of York and Albany (1763-1827), ivory, 3¼ins. The sitter is wearing a scarlet uniform with blue and gold facings, a white cravat and the star and ribbon of the Order of the Garter. Set within a diamond bordered frame. Courtesy Sotheby's.*
B. *L.A. Arlaud, Catherine and Frances Park, ivory, 3⁵/₁₆ins., 1800. Signed: 'Arlaud.' This attractive miniature is one of the few signed works by this artist, whose miniatures are often unrecognised. Courtesy the Bernard Falk Collection, The Royal Pavilion, Brighton.*
C. *F. Ferrière, portrait of an unknown man, ivory, 4⁷/₈ins., c.1830. Notice the tall hat and side whiskers. This is a very good example of Ferrière's work. Courtesy the Bernard Falk Collection, The Royal Pavilion, Brighton.*
D. *E.G. Malbone, portrait of Maria Hayward, ivory, 3⁷/₁₆ins., c.1803. Courtesy the National Collection of Fine Arts, Smithsonian Institution, Washington, D.C.*
E. *E.G. Malbone, a lady identified as 'Henry Bourentheau's aunt', ivory, 3⁷/₁₆ins. This and Plate 95D are fine examples of works by Malbone. Courtesy the National Collection of Fine Arts, Smithsonian Institution, Washington, D.C.*

A

B

C

D

E

F

G

Plate 97A (left). **C.W. Day,** *portrait of an unknown young man holding a paper, ivory, 4¼ins. Signed on the front as well as on the reverse: 'C.W. Day delt / 1825.'* Courtesy E. Grosvenor Paine, U.S.A.

Plate 97B (right). **Mary A. Heaphy,** *after a portrait by Lawrence painted in 1817, Augusta, daughter of the Earl of Westmorland and wife of William, 1st Earl of Lonsdale, ivory, 5¼ins. The miniature is signed in full on the reverse.* Courtesy Christie's.

Ferrière painted miniatures in watercolour and enamel, and executed portraits in pastel and oils. He was a good artist, and most of his works show character. Those painted in watercolour have a lot of gum added, which gives them the impression of oil paintings. His distinguished clientele included a number of Scottish sitters and members of the Buccleuch family. He usually signed: 'F.F.', followed by a date, or: 'F. Ferrière p^t' and: 'Ferrière.' Not all his signatures have an accent on the name. Examples of his work are in the Scottish National Portrait Gallery, the Musée Rath, Geneva, and the Victoria and Albert Museum. A good miniature by him of Frederick, Duke of York was sold at Sotheby's on 10th November, 1969 (Plate 95A), and a fine miniature of an unknown man wearing a top hat is in the Bernard Falk Collection at The Royal Pavilion, Brighton (Plate 95C). A miniature of a young boy painted c.1790, and signed, was Lot 343 in the Heckett Sale at Sotheby Parke Bernet, in New York, on 5th October, 1977.

Plate 96.
A. **E. Nash,** *portrait of an Indian boy, ivory, 2⅛ins., c.1801-1810. Unfinished. Nash did not arrive in India until May 1801 and left in 1810.* Courtesy Sotheby's.
B. **W. Naish,** *Samuel Burgess, ivory, 2¾ins. Another miniature, which is almost identical, represents the sitter's twin brother Joseph and is signed: 'Naish.'* Private Collection.
C. **J. Naish,** *portrait of an unknown officer, ivory, 3ins. Signed on the reverse: 'John Naish.' Miniatures signed with the artist's christian name are rare, and there may well be some confusion between those painted by W. Naish and J. Naish.* Courtesy Sotheby's.
D. **E. Nash,** *the Rev. Samuel Cooper, aged seventy-five, ivory, 3¼ins. Signed on the reverse: 'Mr Saml Cooper / aged 75— / E. Nash pinxit July 28th / 1796.' This is an interesting example of Nash's work. Note the rather stiff way the wig is drawn and the arched eyebrows.* Private Collection.
E. **C. Hayter,** *portrait of an unknown man, ivory, 4ins. Signed and dated on the reverse: 'Charles Hayter / 53 Upper Grafton St / Fitzroy Sq / London. 1822.'* Private Collection.
F. **R. Higs,** *an unknown nobleman, enamel, 2ins. Signed on the reverse: 'R. Higs.' The sitter is wearing a red jacket with a dark collar and white cravat. The star of the Order of the Garter is on his jacket.* Courtesy Sotheby's.
G. **C. Hayter,** *an unknown lady, wife of the sitter in Plate 96E, ivory, 4ins. Signed and dated on the reverse: '1822.' Although not attractive this pair of miniatures are good character studies.* Private Collection.

Plate 97D. **C.W. Day,** *portrait of an unknown boy, ivory, 8½ins. Signed and dated: 'C.W. Day / 1835.' The boy, holding a riding crop, is seated on a rock against a mountainous landscape.* Courtesy E. Grosvenor Paine, U.S.A.

Plate 97C. **Joan Robertson,** *Elizabeth and Sarah Mary, daughters of the Hon. Henry Cavendish, ivory, 7¼ins. Signed in full on the reverse: 'Has / Elizabethae et Rachaelis / Henrici Saraq Cavendish / filiarum effigies / Pinxit car Joan Robertson / AD 1817.' An inscription on the reverse of the frame gives the children's names as Elizabeth and Sarah Mary. This is a good miniature, by a hitherto unrecorded artist, painted in fresh colours with the addition of gum.* Courtesy E. Grosvenor Paine, U.S.A.

Colour Plate 27.
A top left. **Archibald Skirving,** *May Anne Biddulph, second daughter of Michael Biddulph of Ledbury, ivory, 2½ins.*
B top right. **John Smart,** *an unknown man, possibly a relative of Robert Clerk, ivory, 2¾ins. A signed version of this miniature dated: '1792' was in the collection of the late Lord Wharton.*
C centre. **William Wood,** *Lieut. Col. John Dick Burnaby, 1st Foot Guards, ivory, 3½ins., 1805. A tracing and detailed record of colours used, etc., is in Wood's manuscript at the V. & A.M. The sitter came from Lowerby Hall, near Leicester. This is one of the finest miniatures Wood ever painted.*
D bottom left. **Thomas Richmond,** *an unknown man, ivory, 3⅛ins., c.1800.*
E bottom right. **Walter Stephens Lethbridge,** *an unknown lady, ivory, 2⅞ins., c.1820. Signed and inscribed on the reverse: 'W.S. Lethbridge / Pinxit ad vivum / 391 Strand / London.' This is a particularly attractive miniature by Lethbridge.*

Private Collection

Plate 98A (left). **Charlotte Hadfield**, *portrait of an unknown lady, ivory, 2¾ins. Signed and dated on the reverse: 'Char^l Hadfield / London July / 1793.' This is one of the few known examples of the artist's work and is painted in the manner of Cosway, her brother-in-law. Charlotte married William Combe, author of* Dr. Syntax. Courtesy Sotheby's.

Plate 98B (right). **A. Gregory**, *an unknown officer, ivory, 2¾ins. Signed: 'A. Gregory 1821.' This artist is hitherto unrecorded. The miniature is quite well painted.* Private Collection.

Plate 98C. **J.F. Hüet-Villiers**, *portrait of an unknown lady, ivory, 2½ins. Signed and dated: 'Huet-Villiers 1813.'* Courtesy Sotheby's.

Edward Greene Malbone (1777-1807), one of the greatest American miniaturists, came over to this country for a few months in 1801. Miniatures by him are occasionally seen in England and, as few are signed, may well pass unrecognised. His style is reminiscent of Andrew Robertson. Characteristics are the way in which the eyes are painted with the pupils dark and round, and the eyelids and eyebrows clearly delineated. The hair is painted in soft masses and the backgrounds shaded with cross hatching; occasionally he introduced the suggestion of a landscape. He signed: 'Malbone', 'E.G.M.', and 'E. Malbone.' Many of his works are pale in colour. Good examples are in the Smithsonian Institution, Washington (Plates 95D and E).

Works by some of the following lesser known artists are well worth the consideration of the new collector. (The Appendix at the end of this chapter lists other little-known miniaturists of the period.)

Plate 98D (right). **J.B. Sambat**, *an unknown lady, ivory, 2¼ins., c.1780-90. Signed: 'Sambat.' Miniatures by this minor artist are scarce.* Private Collection.

Plate 98E (far right). **H.J. Harding**, *Mrs. Agnew, wife of Patrick Agnew, ivory, 4¼ins. Signed: 'Harding / 1824.'* Courtesy Sotheby's.

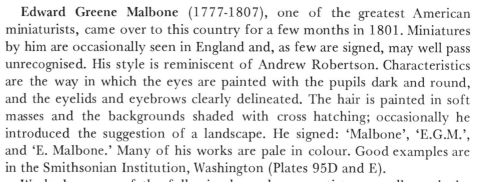

Plate 98F (left). **A.J. Oliver, A.R.A.,** *an unknown man, ivory, 2³⁄₈ins. Signed on the reverse: 'Archer James Oliver pinxt / 27 Air Street Piccadilly. / December. 1799.' Another minor artist whose works are not often seen.* Private Collection.

Plate 98G (right). **Miss Annabella Pigott,** *Lord Adam Gordon (1726?-1801), General 1796, son of Alexander, 2nd Duke of Gordon, ivory, 2³⁄₄ins. Signed on the reverse with the sitter's name, and on another piece of paper inscribed with family details. This portrait, together with others, was sold in 1975 when the artist's christian name was first recorded.* Private Collection.

Walter Stephens Lethbridge (1771/2-1831?) was the son of a farmer, and was born at Charlton, Devon, where he was baptised on 13th October, 1772. He was apprenticed to a house painter, and later assisted a travelling artist. He exhibited at the Royal Academy and Society of British Artists, 1801-1829. He worked in London, Canterbury and Plymouth, and, according to an advertisement in the *Kentish Gazette,* 1805, charged three guineas upwards for his miniatures. Many are of a high quality, and attractive. The modelling of the features is good and the costume recorded in detail. He used opaque white to depict lace, painted the hair with a broad brush stroke, and often shaded the face with a greyish-blue, especially round the eyes and nose and under the chin. An attractive miniature of an unknown lady signed in full on the reverse: 'W.S. Lethbridge / Pinxit ad vivum / 391 Strand / London', is in a private collection (Colour Plate 27E). A pair of good miniatures of Mr. and Mrs. James Octavius Norman, signed in full on the reverse, was Lot 89 at Sotheby's on 2nd June, 1975 (Plates 82B and C).

Plate 98H (left). **F. Morrant,** *portrait of an unknown man, ivory, 2³⁄₄ins., c.1780-90. Signed: F. Morrant / pinxit.' This is by a hitherto unrecorded artist of average ability.* Private Collection.

Plate 98 I (right). **J. Morris Davis,** *miniature of an unknown young man, ivory, 3ins. Signed: I.M.D. / 1811.' It is a good example of the artist's work and is well painted.* Courtesy R. Bayne Powell.

Plate 99A (left). Attributed to **J. Plott,** *William Creech of Edinburgh, bookseller and Lord Provost (d.1815), ivory, 2½ins. Only a small number of miniatures by this artist are known.* Private Collection.

Plate 99B (right). **M. Bingham, Lady Lucan,** *after Kneller, Queen Anne (1665-1714), ivory, 3½ins. Signed with a gold monogram: 'MB.' Painted in the manner of B. Lens.* Private Collection.

Plate 99C. **E. Dayes,** *an unknown lady, ivory, 2⁵/8ins. Inscribed on the reverse: 'Ed Dayes N 5 / King Street Covent / Garden.' Note the large hat decorated with ribbons and perched over a pleated cap.* Courtesy Victoria and Albert Museum.

Henry Jacob Burch, Junior (b.1763) was the son of Edward Burch, R.A. (1730?-c.1814), also a miniaturist. Henry entered the Royal Academy Schools on 25th March, 1779. He exhibited at the Royal Academy, Society of Artists, and Society of British Artists, 1787-1834. On 6th December, 1784, he married Elizabeth Beresford, at St. Mary-le-Bone. In 1793 a fire broke out and destroyed his house in Rathbone Place, leaving them in great distress.

Signed miniatures by Burch are scarce and, as his style varied, not always easy to identify. Some of his works are reminiscent of William Wood whilst others, such as one of a boy signed on the front: 'H. Burch' (in the Alan Evans Collection at the Victoria and Albert Museum), are painted with much more assurance and strength (Plate 83A). A most attractive miniature of the Hon. Frederick Sylvester Douglas, attributed to Burch, was Lot 146 at Sotheby's on 25th November, 1974 (Colour Plate 32B). He painted miniatures in watercolour and oils and executed cameos, intaglios and wax portraits. Some engravings after his works are in the British Museum, and examples of his miniatures are in the Victoria and Albert Museum.

Plate 99D. **W.P.,** *an attractive miniature of an unknown lady, ivory, 3¼ins., c.1780-90. The artist has not yet been identified. The colouring is predominantly green, even on the hair; the draughtsmanship is good and the pose graceful.* Courtesy Sotheby's.

Plate 99E (left). E.W. **Foster,** *an unknown lady, ivory, 3⅞ins. Signed and dated on the reverse: 'Edward Foster / York 1803.' This may have been painted from an earlier portrait as the costume suggests a date of c.1770.* Courtesy Victoria and Albert Museum.

Plate 99F (right). J. **Pastorini,** *miniature of an unknown lady, ivory, 3ins. Sold at the same time as a miniature of the sitter's husband by the same artist, both signed on the reverse and that of the husband dated: '1820.' Good miniatures by Pastorini are scarce. Note the distinct stippling on the background.* Courtesy Christie's.

John (Inigo?) Wright (d.1820) worked in London. His exact date of birth is uncertain. Bénézit identifies him with Inigo Wright, an engraver (c.1745-1820), but this has not been verified. He exhibited at the Royal Academy, 1795-1819, and was friendly with T. Phillips, Hoppner, Lawrence and W. Owen. He married, as his first wife, Priscilla Guise, daughter of a musician who was master of the choristers at Westminster. She had been married previously to a French emigrant who had left her. She did not survive the birth of their son, John William Wright, in 1802 and Wright soon remarried.

He was a good artist who painted his miniatures on both oval and rectangular formats. Some of his works have a yellowish tinge on the face and the shading on the drapery is mauvish. Many of his miniatures are copies of oil portraits after Hoppner, Reynolds, Owen, etc. According to an inscription on the reverse of a miniature he styled himself 'Miniature painter to His Royal Highness the Duke of Kent'. His miniatures are forceful and some give the impression of oil paintings. He used gouache to paint the linen draperies and the hair, and some of his later works are shaded with long hairy strokes on the face. Miniatures of ladies by him are scarce; an attractive one of Lady Raglan, after Lawrence, was sold in the Gilbert Collection at Christie's on 3rd December, 1963 (Plate 83C). One of an unknown lady, in a private collection, is signed and dated on the reverse: 'John Wright / Pinxt / Burlington Gardens corner of Old Bond / St London / 1815' (Plate 83B). Wright committed suicide in 1820. He had several pupils including S.P. Denning. Examples of his work are in the National Portrait Gallery, the British Museum and the Victoria and Albert Museum.

Samuel John Stump (1778-1863) was probably born in America and was called 'the American Stump.' He studied at the Royal Academy Schools from 3rd October, 1796. He exhibited at the Royal Academy, Associated Artists, British Institution, Old Water Colour Society and Society of British Artists, 1802-1849. He painted miniatures, watercolour portraits, landscapes, oil portraits and executed engravings. He worked for the most

Plate 99G. C. **Hardy,** *portrait of an unknown man, ivory, 2¾ins. Signed and dated on the reverse: '1802.'* Courtesy Sotheby's.

A

B

C

D

E

F

G

part in London, but was in Brighton in 1809. Many of his sitters were members of the theatrical profession, including Mrs. Honey and Mrs. Jordan. (Plate 83D.)

Stump was a prolific artist and not all his works are of equal merit: some in fact are rather dull, others well painted and attractive. He often signed his miniatures in full on the reverse, followed by his address and a date such as: 'S.J. Stump Pinxt / No 7 Cork Street / Burlington Gardens / 1816.' One, of an unknown man, was Lot 49 at Christie's on 28th October, 1970; it was

Plate 101A (left). **W. Pether,** *Lord Richard Cavendish (1752-81), ivory, 2³/₁₆ins. Signed: 'W.Pether / 1770.' The sitter was M.P. for Lancaster 1773-80. Edmund Burke writing to the 3rd Duke of Portland in 1781 says: "If ever any one man had Virtues to redeem a bad age it was Lord Richard Cavendish." Miniatures by this artist are scarce.* Courtesy Ivy, Duchess of Portland.

Plate 101B (right). **Joseph Bowring** *(b.c. 1760, d. aft. 1817), self-portrait of the artist, ivory, 2½ins. Signed in monogram: 'JB.'* Courtesy Victoria and Albert Museum, Alan Evans Collection.

signed on the front: 'Stump / 1803' (Plate 83G). One of William Dobell, by Stump, was sold at Sotheby's on 25th November, 1974 (Plate 83F).

Miss Amelia Mary Dietz (fl.1779-1798) is an artist about whom very little is known. She may have been related to Diana Dietz (Mrs. Hill). The only miniature by her that I have ever seen is the one illustrated here from the collection of R. Bayne Powell. It is signed on the reverse: 'Amelia Maria Dietz / 1796' and is an attractive and competent miniature. The painting is soft, and the detail only lightly sketched in (Plate 91E). She exhibited at the Royal Academy, 1782-1798 and from 1788-1798 her address was 41 Broad Street, Soho.

Plate 100.
A. *Miniature of an unknown lady by the artist signing* **V** *in cursive lettering, ivory, 2⅛ins., c.1775-80.* Courtesy Sotheby's.
B. **J.W. Faulkner,** *portrait of an unknown officer, ivory, 3¾ins. Signed on the reverse and bearing his trade card: 'J.W.Faulkner / Portrait & Miniature Painter.' The sitter is wearing a scarlet uniform, and the miniature is well painted.* Courtesy Bonham's.
C. **W.J.L. Hudson,** *one of a pair of miniatures representing two brothers, Robert and Warren Frith, ivory, 3¼ins. This one of Robert is signed and dated: '18(13?).' The technique is reminiscent of works by G. Chinnery.* Courtesy Sotheby's.
D. **P.E. Stroëhling,** *portrait of an unknown lady, ivory, 3¾ins., c.1790-1800. Signed: 'Stroely.' Probably painted on the Continent.* Courtesy Christie's.
E. **R.W. Satchwell,** *Carlo Joseph Doyle, second son of Wellbore Ellis Doyle, ivory, 3ins. Signed and dated in full on the reverse: 'April 1823.' The sitter joined the Coldstream Guards in 1803 and served in the Peninsular War, acting as Military Secretary to Lord Hastings in 1813.* Courtesy Sotheby's.
F. **J.B. van Acker,** *portrait of a young lady, ivory, 2¾ins. Signed and dated: '1824.' The sitter is wearing a mauve dress trimmed with pink ribbons and white lace, and a small cap on her head also tied with pink ribbon.* Courtesy Sotheby's.
G. **G. Slous,** *portrait of an unknown man, ivory, 3ins. c.1800. Signed: 'Slous Pxt.'* Courtesy Sotheby's.

Plate 101C. **J. Bowring,** *portrait of an unknown man in a seascape background, ivory, 3ins. Signed in monogram: 'JB.' This and Plate 101B are good examples of this artist's work.* Courtesy Sotheby's.

Plate 101D. **C. Bestland,** *an unknown lady, ivory, 2¾ins. Signed and dated on the reverse: '1798.'* Courtesy Sotheby's.

Plate 101E. **W. Doyle,** *portrait of an unknown man, ivory, 3¼ins. Signed: 'Doyle.' This is an interesting miniature as few works by Doyle are known.* Courtesy Sotheby's.

Joan Robertson (fl.1817) is an artist about whom I have no information. The only miniature I know by her is the one illustrated of Elizabeth and Sarah Mary, daughters of the Hon. Henry Cavendish. It is inscribed in a copperplate hand on the reverse: 'Has / Elizabethae et Rachaelis / Henrici Saraq Cavendish / filiarum effigies / Pinxit car Joan Robertson / AD 1817.' On the reverse of the frame is a further inscription in a later hand: 'Elizabeth & Sarah Mary ... daughters of the Honble / Henry Cavendish.' The two children are picking flowers in a wood, both wearing white dresses and both with auburn hair. The miniature is well painted and the artist has used a lot of gum with her paint (Plate 97C).

William Naish (c.1767-1800) was born in Axbridge, Somerset. He entered the Royal Academy Schools on 28th November, 1788, aged twenty-one. He had a large practice in London which included many of the theatrical profession. He worked for a time in Bristol. Naish exhibited at the Royal Academy, 1786-1800; he is said to have died at his house in Leicester Square late in 1800. A miniature of a man by Naish, illustrated in Plate 143 in *British Portrait Miniatures*, has been in a private collection for many years. The sitter was unknown until, a few years ago, I came across an almost identical miniature of Samuel Burgess which came from the family (Plate 96B). The sitters were twin brothers, and the earlier miniature represents Joseph Burgess. It is signed on the reverse: 'Naish' in sloping writing. The features of both sitters are shaded with a bluish tint and the eyelids drawn with firm distinct lines. The hair is painted in separate strands, some in a deepish blue. Examples of Naish's work are in the Victoria and Albert Museum.

Sophia H.M. Howell (fl.1781-1788) worked in London and exhibited at the Royal Academy, 1781-1788, as an Honorary Exhibitor. Her exhibits included a self-portrait. A miniature by her of Mrs. Hannay, after A. Plimer,

Plate 101F (left). **R. Fortin,** *portrait of a young girl, ivory, 2⁹/₁₆ins. Signed and dated: 'Fortin 1793', the F and N being in small capitals. The face is shaded with minute stippling. This is at present the only known miniature by this artist.* Courtesy the Bernard Falk Collection, The Royal Pavilion, Brighton.

Plate 101G (right). **Mary Barrett,** *a young boy with a baby, ivory, 3ins. Signed and dated on the reverse: '1799.' This is an attractive miniature and well painted.* Courtesy Victoria and Albert Museum, Alan Evans Collection.

signed in monogram: 'SH', was Lot 127 at Sotheby's on 25th November, 1974. It was not unattractive, but lacked draughtsmanship, and was slightly reminiscent of the work of Mrs. Mee (Plate 88G).

Thomas Arrowsmith (fl.1792-1829) was a native of London. In spite of the fact that he was deaf and dumb, he earned a living as an artist and his works included religious subjects and miniatures. He exhibited at the Royal Academy, 1792-1829, and was apparently working in Lancashire and in Manchester c.1827. Basil Long records seeing a small oil portrait by him which he considered quite good. A drawing on paper of John Nash (b.c.1718) is in the collection of F. Joachim. It is fully inscribed on the reverse and dated 1797 (Plate 75D). A pair of miniatures of a man and a woman by Arrowsmith, are signed on the reverse and dated 1794. The background is shaded in honeycomb strokes rather in the manner of C. Jagger (Plate 82A). His work is not of outstanding merit, but interesting.

Charles William Day (fl.1815-1854) worked in London, Florence, and the West Indies. He was awarded a prize from the Society of Arts in 1815, and exhibited at the Royal Academy, 1821-1854. He published *The Art of Miniature Painting* and *Five Years Residence in the West Indies.* Some of his work is said to be reminiscent of A. Robertson. The only two miniatures by him that I have seen are both in the collection of E.G. Paine, of the U.S.A. One is of a young man in a black coat and white cravat, holding a paper. It is signed on the front: 'C.W. Day delt / 1825', and similarly on the reverse (Plate 97A). The other miniature is of a young boy seated on a rock, holding a riding crop, with mountains in the background. It is signed on the front: 'C.W. Day / 1835.' This latter miniature is more in the manner of Robertson (Plate 97D).

Charles Hayter (1761-1835) was born in Twickenham on 24th February, 1761. His father's christian name is unknown, but his mother's maiden name was Elizabeth Holmes. He entered the Royal Academy Schools on 30th January, 1786, and worked in London and Winchester. In 1788 he married, at St. George's, Hanover Square, Martha Stevenson (1762-1805). Three of

Plate 102A. **J.P. Lambert,** *portrait of an unknown girl, ivory, 4¼ins. Signed on the reverse: 'Lambert (Jas) Powin / July 1825.' The girl is wearing a white low-cut dress with a blue sash. This artist is previously unrecorded.* Courtesy E. Grosvenor Paine, U.S.A.

Plate 102B. **N.N. Carter,** *miniature of an unknown lady, ivory, 3½ins. Signed and dated on the reverse: '1837.'* Courtesy Mrs. E.M. Hamilton.

Plate 102C. **O. Oakley,** *portrait of an unknown lady, ivory, 3½ins. Signed and dated: 'O.Oakley 1829.' This is a good example of costume, with the large hat decorated with feathers over the sitter's curled hair, and a lace-edged bodice partly covered by a cloak.* Courtesy Christie's.

Plate 102D. **W. Haines** *after Hoppner, Admiral Sir Henry Blackwood, K.C.B. (1770-1832), ivory, 4⁵/₁₆ins. Signed on the reverse. This is a fine example of Haines' work. Note the stippling used to shade the face and background.* Courtesy the Bernard Falk Collection, The Royal Pavilion, Brighton.

Plate 103A. Attributed to **W. Read,** *a family of four children and a dog, ivory, 5³/₈ins. c.1790-95. This example is close in style to a few signed miniatures by Read. Courtesy Sotheby's.*

their children, Sir George Hayter (1792-1871), Miss Anne Hayter (fl.1814-1830), and John Hayter (1800-1895), were all artists. Hayter was Professor of Perspective to Princess Charlotte. He executed portraits in crayon and pencil, and painted miniatures. An album of some 440 pencil portraits by him is in the Victoria and Albert Museum; many of the sitters are named. He was the author of *An Introduction to Perspective* and *A New Practical Treatise on Three Primitive Colours.* He died in London on 1st December, 1835. The majority of his drawings are signed on the reverse, but some of his miniatures are signed on the front. Hayter often placed a sketch of the sitter beneath the ivory when beginning a miniature. A pair of miniatures of a lady and gentleman, signed and dated on the reverse: 'Charles Hayter / 53 Upper Grafton St / Fitzroy Sq / London. 1822', are in a private collection. They are both good character studies (Plates 96E and G).

Edward Nash (G?) (1778-1821) was the sixth of eleven children born to Thomas Nash (1743-1809) and his wife, Mary, née Woodbridge. His father was a wealthy merchant of Coventry, although the family had been 'Kentish men' for four hundred years. At his death T. Nash left £96,000 and property in Kent and London. E. Nash exhibited at the Royal Academy, 1800-1820, from London addresses. He was said to have been a pupil or assistant of S. Shelley. He left Portsmouth for India in the *Hercules* on 9th January, 1801, arriving in Bombay in May, 1801. He is reputed to have made money in India, but returned to England in the *Dover Castle* in February, 1810. According to his relatives he was a hunchback and suffered from ill health. He worked for a time in the Lake District, where he knew Coleridge, Southey and Wordsworth, etc.

Some of Nash's work is reminiscent of Shelley and J. Smart, as in the case of Colour Plate 32A, but his style varied. A particularly fine miniature of an Indian boy by him was sold at Sotheby's on 25th March, 1974; it was well drawn and most expressive (Plate 96A). One of the Rev. Samuel Cooper, signed on the reverse: 'Mr Sam¹ Cooper / aged 75– / E Nash pinxit July 28th / 1796' (Plate 96D). It is painted in a rather stiff manner and the draughtsmanship is not as good as that of the Indian boy. Many of his miniatures are unsigned, and are probably not always recognised. He sometimes exaggerated the size of the eyes. He lived from 1811-1818 at 6

Plate 103B. **J. Roberts,** *a young boy, ivory, 2³/₄ins., c.1790-1800. It is a good miniature, the boy wearing a red jacket with a white collar. This artist has not yet been identified with any certainty. Courtesy Christie's.*

Plate 103C. **A.P.**, *portrait of a young boy by an artist who signed: 'AP / 1786.' Ivory, 2¾ins. The miniature is well drawn and attractive.* Courtesy Sotheby's.

George Street, Hanover Square, where Shelley also lived. In his will, dated 31st March, 1817, he left property to his mother; £1,000 to each of his brothers, Thomas and Richard; his casts and figures to his friend, Wm. Haines; wines, liqueurs and £20 to Miss Shelley, for a ring. The rest was to be divided between his brothers and sisters, except for his drawings and miniatures which he left to his brother, William Woodbridge Nash. He died unmarried in London on 3rd January, 1821. Examples of his work are in the Victoria and Albert Museum, and the British Museum.

Miss Mary Anne Heaphy (Mrs. W. Musgrave) (fl.1821-1847) was the daughter of Thomas Heaphy and sister of Elizabeth Heaphy, both miniaturists. She exhibited at the Royal Academy, etc., 1821-1847. In 1832

Plate 103D. **R. Higs**, *portrait of John Jervis, Admiral, Earl of St. Vincent (1735-1823), enamel, 4ins. Signed on the reverse by the artist. Possibly taken from a large portrait.* Courtesy Christie's.

Plate 103E (left). **J.T. Mitchell,** *Mrs. Samuel Marples, née Anne Denton, ivory, 3ins., c.1820. Sold at the same time as a miniature of her husband also by Mitchell.* Courtesy Sotheby's.

Plate 103F (right). **P.N. Violet,** *an unknown young lady, ivory, 3¼ins., c.1780-90. Signed: 'P. Violet.' The sitter appears to be cleaning oysters.* Private Collection.

she married W. Musgrave, the portrait painter, after which date she exhibited under her married name. She was a good artist who worked in the manner of Sir W.J. Newton. In 1847 she was living at 32 Royal Circus, Edinburgh. Works by her are scarce, and those I have seen are attractive. One of Augusta, wife of the 1st Earl of Lonsdale, after a painting by Lawrence, was Lot 37 at Christie's on 2nd June, 1970. It is signed in full on the reverse and is pleasing and well painted (Plate 97B).

It is tempting to go on and on describing the artists who made their contribution to the history of miniature painting during the Georgian period, but there were so many that omissions are inevitable, and my hope is that collectors will continue where I have left off and discover more details for themselves.

APPENDIX

The following artists are amongst those whose works may be found by collectors, and who worked between c.1760 and 1830. An asterisk denotes the fact that the artist has not been previously recorded. To help new collectors, most of the artists listed are represented by an illustration.

A., I., fl.1788.
Acker, Johannes Baptista van, 1794/5-1863 (Plate 100F).
Adam, or Adams, Henry J., ? Eighteenth century.
Aslett, G, b.c.1787
Baine, Louisa, Eighteenth century *(Colour Plate 26B)*.
Barrett, Miss Mary, d.1836 *(Plate 101G)*.
Bestland, Charles, b.1764? *(Plate 101D)*.
Bowring, J., c.1760-d. aft. 1817 *(Plates 101B and C)*.
Burton, W.K., fl.1803-1804 *(Colour Plate 21C)*.
Carter, Noel N., fl.1823-1833 *(Plate 102B)*.
Charles, A., fl.1786-1793.

Collins, W.H., fl.1822-1859.

Cosway, Mrs. Richard, née Maria Hadfield, 1759/60-1838.

Davis, James Morris, fl.1810-1839/40 *(Plate 98 I)*.

Dayes, Edward, 1763-1804 *(Plate 99C)*.

Dillon, Charles, c.1810-1830.

Doyle, W., fl.1826 *(Plate 101E)*.

Faulkner, Joshua Wilson, fl.1809-1820 *(Plate 100B)*.

Fortin, R., fl.1793-1794 *(Plate 101F)*.

Foster, Edward Ward, 1762-1865 *(Plate 99E)*.

Green, Mrs. James, née Mary Byrne, 1776-1845.

*Gregory, A., fl. c.1821 *(Plate 98B)*.

Hadfield, Miss Charlotte (Mrs. William Combes), fl.1793 *(Plate 98A)*.

Haines, William, 1778-1848 *(Plate 102D)*.

Harding, H.J., fl.1823-1824 *(Plate 98E)*.

Hardy, Charles, fl.1802-1817 *(Plate 99G)*.

Hardy, J. (James or Jonathan ?), fl.1809-1810.

Herman, fl. c.1820-1840.

Higs, R., fl.1786-1796 *(Plates 96F and 103D)*.

Hudson, William J.L., 1779-1834 *(Plate 100C)*.

Hüet-Villiers, Jean François Marie, 1772-1813 *(Plate 98C)*.

*Lambert, James Powin, fl. c.1825 *(Plate 102A)*.

Lucan, The Countess of (Lady Margaret Bingham), née Margaret Smith, d.1814 *(Plate 99B)*.

Mitchell, J.T., fl.1798-1830.

*Morrant, F., Eighteenth century *(Plate 98H)*.

Naish, John, Eighteenth century *(Plate 96C)*.

Oakley, Octavius, 1800-1867 *(Plate 102C)*.

Oliver, Archer James, A.R.A., 1774-1842 *(Plate 98F)*.

P., A., fl. c.1786 *(Plate 103C)*.

P., W., fl. c.1789-1790 *(Plate 99D)*.

Parsey, Arthur, fl.1829-1837.

Pastorini, Joseph, c.1775-1839 *(Plate 99F)*.

Pether, William, F.S.A., 1738?-1821 *(Plate 101A)*.

Pigott, Miss Annabella, fl. 1797-1802 *(Plate 98G)*.

Plott, John, F.S.A., 1732-1803 *(Plate 99A)*.

Polack, Solomon, 1757-1839 *(Colour Plate 15F)*.

R., I., fl.1751-1774.

Read, William, fl.1778-1796 *(Plate 103A)*.

Roberts, John, fl.1774-1815 *(Plate 103B)*.

Sambat, Jean Baptiste, c.1760-1827 *(Plate 98D)*.

Satchwell, Robert William, fl.1793-1818 *(Plate 100E)*.

Slous, Gideon, fl.1791-1839 *(Plate 100G)*.

Stroëhling, Peter Edward, 1768-d. aft. 1826 *(Plate 100D)*.

Thick(e), W., fl.1787-1814.

V., c.1778 *(Plate 100A)*.

Violet, Pierre Noel, 1749-1819 *(Plate 103F)*.

Chapter X

The Heyday of Miniature Painting

THE SMALL NUMBER of artists selected for this chapter need no introduction to experienced members of the art world; they represent the flowering of British miniature painting in the eighteenth and early nineteenth century. The inclusion of some of these names may at first seem surprising, as the great masters of this period are usually thought of only in terms of Richard Cosway, John Smart, George Engleheart and Andrew Plimer. To this select gathering I have added Jeremiah Meyer, who was, of course, working slightly earlier than the others, Richard Crosse, Ozias Humphry, William Wood who has, in my opinion, been underrated for some time, and George Chinnery who, although best known for his sketches and paintings, executed some fine miniatures which place him amongst the 'top ten'.

Collectively these artists spanned the years between the reigns of George II and George IV, and in consequence lived through many social and political changes. Fashions altered considerably during those years, and this is particularly noticeable in ladies' hair styles. From c.1760/65 to c.1775 these gradually built up from the simple, upswept arrangement with the occasional bow of ribbon or posy of flowers so popular in the early part of the eighteenth century, to more elaborate constructions which, by c.1770-1780, had risen to extraordinary heights. The *coiffure* was decorated with a variety of ornaments; pads, cushions and supports were used, and the hair was dressed with pomatum, or paste, to stiffen it and hold the powder. This pomatum was made of various ingredients such as hog's grease, tallow or a mixture of beef marrow and oil! It was a tedious and lengthy business to achieve these preparations and good hairdressers were in great demand. From c.1790 high head-dresses were out of fashion, and by the turn of the century ladies wore their hair short, or 'cropped' as it was called, sometimes with a bandeau swathed round the curls. Caps and turbans were popular and by c.1800 larger and stiffer hats of various shapes came into fashion, some with high crowns.

Miniatures are a very good guide to fashion as they show on a small scale what was normally worn, rather than the more stylised fashions dictated in the large portraits or groups. Many of these differences are demonstrated in the illustrations for this chapter.

Men's costume also underwent changes, but these are not so apparent on miniatures and mostly relate to the cut of the coat and waistcoat and to the height and style of the cravat, which by c.1830 was excessively high and bulky. An apt verse is quoted in Cunnington's *Handbook of English Costume in the 19th Century*, p.108:

Each lordly man his taper waist displays,
Combs his sweet locks and laces on his stays,
Ties on his starch'd cravat with nicest care,
And then steps forth to petrify the fair.
                                        At Bath, 1825, *The English Spy.*

During the so-called Regency period of c.1800-1820, ladies' dresses were designed on classical lines, and later in a style that was called 'Gothic'. During the Regency it was said that the only differences between mistress and maid was that the maid wore a cap! A correspondent writing in 1807 remarks that: "for semi-nudity even a shop girl could vie with any Duchess in the land" and that "... the very Abigails have divested themselves of every petticoat in order that the footman or valet may discover the outline of their secret beauties through transparent calico"!

The artists discussed in this chapter were for the most part patronised by the rich and important personages who were at the forefront of society during the gay and frivolous period of Georgian England and the Regency. The Prince of Wales, later George IV, did much to encourage many of the artists of the time, and employed them to paint his own portrait in miniature as well as those of his mistresses. Many portraits and miniatures relating to him are illustrated by J.B. Priestley in his book so aptly entitled *The Prince of Pleasure.* When he was old enough to act independently he took up residence at Carlton House and gathered round him his own set of friends, with whom he enjoyed his leisure hours. Money was to him no object, and as a result he was constantly in debt. He had good taste in art and a great feeling for the overall look of a room, and regardless of cost was constantly adding to his art treasures. Oliver Millar in *The Queen's Pictures* says: "In the annals of the collection George IV's achievements as patron and collector were the most brilliant, sustained and entertaining since the time of the Stuarts."

Richard Cosway, R.A. (1742-1821), whose name is known to any student of art, was one of the most outstanding miniaturists of his day. The son of Richard and Mary Cosway, he was born at Okeford, near Bampton, Devon, where he was baptised on 5th November, 1742. His father, who was of Flemish descent, was headmaster of Blundell's School. The family had emigrated from Flanders during the reign of Elizabeth I, and settled in Tiverton where they established a very prosperous wool business and owned a considerable amount of property in the area. According to Dr. G.C. Williamson, Richard had one brother, William, who became secretary to Nelson, was present at the Battle of Trafalgar, and received a Knighthood. Cosway was educated at Tiverton, which he always regarded as his native place. His family were said to have been great lovers of pictures and to have

Colour Plate 28.
A top left. **William Grimaldi,** *an unknown officer, ivory, 2¾ins. Signed on the front: 'W. Grimaldi A.R. 1793.'*
B top right. **John Barry,** *an unknown man, ivory, 2½ins., c.1800. This is a good illustration of Barry's way of shading the features and painting the hair in a mass.*
C centre. **Richard Cosway, R.A.,** *Mr. Bigland, ivory, 3ins. Inscribed on the reverse: 'Sarah Bigland's hair 1804.'*
D bottom left. **John Cox Dillman Engleheart,** *an unknown lady, ivory, 3³/₁₆ins. Signed on the reverse and dated: '1820.'*
E bottom right. **George Engleheart,** *an unknown lady, ivory, 3⁵/₁₆ins. Signed on the front: 'GE / 1792' (cursive writing).*
Courtesy Bernard Falk Collection, Royal Pavilion, Brighton

Figure 30. Richard Cosway's signature.

possessed some very good ones which Cosway, as a boy, spent many hours copying. He showed unusual talent in art and, assisted by his uncle and a local trader, Oliver Peard, who was his godfather, Cosway was sent to London for some training on the understanding that they would guarantee his upkeep.

The boy was under twelve years of age when he went to London. Graham Reynolds refers to an enamel miniature of a man signed and dated 1753, which he considered was authentic and, as such, an exceptional piece of work for so young a boy. When he arrived in London he was placed at first with Thomas Hudson, who was a Devon man and tutor to Sir Joshua Reynolds. Cosway only remained with Hudson for a few months as for some reason he did not settle with him; being young and over-anxious to get on he probably resented the small jobs required of an apprentice. He took lodgings and attended a drawing school run by William Shipley (1714-1803). The school was in The Strand and was a popular resort for many young artists. It was here that Cosway started on the first rung of the ladder which was to lead him into what proved to be a brilliant career.

From the outset he was determined to become a great artist. When, in 1754, the newly formed Society of Arts offered a premium for the best drawings executed by boys and girls under the age of fourteen, Cosway entered a drawing of a head, representing 'Compassion', and was awarded the first prize of £5 5s. This was one of numerous prizes which he won. In this competition the second prize was won by John Smart, then under twelve years of age. Barbara Marsden, who later married Jeremiah Meyer, won fourth place. Cosway won prizes at the Society of Arts from 1755-1760, and exhibited at the Society of Artists in 1760, and at the Free Society in 1761. On 9th August, 1769, he entered the Royal Academy Schools, and exhibited at the Royal Academy from 1770-1806, becoming A.R.A. in 1770, and R.A. in 1771.

From an early age he began to take commissions from jewellers who wanted fancy miniatures, and from shopkeepers who wanted drawings of

Plate 104A. **R. Cosway, R.A.,** *George IV, when Prince of Wales (1762-1830), ivory, 2½ins. Wearing a plumed hat and white tunic, the ribbon and lesser George of the Garter is suspended round his neck and a red cloak draped over his left shoulder. Set within a pearl-bordered frame surmounted by a crown.* Courtesy Sotheby's.

heads. His original intention was to become a full-scale portrait painter, but he did not excel in this medium and, although he did execute a number of large paintings, he must have realised that his real *métier* was miniature painting, and drawings in pencil and watercolour.

By 1771 Cosway was well established and his popularity was increasing rapidly. He had not been endowed with good looks and was by nature an eccentric and a showman. He had a great love of fine clothes, and grew from a rather insignificant small boy to take his place among the beaux and dandies of the day. His costume was extravagant and ostentatious and this, together with a somewhat monkey-like face, caused him to undergo a great deal of ridicule. Mat Darley, the famous caricaturist, produced an etching calling him 'The Macaroni Miniature Painter', and this name stuck to him. The self-styled 'Macaronis' were the younger members of Almack's Club which was formed about 1765.

In 1773 Cosway proposed to a Miss Woolls, who rejected him. Eight years after, on 18th January, 1781, he married Maria Louisa Catherine Cecilia Hadfield, at St. George's, Hanover Square. He settled a sum of £2,800 on his bride as a marriage gift. Maria had been born in Florence in 1759 of Irish parents. She was a gifted artist, and was elected a member of the Florentine Academy of Fine Arts. Her father, Charles Hadfield, was born in Manchester where his relations were wealthy merchants and manufacturers, from whom neither Charles nor his family seem to have received any financial gain. He died in c.1778 and, at the suggestion of Angelica Kauffmann, his widow and family came to England where they were met by Angelica and taken to her home. Maria entertained great hopes of becoming a leading artist but these were not fulfilled, in spite of the fact that she obtained some patronage. Any money that the family had inherited from her father was soon spent and by the time she married Cosway they were in reduced circumstances. She continued to paint intermittently after her marriage and is said to have copied a number of her husband's miniatures and drawings, but for a time he did not allow her to paint, nor did he approve of her painting for money,

Plate 104B. **R. Cosway, R.A.,** *Mrs. Boswell Preston, ivory, 2¾ins., c.1785-95. This attractive miniature was formerly in the J. Pierpont Morgan Collection.* Courtesy Sotheby's.

359

Plate 104C. **R. Cosway, R.A.,** *John William Hope (1757-1813), banker and merchant, ivory, 3ins. Signed and dated on the reverse: '1796.' Courtesy Sotheby's.*

and she became frustrated. Unfortunately no signed works by Maria have so far come to light, and any assigned to her hand are only attributions.

The Cosways lived in Berkeley Street until 1784, when Richard decided to move into some more palatial premises and obtained part of Schomberg House, in Pall Mall. This move was the beginning of a new era for them. In these rather splendid surroundings they suddenly became the centre of attraction. They held a regular *salon* and entertained a wide circle of notable people; their musical parties and receptions were attended by the Prince of Wales, the Duchess of Devonshire, Horace Walpole, the Marchioness Townshend and many others.

It was at about this time that the Prince of Wales engaged Cosway to paint a portrait of Mrs. Fitzherbert; he was so delighted with the result that many commissions followed, and the fact that he had obtained Royal patronage made Cosway the most sought-after miniaturist in London. He was particularly popular with the members of the Whig Party, who surrounded the Prince and formed the centre of his gay and frivolous society. The fact that Schomberg House and Carlton House were in such close proximity and that, in 1788 and 1789, Cosway was working on a ceiling painting for the Prince of 'Apollo and the Hours', led the gossips to suggest that Cosway had a private means of access to the Prince's apartments. In an age which thrived on scandal and satire all sorts of rumours were put about, and the fact that Cosway was so eccentric gave ample opportunity to those who wanted to poke fun at him.

During the time that Cosway lived in Pall Mall he painted a series of oil portraits of importance for the Earl of Radnor, some of which were engraved. His miniature painting went from strength to strength, and in c.1786 he obtained the much coveted title of 'Miniaturist to the Prince of Wales'. Whilst living in Schomberg House Cosway evidently augmented his income by the purchase and sale of old pictures and antiques. He cleaned the pictures and touched up any defects before selling them to his patrons!

Plate 104D. **Richard Cosway, R.A.** *(1742-1821), self-portrait of the artist, pencil and wash on card, 4½ins. A similar drawing by Cosway is at the N.P.G.* Courtesy Christie's.

Plate 104E. **R. Cosway, R.A.,** *an attractive miniature of Master Bunbury, ivory, 3¼ins. Inscribed and dated: '1802' on the reverse. The sitter was probably the Master Bunbury painted by Reynolds.* Courtesy the late Captain E.B. Woollett.

In 1786 the Cosways were in Paris, where they met Thomas Jefferson (1743-1826), later to become President of the United States. Jefferson became attracted to Maria, and he fell in love with her — details of this attachment are published in *Thomas Jefferson,* by F.M. Brodie, 1974. He kept her letters, and copies of his to her, and these were retained hidden by his descendants until 1945. The Cosways remained in Paris for about six weeks during which time Jefferson and Maria contrived to meet, and they met again in 1787 when Maria went over to Paris alone. In April, 1790, Jefferson had a letter from a friend in London telling him that Maria was expecting a baby, and had been very ill. According to Brodie, Maria had a daughter in June, 1790, and he quotes a letter Jefferson received from Maria on June 11th saying "... No one but God himself can know all I suffered when with child ..." (Williamson gives the baby girl's date of birth as 1789, but this must be an error.) She was named Louisa Paolina Angelica, and was the Cosways' only child; her godfather was General Pasquale de Paoli, and the Princess D'Albany her godmother. According to the Jefferson papers and others, Maria went abroad alone, for the sake of her health, when the child was only a few months old.

By c.1791 Cosway's eccentricities became more marked, and he was attracted to a form of religious fanaticism and curious beliefs. This continued intermittently for the rest of his life. For reasons which are not clear he decided to move from Schomberg House to 1 Stratford Place, Oxford Street, but lived there for a few months only as he was so upset when he was ridiculed in verse by Peter Pindar (John Wolcot), because he had a carved lion standing on a pediment outside the house. Someone affixed the lines to the door of the house:

> When a man to a fair for a show brings a lion,
> 'Tis usual a monkey the sign-pole to tie on!
> But here the old custom reversed is seen,
> For the lion's without, and the monkey's within.

Plate 104F. **R. Cosway, R.A.,** *portrait of a young lady, water-colour on paper, 4½ins., unfinished. This is a good example of Cosway's method of painting the head and lightly drawing in the costume, and may have been a sketch for a finished portrait.* Courtesy Sotheby's.

Cosway moved two doors away to a house where he spent most of his remaining years. Before leaving Pall Mall he sold a large part of his collection of prints and paintings. These were sold by 'Mr. Christie' on March 2nd and 3rd, 1792.

In 1794 Cosway became ill and Maria returned home to look after him and their daughter. Cosway recovered, and Maria must have remained in London for some time. When the child died suddenly at the age of six Cosway insisted on keeping the embalmed body of his daughter in the living room in a marble sarcophagus, and it was only with difficulty that Maria managed to get the body decently interred. Cosway was carried away by all sorts of strange beliefs, imagining that the Virgin Mary had sat to him, and that Charles I had appeared and discussed art with him!

When, in 1811, the Prince became Regent he also became more selective of his immediate circle, and Cosway was dropped and never regained his position in Royal favour. Maria went abroad again for some time, but returned to look after him when his health deteriorated. In c.1821 he had two paralytic strokes which affected his right hand so that he could no longer draw. The house in Stratford Place was larger than they needed and they moved to 31 Edgware Road which was smaller. Cosway sold his collection of pictures and works of art in May, 1821. On July 4th of that year he suffered another stroke whilst out for a drive and died in the carriage before reaching home. He was buried in St. Mary-le-bone Church. He left all his estate to his wife, who was his sole executrix.

Mrs. Cosway, who had always been a devout Catholic, then returned to Lodi in Italy, where she had founded a Convent some years before. This was part of a religious order known as The Lorento Nuns, which had houses in other parts of the world. Maria took a keen interest in the education of her pupils and assisted in the general management of the house. In 1834, Francis I visited the Convent and created her a Baroness in recognition of her work.

In 1830 she made over a sum of £4,000 as a further endowment to the Convent and, before her death, bequeathed to it all her remaining estate.

Apart from visits to other houses of the same order in Rome and Vienna, the Baroness remained at Lodi until she died on 5th January, 1838. She was buried in the Church of Santa Maria della Grazie, attached to the College della Grazie which she had established in 1812. A monument in her memory was erected in the vault of the chapel there.

Cosway is undoubtedly one of the best known miniaturists of the British School, and one whose works have been, and still are, copied in large numbers. From the outset of his career his works were marked by a delicacy and fine modelling which showed him to be an artist of above average ability. His early works are not always recognised as they are painted on a small scale, and often against a dark or buff-coloured background which is not so readily associated with him. Miniatures by him dating from c.1765-1770 are painted with assurance and accurate draughtsmanship, and show promise of the greatness which was to come. Even in these early miniatures the eyes are the thing to look for. They stand out round and clear, and the features are modelled with soft, swift strokes.

In his works painted before c.1780, he had still not achieved his full potential. By this time the size of the ivories used had increased, and this gave more scope for miniaturists to broaden their style. The scale on which miniatures were painted had grown from 1½ins., the normal size when he started, to 3ins. and more by 1785. Cosway used a clear Antwerp blue which is one of the characteristics of his work. Another is that he tended to enlarge the pupil of the eye. He was the artist who first discovered that it was possible to use transparent watercolour on ivory in a way which would allow its natural luminosity to show through. He also developed the use of a 'sky background' which is almost always associated with him. He was a prolific artist, and there can scarcely be any collection of importance which does not contain an example of his work.

His best period was from c.1785-1805, when he painted some of the finest

Plate 104G. R. Cosway, R.A., portrait of an unknown lady, ivory, 2¾ins., 1796. This is a very attractive miniature in perfect condition. The sitter is wearing a white dress and bandeau in her hair, and is painted against a typical Cosway cloud and sky background. Courtesy Sotheby's.

miniatures of the eighteenth century. It was during these years that he started to sign the reverse of his miniatures with a rather pompous Latin inscription. The details vary slightly, but usually read something like this: 'R^{dus} Cosway / R.A. / Primarius Pictor / Serenissimi Walliae', sometimes followed by a date (Figure 30). Some of his drawings are signed in monogram: 'RC', with the 'C' surrounding the 'R'. Not all his works are signed, and any miniature signed on the front should be viewed with suspicion as only a few are genuine. These later miniatures are usually brilliantly executed and drawn with an economy of line. He modelled the features with short grey strokes, which are visible round the eyes and contours of the cheeks, and painted the hair in soft masses. Many of his backgrounds are painted with long parallel strokes, particularly near the edge of the cheek; often these strokes are punctuated with numerous dots or small transverse strokes, each one ending in a small blob of colour. His miniatures are elegant and even the mannerisms of a long neck and enlarged pupil of the eye, which are especially noticeable in his portraits of women, only serve to emphasise his great ability. In portraying men he was equally successful; he painted them with a strength and vitality which is surprising in view of the fact that he was such a fop himself. Not infrequently he used opaque white to indicate the white draperies and this was often shaded with a soft grey, especially on mens' cravats. Cosway executed a number of full length portrait drawings and fancy subjects, many of which are in pencil with only the face painted in watercolour. A large number of his drawings and miniatures were engraved, including ones of himself and his wife. Several self-portraits exist. Two are in the National Portrait Gallery, London, another, wearing fancy dress, is in the National Gallery, Dublin; and a third, executed in pencil and wash, was Lot 25 at Christie's on 18th November, 1969. This latter portrait was sold in the E.M. Hodgkins Collection on 29th June, 1917 (Plate 104D). An attractive one of an unknown lady was Lot 100 at Sotheby's on 25th November, 1974; it was dated on the reverse: '1796', the inscription and signature having been inked over (Plate 104G). A delightful portrait of Master Bunbury, inscribed and dated: '1802' on the reverse, was in the collection of the late Captain E.B. Woollett (Plate 104E). One of George IV when Prince of Wales, in fancy costume and wearing a jewelled and feathered hat, a grey suit slashed with pink, and a scarlet cloak with the blue ribbon and lesser George suspended round his neck, was Lot 48 at Sotheby's on 9th March, 1970 (Plate 104A). A fine miniature of Mr. Bigland by Cosway is in the Bernard Falk Collection at the Royal Pavilion, Brighton (Colour Plate 28C). Examples of his work are in many private collections, including those of H.M. The Queen and the Duke of Portland. Those available to the public are in the Wallace Collection, London, the Fitzwilliam Museum, Cambridge, and the Victoria and Albert Museum. Engravings after Cosway are in the British Museum. (Plates 104B, C and F.)

John Smart (1742/3-1811) is considered to be one of the greatest miniaturists of the eighteenth century, whose miniatures now fetch higher prices than those by Cosway. In spite of diligent research there is still no indication as to his date or place of birth, nor his parentage. *The Gentleman's Magazine* for June 1811, records that Smart, at his death on 1st May, was in his seventieth year, and Cansick's *Monumental Inscriptions* gives his age as sixty-nine at death. From this it seems likely that he was born

Plate 105A. **J. Smart**, *James Bruce (1730-1794), Scottish explorer, ivory, 1½ins. Signed and dated: 'JS / 1776.' Wearing a powdered wig en queue and a lilac coloured waistcoat and jacket. Set within a diamond bordered frame inscribed on the reverse with an account of the expedition across the Nubian Desert. This portrait is now at the N.P.G.* Courtesy Sotheby's.

c.1742/3. It has been alleged that he came from Norfolk, but I have not been able to verify this statement. Nothing is known about his early life or education, nor does he seem to have left any family documents or fee books. The first evidence of his existence was when, in 1755, the Society of Arts held its first competition. He and Richard Cosway entered the section offering premiums for children under fourteen years of age, and Smart's age was noted as under twelve. As has already been mentioned he was awarded second prize, and Cosway first. Smart won the first prize in these competitions for the following three years; his exhibit in 1757 was a chalk drawing of William Shipley, under whom he studied. He exhibited at the Society of Artists from 1762-1783, was elected F.S.A. in 1765, Director in 1772, Vice-President 1777, and President 1778. Smart took a leading part in the affairs of the Society, and in 1777 a medal bearing his portrait was struck and produced in silver and bronze. He exhibited at the Royal Academy, 1797-1811, but curiously enough never received any recognition. Due to the fact that there were several artists named Smart some confusion has arisen regarding entries at the Royal Academy for 1784, and it is now agreed that these were in all probability by another Smart who was not a miniaturist. His earliest known miniatures date from 1760 and as, from the outset, he made a practice of signing his portraits, it is possible to trace his art throughout the whole of his working life.

By his first wife, whose maiden name is unknown, he had three children, John (b.1762), who died young, Anna Maria (1766-1813) later Mrs. Robert Woolf, and Sophia (1770-1793) later Mrs. John Dighton. Their mother eloped with the artist William Pars, A.R.A., who took her to Rome where she died of consumption on 6th June, 1778. After his first wife left him, John Smart formed a connection with a lady called Sarah Midgeley, by whom he had a son, John Smart, Junior (1776-1809), and a daughter, Sarah, both of whom took their father's name. Evidence for this is to be found in

Plate 105B. **John Smart** *(1742/3-1811), self-portrait of the artist, ivory, 1½ins. Signed and dated: 'JS / 1783.' This is the earliest of nine known self-portraits, one, dated 1797, is at the V. & A.M. Courtesy Mrs. H. Kahn.*

Plate 105C. **J.** **Smart**, *after F. Cotes' portrait of 1764, the Hon. Eliza Booth, ivory, 1⅜ins. Signed and dated: 'JS / 1766.' A rare example of Smart copying another artist; it is interesting to note how his style hardly changed throughout his career, all his works being excellent. Courtesy Mrs. Gifford Scott.*

Plate 105D. **J. Smart**, *Samuel Tyssen (1740-1800), ivory, 16/10 ins. Signed and dated: 'JS / 1781.' Set within a diamond bordered gold frame. This is a fine miniature and very colourful. Courtesy the late Lord Wharton.*

Plate 105E. **J. Smart,** *a superb double-sided miniature of William and Maria Burroughs, ivory, 2¹/8ins., c.1780. Both signed 'JS.' The miniatures are contained in a double-hinged gold locket inscribed on the reverse with the sitters' names. The miniatures are in mint condition and amongst the finest to have come on the market. This was reflected in the price they obtained of £16,000 in 1977.* Courtesy Sotheby's.

Plate 105F. **J. Smart,** called *Mrs. Brummell, ivory, 2¹/16ins. Signed 'JS / 1786.' The sitter's upswept hair is dressed with pearls, a curl falling over one shoulder.* Courtesy Sotheby's.

the Guardianship Proceedings of the Court of Chancery for 1790, in which there are references to the arrangements Smart had made for the care, education and maintenance of the children as well as adequate provision for their mother before he left for India in 1785. Robert Bowyer, a miniature painter and Smart's former pupil, was appointed one of Smart's attorneys to supervise the childrens' education and manage his affairs; a house in Water Lane, Fleet Street, was kept for their use. Nothing is known about Sarah Midgeley after this date.

Smart evidently decided to try his luck in India, where artists were said to be making large sums of money. He obtained permission from the East India Company to leave for India taking his daughter, Anna Maria, with him. They sailed on 19th April, 1785, on board the *Dutton,* bound for Madras. On arrival they took up residence in North Street, sometimes known as Middlegate Street, Fort St. George. Many other miniaturists and portrait painters were already in India, including Samuel Andrews, Diana Hill (née Dietz), Charles Shirreff, Johann Zoffany, Tilly Kettle, John Alefounder, and later Ozias Humphry. The latter was the artist most perturbed by Smart's arrival, as he feared it would affect his patronage. In the event, Smart spent almost the whole of his time in Madras where he was kept busily employed as miniature painter to Muhammad Ali, the Nawab of Arcot, and his family. He also painted many of the Government officials and Army officers, as well as English residents, and remained in India for ten years.

On July 11th, 1786, Anna Maria Smart married Robert Woolf of the Madras Civil Service, by whom she had nine children. After her marriage, Smart obtained permission for his other daughter, Sophia, to join him in India. Permission was granted in December, 1788, and she had not been in Madras long before she became engaged to Lieut. (later Lieut. General) John Dighton (1761-1840). She did not survive the birth of their son, John, who was baptised, together with his cousin, Maria Woolf, on 20th May, 1794. Smart spent ten very successful years in Madras, and the only problem was that the Nawab failed to pay all the money owed for his commissions. When Smart left the country, in 1795, 4,114 pagodas were still owing to him, and this debt had still not been settled by 1804.

Apart from short visits to Bombay and Bengal Smart remained in Madras until 27th April, 1795, when he sailed for home on the *Melville Castle*. He was joined by his daughter, Anna Maria, and her family at St. Helena, and arrived at Portsmouth on 19th November. He took up residence at 20 Grafton Street, for which he had been paying rates since 1790. In c.1799 he married, as his second wife, Edith (Vere?). No record of the marriage has been found, and the only authority to supply her name is Dr. G.C. Williamson. On the reverse of the frame of a silhouette, said to be of Smart c.1800, is an inscription: 'Edith / from her husband / John Smarte / Russell Place / Fitzroy Square.' No. 2 Russell Place was the house to which Smart had moved at about this time. The profile does not bear a close resemblance to him, and it may have been of some other member of the family.

On 14th February, 1805, Smart married at St. Mary-le-bone Church, Mary Morton (1783-1851), whom Farington described as a "well disposed woman & Has brought him to habits of regularity in attending Divine Service". Smart was then described as a widower. They had one child, John James (1805-1870). Prior to his last marriage both John Junior and Sarah had been living with their father. In May, 1808, Smart asked permission from the Directors of the East India Company for John Junior to go to India as a miniaturist. He sailed on the *Asia* which arrived in Madras on 11th February, 1809. His time in India was of short duration, for he died only four months later, in June, 1809. After his last marriage Smart settled a considerable sum of money on his daughter, Sarah, who moved to Charlotte Street, not far away from his own house. John Smart, Senior, made his will on 28th April, 1811, in which he made ample provision for his wife and the care and education of John James. He died on 1st May, 1811, after an illness of only nine days, and was buried in St. James's Burial Ground, Hampstead Road, St. Pancras. The inscription placed upon his monument gave his age as sixty-nine years. His widow married, sometime before 1812, John Sidey Caley, and payments were made to her from the executors' account as Mrs. Caley as from that year.

Plate 105G. **J. Smart,** *Mrs. George Aubrey, née Botham, wife of Captain George William Aubrey of the Madras Establishment, ivory, 2⁵/₈ins. Signed and dated: 'J.S. / 1787/I.' An inscription in the case gives the details of the sitter, and the date of her marriage as 19th March, 1786. Courtesy Sotheby's.*

Smart was undoubtedly one of the finest miniaturists of the eighteenth century, and one whose works are greatly sought after. He had an interesting and important clientele, many of whom, as one might expect, were connected with the East Indies. Unlike Cosway, who sought and enjoyed the limelight, Smart was apparently content to live more quietly and his domestic affairs did not, at the time, attract public notice.

Artistically nothing could be less alike than the works of Cosway and Smart. Cosway's style developed from a more modest approach to a broad, free and almost transparent form of painting full of assurance and grandeur, whilst Smart's manner of painting was fully developed from his earliest dated portraits of c.1760, and although as time went on the size of his ivory increased, his meticulous attention to detail and the smooth finish of the entire portrait were to be the hallmarks of his career. His draughtsmanship is superb and the general effect of his portraits harmonious and executed in exquisite colours. He had a natural gift for drawing and his early exhibits, when only a boy of eleven, were ambitious and anatomically accurate. In 1966 Mr. and Mrs. John Starr gave a collection of miniatures by John Smart to the William Rockhill Nelson Gallery of Art, Kansas City. The collection contains an example of his work for every year from 1760 up to 1810, and for the student or collector who has the opportunity to visit the Gallery it is a great experience. The Starrs also own a fine oil portrait of Smart by Richard Brompton (d.1782), painted c.1780. Several self-portraits of Smart exist, and some are illustrated in Foskett, *John Smart The Man And His Miniatures,* 1964, in which a full account of his life is given (Plate 105B).

Smart made a habit of executing small pencil drawings on paper, often lightly coloured, which were probably in most cases preliminary drawings for his miniatures or to be kept by him in case a replica was required. This was a practice used by other artists, including George Engleheart. Besides painting miniatures on ivory, Smart executed some fine finished portraits on paper in pencil and wash (Plates 106A, B, C and D). One of the finest of these is of his grandson, Robert Woolf, Junior, signed and dated 1796. This is in the Huntington Art Gallery, California. It is fully inscribed on the reverse by Smart with instructions of how it was to be displayed: 'To be hung on that side of the room as you stand with your left arm towards the window, otherwise it will appear rougher from the unevenness of the paper it is painted on and always to be viewed in the same manner. Painted by his grandfather / J. Smart / London, July 16th, 1796.'

Some of his other sketches are inscribed on the reverse and an occasional note added about the sitter. They are sometimes signed round the edge of the portrait. His miniatures up to c.1775 were small in size, about 1½ins. This was increased to 2ins. by c.1775, and by c.1790 he used ivories of 3ins. or more. He used a brilliant palette throughout, and his colours have retained their brightness in a remarkable way. One rarely, if ever, sees them faded. His early works are shaded with a slightly bluish tinge, and the draughtsmanship is slightly more tentative. He later used a brick red flesh tint which is quite typical of his work. One unmistakable characteristic is the way he painted the lines and even the crows' feet round the eyes, and drew the eyelashes in minute detail, each lash separate; this is particularly obvious when the portrait is in profile. He seems to have excelled in painting portraits of children which, unlike so many one sees, show character and even mischief. A scintillating pair of miniatures of William and Maria Burroughs, painted by Smart in 1797, was sold at Sotheby's on 19th December, 1977. They are contained in a double hinged gold locket and, because of their superb condition and attractiveness, realised the record sum of £16,000 (Plate 105E).

Smart's miniatures of ladies are both attractive and decorative. He did not resort to elaborate backgrounds or draperies, and only occasionally added a light seascape or landscape. The delightful simplicity of his portraits and his apparently effortless portrayal of his sitters merit him his position among the top rank of his contemporaries. I have only seen one enamel by Smart, and this was executed in exactly the same style as those on ivory and with the same colouring. An outstanding example of Smart's portrait drawings was Lot 82, of Captain Lambe of the *Melville Castle,* sold at Christie's on 2nd June, 1970. It was executed on board when Smart was returning from India, and is fully signed and dated: '1795', with the sitter's name (Plate 106D). An attractive and early portrait of the Hon. Eliza Booth, after a painting by Francis Cotes dated 1764, is in the collection of Mrs. Gifford Scott. It is signed and dated 1766 (Plate 105C).

Plate 105H. **J. Smart,** *an unknown Indian, ivory, 2¾ins. Signed and dated 'JS / 1789 / I.' This is an interesting miniature and a good example of Smart's perfect modelling and portrayal of character.* Courtesy Mrs. Gifford Scott.

Plate 105 I. J. Smart, Colonel Keith Michael Alexander, ivory, 3³/₈ins. Signed and dated: 'JS / 1810.' Wearing scarlet uniform trimmed with silver. This is a late specimen of Smart's work and shows how the quality of his painting never deteriorated. This miniature is now in the Starr Collection, Kansas City. Courtesy Sotheby's.

The new collector needs to be careful when purchasing a miniature attributed to Smart, as both copies and fakes exist. Robert Bowyer and Samuel Andrews are known to have copied or imitated Smart's work and, although the likeness may only be superficial, inaccurate attributions are often made. In the early part of the twentieth century some clever forgeries of Smart's miniatures were executed and are sometimes seen for sale. These fakes are not always easy to detect as they are often signed with Smart's initials or even full signature. Points to look for are the almost three-dimensional modelling which Smart achieved, and the fact that his miniatures never looked harsh. The fakes often look almost too good to be true!

Smart's usual signature is: 'J.S.' in cursive initials, often followed by a date; he also signed: 'J. Smart' in full (rare), 'J. Smart delin', and 'John Smart pinxit.' Those miniatures painted in India had an 'I' placed under the date. Examples of his work are in many private collections, as well as museums, including the British Museum, the Wallace Collection, London, the Victoria and Albert Museum, the Fitzwilliam Museum, Cambridge, and the Ashmolean Museum, Oxford. (Colour Plates 25C, 27B, 31A and 32C and D, and Plates 105A, B, D, F, G, H and I.)

George Engleheart (1750-1829) was one of eight sons born to Francis Englehart (d.1773), a German plaster modeller, and his wife, Anne Dawney, the name being changed to Engleheart after his father died. George is said to have been born in Kew on 26th October, 1750, but when he entered the Royal Academy Schools on 3rd November, 1769, his age was noted as "16 last Nov". He was a pupil of George Barret, R.A., and of Sir Joshua Reynolds, some of whose works he copied. He exhibited at the Royal Academy from 1773-1822, and worked chiefly in London. In 1776 he married as his first wife Elizabeth, daughter of Nathaniel Browne, and the couple went to live in a house in Prince's Street, Hanover Square. The marriage was short-lived, for she died on 29th April, 1779, aged twenty-six.

Plate 106A. **J. Smart,** *Mrs. Wilkes of Madras, pencil on paper, 5¾ins. Signed and dated: 'JS / 1793.' This attractive portrait shows the sitter wearing a tall hat with a plume and swathed with a bandeau. This was in the collection of Mrs. Dyer, Smart's great-granddaughter, sold at Christie's 26th November, 1937. For a copy see Plate 142D.* Courtesy Sotheby's.

Plate 106B. **J. Smart,** *Lieut. General John Dighton (1761-1840), son-in-law of the artist, pencil on paper, 5½ins. Signed and dated: 'J.S. / 1791/ I.' Dighton is wearing the uniform of the East India Company's Madras Infantry. For a copy of this portrait see Plate 142E.* Courtesy Sotheby's.

Plate 106C. **J. Smart,** *Charles, 1st Marquess and 2nd Earl Cornwallis, K.G. (1738-1805), pencil on paper, 7¼ins. Fully inscribed and signed: 'John Smart delineavit / Madras 1792.' At least two finished miniatures of the sitter by Smart exist. This drawing is now at the N.P.G.* Courtesy the late Sir Bruce Ingram, O.B.E.

Plate 106D. **J. Smart,** *Captain Lambe of the Melville Castle, pencil on paper, 6¾ins. Signed in full: 'Jno Smart delint 1795 on board the Melville Castle Captain Lambe.' This is a superb example of Smart's draughtsmanship and almost three-dimensional modelling. Note the lines round the eyes and the distinctly drawn eyelashes.* Courtesy Christie's.

In 1783 Engleheart moved to 4 Hertford Street and in 1785 married as his second wife, Ursula Sarah Browne (d.1817), by whom he had four children, George, Nathaniel, Harry and Emma. From 1775 he kept a fee book, with many tracings of miniatures, and this is still in the family. His sitters were people of fashion and distinction, and in the thirty-nine years covered by the fee book he painted no less than 4,853 miniatures, which must have taken up almost all his time! He numbered among his friends George Romney, William Blake, Jeremiah Meyer, and William Hayley, the poet. Hayley composed several verses in praise of Engleheart, one of which reads:

> Dear Engleheart, with more than magic grace,
> With heavenly aid, you exercise your art;
> You paint my fair one's virtues in her face,
> A gracious Heaven impress them on my heart.

Meyer and Engleheart had much in common; both were of foreign extraction, and had taken up miniature painting as their profession. Both had been pupils of Reynolds and were great admirers of his work.

In 1813 Engleheart retired to his country house, Bedfont, near Hounslow. He had purchased the estate in 1783, and built the house upon it, decorating the interior in Adam style. After his second wife's death he was looked after by his daughter, Emma, but ultimately gave up his house and went to live with his son, Nathaniel, at Blackheath in c.1818, where he died on 21st March, 1829, and was buried at Kew.

His fee book ends in 1813, and although Engleheart continued to paint miniatures and small portraits in watercolour, his output lessened. His fees varied from 3 guineas in 1775, to 20 or even 25 guineas in 1811. The miniatures painted between 1775 and c.1780 are small in size, and are sometimes naïve and not always easy to attribute. His work falls approximately into three phases.

His earliest miniatures are sometimes signed: 'G.E.'; the backgrounds are painted in a darkish buff colour, the shading often being achieved with fine vertical or slanting strokes. The features are modelled with a bluish grey colour, and with a reddish colouring superimposed on a pale flesh tint. From c.1780-1795 there is a marked change in his work; his draughtsmanship is good, his colouring stronger, and his full powers are developing. He still often uses small ivories, and does not always sign his miniatures, but the quality of his work is excellent. Usually no accessories are shown in the background, but his style is very assured and distinctive. The sitter's hair is painted in linear masses, and the corners of the mouth drawn with diagonal grey strokes. The draperies are frequently painted with a zigzag outline of opaque white, and the sitter's large deep blue eyes peer out from under heavy eyebrows. Many of the ladies' miniatures of this period were posed with enormous straw hats embellished with ribbons and flowers (Plates 107C and G). This was in keeping with current fashion. Towards the end of this phase he began to sign his portraits on the front with a cursive: 'E', a practice he continued for some time. His miniatures are elegant; the brush strokes on the face are slightly more hairy than those used earlier, the flesh colour tends to be rather a brownish yellow, and parallel hatching on the draperies is rarer. He took to signing a number of his works in full on the reverse.

B

A

C

D

E

F

G

H

I

His third and last phase, from c.1795 is marked by the use of much larger ivories, about 3-3½ins. in height (Plate 107H). From c.1800 he occasionally used a rectangular format which detracted a little from their charm. Engleheart never descended to flattery in the way Cosway did but painted his sitters as he saw them with a great sense of realism and, in some cases, made no attempt to temper down plain ugliness when he saw it! In his last phase he returned to the use of 'G.E.' as his signature, either cursive or block capitals, followed by a date, and often inscribed on the reverse as well. He copied a few miniatures after Cosway, and was noted for painting 'eye' miniatures, which became popular after he painted Mrs. Fitzherbert's eye for the Prince of Wales. He is thought to have worked in enamel, although no examples are at present known. Two relatives, J.C.D. Engleheart and Thomas Richmond, were his pupils. His works have been frequently copied and faked, and great care is needed in examining works offered as by him, because his style is more easily imitated than that of some artists.

A number of miniatures by Engleheart were exhibited in Edinburgh in 1965, and among them was one of Colonel Charles Erskine of the 92nd Highlanders (d.1801); it was of particular interest as it is the only miniature I know of from which a large portrait was painted. It was copied by Sir Henry Raeburn after the Colonel's death, and the portrait and the receipt are still in the family. Examples of Engleheart's work are in almost every important collection, and may be seen in the Wallace Collection, London, the Fitzwilliam Museum, Cambridge, the Ashmolean Museum, Oxford, the Holburne Museum, Bath, and in the Bernard Falk Collection at the Royal Pavilion, Brighton. (Colour Plates 25E and 30C, D and E, and Plates 107A-I and Plates 111C and D.)

Jeremiah Meyer, R.A. (1735-1789) was really senior to the other miniaturists in this chapter, but his outstanding qualities as an artist warrant him a place among the great painters of the period. He was born in Tübingen, Germany, on 18th January, 1735, and came of an artistic family. His father was portrait painter to the Duke of Würtemberg. He was brought to England by his father when about fourteen years old. He studied at the

Plate 107.
A. **G. Engleheart**, *Stephena Ann Inglis, aged eight, ivory, 3ins. Inscribed round the frame: 'Stephena Ann Inglis aged 8 years 1795.' This portrait is recorded in Engleheart's Fee Book and it was amongst other Inglis family miniatures sold in 1971. Note the attractive bonnet tied with pink ribbon. Courtesy Sotheby's.*
B. **G. Engleheart**, *a very attractive portrait of an unknown girl, ivory, 2⅛ins., c.1780. The sitter is wearing a large pale blue hat decorated with pearls and white plumes. Her white dress is trimmed with blue edging and blue buttons. Miniatures of this quality are rare and it realised £4,200 in 1977. Courtesy Sotheby's.*
C. **G. Engleheart**, *Mrs. Windsor, ivory, 2ins., c.1785. A Mrs. Windsor is recorded in Engleheart's Fee Book for 1784 and 1785. This miniature shows the sitter wearing a blue hat, with plumes, perched saucily on her head. Courtesy Christie's.*
D. **G. Engleheart**, *portrait of an unknown lady, ivory, 2⅞ins., c.1790. The sitter is wearing a white turban over her long curls and a white dress with a lace collar. Painted against a cloud and sky background. Courtesy Sotheby's.*
E. **G. Engleheart**, *an unknown officer, ivory, 3⅝ins. Signed: 'E' (cursive) on the front and signed and dated: '1807' on the reverse. The sitter is wearing the pale uniform of the 8th Light Dragoons (later the 8th King's Royal Irish Hussars). This is a splendid miniature, and one of Engleheart's best works. Courtesy Christie's.*
F. **G. Engleheart**, *a miniature of an unknown lady, ivory, 2⅞ins., c.1790. The sitter is wearing a white dress with a pleated fichu and a pale blue sash. Her fair hair is entwined with a blue and white ribbon. Courtesy Sotheby's.*
G. **G. Engleheart**, *portrait of an unknown girl, ivory, 2¼ins., c.1780-90. This attractive miniature is good for costume, showing the tall wide-brimmed hat trimmed with ribbons and worn over a cap tied under her chin. Ex de la Hey Collection.*
H. **G. Engleheart**, *Mrs. William Saltau, ivory, 3½ins. Signed: 'E' (cursive), on the front and signed and dated: '1802' on the reverse. The sitter is wearing a white dress with lace edging to the bodice, and a coral necklace. Note the short hair style. Courtesy Christie's.*
I. **G. Engleheart**, *Sophia Louisa Dent and her brother Master Charles William Dent with a dog, ivory, 2½ins., 1792. Children of William and Louisa Dent. Double portraits by Engleheart are scarce. Courtesy Sotheby's.*

Plate 108A. **J. Meyer, R.A.,** *portrait of an unknown man, ivory, 1½ins., c.1770.* Courtesy Mrs. T.R.C. Blofeld.

St. Martin's Lane Academy, and Zincke, who was by this time practically in retirement, took him as a pupil from 1757-1758 at a cost of £200, plus £200 for materials. This instruction was presumably the reason why Meyer painted a considerable number of enamels in the early part of his career. He exhibited at the Society of Artists, 1760-1767. In 1761 the Society of Arts awarded him a gold medal for a profile of George III, drawn from memory. Meyer became a naturalised Englishman in 1762, and in the following year married Barbara Marsden (b.1743), herself an accomplished artist and a lover of music. She won premiums at the Society of Arts, 1755-1758. They had at least four children: Mary, whom Reynolds painted as Hebe (she ran away from home when young and was taken back by "Mr. Engleheart", presumably George); Frances Isabella (1784-1815), who married Colonel John Haverfield; William (b.c.1778); and George Charles (1767-1793), who served under the East India Company and blew his brains out in Calcutta on 12th February, 1793. Meyer worked chiefly in London, but was in Chester in 1772 and accompanied Romney to Windsor in 1787. He lived for many years in Covent Garden and occupied successively two houses, one of which had been the home of C.F. Zincke. In 1764 Meyer became miniature painter to the Queen, and painter in enamel and miniature to the King. He was a founder member of the Royal Academy in 1768 and exhibited there from 1769-1783. Besides painting miniatures he executed a few oil portraits. His pupils included Richard Collins and Diana Dietz. Meyer retired to Kew, and was very friendly with Engleheart and William Hayley. He died at Kew in 1789.

In 1772 Zoffany painted a large group of 'The Academicians of the Royal Academy', which included many of the artists whom George III and Queen Charlotte employed, including Meyer. It is still in the Royal Collection, and is illustrated in *The Queen's Pictures,* Plate 124. Early examples of Meyer's miniatures are scarce and few are known before the 1760s, at which time they were no more ambitious than those by N. Hone and others. When, ten years later, ladies' hair styles swept up to dizzy heights and the size of miniatures increased to 3ins. and more, Meyer rose to the occasion and produced some of the most elegant and attractive miniatures of the time. He soon developed a characteristic style that is unmistakable once it has been examined. He used no stippling or broad washes of colours, but modelled the sitter's features with long and short lines, very fine, and crossing one another at all angles. These lines can be seen over the whole surface of the ivory, and even the costume, which is so beautifully painted, is shaded with clusters of vertical lines. Cravats and fichus are emphasised by touches of opaque white, and the high coiffures and sweeping curls are drawn with long brush strokes which interlace in the waves of the hair. Unfortunately he used a fugitive flesh colour which in course of time has faded badly, and few of his miniatures have their original freshness. Carl Winter likened his work to the porcelain of Meissen and Nymphenburg. He drew the mouth and nose in a slightly angular manner, the eyes being rather sunk under the eyelids and often placed quite close together. The lips sometimes protrude slightly. Only a few of his miniatures are signed; some bear a cursive monogram: 'JM', and occasionally he signed on the reverse.

He painted miniatures of several of the Hayley family; three were sold at Sotheby's in 1966, and included Mrs. Thomas Hayley, Mrs. William Hayley

Plate 108B (left). **J. Meyer, R.A.,** *Mrs. William Hayley, née Elizabeth Ball (d.1800), 1st wife of William Hayley the poet, ivory, 2¾ins., c.1770. Elizabeth's upswept hair is decorated with pearls, her pink dress trimmed with a white bow and pearls.* Courtesy Sotheby's.

Plate 108C (right). **J. Meyer, R.A.,** *Lady Dorothy Frankland, enamel, 2¼ins. From the Frankland family collection. Another version of this miniature by Meyer on ivory was sold in 1968. See Colour Plate 29B.* Courtesy Sotheby's.

(Plate 108B), and Thomas Alphonso Hayley as a child. They are fine examples of his work; the one of Mrs. William Hayley being particularly attractive. Both miniatures of these ladies came up for sale again at Christie's on 29th November, 1977.

Considering his popularity, miniatures by Meyer do not come into the sale rooms as often as one would expect. Examples by him are in the collection of H.M. The Queen, and others may be seen at the British Museum, the Ashmolean Museum, Oxford, the Walters Art Gallery, Baltimore, and the Victoria and Albert Museum. An interesting comparison can be made between a sketch on ivory for a miniature of a lady, and a finished version of the same lady on enamel. (Colour Plates 13A, 29B, and Plates 108A-G.)

Richard Crosse (1742-1810) was the second son of John and Mary Crosse (d.1807) of Knowle, near Cullompton, Devon, where Richard was born on 24th April, 1742. He and one of his sisters (out of a family of at least seven children) had the misfortune to be born deaf and dumb. There were four other sons: James (1740-1798), John, Edward (the third child), and Henry. The father was a lawyer and the family members of the landed gentry. Richard took up painting as a hobby and became one of our most successful miniaturists. He won a premium at the Society of Arts in 1758 and went to London, where he studied at Shipley's Drawing School and the Duke of Richmond's Gallery, etc. He exhibited at the Society of Artists, 1760-1796 (becoming a member in 1763), at the Free Society, 1761-1766, and the Royal Academy, 1770-1796. He lived for many years in Henrietta Street, Covent Garden, and attracted many distinguished clients. A MS register of the miniatures he painted between 1775 and 1798 is in the Victoria and Albert Museum, and was published by the late Basil Long in The Walpole Society, Vol. XVII. He is supposed to have been appointed Painter in Enamel to George III in 1789 and if this is correct held the position jointly with R. Collins, in succession to Meyer. It was really Basil Long who first appreciated Crosse's true worth and helped to make accurate attribution of his work. A fine miniature of Sarah Siddons, of whom he painted more than one portrait, is in the Victoria and Albert Museum, who also own his paint

Plate 108D. **J. Meyer, R.A.,** *George IV when Prince of Wales (1762-1830), ivory, 3ins. Wearing the sash and star of the Garter. This is a fine example of Meyer's style, and shows his distinctive brushwork.* Courtesy the Walters Art Gallery, Baltimore, U.S.A.

A

B

C

D

E

box, and a self-portrait of the artist. Due, no doubt, to his affliction Crosse's life was uneventful except for the great tragedy which he sustained when his cousin, Miss Sarah Cobley, with whom he fell deeply in love, rejected him for Benjamin Haydon, father of B.R. Haydon, the painter. Her refusal hurt him so much that he became embittered for the rest of his life and withdrew from society. In c.1786 Crosse retired to Wells to live with Miss Cobley's brother, a prebendary of the Cathedral. The fates decreed that he and Sarah were to meet again on the day before her death in 1807. She had a premonition of her approaching end and made every arrangement for it. She wanted to see her brother once more and she and her son went to Wells, arriving unexpectedly before Crosse could be got out of the way. Not knowing of her visit he entered the room and, seeing her there, rushed over to her, taking her in his arms and uttering totally unintelligible sounds of pent-up emotion. The scene is graphically described by Haydon in his *Memoirs*. His mother died the next day, and Crosse three years later in 1810, at his old home, Knowle, to which he had returned.

Plate 108E. **J. Meyer, R.A.,** *portrait of a young lady, ivory, 3½ins., c.1780.* Ex de la Hey Collection.

Crosse painted miniatures in watercolour and enamel, and oil portraits. His charge varied from 8 guineas for small ones to 15 and 30 guineas for large ones. Although he was not entirely dependant on his earnings he succeeded in amassing quite a considerable sum from his painting, which he invested to bring in additional income. He was a prolific painter and executed about one hundred miniatures in 1777. He painted a particularly charming rectangular miniature of Miss Turner of Uxbridge, which was sold at Sotheby's, Lot 73 on 3rd July, 1961. This portrait is a good example of the period costume, with the large trimmed hat, and hair falling softly over the sitter's shoulders (Plate 109D). Several self-portraits exist, including the one illustrated (Plate 109E), which was sold at Sotheby's some years ago. An early miniature in a private collection, signed in full and dated 1759, almost certainly represents the artist as a young man with one of his brothers, either Edward or James (Plate 109F). His style of painting is easy to distinguish once it has been thoroughly examined for he used, almost invariably, a peculiar greenish-blue tint with which to shade the face, and often this can be seen on the hair and background. The hair on his earlier miniatures is treated rather more in a mass, but the later ones are painted in definite lines. The distinctive way in which he shaded the features, the expression of the eyes and the small shadows under them are all points to look for.

Plate 108F. **J. Meyer, R.A.,** *miniature of an unknown man, ivory, 1⅝ins., c.1780. Set in a gold clasp frame for a bracelet.* Ex de la Hey Collection.

On 9th June, 1969, miniatures of Joseph François Louis, Comte De Lautour, and three of his children were sold at Sotheby's; the miniature of the

Colour Plate 29.
A. **Richard Cosway, R.A.,** *Lady Murray of Elibank, ivory, 2⅞ins. This is an excellent example of a Cosway with the cloud and sky background.*
B. **Jeremiah Meyer, R.A.,** *Lady Dorothy Frankland, ivory, 3ins. The name of the sitter is engraved on the frame. A version of this miniature is illustrated on Plate 108C.*
C. **Andrew Plimer,** *an unknown young boy, ivory, 2⅝ins., c.1800. This is a very colourful portrait by Plimer.*
D. **Nathaniel Plimer,** *an unknown lady, ivory, 3ins. The sitter is wearing a riding habit and plumed hat. The miniature is of outstanding quality for this artist.*
E. **John Downman, A.R.A.,** *Miss Elizabeth Farren, actress, later Countess of Derby (1759?-1829), wife of Edward Stanley, 12th Earl of Derby, ivory, 3ins. This miniature bears an inscription in Horace Walpole's writing: 'Miss Farren / The Incomparable Actress / 1787.' It was Lot 50 at the Strawberry Hill sale, 1842, when it was unattributed.*

Private Collection

Plate 108G. **J. Meyer, R.A.**, *an attractive miniature of Queen Charlotte (1744-1818), ivory, 3¾ins., c.1780. Charlotte Sophia of Mecklenburg-Strelitz married George III in September 1761. This is a superb miniature and shows Meyer's way of drawing the hair in strands, and delineating the features.* Gracious permission of H.M. The Queen.

Comte was by John Smart, and those of his children, Joseph Andrew, Peter Augustus and Amelia, framed together in a hinged oval case, were all painted by Richard Crosse. They are all charming portraits, and among the few I know by him of children (Plates 109B and G). The style of the ladies' coiffure, piled high up on top of the head, suited Crosse to perfection and both he and Jeremiah Meyer obviously enjoyed depicting them like this. He painted at least two large miniatures of Maria, Duchess of Gloucester, based on a portrait by Reynolds, in the collection of H.M. The Queen. One version is in the collection of Mrs. Simon Brett and is an attractive example of this type of his larger miniatures (Colour Plate 31B). There is no evidence to support the theory that he signed his works 'R.C.' on the front, and lack of signatures sometimes makes attribution difficult. His miniatures are well-modelled and refined. Unfortunately, as with Meyer, his carmines were rather fugitive and many of them have faded. One of the finest enamels I know is in the collection of Lord Thomson; it represents one of his brothers (probably Edward) and was exhibited in Edinburgh in 1965, when a number of family miniatures were also shown.

Plate 109A. **R. Crosse**, *an unknown lady, ivory, 1in., c.1780. The sitter's hair is piled high and falling in a coil over one shoulder. She is wearing a pink dress with a white fichu. Mounted in a brooch.* Courtesy Sotheby's.

Plate 109B. **R. Crosse**, *Amelia De Lautour, ivory, 3½ins., c.1793. One of a set of three of the children of Joseph Francois Louis, Comte De Lautour, all painted by Crosse and sold in 1969 (see also Plate 109G). Amelia is wearing a white dress tied with a blue sash. Portraits of children by Crosse are scarce.* Courtesy Sotheby's.

Plate 109C. **R. Crosse.** *The Marchioness of Salisbury (1750-1835), ivory, 3¾ins., c.1784. Mary Amelia was the eldest daughter of the 1st Marquess of Downshire and wife of James Cecil, Earl of Shaftesbury, created Marquess in 1789. This miniature was engraved and published by Richard Harraden in 1790.* Courtesy Christie's.

Plate 109D. **R. Crosse,** *Miss Turner of Uxbridge, ivory, 4½ins. This is a particularly attractive miniature by Crosse and a very good example of costume worn c.1780-85.* Courtesy Sotheby's.

Andrew Plimer (1763-1837) was one of the most prolific artists of the eighteenth century, and one whose work has been copied and faked any number of times. Graham Reynolds, writing in 1952, did not consider his work worthy of being placed beside that of the great artists such as Cosway, but it is in demand by collectors and I feel justified in discussing it in this select group.

Andrew was, like his brother Nathaniel, born at Wellington, Shropshire, where he was baptised on 29th September, 1793. He was the son of a clockmaker, Nathaniel Plimer, and his wife, Eliza. The family owned a clockmaking business in the town to which both boys were apprenticed. As has already been mentioned (under Nathaniel) the boys left home and joined a band of gipsies with whom they toured the country for two years. They arrived in London in 1781, and Andrew succeeded in obtaining a position as a personal servant to Richard Cosway. His duties are said to have included cleaning the studio, grinding and mixing the colours, announcing any callers and making himself generally useful. As is the case with so many artists, few details of his life have been preserved. No further information has been discovered since Dr. G.C. Williamson published his work *Andrew and Nathaniel Plimer.* According to tradition, Cosway discovered Andrew copying one of his miniatures and was so impressed with the result that he at once realised that the boy had artistic ability. He is supposed to have assisted Plimer to obtain further knowledge by allowing him to take lessons. The name of his tutor is not known. He worked for Cosway for some time and always held him in great esteem, describing him as "my beloved master".

Plate 109E (left). **Richard Crosse** *(1742-1810), self-portrait of the artist, ivory, 3¾ins. Sold together with other family miniatures by Crosse in 1960. Other self-portraits exist, one of which is in the V. & A.M.* Courtesy Sotheby's.

Plate 109F (right). **R. Crosse,** *an early miniature of two young men, ivory, 1⅞ins. Signed in full on the reverse and dated: 'Drawn by Richard Crosse / 1759.' The miniature is thought to represent the artist with one of his brothers — Edward, or James; both are wearing mauve jackets and green waistcoats.* Private Collection.

In 1785 Plimer evidently felt sufficiently confident to set up on his own and started a practice in 32 Great Maddox Street, Hanover Square. After a year he moved to 3 Golden Square, which was considered a very fashionable part of London. He exhibited at the Royal Academy, 1786-1830, and was possibly the artist who exhibited at the British Institution in 1819. These were subject pictures and, if they were by Plimer, they are the only ones recorded. In 1796 he moved to 8 Golden Square. He married on 21st February, 1801, at Wicken, Northamptonshire, Joanna Louisa Knight (1774-1861), by whom he had five children, four daughters and a son, who died young. Among their wedding guests were Richard Cosway and his wife and Jeremiah Meyer. Of his children, Andrew (d.c.1813), Joanna (1803-1846), Charlotte (1804-1845), Selina (1809-1841) and Louisa

Plate 109G. **R. Crosse,** *Peter De Lautour, ivory, 3½ins., c.1793. Brother of Amelia (Plate 109B). This is an unusual and attractive miniature of a young boy with his bat and ball.* Courtesy Sotheby's.

Colour Plate 30.
A. **Richard Cosway, R.A.,** *Lady Fairfield, ivory, 2⁹/16ins., c.1795-1800.*
B. **Nathaniel Plimer,** *an unknown officer, ivory, 3ins., c.1795.*
C. **George Engleheart,** *an unknown young man, ivory, 3ins., c.1800. Signed on the front: 'E' and on the reverse: 'G.Engleheart / Pinxit.'*
D. **George Engleheart,** *an unknown officer, ivory, 3¼ins., c.1800. This miniature is in fine condition.*
E. **George Engleheart,** *Mrs. Ann Bell, ivory, 2¾ins., 1795. Listed in Engleheart's Fee Book.*
Courtesy Bernard Falk Collection, Royal Pavilion, Brighton

A

B

C

D

E

Plate 110A. **A. Plimer,** *portrait of an elderly lady, ivory, 1⅞ins. Signed and dated: 'A.P. / 1796.' Plimer seldom signed his miniatures after c.1790.* Courtesy Sotheby's.

Plate 110B. **A. Plimer,** *a lady and child, ivory, 2⅞ins. Signed and dated: 'A.P. / 1786.' This is a good example of Plimer's early signed work.* Courtesy E. Grosvenor Paine, U.S.A.

(d.1864), only the latter married; she became the wife of John Scott, M.D., of Edinburgh, and was the only one of the children to survive her mother. It was at her house in Hawick, Scotland, that Mrs. Plimer died in 1861.

In 1801 the family toured through Devon and Cornwall, and in c.1815 Plimer was working in Exeter. After about three years they returned to London and took up residence in Upper York Street, Montague Square. In c.1820 Plimer seems to have set off on a tour, leaving his family behind. He visited Reading, Brighton, Devon, Cornwall, Dorset, Wales and Scotland. Whilst in Scotland he is said to have obtained a number of commissions by staying with families and painting several of their portraits; this lessened his expenses and he was able to save money. In 1835 he took his family to live

Plate 110C (left). **A. Plimer,** *miniature of an unknown young lady, ivory, 3ins.* Courtesy Christie's.

Plate 110D (right). **A. Plimer,** *a fine miniature of an unknown officer, ivory, 2⅞ins. Wearing scarlet uniform with a white collar and silver epaulettes and froggings.* Courtesy Sotheby's.

at Brighton, and eventually settled in 'Western Cottages'; these were at that time occupied by well-to-do people and were in a fashionable district of the town. He died only two years later and was buried on 4th February at 'Old Hove' aged seventy-four years.

Plimer's sister-in-law, **Mary Ann Knight** (b.1776) was also an artist, who began to paint portraits at the age of twenty-six in order to help to support the family. She had some instruction from Plimer, and it is thought that it was in this way that he met and fell in love with her sister, Joanna. Her work closely resembles that of Andrew Plimer, and as the majority of it is not signed it is possible that some miniatures are wrongly attributed.

At his best Plimer was capable of producing well executed and attractive miniatures, but not all his work is of equal merit. He often painted family groups which are quite effective. His draughtsmanship is inclined to be weak and the pose a little stiff. He was rather better at painting men than women; the portraits of men are stronger and not so idealised.

His work falls into two phases; the earlier examples, up to c.1789, are more natural than those painted later. In this period he frequently signed his miniatures 'A.P.' on the front, followed by a date (Plate 110B); sometimes they were also inscribed on the reverse. In his second phase he did not sign his miniatures, the size of the ivories increased, his palette was more restricted, and the flesh colours inclined to fade. It was marked by a sameness of appearance in both features and costume.

Characteristics of Plimer's work are the elongated necks of the women, long noses, and the treatment of the eyes, which are large and appealing. He used a thin cross-hatching in the background to the left and right of the sitter, and thin cross-strokes of shading in the hair. His portraits of children are superficially pleasing but they tend to look forlorn, and the eyes seem too large for the faces. He often used a dullish brown flesh colour which, when faded, is unattractive. He painted on ivory, vellum, paper and card, and executed portraits in oils as well as miniatures. Portraits of his family, many of which were illustrated by Williamson, are among his best paintings. A self-portrait of the artist was Lot 31 at Sotheby's on 19th October, 1970

(Plate 111B), and a charming one of his daughter, Louisa, was sold at Sotheby's, Lot 79, on 27th January, 1964 (Plate 111A). A good example, of an officer, in his best style was Lot 91 at Sotheby's on 28th July, 1975, and an unusual miniature of a child wearing a wide-brimmed hat is in a private collection (Plate 110G). Examples of his work are in many private collections, and may be seen at the Fitzwilliam Museum, Cambridge, the Ashmolean Museum, Oxford, and the Victoria and Albert Museum. (Colour Plate 29C, Plates 110A, C, D, E and F.)

Plate 110G. **A. Plimer,** *portrait of an unknown child, ivory, 2¾ins., c.1780-85. The sitter is wearing a straw hat trimmed with feathers and a white dress tied with a yellow sash, and holding a striped ball in her left hand.* Private Collection.

William Wood (1769-1810) was born in Suffolk, in or near Ipswich. Nothing is known about his early life or parentage, but he entered the Royal Academy Schools on 16th December, 1785, at the age of sixteen. He worked in London, Bristol and Gloucester. His London addresses include 30 St. James's Place (1792-1794), and 8 Cork Street (1795-1807); he subsequently lived in Golden Square. In my opinion miniatures by him have not for many years had the attention they deserve, and his life and work has tended to be dismissed by authors with only a brief reference. This may be partly because some people find his style difficult to identify and, unless the frames are opened up, no signature is visible. In point of fact, if a collector or student takes the trouble to examine and compare miniatures by Wood he will discover certain characteristics which may make for easier attribution. He was undoubtedly one of the best miniaturists of this period, better than Plimer and in every way comparable with Engleheart and, at times, even Cosway. He painted portraits and subject miniatures as well as a few 'eye' miniatures (see Figure 7), watercolour drawings and landscapes, and executed works in crayons and lithographs. He exhibited at the Royal Academy, British Institution, etc., 1788?-1808. No initial was given for the portrait exhibited in 1788, but it is assumed to be by him. He is known to have copied a few miniatures by Cosway, Engleheart and Smart, but I have never seen an example that I could attribute with certainty. His portraits have an honesty about them and, like Smart's, are well drawn and expressive without any exaggeration. A characteristic is the way in which he painted the backgrounds with short brush strokes, many of which are crossed, and

Plate 111A. **A. Plimer,** *Louisa Plimer later Mrs. Scott, daughter of the artist, ivory, 4½ins. Wearing a low-cut dress edged with lace and a shawl.* Courtesy Sotheby's.

Plate 111B. **Andrew Plimer** *(1763-1837), self-portrait of the artist, watercolour on paper, 6¾ins. Other self-portraits of the artist exist.* Courtesy Sotheby's.

Plate 111C. **G. Engleheart,** *Sir William Charles Farrell Skeffington, Bart., ivory, 4½ins. Unfinished, signed and dated on the reverse: '1792.' Engleheart painted this sitter more than once. It is interesting as an example of an unfinished miniature.* Courtesy Sotheby's.

Plate 111D. **G. Engleheart,** *John Cox Dillman Engleheart (1782/4-1862), aged twelve, painted by his uncle, pencil and wash on paper, 4¼ins. Signed in cursive initials: 'GE.' This is an attractive miniature and one of several executed on paper by Engleheart.* Private Collection.

Plate 112A. **W. Wood,** *portrait of a Chinese boy, ivory, 3¹/8ins. Signed on the reverse: 'No.5727.' The boy was the servant of a certain Mr. Hobson employed by the East India Company. The miniature was exhibited at the R.A. in 1800, and realised £2,300 when it was sold in 1973.* Courtesy Sotheby's.

Plate 112B. **W. Wood,** *an unknown Cavalry officer, ivory, 3¹/8ins. Inscribed on the reverse: 'D.J.D.F. by Will: Wood / of Cork Street / Lond / 1807.' This is a fine miniature by Wood and the stippling he always used can be seen on the background.* Ex de la Hey Collection.

frequently emphasised the shading with small dots of paint which can sometimes be seen even on the hair. He used a pleasing warm flesh colouring and shaded the features with darkish brown strokes. His male sitters often have a rather rubicund complexion, the modelling being achieved by a series of lines crossing each other and a slight shading of brown round the contours of the face and features. One of the finest miniatures I have ever seen of this period of the eighteenth century is by Wood. It represents Lieut. Col. John Dick Burnaby of Lowerby Hall, Leicestershire, wearing the uniform of the 1st Foot Guards, and was painted in 1805 (Colour Plate 27C). Details regarding this miniature are in Volume 3 of William Wood's manuscript, No. 6118.

Wood kept an important MS list of his clients, together with notes and comments regarding the sitters and any alterations made to the miniatures. This is preserved in the Victoria and Albert Museum. From the ledger we learn that he frequently adapted or altered his miniatures as and when the occasion arose, because of some change in the social position of the sitter. In the case of Colonel Burnaby, his notes give details of colours used and an account of the ivory base. He also states that "I did not breathe upon this miniature". The miniature was commenced in September, 1805, and finished in the November of the same year; a tracing of the portrait accompanies the notes. From his records it is evident that he painted several self-portraits, but these never satisfied him and they were frequently destroyed. He also gives important details regarding his study of the durability of pigments used in miniature painting and noted those which, in his experience, deteriorated. From this MS we learn that he painted 1,211 miniatures between 1790 and 1808. This in itself is a clear indication of the demand put upon miniaturists of this period.

The majority of his miniatures are signed on the reverse, with his address and a code number such as: 'D.J.D.F. by Will: Wood / of Cork Street / Lond / 1807.' The City of Liverpool Museum contains a miniature copy by Wood of one of Reynolds' self-portraits, signed on the reverse: 'Sir J. Reyn / after himself / By Will: Wood.'

Miniatures of ladies by Wood are scarcer than those of men; a particularly attractive one of a young lady wearing a bonnet was exhibited in Edinburgh in 1965 (Plate 112C). In 1808 Wood published *An Essay on National and Sepulchral Monuments*. His hobbies included landscape gardening. He had joined the Artists' Volunteer Corps in 18c3, and in 1807 was instrumental in founding the Society of Associated Artists in Watercolours, of which he was the first President, being succeeded after a year by David Cox. The Society survived for only a few years, and was followed by what is called the Royal Institute of Painters in Watercolours.

On 16th July, 1973, an extremely fine miniature by Wood was Lot 73 at Sotheby's. It represented a Chinese boy who had been employed by a certain Mr. Hobson, of the East India Company. It was signed on the reverse, with 'No. 5727', and realised the astonishingly high sum of £2,300 (Plate 112A). A miniature of a lady holding a child, signed and dated on the reverse: '1807', and bearing the Cork Street address, was Lot 98 at Christie's on 3rd October, 1972; it was an uncharacteristic miniature, for Wood, and did not have as much of the dotting on the background as is usual (Plate 112G). In the same sale was a typical example of his work of an unknown man named Zaas, signed on the reverse and dated: '1805' (Plate 112E). Wood died at his house in Golden Square on 15th November, 1810, at the age of only forty-one. Examples of his work are in many private collections, and in the E.B. Greene Collection, Cleveland Museum of Art, Ohio, the Ward Usher Collection, Lincoln, and the Victoria and Albert Museum. (Colour Plate 24E.)

Plate 112C (far left). **W. Wood,** *an unknown lady, ivory, 3ins. This is a particularly attractive portrait of c.1790, the sitter wearing a bonnet held in position by ribbons taken over the top and tied under the chin.* Present whereabouts unknown.

Plate 112D (left). **W. Wood,** called *Mrs. Clide, ivory, 3ins., wearing a white dress and coral necklace. This miniature was at one time attributed in error to Cosway.* Courtesy Sotheby's.

George Chinnery (1774-1852) was born on 7th February, 1774. He was the fifth son of William Chinnery, an amateur painter of 4 Gough Square, Fleet Street, and the grandson of another William Chinnery, a noted writing-master. The family came from East Anglia, but as early as 1620 a branch had become established in Ireland and it was from this side of the family, part of which returned to England in 1642, that George was descended. To most people his art is more closely associated with the large portraits and drawings and scenes of Chinese life, for which he is so well

Plate 112E **W. Wood,** *portrait of a gentleman called Zaas, ivory, 3¼ins. Signed on the reverse and dated: '1805' with the Cork Street address. This is a well drawn and strong portrait and shows clearly Wood's method of 'dotting' in the background.* Courtesy Christie's.

Plate 112G. **W. Wood,** *a lady and her child, ivory, 3½ins. Signed on the reverse and dated: '1807' from the Cork Street address. This is an unusual miniature for Wood who seldom painted a double portrait.* Courtesy Christie's.

Plate 112F. **W. Wood,** *Miss Wood, the artist's sister, ivory, 2¾ins., c.1790-95. The sitter is wearing a white dress and frilled collar, her long hair tied with a bandeau. According to his ledgers Wood painted Miss Wood eight times. Present whereabouts unknown.*

known, than with miniatures. Largely because of the fact that they are practically never signed his ability as a miniaturist has been overlooked. More recently examples of his work have come into the sale rooms, and the best of them are so dramatic that they warrant him a place amongst the top miniaturists of the period. Various articles have been written about his art, but no full-scale biography has yet been attempted.

He is presumed to have had his initial training in painting from his father and entered the Royal Academy Schools on 6th July, 1792, aged nineteen. He exhibited at the Royal Academy from 1791-1846. His early exhibits were of sufficient merit to attract notice and John Williams, alias 'Pasquin', likened his work to that of Cosway. In c.1794 Chinnery went to Ireland, where he painted the portrait of a distant relative, Sir Brodrick Chinnery. He obtained lodgings with James Vigne, a jeweller, of 27 College Green, Dublin, who was said to be connected with the firm of Myre Vigne and Luard, of Threadneedle Street, London. In 1799 Chinnery married his host's daughter, Marianne Vigne, by whom he had two children, a daughter, Matilda, and a son, John. Whilst in Ireland he became acquainted with John Comerford, who may well have influenced him to paint miniatures in a broader and freer style. Something of Comerford's linear shading on the face can be seen on Chinnery's sketch of an Indian ruler, which was Lot 53 at Sotheby's on 15th July, 1974 (Plate 113G). Chinnery is known to have painted miniatures in the early part of his career, and it is doubtful if he painted any after he settled in China in c.1825.

Whilst in Dublin Chinnery was connected with the drawing school of the Royal Dublin Society, and was secretary and treasurer of an exhibition held in Dublin in November, 1799. There is no evidence to support the theory that he was a member of the Royal Hibernian Academy, which was not incorporated until 1823, by which time he was in India. In 1802 Chinnery's marriage had already broken down and he left his wife and children, to return to London with the intention of going to India. He sailed from England on the *Gilwell* on 11th June, 1802, reaching Madras on 21st December of that year, where he was well received and obtained a large number of patrons. Apart from a trip to Calcutta in 1807 and visits to places in the surrounding area, he remained in Madras for the rest of his time in India.

He was joined by his daughter, Matilda, in 1817, and in the following year Mrs. Chinnery arrived, to be joined by their son, John, three years later. By this time Chinnery had had two illegitimate children, Edward Charles and Henry Colin, both born in c.1813. John died in Berhampore in 1822 and in the same year Chinnery forsook his family and went to Serampur, presumably to escape arrest for debt. Three years later his debts had risen to some £40,000 and he fled to China, leaving his wife and daughter behind. He settled at the port of Macao, which he reached on 29th September, 1825, and, apart from short visits to Canton, he appears to have resided there for the remaining twenty-seven years of his life.

Plate 113A. **G. Chinnery,** *an unknown man, ivory, 2½ins. Signed and dated on the reverse: 'GC / 1795.'* Courtesy Brigadier and Mrs. G. Viner.

From an artistic point of view this was probably the most important and productive period of his career. His sketches of views, scenes, market vendors, portraits, etc., filled his days. Many of these he later finished in watercolour and oils. He continued to submit paintings to the Royal Academy, and in 1846 sent a self-portrait (now in the National Portrait Gallery). Other self-portraits exist. He died of apoplexy at Macao on 30th May, 1852, and in an obituary notice in *The Friend of China and Hong Kong Gazette,* 2nd June, 1852, reference is made to his "straitened circumstances".

In 1957 a Chinnery Exhibition was held in Edinburgh, which contained several of his miniatures, including three from the Victoria and Albert Museum. One, of an elderly lady, was signed on the reverse: 'Georgius Chinnery / Pict: London: / Jany 1st 1793'; another was signed 'G.C.' on the reverse and dated 1798. One of a lady and gentleman was inscribed in full on the reverse: 'G. Chinnery pinxt / Comillah Tippesah, Bengal, November 1809.' Occasionally he signed with the monogram 'GC' on the front and, on rare occasions, as in the case of a miniature of Miss MacKenzie, with a double monogram: 'GC EI / 1804.' This was for many years accepted by the authorities as a work by Engleheart, but under high magnification the correct signature was seen and the scales fell from one's eyes — that, of course, it was a work by Chinnery, the initials 'E.I.' referring to the East Indies (Plate 113C).

On 15th July, 1974, an important collection of unfinished sketches and miniatures of members of the D'Oyly family were sold at Sotheby's. Sir John Hadley D'Oyly, 6th Bart., joined the East India Company in 1770. He married in Calcutta a Mrs. Diana Coles, by whom he had two sons; of these, Charles (1781-1845), later the 7th Bart., went to Calcutta in 1797, and was attached to the Governor-General's Office. He was an amateur artist, who

Plate 113B (left). **G. Chinnery,** a miniature of an unknown officer, ivory, 3⁵/₁₆ins. Signed and inscribed on the reverse: 'George Chinnery / Sackville Street / pinxt / 1794.' This is an outstanding miniature by Chinnery and probably one of the finest he ever painted. See Figure 31 for signature. Present whereabouts unknown.

Figure 31 (right). George Chinnery's signature, the reverse of Plate 113B.

Plate 113C. **G. Chinnery,** Miss MacKenzie, ivory, 2⁹/₁₆ins. Signed with a double monogram: 'GC EI / 1804.' This is one of the rare occasions when Chinnery signed a miniature in this way. Private Collection.

had some tuition from Chinnery.

Sir Charles became very popular as an artist, and details regarding his work are given by Dr. Mildred Archer in *British Drawings in the India Office Library*. Among the miniatures sold were two by Chinnery of Sir John Hadley D'Oyly (Plate 113E), an unfinished three-quarter length sketch of Sir Charles D'Oyly (Plate 113 I) and a number of small sketched portraits of the family, all by Chinnery. There were also some miniatures of the family by one of his pupils, Maria Bellett Brown, whose work will be discussed in the next chapter. The collection of sketches of heads was of great importance as they give a good guide to Chinnery's manner of painting, his sweeping brush strokes and the dark deep-set eyes which are a characteristic of his work. One of the finest miniatures by Chinnery that has come on the market was of an officer painted against a cloud and sky background, and inscribed on the reverse: 'George Chinnery / Sackville Street / pinxt / 1794.' It was purchased by Spink & Son, and was superbly drawn and colourful. The dramatic portrayal of the eyes and the shading of the face with thin brush strokes, very much in the manner of Comerford, was a good example of his technique (Plate 113B and Figure 31). Points to look for are a slightly protruding lower lip coloured in bright red, dark shading of the eyes which often have a touch of red in the corner, a dark area behind the sitter's head, the background shaded with blues, greys and browns, and the hair painted in sweeping strokes. A good example of a miniature by Chinnery painted in a slightly softer manner is in the collection of Brigadier and Mrs. Viner, and is signed and dated: 'G.C. / 1795' on the reverse (Plate 113A). Examples of his work are in the Bernard Falk Collection at the Royal Pavilion, Brighton, the National Gallery, Dublin, the National Portrait Gallery, the British Museum, and the Victoria and Albert Museum. (Colour Plate 23B.)

Ozias Humphry, R.A. (1742-1810) was, like Cosway, a native of Devonshire, and both were born in the same year. Humphry was born on 8th September, 1742, the son of George Humphry, a peruke-maker and mercer, and his wife, Elizabeth. Ozias was educated at the local grammar school but in 1757, when he was only thirteen, he went to London to study

390

art under William Shipley. He found London expensive, and told his parents that "the dirt of London rots shoes exceeding fast." He returned home in 1758, and his father died the following year. He had no desire to enter the family lace business and, in 1760, was apprenticed to Samuel Collins at Bath for what was supposed to be a period of three years' training. In the event Collins fled to Dublin in 1762 to avoid his creditors and Humphry was left rather in the lurch. He was in an embarrassing position as he was still legally bound to Collins, but the contract was deemed to be dissolved due to Collins' hasty departure and Humphry set up on his own. His mother had hoped that he would return to help her with the business but his heart was set on painting and, in spite of her pessimism about his success, she gave him a guinea which he asked for to go to Exeter and try his luck! He stayed there for about two months, having obtained some patrons. It was after this that he returned to Bath and was given some rooms at the house of Thomas Linley, the musician, whose daughter, Elizabeth Anne, became the first Mrs. Sheridan. Humphry's time with this family was a very happy one, and they became so attached to him that they named one of the sons after him.

Plate 113D. **G. Chinnery,** *Lady Charlotte D'Oyly, née Thompson, first wife of Sir John D'Oyly, 8th Bart., pencil and wash on paper, 2½ins., c.1805-10. Unfinished sketch.* Courtesy Sotheby's.

Gainsborough was at Bath at this time and painted celebrated portraits of the Linley family. It is possible that Humphry had some instruction from Gainsborough and, being an observant young man, he noted many details concerning Gainsborough's studio technique. Both Gainsborough and Sir Joshua Reynolds urged Humphry to go to London. Humphry was a little reluctant to move again so soon, but on Reynolds' strong advice he left for London in 1764. He was allowed to copy some of Reynolds' pictures and was at first given great encouragement by the master but, rather to Humphry's disgust, he was soon left to stand on his own feet! He succeeded in establishing himself in London and built up a good practice. He exhibited at the Society of Arts from 1765-1771, becoming a member in 1773. He lived for a time in Leicester Square, then moved to 21 King Street, Covent Garden, where he remained until 1771. In 1766 Humphry exhibited a miniature (now lost) of "John Mealing, dressed in scarlet lined with fur". This portrait of Mealing, a well-known model who acted as porter at the St. Martin's Lane Academy, attracted a lot of attention, and was purchased by George III for 100 guineas. His standard rate for a miniature was at that time

A. **John Smart,** *an unknown officer, ivory, 3ins. Signed and dated: 'JS / 1794 / I.' This is a fine example of Smart's Indian period. An unsigned and undated replica of this miniature is in the E.B. Greene Collection (No. 36), at the Cleveland Museum of Art, Ohio.* Courtesy Asprey's.

B. **Richard Crosse,** *after a portrait by Reynolds, Maria, Duchess of Gloucester (d.1807), ivory, 7ins. Other versions of this miniature exist, including one in the collection of the late Colonel G. Warland which showed the sitter with her son and a dog. The original portrait on which these are based is in the collection of H.M. The Queen, and does not have the child or dog.* Courtesy Mrs. Simon Brett.

12 guineas. He had found Royal favour, and in 1767 exhibited a miniature of the Queen, and in 1769 one of the Princess Royal.

Humphry did not possess an easy disposition and was inclined to be conceited and quick-tempered, particularly if there was any suggestion of his having been slighted. This did not make for popularity, added to which he was restless and never settled anywhere for very long. He had a brother, William, with whom he kept in close touch, who became Vicar of Kemsing-cum-Seale (now separate parishes), and Birling, both in Kent and under the patronage of the then Duke of Dorset. In 1773 Humphry and George Romney set off for Italy, and stayed en route at Knole, the home of the Duke of Dorset. The tour was undertaken for reasons of Humphry's health as, in 1772, he had had a severe fall from his horse which damaged his nervous system and affected his eyesight. This had always given some trouble, as he was near-sighted and found focusing for large paintings more difficult.

Plate 113E. **G. Chinnery,** *Sir John Hadley D'Oyly, 6th Bart. (1753-1818), ivory, 4ins. From a collection of miniatures of the D'Oyly family sold in 1974, the majority of which were by Chinnery. Sir John served in Calcutta under the East India Company.* Courtesy Sotheby's.

The trip took him to Rome, Florence, Venice and Naples. His health improved and he was able to copy well-known paintings, and when, in 1777, he returned to London he intended giving up miniature painting and turning his attention to working in oils. He studied in this medium but he was never so successful on a large scale. Having been one of the Directors of the Incorporated Society of Artists who voted for expulsion of the dissident artists who had formed the Royal Academy, relations were strained, and he only made his peace with the Royal Academy in 1779, when he was elected A.R.A., and R.A. in 1791. He served on the hanging committee in 1793 and exhibited at the Royal Academy from 1779-1797.

Being dissatisfied with his earnings he was tempted by the stories of the riches to be made in India to go there and try his luck. He left England on 25th January, 1785, reaching Calcutta early in August. His main worry was the fact that John Smart was in India, and that this would affect his patronage. This fear was unfounded as Smart spent almost all his time in Madras.

Plate 113F (above). **G. Chinnery,** *Marian Greer (d.1814), first wife and cousin of Sir Charles D'Oyly, pencil and wash on paper, 2ins.* Courtesy Sotheby's.

Plate 113G (right). **G. Chinnery,** *portrait of an Indian ruler, watercolour on paper, 3½ins., unfinished. This drawing shows the influence of Comerford in the way the face is shaded.* Courtesy Sotheby's.

Before his departure Humphry was practically engaged to Miss Mary Boydell, whose portrait he painted. The lady was the niece of Alderman Boydell, and it has always been held that the attraction was a mercenary one rather than one of affection. In any case, the attachment was eventually broken off and Miss Boydell returned his correspondence and his presents. Whilst in India Humphry visited Calcutta, Benares and Lucknow, and had a large number of commissions to paint local residents and native princes, including the Nawab of Oudh. He was to discover, as others had done to their cost, that commissions were one thing but payment was another! (Smart suffered in the same way.) Humphry's chief debtor was the Nawab of Oudh, for whom he had painted numerous portraits. The fact that the Indian climate did not agree with him, coupled with the fact that he did not make the money he expected and that he only got part of the sum owed him by the Nawab, made him decide to go back to England. He returned in 1787, a disappointed man, and the experience left him embittered for the rest of his life. His sight and health were deteriorating, and he was only able to continue to paint miniatures for a further five years. He took up residence in London in March 1787, and turned to executing portraits in crayon. His temperament worsened as a result of his disillusionment in India and he became more quarrelsome and argumentative. His attempt to sue the Governor-General, Sir John MacPherson, for the fees due to him for portraits painted in India was unsuccessful, and one way and another he lost much of his confidence. He remained unmarried, but in 1779 a young woman called Dolly Wickers, whose father, William Wickers, was a general shopkeeper in Oxford, bore him a son who was called William Upcott (1779-1845), a family name. The boy had a varied education and was intelligent and good at languages, learning Hebrew, Greek and Latin. He became a bookseller and was placed with Mr. R.H. Evans of Pall Mall, and then with J. Wright of Piccadilly where he worked for three and a half years. He later obtained the post of sub-librarian at the London Institute. He was a keen collector, and became interested in coins, tokens, prints, engravings and autograph letters. This pursuit led him to the discovery of John Evelyn's diary among the Evelyn papers. He kept a lot of information regarding Humphry, whom he always referred to as his godfather. When Upcott died his collection was sold at Sotheby's and realised over £4,000. Many items were purchased by the British Museum and the Bodleian, Oxford.

By 1792 Humphry's sight was so bad that he was obliged to give up miniature painting, and became portrait painter in crayons to the King. His last exhibits at the Royal Academy in 1797 were portraits of the Prince and Princess of Orange. After this his sight failed totally and he spent the remainder of his life in seclusion. He was granted an annuity of £100 by Lord Egremont in exchange for a painting attributed to Raphael. Many letters and notebooks as well as papers by Humphry are preserved in the British Museum. Information regarding Humphry's time in India is given by Sir William Foster, in The Walpole Society, Volume XIX, which contains some interesting illustrations of his portraits.

Humphry died on 9th March, 1810, at 39 Thornhaugh Street, Bedford Square, in lodgings kept by the widow of Henry Spicer, and was buried in St. James's burial ground, Hampstead Road.

His works included miniatures on ivory and paper and small portrait drawings, rather in the manner of Downman, a good example of which is the one illustrated of the unknown young boy (Plate 115B). He also painted portraits in oil and crayon and sometimes executed unfinished sketches of heads, presumably like other artists' preliminary sketches for larger works. Many of his miniatures were copies of oil paintings commissioned by the Duke of Dorset, who was one of his most important patrons.

Plate 113H. **G. Chinnery**, called *The Countess of Orford and her child, ivory, 4¾ins., unfinished. This charming study shows clearly Chinnery's method of painting the sitters' eyes in a dramatic and rather dark way.* Courtesy Sotheby's.

Plate 113 I. **G. Chinnery**, *Sir Charles D'Oyly (1781-1845), son of Sir John Hadley D'Oyly, pencil sketch on paper, 4½ins., c.1805-10. Unfinished.* Courtesy Sotheby's.

B

A

C

D

E

F

G

Humphry was undoubtedly one of the best miniaturists of the eighteenth century, and many of his works show, on a small scale, the close affinity he had with the works of Reynolds; this is perhaps surprising in a period when there was not as much close resemblance between the work of the miniaturist and that of the large scale portrait painter. Humphry's portraits are usually elegant; his early works are small and executed in the style of the other artists of the 1760s, and are obviously influenced by Collins' tuition. The fact that he rarely dated his miniatures makes a chronological assessment difficult, and one has to rely on costume. From the outset his works are marked by his use of rich colours, fine brush strokes, and a perception of character. His early works particularly have the appearance of oil paintings as he used a lot of gum with his paints. Those of women have a rather limpid, clear-cut appearance; individual brush strokes on the face are not so apparent, and the eyebrows are sometimes made up of a number of fine, almost parallel, lines. He used light touches of opaque white in the sitters' hair, and soft brown shading on the faces of his male sitters. The eyes sometimes have a slightly sleepy look. His style developed later into one that was broader and more fully developed, and the size of his portraits increased. He executed a number of half-length, three-quarter length, or even full-length portraits which were more ambitious and showed his desire to become an oil painter. Two fine examples of his larger miniatures are in the collection of H.M. The Queen; they represent Queen Charlotte (Plate 114E), and Charlotte Augusta, Princess Royal (Plate 114G). Many of his miniatures of Indian potentates are of fine quality, including one of The Shah Zada, fully inscribed on the reverse: 'The Shah Zada / Painted at Lucknow / from nature 1786 / by Ozias Humphry' (Plate 115A). This was Lot 30 at Christie's on 8th June, 1971. Other versions of it are known to exist. An attractive one of an unknown lady, from the de la Hey Collection, was exhibited in Edinburgh in 1965 (Plate 114F). An interesting unfinished miniature on paper in pencil and wash was Lot 101 at Christie's on 29th November, 1977. It was fully inscribed on the reverse: 'William Gardiner Esq / Groom Porter at St. James's / an old and faithful Servant / to the Dorset family for whom this portrait was painted / by Ozias Humphry R.A. / 1790' (Plate 115C).

Plate 115A. O. Humphry, R.A., the Shah Zada, ivory, 3¾ins. Inscribed and dated on the reverse: 'The Shah Zada / Painted at Lucknow / from nature 1786 / by Ozias Humphry.' Another version of this miniature exists. Courtesy Christie's.

Plate 114.
A. *O. Humphry, R.A., Sahib Zada, ivory, 3½ins. Inscribed and signed on the reverse: 'Sahib Zada Eldest son / and Presumptive / Heir to Asoph / Ub Dowlah Nabob / Vizier of Oude / Ozias Humphry / R.A. Pinxt / 1786.' This is a delightful study of the young boy. Courtesy E. Grosvenor Paine, U.S.A.*
B. *O. Humphry, R.A., Mary, Countess of Thanet, wife of the 8th Earl of Thanet, ivory, 1½ins., c.1770. Signed in monogram: 'OH.' Other versions of this miniature exist. Courtesy the Nelson Gallery and Atkins Museum, Starr Collection, Kansas City, U.S.A.*
C. *O. Humphry, R.A., portrait of an unknown man, ivory, 1½ins., c.1770. This is typical of the small miniatures painted by Humphry. Courtesy Sotheby's.*
D. *O. Humphry, R.A., Mary Panton (1730-93), second wife of Peregrine, 3rd Duke of Ancaster, ivory, 3¼ins. Signed in monogram and dated: 'OH / 1770.' Courtesy The Duke of Buccleuch and Queensberry, K.T.*
E. *O. Humphry, R.A., Queen Charlotte (1744-1818) wife of George III, ivory, 3½ins. Signed in monogram: 'OH', and signed and dated on the reverse: '1766.' This is one of Humphry's most attractive miniatures, painted five years after the Queen's marriage, at the age of twenty-two. Gracious permission of H.M. The Queen.*
F. *O. Humphry, R.A., miniature of an unknown lady, ivory, 1⁷⁄₈ins., c.1770. Ex de la Hey Collection.*
G. *O. Humphry, R.A., Charlotte Augusta Matilda, Princess Royal, ivory, 4½ins. Signed in monogram: 'OH' and signed and dated on the reverse: 'January 1769.' This charming miniature of the Princess at the age of three is probably the one exhibited at the Society of Artists in 1769. Gracious permission of H.M. The Queen.*

A

B

C

D

Plate 115B. **O. Humphry, R.A.,** *portrait of an unknown boy, pencil and wash on paper, 5¼ins. This is a particularly fine drawing by Humphry, and shows great freedom of draughtsmanship.* Private Collection.

His usual signature was 'OH' in monogram, the 'H' being set within the 'O'; on rare occasions he signed on the reverse: 'O:H: / 1770,' or 'O: Humphry p^t'; others are signed in full on the reverse as has already been indicated. (Colour Plate 16B.)

Examples of his work are in many private collections, and may be seen at the National Portrait Gallery, the Walker Art Gallery, Liverpool (who also have a portrait of George Stubbs by Humphry, executed in gouache and pastel), and the Victoria and Albert Museum. (Colour Plate 16B.)

The eighteenth century was a truly great period for art in every form. Patronage was overwhelming and architects, cabinet makers, porcelain manufacturers and artists all contributed, in their various ways, to produce homes and *objets d'art* which today are amongst our most sought-after treasures.

In miniature painting this is especially true. Artists, such as those

Colour Plate 32.
A. **Edward Nash,** *a young girl, painted in the manner of J. Smart, ivory, 2¾ins. Signed and dated: 'N / 1802.' Painted in India. This interesting miniature is typical of the yellow colouring Nash used.* Courtesy Sotheby's.
B. **Henry Jacob Burch, Junior,** *The Hon. Frederick Sylvester Douglas (1791-1819) as a boy, ivory, 3ins. Set within a pierced diamond frame. This is an exceptionally fine miniature.* Courtesy Sotheby's.
C. **John Smart,** *Major Richard Gomonde, of Madras, ivory, 2½ins. Signed and dated: 'JS / 1790 / I.' A second version of this miniature exists and was once in a double frame together with one of his wife, Susannah Ellerker, both signed and dated by Smart: '1790.'* Courtesy Christie's.
D. **John Smart,** *Anne Woodruff Guidott, later wife of Henry Sealey, ivory, 2⅜ins. Signed and dated: 'J.Smart / 1778.' This ravishing portrait of a beautiful woman in her décolletée dress is an example of a most personal portrait by a brilliant artist.* Courtesy The Royal Ontario Museum.

discussed in this chapter, deserve their honoured place among the many who produced the hundreds of small portraits which now help to fill the cabinets of collectors who find a special interest in this form of art.

Plate 115C. **O. Humphry, R.A.,** *an interesting miniature of William Gardiner, watercolour on card, 4³/₈ins., unfinished. Inscribed and dated on the reverse: 'William Gardiner Esq / Groom Porter at St. James's / an old and faithful Servant / to the Dorset family for whom this portrait was painted / by Ozias Humphry. R.A. / 1790.' Courtesy Christie's.*

Plate 115D. **O. Humphry, R.A.,** *Hyder Beg Khan, ivory, 3⁵/₁₆ins. Signed and dated in full on the reverse: 'Lucknow 1786.' The sitter is referred to as Prime Minister to Asoph Ub Dowlah. Another version of this portrait exists on which the inscription gives the sitter's position as Acting Minister to the Nabob of Oudh. Courtesy Sotheby's.*

Chapter XI

19th and 20th century Artists

AFTER THE DEATH of George IV in 1830 and the comparatively short reign of William IV, Britain moved into what was to be one of the longest reigns in the history of the country. The young Queen Victoria ascended the throne in 1837 and was to live to see changes and discoveries which could never have been dreamed of. In industry and science great advances were made; many of the amenities now taken for granted such as the telephone, electric light, and travel by rail, were developed and by the middle of the century, photography had been invented. This was to have a serious effect on miniature painting and the eventual cause of its decline, both in quality and demand. When it became possible to have large photographs framed and displayed on a desk or table, miniaturists made a valiant attempt to compete by enlarging their format. This was not a success: these large miniatures, which were produced at a time when fashions were all too often rather dark and drab and backgrounds were loaded with dark curtains and furniture, lost the intimacy which had always been the great charm of miniature painting. These larger portraits, good though many of them were, could not defend themselves against the cheaper and popular method of photography.

In spite of this, however, there were still a large number of miniaturists working between c.1830 and 1900, many of whom were capable of producing good works which are now very desirable. Insufficient research has been done on the late nineteenth and early twentieth century miniaturists, and they have not been truly appreciated. It is, in fact, only since sales of 'Victoriana' have begun to take place that they have even been considered collectors' items, and a lot of work still needs to be done to discover more about these later artists. In this chapter I have tried to discuss as many of them as possible, but do not have the space to cover them all and the names of further artists who will be of interest to collectors are included in the Appendix at the end of this chapter, most of them being represented by an illustration.

Although there is only a comparatively small number of contemporary artists who still paint miniatures I think it important to mention some of them, and I have included illustrations of the work of a few members of the Royal Society of Miniature Painters, Sculptors and Gravers, who hold annual exhibitions in London. These artists still follow the tradition set by the great miniaturists of the eighteenth century, when the use of ivory supplanted vellum as a base on which to paint. This, or its modern counterpart, imitation ivory, has remained the most popular background ever since, although some artists use paper or card.

Plate 116B. **W. Bone,** *after an engraving by W. Bromley, Senior, Warren Hastings (1732-1818), enamel, 3¼ins. Courtesy Sotheby's.*

Plate 116A. **C.R. Bone,** *Captain Richard H. King, ivory, 5ins. Signed on the front in monogram and dated: 'CR B. 1830' and on the reverse: 'Portrait of Capt R.H. King, R.N. / Painted by C.R. Bone / 47 Charlotte Street Portman Square / London. 1830.' This is a good example of Bone's paintings.* Courtesy Mrs. E.M. Hamilton.

Plate 116C. **W. Bone,** *an unknown young man, ivory, 3¼ins., c.1830. Signed on the front: 'W Bone' and on the reverse: 'Painted by / William Bone / 15 Berners St. / Oxford St.'* Courtesy F. Joachim.

Plate 116D. **H.P. Bone,** *Louisa Frances Bone, daughter of the artist, enamel, 8ins. Inscribed and signed on the reverse: 'Louisa Frances third daughter of H.P. and Ann Maria Bone / London September 1832 / (Original) Painted by Henry Pierce Bone Enamel Painter to Her Majesty and their Royal Highnesses The Duchess of Kent and the / Princess Victoria.'* Present whereabouts unknown.

Fashions have undergone many changes since the beginning of Queen Victoria's reign and a great number of these can be followed through in the illustrations depicting the miniaturists' art which accompany this chapter. The classical and rather clinging lines of the first quarter of the nineteenth century were followed by low, draped, and tight-fitting bodices which emphasised a slimmer waistline and full skirts. By c.1840 the bodices were often 'long-waisted' and tapered to a point at the front, worn over tight stays and a mass of underclothing with a full and flounced skirt. Pelisse-robes, or over-dresses, were still in use, and bonnets in varying shapes and sizes trimmed with ribbon. The custom of wearing these tight-waisted gowns was one of the reasons that so many young ladies 'sank into a decline'; *The Girls' Book of Diversions* gives instruction on this problem — "How to faint; the modes of fainting should all be as different as possible and may be made very diverting"! Next came the crinoline in its various forms, some so wide that the poor men could hardly stretch over to shake the ladies' hands! By c.1880-1890 the crinoline had been replaced by draped and pleated skirts worn over a large bustle. Tennis and riding became popular activities for the 'fair sex', and riding habits and tennis costumes were designed. For evening wear many of the dresses had long trains, ruched and pleated with bows of ribbon as decoration. In October, 1883, *The Daily News* announced that: "The Princess of Wales has banished the crinoline in spite of Paris". By the end of the nineteenth century the mood had changed again and dresses of a more masculine design were in vogue, worn with fitted and double-breasted jackets; for outdoor wear bonnets or small 'toques' were popular, usually made with small high crowns and trimmed with flowers, or a vertical bow behind. These fashions took us into the twentieth century, and since then they have undergone almost every kind of change, with the pendulum swinging backwards and forwards to earlier styles. Men's costume also changed considerably. Wigs were abandoned for curled or close-cropped hair by c.1835 (the elderly still wearing wigs), side-whiskers were popular, and a high cravat was often worn with a large bow with pointed ends, or a 'scarf neckcloth' kept in position with a tie-pin. Some of the neckwear became very exaggerated and caused a great deal of ridicule. So varied are the different styles of costume that one really needs to study the standard works on the subject, some of which are listed in the bibliography. It is not always as easy to date miniatures of men as those of ladies, because the portraits are often only to the bust and insufficient of the costume is visible for comparison. The chief points to look for are the cut of the coat, and the type of collar or cravat.

The nineteenth century saw a great revival of interest in miniatures painted on enamel. This was largely due to the volume of work done by the various members of the Bone family. Henry Bone's contribution to enamelling has already been discussed, and his tradition was carried on by his sons and one grandson.

Henry Pierce Bone (1779-1855) was born in Islington, and was one of the sons of H. Bone, R.A. He was educated at Tooting, and was taught the art of enamelling by his father, whom he assisted. He entered the Royal Academy Schools on 17th March, 1796, and exhibited at the Royal Academy, Society of British Artists and British Institution, 1799-1855. He was a prolific artist and painted oil portraits early in his career, but is best known for his enamels, many of which were copies from large portraits. His earliest known dated enamel is in the Victoria and Albert Museum, and represents Ralph Allen Daniell, dated 1795. On 14th October, 1805, he married Ann Marie (or Maria) Long, at the church of St. Mary-le-bone. A pair of miniatures of himself and his wife were sold at Christie's on 9th November, 1965. Both were signed and fully inscribed on the reverse: '. . . for his / daughter Elizabeth . . .' The miniature of Mrs. Bone was dated 1849, and that of H.P. Bone, from a drawing by his son, C.R. Bone, dated 1847. His family consisted of four sons and three daughters: George (living c.1879), Henry Thomas, an artist (1807-1827), Charles Richard (1809-c.1880), William, Junior (fl.1827-1851), Louisa Frances, and Emily Elizabeth. The name of the other daughter is unknown. One daughter married Henry Courtney Selous, the painter.

Plate 117. **Joseph Lee** *after Van Dyck, Lady Dorothy Percy (d.1650), enamel, 9½ins. Signed on the front: 'Jo Lee' and on the reverse: 'The effigies of Lady Dorothy Percy / daughter to Henry 9th Earl of Northumberland / and wife of Robert, Earl of Leicester / Ant Van Dyk / Pinxit 1626 / Painted by / Joseph Lee 1832.' This is an exceptionally fine enamel by Lee.* Courtesy Sotheby's.

Plate 118B. **J. Simpson**, *portrait of an unknown lady, enamel on porcelain, 4¼ins., c.1840. Signed on the reverse.* Courtesy Sotheby's.

Plate 118A. **J. Haslem**, *Princess Luise Marie Elisabeth (1838-1923), daughter of Prince Friedrich Wilhelm Ludwig (1797-1888), and his wife Maria Luise Augusta Catherine, of Saxe-Weimar-Eisenach, enamel, 2⅛ins. Signed and inscribed on the reverse: 'H.R.H. The Princess Louise / daughter of the Prince and Princess of Prussia / Aetatis 12 / Painted by John Haslem / after Frans Winterhalter / 1851.' Miniatures by Haslem are scarce. Princess Luise (whose father succeeded as King of Prussia 1861-1888), married on 20th September, 1856, Friedrich I, Grand Duke of Baden (1826-1907).* Courtesy Christie's.

Plate 118C. **W. Essex** *after Lawrence, Arthur Wellesley, 1st Duke of Wellington (1769-1852), enamel, 2½ins. Inscribed and dated on the reverse: '1841.' Sir Thomas Lawrence exhibited the original portrait in 1822. Other versions exist.* Courtesy Sotheby's.

Plate 118D. **W. Corden**, *portrait of an unknown man, enamel on porcelain, 5⅜ins. Signed on the reverse: 'Painted by W. Corden / April 1823.' This is a good example of a miniature on porcelain.* Courtesy R. Bayne Powell.

Plate 118E. **H.P. Bone**, *after G. Hayter, miniature of Matilda Strachan, enamel, 6⅝ins. Fully inscribed on the reverse with the sitter's name and dated: 'London Octʳ 1834.'* Courtesy Sotheby's.

H.P. Bone's work is so close to that of his father that, but for the signature, it is difficult to attribute with accuracy. H.P. Bone almost always signed his miniatures in full on the reverse, often adding the name of the painter if the work was after another artist. Many of his miniatures are very large and in some cases, due to the size, they have cockled slightly in the firing. He was a member of the Associated Artists in Watercolours from 1807-1808. He was appointed enamel painter to the Queen, the Duchess of Kent and the Princess Victoria in 1833, and to Prince Albert in 1841. According to Basil Long, Bone executed a few miniature copies on card. A number of his works are in the Spencer Collection at Althorp. He painted an attractive oblong miniature of his daughter, Louisa Frances, which is fully inscribed and dated on the reverse 1832 (Plate 116D). A good enamel by Bone was Lot 84 at Sotheby's, 10th November, 1969. It was fully inscribed on the reverse: 'Matilda Strachan / London Octr 1834. Painted by Henry Pierce Bone / Enamel Painter to her Majesty & their Royal Highnesses the Duchess of Kent & Princess Victoria / ; from a Picture by G. Hayter' (Plate 118E). Little information seems to have been preserved about his life or that of his family. He died in London on 21st October, 1855.

Like his father he used bright fresh colours, and the majority of his miniatures are good, but towards the end of his life the quality deteriorated slightly and became rather dull and uninspired. Miniatures by him are now very sought after and realise high prices. Examples of his work are in many private collections, and in the Victoria and Albert Museum. (Colour Plate 13D.)

William Bone, Senior (fl.1815-1843) was a son of Henry Bone. He is presumed to have been taught by his father, and exhibited at the Royal Academy and Society of British Artists, 1815-1843. He executed miniatures on ivory and enamel, and a "portrait for a ring". He copied the works of H.P. Bone, and R.T. Bone, and J. Jackson the portrait painter. His

Plate 119A (right). **J. Severn,** *E. Elton Esq., ivory, 3¼ins. Inscribed on the reverse: 'To E. Elton Esqr / from Joseph Severn / Rome April 22nd 1823.' Miniatures by Severn are very rare.* Courtesy B.W. Cave-Browne-Cave.

Plate 119B (far right). **John Cox Dillman Engleheart** *(1782/4-1862), self-portrait, ivory, 3½ins. Signed and dated on the reverse: '1821.' A sketch similar to this miniature and dated the same year was painted by his uncle, G. Engleheart.* Private Collection.

Plate 119C (left). **Sir W.J. Newton,** *portrait of an unknown man, ivory, 3½ins. Signed and inscribed on the reverse: 'Wm J. Newton / Pinxᵗ / 6 Duke Sᵗ / Sᵗ James's / 1812.' This is a well painted and strong portrait by Newton.* Private Collection.

Plate 119D (right). **W.M. Bennett.** *Henrietta, Countess Cathcart, née Mather (d.1872), ivory, 4⅝ins., c.1830. Signed on the reverse: 'W. Bennett Delint / Peebles.' The sitter was the wife of General Charles Murray, 2nd Earl Cathcart. This is an attractive miniature and gives a good idea of period costume.* Courtesy R. Bayne Powell.

miniatures on ivory are usually better than those on enamel. A good example of an unknown young man, is in the collection of F. Joachim. It is signed in full on the front: 'WBone', the first two letters being in monogram (Plate 116C).

William was appointed enamel painter to the King of Hanover in 1842. He seems to have worked from 15 Berners Street, Oxford Street. His work is not as good as that of his father or his brothers, and often the colouring is a little hard. His usual signature is: 'WB' (monogram), 'W. Bone' (the first two letters conjoined), or in full on the reverse. An enamel miniature of Warren Hastings, by Bone, after an engraving by W. Bromley, Senior, was lot 13 at Sotheby's on 25th November, 1974 (Plate 116B). Examples of William Bone's work are in the Wallace Collection, London, the Liverpool Museum and the Victoria and Albert Museum.

William Bone, Junior (fl.1827-1851) was the son of H.P. Bone, and was presumably taught by him. Works by him are scarce, and have never attracted much attention. He copied the works of Constable, Reynolds, Lawrence, Rubens, etc., and, as far as I know, only painted on enamel. He exhibited at the Royal Academy and Society of British Artists, 1827-1851. His early exhibits were of shells and china. Examples of his work are in the Victoria and Albert Museum, and include an enamel portrait of H. Bone, after H.P. Bone, dated 1845. This is illustrated in *A Dictionary of British Miniature Painters,* on Plate 24, no. 74.

Charles Richard Bone (1809-c.1880) was the son of H.P. Bone. He entered the Royal Academy Schools on 21st April, 1828, and was awarded a large silver medal in 1825 by the Society of Arts for a miniature (copy), and another in 1827 for a miniature portrait. He exhibited at the Royal Academy, British Institution, and Society of British Artists, 1826-1848. Charles painted miniatures on ivory and enamel, and was a competent artist. Some of his works show the influence of Lawrence; the draughtsmanship is good, and I have seen at least one which was painted in the manner of

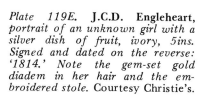

Plate 119E. **J.C.D. Engleheart,** *portrait of an unknown girl with a silver dish of fruit, ivory, 5ins. Signed and dated on the reverse: '1814.' Note the gem-set gold diadem in her hair and the embroidered stole.* Courtesy Christie's.

Andrew Robertson. He sometimes copied the works of old masters: one of Guido Reni's 'Beatrice Cenci' is in the Victoria and Albert Museum, and is signed on the reverse: 'C.R. Bone. Feb^r / 1842.' A fine example of his work is in the collection of Mrs. Hamilton; it represents Captain Richard H. King, and is signed on the front: 'CRB' (monogram) '1830', and on the reverse: 'Portrait of Capt R.H. King. R.N. / Painted by C.R. Bone / 47 Charlotte Street Portman Square / London 1830' (Plate 116A).

William Essex (1784-1869) was another good enamellist of this period. There is no information regarding his early life and training. He exhibited at the Royal Academy, British Institution, Society of British Artists, Old Water Colour Society, etc., from 1818-1864. He painted portraits, and is noted for his paintings of dogs, many of which are set in tie-pins. He copied the works of other artists. He is reputed to have drawn small sketches of dogs on vellum before painting reduced copies on enamel on a gold base and painted under a magnifying glass. He also painted miniatures on ivory, and some flower and historical subjects. He was appointed enamel painter to Queen Victoria in 1839, and to the Prince Consort in 1841. He died at Brighton on 29th December, 1869. The majority of his miniatures are signed in full on the reverse, rather in the manner of the Bone family, with details regarding the sitter and name of the artist if it was a copy. He had a son, W.B. Essex (c.1823-1852), who followed his father's profession. J.W. Bailey (1831-1914), and W.B. Ford (1832-1922) were his pupils. The size of his works varied: some are quite large. A pair of miniatures representing Mr. and Mrs. William Catt was sold at Christie's on 18th November, 1969. They were both fully inscribed by Essex and described as 'My father' and 'My mother'; the date of his birth makes this impossible, as Mr. Catt died in 1853, aged seventy-six, and Mrs. Catt in 1823, aged forty-six; see *Dictionary of British Miniature Painters,* p.264. Possibly he lodged with them or they were in some way responsible for his welfare.

Plate 120A. **W. Egley,** *Harriet, née Thornton (d.1832), wife of John Thornton, 9th Earl of Leven, ivory, 4½ins. Signed in monogram and dated: 'WE / 1828.' Courtesy Christie's.*

Plate 120B. **W. Egley,** *Master Henry Thornton Pearse, ivory, 6ins. Signed and dated on the pillar: 'WEgley (monogram) / 1840' and signed in full and dated: '1840' on the reverse. Standing in a garden with a spaniel puppy. Courtesy Sotheby's.*

Plate 120C. **R. Easton,** *three unknown children, ivory, 4½ins. With a curtain and landscape background. Miniatures by Easton are very rarely signed. Courtesy Sotheby's.*

Plate 120D. **H. Collen,** *portrait of an unknown man, ivory, 3¾ins. Signed on the front: 'H. Collen 1835.' Courtesy F. Joachim.*

Plate 121A. **A.E. Chalon, R.A.,** *Lady Wigram, née Eleanor Watt (1767-1841), 2nd wife of Sir Robert Wigram, by whom she had twenty-three children, ivory, 3¼ins. Signed in monogram: 'AEC. R.A.', the C encircling the A and E. Chalon exhibited miniatures of Lady Wigram at the R.A. in 1819, 1823 and 1826.* Courtesy Christie's.

Plate 121B. **F. Harding,** *portrait of an unknown lady, ivory, 8½ins. Signed and dated: 'F. Harding 1833.' This is typical of interior scenes of the period, with heavy curtain draperies. The sitter's costume is interesting as is her jewellery.* Courtesy F. Joachim.

Plate 121C (above). **W. Barclay,** *portrait of an elderly lady, ivory, 5½ins. Signed and dated: 'WBarclay 1833.' Note the large bonnet, tied under her chin, and a pair of spectacles in her left hand.* Private Collection.

Plate 121D (right). **W. Barclay,** *miniature of an unknown lady, ivory, 5½ins. Signed and dated: 'W. Barclay 1831.' This is another portrait which is interesting for its costume. Note the sitter's large-brimmed hat trimmed with plumes and ribbons and her outer garment edged with fur.* Courtesy Christie's.

An attractive miniature by Essex of the Princess Victoria (later Queen Victoria) is fully inscribed on the reverse; it shows the Princess as a child of five, after a painting by William Fowler, and was painted by Essex in 1858. He must have had a daughter named Hannah (after Mrs. Catt), as a self-portrait, sold at Sotheby's on 17th April, 1961, was inscribed on the reverse: 'Portrait of Wm Essex Enamel Painter to Her Majesty and H.R.H. Prince Albert, 1857. With Father's best love to Hannah.' Examples of his work are in many private collections, and in the Ashmolean Museum, Oxford, the National Portrait Gallery, Dublin, and the Victoria and Albert Museum, (Colour Plate 35B and Plate 118C.)

Joseph Lee (1780-1859) was born on 16th January, 1780, the second son of John Lee of Islington, Middlesex, and his wife, Rachel, née Oldroyd (1740-1822). Joseph is said to have started life in business but, finding that he was unsuccessful in this sphere, turned to art. He is believed to have been self-taught, and to have studied the work of Zincke upon which he based his own. He painted miniatures on enamel and a few portraits in watercolour; some were from life, but the majority were copies from the works of other artists such as Van Dyck, Petitot, Van der Helst, Romney, Boit, etc.

He exhibited at the Royal Academy, 1809-1853, and at the Society of British Artists in 1824, from various London addresses including 21 Seymour Place. By his wife, Anne, who died on 27th February, 1827, he had eight children. In spite of the fact that he was appointed enamel painter to the Princess Charlotte of Wales, and to H.R.H. the Duke of Sussex, he does not seem to have been financially very successful and, towards the end of his life, was receiving an allowance from a nephew, Charles Lee, an architect. He is traditionally supposed to have carried an enamel miniature of Napoleon I in his pocket as a show piece! He died on 26th December, 1859, at 13 Victoria Place, Gravesend. Many of his works are attractive and well-painted, and the colouring pleasing. His enamels are very difficult to attribute accurately and, unless signed, are often wrongly identified. A large miniature of Lady Dorothy Percy, after Van Dyck, was Lot 47, at Sotheby's, on 25th November, 1974. It was signed on the front: 'Jo Lee' and fully inscribed on the reverse: 'The effigies of the Lady Dorothy Percy / daughter to Henry 9th Earl of Northumberland / and wife of Robert, Earl of Leicester / Ant Van Dyk / Pinxit 1626 / Painted by / Joseph Lee 1832' (Plate 117). Examples of his work are in many private collections, including that of H.M. the Queen, and in the Wallace Collection, London, the National Gallery, Dublin, and the Victoria and Albert Museum. (Colour Plate 14.)

A few artists who worked during the nineteenth century painted miniatures on porcelain, and were, as far as I know, all connected in some way with one or other of the china factories. The following three are best known, but there may well be others who are as yet unrecorded.

William Corden (1797-1867) was born at Ashbourne, Derbyshire, on 28th November, 1797. Nothing is known of his early life, nor the date on which he became an apprentice at the Derby China Factory (now the Royal Crown Derby). He was taught to paint landscapes, but turned to painting portraits and figure subjects and finally devoted his time to portrait painting. He executed portraits in oils as well as miniatures on porcelain plaques, ivory and enamel. He left the Derby works in c.1820, having painted, shortly before he left, the greater part of a dessert service with subjects taken from

Plate 122. **G.P. Harding, F.S.A.,** *The Cumberland Family, watercolour on paper, 11½ins. This painting is after part of a contemporary triptych which formerly hung at Appleby Castle. The original was finished in 1646, from family portraits of c.1589. This drawing is signed: 'G.P.Harding fecit', and represents the centre panel of 'The Great Picture' as it is called, of which there was once a second version at Skipton.* Courtesy Sotheby's.

Plate 123A. **M.A. Chalon, (Mrs. Moseley),** *General Sir James R. Steadman Sayer, K.C.B., as a young man, ivory, 4½ins. Signed in full on the reverse: 'J.R.S. Sayer Esq. / 1st Regt Dragoon Guards painted by Mrs. Henry Moseley / 52 Upper Charlotte St. Fitzroy Square.' This is a good miniature by Maria Chalon whose works are well worth acquiring.* Private Collection.

Thurston's illustrations for Thomas Tegg's edition of Shakespeare's plays (1812). Corden worked in the vicinity of Derby, and also in Nottingham. In 1829 he went to Windsor and obtained the patronage of the Marchioness of Cunningham, who introduced him to the Court. He painted a few miniatures for Queen Victoria which were not considered to be very successful but, in spite of this, the Prince Consort sent him to Coburg in 1844 to copy some full size portraits of his ancestors, and in this he was assisted by his son whose name is not recorded. In c.1854 Corden obtained work in the Staffordshire potteries, and later became an assistant to a Mr. Scaife, a miniature painter and photographer. They combined enamelling and photography but this was not a success. Corden retired to live in Nottingham, where he died on 18th June, 1867. A number of his miniatures are illustrated by Gilhespy in *Derby Porcelain,* 1961. A good miniature on porcelain, of an unknown man, is in the collection of Robert Bayne Powell. It is signed on the reverse: 'Painted by W. Corden / April 1823' (Plate 118D).

John Haslem (1808-1884) was born in Carrington, Cheshire, in February, 1808; he received his education locally and was then, at the age of fourteen, sent to an uncle in Derby and became an apprentice to George Hancock at the Derby china works. Haslem practised drawing in his spare time and executed portraits, flowers, etc., and miniatures on enamel and porcelain. He also painted in watercolour, and copied the works of old masters in miniature and a few portraits from life. He went to London in 1835, and became a pupil of E.T. Parris. He exhibited at the Royal Academy and Society of British Artists, 1836-1876. In 1843 he was awarded a silver medal by the Society of Arts. He was patronised by the Royal family, including Queen Victoria, the Prince Consort, the Duchess of Gloucester and the Duke of Sussex. In 1876 he published *The Old Derby China Factory,* which is still a valuable source of reference. He died in Derby in 1884.

Plate 123B. **Sir W.J. Newton,**
an unknown young man,
ivory, 4½ins. Ex. Holzscheiter
Collection.

Miniatures by Haslem are scarce. Those I have seen on either enamel or porcelain have been well painted; he achieved a soft, smooth modelling and drew well. An attractive miniature on enamel of the Princess Louise was Lot 11 at Christie's on 16th November, 1976. It is signed on the reverse in full: 'H.R.H. The Princess Louise / daughter of the Prince and Princess of Prussia / Aetatis 12 / Painted by John Haslem / After Frans Winterhalter / 1851' (Plate 118A). An enamel miniature of Wellington by Haslem is in the Ashmolean Museum, Oxford. It is signed and dated 1852. One of Prince Albert is in the Derby Art Gallery.

John Simpson (1811-d. aft. 1871) was another miniaturist who painted some miniatures on porcelain. Little is known about him but he was presumably related to the William Page Simpson (fl.1859-1877) whose address, 3 Royal Hill, Queen's Road, Bayswater, he shared in various years. Simpson worked at the Minton Porcelain Works from 1837-1847, where he was noted for his figure subjects. In 1847 he left and moved to London where he became a successful miniaturist. He painted portraits on enamel and porcelain from life and from photographs, as well as executing some after the works of other artists such as Lawrence, Sir W.C. Ross and Winterhalter. He exhibited at the Royal Academy and Society of British Artists from a number of different addresses in London, from 1847-1871. In

Colour Plate 33.

A. **Cornelius B. Durham,** *an unknown girl, ivory, 3½ins. Signed on the front: 'CD,' and on the reverse: 'The Little English Girl / Painted by Cornelius Durham.' This was exhibited at the R.A. in 1839.*

B. **George Patten, A.R.A.,** *an unknown lady, ivory, 3⁷⁄₈ins. Signed on the front: 'G. Patten / 1832,' and on the reverse: 'Geo Patten pinxt / 59 Berners St. / Oxford St. / London.'*

C. **Miss Eliza Sharpe,** *Mrs. William Walker, née Elizabeth Reynolds (1800-1876), miniaturist, ivory, 3½ins.*

D. **James Holmes, Junior,** *Lorenzo George Moore, ivory, 4¹⁄₈ins. Signed on the reverse: 'Painted by James Holmes Jun / Sept 1842 / 15 Wilton St / Belgrave Sq.'*

Courtesy R. Bayne Powell.

A
B

C
D

1860 he exhibited an enamel of 'the late Herbert Minton'. He usually signed his miniatures: 'John Simpson', or: 'Simpson' on the reverse, often followed by a date. His miniatures are well painted and colourful, but occasionally lack draughtsmanship. A miniature on porcelain of Queen Victoria after Winterhalter, signed on the reverse and dated 1845, was sold at Christie's on 28th June, 1966. A number of family miniatures including a self-portrait, one of his wife, and one of Ellen Simpson, painted in 1863, are in the Victoria and Albert Museum. A miniature of an unknown lady by him, on enamel and signed on the reverse, was sold at Sotheby's a few years ago (Plate 118B).

William Mineard Bennett (c.1778-1858) was born at Exeter. Nothing is known about his early life, nor when he came to London. He was a pupil of Sir Thomas Lawrence, and exhibited at the Royal Academy, 1812-1816, when his address was 58 Frith Street, Soho. He became a successful artist and painted in oils and executed drawings and miniatures. His interests included music and literature. Bennett must have been working in Scotland in c.1830, as a miniature of Henrietta, Countess of Cathcart, in the collection of R. Bayne Powell, is signed in full on the reverse: 'Henrietta, Countess Cathcart / W. Bennett Delint / Peebles.' It was painted c.1830, and is an attractive example of his work (Plate 119D). In 1835-1844 he was in Paris, where he was decorated by Louis XVIII. Whilst there he was the protégé of Louis Philippe and the Duke of Berry. Bennett returned to England in 1844, and lived at Exeter, where he died at Hill's Buildings, St.

Plate 123C. **M.A. Chalon (Mrs. Moseley),** *Miss Katherine Davy, ivory, 5¼ins. Signed on the reverse and dated: 'Portrait of / Miss Katherine Davy / June 1848 / painted by / Mrs Henry Moseley / 52 Upper Charlotte St— / Fitzroy Square.' Signed miniatures by this artist are scarce.* Courtesy Sotheby's.

Plate 123D. **Sir W.J. Newton,** *Miss Fanny Hunt, ivory, 4½ins. Signed on the reverse and dated: '1837.' This attractive miniature was painted in the year Queen Victoria came to the throne.* Courtesy Christie's.

Sidwells, on 17th October, 1858. Works by him are scarce; those that I have seen have been attractive and well drawn. He sometimes shaded the faces of his sitters with a greenish tone. His usual signature is: 'W.M. Bennett', or: 'WMB', as in the case of one in the Victoria and Albert Museum. Some of his miniatures are circular in shape. Engravings after some of his portraits are in the British Museum.

John Cox Dillman Engleheart (1782/4-1862) was the son of John Dillman Engleheart by his second wife, Jane Parker, and a nephew of George Engleheart, whose pupil and assistant he became. John entered the Royal Academy Schools on 21st June, 1800, when his age was given as eighteen. He copied works by his uncle, Reynolds, Zincke, etc. He exhibited at the Royal Academy from 1801-1828, and is thought to have been working on his own from c.1807. He lived in Birmingham for a time, where he met Mary Barker of Edgbaston whom he married in 1811. They had four daughters and a son, who later became Sir J. Gardner D. Engleheart and died a centenarian in 1923. Engleheart is said to have travelled widely on the Continent. Apparently he gave up miniature painting in c.1828, and settled at Beechholm, Tunbridge Wells, where he remained until his death in 1862.

Many of Engleheart's miniatures are excellent, and painted very much in the manner of his uncle, but after he set up on his own they were slightly weaker and drawn with less assurance. He favoured rather darker colours, and often used a rectangular format. His works are signed either: 'JCDE' (monogram) and on the reverse: 'J.C.D. Engleheart', followed by an address and often a date, or only in full on the reverse. Long records seeing a miniature signed and dated 1812 on the reverse, and with a cursive: 'E' within a heart of gold on the front. He is reputed to have painted some miniatures on enamel but I have never seen any. Many of his portraits are on paper. His miniatures of ladies tend to be rather better than those of men. One of the finest I have seen is of an unknown lady in a landscape, holding a sheet of music; it is painted in strong fresh colours and has pleasing flesh tints. It is fully inscribed on the reverse: 'C Dillman Engleheart / 1826 / Pinxit / 88 Newman Street / London' (Colour Plate 34). A self-portrait in miniature is in the Engleheart family collection, and is signed and dated: '1821' (Plate 119B). A good pair of miniatures of an unknown officer and his wife was Lot 82 at Sotheby's on 22nd February, 1971, and one of a lady in classical dress, holding a bowl of fruit, was Lot 52, at Christie's, on 14th December, 1971 (Plate 119E). Examples of his work are in many private collections, and in the Victoria and Albert Museum, the Glynn Vivian Art Gallery, Swansea, the Liverpool Museum, and the Bernard Falk Collection, the Royal Pavilion, Brighton.

William Egley (1798-1870) was born in Doncaster. He began his career in a London publishing firm, but decided to take up painting. Having had no initial training in art he was self-taught, and had a struggle to gain recognition. He exhibited at the Royal Academy, Society of British Artists, etc., from 1824-1869, from various London addresses, and seems to have remained in London until his death on 19th March, 1870. His work varies a lot; much of it is very good, and reminiscent of Sir William Charles Ross. He usually signed his miniatures in full on the reverse, followed by an address and a date. Occasionally as in the case of one of Harriet Thornton, wife of John, 9th Earl of Leven, which was sold at Christie's on 28th October, 1970,

Plate 124A (left). Attributed to **S.J. Rochard**, *Sir Thomas Makdougall Brisbane, K.C.B. (1773-1860), ivory, 3¼ins. Signed: 'Rochard 1819.' The sitter is wearing the insignia of the K.C.B. and the Peninsular Gold Cross and bar.* Courtesy Sotheby's.

Plate 124B (right). **J.G.P. Fischer,** *George IV, when Prince Regent, ivory, 3ins. This is a fine miniature by Fischer whose works are scarce.* Courtesy National Portrait Gallery, Alan Evans Bequest.

Plate 124C (right). **Sir G. Hayter, K.S.L.,** *an unknown man, ivory, 2⁹/16ins. Signed: 'GH.'* Courtesy Victoria and Albert Museum.

Plate 124D. **F.T. Rochard,** *Miss Blood, ivory, 4¹⁷/32ins. Inscribed and dated on the reverse: 'Peint par Fᶜⁱˢ Rochard / 19 Howland Street / Fitzroy Sqʳᵉ / July 1833.' Unless signed it is difficult to identify the works of F.T. Rochard and those of his brother S.J. Rochard.* Courtesy Victoria and Albert Museum.

Plate 124E. **S.J. Rochard,** *miniature of a young lady, ivory, 5¾ins. Signed and dated: 'Rochard pinxt July 1832.' It is interesting to compare this portrait with Plate 124D.* Courtesy Sotheby's.

418

Plate 125A. **E.E. Kendrick,** *portrait of a young boy, ivory, 2⁷/₈ins. One of a pair, each signed and dated in full on the reverse: '1836.' See Plate 125C.* Courtesy Sotheby's.

Plate 125B. **Anne Hayter,** *Sarah E.C. Fitzclarence, née Gordon, wife of Lord Augustus Fitzclarence and daughter of Lord Henry Gordon, ivory, 4¹/₈ins. Signed: 'Anne Hayter / 1826 / London.' This is an attractive example of the work of an artist whose miniatures are scarce.* Courtesy R. Bayne Powell.

Plate 125C. **E.E. Kendrick,** *a young boy, brother to the child in Plate 125A, ivory, 2⁷/₈ins. Signed and dated in full on the reverse: '1836.'* Courtesy Sotheby's.

he signed in monogram on the front: 'WE / 1828' (Plate 120A). A good one of Master Henry Thornton Pearse, by Egley, was sold at Sotheby's Belgravia on 21st October, 1976; the child is standing in a landscape with a dog at his feet. It is signed, and dated in full on the reverse 1840, and was exhibited at the Royal Academy in 1841, No. 768 (Plate 120B). Egley was married twice but the names of his wives are not known. He had a son, William Maw Egley (1827?-1916), who followed his father's profession. A portrait of Egley by his son is in the British Museum. The Liverpool Museum has eight miniatures by Egley of Queen Victoria and other members of the Royal family, all painted in 1851. They are similar in style to works by Sir W.C. Ross. Other examples are in the Victoria and Albert Museum.

Reginald Easton (1807-1893) was another artist who was self-taught. He started as an engraver, but changed to painting portraits and miniatures in watercolour. He exhibited at the Royal Academy, 1835-1889, and succeeded in building up a good practice. He was patronised by the Royal Family, and was particularly good at painting children. Although we know that he was in Leamington in 1850, living at 4 Somers Place, Easton worked principally in London. His sitters included Prince Christian Victor of Schleswig-Holstein, and the Princesses Victoria, Elizabeth and Irene of Hesse. A miniature of William IV, signed: 'R. Easton', is in the collection of H.M. The Queen.

Easton produced some very attractive miniatures; the features are softly painted and the draughtsmanship good. The sitters' features and costume are delineated in great detail, often against a landscape background with autumn colouring which is more broadly treated with a fuller brush. He shaded the flesh parts with pale, soft, greyish blue strokes, but did not use any stippling. I have seen, in a private collection, a most attractive pair of miniatures of children by him. Examples of his work are in the National Portrait Gallery, and the Victoria and Albert Museum. (Plate 120C.)

Henry Collen (1798-d. aft. 1872) was born at St. Albans. He entered the Royal Academy Schools on 1st September, 1820, and won a silver medal in 1821. He studied under Sir George Hayter, whose work he sometimes copied. Collen exhibited at the Royal Academy and Society of British Artists from 1820-1872. He had numerous important patrons, and was appointed miniature painter to Queen Victoria and the Duchess of Kent. Some of his work is good, but much is of uneven quality. He often used a scraper, particularly in the hair, and painted his sitters against a rather drab background. His most usual signature is one scratched on the front of the miniature, followed by a date, as on the one in a private collection, signed: 'H. Collen 1841', and on the reverse in full (Plate 132E). Sometimes the signature has the: 'H' and 'C' forming a monogram, and at other times he signed in capital letters: 'H. COLLEN'. At least one is recorded where he inscribed the date on the collar of the sitter. A miniature of a lady, signed and dated 1829, was Lot 1 at Sotheby's in Zurich, on 15th November, 1977. One of an unknown man, signed and dated: '1835', is in the collection of F. Joachim (Plate 120D). A number of his works are at Windsor Castle. Some engravings after him are in the British Museum, and miniatures by him are in the National Portrait Gallery and the Victoria and Albert Museum.

Alfred Edward Chalon, R.A. (1780-1860) was a native of Geneva, where he was born on 15th February, 1780, of French descent. He came to London as a young man and entered the Royal Academy Schools on 12th August, 1797, his father having brought him to England when he became a

Plate 125D. **S.P. Denning,** *an unknown man, ivory, 5½ins., c.1825. Signed on the front: 'S.P.D.' This miniature is slightly reminiscent of the works of A.E. Chalon.* Courtesy Mrs. E.M. Hamilton.

Plate 125E. **A. Tidey,** *portrait of an unknown man, ivory, 7½ins. Signed and dated on the reverse: 'Alf Tidey pinx^t 1842.' This is a fair example of the work of an artist who was not of outstanding ability.* Private Collection.

Plate 126. **Sir W.C. Ross, R.A.,** *Lady Augusta Haly-Burton, her children and a dog, ivory, 11ins., c.1840. The portrait is painted on two long sections of ivory, and shows the family seated in a room with a view of a lake and landscape through a window. It is a particularly attractive miniature on this scale.* Courtesy Christie's.

professor at the Royal Military College, Sandhurst. The family settled in Kensington. Chalon had intended to go into commerce but abandoned it for art. He exhibited at the Royal Academy and British Institution, etc., from 1801-1860. In 1808 he became a member of the Associated Artists in Watercolours and, in the same year he and his brother, J.J. Chalon, founded a famous sketching society. The brothers remained bachelors, and kept house together for many years. Alfred was elected A.R.A. in 1812, and R.A. in 1816. He was a very successful artist and was appointed painter in watercolours to the Queen. Besides painting miniatures he also executed subject pictures in oils and is said to have been a witty companion and a clever musician. Some of his portraits on paper are quite large, as in the case of a portrait of Mary Frances, Lady Owen, of Taynton House, Glos., which was exhibited at the Fine Art Society Ltd., in 1977. It measured 13⅜ins. by 11¾ins., and was encased in a large wooden folding frame. The portrait was inscribed: 'A.E. Chalon.R.A. 1830', and inscribed on the mount: 'Jour à droite'. This portrait is a very good example of the prevailing fashion for ladies, with the wide neckline, puffed sleeves, tight waist, and hair piled up in bunches on the top of the head (Plate 131B). A good miniature of Lady Wigram, née Eleanor Watt, by Chalon was sold at Christie's on 18th June, 1974. It was signed on the front in monogram: 'AEC. R.A.', the: 'C'

Plate 127A (above). **G.P. Harding, F.S.A.,** *David Garrick, (1717-79), actor, pencil on paper, 4¼ins. Signed: 'G.P. Harding f.' This is one of Harding's many drawings ,after earlier portraits.* Courtesy Sotheby's.

Plate 127B (right). **Hugh Ross,** *Thomas Parker, watercolour on paper, 9ins. Signed on the reverse of the frame: 'Drawn by / Hugh Ross / 1841.', and in a later hand: 'Thomas Parker / younger brother of Admiral Parker.'* Private Collection.

encircling the: 'AE'. This again is a good guide to the type of headdress and tippet worn at the time (Plate 121A). On 3rd October, 1972, Christie's sold a good miniature of Lady Blunt, which was signed in full on the front: 'A. Chalon'. Chalon died at Campden Hill, Kensington, on 3rd October, 1860, and was buried at Highgate. His work varies a lot in quality, some of his earlier miniatures being among his best. Later he took to using thick touches of opaque white on the lace and costume. A chalk self-portrait of Chalon, as well as other drawings and numerous engravings after him, are in the British Museum. Examples of his work are in many private collections, and in the National Portrait Gallery, and the Victoria and Albert Museum. (Colour Plate 23A.)

William Barclay, Junior (1797-1859) is said to have been a native of London, where he worked mainly as a miniaturist. He entered the Royal Academy Schools on 15th June, 1819, and is thought to have worked for a time in Paris, copying pictures in The Louvre. Barclay was, in my opinion, a clever miniaturist, and one who has not yet had the attention he deserves. I have seen several examples of his portraits in recent years, and all of them have been well-painted and shown character. It has been suggested that he worked in the manner of A.E. Chalon, but I think that his style is much closer to that of Sir W.C. Ross or Maria Chalon (Mrs. Moseley). He used a pink flesh colour, shaded with soft blue brush strokes; the hair is painted with a few swift strokes, but great attention is given to the costume. One fine example of an elderly lady wearing a high, frilly lace cap and lace collar is signed in full: 'WBarclay 1833', scratched on the front (Plate 121C). It was one of a set of three sold together in 1977; the other two were almost certainly this lady's son and daughter and they were all very well-painted. He exhibited at the Royal Academy and Society of British Artists, 1832-1856, and at the Paris Salon, 1831-1859. Examples of his work are in private collections. One, of an unknown lady, signed on the front, is in the Alan Evans Collection at the Victoria and Albert Museum (Colour Plate 20A. See also Plate 121D).

George Perfect Harding, F.S.A. (c.1780-1853) was the son of Sylvester Harding (1751-1809), also a miniaturist. George exhibited at the Royal Academy and Society of British Artists from 1802-1840. Harding is best known for his copies of big portraits and groups, which he executed in London and on visits to large country houses. Many of them were made from oil portraits which he copied in watercolour on card or paper, on a small scale. He was a Fellow of the Society of Antiquaries from 1839-1847. Harding married late in life and had a large family, which he had difficulty in supporting. He became poor and was obliged to sell all his accumulated works. He was a prolific artist, and one frequently sees examples of his works in the sale rooms. A large number were sold at Sotheby's on 16th December, 1974, comprising copies of many full-size portraits, including one of David Garrick, signed: 'G.P. Harding f.' (Plate 127A). There was also a copy of the 'Cumberland Family', after the central panel of 'The Great Picture', a triptych painted for Lady Anne Clifford in 1646 from family portraits of c.1589. This triptych formerly hung at Appleby Castle (Plate 122). Another version (since destroyed) was at Skipton Castle. Both were copied by Harding. He exhibited a self-portrait at the Royal Academy in 1813; it was probably the one which was engraved by J. Brown, a copy of which is in the British Museum. An interesting miniature in the manner of Isaac Oliver, supposedly of the Countess of Pembroke, by Harding, came into my possession recently. It is signed in monogram: 'GPH' (in gold), the letters being conjoined and the monogram encircled with four dots as in the manner of Oliver; it is a key piece as, were it not for the signature, it might well have been taken to be an earlier copy of a seventeenth century

Plate 127C. **J. Fisher,** *an unknown girl, watercolour on paper, 4⁷/₁₆ins. Signed and dated: 'J. Fisher / 1854.' This charming portrait is one of the few known examples by this artist.* **Present whereabouts unknown.**

Plate 127D. **Sir W.C. Ross, R.A.,** *Anker Smith Junior, pencil on paper, 10ins. Signed and dated: 'Mʳ Anker Smith — drawn by W.C.Ross / 1820.' The Smith and Ross families were related. Drawings by W.C. Ross are very scarce.* Courtesy B.W. Cave-Browne-Cave.

miniature. The portrait is well painted and the dress and ruff executed in great detail. This signed example has made it possible to authenticate several other works which had been puzzling experts for some time (Colour Plate 6C). The British Museum and the National Portrait Gallery have a number of small, highly finished watercolour portraits by Harding after other artists.

Sir George Hayter, K.S.L. (1792-1871) was born in London on 17th December, 1792, and was one of the children of Charles Hayter (1761-1835) and his wife, Martha Stevenson. George entered the Royal Academy Schools on 21st January, 1808, at the age of fifteen. In the same year he became a midshipman in the Navy but, in 1809, returned to an artistic career. He exhibited at the Royal Academy, British Institution, etc., from 1809-1859. Although he painted miniatures he is best known for his oil portraits and historical subjects. He was working in Southampton in c.1811, and in the following year became a member of the Associated Artists in Water Colours. He was awarded a premium of £200 by the British Institution in 1815 and went to Italy for three years, and again in 1826. By 1831 he had settled back in England. Hayter was appointed miniature and portrait painter to the Princess Charlotte and Prince Leopold of Saxe-Coburg and, in 1837, portrait and history painter to Queen Victoria, and was knighted in 1842. He was a member of the Academies of Rome, Bologna, Florence, Parma and Venice. Henry Collen was his pupil. His wife, too, is said to have painted miniatures. Hayter died on 18th January, 1871, at 238 Marylebone Road, London. He was a capable artist and drew accurately. Miniatures by him are scarce; they are usually signed: 'G.H.', sometimes followed by a date. There are numerous portrait drawings by Hayter in the British Museum, and engravings after his work. The National Portrait Gallery has drawings and portraits in oils by Hayter, including one of Queen Victoria and some portrait groups.

Miniatures by Sir George Hayter are in the Victoria and Albert Museum (Plate 124C).

Miss Anne Hayter (fl.1814-1830) was the daughter of Charles Hayter, and sister of Sir George Hayter and John Hayter, also a miniaturist. She was awarded premiums by the Society of Arts in 1814 and 1815, and exhibited at the Royal Academy, Old Water Colour Society, Society of British Artists, etc., from 1814-1830. Miniatures by her are rare, so it is difficult to describe her work. An attractive one of Sarah E.C. Fitzclarence, wife of Lord Augustus Fitzclarence and daughter of Lord Henry Gordon, is in the collection of Robert Bayne Powell. It is signed: 'Anne Hayter / 1826 / London' (Plate 125B).

Plate 127E. J. Fisher, an unknown lady, watercolour on paper, 6ins., c.1850. Signed: 'FISHER.' Another fine example by the artist who painted Plate 127C. Private Collection.

Miss Emma Eleonora Kendrick (c.1788-1871) was the daughter of Joseph Kendrick, the sculptor. She took up art and was awarded several prizes by the Society of Arts, and from 1811-1840 exhibited at the Royal Academy, Society of British Artists, Old Water Colour Society and New Water Colour Society. She became miniature painter to Princess Elizabeth of Hesse-Homburg, and to William IV in 1831. Her main works were miniatures and genre subjects in watercolour. In 1830 she published *Conversations on the Art of Miniature Painting*. She died on 6th April, 1871. She was not an outstanding miniaturist, and her draughtsmanship was often poor. Her portraits are usually signed in full on the reverse. Examples of her work are in the Victoria and Albert Museum. (Plates 125A and C.)

James Heath Millington (1799-1872) was born in Cork but spent his early years in England; he seems to have returned to Ireland for a time in 1821 and had rooms in 22 Patrick Street, Cork, where he set himself up as a miniaturist. He moved to Dublin in the same year, where he exhibited a portrait in oils. Millington must have returned to London sometime before the 1st April, 1826, when he entered the Royal Academy Schools where he won several prizes and a silver medal. He exhibited at the Royal Academy,

Plate 128A. **H. Gray,** called *Princess Helena Augusta Victoria (b.1846) daughter of Queen Victoria, ivory, 3⅝ins. This is a delightful study of a child, and bears a facial resemblance to one of Princess Helena painted by Winterhalter. It is signed and dated on the reverse: 'H. Gray 1855.'* Courtesy Donald C. Whitton, California.

British Institution and Society of British Artists, from 1831-1870, and was for a short time curator of the School of Painting at the Royal Academy. He died of a heart disease at 3 Chepstow Place, Bayswater, on 11th August, 1872. Miniatures by him are scarce; those I have seen have all been attractive. He may have been influenced by W. Etty, a fellow pupil at the Royal Academy Schools. Some of his works are reminiscent of the work of Cosway; one of Lady Anne Hudson, daughter of the 1st Marquess Townshend, which was sold at Christie's on 18th February, 1969, is a case in point, and is signed and dated: 'J.H.Millington 1818'. A very pretty miniature of a young girl, signed: 'J.H.M.' on the front, is in the Alan Evans Collection at the Victoria and Albert Museum (Colour Plate 22D). Occasionally he used a scratched signature. Some of his work is in the manner of A.E. Chalon.

Sir William John Newton (1785-1869) was born in London, and was the son of James Newton, an engraver. He was trained as an engraver but took up miniature painting in which he excelled. He is thought to have been a member of an artists' volunteer corps in 1803, and entered the Royal Academy Schools on 15th January, 1807; he exhibited at the Royal Academy and British Institution, from 1808-1863. Newton soon established a good practice, and became popular; his patrons included members of the Royal Family and titled persons, Members of Parliament and fellow artists. In 1822 he married Anne Faulder, by whom he had a son, H.R. Newton, an architect. Newton was appointed miniature painter to William IV and Queen Adelaide in 1833, and painter to Queen Victoria. He was knighted in 1837, the year of her accession. He executed some very large miniatures on big pieces of ivory joined together. These included 'The Marriage of Queen Victoria' and 'The Christening of the Prince of Wales', painted in 1845, which measured 27ins. by 37ins., but this size was not satisfactory owing to the effect change of temperature has on ivory. His work was certainly equal to that of Sir W.C. Ross and A. Robertson, and not inferior as has been suggested. He was a good draughtsman, and painted the flesh with fresh, natural colours modelled with yellowish shadows. His later works are probably better than those executed early in his career. Newton died on 22nd January, 1869, at 6 Cambridge Terrace, Hyde Park, London. He painted portraits in watercolour, miniatures on ivory, and drew portraits in chalk on paper. Two fine miniatures by him were exhibited in Edinburgh in 1965, representing Viscount and Viscountess Cardwell. Both were signed on the reverse and painted in 1838. His signature varies; sometimes it is written in cursive writing on the reverse: 'Wm J. Newton / Pinx^t / 6 Duke S^t / St James / 1812', as on the miniature of an unknown man in a private collection (Plate 119C). Other signatures are: 'W.I.N.' on the front in Roman capitals, or in full on the reverse with details of his appointments to the Royal Family. An attractive miniature of Miss Fanny Hunt, signed and dated 1837 on the reverse, was Lot 16 at Christie's, on 18th June, 1974 (Plate 123D). One of Mrs. Joseph Faulder (possibly a relative) is in the collection of F. Joachim; it is fully inscribed on the reverse: 'Portrait of Mrs. Joseph Faulders / W.J. Newton Pinxit / 8 Argyle Street. 1822.' This illustrates the slightly more tentative style of his earlier work. A collection of his works is at the Glynn Vivian Art Gallery, Swansea, and other examples at the British Museum, National Gallery, Dublin, and the Victoria and Albert Museum.

Simon Jacques Rochard (1788-1872) was the son of René Rochard, and his wife, née Talon. Simon was born in Paris on 28th December, 1788. His father evidently died young, and Simon drew crayon portraits when still a child in order to help to support his widowed mother and her twelve

Plate 128B. **H. Gray** *(1823-98), self-portrait, ivory, 2ins. Probably painted on a light photographic base.* Courtesy Donald C. Whitton, California.

Plate 128C. **Mrs. J.W. Gray,** *née Catherine Geddes (1796-1882), possibly a self-portrait, watercolour on card, 3ins., c.1850. Unlike her other paintings this portrait is painted with stippling and rather loose brush work.* Courtesy Donald C. Whitton, California.

Plate 128D. **Mrs. J.W. Gray, née Catherine Geddes,** *portrait of an unknown young lady, watercolour on paper, 14ins. Signed and dated on the reverse: 'By Catherine Gray 1876.' This is a charming portrait, the sitter is wearing a black dress, her hair tied with pink ribbon.* Courtesy Donald C. Whitton, California.

children. He studied engraving under Pierre N. Ransonnette (1745-1810), and miniature painting under Mille Bonnieu and L.F. Aubry, and is also said to have had some instruction from Isabey and J.F.L. Mérimée. He entered the Académie des Beaux-Arts, Paris, on 16th November, 1813, and copied miniatures for Augustin. He went to Brussels in 1815 to escape conscription: while there he sketched Wellington and the Duke of Richmond. In 1816 Simon came to London with letters of introduction from the Duke of Richmond and Lady Caroline Lamb. He exhibited at the Royal Academy, Society of British Artists and New Water Colour Society, from 1816-1845, and soon became popular; his sitters included the Princess Charlotte, and the Duke of Devonshire. Rochard painted chiefly miniatures, but also executed engravings and painted pictures in oils. His work was influenced by Lawrence and Reynolds. He married Henriette Petitjean, by whom he had a daughter who married an English officer. His wife remained abroad. Rochard became wealthy and collected old masters. In 1846 he returned to the Continent and settled in Brussels, where he exhibited at the Brussels Salon from 1848-1869, at the Paris Salon in 1852, and the Paris Exhibition of 1867. At the age of eighty he married as his second wife Henriette Pilton, by whom he had a son. He was nearly ruined by the failure of Moore's Bank and he died a few days later on 13th June, 1872, at 23 Rue des Douze Apôtres, Brussels.

Rochard was a good miniaturist who used pure, fresh colours and painted with a broad brush stroke. The flesh colours are pink, shaded with yellowish brown. He was one of the artists who used a lot of gum with his paints, and a scraper to indicate the lines in the hair. His brother, F.T. Rochard, also a miniaturist, painted in a very similar manner. Not all his miniatures are of equal quality and some give the appearance of being large pictures on a reduced size. The fact that both brothers tended to sign their miniatures: 'Rochard', without initials, has led to some confusion and identification is sometimes difficult. One of Sir John Rennie, F.R.S., signed and dated 1831, is in the Victoria and Albert Museum. A miniature of a lady, signed and dated July 1832 was lot 372 in the Heckett Collection, sold in New York by Sotheby Parke Bernet on 5th October, 1977 (Plate 124E). The same sale contained as Lot 377 a miniature of John Wheelwright Esq., signed and dated 1853. A good miniature of Sir Thomas Makdougall Brisbane, signed and dated 1819, was Lot 70 at Sotheby's, on 1st June, 1970 (Plate 124A). A miniature set in a hair bracelet, in a private collection, is attributed to S.J. Rochard, although F.T. Rochard is better known for executing miniatures for bracelets (Figure 19a). The British Museum has engraved portraits after S.J. Rochard, and examples of his work are in the Victoria and Albert Museum.

François Theodore Rochard (1798-1858) was born in France, the younger son of René Rochard, and brother of S.J. Rochard. He studied art in Paris, and joined his brother in London in c.1820; he exhibited at the Royal Academy, Society of British Artists, and New Water Colour Society, etc., from 1820-1855, becoming a member of the latter society in 1835. The Society of Arts awarded him a silver medal in 1823 for a copy of a portrait, and another for an oil copy of an historical subject. Like his brother he seems to have had eminent clients, and was patronised by royalty. He painted miniatures, portraits and genre subjects, and was one of the artists who specialised in executing miniatures for bracelets, so that many of his portraits are on a small scale. He married in c.1850 but the lady's name is not recorded. He was so successful that he was eventually able to retire on his savings and live in Notting Hill, where he died in 1858. Mrs. F. Dixon, née Cowell (fl.1851-1875), was his pupil. The miniatures painted by the two Rochards are very alike, and attributions are not always easy. François' work is slightly weaker than that of Simon and lacks something of his panache. François usually signed his works with his initials: 'F.R.' or: 'F.R^{d}', and sometimes he inscribed the portrait in full on the reverse, as in the case

Plate 128E. A. Gray, an unknown lady with a flower, ivory, 7⅞ ins., c.1850-60. This is a competent and colourful miniature by a hitherto unknown artist. The sitter, painted against a landscape background, is wearing a black jacket with a white lace collar over a full blue skirt, her chair draped with a matching shawl. Courtesy Donald C. Whitton, California.

of the one of Miss Blood in the Victoria and Albert Museum. This is signed: 'Peint par F^cis Rochard / 19 Howland Street / Fitzroy Sq^re / July 1833' (Plate 124D). François, like Simon, used a lot of gum with his paints. Some sketches for heads in the Victoria and Albert Museum are by one of the brothers, and the British Museum has engravings after F. Rochard.

Johann George Paul Fischer (1786-1875) was another artist who came from the Continent to work in England. He was born in Hanover, and was the son of an engraver. He became a pupil of H. Ramberg and assisted him to paint portraits, theatrical decorations and wall paintings. Fischer came to England in 1810 and worked chiefly in London and Cheltenham. He exhibited at the Royal Academy and Society of British Artists, from 1817-1852. He may have visited India, c.1848, as one of his exhibits in 1850 was of 'Mirza Mohan Lal, native of Cashmere'. He also exhibited portraits of other sitters connected with India, including one of Major-General Sir Joseph O'Halloran, K.C.B., of the Bengal Service, and 'An officer of the 4th Light Dragoons, Bombay.' He painted members of the Royal Family including Queen Victoria and Queen Charlotte. A good miniature of George IV, when Prince Regent, by Fischer is in The National Portrait Gallery (Plate 124B).

Plate 129A (left). **Maria Bellett Browne,** *Lady Elizabeth Jane D'Oyly, née Ross, 2nd wife of Sir Charles D'Oyly 7th Bart, ivory, 3¾ins., c.1820. Signed: 'MB.' This portrait was part of a collection of family miniatures sold in 1974. Only a small number of miniatures by Mrs. Browne are known.* Courtesy Sotheby's.

Plate 129B (right). **Maria Bellett Browne,** *Sir Charles D'Oyly, 7th Bart (1781-1845), son of Sir John Hadley D'Oyly, ivory, 2¾ins. Husband of the sitter in Plate 129A. Both these miniatures show Chinnery's influence.* Courtesy Sotheby's.

He died in London on 12th December, 1875. His works, which are seldom seen, are not of a very fine quality. His portraits are painted with fresh flesh tints, light shadows, long distinct brush strokes and a fair amount of gum; the backgrounds are often stippled. A miniature of Charlotte Augusta Matilda, Princess Royal, afterwards Queen of Würtemberg, is in the collection of the Bankers, Messrs. Coutts & Co. There are some examples of his work at Windsor Castle.

Stephen Poyntz Denning (1795-1864) is another artist whose works are very rarely seen. His parentage is unknown and he is supposed to have been a beggar boy. He studied under John Wright (d.1820), and exhibited at the Royal Academy, British Institution, Society of British Artists, etc., from 1814-1852. In 1821 he was appointed Curator of the Dulwich Gallery. He worked in London and Dulwich, and painted portraits in watercolour, miniatures, and executed some very good drawings in pencil. He was a talented artist who drew accurately and was able to portray character. Many of his miniatures on ivory are reminiscent of the work of A.E. Chalon. A good miniature on ivory of an unknown man is in the collection of Mrs. Hamilton. It is signed on the front: 'S.P.D', and was painted c.1825 (Plate 125D). Some of his miniatures are signed: 'S.P. Denning', scratched along the lower edge. Several portraits in watercolour are in the British Museum, and the Victoria and Albert Museum has a delightful group of the children of E. Bicknell, signed: 'S.P. Denning pinxit 1841'.

Maria A. Chalon (Mrs. Henry Moseley) (c.1800-1867) is probably best known under her maiden name. She was the daughter of Henry Barnard Chalon, the animal painter of London, whose wife was the sister of James Ward, R.A. Maria was taught art by her father and friends, and had an aptitude for music. She was premiated by the Society of Arts in 1813 and 1818, and exhibited at the Royal Academy from 1819-1840 under her maiden name, and from 1841-1866 as Mrs. Moseley. She also exhibited at the Society of British Artists, 1831-1835, and at the British Institution in 1863. She married Henry Moseley, a portrait painter, in c.1841. In c.1823 she became 'portrait paintress' to the Duke of York. Her sitters included such well-known persons as H.B. Chalon, James Ward, and John Tenniel. In 1851, she exhibited a miniature of her husband. She died in 1867.

Maria's works included miniatures in oils and watercolour, although I have never seen an example painted in oils. Her work is of a very high quality, and she has not yet had the attention she deserves. Some of her miniatures are influenced by the work of Sir W.C. Ross. Those of ladies are attractive and usually elegant. She used a pale pink flesh colour and modelled the features

Plate 129C. **J.W. Childe,** *a young Etonian, watercolour on paper, 7½ins. Signed: 'J.W.Childe.39 Bedford St / Strand.' This is an attractive portrait and well drawn.* Private Collection.

Plate 129E (above). **T.C. Wageman** *after Van Dyck, Charles I and the young Duke of Gloucester, watercolour on paper, 4¾ins. The majority of Wageman's works were pencil portraits for engravings.* Courtesy Sotheby's.

Plate 129D (left). **C.B. Durham,** *miniature of an unknown man, ivory, 6ins. Signed on the reverse and dated: '1835.' This was one of a pair by Durham sold in 1970.* Courtesy Christie's.

with a soft greyish blue. I have seen a number of her miniatures in which the backgrounds have had a mauvish blue colouring. She occasionally painted her sitters against a landscape, or in a panelled room. One of Miss Lee, in a private collection, is fully inscribed on the reverse: 'Portrait of / Miss Lee / painted by / Maria Chalon / July 1840' (Colour Plate 36B). A miniature of General Sir James R. Steadman Sayer, K.C.B., in a private collection, is signed in full on the reverse with her address (Plate 123A). An attractive miniature of Miss Katherine Davy, signed on the reverse and dated 1848 was Lot 90 at Sotheby's on 17th November, 1975; it is a good example of her soft manner of painting (Plate 123C).

Sir William Charles Ross, R.A. (1794/5-1860) was one of the greatest miniature painters of the nineteenth century. He was born in London on 3rd June, 1794/5, and was the son and pupil of William Ross (d. aft. 1842), whose family came from Scotland. Both his sister, Magdalena Ross, and his brother, Hugh Ross, were also miniaturists. William showed artistic ability at an early age, and was awarded prizes at the Society of Arts, 1807-1817, for drawings, historical paintings and original portraits. He entered the Royal Academy Schools in 1808, and won five silver medals. His main work lay in miniature painting, in which he excelled. Ross exhibited at the Royal Academy from 1809-1859. In 1814 he worked as an assistant to Andrew Robertson, to whom he was related on his mother's side. He worked for a time at the Portuguese Court. He was elected A.R.A. in 1838, and R.A. in 1842, and was knighted in the same year. In 1843 he won a premium of £100 in the Westminster Hall competition. Ross established a large practice and his patrons included Queen Victoria, the Prince Consort, their children, and other members of the Royal Family. A number of miniatures by him are

Colour Plate 34.
John Cox Dillman Engleheart, *an unknown lady in a landscape, holding a sheet of music, ivory, 6¼ins. Inscribed on the reverse: 'C Dillman Engleheart / 1826 / Pinxit / 88 Newman Street / London.' This is a particularly fine example of Engleheart's work and unusual in this setting.* Private Collection.

Plate 130B. **C.J. Basebe,** *an unknown officer, ivory, 4¾ins. Signed in full and dated: 'C.J.BASEBE. 1846.' The sitter is wearing the uniform of the 60th Corps (later the King's Royal Rifle Corps), with a crimson belt. This is a fine miniature by a little known artist.* Courtesy Christie's.

Plate 130A. **Miss M. Gillies,** *William Wordsworth (1770-1850) and his wife, Mary, née Hutchinson (1770-1859), ivory, 12ins., 1839. Two versions of this miniature once existed, but one was destroyed by fire.* Courtesy the late Mrs. D. Dickson.

Plate 130C. **W. Booth,** *Ann Ellen Garden (b.1826), Madelina Douglas Garden (b.1828) and Huntley Rothery Garden (b.1827), ivory, 4⅜ins. Signed in full and dated on the reverse: 'W.Booth— Pinxt / 16 Grafton Street Fitzroy Sq / London / August 1833.' Miniatures by Booth are scarce and his work little known.* Courtesy Christie's.

Plate 130D. **G.R. Ward,** *portrait of an unknown lady, ivory, 6½ins., c.1845. The sitter is wearing a white turban with gold tassels and a green silk dress. In her hand is a bouquet of summer flowers. A gold brooch is pinned at her bosom.* Courtesy Sotheby's.

in the collection of H.M. The Queen. He died unmarried on 20th January, 1860, having suffered a paralytic stroke in 1857. Long quotes an assessment of Ross which is as true today as when it was written: "Ross who was an extremely amiable and benevolent man, was one of the greatest English miniature-ptrs, and is likely in the future to be even more appreciated than he is today. He was an exquisite draughtsman and colourist; he designed skilfully, arranged gracefully, and used elaborate finish or bold treatment as required. His miniatures have the appearance of having been ptd. with ease and assurance. His painting-table was so placed that light came down aslant from behind, over his left shoulder, the sitter being in front of him rather to the right."

He was a prolific artist and painted over 2,200 miniatures. A good example of a drawing by him (which are not often seen) is of Mr. Anker Smith, son of Anker Smith, A.R.A., whose sister, Maria, was Sir William Ross's mother. The portrait is inscribed on the front: 'Mr Anker Smith — drawn by W.C. Ross / 1820' (Plate 127D). A fine miniature of Sir John Charles Dalrymple-Hay, 3rd Bart., was Lot 47 at Sotheby's on 29th April, 1974, and an attractive portrait of an unknown young lady was Lot 144 at Sotheby's on 25th November, 1974. This shows to perfection the hair style and fashion of the dresses worn at the time. A charming family group was Lot 85 at Christie's on 22nd March, 1977, when it realised £700. It represents Lady Augusta Haly-Burton, her three children and a dog, seated

Plate 131A. A.E. Chalon, R.A., *an unknown lady, ivory, 37/8 ins., c.1830.* Courtesy Victoria and Albert Museum.

Plate 131B. A.E. Chalon, R.A., *Mary Frances, Lady Owen of Taynton House, Gloucestershire, watercolour on paper, 13 3/8 ins. Signed and dated: 'A.E. Chalon. R.A. 1830' and inscribed on the mount: 'Jour à droite.' This very large and splendid miniature is encased in a wooden frame with folding doors.* Courtesy The Fine Art Society Ltd.

435

Plate 131C. **Edward Lobo Moira,** *Lady Suffield and her child, ivory, 17½ins., c.1857. Signed on the reverse. Lady Suffield was presumably Cecilia Annetta, née Baring, who married in May 1854, Charles Harbord, 5th Baron Suffield, and was Lady of the Bedchamber to Queen Alexandra. The cracks in the ivory due to changes of temperature can be seen in the illustration.* **Courtesy Christie's.**

on a sofa in front of a curtain with a lake landscape in the distance. It is 11ins. high, and painted on two long ivory sections (Plate 126). An attractive small portrait of Queen Victoria, set in a brooch, is inscribed on the reverse: 'London 1840 / Painted by / W.C. Ross. A.R.A. / Miniature Painter / To / The Queen;' it is in a private collection (Figure 20). A number of his miniatures are very large and, unless they are kept carefully, the ivory is liable to crack.

Besides all the portraits he painted in England he was in great demand abroad and worked for Louis Philippe, King of France, Prince Louis Napoleon, the King and Queen of the Belgians, the Empress Eugénie and other notable people. He used a pale flesh tint and shaded the features with soft grey-blue strokes; the hair is drawn in loose masses rather than in detail, and the costume often picked out with opaque white. Some of his sitters are posed against a cloud and sky background, or even a plain soft grey, as in the ones of Louisa Hubbard and the Hon. Maria Margaret Hubbard (Colour Plate 36A and C). An exhibition of 220 of his works was held in London the year of his death, and the complete list published by J.J. Foster, *Miniature Painters British and Foreign,* Volume I. Several artists copied miniatures by Ross, including G. Faija and E. Moira, etc. Examples of his work are in numerous private collections, and museums including the Wallace Collection, the National Portrait Gallery, the British Museum, the Nottingham Art Museum, the Glynn Vivian Art Gallery, Swansea, and the Victoria and Albert Museum.

Hugh Ross (1800-1873) was the son of William Ross and his wife, Maria Smith, and the brother of Sir W.C. Ross and Miss M. Ross. He exhibited at the Royal Academy, 1814-1845, and was awarded prizes by the Society of Arts in 1815, 1816, and 1820. A miniature of Sir W.C. Ross by him is in the National Portrait Gallery. He painted miniatures and portraits in

Plate 131D. **Edward Lobo Moira,** *the Prince Imperial (1856-1879), son of Napoleon III and the Empress Eugenie, ivory, 4½ins. Signed and dated: 'E.Moira ft 1872.' The Prince is wearing the uniform of a Woolwich Cadet.* Courtesy R. Bayne Powell.

Plate 132A. **J.J. Nimmo,** *an unknown lady, ivory, 3¼ins. Signed and dated: 'J.Nimmo 1851.'* Private Collection.

watercolour, some of which were pencil drawings partly coloured. One of these latter portraits by him in a private collection is signed on the reverse: 'Drawn by / Hugh Ross / 1841'. An inscription with the portrait identifies the sitter as 'Thomas Parker / younger brother of Admiral Parker' (Plate 127B).

In 1976, an exhibition was arranged in Salisbury which contained paintings executed by several generations of a family of artists named Gray. Their descendant, Donald C. Whitton of California, had been in touch with me for some time and has kindly furnished me with details which have clarified the relationship of the various members, some of whom had been recorded previously but not identified. The exhibition was called 'The Grays of Salisbury' and was a fascinating insight into the work of the whole family. Those that concern us as miniaturists are as follows.

Plate 132B. **A. Weigall,** *Arthur Douglas Scott as a child, ivory, 2⅞ins., c.1862. The frame is engraved on the reverse: 'Arthur Douglas Scott / 1862 / By Weigall.'* Private Collection.

Mrs. John Westcott Gray, née Catherine Esther Geddes (1796-1882) was the third of five daughters born to Alexander and Harriet Geddes. She was baptised at Alderbury on 9th September, 1798, with her brother, Alexander James. Her father, who was a cousin of Andrew Geddes, the Scottish painter, leased some land on Lord Radnor's estate at Longford Castle, where the children grew up. Her sister, Margaret (also a miniaturist) became Mrs. William H. Carpenter, wife of W.H. Carpenter, Keeper of Prints and Drawings at the British Museum. The family studied art at Longford Castle, and Catherine may have had some training from her sister. On 11th May, 1816, she married John Westcott Gray in the Parish Church at Alderbury, and the couple moved to Bath. Their first child, William John, was born in 1817, and eight others followed, of whom Alfred (b.1820), and Henry (b.1823), were artists and painted miniatures. The Grays moved to London in c.1838. Catherine only exhibited at the Royal Academy three times, in 1844, 1852, and 1857. How much painting she had found time to do in the early part of their marriage is not known. By c.1850 her husband was living in Switzerland, and it is thought that she helped to support herself by painting portraits in watercolour and in miniature. A small miniature on paper, thought to be a self-portrait by her, is in the family, and is a good example of her brush work which, in this case, is free and loosely painted (Plate 128C). A watercolour portrait of a young girl, signed and dated 1876, executed on paper, is a charming example of her work. It is gracefully posed and most appealing, and is the only dated work known by her (Plate 128D). Other examples of her pictures were exhibited, but were on a larger scale. Besides portraits, Catherine executed a few landscapes and was painting up to the end of her life. She died in London on 9th April, 1882.

Alfred Gray (b.1820-?) was the third son of Catherine and John Gray. Little is known about his life, and only a small number of works by him are

Plate 132C. **H. Inman** *and* **T.S. Cummings,** *an unknown man, ivory, 2¾ins. Signed in full: 'Inman and Cummings.' The two artists were partners and often signed their work jointly. Most of their miniatures are in America.* Private Collection.

Plate 132D. **J.J. Nimmo,** *an unknown child, ivory, 4¾ins. Signed and dated: 'NIMMO 1867.' This is an appealing miniature and well painted.* Courtesy F. Joachim.

Plate 132E. **H. Collen**, *portrait of an unknown man, ivory, 3⁵/₈ins. This bears a scratched signature on the front: 'H.Collen 1841', and on the reverse: 'Painted by Henry Collen. Miniature Painter to the Queen & H.R.H. the Duchess of Kent 29 Somerset Street, Portman Square London.'* Private Collection.

Plate 132F. **Annie Dixon**, *Horace Charles George West, son of Sir Algernon Edward West G.C.B. and Mary, née Barrington, as a child, ivory, 3ins. Signed on the reverse and dated: 'May 1861.' The frame is engraved: 'from Victoria R. / Horace Charles George West Aug 26 1861.' The miniature was given by Queen Victoria to Lady Barrington, the child being the grandson of Lady Caroline Barrington who was a woman of the Bedchamber to Queen Victoria.* Courtesy Christie's.

in the family. These date from 1839-1843, and comprise landscapes, drawings and watercolours, eight of which are portraits, mostly on a large scale. An attractive watercolour of his sister, Marion, was exhibited in Salisbury, together with several other drawings and sketches. The only one on ivory is a delightful picture of a young woman holding a flower, painted against a landscape background; the colouring is good, and the black bodice shows well over her pretty blue dress. The draughtsmanship is strong and the modelling achieved with stippling (Plate 128E). Nothing is known about the latter part of Alfred's life, and his date of death is not recorded by the family.

Henry Gray (1823-1898) was the sixth child of Catherine and John. He takes us into the period of photography and in the Salisbury catalogue is

Plate 133.
A. **Mrs. V.V. Butler**, *Winifred Anna, Duchess of Portland, née Dallas-Yorke, wife of the 6th Duke, ivory, 3¾ins., c.1920-25. The Duchess was noted for her beauty and beloved in Nottinghamshire for her work for the miners.* Courtesy Ivy, Duchess of Portland.
B. **Mrs. V.V. Butler**, *Ivy, Duchess of Portland, née Gordon Lennox, when Marchioness of Titchfield, wife of William Arthur Cavendish Bentinck, 7th Duke of Portland (d.1977), ivory, 3½ins., c.1932. Signed: 'V.V.Butler.'* Courtesy Ivy, Duchess of Portland.
C. **A.J. Downey**, *possibly Queen Maud of Norway (d.1938), ivory, 3ins., c.1909. Wearing a diamond and pearl coronet and matching choker necklace.* Courtesy Christie's.
D. **Fanny Way (Mrs. Thacker)**, *Queen Mary (1867-1953), when Duchess of York, formerly Princess Victoria Mary of Teck and later Queen of George V, ivory, 3½ins., c.1895. Signed: 'Fanny Way.'* Private Collection.
E. **Fanny Way**, *George V (1865-1936), when Duke of York, ivory, 3½ins., c.1895. Signed: 'Fanny Way.'* Private Collection.

A

B

C

D

E

Plate 134A. **J. Smart,** *an unknown lady, ivory, 3¼ins. Signed: 'J. Smart 1903', the first two letters in monogram. This artist is hitherto unrecorded.* Private Collection.

Plate 134B. **C.J. Turrell,** *Jessie Percy Butler Phipps, ivory, 3¼ins. Signed and dated: 'C.T. 1885.' The sitter's name is engraved round the frame.* Courtesy F. Joachim.

Plate 134C. **Alyn Williams, P.R.M.S.,** *an unknown lady, ivory, 3ins. Signed and dated: 'Alyn Williams / 1905.' Williams was one of the leading miniaturists of the day.* Private Collection.

described as "Henry Gray, Photo-Miniature Painter". Henry was one of those who took up this form of art and for some forty years painted miniatures on a photographic base. He was born in Salisbury on 8th October, 1823, and entered the Royal Academy Schools in 1846. Almost all his miniatures were from photographs. His self-portrait (Plate 128B) is a typical example of one painted c.1888. An attractive one of a young girl *called* Princess Helena Augusta Victoria, painted in watercolour on ivory, is the best I have seen by him and does not give the impression of having a photographic base at all (Plate 128A). Henry married an Irish girl called Sophia, from County Wicklow; they had no children. Sophia died on 29th December, 1895, and Henry, in St. Mark's Hospital, London, on 21st May, 1898, after a three year struggle with cancer.

Thomas Charles Wageman (1787-1863) was a comparatively minor miniaturist, whose work might be obtained by new collectors. Nothing is known about his life except that he exhibited at the Royal Academy, British Institution, and New Water Colour Society, from 1817-1857, and was a member of the New Water Colour Society, 1831-1832. He held an appointment as portrait painter to the King of Holland. Wageman painted a few miniatures but is best known for his portraits in pencil and watercolour, many of which were engraved. He also painted pictures of animals and fruit, and copied the works of old masters. A number of his sitters were members of the theatrical profession. He died on 20th June, 1863. A miniature of Charles I and the Duke of Gloucester, after Van Dyck, was Lot 100 at Sotheby's on 16th December, 1974 (Plate 129E).

Mrs. Marmaduke Bellett Browne, née Maria Roberts (1786-1828) was the daughter of Arundel Roberts and his wife Mary, née Bellett. She was born in London on 30th December, 1786, and when she was fourteen returned to her mother's birth-place, Sampford Arundel, in Somerset, where she was educated at the local school. She was musical and "a passionate artist" according to her school teacher. At the age of nineteen she accompanied her brother, Arundel, to Calcutta where his business was connected with loading and unloading ships for the East India Company. She had a number of suitors but fell in love with a soldier called Marmaduke Browne, whom she married in Calcutta on 14th March, 1806. They had two sons, Arthur and Tom (two daughters having died in infancy). Her husband became a Lieutenant-Colonel in 1821. Maria never claimed to be anything more than an amateur artist and many of her works were painted as gifts to friends. Her health having broken down in c.1823, she and her husband came back to England. She remained with her mother at Samford, whilst he returned to India. She had a premonition of her approaching death and mentioned it in a letter to her brother in October, 1827, referring to her husband as one "whose equal never lived." She died on 13th February, 1828, and her husband married as his second wife Charlotte Droz, an old friend from Calcutta. He died in 1833.

Mrs. Browne was a close friend of George Chinnery and was almost certainly his pupil, basing her own painting on his work. Detailed information about Mrs. Browne and her connection with Chinnery was published by Richard Ormond in The Walpole Society, Vol. XLIV, together with numerous sketches, and illustrations of Maria's miniatures. The information came largely from family papers to which he had access. Mrs. Browne was said to be a pretty woman, and very lively. Chinnery was obviously fond of her and may possibly even have been in love with her at one time; they were certainly close friends, as is clear from the letters published by Richard Ormond. Most of them are taken up with technical advice on painting and what colours to use.

Plate 134D. G. Faija, *Princess Mary Adelaide, Duchess of Teck (1833-97)*, ivory, 2ins., c.1853, some years before her marriage to Francis, 1st Duke of Teck. She was the mother of Queen Mary. Another version of this portrait by H.T. Wells, dated 1853, is in the Royal Collection. Courtesy Christie's.

An interesting collection of miniatures of the family of Sir John Hadley D'Oyly and others was sold at Sotheby's on 15th July, 1974. Unfortunately some of the information regarding the sitters got confused and I am grateful to Dr. Mildred Archer of the India Office for providing me with the correct identifications. A number were by George Chinnery, others were by Maria Browne and a few by Lady Charles D'Oyly (not, as stated in the catalogue, by Charlotte Thompson, who was the first wife of Sir John D'Oyly, 8th Bart.). One of the large frames containing these miniatures was inset with a portrait by George Chinnery of Sir John Hadley D'Oyly, 6th Bart. (1753-1818); one of his son, Sir Charles D'Oyly, 7th Bart. (1781-1845), by Maria Browne (Plate 129B), together with two other miniatures representing Charles' first wife, Marian, née Greer (his cousin), and his second wife, Elizabeth Jane, herself a miniaturist (Plate 129A), and two more by unknown artists. Sir Charles was a popular and prolific artist who also received some tuition from George Chinnery. A miniature of James Atkinson (1780-1852), Surgeon in the Bengal Medical Service, signed: 'MB Browne', is in the Scottish National Portrait Gallery. Atkinson's wife, Jane, was another of Chinnery's pupils in Calcutta.

Mrs. Browne's miniatures are quite attractive and, although clearly

Plate 134E (left). **E. Jenner Rosenberg,** *Lady Scourfield, ivory, 3¼ins. Signed and dated: 'EJR (monogram) / 92 (1892).' The locket is inscribed on the reverse: 'Lady Scourfield painted by Ethel J. Rosenberg (Mrs) New Bond St.'* Private Collection.

Plate 134F (right). **Rosa Carter,** *miniature of an unknown girl, ivory, 2½ins. Signed: 'R.C.' Presumably copied from an earlier portrait.* Courtesy Sotheby's.

influenced by Chinnery, are painted with a softer touch and without the dramatic effect which he produced.

Alfred Tidey (1808-1892) was born at Worthing on 20th April, 1808, and was one of nine children born to John Tidey (a schoolmaster) and his wife, Elizabeth. One of his brothers, Henry Fryer Tidey (1814-1872), painted watercolours, and possibly a few miniatures. Alfred entered the Royal Academy Schools in 1834, and set up on his own in London. He was not an artist of outstanding merit but succeeded in obtaining the patronage of people of distinction, including Royalty. Details regarding the family have been written up by a descendant, Miss M. Tidey, in *The Tideys of Washington Sussex.* Alfred worked chiefly in London, but also in Jersey and Germany and travelled frequently on the Continent. In 1855 he married Miss Justina Gertrude Campbell, by whom he had three sons, Percy Campbell, Stuart Alexander, and Alfred 'Constable'. Tidey was a member of the Dudley Gallery Art Society. He became friendly with, and received help from, John Constable, whose children he painted. A MS list of Tidey's works is in the Victoria and Albert Museum. He died on 2nd April, 1892, at Glenelg, Springfield Park, Acton.

Some of his miniatures are well drawn and pleasing, but others lack draughtsmanship and are rather dull. One of an unknown man, signed and dated 1842 on the reverse, is in a private collection (Plate 125E). A miniature called 'White Mice' is in the Victoria and Albert Museum.

Mrs. William Walker, née Elizabeth Reynolds (1800-1876) was the second daughter of S.W. Reynolds, the engraver, by whom she was taught to paint. Her sister, Fanny Reynolds, was also a miniaturist. Elizabeth exhibited at the Royal Academy and Society of British Artists from 1818-1850. She married, in 1829 or 1830, William Walker (1791-1867), an engraver, and subsequently assisted him, having engraved in mezzotint herself at an early age. She was appointed miniature painter to William IV and her sitters included five Prime Ministers. She herself was painted by Opie when only a child, and in miniature by a contemporary, Miss Eliza Sharpe (Colour Plate 33C). Her daughter, Marion, was also an artist and exhibited from her mother's address. Elizabeth died on 9th November, 1876, and was buried in the Brompton Cemetery.

She painted miniatures and portraits in oils as well as executing engravings. Her miniatures are scarce; those I have seen have been well painted and attractive. An oil portrait by her of the Earl of Devon is at Christ Church, Oxford, and a miniature of her father, Samuel William Reynolds, is in the National Portrait Gallery.

George Raphael Ward (1801?-1878) was the son and pupil of James Ward, R.A. (1769-1859). George entered the Royal Academy Schools on 30th December, 1822, when his age was given as twenty-two. He was awarded a silver medal by the Society of Arts in 1823, and exhibited at the Royal Academy, New Water Colour Society, etc., from 1821-1864. He was an engraver and also painted miniatures, many of which were copies from works by Lawrence and other artists. In c.1827/8 he married Mary Webb, by whom he had a daughter, Henrietta (1832-1924), who married E.M. Ward, R.A. Ward died in London on 18th December, 1878. His work varied a great deal; some of it is very good and painted in attractive colours. He modelled the features with blue-grey shadows, and painted with minute brush strokes, cleverly blended. Touches of white are often to be found on the nose, eyelids, lips and pupils of the eye. A miniature of an unknown lady signed on the front: 'G.R. Ward delt', was sold at Sotheby's in 1970, and one, of an unknown lady standing against a balustrade with a garden and sky background, was Lot 23 at Sotheby Parke Bernet, Zurich, on 15th November, 1977. It was a good example of his work and painted c.1845 (Plate 130D).

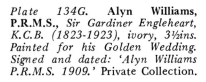

Plate 134G. **Alyn Williams, P.R.M.S.,** *Sir Gardiner Engleheart, K.C.B. (1823-1923), ivory, 3½ins. Painted for his Golden Wedding. Signed and dated: 'Alyn Williams P.R.M.S. 1909.'* Private Collection.

Plate 135A. **G.M. Mather,** *portrait of an unknown lady, ivory, 4¼ins., c.1840. Only a small number of miniatures by this artist are known.* Courtesy Sotheby's.

Plate 135B. **G.M. Mather,** *an unknown lady, ivory, 2¹⁄8ins. Signed on the reverse: 'Painted by G.M. Mather. 1848.'* Private Collection.

Plate 135C. **C. Farrier,** *miniature of an unknown lady, ivory, 4¹⁄8ins., c.1840. Signed on the reverse: 'Painted by / Charlotte Farrier / 7 Smith St. / Chelsea.' This is an attractive miniature by a little known artist.* Courtesy R. Bayne Powell.

Miss Margaret Gillies (1803-1887) was born on 7th August, 1803, in Throgmorton Street, London, and was the second daughter of William Gillies, a Scottish merchant. Margaret was educated by an uncle, Adam Gillies, a judge in Edinburgh, where she knew Sir Walter Scott and other notable people. She returned to London and became a pupil of F. Cruickshank, and later had lessons from Ary Scheffer. She exhibited at the Royal Academy, British Institution, Society of British Artists, Old Water Colour Society (of which she was an Associate Member in 1852), from 1832-1887. She is best known for her miniatures, which are scarce, but also painted portraits in oils and genre subjects. She seems to have had a number of famous sitters including Charles Dickens, Leight Hunt, and William Wordsworth. Miss Gillies painted Wordsworth at her own "earnest request" in 1839. She stayed at Rydal Mount, Ambleside, with the family for over a month, and during that time became great friends with them and painted several miniatures of Wordsworth, and of his wife and daughter, Dora. This latter portrait is at Dove Cottage; others by her of Wordsworth and his wife, and one of Miss Isabella Fenwick, remain in the family. The large double miniature of the poet and his wife is one of two replicas, the original having been destroyed by fire (Plate 130A). Margaret died on 20th July, 1887, at Warren, Crockham Hill, Kent. Some of her miniatures — like that of Miss Fenwick — are charming, but she tended to idealise her sitters, a common fault of many artists. Nevertheless, her miniatures show character and the colouring is generally pleasing. She used a lot of gum with her paints and some of her portraits have rather dark backgrounds. A miniature by her of Leigh Hunt is in the National Portrait Gallery.

Miss Annie Dixon (1817-1901) was born at Horncastle on 12th March, 1817. Nothing is known about her early life or training. She is said to have been a pupil of Sir W.C. Ross. In c.1840 she went to London, and worked at Horncastle, Hull, St. Lawrence, Isle of Wight, and in London. She was one of the artists who travelled about, painting her clients in country houses. Miss Dixon had the patronage of the Royal family, and many of the aristocracy. In 1862 she painted all the Strathmore family. She is traditionally supposed to have once painted a ring on the finger of the Dowager Marchioness of Cambridge, then a child, to keep her quiet whilst being painted! She was very prolific and is said to have painted over one thousand miniatures. Her sitters included Queen Alexandra, as Princess of Wales, and Louisa, Marchioness of Waterford. Miss Dixon died in February, 1901.

Miniatures of children are amongst Annie Dixon's most attractive works. One of Horace Charles West as a child, signed and dated 1861, was Lot 20 at Christie's on 20th June, 1967; this portrait was given by Queen Victoria to Lady Caroline Barrington, a woman of the Bedchamber, whose grandson was the sitter (Plate 132F). She was another artist who used a lot of gum with her paints. Her miniatures are usually signed: 'A.D.', or: 'A. Dixon', often followed by a date, the signature being scratched on the front or signed in full on the reverse. Examples of her work are in the Victoria and Albert Museum.

Plate 135D. **Miss A.H. Laird,** *portrait of an unknown man, ivory, 1⅝ins. Signed and dated on the reverse: 'Painted by A.H.Laird. London, June 1840.'* Private Collection.

Plate 135E. **J. Linnell,** *'Miss Otway as St. Cecilia', ivory, 5ins. Signed and dated: 'J. LINNELL 1827.' Linnell was greatly influenced by W. Blake the poet and painter, and this miniature was no doubt inspired by Blake. Miniatures by Linnell are scarce.* Private Collection.

Plate 135F. **J.W. Jarvis,** *an unknown man, ivory, 2ins., c.1825-30. This artist spent most of his working life in America.* Courtesy Christie's.

Alfred Weigall (fl.1855-1866) was a member of an artistic family, several of whom painted miniatures. He was almost certainly the son of Henry Weigall, Senior, a sculptor, whose address he shared. Alfred exhibited at the Royal Academy, 1855-1866, from various London addresses, including 38 Wimpole Street and 102 Piccadilly. His sitters included members of the Spencer family and a miniature of the Countess Spencer by him is still at Althorp. One of Arthur Douglas Scott as a child is in a private collection; the frame is engraved with the child's name and the date of the portrait, 1862 (Plate 132B). One of Miss Hester Leir, signed: 'Alfred Weigall pinxt 1860', is in the collection of R. Bayne Powell. His portraits show Continental influence, and some are painted against a dark background.

Plate 135G. **F.N. Heigel,** *Henry Everard, watercolour on card, 4⁷/₁₆ins. Signed and dated: 'F.N.Heigel / 1847.'* Courtesy Madam H. Stuart Stevenson.

Cornelius B. Durham (fl.1825-1865) worked in London and exhibited at the Royal Academy and Society of British Artists from 1828-1858. He was awarded prizes at the Society of Arts, 1825-1826, and a gold Isis medal there in 1832. His exhibits included a chalk drawing of animals, and miniatures. He also worked as an intaglio cutter. Some of his works were engraved. It is only in comparatively recent years that Durham's work has become known or even recognised: it is of a very high quality and well worth acquiring. One of the best I have seen (formerly in the possession of the late Captain E.B. Woollett) was of an unknown lady standing by a terraced garden; the frame was surmounted by a coronet, but I have been unable to identify the sitter. It was signed: 'C. Durham'. A miniature of an unknown man by him was Lot 41 at Christie's on 2nd June, 1970; it is signed: 'C. Durham / 1835' (Plate 129D). Durham was a good draughtsman and used pleasing colours; he painted the flesh parts in a soft manner not unlike Ross. The sitters' eyebrows are often slightly arched, and the lips and eyes strongly delineated. His work will, I am sure, be more appreciated as time goes on. (Colour Plate 33A.)

William Booth (1807/8-1845) was a native of Aberdeen. Little is known about him except that he came to London and entered the Royal Academy Schools on 31st March, 1825, when his age was given as seventeen. He exhibited at the Royal Academy and Society of British Artists from 1827-1845, and was awarded a silver medal in 1827. His portraits included one of John Constable: many of his sitters were clergymen and officers, and a large number were of children, who seem to have had a special appeal to him. Some of his works are as large as 10ins. Two miniatures of his sister, Jessie, were sold at Christie's on 23rd May, 1967, and were probably by him. His works are little known; those I have seen are pleasing and painted in the manner of the Scottish school. Some are particularly reminiscent of miniatures by Ross. An attractive group of children was Lot 73 at Christie's

Plate 135H (left). **T. Marshall,** *Mrs. Thomas Marshall (Elizabeth Jane), wife of the artist, ivory, 3¼ins. Signed and dated with initials: 'JM / 1826.' One of a pair, the other miniature being a self-portrait.* Private Collection.

Plate 135 I (right). **G.B. Canevari,** *an attractive miniature of an unknown lady, ivory, 4⁵⁄₈ins., c.1850. Signed: 'G.B.Canevari.' The influence of Sir W.J. Newton can be seen in the way the artist has modelled the face and drawn the hair.* Courtesy Sotheby's.

on 18th April, 1972. It represented Ann, Madelina and Huntley Rothery Garden, when young. Madelina was born in 1828, Huntley in 1827, and Ann Ellen in 1826. The miniature is signed on the reverse: 'W. Booth-Pinxt / 16 Grafton Street, Fitzroy Sq / London / August 1833' (Plate 130C). Three miniatures were loaned to the exhibition at South Kensington in 1865. They included a portrait of his sister, and one on ivory of one of his sons. Booth died in 1845.

C.J. **Basebe** (1843-1879) was one of a family of artists, many of whom painted miniatures. Little is known about any of them except that they appear to have worked in London, and often exhibited from the same addresses. Basebe exhibited at the Royal Academy from 1843-1879, and was probably the C. Basebe who exhibited at the Society of British Artists in 1835. In 1855 he was living at 108 King's Road, Brighton. His sitters included the Marchioness of Bath, Lady Louisa Thynne and a number of other well-known persons. Works by him are scarce. A good one of an unknown officer wearing the black uniform of the 60th Corps (later the King's Royal Rifle Corps), with a crimson belt and black cloak, signed and dated: 'C.J. BASEBE. 1846', was Lot 61 at Christie's on 14th October, 1969. The portrait was painted against a sky background and was of a very high quality; it is the only one by this artist that I have seen. The treatment was reminiscent of the Scottish school (Plate 130B).

John Jules Nimmo (b.c.1830-d. aft. 1881) was born in Paris, and became a pupil of François Meuret. Nimmo painted miniatures and copied the works of old masters. He worked chiefly in Paris, and exhibited at the Salon from 1853-1881. He was in Britain for a time and was working in Edinburgh in 1856, when he was living at 4 Young Street. Works by him are scarce; those I have seen are well painted. A good one of a child holding a rattle is in the collection of F. Joachim. It is signed on the front: 'NIMMO 1867', and is well drawn and expressive (Plate 132D). One of an unknown lady wearing a bonnet, signed and dated: 'J. Nimmo 1851', is in a private collection, and may well have been painted in Scotland (Plate 132A).

A

B

C

D

450

Frederick Harding (fl.1814-1857) worked in London and Totnes. He was awarded premiums at the Society of Arts in 1814 and 1815, and exhibited at the Royal Academy and Society of British Artists from 1825-1857. Pigot's *London and Provincial Directory,* 1834, gives two London miniaturists of this name who may have been identical. He is a minor artist who has not been considered of any great merit, but a miniature of an unknown lady by him in the collection of F. Joachim is rather better than has been suggested. It is signed: 'F. Harding 1833', and is a good example of the costume of the time, and well painted (Plate 121B). His known signatures are 'F.H.', 'F. Harding', 'Fred^k Harding' and 'Fred^c Harding.' He used a rather deep pink flesh colour, and brown shadows. Long mentions seeing a miniature of William IV by Harding.

J. Fisher (fl.1845-1854). Nothing is known about this artist, but I have seen several most attractive miniatures by him which are easily recognisable once his work has been examined. They have all been on paper and signed either: 'FISHER' in sloping capitals (Plate 127E) or, in cursive writing: 'J. Fisher / 1854' (Plate 127C). The colouring is fresh and the draughtsmanship good, and the work slightly reminiscent of Sir W.C. Ross.

James Warren Childe (c.1778-1862) worked in London, and exhibited at the Royal Academy and Society of British Artists from 1815-1853. He is noted for his portraits of actors and actresses, and painted miniatures and small portraits in watercolour. His miniatures are not usually of outstanding quality· but his small watercolours are more attractive, and well executed. One of a young Etonian is signed: 'J.W. Childe' on the left of the portrait and inscribed on the right: '39 Bedford St / Strand', from which address he exhibited from 1837-1853. This is painted against a sky background; the features of the young boy are well modelled, and the general effect is very satisfactory (Plate 129C). Examples of his work are in the Victoria and Albert Museum.

Henry Inman (1801-1846) was born in Utica New York State, on 28th October, 1801, and was the son of English parents who had settled in New York. Few of his miniatures are seen here although he was working in England from 1843-1845, after which he returned to New York where he died on 17th January, 1846. He had his own studio, in partnership with

Plate 136.
A. **J.F. Sharpe,** *portrait of an unknown young lady, ivory, 4½ins. Signed and dated: 'Sharpe / 1854.' This is another well-painted miniature by a little-known artist.* **Courtesy R. Bayne Powell.**
B. **L. Wyon,** *an attractive portrait of an unknown girl, black and red chalk on buff coloured paper, 8ins. Signed twice: 'L. Wyon / March / 1846,' and over her shoulder: 'L. Wyon.' The draughtsmanship is excellent and the features delicately tinted. This artist is hitherto unrecorded.* **Private Collection.**
C. **E. Dalton Smith,** *portrait of an unknown lady, ivory, 7ins. Signed: 'Edwin D. Smith Pxt 1860.' This is a typical example of a large miniature of the period following the trend of photography.* **Courtesy Sotheby's.**
D. **B. Mulrenin, R.H.A.,** *a miniature of Miss Eva Line, ivory, 4¾ins. Signed and dated: 'B:M: / RHA / 49' [1849]. This is an attractive miniature; the sitter is wearing a white dress, and her long ringlets are adorned with a twisted red velvet band.* **Courtesy Sotheby's.**

Colour Plate 35.

A

B

A

B

Colour Plate 36.

C

D

Thomas S. Cummings, and some of their miniatures bear their joint signature as in the case of the one illustrated from a private collection. This portrait of an unknown man is signed in cursive writing near the outer edge: 'Inman & Cummings' (Plate 132C). It is well painted, the background being shaded with a number of long brush strokes. Inman was a founder member of the National Academy, and its first Vice-President. He worked as a miniaturist, portrait painter and lithographer and executed some landscapes. He suffered from failing health from c.1840. While he was in England Wordsworth and Macaulay sat to him. He was in financial difficulties when he died, and an exhibition of his work was arranged in New York to raise funds to support his family.

Edward Lobo Moira (1817-1887) was born at Villa Nova de Foscôa in October, 1817. He came to London and became an actuary at the Portuguese Embassy. He then took up miniature painting and acquired a fashionable clientele, including many Royal personages. He exhibited at the Royal Academy and New Water Colour Society from 1848-1887. After his arrival in England he seems to have spent most of his life in London, but was working at Chislehurst, Kent, from 1878-1885, returning to London in 1886. He died on January 2nd, 1887, probably at 9 Colville Terrace, Bayswater, London. In 1877, he painted the Princess Beatrice for Queen Victoria. A number of his miniatures are in the collection of H.M. The Queen. A very large miniature of Lady Suffield and a child was Lot 109 at Christie's on 29th November, 1977. It is signed on the reverse: 'Edward Lobo Moira.' It is a fine example of this type of miniature but is spoilt because, as so often happens when such a large piece of ivory is used, it has cracked badly in lines. This can be clearly seen in the illustration (Plate 131C). The painting is very much akin to the work of Thorburn, who was one of the last important miniaturists of the nineteenth century.

Colour Plate 35.
A. **John Faed, R.S.A.,** *Mrs. Robertson, née Mary Anne Jean Manson, ivory, 7¹/₁₆ins. Inscribed on the reverse of the frame:* 'JOHN FAED / R.S.A. / PAINTED ON IVORY / This miniature likeness of / my niece Mary Anne / Jean Manson, now the / wife of Captain Robertson of / the 8th (The King's) Foot, was / painted for me in 1854.' *Private Collection.
B. **William Essex,** *after a portrait by George Saunders, William Carr, Viscount Beresford (1768-1854), illegitimate son of George de la Poer Beresford, Marquess of Waterford, became Viscount Beresford in 1823, enamel, 6¼ins. This is a fine example of a work by Essex.* Courtesy Bernard Falk Collection, Royal Pavilion, Brighton.

Colour Plate 36.
A. **Sir William Charles Ross, R.A.,** *The Hon. Maria Margaret Hubbard, eldest daughter of William John, 8th Lord Napier, and wife of John Gellibrand Hubbard, later Lord Addington (d.1896), ivory, 5¼ins. Signed and inscribed on the reverse:* 'Painted by Sir WC Ross.R.A. / miniature painter to / The Queen / 1846. / The Honble Maria Margaret / Hubbard.' *Private Collection.
B. **Maria A. Chalon (Mrs. Henry Moseley),** *Miss Lee, ivory, 4½ins. Inscribed and signed on the reverse:* 'Portrait of / Miss Lee / painted by / Maria Chalon / July 1840.' *Private Collection.
C. **Sir William Charles Ross, R.A.,** *Lady Parish, née Louisa Hubbard (1814-1888), sister of Lord Addington, and wife of Sir Woodbine Parish, K.C.H., ivory, 4¹/₈ins., c.1850. Inscribed on the reverse:* 'Louisa Hubbard. (Lady Parish). / painted by Sir W. Ross—" *Private Collection.
D. **Mrs. John Siree,** *née Clementina Robertson, Miss Cynthia Harcourt, ivory, 5ins. The sitter's name and that of the artist are on the reverse.* Dr. A.K. Brown.

B

A

C

D

E

F

G

Moira did his best to compete with the photograph but this cheap method of catching a likeness had come to stay, and the artists who followed him did so in spite of the odds. They dwindled in number and, with a few exceptions, their work was dull and lacking in any inspiration. There were, however, and still are, artists who kept up a good standard of painting and from these I have selected a few to mention in detail; others will be included in the Appendix to this chapter.

Charles James Turrell (1846-1932) was a popular miniaturist of the twentieth century. He was born in London on 14th January, 1846, the son of Edwin Turrell, an amateur violinist, and exhibited at the Royal Academy and Society of Miniaturists from 1873-1932, from various London addresses. Turrell had a successful career and his distinguished patrons included Queen Victoria, Queen Alexandra, Princess Mary (later Queen Mary), the Queen of Norway, and many others. In 1867 he visited the U.S.A. and painted many of the important people there such as J. Pierpont Morgan and the Vanderbilts. He returned to London in c.1869 but frequently spent his winters in America. He died in White Plains, New York, on 13th April, 1932. Several works by him are in the collection of the Duke of Portland, whose family he painted, including Lieut. General Arthur Cavendish Bentinck. A miniature by him of Jessie Percy Butler Phipps, signed and dated: 'C.T. 1885', is in the collection of F. Joachim (Plate 134B).

Miss Frances Elizabeth (Fanny) Way (Mrs. Arthur Thacker) (1871-1961) was the daughter of William Dwyer Way and his wife, Esther, née Langmead. She was born on 28th March, 1871, at 20 Lloyd Square, Clerkenwell, London. She and her four sisters were educated privately, and Frances later studied at the Crystal Palace School of Art, c.1886, where she was awarded two silver medals for a painting in oils and a drawing. After spending a year in Lausanne at a school of art run by her uncle, C.J. Way, she returned to London and exhibited at the Royal Academy, the Royal Society of Miniature Painters, and the Royal Institute of Portrait Painters, etc., 1893-1921, and at the Paris Salon in 1897. She married Arthur Thacker in 1895, in which year she is recorded under her married name although she exhibited throughout under her maiden name; she always signed her works: 'Fanny Way.' She painted portraits of the Duke and Duchess of York (later George V and Queen Mary), Sir Thomas Somer Vine, Mrs. Langtry, Miss Ellaline Terriss

Plate 137.
A. **Wilson H.G. Crutwell**, *miniature of an unknown lady, ivory, 2½ins., c.1900. Signed in monogram: 'WHGC,' and in full on the reverse. Note the rounded toque and high fur collar.* Courtesy R. Bayne Powell.
B. **Mrs. E.M.D. Collingwood**, *Barbara Collingwood, the artist's daughter, ivory, 2½ins., c.1901. This hitherto unrecorded artist painted some attractive miniatures of her family, and landscapes of the Lake District and abroad.* Private Collection.
C. **F. Coop**, *an unknown man, ivory, 3ins. Signed and dated: 'Fred / Coop / 1903.' This is another hitherto unrecorded artist who followed the fashion of the time and painted over a light photographic base.* Private Collection.
D. **The Misses M. and E. Hall**, *portrait of a young boy, ivory, 3¹/8ins., c.1895-1900. Signed: 'M & E.Hall.' This is at present the only known example of their work.* Private Collection.
E. **G. Hayward**, *miniature of an unknown lady, ivory, 3ins. Signed and dated: 'Gerald S. Hayward 1885.' This artist settled in America where he met with great success.* Private Collection.
F. **Mrs. A.G. Chamberlin**, *an unknown Russian officer, ivory, 3¹/16ins. Signed in full and dated: 'A.G. Chamberlin 1907.'* Private Collection.
G. **Miss E.M. Cannon**, *Miss R.A. Withall, ivory, 3ins., c.1890-1900. Signed: 'E.M. Cannon.' Although lightly sketched in this miniature is attractive.* Private Collection.

Plate 138A (left). **Mabel Lee Hankey,** *The Dowager Lady Brentford, ivory, 3ins., c.1900. Signed: 'Mabel Hankey.' This is a good example of one of the more important miniaturists of this period.* Private Collection.

Plate 138B (right). **F.E.W. Farrar or Farrah,** *portrait of an unknown young lady, ivory, 3½ins., c.1900. Signed: 'F.E.W. Farrar.' The reverse of the frame bears an inscription: 'A Portrait / F.E.W.Farrar (Mrs.).'* Private Collection.

Plate 138C. **E. Horwitz,** *an unknown lady, ivory, 5⅛ins. Signed and dated: 'Horwitz / 1905.' Although loosely painted this miniature is attractive.* Private Collection.

Plate 138D. **C.J. Hobson,** *portrait of an unknown lady, ivory, 5ins. Signed: 'C.J. Hobson 1906.' Note the change in hair style.* Private Collection.

Plate 138E. **C. Devine,** *an unknown lady, ivory, 4½ins. Signed and dated: 'C.Devine / 1894,' the first two letters in monogram. This is a good example of how the hair was swept up into a bun on the top of the head, unlike the later style in Plate 138D.* Courtesy F. Joachim.

Plate 139A (left). **Miss M.C. Smith, R.M.S.,** *Mrs. Reginald Foskett, F.R.S.A. née Daphne Kirk (b.1911), ivory, 3ins. Signed and dated: 'Muriel Smith 1956.' The sitter is the daughter of Lieut. Col. and Mrs. J.W.C. Kirk and wife of the late Dr. R. Foskett, Bishop of Penrith.* Family Collection.

Plate 139B (right). **R.P. Martin,** *an unknown girl, ivory, 3¼ins. Signed: 'R.P. Martin 1901.'* Private Collection.

Plate 139C. **Winifred C. Dongworth,** *Mrs. John William Carnegie Kirk, née Maude Agnes Haynes (1889-1949), watercolour on paper, 6¾ins. Signed and dated: 'WD / 1915.' Wife of Lieut. Col. J.W.C. Kirk, D.S.O., and mother of the author. A sketch for this portrait exists.* Family Collection

Plate 139D. **Lisa De Montfort, R.M.A.,** *called 'General Scarlet', ivory, 3¾ins., c.1960. This is a colourful miniature; the sitter was probably an M.F.H.* Private Collection.

Plate 139E. **L. Ogilvie,** *Lady Mary Baillie Hamilton (b.1934), daughter of the 12th Earl of Haddington, ivory, 3½ins. Signed 'L.OGILVIE.' This is a very attractive and well painted miniature.* Courtesy The Earl of Haddington, K.T.

Plate 140B. **Lisa de Montfort, R.M.S.,** *Lucilla Bayne Powell, daughter of Mr. and Mrs. R. Bayne Powell, ivory, 2¾ins., 1971.* Courtesy R. Bayne Powell.

Plate 140A. **Miss C. Marjory Forbes, V.P.R.M.S.,** *Lucinda Cook, ivory, 3ins., painted in 1976, in which year it was exhibited at the R.M.S. Signed in monogram: 'CMF.'* Courtesy Miss C.M. Forbes.

Plate 140C. **Barbara Owen Baker,** *Flavia Bayne Powell, elder daughter of Mr. and Mrs. R. Bayne Powell, ivory, 2¾ins., 1962.* Courtesy R. Bayne Powell.

and Lord Roberts. Her work varied: the two miniatures of the Duke and Duchess of York are well drawn, but the painting of the backgrounds is rather hesitant (Plates 133D and E). A number of her miniatures are still in possession of the family.

Alyn Williams, P.R.M.S. (1865-1955) was one of the best miniaturists of the early part of the twentieth century. He was born at Wrexham, Wales, on 29th August, 1865, and eventually became a pupil at the Slade School in London, and of J.P. Laurens. He exhibited at the Royal Academy, New Water Colour Society and The Royal Society of Miniature Painters, Sculptors and Gravers (of which he was President), the Paris Salon, and in the U.S.A., from 1890-1914. He had a very successful practice and painted many interesting and important people. He was noted for his interest in guiding the destinies of the R.M.S., and was Vice-President of the Imperial Art League, and a member of the Philadelphia Society of Miniature Painters. A large number of his miniatures are probably in America. His sitters included Queen Alexandra, Edward VII, Mrs. Alyn Williams, and Sir Gardiner Engleheart, K.C.B., a descendant of George Engleheart (Plate 134G). Some of his works are in the Smithsonian Institution, Washington. His portraits of Queen Alexandra and Edward VII are in the Guildhall Gallery, London.

His subjects are well drawn, and the character of his sitters well expressed. One in a private collection, of an unknown lady, is well painted and executed with a soft flesh tint and a cloud and sky background. It is signed and dated: 'Alyn Williams / 1905' (Plate 134C).

Winifred Cecile Dongworth (1893-1975) was an artist about whom little has so far been recorded. She worked in London and the Provinces, and was in or near Cheltenham in 1914, when she painted a portrait of my mother,

Plate 140D. **Miss C. Marjory Forbes, V.P.R.M.S.,** *'Deborah and the Twins', ivory, 3¹/16 ins. diam. Signed in monogram: 'CMF.' This is an attractive family group.* **Courtesy Miss C.M. Forbes.**

Mrs. J.W.C. Kirk (Plate 193C), and one of myself as a child. I have the sketch for my mother's picture which my father carried in his pocket-book throughout the 1914-18 War. Winifred Dongworth was a competent artist; her draughtsmanship was good and her likenesses accurate. The portrait of my mother is on paper, signed: 'WD / 1915', and that of myself on ivory, signed: 'W. Dongworth 1915.' She used fresh colours, and painted the hair in loose waves, with just the slightest suggestion of a scraper when painting on ivory. The features are painted softly, without any stippling. A number of her miniatures were sold in London after her death, but unfortunately I did not see them.

Mrs. Violet Victoria Butler (19th and 20th century) is an artist about whom I have little information except that she was born in London. She is known to me by two very good miniatures in the Portland Collection. One represents Winifred, Duchess of Portland, wife of the 6th Duke (Plate 133A), which is a charming study of one who was noted for her beauty and elegance. The other is equally good of Ivy, Duchess of Portland, wife of the 7th Duke (Plate 133B). This was painted in 1932 when she was Marchioness of Titchfield, and is signed: 'V.V. Butler.' These miniatures are so competent that it is to be hoped that more by her hand come to light, as they are well worth acquiring.

Although a few artists exhibit miniatures at the Royal Academy from time to time, the main annual exhibition of modern work is the one held in the autumn by the Royal Society of Miniature Painters Sculptors and Gravers, at the Mall Galleries, London. I am frequently asked for advice about modern miniaturists and, as the selection of an artist is such a very personal one, I always suggest that people visit this exhibition and decide, from the miniatures on view, whose work most appeals to them. Names and addresses of exhibitors may be obtained from the Secretary, and the artist can then be contacted for further details.

It is mostly from the membership of this Society that I have made a small selection of contemporary artists for inclusion in this chapter. Due to various

Plate 140E. **Mrs. Phoebe Sholto Douglas, R.M.S.,** *Clare Whitaker, ivory, 4½ins. Signed: 'Phoebe Sholto Douglas, R.M.S.,' The artist has succeeded in catching the child's mischievous expression.* **Courtesy Mrs. P. Sholto Douglas.**

circumstances it has not been possible for me to attend these exhibitions recently, and I hope that those members not mentioned will realise that, in a work such as this, my space is limited.

The Royal Society of Miniature Painters was founded in 1895 by Alyn Williams and some of his brother artists, and has given great encouragement to those who still strive to keep the art alive. In the annual catalogue it is stressed that "a miniature portrait to be correct must be painted direct on to the material, without any photographic or lithographic basis". Thus the standard set by the great British artists is still upheld.

Miss Muriel Constance Smith, R.M.S. (b.1903) of Nottingham has been known to me for over twenty-five years and has painted all my family. She is a most versatile artist, and paints portraits in oils, miniatures, watercolours, and executes pencil drawings and drawings in chalk. She has an extraordinary aptitude for catching a likeness, and the portrait she painted in oils of my husband in 1956 is a superb example of her work in that medium, as is the chalk drawing of my daughter, Patricia, executed in 1956. Her miniature of my younger daughter, Helen, has always attracted much attention and is painted in the best tradition of the British school of miniaturists. She works chiefly in Nottingham, but also visits clients in their homes and paints the family there. (Plate 139A.)

Mrs. Lily A. Ogilvie, Hon. R.M.S. (20th century) has been exhibiting at the R.M.S. for many years and is a well known miniaturist. She is now a retired member of the Society, but I am illustrating her charming miniature of Lady Mary Baillie Hamilton (b.1934), daughter of the Earl and Countess of Haddington, painted when she was a girl. It is signed: 'L. OGILVIE', and is a good example of her work (Plate 139E).

Miss Lisa De Montfort, R.M.S. (20th century) is another well known exhibitor at the Royal Society of Miniature Painters. She lives in London, and is represented by a miniature of a Master of Foxhounds called 'General

Plate 140F. **F. Boyd-Waters, R.M.S.,** *an unknown child with a doll, ivory, 3½ins., c.1935-40. Signed: 'BOYD / WATERS.' His portraits of children are particularly good.* **Private Collection.**

Plate 140G. **Mrs. Sheila P. Sewell, A.R.M.S.,** *'Ann', ivory, 2¾ins. Signed: 'P.S.' This attractive miniature was exhibited at the R.A. and R.M.S. in 1976.* **Courtesy Mrs. S.P. Sewell.**

Scarlet', painted in 1960 (Plate 139D), and by a pretty miniature of Lucilla Bayne Powell, daughter of Mr. and Mrs. Robert Bayne Powell, painted in 1971 (Plate 140B). Both these miniatures are good examples of her style.

Barbara Owen Baker (20th century) is not a member of the R.M.S. and I have not, unfortunately, been able to trace her. She painted an attractive portrait of Flavia Bayne Powell in 1962, which is a good likeness and is well modelled and painted against a cloud and sky background (Plate 140C).

Mrs. Phoebe Sholto Douglas, R.M.S. (20th century) lives at Cranbrook, in Kent. She is an artist who succeeds in catching a good likeness and, as in the case of the portrait of Clare Whitaker (Plate 140E), is able to capture all the liveliness and mischief in a child who is enjoying the experience of being painted. Getting good likenesses of children is not easy, as they are seldom still for long! This is a particularly attractive miniature.

Mrs. Sheila P. Sewell, A.R.M.S. (20th century) also comes from Kent, and lives at Orpington. In 1976 she exhibited a portrait of 'Ann' at the Royal Society of Miniature Painters (106 in the catalogue), which is a good example of her work. It is much more dramatic in its approach than many modern miniatures, and is well drawn and has great charm. She favours a looser manner of painting which is most effective (Plate 140G).

Miss C. Marjory Forbes, V.P., R.M.S. (20th century) is well known to all who are interested in the Royal Society of Miniature Painters. She has kindly allowed me to reproduce two of her miniatures which I think illustrate her great ability to paint children. The one of Lucinda Cook was exhibited in 1976, and is signed in monogram: 'CMF' (Plate 140A). The other one, which is circular, is called 'Deborah and the Twins'; it is set in a landscape and also signed in monogram (Plate 140D). Both are good examples of modern miniatures.

Last but not least I must mention **Mrs. Stella Lewis Marks, M.V.O., R.M.S., A.S.M.P.** (b.1889) of London. Stella Marks, née Lewis, was born in Melbourne, Australia, and studied there at the National Gallery School of Art, under F. McCubbin and Bernard Hall. She paints portraits in oils as well as miniatures. After leaving Australia she spent some years in America and many of her works are in the U.S.A. and Canada. Mrs. Marks finally came to England, where she settled and is still actively employed with her painting. She has the distinction of having painted H.M. The Queen from the time of her marriage: Prince Philip commissioned her to paint a miniature of his bride. This was finished only three days before Prince Charles was born! Since then, Mrs. Marks has painted fourteen miniatures of members of the Royal family, including one of the Queen in her Silver Jubilee year.

She has painted Prince Charles, Princess Anne, Prince Andrew, and Prince Edward as children, and one of Prince Charles on the occasion of his twenty-first birthday on 14th November, 1969, in which year he was invested as Prince of Wales. This shows him in the uniform of Colonel-in-Chief of the Royal Regiment of Wales, wearing the blue sash of the Order of the Garter on to which is pinned the Queen's Coronation Medal (Plate 141E).

A miniature of Princess Anne (also painted for her twenty-first birthday) is set against a peacock blue background. The Princess is wearing a dark blue jacket over a white blouse to which is pinned a Wedgwood brooch depicting a horse; her fair hair falls over her shoulders. It is signed on the front with

A

B

D

C

E

Mrs. Marks' usual signature: 'Stella L Marks. R.M.S.' (Plate 141A). Occasionally she adds a date. Her work is, as one would expect, executed with great care and good draughtsmanship, and all the miniatures that I have seen by her have been attractive and worthy of the great tradition set by British miniature painters throughout the years.

In these days when colour photography has become so popular I fear it is nothing more than a pipe dream to hope that the demand for these small portraits may return on a greater scale, and one can only be thankful that there are still a number of twentieth century miniaturists who keep the art alive, and fulfil commissions for those patrons who continue to find pleasure in owning examples of one of the most attractive forms of painting ever nurtured in these islands.

APPENDIX

A further selection of artists painting miniatures in the 19th and 20th centuries.

Miss Joan Ayling, V.P.R.M.S., 20th century.
Frederick Boyd-Waters, R.M.S., 1879-1967 *(Plate 140F)*.
Miss Jennifer Buxton, R.M.S., 20th century.
Giovanni Baptista Canevari, or Canavari, 1789-1876 *(Plate 135 I)*.
Miss Edith Margaret Cannon, fl.1892-1904 *(Plate 137G)*.
Miss Rosa or Rose Carter, fl.1889-1910 *(Plate 134F)*.
Mrs. Amy Gertrude Chamberlin, fl.1895-1911 *(Plate 137F)*.
Mrs. Edith Mary Dorothy Collingwood, 1857-1928 *(Plate 137B)*.
Frederick Boyd-Waters, R.M.S., 1879-1967 *(Plate 140F)*.
Mrs. Phyllis Cooper, A.R.M.S., b.1895 *(Plate 141B)*.
Wilson H.G. Crutwell, fl.1908-1914 *(Plate 137A)*.
Miss Catherine Devine, fl.1892-1894 *(Plate 138E)*.

Plate 141.
A. **Mrs. Stella L. Marks, M.V.O., R.M.S.,** *H.R.H. The Princess Anne, now Mrs. Mark Phillips (b.1950), ivory, 3¾ins., painted in 1972 for the Princess's twenty-first birthday. Signed: 'Stella Marks R.M.S.' In the Royal Collection.* Courtesy Mrs. S.L. Marks.
B. **Mrs. Phyllis Cooper, A.R.M.S.,** *H.M. Queen Elizabeth II, when Princess Elizabeth (b.1926), ivory, 3¹/8ins. Signed in monogram: 'PC,' and inscribed on the reverse: 'Painted by Phyllis Cooper / 1951.' Wearing the uniform of Colonel in Chief of The Grenadier Guards, and the sash of the Order of the Garter.* Private Collection.
C. **E. Rinzi,** *H.M. Queen Victoria (1819-1901), ivory, 4ins., painted in her Diamond Jubilee year, 1897. Signed on the reverse. The Queen is seated on a throne, wearing a small coronet over a veil, a black dress trimmed with lace, and the sash and Star of the Garter. On her right wrist she is wearing a bracelet set with a miniature portrait of Prince Albert, the Prince Consort (1819-1861).* Courtesy Sotheby's.
D. **Kenneth Kendall,** *H.R.H. The Prince Philip, Duke of Edinburgh (b.1921), enamel on porcelain, 4¾ins. Signed and dated on the reverse: 'H.R.H. The Duke of Edinburgh / Kenneth Kendall / Los Angeles / 1971.' The Prince is wearing the uniform of Admiral of the Fleet, with the sash of the Order of the Garter, the Order of Merit, and Campaign Medals. It is interesting to find a modern miniature painted on porcelain.* Courtesy Kenneth Kendall, Los Angeles.
E. **Stella L. Marks, M.V.O., R.M.S.,** *H.R.H. The Prince Charles, Prince of Wales (b.1948), ivory, 3⁵/16ins. Signed: 'Stella L. Marks, R.M.S.' The prince is wearing the uniform of Colonel-in-Chief of the Royal Regiment of Wales with the sash of the Garter, onto which is pinned the Queen's Coronation Medal. The miniature is in the Royal Collection.* Courtesy Mrs. S.L. Marks.

Alfred James Downey, fl.c.1907-1935 *(Plate 133C)*.
Gugliemo Faija, 1803-d. aft. 1861 *(Plate 134D)*.
Mrs. Frederica E.W. Farrar or Farrah, fl.1886-1895/1900 *(Plate 138B)*.
Miss Charlotte Farrier, fl.1826-1875 *(Plate 135C)*.
Miss Rita Foot, 1886-1965.
Miss Margaret and Miss Ethel Hall, fl.1899 *(Plate 137D)*.
Mrs. William Lee Hankey, née Mabel Emily Hobson, d.1943 *(Plate 138A)*.
Gerald S. Hayward, fl.1879-1883 *(Plate 137E)*.
Miss Elizabeth Heaphy, Mrs. Henry Murray, c.1815-1882.
Franz Napoleon Heigel, 1813-1888 *(Plate 135G)*.
Mrs. Edith M. Hinchley, née Edith M. Mason, fl.1902-1914.
Cecil J. Hobson, fl.1896-1914 *(Plate 138D)*.
Emmanuel (Henry?) Horwitz, fl.1901-1914 *(Plate 138C)*.
John Wesley Jarvis, 1780-1839/40 *(Plate 135F)*.
Kenneth Kendall, 20th century *(Plate 141D)*.
Miss Alice or Alicia H. Laird, fl.1840-1865 *(Plate 135D)*.
John Linnell, 1792-1882 *(Plate 135E)*.
Thomas Marshall, 1788-1874 *(Plate 135H)*.
Miss Winifred Marshall, fl.1898-1914.
Miss Rosa P. Martin, fl.1899-1901 *(Plate 139B)*.
George Marshall Mather, fl.1832-1833 *(Plates 135A and B)*.
Mrs. Lilian Mary Mayer, 20th century.
Bernard Mulrenin, R.H.A., 1803-1868 *(Plate 136D)*.
George Patten, A.R.A., 1801-1865 *(Colour Plate 33B)*.
Ernest Rinzi, 1836-1909 *(Plate 141C)*.
Miss Ethel Jenner Rosenberg, fl.1883-1901 *(Plate 134E)*.
Gertrude Sargant, fl.1900.
Joseph Severn, 1793-1879 *(Plate 119A)*.
Eliza Sharpe, 1796-1874 *(Colour Plate 33C)*.
Joseph F. Sharpe, fl.1826-1854 *(Plate 136A)*.
J. Smart, fl.1903 *(Plate 134A)*.
Edwin Dalton Smith, 1800-d. aft. 1866 *(Plate 136C)*.
L. Wyon, fl.1846 *(Plate 136B)*.

Chapter XII

Fakes, Forgeries
and Facts

TO REITERATE THE sentiment expressed by J.T. Barber Beaumont, that "a man who never makes a mistake will never make anything", is perhaps the most apt introduction to this brief chapter. Few people, even if they possess a natural 'flair' for collecting, have not at some time in their lives purchased an article which, in the light of further knowledge, has turned out not to be as good as was at first supposed. On the other hand I could give many examples of collectors having bought, for a modest price, items which have proved to be great bargains. I can recall many instances where I have bought miniatures and other works of art on instinct, and later found out their true value. About thirty years ago very few people were interested in miniatures, and one could buy good examples for a few pounds. This meant that one could afford to take a risk and hope to discover something about the artist or sitter later. In those days I could never afford to spend more than a few pounds, and my only regrets are the things which I did not buy!

One of my best and comparatively early finds was when, in about 1949, I was travelling from Nottingham to Harrogate. I stopped at a 'junk shop' outside Doncaster where, amongst many other things, I saw a few Continental miniatures. I asked the owner if he had any others, and he produced five from a drawer and threw them on his table. After some bargaining I bought them for £20, which at the time seemed a lot of money and I was rather apprehensive as to how I was going to explain this away to my husband when I got home. They included a fully signed and dated miniature by Bernard Lens of the so-called portrait of Mary, Queen of Scots, after the miniature by L. Cross (which I immediately recognised as such); one of Mr. Inigo Thomas, which I found to be by John Barry; and an enamel of Peter the Great after Kneller which, many years later I had opened by a jeweller and found it was signed by C. Boit. The two others were good Continental miniatures, which I eventually sold. I could give numerous instances when I have had similar luck, and many of the circumstances under which treasures are bought are as interesting as the objects themselves. The whole essence of a real collector is the fun he or she derives from poking about looking for items which appeal to him, and then taking them home and, if possible, discovering about them later. It is not always easy to attribute a miniature to a specific artist, but if the portrait is well painted this does not matter. Of the four and a half thousand names listed in my *Dictionary* only a fraction of the artists' work is ever seen; almost every month I make additional notes in my copy as new information comes to my notice and the names of hitherto unrecorded artists are discovered.

Many years ago an old man said to me: "Knowledge, my child, is power";

Plate 142A (left). Possibly **G. Engleheart,** *an unknown man, ivory, 2ins. The miniature has had restoration which makes accurate identification difficult. It is set within a frame of rose diamonds.* Courtesy Sotheby's.

Plate 142B (right). Portrait of an unknown lady after G. Engleheart, ivory, 2ins. Mounted in a dark blue enamel frame surrounded with split-pearls. Courtesy Sotheby's.

this is a true saying, but I think I would add that in collecting one needs a little luck as well — and the chance to be in the right place at the right moment.

There is no easy way to knowledge and, unfortunately, there are as many pitfalls in miniature collecting as in any other field. In endeavouring to assist the new collector to avoid purchasing fakes and forgeries I can only point out some of the elementary precautions which he should take.

The first essential is to be perfectly clear about what is a FAKE, and what is a FORGERY.

A FAKE is something which is produced with the deliberate intention of deceiving people into thinking that it is genuine, and put on to the market to be sold to the unwary. Faked miniatures are not confined to any period, and are to be found representing artists from Holbein upwards. They are not always taken from a specific portrait (although they are usually based on one), are frequently of well known people, and are executed in the style of a particular artist.

A FORGERY, or 'fraudulent imitation' to use the term given in the *Oxford Dictionary,* is a copy made from a genuine original to be passed off as a genuine work of art, or document, etc. In connection with miniatures a forgery is a copy painted by someone from the work of a known artist, to be sold (usually by a dealer) as of the period it indicates. It is a known thing that, early in this century, some unscrupulous dealers employed a skilful miniature painter to do nothing else but copy miniatures from good originals (usually eighteenth century) after Cosway, Plimer, Smart, Engleheart, etc. The dealer was then able to sell the same miniature several times over: one collector got the original, and the rest bought the copies!

There are various differences to look for in assessing the merits of such miniatures, and both fakes and forgeries may be signed or unsigned. Only experience will assist the collector in avoiding them. Some were painted in the period of the sitter, and others are nineteenth and twentieth century

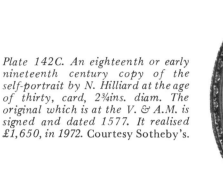

Plate 142C. An eighteenth or early nineteenth century copy of the self-portrait by N. Hilliard at the age of thirty, card, 2¾ins. diam. The original which is at the V. & A.M. is signed and dated 1577. It realised £1,650, in 1972. Courtesy Sotheby's.

copies. The most usual fakes are taken from portraits by well known artists of any period, and many of them have been, and still are, painted on the Continent. I have seen artists sitting all day copying masterpieces in the Louvre, Paris, and the Uffizi and Pitti Palace Florence; many of these miniatures are excellent and, as such, may be enjoyed by many people, but they must not be confused with original works of old masters.

As the reader will have appreciated already, many artists of every age have copied other people's work. These copies were not necessarily executed to deceive anyone, but were frequently done as practice pieces by budding

Plate 142D (left). Mrs. Wilkes of Madras after an original drawing by John Smart, dated 1793. This copy is in pen and ink on ivorine, 3ins., in a carved ivory frame, and was probably executed in the nineteenth century. Compare it with Plate 106A. Courtesy Phillips Son & Neale.

Plate 142E (right). Lieut. General John Dighton, after an original drawing by John Smart, dated 1791. This copy is in pen and ink on ivorine, 3ins., and set in an ornate carved ivory frame. Like Plate 142D, this is probably nineteenth century. Compare it with the original, Plate 106B. Courtesy Phillips Son & Neale.

artists in order to perfect their own technique. Time and time again one reads of miniaturists copying paintings by Van Dyck, Rubens, Reynolds, Lawrence, and many more. Good copies of large portraits or miniatures are not to be despised as long as they are purchased as such; and if the collector buys them because he likes them they are well worth acquiring. Some artists were not good at catching a likeness themselves, but excelled at copying the works of other painters. These copies are genuine works of art and should be accepted on their aesthetic merit.

In the seventeenth century, for example, S.P. Rosse and others made copies of miniatures by Samuel Cooper which are well worth possessing, so long as they are recognised as copies. Enamellists such as the Bone family, and others of a later period, executed miniatures which were almost exclusively copies of the works of portrait painters. These are usually signed and inscribed, and make no attempt to deceive anyone. They are amongst the collectors' items of today.

Plate 143A (left). Portrait of an unknown lady, after Cosway, ivory, 2½ins. Mounted in a frame decorated with blue enamel and split-pearls. Note the dark rather staring eyes and harsh treatment, totally unlike Cosway's painting. Courtesy Sotheby's.

Plate 143B (right). Called Lady Northwick, after A. Plimer, ivory, 2½ins. Set within a blue enamel and split-pearl frame. Points to look for here are the dark, heavily painted eyes and strong delineation of the features. Courtesy Sotheby's.

It must also be remembered that it was not unusual for a miniaturist to paint more than one identical portrait of a sitter (possibly for another member of the family), and it is perfectly possible to find two alike. I remember some few years ago a miniature of Mrs. Siddons by Horace Hone was sold in London, and soon afterwards I had occasion to go to the National Gallery, Dublin, where, to my surprise, I found they had an identical miniature, signed and dated the same year!

Another point to bear in mind was that many families had relations who were good amateur artists who were quite capable of copying miniatures painted by the professional painters, or even attempting the art themselves. An instance of this is provided in the life of *John Harden of Brathay Hall*, p.16, when Jessy Harden, writing to her sister in India, tells her that she has "had her picture painted [in miniature] by her sister Helen and that this is being sent to her". Mention is also made on another occasion of a miniature being copied by one of the family. These portraits are not fakes but genuine copies, often of some merit. A miniature of Lady Blunt is clearly copied

Plate 143C. Portrait of an unknown lady, after Cosway, ivory, 3ins. This is a clever copy of a Cosway, and could easily deceive the unwary. It lacks the panache of his work. The miniature is set within a rose diamond frame. Courtesy Sotheby's.

from an original painting by G. Engleheart. It is inscribed on the reverse: 'This was drawn by / the late Hon'ble Mrs Bruce / who died in Bengal before / she finished it — It is copied from a / painting of a likeness of Lady Blunt — and was / Mrs Bruce's first attempt' (Plate 144C).

What the new collector has got to learn is how to assess the quality of the work he is offered, and this takes time. It is important to have some idea as to whether or not the work one is being offered is of the period suggested. I have frequently been shown so-called Elizabethan miniatures painted on ivory, with the story that they were 'period'. By this time the reader will know that ivory was not used, as a base on which to paint, before the late seventeenth or early eighteenth century. It is essential to examine any possible purchase under a lens to see the quality of the painting, and if there has been any restoration. Fresh paint can usually be discerned as, if it is applied over old pigment, it is often either slightly raised or some discoloration has taken place. In the case of an oil miniature which has been repainted after the original paint has flaked off, one can sometimes see an area from which the paint has gone, leaving the bare copper. The question of the technical analysis of the paints is one that is too complex to deal with here, for the average collector would not be in a position to know how to test them. This is usually the work of experts such as those in the Conservation Department in the Victoria and Albert Museum. It is true that it is possible to tell if the paints used are of the period, and ones which were normally used by a particular artist, but this is not something to be undertaken by the inexperienced.

Another danger that the collector has to be aware of is the possibility of being offered a miniature which is a clever fake, the likeness having been cunningly painted over a photographic base. This method was occasionally used during the Victorian period (and, I suspect, still is). During the late part of the nineteenth century, when photography had become popular, many studios employed artists to hand-tint this type of portrait. It was a cheap way of obtaining a likeness and, for those of the public who merely wanted a coloured photograph, was ideal. Many of these pictures are, unfortunately, now passed off as genuine miniatures, but if the portrait is of either of the types mentioned the base can usually be spotted under magnification. The more difficult ones to be sure about are those copies of earlier periods which, all too often, are so clever that they are difficult to detect. One develops a built-in instinct for recognising this sort of deception which is almost impossible to express in words to anyone else.

Cracked or damaged miniatures should be avoided unless they are of especial interest, as these can rarely be restored satisfactorily; vellum can be laid down more successfully, but ivory is a treacherous substance and, once cracked, is really spoilt.

Plate 143D (left). Called *Lady Wellesley, after Cosway, ivory, 2½ins. Cleverly painted and almost certainly, like all these 'decorative' examples, painted to deceive. Mounted in a rose diamond frame.* Courtesy Sotheby's.

Plate 143E (right). Called *The Hon. Anne Rushout, daughter of Lord Northwick, after A. Plimer, ivory, 2¾ins. This is not like any known portrait by Plimer of the sitter suggested, but is a clever imitation of his work.* Courtesy Sotheby's.

The most obvious FAKES are those which are housed in ivory frames, made of old piano keys, which occasionally have pieces of imitation tortoiseshell let into them to form a design. These are usually Continental, and have old paper from French or German books pasted on the back. They are often signed with fictitious foreign names; some are signed Romney, Reynolds, Gainsborough, Holbein, etc. Others are signed with the names or initials of well known miniaturists such as Cosway, Plimer, Engleheart or Smart, or by Continental artists such as Isabey. Many of these miniatures are in ornate metal frames with scroll or ribboned designs on the top, and the backs covered with embroidered damask. Many of them were painted about the turn of this century, but this type is still being produced on the Continent today.

The really clever fakes are sometimes more difficult to detect. These were, I think, mostly painted in Britain, and are copies of the British School, mounted in eighteenth or nineteenth century gold and silver frames set with precious or semi-precious stones. Miniatures of this type frequently come into the sale rooms and, although some of them are quite attractive, they lack the panache and draughtsmanship of the top artists and are rather harsh, and to the experienced eye stand out like sore thumbs! Others are so clever that accurate attribution is difficult and one has sometimes to give them the benefit of the doubt.

470

Plate 144A. **J.A. Janinet,** *an attractive 'decorative' miniature probably based on some known portrait, ivory, 3³/₈ins., nineteenth century. Signed: 'Janinet.' Miniatures of this quality have an appeal but it is important to realise that they are not period.* Courtesy Sotheby's.

Such fakes are usually catalogued as 'decorative' miniatures; they are purchased either by collectors, who like them for what they are, or by jewellers who can use the frames for more important portraits. A large collection of this type of miniature came up for sale at Sotheby's in July, 1972. The frames were almost all set with precious stones, or enamel and pearls, and were very attractive. The fact that everyone knew that they were fakes was reflected in the prices obtained, which varied from £65 to one at £480. This latter miniature was called 'Mrs. Damer Dawson'; it was after Engleheart, and was mounted in a frame set with rubies and rose-cut diamonds. Another one, of an unknown lady after Cosway, in a pearl and blue enamel frame, is a typical example of this kind of fake. The sitter's eyes are staring, the painting is harsh, and the features look pinched and in no way comparable to the work of Cosway (Plate 143A).

This collection was probably bought in all good faith by someone who was badly advised, for most of the miniatures were painted c.1900.

There are also some quite attractive 'decorative' miniatures, again usually Continental, which appeal to many people who want them to hang on a wall. A pair of these signed: 'Janinet', and painted in the nineteenth century was sold at Sotheby's on 3rd March, 1977. They were in turned metal frames, and were quite pretty (Plates 144A and E).

A typical illustration of the fake miniature in a piano key frame is (Plate 144B). It is a good example of the type of frame I have been discussing, and is being passed off as a genuine portrait of Mary, Queen of Scots. It is signed: 'S. Cooper' and is an imaginative portrait of Mary, based in part on the one by Clouet, and painted with the excessive use of opaque white which is so common on this kind of fake miniature. Another Continental fake is Plate 144D; this is painted with a light wash of watercolour, the details being picked out in opaque white, and has all the crudity of the superficial portraiture used on these miniatures, which, if examined under a lens, lack the quality one is accustomed to seeing on miniatures painted by good artists. The frame in this case is slightly more elaborate, with the tortoiseshell inlay, and the miniature is probably nineteenth century.

Detecting fakes is something one has to learn by experience. If collectors attend the sale rooms and find that certain miniatures catalogued as by well known artists sell for modest sums, the most usual conclusion to draw is that no one thought they were right! There are exceptions to this, and one can sometimes, for no known reason, obtain a genuine miniature cheaply. All sorts of factors have to be taken into account. The sale may be on a wet day and buyers fail to turn up, or dealers and collectors might be away from home, or the catalogue might have come out too late for some collectors to view the sale properly. I have, on occasions, missed bargains and at other times been lucky enough to buy miniatures at a price far lower than expected.

Many people do not understand that there is an accepted formula for describing miniatures in a sale catalogue from which they can tell if there is a serious doubt regarding the attribution. For the benefit of new collectors I set it out here:—

1. If the forename and surname of the artist is given, the assumption is that the auctioneer thinks the miniature is by the artist, e.g. "Miniature of an unknown man by Samuel Cooper."

2. If the surname only of the artist is given, the miniature is thought to be a work of the school of, or by one of the followers of the artist, or in his style and of uncertain date, e.g. "Miniature of an unknown lady by Cosway."

3. 'Signed' means that the miniature has a signature which is a recognised signature of the artist and thought to be right, e.g. "Miniature of a young girl: 'Signed and dated Samuel Shelley / 1800.' "

4. 'Dated' means that the miniature bears a date considered to be correct for the artist, e.g. "Miniature of an unknown man dated: '1799.' "

5. 'Italian School', 'Spanish School', without a date, suggests that the miniature is probably executed at a later date than the style might suggest.

6. Dexter = to the right (looking to the observer's left). Sinister = to the left (looking to the observer's right).

7. 'Called' suggests a doubt as to the identity of the sitter.

8. 'Attributed' normally means that, although it cannot be proved, the work is thought to be by the artist named.

To a new collector sale catalogues can be confusing, and I hope that this information will prove of use, as I have often heard people say "it must be right, it said 'Cosway' in the catalogue" — not realising that this left it in doubt!

Another form of deception which really comes under FORGERIES is the addition of an artist's signature, at a much later date, to a genuine miniature. There have always been collectors who have insisted on buying signed examples of important artists' work and, equally, there have always been people willing to oblige by putting on what looks like a genuine signature. The artists who have suffered from this most frequently are Samuel Cooper, John Hoskins, and Richard Cosway. Sometimes the signature has been added to a miniature which was, in fact, by the artist (who had not signed it), and

sometimes it has been added to a miniature which was, in fact, the work of another hand. An instance of this was when a miniature (now thought to be, possibly, a self-portrait of Thomas Flatman) was sold bearing the signature: 'S.C.' (for Samuel Cooper). It was sold at Christie's on 6th July, 1965, Lot 41; it was signed and dated: 'SC / 1662', and was one of the miniatures exhibited at the National Portrait Gallery in 1974, No. 163, and is in the collection of Eric Hawtin, who has had the false signature removed (Plate 21C). Detecting forgeries is one of the most difficult problems as, all too often, the miniature is genuine and only the inscription false so that it needs knowledge even to begin to make a serious pronouncement.

Another form of deception is that of painting over prints and framing them in eighteenth century frames, or cutting colour plates out of books and placing them in suitable frames. The collector should be able to detect either of these forms of deceit with the aid of a good lens. The best place to look for this imposture on a print is where the colours are light, and do not conceal the printed line or stippling. A few expensive books on miniature painting were published in the early part of this century, and some of the special editions had hand-coloured portraits in them which, I suspect, have on occasions been cut out and framed. Those of miniatures by eighteenth century artists should be easy to spot, as they will be painted on paper instead of ivory. There are other instances, however, where copies of seventeenth century miniatures have been painted separately and the portraits stuck into the pages afterwards. These are very clever, and could easily deceive the uninitiated if they were taken out of the book and framed for sale.

Other difficulties facing a collector or student are assimilating the findings constantly being thrown up by research and learning to adjust to completely new opinions. For instance whilst this book is going through the press information has been uncovered that suggests the possibility of Richard and

D. Gibson being one and the same person!

It is impossible to do more than put before the new collector as many as possible of the various problems which may arise, and hope that this information will be of value in assembling a collection of miniatures which will be rewarding and enjoyed by himself and his friends. Mistakes are bound to be made in the early days, and the important thing to remember is never to pay too much for a miniature – or, for that matter, any other work of art – unless it is fully authenticated by someone with knowledge. Experience has to be bought but it is important not to buy it at too big a price! The true collector is never daunted at making a mistake but is careful not to make the same one again. The fun to be had in forming a collection of any works of art comes from the pursuit of the object – the ultimate 'find', and the enjoyment of adding it to the rest.

I have never set out to look for a particular miniature, or an example of a particular miniaturist; I have always been on the alert and purchased any portraits that appealed to me which I could afford, regardless of the artist. I have never confined my collecting to any period as I believe that every period – even the twentieth century – should be included in a comprehensive collection. Others confine their purchases to either the seventeenth or eighteenth century, but more recently the nineteenth and early twentieth century portraits have become desirable, as I always thought they would. This may be partly due to the upsurge of prices and the fact that early miniatures are now difficult to obtain and very expensive; even the eighteenth century examples have risen sharply in the last few years.

Little research has been done on the miniaturists who worked in the latter years of Queen Victoria's reign and into this century, and only a few names are well known. Many more artists were working then than is realised, and information about them and their work has yet to be discovered.

Armed with the advice which I have endeavoured to supply in this chapter, collectors should set out to learn as much as possible from viewing miniatures in the sale rooms or in any of the museums where they are to be seen, such as the Victoria and Albert Museum, the National Portrait Gallery, the Wallace Collection, London, and museums in the provinces, Scotland and Ireland. They should handle as many as possible in order to train their eyes to see the finer points, such as the way the artists applied their paints, the colours they used, the manner in which they modelled the features, the bases on which they painted and any other characteristics.

When beginning to form a collection it is wise to confine oneself to purchasing miniatures from a reputable dealer at a modest price until one gains experience and confidence. Expensive miniatures should only be bought with knowledge, or with the advice of an expert.

To be a collector one must have a broad outlook. It is a mistake to be swayed by fashion into buying examples by artists whose works are at the top of the market; the wheel always turns and, in my experience, there comes a day when others are at the top, and yesterday's favourite can be bought for less! It only needs two collectors to decide to purchase the works of an artist and the prices go sky high; let one of them drop out and the miniatures by that artist find their true level again.

Although it is more difficult today than it was thirty years ago to pick up bargains, I still believe that they are to be had if one is patient and has the

Plate 144D. A decorative miniature of an unknown lady, Continental, ivory, 3¼ins., nineteenth century, in a frame made of piano keys and tortoiseshell. The painting is superficial and lacking in modelling. Courtesy Phillips Son & Neale.

opportunity to move about the country looking in every shop which might sell a miniature; only bearing in mind what I have said about the importance of being on one's guard against fakes and forgeries and how best to detect them.

I can only hope that the collectors who read this book will get as much pleasure out of their pursuit as I have done, and that they will have the good fortune to discover at least some really good bargains. In my experience one can make friends, often in unexpected places, with whom one can share one's knowledge and triumphs and exchange ideas. My research has taken me all over the world and I have received nothing but kindness from other collectors and museum staff, to whom I am deeply indebted, and without whose help I would never have been able to write this book.

Plate 144E. **J.A. Janinet,** *an attractive Continental 'decorative' miniature probably based on some known portrait, ivory, 3⅜ins., nineteenth century. The miniature is by the same artist as that of Plate 144A.* Courtesy Sotheby's.

Dictionary of
British Miniature
Painters

A

*A., D. See **D., A.**

*A., E. (fl. 1782). See also **E., A.**

Five family miniatures, signed and dated 'A.E. 82.' (1782), were sold at Sotheby's, 12 April 1960. Four represented Sir John Eden of Windlestone and one was of Mrs. Bore of York.

*A., E.A. (fl. 1820)

A miniature of Lady Clifton, signed 'E.A.A.' and dated '1820', said to have been painted by her daughter, was sold in 1962.

*A., M. See **M., A.**

Absolon, John, R.I. 1815–1895

Born in Lambeth in May 1815. Pupil of Ferrigi, an obscure artist. Began by earning a living as a portrait painter; was employed as a scene-painter by the Grieve brothers who worked at Covent Garden and Drury Lane. Exhibited at the R.A., B.I., N.W.C.S., S.B.A., etc., 1832–1889. Painted portraits, scenery, figure subjects, miniatures and book illustrations. Was for a time a member of the Institute of Painters in Oil Colours. Went to Paris in 1835. Married c. 1836.

Became a member of the N.W.C.S. in 1838 and served as its Treasurer for some years. Painted miniatures in Paris, 1838–1839. Helped Thomas Grieve and Telbin to produce the first diorama in 1850. Died 26 June 1895.

Acker, Johannes Baptista van. 1794/5–1863

Born in Bruges, 1 November 1794/5. Was a pupil of J. F. Ducq; gained a considerable reputation as an artist. Went to Paris in 1834 with introductions to Isabey (q.v.) and Saint. After a stay of some years in Paris, he was summoned to Brussels by Leopold I who appointed him miniature painter to the Court. He ranks as one of the best Belgian miniaturists. He was in England for a short time, but returned to Bruges where he remained until his death on 15 June 1863. His work was marked by pure fresh colours mixed with a lot of gum. The flesh colours are pink, with red-brown shading and light blue half tints, the hair being executed in gouache. He signed J. Vanacker and Vanacker often followed by a date. Schidlof records a number of his works. A miniature of Mrs. Sherard, wife of the Rev. P. C. Sherard, and the mother of Lord Sherard, painted on ivory, was lent to the exhibition at the South Kensington Museum in 1865, and was catalogued as by Vanacker.

*Ackerman, Miss Katye. (fl. 1906)

Of Cape Colony, S.A. Exhibited at the R.A. 1906, from c/o Miss Glossop, Wellington, Cape Colony.

Acres, Edward. (fl. 1797–1823)

Of London. Exhibited at the R.A. 1797–1823, from 30 Russell Court. He must not be confused with J. E. Acres (q.v.), who may have been a relation, but who never exhibited from the above address. His sitters included Mr. Taylor of Bath, Mr. S. Smith, Signora Storace, Master C. Acres, his self-portrait (exhibited 1811, No. 570), and in 1812, 'Mary Magdalene'.

Acres, John Edward. d. c. 1826

Of London. Said to have been a student of the R.A., but the list published in Vol. XXXVIII of the *Walpole Society* does not contain his name. He must not be confused with Edward Acres (q.v.) who may have been a relation. Exhibited at the R.A., 1800–1813, his address in 1800 being Great Russell Street. He exhibited a self-portrait in 1802, and portraits of J. March, Esq., Master Acres and Miss S. Acres. He had various London addresses, but never exhibited from the same address as E. Acres (q.v.). In 1802 J. Acres exhibited from 18 Fleet Street, and E. Acres from his usual address, Russell Court. In 1818 went to Sydney, Cape Breton County to see about an inheritance. Was in Halifax, Nova Scotia c. 1815–1816; Sydney, c. 1817 and back to Halifax before 1823. Was painting miniatures at Halifax in 1826; committed suicide there soon after. A miniature of the grandfather of Colonel Davidson of Esher, signed 'J.E.A.' on the reverse, was shown to the V. & A. M. where it was noted that the work was definitely not like that of E. Acres.

*Acret, John F. (fl. 1884–1903)

Of Hampstead. Exhibited at the R.A. and S.M., 1884–1903. Painted miniatures and large paintings in oils. In 1902 painted a portrait of Miss Maas, possibly Edith Maas (q.v.) of South Kensington who exhibited 1890–1909.

*Adam, Henri Albert. 1766–1820. See also **Adams, Henry J.**

Born in Geneva in 1766. Possibly identical with Henry J. Adams (q.v.), although there is no evidence that this artist ever worked in Britain. He died at St. Petersburg in 1820.

*Adams, Chris. (fl. 1905–1914)

Of Reading. Exhibited at the R.A. and S.M., 1905–1914, from Caversham Heights, Reading. Sitters included Lord Reading (Rufus Daniel Isaacs, 1860–1935, 1st Marquess of Reading; Lord Chief Justice, 1913–1921; Viceroy of India, 1921–26; Foreign Secretary, August–October 1931). An example of his work is at the Walker Art Gallery, Liverpool.

*Adams, Henry. See **Adams, Henry J.**

*Adams, Henry J. (fl. 1801). See also **Adam, Henri Albert**

A miniature portrait of Rossini, signed 'H. J. Adams, 1801', was seen by Long who noted that it was painted in French style. This artist is possibly identical with either Henry Adams or Henri Albert Adam (q.v.), an enamellist who worked in the manner of Isaac Adam. Henry Adams signed his work H. or Hy. Adams, followed by a date. A miniature by him, signed and dated '1801' of Mrs. May Gibbs, née Hamer, was recorded by Mr. A. J. B. Kiddell.

Adams, J. (fl. 1815–1817)

Of London. Exhibited at the R.A., 1815–1816. Was working at 3 Ludgate Hill, London until 1817. He exhibited at the R.A. in 1815 as an Hon. Member.

*Adams, Miss Jane. (fl. 1821–1851)

Exhibited at the R.A., B.I., etc. 1821–1851, from various London addresses. Painted figure subjects and, in 1827, exhibited a portrait of Miss Page which may have been a miniature.

*Adams, Miss Lilian. (fl. 1903)

Exhibited at the R.A. 1903, from 18 Rue Magenta, Asnières, Seine, France.

*Adams, William. (fl. 1842)

A miniature of an unknown man, signed and dated '1842', by this artist, is in the V. & A. M. It is well-modelled but rather loosely painted. (Pl. 1: no. 2.)

Addington, Sarah. (fl. 1778). See also **Andrews, Samuel**

Exhibited at the R.A. 1778, from 10 Cheapside, the exhibits being two miniatures. Nothing is known about this artist and for many years all miniatures signed S.A. have been attributed to her. Recent research and the discovery of certain signed miniatures, has made it reasonably certain that works signed in this manner are the work of Samuel Andrews (q.v.). Possibly some miniatures signed S are by her.

Aders, Mrs. E. b. c. 1787

Née Eliza Smith. Of London. Exhibited at the R.A., 1841.

Agar, John Samuel (I). b. 1775. See also **Agar, J. S. (II)**

Of London, b. 1775. Entered the R.A. Schools, as an engraver, 31 December 1792, aged 17. Was awarded a silver medal in 1798. In 1793 the Society of Arts awarded him a silver palette for an historical drawing. Exhibited at the R.A. 1796–1806, from various London addresses, the last one being 59 Stopford Place, Pimlico. In 1810 and 1811 an artist of this name, presumably the above artist, exhibited four religious subjects at the B.I. from the same address. Was possibly identical with the John Samuel Agar (II) (q.v.) who exhibited at the B.I., 1837–1842 and the R.A. 1836–1851, from 9 Portland Place, Hammersmith. Agar painted portraits (including one of his mother, exhibited R.A., 1796), historical drawings and miniatures, but is best known for engravings. Was Governor of the Society of Engravers in 1803. Knew Samuel Woodforde, and is mentioned in the *Woodforde Diaries*, published 1932, pp. 91–92. Two pencil portraits, dated '1801', were seen by Graham Reynolds. Long records a miniature of a man, signed on the reverse 'J. S. Agar/52 Gt Russell St, 1800', which was sold at Sotheby's, 16 June 1927. It was well drawn, the face painted with a soft stippling touch, and was reminiscent of the work of Cosway (q.v.). The shading on the face was predominantly brown, with traces of blue. Long states that he was said to have been living in 1820, and the possibility of there having been another artist of this name (perhaps his son), who worked from his father's address, is not excluded.

*Agar, John Samuel (II). (fl. 1836–1851). See also **Agar, John Samuel (I)**

Exhibited at the R.A. and B.I., 1836–1851 from 9 Portland Place, Hammersmith. Was possibly identical with, or related to, the John Samuel Agar (I) (q.v.) who exhibited at the R.A. 1796–1806, and at the B.I., 1810–1811. Painted chiefly religious subjects and portraits, including at least one which was in the Drawing and Miniature section of the R.A., 1847.

*Agar, L. (fl. 1833)

A miniature of Lord Charles Spencer Churchill, signed and dated '1833', oval, 3⅜ in. high, was noted by Long.

Aikman, William. 1682–1731. See also **Alexander, John**

A Scottish painter, born in Forfarshire (now Angus), 24 October 1682. Alleged to have painted enamel miniatures, but this fact cannot be established, and it is more than likely that there has been some confusion with John Alexander (1686–1760) (q.v.), and that W. Aikman never painted miniatures. According to the catalogue for the South Kensing-

ton

ton Exhibition of 1865, he studied for a time in England and then in Italy, and painted in the manner of Kneller. A portrait on enamel of Frances Worseley, Countess Granville, attributed to Aikman, was loaned to this exhibition. A portrait of W. Aikman by John Bogle (q.v.), from a self-portrait, was also exhibited. W. Aikman died 7 June 1731.

*Aird, Miss Edith. (fl. 1896–1904)
Of London. Exhibited at the R.A. 1896–1904, from 18 Bute Street, South Kensington (1901 and 1902), and from 8 Gerald Road, Chester Square, S.W. (1903 and 1904). Sitters included children of the Rev. Percy Wigan.

*Akers, W. S. (fl. 1821). See also **Akers, William**
Exhibited at the R.A. in 1821, from 10 Mile End Road. Was probably identical with William Akers (q.v.).

Akers, William. (fl. 1826). See also **Akers, W. S.**
Lived in Mile End Road, London in 1826, according to Long, and was probably identical with W. S. Akers (q.v.) who exhibited at the R.A. from 10 Mile End Road in 1821, the exhibits being two portrait miniatures.

*Alais, W. (fl. 1829–1833)
Exhibited at the R.A., 1829–1833, three portraits, possibly miniatures, from 10 Darlington Street, and 65 Kennington Street, Beresford Street, Walworth.

*Alcock. (fl. 1778)
The R.A. catalogues for 1778 give No. 428 as 'Two small heads'. These may have been in miniature.

Alcock, Miss Harriet. See **Easthed, Mrs.**

*Alder, Miss Ruth. (fl. 1910–1914)
Exhibited at the R.A., 1910–1914, from Amoril House, Batheaston, Somerset.

*Aldous, W. (fl. 1824–1825)
Exhibited at the R.A., 1824–1825, from 15 Great Russell Street, Bloomsbury. In 1825 he exhibited a portrait of Mr. Marston, catalogue No. 718. Long and Graves record an artist named Marston, no initial given, as exhibiting in this year, whereas in fact Marston was the sitter and W. Aldous the artist.

Alefounder, John. 1757?–1794
Of London, born 1757? Entered the R.A. Schools 4 October 1776, aged 19 'last Sept'. Possibly the son of a goldsmith and frame-maker. Exhibited at the R.A. 1777–1793. Won awards at the R.A. Schools 1781 and 1784. Executed drawings, a design for a lunatic hospital (1777), portraits in chalk, oil portraits, groups and miniatures. Went to Calcutta, arrived in October 1785. Due to worries connected with his profession he went mad, for a time, but by 1786 had recovered and was painting again. Had to advertise for some of his paints and materials which had been sold during his illness. Richard Miller (portrait painter) lived with Alefounder in Calcutta, December 1788. He died at Calcutta on 20 December 1794, having committed suicide as a result of a fresh fit of insanity. Details about his time in India are recorded by Sir W. Foster, *Walpole Society*, Vol. XIX, pp. 5–7.

*Alexander, J. See **Alexander, John**

*Alexander, John. 1686–1760
A native of Aberdeenshire, born 1686. Painted portraits and miniatures, and a large ceiling at Gordon Castle in 1720. Was in Italy, 1711–1719 (in Florence in 1712). Published a set of engravings after Raphael, some of which were dedicated to Cosmo de Medici. Was a prolific painter. Returned to England in 1719. Took part in the 1745 Rising. Married and had at least one son, Cosmo John Alexander, also an artist. A self-portrait in oil on copper was sold at Sotheby's, 24 October 1960, and is now at the S.N.P.G. It is inscribed in Italian on the reverse, the translation of which is 'John Alexander, a Scotch Painter of Paris, his portrait painted by himself on his arrival (by sea from London) at Leghorn, A.D. 1711, when he was 25 years of age and on his way to prosecute his studies at Florence and Rome.'. Long noted a miniature copy of 'Thomas Guy's portrait, 1721', which was inscribed on the reverse 'J. Alexander'; it was on card and was probably by the above artist. Died near Edinburgh, 1760.

Alken, Henry Thomas. 1785–1851
Born at 3 Dufours Place, near Golden Square, London, 12 October 1785. Son and pupil of Samuel Alken (1756–1815). Exhibited at the R.A., 1801 and 1802. Was a pupil of J. T. Barber Beaumont (q.v.). Painted miniatures early in his career, but is best known for his drawings of sporting subjects. Married at Ipswich, 14 October 1809, Maria Gordon (d. 1841). Lived for most of his life near London. Died in reduced circumstances in 1851.

Allan, David. 1744–1796
Born in Alloa, 1744. This well-known Scottish painter is not usually considered a miniaturist, but the S.N.P.G. have a pencil and water-colour portrait of W. Cullen, M.D., signed and dated '1774'. It measures $3\frac{1}{4} \times 2\frac{3}{4}$ in. A miniature of a man signed 'D. Allan' was No. 811 in the Exhibition of Scottish Art at Burlington House in 1939. Died near Edinburgh, 1796.

Allan, J. McGregor. b. c. 1830. See also **Allen, J. M.**
Schidlof records that the above artist was born c. 1830. Listed by Long as exhibiting at the R.A., 1854–1856. He exhibited in 1854 from 19 Cecil Street, Strand, an oil portrait, and another oil portrait (no address given) in 1855. In the same year (1855) J. M. Allen (q.v.) is given in the R.A. catalogues as exhibiting a miniature portrait and a miniature on enamel from 14 Catherine Street, Strand. In 1856 a J. M. Allan is listed as exhibiting an enamel on porcelain from 27 Park Road, Peckham. This latter exhibit may have been the work of J. M. Allen.

*Allan, Sir William, R.A., P.R.S.A. 1782–1850
Born in Edinburgh, 1782; exhibited at the R.A., 1803–1849. Noted historical painter, apprenticed as a coach painter. Studied at the Trustees' Academy with David Wilkie and John Burnet the engraver. Went to London, imitated Opie, and had great success as a portrait painter. Not usually considered a miniaturist, but the V. & A. M. has a miniature signed 'Wm Allan, June 28. 1805', and the Scottish National Portrait Gallery has a rectangular oil miniature of William H. Murray (1790–1852) catalogued as by Sir William Allan. Died in Edinburgh, 1850.

*Allcock, S. A. (fl. 1821–1822)
Exhibited at the R.A., in 1821 and 1822. In 1821 his address was 45 Carnaby Street when he exhibited a portrait of his father – probably a miniature. In

1822 he exhibited a portrait of a lady, which may also have been a miniature, from 20 Whitfield Street, Finsbury. His initial is given as S in the catalogue and S.A. in the index. Was probably related to J. Alcock who exhibited an architectural drawing from 20 Whitfield Street in 1821.

*Allen, Mrs. (fl. c. 1830)
Worked in England c. 1830. Schidlof refers to a miniature sold in Vienna 6/7 June 1921 of a lady holding a fan and signed 'Mrs. Allen, Ural Park, Perthshire'.

*Allen, G. (fl. 1830)
Exhibited at the R.A. 1830, as an Honorary Member, Catalogue No. 981, 'Portrait of a Lady'; this was in the Antique Academy and may have been a miniature.

*Allen, J. M. (fl. 1855). See also **Allan, J. McGregor**
Exhibited at the R.A. 1855, from 14 Catherine Street, Strand, Master Henry from life, and the Rev. Benjamin Price of Clapham, an enamel. This artist is not recorded by either Graves or Long, but is listed in the R.A. catalogue for 1855 as exhibiting from the above address, when J. M. (McGregor?) Allan (q.v.) is listed separately (no address given). It seems likely that there were two artists, and that the enamel ascribed to Allan in 1856 was in fact the work of J. M. Allen.

Allen, Miss M. (fl. 1807–1813)
Worked in London and exhibited at the R.A., 1807–1813. These exhibits included her self-portrait.

Allen, T. (fl. 1854)
Of London. Exhibited at the R.A. 1854, an enamel portrait.

Allison, F. b. c. 1765
Born in London c. 1765. Exhibited at the Society of Artists 1790, and at the R.A. 1792–1799. Long records having seen an attractive unfinished miniature portrait of a lady, c. 1785, which showed an affinity to the work of Cosway (q.v.), and which, according to an inscription on the reverse, was by the above artist.

*Allison, J. W. (fl. 1908)
Exhibited at the R.A. 1908, from Havelock Villa, Outram Road, Southsea.

Allison, W. (fl. 1817–1819)
Of Southampton and London. Exhibited at the R.A., 1817. Long saw two miniatures of boys by him which were correctly drawn, but uninspiring and rather crudely executed. He painted a portrait of the Duchess of Kent, on ivory, signed 'Allison 1819', which was at one time in a collection in Paris.

*Allnutt, Miss Emily. (fl. 1900–1905)
Exhibited at the S.M. 1900–1903, and at the R.A. 1905, from 10 Clarence Crescent, Windsor.

Allston, Washington, A.R.A. 1779–1843
Born in South Carolina, 5 November 1779; studied at Harvard. Came to England 1801, and entered the R.A. Schools 23 October, aged 21. Exhibited at the R.A. 1802–1819. Visited Paris in 1804; spent four years in Italy. Returned to America 1808, but was back in England 1811. In 1817 revisited Paris with Leslie (q.v.). Was elected A.R.A. in 1818 and returned to America in the same year. Wrote on art, painted portraits, historical, religious and allegorical subjects, and is said to have painted a few miniatures without success. T. Bolton mentions two

miniatures by him as being at the Rhode Island School of Design, and another in Boston. He died in Cambridge, Mass. on 9 July 1843.

*Almond. 18th Century
Painted twenty-two miniatures of family servants for Lord Sackville of Knole, Kent, for 4 guineas a day, in 1783.

*Alvery. 19th Century
A miniature of Captain Charles Beetham by Alvery is reproduced on p. 66 in the *New Edition* of a *House of Letters* by Ernest B. Betham. Long noted that the artist worked until 1813.

Alves, James. 1737/8–1808
Born *c*. 1737/8, probably in Inverness where his family were well known. Was awarded a gold medal by the Edinburgh Society of Arts in 1756, by which time he had gone abroad to study painting. Exhibited at the R.A. 1775–1779. Was evidently in Inverness in 1773, and met Boswell and Johnson. Johnson recalls that he and Alves had met in Rome in 1765 – *Tour of the Hebrides*. John Barker in his diary, 17 April 1778, mentions two Master Nicholags as having sat to Alves. He was eight years in Rome, where he became a bigoted Roman Catholic. Alves worked in London and possibly in Scotland. Painted miniatures, small portraits in crayons and mythological subjects. Died in Inverness 27 November 1808. A miniature by this artist, signed in red 'Alves 1793', was formerly in the collection of Mr. Sidney Hand. It was well painted with a dark background and bluish shading round the face.

Alvey, William Charles. (fl. *c*. 1800–1805)
Probably identical with W. Alvey, a porcelain painter, who was employed at John Coke's factory at Pinxton (founded 1796). The V. & A. M. has a miniature *c*. 1805 which has an engraved card on the reverse 'Miniatures Painted from 2 to 10 Guineas / William Charles Alvey / Miniature Painter / No. 2, Strand / and 12, Middle Row, Holborn.' The face is shaded with a brownish tone and a lot of stippling. Long also mentions having seen a miniature of *c*. 1800 on the back of which was an engraved label bearing a female head with an anchor in her hair and the inscription 'Mr. Alvey / Miniature Painter . . . etc.'

*Ames, Mrs. 18th Century
Advertised as from 60 Bull Street, Birmingham in 1785. 'Takes likenesses of any size 2s to 5s each. Likenesses painted on glass' (*Birmingham Gazette*, 19 September 1785).

Anderson. (fl. 1817). See also **Andersson, Anders Gustaf**
Long records an artist of this name (no initial given) as working in Bell Street, Paddington in 1817. He was probably related to William Anderson who exhibited landscapes and seascapes at the R.A. and B.I., 1787–1834, from 46 and 48 Bell Street, and earlier from Horsleydown, New-Stairs. Schidlof suggests that Anderson was possibly identical with Anders Gustaf Andersson (q.v.) of Sweden, but this seems unlikely.

*Anderson, Miss Winifred. (fl. 1905)
Exhibited at the R.A. 1905, from Holt Side, Farnham, Surrey.

*Andersson, Anders Gustaf. 1788–1833. See also **Anderson**
Born in Sweden in 1788. Painted miniatures and oil portraits. Schidlof suggests that the above artist may have been identical with the Anderson (q.v.)

recorded by Long as working in London in 1817, but this seems unlikely. Died in 1833.

*Andras, Miss Catherine. (fl. 1799–1824)
Of London. Exhibited at the R.A. and B.I., 1799–1824. Was a 'Modeller in Wax to Her Majesty'. In 1800 she exhibited a portrait of T. Plummer, Esq. which may have been a miniature.

*André, David. b. 1684. See also **André, D. E.**
Born in Geneva, 16 May 1684; son of Jean André senior. Painted enamel miniatures early in his career; in 1704 he and his brother, Jean André junior, opened an art school in Geneva. A miniature on enamel dated 1709, and referred to by Long, as by D. E. André (q.v.), was probably by him. It is not known if he ever came to England. Schidlof mentions examples of his work in the Condé Museum, Chantilly and in various sales.

André, Dietrich Ernst. *c*. 1680–1735. See also **André, David**
An enamel miniature, dated '1790', has been attributed to D. E. André, a painter of portraits and historical subjects, who settled for a time in London. This is probably an error, and the enamel was probably executed by David André (q.v.).

André, Major John. 1751–1780
Born in London, 1751. A talented amateur artist. Painted and etched landscapes. Was hanged as a spy by the American forces, 2 October 1780. His self-portrait in miniature, said to have been drawn on the eve of his execution, was engraved by J. K. Sherwin. This portrait may be the one which is now in the Yale University Art Gallery. André is said to have executed some silhouettes which were reproduced in *The Connoisseur*, December 1926, p. 211, and included a self-portrait. A portrait attributed to S. Cotes (q.v.) and alleged to be of the above artist, is in the V. & A. M.

*Andree, Miss. (fl. 1825–1833)
Exhibited at the R.A., 1825–1833, as an Hon. Member, except for 1833, when she exhibited from 47 Hatton Gardens.

*Andrewes, Miss Elizabeth Catherine. (fl. 1900–1909)
Of Folkestone. Exhibited at the Society of Miniaturists, 1900–1909.

Andrews, D.R. 19th century
Exhibited at the R.A. 1820, from 10 Warwick Court, Gray's Inn, a miniature of H. Colewell, Esq. Long records seeing two miniatures by this artist in papier-mâché frames; a trade card at the back of one of them ended with 'N.B. Portraits painted in oil'. The miniatures were not of a very high quality, softly painted, and the drawing rather weak.

*Andrews, Edward William. (fl. 1860–1897)
Of London. Exhibited at the R.A., B.I., etc., 1860–1897. Painted fruit, miniatures, landscapes in water-colour and portrait drawings. His sitters included Professor John Ruskin and Cardinal Manning. He exhibited an etching of this last portrait in 1884. Married Emily J. Harding (q.v.) who exhibited at the R.A., from their address 4 St. George's Square, Regent's Park, 1897–1898, under her maiden name.

Andrews, Samuel. 1767?–1807
Said to have been an Irishman by birth. In 1791 applied to the East India Company for permission to go to Bengal. This application was refused, but he must have found some other way, for he arrived in Madras in the same year. He is probably the Samuel

Andrews who married in July 1795 Janetta Christina Elbracht. In the same year he moved into the house which John Smart (q.v.) had occupied in Madras, and advertised that he would attend to all orders for miniatures. He later moved to Calcutta and was there in 1798. Andrews painted miniatures in water-colour and *en grisaille* with dark backgrounds, often these were brown with the portraits in profile, and were signed on the front 'S. Andrews, Calcutta,' followed by a date, 'S. Andrews / 1807' etc.; some were signed on the reverse. His work has been confused with that of John Smart whose style he imitated, and with Sarah Addington (q.v.) whose initials he shared. Graham Reynolds considers that all miniatures signed S.A. should be attributed to Andrews. He died at Patna, 21 September 1807, aged 40. Schidlof notes miniatures painted with a very pointed brush, the face shaded with greenish shadows, the cheeks and mouth painted with a rather vivid red, which he considers are the work of Andrews and painted between 1780 and 1790. Examples of his work are in the V. & A. M.

*Angus, Miss Maria L. (fl. 1887–1910)
Of London. Exhibited at the R.A., etc., 1887–1910. Painted miniatures and subject paintings in oils and water-colour.

Appleton, Miss H. 19th century
An amateur artist of Brixton Oval. Was awarded a silver Isis medal in 1829 from the Society of Arts for a copy of a portrait in miniature.

*Archer, Edith. (fl. 1901–1905)
Of London. Exhibited at the R.A. 1901–1905, from 3 Elm Row, Hampstead, N.W. (1901), and from c/o Miss Butler, Cromwell Hall, East Finchley, N. London. Painted miniatures and subjects in water-colour.

Arichall, Francis. (fl. 1797)
Of London. Exhibited landscapes and miniatures at the R.A. 1797, from 3 Took's Court, Chancery Lane.

*Arkwright, Miss E. (fl. 1900–1901). See also **Arkwright, Miss Edith**
Of London. Exhibited at the Society of Miniaturists, 1900–1901. Possibly identical with Miss Edith Arkwright (q.v.).

*Arkwright, Miss Edith. (fl. 1884)
Of Brighton. Exhibited at the R.A. 1884, from 4 Denmark Terrace, Brighton. Possibly identical with Miss E. Arkwright (q.v.).

Arlaud, Benjamin. (fl. 1701–1721)
Born in Geneva *c*. 1670 (according to Schidlof); brother of J. A. Arlaud, whose family were clockmakers. Studied art in Geneva and took up miniature painting. Little is known about him, but the high quality of his work speaks for itself. He is thought to have been in England *c*. 1701–*c*. 1714. In the collection of H.M. the Queen of the Netherlands is a miniature of his wife, Jeanne Marie Arlaud (née Walker), painted by his brother, J. A. Arlaud. The inscription on the reverse contains the information that the miniature was painted in London in September 1721 when the sitter was a widow. From this evidence, B. Arlaud's date of death must have been at least ten years earlier than has hitherto been supposed. It is conceivable that he is identical with Benoît Arlaud (q.v.) who is said to have died in London in 1719. A miniature of Field Marshal George Wade, by Benjamin Arlaud, formerly in the Pierpont Morgan Collection, was

said to have been painted in 1731, but this must have been a mistake. He usually signed on the reverse, e.g. 'Benjamin Arlaud Pinxit / 1708'. He often delineated the eyebrows, upper eyelids and the corners of the eyes with red, and shaded the face with a greenish grey. Often the backgrounds are dark grey; his draughtsmanship was very good, and the general effect pleasing. A most attractive miniature of an unknown lady wearing a tricorn hat, red dress, and blue cloak, is in the collection of the Earl of Haddington and was exhibited in Edinburgh in 1965. A good miniature of an unknown man, which was examined by Long, is in my own collection. Examples of his work are in a number of private collections, including those of H.M. the Queen, the Duke of Buccleuch, the Duke of Portland, etc. Others are in the Rijksmuseum, Amsterdam, the National Museum, Munich and the Wallace Collection, London.

Arlaud, Benoit. d. 1719

The above artist is recorded by Benezit as having been born in Geneva. He is said to have worked successively in Amsterdam and London (1707) and to have been the youngest brother of J. A. Arlaud (q.v.). According to Benezit, portraits of the Princess Wilhelmina Charlotte DeGalles, and of the Baron Ezéchiel Spanhemius, were attributed to him. Long suggests that this artist may have been confused with Benjamin Arlaud (q.v.). Said to have died in 1719 in London.

Arlaud, Bernard or Benjamin. (fl. 1793–1825). See also Arlaux and Artaud

Redgrave records the name of this artist as coming from Geneva to London and exhibiting at the R.A., 1793–1800, and again in 1825 from Geneva. As neither the R.A. lists nor the indexes give the artist's christian name, it is impossible to identify this artist. Long may be correct in assuming that he was, in fact, L. A. Arlaud (q.v.). The reference to Benjamin Arland by Graves, and cited by Long, was probably a misprint, as in his Dictionary it is spelt Arlaud. Four miniatures attributed to Bernard Artaud (q.v.) were loaned to the South Kensington exhibition of 1865. These may have been by Bernard Arlaud.

Arlaud, Jacques Antoine. 1668–1746

Born in Geneva, 18 May 1668; son of a watchmaker whose family came from Auvergne; brother of B. Arlaud (q.v.). Gave up a brilliant career in classical studies to devote himself to miniature painting. Studied in Geneva for two or three years and in 1688 went to Paris where he became painter to the Prince Regent who granted him a lodging in his château at St. Cloud. Painted religious and mythological subjects in oils, as well as portraits in miniature. Came to London in 1721 and brought with him a copy of a 'Leda' after Michelangelo, or Correggio, which he is said to have sold for £600. Soon became popular, and he had a letter of introduction to Caroline, Princess of Wales. Said to have been 'loaded with presents' during his stay in England. Knew Sir Isaac Newton. Returned to Geneva 1729 and remained there up to his death in June 1746. A portrait of Arlaud by Largillière is in the Museum in Geneva. He painted at least two miniatures of Prince James Francis Edward Stuart (1688–1766). One is still in the family to whom it was given by the Prince, and is inscribed and dated on the reverse 'Jacobus / Antonius / Arlaud / Pincabat ad / Vivum / Mensis Octobris / ANNO 1702 / Jacobus Rex.' In this miniature the Prince was only 14 years of age; another miniature of him by Arlaud is in the Wallace Collection, London; it shows him as an older man. The former miniature was exhibited in Edinburgh in 1965. His miniatures,

which are painted in gouache on vellum or card are beautifully drawn, and executed in restrained colours. Examples of his work are in the V. & A. M., the Louvre, the Nationalmuseum, Stockholm, and in private collections including those of H.M. the Queen, and H.M. the Queen of the Netherlands. This latter collection contains an interesting and attractive miniature of the artist's sister-in-law, engraved on the reverse of the frame, 'Jeane Marie / Walker. Nee / Dans le Palatinat / veuve de Benjamin Arlaud / Peintre a Londres par / son beaufrere Jacques / Antoine Arlaud / citoyen de geneve / au mois de Septbre / 1721.'.

Arlaud (–Jurine), Louis Ami. 1751–1829. See also Arlaux

Born in Geneva, 13 October 1751; grand-nephew of J. A. Arlaud (q.v.). Was taught by Liotard (q.v.) in Geneva; went to Paris and studied under Vivien, the historical painter. Visited Italy; returned to Geneva in 1778. Practised principally as a miniaturist on ivory, but also painted enamel and watercolour portraits and retouched pictures. Charged from 5 to 25 louis for a miniature. Was a prolific artist. Came to London in 1792 and soon became popular. Was probably the L. R. Arlaud (q.v.) who exhibited at the R.A. 1792, from Chelsea, and thought to be the Arlaud who exhibited miniatures at the R.A. 1793–1800, from different London addresses and, in 1825, a miniature of Joseph Marie Coutet, guide at Chamouni; this last exhibit was said by Redgrave to have been sent from Geneva. Neither the R.A. catalogues nor the indexes give a christian name for these exhibits. L. A. Arlaud painted portraits of Swiss, Frenchmen, actresses and members of the aristocracy. If he was the artist who exhibited at the R.A. in 1796, his entries included Signora Storace, and H.R.H. Princess Sophia of Gloucester. Arlaud was fond of fencing, riding and playing the violin. A. E. Chalon (q.v.), Mlle Liotard, Mlle Jurine and Mme Mayor were said to have been his pupils. He returned to Geneva in 1802 and painted 645 more portraits. Whilst in England he painted several portraits of Prince Edward, Duke of Kent. His work is good, and his miniatures well drawn and pleasing. After his stay in Britain his works show the influence of the English school. Works by him are scarce. He died in Pré-l'Évêque, 8 August 1829. A miniature in my collection, of a Mr. Bryan, is signed 'Arlaud' on the front, in cursive writing. Schidlof mentions others in Geneva including his self-portrait, and a miniature of a lady, signed 'L. Arlaud'. Examples of his work are in the V. & A. M. and the Holzscheiter Collection, Meilen. In the collection of the Duke of Northumberland is an attractive miniature, signed and dated, 'L. Arlaud / 179–' (the last numeral being indecipherable). It represents George Percy, afterwards 5th Duke of Northumberland and his sister Charlotte Percy, afterwards Countess of Ashburnham. This miniature, which is painted on vellum, oblong, and is beautifully executed, shows the sitters as children.

Arlaud, L.R. (fl. 1792)

Of Chelsea. Exhibited at the R.A., 1792. May possibly have been L.A. Arlaud (q.v.). In the index, the name is spelt Arland, and the exhibit No. 303 was entitled 'The Mouse-trap'. The address was given as 12 Grosvenor-row, Chelsea.

*Arlaux. See also Arlaud, Bernard and Arlaud, Louis Ami

A miniature of Mr. William Byrne (1743–1805), the landscape engraver, painted in 1796, was loaned to the South Kensington Exhibition of 1865. It was catalogued as by the above artist, but may have been by Bernard Arlaud (q.v.) or Louis Ami Arlaud (q.v.).

*Armitage, Charles de W. (fl. 1903–1905)

Of London. Exhibited at the R.A. 1903–1905, from 39 Grosvenor Street, Grosvenor Square. His sitters included Captain A. W. H. Lees and Captain C. H. Armitage, D.S.O.

*Armstrong, Miss Caroline. (fl. 1885–1897)

Of London. Exhibited at the R.A., 1885–1897. Painted miniatures and large oil paintings.

Armstrong, S. D. (fl. 1813)

A miniature of a lady, signed in full and dated 'Aug. 1813' on the reverse, and signed 'SDA' in white on the front, was seen by Long. The work was not of any great merit, the face and background both being rather pink.

*Armstrong Carr, Miss. (fl. 1901–1911)

Of London. Exhibited at the R.A., 1901–1911. Painted miniatures and landscapes in oils.

*Arnauld.

An advertisement for a miniature by this artist appeared in The Daily Advertiser, 9 August 1796. 'Lost a miniature painted by Arnauld.' The name may have been a misspelling for Arlaud (q.v.).

*Arnold, Mrs. Annie Merrylees. See Merrylees, Miss Annie R.

*Arnold, Annie R. (fl. 1901–1914). See Merrylees, Miss Annie R.

Exhibited at the R.A. 1901 and 1914. Was probably identical with Mrs. A. M. Arnold who exhibited under that name and under her maiden name of Annie Merrylees (q.v.).

*Arnold, Miss Edith M. (fl. 1910)

Exhibited at the R.A. 1910, from 33 Manor Park, Lee, London, S.E.

*Arnold, Mrs. L. A. (fl. 1908)

Exhibited at the R.A. 1908, from Amwell, Ware, Herts.

*Arnold, Miss Mary. (fl. 1899). See also Arnold, Miss May

Exhibited a miniature of Mrs. T. G. Jackson at the R.A. 1899, from Stamford House, West Side, Wimbledon. Was probably identical with Miss May Arnold (q.v.) who exhibited from the same address in 1898.

*Arnold, Miss May. (fl. 1898–1911). See also Arnold, Miss Mary

Of Wimbledon and Horsham. Exhibited at the R.A. and S.M., 1898–1911. Probably identical with Miss Mary Arnold (q.v.) who exhibited at the R.A. in 1899 from Stamford House, West Side, Wimbledon, from which address Miss May Arnold exhibited in the previous year. Benezit suggests that they were sisters, but this seems unlikely.

Arnold, R. (Reginald Edward?) (fl. 1791)

Of London. Exhibited at the R.A. and Society of Artists 1791, from 123 High Holborn. Exhibited portraits and miniatures on ivory and enamel. Possibly Reginald Edward Arnold, R.B.A., who married Miss Annie Merrylees (q.v.). The V. & A. M. has a portrait of a man, signed 'Arnold'.

Arrowsmith, Thomas. (fl. 1792–1829)

Of London. Was deaf and dumb. Exhibited at the R.A., 1792–1829. Painted religious subjects and miniatures, including ones of Flaxman (q.v.) and the Bishop of Hereford. Said to have been working in Manchester c. 1827. One Thomas Arrowsmith married Elizabeth Carpenter (who was illiterate) at St. Mary-le-bone, 17 September 1812. May have worked in Lancashire. Long saw a small portrait in oil on canvas by him which he thought quite good. An engraved portrait of John Emery, an actor, after Arrowsmith is at the B.M. In 1798 his exhibits included a self-portrait. Long records seeing a miniature of a man painted by Arrowsmith in July 1796; it was not of any great merit, and was a weak imitation of Cosway (q.v.). A miniature of a little girl, signed and dated '1796', is in the collection of E.G. Paine of New York.

*Artaud, Bernard. See also **Arlaud, Bernard**

Four miniatures attributed to Bernard Artaud were loaned to the South Kensington Exhibition of 1865. They may have been the work of Benjamin Arlaud (q.v.).

Artaud, William. b. 1763

Son of a jeweller; entered the R.A. Schools, 31 December 1778 aged '15 24th last March'; was awarded a silver medal 1783, and a gold medal, 1786. According to the R.A. School entries he was sent abroad in 1795. Was awarded silver palettes by the Society of Arts in 1775 or 1776, and in 1777 for drawings after pictures, and in 1782 for historical drawings. Exhibited at the R.A., 1780–1822. Painted figure subjects, portraits in oil, miniatures (one of which was an enamel), historical drawings, etc. Gave evidence in the Delatre v Copley case in the King's Bench, 2 July 1801. Joined an artists' volunteer corps in 1803. He executed an enamel copy of 'The Calling of Samuel' after Reynolds, which was signed on the reverse 'Wm Artaud fecit / 1782'. Several engraved portraits by him are at the B.M.

Arundale, Mrs. Francis. b. c. 1806

Of London and Brighton (1846–1847). Entered the R.A. Schools, 22 April 1829 aged 23. Exhibited at the R.A., 1839–1862.

Ashburnham, Mrs. Denny (Miss Nancy Dickson, later Mrs. T. F. Bancroft)

Née Nancy Dickson; only child of Joseph Dickson of Calcutta. Was a wealthy and beautiful heiress who was brought out by the Duchess of Chandos. Studied Latin, Greek, Hebrew, French and Italian. Painted miniatures. Married firstly T. F. Bancroft (Mrs. Lister, in *Reminiscences Social and Political*, says Samuel Bancroft); was left a widow and married in July 1802, the Rev. Denny Ashburnham (1773–1843), Rector of Catsfield, and Vicar of Ditchling; son of Sir William Ashburnham of Broomham, Sussex. She was found dead, perhaps murdered, in May 1818. Burke does not, as stated by Long, say that she died without issue, but that she left 'with other issue' a daughter, Harriet Alicia. This may have been the daughter said by Mrs. Lister to have been the ward of Lord Lyndhurst.

Ashby, Arthur. (fl. c. 1830)

Was living in Oakhampton Street, Exeter in 1830.

*Ashby, Harry. (fl. 1794–1836)

Exhibited at the R.A., 1794–1836. Said by Schidlof to have been only an average artist. He noted a miniature of a young boy in blue costume, signed 'Ashby pinx. 1814', which was sold in Brussels 27–28 April 1934.

Ashfield, Edmund. d. c. 1700

Said to have been a pupil of Michael Wright. Worked during the latter part of the 17th century, lived at the 'Red Ball' in Holborn Row, Lincoln's Inn Fields; was 'a sober Person and suspected to be a Roman Catholick'. Signed pastels which are small and well executed, date from 1673–1675. He is said to have painted miniatures, but none have been discovered which can be ascribed to him with certainty. A portrait on card 2½ × 3 ins., of La Duchesse de Mazarin, and a drawing in pencil on paper of John, 4th Duke of Somerset and Mar-

quess of Hereford, were catalogued as by him in the Wellesley sale in 1920. Said to have died c. 1700.

*Ashley, Mrs.

Long recorded an artist of this name who was a miniaturist, but did not give any details. She may have been identical with the Mrs. Ashley of London, who exhibited at the Free Society of Artists and the Society of Artists, 1768–1772, and who painted fruit pieces, religious subjects and portraits in crayon and Indian ink; some after Rembrandt. Her portraits included one of 'His late Highness the Duke of York' and 'the King of Denmark'.

*Ashton, William. (fl. 1899–1914)

Of Cheshire. Exhibited at the R.A. 1899–1914, from 19 Euston Grove, Claughton, Cheshire. Painted landscapes in water-colour and, in 1900, exhibited 'A reverie' in the miniature section.

Askew, Richard. (fl. 1781–1786)

Of London, living in March 1781 at 'Coy's Gardens,' Tottenham Court Road. Painted miniatures on enamel. Was employed by James Pearson, glass painter of Westminster, on a window designed by J. H. Mortimer, and offered by the 2nd Earl of Radnor to Salisbury Cathedral, the subject being 'the Elevation of the Brazen Serpent'. Thomas Normansel, whose portrait Askew was painting in 1781, was acquitted of a charge of assault on Askew's wife. Askew later went to Dublin, where he advertised in *Faulkner's Journal*, 16 February 1786.

*Aslett, G. b. c. 1787. See also **Astlett, G.**

Entered the R.A. Schools, 4 January 1806, aged 19. A miniature, signed and dated '1807', oval 3½ in., was sold on 13 November 1962 at Christie's; it was Lot 124 and depicted a gentleman wearing a blue coat and white cravat. A miniature of a lady, signed 'G. Aslett / 1807' is in the collection of Major R.M.O. de la Hey.

Assen, Benedictus Antonio van. c. 1767–c. 1817

Worked in London. Presumably identical with Anthony van Asson, or van Assen, who entered the R.A. Schools, 4 December 1783, aged '16. 12th Inst Decemr', and who obtained a silver medal in 1786. Exhibited at the R.A., 1788–1804. Was an engraver, draughtsman, copyist and miniaturist. A drawing by him is in the Nottingham Castle Museum. Engraved portraits after A. van Assen are in the B.M. A family group of Mrs. Soane and sons, by 'Van Hassen', is in the Soane Museum, and is probably by this artist. Died c. 1817.

Astles, S. (fl. 1827)

Of Worcester. Exhibited a painting of flowers on china, after van Hysum, at the R.A., 1827. An artist of this name worked at the Derby China factory.

Astlett, G. (fl. 1807). See also **Aslett, G.**

Exhibited a triple portrait, possibly a miniature, of Mr. and Mrs. Cannon and Miss Wilton at the R.A., 1807; was doubtless a pupil of C. Hayter (q.v.) from whose address he exhibited. A miniature, signed 'G. Aslett / 1807', is in the collection of Major de la Hey. The two artists may be identical.

*Aston, Lady Willoughby. 18th century

A miniature of Sir Willoughby Aston (died 1772) painted by his wife, is in the collection of Mrs. Louisa Miller. It represents a youngish man in full white wig, blue cloak, white lace cravat, in an ebony case, inscribed on the reverse 'Sir Willoughby Aston painted by his wife, the ebony case turned by herself'.

Athow, T. (fl. 1806–1822)

Worked in London and the provinces. Exhibited at the R.A., 1806–1822. Painted water-colour copies of oil paintings and landscapes. Some of his works may have been miniatures.

*Atkins, Miss Elsie. (fl. 1903–1904)

Of London. Exhibited at the R.A., 1903–1904, from 1 Trafalgar Studios, Manresa Road, London.

Atkins, Miss G. (fl. 1849–1850)

Of London. Exhibited at the Society of British Artists, 1849–1850.

Atkins, James. 1799–1833

Born 1799, son of James Atkins of Stranraer, Scotland, who carried on a business as a coach painter in Belfast, where his son was born; assisted his father with his heraldic painting. Studied at the Belfast Academical Institution, 1814–1818; was under Gaetano Fabbrini. Was awarded a medal in 1818 for a painting in oil. He painted portraits and miniatures. Exhibited at the Institution, where his work attracted attention. The Marquess of Londonderry, and others, sent him to Italy in 1819, where he remained for thirteen years, copying the works of old masters in Rome, Florence and Venice. Exhibited at the R.A., from Rome in 1831 and 1833. In 1832 he went to Constantinople to paint a portrait of the Sultan, and on his way home whilst undergoing quarantine in Malta, he contracted consumption and died there in December 1833.

Aubr(e)y.

Long records this artist as exhibiting at the R.A., 1797 (No. 967), but this must be an error; No. 967 is given in the index as by J. Bowring, and is also catalogued as by J. Bowring. No Aubrey exhibited in that year.

*Augustin, Jean Baptiste Jacques. 1759–1832

Born in St. Dié, 15 August 1759. One of the greatest miniaturists of the French school. Long noted that he came to England, but gave no details, and I have been unable to confirm this fact. He died in Paris 13 April 1832. For further information see Schidlof, pp. 53 and 54. Some of his works were exhibited at the South Kensington Exhibition of 1865.

*Austin, Mrs. (fl. 1835–1838)

Of Bristol. Exhibited at the R.A., 1835–1838, portraits which may have been miniatures. Had addresses in Harford Place, Bristol (1835) and 10 Orchard Street, Bristol (1838).

Austin, Miss Christina. (fl. 1783–1797)

Of London. Exhibited at the Society of Artists 1783–1791, and at the R.A., 1792–1797. Painted miniature portraits, mythological subjects, and drew in red chalk. A miniature by her was lent to the exhibition at South Kensington Museum, 1865.

*Austin, Francis Joseph. 18th Century

Said by Schidlof to have worked in England towards the end of the 18th century. He saw a signed miniature on ivory, c. 1790, painted in the manner of N. Plimer (q.v.).

Austin, Thomas, junior. (fl. 1779)

Of London. Exhibited an enamel portrait at the Society of Artists 1779, from Crown Street, Soho.

*Austin-Carter, Miss Mathilde, R.M.S. b. 1840

Born in Bristol 1840. Daughter of J.H. and Elizabeth Carter (q.v.), both miniaturists. Was a pupil of her mother. Painted subjects in water-colour, but from 1890 confined her work to miniatures on ivory. Exhibited at the S.M. 1900–1907.

Avarne, Mrs. William. 1749–1826

Born in 1749, née Charlotte Hemington, daughter of R. Hemington of Donnington Park, Leicester. Married in 1775 the Rev. Wm. Avarne, private tutor to the Countess of Huntingdon's children. Met many persons in the Countess's circle, and painted a number of clergy. Was a widow in 1784. Exhibited at the R.A. 1793. Had an estate in the Isle of Man, but seems to have lived chiefly in London. Died 1826. Her work was well drawn and showed the influence of Shelley (q.v.) and Engleheart (q.v.), particularly in the manner of drawing curls in the hair. Occasionally she painted in profile. Examples of her miniatures are at the V. & A. M.

*Axford, Miss Edith. (fl. 1906–1911)

Exhibited at the R.A. 1906–1911, from Maycourt, Campden Road, South Croydon. Her sitters included Mrs. Arthur Glegg.

*Ayles, Mrs. Ellen. (fl. 1893)

Of Tilbury. Exhibited at the R.A. 1893, from 2 The Garden, Tilbury. The sitter was the Rev. Canon Colson.

*Ayling, Albert W. (fl. 1843–1892)

Of Guernsey, 1853; London, 1854 and 1880; Chester, 1855–1872; Liverpool, 1886 and Conway, 1892. Exhibited at the R.A., N.W.C.S., etc., 1843–1892. He painted portraits, possibly miniatures; studies of fruit, large oil paintings, water-colours and landscapes. In 1872 'Still pool, N. Wales' (large oil), sold for 21 guineas and, in 1886, 'Waiting for the tide', water-colour, sold for 70 guineas.

*Ayling, John. (fl. 1823–1842)

Of London. Exhibited at the R.A. 1823–1842, from various London addresses. Painted portraits in oil, and a number of other portraits, probably miniatures, which were exhibited in the miniature section including, in 1827, that of John Love, Esq., which was erroneously catalogued as by W. Ayling (q.v.), when it was lent by Mr. J. Love to the exhibition at the South Kensington Museum in 1865 (No. 1038). Had an address at 39 Nutford Place, Bryanstone Square, 1829–1833.

Ayling, W. See also **Ayling, John**

A miniature of Mr. J. Love was catalogued in error as by W. Ayling, when it was lent to the exhibition at the South Kensington Museum, 1865. The entry states that it was on ivory, and painted in 1827. It was identical with the miniature of Mr. J. Love by J. Ayling (q.v.), exhibited at the R.A. in 1827 (catalogue No. 860).

*Aylmer, H.

A miniature painted in the style of a silhouettist was seen by Mr. A. J. B. Kiddell, who thought it was probably the work of an Irish artist. He may have been related to J. Aylmer (q.v.).

Aylmer, John. 1815?–1868

Born 1815? Worked in Dublin. Exhibited regularly at the R.H.A., 1847–1854. Later abandoned miniature painting and became a 'photographic artist'. He died at his house, 6 Hamilton Row, Dublin, on 7 January 1868, aged 53.

B

B., F.L.

An attractive enamel miniature of Charles I after Van Dyck, signed in monogram 'F.L.B.' or 'T.L.B.', is in the collection of H.M. the Queen of the Netherlands. It is softly painted in brilliant colours.

*B., G. 19th century

A well painted miniature of Major Pardoe, J.P., D.L., signed and dated 'G.B. 1843', was in a sale at Sotheby's, 25 July 1966. There was an inscription on the reverse noting that 'Major Pardoe of Lower Park in the County of Worcester, died from a fall from his horse in March 1827, aged 51'. From the costume, the sitter would appear to have been painted c. 1805, and the miniature was evidently painted from an earlier portrait, probably as a memorial. A miniature of a gentleman, signed and dated 'G.B. 1837', was sold at Christie's, 15 October 1963.

B., G. (fl. c. 1780). See also **Bemfleet, G.**

A miniature of a man, signed 'GB' in Roman capitals, was seen by Long; it appeared to date from c. 1780 and may possibly have been by G. Bemfleet (q.v.). The draughtsmanship was not very good, and the face was rather laboriously stippled and had a brownish tone.

B., J. 18th century

Long records having seen a miniature with a stippled background, signed '1768/JB' (cursive monogram). A miniature of a man, signed and dated '1796, JB', was sold at Puttick & Simpson, 31 March 1933.

B., J.H. (fl. 1780)

An amateur artist who exhibited at the R.A. in 1780.

*B., J.J.M. (fl. 1783)

An enamel miniature signed 'J.J.M.B. 1783' was sold at Sotheby's, 9 March 1964.

*B., M.

A miniature signed 'MB' (monogram) and painted in the manner of Mrs. Mee (q.v.) was sold at Sotheby's, 15 May 1930.

*B., P. See **P., B.**

*B., S. (fl. 1787)

I have seen a miniature of the Madonna and Child, signed 'S.B. 1787'. It was oval, 4½ in. high.

*B., T.L. See **B., F.L.**

*B., V. See **V., B.**

*B., W.E. (fl. c. 1750).

A miniature of the Duke of Monmouth, c. 1750, signed 'W.E.B.', was noted by Long.

Babu. (fl. 1765–1775)

Of London. Exhibited miniatures and crayon portraits at the Free Society of Artists, 1765 and, in 1775, at the Society of Artists.

*Bach, Mrs. Alice Guido. (fl. 1909–1910)

Of London. Exhibited at the Society of Miniaturists, 1909–1910. Her sitters included Mrs. Ernst Bach.

Backhoffner, Mrs. Caroline (Miss Derby). b. c. 1810

Born c. 1810, née Caroline Derby. Daughter of William Derby (q.v.) and a sister of Miss Emma Maria Derby (q.v.) with whom she lived before her marriage. Was awarded a silver palette in 1826 by the Society of Arts and, in 1827, a silver Isis medal for a chalk drawing of a bust. Obtained a similar award in 1828 for an oil painting from a bust and, in 1829, for a miniature (a copy). In 1832 she won a large silver medal for a water-colour portrait. Exhibited at the R.A., S.B.A., etc., 1830–1835. Married between 1832 and 1835. Her exhibits up to 1833 were under her maiden name and, in 1835, under 'Mrs. Backhoffner, late Miss Derby.'

*Backhouse, Mrs. (fl. 1846–1882)

Née Margaret Holden. Of London. Exhibited at the R.A., etc., 1846–1882. Painted portraits and figure subjects. Her earlier exhibits were in the drawing and miniature section; some of these portraits could have been miniatures. Her daughter, Miss Mary Backhouse, later Mrs. W. E. Miller, was also an artist and exhibited at the R.A., from her mother's address, 2 Whitley Villas, Caledonian Road, for some years.

*Badcock, Mrs. E. B. (fl. 1907–1913)

Of London. Exhibited at the R.A., 1907–1913. Her sitters included H.R.H. Princess Louise of Argyll and the Duke of Argyll.

*Badcock, Miss Isabel B. (fl. 1905–1914)

Exhibited at the R.A. 1905–1914, from Somerleaze, Wells, Somerset. Exhibits included miniatures and subject paintings in water-colour. Her sitters included Captain G. W. Probert. Was probably identical with the artist who exhibited at Suffolk Street, etc., from Ripon, 1886–1889.

*Bailey, Mrs. Ethel Porter-. See **Porter, Miss Ethel**

Bailey, G. (fl. 1786–1797)

Of London. Exhibited at the R.A. 1786–1797, from various London addresses. Painted miniatures and a few portraits which may have been small, but were not exhibited in the miniature section.

Bailey, John William. 1831–1914

Born in London, 27 April 1831; son of a tanner. Educated in Stratford-on-Avon. Was a pupil of W. Essex (q.v.) whom he assisted until the latter's death. Exhibited at the R.A. and S.B.A., 1859–1889. Painted enamels of dogs and portraits, etc., many being copies, Worked at Buckingham Palace and for the Rajah of Kolapore (in England). Collaborated for a short time with W. C. Bell (q.v.). He usually signed on the reverse, 'J. W. Bailey', followed by a date. His works lacked some of the finish of those of W. B. Ford (q.v.), but were more lively. He was married and had eight children, of whom his son, Arthur Alexander, was his pupil. He died 20 May 1914, aged 83. The R.A. catalogues for 1862 and 1863 give his initials as T. W. Bailey; this must be a misprint, as the exhibit for 1862, of Lady Nugent, an enamel after Lawrence, is now at the Ashmolean, and signed on the reverse.

*Bailey, Miss Mildred B. (fl. 1895)

Exhibited at the R.A. 1895, from 78 Mountview Road, Stroud Green, N. London. The sitter was Mrs. Gertrude Lock.

*Bailey, T. W. (fl. 1862–1863). See also **Bailey, John William**

The R.A. catalogues for 1862 and 1863 record a T. W. Bailey. This was probably a misprint for J. W. Bailey (q.v.).

Bailey, Thomas. (fl. *c.* 1840)

Painted portraits and landscapes; was a professor of miniature painting. Worked from Seller Street, Chester in 1840.

Bainborough, William. See Bamborough, William

*Baine, Louisa. 18th century. See also **Bone, Louisa**

This artist is known only by a miniature, in my collection, of Sir George Berkeley, which is inscribed on the reverse of the gold locket, 'Sir George Berkley / by Louisa Baine'. The miniature is oil on ivory, and in the manner of Leakey (q.v.). I have seen three family miniatures in a private collection which were undoubtedly by the same hand. They were well painted and had a slightly brick red flesh colouring as in the case of the one in my collection, which depicts the sitter in scarlet uniform of the 18th century. It is possible that the artist's name was wrongly inscribed and that it was the work of Louisa Bone (q.v.).

Baines, Miss Catherine. (fl. 1857–1860)

Of London. Exhibited enamels at the R.A., 1857–1860. She executed studies from nature, enamels after Landseer and, in 1859, a portrait miniature of E. M. Baines, Esq., enamel on porcelain.

*Baker, Miss Eve. (fl. 1909)

Exhibited at the R.A. 1909, from Albany Studios, Charing Cross, Glasgow.

*Baker, J. (fl. *c.* 1785)

According to *Adam's Weekly Courant*, 17 May 1785, a miniaturist of this name had apartments in Chester.

*Baker, Miss Julia. (fl. 1901–1910)

Of 27 Hollywood Road, London, S.W. Exhibited at the R.A., 1901 and 1910.

*Baker, Miss Martha Susan. 1871–1911

Born in Evansville, Indiana, 20 December 1871. Studied at the Chicago Art Institute. Painted miniatures and subjects in oil and water-colour, as well as executing some murals. Exhibited at the R.A. 1908, from 70 bis Rue Notre Dame des Champs, Paris and at the Paris Salon, 1909. Died in Chicago, 1911.

Baker, Miss Mary. (fl. 1834–1856)

Of London. Awarded premiums by the Society of Arts in 1834 and 1837. Exhibited miniatures, etc., at the R.A., 1842–1856. An oil painting by her is in the V. & A. M.

*Baker, Mrs. Sophia de Chair. (fl. 1902–1906)

Worked in Surrey and London, and exhibited at the Society of Miniaturists, 1902–1906. Sometimes indexed under De Chair.

*Baker, Miss Violet. (fl. 1904–1910)

Of Oxford. Exhibited at the Society of Miniaturists, 1904–1910.

*Balaca, José. 1810–1869

Born in Cartagena in 1810. From 1836 was a pupil at the School of Painting in Madrid. Established himself in Lisbon in 1844 as a portrait painter and miniaturist. He travelled extensively and spent some time in England and France. Settled in Madrid and exhibited there from 1852. His sitters included the Queen of Portugal. Died in Madrid, 19 November 1869.

*Baldrey, John K. b. 1750? d. after 1821

Said to have been born *c.* 1750. Worked in London and Cambridge from *c.* 1780. Chiefly noted as an etcher and draughtsman, but also painted portraits in water-colour. Schidlof records a portrait on card, signed on the reverse 'by Jn Baldrey del. 1807 Cambridge'. Died probably in Hatfield after 1821.

Baldwin, Benjamin. (fl. 1826–1847)

Of London. Working in 1826 at 2 Hanway Street, London. Exhibited at the R.A. 1842–1845, from 46 and 27 Rathbone Place. In 1845 he exhibited a portrait of the Duke of Brunswick. A pair of miniatures of a lady and gentleman, signed on the reverse and dated '1847' (4¼ in. rectangular), were sold at Christie's, Lot 17, on 10 April 1962.

Ball, I. (fl. 1765)

A miniature signed 'I. Ball 1765' was sold at Sotheby's, 18 July 1929.

*Ballantyne, Miss Jean (Mrs. A. Lowis). (fl. 1906–1910)

Of London. Exhibited at the R.A., 1906 and 1910. Exhibited under her maiden name. Her sitters included Captain Ballantyne, 19th Bengal Lancers.

Ballard, James. d. 1792

An Irish artist who was a pupil in the Dublin Society's Schools where he obtained prizes in 1753, 1754 and 1756. Exhibited in Dublin, 1766–1777. Was a drawing teacher of some repute for many years. In 1766 he was living in Bull Lane and, from 1767–1777, in Mary's Abbey. He died in 1792. Some of his works were engraved including a portrait of Dean Swift. A miniature of a lady, signed and dated '1768', is in the National Museum, Dublin.

*Ball-Hughes, Miss Georgina. (fl. 1889)

Of London. Exhibited at the R.A. 1889, from 5 Lyndhurst Road, Hampstead. Her sitter was Trevor, eldest son of Henry S. Hume, Esq.

Ballinger, Thomas. (fl. *c.* 1810–1826)

Of London. A miniature signed on the reverse with the address 6 Middle Row, Holborn, *c.* 1810 was seen at the V. & A. M. In 1826 Ballinger was working from 91 Strand, London.

*Bally, Miss Gladys M. (fl. 1903)

Of London. Exhibited at the R.A. 1903, from 6 Queen's Mansions, Brook Green.

*Bamborough, William. 1792–1860

Born in Durham, 1792. Went to America in 1819 and settled in Columbus, Ohio. Was a friend of J. J. Audubon with whom he travelled between 1824 and 1832. Said to have been in Shippenport (1830), Louisville (1832). Was living in Columbus, 19 September 1850 with his wife, Lucy (born *c.* 1811 in Pennsylvania), and a daughter Mary (born *c.* 1844 in Ohio). Painted portraits, some of which may have been miniatures. Long records the name as Bainborough, but this appears to be a mistake. Died 1860.

Bancks or Banks, Charles. (fl. 1738–1792)

A Swede who, according to Redgrave, came to England as a young man in 1746. Exhibited a miniature of 'Diana & Endymion' at the R.A. in 1792, from Portland Row, Portland Place, London. Not to be confused with Charles Banks, the sculptor, who was working at the same period. A drawing by him, executed in Indian ink on card, of a lady, and signed on the reverse 'C. Bancks fecit, 1756', is

at the V. & A.M. The B.M. has a portrait of Michael Descazeaux du Hally engraved by Beauvais in 1747 after Bancks. McArdell engraved a self-portrait of Bancks, prints of which are in the B.M.

Bancroft, Mrs. T. F. See Ashburnham, Mrs. Denny

*Banford, James. b. 1758

Born 7 May 1758 at Berkeley, Gloucestershire. Son of Thomas Banford, goldsmith, and grandson of Thomas Banford senior, goldsmith, of London. His uncle and godfather worked for the Chelsea China Factory, 1747–1751. James Banford junior was apprenticed to Richard Compton of Bristol, 1773. Worked at the Chelsea Factory, 1781–4; Derby, 1786–95; and Bilston, 1791. Said by Long to have painted miniatures.

*Bannister, Miss Isabel. (fl. 1910)

Of London. Exhibited at the Society of Miniaturists, 1910.

Barber and Giles. (fl. 1762). See also **Giles, James**

Exhibited enamel miniatures at the Society of Artists, 1762.

Barber, Christopher. 1736/8–1810

Born *c.* 1736/8. Exhibited at the Society of Artists (of which he was a member), 1763–1765; at the Free Society of Artists, 1763–1769 and at the R.A., 1770–1808. Painted portraits in oil and water-colour, miniatures (some copies) and heads in chalk, subject pictures, landscapes, etc. Was fond of music. Painted a self-portrait aged 70 years. Died in Great Marylebone Street, London, 8 March 1810.

Barber, John Thomas. See Beaumont, John Thomas Barber

Barber or Barbor, Lucius. d. 1767

Worked in London; said to have been a Swede. Exhibited at the Society of Artists, 1763–1766. Painted portraits in oil and water-colour as well as miniatures, some of which were on enamel. An enamel portrait of Lord Edward Bentinck, in the collection of the Duke of Portland, is signed on the reverse 'L. Barber ad Vivum pinx[t] 1749'. The Society of Artists gives his name as Barbor. He lived in the Haymarket. Although Long records his date of death as 7 November 1767, he is probably identical with the artist whose death is recorded in *Lloyd's Evening Post*, 2 November 1767 – 'Mr Barber, painter Haymarket. Died 31. Oct 1767'. His widow is said to have been left in distressed circumstances. He signed with cursive initials in monogram LB, B and in full. His work was good and rather smoother than that of Zincke's (q.v.). He used a greenish tone in shading the background. There may have been some confusion between the work of this artist and that of R. Barber (q.v.), and it is probable that the copy made for Mrs. Delany, and mentioned by Long, was in fact the work of R. Barber. A miniature of an unknown lady, signed 'B' on the front, is in the National Gallery, Dublin; it is very attractive.

Barber, Rupert. (fl. 1736–1772)

Son of Jonathan Barber, a woollen draper in Capel Street, Dublin, and his wife, Mary Barber, the poetess, who was a friend and protegée of Swift. Was sent to study in Bath *c.* 1736. Returned to Dublin by 1743 where he practised as a miniature painter on enamel. Was befriended by Mrs. Delany and given a house at the end of the garden at Delville, near Dublin. Painted several miniatures of her on enamel. Was in London, 1748 and Bath, 1752. Executed an enamel miniature of Mrs. Donnellan.

Besides miniatures he painted portraits in oil and experimented in glass-making. Was awarded a premium by the Dublin Society in 1753 for making phials and green glass. Married in March 1742 a Miss Wilson, 'a very pretty and prudent woman' according to Mrs. Delany, by whom he had a daughter and a son who studied in the Dublin Society Schools before becoming an officer in the artillery. In 1772 he appears to have been involved in a project with a distillery by which he incurred a heavy debt. He was in Dublin up to 1772, but the date of his death is not known. He painted an enamel miniature of William Thompson, a Dublin beggar, aged 114, in 1744 which was exhibited at the Burlington Fine Arts Club Exhibition of 1887, and sold at Sotheby's on 11 December 1958, in the Dyson Perrins Collection; it was inscribed on the reverse 'Gulielms Thompson Mendicans Dublini Ann. 1744, Aetat 114. R. Barber Pinxt.' A black chalk drawing, $12 \times 8\frac{1}{2}$ in., sold at Sotheby's, 4 May 1921, was a sketch for this miniature. It is possible that there has been some confusion between the work of this artist and that of L. Barber (q.v.).

*Barber, W. T. Scott. (fl. 1893–1901). See also **Barber, William Thompson**

Of Clifton, Bristol and Florence. Exhibited at the R.A., 1893–1901. Possibly identical with William Thompson Barber (q.v.) who exhibited at the R.A., 1876–1885.

*Barber, William Thompson. (fl. 1876–1885). See also **Barber, W. T. Scott**

Of Bristol (1876) and London. Exhibited at the R.A., 1876–1885. His sitters included H.R.H. the Princess Christian of Schleswig-Holstein. May have been identical with W.T. Scott Barber (q.v.) who exhibited at the R.A., 1893–1901.

Barbier, G. P. (fl. 1792–1795)

Of London. Exhibited portraits and landscapes at the R.A., 1792–1795. A portrait of John Steers, Esq., in crayons, tinted, and stated to be signed 'P. Barbier, 1793', was exhibited at the South Kensington Museum, 1865.

Barbor, Lucius. See **Barber, Lucius**

Barclay, Hugh. 1797–1859. See also **Barclay, William, junior**

A miniature formerly in the Hand Collection bears a scratched signature 'H. Barclay 1837'. Schidlof suggests that these two artists are identical in view of the fact that the dates of birth and death are the same for both. Redgrave gives the name as Hugh Barclay, 1797–1859, and the D.N.B. only mentions William Barclay (q.v.), giving the same dates. If the miniature referred to from the Hand Collection bears the signature H. Barclay, there must have either been two artists, or one who signed himself either H. Barclay or W. Barclay. In which case both or one of them worked in London and Paris, and made copies in the Louvre of the paintings of old masters, as stated by Long and others. The above artist is catalogued in the index as exhibiting at the South Kensington Exhibition of 1865. No catalogue number is given and there may be some confusion with the Hugh Barclay who loaned portraits by W. Barclay to the exhibition.

Barclay, William. (fl. 1764-1769)

Of Tottenham, London. Exhibited at the Free Society of Artists, 1764-1769.

Barclay, William, junior. 1797–1859. See also **Barclay, Hugh**

Said to have been born in London where he worked as a miniaturist. Entered the R.A. Schools, 15 June 1819, aged 22. Long and others state that he worked for a time in Paris, and copied pictures in the Louvre, but Schidlof suggests that there has been some confusion and that the details given for Hugh Barclay (q.v.) should be given to this artist who, he says, was a clever miniaturist and worked in the manner of Chalon (q.v.). He exhibited at the R.A., 1832–1856 and at the Paris Salon, 1831–1859. He is listed as William Barclay junior in the R.A. School's Council Minutes, and may have been the son of W. Barclay (q.v.). He used a pink colouring for the flesh parts, and painted the shadows in clear blue; the hair and clothes are executed with a few swift strokes. Some of his works are at the V. & A. M. and at Windsor Castle. Miniatures by him were loaned to the South Kensington Exhibition of 1865.

Barfoot, J. R. (fl. 1830–1856)

Of London. Exhibited at the R.A., 1830–1856. The exhibit ascribed to him in 1857 was in fact that of his son, J. W. Barfoot junior (q.v.). He painted portraits (including one of his son, exhibited in 1853), flower pieces, etc. His son was a miniaturist and may have been confused with his father.

*Barfoot, J. W., junior. (fl. 1852–1857)

Undoubtedly the son of J. R. Barfoot (q.v.). Exhibited at the R.A. 1852–1857, from 1 Gainsford Place, Richmond, his father's last address. Painted miniatures.

Barker, Robert. 1739–1806

Born in Kells, County Meath, Ireland in 1739. Said to have set up in business in Dublin and, having failed in this project, took up miniature painting; was not very successful and went to Edinburgh where he practised as a portrait painter and miniaturist. Invented a system of painting panoramas of curvilinear perspective which he taught. The view of Calton Hill, Edinburgh, first suggested the idea and, in 1787, assisted by his son Henry, then a boy of about 12, he made drawings of a half circle view of the hill, eventually completing a whole circle view of Edinburgh. This was exhibited in Edinburgh and later, in 1788, in London. It was such a success that he painted several other views in this way. He married a daughter of Dr. Aston of Dublin, by whom he had two sons: Thomas Edward who worked with his father, and Henry Aston Barker who was born in Glasgow in 1774 and who assisted his father with his panoramic views. He died in West Square, Lambeth, 8 April 1806.

*Barkley, Charles

A rectangular miniature, signed 'Chas Barkley / Miniature Painter Strand', was seen by Long and noted to have been painted in the manner of Keman (q.v.).

*Barlow, Francis. 1626–1702

Born in Lincolnshire in 1626; was a pupil of William Sheppard. Not usually thought of as a miniaturist; noted for painting and engraving and was particularly good at representing animals, birds, fish, etc. Published etchings, painted ceilings and designed monuments for Westminster Abbey. His only known miniature is a portrait in oil on prepared paper of Humphry Dove, $2\frac{1}{4} \times 2$ in. This portrait is in the V. & A. M. and is inscribed on the reverse 'Vera effigies, Humfredi dove Anno etatis suæ Quadragesimo a ffr Barlow depicta'. It was exhibited at Edinburgh in 1965. Barlow died in 1702.

Barnard, Philip Augustus. (fl. 1840–1884)

Of London and Southampton (1845). Exhibited at the R.A., 1840–1884. Painted portraits in oil and miniatures. Married Hebe Saunders who exhibited under the name Mrs. Hebe Barnard (q.v.). Schidlof mentions a miniature by him of Maud Legh of Lyle Park, Cheshire, signed on the reverse 'P. A. Barnard Pinxt', and another signed 'Barnard'. His last address was 131 Regent Street, London, from which address his son W. S. Barnard (q.v.) also exhibited at the R.A.

Barnard, Mrs. Philip Augustus (Miss Hebe Saunders). (fl. 1852–1857)

Née Hebe Saunders. Wife of P.A. Barnard (q.v.). Exhibited at the R.A., 1852–1857. Painted miniatures. The R.A. exhibits are under her married name. A miniature of an unknown lady, inscribed on the reverse 'Painted / by H. Saunders / 34 Berners Street / Oxford St / London', was seen by me in 1967. It was well painted and expressive.

*Barnard, Walter Saunders. 1851–1930

Born in 1851. Probably the son of P. A. Barnard (q.v.) and his wife, née Hebe Saunders (q.v.), from whose address he exhibited at the R.A. in 1883. Said to have married a French lady of noble birth by whom he had two children. The wife's family objected to the marriage and gave Barnard money to return to England. He never heard from his wife again, nor his children. Was a clever artist, but not financially successful. Was a friend of Mr. Nathaniel Myers of Essex Road, Islington who gave him commissions. Dickens sat to him as a young man; he valued this portrait so much that he refused £70 for it and went hungry rather than part with it. The Morning Post, 10 January 1930, records that he was knocked down by a bus near The Angel, Islington, and died in hospital. The miniature was found in his pocket.

*Barnard, Mrs. William (Miss Emily Cummins). (fl. 1900–1905)

Née Emily Cummins. Born at Woodville, Cork. Studied at Munich under Wilhelm von Kaulbach. Married William Barnard of Valparaiso and spent six years in South America. After her husband's death she returned to England and took up art as a profession, her first sitter being Sir Frederick Milner, Bart. Her other sitters included Winifred, Duchess of Portland, wife of William Arthur, 6th Duke of Portland, and Lady Victoria Cavendish-Bentinck who was painted by her in 1900. Exhibited at the S.M., 1900–1905. Some of her works were reproduced in The Woman at Home, August 1906. The foregoing information was recorded by R. W. Goulding. This artist is possibly identical with the Mrs. J. L. Barnard recorded by Graves as exhibiting at Suffolk Street and the N.W.C.S., 1881–1886.

*Barnes, Miss Isabella. (fl. 1890–1910)

Of London. Exhibited at the R.A., etc. 1890–1910, from 4 Garden Studios, Manresa Road, S.W.

Baron, Jeffery. (fl. c. 1825–1828)

A drawing master; painted miniatures, portraits and landscapes. Was working c. 1825–1828 at Rochdale where, in 1825, his address was Drake Street.

Barou, Mrs. (fl. 1796-1801)

Of London. Exhibited at the R.A., 1797-1801. A miniature said to be of Charlotte G. Walton and signed on the reverse 'Mrs. Barou St Alban's St,/ Pall Mall/No. 33/1801' was seen by Long, who thought it quite good. Her work slightly resembles that of A. Plimer (q.v.) and J. Wright (q.v.). Some of her colouring was reminiscent of that used by Cosway (q.v.).

*Barrable, Miss Millie. (fl. 1883–1886)

Of London. Exhibited at the R.A., 1883–1886. Possibly related to Mrs. T.J. (Amelia) Barrable (q.v.).

Barrable, Mrs. T. J. or I. J. (Amelia). (fl. 1847–1880)

Of London. Exhibited at the R.A., 1847–1880. The R.A. catalogues, 1848, give her initials as I.J. and not T.J., as given by Graves and Long. In 1852 Mrs. S. G. Barrable is listed in the R.A. catalogues (Mrs. J. G. Barrable in the index), from the same address as Mrs. I. J. Barrable exhibited from in 1848. The miniatures listed by Long, of Mrs. Frederick Robertson of Brighton and Mrs. William Gladstone, were both exhibited in this latter year by Mrs. S. G. or J. G. Barrable who may have been identical with Mrs. I. J. Barrable.

Barret, Edward. (fl. c. 1790)

Was working at Dublin in 1790. Nothing else is known about this artist.

Barret or **Barrett, Miss Mary.** d. 1836

Daughter of George Barret, R.A. Was a pupil of Romney and possibly also of Mrs. Mee (q.v.). Exhibited at the R.A., 1797 and 1800. Became a member of the O.W.C.S. in 1823. Resided in London with her brother G. Barret junior. Painted miniatures, still life and birds. Died in 1836. Examples of her work are at the V. & A. M. and N.P.G. She signed on occasions M. Barrett Pinx' using two t's. She shaded the faces of her sitters in red and used stippling on the eyeballs, long fine lines to model the face, opaque touches were painted on the hair, and the sky backgrounds were painted with horizontal lines. The sitters' coats were painted with rather thick pigment. Two miniatures by her are reproduced by O'Brien. She was probably the artist who advertised in *The Exeter Flying Post*, 2 May 1799: 'Striking likenesses in Profile of the Honorable Lord Duncan, neatly painted on superfine wove vellum paper, may be had of M. Barrett. Miniature profile painter on the New Bridge Exeter, at two shillings and six pence each. Vivant Rex et Regina. N.B. Striking likenesses painted in miniature and profile, shaded from three shillings and six pence, to one guinea. Time of sitting for profile one minute.' Miniatures by Miss Barret were loaned to the exhibition at South Kensington in 1865.

Barret, Michael. (fl. 1777–1797)

Became a pupil at the Dublin Society Schools 1777. Took up miniature painting, some of which were copies taken from large portraits. Three well-executed miniature copies of portraits, dated '1797', are mentioned by Strickland.

Barrett, Miss Mary. See **Barret, Miss Mary**

Barrilli, Signor. (fl. 1783)

Exhibited a miniature, a battle scene, at the Free Society of Artists, 1783 and a view of a seaport (not apparently a miniature).

*Barron, Miss Olive M. (fl. 1902)

Exhibited at the R.A. 1902, from Taplow House, Buckinghamshire.

*Barrow, Mrs. E. (fl. 1829)

Of 7 Charlotte Street, Rathbone Place, London. Exhibited at the R.A., in 1829, a 'Portrait of a young lady', possibly a miniature.

*Barrow, Mrs. Fanny. (fl. 1904)

Exhibited at the R.A. 1904, from Fretherne, Bays Hill, Cheltenham.

*Barrow, J. (I). (fl. 1797–1813)

Only one artist of this name is recorded by Long, but it would appear that there were, in fact, three artists of this name, all of whom exhibited at the R.A. This artist exhibited at the R.A. 1797–1813, from 17 Spann's Buildings, St. Pancras, London. In 1797 he is listed in the index, but not in the catalogue. Painted miniatures, portraits, figure groups and drawings, but not enamels.

Barrow, J. (II). (fl. 1807–1836)

This artist must not be confused with the J. Barrow (I) (q.v.) who exhibited at the R.A. 1797–1813, from 17 Spann's Buildings, since in 1807 J. Barrow (II) exhibited at the R.A., from 1 Weston Place, St. Pancras and, in 1813, both artists exhibited at the R.A., from their respective addresses. He was probably the father of J. Barrow junior (q.v.) who also painted miniatures. He exhibited at the R.A., 1807–1836 and executed miniatures, enamels, and drawings. One of these artists exhibited at the S.B.A., and was a member. In 1828 and 1829 his address was 26 Denton Street, St. Pancras; in 1831 he exhibited an enamel of 'St. Francis' after Murillo and, in 1835, from 29 Burlington Arcade, he exhibited a portrait, possibly a miniature, of Mrs. Hancock; in 1836 he exhibited a portrait of Mr. Jonas Hancock, possibly her husband, in the Drawing and Miniature section.

*Barrow, J., junior. (fl. 1815–1825)

Of London. Probably the son of J. Barrow (II) (q.v.) from whose address, 1 Weston Place, St. Pancras, he exhibited at the R.A., 1815–1825. The exhibits were probably miniatures.

Barrow, Mrs. Janet. See **Ross, Miss Janet**

Barrow, Thomas. 1737–1822

Long records two artists of this name, but later information came to his notice which established that they were one and the same person. Thomas Barrow was the son of Matthew Barrow of Great Eccleston. Born January 1737, he studied for a time under Romney from whose address he exhibited in 1770. Exhibited at the Free Society of Artists, 1769 (a miniature of a lady); the Society of Artists, 1770–1775 and at the R.A. 1792–1801. He exhibited from London addresses, 1769, 1770, 1792–1798; York, 1771–1775; Egham, Surrey, 1801. Long records him as exhibiting up to 1819, but the entry for that year was 'Roman weights (brass) 400 B.C.' from Southall, Middlesex. This was probably the work of another T. Barrow, engraver, who entered the R.A. Schools, 19 November 1790, aged 19. Thomas Barrow painted portraits, miniatures and landscapes, and executed at least one portrait drawing. He died in 1822 and was buried in the Parish Church of St. Michael's-on-Wyre, Lancs. A Thomas Barrow is recorded as having executed views of the ruins of Trinity Church in New York City, 1780.

Barry, G. (fl. 1793–1800).

Of London. Exhibited at the R.A., 1793–1800.

Barry, John. (fl. 1784–1827)

Of London. Exhibited at the R.A., 1784–1827. Little is known about this artist who painted some excellent miniatures and whose work has not always had the attention which it deserves. He painted miniatures and domestic subjects. May have been the John Barry, bachelor, who married Elizabeth

Screech at St. Mary-le-bone on 4 October 1792. Reference to this marriage is in *The Harleian Society*, Part V, p. 18, 1923. His works included portraits of the Rev. John Wesley, Miss De Camp and Mr. Bannister, etc. He appears to have had two distinctly different styles. Characteristics are the angular eyebrows, almost vertical brushstrokes on the faces, the rather mass-like appearance of the treatment of the hair. Many of his miniatures have a brownish shading, whilst others are painted in fresh colours. He seldom signed his work which is often confused with that of T. Hazlehurst (q.v.). Miniatures by him were loaned to the South Kensington Exhibition of 1865. A miniature of a lady, c. 1787, is at the Nottingham Art Museum and is signed 'Barry / pinx'. One in my collection, of Inigo Thomas, Esq. is in brilliant condition and has none of the brownish shading so frequently seen on his work. The sitter's second wife was the Hon. Frances Anne Broderick. Examples of Barry's work are in the V. & A. M.

*Bart, T. (fl. 1816)

Exhibited at the R.A. 1816, from Liverpool 'Portrait of an Irish prelate', possibly a miniature as it was in the drawing and miniature section.

*Barter, Miss Lily. (fl. 1906–1909)

Of London. Exhibited at the R.A. 1906, from 47 Franconia Road, Clapham and at the Society of Miniaturists, 1908–1909.

Bartholomew, Mrs. Valentine. 1800–1862

Née Anne Charlotte Fayerman. Born in Loddon, Norfolk, 28 March 1800. Exhibited at the R.A., B.I. and S.B.A., 1826–1862. Was an authoress and wrote plays, poems and published a farce, *It's Only My Aunt*, in 1825. Painted miniatures, figures and flowers. Married, in 1827, Walter Turnbull, a musical composer (died 1838). She published, in 1840, *Songs of Azreal* and other poems. In the same year married Valentine Bartholomew, the flower painter. Mrs. John Charretie (q.v.) was her pupil. She died in London, 18 August 1862 and was buried in Highgate.

*Bartlett, Miss E. Evelyn (Mrs. Crailsheim). (fl. 1905–1906)

Of London. Exhibited at the Society of Miniaturists, 1905–1906.

*Bartolozzi, Francesco, R.A. 1727–1815

This famous engraver is not usually thought of as a miniaturist, but Mr. A. J. B. Kiddell noted a miniature painted in sepia as being a signed work by him. He was born in Florence and came to England in 1764; exhibited at the R.A., etc., 1765–1799. Executed crayons, drawings and engravings including portraits. Benezit also notes that he painted miniatures successfully.

Barton, Mrs. See also **Barton, Mrs. W.**

Long records having seen a miniature by Mrs. Barton of 20(?) Monday Street. Probably identical with Mrs. W. (Matilda) Barton (q.v.).

*Barton, Mrs. W. (Matilda W.). (fl. 1888–1889). See also **Barton, Mrs.**

Of London. Exhibited at the R.A. 1888–1889, from 23 Cathcart Road and 17 Bolton Studios. Possibly identical with the Mrs. Barton (q.v.) referred to by Long.

Barton Smith, Mrs. Kathleen Kavanagh. 1878–1970

Née Haynes, born 5 September 1878; elder

daughter of Colonel Frederick Hutchinson Haynes of the 21st Hussars and his wife, Kathleen, née Kavanagh. Educated privately; took up art as a hobby and painted miniatures and landscapes. Painted from life and photographs. A miniature by her of her husband, Brigadier General George Barton Smith, C.B., C.M.G. (died 1921), is still in the family, together with one of a dog. I have in my collection a miniature copy of an earlier portrait of my great-grandmother, painted by Mrs. Barton Smith who was her grandchild. She was eventually obliged to give up miniature painting due to eyestrain and lived with her daughter, Mrs. G. U. Averdieck, near Harrogate. Died 1970.

*Basébé, Athelstane. (fl. 1882–1899)
Of London. Exhibited at the R.A., 1882–1899. Had addresses at 199 Brompton Road and Oakcroft, Watford. Was undoubtedly related to C. J. Basébé (q.v.) and probably related to C. E. Basébé (q.v.) and E. Basébé (q.v.).

Basébé, C. (fl. from 1835). See also **Basébé, C. J.**
Exhibited at the S.B.A. from 1835, and was probably identical with C. J. Basébé (q.v.) who exhibited at the R.A., 1843–1879. The R.A. catalogues occasionally give the initial C in the index, but C. J. in the catalogue entry, which is confusing. Long records that he worked in the manner of Lawrence and used an oil technique.

*Basébé, C. E. (fl. 1878–1882)
Of London. Exhibited at the R.A., 1878–1882. Was undoubtedly related to the other artists of this name.

*Basébé, C. J. (fl. 1843–1879). See also **Basébé, C.**
Of London and 108 Kings Road, Brighton (1855). Exhibited at the R.A. 1843–1879, and was probably identical with the C. Basébé (q.v.) recorded by Long as exhibiting at the S.B.A. from 1835. Was undoubtedly related to A. Basébé (q.v.) whose address, 199 Brompton Road, he shared, 1878–1879, and probably related to the other artists of this name (q.v.). His sitters included the Marchioness of Bath, Lady Louisa Thynne, the Hon. Mrs. Vivien, Lady Bridget Bouverie, Lord Sudeley, Miss Fielding, daughter of Lady Fielding, etc. For some years his address was in Pratt Street, Camden Town.

*Basébé, Ernest. (fl. 1886)
Of London. Exhibited at the R.A. 1886, from c/o J. B. Smith, 117 Hampstead Road. Graves states that this exhibit was an enamel, but this is not recorded in the R.A. catalogues. May have been related to the other artists of this name.

*Basébé, Harold E. (fl. 1876–1881)
Of London. Exhibited at the R.A. 1876–1881, from addresses in Camden Town, Holloway and Brompton Road. Undoubtedly related to A. Basébé (q.v.), C. J. Basébé (q.v.) and C. E. Basébé (q.v.) who all shared the same address, 199 Brompton Road. May have been related to E. Basébé (q.v.).

Bass, W. (fl. 1807–1818)
Of London. Exhibited figure subjects and portraits at the R.A., 1807–1818. He is said to have worked at Hinckley and Leicester.

*Bate. (fl. 1810). See also **Bate, W. J.**
Exhibited an enamel of Sadeler, the engraver, after Van Dyck, at the B.I. in 1810 from 52 Margaret Street, Cavendish Square. No initial was given, but it was stated that the artist was 'Painter in enamel to H.R.H. Princess Elizabeth'. He was probably identical with W. J. Bate (q.v.) who lived at the same address. Miniatures by an artist of the name Bate (no initial given) were loaned to the South Kensington Exhibition of 1865. These may have

been by one of the artists of similar name who follow this entry. The National Gallery, Dublin, contains two miniatures signed 'Bate', details of which are given under W. J. Bate (q.v.).

Bate, Francis. b. *c.* 1761. See also **Bate, James**
Born *c.* 1761. Painted landscapes and is noted by Strickland and Long as a miniaturist. Exhibited landscapes at the R.A. and B.I., 1804–1832. Possibly a relative of William Bate (q.v.) from whose address, 36 Brownlow Street, Long Acre, London, he exhibited, 1806–1811. His only known exhibits did not include miniatures. In 1821 he was living at 29 Westmoreland Street, Dublin, according to Strickland, who noted that he was then aged sixty. It is possible that James Bate (q.v) and this artist have been confused, as J. Bate was also in Dublin in 1821, and was also aged sixty. A miniature portrait of Mr. F. Bate was exhibited at the R.A. in 1810, and catalogued as by Murphy, although the artist's name is not in the index.

Bate, James. b. 1761? See also **Bate, Francis**
Worked in Dublin. Lived in 1821 at 29 College Green and was then aged sixty. In view of the fact that Francis Bate (q.v) only exhibited landscapes and that no miniatures are at present known to be by him, it is possible that Strickland has confused information, relative only to this artist, with that of F. Bate, both of whom were stated to be in Dublin in 1821 and to have been aged sixty.

Bate, M. N. (Martin Newland?) b. 1783?
Exhibited at the R.A., 1821 from 56 Upper John Street, Fitzroy Square. Was possibly identical with Martin Newland Bate who entered the R.A. Schools, 2 July 1801, aged 16.

Bate, S. (fl. 1809–1810)
Exhibited as an Hon. Member at the R.A., 1809 and 1810 (two miniatures).

Bate, W. H. b. *c.* 1789. See also **Bate, William**
Born *c.* 1789. Entered the R.A. Schools, 21 January 1808, aged 19. Exhibited at the R.A., 1808–1827. Possibly the son of W. Bate (q.v.) and brother of T. Bate, all three artists exhibiting from the same address, 36 Brownlow Street, Long Acre. In 1817 he is described as 'Painter to H.R.H. Princess Elizabeth' when he exhibited a portrait of Mrs. E. Musters (possibly a miniature) from Dameshed, Dublin. In 1827 he exhibited a portrait of his mother (possibly a miniature) from 14 Upper St. Martin's Lane. He painted portraits as well as miniatures, and exhibited two landscapes at the B.I. in 1811; one of 'Milbank, Thames' was probably identical with the exhibit listed under T. Bate at the R.A., in 1809.

Bate, W. J. (fl. 1806–1808). See also **Bate**
Exhibited at the R.A., 1808, an enamel miniature after Carlo Dolci of the Head of Christ. A miniature on ivory of an officer was sold at Sotheby's, 24 November 1926; it was signed on the reverse 'Painted by / W. J. Bate of London / at York / Jany. 1806'. This is probably the one exhibited at the Exhibition of British Portrait Miniatures in Edinburgh 1965, catalogue No. 351, from the collection of Major R.M.O. de la Hey. The artist's address was given as 52 Margaret Street, Cavendish Square. Possibly identical with the artist Bate (q.v.) (no initial given) who exhibited at the B.I. in 1810 from this address and was described as 'Painter in enamel to H.R.H. Princess Elizabeth'. Assuming that the artist W. J. Bate is identical with Bate (no initial), two miniatures in the National Gallery, Dublin are probably by him. One of Robert, Viscount Castlereagh, is inscribed on the reverse '1822 / Painted by /

Bate / Painter in Enamel / to H.R.H. Princess Elizabeth.' The other, of an unknown lady, is inscribed on the reverse 'Enamelled / by / Bate / Painter in Enamel / to H.R.H. Princess Elizabeth / 1811'. This latter miniature is softly painted with a slightly yellowish flesh tint.

Bate, William. d. *c.* 1845. See also **Bate, W. H.**
Came of a family who, for several generations, had been watchmakers and jewellers in Dublin. Possibly the son of William Bate, jeweller, died 1783. The marriage of a William Bate, described as a watchmaker and jeweller, is recorded. Little is known about his life, but he appears to have had a good practice both in London and Dublin. Exhibited at the R.A., 1799–1807 and in 1819 in Dublin. Painted miniatures in water-colour and enamel. Was Painter in Enamel to the Princess Elizabeth and the Duke of York. He must have died before 10 June 1845 when his effects, including pictures and miniatures, etc., were sold. Signed WBate, the first two letters being joined, and W. Bate. Long suggests that he was identical with W. H. Bate (q.v.), but this seems unlikely as he must have been established in Dublin for some time before he exhibited in London, and W. H. Bate was born in 1789. His London addresses were: 1799, 5 Great Bartholomew Close; 1800, 32 Brook Street, Holborn; 1801, 172 Strand; 1802, 163 Strand; 1806, 8 Gerrard Street, Soho; and 1807, 36 Brownlow Street. The *Leeds Intelligence*, 6 September 1802, recorded that 'Mr. Bate, miniature painter of 163 Strand, London, is staying at Leeds.' A miniature of a man, signed on the reverse 'Painted by / W. Bate. Painter in / Enamel / To H.R.H. / Princess / Elizabeth / 1814', is reproduced by Schidlof, Pl. 36. Two miniatures by W. Bate are in the National Gallery, Dublin. One of Frederick, Duke of York, is inscribed on the reverse '1827 / Wᵐ Bate Painter / in Enamel to H.R.H. / Princess Elizabeth / and his late R.H. The Duke of York'. The other is signed on the reverse in cursive lettering 'W. Bate 1832' (the first two letters being conjoined).

*Bates or Bate, Thomas or T. (fl. 1809)
A miniature painted on glass of Major General Thomas Fairfax, signed 'T.B.', in monogram, on the front, and inscribed on the reverse with the name of this artist, was seen at the V. & A. M. The R.A. catalogues of 1809 contain a T. Bate in the index and catalogue, but the exhibit, 'View on the Thames near Milbank', may have been by W. H. Bate (q.v.) who exhibited a landscape of the same view at the B.I. in 1811.

Bates, W. E. b. 1812
Born in 1812. Worked in London. Exhibited at the R.A., B.I. and S.B.A., 1847–1872. Painted small landscapes and sea pieces, and is said to have executed an enamel portrait of Thomas Moore (poet) and a small portrait on canvas of the Marquess of Anglesey, both having been painted for Lady Morgan.

*Bath, Luke. (fl. 1664–1698)
Was working in Dublin as a 'limner' in the latter part of the seventeenth century, and was a member of the Painter-Stayners and Cutlers, the Guild of St. Luke. His son, George, was baptised in 1664 in St. John's Church. In 1687 he is recorded as living in Fishamble Street.

*Batley, Mrs. Mabel T. (fl. 1908–1913)
Of London and Dorchester. Exhibited at the R.A., 1908 and 1913.

*Batoni, Baron Pompeio Girolamo de. 1708–1787

Born in Lucca, 25 January 1708. Exhibited at the Society of Artists, 1778 from Rome. Best known for historical and mythological paintings. Studied miniature painting under Conca. A miniature of 'Mr. O'Hara' by this artist was loaned to the South Kensington Exhibition of 1865 when the name was given as Pompeio Battoni. Although he exhibited at the Society of Artists, there is no evidence that he worked in Britain. Died in Rome, 4 February 1787.

Battam, Thomas. c. 1810–1864

Of London. Born c. 1810. Exhibited three enamel copies at the R.A., 1833–1840. Worked from 1834 in the Copeland porcelain factory. Was founder and president of the Crystal Palace Art Union. Died in Notting Hill, London, 28 October 1864.

*Battiscombe, Miss E. Dora. (fl. 1910)

Of Hereford. Exhibited at the Society of Miniaturists, 1910. Her sitters included Lady Gardner.

*Battley, J. V. (fl. 1825–1827)

Of 21 Great Russell Street, Bloomsbury. Exhibited at the R.A., 1825–1827. Painted portraits, some of which may have been miniatures.

*Battoni, Pompeio. See **Batoni, Baron Pompeio Girolamo de**

*Batty, Mrs. (fl. 1822)

Evidence of the existence of this artist is to be found in a letter from Maria Edgeworth (Edgeworth family papers) from Grove House, Kensington (the home of Lady Elizabeth Whitebred), to her stepmother on 27 January 1822.

'. . . After dinner Lady E. W. showed us a miniature picture which Mrs. Batty has done of her & another of Mr. Batty – Mr. Batty's is beautifully painted & she has turned him into a fine Spanish looking gentleman with a cloak over one shoulder – Lady E. W. is not nearly so well – It is like her and attractive – (half length) – arm leaning on the arm of her chair & hand hanging very like her attitude – but the expression of the countenance is wanting & the mismanagement of shade makes her face look as if it wanted washing – Lady E. W. kind soul – was sorry we cd not like it – on Mrs. Batty's account because she is now taking miniature likenesses to earn money for her family – Lawrence (the painter) said he admired it which is of rather more consequence than our liking it – Mr. Batty is gone off – where do you guess Honora? To live with Lord Bute – who dotes on him & his only complaint is that Lord Bute will not let him have time enough to himself he is so fond of his company – Lord B. moreover gives him something for his company per annum. I don't know how much – But poor man he was glad to accept of this situation he pined and waisted almost to a shadow Lady E. says because he could do nothing for the support of himself or his children & he saw his wife working her fingers almost off all day – Eleven children to support: I did not understand that they were so poor when we were here before . . .' Mrs. Batty is mentioned by the Edgeworths in 1819, but she was not painting then.

*Baumgarten, Miss Constance. (fl. 1906)

Of London. Exhibited at the R.A. 1906, from 6 Elers Road, Ealing.

Baxter, Charles. 1809–1879

Born in Little Britain, London, March 1809; son of a bookclasp maker. Began as a bookbinder, but later studied under George Clint, A.R.A. (q.v.). Painted miniatures, oil portraits and subject pieces and sketches. Exhibited at the R.A., S.B.A., etc.,

1834–1879. Joined the Clipstone Street Society in 1839. Became a member of the S.B.A., 1842. In 1843 he exhibited from Edinburgh and his address was St. Michael's Chambers, near the Abbey. Died in Lewisham, 10 January 1879. The V. & A. M. has an oil painting by Baxter.

Baxter, George. 1804–1867

Born in Lewes, 31 July 1804. Invented a new method of printing in colours, the results being called 'Baxter Prints'. Known as a miniaturist only by a miniature of the christening of the Prince of Wales, exhibited at the R.A. 1845, from 11 Northampton Square. Long saw a miniature, signed vertically 'G. Baxter 1833'; it was painted with a bluish flesh shading, and may have been by this artist. Died in Sydenham, 11 January 1867.

*Baxter, Miss Martha Wheeler. b. 1869

Born in Castleton, U.S.A., 1869. Was a pupil of the Pennsylvania Academy of Fine Art and of the Art Students' League, New York. Also studied in Paris and Venice. Exhibited in Paris in 1900 and at the R.A. 1901, from Messrs. Brown Shipley & Co., 123 Pall Mall.

Baxter, Thomas. 1782–1821

Born in Worcester, 18 February 1782. Exhibited at the R.A., 1802–1821. Painted fruit, flowers, landscapes and miniatures on porcelain after Reynolds and others. Was in Swansea, 1816–1819 and was charging 'from 3 guineas for miniature portraits'. Drew for Britton's *Salisbury Cathedral*. Went to London but did not succeed in obtaining regular employment. Died in London, 18 April 1821. Information about this artist may be found in W. B. Honey's *English Pottery and Porcelain*.

*Bayes, Miss Jessie. (fl. 1905–1912)

Sister of Gilbert Bayes, sculptor. Member of the Church Crafts League. Exhibited at the R.A., 1905–1912. Painted miniatures, subject paintings in oil and water-colour, including illuminations and frescoes.

*Baydon, Miss Freda. (fl. 1910–1914)

Exhibited at the R.A. 1910–1914, from 100 Queen's Road, Richmond, Surrey.

*Bayley, Miss Elsie M. (fl. 1908)

Exhibited at the R.A. 1908, from The Long Cottage, Knaresborough, Yorks.

Bayley, G. (fl. 1791)

Exhibited at the R.A. 1791, from 56 Lower Brook Street, Grosvenor Square. Said by Graves (R.A.) to be identical with G. Bailey (q.v.), but there is not so far evidence for this assumption.

*Baynes, J. (fl. 1805)

Exhibited at the R.A. 1805, from 73 Castle Street, nr. Berners Street. The title was 'A hermitage', but it was in the miniature section.

Beale, Anne. (fl. 1821)

A miniature signed 'A.B. 1821', was illustrated by Hand as representing the work of Anne Beale about whom nothing is known. The sitter is said to be a member of the artist's family. A miniature of a young Scotsman, by the above artist, signed with initials and dated '1821', was Lot 77 at Christie's, 17 July 1962.

Beale, Bartholomew, 1655/6–1709

Baptised 14 February 1655/6; second son of Charles Beale senior (q.v.) and Mary Beale (q.v.). Studied under Flatman (q.v.). Painted portraits in oil and water-colour, some of which may have been miniatures; assisted his mother with painting the

draperies in her pictures. Gave up art and studied medicine under a Dr. Wydenham. Practised in Coventry where he died. Flatman and Mary Beale both painted his portrait.

Beale. Charles, senior. 1631–1705

Son of one Bartholomew Beale (obituary, 1666) of Gray's Inn. Charles was lord of the manor of Walton-on-Thames and officer of the Board of Green Cloth. Married Mary Craddock (q.v. under Beale, Mrs. Mary) on 8 March 1651; had two sons, Charles and Bartholomew (q.v.) both painters. Beale was an amateur painter and maker of artist's colours, and was probably the artist mentioned by W. Sanderson in his *Graphice*, 1658, as painting miniatures in oil. He accepted a gratuity from Samuel Pepys, 13 July 1660. Kept notebooks up to 1681. Over thirty of them existed, one of which is at the N.P.G. Vertue quoted from them. His signature, CB in monogram, resembled that of his son, C. Beale junior (q.v.). Died in Coventry.

Beale, Charles, junior. 1660–1714

Born 28 May 1660; son of Mary Beale (q.v.) and Charles Beale senior (q.v.). Pupil of his mother whom he assisted from an early age with the backgrounds and draperies of her paintings. He became a pupil of Flatman (q.v.) in 1677, after having been attracted to the art world through seeing Lely's collection, who painted him when he was 14. His father's account books record a payment of £3 to Flatman, a sum he was to work out, and the purchase of 'abortive skins' for his work, and £1 15s. for a desk for him to work at. He painted in oil and water-colour as well as executing drawings in red chalk. He is said to have had to give up miniature painting due to eye strain, and to have continued to paint in oil. Dated miniatures by him are known from 1679–1688. His best works are those which are copies of oil paintings in miniature, and his draughtsmanship and scratchy-hatching, as in the case of the miniatures of the Earl and Countess of Lauderdale at the V. & A. M., are proof that his eyesight was not good enough for miniature painting. He signed B and C.B. in monogram, which consisted of a C clinging to the vertical stroke of a B, and curving round at the bottom to form the rest of the B. He died at the house of Mr. Wilson, a banker, near St. Clement's Church in the Strand in 1714. Being in his debt, many of his pictures remained in Wilson's possession. Examples of his work are in the V. & A. M., the B.M., and the Fitzwilliam Museum, Cambridge. The Pierpont Morgan Library, New York, contains a book of drawings with the inscription 'Charles Beale 1st Book 1679'. A miniature of Archbishop Tillotson (probably that of 1680 recorded by Vertue as being from life) is at Windsor Castle. Earl Beauchamp has four miniatures attributed to Beale, including that of Mrs. Ann Guidott Jennens, signed 'B'. This miniature and that of an unknown man from the collection of Major R.M.O. de la Hey were exhibited in Edinburgh in 1965. Other miniatures by him are in the collection of the Duke of Portland and the Duke of Buccleuch.

Beale, Mrs. Mary (Miss Craddock). 1633–1699

Née Craddock, daughter of the Rev. John Craddock, rector of Barrow, Suffolk, where she was baptised on 23 March 1633, and of Dorothy, his wife. The family had many connections in Suffolk, one branch having settled in Wickhambrook near Bury St. Edmunds. Mary is said to have been a pupil of Robert Walker and to have had some instruction from Sir Peter Lely, whose work she copied as well as that of Van Dyck. On 8 March 1651 she married Charles Beale (q.v.), lord of the manor of Walton-on-Thames, an officer of the Board of Green Cloth and an amateur painter and maker of artists' colours. They had two sons, Charles and Bartholomew (q.v.). Through the marriage of her husband's cousin, Alice, to Dr. Samuel Woodford, a friendship sprang up between the families. Charles Beale junior (q.v.), who suffered from bad eyesight, assisted his mother with the backgrounds and draperies of her portraits. She is best known for her portraits in oil, but evidently executed some miniatures, including one in the collection of Earl Beauchamp, of Henry Somerset, Duke of Beaufort, which is signed 'MB' (monogram) and dated '1674'. It is painted in the manner of Flatman's early work, and is one of the few which is known with certainty to be by her. One of Charles II and another of William III in my own collection are attributed to her. She had a distinguished clientele, was considered to be of an amiable disposition, and mixed well in both learned and artistic circles. She executed some works in crayon. Was said to have led an industrious life; wrote a *Discourse on Friendship*. Died in Pall Mall, London on 8 October 1699 (not on 28 December 1697 as stated by Walpole) and was buried in St. James's Church, Piccadilly. As so few miniatures by her are known, it is difficult to assess her work in that field, but one characteristic seems to be the way she painted curls in rather pronounced rounds. Some of her works, including portraits of her two sons, were exhibited at the South Kensington Exhibition of 1854. Four miniatures by this artist were exhibited in Edinburgh in 1965.

*Beare, William

A square miniature of 'The Miracle of the Fishes', signed 'William Beare', is in the MSS inventory of Charles I's catalogue. (Not in Van Der Doort.)

Beatherd. (fl. 1782)

Exhibited a miniature of a gentleman at the Free Society of Artists, 1782.

Beaumont, Miss Anne. See **Pierce, Mrs. W.**

Beaumont, John Thomas Barber, F.S.A., F.G.S. 1774–1841

Born in Marylebone, London, 21 December 1774. Was connected with the Beaumont family and took the additional name of Beaumont c. 1820. Entered the R.A. Schools under the name of J. Barber on 14 October 1791, aged 17. Won awards from the Society of Arts, 1791, 1793, 1794, 1795 and three medals at the R.A. Schools. These awards were for historical subjects, academy figures and a drawing from a cast. He took up miniature painting in 1784. Exhibited at the R.A., 1794–1806. Obtained a distinguished clientele, painted portraits of the Royal family; was appointed miniature painter to the Duke of Kent and the Duke of York, and is described as miniature painter to Prince Edward in the R.A. catalogue, 1799. Published and illustrated *A Tour Through South Wales* in 1803. During the Napoleonic invasion he wrote tracts about arming the people and organised a rifle corps called the 'Duke of Cumberland's Sharp-shooters'. Was evidently a good shot himself, three silver cups won by him being bequeathed to the V. & A. M. by a grand-daughter, Lady Sarah Augusta Lane (the cups were declined). Founded the Provident Institution in 1806 and was also founder and, until his death, managing director of the County Fire Office and the Provident Life Assurance Company. Was also founder of the Beaumont Institution, Beaumont Square, Stepney; the square is named after him. Served on a Grand Jury, 1809. About 1820 was appointed a magistrate for Middlesex and West-

minster. Died at his official residence in Regent Street, London, 15 May 1841, and was buried at Stepney in a coffin he had ordered to be prepared long before with 'Kyan's process' for preventing dry-rot. Henry Alken (q.v.) was his pupil. He left less than £60,000, out of which he endowed the Beaumont Institute with £13,000, the remainder going to his children. He signed his works I T B in front and often in full on the reverse. His style varied a lot and is not easy to describe. Miniatures by him are in the V. & A. M. Some of his works were loaned to the South Kensington Exhibition of 1865.

Beaurepaire, Mlle. de. (fl. 1816–1819). See also **Chaceré de Beaurepaire, Mme. and Gaillard, Mme.**

Possibly the daughter of (or identical with) Mme. Chaceré de Beaurepaire (q.v.). Exhibited at the R.A. 1816–1819, from various London addresses. Her exhibits included a portrait of Benjamin West, Esq., P.R.A. in 1817, and a sketch of Miss Burchell in 1819.

Beaurepaire, Mme. de. See **Chaceré de Beaurepaire, Mme. and Gaillard, Mme.**

Beauvais, John. (fl. 1757–1773). See also **Beauvais, S.**

According to Redgrave this artist was born in France but came to England where he settled and was working in London c. 1757. He was awarded a premium by the Society of Arts, 1765. He was undoubtedly related to, or identical with, Simon Beauvais (q.v.). John is recorded in Smith's *Life of Nollekens* as a constant attendant at Langford's Auctions, and was noted for his dirty person, but he nevertheless regularly presented himself at Court. Said to have worked in Bath and Tunbridge Wells. Mortimer's *Universal Directory*, 1763, p. 4 cites a 'Beauvois – Miniature Painter and Dealer in Capital Prints and Drawings. Opposite Long's – court, in St. Martin's – Street, Leicester-Square.' Dr. Williamson (*H.P.M.*, Vol. 1, p. 184) calls him Simon Beauvais and cites advertisements issued by Beauvais in 1757, etc. Long quotes a further advertisement as follows: 'Mr. Beauvais, well known at Tunbridge Wells to several of the Nobility and Gentry for taking a striking Likeness, either in Water Colours or India Ink, Miniature Pictures copied by him from large Pictures, to any Size, and Pictures repaired if damaged. He also teaches by a peculiar Method Persons of the least Capacity to take a Likeness in India Ink, or with black Lead Pencil, in a short Time. To be spoke with at Mr. Bryan's, the Blue Ball, St. Martin's Street, Leicester Fields, from Eleven to One o' Clock.' (Dated 1773 in MS.) These advertisements, etc. may refer to one or other (if there are two) of the artists of this name.

Beauvais, Simon. (fl. 1761–1778). See also **Beauvais, J.**

Probably born in France. Undoubtedly identical with, or related to, John Beauvais (q.v.). Graves records this artist as exhibiting at the Society of Artists and the Free Society, 1761–1778, and that he was elected F.S.A., 1771. Long disputed the existence of this artist since in the original catalogues which he consulted the name was given as 'Mr. Beauvais' without an initial, and he could find no contemporary evidence for the name Simon. A John Beauvais was however cited by Redgrave as gaining a premium from the Society of Arts, 1765, and he concluded that there had been a mistake and gave all the known information under John Beauvais. In the review of Long's *British Miniaturists* in *The Connoisseur* (February 1930, p. 112), the reviewer states that 'there is contemporary evidence regarding Simon, for his name appears in a very scarce printed "List of the Society of Gt. Britain", in my possession, which, judging from the internal

evidence, appears to have been issued between the close of the 1772 exhibition and the opening of that for 1773. In this roll, Simon Beauvais is noted as a member of the Society while "John" is not given, so the exhibits must certainly be given to the former artist.' From this it would appear that Graves was correct in attributing the exhibits to Simon Beauvais, whilst the possibility cannot be excluded that there were two artists. The advertisements quoted under John Beauvais may refer to this artist. Benezit records his name as Simon de Beauvais.

Beckett, Isaac. 1653–1719

Born in Kent, 1653. Was apprenticed to a calico printer. Became one of the first English mezzotint-engravers. Noted for engraved portraits. Died in 1719. A good plumbago portrait of the Earl of Feversham was lent to the Manchester miniature exhibition of 1926.

Beckford, Miss Harriet. (fl. 1803–1809)

Daughter of Peter Beckford (1740–1811), and his wife Louisa Pitt, daughter of Lord Rivers. Member of the Academy of Fine Arts, Florence, 27 September 1797. Mr. Ernest Salaman had in his collection a circular miniature of Lady Hamilton, signed in white along the edge 'Harriet Beckford . . . 1803'. It was painted in brown and buff tones. Schidlof records a miniature of a young girl, in a private collection, signed 'H. Beckford / A° 1809'.

Bedford, Anna Maria, Duchess of. See **Tavistock, Marchioness of**

*Bedford, Herbert. (fl. 1908–1912)

Of London. Exhibited at the R.A., 1908 and 1912. The sitter in 1908 was Mrs. Landon Ronald.

Beech, James. (fl. 1830–1839)

Of London. Exhibited at the R.A., 1830–1839. His addresses were as follows: 1830, London Road, Leicester and Miss Linwood's rooms, Leicester Square; 1831–2, 34 Hercules Buildings, Lambeth; 1839, 15 Allen Street, Hercules Buildings, Lambeth.

Beechey, Lady (Miss Anne Phyllis Jessop). 1764–1833/4

Née Anne Phyllis Jessop. Born at Thorpe, nr. Norwich, 3 August 1764. Second wife of Sir W. Beechey, R.A. Exhibited at the R.A. 1787, from Norwich under her maiden name, and under her married name, 1795–1805. H. Berne (q.v.) and H. Burch (q.v.) both exhibited paintings of her. She died in 1833 or 1834, not 1839 as has been stated. Painted miniatures and executed drawings.

*Beerski, Count John de. d. 1869

A Russian nobleman and the owner of an estate near Moscow who, on the accession of the Emperor Nicholas, was obliged to leave Russia on account of his liberal views. Being ruined by his enforced exile he took up miniature painting and lived in Paris, Hamburg and London. Some of his works were exhibited at the Great Exhibition in 1851 and obtained first class honours. He emigrated to America in 1859 and died in Rochester, U.S.A. in 1869.

Beetham or Betham, Miss Jane (Mrs. John Read). (fl. 1794–1815)

Of London; eldest daughter of Edward Beetham, actor, scene-painter, writer and publisher, of Fleet Street, London. Cousin of Matilda Betham (q.v.). Exhibited at the R.A., 1794–1814. Pupil of John Opie (q.v.) whose affection for her led to his separation from his wife. Opie painted her portrait.

After his divorce in 1796 he wanted to marry her, but she married *c.* 1797, a rich elderly solicitor, John Read. Seems to have spelt her maiden name Betham and Beetham. Her exhibits 1808–1814 were under her married name. Her daughter, Cordelia, bequeathed valuable property to the Brompton Consumption Hospital where there is a portrait of Jane Beetham. She painted miniatures, large oil portraits and figures.

Beffin, Miss. See Biffin, Miss Sarah

Begbie. (fl. 1767)

A small miniature of a lady signed on the reverse 'Begbie / 1767', was noted by Long. The lady was in contemporary costume, but wearing a ruff. The work was fairly good.

*Behenna, Mrs. Kathleen. (fl. 1897)

Of London. Exhibited at the R.A. 1897, from 1 Montague Mansions, Portman Square. The miniatures were of J. W. Barclay, Esq. and H.R.H. Princess Louise, Marchioness of Lorne. According to Benezit, she was born in Scotland. Her husband's christian name was Arthur.

Behn, Andreas von. 1650–1713?

Born in Christianopel, Sweden, 1650; worked in Sweden from 1677–1710 or 1711; was appointed miniature painter to Queen Ulrika Eleonora. Painted principally miniatures on vellum and enamel; was influenced by Ehrenstrahl. May have visited England. The V. & A. M. has a miniature by him, signed on the reverse and dated '1704', of Robert Benson, Baron Bingley. Examples of his work are in the Nationalmuseum, Stockholm and the Museum at Gothenburg. He was a dwarf and father of dwarfs.

Behnes, William. *c.* 1795–1864

Born *c.* 1795; son of a German piano-maker who had settled in London. Was taken by his father to Dublin; studied at the Dublin Society Schools. Returned to London; entered the R.A. Schools, 23 March 1813, aged 18. Won silver medals 1816, 1817, 1819. Exhibited at the R.A., 1815–1863. Drew portraits on vellum and in crayons, painted portraits in miniature and oil, became an eminent sculptor. Died in the Middlesex Hospital, 3 January 1864. Miniatures by him are scarce, but he is recorded as a miniaturist in the *Annals of the Fine Arts*, II, p. 567, when he was working at 23 Charles Street, Middlesex Hospital. A miniature by him of 'The late Thomas John Crockford, Esq.', signed and dated, drawn in crayons, in '1815', was loaned to the South Kensington Exhibition of 1865.

Belanger, Louis. 1756–1816

Born in Paris, 25 August 1756 (according to Th. B., 1736). Worked in Switzerland, Italy and England. Exhibited at the R.A., 1790 and 1797 and in Sweden from 1798 (where he was Court Painter). Was a pupil of Louis Moreau. Was painter to the Duke of Orleans in 1790. Died in Stockholm, 16 March 1816. Painted landscapes in gouache, some of which were small enough for boxes.

*Belcamp or Belkamp, Jan van. d. 1653

A Dutch miniature painter, recorded by Schidlof as having executed miniature copies of old masters and to have died in London in 1653.

Belisario, Isaac M. (fl. *c.* 1834). See also **Belisario, J. M.**

Long records the above artist as working in 1834 at 12 Finsbury Chambers, London. Possibly identical with J. M. Belisario (q.v.) who exhibited at the R.A. 1815–1831, from various London addresses, and painted chiefly landscapes, but exhibited a portrait of a lady (possibly a miniature) at the R.A. in 1831.

*Belisario, J. M. (fl. 1815–1831). See also **Belisario, Isaac M.**

Of London. Exhibited at the R.A. and O.W.C.S., 1815–1831. Painted landscapes and, in 1831, exhibited a portrait of a lady (possibly a miniature). May have been identical with the Isaac Belisario (q.v.) mentioned by Long.

*Bell, Mrs. Gladys K. M. (fl. 1910–1914)

Of London. Exhibited at the R.A., 1910–1914. Painted portraits in miniature.

Bell, J. H. or I. H. (fl. 1798–1808)

Pupil of J. S. Copley (q.v.). Schidlof gives his initials as I. H. which may be a misprint. Lived at 2 Wood Street, Bath, 1798–1808. Painted historical subjects, portraits and miniatures, and drew full-length portraits in black and white, with the flesh parts tinted. Was also a drawing master.

*Bell, Miss Jane Campbell. (fl. 1850–1863)

Of London. Exhibited at the R.A., etc., 1850–1863. Painted figures and, in 1863, exhibited a portrait of a lady, which may have been a miniature, from 33 Grove End Road, St. John's Wood.

*Bell, Miss Lucy Hilda. (fl. 1889–1914)

Of Hampstead, London. Exhibited at the R.A. and N.W.C.S., etc., 1889–1914. Painted miniatures and studies of fruit and flowers in water-colour.

Bell, Lady (Maria). See Hamilton, Miss Maria

*Bell, Miss Mary M. (fl. 1903)

Of Edinburgh. Exhibited at the R.A. 1903, from 72 Great King Street, Edinburgh.

*Bell or Bel, Rodolphe. d. 1849

Born in Payerne, Switzerland; was a pupil of Isabey (q.v.). Exhibited at the Paris Salon, 1822–1824; said to have worked in England for a short time, but this fact has not been confirmed. Painted some English sitters. Schidlof lists a number of his works. The E. Holzscheiter Collection, Meilen, contains a number of excellent works by him. Died 1849.

Bell, Mrs. Thomas. See Hamilton, Miss Maria

Bell, William. 1735?–*c.* 1804

Said to have been born in Newcastle-on-Tyne *c.* 1740. Long identifies him with W. Bell who studied at the R.A. Schools after going to London in 1768. The R.A. records show that he was admitted on 30 January 1769 when his age was given as 34, thus making his date of birth 1735; he was awarded a gold medal there in 1771 for a painting of a mythological subject. Exhibited at the R.A. and Free Society of Artists, 1775–1776. Was in Newcastle in 1775. Long, in his annotations, suggests that he may have been the William Bell who married Mary Ann Ward at St. Mary-le-Bone, 16 May 1804, but it is more likely that this was an artist of the same name who entered the R.A. Schools, 8 April 1778 when his age was given as '23 next May'. Long records seeing a miniature depicting Queen Elizabeth inscribed on the reverse 'by William Bell, 1800'; he thought it well painted, in a soft manner. Was patronised by Lord Delaval for whom he painted views and whole length portraits. Said to have died *c.* 1804.

Bell, William Charles. *c.* 1830/1–1904

Born *c.* 1830/1. Of London. Studied in Geneva under Gaspard Lamunière. Exhibited at the R.A., 1870–1894. Collaborated for a time with J. W.

Bailey (q.v.). Lived for some years at 33 Welbeck Street and later moved to various London addresses. Was for 50 years enamel painter to Queen Victoria who gave him a pension which was continued by Edward VII. Bell died at Hampstead, 25 September 1904. Many of his works were set in jewels. A miniature signed 'W. C. Bell, May 1851' and painted *en grisaille* with a blue tone, was seen at the V. & A. M. where there are examples of his work. Enamel miniatures of Queen Victoria and of Prince Albert, both signed 'Bell 1866', are reproduced in Nachemsohn's *Signed Enamel Miniatures*, p. 31. A miniature of Victoria, Princess Royal, as a child, is in the collection of H.M. the Queen.

Bellamy, N. (fl. 1659)

A plumbago and Indian ink miniature of Oliver Cromwell, on vellum, signed and dated '1659', was Lot 23 in the Wellesley sale at Sotheby's, 28 June 1920; it was rectangular, $6\frac{3}{4} \times 9$ in. Nothing else appears to be known about this artist.

Bellew, Captain. (fl. 1764–1767)

Of London. Exhibited at the Society of Artists, 1764–1767 as an Hon. Exhibitor. Executed 'A View of Havanna' in Indian ink, miniatures, some from life, and a landscape.

Bellingham. (fl. 1766–1767)

Of London. Exhibited at the Society of Artists, 1766–1767.

Bemfleet, G. (fl. 1772–1790). See also **B., G.**

Of London. Painted in oil and enamel and engraved gems. Exhibited at the Society of Artists, 1772 and at the R.A., 1788–1790. Long recorded that an artist named Bemfleet died in 1837. He may have been identical with this artist.

Benbridge, Henry. 1744–1812

Born in Philadelphia, 20 May 1744. Was a pupil of Mengs and Battoni in Italy; commissioned by Boswell to paint a portrait of General Paoli. Came to London, 1769; met Benjamin West (q.v.). Exhibited at the R.A. 1770, from Panton Square. One of the two portraits exhibited is said to have been of Benjamin Franklin, but the R.A. catalogues do not record the names. Returned to America, 1770. Was in Charleston, 1779 and subsequently lived in Norfolk, Virginia and Philadelphia. His wife is said to have been a miniaturist and may have been the artist who painted 17 miniatures which were exhibited at Charleston in 1935, catalogued under his name. Died in Philadelphia, February 1812. Some of his work is reminiscent of that of O. Humphry (q.v.). A miniature by him is in the Metropolitan Museum, New York.

*Benham, Miss Maude. (fl. 1897–1898)

Of The Studio, 132 Sloane Street, London. Exhibited at the R.A., 1897–1898. Her sitters included Miss E. Garland.

Benner or Bennet. (fl. 1820)

A large stippled miniature, signed Benner or Bennet and dated '1820', was noted by Long as being in the National Museum, Munich. The artist was probably identical with Henri Benner (1776–*c.* 1829) who was born in Mulhouse, Alsace. There is no evidence that Benner ever worked in Britain.

*Bennet, Lord George Montague. (fl. 1885–1891)

Of London. Exhibited at the R.A., 1885–1891. His sitters included Princess Victoria of Teck, the

Duchess of Leinster, the Grand Duchess Elizabeth of Russia, Lady Colin Campbell, the Duchess of Wellington, Miss Dorothy Chandos Pole and many other distinguished sitters.

*Bennett, Miss Ethel G. (fl. 1895–1907)

Of London. Exhibited at the R.A., 1895–1907.

*Bennett, Miss Florence Emily. (fl. 1903–1914)

Of London. Exhibited at the R.A., 1903–1914, the Paris Salon in 1905 and the Society of Miniaturists, 1903–1905.

Bennett, R. S. (fl. 1845–1848)

Of London. Exhibited at the R.A., 1845 and 1848; possibly identical with R. S. Bennett who exhibited from Cheltenham in 1889, the address being Delia-cottage, St. Mark's, Cheltenham.

Bennett, William Mineard. c. 1778–1858

Born in Exeter c. 1778. Was a pupil of Sir Thomas Lawrence (q.v.). Exhibited at the R.A., 1812–1816. The R.A. catalogues and index of 1812 give his initials as M.N. when he exhibited a self-portrait. His address was consistently 58 Frith Street, Soho. Was a successful artist and painted portraits in oil, drawings and miniatures. Settled in Paris, 1835–1844 where he was decorated by Louis XVIII. Whilst in Paris he was the protégé of Louis Philippe and the Duke of Berry. Returned to England in 1844 and lived in Exeter where he died at Hill's Buildings, St. Sidwells, 17 October 1858. Was interested in music and literature. Some of his miniatures were circular; he signed W. M. Bennett / Delt 1809, W. M. Bennett and W.M.B. The shading of the face of his sitters is sometimes greenish. The B.M. has engraved portraits after his work. A self-portrait was engraved by S. Freeman and published in *The Monthly Mirror*, 1808. A miniature by him is in the V. & A. M.

Benninck, Bening or **Beninc, Levina.** See **Teerlinc, Levina**

*Benoist (Benoît), Antoine. 1632–1717

Born in Joigny, 24 February 1632. Painted portraits and miniatures, executed wax busts, medallions, stone statues (for the Tuileries), and a marble décor for a fountain at the Arc de Triomphe; worked with Legros and Masson. Became an Agrée of the Académie Royale in 1663 and a member in 1681. Was commissioned between 1643–1704 to paint a series of twenty miniatures of King Louis XIII, King Louis XIV and members of the Royal families (eleven of them being of Louis XIV himself). These portraits are now at the Bibliothèque Nationale. Was summoned to England in 1684 and modelled wax busts of James II and principal persons at Court. Exhibited at the Paris Salon of 1699. Died in Paris, 8 April 1717. Two oil portraits by him are in the Louvre.

*Benson, Miss Nellie. (fl. 1897–1901)

Of London. Exhibited at the R.A., 1897–1901. Painted miniatures and executed drawings and water-colours of flowers.

*Bentley, Mrs. See **Smith, Mrs. Lucy Bentley**

Benwell, Miss Mary. See **Code, Mrs.**

Berczy, I. A. (fl. 1790)

Of Florence and said to be a member of the Florence Academy. Exhibited a miniature entitled 'Portrait of an artist' at the R.A. 1790, from 28 Pall Mall. His wife exhibited two Tuscan interiors in the same exhibition.

*Berg, Hans Johan Fredrik. 1813–c. 1874

Born in Nasne, Norway, 25 December 1813. Studied in Christiana from 1835 and later in Copenhagen and Paris. Said to have lived towards the end of his life in Paris and London. Painted genre subjects in water-colour, many of which were copies after old masters. Painted portraits in oil and miniatures. Schidlof records a miniature of a lady, on ivory, signed 'H. J. F. Berg 1845'. Died c. 1874.

*Bernam, Miss Charlotte A. (fl. 1902–1907)

Exhibited at the R.A. 1902–1907, from Whiteleafe, Surrey. Her sitters included Gladys, daughter of Dr. Henry Bernam, and Mrs. John Spencer-Lovell.

*Berndes, Anton Ulrik. 1757–1844

Born in Ramshall, Sweden, 15 June 1757. Was a pupil of G. Lundberg and probably of C. Hoyer (q.v.). Said to have studied in England in 1794. Painted miniatures on ivory and enamel, and was the author of a work on the technique of miniature painting (published in Sweden on his return in 1799), and a treatise on the harmony of colours. He also executed engravings. Schidlof considered his early works were influenced by Hall (q.v.) and were painted with warm colours. Those painted after his visit to England showed the influence of G. Engleheart (q.v.) and the backgrounds were hatched in parallel strokes. The Nationalmuseum, Stockholm, contains a collection of 681 drawings and miniatures by Berndes, chosen by the artist himself, and 26 from the Wincander Collection. These are signed 'Berndes' or 'A. U. Berndes'. They include a self-portrait of the artist on enamel, signed 'A. U. Berndes 1804'. He died in Stockholm, 11 April 1844.

Berne, H. (fl. 1800)

Exhibited at the R.A., 1800; the portraits were of S. Lyons, Esq., the Earl of Caernarvon, Warren Hastings, Esq., Lady Beechey and child, His Grace the Archbishop of York and an enamel miniature of a lady, catalogue No. 896; this artist is not listed in the index.

Bernede. (fl. 1797)

Of London. Exhibited a miniature portrait of a gentleman at the R.A. 1797, from 22 Maddox Street, Hanover Square.

Berrac, G. (fl. 1792–1797)

Of London. Exhibited at the R.A., 1797, a self-portrait and a portrait of a gentleman, from 29 New Street, St. Martin's Lane. A miniature signed 'G. Berrac, 1792', 8½ in., was Lot 131 at the Hayter sale in Vienna in 1934. Schidlof notes a miniature of a lady signed 'Berrac' which was sold in Lucerne in 1934, and another of a man, signed 'G. Berrac 1797', sold in Antwerp, May 1935.

*Berry, Miss Lilian. (fl. 1907)

Of London. Exhibited at the R.A. 1907, from 84 Broadhurst Gardens, South Hampstead.

Bertrand, Miss. (fl. 1800). See also **Bertrand, Miss M.**

Of London. Exhibited at the R.A. 1800, from 5 Upper John Street, Golden Square, a frame containing four miniatures. Long and Schidlof, possibly following Graves (*R.A.*), suggest that she was identical with Miss Mary Bertrand (q.v.) who painted oil portraits and figures which she exhibited at the R.A., 1772–1776. No artist of this name exhibited at the R.A., between 1776 and 1800, when Miss Bertrand (no christian name) is the one referred to. In view of the gap of twenty-four years, it seems probable that Graves may have been in error in attributing all the entries (1772–1800) to Miss Mary Bertrand.

*Bertrand, Miss Mary. (fl. 1772–1776). See also **Bertrand, Miss**

Of London. Exhibited at the R.A. 1772–1776, from Mr. Bertrand's, 12 Stewart Street, Spital-field, and 'Mr. Chamberlain's'. Painted oil portraits and figures. Graves and others have identified her with a Miss Bertrand (no initial given) who exhibited at the R.A., in 1800 from 5 Upper John Street, Golden Square. In view of the time lapse of twenty-four years, and the fact that Mary Bertrand is not known to have painted miniatures, it is unlikely that these two are identical.

*Besche, Lucien. (fl. 1883–1885)

Of Stoke. Exhibited at the R.A., 1883–1885. One miniature was of the Marchioness of Stafford.

Bestland, Charles. b. 1764?

Of London. Possibly Cantlo (Cantelowe?) Bestland who entered the R.A. Schools, 25 March 1779, aged '16 next April', when he was listed as a painter. Exhibited at the R.A., B.I. and S.B.A., 1783–1837. Painted portraits, miniatures, some of which represented allegorical and other figure subjects, and copied oil portraits in miniature. The Ashmolean Museum, Oxford has a miniature copy by Bestland, after G. Stuart, of a ¾-length portrait of Reynolds. The V. & A. M. has a small, full-faced miniature of a child, signed 'C. Bestland, 93', along the edge. This is an attractive miniature and suggests Cosway's influence. Also in the V. & A. M. is an Indian ink portrait of a man in 18th-century costume by Bestland. This latter miniature was thought by Long to be the work of Cantelowe Bestland, an engraver, who may have been identical with the above artist. The B.M. has four engraved portraits after Bestland.

Betham or **Beetham, Miss.** (fl. 1811–1812). See also **Betham** or **Beetham, Miss M. M.**

Long records a Miss Betham and suggests that she may have been identical with either Miss J. Beetham (q.v.) or Miss M. M. Betham (q.v.). Miss Betham or Beetham exhibited at the Associated Artists, 1811–1812. She could not have been Miss J. Beetham (later Mrs. Read) as this artist was exhibiting under her married name of Read from 1808–1814. The R.A. catalogues, however, list a Miss Betham as exhibiting, 1804–1816, and the type of exhibits and addresses are identical with those of Miss Mary Matilda Betham (q.v.). The Miss Betham who is recorded by Long as living at 64 Upper Charlotte Street, Fitzroy Square, in 1817, was probably also Miss M. M. Betham who exhibited from this address in 1816.

Betham, Miss Jane. See **Beetham, Miss Jane**

*Betham or **Beetham, Miss M.** (fl. 1807–1808)

Exhibited as an Honorary Member at the R.A., 1807 and 1808. Painted miniatures and drawings. A miniature of her was exhibited at the R.A. in 1805 by Miss M. M. Betham (q.v.).

Betham or **Beetham, Miss Mary Matilda.** 1776–1852. See also **Betham, Miss**

Born 1776. Cousin of Jane Beetham (q.v.). Eldest daughter of the Rev. William Betham of Stonham Aspel, Suffolk. Was self-taught as a miniaturist. Wrote poems, etc. and was friendly with Lamb, Southey and Coleridge. Exhibited at the R.A., 1804–1816 where she is listed as Miss Betham; some of her exhibits at the R.A. were exhibited in subsequent years at the B.I., 1808–1811, under Miss Mary Matilda Betham, of the same addresses. A Miss M. Betham (q.v.) exhibited in 1807 and 1808 as an Honorary Member of the R.A. at the same time as the above artist, and was probably another member of the family since, in 1805, her portrait in miniature was exhibited at the R.A. by Miss M. M. Betham. Miss M. M. Betham was working from 64 Upper Charlotte Street, Fitzroy Square in 1816 when she exhibited for the last time at the R.A. Died 1852.

*Bethell, P. (fl. *c.* 1851)
Worked in London mid-19th century. Possibly the son of James Bethell who exhibited portraits and historical paintings at the R.A., 1827–1835. Schidlof reproduces a miniature of two ladies, one holding a dog, which is signed 'P. Bethell / 1851'.

Bettes, John (II). b. *c.* 1530
Born in London *c.* 1530. Was an engraver and miniature painter in the reign of Queen Elizabeth I. Said to have been taught by Hilliard (q.v.). Painted an oil miniature of the Queen which gave her satisfaction. Engraved vignettes for Hall's *Chronicle*. No miniatures have been attributed to him with absolute certainty, although several are said to be by him. One, painted in oil, of Gaspard de Coligny (1517–1570), in the collection of Earl Beauchamp, is attributed to him, and several in the collection of the Duke of Buccleuch have been attributed to him. A miniature of Catherine de Medici (1519–1589) was lent to the exhibition at the South Kensington Museum in 1865. It was painted in oil and inscribed '56' and '1581', and signed 'B'. There were probably two artists named John Bettes, one of whom died before 1576 (John Bettes I). The attribution of work to the artist John Bettes (II) according to signatures with a letter B, or monogram I.B., can be only tentative at present. A large portrait in oil on a panel of an Unknown Girl, signed 'I.B.' and inscribed 'Ætatis Suae 20, 1587', reproduced by Miss Auerbach (Pl. 234), is a splendid example of an Elizabethan portrait. John Bettes (II) may be identical with a 'picture maker' who was living in Grub Street, London in 1599. He was said to have been one of the best known English painters of his time. For further information see Auerbach, *Nicholas Hilliard*, pp. 263–5.

Bettes, Thomas. 16th century
Brother of John Bettes (II) (q.v.). A miniature, formerly in the Pierpont Morgan Collection (Lot 4 when the collection was sold in 1935), was attributed to this artist. It was of John, 1st Earl of Bristol, nearly full face, with auburn beard and moustache; he wore a green doublet embroidered with a pointed lace collar and a brown jewelled hat. The background was blue, and the portrait signed with a monogram.

Betts, Miss S. (fl. *c.* 1830–1840)
A miniature *c.* 1830–1840, inscribed on the reverse 'Miss S. Betts / artist from / Shipton', is recorded by Long.

*Beves, Mrs. Helen C. (fl. 1900–1902)
Of London. Exhibited at the R.A. and S.M. 1900–1902, from 8 Holly Village, Highgate.

*Biard, T. or **J.** (fl. 1824–1825)
Of London. Exhibited at the R.A., 1824–1825, portraits and subject paintings, some of which may have been miniatures. The sitters included Miss Frances Ebers, Signor Puzzi and Mme Caradori. His address in 1825 was 84 Dean Street, Soho.

Bickham, George. *c.* 1680–1769
Of London. Exhibited at the Free Society of Artists, 1761–1769; said to have been a member. Was a writing master and engraver, drew portraits from life, possibly in plumbago, wrote on penmanship, painting, etc., and made some book engravings. Some of his engravings were after T. Forster (q.v.),

B. Lens (q.v.), Rembrandt, Rubens, etc. His stock in trade, plates, etc., were sold in 1767. His son, George Bickham junior, was also an engraver. Bickham died at Richmond in 1769.

*Biddle, Robert Stone. d. *c.* 1857/8
A native of Wootton-under-Edge, Gloucestershire. Painted miniatures and silhouettes; went to America and settled in Philadelphia by 1834 where he appears to have remained until his death. According to Groce and Wallace he was listed as a portrait painter between 1839 and 1846; in 1848 as a druggist and, in 1852 as 'China Store'. He died in Philadelphia *c.* 1857 and his will was proved on 20 January 1858.

Biffin or **Beffin, Miss Sarah.** 1784–1850. See also **Wright, Mrs. E. M.**
Born at East Quantoxhead, nr. Bridgwater, 25 October 1784; daughter of Henry and Sarah Biffin. Baptised 31 October 1784. Her father was a farm labourer. Sarah was born without hands, arms or feet. She showed an early aptitude for art and taught herself to paint using her mouth to hold the brush, and executed sketches and miniatures. According to her obituary in *The Art Journal*, 1850, she had instruction from a Mr. Dukes who persuaded her parents to allow her to tour the country where she was exhibited as a freak and genius combined. She bound herself to Mr. Dukes by a written agreement to give the whole of her time and exertions, and for that purpose to remain for a term of years in his house. For this she was paid £5 per year and her keep, and the public paid 1/– or 6d. to see her, and she painted miniatures at three guineas each, although she still received no extra salary for this. A handbill informing the public of her talents stated that 'This Young Lady was born deficient of Arms and Hands; she is of Comely Appearance, twenty-five Years of Age and is only Thirty-seven Inches high; she displays a Great Genius and is an admirer of the fine Arts.' The notice, which was for Fairs at Mitcham, Parsons Green, Peckham and Edmonton, goes on to say that she could sew, embroider, draw landscapes, paint miniatures, etc. 'all of which she performs principally with HER MOUTH'. Apparently the Earl of Morton saw her finishing a miniature at Bartholomew Fair and was so impressed with her work that he ordered one of himself, and according to tradition, took the portrait away between each sitting to prove that there was no deceit. Having been convinced that she was genuine, he was delighted with the miniature and showed it to George III who was so touched to hear that she was being so exploited that he commanded an artist called W. M. Craig (q.v.) to tutor her. This tuition improved her painting considerably and, in 1821, whilst living in the Strand, London, she was awarded a silver medal for an historical miniature by the Society of Arts. The Earl of Morton apparently offered her financial assistance in order that she might leave Mr. Dukes, but she refused to avail herself of the offer, and preferred to remain with Mr. and Mrs. Dukes. According to the article in *The Art Journal*, she lived with the Dukes for nearly sixteen years and, during that time, was treated as one of the family. Miss Biffin exhibited at the R.A., 1821–1850. She worked in London, Birmingham, Brighton and Brussels (1821). Towards the end of her life she moved to Liverpool and took rooms in a house in Duke Street. She received the patronage of members of the Royal family, including George III, George IV, William IV, Queen Victoria and Prince Albert. Married, in 1824, a Mr. Wright; the marriage was not a success and Wright left her, and is said to have taken what money she had, and made no attempt to provide for

her. She was said to have had a nice disposition. For many years she managed to support herself by her art, but after the death of the Earl of Morton, found it more difficult to obtain orders. By 1846 she was in failing health and was left in very reduced circumstances. A number of notable persons, including the Queen Dowager, the Duchess of Kent, the Duchess of Gloucester, Jenny Lind and members of the family of R. Rathbone, etc. raised a subscription list which enabled her to live reasonably comfortably in her remaining years. George Long (grandfather of Basil Long) once visited her and was most impressed by her courage. She is referred to by Dickens in *Little Dorrit*, Chapter XVIII: 'Mr. Merdle came creeping in with not much more appearance of arms in his sleeves than if he had been the twin brother of Miss Biffin.' She died in her lodgings in Duke Street, Liverpool on 2 October 1850 and was buried in St. James's Cemetery. An epitaph giving details of her courageous life was placed on her grave by those who knew her. It recorded her date of birth as 25 October 1784, not 15 October as recorded by Long, and paid a tribute to her 'versatile conversation and agreeable manners'. Long recorded seeing a miniature which she had painted in Brussels, signed on the reverse and dated 'Nov 1822'. In 1960 I saw a pair of miniatures of an unknown lady and gentleman, each signed on the reverse 'Painted by / Miss Biffin / 1817 without hands'. The painting, although a little stiff, showed talent; the backgrounds were buff-coloured, the eyes painted with the upper lids strongly delineated in a sharp curve, with touches of red in the corner and at the nostrils. A portrait of Miss Biffin seated at a round table was painted by A. R. Burt (q.v.). Her self-portrait was lent by the Rev. J. Beck to the exhibition at the South Kensington Museum in 1865; it was painted at Brighton *c.* 1837. Examples of her work are in the Hornby Art Library, Liverpool. A good miniature of an unknown man is in the collection of R. Bayne Powell, Esq. The case is inscribed on the reverse 'By Sarah Wright / née Biffen of Liverpool / born without hands Painted with her mouth / 1784–1850.' A miniature by her of the Rev. William Pateshall, B.A., is at the V. & A. M.

*Bilford or **Beckfordt, Marke.** (fl. 17th century)
Worked *c.* 1610 and is known to have painted Prince Henry.

*Bill, Miss Mary Florence. (fl. 1903–1913)
Of London. Exhibited at the R.A., 1909–1913 and in Paris, 1903–1905. Painted miniatures and subjects in oil.

*Billups-Lee, Jonathan Edwin. 1843–1902
Born in 1843. Father of J. E. Billups-Lee, painter to continental Royalties. Was a Governor of Dr. Bushell's Hospital, Goosenargh, Preston, Lancs. This information was noted by Long. He died in 1902.

Bindon, Francis. *c.* 1700–1765
Of Ireland. Born in Limerick *c.* 1700; fourth son of David Bindon of Cloney, County Clare, and his wife, Dorothy, née Burton. Studied painting and architecture during his travels in Italy and elsewhere. Had many notable patrons including Dean Swift. Painted portraits and designed buildings. No evidence is so far forthcoming that he painted miniatures. One on enamel of Dean Swift, inscribed on the reverse 'Rev J. Swift, D.D., / F. Bindon Pinx (?)', in the collection of the Duke of Buccleuch, is probably after one of his portraits. Strickland suggests that it may have been executed by R. Barber (q.v.). He died on 2 June 1765. This portrait of Dean Swift was loaned to the South Kensington Exhibition of 1865.

Bingham, Lady Margaret. See **Lucan, Countess of**

Birch, S. (fl. 1773–1775)

Exhibited an 'Ecce Homo' in miniature and landscapes in human hair at the Society of Artists, 1773–1775, as an Honorary Exhibitor from 4 Old Bond Street.

Birch, Thomas. 1779 or 1787–1851

Born in London, 1779 (according to Fielding and Groce and Wallace) 1787 (Long). Son of W. R. Birch (q.v.). Went with his father to Philadelphia in 1794. From 1799–1800 they worked together as William Birch & Son, designing, engraving and publishing views of Philadelphia. Thomas was noted for marine views, winter scenes, landscapes, historical subjects, small profile portraits and miniatures. Was a frequent exhibitor at the Society of Artists and the Pennsylvania Academy and the American Academy, etc. Was an Associate of the National Academy and a member of the Pennsylvania Academy. Died in Philadelphia, 14 January 1851.

Birch, William Russell. 1755–1834

Born in Warwick, 9 April 1755. Pupil of H. Spicer (q.v.) from whose house, 11 Henrietta Street, Covent Garden, he exhibited two enamel mythological subjects at the Society of Artists in 1775. Exhibited at the R.A., 1781–1794. Was awarded a silver palette by the Society of Arts in 1784. Copied portraits by Reynolds in miniature, executed enamel miniatures, engravings and invented new colour for the use of enamellists; published, in 1791, a book of engravings called *Délices de la Grande Bretagne*. In *c.* 1794 he went to America with a recommendation from Benjamin West. Settled in Philadelphia where he died 7 August 1834. Painted copies on enamel of a portrait of Washington by Gilbert Stuart, and other enamels. Published views of Philadelphia and of American country houses. Wrote an autobiography. Signed W. Birch followed by a date; W. Birch / No 27 / James Street / Covent Garden / London; and Wm Birch, etc. His work was good and his draughtsmanship excellent. A large oval enamel of Lord Mansfield, signed and dated '1793', after Reynolds, is at the Ashmolean Museum, Oxford. His best known engraving is that of a view from Cosway's (q.v.) breakfast room, Pall Mall, after Hodges and Cosway. A small rectangular enamel with women bathing, signed 'W. Birch 1784', is at the V. & A. M. Several other enamels are recorded by Long. His son, Thomas Birch (q.v.), assisted him in America. A miniature by him was loaned to the South Kensington Exhibition of 1865

Bird, Mrs. See **Essex, Miss Hannah**

***Bird, Miss Constance.** (fl. 1909–1914)

Of Liverpool. Exhibited at the R.A. 1909 and 1914, from 4 Riverside Road, Aigburth, Liverpool.

Bird, Miss E. (fl. 1793–1803)

Of London. Exhibited at the R.A. 1793–1803, from 3 Bartlett's Buildings, Holborn.

Bird, Edward, R. A. 1772–1819

Born in Wolverhampton, 12 April 1772; the son of a clothier. Apprenticed to a tea-tray maker; painted trays with landscapes, fruit and flowers. Moved to Bristol where he set up as a drawing master; painted miniatures and scenery for a pantomime. Exhibited in Bath, 1807. Went to London; exhibited at the R.A., 1809–1818. Became A.K.A. in 1812 and R.A. in 1815. In 1814 he crossed from Dover to Calais on the same boat as Louis XVIII whose portrait he painted. Was best known for his

historical and other figure subjects in oil. Bird was appointed historical painter to Princess Charlotte. One Edward Bird married Elizabeth Sabberton at St. Mary-le-Bone, 27 January 1802, and a man of the same name married Anne Reddel on 21 June 1807. He died in Bristol, 2 November 1819. The Duke of Sutherland purchased his 'Chevy Chase' for 300 guineas.

***Bird, William** (fl. 1901–1911)

Of London. Exhibited at the R.A. and S.M., 1901–1911. Sitters included his wife, Mrs. William Bird.

***Birnbaum, Millicent (Mrs. A.).** (fl. 1906)

Of London. Exhibited at the R.A. 1906, from 53 Marlborough Hill.

Birnie, Archibald. (fl. 1820–1823). See also **Birnie, Archibald D.**

Working in 1820 at Nether Kirk Gate, Aberdeen. Was at Inverness in the spring of 1822 and returned in 1823; conducted drawing classes at 79 Church Street, Inverness. Visited Elgin, Forres and Tain. Possibly identical with Archibald D. Birnie (q.v.) who was working at 14 Pierpoint Row, London in 1834.

Birnie, Archibald D. (fl. 1834). See also **Birnie, Archibald**

Possibly identical with Archibald Birnie (q.v.). Portrait and miniature painter. Working in 1834 at 14 Pierpoint Row, London.

Birrell, Miss. See **Burrell, Miss**

Bischoff, F. H. (fl. 1823–1849)

Of London. Exhibited at the R.A., 1823–1849. His address in 1823 was 176 Sloane Street, Knightsbridge.

Bishop, Thomas. *c.* 1753–1833?

Studied medicine. Lived in London and Paris (1779, etc.). Exhibited at the R.A. 1787–1798, from London addresses. Was in Paris in 1789 at the beginning of the Revolution, and in Portugal when the French invaded it. Went to Philadelphia in 1811 and exhibited there in the same year. He exhibited at the Pennsylvanian Academy and took a leading part in its formation, and also exhibited at the Artists' Fund Society. His daughter, Angelica Bishop, portrait painter, lived with him. Bishop is said to have died in 1833. Some of his exhibits were of flowers. An enamel copy of a portrait of Inigo Jones, signed on the reverse 'T. Bishop pinx / Paris 1779', is in the collection of the Duke of Buccleuch. The T and B form a cursive monogram.

Bisset, James. 1760/2–1832

Born in Perth *c.* 1760 or *c.* 1762. Apprenticed to an artist in Birmingham. Was practising in Newmarket 1785, and was in Caroline Street, Birmingham, 1793–1795. Produced medallions and worked in Birmingham where he kept a Museum *c.* 1800. Engraved and illustrated, with emblematical and topographical designs, his own *Poetic Survey round Birmingham*, 1800. Opened a museum and picture gallery in Leamington in 1812, and died there, 17 August 1832.

Bisson, Jacques. d. 1737

Worked in Paris. May have worked in England. A miniature of Pope by him is in the Ward Usher Museum, Lincoln. A miniature on card of a man, signed 'Bisson pinxit 1722', was sold at Sotheby's on 26 November 1962. He died in Paris on 8 February 1737.

Black, R. A. (fl. 1852)

Long notes having heard of an inferior miniature by R. A. Black, 1852.

***Blackburne, Miss Helena.** (fl. 1880–1899)

Of London. Exhibited at the R.A., N.W.C.S., etc., 1880–1899. Painted miniatures, subject pictures in water-colour and oil and large oil paintings of flowers.

Blackmore, Miss Isabel. (fl. 1836–1853)

Of Dulwich, London and Brighton (1851). Exhibited at the R.A. and S.B.A., 1836–1853. Was awarded a medal for a miniature by the Society of Arts in 1838. A miniature by her of the wife of Fletcher C. Norton was lent to the exhibition at the South Kensington Museum in 1865.

***Blackmore, J.** (fl. 1833–1841)

Of London. Exhibited at the R.A., etc., 1833–1841. Painted portraits, some of which may have been miniatures as they were in the drawing and miniature section.

***Blades, Miss Daisy.** (fl. 1889–1891)

Of Folkstone. Exhibited at the R.A. 1889–1891, from 5 Manor Road and 4 Cherlton Place, Folkstone. Her sitters included H.R.H. Princess Victoria of Teck and Lady Anne Brownlow.

***Blaikley, Alexander.** 1816–1903

Born in Glasgow, 1816. Painted landscapes, subject paintings and portraits, some of which may have been miniatures. Worked in London and exhibited at the R.A., B.I., etc., 1842–1867. One of his sitters was Mrs. George St. John Mildmay. Died in London, 1903. The S.N.P.G. have chalk drawings by him of Lady Charlotte Bury, Sir Charles Colville and Mrs. D. O. Hill.

Blake, William. 1757–1827

Born 28 November 1757. Entered the R.A. Schools, 8 October 1779, aged '21 28th last Nov.'. An eccentric genius, poet, engraver, painter and mystic. Details of his life are given in G. Keynes' *Bibliography of William Blake*, 1921; Figgis, *The Paintings of William Blake*, 1925 and A. G. B. Russell, *The Letters of William Blake*. In 1801 he was said to be working hard painting miniature portraits for orders that Haley, Flaxman and Butts obtained for him. Died in London, 12 August 1827.

Blakeney, Miss Charlotte. See **Ward, Mrs. Charlotte Blakeney**

***Blampey, Frederick.** (fl. 1902–1903)

Of London. Exhibited at the Society of Miniaturists, 1902–1903.

Blanchard, Miss. (fl. *c.* 1817). See also **Blanchard, Miss Ann**

Was a student at the British Institution in 1817 and made miniature copies of pictures by Reynolds. Was possibly identical with Lily Blanchard who married Blanchard Jerrold (according to Long) or may have been identical with the Miss Ann Blanchard (q.v.) who exhibited at the R.A., 1816–1824.

***Blanchard, Miss Ann.** (fl. 1816–1824). See also **Blanchard, Miss**

Exhibited at the R.A., 1816–1824, portraits and studies in the Antique Academy, some of which may have been miniatures. Possibly identical with Miss Blanchard (q.v.) (no initial).

*Blanchard, J. (fl. 1818)

Exhibited at the R.A. 1818, as an Honorary Exhibitor. The portraits may have been miniatures.

*Blankley, Miss Edith. (fl. 1906–1907)

Of London. Exhibited at the Society of Miniaturists, 1906–1907. Her exhibits included an eye miniature.

Blenkinsop, W. (fl. 1824)

Long notes having seen an inferior miniature by this artist and later saw one signed 'W. Blenkinsop / Pinxt / 1824'. A miniature of Mrs. Henry Reeder (1798–1873), née Mary Ann Laing, wife of Dr. H. Reeder of Edinburgh, is in the V. & A. M.

Bloomfield, John. 1764–1808

Of Dublin. Born in Ship Street in 1764. Entered the Dublin Society Schools as a pupil and later went to England where he had a practice as a miniaturist. In 1784 he advertised from 125 Capel Street, Dublin that he would 'paint portraits, – bracelet, locket, or any size – from one to five guineas each.' In 1784, according to the *Adam's Weekly Courant*, 21 December, he had apartments in Chester. Bloomfield was a man of considerable and varied talents and an entertaining companion. He fell on bad times and this brought him to a debtor's prison where he died suddenly on 21 September 1808.

*Blume, Miss Rosey. (fl. 1907–1910)

Of London. Exhibited at the R.A. 1909, from 6 Talbot Square, Hyde Park. The sitter was Mrs. Stanley Richards. Exhibited at the S.M., 1907–1910.

*Blundell, Mrs. Grace E. M. (fl. 1893–1894)

Exhibited at the R.A. 1893–1894, from 2 Victoria Mansions. Painted miniatures and portraits in water-colour. Her sitter in 1894 was Mildred, daughter of Sir Alexander and Lady Taylor.

*Blyth, Mrs. Dora (Miss Fenton). (fl. 1906–1910)

Exhibited at the R.A., 1906–1910; from 1907 exhibited from 92 Marlborough Avenue, Hull.

*Bocquet, E. (fl. 1817–1849)

Of London. Exhibited at the R.A., B.I., etc., 1817–1849. Painted landscapes, portraits, figures and miniatures. A miniature said to represent W. Mouthing, Esq., signed on the reverse 'E. Bocquet, 6 Paradise Row, Lambeth', was seen by the V. & A. M. who noted that it was moderately good. It was probably identical with the portrait catalogued as W. Moulting, Esq. by E. Bocquet which he exhibited at the R.A. in 1818 from the above address. He did not exhibit at the R.A. after 1846.

Bode, Lewis. (fl. 1772–1783)

Of Egham (1772) and London. Exhibited at the Society of Artists and Free Society of Artists, 1772–1783.

Bogardus, Mrs. J. (fl. 1839)

Of London. Exhibited at the R.A., 1839. Three of her exhibits were portraits of children.

*Boger, Mrs. D. (Amy C.). (fl. 1904–1905)

Exhibited at the R.A. 1904, from Farnborough, Hants. and, in 1905, from Millbrook, Cornwall.

Bogle, John. 1746?–1803

Born *c.* 1746; son of an excise officer, John Bogle and his wife, Mary Graham (died 1787), whose brother was the 'Beggar Earl of Menteith'. The Earldom of Menteith became dormant on the death of the 8th Earl, 12 September 1694, and the right of succession was obscure. William Graham, younger son of William Graham of Edinburgh, assumed the title of 9th Earl and voted at election of Peers from

1744–1761. His right to use the title was prohibited by order of the House of Lords, 2 March 1762, in spite of which he continued to use it and was known as the 'Beggar Earl' as he had to subsist on charity. Mary and John Bogle senior had three children, John and two daughters. John was considered heir presumptive, but never made any claim to the title. The earldom is now extinct. Bogle studied at the drawing school in Glasgow which had been formed in 1753 by the brothers Foulis. He subsequently practised as a miniaturist both in Edinburgh and London. He married in New North Parish, Edinburgh, 6 August 1769, Marion Wilson (described as the beautiful May or Mennie Wilson), daughter of James Wilson, a merchant whose family came from Spango, Uppermost Nithsdale. From 1769–1770 Bogle exhibited at the Society of Artists from Edinburgh, after which time he went to London. Exhibited at the R.A., 1772–1794 (not 1774 as recorded by Long and Schidlof). His address was No. 1 Panton Square, London. In May 1790 he accompanied Fanny Burney to Warren Hastings' trial in the Great Hall of Westminster. He returned to Edinburgh in 1800 where he remained until his death in *c.* 1803. His will describes him as 'formerly of Panton Middlesex, but late of the City of Edinburgh'. It was drawn up on 9 December 1786 in the Parish of St. James's, Westminster and was witnessed by George Crozier and John Irving. He left his estate to 'my dear wife Mary' who was sole executrix. He exhibited a self-portrait at the R.A. in 1772 and one of 'the late Dr. W. Hunter' in 1785. His work has not always had the appreciation it deserves; many of his miniatures, particularly the large ones, are among the best of the period. His colouring is soft, and he painted with a minute stippling which, particularly in the treatment of the hair, produces a curiously woolly effect when viewed under a lens. His miniatures have a certain charm without being spectacular. The majority of them are small in size; his portrait of Commodore Johnstone (1730–1787) being an exception. It is signed on the front 'I. Bogle/Pinxt', and is in the collection of E.G. Paine of New York, who lent it to the Edinburgh Exhibition, 1965. It is probably one of his finest works. His usual signature was Bogle, I. Bogle, I. B. (neatly written) or I.B. (Roman capitals) followed by a date in many cases. Examples of his work are in the V. & A. M. and the National Galleries of Scotland, as well as in many private collections. Miniatures by him were loaned to the exhibition at South Kensington, 1865 and the Edinburgh Exhibition, 1965.

Bogle, J. H. 18th century

An 18th-century miniature on ivory representing a man in a plum-coloured suit, with an inscription scratched on the background 'Sam¹ Foote / Born at Truro / Aug¹ 24–1721 / J [?I]–H–Bogle / Pinxt', is at the Holburne Museum, Bath. It is a good miniature, the stippling on the face being reminiscent of the work of Gallaway (q.v.).

Boit, Charles. 1662–1727

Born in Stockholm in 1662; son of Charles Boit, a French salt manufacturer, silk merchant and tennis instructor, and his wife, Marie Creveleur of Calais. Baptised in Stockholm, 1662. Was apprenticed to a goldsmith in Stockholm, 1677–1682. Spent three months in Paris and visited Gothenburg; married a girl née Flitzberg; returned to Stockholm in 1685. Said by Vertue to have studied portrait enamelling under Israel Karlsteen, but Graham Reynolds in *English Portrait Miniatures* points out that he may have been the pupil of Signac or of Elias Brenner and Andreas von Behn (q.v.)

who were, after Signac's death in 1684, the only two enamellists working in Sweden. Came to England in 1687; was in London *c.* 1690 and on the advice of Dahl devoted himself to enamelling and was appointed Court enameller to William III. Alleged to have become engaged to a country gentleman's daughter and to have been imprisoned in England for two years. 1699 saw him in Holland and, in 1700, he obtained commissions at the Elector's Court in Düsseldorf and he worked in Vienna where he painted a large enamel of the Emperor's family. In 1703 he returned to London and Prince George of Denmark encouraged him to attempt a large enamel to depict the 'Battle of Blenheim 1704, with the Duke of Marlborough being led to Queen Anne and her Court by Victory'. In spite of an advance payment by the Treasury of a thousand pounds and the help of many assistants, the task proved too great for him and the work was never completed. Correspondence between Boit and Robert Harley, Earl of Oxford and Lord High Treasurer, is at Welbeck in which Boit presses for further advances of money for the painting. On the death of Queen Anne in 1714, the project was no longer popular and the Treasury demanded repayment of their expenditure. As, by this time, Boit had got into debt, he fled the country to France where he obtained employment at the French Court, became an Agrée of the Académie Royale and was employed by Peter the Great of Russia. Was in Dresden, 1719–1720. He is thought to have married three times; his last wife being Anne Marguerite Williart. Rosalba Carriera (q.v.) executed a portrait of Mme Boit at Paris in August 1720 and accompanied her to the theatre. His pupils included C. F. Zincke (q.v.), Martin van der Meytens (q.v.), John Milward (q.v.), Frederic Peterson (q.v.) and Humfrey Wanley (q.v.), the Earl of Oxford's Librarian. Joseph Lee (q.v.) copied his work. He died in debt in the Rue du Petit-Bourbon, Paris, 5/6 February 1727, leaving his wife and five children. Boit showed great ability in his technique; his drawing was good and his colours pleasant. One of his earliest known works, a miniature of a lady, signed and dated '1693' and inscribed in full on the reverse 'C. Boit p i . . / Coiventry / 1693', was sold at Sotheby's, 3 July 1961. The sitter may have been Sarah Middleton, 2nd wife of Robert Harley, 1st Earl of Oxford. Many of his works are rather large, as in the case of the enamel of Queen Anne and Prince George of Denmark, in the collection of H.M. the Queen; it is inscribed on the reverse 'Anna D:G: Angel: scot Franc: & Hiber: Regina &c / & his Royal Highness George Prince of Denmark / C. Boit Pinx: Anno 1706'. It is 10 × 7½ in. and was exhibited in Edinburgh in 1965. An interesting enamel of the 1st King of Sardinia, signed on the reverse, from the collection of Lord Methuen, was in the same exhibition. He sometimes signed C.B. (monogram). He frequently used pink and yellow and some of his work was smoother than that of Zincke's, and the dots less noticeable. The reverse side of some of his miniatures are often rather rough, whereas those of Zincke's are invariably smooth. The Duke of Portland's collection contains a fine miniature of Henrietta, Countess of Oxford, signed 'C. Boit ft', after Kneller, the receipt for which is recorded by Mr. Goulding in the *Walpole Society*, Vol. IV, p. 145: '7 May 1715. To Mr. Boite for an Enamel of Lady H. Harley £25.' Examples of his work may be seen at the V. & A. M., the N.P.G., the Ashmolean Museum, Oxford, The Louvre, The Rijksmuseum, Amsterdam, The Royal Museum, Stockholm and in many private collections. Several of his miniatures were loaned to the South Kensington Exhibition of 1865.

*Bolton, Miss Alice. (fl. 1900–1909)

Of London. Exhibited at the Society of Miniaturists, 1900–1909. Her sitters included Miss Phyllis Dare.

*Bolton, J. N. (fl. 1906)

Exhibited at the R.A. 1906, from 89 High Street, Warwick. The sitter was the Viscountess Helmsley.

*Bolton, Mrs. R. (Louisa) (fl. 1881–1891)

Exhibited at the R.A. 1881–1891, from Myrtle Cottage, Shepton Mallet and from Belgrave House, 2 Newport Road, Cardiff. One of her miniatures, entitled 'Winter', sold for fifteen guineas in 1881.

*Bond, Mrs. Elizabeth. d. 1897

This artist was recorded by the late Basil Long as having painted miniatures as a hobby whilst looking after her daughter, Lizzy, who lay for 40 years on her face, crippled. She was a niece of Aubrey Smith, the actor. Died 1897.

Bone, Charles Richard. 1809–c. 1880

Born 1809; son of Henry Pierce Bone (q.v.). Entered the R.A. Schools, 21 April 1828, aged 19. Was awarded a large silver medal in 1825 by the Society of Arts for a miniature portrait (copy) and, in 1827, for a miniature portrait. Exhibited at the R.A., B.I. and S.B.A., 1826–1848. Was in Rome 1832–1833, when he probably painted the portraits of Penry Williams and John Gibson, the sculptor (exhibited in 1835). Painted miniatures on ivory and enamel. He lent some enamels to an exhibition at the South Kensington Museum in 1874. Died sometime before 1880. His work shows the influence of Sir T. Lawrence (q.v.) and Cosway (q.v.). A small enamel copy of Guido Reni's 'Beatrice Cenci', signed on the reverse 'C.R. Bone. Feb^r / 1842', and some Italian costume studies, are in the V. & A. M. An attractive miniature, said to be of the Duchess of Kent, signed 'C.R. Bone' in blue, parallel to the edge, is in the collection of Major R.M.O. de la Hey. Two miniatures by C. R. Bone were in the O'Brien Collection.

Bone, Henry, R.A. 1755–1834

Born in Truro, 6 February 1755; son of a woodcarver and cabinet-maker. Painted china for Cockworthy in Plymouth; was apprenticed to R. Champion, 23 January 1772 at Bristol; the factory failed in 1778. In c. 1779 Bone settled in London. On 21 January 1779 he married Elizabeth van der Meulen, by whom he had a number of children: H. P. Bone (q.v.), P. J. Bone (q.v.), Robert Trewick Bone (q.v.), William Bone senior (q.v.), Thomas Mein Bone (b. 1798, said to have gone into the army), Samuel Vallis Bone (q.v.) and probably one further child, a daughter, whose name is not known. Began to execute enamels in 1780, most of them being copies. Exhibited at the R.A., B.I. and S.B.A., 1781–1834, and at the Free Society of Artists, 1783. Resided mainly in London but also toured the country, especially in the West. Was in Truro in 1796. Had collections of his enamels on view at his house in Berners Street, London. Bone painted designs for lockets, watches and jewellery. His miniatures on ivory were mostly originals. Was patronised by George III, George IV and William IV. Obtained large prices for his work, the highest being 2,200 guineas for his framed 'Bacchus and Ariadne' which was sold in 1811, and 600 guineas for a copy of a painting after Da Vinci. Was encouraged by Dr. John Wolcot (Peter Pindar) whose portrait he exhibited in 1794. Two miniatures of Dr. Wolcot by Bone exist; one on ivory is at the V. & A. M. and another, on enamel, was sold at Christie's, 21 November 1967; both are signed and dated '1793'. Eighty-five enamels by him of well-known characters

in the reign of Queen Elizabeth were exhibited at the S.B.A. in 1834. Bone was said to have been a 'worthy, kind, liberal and affectionate man'. Richard Dagley (q.v.) worked with him for a time. A miniature of his son, William, by him was illustrated in *The True Porcelain* by H. Owen. A pair of enamel miniatures by him were sold at Christie's on 9 November 1965. One of these was catalogued as of Miss P. J. Bone, signed and dated on the reverse 'P. J. Bone, born / 21.Jany.1785 / H. Bone pinxt / April 9 1788'. Since his son, P. J. Bone (q.v.), was born 21 September 1785 (see Long), this may, in fact, represent him aged three years, and not a sister about whom nothing is known. The miniature fetched 650 guineas. The other was a portrait of a child (catalogued as possibly another daughter), signed on the reverse 'H. Bone Pinxt / April 6th 1784'. It fetched 480 guineas. A portrait of his wife by him is in the V. & A. M. Henry Bone executed two miniatures of himself in enamel, after Opie. Both are fully inscribed on the reverse. One dated '1828' was sold at Christie's, 27 February 1968 (rectangular) and the other, dated '1830', (oval) is at the N.G., Dublin and was formerly in the Nachemsohn Collection. His portrait by Opie is in the N.P.G., London. In 1832 his sight failed and he died of paralysis at 6 Clarendon Street, Clarendon Square, Somers Town, 17 December 1834. Said to have received a pension from the R.A., after his sight failed. Was a prolific artist and he and the rest of the family gave fresh impetus to the interest in enamel miniatures. In spite of the fact that most of his miniatures were copies, he was a good artist who drew well and used fresh natural colours. His miniatures on ivory (which are scarce) are frequently signed HB in Roman letters, conjoined; occasionally he adopted the same method on his enamels but these were usually inscribed and signed in great detail on the reverse, as on one of John Philip Kemble, inscribed on the reverse 'John Philip Kemble / from a picture by Sir Willm Beechey, R.A. / Portrait Painter to her Majs / Henry Bone Pinxit / August 1798'. This miniature was in the collection of the late Warren Lowenhaupt of Yale, U.S.A. and was lent to the Edinburgh Exhibition, 1965. Among the miniatures exhibited at the R.A., were those of his wife (1781), the Princess Amelia, Princess Mary, Princess Sophia of Gloucester, the Prince of Wales, Queen Charlotte, George III, Warren Hastings, 'the late J. Clements, Esq.' (after J. Smart (q.v.)), Reynolds, Benjamin West, Farington, Opie, Mrs. Siddons, Ozias Humphry (q.v.) (after Romney), etc. His last exhibit at the R.A., in 1832 was of H.M. Charles X, King of France, after Gerard, 'Painted by His Majesty's command, and presented by him to the Dowager Marchioness of Salisbury' (the enamel was painted in 1829). Examples of his work are in many private collections and in the V. & A. M., N.P.G., N.G., Dublin. The Fitzwilliam Museum, Cambridge; The Louvre and the Bristol Art Gallery have enamel portraits of Henry Bone and his wife. A number of his miniatures were exhibited at the South Kensington Museum, 1865.

Bone, Henry Pierce. 1779–1855

Born in Islington, 6 November 1779; son of H. Bone, R.A. (q.v.); educated at Tooting and had instruction in the art of enamelling by his father whom he assisted. Entered the R.A. Schools, 17 March 1796, aged 16. Exhibited at the R.A. and B.I., 1799–1855. Painted a large number of enamel portraits, many of which were copies of pictures; also painted in oil up to 1832. His earliest known enamel is of Ralph Allen Daniell, dated 1795, in the V. & A. M. He married Ann Marie (or Maria) Long of St. James's, Clerkenwell at St. Mary-le-bone, 14

October 1805. A pair of miniatures of himself and his wife were sold at Christie's, 9 November 1965; they were inscribed in full on the reverse: 'Ann Marie / Wife of Henry Pierce / Bone, Enamel Painter / to Her Majesty, Prince / Albert & Painted by H.P.B. from Life, for his / Daughter Elizabeth / May 1849', and 'Henry / Pierce Bone, Enal. / Painter to Her Majesty / H.R.H.P. Albert, H.M. Queen . . . . / July 1847. Painted by him / for his daughter Elizabeth / from a drawing by / his Son Chas Rd / Bone'. Bone is thought to have been a member of an artists' volunteer corps in 1803. Was a member of the Associated Artists in Water-Colours from 29 July 1807 to 24 June 1808. In 1833 he was appointed enamel painter to the Queen, the Duchess of Kent and the Princess Victoria and, in 1841, to Prince Albert. His family consisted of George Bone (living c. 1879), Henry Thomas Bone (an artist), 1807–1827, Charles Richard Bone (q.v.), William Bone junior (q.v.), Louisa Frances Bone (q.v.) (third daughter), Emily Elizabeth and another daughter whose name is at present unknown. A daughter of H. P. Bone married Henry Courtney Selous, the painter. Bone worked in the manner of his father and, but for the signature, it is difficult to tell their work apart. H. P. Bone almost always signed in full on the reverse. Died in London on 21 October 1855. Examples of his work may be seen in the V. & A. M. and are in many private collections. One of Lady Dorothy Sidney, Countess of Sunderland, after Van Dyck, in my collection, was exhibited in Edinburgh, 1965; the original for this painting is at Althorp. Long records that Bone is said to have executed a few well-painted miniature copies on card. Many works by H. P. Bone were lent to the exhibition at the South Kensington Museum, 1865, including several of the Spencer family. One of George John, 2nd Earl Spencer, K.G., on enamel, was painted at Althorp in October 1833 'for Lord Viscount Althorp' partly from a picture by Venables, partly from life and endorsed with the following: 'Very like, Althorp, Fred Spencer'. A miniature of his daughter, Louisa Frances, was seen by me at the Scottish Antique Dealers' Fair, Edinburgh, 1967. It was inscribed on the reverse 'Louisa Frances, third daughter of H.P. and Ann Maria Bone / London, September 1832 / (original) Painted by Henry Pierce Bone Enamel Painter to Her / Majesty and their Royal Highnesses the Duchess of Kent and the / Princess Victoria'.

Bone, Louisa Frances. (fl. 1844). See also **Baine, Louisa**

Third daughter of H. P. Bone (q.v.). Exhibited at the R.A., 1844. A large miniature in enamel, 8 × 10 in., executed by her father, was exhibited at The Scottish Antique Dealers' Fair, Edinburgh, 1967. It was inscribed on the reverse 'Louisa Frances, third daughter of H.P. and Ann Maria Bone / London, September 1832 / (original) Painted by Henry Pierce Bone Enamel Painter to Her / Majesty and their Royal Highnesses the Duchess of Kent and the / Princess Victoria'. A miniature of Sir George Berkeley, in my collection, is inscribed on the back of the frame as by Louisa Baine (q.v.), but may conceivably be by Louisa Bone.

Bone, Lieutenant Peter Joseph. 1785–1814

Born 21 September 1785; son of H. Bone (q.v.). Was awarded a silver palette by the Society of Arts in 1800–1801 for drawing of outlines. Exhibited at the R.A., 1801, a portrait of a young lady on enamel. Joined the army and died from wounds near Toulouse, 1814. A miniature of Dr. Wolcot was in the Nachemsohn Collection and was inscribed on the reverse 'Doctor Wolcot, painted in enamel after a picture by John Opie, R.A., by Peter Joseph Bone, May 1801'.

*Bone, Robert Trewick. 1790–1840?

Born in London, 24 September 1790; son of Henry Bone (q.v.) by whom he was taught art. Painted studies from nature, historical paintings, landscapes and miniatures on enamel. Exhibited at the R.A. and B.I., 1813–1841. He belonged to a Sketching Society. The Liverpool Museum has an enamel miniature by him of a nude female entitled 'The Bath'. He died 5 May 1840, according to Redgrave and others. If so, the exhibit at the B.I. in 1841 must have been posthumous, or the date given by Redgrave incorrect. An enamel miniature of R. T. Bone is in the National Gallery, Dublin, and is inscribed on the reverse 'Rob. Trewick Bone / Painted in enamel by William Bone / after the original / by H. P. Bone / 1834'.

*Bone, Samuel Vallis. (fl. 1819–1824)

Son of Henry Bone (q.v.). Exhibited landscapes at the R.A. and B.I., 1819–1824. An enamel miniature of a Chinese girl, set in a brooch and signed 'SVB' was noted by Long in 1936.

Bone, William, senior. (fl. 1815–1843)

Son of Henry Bone, R.A. (q.v.). Exhibited at the R.A. 1815–1843, including portraits of Henry Bone, the King of Hanover and a portrait for a ring. Copied the work of H. P. Bone (q.v.), R. T. Bone (q.v.), J. Jackson (q.v.). He was appointed enamel painter to the King of Hanover in 1842. He painted miniatures on ivory and on enamel. He signed WB (in monogram), WBone, the first two letters conjoined, and in full on the reverse. His work was not quite as good as that of his father or his brothers, and the colouring is a little hard; his works on ivory are better than those on enamel. Worked from 15 Berners Street, Oxford Street. An enamel miniature of Prince Rupert of Bavaria after Van Dyck is at the V. & A. M.; it is signed on the reverse 'Painted in enamel by Willm Bone'. A miniature of H. Bone by W. Bone is in the collection of J. B. Robertson of Perthshire. The artist is seated, holding a book, on the spine of which are the initials 'HB', and on the cover, the title 'Elizabeth Gallery', obviously relating to the eighty enamels painted by H. Bone of Elizabethan personages. Some of his miniatures were loaned to the South Kensington Exhibition of 1865, including one of Henry Bone, R.A., signed and dated '1828'. Examples are at the V. & A. M., the Wallace Collection, the Liverpool Museum, etc.

Bone, William, junior. (fl. 1827–1851)

Son of H. P. Bone (q.v.). Painted enamels after Constable, Lawrence, Reynolds, Rubens, etc. Exhibited at the R.A., 1827–1851. His early exhibits were of shells and china. Two enamel plaques by W. Bone junior are at the V. & A. M., and an enamel portrait of H. Bone (q.v.), dated '1845', by W. Bone junior, after H. P. Bone.

*Bonnor, Miss Rose D. (fl. 1901–1913)

Of London. Exhibited at the R.A., 1901–1913. Painted miniatures, portraits and subjects in oil.

Boot, Miss Charlotte. (fl. 1847)

Of London. Exhibited at the R.A. 1847, from 17 Euston Place, Euston Square.

*Booth, Miss Dorothy. (fl. 1904–1909)

Of London. Exhibited at the Society of Miniaturists, 1904–1909.

Booth, Joseph. d. 1789

Worked in England and Dublin. Was a clever mechanic and invented the Polygraphic Art, a method of reproducing oil paintings. He also made inventions in connection with woollen manufacture. Was in England for a time and is described as a portrait painter of Lewisham, Kent. He practised in Dublin from c. 1770 up to his death in 1789.

Booth, William. 1807/8–1845

Born in Aberdeen, 1807 or 1808. Entered the R.A. Schools, 31 March 1825, aged 17. Worked in London and exhibited at the R.A. and S.B.A., 1827–1845. Awarded a silver medal. 1827. His portraits included one of John Constable. Said to have been good at painting portraits of women and groups of children. His work was well drawn, and was reminiscent of the works of Ross (q.v.). He used a lot of gum with his paints. Some of his miniatures were as large as ten inches. Two miniatures of his sister, Miss Jessie Booth, probably by William Booth, were Lots No. 38 and 39 at Christie's, 23 May 1967. They were reminiscent of the work of E. Robertson (q.v.). Three miniatures by him were loaned to the South Kensington Exhibition of 1865. They included a portrait of one of his sons and one of his sister dated '1843'.

Borckhardt, C. (fl. 1784–1810)

Of London. Exhibited at the R.A. and B.I., 1784–1810. Executed miniatures, oil and crayon portraits and figure subjects. His sitters included Mrs. Moser, Josia Boydell and H. Ashby. Some of his portraits were engraved. Was working in Maidstone, 1 July 1800. A miniature of a man, signed 'Borckhardt, fecit', in white along the edge, is at the V. & A. M. It has a greenish colouring and there is a fair amount of stippling and some scratching. It is of fairly good quality.

Borden. (fl. 1806)

A snuff-box with a miniature of a lady in the lid, signed 'BORDEN 1806', was sold at Christie's, 22 March 1922, Lot 114.

Bordier, Jacques. 1616–1684

Born in Geneva, 23 August 1616. Friend of Jean Petitot (q.v.) with whom he is said to have collaborated for 35 years. It has been said that Bordier painted the hair, costume and backgrounds of the miniatures, whilst Petitot painted the flesh parts. The date on which Bordier came to England is not known, nor do we know when he and Petitot first met but recent research by R. W. Lightbrown published in The Connoisseur, June 1968 pp. 82–91, established the fact that by August 1638, when he left for Italy, Bordier had already been 'many years in the service of Charles I and his Queen together with his compatriot and partner Jean Petitot'. By 1640 Bordier and his cousin Joseph were arrested and held prisoners in Milan. Sir Theodore Turquet de Mayerne interceded on their behalf with the Spanish ambassador, but without success, and in 1641 Queen Henrietta Maria intervened personally through Conte Carlo Rossetti, her Papal Agent. Soon after this it was known that Bordier had escaped from the Holy Office of Milan. He may have returned to England after his escape, and before going to Paris. In 1651 Bordier married Anne Madeleine Cuper, whose sister had married Petitot. Their daughter married the younger Petitot (q.v.). From 1668 he was a secret agent of the Genevese Government in Versailles. Earl Beauchamp has an enamel group of Louis XIV, Madame de la Vallière and Mme de Montespan which is attributed to J. Bordier. An attractive enamel portrait of a lady, signed 'J.B.', was sold in the Ashcroft Collection at Sotheby's, 7 May 1946. This latter miniature was sold again on 11 November 1947.

*Bordier, Pierre. 17th century

Son of Augustin Bordier, a Genevese goldsmith and cousin of Jacques Bordier (q.v.). According to the catalogues of the South Kensington Exhibition of 1865, he was the assistant and brother-in-law of Jean Petitot (q.v.) and remained in England when the latter left the country. An enamel portrait by him of the poet John Gay was loaned to this exhibition. Although P. Bordier is said to have worked in England, the statement that he was the brother-in-law of J. Petitot is presumably incorrect and should refer to J. Bordier.

*Bosanquet, J. E. (fl. 1852–1861)

Of Cork. May have painted portraits and miniatures c. 1852. Painted chiefly local views in water-colour and occasionally in oil. Had a photography business in Patrick Street, Cork. Exhibited at the R.H.A., 1854 and 1861. His work was not of any great merit.

*Bosset, J. B. (fl. 1778). See also Bosset, John F.

Listed as exhibiting at the R.A. 1778, from 33 Greek Street, Soho, but probably identical with J. F. Bosset (q.v.).

Bosset, John Frederick. 1754–1838. See also Bosset, J. B.

Born in Neufchâtel, Switzerland, 1754. Came to London and exhibited at the R.A., 1778–1780. Some of his entries are catalogued under J. B. Bosset (q.v.), probably in error. He later returned to Neufchâtel where he remained until his death in 1838. The Museum of Neufchâtel has several miniatures by him.

*Bostock, John. b. c. 1808

Entered the R.A. Schools, 31 March 1825, aged 17 years. Painted portraits and genre subjects. Exhibited at the R.A., B.I. and O.W.C.S., 1826–1869. Worked somewhat in the style of Newton (q.v.) and Andrew Robertson (q.v.).

*Bott, Thomas J. 1829–1870

Born in Hyde, nr. Kidderminster, 1829. Worked at the Worcester porcelain factory. Painted in enamel on porcelain. Exhibited at the R.A., 1857–1860. His exhibit in 1860 was in the miniature section and was 'The Holy Family after Raphael'. Died 13 December 1870 in Worcester.

Boulger, Thomas. (fl. 1761–1788)

An Irish artist. Studied in Dublin under F. R. West and Mannin in the Dublin Society Schools. Worked in Dublin and Portarlington. Painted miniatures and flower portraits, and taught drawing and painting. Was given a premium by the Dublin Society. Exhibited at the Society of Artists in William Street, Dublin, 1769–1771. Miss Forster (q.v.) of Dublin was one of his pupils.

*Boullemier, Antonin. (fl. 1881–1882)

Of Stoke-on-Trent. Exhibited at the R.A., 1881–1882. Painted a miniature of the Hon. Adelaide Cavendish, after Sir W. C. Ross (q.v.).

Bourlier, Mlle (Marie-Anne?). (fl. 1800)

Of London. Exhibited at the R.A., 1800. Painted pictures and miniatures from 15 Charlotte Street, Bloomsbury. Benezit records the name of this artist as Marie-Anne and states that she exhibited until 1812, but I can find no evidence of this.

*Bourne, Miss Norah B. (fl. 1907–1914)

Of London. Exhibited at the R.A. and S.M., 1907–1914. Her sitters included Magdalene, daughter of Wykeham Bourne, Esq. and Mrs. Colin Simpson.

*Bouton, G. G. (fl. *c.* 1770–1780)

I have seen an attractive miniature of a lady, *c.* 1770/80, signed 'G. G. Bouton'. It was well painted. Possibly identical with Guillaume Gabriel Bouton (1730–1782), born in Cuxac d'Aude and died in Chartres.

Bouton, Joseph Marie. 1768–1823

Born in Cadiz, 1768. Worked in Paris, 1790–1803. Was miniature and Court painter to Charles IV of Spain. Said to have worked for the Holland family in Spain between 1802–1808. Exhibited at the R.A., from London addresses, 1816–1819. His initials are given as J.I. and J. in the R.A. catalogues. Graves confuses him with C. M. Bouton and states that he exhibited in 1840 which is incorrect. His sitters included his sister-in-law; 'Boneparte'; H.M. Maria Louisa, Queen of Spain with a bust of Charles IV; H.R.H. Princess Charlotte of Wales; H. E. Count Lieven (Russian Ambassador); and Countess Enalie, etc. Died in Chartres, 1823. Was a good miniaturist; used pink tinted with yellow for his flesh colours and grey-greenish or brown shadows. Used long close brush strokes; often painted the backgrounds in gouache. Several works by him are listed by Schidlof. A miniature signed 'Bouton' is in the Musée des Arts Décoratifs, Paris.

*Bouvier. (fl. 1804–1805)

Two miniatures by this artist are in the collection of the Duke of Northumberland; one represents Isabella, Countess of Beverley, circular on ivory, signed 'Bouvier P^t / 1804', and the other is of her son, the Hon. Algernon Percy (1779–1833), also circular, signed 'Bouvier / 1805'. A number of artists of this name are recorded by Benezit, some of whom worked in England. The one who is known to have been a miniaturist is Pierre Louis Bouvier (1766–1836) of Geneva, but I have not found any evidence that he came to England. The above artist evidently knew the Northumberland family and the Hon. Algernon Percy (q.v.) was certainly his pupil, for among the family miniatures at Alnwick are three by him all painted in the manner of Bouvier, including a copy after him of the miniature of Isabella, Countess of Beverley. Bouvier's work is attractive and finely finished, his colours are fresh and his draughtsmanship good.

*Bouvier, Augustin or **Augustus Jules.** *c.* 1825–1881

Born in London *c.* 1825. Of French extraction. Studied at the R.A., and in France and Italy. Exhibited at the R.A., B.I., N.W.C.S., etc., 1845–1881. Worked chiefly in England. Painted miniatures, subject pictures and water-colour portraits. Schidlof notes a portrait in water-colour which is painted with soft shades and was attractive. Other works he saw were rather idealistic and lacked expression. He records a portrait, signed 'Aug. Bouvier 1852', the year in which he first exhibited at the R.A., from 28a Howland Street, Fitzroy Square. J. Bouvier and U. Bouvier also exhibited from this address and other artists of this name (presumably related) exhibited from other London addresses. Died in London, 1881.

*Bowden, Miss Violet L. (fl. 1905–1908)

Of London. Exhibited at the R.A. and S.M., 1905–1908, from 740 Fulham Road, London. The sitter in 1908 was Mrs. David Smith.

*Bowen. (fl. *c.* 1800)

A Mr. Bowen advertised that he painted miniatures on ivory at £1 1s. each from 4 Spring Gardens, (*Johnson's Gazette*, 2 March 1800).

Bower, Lewis. (fl. 1761–1775)

Of London. Exhibited flower pieces and landscapes in water-colour at the Free Society of Artists 1761, and a miniature of a lady at the Society of Artists, 1775. In the latter year he exhibited a water-colour painting of 'Roses' at the R.A., from 14 Millman Street, Bedford Row.

Bowerman, Richard. b. *c.* 1770. d. after 1832

An obscure Irish artist. Practised in Dublin as a miniaturist and portrait painter. Was a pupil in the Dublin Society Schools, 1782. Nothing is known of him after 1832.

Bowring, Benjamin. b. 1751

Of London. Entered the R.A. Schools, 7 December 1770 when his age was noted as '19 last August'. Obtained a silver medal, 1773. Exhibited miniatures and small oil portraits at the R.A., 1773–1781.

Bowring, Joseph. b. *c.* 1760. d. after 1817

Of London and Eton. A little known artist who shared the same initial as J. Bogle (q.v.). Exhibited at the R.A., 1787–1808. Painted miniatures, portraits in oil and water-colour. From 1793–1817 was working at Dove Court Pavement, Moorfields. Signed with a monogram JB, the J often extends in either direction over the vertical stroke of the B. He used a minute stippling. Long considered his work to be good. An engraved portrait, published 1807, of J. Stephens, after Bowring, is at the B.M. A miniature of a young lady in a pink dress, painted on ivory, and signed on the reverse 'Joseph Bowring pinxt. Eton 1785', was sold in Brussels, 27–28 April 1934. Several of his works are listed by Long. Two miniatures by him are in the collection of Major R.M.O. de la Hey. (Pl. 25: no. 78.)

Bowyer, Robert. *c.* 1758–1834

Born *c.* 1758. Was self-taught and began by painting his own portrait for his sweetheart, Mary Shoveller, whom he eventually married. Was a pupil of John Smart (q.v.) with whom he was closely associated and for whom he acted as attorney when Smart went to India and became guardian to his two illegitimate children, Sarah and John Smart junior (q.v.). Exhibited at the Free Society of Artists in 1782 and at the R.A., 1783–1828. Had a distinguished clientele including the Duke of Clarence and Lady Hughes. His portrait of Dr. Francis Willis was engraved by Fittler in 1789. Advertised in *The Lincoln, Rutland and Stamford Mercury*, 20 March 1789. Succeeded J. Meyer (q.v.) as miniature painter to the King and Queen and the Royal family in 1789. Published works which included *Fac-similes of Water Colour Drawings*, 1825 and was partly responsible for an illustrated *History of England*. Was a Baptist and a supporter of the anti-slavery movement. His daughter, Mary Ann Bowyer, married John Crofts at St. Mary-le-bone, 8 June 1797. Portraits of Bowyer and his wife by Opie are reproduced in Ada Erland's *John Opie and his Circle*. Bowyer is known to have copied some of Smart's works and these sometimes pass as authentic works by Smart. They are not of his quality, are superficially not unlike his technique. A miniature by Bowyer of Sir John Webb, signed 'R.B. 1786', after a miniature by J. Smart, painted in 1784, was lent to the exhibition at the South Kensington Museum, 1865. The miniature was seen by Long who thought it only a fairly good imitation of Smart's work. He advertised from Berners Street in *The Times*, 17 January 1792, as Miniature Painter to the King, and in *Johnson's Gazette*, 28 December 1800. Died in Byfleet, 4 June 1834. (Pl. 25: no. 79.)

*Boyd, Mrs. J. A. (Janet). (fl. 1895–1906)

Exhibited at the R.A. and S.M. 1895–1906, from addresses in Northumberland and Durham. Ex-

hibited in Paris, 1897–1899. Her sitters included Evie, grand-daughter of Sir Charles Mark Palmer, Bart.

*Boyd, Miss Myra. (fl. 1906)

Of London. Exhibited at the R.A. 1906, from 35 Ovington Street, Chelsea. Possibly identical with the Miss Myra Boyd recorded in Benezit who was born at Pittsburg, Pennsylvania; studied in Paris.

*Boyd-Waters, Frederick, R.M.S. 1879–1967

Born in Guelph, Ontario, Canada, 1879; son of a business man. Left Canada *c.* 1899 for San Francisco where he trained at the Mark Hopkins Institute. Went to Paris and studied at Julians. He painted still-life, figure subjects, flower pictures, portraits and miniatures. Served during 1914–1918 war in The Artists' Rifles Corps; the fact that he was dyspeptic prevented him from serving overseas. Married Miss Mildred Jessie Burt (born 1884) at Weymouth, 26 January 1921. Visited America, 1928–1929, sponsored by a family from South Carolina. Lived in the south of France for many years. Exhibited at the Paris Salon and at the R.M.S. Left France for England just before the outbreak of war in 1939. Studied the art of old masters and copied many works of Holbein, Cooper, Cosway, etc. (q.v.). Died near Hawkshead, Westmorland, 5 September 1967 and was survived by his widow, who still has a large collection of his miniatures and flower paintings. From the works I have seen, Boyd-Waters seemed to be particularly good at painting portraits of children. He succeeded in capturing the likeness of his sitters with the minimum number of strokes and used no stippling. He signed vertically in capital letters, encased by lines:

B	W
O	A
Y	T
D	E
	R
	S

*Boyes, Miss Gertrude H. (fl. 1906)

Exhibited at the R.A. 1906, from West Hill House, Beverley, Yorks.

*Boyle, Mr. (fl. 1783)

This artist painted a miniature of Frances Burney and Madame d'Arblay in June 1783. He was probably an amateur and he and his wife were keeping the miniature for themselves. Reference to this is to be found in *The House in St. Martin's Street*, 1907, pp. 338–9, by C. Hill.

*Boyle, Miss Kathleen. (fl. 1904–1908)

Of London. Exhibited at the Society of Miniaturists, 1904–1908.

*Boze, Joseph. 1745–1825

Born at Martigues, 1745. Benezit gives his dates as 1744 to 17 January 1826. Exhibited at the Salon of the Correspondence, 1782–1791. Executed portraits in oil, pastel, and painted miniatures. Through the influence of his wife (née Bresse de St. Martin) had access to the Court. Painted portraits of Louis XVI, Marie-Antoinette, Robespierre and Mirabeau. Became official painter and held the title of War Painter by appointment. Became involved in politics and, in October 1793, was imprisoned as a suspect. Was released on his wife's testimony and went to Holland and thence to England. Returned to France in 1798. Took up his position as official painter to the Royal family and was given the title of Count by Louis XVIII. Schidlof and Benezit list a number of portraits by this artist. He died in Paris, 25 January 1825. Painted brown shadows and bluish half-tints and used a rather dirty yellow colouring. Tended to exaggerate the height of the skull of his sitters.

*Bracewell, W. T. (fl. c. 1820)

Long records having seen a miniature, $3\frac{1}{8} \times 3$ in., of an old woman in a cap and white fichu c. 1820, signed 'W.T. Bracewell / Pinxit'. It was quite good. The face was shaded in grey.

*Brackenburg, Miss Georgina A. (fl. 1891–1905)

Of London. Exhibited at the R.A., etc., 1891–1905, including portraits of Viscount Dillon and Lord de Mauley.

*Bradford, C. (fl. 1829)

Of 216 Tottenham Court Road, London. Exhibited at the R.A. in 1829 two portraits of a 'child of Mr. and Lady Maria West' which may have been miniatures.

Bradley, John. b. 1787

Entered the R.A. Schools, 7 January 1814, aged 27 years. Exhibited at the R.A. 1817–1843, from 54 Pall Mall. His sitters included Miss Wetham of the Theatre Royal, Bath. Schidlof mentions a miniature of a lady by him, on ivory, signed on the reverse '1841 / Painted / by J. Bradley / of Coolport' (Coalport?). It was well painted, the features finely executed in fine crossed soft brush strokes. The colouring was warm and pleasing.

Bradley, William. 1801–1857

Of Manchester. Born 16 January 1801; was left an orphan at the age of three. Began work as an errand boy. At sixteen was painting portraits in oil and miniatures, as well as teaching drawing at Manchester, having been a pupil of Mather Brown (q.v.). Came to London in 1823 and exhibited at the R.A., 1823–1845. Due to failing health he returned to Manchester in 1847 and died there in poverty, 4 July 1857. Long noted that he was also a pupil of Charles Calvert (1785–1852) and worked in his studio in Manchester. Was friendly with Wm. Faulkner. Said to have married Calvert's eldest daughter in 1833 and to have returned to London a few months afterwards. His works show French influence; they are expressive and well modelled; the faces painted with crossed strokes. Schidlof records a miniature by him signed 'March 24th 1822 / W. Bradley'. Oil portraits by Bradley are in the City Art Gallery, Manchester and the V. & A. M. and N.P.G., etc.

*Brady, Miss Kathleen H. (fl. 1899–1907)

Exhibited at the R.A. and S.M. 1899–1907, from Cowbitt, Spalding.

Braine, Mrs. b. c. 1780/83. d. after 1855. See also **Briane, Mrs. Elizabeth Ann(e)**

Of London. Exhibited at the R.A., B.I., etc., 1850–1855. It has been suggested that she was identical with Mrs. Briane (q.v.), but this seems unlikely as her name was consistently spelt Braine and there would have been a gap of fifteen years between the exhibits. Some of her miniatures were lent to the exhibition at the South Kensington Museum in 1865 by the Countess of Caledon whose family she painted. It was noted that the artist was over 70 years of age when the miniatures were painted. They were of the Earl of Caledon, Lady Jane Alexander and the Hon. Walter Alexander. Her portraits of the last two sitters were exhibited at the R.A. in 1853 and, if they were painted in the same year, would make her date of birth c. 1780. According to the South Kensington catalogue, she was living in 1852 aged 72. In 1855 she exhibited portraits of Mrs. R. P. Braine and Master Philip Braine.

*Braine, Miss Alice. (fl. 1902–1911)

Of London. Exhibited at the R.A. and S.M. 1902–1911, from 15 and 27 Bartholomew Road, Campden Road.

Braine, Thomas. b. 1769

Of London. Born 1769. Entered the R.A. Schools, 27 March 1788, noted as '18. Dec 21st last'. Exhibited at the R.A., 1791–1802. Painted historical and mythological subjects, portraits and miniatures. In 1793 he exhibited a design for the centre panel of a curtain for the Theatre Royal, Edinburgh. An engraving of Mrs. Bennet the authoress, from a miniature by Braine is in the V. & A. M. A charming miniature of a boy stated to be signed on the reverse 'T. Braine, pinxt 20 George St., Hanover Sq.', was illustrated in *The Connoisseur*, XLV, 1916. W. Braine junior exhibited an architectural drawing at the R.A. in 1813, and was possibly his son.

*Bramson, L. (fl. 1821)

Worked in England c. 1820, according to Schidlof, who records that in the catalogue of the Davidson sale, Perl, Berlin, 27–28 November 1924, No. 84 was of a man in blue, signed 'L. Bramson pinx 1821 October 20'.

*Brandling, H. C. (fl. 1850). See also **Brandling, Henry**

Exhibited at the R.A. 1850, from 34 Fitzroy Square, in the drawing and miniature section, including a portrait of Miss E. Brandling. May have been identical with H. Brandling (q.v.).

Brandling, Henry. (fl. 1847–1856). See also **Brandling, H. C.**

Of London. Exhibited at the R.A., O.W.C.S., etc. 1847–1856, from 5 Newman Street. Became an Associate of the O.W.C.S. in 1853. May have been identical with H. C. Brandling (q.v.).

*Brandon, Lionel. (fl. c. 1840)

Long recorded seeing a rectangular miniature of a man c. 1840 by this artist. He did not consider it of a very high quality. He was also told of a miniature of the Duke of Hamilton said to be by Brandon.

Branwhite, Nathan. 1813–1894

Born at Bristol in 1813; son of N. C. Branwhite (q.v.). Was closely associated with W. J. Müller (q.v.). A miniature by him of Müller, executed in Indian ink, is at the Tate Gallery. The frontispiece to N. N. Solly's *Memoir of the Life of William Müller*, 1875, is a reproduction of a water-colour portrait of Müller by 'Branwhite of Bristol'. This may well have been the work of his father, N. C. Branwhite, who had a large practice in Bristol. Charles Branwhite, his brother, was also influenced by Müller and became a landscape painter. Died in 1894.

Branwhite, Nathan Cooper. 1775–1857. See also **Branwhite, Nathaniel**

Born in Lavenham, Suffolk, 1775; eldest son of Peregrine Branwhite, a minor poet, and his wife Sarah Brooke. Became an engraver and miniature painter. Was a pupil of Isaac Taylor junior (q.v.). Exhibited at the R.A. 1802–1828, from various addresses in London and Bristol, including 1824–1825, 1 College Green. Was the father of Charles Branwhite and Nathan Branwhite (q.v.). Was possibly identical with, or related to, the Nathaniel Branwhite (q.v.) who was living at Trelawny Place, Cotham, Bristol, 1830–1831, and at 1 College Green in 1833. His sitters included the Dean of Bristol and Dr. Spurzheim. He executed small portraits in Indian ink. The R.A. catalogues, 1802–1819, give his initial as N. and 1822–1828, as N.C. He is said to have omitted his second initial when signing en-

gravings. A miniature of Henry William Branwhite by this artist was sold at Sotheby's, 29 January 1968. The sitter may have been his brother. Died in 1857.

Branwhite, Nathaniel. (fl. 1830–1833). See also **Branwhite, Nathan Cooper**

Possibly identical with Nathan C. Branwhite (q.v.). In 1830–1831 he was living at Trelawny Place, Cotham, Bristol and, in 1833, was at 1 College Green, Bristol, from which address N. C. Branwhite also exhibited.

*Brebner, Miss E. M. (fl. 1909–1914)

Of London. Exhibited at the R.A., 1909 and 1914. Her sitters included Lady Rodney.

Breda, Carl Fredrik von. 1759–1818

Born in Stockholm, 16 August 1759; was in London, 1787–1796. Painted portraits in oil, some of which were almost miniature size, e.g. $5\frac{1}{2}$ in. Died in Stockholm, 1 December 1818. Said to have been a pupil of Sir Joshua Reynolds. Was nicknamed 'the Swedish Van Dyck'. Exhibited at the R.A., 1788–1796. Given as R.A., 1791. Exhibited a portrait of 'the late Sir Joshua Reynolds' in 1792. Did not exhibit miniatures.

*Bremer, Miss M. Leonore. (fl. 1903–1906)

Of London. Exhibited at the R.A. 1903 and 1906, from 2 Trinity Road, Tulse Hill, S.W.

Brewer, Mrs. Ann. (fl. 1763–1780)

Of London. Wife of John Brewer (q.v.). Exhibited miniatures and other subjects at the Free Society of Artists and Society of Artists, 1763–1780, including, in 1772, a miniature of one of her children.

Brewer, John. (fl. 1763–1779)

Of London. Husband of Mrs. Ann Brewer (q.v.). Exhibited water-colour landscapes and miniatures at the Free Society of Artists, 1763–1779. Undoubtedly the father of John James Brewer, also an artist, who exhibited from the same address as that of Mr. and Mrs. John Brewer, 13 Broad Court, Long Acre, and is described as 'Master Brewer'.

Brewer, Julian C. (fl. 1855–1876)

Of Plymouth (1855–1857), Bath (1859) and Norwich (1876). Exhibited at the R.A., 1855–1876.

Brewer, Mrs. Mary. (fl. 1848–1874). See also **Jenkins, M.**

Daughter of J. Jenkins, a Welshman who resided in London. Possibly the M. Jenkins (q.v.) who exhibited a portrait of Miss Jane Jenkins at the R.A., in 1830 from 6 Red Lion Square, from which address Miss J. Jenkins also exhibited at the R.A. Long noted that her husband's name was Robert, son of Mrs. A. Brewer (q.v.), but relatives gave his name as Marmaduke Brewer of Newport, Monmouthshire, and said that she was his second wife. She exhibited at the R.A. 1848–1853, under her married name from 4 John Street, Worcester. Her sitters included Dr. Turley of Worcester and W. H. Bishop, Esq. of the same city, as well as Caroline Georgina, younger daughter of Thomas Heaphy (q.v.), and William, Gerald and Albert, sons of the Hon. the Rev. Chetwynd Talbot. J. C. Hook, marine painter, was one of her pupils. She painted architectural subjects, portraits and miniatures. Visited Italy. Was living at Tuxfield, April 1874. Her daughter is said to have been a governess. A portrait of Mrs. Jackson, inscribed on the reverse 'Portrait of Mrs. Jackson April 1838 by Mary Brewer, Newport, Monmouthshire', is reproduced in O'Brien. A stepson of Mrs. Brewer married a daughter of R. H. Jackson. A miniature of J. Jackson, R.A. (q.v.) by Mrs. Brewer is in the V. & A. M. It shows character and is well drawn.

Briane, Mrs. See also **Briane, Mrs. Elizabeth Ann(e)**
Exhibited at the R.A. 1811–1835.

Briane, Elizabeth. (fl. 1830). See also **Briane, Mrs. Elizabeth Ann(e)**
Was at 5 Regent Street, Cheltenham, in 1830. Probably identical with Mrs. E. A. Briane (q.v.).

Briane, Mrs. Elizabeth Ann(e) (Miss Paye). (fl. 1798–1807). See also **Braine, Mrs.**
Née Elizabeth Ann(e) Paye. Worked in London; daughter of Richard M. Paye (q.v.). Exhibited at the R.A. 1798–1807, under her maiden name from 48, 49 and 39 London Street, Fitzroy Square and other London addresses; probably identical with Mrs. Briane (q.v.) who exhibited at the R.A., 1811–1835 and Elizabeth Briane (q.v.) who was at 5 Regent Street, Cheltenham in 1830. She appears to have had a distinguished clientele and painted, among others, miniatures of Miss De Camp, the Duchess of Beaufort, the Marquess of Hartington and Mrs. Siddons (exhibited 1806). M. R. Paye, who was evidently a relation, exhibited from the same address and, in 1801, exhibited a portrait of Miss E. Paye. Long records seeing a miniature with the following inscription on the reverse: 'Mrs Pole Carew / 1808 / painted by Mrs Bryane / formerly Miss Paye'. She may also have been identical with Mrs. Braine (q.v.), but this seems unlikely. A miniature of Mrs. Jeremiah Meyer, née Marsden, by this artist (Miss Paye), dated '1802', is at the Ashmolean Museum, Oxford. Her draughtsmanship was good and at least one miniature showed slight influence of the work of Sir Thomas Lawrence (q.v.). Long noted that others were slightly in the manner of Daniel (q.v.) of Bath.

*Bridges, Miss Amy F. (fl. 1903)
Exhibited at the R.A. 1903, from Mount Sandford, Southborough, Kent.

Bridgman, Miss May (Mary). (fl. 1906–1913)
Of London. Exhibited at the R.A. 1906–1913, from 49 Winterbrook Road, Herne Hill and, in 1906, and 1907, exhibited under the name of Mary Bridgman.

Bridport, Hugh. 1794–c. 1868
Born in London, 1794. Entered the R.A. Schools, 24 November 1815 aged 21. Studied under C. Wilkin (q.v.). Exhibited at the R.A. 1813, from Wilkin's address, Charlotte Street, Buckingham Gate. Emigrated to America in 1816 on the advice of T. Sully (q.v.). He and a brother opened a drawing academy in Philadelphia, 1817. Lived chiefly in Philadelphia but worked in other parts of America also. Exhibited 1817–1845 at the Pennsylvania Academy and Artists' Fund Society. Painted miniatures, portraits in oil, and water-colour landscapes besides executing engravings. Was highly thought of. Died in Philadelphia. Was still on the Philadelphia City Register in 1868. M. Bolton gives a list of works by Bridport. Examples of his art are in the Pennsylvania Academy of Fine Arts.

*Brigden, Miss Margaret. (fl. 1902–1904)
Exhibited at the R.A. 1902–1904, from 65 Dyke Road, Brighton.

*Briggs. (fl. c. 1785)
This artist is referred to in the *Walpole Society*, Vol. XIX, p. 10. An advertisement appeared in *The Calcutta Journal*, 31 March 1785, notifying the public that 'Mr. Briggs had removed from Hurrinburry Street, Calcutta to a house near the New Court House, lately occupied by Henry Richardson, and would continue finishing miniature pictures, likewise, in hair work.' No further information is so far available about Briggs.

Brighty, G. M. (fl. 1809–1827)
Of London. Exhibited at the R.A., 1809–1827. Painted portraits, miniatures and subjects, including the 'burning of Drury Lane Theatre', 24 February 1809. Executed engravings. A portrait in water-colour, representing the picture dealer, C. G. Dyer, dated '1816', is in the B.M.

Brimmer, Miss Anne. (fl. 1846–1857)
Of London. Exhibited at the R.A., 1846–1857. Her first exhibit from 6 Robert Street, Hampstead Road, was of her brother. She remained in the same street throughout her career.

*Brisley, Miss Ethel C. (fl. 1908–1913)
Of Bexhill and London. Exhibited at the R.A., 1908–1913. Amongst her exhibits was a self-portrait in 1913.

*Broadhead, Miss Marion E. (fl. 1907–1912)
Exhibited at the R.A. 1907–1912, from 100 Clarence Road, Longsight, Manchester. One of her exhibits in 1912 was a self-portrait. Executed paintings and engravings. Studied and exhibited in London and Paris.

Broadhurst, John, junior. (fl. 1775–1778)
Of London. Exhibited at the Society of Artists, 1776–1778. *The Daily Advertiser*, 29 May 1775, gives his address as near the Dog and Duck, St. George's Fields. In 1776 he was advertising from 107 Salisbury-court, Fleet Street as painting miniatures for rings, bracelets, etc. from one to two guineas each.

Brocas, James. 1754–1780
Of Ireland. Born probably in Dublin, 1754; fourth son of Robert Brocas and brother of Henry Brocas senior. Painted miniatures and portraits in oil and crayon. Advertised his ability to take likenesses in profile at half-a-crown each. Was a pupil at the Dublin Society Schools where he obtained prizes in 1772 and 1773. Later lived at 64 Dame Street where he practised as a portrait and miniature painter. Married in 1777 and advertised in *Freeman's Journal*, 28 February 1778, and 3 March 1778, that he had returned to Dublin. Some of his silhouettes were full length. He died in September 1780, aged 25 and was buried on 4 September 1780 in St. Andrew's Churchyard. Several of his family were artists in Dublin.

*Brock, Thomas A. (fl. 1904)
Exhibited at the R.A. 1904, from Arandine House, Madingley Road, Cambridge.

Brockmer, John. (fl. 1758–1776)
Of London and Bath. Was working in Bath, 25 September 1758 (*Bath Journal*). Exhibited at the Society of Artists 1762–1776, from London addresses. Painted miniatures and executed portraits in crayon and Indian ink; taught drawing. Advertised that he painted portraits for cabinet pieces, bracelets, rings, etc. Was in Bath in 1772. Walpole described one of his miniatures as very bad.

Brocky, (Charles Karoly). 1807–1855
Born at Temesvar, Hungary, 22 May 1807; son of a theatrical hairdresser; began life with strolling players; was a servant in a cook's shop and assistant to a barber. Studied art in Vienna in 1823 where he was a pupil of Johann Ender and Daffinger. After visiting Italy he returned to Vienna; was in Paris in 1837 and settled in London in 1839. Exhibited at the R.A., B.I. and N.W.C.S. (of which he became a member in 1854), 1839–1855. Painted miniatures, portraits in oil and drew pencil portraits and religious subjects. Died in London, 8 August 1855. Queen Victoria sat to him. He was a good artist

whose work showed the influence of Daffinger. He used a pink colouring for the flesh parts, and brown-red shadows which he painted in bold crossed brushwork. He used a scraper in the hair which was painted boldly. The background, which is usually a cloudy sky, is painted with almost horizontal hatchings which cross each other. The V. & A.M. and B.M. have examples of his work.

*Broff, J? (fl. 1786)
A miniature, signed 'J(?) Broff, / 86', (1786) is in the collection of R. Bayne Powell, Esq. The shading of the face has a brownish tinge, but the miniature is well painted and attractive. The painting is reminiscent of the work of Shelley (q.v.).

*Brome, Charles. 1774–1801
Of London and Suffolk. Entered the R.A. Schools, 29 March 1790, aged 16¼, when he was listed as an engraver. Exhibited at the R.A., 1798–1801. Besides engraving, he painted portraits, scenes and miniatures. His exhibits included portraits of Mr. and Mrs. Brome in 1801. Long records having seen a miniature of Mrs. Arabella Proby, née Waller, signed 'Chas. Brome pinxit / Higham / Suffolk / January 1800'. He considered it to be of fairly good quality; there was a bluish tinge on the face. A miniature of a gentleman by this artist, signed and dated '1799', was Lot 35 at Sotheby's, 6 November 1967. The artist's address was given on the reverse as Higham, Suffolk. He died in London in 1801.

Bronckhorst or Bronkhorst, Arnold or Arthur van. See **Brounckhurst, Arnold or Arthur van**

Brooke, Miss. (fl. 1807)
Of Cork Street, London. Awarded a silver medal in 1807 by the Society of Arts for a miniature painting of Angelica and Medoro.

*Brooke or Brookes, P. (fl. 1740–1749)
A miniature of a gentleman, signed on the front 'PBrooke / p.1749', was seen by me in 1966. The first two letters are joined in monogram and the miniature painted in the manner of Lens (q.v.), but without his draughtsmanship; the background and clothes are painted in gouache on ivory which was only visible on the face. The face was shaded with a loose stippling and a scraper had been used on the hair. The signature was painted in yellow on a dark grey background. A miniature of a young man, signed and dated 'P. Brookes, 1740', on ivory, is at the V. & A. M. The two artists were probably identical, as the miniatures appeared to be by the same hand, the one at the V. & A. M. being of a higher quality. This artist may have been an amateur.

Brooman, Mrs. 17th century
Said by Sanderson in his *Graphice*, 1658, p. 20, to have been a painter in oils. Her works are thought to have been miniatures.

*Brophy, A. Finn. (fl. 1876–1898)
Exhibited at the R.A. etc., 1876–1898, from 11 Rathbone Place.

Brounckhurst or Bronckhorst, Arnold or Arthur van. (fl. 1565–1598)
A Flemish artist who is known to have lived in Britain from c. 1565 onwards. He and his cousin, Cornelius Devosse, were sent by N. Hilliard (q.v.) to prospect for gold in Scotland in 1572 under a special patent or licence. Van Bronkhorst, as his name is spelt in Scotland, found gold, but the Earl

of Morton, who was Regent, would not allow him
to take it out of Scotland, and in 1580 van Brounckhurst was made 'one of his majesties sworne servants at ordinary in Scotland, to draw all small and
great pictures for his Majesty'; i.e. the young James
VI. He received £64 for painting three portraits and
100 marks in gratitude for coming to live in Scotland. In 1598 'Arnolde' is mentioned by Francis
Meres amongst the important contemporary
painters, and this is the last documentary evidence
so far available. An oil portrait representing Oliver,
1st Baron St. John of Bletso, signed in neat Roman
letters 'AR. BRONCKORST FECIT. 1578', which
had been wrongly identified for some years, was
rediscovered about ten years ago and is reproduced
on Pl. 266 in *Nicholas Hilliard* by Auerbach. Other
examples of oil portraits and miniatures may tentatively be assigned to him, including one of William
Cecil, Lord Burghley, in the collection of the Duke
of Buccleuch, and one of James I (James VI of
Scotland) at the Hague, which is not unlike the oil
portrait by him of the boy king in the S.N.P.G.
This Gallery also contains an oil portrait of James
Douglas, 4th Earl of Morton by this artist, and an
oil portrait of the Earl of Arran (died 1578) in the
collection of the Duke of Hamilton is probably by
him.

*Brounower, Sylvester. d. *c.* 1699 or 1700
Practically nothing is known about this artist who
was apparently employed, possibly as a secretary,
by the eminent philosopher John Locke (1632–
1704). A plumbago portrait of Locke by Brounower was purchased by the N.P.G.; it is signed 'S.
B. Fecit'. He must have been a talented artist and
one can only regret that so far no other examples
of his work have come to light. Letters including
some from his wife *c.* 1699 or 1700, acquainted
Locke 'with my greate lose in the Death of my deare
and loveing Husband'. The miniature of Locke, by
Brounower, is probably the one mentioned by Long
as being engraved by J. Nutting.

*Browing, J. See Bowring, J.
Schidlof records a J. Browing in error. The R.A.
catalogues, 1787, give the spelling as Bowing. The
artist was in fact Bowring (q.v.).

Brown. (fl. 1771)
Of Yarmouth. Exhibited at the Society of Artists,
1771. Possibly the Mr. Brown who advertised in the
Leeds Intelligence, 5 June 1797: 'Miniature Painter.
Mr. Brown is staying a short time longer. Price 2
guineas.'

Brown, Miss. (fl. 1783)
Exhibited at the Society of Artists 1783, as an
Honorary Exhibitor.

Brown, Miss. (fl. 1805–1812)
Of London. Exhibited at the R.A., 1805–1812.
Probably the daughter of W. Brown, gem engraver,
and sister of Miss M. C. Brown, Miss L. H. Brown
(q.v.) and Miss A. Brown, who all exhibited from
51 Green Street, Grosvenor Square, in 1801 and
1805. W. Brown and Miss Brown both exhibited
in 1809 from 58 Green Street, Grosvenor Square.
Miss Brown painted miniature portraits and fancy
heads, etc. There is no evidence that she was Miss
E. Brown as stated by Graves (*R.A.*).

*Brown, Miss E. Betts (Mrs. Boese). (fl. 1907–1908)
Of Surrey and London. Exhibited at the R.A.,
1907 and 1908.

*Brown, Miss Ella. (fl. 1895)
Exhibited at the R.A. 1895, from Bryn Hyfryd,
Harrow. The exhibits were three miniatures.

*Brown, Miss Frances Emily. (fl. 1900–1907)
Exhibited at the R.A. 1900–1907, from 4 Anglesea Road, Kingston-on-Thames and Shangton,
Claygate, Surrey. Her sitters included Miss Madeline Forsbrey.

Brown, George. (fl. 1825–1839)
Of London. Exhibited at the R.A., 1825–1839. A
miniature of Lord Byron, signed and dated '1826',
was sold at Christie's, 7 November 1961. He exhibited miniature portraits of Miss E. Harding as
Psyche, William Chappell, Esq. and Frederick
Salmon, Esq.

Brown, George Loring or **Claude.** 1814–1889
Born in Boston, U.S.A., 2 February 1814.
Apprenticed to a wood-engraver. Painted landscapes, portraits, miniatures and was an etcher,
wood-engraver and lithographer. Was in Boston,
1834–1836, New York City, 1837 and in Shrewsbury,
Worcester and Boston, 1838. From *c.* 1839–1859
he visited London, Florence and Rome. Returned
to America and was in New York City in 1862 and
Boston, 1864. Exhibited at the Boston Athenaeum
(1834–1874), the National Academy (1837–1866),
the Apollo Association and American Art Union
(1839–1852), the Pennsylvania Academy and
Artists' Fund Society (1836–1864) and the Maryland Historical Society (1848–1853). Died at
Malden, Mass., 25 June 1889.

*Brown, Ida. (fl. 1858)
Amateur artist; first cousin of the mother of
William Arthur, 6th Duke of Portland. A sketch in
lead pencil on paper of William John Arthur
Charles James Cavendish-Bentinck, afterwards 6th
Duke of Portland, K.G., aged 2 months, is in the
collection of the Duke of Portland. It is inscribed
on the reverse by Lady Hawkins-Whitshed with the
name of the subject and artist 'sketched from life by
Ida Brown – Kinnaird, Feby. 28th (18)58'.

Brown, J. (fl. 1803)
Of Richmond. Exhibited a miniature of his father
at the R.A., 1803. Possibly identical with J. Browne
of Richmond who exhibited a portrait of his mother
(possibly a miniature) at the R.A., 1816. A John
Brown advertised in *The Calcutta Gazette*, 24
October 1793, stating that he had lately arrived in
India and offered engravings for sale. Advertised,
17 April 1794, as an engraver and miniature painter,
executed miniatures for bracelets, lockets, etc. for
128 sicca rupees each. Raffled engravings, won
30,000 rupees in a lottery, 1795. Engraved a portrait
of Hugh Boyd by Home, published, 1795. Subsequently offered to teach drawing and miniature
painting.

Brown, John. 1749–1787
Born 1752 in Edinburgh; son of Samuel Brown,
a jeweller and watchmaker. Had a good education
and studied painting under Alexander Runciman.
Was in Italy and Sicily from 1771–1781 in the company of David Erskine, Mr. Townley and Sir W.
Young. Painted miniatures, highly finished pencil
portraits, pen drawings, made a few etchings and
wrote on music. Was probably the Brown who
married, 2 February 1786, Miss Mary Espline, both
of New Kirk Parish, Edinburgh. Mary was the
daughter of Charles Espline, merchant. Went to
London, 1786 and in the same year exhibited at the
R.A. Died at Leith, 5 September 1787, after
returning by ship from London. His wife survived
him. Examples of his work are in the S.N.P.G.
including a miniature in pencil of David Deuchar
(1743–1808), Seal Engraver, and a portrait by him
of Alexander Runciman, drawn in pencil from life,
1785. This miniature was loaned to the South
Kensington Exhibition of 1865.

Brown, Miss L. H. (fl. 1801–1804)
Of London. Exhibited at the R.A., 1801–1804.
Had a number of Scottish patrons, including Ensign
M'Kenzie of the 78th Regiment, Mrs. Campbell
(not a miniature), Miss Stewart, etc. Was probably
a daughter of W. Brown, gem engraver, and sister
of Miss M. C. Brown, Miss A. Brown and Miss
Brown (q.v.), who all exhibited from 51 Green
Street, Grosvenor Square.

Brown, Mather. 1761/2–1831
Born in Boston, U.S.A., 5/7 October 1761 (or
1762?); son of a clockmaker. Came to Paris and
London *c.* 1780. Entered the R.A. Schools, 7
January 1782, noted as '19, 5th last Oct.'. Taught
painting at Liverpool, Bath, Bristol, etc. Exhibited
at the R.A., 1782–1831. Is best known for his oil
portraits but is known to have painted miniatures.
Died in London, 1 January 1831 or 25 January 1831
(according to Groce and Wallace).

Brown, 'Mysterious'. (fl. *c.* 1812)
Presumably born in England. Later went to New
York where he was working in 1812. Painted
miniatures and drew portraits in chalk. Nathaniel
Rogers was his pupil. Brown was thought to be an
assumed name, but Groce and Wallace suggest that
he may have been identical with Uriah Brown, a
miniature painter who worked in Salem, Mass.,
1805 and New York City, 1808.

Brown, Peter. (fl. 1766–1791)
Of London. Was a member of the Society of
Artists, 1766 and, in 1767, was given assistance
from its funds. Exhibited at the R.A., 1770–1791.
Painted landscapes, animals, birds, shells and insects. From *c.* 1781 specialised in flower paintings
and became botanical painter to the Prince of
Wales. In 1772 he exhibited a miniature of the Holy
Family at the R.A. A miniature signed 'PB *c.* 1760',
in which the top of the P enveloped the top of the B,
both letters having the same downstroke, was sold
in 1931. It was not outstanding; there was some
hatching in the shading of the face.

Browne, Alexander. 17th century
Practised as a limner, etcher and mezzotint-
engraver in London during the reign of Charles II.
His sitters included Charles II, Countess Stewart
and the Prince of Orange. Published in 1660 a
translation of O. Fialetti's *Whole Art of Drawing,
Painting, Limning and Etching* and, in·1669 and
1675, *Ars Pictoria* in which he is described as a
'Practitioner in the Art of Limning'. In 1677 he
published *A Compendious Drawing-book*. Began
teaching Mrs. Pepys to limn, 7 May 1665, and
dined at Pepys' house, 9 May 1665, and again on 28
May 1666; accompanied Pepys from Erith to
Greenwich by the light of a lantern, discoursing on
painting, 3 September 1665. Pepys was apparently
upset by his familiarity in his household. Taught
Margaret, daughter of Sir William Penn. Was a
picture dealer. Pepys noted purchasing his book
Ars Pictoria for 20 shillings on 27 May 1669. An
engraved portrait of him after a painting by Jacob
Huysmans is the frontispiece of the book. Browne's
name appears in the catalogue of the South Kensington Exhibition, but no catalogue number is
given.

Browne, Mrs. H. (fl. 1830–1841)
Of London. Exhibited at the R.A. and S.B.A.,
1830–1841.

Browne, J. See Brown, J.

Browne, M. B. See Browne, Mrs. Marmaduke

Browne, Mary. See **Evelyn, Mrs. John**

Browne, Mrs. Marmaduke Bellet. 1786–1828

A miniature of Dr. James Atkinson (1780–1852) by the above artist is in the S.N.P.G., Edinburgh. It is signed on the front 'MB Browne' and on the reverse 'Mrs. Browne / Pinxit / James Atkinson Edinb'. A piece of paper placed behind the miniature has an inscription which reads: 'Painted by Mrs. Marmaduke Browne, Calcutta'. The miniature is painted on ivory, not on copper as is stated by Long. Schidlof records seeing a miniature in a private collection of the Marchioness of Hastings, signed 'M.B. Browne'.

Browning. (fl. c. 1820)

A miniature inscribed 'Mrs. Bramonson, Picture taken by Browning at Bath. June 1820.', was sold in London in 1978.

Brownover, S. See **Brounower, Sylvester**

*Brownrigg, Miss Edith J. D. (fl. 1902–1904)

Of Portrush, Co. Antrim. Exhibited at the R.A., 1902–1904.

*Brueton, Frederick. (fl. 1903–1907)

Of Brighton and Bridgwater, Somerset. Exhibited at the R.A., 1903–1907. Painted miniatures and landscapes in oils.

Brummell, George Bryan. 1778–1840

Born 7 June 1778 in the Parish of St. Margaret's, Westminster. Son of William Brummell and his wife, née Richardson, youngest daughter of the Keeper of the Lottery Office. Known as 'Beau Brummell'. Educated at Eton and Oxford. Became a friend of the Prince of Wales and a leader of fashion. Was a clever painter. A miniature of the Countess of Essex which he painted and gave to her is mentioned in an anecdote on p. 22 of A. Story's *James Holmes and John Varley*, 1894. Brummell was ruined by gambling; went to France and died in reduced circumstances in Caen, 30 March 1840.

Brunel, Sir Marc Isambard. 1769–1849

Born at Hacqueville, Normandy, 25 April 1769. A noted engineer. Lady Hawes lent what was reputed to be a miniature self-portrait of Brunel to the exhibition held at South Kensington Museum, 1865; it was said to be on ivory and signed 'M. I. Brunel'. Died in London, 12 December 1849.

*Brusetti, Joseph Anthony. d. 1779

This artist was noted by Strickland. He is said to have been a limner who died at Longhrea in September 1779.

Bryan. 17th century. See also **Bryan, Edward**

A limner referred to by George Vertue on p. 69 (60) of *Add. MS 23070* in the B.M. Possibly identical with Edward Bryan (q.v.).

*Bryan, Edward. (fl. c. 1679). See also **Bryan**

Strickland refers to this artist and says that his name appears in the parish registers of St. Michan's, Dublin in 1679. He may have been the Bryan (q.v.) noted by Long, from Vertue's *Add. MS 23070* in the B.M.

Bryan, John. (fl. 1786–1795)

Of London. Exhibited miniature portraits and sea pieces at the R.A., as an Honorary Member, 1786–1790, and at the Society of Artists, 1790–1791. In 1795 he was living at Stations Court, Ludgate Street. In 1790 he was listed as an honorary exhibitor at the Society of Artists from Union Place, Lambeth.

*Brynmor-Jones, Mrs. D. (Florence). (fl. 1898–1904)

Of London. Exhibited at the R.A. 1898 and 1904, from 27 Bryanston Square.

*Buchanan, Miss Inez. (fl. 1903–1913)

Of London. Exhibited at the R.A. 1903–1913, from 91 Elgin Crescent, Notting Hill and 8 Palace Mansions, Addison Bridge, 1912 and 1913. She painted miniatures and figure subjects.

Buck, Adam. 1759–1833

Born in Cork, 1759; the elder son of Jonathan Buck, a silversmith in Castle Street. Practised for some years in Cork, painting miniatures and small portraits in water-colour. Said to have worked in Dublin. Went to London in 1795 and exhibited at the R.A., B.I. and S.B.A., 1795–1833, and at the R.H.A., 1802. Besides painting, he taught portraiture and drawing. Many of his drawings of fancy figure subjects have been engraved and a series of coloured aquatint plates produced to illustrate Sterne's *Sentimental Journey*. Wrote a work on *Paintings on Greek Vases*, published 1811. Had numerous London addresses: 1795–1798 he was at 174 Piccadilly; was in Frith Street, 1799–1802 and, in 1813–1820, in Bentinck Street, after which time he moved frequently. He died at 15 Upper Seymour Street in 1833 and was survived by his wife and two sons, Alfred and Sidney (q.v.), the latter following his father's profession. Some of his miniatures and water-colours are very good and he was undoubtedly a better artist than his brother, F. Buck (q.v.). His technique varied a great deal; the flesh colours being rather pink. He used short and long strokes for the shading and occasionally used a scraper on the background and in the hair. He executed small full length portraits in water-colour or wax crayons, lightly tinted, usually in profile. I have seen small water-colour portraits which are well painted and attractive. He occasionally did decorative work for furniture. His own self-portrait is at the V. & A. M. and is dated '1804'. He often signed his work on the front A. Buck, sometimes in cursive letters and sometimes in Roman letters; some works are signed on the reverse, and he often added a date. Examples of his work are in the V. & A. M., the N.P.G., the B.M. and the National Gallery, Dublin. Two miniatures by him were loaned to the South Kensington Exhibition of 1865.

Buck, Frederick. 1771–c. 1839/40

Born in Cork, 1771; son of Jonathan Buck and brother of A. Buck (q.v.). Probably the F. Buck who was a pupil of the Dublin Society Schools in 1783. Had a large practice in Cork, living in 1787 at Fen's Quay, 1795 in Mardyke Street and, in 1810 (and for some years after), in Buckingham Square. During the Peninsular War, when Cork was a busy port of embarkation, his services were in great demand to paint portraits of officers. In order to keep pace with the demand, he kept a supply of painted ivories to which he added the heads and regimental facings as required. His work is not as good as that of his brother and the features are often badly drawn and modelled; he used a rather hot colouring which is an unmistakable characteristic of his work which looks hard and reflects the haste with which he so often painted. He sometimes painted cloudy sky backgrounds on the reverse of the ivory which he left white on the front. Examples of his work are in the V. & A. M. A fine miniature by F. Buck is in the collection of R. Bayne Powell, Esq. It represents Gaynor Barry of Hillbarry, Co. Dublin and was painted in 1780.

*Buck, Miss Lilias. (fl. 1902)

Exhibited at the R.A. in 1902 from 11 Park Place,

Weston-super-Mare. Painted portraits and miniatures.

Buck, Miss Sarah. (fl. c. 1790)

A miniature of Sir Joshua Reynolds by the above artist, and probably after a self-portrait, was seen at the Castle Museum, Norwich. It is inscribed on the reverse: 'Sr Joshua Reynolds / from Nature / by / Sarah Buck', and on the back of the frame: 'Portrait of Sir Joshua Reynolds / painted from life shortly / before his death in February / 1792 by Sarah Buck'. This latter inscription is in all probability inaccurate. The miniature is attractive and well painted. The owner has in her possession a self-portrait of Sarah Buck, whom she states later became Mrs. Baxter, and a medal enamelled on one side and inscribed in gilt 'ATRIBVTE TO GENIVS. MDCCXC. FROM THE / UNITED FRIARS / NORWICH / No 1'. On the reverse is engraved 'To Sarah Buck / For / a Painting / in Oil'. An artist named Mrs. Baxter exhibited a portrait at the R.A., in 1791 as an Hon. exhibitor. This latter artist was presumably identical with the Mrs. Baxter who worked in India c. 1792 and is referred to in the *Walpole Society*, Vol. XIX, pp. 9–10.

Buck, Sydney or **Sidney.** (fl. 1839–1849)

Son of Adam Buck (q.v.). Followed his father's profession. Exhibited at the R.A., etc., 1839–1849. Painted landscapes, miniatures and domestic subjects. A miniature, formerly in the O'Brien Collection, was signed 'Syd F. Buck Delt. Feby 1850'.

*Buckingham, Miss Ethel (Mrs. C. Havers). (fl. 1893–1901)

Exhibited at the R.A., 1893–1901. Painted portraits, miniatures and animals. Had addresses at 3 Meadow Studios, Bushey and 51 Earlham Road, Norwich.

Buckler, William. (fl. 1836–1856)

Of London. Exhibited at the R.A. and B.I., 1836–1856. Painted historical pictures, portraits and miniatures. His sitters included the children of H. E. the Belgian Ambassador, the Baroness Le Despencer and the Rt. Hon. the Lady Portman. Schidlof records seeing two miniatures painted on card, signed and dated '1850' and '1842', which were sold in Nice in 1942.

*Buckley, C. F. (fl. 1841–1869)

Exhibited at the R.A., 1841–1869. Painted landscapes but executed a portrait miniature of John Ashburner, 7th Bart., signed in full with the address '17 King William Street, City'. This was sold at Sotheby's, 1964.

*Buckley, Miss H. Blanche. (fl. 1896–1914)

Exhibited at the R.A. 1896–1914, from Hampton Wick and 26 Bolton Studios, London. Painted portraits, fancy subjects and studies. Her sitters included the Bishop of Sodor and Man and Anthony and Arthur, sons of Arthur Pilkington, Esq.

Buckley, John. (fl. c. 1835)

An Irish artist who practised at Cork about the middle of the nineteenth century. Painted miniatures, portraits and landscapes. Was not considered of any importance. A silhouette portrait of him painting at his easel was done in 1835 by A. Edouart and is in the National Gallery of Ireland. Long recorded seeing a miniature of a lady who lived near Cork, signed 'IB' (Roman monogram with a tall I) '/1828'.

*Buckman, Percy. (fl. 1886–1935)

Of London and Lewisham. Exhibited at the R.A., N.W.C.S., R.M.S., etc., 1886–1935, from 8 Portland

Place, Kensington and 50 Clarendon Road, Lewisham. Painted miniatures and landscapes in oil and water-colour. Was joint author with Dr. G. C. Williamson of *The Art of the Miniature Painter*, 1926.

Buckner, Richard. (fl. 1840–1879)

Worked at Chichester; was in Rome, 1846 and residing in London from 1847. Exhibited at the R.A., B.I. and S.B.A., 1840–1879. Painted miniatures, portraits and genre subjects. Some of his work was engraved. He had a fashionable clientele. Long considered his work to be pretty and delicately painted. A miniature on ivory of a girl, signed along the edge 'R. Buckner', was seen by Long, the signature being scarcely visible until the ivory was held against the light. The B.M. has engraved portraits after Buckner.

*Bucknill, Miss Julia B. (fl. 1905–1911)

Exhibited at the R.A. 1905–1911, from Hylands House, Epsom. Her sitter in 1905 was the Hon. Mr. Justice Bucknill.

Bulfinch or **Bullfinch, John.** (fl. 1660–1680)

Executed small copies of portraits in Indian ink, one of Sir Christopher Mingh or Myngs is at the B.M. The B.M. have a memo book, 1701–1728, of John Bulfinch, print seller. The N.G., Dublin has copies in Indian ink by this artist after Cooper (q.v.) and Kneller.

Bulkeley, John. (fl. *c.* 1834)

Painted portraits and miniatures; was working at 37 Rathbone Place, London, in 1834.

Bulkeley, Samuel. 18th century

A miniature of George Frederick Handel (1685–1759), musical composer, and executed in plumbago by this artist, is in the V. & A. M.

Bulkley, William. (fl. *c.* 1834)

Painted portraits and miniatures; was working at 6 Paddington Green in 1834.

Bull, Richard. (fl. 1777–1809)

An Irish artist, probably born in Dublin. Was admitted to the Dublin Society Schools, 1769; studied under Jacob Ennis. Exhibited in Dublin from 1777–1780. Executed portraits in hair and miniatures for which he charged two guineas. Went to London *c.* 1790 and exhibited at the R.A., 1794–1809. From 1795–1806 he lived at 101 Pall Mall. His name does not occur after 1809. His sitters included the Prince of Wales, the Duke of York, Lord Moira, Lord Nelson, Kemble, etc. Sir Martin Archer Shee painted his portrait and this was exhibited at the R.A., 1795 when it was called 'Portrait of an Artist'. He signed R. Bull with a date, or Bull. Long noted that he used numerous parallel dots in the background. A miniature signed 'R. Bull' and dated '1787', was sold at Christie's, 27 June 1961. A miniature of an unknown man, signed 'R. Bull / 1799', is in the V. & A. M. An attractive miniature of an unknown lady, signed 'Bull', is in the collection of Major R.M.O. de la Hey.

Bullar, T. or **J.** (fl. *c.* 1805)

Long notes having seen an apparently British miniature of a man *c.* 1805, signed 'T' or 'J Bullar', the letters of the signature being separate. The features were rather hard and there were distinct lines on the forehead and a bluish shading on the face.

*Bulley, Miss G. E. (fl. 1909–1914)

Of London. Exhibited at the R.A. 1909–1914, from 9 Walton Place, Pont Street. Her sitters included Miss Honora Sanford and 'P. L. G. Walker, Esq., Lieut. 7th Hussars'. The artist was possibly identical with Miss Georgina E. Bulley, the sculptress, who exhibited at the R.A. from 1880.

Bullfinch, John. See **Bulfinch, John**

Bullock, Miss Anne. See **Carwardine, Mrs. John**

Bullock, George Grosvenor. (fl. 1827–1859)

Of London. Exhibited at the R.A. and B.I., etc., 1827–1859. Working in 1834 at 121 Strand, London. Painted portraits, still-life and miniatures (one or more in oil).

Bulwitz. (fl. *c.* 1784)

A German artist said by Dr. G. C. Williamson to have been working as a miniaturist in London in 1784.

*Bunbury, Harriett. 19th century

A miniature of Selina Bunbury (1802–1882) by this artist is in the N.G., Dublin. The miniature is rather stiff and not of outstanding merit.

*Burbury, Miss A. Dorothy. (fl. 1905–1909)

Of London. Exhibited at the R.A. and S.M. 1905–1909, from 17 Upper Phillimore Gardens. The sitter was Miss Brenda Coward.

Burch, Edward, R.A. 1730?–*c.* 1814

Of London. Entered the R.A. Schools, 2 September 1769. Was awarded premiums at the Society of Arts, 1762, 1763, and 1765. Studied at the St. Martin's Lane Academy. Exhibited at the Society of Artists, 1760–1769 and at the R.A., 1770–1808. Became A.R.A. in 1770, R.A., 1771 and librarian to the R.A., 1794. Was a sculptor, medallist, a good gem engraver and also painted miniatures and exhibited an enamel at the R.A., 1792. Was on the Hanging Committee of the R.A., 1793. Married, as a widower, Mary Borckhart of St. Pancras, Middlesex at St. Mary-le-bone, 24 December 1793, she being a widow. Became nearly blind and died at Brompton in or before 1814 in which year his son, H. Burch (q.v.) exhibited a portrait of 'the late E. Burch'. Examples of his work are in the V. & A.M.

Burch, Henry Jacob, junior. b. 1763

Born 1763. Of London. Son of Edward Burch (q.v.). Entered the R.A. Schools, 25 March 1779, aged '16 last Dec.'. Exhibited at the R.A., Society of Artists and S.B.A., 1787–1834. Married Elizabeth Beresford, spinster, at St. Mary-le-bone, 6 December 1784. H. J. Burch, Elizabeth Burch and Elizabeth Anne Burch were witnesses at the marriage of Knightly Adams and Sarah Beresford, 22 April 1808. In 1793 a fire broke out and destroyed his house in Rathbone Place, 'The situation of Mrs. Burch was distressing beyond description'. Burch exhibited a portrait of his father in 1814. He signed H. Burch in Roman letters which were sometimes separate, and at other times conjoined. Some of his work is very attractive and is reminiscent of that of W. Wood (q.v.). He painted miniatures in watercolour and oil and executed cameos, intagli and wax portraits. Examples of his work are in the V. & A.M. and the B.M. has engravings after his portraits.

*Burgess, Miss Eliza Mary. b. 1878

Born in Walthamstow, Essex, 2 March 1878. Exhibited at the R.A. and R.M.S. 1900–1914, from

18 Addison Road and 9 Cedars Avenue, Walthamstow. Painted miniatures and portraits and fancy subjects in water-colour. Her sitters included Peter, son of Captain W. Llewellen. Was a member of the R.M.S. and of the Royal West of England Academy. An example of her work is at the Walker Art Gallery, Liverpool.

Burgess, James Howard. (fl. 1830–1846)

Exhibited at the R.H.A. from 1830. Worked in Belfast, Dublin and Carrickfergus. May have been the James Burgess who was at 1 Johnson Street, Horseferry Road, Westminster, 1851, noted in the catalogue of the Great Exhibition as cutting flower pictures with paper. J. H. Burgess executed miniatures, water-colours, landscapes, book illustrations and lithographs. In 1846 he was awarded a prize of ten pounds by the Royal Irish Art Union for a lithograph of Matthew Kendrick's *The Great Britain on Shore in Dundrum Bay*.

*Burgess, Miss Jessie M. (fl. 1907–1910)

Exhibited at the R.A. 1907–1910, from Shenfield, Brentwood, Essex.

Burgess, John. b. 1783?

Long records this artist as having lived at 24 or 34 Nassau Street, Dublin in 1812. He was elected a member of the Irish Society of Artists. Came to London and was probably identical with John Burgess who entered the R.A. Schools, 23 August 1813, aged 30. Exhibited at the R.A., S.B.A., O.W.C.S. and N.W.C.S. 1816–1840, from various London addresses. His exhibits included miniatures, sketches and a view of the Houses of Parliament burning (1839). Was a good miniaturist whose work at times is reminiscent of A. Robertson (q.v.). He used fresh colours mixed with gum and was a good draughtsman. Two miniatures by him are in the V. & A. M. They represent Thomas Constantinus Brooksbank (1779–1850) and his wife, Elizabeth, née Smythers. They are signed respectively, on the front 'I. Burgess' and on the reverse 'J. Burgess August 1816'; and on the reverse 'Jⁿ Burgess August 1816'.

*Burgess, John Bagnold, R.A. 1830–1897

Born in London, 1830. Exhibited at the R.A., B.I., etc., 1850–1893. Is best known for his figure subjects and portraits, but may have painted some miniatures at the outset of his career. Was a pupil of J. M. Leigh. Died in London, 1897.

Burgess, William. (fl. 1762–1791)

Of London. A drawing master. Exhibited at the Society of Artists and the Free Society of Artists, 1762–1791. Noted principally for landscapes and portraits in chalks, but also executed miniatures and small portraits in black lead. There was also a drawing master by the name of Thomas Burgess in Duke Street, Lincoln's Inn Fields in 1763, from which address William Burgess exhibited a self-portrait at the Society of Artists in 1762.

*Burghers or **Burgers, Michael.** b. *c.* 1640

Born in Holland *c.* 1640. Worked in Oxford *c.* 1676. Engraved portraits from his own drawings and those of Loggan (q.v.), W. Crowne, etc. Worked until *c.* 1723. Long recorded seeing a plumbago drawing of Archdeacon Welchman of Cardigan (1665–1739), inscribed 'Burges, Delineart'. Benezit illustrates his monogram MB.

Burke, C. d. 1801

An Irish artist of some repute who worked in Cork. Died January 1801.

Burlin, Richard. (fl. *c.* 1828)

Was working in 1828 at Fold's Road, Little Bolton, Bolton, Lancs.

Burman, J. *c.* 1773–1846

Of Birmingham. Painted miniatures in Birmingham from *c.* 1806–1846. Worked in Stratford-on-Avon and in the neighbourhood. His obituary in *The Birmingham Journal* stated that he charged £1 and upwards for his miniatures, and died 4 April 1846 at Great Colmore Street in his 73rd year, and that he had been a miniature painter in Birmingham for 'upwards of 40 years'. His work was not outstanding. A miniature of an officer, signed 'BURMAN', *c.* 1820, is in the collection of E. G. Paine of New York.

Burne, H. See **Byrne, H.**

*Burns. (fl. 1793)

Worked in England towards the end of the 18th century. Schidlof records seeing, in 1957, a miniature portrait of a man, signed 'Burns 1793'. It was not of any great merit and was painted with so little colour that it had the effect of being executed *en grisaille*.

*Burns, Miss Lilian. (fl. 1908–1911)

Of London. Exhibited at the R.A., 1908–1911. Her sitters included Lady Markham, Sir E. J. Poynter, Bt., P.R.S., Mrs. Poynter and Lieut. Col. Frank Dugdale, C.V.O.

*Burrard, Lady. (fl. 1847–1849)

Schidlof records seeing in a private collection a miniature of Queen Victoria, signed on the reverse: 'Painted by / Lady Burrard (Lyndhurst) / for the benefit of the R.S.H. Infirmary / July 21st 1849 / Lyndhurst'. He gives the name as Burrard-Lyndhurst, but this is probably a mistake. The Burrard family were well known in Hampshire. She may have been the wife of Sir George Burrard, 4th Bart., M.P. for Lymington. He married 3 January 1839, Isabella (died 1876), daughter of Sir George Duckett, 2nd Bart. A miniature of Mrs. Minnie Taunton, née Barber, is in the collection of R. Bayne Powell, Esq. It is inscribed on the reverse 'Painted by Lady Burrard 1847', and signed on the front 'L'(?), the second letter being indecipherable.

Burrell or **Birrell, Miss.** 19th century

In the *History of Burley-on-the-Hill, Rutland* by Pearl Finch, 1901, a miniature portrait of Charles Fielding, R.N., is mentioned in Vol. II, p. 13, as being by Miss Burrell, and there is a reproduction of it in Vol. I, f.p. 310, as 'by Miss Birrell'. From the illustration, the portrait would appear to be early 19th century.

*Burrell, Mrs. H. Théonie. (fl. 1902–1913)

Exhibited at the R.A. and S.M. 1902–1913, from Neville Cottage, Newcastle-on-Tyne.

Burrell, Joseph Francis. b. 1770

Born in 1770. Exhibited at the R.A. 1801–1807, from 7 Rathbone Place, London. His exhibits were landscapes and, in 1807, a miniature of 'Master Banks, a noted beggar, and the artist's daughter'. Said to have been living in 1834 at 9 Great Titchfield Street. Mr. Rubens, in his article in the *Jewish Historical Society*, 1958, notes that this artist must have been the 'little Jew . . . a clever sensible creature' who gave lessons to Sir Walter Scott; this is recorded in *The Journals of Sir Walter Scott*, 1825–6, 1939, Vol. I, p. 118. Burrell came from Prussia where his father had been a commissary in the army of Frederick the Great. According to the

Harleian Society records, he married on 13 August 1801, Mary Blake (widow) at St. Mary-le-bone. Examples of his work are in the V. & A. M., including some landscapes and miniatures, one of which is inscribed on the reverse 'Colonel Thos Poole / Aged 55 years. / Painted the 6th of April 1813 / by Jos. Fran. Burrell / 17 Soho Square'. It is possible that Miss Burrell (q.v.) may have been his daughter. His work is slightly reminiscent of the work of Smart (q.v.), but the faces of the sitters are more coarsely stippled; the drawing is good. The B.M. has an engraved portrait of Dr. Joseph Jenkins, after Burrell

*Burrell, Miss Sermonda. 20th century

Was a member of the Society of Miniaturists.

Burt, Albin Roberts. 1783–1842

Born 1 December 1783, probably in Wales; son of Harry Burt and his wife, Mary, née Roberts; brother of Henry Frederick Burt (died 1807), Secretary to Lord Nelson. His mother was intimate with Emma Hamilton. Began life as an engraver and was a pupil of Robert Threw and Benjamin Smith. Exhibited at the R.A., 1807 and 1830. Worked in Bath and Worcester (1812), Birmingham and Warwick (1814), Oxford (1817 at 113 High Street), London (1805, 1814, 1820, 1830), Chester (*c.* 1810–1830 at Mrs. Hunter's, Northgate), Reading (1832) and Southampton (1834 at 14 Albone Bar and 51 Albone Bar). Executed shell and stone cameos, portraits, miniatures and engraved and stippled a portrait of Francesco Bianchi after Chinnery (q.v.). Married in 1810, Sarah Jones, by whom he had eight children. He died in Reading, 1 March 1842. A miniature profile, signed 'A. R. Burt / Warwick / August 1814', was sold at Sotheby's, 1962. Had a printed advertisement on the back of some of his profiles stating that he had a 'New invented machine by which the most accurate likenesses can be taken. Can with confidence recommend his portraits to the public, especially as the practice of many Thousands has given his Pencil a facility that enables him to afford the coloured Profiles at / Half-a-Guinea each / and more finished at 1 Guinea'. He signed his works Burt followed by a date, or A. R. Burt followed by a date and place. He charged 3 guineas upwards for miniatures on ivory and from 5 to 10 guineas for full-length portraits.

*Burt, Mrs. Lily. (fl. 1901–1902)

Of Stoke Poges, Slough. Exhibited at the Society of Miniaturists, 1901–1902. She exhibited a self-portrait in 1902.

*Burt, Miss Maria or **Marie C. E. (Mrs. Simpson).** (fl. 1872–1883)

Born in Caton Town, Bedfordshire. Worked in Willesden. Exhibited at the R.A., under her maiden name, 1872–1880 and under her married name, Mrs. Simpson, 1882–1883.

Burt, W. (fl. *c.* 1830)

An artist of this name is recorded by J. J. Foster as having worked in the provinces at this period. Schidlof records a miniature of a young lady, on ivory, signed 'W. Burt 1829', which was sold in Vienna in 1934.

*Burton, Miss Aileen G. (fl. 1910–1911)

Exhibited at the R.A. 1910 and 1911, from St. Saviour's Vicarage, St. Albans and 35 Cochrane Street, St. John's Wood.

Burton, Sir Frederic William, R.H.A., F.S.A. 1816–1900

Born 8 April 1816 at Corofin House, Co. Clare; the third son of Samuel Frederick Burton, an

amateur painter, and his wife, Hannah Mallet. Loved art from an early age and was a pupil of the Brocas brothers in Dublin and was influenced by G. Petrie. Progressed rapidly and painted miniatures, portraits in water-colour, landscapes and figure subjects. His miniatures were often painted on large sheets of ivory and, according to Strickland, 'were finely modelled, boldly painted and rich in colour'. In 1837 he exhibited at the R.H.A.; was elected an Associate in the same year and a Member in 1839. He exhibited regularly until 1854 and later when he was living in London. He exhibited at the R.A., O.W.C.S., etc., 1842–1882. Burton visited Germany several times and painted copies for the King of Bavaria. In 1855 he was made an Associate of the O.W.C.S. and a Member in 1856, but resigned in 1869. Was made a Director of the N.G. in 1874, after which time he ceased to paint. He was knighted in 1884 and died unmarried at 43 Argyll Road, Kensington, 16 March 1900 and was buried in Dublin. The N.G. Ireland has drawings by Burton. He mixed a lot of gum with his paints which made them bright. Schidlof mentions a miniature of a lady, on ivory, signed on the reverse 'Frederic Wm Burton R.H.A.' and dated '1836'.

Burton, W. (fl. 1803). See also **Burton, W. K.**

Long records having seen a miniature of an officer with a sky background, signed and dated '1803'. The miniature was good with hatched background and face modelled with short brush strokes. The artist may have been identical with W. K. Burton (q.v.) who exhibited at the R.A., 1803–1804.

*Burton, W. K. (fl. 1803–1804). See also **Burton, W.**

Exhibited miniatures at the R.A., 1803 and 1804. The first exhibit was a 'Portrait of an Officer of the light Cavalry', and may have been the one noted by Long under W. Burton (q.v.). In 1804 he exhibited 'A portrait of an artist' as an Honorary Member.

Busby, J. L. See **Busby, T. L.**

Busby or **Bushby, T. (or J.) L.** (fl. 1804–1821)

Of London. Possibly related to C. A. Busby, an architect. Exhibited at the R.A., etc., 1804–1821. Possibly identical with Thomas, Lord Busby, engraver. Benezit states that he exhibited at the R.A., and Suffolk Street, 1804–1837, but only one T. L. Busby is recorded in the R.A. catalogues. The name is spelt Bushby in 1804 and J. L. Busby is recorded (probably identical) in 1808. No artist of this name exhibited at the R.A., 1821–1837.

Bushe, Letitia. d. 1757

An Irish artist, daughter of Arthur Bushe of Dangin, Co. Kilkenny, Secretary to the Commissioners of the Inland Revenue, and his wife, Mary, daughter of John Forth. Letitia was an intimate friend of Mrs. Delany with whom she frequently stayed and who mentioned her in her letters as a 'gay, good humoured, innocent girl, without the least conceit of her beauty . . . she paints delightfully'. She drew a view of Deville in 1754; this, and a self-portrait, engraved by Joseph Browne, are both reproduced in *Letters of Mrs. Delany* by Lady Llandover. She died in Dawson Street, Dublin, 17 November 1757 and was buried in St. Andrew's Church. A miniature by her, painted on ivory, of the Hon. Mrs. Mary Hamilton in the guise of a shepherdess, is signed 'L. Bushe fecit 1735'. One of her miniatures was a small rectangular landscape of an Italian view (probably a copy), signed 'L. Bushe Fecit 1732'.

*Butchart, Miss Theresa. (fl. 1910–1911)

Exhibited at the R.A. 1910 and 1911, from Armadale, Barrow-in-Furness. Her sitter in 1911 was Mrs. T. F. Butler.

*Butler, Miss Frances E. (fl. 1907–1911)

Of London and Rugby. Exhibited at the R.A., 1907–1911.

Butler, Mrs. Penelope. See Carwardine, Miss Penelope

*Butler, William. (fl. c. 1850)

A miniature of an officer c. 1850, signed 'W.B.', is said to be by this artist. See O'Brien Pl. 46, fig. 3.

*Butson, Miss Norah. (fl. 1891–1902)

Exhibited at the R.A. 1891 and 1902, from Coxlease, Stoner, Henley-on-Thames. Executed portraits in oil and miniatures.

*Butterworth, Mrs. Margaret. (fl. 1894). See also **Butterworth, Miss Winifred M.**

Exhibited at the R.A. 1894, c/o Mrs. Bengough, 8 Wilton Place, Belgrave Square. Painted miniatures and fancy subjects. Possibly identical with Miss Winifred M. Butterworth (q.v.).

*Butterworth, Miss Winifred M. (fl. 1901). See also **Butterworth, Mrs. Margaret**

Exhibited at the R.A. 1901, from 53 Pultney Street, Bath. Possibly identical with Mrs. Margaret Butterworth (q.v.).

*Buttery, T. or J. (fl. c. 1815)

A miniature of a woman c. 1815, signed on the reverse 'T [or J] Buttery / Miniature / painter / St Albans', was seen by Miss E. Clifford Smith on 20 March 1967. It was not of outstanding merit.

*Byres. 19th century

Long noted a miniaturist of this name who was an English banker in Rome.

Byrn. (fl. 1808). See **Byrne, Charles**

Exhibited at the R.A., 1808, a miniature portrait of a lady. No initial or address of the artist is given, but Graves identifies him as C. Byrne (q.v.).

Byrne, Charles. 1757–c. 1810. See also **Byrn**

Born in Dublin, 1757; became pupil, assistant and interpreter to S. T. Roche (q.v.). Had his own practice at 19 Suffolk Street and c. 1791 was employed by Hutchinson, a jeweller, in Dame Street, to paint miniatures for customers. Worked in London for a short time. Exhibited at the R.A. 1800, from 18 Fleet Street, a portrait of Master Byrne. Gave up painting sometime before his death. Became insane. Died in Dublin c. 1810. His self-portrait in miniature is at the N.G., Dublin.

Byrne, Daniel. (fl. 1840–1880)

Exhibited at the R.A. 1840–1880, from 5 Southampton Street and Brighton (1853). Schidlof records an important miniature of a lady with a child in its cradle, landscape background, on ivory, signed 'Byrne 1845'.

Byrne or Burne, H. (fl. c. 1678)

The only examples of this artist's work at present known are in the collection of the Duke of Portland. They represent Henry Cavendish, 2nd Duke of Newcastle, K.G., signed 'HB', and his wife, Frances Pierrepont, Duchess of Newcastle, his son Henry Cavendish, Earl of Ogle and his daughters, Lady Margaret and Lady Catherine Cavendish, the latter four portraits being unsigned. All these miniatures were painted in 1678; evidence for this is quoted by R. W. Goulding 'in the book of weekly dispersment's of the Duke's Steward, Thomas Farr,

under date 20 July 1678, is the following entry – "To Mr Byrne ye limbner as *Per* acqt. £36:01:06, drawing 8 pictures" '. Six of these eight limnings were at Welbeck 19 November 1695, for in an inventory of this date it is recorded that 'six Pictures in Black frames Drawn by Mr. Burne were hanging in the Dutchesse Dowager of Newcastle's Clossett of Busynesse'. It has been suggested that this artist was a pupil or imitator of Des Granges (q.v.). He painted cravats with clearly defined patterns and intensified the effect by using specks of black paint.

*Byrne, K. 18th century

A miniature by the above artist, who appears to be hitherto unrecorded, was Lot 46 at Sotheby's, 11 November 1968. It is signed on the front in cursive lettering 'K. Byrne'. The miniature was quite attractive and the sitter painted against a cloud and sky background.

Byrne, Miss Mary. See Green, Mrs. James

C

C. (fl. 1759)

A miniature portrait on ivory of a lady, stated to be signed 'C. 1759', was lent by Lord Leigh to the exhibition at South Kensington Museum, 1865. A small oil portrait of the Duke of Buckingham, signed 'C.', was in the collection of the Earl of Denbigh.

*C., E. See E., C

*C., H. See H., C

*C., I. 18th century

Long saw a photograph of a miniature of a man, signed 'I.C. 1795', which he thought was possibly Scottish. It was not of very high quality.

*C., R.O. (fl. c. 1800). See also **O., C.R.**

Lady Liddell had a miniature c. 1800, signed 'C^{R}O'.

C., T. See also T., C.

A good miniature of c. 1775, signed 'T.C.' or 'V.C.', of a boy, half length, with a dog, was seen by Long; it bore some resemblance to the work of N. Hone (q.v.). A miniature of a lady, signed 'C.T.' and dated '1897', oval, 3⅝ in., was sold at Christie's, 10 April 1962, and a portrait on ivory of Sir John Aubrey, Bart., and stated to be signed 'C.T.' or 'T.C.', was lent to the exhibition at the South Kensington Museum, 1865. A miniature of a man in a blue coat, signed 'T.C.', is now in the Holburne Museum, Bath. One of an unknown man, signed and dated 'T.C. 1767', is in the collection of E. G. Paine of New York.

C., V. See C., T. and V., C.

C., W. See Claret, William

Cabaliere, John. d. 1780

Began life as a wine merchant in Bond Street, but developed an aptitude for art and was distinguished by his skill as a miniaturist. Died 12 June 1780.

*Caird, Mrs. (fl. c. 1823)

I have in my collection a miniature by the above

artist, inscribed on the reverse 'Mrs. Caird / about 1823'. The miniature represents Henry VIII, Mary I (his daughter) and Will Somers, the Court Jester, holding a dog. The original of this painting is in Lord Spencer's collection at Althorp. The picture is a composite one executed by an unknown 16th-century artist of the English school; the portrait of Henry VIII is after Holbein, Mary I is after Mor and the portrait of Somers is possibly from life. It has been suggested that it was made for Somers on his retirement from Royal service. Mrs. Caird is said to have come from Edinburgh and I can find no other information regarding her.

Caldicate. 17th century

A miniature of Thomas Sackville, 1st Earl of Dorset, died 1608, was lent to the exhibition at South Kensington Museum, 1865 by the Countess of Caledon. It was catalogued as by this artist and was evidently a good miniature.

Caldwall or Caldwell, John. c. 1738–1819

Born c. 1738. Said to have been born in London, although Long gives his place of birth as Scotland. Brother of James Caldwell, an engraver. Practised as a miniaturist in Scotland, executed crayons and miniatures. Lived for some time at Blackfriars Wynd (*Edinburgh Directory*, 1793/4), and in the Canongate until 1816. Died February 1819 when, according to a note in the S.N.P.G., he was in his 81st year. A miniature of an unknown man, signed on the reverse on a piece of paper 'Caldwall', is in the V. & A. M.

*Caldwell or Caldwall, James. (fl. 1809–1830)

This artist, who may have been related to either John Caldwall (q.v.) or James Caldwell, the engraver, was noted by Long as having been referred to as a miniature painter from 1809–1830 at New Street, Canongate, Edinburgh.

Campbell, Colin. (fl. 1820)

Working in 1820 at 187 High Street, Edinburgh. No further information about this artist is available.

*Campbell, Miss Doris H. (fl. 1910)

Of London. Exhibited at the R.A. 1910, from 12 Dene Mansions, West Hampstead.

Canavari or Canevari, Giovanni Baptista. 1789–1876

Born in Genoa, 4/11 March 1789. Worked in Leghorn, Florence and Lucca, and later in Turin, Rome and probably London. Joined the Imperial Guard in Florence and took part in the war against France. On his return to Italy he continued miniature painting and was patronised by many noble families and King Carlo. Settled in Rome in 1824. Exhibited at the R.A., 1853–1854 (Long) or, to give Schidlof's dates, 1848–1871. The exhibit in 1848 is listed as by Canavan, and that of 1849 as by Canavris, both of Rome. These artists were probably identical with the above. He painted portraits in oil, pastels and water-colours. Died in Rome, 11 June 1876. Schidlof notes that before his death he offered a large number of his drawings and sketches to the Academy of St. Luc, Rome. His work shows the influence of some of his English contemporaries, particularly Sir W. J. Newton (q.v.). He used warm colours and the brushwork was soft with a lot of gum with the paint.

*Cannon, Miss Edith Margaret. (fl. 1892–1904)
Exhibited at the R.A. and S.M., etc. 1892–1904, from 7 Windsor Road, Ealing.

Capes, Mrs. See **Weigall, Miss Julia**

Carandini, Paolo. 17th century. See **Cross, P.**
For many years miniatures signed 'P.C.' were attributed to either Carandini or Penelope Cleyn (q.v.), but it has now been established that they are the work of P. Cross (q.v.). No evidence is forthcoming to support the theory that Carandini ever came to England, and a contemporary writer speaks of him as dead in 1673.

Carbonnet, John Baptist. (fl. c. 1795)
Long saw three miniatures signed on the reverse by this artist: 'By / John Baptist / Carbonnet'; they dated from c. 1795 and were in French style, weakly drawn and unattractive. From the inscription it seemed likely that the artist worked in England. Schidlof mentions a miniature by him which was lent to the Berlin Exhibition, 1906.

Carbonnier, Mrs. (fl. 1825)
Of 64 George Street, Portman Square, London. The Society of Arts awarded her a large silver medal for a miniature portrait in 1825. She may have been the wife of Casimir Carbonnier (q.v.).

Carbonnier, Casimir. 1787–1873
Born in Beauvais, 24 May 1787; was a pupil of Augustin van den Berghe, David and Ingres. Exhibited at the Paris Salon, 1812. Worked in London and exhibited at the R.A., B.I., etc., 1815–1836. Painted miniatures, portraits and figure subjects and executed engravings. Painted pictures for the Queen of Naples. Some of his portraits were engraved. Returned to France in 1836 and entered the community of the Lazarists c. 1839. Was known as 'Frère François'. Executed decorations for a chapel in the Rue de Sèvres, Paris. He died in Paris, 20 March 1873. May have been the husband of Mrs. Carbonnier (q.v.). The B.M. has engraved portraits after Carbonnier.

*Carew, Anna Maria. (fl. 1662)
Was a miniature painter to Charles II. Made miniature copies of pictures. Noted in *The Connoisseur*, LIII, 1919, p. 165 by E. Alfred Jones. According to some old official documents which the author was studying, Anna Maria Carew was 'employed for copying the king's pictures in miniature'. She was granted a pension of £100 a year on 8 February 1662, and ten days later this was increased to £200.

Carey, William Sheridan. c. 1795–1821
Born c. 1795. Possibly the son of William Paulet Carey of Ireland. Died 5 June 1821 at Kensington Gravel Pits in his 26th year.

*Cargill, Miss Amy. (fl. 1899)
Exhibited at the R.A. 1899, from 26 Harrington Road, South Kensington. Her sitter in that year was Vyvian, daughter of Charles Pilman, Esq.

*Carin, Miss Marie. (fl. 1889)
Of 51 Rue Palikao, Lille. Exhibited three miniatures at the R.A., 1889.

Carlile, Anne. See **Carlisle, Anne**

*Carlill, Mrs. Stephen B. (Mary). (fl. 1895–1896)
Exhibited at the R.A. 1895–1896, from King's Langley, Herts. Wife of Stephen B. Carlill who also exhibited at the R.A.

Carlin, John. 1813–1891
Born in Philadelphia, 15 June 1813. Was deaf and dumb. Studied at the Pennsylvania Institute for the Deaf and Dumb, 1821–1825. Studied drawing under John Rubens Smith and painting under John Neagle between 1833 and 1834. Was a miniaturist, portrait, genre and landscape painter, as well as an author. Exhibited as a resident of Philadelphia at the Artists' Fund Society, 1835–1838. Came to Europe; was a student at the British Museum in London, 1838 and became a pupil of Delaroche in Paris. Returned to America, 1841 and settled in New York City. Exhibited at the American Institute, the National Academy, etc. from 1835–1886. After the advent of photography he devoted most of his time to genre and landscape painting. He had many friends, and the *New York Tribune*, at the time of his death in his 78th year, 23 April 1891, quoted the following lines from his *Mute's Lament*:
My ears shall be unsealed and I shall hear;
My tongue shall be unbound and I shall speak.

Carlisle or **Carlile, Mrs. Joan (Anne),** 1606?–1679
Miniature painter during the reigns of Charles I and II; was patronised by the former who is said to have made her a valuable gift of ultramarine. Painted miniature copies of oil pictures in the manner of P. Oliver (q.v.) and made copies of paintings after Italian masters. Mentioned by De Piles, p. 361 (2nd Edition), who describes her as Mrs. Anne Carlisle, and in the Turquet de Mayerne MS at the B.M. she is described as 'Mademoiselle Carlile'. The N.P.G. has an oil portrait of Sir Thomas and Lady Browne which is ascribed to her. See *Burlington Magazine*, Sept. 1954. Vol. XCVI, pp. 275-7.

*Carlisle, Miss Mary Helen. (fl. 1891–1913)
Of London. Exhibited at the R.A., 1891–1913. Executed miniatures and oil paintings of flowers.

Carlsten or **Carlsteen.** See **Karlsteen**

Carlyle, J. (fl. 1816). See also **Carlyle, Thomas**
This artist is only known by a miniature on ivory of John Lowry which is at the Tullie House Museum, Carlisle. It is inscribed on paper on the reverse 'John Lowry / Taken / at the age of / 13 in Carlisle / by J. Carlyle / 1816'. The sitter is painted in profile against a pale sky background. The face is softly painted, the eyelashes strongly delineated. No stippling is used. He may have been identical with, or related to, Thomas Carlyle (q.v.).

*Carlyle, Thomas. (fl. 1812–1837). See also **Carlyle, J.**
This artist is possibly identical with, or related to, J. Carlyle (q.v.). Worked in Liverpool and possibly in Ireland. A miniature of a lady illustrated by O'Brien, Pl. 74, Fig. 3, is signed 'T. Carlyle 1837'. On the back of the miniature part of an envelope is affixed on which is inscribed 'To T. Carlyle Brennan's, Scotch Street, Dungarvon'. This is the redirected address, the first one being 86 Bald Street, Liverpool. As the miniature was purchased in Ireland there is every possibility that he worked there. A miniature of Lady Burell, signed 'T. Carlyle 1836', was sold in Vienna in April 1922. A miniature of Lieut. John McKibbin, on paper, signed and dated 'Thos. Carlyle 1812', is in the collection of E. G. Paine of New York.

Carmichael, James. (fl. 1767–1774)
Of London. Executed miniatures and portraits. Exhibited at the Society of Artists, 1767 and 1774.

*Carmichael, Lady Margaret. d. 1727
Daughter of the 2nd Earl of Hyndford and wife of Sir John Anstruther. An attractive miniature self-portrait in the manner of Rosalba Carriera (q.v.) is in the Carmichael House Collection.

Carné, H. de. (fl. 1801–1821)
Of London. Exhibited at the R.A., 1801 and 1821.

*Carney, Sir Richard. d. 1692
Son of Edward Carney, tailor of Dublin. Recorded by Strickland as a limner. Was appointed herald in 1658 and 'Principal Herald of Arms of the whole Dominion of Ireland' in 1655. Held several appointments after the Restoration and was knighted in 1684. Was a portrait painter as well as a herald. Died 1692.

Carpenter, J. (fl. 1837–1855)
Of London. Exhibited at the R.A., 1837–1855. Possibly the husband of Mrs. James Carpenter (q.v.).

Carpenter, Mrs. James. 19th century
Possibly the wife of J. Carpenter (q.v.). A miniature on ivory of two nieces of the artist was lent to the exhibition at the South Kensington Museum in 1865.

Carpenter, Miss Jane Henrietta. (fl. 1847–1857)
Of London; daughter of W. H. Carpenter of the B.M. and of Mrs. William Carpenter (q.v.) by whom she was taught, and sister of Wm. Carpenter junior (q.v.). Exhibited at the R.A., 1847–1857. All members of this family exhibited from the B.M.

*Carpenter, Mrs. William H. (Miss M.S. Geddes). 1793–1872
Née Margaret Sarah Geddes; born in Salisbury in 1793; daughter of a Captain Geddes and sister of Mrs. William Collins (wife of the artist William Collins, R.A.). Studied art from Lord Radnor's collection at Longford Castle. Obtained prizes from the Society of Arts including a gold medal. Went to London in 1814 and exhibited at the R.A. and B.I. under her maiden name, 1814–1817 and from 1818–1866 as Mrs. William Carpenter. Her husband was W. H. Carpenter, Keeper of Prints and Drawings at the B.M., upon whose death, in 1866, Queen Victoria conferred upon her a pension of £100 per annum. Her daughter, Miss J. H. Carpenter (q.v.) and her son, Wm. Carpenter junior (q.v.) were probably taught art by her. Painted fancy subjects and miniatures in oil, water-colour and crayons. She exhibited from various London addresses including the B.M. She exhibited a portrait of R. Henton Wood, Esq., M.R.C.S., at the R.A., in 1862; this may have been a miniature. Her work is said to have been influenced by that of Sir T. Lawrence (q.v.). A portrait of Henrietta Shuckburgh and a self-portrait, both from water-colours in the B.M., are reproduced on p. 96 of *Women Painters of the World*, 1905. Examples of her work are in the N.P.G.

*Carpenter, William, junior. (fl. 1862)
Exhibited a portrait of a lady from Boston, U.S.A., at the R.A., in 1862. Undoubtedly the son of W. H. Carpenter and Mrs. W. Carpenter (q.v.) and brother of Miss J. H. Carpenter (q.v.).

*Carpentier. (fl. 1743)
Of London. The name of this artist appears in *The Daily Advertiser*, 7 February 1743, advertising from Mr. Cheek's Apothecary, Bow Street, Covent Garden. Possibly identical with the artist of this name listed by Schidlof, who worked in France in

505

the 18th century. A portrait of a lady, on enamel, signed 'Carpentier Rotomagus 1761', was in the David-Weill Collection, Paris.

*Carr, Miss Edith. b. 1875

Born 24 February 1875 in Croydon. Exhibited at the R.A., 1907–1914. Was a pupil of the Croydon School of Art and studied in Paris where she exhibited at the Salon.

Carr, Henry. (fl. 1770–1798)

Entered the R.A. Schools, 24 February 1770. A miniature on ivory of a man in a blue coat and signed along the edge 'H. CARR 1789', was seen by Long who considered the miniature of some merit; the sitter was a member of a noted Scottish family. According to a note made by C. F. Bell, H. Carr copied a miniature of John Thomas Stanley, later Sir John Stanley, and eventually 1st Lord Stanley of Alderley (1766–1850). The portrait was painted by Carr in 1798 when the sitter's sister wrote to his wife for hair to mount with it.

Carrick, Thomas Heathfield, 1802–1874

Born in Upperby, nr. Carlisle, on 7 April 1802. According to one of his obituary notices, his father was John Carrick, a glass and china merchant; Long, however, states that his father (no name given) was a cotton mill owner. Was educated at the Carlisle Grammar School. Carrick quarrelled with his family and left home; worked with a chemist in Carlisle and later had his own business. Taught himself miniature painting and was one of the artists who introduced the method of painting miniatures on marble; J. F. M. Hüet-Villiers (q.v.) also being an exponent of this method. Worked in Carlisle, Newcastle, Scarborough and London. Exhibited at the R.A. from 1841–1866. Received a medal from the Prince Consort in 1845 for inventing the method of painting on marble. Some of his miniatures were painted after photographs, or had a photographic base. His obituary states that he had a photographic business in Regent Circus, London. Was a friend of Dickens, Lover and Jerrold and included among his sitters Thomas Allom, Charles Kean, Daniel O'Connell, Samuel Rogers, William Wordsworth, Sir John Russell, the Earl of Carlisle and Longfellow. He is said to have been friendly with T. M. Richardson junior and to have painted the faces in a picture by him. Carrick gave up miniature painting in 1868 and retired on a Turner Annuity to Newcastle where he died on 31 August 1875. He was a good artist and an accurate draughtsman, and able to express the character of his sitters. An article published in *The Cumberland News*, 20 October 1967, records that 'the animation of his portraits was due to his own lively conversation during sittings, indeed he made Thomas Carlyle laugh so much that his wife was sure the portrait would not be characteristic of the "Sage of Chelsea".' He painted boldly in crossed brush strokes with dark brown shading; the faces are painted with a soft pink or orange, the eyebrows hardly visible. He also used a grey-blue shading and tended to bow the mouths of his sitters. His self-portrait on marble is in the Tullie House Museum, Carlisle; it portrays him seated at a table with his palette beside him. The artist is painted against a greenish-grey background, and the miniature is a fine example of his work. In the same Museum there is a portrait of James Steel, of the *Carlisle Journal*, also by Carrick. A fine miniature of William Wordsworth belongs to the poet's family; it is inscribed on paper on the reverse: 'No I. William Wordsworth / T. Carrick / 43 Upper Seymour Street / Portman Sq'. A pair of miniatures by Carrick were sold at Sotheby's, 6 November 1967. Two miniatures by him are in the V. & A. M., and the B.M. has en-

graved portraits after his work. His miniature of William Farren was loaned to the exhibition at South Kensington, 1865.

Carriera, Rosalba. 1675–1757

It has always been alleged that this famous Italian miniaturist and pastellist visited England and Ireland, but the fact has never been established. She was born in Venice, 1675 where a number of her works may be seen. Her introduction of ivory as a base on which to paint revolutionised miniature painting and is of great significance to the history of the art. Bernard Lens III (q.v.) was responsible for introducing it into England in the early part of the 18th century. A miniature said to be of Lady Mary Wortley Montagu, in my collection, and of which there is a second version in the collection of Earl Beauchamp, is on vellum, and inscribed on the reverse 'Lady Wortley Montagu / by Rosalba'. Due to failing eyesight she was obliged to give up painting miniatures and paint large portraits in crayons. Died in Venice, 1757. A characteristic of her work is pure fresh colours, often a dress or cloak of bright blue, and paintings of ladies are frequently depicted with flowers, including a rose, which she appears to have used as a symbol. A self-portrait of the artist is in the collection of the Duke of Portland, and another in the collection of Earl Beauchamp.

*Carroll, W. (fl. 1799)

Lot 69 sold at Sotheby's, 15 June 1933, included a miniature on card by 'W. Carroll, 1799'. The above artist was possibly identical with an obscure Irish painter, William Carroll, recorded by Strickland, and who exhibited at the R.A., 1790–1793. His exhibits were landscapes and subject paintings.

*Carroll, William. (fl. 1895)

Of London. Exhibited at the R.A. 1895, from 4 West Hampstead Studios, Sheriff Road, N.W. The exhibit was of Miss Henrietta Hill.

*Carse, Alexander. (fl. 1809–1830)

Long records that a miniature painter of this name worked from 55 Princes Street, Edinburgh, 1809–1830. He may have been identical with, or related to, Alexander Carse (died *c*. 1838) who was noted for his genre paintings; this latter artist exhibited in Edinburgh, 1808–1836, and at the R.A. and B.I., 1812–1820. He was born in East Lothian and was a pupil of David Allan (q.v.). Said to have died in London.

Carstairs, L.

An enamel miniature of Queen Caroline (1682–1737), catalogued as by L. Carstairs, was lent by the Duke of Devonshire to the B.F.A. Club exhibition, 1889.

*Carter, Miss A. (fl. 1868)

Exhibited at the R.A. 1868, from 20 Johnson Place, Harrow Road; may have been the daughter of Mr. and Mrs. J. H. Carter (q.v.) who exhibited from the same address.

*Carter, Miss Amy J. (fl. 1895–1896)

Exhibited at the R.A. 1895–1896, from Stamford House, 428 Fulham Road. Her sitters included Lord Amherst of Hackney and Mrs. John Walker.

*Carter, Miss Christian. (fl. 1910–1914)

Exhibited at the R.A. 1910–1914, from The Cottage, Falconer Road, Bushey, Herts. Her sitters included Mr. and Mrs. John Herkomer and Mrs. M. A. Carter.

Carter, Mrs. Elizabeth. See Carter, Mrs. J. H.

*Carter, Miss Gertrude H. (fl. 1902)

Exhibited at the R.A. 1902, from The Grange, Howden, E. Yorkshire. Her sitters included Mark H. Carter, Esq.

*Carter, J. (fl. 1835–1844)

Exhibited at the R.A. 1835–1844, from 21 Aldenham Terrace, St. Pancras Road. His first exhibit was called a 'sketch from life', and was possibly a miniature. He executed architectural drawings, landscapes and probably miniatures. Not to be confused with J. H. Carter (q.v.) of the same period who exhibited from Leadenhall Street, etc.

Carter, J. H. (fl. 1839–1856)

Of London. Exhibited portraits, etc. at the R.A. 1839–1856, from 20 Johnson Road, Harrow Road and from Leadenhall Street. As these portraits were exhibited with the miniatures and drawings, it is possible that they were miniatures. A miniature portrait of J. H. Carter by his wife was exhibited at the South Kensington Museum in 1865. The B.M. has an engraving after Carter.

Carter, Mrs. J. H. (Elizabeth). (fl. 1839–1867)

Wife of J. H. Carter (q.v.). Worked in London and Torquay (1862). Exhibited at the R.A., 1839–1867. In 1868 a Miss A. Carter is recorded as exhibiting at the R.A., from 20 Johnson Place, Harrow Road, from which address Mrs. J. H. Carter was exhibiting; she may have been her daughter. A miniature of a lady, signed and dated on the reverse 'Mrs J. H. Carter July 31st (18)48', and painted in the manner of Sir W. C. Ross (q.v.), is in the collection of Miss Edwina Clifford Smith of London. Mrs. Carter loaned some of her miniatures to the South Kensington Exhibition, 1865 including one of her husband painted in 1845. The index for the Exhibition records her name as Elizabeth.

Carter, Miss Matilda. b. *c*. 1815–1891

Of London, born *c*. 1815 (according to Schidlof). Exhibited at the R.A., 1839 and 1849. Was probably the daughter of J. H. Carter and Mrs. J. H. Carter (q.v.) from whose address she exhibited. Said to have died in September 1891.

Carter, Noel N. (fl. 1823–1833)

Of London. Exhibited at the R.A., 1823–1833. Painted portraits and miniatures including several portraits of officers. A water-colour portrait of a child on large paper is signed 'Noel Carter / 1823' and is not of a high quality. His work shows a strong French influence.

*Carter, Miss Rosa. (fl. 1889–1910)

Exhibited at the R.A., S.M., etc. 1889–1910, from various London addresses. Painted fancy subjects, portraits and miniatures. A miniature of Sir Frederic Leighton, P.R.A., by the above artist, is in the N.P.G.

*Cartwright, Mrs. Gertrude A. (fl. 1908–1910)

Of London. Exhibited at the Society of Miniaturists, 1908–1910.

*Caruson, S. (Stefano?). (fl. 1831–1839)

Exhibited at the R.A. 1839, a miniature portrait of two children. A miniature by this artist was No. 2724 at the exhibition at South Kensington Museum, 1865; it was of an unknown lady, painted in 1831. He worked in Naples and London. Several of his works are mentioned by Schidlof, p. 131, Vol. I. He appears to have signed Caruson, sometimes followed by a date, or inscribed on the reverse with the sitter's name.

Carwarden, John. (fl. *c*. 1636)

Frances, Countess of Thanet, writing to her son-in-law, Sir Edward Dering, in 1636, recommends the bearer, Mr. Carwarden: 'an able man by the reporte of yᵉ Country (and in parte I cann speake by experience) to take ye face of my daughter Elizabeth . . . If you shall have any occasion to use a limner. . . .'. This is recorded in the *Stowe MSS*: 243 f. 121. A portrait of Christopher Simpson by Carwarden (painted in 1659) was engraved by Faithorne (q.v.).

*Carwardine, Mr. (fl. 1771)

A Mr. Carwardine, miniature painter of Golden Square, married Miss Holgate of Halstead, Essex (*The Gazette*, 13 August 1771). This artist is probably identical with the Carwardine (no initial given) who exhibited at the Society of Artists, 1771–1772. The exhibits were both portraits and the address in 1772 was James Street, Golden Square.

Carwardine, Mrs. Anne. See **Carwardine, Mrs. John**

Carwardine, Mrs. John. (fl. *c.* 1730). See also **Carwardine, Mrs. Thomas**

Née Anne Bullock of Preston Wynn. Married John Carwardine of Thinghills Court, Withington, Herefordshire *c.* 1730. May have been identical with Mrs. Thomas Carwardine (q.v.) and 'Mrs. Carwardine' who exhibited at the Society of Artists in 1761 and 1762 respectively. A Mrs. Carwardine, miniature painter, was living in Rathbone Place, Soho, London in 1763. John Carwardine ruined the family estates and Anne and her six children, one of whom was Penelope Carwardine (q.v.), also a miniaturist, had to earn their living.

Carwardine, Miss Penelope. *c.* 1730–1801. See also **Cotes, Miss Penelope**

Born *c.* 1730; eldest of six daughters of John Carwardine of Thinghills Court, Withington, Herefordshire by his wife, Anne Bullock, of Preston Wynn. Her father was evidently reckless and extravagant and, as a result, the family were ruined and Penelope took up miniature painting to earn her living. By the age of 24 she had established herself, and *c.* 1772 she married a Mr. Butler who was organist at Ranelagh, St. Margaret's and St. Anne's, Westminster. For many years miniatures painted between 1750 and 1765, and signed P.C., have been attributed alternatively to Penelope Cotes (q.v.), the supposed sister of Francis and Samuel Cotes (q.v.), or to Penelope Carwardine. There is no documentary evidence to establish the existence of P. Cotes, and no mention is made of her in F. Cotes' will in 1770. No artist of this name occurs among the list of exhibitors for 1760 onwards, or in contemporary accounts. In the absence of any such proof, it seems reasonable to regard all miniatures of this period as the work of P. Carwardine. To strengthen this belief, miniatures in the possession of the Carwardine family closely resemble the works previously known, which are signed P.C. If this is so, the assertion that P. Carwardine was taught by O. Humphry (q.v.), may not be correct, as she had been working for a number of years before Humphry set up on his own in 1762. It is true that he did paint a miniature of her in 1767, and it is possible that she studied his style in order to improve her own, but he could not have guided her early work, which had more affinity to the work of Lens (q.v.), mingled with that of a more modern approach. She ceased to paint miniatures after her marriage, as far as we know, and died childless *c.* 1800, her husband having predeceased her. The portrait of her by O. Humphry is reproduced f.p. 78 in Dr. Williamson's *Ozias Humphry, R.A.*, 1918. A miniature of Maria Gunning, afterwards Countess of Coventry (1733–1760), signed and dated

'1757', is in the Wallace Collection, London.

*Carwardine, Mrs. Thomas (Anne). (fl. 1761–1762). See also **Carwardine, Mrs. John**

Exhibited miniatures at the Society of Artists, 1761–1762. Possibly identical with Mrs. John Carwardine (q.v.).

Cary. 17th century

An artist of this name is referred to by W. Sanderson in *Graphice*, 1658 'for miniature or limning, in water-colours . . . Coopers and Cary'. Cary is also mentioned in an inventory of the Wittenhorst Collection in the Netherlands.

*Case, Miss Norah. (fl. 1906–1910)

Of Berkhampsted, London and Lambourne, Berks. Exhibited at the R.A., 1906–1910.

*Castle, T. Charles H. (fl. 1890–1891)

Exhibited at the R.A. etc., 1890–1891, from 23 Bardolph Road, Tufnell Park.

*Catani, Ugo. (fl. 1904–1905)

Of London and Florence. Exhibited at the R.A. and S.M., 1904–1905, from 18 Kensington Court Place, London.

Caton, Miss M. (fl. 1808)

Exhibited at the R.A. 1808, as an Honorary Member.

Caulfield, J. (fl. 1792)

Of London. Exhibited at the R.A., 1792.

*Caulfield, The Hon. Rachel. (fl. 1904–1914)

Of London. Exhibited at the R.A. 1904–1914, from 15 Warwick Gardens, Kensington. Her sitters included Capt. Nelson Ward, R.N., M.V.O. and Lady Camilla Fortescue.

*Cavalier, J. (fl. 1688)

A miniature painted on ivory relief and described as a portrait of S. Pepys by J. Cavalier, 1688, was seen by Long in 1930.

*Cawse, Miss Clara. (fl. 1841–1867)

Of London. Exhibited at the R.A. and B.I., etc., 1841–1867. Painted figure subjects and miniatures.

*Cazalet, Miss Agnes. T. (fl. 1907–1910)

Exhibited at the R.A. 1907–1910, from Neva, Westgate-on-Sea, Thanet.

Cazenave, M. de. See **Cazenove, Simon de**

Cazenove, Simon de. (fl. 1856–1875)

Of London. Exhibited at the R.A., etc., 1856–1875. At the R.A. he is listed as M. De Cazenave. His exhibits included a self-portrait.

*Chaceré de Beaurepaire, Mlle. See **Beaurepaire, Mlle. de**

*Chaceré de Beaurepaire, Mme. (fl. 1804–1822). See also **Gaillard, Mme.** and **Beaurepaire, Mlle. de**

This artist exhibited at the R.A. in 1804, 1820 and 1822. The two earlier entries give no address but, in 1822, she was at 30 Portland Street, Oxford Street. According to Long's notes she was at Bath in 1811 (34 Gay Street) and 1821 (3 Montpelier). In the R.A. catalogues she is styled as Mme de Beaurepaire, but Benezit gives her full name as above. She may have been identical with Louise Chaceré de Beaurepaire who married and worked with René Gaillard, the French engraver. If so, on his death in 1790 she seems to have reverted to her maiden name whilst retaining the style Madame. Exhibited at the Paris Salon, 1798–1822 (the first

exhibit being of one of her daughters), under her maiden name, and in 1833 under the name of Gaillard. Was a pupil of Augustin (q.v.).

*Chadwick, Miss Luie. (fl. 1902–1908)

Of London. Exhibited at the R.A. and S.M. 1902–1908, from 5 Branch Hill, Hampstead Heath.

Chair, R. B. de. (fl. 1783–1785)

Exhibited at the R.A., 1785 (Honorary Exhibitor). He signed his work R.B.D. followed by a date. He may well have been of French origin and worked in the manner of the French school of miniaturists. He seems to have painted chiefly in profile. Three miniatures by him are reproduced in O'Brien, Pl. 77, Figs, 1, 2 and 3. They represent a family; each miniature is signed on the front 'R.B.D. 1783'; de Chair did not exhibit in 1865 as stated by Schidlof.

*Chalker, Miss Cissie (Mrs. J. Fison). (fl. 1890–1898)

Of Bath and Norfolk. Exhibited at the R.A. 1890–1898, from Belle Vue House, Bath, and in 1898, from The Red House, Thetford, Norfolk. Undoubtedly the sister of Miss Sophia Chalker (q.v.). Her exhibits included a portrait of her sister; the children of J. W. Chalker, Esq.; Violet, daughter of A. Johnston, Esq.; Miss Marie Castellian; Mrs. J. A. W. Ricketts; Jack and Roy, sons of J. E. Martin, Esq.; Miss Deane; Betty, daughter of the late W. Chalker, Esq.; Mrs. Henry Chalker; Lady Fairbairn, and Hope, eldest daughter of H. F. Clutterbuck, Esq. Her married name is given in 1898 as Mrs. J. Fison.

*Chalker, Miss Sophia. (fl. 1888–1889)

Of Bath. Undoubtedly the sister of Miss Cissie Chalker (q.v.) whose address, Belle Vue House, Bath, she shared. Exhibited at the R.A., etc., 1888–1889. The exhibit in 1888 was a portrait of her father.

Chalon, Alfred Edward, R.A. 1780–1860

Born in Geneva, 15 February 1780, of French descent. Entered the R.A. Schools, 12 August 1797, aged 17, having been brought to England in 1789 by his father who became a professor at the Royal Military College, Sandhurst, and later settled in Kensington. Chalon was intended for a commercial career, but abandoned it for art. Exhibited at the R.A., and B.I., etc., 1801–1860. His sitters included Queen Victoria, Princess Charlotte of Wales, the Duchess of Kent, etc. In 1808 he became a member of the Associated Artists in Water-Colours and in the same year he and his brother, J. J. Chalon (q.v.), founded a famous sketching society. He was elected A.R.A., 1812 and R.A., in 1816. He had great success as a painter of water-colours and miniatures, and was painter in water-colour to the Queen. He also painted subject pictures in oil. He and his brother were both bachelors and kept house together for many years. He was said to have been a witty companion and a clever musician. He died in Campden Hill, Kensington, 3 October 1860, and was buried at Highgate. His miniatures varied in quality, his earliest often being his best. He was particularly good at painting ladies. Some of his later works often have rather thick touches of white on the lace, etc. Many of his works are signed in monogram AEC, but he occasionally signed A. E. Chalon in the upper right hand corner, or on the reverse, e.g. Painted by / Alfᵈ Edwᵈ Chalon / R.A. / London 1830. Examples of his work are at the V. & A. M.. B.M.. and N.P.G., and in private collections including those of H.M. the Queen, the Earl of Powis, etc. The B.M. has a chalk self-portrait of Chalon as well as other drawings and numerous engravings after him. Several miniatures by him were lent to the South Kensington Exhibition, 1865. A miniature of an unknown lady in the collection of Major R. M. O. de la Hey was exhibited in Edinburgh in 1965.

Chalon, John James, R.A. 1778–1854

Born in Geneva, 27 March 1778; brother of A. E. Chalon (q.v.). Entered the R.A. Schools, 3 October 1796, aged 18. Painted landscapes and is known only as a miniaturist by a full length enamel portrait, 3½ × 2¾ in., of Mme de la Vallière as the Magdalen. This portrait was formerly in the H. C. Bonn Collection (1884). Died in Kensington, 14 November 1854.

Chalon, Miss Maria A. See **Moseley, Mrs. Henry**

Chamberlain. (fl. 1779)

Exhibited at the Free Society of Artists, 1779.

*Chamberlin, Mrs. Amy Gertrude. (fl. 1895–1911)

Of London. Exhibited at the R.A. and S.M., 1895–1911.

*Chambers, Mrs. Norah. (fl. 1900–1906)

Exhibited at the R.A. and S.M. 1900–1906, from Currabinny, Epsom and from 9 Lansdowne Crescent, London. Her sitters included Dr. Clement Daniel and Miss Winifred Malan.

*Chambers, Miss Ruby. (fl. 1905)

Of London. Exhibited at the R.A. 1905, from 42 Pembroke Square. Her sitter was Mrs. Charlie Piggott.

Chambrulard, J. de. 1764–1847

Born in Langres, France, 4 May 1764. Was working in London for a few years and exhibited at the R.A., 1799–1802. Returned to Langres and became Vice-President of the Société Historique et Archéologique there. Died 6 June 1847. A miniature copy on ivory of St. John the Evangelist, after a painting by Domenichino, is at the Museum in Langres.

Chancellor, George. 1796–1862

Born in Dublin in 1796. Son of John Chancellor, watch-maker of 55 Lower Sackville Street, Dublin. Succeeded to his father's business. Was devoted to art and painted landscapes and miniatures. Exhibited in Dublin, 1817–1829; many of the exhibits were miniatures. He died at his father's address on 5 October 1862, and many of his miniatures remained in the possession of the family.

Chandepié de Boiviers, J. C. (fl. 1800–1827)

Born in Jersey. Was a pupil of David. Exhibited at the Salon at Paris, 1800–1817, whilst living there. Was in London and exhibited at the R.A., 1819–1823. Exhibited at the Salon again in 1827.

Chandler, John Westbrooke. 1763?–1804/5

Natural son of Lord Warwick; probably the John Chandler who entered the R.A. Schools, 12 November 1784, aged '21 1st May'. Exhibited at the R.A., 1787–1791, whilst living in London and, in 1791, from Warwick Castle. Worked in Aberdeenshire c. 1800 and was later in Edinburgh. Attempted to commit suicide. A life-size portrait of Elizabeth Cavendish, Duchess of Devonshire, by this artist, is in the N.P.G. Died in confinement c. 1804/5. Some of his work was engraved. The B.M. has engravings of portraits by him.

Chantrey, Sir Francis Legatt, R.A. 1781–1842

Born at Norton, nr. Sheffield, 7 April 1781. Famous sculptor, but also executed miniatures, drawings in black lead and crayon portraits, in Sheffield and London. Miniatures by him are scarce. He exhibited sculpture at the R.A., 1804–1842. Was painting miniatures in Sheffield in 1802. A miniature portrait of Earl Brownlow by him was in the Burdett Coutts Collection, and was in a case enclosing a letter from Lady Chantrey to Miss Coutts, July 1851. He is also known to have painted miniatures of John Law, Joseph Law and T. A. Ward. These are mentioned by John Holland in *Memorials of Sir Francis Chantrey, R.A.*, 1851. Died in London, 25 November 1842. A portrait of Chantrey with a bust of George IV, painted by A. Robertson (q.v.), signed and dated 'A.R. (monogram) 1831', is in the collection of H.M. the Queen and was exhibited in Edinburgh in 1965.

Chantry, N. (fl. 1797–1836)

Of London. Exhibited miniatures and other portraits, landscapes, etc. at the R.A., 1797–1836. The exhibits for 1797 were two portraits in wax.

*Chaplin, Miss Adrienne L. (fl. 1904)

Exhibited at the R.A. 1904, from Beechwood, Deal, Kent.

*Chapman, Miss Anne H. (fl. 1897)

Exhibited at the R.A. 1897, from Walpole St. Margarets, Middlesex.

*Chappell, Graham or **Chappel, G.**

Possibly the G. Chappel, Esq. (Honorary Exhibitor) whose portrait of the Rev. E. Robson was exhibited at the R.A., 1804. A miniature in the catalogue of the Bemrose Collection of a man with a beard was described as by Graham Chappell.

*Chardon-Debillemont, Mme. G. See **Debillemont-Chardon, Mme. Gabrielle**

Charles, A. (fl. 1786–1793)

Worked in London towards the latter part of the 18th century. Painted miniatures which, according to Long, were of poor quality, and silhouettes which were of considerable merit. Was appointed painter to the Prince of Wales in 1793. Charged from 3 to 25 guineas and stated that he had 'studied in the Italian, Flemish, and all the great Schools', and called himself 'Royal Academician', which he was not. A miniature of an unknown young man by Charles is in the collection of Earl Beauchamp; the work is rather naive. The Duke of Buccleuch has a miniature of a man, signed 'by Charles' along the edge. Fanny Burney refers to Charles in her Diary. A miniature of an unknown officer in my collection is inscribed on the reverse 'improv'd / by Mr Charles / Miniature Painter / to his Majesty'.

*Charlton, Mrs. John (Miss Edith M. Vaughan). (fl. 1894–1914)

Née Vaughan, wife of John Charlton. Exhibited at the R.A. 1894–1914, from London and Hillcroft, Farnborough, Kent. Her sitters included Lady Blanche Somerset, daughter of the Duke of Beaufort, the Duchess of Beaufort and Enid and Dornie, daughters of Dr. Scanes Spicer.

Charman. (fl. c. 1805)

Long records having seen a large miniature on ivory, c. 1805, of a naval officer. A frame-maker's card on the back gave the name of 'Charman / George St, Adelphi'. This may, or may not, be the name of the artist.

Charpin or **Charpine, Miss E.** (fl. 1761–1767)

Of London. Probably the daughter of an artist of the same name who exhibited from the same address. Exhibited at the Society of Artists, 1761, her own portrait profile and three other miniatures; and at the Free Society of Artists, 1762–1767, miniatures in enamel and water-colour, one in the style of Sir Peter Lely.

Charretie, Mrs. John. 1819–1875

Born in London, 5 May 1819. Née Anna Maria Kenwell. Pupil of Mrs. V. Bartholomew (q.v.). Married in 1841 Captain John Charretie (died 1868). Exhibited at the R.A., B.I., etc., 1842–1875. Painted miniatures, water-colour flower pieces and genre subjects and, after her husband's death, taught herself to paint in oil. She exhibited a miniature of Blanche, daughter of Lord Charles Beauclerc, at the R.A., in 1860. A miniature of Lord Charles Beauclerc and one of Miss Crampton (both painted by herself), were lent by Mrs. Charretie to the exhibition at the South Kensington Museum, 1865 when her address was 11 Hornton Street, Campden Hill. Died in Kensington, 5 October 1875.

*Chartran, Théobald. 1849–1907

Born in Besançon, 20 July 1849. Studied in Paris and Rome. Exhibited at the R.A., Grafton Galleries, etc., 1881–1892. Was a well-known French artist who painted oil portraits, subject pictures and miniatures. In 1883 his address was c/o Mr Blenkinsop, 12 Tavistock Street, Covent Garden, when the exhibits were miniatures of Geoffrey, George and Sidney, children of T. Gibson Bowles, Esq., whose portrait he painted in oil, exhibited at the R.A., 1881. Was awarded many medals and was made Chevalier of the Legion of Honour. Died Neuilly-sur-Seine, 18 July 1907.

Chase, G. (fl. 1797–1811)

Of London. Exhibited at the R.A., 1797–1811. An engraving of a portrait of the Rev. Wm. Walker, after Chase, is at the B.M.

*Chateaubourg, Le Chevalier de, or **Dechateaubourg, Chevalier de.** b. c. 1765

Born in Nantes, c. 1765. Long records that he came to London for two years in 1792. Benezit gives his information under the name Dechateaubourg, and that he was a pupil of Isabey (q.v.). Worked in Germany and Russia. Exhibited at the Academy of Berlin 1798, and at the Paris Salon in 1804, 1808 and 1812, in which latter year he exhibited the portraits of his children. Said to have settled in Nantes c. 1809–1837 where he was awarded a prize in 1825. A number of his works are recorded by Schidlof, pp. 142–3, Vol. I.

Chatfield, Mrs. See **Derby, Miss Emma Maria**

Chauncey, Miss M. S. (fl. 1835)

Of London. Exhibited at the R.A. 1835, from 24 Seymour Place, North Euston Square. No. 776 is given to her in the index, but catalogued as by Miss M. Chalon (q.v.).

Cheesman, J. (fl. 1798). See also **Cheesman, Thomas**

Of London. Exhibited at the R.A., 1798, a miniature head of a Bacchante from 40 Oxford Street. May have been identical with T. Cheesman (q.v.).

Cheesman, Thomas. 1760–c. 1834. See also **Cheesman, J.**

Of London; born 1760. Entered the R.A. Schools, 19 November 1790. Chiefly known as an engraver, but also executed miniatures and figure subjects. May have been identical with J. Cheesman (q.v.) who exhibited at the R.A. in 1798. Was one of Bartolozzi's best pupils. Was awarded a premium by the Society of Arts, 1781. Exhibited at the R.A., (1798?) or 1802–1820, and at the B.I., 1811–1829. A portrait of him by Bartolozzi is at the N.P.G. Died in London c. 1834.

*Cheney, Mrs. (fl. 1815–1820)
Long noted a miniature by this artist c. 1815–1820.

Chéron, Louis. 1660–1713/5
Born in Paris, 2 September 1660; son of Henri Chéron who was also a miniaturist. Came to London in 1695 where he remained until his death in c. 1713. Was an engraver and historical painter. A miniature formerly in the collection of the late Pierpont Morgan was attributed to him.

Chesters or Chester, S. (fl. 1845–1857). See also Chesters, S.
Of London. Exhibited at the R.A. etc., 1849–1857, from 1 Bloomfield Road, Maida Hill. Painted portrait miniatures on enamel, some of which were from life, and copies of old masters on porcelain. Exhibited a self-portrait in 1853. Possibly identical with S. Chesters (q.v.) who exhibited a miniature at the R.A. in 1885 from Scarborough. A miniature of an unknown lady, signed and dated '1845', was seen by the V. & A.M. and Long records one of an old man, on porcelain, which has a lot of stippling on the face and background.

*Chesters, S. (fl. 1885). See also Chesters or Chester, S.
Exhibited a miniature of an unknown lady at the R.A. in 1885, from Rydal Villas, Avenue Road, Scarborough. Possibly identical with Chesters or S. Chester (q.v.).

Childe, James Warren. c. 1778–1862
Born c. 1778. Worked in London. Exhibited at the R.A. and S.B.A., 1815–1853. Painted portraits of actors and actresses. Some of his children were artists. He signed Childe, J. Childe and sometimes J. W. Childe on the reverse. His work was not of outstanding merit. The B.M. have some engravings after Childe. Died at Scarsdale Terrace, Kensington, 19 September 1862, aged 84. Four miniatures by him are reproduced by O'Brien, Pl. 93, Figs. 5, 6, 7 and 8. A miniature by him was loaned to the South Kensington Exhibition, 1865. Two examples by this artist of Bertie Bertie Matthew painted 1844 and Jane Bertie Matthew, 1841, are at the V. & A. M.

Childe, Miss Maria Louise. (fl. 1839–1846)
Of London. Probably a daughter of J. W. Childe (q.v.) whose address she shared. Exhibited at the R.A., 1839–1846. A portrait of her by J. W. Childe was exhibited at the R.A., 1852.

*Childers, Mrs. Hugh (Eleanor). (fl. 1908–1910)
Of London. Exhibited at the R.A. and S.M. 1908–1910, from 6 Hereford Square, S.W. In 1910 her sitter at the R.A. was the Very Rev. Dr. Eliot, Dean of Windsor.

Childs, Miss Julia. (fl. 1851–1864)
Of London. Exhibited at the R.A. and S.B.A., etc., 1851–1864. Painted still-life, studies from nature and miniatures. A miniature by her of her mother, painted in 1853, was exhibited at the South Kensington Museum, 1865. In 1851 she was living at 12 Amwell Street, Pentonville and, in 1859, at 20 Soley Terrace, Pentonville.

Chinnery, George. 1774–1852
Born 7 February 1774 at 4 Gough Square, Fleet Street, the fifth son of William Chinnery, an amateur painter and grandson of another William Chin-

nery, a writing master of some note. The family originated in East Anglia, but as far back as 1620 a branch had become established in Ireland, and it was from this side of the family, part of which returned to England in 1642, that this artist descended. His father exhibited at the Free Society of Artists in 1764 and in 1766, and it was no doubt he who gave George Chinnery his early tuition in art. Chinnery entered the R.A. Schools, 6 July 1792, aged 19. Exhibited at the R.A., 1791–1846. His earliest exhibits were sufficiently good to be noticed and John Williams, alias 'Pasquin', likened his work to that of Cosway (q.v.). In 1794 or 1795 Chinnery went to Ireland where a distant relative, Sir Brodrick Chinnery, lived and whose portrait he painted. He lived at the house of a jeweller called James Vigne of 27 College Green, Dublin who was connected with the firm of Myre, Vigne and Luard of Threadneedle Street, London. Chinnery's father had numerous friends in Ireland and no doubt George hoped that these might assist him in his career. In 1799 he married Marianne Vigne, daughter of his host, by whom he had two children, a daughter Matilda and a son John. He became acquainted with John Comerford (q.v.) whose broader and more flowing style may well have influenced his work in miniature. Although he painted a limited number of miniatures, he is best known for his large portraits, drawings and paintings of Chinese scenes and people, landscapes and pen and ink drawings. Only fragments of information are available about his life and there was a revival of interest in his work when the Chinnery Exhibition was held in Edinburgh and London in 1957. Although Chinnery was connected with the drawing school of the Royal Dublin Society, and was secretary and treasurer of an exhibition held in Dublin in November 1799, there is no evidence, as is often claimed, that he was a member of the R.H.A., which was not incorporated until 1823, twenty-one years after he had left for India. In 1802 Chinnery, whose marriage by this time had apparently broken down, left his wife and two small children and returned to London with the intention of sailing for India where his family had a well-established firm, Chase Sewell and Chinnery of Madras. He sailed from England in the *Gilwell* on 11 June 1802, reaching Madras, 21 December of that year. Was well patronised and kept fully employed. In June 1807 he went to Calcutta and, apart from intervals of travel to the surrounding areas, he remained there for the rest of his time in India. In 1817 his daughter Matilda was given permission to join her father and the following year Mrs. Chinnery arrived, to be joined by their son John three years later. Chinnery in the interval had had two illegitimate children, Edward Charles and Henry Colin, both born c. 1813. His son John died at Berhampore in 1822 and in the same year Chinnery left for Serampur, presumably to escape arrest for debt, and three years later left India, leaving behind his wife and debts amounting to some £40,000. He settled in China, landing at the port of Macao on 29 September 1825 where, apart from short visits to Canton, he lived for the remaining twenty-seven years of his life. This was probably the most successful and productive period of his career. He filled his days sketching views, scenes, market vendors, portraits, etc., which he later finished in water-colour and oil. Chinnery continued to submit pictures to the R.A., and, in 1846, sent a self-portrait (now in the N.P.G.). There is no evidence that he painted miniatures after he left India. He died at Macao of apoplexy on 30 May 1852. The obituary notice in *The Friend of China and Hong Kong Gazette* of 2 June 1852, refers to his 'straitened circumstances'. Among the miniatures at the Chinnery Exhibition, 1957, were those

of Elizabeth, Lady Tuite, signed and dated '1796'; Sir John Taylor, K.C.B., c. 1798; Miss Jeffreys, c. 1798; Mrs. Siddons and child (identification doubtful), signed 'G. Chinnery E.I. 1803'; and a portrait of a Naval Officer, signed with a monogram 'G.C.', and a portrait of an unknown elderly lady, inscribed on the reverse 'Georgius Chinnery / Pict: Lond: / Pinxit / Jany 1st 1793'. This latter miniature was loaned to the exhibition in Edinburgh, 1965 by the V. & A. M. Chinnery's style varied and his works, which were frequently unsigned, are not always easily recognised. I have in my collection a miniature of Miss Mackenzie formerly attributed to George Engleheart (q.v.) which is the only example I know signed with a cursive double monogram, 'G.C.' 'E.I.' / '1804'; the initials E.I. after the signature stand for East India. In this portrait, as with others I have seen, the artist has given the sitter a slightly protruding lower lip, coloured in a bright red; the eyes are darkly shaded and the hair painted in dark sweeping strokes more in the manner of an oil painting; there is red in the corner of the eyes, and the face is well modelled with soft shading; the background is shaded with blues, greys and browns, with a dark area behind the sitter's head and shoulders. The N.G. Dublin has a charming miniature of Charlotte, Countess of Dysart, which was painted by Chinnery for her sister, H.R.H. the Duchess of Gloucester, in 1793, from a crayon drawing. Examples of Chinnery's work are in the V. & A. M., N.P.G. and B.M.

Chippindale, Mary. (fl.1835)
A miniature of a young lady signed 'Mary Chappindale/fecit.', was seen by me in 1978.

*Chisholm, Alexander, F.S.A. 1792/3–1847
Born c. 1792 in Elgin, Scotland. Was intended by his father to be a weaver and worked at a loom for some time at Peterhead. Not liking this occupation, whilst only a boy, he walked to Aberdeen where his portrait drawings were noticed and he was given encouragement in this art. When about twenty years of age he went to Edinburgh and received the patronage of Lord Elgin and the Earl of Buchan. Was for some time an assistant in the Trustees' Academy where he met and married Susanna Stewart Fraser; they moved to London in 1818. Exhibited at the R.A., B.I., O.W.C.S., etc., 1820–1847. Chisholm is best known for his paintings of historical subjects and romances; he also painted a number of portraits, and Long notes having seen a miniature which he stated was painted by him. He suffered from ill-health and died at Rothesay, 3 October 1847.

*Chisholm, Miss Annie. (fl. 1890–1903)
Of London. Exhibited at the R.A. and N.W.C.S., 1890–1903. Painted miniatures and water-colours.

Chrestien or Chretien, Jacob. See Christian, Jacobus

Christian, Mrs. Edward (Eleanor E.). (fl. 1843–1854)
Of London. Exhibited at the R.A., 1843–1854.

Christian, Jacobus
The Duke of Portland possesses an oil miniature on copper of William III, after Kneller, signed 'Jacobus Christian'. According to Mr. Goulding two persons named Jacob Chrestien or Chretien were naturalised respectively in 1696 and 1700.

*Christie, Alexander, A.R.S.A. 1807–1860
Born in Edinburgh, 1807. Began his career in a writer's office. After serving his apprenticeship he practised for some time as a lawyer. Was keen to

become an artist and when he was 26 years old studied under Sir W. Allan (q.v.) at the Trustees' Academy of which he became a Director in 1845. Went to London for a time, then finally settled in Edinburgh. Was elected A.R.S.A. in 1848. T. Faed and J. Macdonald were his pupils. Exhibited at the R.A., 1853 and at the B.I., 1838–1840. Known as an historical and subject painter, but a miniature of an unknown lady, signed on the reverse 'A. Christie 1832', was seen at the S.N.P.G. He died on 5 May 1860. (Pl. 45: no. 138.)

*Christie, Thomas. (fl. *c*. 1830)
A miniature *c*. 1830 by this artist was seen by Long.

Chubard. (fl. 1763). See also **Chubbard, Thomas**
Exhibited at the Society of Artists, 1763. Probably identical with Thomas Chubbard (q.v.).

Chubbard, Thomas. *c*. 1738–1809. See also **Chubard**
Born *c*. 1738. Of Liverpool; probably a son of Captain John Chubbard, a mariner. Possibly the Chubard (q.v.) who exhibited at the Society of Artists, 1763 and identical with the Chubbard who exhibited at the Society of Artists, 1772–1773, and at the Free Society of Artists in 1771. Exhibited at the Liverpool Society of Artists, 1774 and at the Society for Promoting Painting and Design in Liverpool, 1784, and was Visitor to the Society and exhibited, 1787. Painted landscapes, genre subjects, portraits and still life in oil, water-colour and crayons besides painting miniatures. Taught painting. Died at his house in King Street, Soho, Liverpool, 30 May 1809 and was buried in St. George's Church. Signed his miniatures T.C. A circular miniature painted *c*. 1780 and signed 'T.C.' is reproduced by O'Brien, Pl. 20, Fig. 3.

Churchman, John. d. 1780
Of London. Described as an artist of some ability. Died in Russell Street, Bloomsbury, 5 August 1780.

Cipriani, Francis. (fl. 1787)
Probably a son of J. B. Cipriani. A large oval mythological miniature in Cipriani's manner was signed 'Franciscus Cipriani' on the reverse and dated '1787'.

Clack, Richard Augustus. (fl.1838)
A miniature of Lady Baker signed 'R.A. Clack delt 1838', 67 Charlotte St., Portland Place, London, was seen in London.

Claret, William. d. 1706
Pupil of Lely whose style he imitated. Painted portraits in oil and is thought to have painted miniatures as Earl Spencer has one of Louise de Kéroualle, Duchess of Portsmouth, *c*. 1670, signed in a greyish white with a monogram 'WC' (two Vs crossing, and a C joined to the last stroke of the second V). The face is painted with long hairy brown strokes and shaded with brown. Claret died at his house in Lincoln's Inn Fields in 1706. Details about this artist are recorded by Vertue, *Walpole Society*, Vol. XVIII, pp. 35, 36. He says that 'Mr Claret lived many years a Widower. & left, when he died having no Children, all he had by will. to an old house^{per} he had, that lived with him forty years or upwards'. I know of a miniature of a lady *c*. 1670 in a private collection, signed 'WC', which is undoubtedly by this artist.

*Clark, Miss Dorothy M. (fl. 1903)
Of London. Exhibited at the R.A. 1903, from 19 Cavendish Road, St. John's Wood.

Clark, Miss E. (fl. 1799–1800)
Of London. Exhibited at the R.A., 1799. An advertisement in *The Morning Herald*, 3 July 1800, gives her address as 4 Cockspur Street and states that she was the great grand-daughter of Theodore King of Corsica.

Clark, J. W. (fl. 1824)
Of London. Exhibited an enamel portrait from life at the R.A., 1824.

Clark, John Heaviside. *c*. 1771–1863
Born *c*. 1771, probably in Scotland. Exhibited at the R.A., from 1812–1832. Was in London, 1802–1832. Best known as a landscape painter and engraver and presumably executed some miniatures as he gives instruction on the subject in his *Elements of Drawing and Painting* (1851 edition). Published several books on painting. Died in Edinburgh, October 1863.

*Clark, John Stewart. (fl. 1901–1911)
Exhibited at the R.A. 1901–1911, from Newcastle-on-Tyne and Gateshead-on-Tyne.

*Clark, Miss Louisa Campbell. (fl. 1887–1891)
Of London. Exhibited at the R.A. 1887–1891, from London addresses. She exhibited a miniature of her mother in 1890. This artist was possibly identical with Louise Campbell Clark (q.v.).

Clark, Miss Louise Campbell. (fl. *c*. 1830)
Worked in England *c*. 1830. Schidlof records a miniature sold in Vienna, 5/6 June 1934, No. 50; the mother of the artist, on ivory, signed on the reverse: 'Ann . . . Clark, painted by her youngest daughter Louise Campbell Clark'. This artist was possibly identical with Louisa Campbell Clark (q.v.).

*Clarke, Miss Alice Dolores. (fl. 1908–1910)
Of London. Exhibited at the Society of Miniaturists, 1908–1910.

*Clarke, Miss Emmeline Thornton. (fl. 1896–1910)
Of London. Exhibited at the R.A. and S.M., 1896–1910. She painted miniatures and studies in water-colour.

*Clarke, Mrs. Gertrude C. (fl. 1910–1914)
Of Burton-on-Trent, and Edgbaston. Exhibited at the R.A., 1910–1914.

Clarke, H. (fl. 1834)
Of London. Exhibited at the R.A., 1834.

*Clarke, Miss Minnie E. (fl. 1892–1901)
Of London. Exhibited at the R.A., etc., 1892–1901.

Clarke, T. (fl. 1799). See also **Clarke, Theophilus**
Probably the Theoph. Clarke who entered the R.A. Schools, 22 March 1793, aged 17. A miniature portrait of Mrs. Scott, stated to be signed 'T. Clarke, 1799', was exhibited at the South Kensington Museum, 1865.

*Clarke, Theophilus, A.R.A. b. 1776. See also **Clarke, T.**
Exhibited at the R.A., 1801–1810. Entered the R.A. Schools, 22 March 1793, aged 17. Probably identical with the T. Clarke (q.v.) mentioned by Long. Was a portrait painter and may have executed a few miniatures.

*Clarke, W. (fl. 1780)
Of Chester. May have executed miniatures and advertised that he did likenesses in hair, *Adam's Weekly Courant*, 19 September 1780.

Clarkson, A. (fl. 1835–1836)
Of London. Exhibited at the R.A., 1835–1836. His address in 1835 was 13 Dorset Terrace, Clapham Road.

*Claxton, Miss Adelaide (Mrs. G. G. Turner). (fl. 1860–1876)
Of London. Daughter of Marshal Claxton. Exhibited at the R.A., etc., 1860–1876. Married George Gordon Turner some time after 1867, in which year she exhibited from her father's address, 4 Burlington Gardens, Bayswater, from which address Miss F. Claxton also exhibited at the R.A. Painted subject paintings in water-colour, executed drawings and, in 1863, exhibited a portrait of a gentleman which may have been miniature.

Clayton, Samuel. 19th century
An Irish artist. Eldest son of Benjamin Clayton, an engraver, and brother of Benjamin junior and Robert who all followed their father's profession. Samuel also painted miniatures. He married twice, in 1800 and 1807. While still a young man he emigrated to Sydney where he was in business.

*Clayton Jones, Mrs. Marion Alexandra. b. 1872
Born 23 November 1872. Exhibited at the R.A. and S.M. 1907–1913, from Silverton House, nr. Exeter.

*Cleeve (Sotto?)
Long noted a triple miniature after Füger, by Cleeve, and thought the work good. A miniature of Sotto Cleeve, painter, after a self-portrait, was painted on enamel by J. H. Hurter (q.v). and was No. 40 at the South Kensington Exhibition, 1865. No. 42 in the same exhibition was of Sotto Cleeve's wife, after Cleeve, also an enamel by Hurter.

Clein. See **Cleyn**

*Clement, G. R. (fl. 1827)
A miniature of a young boy, painted against a landscape background and inscribed 'G. R. Clement 1827', was illustrated by O'Brien, Fig. 3, Pl. 49.

Clements or Clement, James. (fl. 1818–1831)
Of London and Worcester (1822–1831). Exhibited at the R.A., 1818–1831. In the R.A. catalogue for 1830 his name is spelt Clement, but this may have been an error, as otherwise his name is consistently spelt Clements. He exhibited a group of himself, his wife and a child at the R.A. in 1831. He may have been identical with the James Clement, a miniaturist, who was living at 62 Broad Street, Worcester in 1828. I have seen a profile miniature of a man, painted in water-colour on card, which was inscribed on the reverse 'Painted by / James Clement, Worcester / 1821'.

*Clench, Miss Ada L. (fl. 1908–1910)
Of Folkestone and Blandford, Dorset. Exhibited at the Society of Miniaturists, 1908–1910.

Clerc, Jakob Friedrich le. See **Leclerc**

*Cleve, Miss J. (Mrs. W. Whately). (fl. 1902)
Was a member of the Society of Miniaturists in 1902.

Cleyn, Charles. 17th century
Cleyn, Francis
Cleyn, John
Cleyn, Magdalen

Cleyn, Penelope. See also **Cross, P.**

Cleyn, Sarah

Children of a German artist, Franz Cleyn (born 1582, died 1658), who worked at the Mortlake tapestry factory. All six children are said to have been miniature painters, but little information is known about them. For many years miniatures signed P. C. were attributed to either Penelope Cleyn or Paolo Carandini (q.v.), but there is no evidence to support this theory, and all miniatures of this period, signed in this way, are now thought to be the work of P. Cross (q.v.). The alternative spelling of the family name is Clein.

*Clink, Miss Edith L. (fl. 1896–1913)

Of London and Littlehampton. Exhibited at the R.A., 1896–1913. Probably related to Miss Isabelle M. Clink of the same address who exhibited an oil painting in 1897. Miss E. L. Clink was in Littlehampton, Sussex in 1903.

Clint, George, A.R.A. 1770–1854

Of London. Born 12 April 1770 in Brownlow Street, London; son of a hairdresser. Appears to have been employed by a fishmonger, an attorney and as a house painter. Was a miniaturist, portrait painter and mezzotint engraver. Exhibited at the R.A., B.I. and S.B.A., 1802–1845. Was elected A.R.A. in 1821; resigned after a disagreement in 1835. A number of his portraits represented actors and actresses, some in character. He was married and had nine children of whom Alfred was an artist and Scipio a medallist. His wife died in 1807. He died at Pembroke Square, Kensington, 10 May 1854.

Clonney, James Goodwyn. 1812–1867

Born in Liverpool, 28 January 1812. Was a genre and miniature painter. Went to America as a young man and established himself in New York City c. 1834. From c. 1841 he devoted most of his time to painting genre subjects. From 1842–1852 he lived at New Rochelle, New York, and later at Cooperstown, New York. Exhibited frequently at the National Academy of which he became an Associate, etc. Died in Binghampton, New York, 7 October 1867.

Clothier, Robert. (fl. 1842–1865)

Of London. Was in Liverpool, 1854. Exhibited at the R.A. and B.I., 1842–1865. His exhibits included a miniature for a bracelet. Painted historical and genre pictures as well as portraits in oil and miniatures.

*Clow, J. or **Clows, John.** (fl. 1837–1840/50)

Thought to be British. Worked at Halifax, Nova Scotia, 1837 and 1840. Possibly identical with John Clows, an English engraver, recorded by Groce and Wallace as being 60 when the 1850 census was taken in New York City.

*Clunas, Laura B. S. (Mrs. H. Fidler). (fl. 1904–1910)

Of Hertfordshire and Abbots Ann, Andover. Exhibited at the R.A., 1904–1910.

*Clutterbuck, C. (fl. 1825–1842) See **Clutterbuck, Charles Edmund.**

Clutterbuck, Charles Edmund. 1806-1861

Born in London, 3 September, 1806, third son of Edmund Clutterbuck, tobacconist of Lewisham and Susanna née Toplis. Presumably identical with C. Clutterbuck (q.v.). Lived at Bridge Street, Lambeth 1820-1827. Exhibited miniatures at the R.A. and Suffolk Street. Married Hannah Kinlock in 1828 by whom he had a son Charles Edmund junior, a stained

glass artist and Robert Hawley Clutterbuck who became a clergyman.

*Coad, Miss Kathleen E. (fl. 1894–1910)

Of London. Exhibited at the R.A., 1894 and 1910. Painted miniatures and historical subjects.

Coater

A miniature portrait of John Law (1671–1729), was lent by the Earl of Derby to the exhibition at the South Kensington Museum, 1865. It was catalogued as by Coater about whom nothing is known.

*Cobb, Mrs. Emily J. (fl. 1890)

Of London. Exhibited at the R.A. 1890, from 4 St. Lukes Road, Westbourne Park.

*Cobbe, Miss Ethel L. (fl. 1907–1912)

Of London. Exhibited at the R.A. and S.M. 1907–1912, from 20 St. George's Road, Eccleston Square.

Cochran, John. d. after 1855

Of London. Exhibited at the R.A., 1821 and 1823, and at the S.B.A., until 1827. Was best known as an engraver. Had a distinguished clientele including Queen Victoria, William IV and the Duke of York.

*Cockburn, Miss Maud L. (fl. 1894–1895)

Exhibited at the R.A. 1894–1895, from Ryslau, Brondesbury, N. London.

Cockburn, Ralph. b. 1779?

Son-in-law of Ralph Kirtley, a servant of Sir Joshua Reynolds. Possibly the R. Cockburn who entered the R.A. Schools, 26 August 1797, aged 18. Exhibited at the R.A., etc., 1802–1812. Painted miniatures, portraits and domestic subjects. In 1813 became curator of the Bourgeois Collection (Dulwich College Gallery). Published, c. 1830, colour aquatints of pictures in the Dulwich Gallery. Recorded as a miniaturist in *Annals of the Fine Arts*, II, p. 569. Was noted by Farington in his *Diary*, Vol. VII, p. 141.

Code, Mrs. (Miss Mary Benwell). (fl. 1762–1791)

Of London. Née Mary Benwell. Exhibited at the Society of Artists, 1762–1791 and at the R.A., 1775–1791. Worked in London; painted portraits in miniature, crayon and oil. Married c. 1782 an officer named Code; purchased his promotion. Was living in retirement at Paddington in 1800. She painted a miniature self-portrait which was signed 'Maria / Benwell / 1779'. An example of her work is at the V. & A. M. A portrait by her of Queen Charlotte was engraved by Houston. (Pl. 46: no. 140.)

Cohen, Miss A. (fl. 1833)

Of London. Exhibited at the S.B.A., 1833.

*Colborne, Miss Theo E. (fl. 1909)

Of London. Exhibited at the R.A. 1909, from 35 Rossetti Mansions, Chelsea. Her sitter was the Very Rev. W. Skipton, Dean of Killala.

Colclough, W. (fl. 1847)

Of Church Street, Burslem. Exhibited an enamel landscape at the B.I., 1847. Was described as an enamel painter.

Cole, Miss A. (fl. 1855–1856). See also **Cole, Miss A. M.**

Of London. Exhibited at the R.A. 1855 and 1856, from 5 Queen's Square, Bloomsbury and was possibly identical with Miss A. M. Cole (q.v.) who also exhibited from that address. Her exhibit in 1856 was of 'Jessie, the artist's sister'.

*Cole, Miss A. M. (fl. 1861–1872). See also **Cole, Miss A.**

Of London. Exhibited at the R.A. 1861–1872, from 5 Queen's Square, Bloomsbury and, in 1870 and 1872, from Belvedere House, Bexley Heath, Kent. Possibly identical with Miss A. Cole (q.v.).

Cole, Miss Augusta. See **Samwell, Mrs.**

*Cole, Miss Dorothy. (fl. 1907)

Exhibited at the R.A. 1907, from King's Ride, Richmond, Surrey. Her sitter was Mrs. J. B. MacEwen.

*Cole, Miss Emily E. 19th century

Sister of the Misses Augusta and Mary Ann Cole (q.v.) and of Miss Ellen Cole, also an artist. A miniature of a gentleman wearing 17th-century costume was sold at Christie's 21 February 1961, when it was catalogued as by the above artist.

Cole, M. E. (fl. 1832)

Of London. Exhibited at the R.A. 1832, from 33 Red Lion Square, London. The exhibit was of 'Dorria Damiania'.

*Cole, Miss Mary Ann. (fl. 1842–1872)

Of London. Sister of Augusta and Emily Cole (q.v.) and of Ellen Cole. Exhibited at the R.A. and B.I., etc., 1842–1872. Painted figure studies and portraits and at least one miniature. This exhibit was of Miss Julia Laurance, who had also been painted in miniature by Miss Augusta Cole. Apart from 1853 her address was consistently 57 Upper Norton Street, Portland Place.

*Cole, William. 18th century

A miniature of a man in the manner of A. Buck (q.v.) (rectangular) was seen by me in 1960. It had a label on the back which was inscribed 'pt by Wm Cole, bought from the sitter's family of Chester'.

*Coleridge, Miss Maud. (fl. 1893–1901)

Of London. Exhibited at the R.A., S.M., etc., 1893–1901. Her exhibit in 1898 was of the 'Late Lord Chief Justice of England'. Her brother, the Hon. Stephen Coleridge, was also an artist.

Coles, H. (Henry?). b. 1797?

Of London. Probably the Henry Coles who entered the R.A. Schools, 8 January 1818, aged 21. Exhibited at the R.A., 1819–1820.

Colison, Alexander. (fl. 1630?)

In the collection of Earl Beauchamp there is a good oil miniature on copper of a man in a brown coat with a lawn collar edged with lace. His left hand fingers a locket. This miniature is signed and dated 'Alexandre Colison, Anno 1630 V . . . 0.4.'. This may refer to either the sitter or the artist.

Collen, Henry. b. 1798. d. after 1872

Born in St. Albans (according to Schidlof). Entered the R.A. Schools, 1 September 1820, aged 22 years; obtained a silver medal in 1821. Was a pupil of Sir George Hayter (q.v.). Worked in London and at St. Albans (1861–1872). Exhibited at the R.A. and S.B.A., 1820–1872. Was miniature painter to Queen Victoria and the Duchess of Kent, and had a distinguished clientele. He was a good artist but his work was of uneven quality. He used a scraper, particularly in the hair, and usually signed with a scratched signature on the background, sometimes parallel with the edge of the miniature; the H and C frequently form a monogram. Some of his miniatures are signed H COLLEN, and Long records one on which the date, 1820, is placed on the collar of the sitter. A number of his works are at Windsor Castle. Some of his portraits were after the works of Hayter, Lawrence (q.v.), etc. A miniature of the Countess of Warwick, by Collen, 1825, after Hayter, is in the Wallace Collection, London. Some engravings after Collen are in the B.M. Miniatures by him were lent to the South Kensington Exhibition, 1865 including one of Queen Victoria and one of the 'Late Charles Mayne Young, the Tragedian, 1824', this latter miniature being lent by the artist. Examples of his work are in the V. & A. M., the N.P.G. and the Wallace Collection.

*Colles, Mrs. E. A. G. (fl. 1907–1910)
Of London. Exhibited at the Society of Miniaturists, 1907–1910.

*Collett, Miss Sophia E. (fl. 1889–1895)
Of Bury St. Edmunds (1889) and London. Exhibited at the R.A., 1889–1895.

*Collie, Miss Katharine. (fl. 1906)
Exhibited at the R.A. 1906, from South Road, Waterloo, Liverpool.

*Collier, Alexander. (fl. 1889–1892)
Of Southampton and London. Exhibited at the R.A., 1889–1892. Painted miniatures and fancy subjects.

*Collier, Joyce. (fl. 1906)
Of London. Exhibited at the R.A. 1906, from 69 Eton Avenue. Her sitter was Mrs. Bowman Porter. Undoubtedly related to the Hon. John Collier (1850–1934), portrait painter, who exhibited at the R.A., from the same address.

*Collingwood, Mrs. E. M. D. (fl. 1901–1911)
Of Lancashire. Exhibited at the R.A. and S.M. 1901–1911, from Lanehead, Coniston, Lancs.

*Collins, Mrs. (fl. c. 1777–1778). See also **Collins, Mrs. John**
Possibly the wife of John Collins (q.v.), and a noted beauty. Advertised herself as follows: 'By H.M. Letters patent. Late pupil and assistant to Mrs. Harrington who has the honour of taking profiles of the Royal Family &c is now making a tour of the whole Kingdom, having purchased a moiety of that Lady's Patent. Price 2s 6d. Time of sitting three minutes. Coventry, Warwick, Wolverhampton, Litchfield & Derby will be visited.' She advertised in the *Birmingham Gazette*, 6 January 1777; the *Leicester & Nottingham Journal*, 24 May 1777; the *Bristol Journal*, 14 February 1778. Benezit gives her christian names as Elizabeth Joanna and states that she executed book illustrations.

*Collins, Humphrey. (fl. c. 1773)
Long recorded having seen a miniature signed 'Humphrey Collins / Historical portrait / Engraver / and / miniature painter'. The portrait was softly painted with a slightly brown tinge.

Collins, John. d. 1808
Born at Bath. Said to have painted miniatures in profile. Went on the stage appearing in Bath and later in Dublin and London. Settled in Birmingham, 1793 and became one of the proprietors of the *Birmingham Chronicle*. His wife was a noted beauty and painted miniatures in profile. A portrait of Collins in Indian ink, tinted and signed 'J.C.B.', is at the B.M. and was engraved in aquatint. He died in Birmingham 2 May 1808. His wife may have been identical with the Mrs. Collins (q.v.) who advertised in Birmingham in 1777.

*Collins, Mrs. John. See also **Collins, Mrs.**
Wife of John Collins (q.v.). A noted beauty; painted miniatures in profile; possibly identical with Mrs. Collins (q.v.).

Collins, Richard. 1755–1831
Born in Gosport, 30 January 1755. Was apprenticed to a mercer. Entered the R.A. Schools, 4 October 1776, aged '21, 30th last Jany'. Exhibited at the R.A., 1777–1818. Pupil of Plott (q.v.), Humphry (q.v.) and Meyer (q.v.). Copied pictures at Petworth in 1798. Held an appointment as principal portrait painter in enamel to George III from 1789. Was patronised by members of the Royal family and the Court. Collins lodged for some time with Humphry who recorded in a manuscript memoir some details about his friend's career. According to Humphry, Collins only painted portraits of members of the Royal family from 1788–1791, but that later he took up public practice again. As he rarely signed his work, attribution is difficult. He painted on ivory and enamel and his portraits are well painted, his brush strokes being so blended as to make them indistinguishable. He married a Miss Scale, who died in 1788, leaving one daughter. From Humphry's notes we learn that it was because of his grief at her death that George III felt sorry for him and had him appointed as his Enamel Painter in spite of the fact that Bowyer (q.v.) and R. Crosse (q.v.) had already been appointed to the same office. Said to have retired on his savings to Pershore, 1811, and to have returned to London c. 1828. Died in London, 5 August 1831. Examples of his work are at the V. & A. M., including one of George III and one of the Duke of Sussex when a boy, signed on the reverse 'R^d Collins pinxt / 1789 / Portrait Painter / in Enamel to / His Majesty'. Examples of his work are also at the B.M., Windsor Castle and in other private collections. A fine miniature of an unknown lady is in the Rijksmuseum, Amsterdam, signed on the reverse by the artist.

Collins, S., junior. (fl. 1829–1833)
Of London. Exhibited at the R.A. and S.B.A., 1829–1833. One miniature is known to have been in oil. Possibly a son of Samuel Collins (q.v.).

Collins, Samuel. 1735?–1768
Born in Bristol; son of a clergyman; was trained as an attorney, but evidently forsook this profession for art. By the middle of the eighteenth century he had established himself in a good practice in Bath. Painted miniatures in water-colour and enamel. He was described by Nollekens as a 'very indifferent miniature painter and what was worse, a man of gay and expensive habits'. These evidently got him into debt and he went to Ireland in 1762, leaving Humphry (q.v.), who had been his pupil, to succeed to his practice. Collins had a good practice in Dublin where he remained until his death at his house in Summer Hill in October 1768. In the absence of documentary evidence, it is difficult to ascribe miniatures to him with absolute certainty, and some signed S.C. are probably the work of S. Cotes (q.v.). A miniature signed and dated 'S C 1755' was seen by Mr. A. J. B. Kiddell and must have been one of his early works. The V. & A. M. has a small miniature signed 'Collins' and dated '1763'. The letters of the signature are all separate. It is of a member of an Irish family, wearing a blue and red uniform; the drawing is accurate and the face softly painted with short strokes. Miniatures signed by S. Cotes appear to have the initials S. C. made up of several strokes, rather than smooth initials as in the case of Collins. A journeyman, Samuel Collins, was employed by Paul de Lamerie who was making a bequest in 1751. Two miniatures

by him (including one of George III) were lent to the South Kensington Exhibition, 1865.

Collins, W. H. (fl. 1822–1859)
Of London. Exhibited at the R.A., 1822–1859.

Collis, Isaac. (fl. c. 1778)
Painted profile miniatures in oil. In 1778 opened a print shop and lottery office at No. 13 Capel Street, Dublin. Charged £2 5s. for full-length miniatures and £1 2s. 9d. for half-length. Had a partner called Campbell. Painted transparencies for shops.

*Collyer, Miss Edith N. (fl. 1905–1914)
Exhibited at the R.A. 1905–1914, from 6 Foxley Lane, Purley, Surrey.

*Collyer, Miss Kate Winifred (Mrs. Benjamin Walker). (fl. 1891–1914)
Of Leicester and Birmingham. Exhibited at the R.A. and S.M., 1891–1914. Married Benjamin Walker, about 1902, and exhibited under her married name after this date. Her sitters included her son, Joseph Walker, Lady Chamberlain, Sir William Gilstrap, Bart., the Hon. Eleanor Rolls (daughter of Lord Llangattock) and Miss Dorothy A. Satchwell.

*Collyer, Miss Mildred H. (fl. 1894–1914)
Of London. Exhibited at the R.A. 1894–1914, from various Chelsea addresses. Executed miniatures, large oil paintings and landscapes in watercolour. Her sitters included Captain Ernest Troubridge, R.N., C.M.G., M.V.O.

*Colthurst, Francis Edward. b. 1874
Born in Taunton, Somerset, 28 July 1874. Exhibited at the R.A. 1903–1912, from Northfield House, Taunton and 6 Scarsdale Studios, Stratford Road, Kensington. Painted miniatures, landscapes in oil and water-colour.

*Colthurst, Miss G. A. Buller. (fl. 1910)
Of London. Exhibited at the Society of Miniaturists, 1910.

*Colyers, Mrs.
A miniature of General Steele (rectangular, 3¼ in.) was sold at Christie's, 15 October 1963.

Combe, Miss E. (fl. 1834–1840)
Of London. Exhibited at the R.A. and S.B.A., 1834–1840.

Comelera, M. (fl. 1834). See also **Comolera, Mme. Melani de**
Long records this artist as working at 2 Wigmore Street, London in 1834. She may have been identical with Mme. M. de Comolera (q.v.).

Comerford, Mrs. (fl. 1801)
Exhibited a portrait of a gentleman at the R.A. 1801, from 4 Gerrard Street, Soho, London.

Comerford, John. c. 1770–1832
Born in Kilkenny c. 1770; son of a flax-dresser. Little is known about his early life; he is said to have acquired his knowledge of art by copying pictures in Kilkenny Castle, Waterford and Carrick-on-Suir, etc. Must have visited Dublin before 1793 when he advertised in the *Leinster Journal*, 29 June that he had arrived in Kilkenny from Dublin. Said to have been a pupil at the Dublin Society of Arts. Strickland does not record this, but does remark that Comerford was unknown to the Dublin public until he exhibited two miniatures at the Artists Exhibition in Dame Street, Dublin in 1800. *The Hibernian Journal* went so far as to remark that he was an artist 'whom we never saw or even before so much as heard of', and went on to express a note of

admiration at his work. He exhibited in Dublin from 1800–1813 and at the R.A., 1804 and 1809. From 1802–c. 1817 his address was 27 Dame Street, after which he moved to 2 Leinster Street where he remained for most of the rest of his life. Comerford and Chinnery (q.v.) met, and the latter was probably responsible for Comerford entering the exhibitions which he was organising. Up to about this time Comerford had painted portraits in oil as well as miniatures, but he gave this up and confined himself entirely to executing miniatures and small portraits in chalk or pencil. In 1811 he was a member of the committee of the Dublin Society of Artists and its Vice-President. He was strongly opposed to the formation of an Academy in Ireland and thought artists should learn from nature, as he had done. He was financially successful and popular among his friends. Shortly before his death he moved to 28 Blessington Street and after two apoplectic seizures he died suddenly at his house on 25 January 1832. He had an only daughter to whom he left about £500 per annum. His pupils included J. Doyle (q.v.) and T. C. Thompson (q.v.). His work is often slightly reminiscent of oil paintings. Some of his miniatures are painted with a loose brushwork almost as if they had been painted quickly. He often used a brownish shading on the flesh parts, with a little blue to darken it in places; he also used the scraper. Examples of his work are in the V. & A. M. and N.G., Dublin. A miniature in my collection of Captain Samuel Lamb (previously illustrated as an unknown officer) is one of the finest examples I have seen. He sometimes signed in full on the reverse, followed by a date. Miniatures by him were lent to the South Kensington Exhibition, 1865 and to the exhibition in Edinburgh, 1965.

*Comolera, Mme. Melani de. (fl. 1826–1854). See also **Comelera, M.**

Of London. Exhibited at the R.A., B.I., etc., 1826–1854. Possibly the M. Comelera (q.v.) mentioned by Long. Painted flowers, fruit, etc. and was Flower Painter to Queen Victoria and the Queen Dowager (Queen Adelaide). Some of her exhibits were probably miniatures; she also painted on china. Benezit records that she exhibited in Paris, 1816–1818.

Condé, Pierre. d. after 1840

Of London. Exhibited at the R.A., 1806–1824. Was an engraver and miniaturist. According to Schidlof he died after 1840.

*Conder, Miss Helen L. or E. (fl. 1890–1901)

Of London. Exhibited at the R.A., N.W.C.S., etc., 1890–1901. Undoubtedly related to, or identical with, Miss Louise Conder (q.v.) who exhibited from the same address.

*Conder, Miss Louise. (fl. 1899–1912)

Of London. Exhibited at the R.A., 1899–1912. Was undoubtedly related to, or identical with, Miss Helen L. Conder (q.v.) who exhibited from the same address, Warwick Studio, South End, Hampstead.

Condy, Nicholas Matthews. c. 1799–1851

Born at Plymouth, c. 1799. Started his career as a miniaturist but later took to painting landscapes and marine subjects in oil and water-colour, for which he is best known. Exhibited at the R.A. 1842–1845, from Plymouth and London. Died at Plymouth, 20 May 1851.

*Congers, Mrs. (fl. c. 1830)

Of Copt Hall, Essex. Noted by Long as working c. 1830.

*Connell, Miss Dora M. (fl. 1909)

Of London. Exhibited at the R.A. 1909, from 58 Grove End Road, N.W. Her sitter was the Rev. R. J. Campbell.

*Connell, Miss Janet. (fl. 1890–1908)

Of London. Exhibited at the R.A., 1890–1908. In 1892 she exhibited a miniature of Miss Ellen Terry. Amongst her other sitters was Sir Malcolm Morris, K.C.V.O.

Connell, John Minton. (fl. 1830–1882)

An Irish artist, born at Cork where, from c. 1830, he practised miniature painting for many years. Was living at 5 Fitton Street, 1832–c. 1852, and charged from one to twenty guineas for his works. Exhibited at the R.H.A., etc., 1852–1881. Was settled in Dublin, 1879 and held an appointment as miniature painter to the Duke of Marlborough, Lord Lieutenant. Exhibited a miniature of the Empress of Austria (1880) and of Dr. P. Crampton Smyly (1881). Died in Dublin c. 1882.

*Connolly, Peter. (fl. c. 1821)

Strickland lists this artist as a limner practising in Dundalk c. 1821.

Connor, Joseph. (fl. 1779–1786). See also **O'Connor, Joseph**

Of Cork. In c. 1779 painted miniatures for 16s. 3d. each and advertised that he executed 'all manner of miniatures and frames in hair for bracelets, rings and lockets'. Was probably identical with the artist of that name who was living in Crampton Court, Dublin in 1786. Possibly identical with Joseph O'Connor (q.v.).

Contencin, Peter. (fl. 1797–1819)

Of London. Had an address at 32 Chester Place, Kensington. Exhibited at the R.A., 1797–1819. Painted at least one miniature (of a lady), landscapes as well as portraits in oil.

*Conway, Miss Anne Seymour. See Damer, The Hon. Mrs. Anne Seymour

*Cook, Mrs. Alice M. (fl. 1907–1914)

Of London. Exhibited at the R.A. 1907–1914, from 21 Oxford Road, Kilburn. Exhibits included miniatures and subjects in water-colour and oil. Probably the wife of Walter F. Cook (q.v.) who exhibited from the above address, 1904–1914.

*Cook, Miss Ellinor E. (fl. 1905)

Of London. Exhibited at the R.A. 1905, from 117 Finchley Road, N.W.

*Cook, Miss Ethel M. (fl. 1902)

Of London. Exhibited at the R.A. 1902, from 17 Keppell Street, Russell Square.

*Cook, Miss Hilda V. (fl. 1909–1914)

Exhibited at the R.A. 1909–1914, from Ashford Farm, Ashford, Middlesex.

*Cook, Miss Nelly E. (fl. 1887–1900)

Of London. Exhibited at the R.A. 1887–1900, from 60 Alexandra Road, South Hampstead. Painted flowers; some of her exhibits were in the miniature section.

*Cook, Walter F. (fl. 1894–1914)

Of London. Exhibited at the R.A., 1894–1914. Painted portrait and subject miniatures, and executed etchings, drawings and engravings. Probably

the husband of Alice M. Cook (q.v.) who exhibited from the same address, 1907–1914.

Cooke. (fl. c. 1801)

Referred to by Farington in his diary for 5 February 1801 as having resided for several years at Bath. Was a pastellist, drawing-master and miniaturist.

Cooke, John. c. 1778–1805

Born c. 1778, probably in Dublin. Studied at the Dublin Society Schools. Worked as a miniaturist in Dublin from c. 1796. Exhibited with the Dublin Society of Artists, 1800–1803. Died in Charlotte Street, Dublin, in December 1805. His usual signature is J. Cooke, followed by a date. A miniature of an unknown man, signed on the front 'Cooke / pinx / 1800', is in the N.G., Dublin. The draughtsmanship is good and the painting soft. Another example of his work is in the V. & A. M.

*Cooke, R. (fl. 1812–1814)

Exhibited at the R.A. 1812–1814, from 12 Greek Street, Soho. The exhibit for 1812 was a miniature self-portrait on enamel. That for 1814 was a miniature of Mr. G. F. Cooke. Possibly identical with the Cooke (no initial given) (q.v.). A Mr. G. F. Cooke celebrated comic actor, is noted by Benezit under John Corbett (q.v.) who executed a portrait of him.

*Cookesley, Mrs. Margaret Murray. (fl. 1884–1912)

Of London. Exhibited at the R.A., N.W.C.S., and S.M. etc., 1884–1912. Painted subject pictures and portraits in oil and water-colour and miniatures. Her sitters included William Cookesley (possibly her husband), the Hon. Mrs. Claud Portman, the Countess of Chesterfield, etc. Many of her paintings were of Egypt.

*Cooking, Mr. (fl. c. 1820)

A miniature of an officer of c. 1820 by the above artist was Lot 42 at Sotheby's 14 July, 1969. The reverse of the miniature bore the artist's trade label giving the address as 5 West Rose Street, New Town, Edinburgh, and stated that 'he continued to paint striking Likenesses, high-finished, from One to Five Guineas'. This artist appears to be hitherto unrecorded.

Coop, Frederick. (fl. 1903)

I have seen four miniatures all signed and dated 'Fred/Coop/1903'. They represented a father, mother and two boys and were well painted.

Cooper, Alexander. c. 1605-1660

Born 1609, London. In the registers of the Guildhall Library (Guildhall MS 5685) there is an entry for 1 September 1607 for the marriage of 'Richard Cowper of the parish and Barbara Hoskens' at St. Nicholas Cole Abbey: Barbara was the sister of John Hoskins (q.v.). Alexander and Samuel (q.v.) were the sons of Richard and Barbara, Alexander being baptised on 11 December 1609 at St. Nicholas Church. (His brother Samuel was said to have been born in 1609 but details of his baptism have not been found thus making this date uncertain.) Early authorities give his Christian names as Abraham Alexander, but no evidence for this is forthcoming, and he is usually referred to as Alexander. He and Samuel were brought up by their uncle, John Hoskins, when presumably they were orphaned as young children. It has also been suggested that his father might have been John Cooper or Coperario, the King's Lutanist, which would account for his brother's mastery of that instrument. On the other hand, the names Cooper, Cowper or Kuyper, frequently occur among the Dutch refugees who were in London at that time. There appears to be no evidence to support Dr.

Williamson's statement that he was a 'Jew portrait painter', and Alfred Rubens, in his notes on early Anglo-Jewish artists, *Jewish Historical Society*, Vol. XVIII, p.104, doubts the accuracy of this statement. Besides any instruction given to him by his uncle, John Hoskins, it is traditionally believed that Cooper had some training under Peter Oliver (q.v.) and it may well be that his early work, where he painted his sitters against a lilac or other unusual background, was influenced by Oliver; J. Sandrart, in his *Academia Noblissimae Artis Pictoriae*, 1683, p.312, states that he was by far the most celebrated pupil of Peter Oliver and that he visited Sandrart in Amsterdam (before 1642), who showed him some of his own work and that Cooper in turn showed him some of his portraits of personages in the English Court. Sandrart noted that they 'certainly abounded in all the requisites of the most perfect gummed painting'. This suggests that Cooper may have returned to England between 1633 and 1642, but no works by him of this period of his life are at present known to have been painted in England. Cooper apparently went to Holland in c.1631; evidence for this is to be found in the inscription engraved on the reverse of the miniatures by him in the collection of the Countess of Craven, representing the King and Queen of Bohemia and William, Lord Craven, who fought in their cause. He painted a series of portraits of the Bohemian Royal family, depicting the King and Queen and seven of their children. These portraits, framed together in a chain, are in the Kaiser Friedrich Museum, Berlin. Cooper was in the Hague, 1644–1646 and in Sweden from 1647–1657 where he was appointed by Queen Christina to the office of Court Painter, which office he also held under Charles X who succeeded her on her abdication in 1654. An invoice of 1655 or 1656 shows that he went to work for the King of Denmark, probably in Copenhagen. Six miniatures of this period by Cooper are in the Rosenborg Castle, Copenhagen. They are all painted on vellum on blue backgrounds, and set into rich enamel lockets on the reverse of which are monograms and the date 1656. They represent, Frederick III, Queen Sophie Amalie, Christian V, (when Prince), Princess Frederikke Amalie (1649–1704), and Princess Wilhemine Ernestine (1647–1706). His annual salary as Court Painter was nominally 1200 daler, but this seems to have failed to mature and, in 1652, he was obliged to petition for eighteen months arrears of salary as he was ill and bed-ridden. This petition evidently failed to produce any results and, in 1654, he was obliged to approach Prince Charles Gustavus for two years arrears of pensions and money due to him for six and a half years' work over and above this. The fact that, unlike so many artists who came to England, Alexander Cooper went abroad, means that it is in Amsterdam, the Hague, Stockholm, Gothenburg, etc. that we must seek his work. He numbered among his friends the philosopher Descartes. He is said to have died in Stockholm in 1660 and, according to records quoted by Dr. G. C. Williamson, his death took place 'at his rooms in the inner quarter of the city, alone, while at work, and with his brush in his hand'. Only a small number of miniatures authenticated by his signature, AC, are known; the signature is to be found in black and gold. Other miniatures are attributed to him from time to time on style and technique. Signed ones are in the collections of H.M. the Queen of the Netherlands, the Countess of Craven, the V. & A. M., the Kaiser Friedrich Museum and the Nationalmuseum, Stockholm. A miniature said to be of Prince Rupert, but possibly of his brother, Charles Louis, Elector Palatine, is in the collection of H.M. the Queen. He was a fine artist and his works are delicately finished, the hair of his sitters being lighted so that it gleams like the

sheen of silk. The highlights on the costume are treated with the same brilliance. He painted miniatures from life as well as executing miniature copies of oil portraits, and landscapes, said to have been painted in water-colour. A miniature attributed to him of Christina, Queen of Sweden (oil on copper) was loaned to the South Kensington Exhibition, 1865. The miniature of Prince Rupert, already mentioned, was exhibited in Edinburgh, 1965. The pair of miniatures in the collection of H.M. the Queen of the Netherlands represent an unknown man and an unknown woman; both are signed 'A. C.' (block letters) on the front, and have mauve backgrounds.

*Cooper, Miss Bessie. (fl. 1902)
Of London. Exhibited at the R.A. 1902, from c/o C. Jordan, Esq., Inner Circle, Regent's Park.

*Cooper, Miss Catharine C. (fl. 1903)
Exhibited at the R.A. 1903, from The Vicarage, Robin Hood's Bay, Yorks. Her sitter was Irene, daughter of Lady Elphinstone.

*Cooper, Lady Charlotte Barbara Ashley. 1799?–1889
Daughter of the Earl of Shaftesbury. Married in 1824 Henry Lyster, Esq. of Rowton Castle, Shropshire. Long records a good family miniature painted by her.

*Cooper, Mrs. Emma (C.B.). b. 1837
Born 1837 in Hertfordshire, née Emma Wren. Worked in London. Exhibited at the R.A., O.W.C.S., S.M., etc., 1872–1901. Pupil of John Leech and W. Garland. Married in 1858. Schidlof records that she took part in various exhibitions from 1865. Painted miniatures, fancy subjects and bird life. The R.A. catalogues always record her as Mrs. E. Cooper, but Graves gives her initials as C. B. (probably her husband's).

*Cooper, Miss Florence M. (fl. 1887–1914)
Of London. Exhibited at the R.A. and S.M., 1887–1914. Painted religious subjects and portrait miniatures. Her exhibit in 1901 was of the Marchioness of Granby. Also exhibited portraits of the Marchioness of Anglesey and Lady Diana Manners.

Cooper, Gibbons. (fl. 1834)
Was working at 15 George Street, New Road, St. Pancras, London in 1834.

*Cooper, Miss I. (fl. 1900–1901)
Of London. Exhibited at the Society of Miniaturists, 1900–1901.

Cooper, J. (fl. 1688)
Lot 123 on the eighteenth day of the Strawberry Hill sale, 1842 was described as 'A highly finished miniature by J. Cooper, 1688'.

*Cooper, Miss Lena. (fl. 1902)
Was a member of the Society of Miniaturists, 1902.

*Cooper, Miss Louisa. (fl. 1879)
Of Hartwells, Pinkney's Green, nr. Maidenhead. Exhibited a portrait of 'H.R.H. the late Princess Alice' at the R.A., 1879.

Cooper, Richard. (fl. 1793–1799)
Of London. Exhibited at the R.A., 1793–1799. Evidently worked in the provinces as Long saw a miniature in Bath, on the reverse of which was his printed card on which he described himself as 'from London'. The miniature was of no outstanding merit. Schidlof records a Richard Cooper, but appears to have confused the biographical details of Richard Cooper, engraver, born c. 1730, died 1820, and who was a pupil of Le Bas, and another Richard Cooper, 1740–1814, who painted landscapes (see Benezit, p. 618). Cooper exhibited from 30 Russell Court, London. Mr. A. J. B. Kiddell saw a miniature by this artist which he considered of only average ability; it was somewhat continental in style and had a trade card on the reverse which read:

> Richard Cooper
> Miniature Painter
> From London.

Begs to inform the Nobility, Gentry, and others, that he continues to take likenesses at 2 guineas each At his Appartments near the Artichoke, under Bank, St Augustine's Place, Bristol.

He adds that 'Ladies and Gentlemen may depend on a good likeness' and that he had been a student at the Royal Academy and had exhibited for several years successively.

Cooper, Samuel. 1609?–1672
Born in London in 1609 and brought up together with his brother, under the 'care and discipline' of their uncle, John Hoskins (q.v.) by whom they were taught painting. Samuel Cooper was undoubtedly one of the greatest, if not the greatest, miniaturist of the British school, and many would claim that he was the greatest in Europe. Only scanty information is available about his life, and it is his art which will live for ever. Cooper was a man of varied gifts, being a keen musician, a good linguist and a great traveller. He is known to have visited France and Holland and may have been in Germany. The year in which he and his brother went to live with their uncle is not known, but Samuel evidently remained with Hoskins for some years, for he was still with him in 1634 when Sir Theodore Turquet de Mayerne visited him and procured from him a recipe for preparing lead white. As far as is known, this Document, which is preserved in the Mayerne manuscripts in the B.M., is the only one that exists in Cooper's own handwriting, apart from the inscriptions on his miniatures. Between 1635 and 1642 few of his works can be traced, and it is fair to assume that it was probably during this period that he was abroad. From 1642 he was living in Henrietta Street, Covent Garden and, from then onwards, there is a continuous record of signed and dated miniatures which convey to us all we want to know about his artistic merit, which never faltered up to his death. One of his earliest recorded works is of Elizabeth Cecil, Countess of Devonshire (1620–1689); it is signed and dated 'Sa Cooper pinxet A°: 1642', and is in the collection of the Marquess of Exeter. The miniature is charming in its simplicity and was one of the twenty-nine miniatures by Cooper exhibited in Edinburgh, 1965. Cooper was so highly estimated as an artist that he was patronised by Charles II and his court as well as by Oliver Cromwell and members of the Commonwealth. His unfinished sketch of Cromwell in the collection of the Duke of Buccleuch is one of his most famous works. When Charles II was restored to the throne Cooper was soon established as the principal miniaturist and in 1663 was appointed the King's

limner at a salary of £200 a year and certain perquisites. His salary, in fact, was not paid in full and an order was eventually given, granting him payment of the arrears plus £200 p.a. Cooper's wife was Christina, daughter of William Turner of York, and an aunt of Alexander Pope, the poet. A very attractive, unfinished portrait of her is in the collection of the Duke of Portland. Nothing more is known of her except that after her husband's death she was his sole executrix. She was granted an annuity of £200 by Charles II in return for 'several pictures or pieces of limning of a very considerable value', but this pension, like many others, soon fell into arrears and she was obliged to petition for its payment in September 1676. The majority of Cooper's miniatures were painted from life, but he executed a few after the works of other artists including Van Dyck. Samuel Pepys refers to Cooper in his Diary of 1668 when he was painting Mrs. Pepys for which she had at least nine sittings. Pepys was not satisfied with the likeness but found Cooper good company and was delighted by his skill in music. Cooper had a wide circle of acquaintances which included John Aubrey, Samuel Butler, John Evelyn, John Hayls, Thomas Hobbes, John Milton and Sir William Petty. He was working until a few days before his death and was busily employed with commissions from a number of people including Charles II and the Duke of York, and was asked to hasten a portrait of Lady Exeter only a month before his death, which took place on 5 May 1672. He was buried in Old St. Pancras Church. In his will he made various bequests to John Hoskins the younger (q.v.) and others. His wife died on 24 August 1693 and was buried with her husband. Charles Beale (q.v.), writing in his diary, recorded that on 'Sunday, May 5, 1672, Mr. Samuel Cooper, the most famous limner of the world for a face, died.' One of his finest qualities as a painter was his ability to portray character and the features are modelled with greater dexterity than those of earlier periods. Whereas in the past miniaturists had painted with a detailed technique which had more affinity with the work of illuminators, Cooper abandoned this style and painted with a broader and freer brush stroke, more usually associated with that used by painters of oil portraits. It is interesting to note his method of getting the best lighting for shadows; he arranged a candle high overhead and to one side so that the shadows fell on the sitter's face in such a way as to bring out the modelling to the full. He used a rather strong reddish brown on the flesh parts, instead of pinker tones previously used. Unfortunately, in some cases, the carmines have faded, but despite this the harmony and blending of his colours endows his work with a richness that is only matched by the power and depth of his draughtsmanship. He executed portraits in crayon and pencil and is said to have painted in oil as well as water-colour, although no oil portraits have been found which can with certainty be said to be by him. His signature was usually SC either in separate letters or in monogram, followed by a date, S. Cooper, Sa Cooper pinxet, etc. The letters are to be found in gold and also in dark brown or grey on the background. Like his predecessors, he painted on vellum laid onto card, the size varying up to 3 in. or more in ovals, and considerably larger in rectangular format, e.g. William Cavendish, Duke of Newcastle (1592–1676), after Van Dyck, which measures 13⅝ × 9½ in. One of the most important of the large portraits is the recently discovered miniature of Cosimo de Medici, signed in monogram as if incised, on vellum, 20.9 × 17.1 cm. Mr. Oliver Miller in *Apollo*, January 1965, p. 2, 'Notes on British Art', describes how this miniature, which was thought to have been lost, was discovered standing on a shelf in the office of

the Director of the Gabinette dei Designi in the Uffizi, Florence. This portrait was painted in London when the Prince visited England in 1669. It was not finished until 1670 when by 5 December of that year Cooper was paid £150 and the portrait had been sent to Florence. The unusually high price for the miniature is explained by the fact that it is five times larger than Cooper's usual portraits, for which his usual charge was about £30. Of the few crayon drawings that have survived, the most notable is that of Thomas Alcock, which is preserved in the Ashmolean Museum, Oxford, on the back of which is an inscription which reads: 'This picture was drawne for mee at the Earle of Westmoreland's house at Apethorpe in Northamptonshire by the Greate (tho' little) Limner, the then famous Mr. Cooper of Couent Garden; when I was eighteen years of age. Thomas Alcock, Preceptor.'. By far the greater number of Cooper's best works are still in private collections such as those of H.M. the Queen, the Duke of Portland, the Duke of Buccleuch, the Duke of Richmond and Gordon, the Duke of Rutland, the Marquess of Exeter, Major R.M.O. de la Hey and many more. Those accessible to the public are in the V. & A. M.; the N.P.G.; the Wallace Collection; the Fitzwilliam Museum, Cambridge; the Ashmolean Museum, Oxford; the Rijksmuseum, Amsterdam; the Nationalmuseum, Stockholm; the Cleveland Museum of Art, Ohio; and many others. More detailed information may be found in Basil Long's *British Miniaturists*, J. J. Foster's *Samuel Cooper* and Graham Reynolds' *English Portrait Miniatures*. Examples of his work were loaned to the exhibition at South Kensington, 1865 and to the Edinburgh Exhibition in 1965.

Cooper, T. (fl. 1845)
Of London. Exhibited at the R.A., 1845.

Coote or **Cootes, Miss Sarah.** (fl. 1777–1784)
Of Clerkenwell. Exhibited at the Society of Artists, 1777–1780 and at the R.A., 1781–1784. Executed miniatures and crayon portraits.

Copeland, G. (fl. 1835)
Exhibited at the R.A., 1835.

Copley, John Singleton, R.A., F.S.A. 1737/8–1815
Born in Boston, Mass; probably 26 July 1738 (Copley exhibition catalogue 1965) or 3 July 1737 (Long); son of Richard and Mary Copley of Irish descent. His father owned a tobacco shop on Long Wharf, Boston, and died before the boy was ten years old. His mother married in May 1748 Peter Pelham, a mezzotint engraver, portrait painter and schoolmaster. Copley undoubtedly watched his stepfather at work, and when three years later, in 1751, he died, was left with Pelham's studio and the equipment for making mezzotints and paintings. In 1753 Copley produced a mezzotint portrait of the Rev. William Welstead which he made by altering a plate used by Pelham, of the Rev. William Cooper, made in 1743. Is best known for his portraits in oil, pastels and historical and other subjects. His miniatures, with the exception of a few, seem to date before 1769. He was influenced by Joseph Blackburn who went to Boston in 1755. Some of Copley's miniatures are reproduced in the catalogue of the Copley Exhibition held in America in 1965. His miniature of Deborah Scollay c. 1762 (reproduced in the catalogue) is thought to be his earliest known work in miniature on ivory. He exhibited at the Society of Artists 1768–1772, from Boston, New England and at the R.A., B.I., etc., 1776–1812. He is known to have obtained his gold and silver miniature frames from Paul Revere and Nathaniel Hurd. Copley married on 16 November 1769

Susanna Farnham Clarke (daughter of Richard Clarke, agent of the East India Company and a wealthy merchant), by whom he had five children: Clarke, who died young, Elizabeth, John Singleton junior, Mary and Susanna. He worked in New York in 1771 returning to Boston in 1772. In June 1774 Copley left America never to return. He sailed for England and later visited Rome, Paris, Naples, Pompeii, etc. He returned to London in October 1775 and lived in Leicester Square. Became A.R.A., 1776; R.A., 1799. Towards the end of his life he lost his popularity and his faculties deteriorated. He had a stroke and died a month later on 9 September 1815. His son, John Singleton (1772–1863), became Lord Lyndhurst, thrice Lord Chancellor of England. Miniatures by him are rare; those I have seen are of a very high quality; those of Samuel Cary and Mrs. Samuel Cary, painted c. 1769, are reproduced on p. 55 of the Copley catalogue, 1965/66. He did not always sign his miniatures; when he did, as in the case of his portrait of Mrs. Cary, the signature is 'JSC' (monogram) the J and S being encircled by the C. Examples of his miniatures are in the Worcester Art Museum, U.S.A., the Boston Art Museum, U.S.A. and in private collections. His self-portrait is reproduced Pl. IX in *American Miniatures* by Whele. Some of his miniatures are executed in oil on copper. Drawings by Copley are in the B.M. and the V. & A. M. A miniature by him of Sir George Jackson Ducket, Bt., M.P., was loaned to the South Kensington Exhibition, 1865.

Coques or **Cockx, Gonzales.** 1614–1684
Born in Antwerp, 8 December 1614. Celebrated Flemish painter. Recorded as having worked for Charles I and may possibly have lived for a time in England. Was influenced by the work of Van Dyck. Painted small oil portraits and miniatures. A miniature by him is at the museum at Malines, Belgium. Died 18 April 1684. An oil miniature, said to be a self-portrait, is in the Rosenbach Library, Philadelphia.

Corbaux, Miss Fanny. See **Corbaux, Miss Marie F. C. D.**

Corbaux, Miss Marie Françoise Catherine Doetter or **Doetger.** 1812–1883
Born in 1812. Probably a daughter of Francis Corbaux, F.R.S., author of *Dictionnaire des Arbitrages des Changes*. Known as Fanny Corbaux. Studied at the N.G. and B.I., and took up painting when her father became poor. Executed miniatures, portraits and figure subjects in oil and water-colour. The Society of Arts awarded her a large silver medal for a miniature portrait in 1827 and in, 1829, a large silver Isis medal for an original historical composition in water-colour. In 1830 she won a further award of a gold Isis medal for an original miniature portrait. Exhibited at the R.A., 1829–1854 and at the S.B.A. (Honorary Member, 1830) and N.W.C.S. (a member, 1839). Illustrated Moore's *Pearls of the East*, 1837, etc. Wrote on subjects relating to Biblical history. In 1871 she was granted a pension of £50 from the Civil List. She died in Brighton, 1 February 1883. The B.M. has some engraved portraits after her work. Her sister, Louisa or Louise Corbaux exhibited at the R.A., 1828–1881. One of these exhibits was from the same address as the above artist, i.e. 5 Hercules Buildings, Lambeth in 1833. Miss Fanny Corbaux loaned a portrait of her father by J. B. J. Augustin (q.v.) to the South Kensington Exhibition, 1865.

Corbett, John. 1777?–1815
An Irish artist; son of Daniel Corbett, the engraver, of Cork and brother of Daniel Corbett

junior, a dentist. Had an aptitude for art and was sent to London where he entered the R.A. Schools, 'Feb. 3rd 1798 age 21'; became a pupil of James Barry, R.A. Returned to Cork and acquired a good practice. Painted portraits both in oil and miniature and showed talent in historical painting. Had musical accomplishments and a fine voice. His convivial disposition is said to have contributed to his death of brain fever in February 1815 at the age of only 36. Some of his portraits were engraved. A self-portrait of the artist as a young man is illustrated in Strickland, Pl. XV. Engraved portraits after Corbett are in the B.M.

*Corbould, Alfred Chantry, R.B.A. (fl. 1878–1910)
Of London. Exhibited at the R.A., N.W.C.S., S.M., etc., 1878–1910. Executed illustrations for *Punch*. As far as I know, his exhibits at the Society of Miniaturists were subject drawings, not portraits.

*Corbould, Edward Henry. 1815–1905
Born in London, 5 December 1815. Exhibited at the R.A., B.I., S.B.A. and N.W.C.S., 1835–1880. Well-known painter, illustrator and sculptor. Painted figure subjects and portraits in water-colour and miniatures. Schidlof mentions a miniature painted by him of his great-granddaughter, Mrs. Weatherley, which is still in the family. A portrait by him of Prince Albert was lithographed by R. J. Lane (q.v.). In 1851 he was appointed to teach Queen Victoria's children to paint in water-colour, and executed their portraits. A miniature of Mrs. Julia Seaton, signed 'Edward Henry Corbould June 1857', was sold in Vienna, 6–7 June 1921. Died 18 January 1905.

Corbould, Richard. 1757–1831
Born in London, 18 April 1757. Entered the R.A. Schools, 21 March 1774, aged '17. 18th last April'. Exhibited at the R.A., 1777–1811 and at the S.B.A., until 1817. Painted on porcelain and executed miniatures on enamel and ivory, as well as painting landscapes, allegorical subjects and drawing book illustrations and historical subjects. Painted in oil and water-colour. Died at Highgate, 26 or 27 July 1831 and was buried in the ground of St. Andrew's, Holborn, Gray's Inn Road. Had two sons Henry and George who followed his profession. A miniature of Lieut. General Cleveland (d. 1794), seen by Long, 1926, and indistinctly signed, was probably by him. The B.M. has a few engraved portraits after R. Corbould. His great-great-granddaughter, Miss Lily Haywood (q.v.), exhibited a portrait of the artist's wife at the Society of Miniaturists, 1905, copied from an enamel on gold, painted by Bone (q.v.) in 1786.

*Corbould-Ellis, Mrs. Eveline or **Evelyn.** (fl. 1898–1913)
Of London. Exhibited at the R.A. 1898–1913, from various London addresses and from Cromwell Lodge, Stevenage, Herts. Her sitters included Lady Douglas Galton and Gwendolen Margaret Evans, daughter of the Solicitor-General, and Master Leslie Corbould-Ellis.

Corden, William. 1797–1867. See also **Corder, W.**
Born at Ashbourne, Derbyshire, 28 November 1797. Was apprenticed at the Derby China factory and was taught to paint landscapes; he later turned his attention to painting portraits and figure subjects and finally devoted himself to portrait painting. He painted portraits in oil, as well as miniatures on porcelain plaques, ivory and enamel. Exhibited at the R.A., 1826–1836 and was probably identical with the W. Corder (q.v.) who exhibited an enamel at the R.A. in 1825. Left the Derby works c. 1820

having painted, shortly before he left, the greater part of a dessert service with subjects copied from Thurston's illustrations for Tegg's edition of Shakespeare's plays (1812). Worked in Derby and the vicinity and also in Nottingham. In c. 1831 he was engaged to paint some of the subjects on part of a service for William IV. Corden went to live at Windsor in 1829 and had the patronage of the Marchioness of Cunningham who gave him employment and introduced him to the Court. He painted a few small enamel portraits for Queen Victoria, but they were not considered to be very successful. In 1844 the Prince Consort employed him to copy several full size portraits of his ancestors, and Corden went to Coburg for the purpose and was assisted by his son. In c. 1854 Corden obtained work in the Staffordshire Potteries and later assisted a Mr. Scaife (q.v.), a miniature painter and photographer, in combining enamelling and photography; this was not a success and Corden went to live in Nottingham. He died there on 18 June 1867, aged 70. Gilhespy, in *Derby Porcelain*, records a number of miniatures on porcelain plaques; some of his miniatures are illustrated on Pl. III.

Corder, E. (fl. 1828)
Of London. Exhibited at the R.A. 1828, an enamel portrait of Mrs. Williams from 38 Hatton Garden.

Corder, W. (fl. 1825). See also **Corden, W.**
Of London. Exhibited an enamel portrait on china of Miss F. H. Kelly, Theatre Royal, Covent Garden, at the R.A., 1825. May have been confused with W. Corden (q.v.).

*Cordier, Mlle. A. Deville. (fl. 1860–1882)
Of Paris. Exhibited at the R.A., 1860–1882. Painted portrait miniatures and figure subjects.

*Corey, Mrs. Linda W. (fl. 1904)
Of London. Exhibited at the R.A. 1904, from Ontario, Cole Park, Twickenham. Her sitter was Mrs. Charlesworth.

Corking. 18th century
A miniature of a man in the manner of Hobday (q.v.) was lot 82 at Christie's 1 October 1974. The miniature was inscribed on the reverse 'Self portrait by Corking'. There was a partly legible signature.

*Corkran, Miss Henrietta L. d. 1911
Of London. Exhibited at the R.A., 1872–1903; her last addresses were 45 Mecklenburg Square and c/o B.V. Head, Esq., British Museum. Executed miniatures and subjects in water-colour. Died 17 March 1911.

*Cormack, Mrs. Minnie. (fl. 1892–1906)
Née Everett. Of London. Exhibited at the R.A., 1892–1906; her addresses included Pomona House, New King's Road, Fulham. Executed engravings and painted miniatures, and pictures in oil.

Cormack, Neil. b. 1793?
Brother of the Rev. John Cormack, minister of Stow. Entered the R.A. Schools, 9 August 1816, aged 23 years; author of an account of female infanticide in Gujarat, and other works. Applied, 29 April 1818, to the Court of Directors of the East India Company for permission to go to Bombay and practise his profession as a miniature painter. He gave the Earl of Fife and Mr. Charles Forbes, M.P. as his securities. Permission was granted and he sailed from Liverpool, 27 June 1818 in the *Hannah* and reached Bombay, 30 October 1818. In

1823 he went to Madras, but does not appear to have stayed long, and is recorded as living in Bombay, 1819–1827. He must have returned to Madras c. 1831 and advertised from 10 Stringer Street on 27 January that he was willing to paint miniatures and sell drawing materials. On 31 March he advertised again that he had moved to a garden which was opposite the Pantheon and formerly owned by Dr. Filson. He stated that he had reduced his charges to 'thirty pagodas and upwards, according to style'. He was living in Madras up to 1837 after which date nothing is known about him.

Cornelisz, Lucas. 1493/5–1552
Born in Leyden, 1493 or 1495; son and pupil of Cornelis Engelbrechtsz. Called 'de Kok', or 'Kunst'. Worked as a cook. Came to England c. 1527 with his wife and seven or eight children. Said to have been painter to Henry VIII and to have taught Holbein (q.v.) to paint in water-colour. Walpole asserted that he excelled both in oil and miniature painting; he may have painted in distemper. *The Burlington Magazine*, Vol. XVI, 1910, f.p. 154, reproduces a circular oil portrait of Sir T. Wyat, attributed to this artist. Died in Leyden, 1552.

Cornman, H. (fl. 1782–1821)
Of London. Exhibited at the Free Society of artists, 1782 and at the R.A., 1799–1821. Was a miniaturist, sculptor and wax modeller.

*Corrie, Miss Jessie E. (fl. 1906–1910)
Of Alresford, Hants. Exhibited at the Society of Miniaturists, 1906–1910.

Coslett, R. G. (Roderick?). b. 1785?
Of London. Probably the Roderick Coslett who entered the R.A. Schools, 12 November 1802, aged 17 years. Exhibited at the R.A., 1808–1827. His sitters included Sir W. W. Doveton; the Rev. J. Hall; Miss Fitzgerald; Washington Ashby and the Rev. H. G. Watkins. He painted portraits, miniatures and executed subject drawings.

Cosse or **Cossé, Lawrence Joseph.** b. 1759?
Worked in Düsseldorf and London. Noted by Long as Laurence J. Cosse, but probably identical with Lawrence Joseph Cosse who entered the R.A. Schools '3rd Dec. 1784. age 26, April 1784'. Obtained a silver medal in 1788. Painted miniatures, genre subjects, interiors, landscapes, etc. Exhibited at the R.A., B.I., etc., 1784–1837.

Costa, Catharina da. (fl. 1712–1730)
Daughter of Ferdinando Mendez, a Jewish doctor from Portugal. Was for some years a pupil of Bernard Lens (q.v.); made copies of the works of Rubens, Van Dyck, etc.; also painted portraits of her family, two of which are in the Jewish Museum, London. One is of her son Abraham and is an early example of painting on ivory, which technique she would have learnt from Lens; it is a combination of oil paint on the background, gouache for the costume and hair, and transparent water-colour for the features and hands. It is signed 'C da Costa 1714'. The other is signed and inscribed on the reverse 'Mr Salvadore. Catherine Da Costa Fecit Feb. Ye 13th 1720'. The sitter was probably Francis (Jacob) Salvadore, merchant of Lime Street, London. A portrait miniature by C. Da Costa, of Mary Queen of Scots after a miniature painted by B. Lens, after an earlier portrait, is at Ham House.

Costa, De. (fl. 1827)

Long refers to having seen a rectangular miniature of a girl, painted on ivory, and probably after Lawrence (q.v.), c. 1827, signed in gold 'De Costa'.

Costello, Miss Louisa Stuart. 1799–1870

Born in England in 1799; the daughter of Captain James Francis Costello of the 14th Foot, a native of County Mayo. When barely sixteen, her father died and she was obliged to take up painting in order to help support her mother and brother. Settled in Paris where she painted miniatures. Removed to London c. 1820. Exhibited at the R.A., 1822–1839. Was pretty, with an engaging personality, and made many friends, including Sir Francis and Lady Burdett who helped and encouraged her. Published *Songs of a Stranger* and, in 1835, *Specimens of the Early Poetry of France*, dedicated to Thomas Moore. This established her in the literary world and she gave up painting for literature. Maintained her brother at Sandhurst. Published *Rose Garden of Persia* which she illustrated. Lived in Brighton, 1833–c. 1839, and after her brother died in 1865, went to live in Boulogne. Was given a small pension from the Burdett family and one from the Civil List. Died of cancer, 24 April 1870 and was buried in the cemetery of St. Martin.

Cosway, Maria. See Cosway, Mrs. Richard

*Cosway, R. B.

A small full-length portrait of a lady, signed 'R. B. Cosway / 08' (1908), was seen by me in 1967 in Edinburgh. It was executed in pencil and wash, the face being tinted; the draughtsmanship was good and the painting attractive.

Cosway, Richard, R.A. 1742–1821

Born in Okeford, nr. Bampton, Devon, 5 November 1742; son of Richard and Mary Cosway, his father being headmaster of Blundell's School, Tiverton. The family was of Flemish descent who established a prosperous woollen business and owned a considerable amount of property. Cosway was attracted to art from an early age, and copied many of the family pictures. Was sent to London before he was twelve where he studied under Thomas Hudson and at Shipley's drawing school. Was awarded prizes at the Society of Arts in 1755–1760. Exhibited in 1760 at the Society of Artists and, in 1761, at the Free Society of Artists. Entered the R.A. Schools, 9 August 1769. Exhibited at the R.A., 1770–1806. Became A.R.A., 1770 and R.A., 1771. In 1773 fell in love with Miss Wools (afterwards Mrs. Bullock). On 18 January 1781 married Maria Louisa Catherine Cecilia Hadfield (Cosway, Mrs. R. q.v.) at St. George's, Hanover Square, London. He settled £2,800 on her. She copied many of her husband's works. Their only child, Louisa Paolina Angelica, was born in 1789 and died suddenly in 1796. Cosway became a fashionable miniaturist and obtained the patronage of the Prince of Wales. He was an eccentric, foppish in his attire, small in stature, superstitious and inclined to mysticism. He collected drawings by old masters; held brilliant receptions at Schomberg House, Pall Mall, but moved, in 1791, to what is now 21 Stratford Place, Oxford Street. Early in his career he painted large portraits in oil, executed drawings (some of which were tinted), but chiefly, as time went on, miniatures on ivory and a few on enamel. Was in Paris, 1785 and 1790–1791. Gave some cartoons by Giulio Romano to the Louvre. In c. 1786 he obtained the coveted honour of being made Miniature Painter to the Prince of Wales with

whom he was on very friendly terms. When the Prince became Regent in 1811 he became more selective of his immediate circle and Cosway was dropped and never regained his position. After two strokes in c. 1821 he became partially paralysed and he and his wife moved to 31 Edgware Road. On 4 July 1821 he suffered another attack whilst out for a drive and died before he could be got home. He was buried in St. Mary-le-bone Church. Cosway is probably one of the best known miniaturists of the British school and one whose work has been, and still is, copied in large numbers. His early works were painted on a small scale, the backgrounds frequently plain. From the start his miniatures were painted with a delicacy and fine modelling which was a characteristic of his work. He was a prolific artist and able to produce likenesses with a minimum of soft swift strokes. He tended to enlarge the pupil of the eye and, by c. 1785, by which time the use of larger ivories (3 in. or more) was popular, he had developed the technique of using transparent pigments which, when floated on to the ivory, allowed its natural luminosity to show through. He also developed the use of 'sky backgrounds' which soon became popular, and a clear Antwerp blue is another characteristic of his work. His best period was c. 1785–1805. He modelled the features with short grey strokes which are visible round the eyes and contours of the cheeks, and painted the hair in soft masses. On the background, particularly near the edge of the cheek, away from the spectator, long parallel strokes may be seen, often punctuated by numerous dots or small transverse strokes, each one ending in a small blob of colour. His miniatures are not by any means always signed, and any portrait signed on the front should be viewed with suspicion. When he did sign, it was either in monogram (with a C surrounding an R) on a drawing, or on the reverse of miniatures in full, with long flowery inscriptions, most of them in Latin. A typical inscription would be: R^d Cosway / Pinxit / 1764, or Rdus Cosway / R.A. / Primarius Pictor / Serenssimi Walliae / Principis / Pinxit / 1794. Schidlof states that he was styled Sir Richard Cosway, but this was not the case. Examples of his work may be found in many private collections including those of H.M. the Queen, Lord Methuen and Major R. M. O. de la Hey. Those available to the public are in the V. & A. M., the Wallace Collection and the Fitzwilliam Museum, Cambridge. The B.M. has drawings by Cosway and numerous engravings after his work. I have seen a hitherto unrecorded self-portrait of Cosway in the N.G., Dublin. It is well drawn; he is wearing fancy dress with a ruff and is hatless. The miniature is set in a pearl frame. Several miniatures by him were loaned to the South Kensington Exhibition of 1865 and to the Edinburgh Exhibition of 1965. For a full account of his works see Basil Long's *British Miniaturists*, pp. 94–101 and Dr. G. C. Williamson's *Richard Cosway*.

Cosway, Mrs. Richard (Miss Maria Hadfield). 1759/60–1838

Née Maria Louisa Catherine Cecilia Hadfield. Born in Italy c. 1759/60, probably in Florence; daughter of an Irish hotel-keeper. Educated at a convent. Studied art in Rome, becoming a member of the Academy in Florence in 1778. In 1779 after her father's death she came to England at the suggestion of Angelica Kauffmann (q.v.) and obtained work as a miniaturist, but in spite of this she and her family were in reduced circumstances when she married Richard Cosway (q.v.) on 18 January 1781 at St. George's, Hanover Square. Exhibited at the R.A., 1781–1801. Executed many drawings, some of which were engraved by Bartolozzi (q.v.)

and others. Painted figure subjects in oil and copied a number of her husband's works. Travelled extensively; accompanied her husband to Paris, visited Rome with her brother, George Hadfield, an architect, in 1790. Whilst in Paris, in 1802, she met Mrs. Damer and is said to have undertaken to draw every picture in the Louvre. Was in Lyons in 1803. The Cosways had one child, Louisa Angelica (1789–1796), whose godfather was General Paoli. Was in Milan in 1811 and, in 1812, founded a college in Lodi which she turned into a convent in 1830, having retired there after her husband's death in 1821. Acted as hostess for her husband at the gay parties held at their house in Pall Mall which were attended by the Prince of Wales, the Duchess of Devonshire, etc. Mrs. Cosway looked after her husband towards the end of his life when he became ill. Writing from Lodi in 1824 she says she is still attached to England and has 55 children entrusted to her care. The Emperor Francis I made her a baroness in 1834. She died at Lodi, 5 January 1838. Her sister, Charlotte Hadfield, married William Combe, the comic poet, noted for his *Tours of Dr. Syntax*, etc. Without documentary evidence of signed works by her, attribution is difficult and her miniatures and drawings probably pass unrecognised. The Leeds Art Gallery has an oil portrait of Maria Cosway, said to be by her. W. Birch (q.v.) executed a well known engraving of Cosway's studio in Pall Mall, showing Mrs. Cosway, and numerous portraits have been said to represent her. Dr. Williamson reproduces portraits of her including a marble bust of her as an old woman, and photographs of the college at Lodi, in his work *Richard Cosway, R.A.* For more details see this work and Basil Long's *British Miniaturists*. Three miniatures by her were loaned to the exhibition at South Kensington in 1865. Her self-portrait was engraved by V. Green.

Cotes, Francis, R.A. 1725?–1770

Born in London, 1725? Brother of Samuel Cotes (q.v.). Noted portrait painter in oil and pastel. Not usually regarded as a miniaturist except for a portrait of John Russell, R.A., reproduced by Dr. G. C. Williamson on p. 8 of his *John Russell, R.A.*, 1894, and said to be from a miniature by Cotes. Exhibited at the R.A., 1760–1770. Died in July 1770.

Cotes, Miss Penelope. See Carwardine, Miss Penelope

Although for many years a large number of miniatures signed P. C. have been attributed to either Penelope Cotes or Penelope Carwardine (q.v.), there is not, so far, any documentary evidence of Penelope Cotes' existence. The late Mr. Carl Winter pointed out in 1931 that there were neither documents of her birth nor mention of her in the will of Francis Cotes (q.v.) to prove that she was his sister. Her name does not occur among the list of contemporary exhibitors in this period. Penelope Carwardine certainly painted miniatures and from those works still in the possession of the family, it would seem that unless any fresh evidence is forthcoming, all miniatures signed P. C. of this period should be regarded as the work of Penelope Carwardine.

Cotes, Samuel. 1734–1818

Born in London, 1734; younger son of an ex-Mayor of Galway who had become an apothecary in Cork Street, London. Was trained in this trade but was taught art by his brother, F. Cotes (q.v.) and took up miniature painting on ivory and enamel, and executed pastel portraits. Exhibited at the Society of Artists 1760–1768, and at the R.A. 1769–1789. Was living in Cork Street, 1763 and is said to have worked in Bath. Was married twice;

his only child died in infancy; his second wife, Sarah Shepherd or Sheppard (died 1814), was an amateur painter. Letters written by Cotes to her, 5 May 1808 and 14 December 1813, were published in *Highlights on Chelsfield Court Lodge* by A. T. Brown, privately printed in Liverpool, 1933. Cotes ceased to paint before 1807. Died in Paradise Row, Chelsea, 7 March 1818. A certain amount of confusion has arisen over attribution due to the fact that a mysterious Sarah Coote (exhibited, 1777–1784) about whom nothing is known, shared the same initials as Samuel Collins (q.v.) and Samuel Cotes. Until any further information is available, any miniatures bearing the initials S. C. and dated after 1768 are attributed to Cotes, and a number of others signed and dated as far back as 1757 have also been assigned to him. As the size of the ivories increased Cotes seems to have striven after greater boldness of effect. He used opaque colour in broken touches on the hair, as well as on the lace edging of costume and cravat. Recent research suggests that his signature S. C. was often made up of several strokes, rather than a smooth signature used by Collins. Examples of his work are at the V. & A. M., one of them being signed 'S. Cotes / 1766'.

*Cotes, Mrs. Sarah. See Shepherd, Sarah

*Cotman, S. (fl. 1854)
Schidlof refers to this artist as having worked in London in the middle of the 19th century and mentions a portrait signed on the reverse 'Painted by Mrs. Green 1819. Exhibited Soc. of Arts Gallery 1820, copied by S. Cotman 1854'.

Coton, M. (fl. *c.* 1790)
Long records seeing a large set of monochrome miniatures on ivory of the Kings of England, etc. One (Charles I) was signed 'M. Coton'. They evidently dated from *c.* 1790 and were copied from engravings by Vertue (q.v.). They were not of any great merit and may have been executed by an artist named Coton who exhibited an intaglio at the R.A. in 1782.

*Cotton, Miss. (fl. 1810)
Long records having seen in 1930 a miniature of a young girl inscribed 'Miniature / of my early / playmate, Mp Agnes / Casarmajor, age 9 yrs / painted / by my governess / Mips Cotton, Janry 1810 / for her to my Nurse / Bickley on her / leaving my mother's / care for Mips / Jame's / School / T. Well' (Tunbridge Wells). The miniature was good but the face was slightly pink. Miss Cotton of Chicheldy exhibited flowers, 1815–1822 at the R.A. and O.W.C.S., and may have been identical with the above artist.

*Cotton, Thomas. (fl. 1650)
Son of Ralph Cotton, picture maker of Dublin. Recorded in the muniments of the city of Dublin as being admitted to the franchise in 1650 as a limner.

*Coudert, Mrs. Amalia. See Küssner, Miss Amalia

*Cougnard, Miss Augusta. (fl. 1886–1892)
Of London. Exhibited at the R.A., etc., 1886–1892. Her sitters included W. Spencer Stanhope, Esq. and Miss C. Spencer Stanhope.

*Couldwell, Miss Agnes M. (fl. 1908)
Of Garforth, nr. Leeds. Exhibited at the R.A., 1908.

Cour, B. de la. See De la Cour, Benjamin

*Court. (fl. 1836). See also **Court, William**
Exhibited at the R.A. in 1836, from 14 Rue de l'Ancienne Comédie and from 108 Jermyn Street (no initial given). Possibly identical with William Court (q.v.).

Court, William. (fl. 1785–1823). See **Court**
Of London. Exhibited at the R.A., 1785–1823; possibly identical with the Court (q.v.) (no initial given) who exhibited in 1836 from 14 Rue de l'Ancienne Comédie and from 108 Jermyn Street; the exhibits were not miniatures. His most consistent address was 62 Paddington Street, Marylebone.

Courtney, F. (fl. 1835–1841)
Of London. Exhibited at the R.A., 1835–1841.

Cousins, Samuel, R.A. 1801–1887
Born at Exeter, 9 May 1801. Was a famous engraver. Painted miniatures in London and Brussels *c.* 1826. Exhibited at the R.A., 1837–1880. Was made an Associate Engraver in 1836, but does not seem to have exhibited that year. Long records seeing a good miniature by him of an unknown lady. Died in London, 7 May 1887.

Couzens, Charles. (fl. 1838–1875)
Of London. Exhibited at the R.A., 1838–1875. His exhibits included portraits of H.R.H. Princess Mary of Cambridge, H. W. Phillips and several Anglo-Greek sitters as well as members of London society. A miniature of Gilbert A. a Beckett, by Couzens, is in the N.P.G.

*Coward, Miss C. Brenda. (fl. 1910)
Of London. Exhibited at the R.A. 1910, from 10 Melbury Court, Kensington.

*Cowderoy, Miss Kate E. (fl. 1905–1914)
Exhibited at the R.A. 1905–1914, from The Retreat, Hillside Road, Bushey, Herts. One of her sitters was Miss Margaret Dockerill (q.v.) who exhibited at the R.A., 1900–1904. Others included Miss Ethel P. Cowderoy, Winifred E. Cowderoy and Phyllis Cowderoy. She also exhibited in Paris in 1909.

*Cowell, Miss Fan. (fl. 1903)
Exhibited at the R.A. 1903, from Ash Lea, Stanks, Leeds.

Cowell, Miss Grace Charlotte. See Dixon, Mrs. F.

*Cowper, Miss Gertrude (I.J or T). (fl. 1900–1903)
Of London. Exhibited at the R.A. 1900–1903, from various London addresses. Possibly Gertrude I.J or T Cowper as her name appears with these three initials in the R.A. catalogue.

Cox, David. 1783–1859
Born 29 April 1783. Famous water-colour painter, not usually regarded as a miniaturist, but was apprenticed to a miniaturist named Fielder (? the name is uncertain) at Birmingham who painted miniatures for lockets and boxes. The only known miniature by Cox was that in the collection of the Rev. H. G. Hills which was on loan to the V. & A. M. in 1929. A miniature landscape on mother-of-pearl attributed to him was on loan in 1928 at the Christchurch Mansion Museum, Ipswich. Died 7 June 1859.

*Cox, Miss Dorothy. (fl. 1899–1906)
Of London and Croydon. Exhibited at the R.A., 1899–1906. Executed miniatures and subjects in water-colour. According to Benezit her married name was Lewis.

*Cox, Miss Louisa E. (fl. 1874–1888)
Of St. James Street, Nottingham. Exhibited at the R.A., 1874–1888.

Cox, Miss S. (fl. 1824)
Of London; lived at 22 Nottingham Street. Awarded a silver palette by the Society of Arts in 1824 for a miniature portrait (copy) and a large silver medal for a drawing from a bust.

*Cox, Thomas. 19th century
A miniature was noted in 1950 in a Bournemouth catalogue. It was described as follows: 'Miniature on ivory of Miss E. B. Miller (a child of 2–3 years). Oval $2 \times 1\frac{3}{4}''$ $\frac{1}{2}$ length, painted by Mr Thomas Cox Miniature painter; whose engraved label is on the back of the frame, bright, good state, in a 19th c hand is written "Darling Loggie" on back'. A miniature of George Bradnock Stubbs *c.* 1830 was seen at Sotheby's in 1967. On the reverse of the portrait was a trade label which read:

Mr Thomas Cox
Miniature Painter
4 Warston Lane
Birmingham

The miniature was not of very good quality; the mouth was shaded with blue and there were heavy lines under the eyes.

Craddock, Miss Mary. See Beale, Mrs. Mary

*Craft or Croft, William (Hopkins?). *c.* 1730/5?–1811. See also **Craft or Croft, William Hopkins**
Born *c.* 1730/5? His date of birth and parentage are unknown. He is at present identified with William Hopkins Craft (q.v.) or Croft, also an enameller and possibly the brother of Thomas Craft who painted at the Bow Factory. An artist named William Craft entered the R.A. Schools, 4 November 1774, aged 39; if he was identical with W. H. Craft, this would make his date of birth *c.* 1735. Aubrey J. Toppin, in his paper to the English Ceramic Circle, 1959, identifies him with William Craft or Croft of Tottenham, born *c.* 1730, who obtained a marriage licence from the Bishop of London, 25 July 1757, when he was described as 'William Croft, of the parish of Tottenham High Cross, in the County of Middlesex, Bachelor, of the age of 21 upwards to marry Sarah Wood, of the same parish, 21 years and upwards'. The marriage took place at Tottenham on 15 September 1757 when the name was entered as Craft. A son, Thomas, was born *c.* 1771 (died 1796), whose wife, another Sarah, proved his will in which the spelling of the name is Craft, as on the burial entry, but on a monumental inscription the spelling is Croft. Thomas left £20 to his sister Hannah who was baptised, 10 December 1760, and married John Bowstreed, 21 January 1777. W. H. Craft was apparently working for Wedgwood in partnership with David Rhodes for a few years from 1768 and before that had worked in Paris. Evidence for the additional name of Hopkins is to be found on receipts of this period. W. Craft exhibited at the R.A., 1774–1781 and from 1794–1795; in all the entries the initials are only W, and (with the exception of a pair of large enamel plaques of George III and Queen Charlotte, signed 'W. H. Craft, 1773', in the B.M.) examples painted before 1782 were signed W. Craft. It is conceivable that there were two artists, possibly related, one of whom was W. Craft and the other W. H. Craft. Many of the enamels executed by W. H. Craft are over-large to be classed as miniatures. His decorative compositions include an oval plaque of 'The Judgement of Paris' signed 'W. Craft 1782', 'The Goddess of the Arts' signed 'W. H. Craft' (Nachemsohn Catalogue), and a large oval plaque of a rustic scene in

the manner of Bouchier, signed 'W. Craft', in the B.M. An ambitious work of *c.* 1798 commemorates the Naval Heroes of that period, with names and dates of their victories. These were Earl Howe, Earl St. Vincent, Viscount Duncan and Baron Nelson; Britannia is seated, pointing to a triumphal column, and a lion is trampling on the Tricolor flag, etc. It is signed 'W. H. Craft, invt et fecit'. (Nelson did not become Viscount Nelson until 1801.) Long gives Craft's date of death as 1805?, but if the two artists are identical, W. H. Craft was admitted to the Charter House as 'Mr. Croft, Pensioner' (a Poor Brother), 15 June 1810. He died there on 20 January 1811 and was buried in the Charter House burial ground on 24 January as Wm Hopkins Croft, Poor Brother, aged 80. *The Gentleman's Magazine* gives the information: 'Aged 80, Mr. Croft, formerly a Painter, but latterly on the Establishment of the Charter House. He was suddenly taken ill on Clerkwell Green, and being conveyed home in a coach, expired on entering his apartment'. It has been suggested that he may have been related to Herbert Croft, one of the Clerks in Chancery. The question of the alternative spelling and whether or not there were two artists cannot, at present, be resolved. Craft painted portraits and subject pieces on enamel, as well as clock-faces and landscapes. At times his work is hesitant, and often the colouring tends to be a little harsh, but nevertheless his work is good. A miniature of an 'Unknown Lady', exhibit No. 290 at Garrards, June 1961, was of exceptional quality. It was dated '1781'. A large enamel portrait of Sir William Hamilton, signed 'W. H. Craft, 1802', is in the B.M., and a similar plaque, also signed and dated '1802', was sold at Sotheby's, 1 March 1965, and a third is in the Ashmolean Museum, Oxford. Several examples of his work are in the N.G., Dublin including a self-portrait, signed on the front 'Craft 1780' and on the reverse 'Portrait / of / W. Craft / Enamel Painter / 1780'. This miniature was formerly in the Nachemsohn Collection. A miniature, still in the Spencer Collection, of Lavinia, Countess Spencer, and her son, John Charles, Lord Althorp, after the picture by Sir Joshua Reynolds at Althorp, signed and dated 'W. H. Craft fec^t 1787', was loaned to the South Kensington Exhibition, 1865.

Craft or Croft, William Hopkins. (fl. *c.* 1768). See also **Craft or Croft, William**

This artist is at present considered to be identical with William Craft (q.v.) or Croft, but the possibility cannot be excluded that there may have been two artists. William Hopkins Craft was in partnership with David Rhodes, for a few years from *c.* 1768, when they were employed by Wedgwood in London, and if the artists are identical it must have been at this time that he assumed the additional christian name of Hopkins. Evidence for this is to be found on receipts of this period.

*Craig, Mr. (William? junior). (fl. 1786). See also **Craig, William Marshall**

Possibly the son of W. M. Craig (q.v.). *The Manchester Chronicle* for 18 February 1786 advertised that 'Mr Craig jun' has set up in Manchester to do miniature painting and drawing, having been instructed by his father 'the ablest artist in London'. This may have been the W. Craig junior who exhibited at the R.A., 1801–1806, and who shared the family address of Charlotte Street, Rathbone Place.

*Craig, Miss Clara E. (fl. 1903–1908)

Of London and Bournemouth. Exhibited at the Society of Miniaturists, 1903–1908.

*Craig, J. K. (fl. 1819–1821)

Exhibited at the R.A., 1819–1821. Probably a son of W. M. Craig (q.v.) from whose address, 124 Oxford Street. he exhibited at the R.A. in 1821. The exhibits were portraits of Mr. and Mrs. Barker and of W. Kershaw, Esq., and were probably miniatures.

Craig, William Marshall. (fl. 1787–1827)

Said to have been the brother of James Craig, an Edinburgh architect. Exhibited in Liverpool, 1787, worked in Manchester, 1788, London *c.* 1791 onwards. Exhibited at the R.A. 1788–1827, and at the Associated Artists in Water-Colours, 1808–1812, becoming a member in 1810. Was appointed painter in water-colour to the Queen and miniature painter to the Duke and Duchess of York. Painted miniatures, portraits, landscapes, figure subjects in oil as well as water-colour, drawings and book illustrations. W. Craig junior (q.v.) was probably his son; several other artists of this name were certainly related, and all exhibited at times from 88 Charlotte Street, Rathbone Place. *The Manchester Chronicle*, 18 February 1786, advertised 'Mr Craig (Junior) Miniature Painting and Drawing. Instructed by his Father & the ablest artist in London. Sets up in Manchester.' This presumably refers to W. M. Craig's son, W. Craig Junior. J. K. Craig (q.v.), who was probably another son of W. M. Craig, exhibited in 1821 from the same address, 124 Oxford Street. Drawings by Craig are in the V. & A. M. and the B.M., who also have numerous engraved portraits after him. A miniature of an officer, signed on the reverse and dated '1815', is in the V. & A. M.

Cramer, R. (fl. 1802–1811). See also **Creamer, R.**

Of London. Worked in Leicester, 1807–1808. Exhibited at the R.A., 1802–1811. Painted a number of military and naval officers. Possibly identical with R. Creamer (q.v.) who exhibited at the R.A. in 1797, from 6 Coleman Street five portraits, probably miniatures.

*Crampton, Miss Maude M. (fl. 1896)

Exhibited at the R.A. 1896, from 2 North Parade, Queen Ann's Place, Bootham, York.

Cranch, John. 1751/7–1821

Born in Kingsbridge, Devon, 12 October 1751 or 1757. Was a clerk at Axminster; taught himself drawing. Came to London and was befriended by Reynolds. Exhibited at the Society of Artists, 1791 and at the B.I., 1807–1808. Best known as a painter of genre subjects and poker pictures, but is cited as a miniaturist in the *Annals of the Fine Arts*, II, p. 570, 1817. He died in Bath in February 1821. I have found no evidence that Cranch exhibited at the R.A. as recorded by Benezit.

Crane, Thomas. 1808–1859

Born at Chester, 1808; had two brothers, also artists. Entered the R.A. Schools, 31 March 1825, aged 17. Was given assistance by a Manchester patron and went to London, 1824. Won a gold medal at the R.A. Schools. Said to have returned to Chester in 1825, but this does not agree with his entry into the R.A. Schools. Exhibited at the Liverpool Academy, 1832; became an Associate, 1835 and a Member, 1838. Was living in Liverpool, 1838, but removed to London after his marriage in 1839. Exhibited at the R.A., B.I. and S.B.A., 1842–1858. Lived for a time at Leamington, returned to London and then lived for twelve years at Torquay, returning to London, 1857. Walter Crane (1845–1915) was his son. He died at Westbourne Park, July 1859.

*Crawford, Mrs. Fanny. (fl. 1909–1910)

Of Ashton-under-Lyne and Hampton-in-Arden. Exhibited at the Society of Miniaturists, 1909–1910.

*Crawfurd, Mrs. Charlotte Annabella. (fl. 1831)

An amateur miniaturist working *c.* 1831 possibly in India. Wife of Colonel Gavin Ralston Crawfurd.

*Crawshay, Miss Constance M. (fl. 1902–1904)

Of London. Exhibited at the Society of Miniaturists, 1902–1904.

*Creamer, R. (fl. 1797). See also **Cramer, R.**

Exhibited at the R.A. 1797, from 6 Coleman Street, five portraits, probably miniatures. Possibly identical with R. Cramer (q.v.).

Crease, Harold. b. 1788?

Exhibited at the R.A., 1812. Was probably identical with the artist of this name who entered the R.A. Schools, 26 February 1811, aged 23 years. Long recorded seeing a rather inferior miniature said to be of William Cobbett, executed by Crease, when the former was in prison. The face was smoothly painted and the shading was reddish. A miniature said to be of the Rev. Joseph Hughes, first Secretary of the British and Foreign Bible Society, was Lot 149 at Christie's, 22 March 1922. The B.M. has an engraved portrait of the Rev. Thos. Waters, after H. Crease.

*Credoe, Harold. (fl. 1812)

A miniature by the above artist of Charles James Fox (1749–1806), painted in 1812, is in the collection of Kenneth Guichard, Esq. The miniature is quite well modelled, the shading of the face is rather dark and is painted in greys, browns and blues.

*Creige. (fl. 1805)

A miniature portrait of Robert Burns was catalogued as by Creige at a sale in 1805.

Creke, W. (fl. 1803–1824)

Of London. Exhibited at the R.A. and S.B.A., 1803–1824. Painted enamel copies of old masters and rustic subjects.

Crellin, H. N. (fl. 1819–1825)

Of London. Was awarded a premium at the Society of Arts, 1819. Exhibited at the R.A., 1825.

Crew, Miss. (fl. 1833)

Of London. Exhibited at the R.A., 1833.

*Crisp, Miss Lucy Mary. (fl. 1908–1911)

Of London. Exhibited at the R.A. and S.M. 1908–1911, from 92 Goldhurst Terrace, South Hampstead.

*Cristall, Miss Anna. (fl. 1888)

Of London. Exhibited at the R.A., 1888.

*Crocket, Douglas G. (fl. 1901–1908)

Of London and Sussex. Exhibited at the R.A., 1901–1908. Painted miniatures and landscapes in water-colour. Probably related to H. E. Crocket who exhibited oil paintings from the same address in 1901 and 1908.

Croizier or Croisier (J?). (fl. 1815–1825)

Of London. Exhibited at the R.A., 1825. Probably the J. Croizier who worked in France during the early part of the 19th century and possibly the artist who painted two miniatures which were exhibited in Paris, 1906 and attributed to Mlle. Anne Croisier, an engraver. J. Croizier was working in Strasbourg in 1815, but was in London by 1825.

Crombie, Benjamin W. 1803–1847
Born in Edinburgh, 19 July 1803; son of a solicitor. Best known for his lithographs and for a series of etchings of Edinburgh characters, but also painted miniatures. Died 1847.

*Crombie, Miss Ethel. (fl. 1900–1910)
Of York. Exhibited at the Society of Miniaturists, 1900–1910.

*Cromer, Dr. Walter (or Abercrombie?). (fl. 1544)
Doctor to Henry VIII whose real name was thought to be Abercrombie. Evidence for the existence of this artist comes from a sale catalogue of Myers & Co., New Bond Street in 1934. Item No. 196 was called 'The Cromer Prayer Book' which contained six almost full page miniatures, including one of himself and his wife, three other pages and nine (evidently smaller), making eighteen pages altogether. The catalogue gave the following information: 'Dr Walter Cromer (a Scot) m. Alice . . . . XVe XXVIII et ano R R Henrich Octani XX. The IIIde daye of August.' Apparently he received £20 from the King, July 1544 and was said to be Doctor to Mary Queen of Scots in 1544. The armorial bearings on the prayer book were similar to those of the Abercrombie family.

*Crompton, Miss M. A. E. (fl. 1906)
Exhibited at the R.A. 1906, from Y.M.C.A. Buildings, Eastbank Street, Southport.

*Crompton, Oswald. (fl. 1908–1911)
Of Sunderland. Exhibited at the R.A. 1908 and 1911, from 13 Amberley Street, Sunderland. Painted miniatures and, in 1911, exhibited 'The Miracle at Lourdes' on enamel which was in the Sculpture section.

*Cross, John. 17th century
A contemporary miniature of Sir Isaac Newton (1642–1727), signed in monogram 'JC', is in the collection of the Marquess of Exeter and, according to family records, was painted by John Cross.

*Cross(e), Peter. *c.* 1645-1724
It is now believed that **Lawrence and Peter Cross** are one and the same artist; and Peter's date of death as 1724 (a date previously given to Lawrence) has been established by Mary Edmond (*Burlington Magazine* CXXXI 1979). Peter Cross was probably of French extraction, the family name being 'de crosse'. His parents, Anthony and Margaret Cross(e) were married early in 1616 and had a family of seven children, of whom Peter was the youngest, born about 1645. The family settled in London at the sign of the 'Golden Cross' in the parish of St. Edmund, Lombard Street. Anthony Crosse died in 1651 or 1652 having become a man of considerable wealth. Peter was then only a child and his father's executors were instructed to apprentice him to a 'fitting trade' when he was old enough. He must have shown an aptitude for art and had some instruction in limning. The suggestion that Samuel Cooper (q.v.) may have taught him has been put forward, and later in life Peter and his family had a studio at the sign of the 'Blue Anchor' in Henrietta Street close to the Coopers' residence.
Peter married Arabella Burman on 23 September 1667 at St. Margaret's Westminster. They too had seven children. Arabella died in 1700 and Peter later married his brother-in-law's widow, Elizabeth Burman on 3 February, 1713. She died the following

year and was buried at St. Paul's Covent Garden on 3 December. Peter was infirm when he made his will in 1721 and eventually moved to the house of his youngest daughter Elizabeth, where he died. He was buried on 3 December 1724. For many years the existence of an artist signing P.C. had been known, and works thus signed had been attributed to either Penelope Cleyn (q.v.) or Paolo Carandini of Modena (q.v.). In 1935 the whole position was clarified when a miniature of Mr. William Gore came into the saleroom and was bought by the V. & A. M. It was signed 'P.C.' in monogram, and in pencil on the reverse, 'Mr. Willm. Gore Picto(r)/P. Cross fecit 1670', followed by a flourish. This discovery was fully discussed by Graham Reynolds in *English Portrait Miniatures*, pp.90-92, and enabled the experts to compare the work with others signed in this way and reassess them. The late Carl Winter records this artist's name as Peter. Examples of his known work date from 1661. One in my collection of Mr. Carter is signed 'P.C.' and dated '1716'. Another in my collection is of a young woman whose face is framed to perfection by a lace wimple tied with a black ribbon under her chin. The hair is well painted, a glossy sheen being visible and tiny downward strokes can be discerned round the edge of the face. Cross is undoubtedly one of the best artists of the latter half of the 17th century and at the beginning of the 18th century. He is known to have spelt his name with or without an e, and the generally accepted spelling is Crosse. His style has more affinity to the method adopted on the Continent rather than that of the British school. He was a collector of miniatures and his cabinet contained works by Hoskins and Cooper (q.v.). Vertue records seeing no less than twelve miniatures by Cooper in the collection which was sold at Crosse's house, 'The Blue Anchor', Henrietta Street, Covent Garden on 5 December 1722. Several were bought by Edward, Lord Harley, including the portrait of Sir Frescheville Holles, and the famous unfinished miniature of Cooper's wife; these are both at Welbeck. The earliest recorded work by Crosse, which is signed and dated, is a chalk drawing of the Duke of Monmouth, at Windsor Castle, and judging from the costume, some of his miniatures probably date from *c.* 1675. According to Vertue he was still active in 1723. He had a distinguished clientele and was responsible for restoring a portrait of Mary Queen of Scots for the Duke of Hamilton. Being told to make it beautiful, and not knowing what the miniature originally looked like, he painted the shape of the lady's face round, a feature which it was subsequently discovered, she did not possess. The so-called portrait of the Queen was frequently copied by B. Lens (q.v.) and others. He died aged over 70 in October 1724. His miniatures are not often dated; his normal signature is LC (usually a cursive monogram with the C attached to the stalk of the L), L.C. in monogram followed by a date (rare), or L.C.f. (for fecit); occasionally his works are signed on the reverse. He used a slightly sombre colouring, the backgrounds often being plain brown or reddish, with the occasional addition of curtaining draped to one side. He shaded with a minute stippling which he applied in varying shades of red, blue and green to model the face. It was a form of *pointilliste* which was practised on a much wider scale in the following century. Examples of his work are in the V. & A.M., the Wallace Collection, the N.P.G. the S.N.P.G. and many private collections, including those of H.M. the Queen, the Duke of Portland, the Duke of Buccleuch, Earl Beauchamp, Earl Spencer and the Duke of Devonshire. Several miniatures by Crosse were exhibited in Edinburgh in 1965.

Crosse, Richard. 1742–1810
Born 24 April 1742 at Knowle, nr. Cullompton,

Devon where his family had lived for many years. Second son of John and Mary Crosse. Born a deaf mute, he took up miniature painting as a hobby. Won a premium at the Society of Arts in 1758 and went to London to study at Shipley's Drawing School, and the Duke of Richmond's Gallery, etc. Exhibited at the Society of Artists, 1760–1791 (becoming a Member, 1763), the Free Society of Artists, 1761–1766 and the R.A., 1770–1796. He was appointed Painter in Enamel to George III. Lived for many years until *c.* 1796 in Henrietta Street. Crosse was an outstanding artist and had a distinguished clientele including the Prince of Wales and the Dukes of Cumberland and Gloucester. Was a prolific worker and painted about one hundred miniatures in 1777. Several self-portraits exist, one of which is at the V. & A. M. and another in the family collection. This contains interesting and superbly painted miniatures of other members of the family, including James Crosse, his brother, who looked after him for many years, and Mrs. Mary Crosse, his mother. He fell in love with his cousin, Miss Sarah Cobley, who refused his offer of marriage and married Mr. Haydon, father of B. R. Haydon, the painter. This left him embittered and B.R. Haydon gives a pathetic account of his meeting with his old love just before her death and while Crosse was living with her brother, Prebendary Cobley, at Wells. He charged from 8 to 30 guineas for a miniature according to size, and is not thought to have painted after April 1798. He was of independent means and had good investments which brought him in additional income. He painted portraits in oil and miniatures in water-colour and enamel. There is no evidence to support the theory that he signed his miniatures R.C. on the front; in fact, owing to lack of a signature, many of his works pass unattributed. His style is easily distinguishable once examined; he invariably used a peculiar greenish-blue tint which can be seen in the shading of the features, and often on the hair and background. In his early works he drew the hair rather in a mass, but later painted it emphasising the individual strands. His miniatures are well modelled and refined. Unfortunately some of his colours are fugitive and many of his miniatures have faded. One of his finest enamels is of one of his brothers (probably Edward); this was exhibited in Edinburgh in 1965 and is in the collection of the Hon. Kenneth Thomson of Canada. Some of his works were engraved. He died in his old home near Cullompton in May? 1810. A number of family miniatures by him were lent to the Edinburgh Exhibition, 1965. Examples of his work are at the V. & A. M. and in many private collections. For further information see *Walpole Society*,

Crosse, Lawrence. See Cross(e), Peter

Crouch, W. (fl. 1774–1776)
Of London. Exhibited at the Free Society of Artists, 1774–1776. Painted portrait miniatures and religious and mythological subjects.

*Crowdy, Miss Constance E. (fl. 1909–1910)
Of Reading and Hope Cove, nr. Kingsbridge, Devon. Exhibited at the Society of Miniaturists, 1909–1910.

Crowe, Stephen. b. 1812
An Irish artist, born at Kilkenny, 1812. Entered the Dublin Society Schools, 1825. After a short apprenticeship set up his own practice as a miniature painter in Grafton Street, moved in 1828 to 16 Suffolk Street. Exhibited at the R.H.A., 1826–1848. He obtained a large practice and painted a considerable number of miniatures. Not all were of a high quality but at best his work was well

modelled and carefully painted. He was undoubtedly related to T. Crowe (q.v.) who exhibited from the same address.

Crowe, Thomas. (fl. *c.* 1834)

Probably Irish. Worked in Dublin from 16 Suffolk Street, the same address as that of S. Crowe (q.v.). May have been the T. Crowe of London who exhibited at the R.A., 1854–1855. Long recorded having seen a miniature signed 'T Crowe / Kilkenny, Feby 1834'. This was probably the same one noted by Schidlof. It was well drawn, but the features were slightly stiff; the shadows on the flesh parts were painted with a yellowish tinge and the curls of the hair were painted in parallel strokes, the effect being rather unnatural.

*Crowhurst, Miss Julia M. (fl. 1899–1910)

Of London. Exhibited at the R.A. and S.M. 1899–1910, from 38 Gower Street.

Croy. See **Le Croy**

*Cruikshank, Miss Catherine Gertrude. (fl. 1868–1889)

Undoubtedly one of the children of F. Cruikshank (q.v.). Exhibited at the R.A., etc. 1868–1889, from various London addresses. Painted portrait miniatures and subjects.

Cruickshank, Frederick. 1800–1868

Born 1800. Was a native of Aberdeen and lived for a time in Manchester with some of his family. Pupil of Andrew Robertson (q.v.). Exhibited at the R.A. and S.B.A., etc., 1822–1860. Worked in Scotland at country houses. Painted miniatures and water-colour portraits. Married Miss Catherine Baly by whom he had six children: Harry, Anne, Gertrude, Grace, Agnes and Dorothea Blanche (living in 1933 in Lordship Lane, Dulwich, aged 84). Cruickshank lived in Portland Place or Great Portland Street, in some style. Mrs. F. Dixon (q.v.) and Margaret Gillies (q.v.) were his pupils. His miniatures were good and show the influence of A. Robertson. He signed F.C. followed by a date. A miniature by him and a water-colour portrait are at the V. & A. M. Died 1868. His daughters, Miss Catherine Gertrude and Miss Grace Cruickshank (q.v.) were both miniaturists.

Cruickshank, Miss Grace. (fl. 1860–1894)

Of London. Daughter of F. Cruickshank (q.v.). Worked in Manchester, 1863–1867. Exhibited at the R.A., 1860–1894.

*Cruickshank, William. (fl. 1866–1886)

Of London. Exhibited at the R.A. and Suffolk Street, 1866–1886. Painted miniatures, landscapes and still-life in oil and water-colour. His work was executed with care and the detail was good.

Cruikshank, Robert Isaac or Isaac Robert. 1789–1856

Of London, born in Duke Street, Bloomsbury, 27 September 1789; son of Isaac Cruikshank and brother of George Cruikshank. Was a midshipman in the East India Company. Later devoted himself to miniature painting, book illustrations and caricatures. Died 13 March 1856. Some of his drawings are at the B.M.

*Crutwell, Wilson H. G. (fl. 1908–1914)

Exhibited at the R.A. 1908–1914, from Oxford Lodge, St. Leonards Road, Surbiton. His sitters included Mrs. A. Stuart.

Cubitt, Thomas. b. *c.* 1757

Of London. Entered the R.A. Schools, 2 July 1773, aged '16 31st March last'. Exhibited at the R.A., 1775 and at the Society of Artists, 1776 and 1778. Painted portraits and miniatures.

Cullen, D. (fl. 1819)

Of London. Exhibited at the R.A. 1819, from 36 Poultry.

*Cullen, Frederick. (fl. 1900–1911)

Exhibited at the R.A. 1900–1911, from Latchmoor, Gerrard's Cross, Slough. Executed miniatures and large oil paintings. His sitters included E. W. Tait, Esq. and J. Fairbank, Esq.

Cullen, John. 1761–1825/30

Born in 1761. Of Dublin; son of E. Cullen, a box-keeper at the Crow Street Theatre. Studied at the Dublin Society Schools where he won a prize for figure drawing in 1775. Was later a pupil of H. D. Hamilton, the pastellist. Exhibited in Dublin, 1800–1817. Executed miniatures and crayons. His sitters included Gerald Macklin, State Surgeon, and Richard, 3rd Viscount Powerscourt; this latter portrait was in the manner of Hamilton. Died between 1825 and 1830.

Cumberland, George. 1763?–1848. See also **Cumberland, George, junior**

Worked in London and Bristol. Probably identical with the artist of that name who entered the R.A. Schools, 30 November 1772, aged '19 yrs 27th Nov last'. Was, for a time, an insurance clerk. Exhibited at the R.A., 1773–1777. Executed miniatures and landscapes, figure subjects, etchings and lithographs, besides writing books on subjects connected with art. Some of his works were engraved. Graves gives three artists of this name, one being George Cumberland junior (q.v.). This leaves some doubt as to identification, but until any further information is available, it is not possible to clarify the matter. In 1782 a G. Cumberland exhibited at the R.A. as an Honorary Member; his exhibits were not miniatures. Died 1848.

*Cumberland, George, junior. See also **Cumberland, George**

Possibly related to, or identical with, George Cumberland (q.v.). A miniature of the 1st Marquess and Marchioness of Exeter, painted against a landscape background, had an engraved label on the reverse: 'Scenes Chiefly Italian / G. Cumberland, Jnr.', when it was sold at Sotheby's in 1966. The 10th Earl of Exeter was created 1st Marquess of Exeter on 4 February 1801.

*Cumming, Miss Constance H. (fl. 1895–1910)

Exhibited at the R.A. 1895–1910, from The Hall, Dedham, nr. Colchester; The Apiary, Bushey, Herts and Freston Hill, Ipswich.

*Cumming, Mrs. Marion G. (fl. 1907–1908)

Of London. Exhibited at the R.A. 1907 and 1908, from 6 Worple Avenue, Wimbledon. Her sitters were Lieut. General Sir Bryan Milman, K.C.B. and Mrs. Cortlandt Angelo.

Cummings, Thomas Seir. 1804–1894

Born at Bath, 26 August 1804; son of Charles and Rebecca Cummings. Shortly after his birth the family moved to Bristol and, whilst Thomas was only a child, to America. Received encouragement in art from Augustus Earl (traveller and painter) when about 14 years old and was placed in a drawing school run by J. R. Smith. In 1821 he went as a pupil to Henry Inman (q.v.) and after three years was taken into partnership. Painted miniatures and

portraits in oil and water-colour. His main work was in miniature. Married an English girl named Jane Cook in 1822 who bore him fourteen children. Inman retired in 1827 and Cummings and some other artists formed an academy which, in January 1826, became the National Academy of Design of which Cummings was treasurer, 1827–1865, vice-president, 1850–1859 and chairman of the committee responsible for erecting the first building of the Academy. The University of New York City appointed him as drawing teacher. Died in Hackensack, New Jersey, 4 September 1894. Examples of his work are in the Metropolitan Museum, New York and the Brooklyn Museum.

*Cummins, E. L. (fl. 1863)

Of Darmstadt. Exhibited at the R.A., 1863.

*Cummins, Miss Emily. See **Barnard, Mrs. William**

*Cundy, Miss Alice Langford (Mrs. R. Speaight). (fl. 1898–1914)

Of London. Exhibited at the R.A., 1898–1914. Married *c.* 1906, in which year is recorded as Mrs. R. Speaight in the index. Her husband was probably the Richard N. Speaight, Esq. whose miniature she exhibited in 1909. Her sitters included the Dowager Marchioness of Ormonde and Lord Wendover.

Cunningham, H. F. (fl. 1846–1853)

Of London. Exhibited at the R.A., 1846–1849. Was working in 1853. Signed HFC.

*Curnock, James. 1812–1870

Born in 1812. Of Bristol. Exhibited at the R.A. and S.B.A., 1847–1862. Painted portraits and genre subjects. Long records having seen a self-portrait in miniature inscribed 'James Curnock artist / painted by himself'. He died in Bristol, 1870.

*Currie, Miss

An oval miniature on ivory of Charles Dickens as a young man was painted by Miss Currie and illustrated from an edition of the *Pickwick Papers* in a book catalogue published by H. Sotheran in 1936.

Curtis, Miss Sarah. 1676–1743

Born 1676. Sarah Curtis; married (as his first wife) Dr. Benjamin Hoadley (1676–1761), later Bishop of Winchester. Was a pupil of Mrs. Mary Beale (q.v.). Painted portraits and, according to J. J. Foster, miniatures, although no evidence for this has so far come to light. A large portrait of her husband by this artist is at the N.P.G.

D

D., A. (fl. 1764)

A small miniature of a man with a gold background signed 'A.D. / 1764' is in the collection of Major R. M. O. de la Hey. It is slightly in the manner of Shelley (q.v.).

D., C. See **Dixon, Charles**

D., E. 17th century

An enamel miniature of a lady was sold as lot 127D at Sotheby's 30 November 1921, and was inscribed on the reverse 'E.D.p^s Coven– / try,

October. yᵉ 5. / ∿ 1693. ≅' It was in the manner of Petitot (q.v.) but not well drawn.

D., E. 18th century

An enamel miniature of a lady signed 'E.D.' is at the V. & A. M., and a copy of a portrait of Mary Tudor is in the collection of the Dowager Viscountess Galway.

D., N. (fl. 1745–1763)

A fairly good miniature of an unknown man c. 1745–1750 in a plum coloured coat, signed 'ND' in monogram was sold at Sotheby's 30 November 1921 and Long saw a good miniature of a man c. 1763, signed in the same way. The Derby Museum have two miniatures signed 'ND' conjoined.

*D., R.B. See **Chair, R. B. de**

D., S. (fl. 1776)

A miniature of a lady holding a painting of part of a skeleton (tall oval), inscribed 'How changed!' and signed 'SD pinx / 1776' is in the City of Liverpool Museum.

D., W. (fl. 1770). See also **Dufour, William**

A good miniature on ivory of an unknown man c. 1770, signed 'WD / P.' (possibly Pinxit) was seen by Long. The above artist may have been identical with W. Dufour (q.v.).

Dackett, T. (fl. 1684)

A portrait of a man drawn in plumbago on vellum (4¾ in. × 3¾ in.) and inscribed 'T. Dackett fe: ad: vivum, 1684.' is at the B.M. Nothing further is known about this artist.

*D'Aeth, Mrs. Eleanor H. (fl. 1896)

Of Eythorne House, nr. Dover. Exhibited at the R.A., 1896. Her sitters included the Rev. Walter Sneyd and Mrs. Sneyd, of Keele, Staffs. and Capt. Hughes D'Aeth, late Royal Scots Fusiliers.

Dagley, Richard. c. 1765–1841

Born c. 1765 (according to Benezit). An orphan educated at Christ's Hospital. Apprenticed to a jeweller named Cousins, whose daughter he married. Exhibited at the R.A., B.I. and S.B.A. 1785–1833. Painted enamel miniatures and allegorical subjects for jewellery, and became a good artist in watercolour, and a medallist. Worked for a time with Henry Bone (q.v.). Exhibited from Doncaster in 1797. Author of *Gems selected from the Antique* in 1804 and other works. Illustrated *Flim-flams*, a book by the elder D'Israeli. Went to live in Doncaster where he taught drawing, but this was evidently unsuccessful and in 1815 he returned to London where he devoted himself to painting domestic subjects, portraits and illustrations. He died in 1841.

*Dagoty (C. O'Connor?). (fl. 1815)

I was shown a good miniature of a man (oval) in a papier-mâché frame, signed and dated '1815'. Schidlof lists two artists of this name, Julia Gautier-Dagoty, working 1832, and Pierre Edouard Gautier-Dagoty (1775–1871). The miniature I saw had the name C. O'Connor inscribed before the Dagoty, which could have been either the sitter or the artist's name.

Dahl, Michael. 1656–1743

Born in Stockholm 1656. This famous Swedish artist and portrait painter who worked in England can hardly be regarded as a miniaturist, but Horace Walpole evidently had a miniature self-portrait by him. Died in London 1743.

*Dakin, Miss Rose M. (fl. 1906–1910)

Of Grappenhall, Cheshire. Exhibited at the Society of Miniaturists 1906–1910.

*Dale, Miss Emily L. (fl. 1902–1903)

Of the Knoll, Peppard, Henley-on-Thames. Exhibited at the R.A., 1902–1903.

*Dale, Miss Margaret H. (fl. 1910)

Exhibited at the R.A. 1910, from The Lowry, Archers Road, Southampton.

Dalton, Edwin. (fl. 1818–1844)

Exhibited at the R.A., 1818–1844. Was awarded a silver palette by the Society of Arts in 1824. Said to have worked in Philadelphia in 1827. Married Miss Magdalena Ross (q.v.) in 1841/2. Long noted that all the examples of this artist's work seemed to have an intense expression. The B.M. have a lithograph portrait of Sir Harry Smith, by and after E. Dalton.

Dalton, Mrs. Edwin. See **Ross, Miss Magdalena**

*Dalton, Miss Maud. (fl. 1906–1913)

Of London. Exhibited at the R.A. 1906–1913, from Eskhaven, East Heath Road, Hampstead and 26 Belsize Lane, Hampstead. Her sitters included Mrs. C. N. Dalton. Possibly identical with the artist of this name who exhibited at the Salon des Artistes Français, 1933–1938.

*Dalziel, Caroline Anna. (Mrs. C. A. Rose). (fl. c. 1890–1914)

Studied at the Edinburgh School of Art c. 1890. Painted landscapes, water-colours, copies of oil paintings, country scenes and miniatures. I have seen family miniatures dating from 1904–c. 1914. They were well painted. She was particularly good at painting children. Signed C.D. and C.R. in monogram. Exhibited in Aberdeen. A miniature of Lilias R. Carmichael was inscribed 'Christmas 1906 /by Caroline A. Dalziel.'

*Damer, The Hon. Mrs. Anne Seymour. c. 1749–1828

Née Anne Conway. Born c. 1749, only child of Field Marshal Henry Seymour Conway, by his wife Lady Caroline Campbell. Exhibited at the R.A. 1785–1818, as an Hon. Member (sculptures only). Was a noted beauty and talented sculptress, also said to have painted miniatures. Was a great favourite of Horace Walpole who left her his executrix and residuary legatee and the use of Strawberry Hill for life, together with a legacy of £2,000 for its upkeep. Married John Damer on 14 June 1767 (he committed suicide in 1776). She has been erroneously described as Dawson Damer, but the additional name of Dawson was only assumed at a later date by her husband's cousins, the second and third sons of the 1st Earl of Portarlington. She was painted by Reynolds and a fine miniature of her by J. Meyer, R.A. (q.v.) in the collection of E. G. Paine of New York, was exhibited in Edinburgh in 1965. She died in London on 28 May and was buried at Sundridge, Kent.

Dampier(e), ? E. (fl. 1784–1786)

Exhibited at the R.A. 1784–1786, as an Hon. Exhibitor. His name is spelt Dampiere in 1785.

Dance, George. (fl. 1821–1829)

Of London. Exhibited at the R.A., 1821–1829. Was probably related to George Dance, R.A. and to Nathaniel Dance, R.A. (q.v.). Was at one time living near W. Dance, jun. (q.v.) at Holloway and at Pavement, Moorfields.

*Dance or **Dance Holland, Nathaniel, R.A.** 1734–1811

Born in London 1734. Well known portrait and subject painter. Later took the additional name of Holland; was created baronet in 1800. Is not usually considered a miniaturist, but a miniature portrait of David Garrick, as Richard III, sketched from the pit, was exhibited at South Kensington in 1865. The same exhibition contained three miniatures ascribed to Dance (no initial given); they represented Mr. Benjamin Lacam, Mrs. Lacam (c. 1780) and Mr. Andrew Lacam (c. 1760); these may possibly have been by W. Dance (q.v.). A miniature portrait of Peter Van Der Faes, oil on copper, 4½ in. was attributed to N. Dance when it was sold at Christie's 15 October 1963. Dance died at Cranborough House, nr. Winchester, 15 October 1811.

Dance, W. (William?). (fl. 1780)

Of London. Possibly the William Dance who entered the R.A. Schools 16 March 1773. Exhibited at the Free Society of Artists 1780. The exhibition at the South Kensington Museum 1865 contained three miniatures ascribed to Dance (no initial given). They may have been by the above artist or by Nathaniel Dance, R.A. (q.v.). A portrait entitled 'The Late Wm. Dance, of Holloway, in his 89th year' by W. Dance junior (q.v.), was exhibited at the R.A. in 1856.

Dance, W., junior. (fl. 1819–1859)

Of London. Exhibited at the R.A., 1819–1859. Probably related to George Dance, R.A. (from whose address he consistently exhibited in the early years) and to Nathaniel Dance (q.v.), W. H. Dance and W. Dance (q.v.), portraits of whom he exhibited.

Danckert, Hugh. b. 1826

Born 1826. Son of a Cork wine merchant. Painted oil portraits and miniatures in Cork. His work was not of outstanding merit.

*Dangerfield, Miss Agnes. (fl. 1894)

Exhibited at the R.A. 1894, a portrait of Sir Benjamin Baker, K.C.M.G. from 40 Central Hill, Upper Norwood.

*Daniel or **Daniell, Miss.** (fl. 1825–1840). See also **Daniel, Miss A.S.W.**

A Miss Daniel exhibited at the R.A. intermittently between 1825–1840 from Oxford Street and the Strand. She had been identified by Graves and Long as being Miss A. S. W. Daniel (q.v.) but the R.A. catalogues do not give any initials for Miss Daniel who only appears to have painted miniatures. A Miss A. S. W. Daniel exhibited at the B.I. in 1852 and 1853, from the Royal College of Surgeons; the exhibits were not miniatures, but subject pictures, and the change in subject and the lapse of time between 1840 and 1852 suggest that there were two artists and that Miss A. S. W. Daniel may not have been a miniaturist. Miss Daniel's exhibits included Kneller Smart, Esq., a self-portrait (exhibited 1824) and one of her sister in 1832. Her name was sometimes spelt Daniell.

Daniel, Miss A. S. W. 19th century. See also **Daniel, Miss**

The above artist exhibited at the B.I. in 1852 and 1853 from the Royal College of Surgeons; the exhibits were subject pictures not miniatures. Graves and Long identified her with Miss Daniel (q.v.) who exhibited at the R.A., 1824–1840 (not 1845 as stated previously), but no initials are given in the R.A. catalogues and as Miss Daniel only painted miniatures, it is possible that there has been some confusion and that there were two different artists.

Daniel, Abraham. d. 1806

Of Bath and Plymouth. Son of Nochaniah Daniel of Bridgwater, Somerset. One of a family of three brothers, of whom Joseph (q.v.) was also a miniaturist. As both brothers worked at Bath, where they appear to have set up in opposition and both claimed to be 'Mr. Daniel' this has led to difficulty in attributing their works. All three sons are said to have received instruction from their mother who was described as an 'ingenious woman'. Abraham worked as an engraver, miniaturist and jeweller. In 1779 Samuel Hart (q.v.) was apprenticed to Daniel to study miniature painting and engraving. The only known signed work by Daniel is that of Rabbi Moses Ephraim of Plymouth, illustrated in the *Jewish Historical Society*, Vol. XVIII. Although Daniel practised chiefly at Plymouth he returned to Bath from time to time and advertised in the *Bath Chronicle*. It is impossible to be certain which of the two brothers was responsible for the various advertisements as no christian names were given, although the addresses differed. Abraham Daniel died in Plymouth on 11 March 1806. By his will which was taken down on his death-bed by Samuel Hart, he left legacies to his mistress and two illegitimate sons and £20 to the charity of the Plymouth Synagogue. His estate was valued at £1,500 and the residue was left to his two sisters Rachel Nathan and Rebecca Almon, both of Plymouth. It is at present impossible to distinguish between the work of Abraham and Joseph Daniel as no signed works by Joseph have so far come to light; for the present, therefore, all miniatures painted with clearly marked characteristics which have come to be associated with 'Daniel of Bath' are assigned to Abraham. The style of painting is easily recognisable once it has been studied, the hair is painted softly, in large masses, without much detail, the eyes are large and usually wide open, the eyelids strongly delineated, and the features shaded so as to emphasise the modelling of the cheeks and nose; the mouth is clearly defined and the general effect of the work is that it has a slightly glossy appearance, due to the use of gum with the pigments. I have seen several miniatures in this style which were of outstanding merit and which would warrant the artist a place among the best eighteenth-century miniaturists. The Ernst Holzscheiter Collection (Meilen), Zurich, contains three miniatures attributed to Abraham Daniel. Two of them are typical of the style usually considered to be that of Abraham, whilst a third, of a man in a red coat, is unlike the other two, the painting being much tighter and more detailed; it may possibly be by Joseph Daniel (q.v.). Works attributed to Daniel are in the V. & A. M., the Holburne Museum, Bath, and the Victoria Art Gallery, Bath, as well as in many private collections. A fine example of an officer, by Abraham or Joseph Daniel was sold at Christie's 21 November 1967 when it realised £300. Miniatures attributed to Daniel were exhibited at the South Kensington Museum 1865 and in Edinburgh 1965. For further information see the *Jewish Historical Society*, Vol. XVIII, by A. Rubens, F.S.A., pp. 105–108.

Daniel, Joseph. *c.* 1760–1803

Born *c.* 1760, son of Nochaniah Daniel of Bridgwater, Somerset and brother of Abraham Daniel (q.v.) and Phineas (a watchmaker, silversmith and engraver). All three brothers received instruction from their mother, who, according to Samuel Hart (q.v.) was 'a very ingenious woman'. Joseph appears to have worked in Bristol, Bath and London and was a jeweller, engraver and miniaturist, besides working in crayons and oil and executing pictures in hair. From 1777 he was in Bristol, living at Clare Street, from which address

he exhibited a miniature of a 'Jew Rabbi' at the Society of Artists in 1783. In 1799 he exhibited at the R.A., from 17 New Bond Street, London, the exhibits being five miniature portraits. He appears to have made Bath his centre as he can be traced through the Rate Books and Directories as well as in numerous advertisements in the *Bath Chronicle*, which on 11 April 1796 announced his recovery from 'a most serious illness'. The wording of the announcement in which he is described as 'our first artist as a Miniature painter' etc. gives some indication of the reputation he had established. Daniel continued to suffer ill health and died in Bath on 29 August 1803, leaving a widow and one son John, who were living at Exeter in 1806. He also left a number of illegitimate children at Bristol, where he had an address up to 1792. His obituary in *Felix Farley's Bristol Journal*, 3 September 1803 read as follows: 'On Monday last died after a painful and lingering illness, which he bore with the utmost fortitude for upwards of 13 months Mr. Joseph Daniel aged 43 years; long an eminent miniature painter of this city and of Bath'. Owing to the fact that no signed miniatures by this artist are at present known, all works with certain characteristics which have come to be associated with 'Daniel of Bath' are attributed to his brother Abraham. The Ernst Holzscheiter Collection (Meilen), Zurich, contains among others a miniature of a man in a red coat which may possibly be by Joseph. The style of painting is much tighter and more detailed than that usually considered to be the work of Abraham. For further information see the *Jewish Historical Society*, Vol. XVIII, 1958, by A. Rubens, F.S.A., pp. 105–108.

*Daniel, Mary (Mrs. C. Bampfyde). (fl. 1900)

Of London. Exhibited at the Society of Miniaturists 1900.

Daniell, Miss S. S. See Gent, Mrs.

*Daniels, George. (fl. 1884–1894)

Exhibited at the R.A. 1884–1894, from 35 Malvern Road, Dalston. Executed drawings in pen and ink, and miniatures.

Daniels, Maria. (fl. 1834)

Of London. Working at 69 Oxford Street in 1834.

Daniels, William. 1813–1880

Born in Liverpool, 9 May 1813. Was the son of a brickmaker and was working at this trade at an early age; received little education. Was apprenticed to a wood-engraver. Took up painting and executed oil portraits, miniatures, small full-length portraits in oil, still-life and genre subjects. Died in Everton, Liverpool, 13 October 1880. Five oil portraits by Daniels are at the V. & A. M. including those of Charles Kean and George Stephenson. They are not of a very high quality.

Danvers. 17th century

The only known example of the above artist's work is a miniature copy on card of Barbara, Duchess of Cleveland, signed on the reverse 'By Danvers'. The quality of the portrait was such as to warrant Danvers a place among the best of the late 17th century miniaturists. The portrait was illustrated by Sidney Hand, in *Signed Miniatures*, 1925. A portrait of a Mr. Danvers, painted 1683 by L. Crosse (q.v.) is in the Ashmolean Museum, Oxford.

*Danvers, H. (fl. 1830)

Schidlof refers to having seen works by this artist of about 1830 and considered them to be well executed.

Darbishire, Sophia. (fl. 1834)

Probably of Bolton. Long refers to a rectangular miniature painted by this artist in January 1834, of Mrs. Ashworth Clegg, née Elizabeth Darbishire, daughter of Samuel Darbishire of Bolton. The miniature was correctly drawn and of some merit.

D'Arce, Miss C. (fl. 1814)

Exhibited at the R.A. 1814, portraits of herself and two sisters.

Darcey. (fl. 1778–1792)

Practised as a miniature painter at Portsmouth 1778. Was in his youth a companion of Thomas Stothard, R.A. Accompanied the embassy—presumably Lord Macartney's of 1792—to China. Appears to have executed many drawings illustrating the Court and customs of that country.

Darell, Carl Fredrik M. b. *c.* 1800

Of Sweden. Born in Stockholm *c.* 1800. Caricaturist, miniature painter and lithographer, known to be working in 1838. In March 1839 was condemned to life imprisonment for forgery, but escaped and came to England. One account says he was hanged for another forgery, and another that he was still living in 1890.

Darling (W). (fl. 1762)

An artist of this name exhibited a drawing in miniature at the Society of Artists 1762. Benezit records this artist's initial as W, and states that he was an engraver.

*Darnell, Miss Dorothy. (fl. 1904–1914)

Of London. Exhibited at the R.A. and S.M. 1904–1914, from 25 Campden House Road, Kensington.

*Darney, Miss Lilian D. (fl. 1891–1894)

Exhibited at the R.A., 1891–1894. Probably a Scottish artist as she exhibited from Park Place, Kinghorn, Fife (1891) and Sherwood, Colinton, Midlothian (1892.)

Dartiguenave, Victor. (fl. 1838–1854)

Exhibited at the Paris Salon 1838–1841 and at the R.A., 1841–1854, whilst living in London. Painted miniatures, figure subjects, pastel portraits, etc. A lithographed portrait of R. B. W. Wilson, after this artist, is at the B.M.

Darvall, Henry. (fl. 1848–1889)

Of London, and, from 1875, Venice. Exhibited at the R.A., B.I. etc., 1848–1889. Painted principally figure subjects and landscapes, but at least one miniature is known—that of Henry Crabb Robinson which is at the N.P.G.

*Daugars, Madame. (fl. 1852–1879)

Exhibited at the R.A. etc. 1852–1879, from Sydenham and 30 St. John's Wood Park. Painted figure subjects and miniatures.

*Davey, Miss Edith Mary. (fl. 1910–1935)

Of London. Exhibited at the R.A., 1910 and 1911 and in Paris 1928–1935. Was a pupil of Gerald E. Moira (q.v.).

*Davidson, Mrs. Bruce (Georgiana). (fl. 1905–1907)

Of Bath. Exhibited at the Society of Miniaturists 1905–1907.

*Davies, Miss Aimée M. (fl. 1907–1914)

Of London. Exhibited at the R.A. 1907–1914, from 51 Tregunter Road, South Kensington and 60 Schubert Road, East Putney. Her sitters included Eileen, daughter of the Rev. C. G. Rivett-Carnac.

*Davies, Arthur. (fl. 1909)

Exhibited at the R.A. 1909, from Sandford Villa, College Road, Cheltenham.

Davies, E. M. See also Davis or Davies, J. M.

This artist is recorded by Foster, Long and Schidlof as having exhibited at the R.A. in 1840, but this must be a mistake as the original R.A. catalogue of that year gives no such artist; it does, however, record a J. M. Davies in this year and in 1820 J. M. Davies in the index (no address) and J. M. Davis (q.v.) in the catalogue entries. It would appear, therefore, that all three of the above artists were identical.

Davies, I. S. or J. S. (fl. c. 1825)

An inferior miniature of a lady c. 1825, with a cursive signature 'I. S. Davies' (in white) is at the V. & A. M. The shading of the flesh is in a green tone.

*Davies, J. M. See Davis, J. M. and Davies, E. M.

*Davies, Miss Minnie M. (fl. 1884–1890)

Of London. Exhibited at the R.A., etc. 1884–1890, including a miniature of her mother.

*Davies, Norman Prescott, R.B.A., A.R.C.A. (fl. 1880–1893)

Of Eversley House, Isleworth. Exhibited at the R.A., N.W.C.S. etc., 1880–1893. Painted domestic and fancy subjects as well as miniatures.

*D'Avigdor, Miss Estelle. (fl. 1890–1896)

Of London. Exhibited at the R.A., 1890–1896. Painted subject pictures and portrait miniatures. Her sitters included Mrs. Ernest Franklin, George A. Crawley, Esq., and Mrs. Arthur Lucas.

Davis, H. (fl. 1832)

Of London. Exhibited at the R.A., 1832. The portraits were of Miss M.A. Jarrett and Mr. J. Jenkins.

Davis, J. (fl. c. 1795–1812)

Of London. Exhibited at the R.A., 1799–1812. A miniature of a man c. 1795 inscribed on card 'Davis no 46 Upper Rathbone Place' was seen by Long in 1931. The exhibit of 1799 was a self-portrait. Presumably related to J. P. Davis (q.v.) from whose address he exhibited in 1812. Painted portraits and figures in oil (large) as well as miniatures.

Davis or Davies, James Morris. (fl. 1810–1839/40). See also **Davies, E. M.**

Of London. Exhibited at the R.A., 1810–1839 or 1840? Undoubtedly identical with E. M. Davies (q.v.) recorded by Long and others as having exhibited at the R.A., in 1840. The catalogues show no such artist, but record a J. M. Davies who was probably identical with J. M. Davis. In 1820 J. M. Davies is recorded in the index and J. M. Davis in the catalogue entries; it would appear, therefore, that all three of the above artists were identical. J. M. Davis exhibited from several London addresses including 33 Gerrard Street; 10 North Crescent, Bedford Square and 31 Upper Gower Street, Bedford Square. A miniature of Lady Onsley was sold at Christie's 5 November 1968 and provided evidence for J. M. Davis's christian names. It was inscribed on the reverse, 'Portrait of / Lady Onsley / Painted by / Jas Morris Davis / at Boulogne Sur Mere / Completed on the / 4th May 1838'. The miniature was painted with strong brush strokes and was slightly reminiscent of the work of W. Wood (q.v.). Davis used pure fresh colours, blue half-tints and deep red-brown shadows. He mixed a large amount of gum with his paints. His sitters

included members of his family, Sir J. S. Yorke, K.C.B., and 'H. M. Louis Philippe, King of the French'. Schidlof records seeing in a private collection a miniature of James Brown, signed on the reverse, 'painted by Jas M. Davis / April 1832'.

Davis, John Pain, R.C.A. 1784–1862

Was born in 1784. Called 'Pope' Davis. Exhibited at the R.A., B.I., N.W.C.S. etc., 1811–1844. Was in Rome 1824 and painted a picture of the 'Talbot family receiving the Benediction of the Pope'. Was awarded a premium by the B.I., in 1825. Was a friend of B. R. Haydon and according to Long, an enemy of the Royal Academy. Published a criticism on the Royal Academy and National Gallery 1858, and *Thoughts on Great Painters*. Painted portraits, subject pictures and miniatures. Died on 28 September 1862. The *D.N.B.* gives his christian names as John Philip but this does not accord with any other authorities. Works by him (not miniatures) are in the V. & A. M. and the N.P.G.

Davis or Davies, John Scarlett. 1804–1845

Born at Leominster 1 September 1804, son of a watchmaker. Entered the R.A. Schools 25 November 1820 aged 16 years. In the Council minutes his name is spelt Davies. Awarded a silver palette by the Society of Arts 1816 and another in 1820 for an engraving. Exhibited at the R.A., B.I. and S.B.A., 1822–1844. Studied at the Louvre 1829. Was at Florence in 1834 and Amsterdam 1841. Painted interiors, street views, miniatures (chiefly of his family), lithographed heads after Rubens and views of Bolton Abbey. He painted at least three self-portraits. Died in London 1845.

Davis, 'Pope'. See Davis, John Pain

Davis, Miss Sara. (fl. 1846–1855)

Of London. Exhibited at the R.A. etc., 1846–1855. Undoubtedly related to R. B. Davis, also an artist. They both exhibited from 9 Bedford Place, Kensington.

*Davison, Miss Minnie Dibden. (Mrs. C. Spooner). (fl. 1893–1903)

Of London. Exhibited at the R.A., 1893–1903. Painted portraits in oil, miniatures and subjects in water-colour. Her address from 1900 was Eyot Cottage, Chiswick. Her sitters included Charles Spooner, Esq., presumably her husband. She exhibited at the R.A. in 1903 under her married name.

*Daviss, Mrs. Jessica. (fl. 1898)

Of 19 Leathwaite Road, Clapham Common. Exhibited at the R.A., 1898.

Davy, Robert. c. 1735–1793

Born at Cullompton, Devonshire c. 1735. Studied art in Rome. Returned to England c. 1760. Exhibited at the Society of Artists 1762–1770 and at the R.A., 1771–1782. Taught drawing at a ladies' school in Queen Square, London, and at the Royal Military Academy at Woolwich. Executed miniatures, crayon portraits etc. and copied pictures. He was knocked down and robbed near his home in John Street, Tottenham Court Road, and died a few days later, 28 September 1793. An engraved portrait of J. Arnold after R. Davy is at the B.M.

Dawe, Elizabeth. 19th century

Said to have been a niece and pupil of William Grimaldi (q.v.) and to have lived at his home. A self-portrait of the artist (water-colour) in a white decolleté dress, and wearing a white kerchief round her head, holding a hurdy-gurdy, was Lot 306 in the Pierpont Morgan sale at Christie's 24 June 1935.

It was stated to have come from the Grimaldi family. This miniature was sold again at Christie's on 20 June 1967 when it realised 110 guineas.

*Day, Alexander, senior. 18th century. See also **Day, Alexander, junior,** and **Day, Thomas**

Not to be confused with Alexander Day junior (q.v.) noted by Long. Recent research by Mr. Francis Watson and Mr. Brinsley Ford has established the fact that there were two artists named Alexander Day, both of whom lived for some years in Rome, and who may have been father and son, although there is so far no proof of this. Alexander Day senior was a pupil of O. Humphry (q.v.); this fact is to be found in Hayward's list of British artists in Rome in 1774. Day was evidently acquainted with Humphry in London, as he witnessed a document for him on 2 February 1773. On 7 January 1774 Day wrote to Humphry from Turin thanking him for the offer of one of his rooms in Rome, which he accepted with pleasure. Evidence that he was a miniaturist is to be found in Lord Herbert's notes (26 September 1779) of British artists working in Rome, 1790, and in *Farington's Diary*, Vol. III, p. 53, February 1st 1805. 'Mr. Day (Miniature), Arco della Regina'. Day was evidently in Rome from 1774–c. 1787, assuming that all the references refer to A. Day senior. Besides being a miniaturist, Day was a picture dealer.

Day, Alexander, junior. 1773–1841. See also **Day, Alexander, senior,** and **Day, Thomas**

Said to have been born in Somerset 1773. Possibly the son of Alexander Day senior (q.v.). It is now known that there were two artists named Alexander Day, both of whom worked in Rome. The elder A. Day was a miniaturist and whilst it is possible that the above artist may have painted miniatures, there is so far no proof of this, and he is known only as a portrait painter, sculptor, medallist and dealer. If he was the son of Day senior, he must have been taken to Italy as a child, as, in *Letters of George IV* edited by A. Aspinall, 1938, he is described as originally a portrait painter having resided 'near 40 years' at Rome. Long drew the erroneous conclusion that the Day referred to was Thomas Day (q.v.) who, so far as is known, never went to Italy. A. Day junior returned to London c. 1816 and exhibited at the Royal Mews Gallery, Charing Cross. He is said to have died in Chelsea in January 1841. He imported works of old masters into England, some of which are in the N.P.G.

Day, C. (fl. 1821)

Of London. Exhibited at the R.A. 1821, an enamel copy of a portrait of Napoleon after Toffanelli, from 43 Devonshire Street, Queen Square. A lithographed portrait of Mrs. Beverley, after C. Day, is in the B.M.

Day, Charles William. (fl. 1815–1854)

Worked in London, Florence and the West Indies. In 1815 he won a prize from the Society of Arts. Exhibited at the R.A., 1821–1854. Was in Florence in 1830. In 1852 published *The Art of Miniature Painting* and *Five Years Residence in the West Indies*. His exhibits included portraits of his wife, and Miss A. C. Flayerman. His work recalls that of A. Robertson (q.v.). He used clear colours but the faces lack expression. Schidlof records a miniature of Francis John Brown, aged 79, painted on ivory and signed 'Day 1832'; it was possibly by this artist.

Day, Miss Frances S. (fl. 1838–1858)

Of London. Exhibited at the R.A. and S.B.A.,

1838–1858. Won a prize at the Society of Arts in 1839. Painted miniatures, some of which were for brooches, lockets and bracelets.

*Day, John or **'MacGilp'.** c. 1732–1807. See also **Day, Thomas**

Recent research by Mr. Francis Watson and Mr. Brinsley Ford has established the fact that the artist called MacGilp Day was not, as has always been supposed, Thomas Day (q.v.), or either of the Alexander Days (q.v.), but an unknown artist called John Day. The matter was ventilated in the *Times Literary Supplement*, 17 November 1966 by Mr. Watson. It appears that Mrs. Mary Day, widow of the above artist, applied for assistance to the R.A. in 1808. This is mentioned by Farington, without the christian name being given. The Royal Academy lists of benefactions show that on 11 April 1807 Mr. John Day received a benefaction of £31.10., which was not repeated in subsequent years, and that Mrs. Mary Day, his widow, was given a charitable payment of 5 guineas in August 1808, which was repeated with variations in value until 1813, when the sum of an extra 8 guineas was given to her to 'procure a situation for her son'. Her name does not appear after 1819. John Day was not a miniaturist so far as is known, his chief work being preparing vehicles for varnishes. He lived in the same house as Gavin Hamilton and was in Rome for about ten years (1756–1765). He died in or about December 1807 aged 75. *Farington's Diary*, 28 June 1808, records the fact that he had been employed by the Duke of Bedford and Sir Henry Mildmay, and that they had supported him during the last three years of his life. Sir Henry Mildmay placed two of his daughters as apprentices and paid 100 guineas for them. All this latter piece of information has, in the past, been erroneously given to Thomas Day (q.v.).

*Day, K. (fl. c. 1820)

I have seen a miniature of a lady c. 1820 signed 'K.Day'; it was painted in a continental style.

*Day, T. F. (fl. 1844)

Of 26 Francis Street, Newington-Butts. Long records seeing a miniature silhouette by the above artist which was signed and dated '1844'.

Day, Thomas. c. 1732?–1807? See also **Day, Alexander, senior, Day, Alexander, junior,** and **Day, John**

Said to have been born in Devonshire c. 1732, and to have had originally some private means. Has been confused with Alexander Day senior (q.v.) and Alexander Day junior (q.v.) as well as with an unknown artist named John Day (q.v.). Graves identified him with the Day who exhibited at the Society of Artists 1768–1783, and the Free Society of Artists 1768–1771. He is said to have been a pupil of O. Humphry (q.v.) and D. Dodd (q.v.). Graves lists a miniature by him exhibited at the Society of Artists 1768 'At Mr Humphrey's, King St, Covent Gdn'. In 1772 he is given as 'Late pupil of Mr Humphry's, at Mr Blake's, Cook's Court, Carey St'; in 1778 he exhibited two crayon portraits from 'T.Day, Brakes Place, nr. Romford, Essex'. From 1768–1771, a Master Day and a Mr. Thomas Day exhibited from 'Mr Dodds, Great Portland St.' All these exhibits have been assigned to Thomas Day, but in view of the confusion which has arisen, it is possible that they were not all by the same artist. Mr. Francis Watson and Mr. Brinsley Ford have, through their research, proved conclusively that Thomas Day was not 'MacGilp Day' as has always been supposed, but that the artist who earned that nickname was one John Day (q.v.) who was not, as far as is known, a miniaturist. It is known that

Alexander Day senior (q.v.) was a miniaturist and a pupil of Humphry, and whilst it is possible that both he and T. Day were Humphry's pupils, it may be that Graves confused the two men and that some of the information given under T. Day's exhibits at the Society of Artists, relates to A. Day; and that, under the Free Society of Artists, to T. Day, and that the latter was a pupil of Dodd's and not of Humphry's. There is no evidence that T. Day ever went to Rome, and his name does not appear on any lists of residents at that period. He exhibited at the R.A. 1773–1788, from various addresses including Little Tichfield Street, Cavendish Square, and Brentwood, Essex, etc. He painted miniatures, views, water-colour landscapes and executed crayon drawings. T. Day signed T.D., T. Day / 1794; often the initials were cursive, sometimes the signature was placed along the edge of the miniature. Some of his work showed Smart's (q.v.) influence, and Long records a pastel which was reminiscent of the work of Russell. Examples of his work are at the V. & A. M. A miniature of an unknown lady signed and dated 'TD 1783' from the collection of Major R. M. O. de la Hey, was exhibited in Edinburgh in 1965. Long notes that there was another portrait painter named T. Day, and that two copies executed by him in 1819 and 1820 were at one time in the Government House, Madras. T. Day's date of death which is given as c. December 1807, may be an error, and should relate to J. Day whose widow applied to the R.A. for financial assistance in 1808. J. Day was the artist who was supported financially for the last three years of his life by the Duke of Bedford and Sir Henry Mildmay, who also assisted his two daughters to obtain apprenticeships. This information was hitherto erroneously given to Thomas Day's family.

Day, Mrs. W. C. (fl. 1847)

Of London. Exhibited at the R.A. 1847, a portrait of Mr. W. C. Day, presumably her husband, from 66 Upper Ebury Street, Pimlico.

Dayes, Edward. 1763–1804

Was born 6 August 1763. Entered the R.A. Schools 6 October 1780 aged '17, 6th last Aug.' Was a pupil of W. Pether (q.v.). Exhibited at the R.A. 1786–1804 and at the Society of Artists, 1790–1791. Noted chiefly for landscapes and figure subjects and was a mezzotint engraver as well as a miniaturist. He taught drawing, Thomas Girtin being one of his pupils. He held the appointment of draughtsman to the Duke of York. His wife, Mrs. Edward Dayes (q.v.) was also a miniaturist. He committed suicide in May 1804. Was the author of *An Excursion Through Derbyshire and Yorkshire*, *Instructions for Drawing and Colouring Landscapes*, and *Professional Sketches of Modern Artists*. Works by him are scarce. He signed E. Dayes or Ed. Dayes (cursive), followed by a date and occasionally an address. Examples of his work are in the V. & A. M. and include a portrait of an unknown lady c. 1785, wearing a large hat and painted in the manner of George Engleheart (q.v.). A miniature by him was loaned to the South Kensington Exhibition 1865.

Dayes, Mrs. Edward. (fl. 1797–1800)

Wife of Edward Dayes (q.v.) who predeceased her. Exhibited at the R.A., 1797–1800.

Deacon, James. d. 1750

A gifted musician and draughtsman, took up miniature painting. In 1746 took the house previously owned by C. F. Zincke (q.v.) in Tavistock Row, Covent Garden. Caught jail-fever whilst attending as a witness at the Old Bailey in 1750; this resulted in his death and that of the judge, the

Lord Mayor and others. Died 21 May 1750. The B.M. has portraits of Samuel Scott and his wife executed in Indian ink by Deacon.

*Dean, J. (fl. 1791)

The name of this artist is recorded in the *Walpole Society*, Vol. XIX, p. 24. He advertised in the *Calcutta Gazette*, 13 October 1791, 'Miniature and crayon painting by J. Dean, who begs leave to inform those gentlemen and ladies of Calcutta that wish to have their likeness in either of those branches, that he is just arrived on the "*Hunter*".' He stated that his terms were moderate and that a likeness could be depended on. Nothing further is known about him. Perhaps identical with the John Dean(e) who exhibited at the R.A. 1789–1791, from Bentinck Street, and at the S.A. 1773–1778, from Salisbury Street, Strand ('a pupil of Mr. Green'). His exhibits included portraits in oil and chalk, figures, and mezzotints. The last date coincides with that of his departure for India.

Dean, T. A. (fl. 1818–1824)

Of London. Exhibited at the R.A., 1818–1824, including a self-portrait in 1818. He painted miniatures and executed engravings.

*Deane, Miss Dorothy. (fl. 1907)

Exhibited at the R.A. 1907, from Newlands, Surbiton. Her sitters included Josephine, daughter of the Rt. Hon. Sir H. M. Durand, G.C.M.G.

*Deane, Miss Emmeline. (fl. 1879–1934)

Exhibited at the R.A., 1879–1903; had addresses at 20 Sion Hill, Bath, Cheney Court, Box, Wilts, and 54a Bedford Gardens. Executed figures, studies and miniatures. A large portrait of Cardinal Newman by this artist is in the N.P.G.

*Deanes, Edward. (fl. 1860–1912)

Of London. Exhibited at the R.A., B.I. etc., 1860–1912, from various London addresses, including 22 St. John's Wood Road. Husband of Mrs. H. Christabella Deanes (q.v.). Painted figure subjects, miniatures and executed drawings. His sitters included Lady Peyton and G. J. Thursby, Esq.

*Deanes, Mrs. H. Christabella. (fl. 1887–1897)

Of London. Exhibited at the R.A., 1887–1897. Painted portraits and miniatures, including one of the Rev. Sir J. L. Hoskins, Bt., in 1895, from the family address 22 St. John's Wood Road. Wife of Edward Deanes (q.v.).

Deare, Thomas. (fl. 1769–1781)

Of Liverpool; lived in Castle Street 1769–1781. Was a silversmith and miniature painter. Probably identical with the Tax Collector and Jeweller also of Castle Street, who was father of the sculptor John Deare (1759–1798).

*de Bathe, Miss Dora. (fl. 1910)

Of London. Exhibited at the R.A. 1910, from 50 Grove End Road, N.W.

*Debillemont-Chardon, Madame Gabrielle. b. 1860

Born in Dijon, 26 September 1860. Daughter of the composer J. J. Debillemont. A noted French miniaturist who exhibited at the Salon from the age of 16, and at the R.A. and S.M., 1897–1910. Her exhibits included a portrait of her grandmother. She ran a well-known school of art in Paris which attracted pupils from France, England, America and Sweden. Published a treatise on miniature painting in 1903. I have not been able to ascertain whether or not this artist worked in England. Examples of her work may be found in the Museum of Dijon, the Luxembourg Museum, Paris, and the

Walker Art Gallery, Liverpool. (Pl. 76: no. 215; Pl. 77: no. 216.)

* De Caselli, Paul Frederick. (1803 – 1817)

Born in Basle, and in 1803 went out to paint in India, becoming a popular artist. In 1805 he married Petronille de Meuron-Motiers at Mysore and in 1812 migrated to Pondicherry where he died on 23 May 1817. A miniature by him is in the collection of Kenneth Guichard Esq. It is said to represent a Dr. Walls, and is signed on the front, 'De Caselli, Madras 1805'. From this example his work is typically Continental, the features are painted with a smoothness reminiscent of enamelling.

*De Castro, Miss Mary B. (fl. 1892–1897)

Exhibited at the R.A. 1892–1897, from Mortlake and 6 William Street, Lowndes Square. Her sitters included Muriel, youngest daughter of Daniel de Castro, Esq., and D. de Castro, Esq., no doubt identical with the father of Muriel and possibly her own father.

*De Chair, R. B. See **Chair, R. B. de**

*De Chair Baker, Mrs. Sophia. See **Baker, Mrs. Sophia de Chair**

*Dechateaubourg. See **Chateaubourg, Le Chevalier de**

*De Cool, Madame Delphine. (fl. 1879–1881)

Of 89 Rue de Rennes, Paris. Exhibited at the R.A., 1879–1881. Painted enamel miniatures from life and from old masters.

De Geer, Ignatio. See **Du Geer, Ignatius**

De Grange. See **Des Granges**

Dehaussy, Jean Baptiste Jules. 1812–1891

Born in Peronne (Somme) 11 July 1812. Was a pupil of his brother Auguste Dehaussy, and of Theophile Fragonard. Exhibited at the Paris Salon 1836–1890. Went to London in 1848 and exhibited at the R.A., B.I. etc., 1848–1851. Returned to Paris 1852; lived in Italy 1869–1871. Died 16 July 1891.

De la Cour or **Delacour, Benjamin.** (fl. 1818–1843)

Of London. Probably the Benjamin Delacour who entered the R.A. Schools 13 March 1818 aged 23. Exhibited at the R.A., 1818–1843. An engraved portrait of Jas. Barnett after B. de la Cour is at the B.M. He died of lockjaw after driving a rusty nail into his hand. This last information was obtained by the V. & A. M. from a relative of the artist.

*Delacour, William. (fl. c. 1753)

A William Delacour, limner, is mentioned by Strickland as advertising in September 1753 that he had moved from Ormonde Quay to College Green, Dublin, near the Parliament House.

*De La Croix or **De Lacroix, Madame.** (fl. 1874–1880)

Of London. Exhibited at the R.A., 1874–1880.

Delahante or **De la Hante.** (fl. 1798–1799)

Of London and Paris. Exhibited at the R.A., 1798–1799. A miniature by Delahante of a grand-daughter of Louis XV is at Windsor Castle; the eyes are rather exaggerated and it is French in style.

De la Monnière Hervé, F. See **Hervé, Francis**

De la Monnière Hervé, Rosa. See **Hervé, Rosa de la Monnière**

*De la Morinière, F. See **Morinière, F. de la**

Delamotte or **De la Motte, George Orleans.** (fl. 1809–1830)

Son of William Delamotte, the landscape painter. Exhibited a landscape at the R.A. 1809, from his father's address, Great Marlow, Bucks. Long records seeing a rectangular miniature of a lady signed 'George Orleans Delamotte fecit Jany 1821'. He noted that it was in the manner of A. E. Chalon (q.v.). Delamotte was working at 7 Sydney Buildings, Bath in 1830.

Delany, Mrs. (Miss Mary Granville). 1700–1788

Née Mary Granville. Born 14 May 1700 at Coulston, Wiltshire. Daughter of Bernard Granville. Married firstly Alexander Pendarves (died 1724) of Rosecrow, nr. Falmouth on 17 February 1717/18, he being then nearly 60 years of age. She married again in June 1743 Dr. Patrick Delany (1685?–1768), an Irish divine. She was a clever amateur artist and painted flowers, oil portraits etc., and a few miniatures, including a miniature copy of a self-portrait of Letitia Bushe (q.v.) in which the hair and part of the costume were worked in hair. One of her great friends was the Duchess of Portland. She knew Swift, Pope, Fanny Burney, etc. Benezit records that she was taught by Bernard Lens III (q.v.). Her portrait was twice painted by Opie. She died 15 April 1788. An enamel miniature of Dr. Delany, by an unknown artist, is in the N.G. Dublin.

*De Lisle, Miss Edith Fortunée Tita. 1866–1911

Born in 1866. Of London. Exhibited at the R.A., 1899–1905. Painted miniatures and fancy subjects. The N.P.G. has a miniature of Dionysius Lardner by the above artist painted in oil on wood. Long attributes this miniature in error to Madame de Lisle (q.v.) who exhibited at the B.I. in 1832. She may have been the artist's mother. Died in 1911.

De Lisle, F. See **Lisle, Madame F. de**

*De Lisle, Miss Georgina L. (fl. 1897–1898)

Exhibited at the R.A. 1897–1898, from Ivydene, Cranbrook Road, Wimbledon. Her exhibits included one of Evelyn De Lisle.

*Delves-Yates, Miss L. See **Yates, Miss L. Delves-**

*De Merbitz, Mlle. Marguerite P. (fl. 1895–1906)

Of 11 Rue de Penthièvre, Paris. Exhibited at the R.A., 1895–1906. Her sitters included Sir Edmund Monson, late H.B.M. Ambassador at Paris and La Comtelle de Montholon.

Dempsey, J. (fl. c. 1830–1850)

Of London. Was principally a silhouettist but also executed miniatures on card. Had a studio at 30 Manchester Street, London, but worked at Manchester, Liverpool, Birmingham, Dublin, Limerick, Edinburgh, Aberdeen, Dundee, Glasgow, Leeds, Bristol, Bath etc. His signatures were 'J. Dempsey, miniature painter', and 'J.D.' the J looking slightly like a T.

Dendy, W. (Walter C.). (fl. 1842–1850)

Of London. Exhibited at the R.A., 1842–1850. Long records this artist as exhibiting at the R.A., 1848–1850. He was presumably identical with the W. Dendy who exhibited landscapes 1842–1843 from 33 Newman Street and 1849–1850 (miniatures) from other London addresses. Graves gives his name as Walter C. Dendy.

Denham, Mrs. d. c. 1782

Of London and Greenwich. Exhibited at the

Society of Artists and Free Society of Artists 1767–1775 and at the R.A., 1771. Her exhibits included miniatures (one of which was in oil), oil portraits, portraits in water-colour and likenesses in human hair. One of her exhibits was 'Mrs Denham's present and future resemblance' and another was of General Paoli. From a letter published in *The Connoisseur*, Vol. LXXXVII, 1931, it would appear that the above artist invented a method whereby her miniatures could be supplied with a variety of costume. It is difficult to be certain what material she used for this purpose, but the following advertisement appeared in the *Public Advertiser*, 11 February 1771. 'To the nobility and Gentry. Advertising is not common or consistent with so noble an art as that of painting; but Mrs. Denham, miniatures paintress, has been strongly persuaded by many ladies to make it public at this juncture that she dresses her miniatures in fancied dress, masks and masquerade dresses, to take off and put on at pleasure. Gentlemen and ladies may have as great a variety of dresses as they choose to one picture. The dresses will wash when dirty ... According to Schidlof she died c. 1782.

Denholm, James. 1772–1818

A Scottish artist born in 1772; taught at Glasgow Drawing and Painting Academy, Argyle Street. Was a member of the Glasgow Philosophical Society from 1803, and President 1811–1814. Author of topographical works on Glasgow etc. Was practising as a miniaturist and landscape painter at M'Ausland's Land, Trongate, Glasgow, in 1801. Died at Glasgow 20 April 1818.

*Denison, Miss Clare. (fl. 1905)

Exhibited at the R.A. 1905, from 4 Headingley Terrace, Leeds.

Denman, J. Flaxman. (John?). b. 1808?

Was awarded a premium by the Society of Arts in 1822. Entered the R.A. Schools 31 March 1825 aged 17. Exhibited at the R.A. 1839, from a London address.

Denning, Stephen Poyntz. 1795–1864. See also **Dimming, S. P.**

Born in 1795. Said to have been a beggar boy. Became a pupil of J. Wright (q.v.). Worked in London and Dulwich. Exhibited at the R.A., B.I., S.B.A., 1814–1852. Was appointed Curator of the Dulwich Gallery in 1821. Painted portraits in water-colour and executed miniatures and pencil drawings. Was a good artist and a perfect draughtsman. I have in my collection a half-length drawing of George Vincent by him which shows great character and is well drawn. Several portraits in water-colour are at the B.M. and the V. & A. M. has a superb group of children of the family of E. Bicknell, signed 'S. P. Denning, pinxit 1841'. Many of his miniatures are on ivory and have a slight affinity to the work of A. E. Chalon (q.v.). Often signed his miniatures S. P. Denning, scratched along the edge. Two miniatures by him were loaned to the South Kensington Exhibition 1865. The above artist may have been identical with the S. P. Dimming (q.v.) mentioned by Schidlof.

*Dennis, Miss Ada. (fl. 1896)

Of Chester. Exhibited at the R.A. 1896, from 47 Nicholas Street, Chester. Probably identical with the artist who exhibited at Suffolk Street 1891–1893.

Dennis, G. (fl. c. 1800–1816)

Long records having seen a miniature of c. 1800, on the back of which was a printed label 'G.

Dennis, Miniature Painter, No 9, George St, Dock' (i.e. Plymouth Dock). I have seen a miniature of a man in Naval uniform on the reverse 'G. Dennis, artist, Ex on Sept 1816.' It was well painted, and had grey, brown and blue shading on the face.

Dennis, J. (fl. 1823–1831)

Was living at 265 Fore Street, Exeter in 1823 and was known to be working at Exeter in 1831.

Denny, Stephen. (fl. 1814)

A miniature of an unknown Scotsman signed in full and dated '1814', was in the E. Grosvenor Paine Collection.

*Dent, Rupert Arthur. (fl. 1884–1909)

Exhibited at the R.A. 1884–1909, from Wolverhampton and Berkeley Villas, Pittville Gates, Cheltenham. His exhibit in 1909 was of 'the late William Dent, Esq.'

Denton, W. (fl. 1792–1795)

Of London. Exhibited at the R.A., 1792–1795.

De Quelen. See **Quelen, De**

Derby, Alfred Thomas. 1821–1873

Born in London 21 January 1821; the son of W. Derby (q.v.). Said to have studied at the R.A. Schools. Was awarded a premium by the Society of Arts, 1836. Exhibited at the R.A., B.I. etc., 1839–1872. Painted miniatures, portraits in oil and water-colour, subject pictures and copies after Landseer, etc. Died after a long illness 19 April 1873. This artist lent two miniatures to the exhibition at South Kensington Museum 1865—Mrs. Graham, wife of General Graham, afterwards Lord Lynedoch (after Gainsborough) and one of the late Mrs. W. Derby, on paper. His sisters Miss Caroline Derby and Miss Emma Derby (q.v.) were also miniaturists.

Derby, Miss Caroline. See **Backhoffner, Mrs.**

Derby, Miss Emma Maria (Mrs. Chatfield). (fl. 1835–1838)

Daughter of William Derby (q.v.) and sister of Alfred Thomas Derby (q.v.) who all exhibited from 12 Osnaburgh Street, Portland Place. Won several prizes for miniatures at the Society of Arts 1835–1838. Married a Mr. Chatfield, possibly Edward Chatfield (1802–1839), a pupil of B. R. Haydon. Schidlof states that she won prizes at the Society of Artists but this is an error.

Derby, William. 1786–1847

Born in Birmingham 10 January 1786. Was a pupil of Joseph Barber in Birmingham, but by 1808 had settled in London. Exhibited at the R.A., B.I., O.W.C.S., N.W.C.S. etc., 1811–1842. Painted miniatures, portraits in oil and water-colour, some of which were small water-colour copies of portraits, subject pictures, etc. Some of his works were engraved. Recovered from an attack of paralysis in 1838. Died in Osnaburgh Street, Regent's Park on 1 January 1847, leaving a widow and eight children, of whom Alfred, Caroline and Emma Maria (q.v.) were miniaturists. Examples of his work are at the B.M. and V. & A. M. Six miniatures by him were lent to the South Kensington Museum Exhibition in 1865. Five of these were copies after earlier portraits executed c. 1840 and 1850 on card and of Lucy Smith Stanley, Lady Strange; Edward, 12th Earl of Derby; Lady Elizabeth Hamilton; Elizabeth Gunning, Duchess of Hamilton; and Edward, 13th Earl of Derby, K.G. with Lady Charlotte Stanley, after a painting by Romney. The sixth was a port-

rait in water-colour of John Flaxman (1755–1826) drawn from life. A miniature of Adam, 1st Viscount Duncan, after Hoppner, is in the S.N.P.G. Edinburgh.

*Derry, Mrs. Anne. (fl. 1903)

Of London. Exhibited at the R.A. 1903, a portrait of the Marchioness of Headfort.

*Derry, Miss Constance M. (fl. 1899)

Exhibited at the R.A. 1899, from Woodlands, Tooting Common.

Des Granges, David. 1611/13–c. 1675

Baptised in London 24 May 1611 or 20 January 1613, as a Huguenot; son of Samson Des Granges of Guernsey and his wife Marie Bouvier. Subsequently became a Roman Catholic and was associated for a time with French Dominicans. Began his career as an engraver and in 1628 engraved the painting of 'St. George and the Dragon' after Raphael. Was given employment by Charles I and Charles II, and accompanied the latter to Scotland in 1651; was appointed His Majesty's limner in Scotland in that year. Said to have been a friend of Inigo Jones, whose miniature he painted. Two portraits are known to exist, one is in the collection of the Duke of Portland and the other in the collection of the Duke of Devonshire. His earliest known dated miniature is that said to represent Catherine Manners, Duchess of Buckingham, at Windsor Castle; this portrait is signed 'D D G' in a triangle, and dated '1639'. A signed miniature of an unknown lady, by Des Granges, is in the V. & A. M.; it depicts the sitter in a costume of c. 1630. In 1640 he executed what is considered to be one of his finest works—the miniature copy of Titian's *Marquis del Guasto with his Mistress*, the original of which is in the Louvre. Two other miniatures after this painting exist, one by Peter Oliver dated '1629' is at Windsor Castle, and the other by Richard Gibson dated '1640' is in the collection of the Duke of Portland. At least one large painting by this artist is known to exist; it is 'The Saltonstall Family', and is in the collection of Sir Kenneth Clark. The colouring of the whole painting is predominantly red, the children are well drawn, but the father is placed in rather an angular pose. In 1671 due to increasing years, ill health and failing sight, he was unable to support himself or his children and was obliged to rely on charity. He sent a petition to Charles II for £72 which was still owing to him for thirteen portraits (not all necessarily miniatures). The Treasury Papers 1557–1696, item 25, record this petition which was put to the Lords of the Treasury, 11 November 1671. A list of works was appended to it which included—'One picture of Your Majesty *in small*, delivered to the French Marquess who came to Your Majesty at St. Johnston's in 1651 . . .' This was probably the miniature signed and dated 'DDG 1651' which was exhibited in Edinburgh in 1965 from the collection of T. Cottrell-Dormer, Esq. In the Treasury Papers his name is spelt 'de Grange'. He died c. 1675. Although his work varied, much of it was of very high quality. He painted a large number of miniatures after the works of other artists, such as Hoskins (q.v.), Titian, etc. He usually signed with his initials DDG arranged in a triangle. R.W. Goulding gives a list of some of Des Granges' works in *Welbeck Abbey Miniatures, Walpole Society*, Vol. IV. Examples of his works are in the V. & A. M., Ham House, the N.P.G., and many private collections including those of H.M. the Queen, the Duke of Portland, the Duke of Buccleuch, the Earl of Haddington, Earl Beauchamp, T. Cottrell-Dormer, Esq. Examples of his works were loaned to the exhibition at the South

Kensington Museum 1865, including a portrait of Catherine of Braganza, Queen of Charles II, dressed as a pilgrim, holding a staff and wearing a wide hat; it is signed 'D.D.G.' The Edinburgh Exhibition 1965 also contained miniatures by him.

*Deshayes. (fl. c. 1820)

This artist is referred to by Schidlof who records seeing a miniature c. 1820, of a little boy in blue, signed 'Deshayes'. The miniature was painted in English style, with a lot of gum mixed with the colours.

*De Solomé, Antoine. (fl. 1848–1868)

Of London. Exhibited at the R.A., 1848–1868. Executed crayon portraits, some of which may have been miniatures. In 1861 he exhibited a portrait of Lady Georgiana Hamilton. A miniature by him, signed and dated, in crayons was loaned to the South Kensington Exhibition 1865.

*Desprez, Mrs. Lilian. (fl. 1898–1901)

Of Streatham. Exhibited at the R.A. and S.M., 1898–1901.

*De St. Aubin. (fl. 1795). See also **St. Aubin, J. de** and **St. Aubin, Augustin de**

The above artist (no initial given) exhibited at the R.A. 1795, from 47 Berwick Street, London. He was possibly identical with J. de St. Aubin (q.v.) or Augustin de St. Aubin (q.v.).

Deuent, J. (fl. 1808)

Of London. Exhibited at the R.A. 1808, from 4 Queen's Court, Queen Street.

*Devine, Miss Catherine. (fl. 1892–1894)

Of Chelsea. Exhibited at the R.A. 1892–1894, from 54 Glebe Studios, Glebe Place. Painted miniatures and water-colours.

*Devis, A. W.

A portrait in miniature painted on glass was sold at Christie's 22 May 1936. The artist may have been Arthur William Devis (1763–1822).

Devoto, James. (fl. c. 1730)

Two portraits in pencil on vellum c. 1730 and both signed in full by the above artist, are in the B.M.

De Wilde, Samuel. 1748/51–1832

Born in Holland 1 July 1748? or 1751. Brought to England as an infant. Entered the R.A. schools 9 November 1779 when his age was noted as '28. 1779', pointing to his year of birth being 1751. Exhibited at the R.A., Society of Artists, B.I., S.B.A. etc., 1776–1832. Painted in oil, water-colour and chalk and executed miniatures, portraits and figure subjects. Many of his works were of actors or scenes from plays. He died in London 19 January 1832 and was buried in the ground of Whitefield's Tabernacle, Tottenham Court Road. Some of his works were engraved and may be seen at the B.M. The V. & A. M. has chalk and water-colour portraits by De Wilde.

*Dewime, (P?). (fl. 1766–1787?)

No. 142 in the exhibition at the South Kensington Museum, 1865, was a miniature of the Marquis de Belcourt, said to have been signed 'Dewime P. 1787'. Nothing is known about this artist and he may not have worked in Britain. Schidlof mentions a miniature of a young man in a mauve costume, on ivory, signed 'Dewime 1766'.

*Dick, Miss Catherine M. (fl. 1908–1910)

Of London. Exhibited at the Society of Miniaturists 1908–1910.

Dickinson. (fl. 1809–1811)

Of Bath. Was living c. 1809–1811 at St. James's Parade, Bath.

Dickson. (fl. 1772–1774)

Of London. Exhibited at the Society of Artists, 1772–1774. These exhibits included a self-portrait.

Dickson, J. (fl. 1842)

Of London. Exhibited at the R.A. 1842, from 3 Bentinck Terrace, Regent's Park.

Dickson, Miss Nancy. See **Ashburnham, Mrs. Denny**

Diemar. (fl. 1766–1769). See also **Diemar, Benjamin**

Of London. Exhibited at the Society of Artists 1766–1769. Probably identical with Benjamin Diemar (q.v.).

Diemar, Benjamin. 1741–1790? See also **Diemar**

Born in Berlin in 1741. Of London and Cambridge, 1783. Exhibited at the R.A., 1776–1783. Pupil of his brother Nathaniel at Paris 1762, later at Rome; came to England and was probably identical with the Diemar (q.v.) referred to by Long as exhibiting at the Society of Artists 1766–1769. A Mrs. Diemar was a print seller in the Strand until 1799. According to Benezit he painted historical subjects and landscapes and died in Birmingham 1790.

Dietz, Miss Amelia Mary. (fl.1776–1798)

Of London. Awarded a premium by the Society of Arts in 1779. Exhibited at the R.A., 1782–1798. Exhibited 1788–1798 from 41 Broad Street, Soho. May have been related to Miss Diana Dietz (q.v.). A painting of flowers in water-colour, exhibited at the Society of Artists 1776, is catalogued under Miss Diana Dietz (q.v.) from 'Mr. Dietz, Jeweller, Angel Court, Windmill St'. but Graves (S.A.) suggests that it may have been by Miss Amelia Mary Dietz.

Dietz, Miss Diana (Mrs. Diana Hill and later **Mrs. Harriott).** d. 1844

Of London and India. Won an award at the Society of Arts 1775. Exhibited as Miss Diana Dietz at the Society of Artists 1775 and possibly in 1776. This last exhibit, of flowers, may have been by Miss A. M. Dietz (q.v.). Her address in 1775 was Angel Court, Great Windmill Street. Exhibited at the R.A. 1777–1780, under her maiden name, and in 1785 as Mrs. Hill (Hon. Exhib.). Married sometime before 1785 and in the same year was granted permission to go to India as a portrait painter. Lived in Calcutta; said to have been a pupil of J. Meyer (q.v.). Painted miniatures, flower pieces (?) and a bracelet in human hair. Details of her time in India are given in the *Walpole Society*, Vol. XIX, pp. 39, 40. Ozias Humphry (q.v.) described her as a 'Pretty widow with two children' on 15 November 1786, and said that she was 'the daughter-in-law of Mrs. Hill of Newman Street, and a relative and friend of Miss Lenquets'. He was so alarmed at her popularity that he felt that he would 'rather have all the male painters in England landed in Bengal than this single woman'. She obtained many patrons in India and was evidently in great demand. On 15 November 1788 she married as her second husband, Lieutenant Thomas Harriott, of the 1st Native Infantry, by whom she had two sons, William Henry (died 4 November 1839), who painted in water-colour and married Sibella Mary Hunter, by whom he had a daughter Sibella

Christina (also an artist), and Thomas George (died 18 July 1857) of the Royal Staffs Corps. Mrs. Hill may have been the sister of Miss Sophie Dietz, who went to Bengal whilst she was there and who had as one of her securities Mrs. Elizabeth Hill of Newman Street (presumably Mrs. Hill's mother-in-law) who had acted in the same capacity for Mrs. Hill. Thomas Harriott retired from the Service in 1806 and returned to England, presumably accompanied by his wife and children, and lived at West Hall, Mortlake, where he died 19 April 1817, aged 64. His wife died at Twickenham on 10 February 1844. Her signature varied, sometimes it is D H followed by a date, and at others, Hill, or Mrs D Hill. Works executed before her marriage are either unsigned, or signed DD, initials she shared with Daniel Dodd (q.v.). The quality of her work varies; some of her flesh tints are rather pink. Examples of her work are in the V. & A. M. including a miniature of her second husband, Lieut. (later Major) Thomas Harriott, signed 'DH / 1791'. A miniature of an unknown girl from the same collection is of outstanding merit. The dark complexion of an evidently half-caste girl is dramatically set off by her large white mob cap. Miniatures by her were exhibited in Edinburgh 1965.

*Diez, J. (fl. 1842)

Of London. Exhibited at the R.A. 1842, from 13 Cornhill, portraits, presumably miniatures, of Queen Victoria, Prince Albert, the King and Queen of the Belgians, Princess Mary, and Princess Sophia. Undoubtedly related to S. Diez (q.v.) who exhibited from the same address in 1842.

Diez, S. (fl. 1842). See also **Diez, Samuel Friedrich**

Of London. Presumably a relative of J. Diez; both exhibited from the same address (13 Cornhill) at the R.A., 1842; the portraits exhibited by S. Diez were of H.R.H. Princess Sophia, and the Duke of Wellington. Possibly identical with Samuel Friedrich Dietz (q.v.) who is known to have been in London in 1842.

*Diez or **Dietz, Samuel Friedrich.** 1803–1873. See also **Diez, S.**

Born in Neuhausen near Sonneberg 19 December 1803. Probably identical with the S. Diez (q.v.) who exhibited at the R.A. 1842, and became painter to the Court of Meiningen in 1832. Had a distinguished clientele and painted portraits of many persons in Germany, Russia (1840), France, England (1842) and Belgium (1851). Executed many portraits in pencil, heightened with water-colour. Published 300 of them in steel engraving. Painted historical and genre subjects. Examples of his work are at the National Gallery, Berlin. Died in Meiningen on 11 March 1873.

Digby, Simon, Bishop of Elphin. d. 1720

Son of Essex Digby of Dromore, Ireland; educated at Trinity College, Dublin. Became Rector of Dunshaughlin and Chaplain to the Earl of Ossory in 1668; Bishop of Limerick in 1678 and Bishop of Elphin in 1691. Digby was an accomplished miniaturist who painted many of the leading men of the day including Bishop Tillotson, Lord Capel and Henry, Lord Sidney. Digby died at Lacken, County Roscommon on 7 April 1720 and was buried on 20th 'in the church of Tosara (Mount Talbot) in the said county, together with his Lady who died a few days after him'. A miniature said to be of the Earl of Arran by Digby was exhibited in Edinburgh 1965 from the collection of Major R. M. O. de la Hey. A family group representing the artist and his family is reproduced in Strickland. A miniature of John Hough, Bishop of Worcester, by Digby, is in

the N.P.G. A miniature of Bishop Tillotson is in the N.G. Dublin

Dighton, Richard. 1795–1880

Born in London in 1795, son and pupil of Robert Dighton (q.v.). Drew and etched portraits and caricatures and executed miniatures. Died in London 13 April 1880. Long records seeing a large oval miniature executed on paper or card of c. 1827–1830. The sitter was an unknown man, and the miniature was signed 'Richd Dighton'. Examples of his work are at the B.M. and N.P.G., the latter Gallery having his self-portrait.

Dighton, Robert. c. 1752–1814

Born in c. 1752. Entered the R.A. Schools 24 February 1772. Exhibited at the R.A. and the Free Society of Artists, 1769–1799. Executed miniatures, portraits in black lead, and etchings. Noted for his caricatures, mostly satirical, of lawyers, officers and actors. According to a note in the *British Gazette* 31 May 1801, he had been established 'for 12 years past at 12 Charing Cross'. Was related to Denis Dighton (military painter to H.R.H. the Prince Regent), who exhibited at the B.I. from the same address, 4 Spring Gardens, in 1811 and at which address Robert Dighton died in 1814. His son Richard Dighton (q.v.) followed his father's profession. Examples of his work are in the N.P.G. and the B.M. has numerous engraved portraits after him.

Dillon, Charles G. (fl. 1810–1830). See also **Ditton, C. G.**

Of Plymouth. I have seen a good miniature of a young boy by this artist inscribed on the reverse on a printed card, 'Joseph Sambell / when 4 years / of age / 1810'; the printing was as follows: 'Dillon Miniature Painter & Engraver / 52 St Aubyn Street, Dock. / Profile likenesses in va Styles'. The miniature was well painted and strongly delineated round the nose and mouth, and the veins were painted on the eyeballs. The eyelashes were very distinct and the eyes were large and appealing. The general appearance of the work was in the manner of Edridge (q.v.). In 1830 Dillon was working at 6 Union Street, Plymouth. The B.M. has engraved portraits after Dillon.

Dillon, P. (fl. 1802–1815)

An Irish artist; was working in Dublin in the early part of the nineteenth century. He exhibited at Parliament House in 1802, Allen's in Dame Street in 1804 and at the H.S.A., in 1815. He executed miniatures, engravings and etchings. Long recorded that he may have worked at St. Helier, Jersey.

*Dimming, S. P. See also **Denning, S. P.**

The above artist is recorded by Schidlof as working in England in the early part of the 19th century. He mentions a miniature sold in Brussels in 1934 as being signed 'S. P. Dimming Pinxit 1816'. The signature may have been mis-read and the artist identical with S. P. Denning (q.v.).

*Dismore, J. S. (fl. 1893)

Of Gravesend. Exhibited at the N.W.C.S., 1893. Possibly identical with Jessica Stewart Dismorr recorded by Benezit.

*Ditton, C. G. See also **Dillon, C. G.**

A miniature said to have been signed by this artist was sold at Sotheby's 1926. It may have been by C. G. Dillon (q.v.).

Dixon. (fl. 1771)

Of London. Exhibited a portrait of a lady in miniature at the Society of Artists 1771, from 'Mr. Murray's, perfumer, Brewer St.' Was presumably related to the Miss Dixon who exhibited from the same address at the Society of Artists in the same year, the latter's exhibit being a portrait of a boy.

Dixon, Miss Annie. 1817–1901

Born at Horncastle 12 March 1817. Went to London c. 1840; worked at Horncastle, Hull and St. Lawrence, Isle of Wight. Exhibited at the R.A., 1844–1893. Was patronised by the Royal Family and had an aristocratic clientele. Went to paint at country houses. Said to have been a pupil of Sir William Ross (q.v.). Painted all the Strathmore family in 1862. A story is told of her that she once painted a ring on the finger of the Dowager Marchioness of Cambridge, then a child, to keep her quiet whilst painting. Painted over 1,000 miniatures, including ones of Queen Alexandra as Princess of Wales, and Louisa, Marchioness of Waterford. Long records that she was described by a man who had known her as 'small, dowdy and dressed in black'. She died in February 1901. She used a lot of gum with her paints and signed A.D. or A. Dixon, often followed by a date. I have, in my collection, a miniature of Lady Lucy Home, wife of the 11th Earl, by the above artist signed on the front 'A.D. 1872', the signature being scratched on the paint, and on the reverse 'The Countess of Home / Painted by / A. Dixon. 1872'. This miniature is probably the one exhibited at the R.A. in 1873, when the name is given as Lady Horne. Examples of her work are at the V. & A. M. and in many private collections including those of H.M. the Queen and the Duke of Northumberland. Several miniatures by her were loaned to the South Kensington Exhibition 1865.

*Dixon, C(harles?). (fl. 1748–1798)

The identity of the artist who signed C.D. was established as C. Dixon, by Charles Coleman Sellers, the American scholar, in 1955, when he wrote an article in *Proceedings of the American Philosophical Society*, Vol. 99, No. 6, December 1955. The article contains a reproduction of a miniature of Benjamin Franklin, painted by C. Dixon, c. 1757, when Franklin was living at 7 Craven Street, nr. Charing Cross, London. Writing to Mrs. Franklin soon after his arrival, Franklin says, 'I wrote you by Man of War lately sailing for New York & sent you my Picture in Miniature'. Two months later he wrote to his wife again and sent another portrait of himself, noting in a postscript, 'P.S. When you write to Boston, give my love to sister Jenny (Mrs. Jane Mecom) as I have not often time to write to her. If you please, you may send her the enclosed little picture.' The whereabouts of Mrs. Franklin's miniature is unknown, but the replica which was given to Mrs. Mecom is the one illustrated by Mr. Coleman Sellars. It is signed 'C.D.' on the front and inscribed 'Franklin' on the reverse. The miniature descended in the family until in 1943 it was gifted to the Museum of Fine Arts, Boston. The payment by Franklin for the original miniature is recorded in his accounts—'Oct. 31, 1757; paid Mr. Dixon for B.F.'s picture £6.6.0.' Basil Long described several works by C.D. and suggested that he may have worked in the provinces, or in Scotland. Dixon's self-portrait is in the V. & A. M.; it is signed in gold 'C.D. / Se ipse / P / 1748'. The miniature is well painted and expressive and is slightly reminiscent of the work of Lens (q.v.). Also in the V. & A. M. is a miniature of an unknown Divine signed in black 'C.D.' (cursive). The artist had used a lot of

white in the hair. A miniature of an officer signed and dated, 'C.D. 1798' was noted by Mr. A. J. B. Kiddell in 1961. Miniatures of Janet, Countess of Hyndford (1727–1807) and of John, 3rd Earl of Hyndford (1701–1787) both signed C.D. are in the Carmichael House Collection. An attractive miniature traditionally supposed to be Frederick, Prince of Wales, signed 'C.D.' is in the collection of H.M. the Queen; the identification of the sitter is doubtful and the portrait may represent either George III when young, or one of his brothers.

Dixon, Mrs. F. (Miss Grace Cowell). (fl. 1851–1875)

Née Grace Charlotte Cowell; married c. 1851/2. Exhibited from London, Brighton (1854–1855), York (1856) and Manchester (1860) and again from York in 1872. Exhibited at the R.A. and S.B.A., 1851–1875. Was a pupil of F. Cruickshank (q.v.) and F. Rochard (q.v.). Executed chalk portraits and miniatures.

Dixon, Frederick Henry. (fl. 1831–1842)

Of London. Exhibited at the R.A., 1831–1842.

Dixon, John. d. 1721

Said to have been the son and grandson of artists who painted oil portraits in Lely's studio. Executed pastel portraits from life and from pictures by other artists. Is supposed to have painted some miniatures. Died in Thwaite, Norfolk; was buried there 14 March 1721. The *D.N.B.* confuses him with N. Dixon (q.v.). The miniature of the 'Wise Men making their Offering' at Burghley House, which is mentioned by Long and Williamson, is by N. Dixon (q.v.) not J. Dixon.

Dixon, John. (fl. 1819–1822)

Was living at 7 Northumberland Place, Bath, in 1819–1822.

*Dixon, Miss May. (fl. 1904)

Of Harlow, Essex. Exhibited at the R.A. 1904. Her sitters included Lily, daughter of John Dixon, Esq.

Dixon, Nicholas. (fl. c. 1660–1708)

Occasionally erroneously called Nathaniel Dixon. Was working from c. 1660. Practised in London and lived for some time in the Parish of St. Martin-in-the-Fields. Was an important miniaturist who had a distinguished clientele; was for some years 'Limner' to Charles II, in succession to Samuel Cooper (q.v.) and Keeper of the King's Picture Closet. Had an official annuity of £200, which was not paid with any regularity. From documents found in Florence it is known that he had a lottery in 1684/5 of 'excellent miniature paintings'. In 1698 he started a lottery called the 'Hopeful Adventure'; the total sum of £40,000 was involved which was to be divided into prizes ranging from £3,000 to £20, together with a collection of pictures and limnings which were to be seen at his house. The venture was not a success and by 1700 he was obliged to mortgage 70 miniatures, probably those mentioned in the lottery, and 30 of which are now in the collection of the Duke of Portland at Welbeck. A deed of sale is preserved from which it appears that on 23 November 1700 'Nicholas Dixon of the Parish of St. Martin's-in-the-Fields in the County of Middlesex, Gentleman, mortgaged his limnings, 70 in number'. These were transferred to John Holles, Duke of Newcastle for £430 on 14 February 1707/8. Dixon evidently never recovered from his financial embarrassment, and according to Vertue he died in the King's Bench Walk, where he was avoiding prosecution. His usual signature was N D in mono-

gram, the right hand stroke of the N forming the left-hand stroke of the D. Little is known about his life, but from his early work, c. 1660, one can surmise that he may have been taught by Hoskins (q.v.). He used a reddish brown flesh colour and painted the eyes of his sitters half closed and rather elongated with a shadow of uniform thickness under the top lid. One of his most outstanding works is a large cabinet miniature of Anne, Countess of Exeter and her brother William, later 1st Duke of Devonshire, and a black page. It is rectangular $6\frac{3}{4} \times 7\frac{1}{4}$ in. and signed and dated 'ND' (monogram) 1668. It is owned by the Marquess of Exeter and was one of seven miniatures by this artist exhibited in Edinburgh in 1965. Examples of his work are in the V. & A. M. and many large private collections such as those of H.M. the Queen, the Duke of Portland, The Marquess of Exeter, Earl Beauchamp and others. Two miniatures by him were loaned to the South Kensington Exhibition 1865, when his christian name was given erroneously as Nathaniel. Lists of works attributed to Dixon are given by R. W. Goulding in *Welbeck Abbey Miniatures*, and by J. J. Foster in *Samuel Cooper*. (Col.

Dixon, William. (fl. 1791–1818)

Possibly the son of Thomas Dixon, a hosier of Cork Hill, Dublin, and a brother of John, Samuel and Thomas Dixon, artists and engravers. Was working in Dublin 1791–1798 and was probably the William Dixon who was living at 43 Cuffe Street in 1815 and 29 Dawson Street in 1818 (not 39 Dawson Street in 1816 as stated by Long), where he had a haberdashery business combined with that of a portrait and miniature painter.

Dixon, William. b. 1774?

Of London. Possibly the William Dixon who entered the R.A. Schools 11 December 1789 aged 15 years. Exhibited at the R.A., 1796–1824. Painted miniatures, shipping subjects and portraits. Exhibited a portrait miniature of his mother in 1803.

*Dobson, William. 1610–1646

Born in London in 1610. Apprenticed to Robert Peake (q.v.). Noticed by Van Dyck who introduced him to the King. After Van Dyck's death, Dobson was said to be serjeant painter to Charles I. Dobson painted portraits and historical pictures. An oil miniature on copper of Sir Charles Cottrell, painted c. 1645 is in the collection of T. Cottrell-Dormer, Esq., and was exhibited in Edinburgh in 1965. A miniature of John, Lord Digby (oil) attributed to the above artist was loaned to the South Kensington Exhibition 1865.

Docke. (fl. 1763–1767)

Of London. Exhibited at the Society of Artists 1763–1767, from addresses in Covent Garden.

*Dockerhill, Miss Margaret. (fl. 1900–1904)

Of 5 Meadow Studios, Bushey, Herts. Exhibited at the R.A., 1900–1904. Executed miniatures and portraits in water-colour. Her sitters included Miss Emily G. Dockerill and Mrs. de Montmorency.

Dodd, D. P. (fl. 1768–1778)

Of London. Possibly a son or brother of Daniel Dodd (q.v.). Exhibited at the Free Society of Artists 1768–1778. Painted heads, figure subjects, landscapes and miniatures; worked in oil and crayons. Is described in the R.A. catalogue alternately as 'Master Dodd', 'D. P. Dodd of 3 Old Bailey' and 'Mr Dodd, Jun.'.

Dodd, Daniel. (fl. 1752–1780)

Of London. Exhibited at the Society of Artists and the Free Society of Artists 1761–1780. Was a member of the Society of Artists, 1780. Painted flower pieces, portraits in oil and crayon and pictures of historic interest besides painting miniatures. His works included 'The Royal Procession to St. Paul's', etc., and illustrations for Harrison's Novelists. Traditionally said to have taught John Smart (q.v.) and whilst this is not impossible there is a likelihood that some confusion may have arisen and it may have been one of the other artists named John Smart. Certainly J. Smart Jun. (q.v.) could not have been taught by him in 1770, the year in which a J. Smart Jun. is given as a 'pupil of Mr Dodd' at the Free Society of Artists, as Smart was not born until 1776. He is said to have taught T. Day (q.v.). The *Daily Advertiser*, 28 November 1752, contains the information that Dodd had etched the portrait of Mr. Leveridge, in the manner of Rembrandt, and gave his address as 'The Rising Sun', Lemon Street, Goodman's Fields. As Dodd shared the same initials as Diana Dietz (q.v.) and both appeared to have signed D.D. their works may sometimes be confused. Examples of his work are in the V. & A. M. and the B.M. has engravings after his work. The above artist may have been related to D. P. Dodd (q.v.).

Dodd, Miss M. (fl. 1830–1831)
Of Bristol. Exhibited at the R.A., 1830–1831. Painted oil portraits and miniatures, from 10 Sion Place, Easton Road, Bristol.

Dodd, P. G. (fl. 1825–1836)
Of London. Exhibited at the R.A. and S.B.A. etc., 1825–1836. According to Schidlof he was a London goldsmith and jeweller as well as a miniaturist. From 1825–1836 his address was 25 Leadenhall Street. Benezit records that he also painted portraits.

***Dolben, Mrs. Frances (Miss).** (fl. 1806)
Self-styled Mrs. but really Miss. Amateur artist, friend of Mary Anne Knight (q.v.) who painted her portrait in February 1806. She painted Lady Harriet Williams Wynne (at Belvoir Castle).

Donaldson, John, F.S.A. 1737–1801
Born in Edinburgh in 1737, son of a glover. The family were evidently poor and whilst very young he supported himself by copying engravings and executing miniatures in Indian ink. Was awarded premiums by the Edinburgh Society of Arts 1757 and 1758. Went to London and exhibited at the Free Society of Artists 1761–1774, becoming a member of the Society of Artists in 1764. Was awarded premiums by the Society of Arts 1764 and 1768. Exhibited at the R.A., 1775 and 1791. Painted miniatures on ivory and enamel, painted on Worcester porcelain, drew in black lead, executed some portraits and historical subjects as well as etchings. A man of unsettled habits, he took up chemistry and patented a method of preserving vegetables and meat. Published a volume of poems, 1786 and an essay on the *Elements of Beauty*, 1780. He was a dreamer and idealist and most unpractical. Would have been destitute but for the kindness of his friends. Died 11 October 1801 and was buried in Islington Churchyard. The N.G. of Scotland have a miniature of a lady by Donaldson, signed in a neat hand on the front with a cursive 'J.D.' and dated '1787'. This miniature was loaned to the exhibition in Edinburgh 1965. The face is shaded with a bluish-grey, especially round the eyes, and a deeper bluish-grey is apparent on the hair which is drawn in lines made partly by the use of a scraper and partly with opaque white. The flesh colour is rather pink and white and the red on the lips has retained its brilliance. Superficially it is slightly like the work of J. Downman (q.v.).

Donaldson, T. (fl. 1795)
Of London. Exhibited at the R.A. 1795 (not a miniature), from 13 Tavistock Row, Covent Garden. The exhibit was a portrait. Long suggests that he may have been identical with J. Donaldson (q.v.) who was living at 4 Southampton Street, Covent Garden in 1791 or Thomas Donaldson of Edinburgh, who was awarded premiums by the Edinburgh Society of Arts in 1756 (when under 16 years of age) and again in 1757.

Dongworth, Winifred Cecile. 1893–1975
Exhibited at the R.A., and in the provinces and worked for some time in and around Cheltenham. Was a good artist who used clear fresh colours. Many of her works are signed in full and dated. She painted miniatures and small watercolour portraits on paper.

Donkin, Miss. (fl. 1821)
Of Bath. Long saw a rather poor quality miniature which bore an inscription on the reverse stating that it had been painted by 'Miss Donkin, of Bath, Feb. 1821'. Schidlof also mentions a miniature signed on the reverse 'By Miss Donkin at / Bath. Feby 1821'. Her work was not of outstanding merit; some of it was in the manner of Mrs. Mee (q.v.).

***Donne, Walter J.** (fl. 1885–1902)
Of London and Scarborough. Exhibited at the R.A., 1885–1902. Painted landscapes in watercolour, subject pictures in oil, and at least one miniature, which he exhibited at the R.A., 1897.

***Doray, E.** (fl. 1799–1865?)
A miniature by him was loaned to the South Kensington Exhibition 1865. This was signed and dated '1799'. Benezit records an artist of this name who worked in London c. 1865.

Dorman. (fl. 1768)
Of London. Exhibited a miniature at the Free Society of Artists 1768, the exhibit being 'Diana and her nymphs'.

Dotchen, John. (fl. 1772–1774)
Of London. Exhibited at the Society of Artists 1772–1774. Executed architectural drawings and at least one miniature in Indian ink.

Douglas, Miss Archibald Ramsay. 1807–1886
Of Edinburgh. Born 23 April 1807, daughter of W. Douglas (q.v.). Exhibited at the R.A. 1834–1841. Lived at 13 Hart Street, Edinburgh, where she died 25 December 1886.

***Douglas, Mrs. Hope.** (fl. 1910–1914)
Of Cornwall and Lutterworth. Exhibited at the R.A., 1910–1914.

***Douglas, Mrs. J. (Anna/Anne).** (fl. 1901–1911)
Of Chilworth, Surrey, and London. Exhibited at the R.A. and S.M., 1901–1911. Painted miniatures and landscapes in water-colour.

***Douglas, Miss Mabel M.** (fl. 1904–1912)
Of St. Ives, Cornwall. Exhibited at the R.A., 1904–1912. Her sitters included Kitty, daughter of Sir Edward Hain.

Douglas, William. 1780–1832
Born in Fife 14 April 1780; descended from the Douglas family of Glenbervie. Brought up in Edinburgh and was a pupil of Robert Scott, the

engraver. Exhibited at Edinburgh 1808, 1809, and at the R.A. 1818–1826. Worked in Edinburgh. Executed miniatures (including some of animals) and engravings. Held a curious appointment as miniature painter in Scotland to H.R.H. Prince Leopold of Saxe-Coburg. Died at Hart Street, Edinburgh, 30 January 1832, leaving a widow, two sons and a daughter, Miss A. R. Douglas (q.v.). A miniature of Mary, Dowager Lady Molesworth, painted on ivory, 1809, by Douglas, was lent to the South Kensington Exhibition 1865. Schidlof mentions two miniatures sold in Amsterdam in 1924, signed on the reverse 'W. Douglas Edinburgh Pinxit 1816'. The B.M. has an engraved portrait of the Rev. H. Gray after W. Douglas.

***Douin.** (fl. c. 1840)
A miniature of c. 1840, signed 'Douin', was seen by the S.N.P.G.

***Douton, Miss Isabel F.** (fl. 1904–1914)
Of London. Exhibited at the R.A. 1904–1914, from 35 Blomfontein Road, Uxbridge Road and 24 South Audley Street. Executed miniatures and portraits in water-colour. In 1910 her exhibit was of 'Isabel, daughter of R. F. Douton Esq.', possibly a self-portrait.

***Dove, Miss Greta.** (fl. 1908)
Exhibited at the R.A. 1908, from Pinner Hill, Pinner, Middlesex.

***Doveton, Anne.** (fl. 1826)
A miniature by this artist, signed and dated '1826' was recorded by Mr. A. J. B. Kiddell.

Dowling, J. (fl. 1839–1872)
Of London. Exhibited at the R.A., 1839–1872.

Dowling, Miss Mary. (fl. 1845–1846)
Of London. Exhibited at the R.A. 1845–1846, from 38 Foley Place, from which address J. Dowling (q.v.) also exhibited.

Downman, John, A.R.A. 1750–1824
Born in 1750, son of Francis Downman, an attorney and his wife Charlotte, née Goodsend. Was educated at Ruabon, N. Wales. Said to have been sent to Chester and then to Liverpool to learn drawing. Went to London and entered the R.A. schools 17 March 1769. Studied under B. West (q.v.). Exhibited at the Free Society of Artists 1768 and at the R.A., 1770–1819. Worked in London, Plymouth, Exeter, Chester, Cambridge, etc. Is best known for his delightful small portraits in water-colour and miniatures, although these latter are scarce. He also painted oil portraits and historical pictures; some of his works were executed in chalk. Downman's miniatures are painted in the same manner as his water-colour portraits; they are very attractive but as they are not usually signed often pass unrecognised. He died in Wrexham 24 December 1824. A miniature of an unknown lady, by him, was sold at Sotheby's on 21 November 1960 and realised £60. Examples of his work are in the V. & A. M. and B.M., the Wallace Collection and private collections including that of Major R. M. O. de la Hey. Miniatures by him said to be signed and dated were exhibited at South Kensington 1865 and one from the de la Hey collection in Edinburgh 1965.

Doyle, John. 1797–1868
An Irish artist born in Dublin 1797, the son of a business man. Entered the Dublin Society Schools at an early age and was awarded a medal there in 1805. Was a pupil of Gaspare Gabrielli and of J. Comerford (q.v.). Exhibited at Dublin 1814–1821

and at the R.A., 1825–1835. Painted portraits, but is best known for his paintings of horses. Went to London *c.* 1821 where he painted portraits and miniatures. Executed drawings for engravings etc., and was well known as a political caricaturist. He married Marianne, daughter of James Conan of Dublin, by whom he had four sons who inherited his artistic talent and are noted by Strickland—James William Edmund, Richard, Henry Edward and Charles. Sir Arthur Conan Doyle, the writer, was his grandson. He died 2 January 1868. Doyle signed his works '**HB**', in order to conceal his identity. The monogram was formed of two ID's, one above the other. Many of his drawings are at the B.M.

Doyle, W. (fl. 1826). See also **Doyle, William M. S.**
Of 229 High Holborn, London. Exhibited an enamel miniature of 'the late John Crace Esq.,' after Hoppner at the R.A., in 1826. Identified by Schidlof as William M. S. Doyle of Boston (1769–1828) who painted miniatures on ivory and enamel.

*Doyle, William M. S. 1769–1828. See also **Doyle, W.**
Born in Boston in 1769, the son of a British Army officer who was stationed there. Worked in America and said by Schidlof to have worked in England. Painted miniatures on ivory and on enamel. Schidlof identifies him with the W. Doyle (q.v.) who exhibited an enamel portrait at the R.A. in 1826. A miniature signed 'Doyle 1814' is in the Metropolitan Museum, New York. Died in Boston, May 1828.

*Drake, Miss Elizabeth. (fl. 1902–1906)
Of 55 Roebuck Road, Rochester, and Hampstead. Exhibited at the R.A., 1902–1906. Her exhibit in 1906 was not a miniature but was of Henry VII Chapel, Westminster Abbey.

Drake, Nathan. (fl. 1751–1783)
Son of a Vicar Choral of York Minster, and father of Nathan Drake (born 1766), the essayist and physician. Was a member of the Society of Artists in 1771 and exhibited there in the same year from London, and in 1773–1776 from York. In 1783 he exhibited at the Free Society of Artists from London. Painted portraits, landscapes and miniatures and published a view of Boston, Lincs. in 1751. Some of his works were engraved and may be seen at the B.M.

*Drew, Herbert J. (fl. 1900–1911)
Of London. Exhibited at the R.A. and S.M. 1900–1911, from various London addresses. Painted miniatures and subjects in water-colour.

*Drew, Miss Mary. (fl. 1880–1901)
Exhibited at the R.A. etc. 1880–1901, from Cravenhurst, Seaford, Sussex. Painted miniatures, genre subjects and portraits.

Droege, Friedrich. b. 1801
Born in Hanover in 1801. Exhibited at the Academy of Berlin 1828–1846. Was miniature painter to the King of Prussia. Came to London where he settled and exhibited at the R.A., 1851 and 1854. Was a very good artist who painted with fresh colours and used such a fine stroke that it is difficult to see the brushwork, even with a magnifying glass; the effect is of an enamel. Schidlof records seeing a miniature of a Prussian Prince signed 'Dröge pinx. Berlini 1833'.

*Drucker, Miss Amy J. (fl. 1899–1914)
Of London. Exhibited at the R.A. 1899–1914, from various addresses in London. Painted minia-

tures and studies in oils. Amongst her sitters was H.R.H. Prince Henry (born 1900). Studied in Paris for a time.

Drummond, Miss E. Ellen. (fl. 1836–1860)
Of London. Probably a daughter of Samuel Drummond (q.v.) from whose address she exhibited in 1836. Exhibited at the R.A., 1836–1860. Graves, Long and Schidlof all give her name as F. Ellen, but the R.A. catalogues give her initials as E. Ellen. She was undoubtedly the sister of the Misses Rose Emma, Jane, Eliza and Rose Myra Drummond (q.v.) and painted portraits of Rose Myra which she exhibited at the R.A., in 1854 and 1859.

Drummond, Miss Eliza. See Effingham, Countess of

Drummond, Miss Eliza Anne. (fl. 1820–1843)
Of London. Probably a daughter of Samuel Drummond (q.v.) from whose address she exhibited in 1820 and 1821, and sister of the Misses Jane, Rose Emma, Rose Myra and E. Ellen Drummond (q.v.). Exhibited at the R.A., N.W.C.S., B.I. etc., 1820–1843. Won a premium at the Society of Arts in 1822 and 1823. A pastel of Charles John Kean is in the N.P.G.

Drummond, Miss F. Ellen. See Drummond, Miss E. Ellen

Drummond, Miss Jane. (fl. 1819–1833)
Probably a daughter of Samuel Drummond (q.v.) and sister of the Misses E.A., R.E., R.M., and E.E. Drummond (q.v.). Exhibited at the R.A., 1819–1833. The Society of Arts awarded her a silver medal for a fixed crayon portrait in 1821 and the silver Isis medal in 1826, for a miniature portrait. Worked from addresses in Rathbone Place, etc., London, and was in Calcutta in 1833. She was an artist of only average ability. Many of her sitters were from the theatrical profession.

*Drummond, Mrs. John. (fl. *c.* 1790)
A miniature painted in the manner of C. Shirreff (q.v.) and inscribed on the reverse 'Mrs John Drummond / New Street / Spring Gdns.' *c.* 1790, was seen by Long.

Drummond, Miss Rosabella. (fl. 1898–1905)
Of 18 Rawlinson Road, Oxford, and London. Exhibited at the R.A., 1898–1905. Painted fancy subjects in oil and portrait miniatures.

Drummond, Miss Rose Emma. (fl. 1815–1837)
Of London. Probably a daughter of Samuel Drummond (q.v.) from whose address she exhibited 1815–1819 and sister of the Misses E. Ellen (q.v.), Jane, Eliza Anne, and Rose Myra Drummond (q.v.). Exhibited at the R.A., N.W.C.S. etc., 1815–1837. In 1823 was awarded a silver medal by the Society of Arts for an historical composition (not in miniature). Painted numerous actors and actresses, including Garrick (in 1825).

Drummond, Miss Rose Myra. (fl. 1833–1849)
Of London, probably a daughter of Samuel Drummond (q.v.) from whose address she exhibited 1833–1837, and sister of the Misses Jane, Eliza Anne, E. Ellen and Rose Emma Drummond (q.v.). Exhibited at the R.A., and B.I., 1833–1849. Painted miniatures and theatrical portraits as well as at least one portrait sketch. She normally exhibited under the christian name of Myra.

Drummond, Samuel, A.R.A. 1765–1844
Born in London 25 December 1765, son of a partisan of Prince Charles Edward (the Young

Pretender). Drummond ran away to sea but later devoted himself to art. Exhibited at the R.A., B.I. 1791–1844, from London addresses apart from 1798 when he was at Maidstone. Was elected A.R.A. in 1808. Executed portraits in oil and crayon, historical subjects and miniatures; was also a lithographer. A miniature portrait of Elizabeth Fry is at the N.P.G., who also have oil portraits by him. Engravings after some of his works are at the B.M. Died in London 6 August 1844.

*Drummond, W. (fl. 1831–1852)
Of London. Exhibited at the R.A., B.I. etc., 1831–1843. Executed figure subjects and in 1843 a portrait of Mrs. Dodd, at the R.A., in the drawing and miniature section, from 62 Welbeck Street.

*Drury, Mr. (fl. 1744)
A Mr. Drury, miniature painter, was working in London in 1744, and was at Mr. Applin's, Haberdasher, the 'White Ball' in Jermyn Street, according to the *Daily Advertiser* of that year.

Drury, Franklin. d. *c.* 1771
An Irish artist; son of Thomas and Rebecca Drury of Dublin. Worked in Dublin but little is known about his life or works. The *Poetical Works* of the late Rev. Samuel Shepherd, published in 1790, contain verses on Drury's inability to paint the likeness of Miss Doro Burgh.

> Drury, thy pencil skill'd to trace
> With Rival art less finished forms;
> In vain attempts with equal grace
> To imitate Dorinda's charms.

He died at Powerscourt, Co. Dublin in either December 1770 or January 1771, in which parish his brother the Rev. John Drury was Vicar. Strickland gives the month he died as February 1771, but Long states that his death was announced in Hoey's *Dublin Mercury*, 3–5 January, 1771.

Drury, Richard. b. *c.* 1791
Was born *c.* 1791. Entered the R.A. Schools 31 October 1821 aged 30 years. Was a drawing master and miniaturist in Manchester in 1828 when his address was 27 George Street, Oxford Street, and in 1845, 63 George Street, York Street.

*Dubisson, Walter. (fl. 1878–1879)
Of London. Exhibited at the R.A. 1878 and 1879, from 10 Harrington Square, Hampstead Road. His sitters were Miss Neilson and Miss Darwood.

Dubisson, William C. (fl. 1821–1834)
Of London. Exhibited at the R.A. 1821, from 113 Strand. In 1834 his address was 85 Regent's Quadrant, London. His sitters included Signor Roveni and Mrs. Bellchambers.

Du Blaisel, Miss H. (fl. 1812–1813)
Of London. Exhibited at the R.A., 1812–1813.

Dubois, Frédéric. (fl. 1780–1819)
Of Paris. Exhibited at the Paris Salon de la Correspondance 1780, at the Salons du Louvre 1795–1804, and at the R.A., 1818–1819. Worked in Russia 1804–1818 and became a member of the St. Petersburg Academy. Some of his works were engraved. A number of his works are listed by Schidlof. He was a good draughtsman who used fresh colours and painted with a small cross stroke. His most usual backgrounds are painted in rather dark gouache, but towards the end of his career he painted them in the manner of the English school and executed the backgrounds in parallel hatching. A miniature of a lady signed 'Dubois' in pencil is in the Louvre. He also signed his works F.D. and F. Dubois.

Dubois or **Du Bois, Simon.** 1632–1708

Born in Antwerp July 1632, son of Hendrick Dubois, Jun., a Flemish painter. Was at Rotterdam for many years and was a pupil of Berghen and Wouwermans. Went to Italy; returned to Haarlem. He and his brother Eduard went to London *c.* 1680. Painted oil miniatures and portraits. He died in London May 1708. Works by this artist are scarce. A pair of oil miniatures of William III and Mary II, oval $1 \times \frac{7}{8}$ in. are in the collection of the Duke of Portland. They were purchased by Edward Harley, 2nd Earl of Oxford 13 October 1726 from Bernard Lens (q.v.). Another oil miniature by him signed and dated '1682' is at the Fitzwilliam Museum, Cambridge.

*Dubourjal, Savinien-Edmé. 1795–1865. See also **Dubourjal, T. S.**

Of Paris. Born 12 February 1795. Entered the École des Beaux-Arts August 1819, pupil of Girodet. May have been identical with the T. S. Dubourjal (q.v.) who exhibited at the R.A., 1838. Painted miniatures and portraits in water-colour. Visited America 1844. Was working in Boston in 1846 and in New York 1847–1848 where he exhibited at the National Academy of Design exhibitions. He was a friend of the artist G. P. A. Healy. Returned to France in 1848 after which time, due to failing health, he was obliged to rely on the support of Healy. His year of death has been given as 1853 but in Healy's biography by De Mare it is stated that he died in Paris 8 December 1865.

Dubourjal, T. S. See also **Dubourjal, S.-E.**

Of London. Exhibited at the R.A., 1838. Possibly identical with S.-E. Dubourjal (q.v.). The exhibit was a study of a head, and the initials given in the catalogue are T. J. Dubourjal and in the index, T. S. Dubourjal.

*Duchesne, Jean-Baptiste-Joseph. 1770–1856

Born at Gisors 20 December 1770. Son of the sculptor J. B. Duchesne. Painted miniatures on ivory and enamel. Worked in Paris where he died 23 December 1856. He may not have worked in Britain but Schidlof records that he painted a series of enamels after Sir W. C. Ross (q.v.) for Queen Victoria. Examples of his work are rare.

*Dudley, Mrs. Ruth M. (fl. 1903–1909)

Of Devonport, S. Devon, Essex and London. Exhibited at the Society of Miniaturists, 1903–1909. Was the wife of Captain Dudley, Royal Artillery.

Dudman, R. (fl. 1797–1801)

Of London. Exhibited at the R.A. 1797, from 41 Strand. Advertised in the *Morning Chronicle*, 17 April 1797 – 'Late of Strand, now of 17 Salisbury Street. Late pupil of Sir Joshua Reynolds.'

Dudman, W. (fl. 1801)

Of London. A miniature by the above artist of an officer, was signed in full and dated '1801'. It was in the E. Grosvenor Paine Collection.

Dufour, William. (fl. 1763–1770). See also **D., W.**

Of London. Exhibited at the Free Society of Artists 1765 and at the R.A., 1770. A good miniature of a man, signed 'W: Dufour / 1763' is at the V. & A. M. Angelini, a sculptor, exhibiting in 1775 gave his address as 'At Mr. Dufour's, Berwick Street'.

Du Geer or **De Geer, Ignatius.** d. 1751

Was working at Dublin as a miniaturist in the early part of the eighteenth century. Acted at the Theatre Royal, Dublin. His death was recorded in *Faulkner's Journal* – 'Last Saturday' (i.e. 13 January

1751) 'died Mr Du Geer, a very eminent Painter in Miniature, well known for his simplicity of manners and very inoffensive behaviour'. A miniature of a man signed 'Igna de Geer pinxit' was sold in Geneva 26–27 April 1920 and a miniature of a man in armour *c.* 1720, inscribed in gold along the edge 'Ignatio de Geer. Pinxit, after Sir Godfrey Kneller' was sold at Sotheby's 21 March 1935. These miniatures were presumably by the above artist whose name is given as 'de Geer' by Benezit and Schidlof. A miniature of an unknown man, painted after Kneller and signed 'Ignatio de Geer' is in the collection of the Earl of Haddington.

*Du Guernier, Alexandre, or **Guernier, Alexandre du.** 1550?–1620?

A French Protestant. Painted miniatures; fled to England during the religious wars. Returned to Paris where he was a successful miniaturist and the father of a family of miniaturists. Schidlof gives the above artist the additional christian name of Louis (the elder), but the biographical details of the Du Guernier family appear to be obscure and Louis Du Guernier (q.v.) is described as 'the elder' by Benezit.

*Du Guernier, Louis. 1614–1659

Born in Paris 14 April 1614; son of Alexandre (Louis) Du Guernier (q.v.) and elder brother of Pierre Du Guernier. Said to have been a pupil of J. Toutin. Was a very successful miniaturist and one of the founder members of the French Royal Academy of Painting. Married in 1648, Marguerite Ducloux, daughter of a goldsmith. Painted most of his miniatures on vellum, but also executed some on enamel. In 1648 he painted a prayer book for Duke Henri du Guise, in which the ladies of the Court were depicted as saints. It is not certain that he worked in England but he certainly painted English sitters. He died in Paris 16 January 1659. His works are excellent and the draughtsmanship good; the hair is well painted, a characteristic being the large amount of white used in the shading; the flesh tints are pinkish brown, the eyes sometimes appear to be half closed, with a strong light on the lower lid. The general appearance of his work is reminiscent of that of Des Granges (q.v.) or Gibson (q.v.). Some of his works are signed L D G. with a date, or LDG in monogram, others are signed Du Guernier / pinxit, followed by a date. It is possible that the miniatures painted by Louis and Pierre Du Guernier are sometimes confused where there is no initial. Examples of his work are in the V. & A. M.; the Rijksmuseum, Amsterdam; the collection of H.M. the Queen of the Netherlands; and the Edward B. Green collection, Cleveland, Ohio. An enamel miniature of Louise Henriette, Princess of Orange Nassau, in the collection of H.M. the Queen of the Netherlands, is signed on the reverse 'Le 28 dec: Du Guernier fecit 1643'. A miniature of Lord Cavendish, signed 'Du Guernier Pinxit. 1638' is in the collection of the Marquess of Exeter.

*Du Guernier, Pierre. 1624–1674. See **Du Guernier, Louis**

Dukes, Emanuel

Lived in 1830 at Church Street, Basingstoke. Painted miniatures, portraits, landscapes and historical subjects.

*Dumas, Miss Alice Dick. b. 1878

Born in Paris 4 January 1878. Exhibited at the Salon des Artistes Français 1903, and at the R.A. 1907 and 1908, from 2 Rue Gaillard, Paris.

*Dunbar, Miss Hilda C. (fl. 1907–1914)

Of Sydenham, London. Exhibited at the R.A., 1907–1914. Her sitters included her mother and Miss Helen Dunbar.

Dunlap, William. 1766–1839

Born 17 or 18 February in Perth, Amboy, New Jersey. Came to England in 1784 and studied in London under B. West (q.v.). Had executed a crayon portrait from life of George Washington as early as 1783. Returned to America in 1787; painted a number of portraits as well as miniatures and became an art historian. According to Wehle he was the first important native American dramatist. Was for a time an itinerant miniaturist, but after 1813 painted chiefly oil portraits and large religious paintings. Was appointed Librarian and keeper of the American Academy in 1817 and helped to found the National Academy, holding office as Treasurer and Vice President. His last years were spent in poverty and ill-health, during which time he continued to write histories of the American theatre, etc. He died in New York on 28 September 1839. The Metropolitan Museum, New York, owns portraits of Mr. and Mrs. John Connant by him.

Dunn, Andrew. (fl. 1800–1820)

Studied at the Dublin Society Schools and was a pupil of F. West. Worked in Waterford and Kilkenny before going to London. Returned to Ireland in 1808 where he apparently hoped to set up a practice, and held an exhibition at the Royal Dublin Society House. He was evidently unsuccessful in establishing a practice in Ireland and went back to London in the same year. Exhibited at the R.A., 1809–1818 and at the Society of Artists, Dublin 1809–1819 from various London addresses. Painted portraits and miniatures and had a distinguished clientele. Was living at 16 Norton Street, Fitzroy Square in 1820 after which date nothing is known about him. His sitters included the Archbishop of Dublin, the Archbishop of Cashel, the Earl of Arran and in 1811 he exhibited a portrait of Princess Charlotte of Wales. A miniature in my collection of Sir Joseph Banks is signed and dated 'A. Dunn / 1809' on the front in cursive writing; the face is expressively drawn and the miniature well painted. This portrait was exhibited in Edinburgh 1965. An attractive pair of miniatures of a young boy and his sister were sold at Christie's 13 December 1966. The portrait of the boy is signed in cursive letters 'ADunn'. The B.M. has an engraved portrait of Dr. T. Young after a miniature by A. Dunn.

Dunn, John. (fl. 1801–1841)

An Irish artist who practised in Dublin where he exhibited at intervals from 1801–1810. Painted portraits and miniatures, as well as drawings. In 1841 he was living at 2 Park Street, Dublin. He has been erroneously identified with N. F. Dun (1764–1832) who worked at Naples etc., and signed Dun.

Dunn, Michael. (fl. *c.* 1819–1834)

Was a pupil at the Dublin Society Schools where he won a prize in 1819. Probably the artist of this name who was working at Clonmel *c.* 1824 and in Dublin 1833–1834. Painted portraits and miniatures. A copy of a portrait by him after M. Strolling was seen by Long in 1930. Exhibited at the R.H.A., in 1833 and 1834.

Dunthorne, John, senior. (fl. 1784–1786)

Of Colchester. Exhibited at the R.A., 1784–1786. His work has an affinity to that of J. Bogle (q.v.). An engraving of the Rev. J. King, after Dunthorne, is at the B.M.

Durham, Cornelius Bevis. (fl. '825–1865)

Of London. Exhibited at ⸴ R.A., and S.B.A., 1828–1858. Won awards at the Society of Arts 1825–1826 and a gold Isis medal in 1832. These awards included a chalk drawing of animals and a portrait miniature. Worked as a miniaturist and intaglio cutter. Some of his works were engraved. Was apparently still alive in 1865 when 'Mr Cornelius Durham' lent some miniatures by 'Cornelius Durham' to the exhibition at the South Kensington Museum. Benezit records that he painted the portraits of the musician John Parry, and of Lady Cecilia Catherine Gordon Lennox (daughter of the Duke of Richmond). The R.A. catalogues for 1827 list an E. Durham as exhibiting from 17 Arundel Street, Strand (the same address as the above artist in subsequent years). The exhibit was an intaglio and he may have been identical with Cornelius B. Durham, the initial being a misprint. A fine miniature of an unknown lady, signed on the front, 'C. Durham' in gold, was in the possession of Captain E. B. Woollett. The quality of this miniature places the artist among the higher ranks of those working in the nineteenth century. A good miniature of Mrs. Burton Phillipson, née Thorpe, of Chippenham Park, by the above artist is in the collection of R. Bayne Powell, Esq. It is signed on the front 'C.D' (vertically) and inscribed on the reverse 'Painted by C. Durham. 1849'. (Col. Pl. XXⱽ   00· Pl.

*Durham, W. H. (fl. 1890)

Of 6 Myrtle Grove, Sydenham. Exhibited at the R.A., 1890.

*Duthier, A. C. (fl. 1814)

A miniature of a lady signed and dated '1814', rectangular, 5½ in, was lot 135 at Christie's 13 November 1962.

Du Thuillay, Lewis. (fl. 1765–1774)

Of London and Chelsea. Exhibited at the Free Society of Artists 1765–1774. Painted portraits and religious subjects and paintings after old masters. Many of his works were enamels, one of which was of the King of Poland.

Dutton, Miss. (fl. 1830–1858)

Of London. Exhibited at the R.A. 1830–1856, and at the Society of Female Artists 1858. Her addresses included 5 Hart Street, Bloomsbury; Claremont House, Stockwell Private Road, Clapham Rise; and 3 Brixton Hill Terrace. Her sister Mrs. Charles Pearson (formerly Miss Mary Martha Dutton) also exhibited at the R.A., and B.I., 1821–1842 (not miniatures) from the family address, 5 Hart Street. Graves, in his *Dictionary of Artists*, has confused the information regarding the two sisters and assumed they were identical. Miss Dutton was a prolific artist and her sitters included her sister, Mrs. Charles Pearson, Charles Pearson (presumably her brother-in-law) and the Baroness Audlace.

Duval, Charles Allen. 1808–1872

Born in Ireland in 1808; went to sea, but later took up painting. Went to Manchester c. 1833 where he worked for many years. Exhibited at the R.A., 1836–1872 and at Manchester and Liverpool. Painted principally portraits and figure subjects, but is also known to have painted miniatures. Was an engraver and lithographer, and was said to have been a witty writer. Had a large practice in Liverpool and Manchester and also worked in London; was said to have been a good artist. He lent a miniature of a lady, painted by himself, to the exhibition

at the South Kensington Museum 1865; his name was then recorded in the catalogue as Du Val. Died in Alderley, Cheshire, 14 June 1872. The B.M. has engraved portraits after Duval. A portrait in water-colour by Duval of Thomas Milner-Gibson is in the N.P.G.

*Duvergé, Madame Yseult K. (fl. 1890–1912)

Of Anjou, Claremont Road, Surbiton. Exhibited at the R.A., 1890–1912. Her sitters included 'the artist's sister', Mrs. Philip Dyson, Mrs. Hope Price and Mrs. Harry Snowden.

Duvigneaud. (fl. 1797)

Of London. Exhibited at the R.A. 1797, from 364 Oxford Street, a frame containing five portraits.

Dyce, William, R.A. 1806–1864

Born 19 September 1806. Noted painter of figure subjects; said by Dr. G. C. Williamson to have painted a few miniatures. Died 14 February 1864.

Dyck, Sir Anthony van. 1599–1641

Born in Antwerp 1599. Although works said to be by him were exhibited at the South Kensington Museum in 1865, it has never been established that this great artist painted miniatures. Died in London 9 December 1641.

Dyer, Miss E. A. (fl. 1828)

Of Didmarton, Gloucestershire. Was awarded a silver Isis medal by the Society of Arts in 1828 for a miniature copy of an historical subject.

Dyer, G. (fl. 1821–1847)

Exhibited at the R.A., 1821–1847. Worked in London, Brighton (in 1822) and Worthing (1826).

Dyer, G. E. O. (fl. 1835)

Possibly identical with or related to G. Dyer (q.v.) and exhibited at the R.A. 1835, from addresses in the Old Kent Road. His sitters were William Hardy, Esq., an unknown sailor, and a portrait of an unknown lady.

Dyke, Richard. (fl. 1819–1820). See also **Dyke, Richard William**

Possibly identical with Richard William Dyke (q.v.). Was working in 1819 at Dyke Road, Belfast and c. 1820 at 5 Castle Street, Belfast.

Dyke, Richard William. (fl. 1787–1815). See also **Dyke, Richard**

Entered the Dublin Society Schools 1787. Was awarded medals in 1788 and 1789 for drawings. Went to Belfast and executed small portraits in water-colour and crayons, for which he charged one guinea each. Returned to Dublin and exhibited a miniature at the H.S.A., in 1815 from 14 Crampton Court. Possibly identical with Richard Dyke (q.v.).

E

Σ.

An enamel miniature of a lady, said to be Elizabeth Chudleigh, Duchess of Kingston (1720–1788), is in the V. & A. M. It is signed 'Σ', which probably represents the Greek Sigma, i.e. the letter S. If this assumption is correct, the artist presumably signed in this way to conceal his identity. The miniature is well painted and attractive and is typical of the British school of that period.

E. 18th century

An enamel miniature in the style of Zincke (q.v.) signed 'E' on the reverse is in the collection of Major R. M. O. de la Hey. It has red dots on the face and is tightly painted.

E., A. (fl. 1782?–1806). See also **A., E.**

Exhibited a miniature at the R.A., 1806. Four miniatures of the family of Sir John Eden of Windlestone were sold at Sotheby's 12 April 1960. One of Mrs. Bore of York, was signed and dated 'A.E. 82' (1782). They were possibly by the above artist whose identity is unknown.

*E., C. 18th century

A miniature portrait on ivory and signed 'C.E.', of the Bishop of Bangor, is in my collection. This may possibly be of John Moore (1730–1805), Bishop of Bangor, 1775–1783, and Archbishop of Canterbury, 1783–1805. The painting is slightly hesitant and, although adequate, is not of outstanding merit.

E., G. See also **Engleheart, George**

I have seen a number of miniatures signed G.E. often in Roman lettering or cursive capitals and painted between 1760 and 1770, which are undoubtedly the early works of George Engleheart (q.v.). The Engleheart Family Collection contains several examples of this period, and one in my collection represents a child of c. 1760 and is signed G.E. in white (cursive). These works are weaker than those normally associated with Engleheart and therefore usually pass unrecognised. Three miniatures signed in this manner are in the V. & A. M.

*E., J.I.

A family miniature of John Kirkman born 20 September 1778, died 19 October 1842, signed 'J.I.E.' was seen by F. Gordon Roe. It was well painted.

*Earl(e), James. 1761–1796

Born in Massachusetts, 1 May 1761, brother of Ralph Earl(e) (q.v.) with whom he may have been confused. Painted portraits and miniatures; came to London when a young man and entered the R.A. schools 24 March 1789 aged 27 years. Exhibited at the R.A., 1787–1796. Returned to America in 1794 and intended to settle in Charleston but had an attack of yellow fever from which he died 18 August 1796. His son Augustus Earl was also an artist.

Earl(e), Ralph. 1751–1801

Of Worcester County, Massachusetts, born 11 May 1751. Fled to England 1778 due to his Loyalist sympathies. Studied in London under Benjamin West (q.v.) in 1782. Exhibited at the R.A., 1783–1785. Painted portraits in oil and historical subjects and may have painted miniatures. Was intemperate. Returned to America 1785 leaving his wife and children behind. Died at Bolton, Connecticut 16 August 1801. May have been confused with his brother James Earl(e) (q.v.) who painted portraits and miniatures.

*Earle, Miss Kate. (fl. 1887–1914)

Of London. Exhibited at the R.A. etc., 1887–1914. Executed miniatures and oil paintings. Her sitters included Lady Lilford.

*Earnshaw, Mrs. Mary Harriot. (fl. 1888–1900)

Of London. Exhibited at the Society of Miniaturists etc., 1888–1900.

East, J. B. (fl. 1818–1830)

Of London. Exhibited at the R.A., 1818–1830. Was awarded a silver medal by the Society of Arts in 1818 for a miniature copy after Guido Reni.

Painted miniatures and subject pictures. The artist's sitters included Lady Emily Herbert, Lady Harriet Herbert, 'Mr Nasmyth' and Lord Porchester.

Easthed, or Easthead, Mrs. Harriet (Miss Alcock). (fl. 1832–1836)

Of London. Exhibited at the R.A., 1832–1835 from Herne Hill and Dulwich under her maiden name, and in 1836 under her married name. Long records her name as Easthead, but the catalogue gives it as Easthed.

*Easther, Miss Charlotte. (fl. 1902)

Of London. Exhibited at the R.A. 1902, from 57 Bedford Gardens, Kensington.

*Eastman, Frank Samuel. b. 1878

Of London, born 27 April 1878. Exhibited at the R.A. 1908–1914, from 14 Edith Villas, West Kensington. Painted miniatures and subjects in oil. Husband of Mrs. Maud Eastman (q.v.). Was a pupil at the Croydon School of Art and in 1899 of the R.A. Schools. Obtained a prize in 1902 for a decorative mural.

*Eastman, Mrs. Frank S. See Mair, Miss Maud

Easton, Reginald. 1807–1893

Was born in 1807; self taught. Started as an engraver but later took up painting portraits and miniatures in water-colour. Exhibited at the R.A., 1835–1887. Became a fashionable artist and was particularly good at painting children. He was patronised by the Royal Family and had an aristocratic clientele. Worked principally in London but in 1850 was living at 4 Somers Place, Leamington. Died in 1893. Many of his works are very attractive, the features are softly painted, and the draughtsmanship good. His sitters included Prince Christian Victor of Schleswig-Holstein, and the Princesses Victoria, Elizabeth and Irene of Hesse, Mrs. Baillie Hamilton, Lady Mary Herbert, etc. A miniature copy of Miss Curran's portrait of Percy Bysshe Shelley, by R. Easton, was loaned to the South Kensington Exhibition 1865. A miniature of William IV, signed 'R. Easton' is in the collection of H.M. the Queen. An attractive miniature of an unknown lady was exhibited in Edinburgh 1965. There is also an example of his work at the V. & A. M.

*Eaton, Miss Maria. (fl. 1905–1914)

Of Manchester and London. Exhibited at the R.A. and S.M., 1905–1914. Executed miniatures and flowers in water-colour. Her sitters included Edwin Waugh, the Lancashire poet, George Bernard Shaw and Signora Caruso. Possibly identical with Maria Eaton, an engraver, who is recorded by Benezit.

Eckstein, John (Johann). d. after 1805

Born at Strelitz. Studied art in London. Won prizes at the Society of Arts 1761 and 1764. Exhibited at the R.A., 1770–1802. Worked in London and, c. 1792, Birmingham. Was a sculptor, painter, miniaturist and lithographer. Had the same address for a time as George Paul Eckstein, sculptor. Engravings after Eckstein are at the B.M. A miniature of Captain Rodney Kempt (died 1815) signed 'Eckstein', is at the V. & A. M. Eckstein's oil portrait of Sir William Sidney Smith is at the N.P.G.

*Eden, The Hon. Emily. 1797–1869

Born in Old Palace Yard, 3 March 1797. 7th daughter of William Eden, 1st Baron Auckland. Went to India 1835–1842. Published in 1844,

Portraits of the Princes and Peoples of India, novels, etc. Lived at Eden Lodge, Upper Grove, Kensington. Held coffee-mornings for celebrities of the day. Was a pupil of David Cox (q.v.).

Edenberger, J. N. (fl. 1773–1776)

Born at Baden. Worked for most of his life at the Hague where he was a member of the Painter's Guild, 1773. Came to England but was back at the Hague by 1776. A miniature of a group of four children in a landscape, signed 'Edenberger' was noted by Schidlof.

Edgecumbe, Richard. 17th century

This artist appears to be unrecorded except for lot 21 on the 22nd day of Horace Walpole's sale at Strawberry Hill, and which included 'a miniature of Charles II; by Richard Edgecumbe, a very early specimen of the artist'.

*Edgeworth, John. (fl. c. 1719)

An early eighteenth-century artist of Dublin. Baptisms are recorded of the children of 'John Edgeworth, Limner' and his wife Margaret, in the Parish Registers of St. Michan's, 1719.

*Edmeads, Mrs. John. See Grimaldi, Miss Louisa Frances

*Edmonds, Mrs. Courtenay. (fl. 1902–1903)

Of Exeter. Exhibited at the Society of Miniaturists 1902–1903.

*Edmunds, Miss Nellie M. Hepburn, V.P.R.M.S. (fl. 1895–1914)

Exhibited at the R.A., R.M.S., S.M. 1895–1914, from 23 South Croxted Road, West Dulwich and 79 Casewick Road, West Norwood. Her sitters included Mrs. William Rathbone, Doris and Barbara, daughters of Major Balfour, Mrs. Henry Barber and Alice, Countess of Chichester. The V. & A. M. has a miniature by the above artist of Miss Eileen Marshall in early Victorian dress, signed and dated 'N. H. Edmunds / 12' (1912).

Edridge, Henry, A.R.A. 1768–1821

Born in Paddington 12 October 1768, son of a Westminster tradesman. Was apprenticed to W. Pether (q.v.), the engraver. Entered the R.A. Schools 7 January 1784 'age 15 12 Oct. last' (this date does not accord with August 1769 as stated by Long). Awarded a silver medal in 1786; was permitted to copy some of Sir Joshua Reynolds's pictures in miniature. Exhibited at the R.A., 1786–1821. Visited France 1817 and 1819. In 1820 was elected A.R.A. His friends included Dr. Monro, Sir George Beaumont and the artists T. Hearne and J. Farington. Painted landscapes, portraits in water-colour and at least one small oil portrait (sold at Christie's 24 February 1933), miniatures on ivory and paper. His early miniatures were chiefly on ivory and afterwards he drew with black lead or Indian ink on paper. This method was later abandoned and he drew the figure in lightly and finished the face and sometimes the costume elaborately in water-colour. He died in Margaret Street, Cavendish Square, London on 23 April 1821. He did not always sign his work; when he did it was usually H.E. either separately or in monogram, often followed by a date. Occasionally he inscribed in full on the reverse as in the case of one in the Liverpool Museum, 'Painted 1793 by Henry Edridge Dufours Place Broad St., Golden Square.' This miniature has a look of Shelley's (q.v.) work. Sometimes he painted a blue shading under the eye, on the upper lip, and a sharp shadow under the nose. Examples of his work are at the V. & A. M., B.M., N.P.G. etc. His

works are elegant and attractive. Several of his miniatures were loaned to the South Kensington Exhibition 1865. Edridge drew a small portrait of William Wordsworth in 1806 when the poet was aged 36. This has been reproduced in works on Wordsworth. I have seen, in a private collection, a fine miniature on ivory of a judge by Edridge signed 'HE'.

*Edwards, Miss Annie or Anne. (fl. 1906–1914)

Of Paris and Leamington. Exhibited at the R.A., 1906–1914. Her sitters included Olive, daughter of Major K. Chesshyre Molyneux.

Edwards, Edward, A.R.A. 1738–1806

Born in Castle Street, Leicester Square, London, 7 March 1738, son of a chairmaker and carver. Educated at a French School in London; worked for an upholsterer. Entered a drawing school and in 1759 was a pupil at the Duke of Richmond's Gallery. Entered the R.A. Schools 30 January 1769 aged 31 years. Exhibited at the Society of Artists and the Free Society, the R.A., and B.I., 1766–1806. Became A.R.A. in 1773 and was professor of perspective at the R.A. Taught drawing in London; was author of *Anecdotes of Painters*. Painted landscapes, portraits and figure subjects and painted at least one miniature copy from a picture. He exhibited his self-portrait at the Society of Artists in 1768. Died in London 10 December 1806. A miniature copy of Arthur, Prince of Wales, eldest son of Henry VII and Elizabeth of York (1486–1502) painted by Edwards in 1781 was lent to the exhibition at the South Kensington Museum in 1865. Engraved portraits after E. Edwards are in the B.M.

Edwards, Frances. b. 1786

Of London. Entered the R.A. Schools 1808 aged 22 years. Exhibited a self-portrait at the R.A. 1813, from 27 Great Suffolk Street, Blackman Street, Southwark.

*Edwards, G. H. (fl. 1901)

Of London. Exhibited at the Society of Miniaturists 1901. Was possibly identical with either George Hay Edwards of Putney, who exhibited landscapes at the R.A., or George Henry Edwards who exhibited subject pictures at the R.A., from Camden Street, London.

*Edwards, Mrs. Inez C. S. (fl. 1902)

Of Marlow, Buckinghamshire. Exhibited at the R.A. 1902, from Sunnybank, Marlow. Her sitter was Mrs. Hugh Inglis.

*Edwards, J. (fl. c. 1814–1820)

This artist is known only by two porcelain plaques enamelled with scenes, owned by the City of Liverpool Museum. These were once in the Joseph Mayer collection and were in the 1867 inventory when they were catalogued as by J. Edwards. Mr. A. Smith, Keeper of Ceramics and Applied Art at the City of Liverpool Museum, informs me that he recently met a descendant of the artist who told him that Edwards was under apprenticeship to John Flaxman (q.v.) at Wedgwood, and that he had gone to Liverpool to take up an engagement as ceramic art modeller with the Herculaneum factory. Among the Entwistle Papers in the Liverpool Record Office, there is a reference to a manuscript by John Edwards and his son James Edwards (one time manager of the Herculaneum Pottery). This manuscript is now lost, as is also a notebook entitled *The Advantages of Establishing Pottery Works in Liverpool*, by John Edwards compiled c. 1795–1800. The porcelain plaques appear to date c. 1814–1820.

*Edwards, Miss Mabel. (fl. 1909–1914)

Of Pinner and London. Exhibited at the R.A. 1909–1914, from The Grange, Royston Park, Pinner and 3 Powis Square. Executed miniatures and oil paintings.

Edwards, R. (fl. 1849–1851)

Of Leicester. Said to have exhibited enamels at various exhibitions 1849–1851.

*Edwards, Miss R. Spencer. (fl. 1905)

Exhibited at the R.A. 1905, from Abbotsleigh, Freshford, Bath. Her sitter was Lieut. Colonel Spencer Edwards.

Edwards, T. (Thomas?). (fl. 1816)

Of London. Exhibited at the R.A., 1816. A miniature of a man, called Sir Eyre Coote, signed and dated by Thomas Edwards, 1816, is in the collection of E. G. Paine of New York and is possibly by the above artist.

Edwards, W. H. (fl. 1817)

Working in London 1817. Probably identical with the artist of this name who exhibited at the R.A., and S.S., 1793–1850 (fruit pieces, according to Graves). The R.A. catalogues for 1817 give his address as Clapham Rise. His wife also exhibited fruit pieces at the R.A.

Effingham, Eliza, Countess of (Miss Drummond). d. 1894

Only daughter of General Sir Gordon Drummond, G.C.B. Married Henry, 2nd Earl of Effingham 18 August 1832 by whom she had six children. Long records having seen miniature portraits by her copied from works by Lawrence and Carlo Dolci. The miniatures were painted with considerable skill and suggested that she had a good technical knowledge and was a practised hand. She died on 27 February 1894.

*Egan, William. (fl. 1850)

A miniature of an elderly lady inscribed on the reverse 'Painted by William Egan 1st June 1850 an domino' is illustrated by O'Brien. Nothing more is known about this artist.

Egerton, Miss Jane Sophia. (fl. 1844–1856)

Of London. Exhibited at the R.A., 1844–1856. Her sitters included the sons of Baron Lionel de Rothschild.

Egley, William. 1798–1870

Born in Doncaster 1798. Worked in a London publishing house, but decided to take up painting; was self-taught and had a struggle to obtain a good practice. Exhibited at the R.A., etc., 1824–1869. Succeeded in acquiring an aristocratic clientele. Married twice and had a son, William Maw Egley (q.v.) who followed his father's profession. His addresses included 47 Cirencester Place (1825), 15 Buckingham Street, Norton Street nr. Portland Place (1831) and 9 Montague Street, Portman Square (1860–1862). Died in London 19 March 1870. He worked slightly in the manner of Sir W. C. Ross (q.v.) but his painting appears more laboured and harder. Egley usually signed in full on the reverse followed by an address. Five miniatures by him were loaned to the exhibition at the South Kensington Museum 1865; they included portraits of Lady Burleigh and Lord Churchill. A portrait of William Egley, by his son W. M. Egley (q.v.) is in the B.M. The V. & A. M. have miniatures by Egley painted 1849–1850 and other examples are at the City of Liverpool Museum. A miniature of Miss Browne as a child, signed on the reverse 'Daughter of / Captain G. Browne / Painted by / William Egley / 8 Montagu Street / Portman Sq / London /

April 30th / 1858' is in my collection. One of Master Browne, as a child, presumably her brother, was sold at Sotheby's on the same day as the above, 11 December 1967.

*Egley, William Maw. 1827?–1916

Was born in 1827?, son of W. Egley (q.v.) from whose address he exhibited at the R.A., B.I. etc., 1843–1898. A miniature of A.S. Melville, Esq. was inscribed on the reverse, 'painted by William Maw Egley jun. 75 Connaugh Terrace, Hyde Park, Jan 13. 1849'. Died 1916. A portrait of W. Egley by his son, W. M. Egley, is in the B.M. There is also an example of his work at the V. & A. M.

Einslie or Einsle, S. (fl. 1785–1808)

Of London. Exhibited at the R.A., 1785–1808. Painted portraits, miniatures and executed mezzotints, some of which were copied from the works of Gainsborough and Hoppner. An S. Einsle, possibly a son, was premiated by the Society of Arts in 1819. The B.M. has an engraving after S. Einslie, and mezzotint portraits by him.

*Eley, Miss Frances. (fl. 1890)

Of London. Exhibited at the R.A., 1890. The portraits were of the Viscountess Raincliffe, and the Hon. Mrs. Algernon Bourke.

*Elias, Mrs. A. (Emily). (fl. 1882–1910)

Of London and Paris. Exhibited at the Salon 1882–1890 and at the R.A., S.M. etc., 1884–1910. Was the wife of Alfred Elias who exhibited oil paintings at the R.A. Must not be confused with Miss Annette Elias who also exhibited oil paintings. Painted miniatures and pictures in oil.

Elizabeth, Princess. 1770–1840

Born at Buckingham House May 1770. Daughter of George III. Painted portraits as well as mythological and allegorical designs, some of which were engraved. Drew with accuracy and taste; showed the influence of Mrs. Mee (q.v.). Married the Prince of Hesse-Homburg in 1818 and died at Frankfurt 10 January 1840. A portrait of her after W. M. Craig (q.v.) was reproduced in the *Lady's Monthly Museum*, August 1806, f.p. 49. A miniature by her of Lady Charlotte Finch is in the collection of H.M. the Queen.

*Ellis, Miss Beryl M. J. (fl. 1903–1910)

Of Shadingfield Hall, Wangford, Suffolk. Exhibited at the Society of Miniaturists 1903–1910.

*Ellis, Mrs. Edith Kate. (fl. 1906–1914)

Of Eaglescliffe, Co. Durham and Bedford. Exhibited at the R.A., 1906 and 1914. Sitters included Dr. Campbell Smith and Mrs. Bamford Emerson.

*Ellis, Mrs. Evelyn Corbould. See Corbould-Ellis, Mrs. Eveline

Elouis, Jean Pierre Henri. 1755–1840/3

Born in Caën 20 January 1755. Of German descent. Was a pupil of Restout and Lefèvre. Entered the R.A. Schools 29 October 1784 aged '29, 20th Jany last'. Won a silver medal in 1786. Exhibited at the R.A., 1785–1787. Went to America c. 1787 and worked at Annapolis, Baltimore and Philadelphia. His miniatures of George and Martha Washington were probably painted during his time in Philadelphia. Travelled with Humboldt from c. 1799–1804 to Mexico and South America. Returned to France in 1807. Exhibited portraits in oil at the Paris Salon 1810–1819. Was appointed curator at the Caën Museum 1814. Worked in a continental style and used good fresh colours. Died in Caën 23 December 1843 (according to Long) or 1840, according to

Schidlof and Groce and Wallace. A miniature of a lady, signed and dated 'London, 1786' is in the collection of E. G. Paine of New York.

*Elwes, Miss Eleanor M. (fl. 1903–1906)

Exhibited at the R.A. 1903 and 1906, from 35 Baring Road, Lee, S.E. and from 26 Rue Comte du Marois, Gaad, Belgium.

Emdin, G. (fl. 1817–1818)

Of London. Exhibited at the R.A., 1817–1818. Examples of his work are at Windsor Castle. He exhibited a self-portrait in 1817 and a portrait of Mr. J. Emdin in 1818.

Emrich, C. (fl. 1701)

A pair of enamel portraits of the Duke and Duchess of Marlborough, one said to be signed 'C. Emrich fec: Ao 1701' are at the Bayrisches Nationalmuseum, Munich. It is not certain that this artist ever worked in England, but in view of his subjects this is a possibility.

*Emslie, Rosalie M., R.M.S. (Mrs. A. E.) d. c. 1932

Of London and Sevenoaks. Exhibited at the R.A., N.W.C.S., S.M., R.M.S. etc., 1888–1914. Executed miniatures and subjects in water-colour. She was a prolific artist and had a distinguished clientele which included Madame Melba, Lady Mather and her family, Maud and Ethel daughters of Sir David Solomons, Bart., and Laurence John, son of George Cadbury, Esq. Married Alfred Edward Emslie, also an artist. Died c. 1932.

*Enfield, Miss Mary P. (fl. 1892–1914)

Exhibited at the R.A. 1892–1914, from Bramcote, Nottingham. Her sitters included Mrs. Herbert Churchill and Mrs. Astle.

*Englefield, Arthur. b. 1855

Born in London 1855. Worked in London, St. Albans and Gloucester. Exhibited at the R.A. etc., 1891–1904. Painted miniatures, portraits in water-colour and flowers in oil.

Engleheart, George. 1750/5–1829. See also **E., G.**

One of eight sons born to Francis Englhart (died 1773), a German plaster-modeller and his wife Anne Dawney. Said to have been born in Kew 26 October 1750 but when he entered the R.A. Schools on 3 November 1769 his age was noted as '16 last Nov.'; if this is correct it makes his date of birth November 1753. Was a pupil of George Barret, R.A., and of Sir Joshua Reynolds, some of whose work he copied in miniature. After his father died, the spelling of the name was changed to Engleheart. Exhibited at the R.A., 1773–1822. Worked chiefly in London at Shepherd Street, Hanover Square (1773) and Princes Street, Hanover Square (1776), in which year he married as his first wife, Elizabeth, daughter of Nathaniel Browne. She died 29 April 1779 aged 26. In 1783 he moved to Hertford Street and in 1785 married Ursula Sarah Browne (died 1817) by whom he had four children, George, Nathaniel, Harry and Emma. Kept a fee book from 1775 and many tracings of miniatures. Knew Romney, William Blake, W. Hayley, and J. Meyer (q.v.). Retired in 1813 to his country house at Bedfont, near Hounslow, after which he only painted a small number of miniatures and water-colours. Was looked after by his daughter, Emma, after his second wife's death, and ultimately gave up his house and lived with his son Nathaniel at Blackheath, c. 1818. He died there 21 March 1829 and was buried at Kew. His work falls approximately into three phases. His earliest miniatures were signed G.E. on the front, the draughtsmanship was often unsure and his full style had not yet developed. The size of his miniatures of this period were usually small and the backgrounds, as in the case of one of a child, in my collection, were a darkish buff colour, the shading often being obtained by fine vertical or slightly slanting strokes, and the application of opaque white to indicate the highlights on the hair and face. The faces were modelled by the use of bluish grey and reddish shading superimposed on a pale flesh tint. From *c.* 1780–1795 there was a marked change; his full powers developed, his colouring became strong, his draughtsmanship was good and although he still used small ivories, the quality of the work was excellent. No accessories are usually shown in the background and often the portraits were not signed. Characteristics of this period are large deep-set eyes, set under rather heavy eyebrows, the hair drawn in lines rather than in masses and diagonal grey lines at the corner of the mouth. The draperies are picked out in opaque white. Towards the end of this period he began to sign with a cursive E on the front, followed by a full inscription on the reverse including his address. From *c.* 1795 the size of his miniatures was 3 in.–3½ in. or more; his practice of signing with an E continued. He was then at the height of his power. His miniatures were elegant and attractive, and he was a prolific worker. The brush-strokes on the face are slightly more hairy than in his earlier work, the flesh colour being rather brownish yellow and parallel hatching on the draperies rarer. A typical signature on the reverse would be – George Engleheart / Hertford Street / Mayfair / 1812. From *c.* 1800 onwards he frequently used a rectangular format and did not attempt to flatter his sitters, but painted them as he saw them. In this last phase he signed G.E. either cursive or in block letters, followed by a date and occasionally inscribed on the reverse as well. He was one of the great artists of the eighteenth century. Engleheart painted a few copies of miniatures by Cosway (q.v.) and was noted for executing 'eye miniatures'. Two relatives, J. C. D. Engleheart (q.v.) and T. Richmond (q.v.) were his pupils, and both artists worked in his style. Although no examples are at present known, he certainly worked in enamel, for I have seen his artist's equipment which contains numerous enamelled plates on which he had experimented with various colours. Dr. Williamson refers to at least two works in this medium and there is an entry in Engleheart's fee book for 10 December 1778 'a lady copied in enamel'. A number of miniatures by Engleheart were exhibited in Edinburgh in 1965, including those of Elizabeth, his first wife, and Millicent Dillman Engleheart, from the collection of Mrs. F. H. A. Engleheart. Among others loaned was one of Colonel Charles Erskine, 92nd Highlanders (died 1801) from the collection of Mrs. Hugh Bowlby. It is of particular interest as it was from this miniature that a large portrait was painted by Raeburn after Colonel Erskine's death in Egypt; this portrait, together with the receipt are still in the Bowlby family. This is probably one of the few examples where a large portrait has been painted from a miniature. Colonel Erskine was painted by Engleheart in 1795 and 1800. Several miniatures by him were also loaned to the South Kensington Exhibition 1865. For information regarding this artist I am indebted to the Engleheart family who allowed me access to the family papers, which contained many sketches and tracings of his miniatures. Examples of his work are in the V. & A. M., the Wallace Collection, the Fitzwilliam Museum, Cambridge, the Ashmolean Museum, Oxford, the Holburne Museum, Bath, and many private collections including those of H.M. the

Queen, Earl Beauchamp, R. Graham, Esq., and many more. For further information see *George Engleheart* by Dr. G. C. Williamson, 1902.

Engleheart, John Cox Dillman. 1782/4–1862

Born 1 January 1784 (according to a tablet in Kew Church), or 1782, if the date given in the R.A. Schools is correct. Son of John Dillman Engleheart, by his second wife Jane Parker, and a nephew of George Engleheart (q.v.) whose pupil and assistant he became. Entered the R.A. Schools 21 June 1800 when his age was noted as 18. Copied works by his uncle, Reynolds, Zincke (q.v.) etc. Exhibited at the R.A., 1801–1828. Was probably working on his own from *c.* 1807. Worked for a time in Birmingham and married Mary Barker of Edgbaston, Birmingham, in 1811. Travelled widely. Appears to have ceased painting miniatures about 1828. Settled in Beechholm, Turnbridge Wells, where he lived until his death in 1862. Had four daughters and a son, Sir J. Gardner D. Engleheart, K.C.B., who died a centenarian in 1923. The works of J. C. D. Engleheart vary in quality, some of his miniatures are very like the ones painted by G. Engleheart but when he began to work independently his miniatures were slightly weaker and painted with a less vigorous brush-stroke. He used slightly darker colours and favoured a rectangular format. He signed on the front and back of his work, sometimes both, e.g. JCDE (monogram) and on the reverse 'J. C. D. Engleheart' followed by an address and often a date. Long notes one signed with a cursive E within a heart of gold. He is said to have painted some enamel miniatures but none are known. Many of his works were on paper. Examples of his work are at the V. & A. M., the Liverpool Museum and the Glynn Vivian Art Gallery, Swansea, as well as in many private collections. Six miniatures by him were loaned to the exhibition in Edinburgh 1965, including some family ones and a self-portrait of the artist. A good miniature of an unknown lady signed on the reverse 'J. C. D. Engleheart / 1822 70 Berners St., London' is in the collection of R. Bayne Powell, Esq.

Engleheart, William Francis S. b. 1780

Of London. Entered the R.A. Schools 14 December 1798 aged 18. Exhibited at the R.A. 1801, from 7 Shepherd Street, Mayfair. Undoubtedly related to George Engleheart (q.v.), probably his nephew. Several members of the Engleheart family are known to have lived in Shepherd Street where George Engleheart had a studio 1773–1776. According to information supplied to me by the Engleheart family George Engleheart had an elder brother Francis (died 1780) who had two sons – the younger of whom, William, was an artist; said to have died young. He was undoubtedly identical with the above artist, as an Engleheart family miniature of a man signed 'WE' (cursive) and inscribed on the reverse 'Wᵐ Fˢ Engleheart / pinxt May 10 / 1800' is in the collection of W. A. Twiston Davies.

*Ensor, Mrs. M. M. Ricardo. (fl. 1903–1905)

Of Shoreham, Sussex, Exhibited at the Society of Miniaturists 1903–1905.

*Epinette, Mlle. (fl. 1881)

Of London. Exhibited at the R.A. 1881, from 6 St. James's Terrace, Regent's Park, London. Probably identical with Marie Epinette, who was born in Rouen and exhibited at the Salon in 1875. Graves records Mlle. Epinette as a miniaturist but the exhibit in 1881 was a portrait which was in the Drawing, Etching and Engraving section.

*Ertz, Mrs. Ethel Margaret Horsfall. b. 1871

Born 19 January 1871. Exhibited at the R.A. 1901–1913, from c/o the Kensington Fine Art Society, 26 Alfred Place, West Kensington; Kingsbridge, Devon; and Pulborough, Sussex. Executed miniatures and landscapes in water-colour. According to Benezit her maiden name was Horsfall. She was the wife of Edward Frederick Ertz, painter, illustrator and etcher.

Essex, Mrs.

Two copies of portraits after Reynolds, of which at least one was a miniature, were sold at Knight, Frank and Rutley's 14 December 1911 and catalogued as by Mrs. Essex.

Essex, Alfred, d. 1871

Brother of William Essex (q.v.). Published in June 1837 an article on the art of painting in enamel, in the *London and Edinburgh Philosophical Magazine*. He prepared plates for C. Muss (q.v.) and plates and colours for W. B. Essex (q.v.). Emigrated to South Africa where his daughter Harriet married Wm. Rathbone in 1852. Essex died in South Africa in 1871.

Essex, Miss Hannah (Mrs. Bird). (fl. 1854–1856)

Daughter of William Essex (q.v.). Exhibited at the R.A., B.I. 1854–1856, from W. Essex's address. Painted enamel copies of flower pieces after Veerendael. She later became Mrs. Bird.

Essex, Sarah, Countess of. See Malden, Lady

Essex, William. 1784–1869

Born in 1784. Exhibited at the R.A., B.I., S.B.A., O.W.C.S. etc., 1818–1864. Painted portraits and dogs in enamel. Many of his portraits were copied from works by other artists. He is reputed to have made small drawings of dogs on vellum and then executed reduced copies in enamel on gold, painted under a magnifying glass; he also painted miniatures on ivory and some flower and historical subjects. In 1839 he was appointed enamel painter to Queen Victoria and in 1841 to the Prince Consort. Was one of the best enamellists of the period and used clear fresh colours. Died at Brighton 29 December 1869. Long noted that a Miss Emily Essex was a descendant. Most of his miniatures are signed in full on the reverse, often with an inscription similar to that on one in my collection, of Princess Victoria (later Queen Victoria), i.e. 'H.R.H. Princess Victoria / age 5 yrs from the origl / picture by Wm. Fowler / Painted by W. Essex 1858 / Enamel Painter to Her Majesty / & H.R.H. Prince Consort'. This miniature was exhibited in Edinburgh in 1965. Seven miniatures by Essex were exhibited at the South Kensington Museum 1865. J. W. Bailey (q.v.), W. B. Ford (q.v.) and his son W. B. Essex (q.v.) were his pupils. His format varied from ones that were quite small to others that were large. A self-portrait of the artist was lot 38 at Sotheby's 17 April 1961. It was inscribed on the reverse 'Portrait of Wm. Essex, Enamel Painter to Her Majesty and H.R.H. Prince Albert, 1857. With a Father's best love to Hannah'. A pair of miniatures representing Mr. and Mrs. William Catt were sold at Christie's 18 November, 1969 when they were said to be by 'their son, W. Essex'. The date of Essex's birth makes this impossible as he was only seven years younger than either of the Catt's, but the miniatures were inscribed, ' "My Father" / William Catt / Obt Mar.4 1853 / aged 76 yrs / Painted by W.Essex.Enl. / pr. to Her Majesty &c / 1855' and ' "My Mother / Hannah" Catt / Obt. Jany.19 1823 / aged 46 yrs / Painted by W.Essex Enl / pr. to Her Majesty &c / 1855'. From this it would appear that he must have at least shared a home with the Catt's or been indebted to them in some way for his upbringing. Examples of his work are at the V. & A. M., the Ashmolean Museum, Oxford, the N.P.G. Dublin and a number of private collections including that of the Duke of Northumberland.

Essex, William B. *c.* 1823–1852

Was born *c.* 1823. Son of William Essex (q.v.). Exhibited at the R.A., B.I., and S.B.A., 1845–1851. Was an enamellist like his father. Died in Birmingham 19 January 1852. Painted mythological, historical and religious pictures as well as miniatures and portraits. Exhibited a miniature of his father in 1847.

*Etherington, Miss Lilian M. (fl. 1884–1901)

Of London. Exhibited at the R.A. etc., 1884–1901. Painted oil subjects and in 1899 exhibited in the miniature section.

*Eusebi, Luis. (fl. *c.* 1815–1830)

A Spanish artist; worked in Madrid from *c.* 1815–1830. Toured Europe during which time he visited England. Returned to Madrid where he became 'Pintor de Camara'. Was an art historian and held a position as Keeper of the Madrid Museum.

Evans, John T. (fl. 1809)

Worked in England, Ireland and Philadelphia (1809). Painted miniatures and water-colour views.

Evelyn, John. 1620–1706

Born at Wotton, Surrey, 31 October 1620. Notable diarist and author. Noted by Pepys in his Diary for 5 November 1665 as having executed paintings in 'little; in distemper, Indian incke, water colours, graveing; and, above all, the whole secret of Mezzo-tinto.' This suggests that both he and his wife Mary (q.v.) painted miniatures. Died 27 February 1706.

Evelyn, Mrs. John (Miss Mary Browne). *c.* 1635–1708/9

Née Mary Browne, born *c.* 1635, daughter of Sir Richard Browne of Sayes Court (and for some time ambassador in Paris). Was well-read, and executed etchings, water-colours and miniatures. Married John Evelyn (q.v.) in Paris 27 June 1647 and bore him eight children; was said to be 'attentive to the domestic concerns of her household, and a most affectionate mother'. John Evelyn refers in his Diary, 11 May 1661, to her having 'presented to his Majesty the Madonna she had copied in miniature from P. Oliver's painting, after Raphael, which she wrought with extraordinary pains and judgment. The King was infinitely pleas'd with it, and caus'd it to be plac'd in his cabinet amongst his best Paintings.' She died in London 9 February 1708/9, in her 74th year and was buried at Wotton. A portrait of her by Nanteuil painted in Paris 1650 is engraved as the frontispiece to Vol. II of the 1854 edition of *The Diary of John Evelyn.*

*Everitt, Walter. (fl. 1905–1911)

Of London. Exhibited at the R.A. 1905–1911, from 55 Baker Street. His sitters included the Lord Chief Justice, the Lord Bishop of London, the Hon. Mrs. St. Clair and the Rt. Hon. Sir H. H. Cozens-Hardy, Master of the Rolls, later 1st Baron Cozens-Hardy, Henry Tollemache, Esq., and J. Murray Kennedy.

Everton, Dora.

An attractive miniature after John Smart (q.v.) of Elizabeth Townsend as a girl is in the Latter-Schlesinger Collection, New Orleans.

*Eves, Miss Elsie M. (fl. 1909–1911)

Of London. Exhibited at the R.A. 1909 and 1911, from 2 Winchester Avenue, Brondesbury. Her sitters included the children of G. Woolstone, Esq.

*Evezard, Miss Alice. (fl. 1905)

Exhibited at the R.A. 1905, from 9 Augusta Road, Ramsgate.

Ezekiel, Ezekiel Abraham. 1757–1806

Born in Exeter, 1757, son of Abraham Ezekiel, a Jewish goldsmith. Was apprenticed as a jeweller, during which time he made an etching after a landscape drawing. From 1788 onwards he engraved portraits after Opie and others. Was an optician, goldsmith and print-seller as well as being in great demand as a miniaturist. Was also a good scholar and linguist. He died of dropsy after a long illness on 14 December 1806. One of his pupils was J. Frost (q.v.). Some engravings after Ezekiel are in the B.M. His son, Solomon Ezekiel (1781–1867) was an author. The V. & A. M. has one of his trade cards which was reproduced in the *Jewish Historical Society,* Vol. XVIII.

F

F., C. (fl. *c.* 1778). See also **Forrest, C.**

Miniatures signed with cursive initials 'C.F.' and dated *c.* 1778 were seen by Long; the size of the miniatures was small and they were quite well painted without being first rate. They were slightly reminiscent of the work of N. Hone (q.v.). One which represented a Captain Fisher had the ear drawn rather too large, the hair was opaque grey, and the face painted with a buff-colour, shaded with grey and brown, blended hatching and a greenish-grey background. The miniatures may have been the work of C. Forrest (q.v.).

F., M. (fl. 1790–1795)

A miniature signed with the above initials is in the Musée Dobrée at Nantes. It shows the influence of Cosway (q.v.). A miniature of an officer signed 'M.F. *c.* 1790' with a stippled background was sold at Christie's 29 July 1925, and Long saw a miniature in a private collection signed 'M.F.' (in Roman monogram) *c.* 1795. There was a lot of hatching on the background and on the coat.

*F., T. (fl. 1729–1730)

A miniature signed in monogram ⅂F *c.* 1730 was sold at Sotheby's 15 June 1933 and another, similarly signed, *c.* 1729, was also seen by Long.

*F., T.H. (fl. 1805)

A miniature of a gentleman signed 'T.H.F.' and dated '1805' was lot 125 at Christie's 13 November 1962.

*F., W. (fl. *c.* 1812). See also **Foster, William**

A miniature portrait in oil *c.* 1812 signed 'W.F.' was shown to Long who noted that it was painted in the style of Wm. Foster (q.v.).

Faber, John. *c.* 1650/60–1721

Born in the Hague *c.* 1650 or *c.* 1660. Executed pen-and-ink portraits on vellum in the manner of engravings; was also a mezzotint portrait engraver. Came to England *c.* 1687 and settled in London; lived at Fountains Court, Strand. His son John Faber Jun. (*c.* 1684–1756) was also a well-known

engraver. Died in Bristol May 1721. Faber was a very good artist, his miniatures were executed in plumbago, Indian ink and wash, and pen-and-ink. His signatures were J. Faber, and I. Faber, often followed by an inscription and a date; one of William III, in the V. & A. M. is signed 'J. faber cum penna Dei:ᵗ Aº 17–02', another also in the V. & A. M. of Admiral Sir George Rooke (1650–1709) is signed 'J.Faber Delineavit ∼ in / Aº 1705 Chatham / 18ᵗʰ of August'. A number of works by Faber and his son were in the Wellesley sale at Sotheby's in 1920, including one of Charles I inscribed 'Carolus I.Mag: Brit: Fr: Hib: Rex. Done from yᵉ Original Painting in the Possession of yᵉ Honᵇˡᵉ George Clarke in Oxford. by J: Faber.' Examples of his work are in the B.M., the Rotterdam Museum and the N.G. Dublin, which has a miniature of the Earl of Athlone signed and dated 'J.Faber / 1703'. Miniatures by him were loaned to the exhibition at South Kensington 1865.

Fabian, John. (fl. 1762–1763)

Worked in London. Exhibited at the Society of Artists in 1762. Painted miniatures in enamel and water-colour. In 1763 was living at Mr. Tacet's in Meard's Court, Dean Street, Soho. An engraving after Fabian of the Rev. George Carr (1705–1776) is at the B.M.

*Fabian, M. (fl. *c.* 1774)

Advertised in the *Edinburgh Evening Courant,* 4 June 1774, that he could preserve miniatures from fading by a 'peculiar and only effective method invented by Mr M. Fabian at Mr Patterson's in the exchange Edinburgh. Miniatures in oil and water-colour preserved for 5 gns.'.

Facius, George Sigmund, and **Johann Gottlieb.** b. 1750. d. after 1802

The above artists, born in Ratisbonne *c.* 1750, were twin brothers who were inseparable, and whose work was identical. They studied firstly in Brussels, where their father was the Russian consul, and later went to London, in 1776, where they settled. They were engravers. In 1785 and 1788 either one or both artists exhibited at the R.A., in each case the initials were given as J.G.S. Facius, and both exhibits were described as 'portrait of an artist'. The miniatures may have been the combined work of both brothers. Some of their works were after Benjamin West (q.v.) and Angelica Kaufmann (q.v.).

Faed, James. 1821–1911

Born 4 April 1821 at Burley Mill, Kirkcudbrightshire; son of a millwright, and younger brother of John Faed (q.v.). Best known for his landscapes in oil, genre subjects, etc.; also painted a few miniatures and executed some engravings. Exhibited at the R.A., 1855–1904. Lived in Edinburgh from 1856. Died 24 September 1911. His exhibit at the R.A. in 1855 was of his other brother, Thomas Faed, the painter. His son James Faed jun. (fl. 1880–1900) was also an artist. The only miniature at present known by James Faed sen. is in my collection, and represents Miss Mary Duncan, daughter of Thomas Duncan, A.R.A., R.S.A., (1807–1845). This is an attractive miniature, of the sitter as a young girl, painted in profile against a blue background. It is inscribed on the reverse, 'N. 2 portrait of Miss Mary (Duncan) / James Faed Senʳ / 7 Barnton Terrace / Edinburgh'.

Faed, John, R.S.A. 1819/20–1902

Born at Burley Mill, Kirkcudbrightshire 1819/20, son of a millwright and elder brother of James Faed (q.v.). Took up miniature painting at an early age and showed more than average talent. Wandered about from place to place executing paintings, but in 1841 went to Edinburgh and was at 5 York Place. Exhibited at the R.S.A., 1841–1895, became A.R.S.A. 1847, and R.S.A. in 1851. Went to London in 1862, exhibited at the R.A. etc., 1855–1893. Returned to Scotland in 1880. Painted miniatures early in his career and later painted principally figure subjects and outdoor scenes. He had a number of children of whom four became artists. Died at Ardmore, Gatehouse of Fleet, 22 October 1902. His miniatures are scarce and as he did not always sign his work, may pass unrecognised. He was an excellent artist and his work somewhat resembles that of Sir W. C. Ross (q.v.). A miniature in my collection, of Mrs. Robertson née Mary Anne Manson, is one of the most attractive nineteenth-century miniatures that I have seen. The draperies, green silk dress edged with mauve ribbon, and shot-silk shawl are perfectly painted and the features of an obviously serene and beautiful woman are drawn and painted with a delicate touch. I do not know of any of his work available to the public, other than a large painting called 'The Evening Hour' depicting figures, which is in the N.G. Edinburgh.

*Faesch, Johann Ludwig Wernhard. *c.* 1738–1778
Born in Basle *c.* 1738. Worked as a miniaturist and designer in Paris and London. Painted portraits of members of the theatrical profession in their roles. Died in Paris 20 May 1778.

*Fagnani, Miss Nina. (fl. 1892)
Born in New York. Possibly the daughter of Giuseppe (Joseph) Fagnani (1819–1873). Exhibited at the R.A. 1892, from 14 Rue Lauriston, Paris.

Fahey, James. 1804–1885
Born at Paddington 16 April 1804. Exhibited at the R.A., B.I., N.W.C.S., etc., from 1825–1885. Studied engraving under his uncle John Swaine, and was a pupil of G. Scharf (q.v.). Studied in Paris. Became a member of the N.W.C.S. (now R.I.) in 1834 and was its secretary 1838–1874. Taught drawing at the Merchant Taylors' School from 1856. Executed portraits and landscapes and, according to a directory of 1830, painted miniatures when working at 280 Strand. Died at the Grange, Shepherd's Bush Green, 11 December 1885.

Faija, Guglielmo. 1803–d. after 1861
Born in Palermo 21 March 1803. Pupil of Comte at Naples and of F. Millet at Paris. Exhibited at the Paris Salon 1831–1837, after which time he was in London and exhibited at the R.A., 1838–1848. He painted miniatures on ivory, portraits in watercolour, and enamels. Was a good artist who worked slightly in the manner of Sir W. C. Ross (q.v.) whose works he frequently copied. Was patronised by the Royal Family and a number of his miniatures are at Windsor Castle. His last dated miniature so far recorded is of the Prince Consort, dated '1861' and painted from a photograph taken fourteen days before the Prince's death. He signed G. Faija, and Faija, often followed by a date.

Faithorne, William. *c.* 1616–1691
Born in London *c.* 1616, studied painting and engraving under Robert Peake (q.v.) and under an engraver, John Payne. Joined the Royalists in the Civil War, was taken prisoner at Basing House, 1645 and was imprisoned at Aldersgate where he executed engravings. Was a more skilful draughtsman than many of his predecessors and wherever possible drew his subjects from life. Was banished

to France where he is said to have been a pupil of Philippe de Champaigne and Nanteuil. Returned to London *c.* 1650 and for a time shared a house with W. Hollar (q.v.). Sold prints by himself and others in a shop near Temple Bar. In 1662 he published *The Art of Graveing and Etching*. Pepys mentioned buying prints from him. Left his shop *c.* 1680 to devote himself to drawing and engraving portraits. Executed chiefly crayons from life but also drew in plumbago and painted miniatures. De Piles in his *Art of Painting* says, 'He was also a great proficient in graving, as likewise in painting, especially in miniature, of which there are many instances now in England.' Was a friend of T. Flatman (q.v.) who composed some verses in his praise. He married Mary, daughter of Captain Grand or Cround, by whom he had two sons and a daughter. His wife predeceased him. He died in Printing House Square, May 1691 and was buried in St. Anne's Church, Blackfriars. John Fillian and Thomas Hill were his pupils. Original works by him are rare. Examples may be found at the B.M., the Bodleian Library, Oxford, which has a portrait of the Hon. R. Boyle by him, and the Ashmolean Museum, Oxford, which contains his superb portrait of John Aubrey (1626–1697). This miniature is executed in black lead and Indian ink on vellum, with the addition of red chalk in the flesh tints. It is dated 1666, and although it is not signed it is authenticated by an engraving. The miniature was given by the artist to the subject, and by him to the Museum. For further information see article by C. F. Bell and Mrs. R. Poole, *Walpole Society*, Vol. XIV, pp. 49–55.

*Falcke, Miss Gladys L. (fl. 1904–1910)
Of Birmingham. Exhibited at the R.A., 1904–1910.

Falconet, Pierre Étienne. 1741–1791
Born in Paris, 8 October 1741, son of the sculptor E. M. Falconet. Came to London 1766 to study painting under Reynolds. Won a premium at the Society of Arts 1766 and 1768. Entered the R.A. Schools 14 February 1769. Exhibited black lead portraits at the Society of Artists 1767–1772; was elected F.S.A. in 1771. Exhibited at the R.A., 1773. Went to St. Petersburg and painted oil portraits for the Empress Catherine and others. Married M. A. Collot, a sculptress, 30 January 1777. In 1778 he returned to Paris, was separated from his wife, and died in Paris 25 June 1791. Although not strictly a miniaturist he executed small pencil portraits of artists and others in which the face was slightly tinted. The B.M. has some engravings after Falconet, and two portrait drawings by him, signed 'P.F.del.1768'.

Fallon, A. D. (fl. 1828)
Exhibited at the R.A., 1828.

Fane (I). (fl. 1776)
An English artist who lived at Staines. Exhibited at the R.A., 1776. The R.A. catalogues for 1776 give his address as Dean Street, St. Ann's (presumably Soho).

Fane (II). (fl. *c.* 1840)
A miniature at the Metropolitan Museum, New York, bears the inscription 'The English Artist / Fane / by himself'. This has been attributed to Fane (I) (q.v.), but as the costume appears to be *c.* 1840, the attribution is impossible, and the miniature must have been the work of another artist of this name.

Fanshawe, Miss Althea. 1759–1824
Born 11 February 1759, daughter of Simon Fanshawe of Dengie. Was an amateur artist who had private means; wrote verses and religious books and executed embroidery. A miniature self-portrait of the artist was seen by Long. She died after a life of suffering from fits and gout, 20 April 1824. She signed her work A.F. in monogram.

*Farhall, Miss Hilda M. (Mrs. Sare). (fl. 1905–1910)
Of Sutherland and London. Exhibited at the R.A., 1905–1910. Her sitters included J. H. Sare, Esq. She exhibited under her maiden name up to 1908.

Farington, Frances Ann
Possibly a relation of Joseph Farington, R.A., (1747–1821), whose miniature portrait by her after Sir W. Newton (q.v.) was sold at Puttick and Simpson's 11 November 1921.

*Farquhar, Miss Lizzie Boly. See **Vivian, Mrs. Comley (Lizzie)**

*Farrah, Mrs. F. E. W. (fl. 1900–1904). See also **Farrar, Frederica**
Of London. Exhibited at the Society of Miniaturists 1900–1904.

*Farrar, Mrs. Frederica Emily Wood née Payne, A.R.W.S. b.1870, wife of Ernest Farrar. See also **Farrah, Mrs. F.E.W**
An attractive miniature of an unknown young lady, executed by the above artist *c.* 1900, is in my collection. It is signed 'F.E.W.Farrar.'; an inscription on the reverse of the frame reads 'A Portrait / F.E.W.Farrar (Mrˢ)'. The miniature is painted in soft colours with a sky background. The artist may be identical with Mrs. F. E. W. Farrah (q.v.).

*Farren, Miss Jessie. (fl. 1886–1895)
Of Scarborough and London. Exhibited at the R.A., 1886–1895. Possibly related to Robert Farren, also of Scarborough, who exhibited at the R.A. in 1889.

Farrer, Henry. (fl. *c.* 1826)
Lived in Euston Street, London. Possibly the son of T. Farrer (q.v.) and identical with the Mr. Henry Farrer who lent miniatures to the exhibition at the South Kensington Museum 1865; they were 'Mrs. Farrer' by H. Farrer, and 'Master Farrer' by Henry Farrer. A good miniature of a lady signed with a scratched cursive signature 'H. Farrer 1826' is in the collection of Major R. M. O. de la Hey. A mezzotint of Denvil, an actor, after Farrer is at the B.M.

Farrer, T. (fl. 1805?–1820)
Of London. Exhibited at the R.A., 1805?–1820, or 1815–1820. The exhibit in 1805 is listed as by this artist in the index but catalogued as by J. C. D. Engleheart (q.v.). Farrer's name does not appear again until 1815. Some of his exhibits were of members of the theatrical profession. Undoubtedly related to H. Farrer (q.v.) who may have been his son, both of whom lived in Euston Street, London, as did L. H. Farrer and J. H. Farrer, also artists.

Farrier, Miss Charlotte. (fl. 1826–1875)
Of London. Exhibited at the R.A., B.I. etc., 1826–1875. Undoubtedly related to Robert Farrier (q.v.) as both artists exhibited from the same addresses, which included 6 Wellesley Street, Chelsea, and 7 Smith Street, Chelsea. Her sitters included Lady

Boyce, The Countess of Cork, the Hon. Ashley Ponsonby, the Dowager Lady Croft, Lady Parke and members of the Pilkington family. She was a prolific artist.

Farrier, Robert. 1796–1879
Born in Chelsea 1796. Entered the R.A. schools 15 January 1820 aged 24. Exhibited at the R.A., B.I., N.W.C.S. etc., 1818–1872. Painted miniatures, domestic subjects and scenes from schoolboy life. Pigot's *London and Provincial Directory* for 1834 gives two artists of this name, one a portrait painter at 6 Wellesley Street, Chelsea and the other a miniature painter at 2 Pelham Place, Chelsea. Farrier died in Chelsea 1879. Undoubtedly related to Miss Charlotte Farrier (q.v.). The V. & A. M. has paintings (not miniatures) by Farrier.

Faucigny. (fl. 1797)
Of London. Exhibited at the R.A. 1797, from 140 Oxford Street. His sitters included 'The Elector of Mentz' and a French gentleman.

Faulkner, Joshua Wilson. (fl. 1809–1820)
Born in Manchester. Exhibited at the R.A., and the Liverpool Academy 1809–1820. Painted portraits and miniatures and was a member of the Liverpool Academy. His brother Benjamin Rawlinson Faulkner (1787–1849) was a portrait painter. Worked slightly in the manner of Daniel (q.v.) of Bath. An engraving of C. M. Young, an actor, by S. Freeman 1807 after J. W. Faulkner, is at the B.M.

*Faulkner, Miss Nina. (fl. 1892)
Of London. Exhibited a miniature of Miss Eveline Faulkner at the R.A. 1892, from 7 Hyde Park Mansions, N.W.

Favard, Ville, or **Villefavard?** (fl. 1794–1797)
Of London. Exhibited at the R.A., 1794–1797. Exhibited 1794–1795 and 1797, from 67 Margaret Street, Cavendish Square, and in 1796 from 125 The Strand, when his initial was given as P. Favard in the catalogue.

*Fawkes, Miss Madeline C. (fl. 1909–1911)
Exhibited at the R.A. 1909 and 1911, from Elmfield, Cheltenham. Exhibited miniatures and subjects in oil.

Fayerman(n), Miss Anne Charlotte. See Bartholomew, Mrs. Valentine

*Fayram, John. (fl. *c.* 1743)
The *Daily Advertiser*, 24 December 1744, refers to a John Fayram, limner, St. James's 'lately deceased' who executed drawings in crayon.

*Fayrer, Miss Ethel. (fl. 1902–1903)
Of Macclesfield, Cheshire. Exhibited at the R.A., 1902–1903. Her sitters included Nora Griffin and Eva Mary, daughter of Lieut. A. Trevor Dawson, R.N.

Fearson, J. See Frearson, John

*Fellowes, Mrs. P. (Madeline). (fl. 1903–1905)
Of Winchester and Brussels. Exhibited at the R.A., 1903 and 1905.

*Fenton, Miss Dora. See Blyth, Mrs. Dora

Ferg, Frans de Paula. 1689–1740
Born in Vienna 2 May 1689. Went to Germany 1718; settled in London *c.* 1720. Painted landscapes, genre subjects and executed etchings. A painting on silver 2¼ × 4 in. of the 'Building of Soloman's Temple' was sold at Christie's March 1885 and

catalogued as by 'P.Ferg.' Benezit records that he died in London in 1740.

Ferguson, James. 1710–1776
Born in Banffshire 25 April 1710 of poor parents. Had no education other than learning to read. Worked for a farmer and discovered that he had an aptitude for mathematics; studied the stars whilst looking after the sheep. Showed a talent for drawing and was sent by friends to study in Edinburgh. Drew miniature portraits in Indian ink. Worked in Edinburgh and London. Became known as 'Ferguson the astronomer'. Advertised that he drew pictures in 'China ink' for 12/6 and 15/- in 1752. The following notice appeared in the *Daily Advertiser* 27 November 1746, 'Mr. Ferguson limner in China ink, has removed from Compton Street to the White Perriwig next door to the Golden Ball in Gt. Pultney St. near Golden Sq. where he draws pictures as usual for nine shillings or goes abroad to do them for ½ guinea'. He died in London 16 November 1776. Several miniatures by him were in the Wellesley sale at Sotheby's in 1920. His works are rather precise and neatly executed; they are not, as far as I know, ever signed, and are not always recognised. Examples of his work are in the V. & A. M.

*Fernal. (fl. 1782). See also **Fernell, John**
Was a seal engraver; according to the *Adam's Weekly Courant* he worked in Chester 4 June 1782. May have painted miniatures. Possibly identical with the J. Fernell (q.v.) of Liverpool.

*Ferneley, Miss Edith Helen. (fl. 1900–1902)
Of London. Exhibited at the R.A., 1900–1902.

Fernell, John. (fl. 1824–1839). See also **Fernal**
The above artist was working in Liverpool 1824–1839. In 1828 he was living at 54 Paradise Street. He may have been identical with the Fernal (q.v.) who was in Chester in 1782.

Ferrand, Jacques Philippe. 1653–1732
Born at Joigny, Yonne, 25 July 1653, son of a physician. Was a pupil of Mignard and Samuel Bernard. Employed at Court and was a member of the Académie Royale. Travelled in Germany, England and Italy. Was an enamellist and published a work on the subject – *L'Art du Feu ou de Peindre en Email.* Died in Paris 5 January 1732. A portrait of Ferrand, by Largielliere, is said to be in the Museum of Rheims.

Ferrière, François. 1752–1839
Born in Geneva 11 July 1752. Studied art in Paris 1770; returned to Geneva where he married. Came to England 1793. Exhibited at the R.A., B.I., 1793–1804 and 1817–1822. Was a successful and prolific painter and was patronised by the Royal Family. In 1804 he went to St. Petersburg and Moscow (*c.* 1810). Lost all his fortunes in the French invasion 1812. Returned to St. Petersburg where he was made a member of the Academy in 1813. Was back in England 1817. From 1819 onwards he describes himself in the R.A. catalogue as 'Portrait Painter to Her Imperial Majesty the Dowager Empress of all the Russians, and to the Grand Dukes Nicolas and Michael, Professor of the Academy of Painting at Geneva, and Associate to that of St. Petersburg.' Returned to Geneva in 1822 and worked there until 1835. In 1836 he retired and settled in Morges where he remained until his death 25 December 1839. He painted portraits in pastel and oil and executed miniatures, some of which were in enamel. Ferrière was a good artist and his works express character. Some of his miniatures are painted on paper and some are in profile; his works painted in water-colour have a lot of gum

mixed with the paint so that the effect is that of oil painting. He usually signed F. F. followed by a date or F. Ferrière p¹, followed by a date, and Ferrière followed by a date. Long says he signed without an accent on his name. My copy of the R.A. catalogue for 1795 contains annotations giving his sitters which include 'Mr. Sandby' (possibly Paul Sandby), Lady E. and Lady C. Montague and Mrs. Ferrière. He exhibited a miniature self-portrait in 1801 and a large self-portrait in 1818. He had a distinguished clientele which included a number of Scottish sitters among whom were the Countess of Dalkeith, Lord Scott and Lady Ann Montague. Examples of his work are at the V. & A. M., the S.N.P.G., and the Musée Rath, Geneva. Miniatures by him of Admiral Richard, Earl Howe, James Wauchope and Major General Ramsay, were exhibited in Edinburgh in 1965.

Ferrière, Louis Ami. 1792–1866
Born 21 September 1792 in Geneva, son of F. Ferrière (q.v.); came to England in 1794, where he was educated and became a naturalised Englishman. Followed his father to Russia. Returned to England 1810. Was employed for twenty-two years at the War Office. Married on 9 January 1815, Cecilia (born 1797), daughter of P. N. Violet (q.v.). Exhibited at the R.A., 1817–1828, including a portrait of his son in 1826. Became British Consul in Tunis. Lived for five years in Geneva where he exhibited in 1837. Ferrière died in 1866 leaving a widow, who died on 28 August 1880. His sitters included the Hon. Miss Arundell, Mr. Beverley, Surgeon and Naturalist 'to the Expedition lately set off to the North Pole.' A miniature of A. W. Töpffer by Ferrière is in the Musée Rath in Geneva. An engraved portrait of the Countess of Lovelace, after Ferrière, is in the B.M.

Ffoulkes, Mrs. John Powell (Miss Caroline Jocelyn). 1779–1854
Was born 3 April 1779, née Caroline Mary Jocelyn, second daughter and heiress of Captain Robert Jocelyn, R.N. of Stanstead Bury House, Herts., and Bryn of Barcut, Denbighshire, as well as Maes y Coed, Flintshire. Studied under Cosway (q.v.); married John Powell Ffoulkes of Eriviat, Denbighshire. Died 19 March 1854.

Field, or Fielder. d. 1800
Worked in Birmingham. His name may have been Fielder. Painted portraits on snuffboxes, jewellery, etc., and taught David Cox (q.v.). He committed suicide in 1800.

Field, Robert. 1769–1819
Possibly born in Gloucester *c.* 1769 Entered the R.A. Schools 19 November 1790 aged 21, as an engraver. Lived in London until 1793 or 1794, when he sailed for Baltimore. Was in New York in 1794, Philadelphia 1795; drew portraits of Washington and his wife; worked in Boston, Baltimore, etc., and Halifax, Nova Scotia, *c.* 1808, where he painted a number of portraits in oil, including one of the Governor General, Sir John Cope Sherbrooke. Exhibited a portrait of Sir A. Cochrane, K.B. in 1810 from Halifax, N.S. Was one of the best American miniaturists of his time. His work is finely executed and painted in pastel shades with a soft brush stroke. Went to Jamaica in 1816 and died there on 9 August 1819 of yellow fever. Field was said to have been a handsome man, fond of music, a good conversationalist, a sturdy loyalist and a member of the Church of England. Some of his miniatures were copied from portraits. Examples of his work are in the Metropolitan Museum, New York. An oil portrait by him of Bishop Inglis is in the N.P.G.

He engraved a portrait of George Washington after a miniature by Walter Robertson (q.v.).

Field, S. (fl. 1803)

Exhibited at the R.A., 1803.

Fielding, Nathan Theodore. (fl. 1770–1818)

Lived near Halifax, later worked in London and c. 1802 at Keswick and Ambleside. In 1809 he was at Manchester. Exhibited at the Society of Artists 1791 and the Free Society of Artists 1770 and 1772, and at the B.I., O.W.C.S. etc., till 1818. Painted oil portraits and landscapes as well as miniatures. Was well patronised by the gentry of Yorks. and Lancs. His son, Copley Fielding, became a notable landscape painter in water-colour. The V. & A. M. has a miniature portrait of an unknown man by Fielding; it is rather loosely painted. A miniature of Henry Heaton, Mayor of Doncaster (died 1821) is also in the V. & A. M.; there is a considerable amount of opaque white on the hair and cravat. Long records the order of his christian names as Theodore Nathan, but the *D.N.B.*, and Graves in his various works record his name as Nathan Theodore Fielding.

*Figgis, Miss Kathleen E. (fl. 1904–1912)

Of London. Exhibited at the R.A., 1904–1912. Painted miniatures, subjects and portraits in oil and water-colour.

*Fildes, Miss Lucy. (fl. 1903)

Of Sale, nr. Manchester. Exhibited at the R.A. 1903, from Studio, Tatten Buildings, Sale.

*Finch, Francis Oliver. 1802–1862

Of London. Was born in 1802. Exhibited at the R.A. and O.W.C.S. (of which he was a member) 1817–1862. Painted landscapes, but according to a note by Long, showed ability as a miniaturist. Died in 1862.

Finch, Miss H.

An amateur artist. Known only by a miniature copy of a female head noted by Pearl Finch in *History of Burley-on-the-Hill, Rutland*, 1901, Vol. II, p. 22.

Finch, R. (fl. 1795)

Of Southwark. Exhibited at the R.A. 1795, from Long Land, Southwark. The exhibit was catalogued as a portrait of a gentleman; in my copy of the catalogue Duveen noted that the sitter was Mr. Gray.

*Finch, Madame Renée. (fl. 1907–1908)

Of London. Exhibited at the R.A. and S.M., 1907–1908, from 18 Bath Road, Bedford Park.

*Findlater, Countess of. (fl. 1779)

A miniature self-portrait of her painted in 1779 was seen by Long.

Finlayson, John. c. 1730–c. 1776

Was born c. 1730. Of London. Exhibited at the Free Society of Artists 1762–1763 and at the Society of Artists 1768. Painted miniatures in water-colour and enamel, and executed engravings. Awarded a premium by the Society of Arts in 1764 for an enamel painting, and a gold palette and thirty guineas for a mezzotint in 1773. Died in c. 1776.

Finn, Henry James William. 1787–1840

Born in Sydney, U.S.A., 17 June 1787. Was brought up in New York, where he studied law. Later became an actor and miniature painter. Toured England c. 1811 with a company of actors; acted in Philadelphia in 1817; played in New York in 1818: spent several years in Savannah. Was in England in 1821, painting miniatures and acting. Settled in Boston in 1822 where he continued to act and paint; he exhibited at the Boston Athenaeum 1830–1833. He died on 13 January 1840, when the steamer Lexington was burnt in Long Island Sound.

Finney, Samuel. 1718/19–1798

Born at Wilmslow, Cheshire, 13 February 1718/19, son of Samuel Finney of Fulshaw and his wife Esther, née Davenport. Studied law in London c. 1740, and became an Attorney, but gave it up for painting. Exhibited at the Free Society and Society of Artists 1761–1766; was a member of the latter Society. Married as his first wife, Martha Foster, of Hereford. Worked for clients in Bath and Bristol etc. Painted large portraits and miniatures on ivory and enamel. Early in his career he executed portraits in Indian ink. Was appointed Enamel and Miniature painter to Queen Charlotte on 31 December, 1763. According to Finney's notes (Chester Record Office), he was presented by the Queen's order with 'the King's and Queen's picture in large, painted by Mr Ramsey'. Lived for a time on the south side of Leicester Square. Was a successful artist and had a distinguished clientele. Retired to Fulsham, Cheshire, in 1769, and became a Justice of the Peace. Died in 1798 and was buried at Wilmslow. Was survived by his second wife Ann, to whom he left the first choice of his drawings, pictures and plasters etc. Finney was a good artist who worked in the manner of Lens (q.v.). His miniatures are usually elegant. He used stippling on some of his backgrounds and in the shading of the face. Several miniatures of unknown ladies by this artist are in the collection of E. G. Paine of New York. An attractive miniature of an unknown girl in a hat, by Finney, is in the collection of Major R. M. O. de la Hey. A collection of five family portraits traditionally said to be by Finney were datable from c. 1750–1755.

Finucane, Matthias. (fl. c. 1798)

Possibly of Guernsey. A miniature of a man, c. 1798, signed almost vertically 'FINUCANE' was seen by Long, who says that its effect was obtained by colour and contrasts rather than by modelling; the face was pale and the nose and eyelids etc., outlined with brown, and grey shading. The background was partly stippled and partly hatched. Two signed drawings of 1798 by this artist were seen at the V. & A. M.; one was of Lady Dalrymple. Miss J. Beetham (q.v.) exhibited a portrait of a Mr. Finucane at the R.A., in 1805. A miniature of General Sir Thomas Bradford, at the age of 20, signed on the front vertically, 'By Matthias Finucane Guernsey, May 1798' was noted at Sotheby's. A miniature of an officer by Finucane was formerly in the Hand collection.

Fischer, Johann Georg Paul. 1786–1875

Born in Hanover 16 September 1786, son of an engraver. Was a pupil of H. Ramberg and assisted him to paint portraits, theatrical decorations and wall paintings. Came to England in 1810. Worked principally in London and Cheltenham. Exhibited at the R.A. and S.B.A., 1817–1852. May have visited India c. 1848 as one of his exhibits in 1850 was a native of Cashmere. Painted members of the Royal Family including Queen Victoria and Queen Charlotte. Died in London 12 December 1875. He signed I. Paul Fischer, Paul Fisher, P. Fisher and I. P. F. The carmines he used were fresh with light shadows and he used long and distinct brush strokes, and a fair amount of gum with his paint. Some of his works are at Windsor Castle. The B.M. has examples of his work including two small pencil portraits and an engraving after him. He lent a miniature by himself of H.M. George IV and one of H.R.H. the Duke of Kent, 1818, both on ivory, to the exhibition at the South Kensington Museum 1865.

Fischer, Leopold. b. c. 1813, d. after 1864

Born in Vienna 1813, where his father was a painter in the porcelain factory. Entered the Vienna Academy c. 1828 and exhibited there 1832–1847, and at the Oesterreichischer Kunstverein from 1850–1864. Travelled in Italy and came to London. Exhibited at the R.A., 1854. Painted miniatures and portraits in water-colour. Used fresh pure colours. Signed L. Fischer and Leopold Fischer. Several of his works are listed by Schidlof. His sitters included the Rev. George Hills, the Hon. Mary Catherine Stanhope (daughter of the Rt. Hon. Viscount Mahon), the Hon. Philip James Stanhope (son of the Rt. Hon. Viscount Mahon) the Countess of Erdoby, and the two younger children of the Rt. Hon. Lord Henniker.

Fisher. See also **Fisher, J. (I)**

Of Bristol. May have been identical with J. Fisher (I) (q.v.). Taught John Syer (1815–1885) at Bristol when Syer was a young man.

*Fisher, Alexander. (fl. 1886–1914)

Of London. Exhibited enamels at the R.A. etc., 1886–1914. His addresses included Warwick Gardens, Kensington and St. Mary Abbot's Place, Kensington. His exhibits included miniatures, portraits, sculptures and a book cover in enamel.

Fisher, G. (fl. 1849)

Of London. Exhibited at the R.A., 1849. The exhibit was a portrait of the Hon. Mrs. Baillie.

Fisher, J. (I). (fl. 1849–1858). See also **Fisher, J. (II)** and **Fisher**

Of Bristol and Clifton. Exhibited at the R.A., 1849–1858. May have been identical with the artist Fisher (q.v.) who taught J. Syer. He exhibited a self-portrait at the R.A., in 1849. Was possibly identical with J. Fisher (II) (q.v.).

*Fisher, J. (II). (fl. 1845–1854). See also **Fisher, J. (I)**

I know of three miniatures all signed 'J. Fisher' in cursive writing and followed by a date, the first two letters of the signature being conjoined. They represent an unknown lady dated '1845', and two attractive young girls, possibly her daughters, both dated '1854'. The portraits are executed in water-colour on paper and are all superbly drawn, and full of character. The colouring is fresh and clear and the work is reminiscent of that of Sir W. C. Ross (q.v.). The portrait of the lady shows her in a black dress wearing an attractive gauze cap, one girl is wearing a black habit and a black hat with feathers, and the other is dressed in blue with a pink bow tying her lace collar. The two former miniatures are in my collection and the latter in the collection of Miss A. Warner. The artist may have been identical with J. Fisher (I) (q.v.) about whom little is known.

*Fisher, Miss Margaret D. (fl. 1900–1901)

Of London. Exhibited at the Society of Miniaturists 1900–1901.

*Fisher, Miss Vaudrey. (fl. 1910–1913)

Of London. Exhibited at the R.A., 1910–1913. Painted miniatures and subjects in oil.

*Fison, Mrs. J. See **Chalker, Miss Cissie**

*Fitzgerald, Mrs. Annie. (fl. 1888)

Of Old Charlton, Kent. Exhibited at the R.A., 1888.

Flatman, Thomas. 1635–1688

Born in London 1635, son of a clerk in Chancery. Educated at Winchester and New College, Oxford, where he was elected a Fellow in 1656. Was admitted to the Inner Temple 31 May 1655 and called to the Bar 11 May 1662. On 11 December 1666 the King requested the University of Cambridge to admit him as M.A. Took up art and became a very distinguished miniaturist, besides painting oil portraits and publishing a volume of poems and songs, in 1674. Shared a house for a time with Samuel Woodford. Was a friend of Charles and Mary Beale (q.v.) and painted them and their children in 1661. Taught their sons Charles and Bartholomew Beale (q.v.). Remained a close friend of the Beale family and wrote numerous letters of an effusive nature to Charles Beale, sen. His artistic temperament is revealed in his writings, and he appears to have had alternating periods of elation and depression. Flatman was of an earnestly religious temperament and was related to Sancroft, Dean of St. Paul's, and later Archbishop of Canterbury. He married a rich girl 26 November 1672 and Anthony à Wood remarks that he was 'smitten with a fair virgin and more with her fortune.' The son of this marriage died before his father. Flatman had an estate in Tishton, near Diss, Norfolk, but appears to have lived in Three-leg Alley, St. Bride's, London. His circle of friends and acquaintances included Walton, Cotton, Faithorne (q.v.), Purcell, Blow, etc. His earliest known miniatures are dated 1661, and Goulding lists ten signed and dated miniatures between 1661 and 1683. His work shows the influence of Samuel Cooper (q.v.) particularly in the earlier miniatures which show the characteristics of the duller type of Cooper's portraits. Examples of this period are signed and dated portraits such as those of Samuel Woodford, 1661 (in the Fitzwilliam Museum, Cambridge), an unknown man dated '1662' and Charles Beale, sen., both in the V. & A. M. These examples are good but uninspired portraits, painted in a more hesitant manner than Flatman's later works. They tend to have a brownish flesh colour which is unattractive. Often his miniatures have a sky background, the blue being harsher than that used by Cooper. In maturity Flatman painted with assurance and brilliance and it is not surprising that his works have often been identified with Cooper's, or even had Cooper's initials added at a later date. His self-portrait dated 1673, formerly in the collection of the Duke of Buccleuch, was presented to the V. & A. M., in memory of the late Basil Long. It is brilliantly executed and cleared up the hitherto obscure problem of iconography. The matter was fully ventilated by Mr. Reynolds in the *Burlington Magazine*, March 1947, pp. 63–67. Comparison between the works of Flatman and Cooper reveals that the coarseness so often visible in Flatman's portraits is unlike anything produced by Cooper. The finest pair of miniatures executed by Flatman are, in my opinion, those of Sir Henry and Lady Langley, of the Abbey, Shrewsbury, from the collection of the Earl of Powis; they are both signed 'TF' and were among nine works by Flatman exhibited in Edinburgh 1965. His signature varied from TF (monogram) to T.F. in separate letters. Many of his miniatures are unsigned. Examples of his work are to be found in most of the great collections, including those of H.M. the Queen, the Dukes of Buccleuch and Portland, and Earl Beauchamp, besides the V. & A. M., the Fitzwilliam Museum, Cambridge and the Wallace Collection, London. Several miniatures by him were loaned to the South Kensington Exhibition of 1865.

Flavelle, William. b. *c.* 1786

Born in Dublin *c.* 1786, of a Huguenot family which had settled in the north of Ireland. Studied at the Dublin Society schools; worked in Dublin. Executed miniatures and engravings. He and his wife Julia had two sons, Thomas and Henry Erasmus Flavelle; Thomas was a gem and seal engraver, and Henry a silversmith. His brother, Henry, was a dentist in Dublin. Was possibly alive as late as 1820.

*Flaxman, John, R.A. 1755–1826

Was born in 1755. This famous sculptor is not usually regarded as a miniaturist, but a self-portrait catalogued as by him was lent to the exhibition at the South Kensington Museum 1865. He exhibited at the Free Society of Artists, the Society of Artists and the R.A., 1767–1827 (the last exhibit being entered after his death). Died in 1826.

Flaxman, Miss Mary Ann. 1768–1833

Was born in 1768. Half-sister of John Flaxman, R.A. (q.v.), the sculptor. Worked on the continent as a governess. Was living at Flaxman's house from 1810 till her death in 1826. Exhibited at the Society of Artists 1790 and at the R.A., 1786–1819. Painted mythological subjects, miniatures, and executed wax portraits and drawings. Some of her works were engraved by William Blake (q.v.). A miniature of her, which may be a self-portrait, is at the N.P.G. Died in 1833.

Flaxman, William. *c.* 1753–1795?

Born in York (?) *c.* 1753. Elder brother of John Flaxman, R.A. (q.v.) who worked in London. Exhibited at the Free Society of Artists 1768 and at the R.A., 1781–1793. Executed wax portraits and may have attempted miniatures, for in 1785 he exhibited two portraits in the miniature section. Died in 1795?

Fleischmann, Adolph. (fl. 1851)

Probably German or Austrian. Worked in London. Exhibited a portrait of the 'Prince of Nepaul' at the R.A., 1851. Schidlof mentions two artists of this name who worked on the continent, Friedrich Fleischmann and Georg Fleischmann. In 1851 he gave his address as 43 Gerrard Street, Soho.

*Fleming, William J. (fl. 1887)

Of Leeds. Exhibited at the R.A., 1887. His sitters included 'the late George Cruikshank Esq.'

*Fletcher, Miss Annie G. (Mrs. E. J. Houle). (fl. 1895–1914)

Exhibited at the R.A. 1895–1914, from various London addresses. Painted miniatures and portraits in oil. Exhibits included a portrait in oil of the late General Sir Michael Biddulph, G.C.B., R.A., Black Rod; Mrs. Mullens; and Miss Hilda Marion, and Arnold, children of W. Wolfe Fletcher, Esq.

*Fletcher, Miss Hilda M. (fl. 1907)

Exhibited at the R.A. 1907, from Marlingford Hall, nr. Norwich.

Flight, J. (Joseph?). (fl. 1802–1806)

Of London. Exhibited at the R.A., 1802–1806. An engraved portrait of Alexander Bengo, published in 1814, after Flight, is at the B.M. His sitters included Mr. C. Townley, and Mr. Palmer of Drury Lane. The above artist was probably identical with Joseph Flight who entered the R.A. Schools 10 October 1794 aged 17.

*Flower, Noel. (fl. 1898–1909)

Of London. Exhibited at the R.A. 1898–1909, from various London addresses including 17 Holland Park Road, Kensington, from which address Ernest B. Lloyd exhibited a portrait of Kathleen Flower. Painted portraits, historical and genre subjects as well as miniatures. In 1900 he exhibited an oil portrait of Major Lamorock Flower, at the R.A.

Foldsone, Miss Anne. See **Mee, Mrs. Joseph**

Foldsone, John. d. *c.* 1783

Of London. A portrait painter and copyist of pictures. Exhibited at the Society of Artists and the R.A., 1769–1783. His only known miniature is of an unknown lady painted on ivory and signed 'foldsone pinxt' in the collection of the Duke of Bedford.

*Follett, Annie. (fl. *c.* 1830)

I have seen a rectangular miniature on ivory of a child, *c.* 1830 signed on the reverse 'Annie Follett, Duke St.'. It is quite attractive but loosely painted.

*Fontaine, H. (fl. 1826)

A rectangular miniature by H. Fontaine, signed and dated '1826' was sold at Sotheby's 5 June 1967. The sitter, William Emery, was an underwriter at Lloyds. The artist does not appear to have been previously recorded; he may have been related to George Fontaine, painter, who entered the R.A. Schools 20 March 1795 at the age of 19. The miniature was well painted, depicting the sitter almost half-length, wearing a dark blue coat, yellow vest and black cravat.

*Foot, Miss Rita. 1886–1965

Born in Dublin 8 October 1886. Was a pupil of Miss Liza Hallam in Dublin. Exhibited at the Royal Hibernian Academy. Executed most of her work before 1914. She died 28 August 1965. A miniature by her of the Rev. Ralph Michael Lanyon Westropp (born 1907) as a child, is signed and dated, 'Rita Foot / 1912' and is in the possession of the sitter. He is wearing a sailor costume and is painted against a sky blue background. It is well painted and expressive. Her brother, Major General Foot, lives in Dublin.

Foottit, Harrison. (fl. 1772–1774)

Of London. Exhibited at the R.A., 1772–1774. Was apparently still practising until nearly the end of the century. His sitters included Mrs. Punster.

*Forbes, Miss Rachel H. (fl. 1907–1914)

Of London. Exhibited at the R.A. 1907–1914, from 9 Campden Mansions, The Mall, Kensington, and from 18 Cathcart Road, South Kensington.

*Forbes-Robertson, Miss Margaret. See **Robertson, Miss Margaret Forbes**

Ford, Charles. 1801–1870

Of Bath. Born in 1801. Exhibited at the R.A. 1830–1856, from various addresses in Bath. Was an associate of Wordsworth and Hannah More, and according to O'Brien was a pupil and friend of Sir Thomas Lawrence (q.v.). Was in his day one of the principal miniaturists at Bath. He may possibly have been related to Charles Ford, an ironmonger of Bath. He painted miniatures on ivory and portraits in water-colour. His portraits are expressive, the upper eyelids, nostrils and upper lip being strongly delineated and the costume painted with loose brush work. He mixed a lot of gum with his paints. A miniature of Colonel Robert Hall, formerly in the O'Brien collection, is inscribed on the reverse 'By C. Ford painted at Bath 1835'; the strokes modelling the face are well blended, the shading of the complexion being rather reddish. Many of his miniatures are rectangular. His sitters included Lord Weston, Sir William Cockburn, Bart., and Mr. Thomas Gill, Mayor of Bath. At the Pierpont Morgan sale, 24 June 1935, Lot 340 was a miniature by C. Ford of Miss Harriett Mellon, the celebrated actress. A miniature of Sir William Herschel, Bart., by Ford (1860), after L. Abbot, is in the

Holburne Museum, Bath. Examples of his work are in the Victoria Art Gallery, Bath, and the B.M. has an engraved portrait of Dr. J. W. Howell, after Ford.

Ford, J. E. (fl. 1793–c. 1830)

Of London and Cape Town. Exhibited at the R.A., 1793–1797, from 15 Camomile Street. Painted portraits and miniatures. In my set of the original catalogues of the R.A., which once belonged to Duveen, the latter noted that the portrait exhibited in 1795 was of 'Mr Ford'. In the same year he exhibited a miniature of a gentleman. A miniature of a boy in a tunic, signed 'J. E. Ford, 1824', was seen by Mr. A. J. B. Kiddell. He was working at Cape Town c. 1830. Schidlof mentions this artist and records a miniature of an officer signed on the reverse 'J. E. Ford / Cape Town' and one of a lady signed on the reverse 'J. E. Ford 1828'. He drew with accuracy and worked in noticeable crossed brush strokes, painting the accessories in gouache.

Ford, John. (fl. 1764–1776)

Of Bath and London. Exhibited at the Free Society of Artists 1764–1776. Was a sculptor and painted portraits and miniatures. Was probably identical with the John Ford who exhibited at the R.A., in 1779, from 8 Chapel Street, Bedford Row. The exhibits were two enamels, one of 'His Majesty' and the other of a lady.

Ford, William Bishop. 1832–1922

Of London; born in Whitfield Street, off Tottenham Court Road, 1832. Was a pupil of William Essex (q.v.) whom he assisted for ten years. Attended the Somerset House School of Design in 1847, and won prizes there. Exhibited at the R.A. etc., 1854–1895. Painted in enamel on porcelain, copper and gold. Executed paintings on porcelain for the Minton factory which were shown at the Paris Exhibition of 1855. Copied portraits of Scott, Garrick, etc. and copied pictures, heads of animals, etc. King Edward sat to him in 1902. Died in 1922. He usually signed W. B. Ford or W. Ford. His work is painted in the manner of Essex (q.v.) and is carefully executed. A self-portrait of the artist is in the V. & A. M., and is inscribed on the reverse 'Willm. B. Ford b. May 3rd 1832 as a token of affection for his first and only love, Janey, 1860'. The miniature is enamel on metal. An enamel miniature of Prince Albert (later Edward VII), formerly in the O'Brien collection, is inscribed on the reverse 'H.R.H. Albert Prince of Wales W.B.Ford pinx, 1865'. The V. & A. M. has some paintings on porcelain by Ford.

*Foreman, Miss Agnes Emily. (fl. 1910–1912)

Of Pembury, nr. Tunbridge Wells, Kent, and Crowborough, Sussex. Exhibited at the R.A., 1910 and 1912. Her sitters included Dorothy, daughter of the Rev. A. Capes Tarbolton. In 1910 she exhibited a portrait of her father.

Formby, John. (fl. 1774)

Of Liverpool. Exhibited at the Liverpool Society of Artists 1774. Painted miniatures and executed portraits in human hair.

Forrest, Miss B.

Graves, Long and Schidlof list the above artist as exhibiting at the R.A., in 1855 but I have been unable to trace her either in the index or the catalogue.

Forrest, Charles. (fl. 1765–1787). See also **F., C.**

Was admitted as a pupil to the Dublin Society

schools in 1765. Exhibited at the Society of Artists in William Street, Dublin 1771–1780 and at the Society of Artists in London in 1776. Executed chalk portraits, miniatures and water-colour landscapes. Was awarded a premium by the Dublin Society in 1772 for a drawing in chalks.

Forrest, Ion B. or **John B.** c. 1814–1870

Born in Aberdeenshire c. 1814. Was apprenticed to Thomas Fry, a London engraver. In 1837 he went to Philadelphia to engrave for the N.P.G. Also painted miniatures. May have been identical with J. B. Forrest of 46 Dean Street, London, who won awards for engraving at the Society of Arts in 1826–1827. Died in Hudson County, New Jersey in 1870.

*Forrest, J. B. See **Forrest, Ion B.**

Forster, Miss. 18th century

Of Dublin. Sister of John Forster (fl. 1773–1780), a landscape painter. Was a pupil of Thomas Boulger (q.v.). Exhibited at the Society of Artists in Dublin.

Forster, The Hon. Misses. fl. 19th century

Were apparently taught miniature painting by Miss E. E. Kendrick (q.v.).

Forster, C(harles). (fl. 1821–1847). See also **Foster, Charles**

Of London. Exhibited at the R.A., 1828–1847. Painted portraits, some of which were probably miniatures. Probably the father of Charles Forster, jun., (q.v.) and also of Robert E. Forster (q.v.). May have been identical with Charles Foster (q.v.). Long records seeing a profile miniature on card, signed and dated 'Jan. 1821' on the reverse. His sitters included Miss W. Halthorn; the Duchess of St. Leu, ex-Queen of Holland; Mr. Anderson of the Theatre Royal (in character); Captain Roper; and Miss Louisa Forster. His exhibit in 1847 was an architectural drawing. C. Forster, jun. (q.v.) exhibited from his address, 24 Grafton Street, in 1840, and R. E. Forster (q.v.) in 1838.

Forster, Charles. (fl. 1709–1717)

Probably a son of T. Forster (q.v.) in whose manner he worked, though with less ability. Executed plumbago miniatures. The V. & A. M. has a plumbago miniature of a youth signed 'C: Forster / Delin / 1711'. A plumbago drawing of the Duchess of Marlborough, after Kneller, signed 'Charles Forster' and dated '1709' was at one time in the Bodleian Library, Oxford.

Forster, Charles, junior. (fl. 1835–1855)

Of London. Probably the son of C. Forster (q.v.) from whose address he exhibited in 1840. Exhibited at the R.A., 1835–1855. Won a silver Isis medal from the Society of Arts in 1836 for an original miniature. Was undoubtedly related to R. E. Forster (q.v.) who also exhibited from the family house at 24 Grafton Street.

*Forster, Miss Emma. 1800–1848

Was born in 1800. Married Ambrose Poynter and was grandmother of C. F. Bell, M.A. Painted miniature copies of old masters. Died in 1848.

Forster, Robert E. (fl. 1835–1855)

Of London. Probably the brother or uncle of Charles Forster jun. (q.v.) whose address he shared in 1838. Exhibited at the R.A., 1838–1855.

Forster, Thomas. b. c. 1677

An artist about whose life nothing is known except that he executed plumbago miniatures of

outstanding quality. That he was born c. 1677 can be deduced from an entry by Vertue which reads: 'the head of Mr. Foster done by himself on vellum aeta 31 1708, ditto his sister, sold to Mr Glynn'. Dated examples of his work range from 1690–1713. This would mean that he excelled as a draughtsman at the early age of thirteen. He evidently had a distinguished clientele and may have worked in Ireland. Forster was probably one of the greatest 18th-century draughtsmen who executed plumbago miniatures. His portraits are very highly finished, full of character, and elegant. Several of the costumes in his portraits of ladies are identical in folds and other details. He signed T. Forster, Thos Forster delin, T. Forster del; and Tho.fforster. Examples of his work may be seen at the V. & A. M., B.M., the City of Liverpool Museums and the Holburne Museum, Bath. Many of his works were engraved, some are at the B.M. including an alleged self-portrait. A fine plumbago miniature of an unknown General, signed and dated 'T. Forster Delin 1699' from the collection of Miss D. M. Kleinfeldt, was exhibited in Edinburgh in 1965. The Duke of Portland has a superb portrait of William III by Forster signed on the front 'Tho. Forster / delin' and dated, in error, '1074' (1704). Lists of portraits by Forster may be found in *The Welbeck Abbey Miniatures* by R. W. Goulding, *Samuel Cooper* by J. J. Foster and the *Walpole Society*, Vol. XLV, article by C. F. Bell and Mrs. R. L. Poole. A large number of miniatures by him were exhibited at the South Kensington Exhibition 1865.

Fortin, R. (fl. 1793–1794)

Exhibited at the R.A., 1793 and 1794; may have been a son of A. F. Fortin (1763–1832) a French artist who exhibited at the R.A., 1790 and whom Graves wrongly identifies with R. Fortin. A miniature in the Bernard Falk collection, of a child in a straw hat lined with green and wearing a white dress with a green sash, and a foliage and sky background, was signed vertically, high up on the left 'FortiN / 1793' the F and N being small capitals and the t tall. It was not an outstanding miniature; the face was shaded with a minute stippling, with definite lines at the upper eyelids.

*Foster, Miss A. M. (fl. 1910)

Of London. Exhibited at the R.A. 1910, from 6 Bridge Avenue, Hammersmith.

*Foster, Annett. (fl. 1819)

A miniature signed 'painted by Annett Foster, 1819' was seen by Long, who noted that it was done with rather scratchy hatching.

Foster, Charles. (fl. 1826). See also **Forster, Charles**

Was working in 1826 at 75 Cheapside, London. May have been identical with Charles Forster (q.v.).

*Foster, Miss Dorothea. (fl. 1900)

Exhibited at the R.A. 1900, from Beechwood, Halton, Leeds. Undoubtedly related to Gilbert Foster who exhibited large oil paintings and watercolours from the same address in 1900.

Foster, Edward Ward. 1762–1865

Born in Derby, 8 November 1762, son of a gentleman of means. Held a commission in the Army as a young man but took to painting, and, having good connections, became miniature painter to Queen Charlotte and the Princess Amelia, and had apartments at Windsor. Returned to Derby after the death of his Royal patrons and worked there for many years. Was at Huddersfield 1825. Towards the end of his life he executed silhouettes, painted in a brownish-red, sometimes heightened with gold. He also composed educational charts which were used in schools. Was married five times and may have had a son who was an artist and called 'Foster junior of Liverpool', and who was working in Greece in or before 1812. Received £60 from Queen Victoria on his hundredth birthday. He died 12 March 1865. One of his daughters was living in Liverpool in poor circumstances in 1907. Two water-colour portraits in profile and said to be by him, are at the V. & A. M., and also a miniature of a lady signed in ink on the reverse 'Edward Foster / York' and dated '1803'.

Foster, John. (fl. 1828)

Was living in 1828 at Castle Hill, Richmond, Yorks.

*Foster, Myles Birket, R.W.S. 1825–1899

Born 4 February 1825. The above artist is best known for his domestic scenes and landscapes with rustic figures. He was one of the most popular and successful artists in water-colour, being an early exponent of the stippled method of water-colour painting. He is not usually considered a miniaturist but the V. & A. M., has a miniature by him signed 'BF' in monogram and inscribed on the reverse 'Anne aged 18 / painted by Birket Foster'. It is painted on card. Died 27 March 1899.

Foster, William. d. 1812. See also **F., W.**

Exhibited at the Society of Artists, R.A., B.I. etc., 1772–1812. Some of his portraits were of actors and actresses. Possibly the artist who signed W.F. Died in 1812. The B.M. has two drawings by him, one of which is a small portrait in pencil and water-colour signed 'W.Foster, 1811'. Another miniature by him showed the influence of Cosway (q.v.).

Foulis, R. (fl. c. 1819)

Worked in Edinburgh and London. In c. 1819 went to Halifax, Nova Scotia, where he had a drawing school. Painted miniatures and oil portraits.

Foulon or **Foullon, Mme. Lucille.** 1775–1865

Née Vachot. Born at Le Havre in 1775. Pupil of Robert Lefèvre. Painted portraits in oil and miniature, and exhibited at the Paris Salon 1793–1822. Came to London and exhibited at the R.A., in 1837. Evidently returned to France and died at Antibes 3 February 1865.

*Fountain, Miss Muriel D. (fl. 1909)

Of London. Exhibited at the R.A. 1909, from 63 Middleton Road, Bowes Park. Her sitter was Miss Charlotte Allan.

Fowler, Mrs. (fl. 1845–1853)

Of London. Exhibited at the R.A. 1845–1853, from 1 Brompton Terrace, Brompton and 411 Oxford Street. Her sitters included Mrs. J. Salway and Miss Fanny Sternbridge.

*Fowlis, James. (fl. 1805)

Of Edinburgh. Living in 1805 at 37 Hanover Street. This artist was noted by Long. Possibly identical with James Foulis (1770–1842), an amateur artist who executed large paintings.

Fox, Charles. 1749–1809

Born at Falmouth in 1749. Showed aptitude for literature and drawing at an early age. Started life as a bookseller but after losing all his possessions in a fire, he took up art and travelled on foot in Scandinavia and Russia. Painted landscapes from his sketches, and portraits. Studied Oriental languages, translated Persian poems and wrote a journal on his travels which was never published. Died at Villa Place, Bathwick, Bath, 1 March 1809.

An example of his work, signed 'CF' and dated '1788' is at the V. & A. M.; it is inscribed 'C.Fox pinxt / Bristol / 1788' on the reverse.

Fox, Charles. 1794–1849

Born at Cossey Hall 17 March 1794. Pupil of John Burnet (engraver). Of London. Exhibited at the R.A. 1836–1837, from 2 Whitehead's Grove, Chelsea. His sitters included Alan Cunningham, Esq., and Lieut. Joseph Cunningham, Bengal Engineers. Died in Leyton 28 February 1849. Best known as an engraver. A miniature of an officer of the 55th Foot, signed 'Fox, PXT' is at the V. & A. M.

*Fox, Miss Florence. (fl. 1887–1903)

Of London and Slinfold, Sussex. Exhibited at the R.A. and S.M., 1887–1903. Her sitters included the Earl of Pembroke and Miss Brenda Fox.

Fox, John. (fl. 1830–1846)

Of London. Exhibited at the R.A., 1830–1846. Long records seeing an oval miniature of c. 1830 of a man with the above artist's name and address, 29 Poultry, pencilled on the reverse. His first exhibit in 1830 was from this address where he remained until 1840 when he moved to 77 Cheapside from which address he exhibited up to 1846. A miniature of an unknown lady, signed on the reverse in pencil, with the Cheapside address, was Lot 13 at Sotheby's 29 January 1968. His sitters included Mrs. Fox, R. A. Fox, Esq., and A. Wanderer, Esq.

*Fox, Miss Louisa B. (fl. 1905–1913)

Of London. Exhibited at the R.A. 1905–1913, from Ben Lomond House, Hampstead.

*Fox, T. (fl. 1761)

A miniature, signed and dated '1761' by the above artist was Lot 75 at Christie's 24 November 1964.

Fox, T. M. (fl. 1843–1846). See also **Fox, Thomas**

Of London. Exhibited at the R.A., 1843–1846. Possibly identical with Thomas Fox (q.v.).

Fox, Thomas (fl. 1833 – 1838). See also **Fox, T. M.**

Of London. Exhibited at the R.A., 1834; possibly identical with T. M. Fox (q.v.) who exhibited at the R.A., 1843–1846, as both lived in the same road. Long records having seen a miniature signed 'Painted by Thos Fox / Miniature Painter / 5 Grenada Terrace / Commercial Road / London / Jan 29 / 1834.' A miniature of a boy dated '1833' is mentioned by Schidlof.

*Foy, William. b. 1789 ?

A miniature portrait of Washington Irving, the author, was Lot 341 in the Pierpont Morgan sale 24 June 1935 and catalogued as by W. Foy. The above artist was probably identical with the William Foy who entered the R.A. Schools 12 November 1814 aged 25.

*Frain, Robert. (fl. 1830)

The above artist, who is hitherto unrecorded, is known only by a good miniature of an unknown officer which was sold at Christie's on 25 June 1968. It is signed and dated on the reverse 'Painted / by / Robert Frain / Edinburgh / Decr. 1830'. The miniature is well painted and colourful; it shows the influence of Raeburn and A. Robertson (q.v.); the lighting behind the head is dark and that on the face dramatic.

*Franasco, J. (fl. c. 1730)

The Derby Museum has a small painting of an interior c. 1730 by the above artist. The manner in which it has been painted suggests the technique of a miniaturist.

Francata. 17th century

An Italian artist, said to have attained considerable reputation by painting miniatures in pen and ink. He is reputed to have drawn James II and his Queen, as well as members of the Court.

Francis, (Mr?). (fl. 1797)

Exhibited at the R.A. 1797, from 14 Holborn. The exhibit was catalogued as 'Portrait of himself'. Long suggests that the above artist may have been identical with Miss Francis (q.v.) but if the catalogue is correct this is impossible.

Francis, Miss. (fl. 1799)

Exhibited at the R.A., as an Hon. Member in 1799. Schidlof suggests that the above artist may have been identical with the Francis (no initial given) recorded by Long as exhibiting at the R.A., in 1797, but this is impossible as the R.A. catalogues give the exhibit as 'portrait of himself'.

Franti

An artist known only by a miniature on ivory of George IV when Prince of Wales, catalogued as by this artist when it was exhibited at the South Kensington Museum in 1865.

Frearson or **Fearson, John.** (fl. 1786–1831)

Of London. Exhibited at the R.A., B.I., 1786–1831. Painted religious subjects, figure subjects, interiors and views, besides miniatures which were among his early exhibits. His name is spelt both ways in the R.A. catalogues. He was presumably identical with the John Frearson who entered the R.A. schools on 5 April 1786, aged 24.

Frederick, William. b. c. 1796

Was born c. 1796. Entered the R.A. Schools 5 November 1818 aged 22 years. He was living in 1828 at Mill Hill, Leeds. Painted portraits and miniatures. Was described as a 'chaste sweet painter of portraits, dead game and small moonlights'. Two oil paintings by him, one of which was a portrait group, were exhibited in Leeds in 1926. A miniature in oil on ivory of Thomas Gatliff is signed on the reverse 'Painted by W. Frederick 1831 / Leeds'. It is slightly reminiscent of the work of Sir W. C. Ross (q.v.). The B.M. has an engraving of B. H. Allen, 1831 after W. Frederick.

Freeman, Miss Anna Mary. d. after 1859

Born in Manchester, daughter of an American artist (probably George Freeman (q.v.)). Went to America when very young. Painted miniatures, wrote poems and stories and was an elocutionist. Was still living in 1859.

Freeman, George. 1787/9–1868

Born 21 April 1787/9 at Spring Hill, Connecticut, son of a farmer. Came to Europe and studied at Paris and London. Worked at Bath and Manchester and was probably the father of Anna Mary Freeman (q.v.). Painted miniatures on ivory and porcelain, some of which were large. His sitters included William IV, Queen Victoria, and Prince Albert. Returned to America in 1837; was back in England 1841 and died at Hartford, Connecticut 7 March 1868. Examples of his work are at the V. & A. M.

Freese, N. (fl. 1794–1814)

Of London. Exhibited at the R.A., 1794–1814. Probably joined an Artists' Volunteer Corps in 1803. In 1814 exhibited a portrait of Lieut. G. F. Freese, who fell at the storming of Salamanca.

J. Freese, who exhibited at the R.A. 1811 and who worked for the Duke of Cambridge, was probably a relation of this artist. He often used a small label on the reverse of his miniatures which reads 'Freese / Miniature Painter / No 411 Strand / London'. His work is not outstanding but at best it is reminiscent of that of J. C. D. Engleheart (q.v.). A miniature of a Naval Officer, signed and dated '1808' is in the collection of E. G. Paine of New York. A miniature of an unknown man, by him, is at the Fitzwilliam Museum, Cambridge.

*French, Jinnie K. (fl. 1901)
Exhibited at the R.A. 1901, from 15 Lower Pembroke Street, Dublin. Her exhibit was a case of eight miniatures.

*French, Robert. (fl. c. 1720–1740)
A miniature on vellum, the subject wearing the costume of c. 1720, signed 'R. French. Pinxit. A.D. 1740' and another of a Bishop painted in the manner of L. Crosse (q.v.) with reddish stippling on the face, were seen by Sotheby's.

*Friedenson, Mrs. A. (Lily). (fl. 1909)
Exhibited at the R.A. 1909, from Thruxton, Andover, Hants. Probably the wife of Arthur Friedenson who exhibited landscapes in oil at the R.A., and was at the same address in 1909.

*Friedlander, Miss Gertrude. (fl. 1909–1910)
Of London. Exhibited at the Society of Miniaturists 1909–1910.

Frieman, J. (fl. 1799). See also **Fruman, I. or J.**
Of London. Exhibited at the R.A. 1799, a miniature portrait of Mr. and Mrs. Barbot, from 5 Great Pulteney Street, Golden Square. Possibly identical with J. Fruman (q.v.).

Frith, J. (fl. 1819). See also **Frith, John**
Of Croydon. Exhibited at the R.A., 1819. Possibly identical with John Frith (q.v.). His work was of no great merit. His sitters were Mrs. Hewson, and C. Armstrong, Esq., and his addresses given as Croydon and 7 St. Martin's Court.

Frith, John. (fl. 1834). See **Frith, J.**
Possibly identical with J. Frith (q.v.). Was working in 1834 at 7 Cornhill, London. Painted portraits and miniatures.

Frost, J. (fl. 1807)
Was working at Exeter as a miniaturist and engraver in 1807. Senior pupil of Ezekiel (q.v.).

Frost, James. (fl. 1766–1783)
Of London and Wandsworth. Exhibited at the Free Society of Artists 1766–1783. Painted miniatures, but chiefly executed landscapes, seascapes, figure subjects and drawings.

*Froste, M. H. (fl. c. 1830–c. 1850)
Recorded by Schidlof as working in England c. 1830. A portrait of a man wearing a black costume, on a terrace, painted on card and signed 'M. H. Froste pinxit', was sold in Brussels 27–29 June 1935.

*Fruman, I. or J. (fl. 1807). See also **Frieman, J.**
Several miniatures by this artist are at the V. & A. M. They include a miniature of Charles Augustus Busby signed on the reverse 'J. Fruman Pinxt / London', dated 'July 1807', two youths of the Busby family and a pair of miniatures of Mr. and Mrs. John Pusey Wint of Jamaica, painted c. 1807, probably in London. His work is slightly reminiscent of that of J. C. D. Engleheart (q.v.). The artist may have been identical with J. Frieman (q.v.).

Fry, M. W. (fl. 1825)
Of Manchester. Painted miniature portraits and transparencies. In 1825 his address was 5 Back Street, King Street, Manchester.

Frye, Thomas. 1710–1762
An Irish artist born in or near Dublin 1710. Went with Herbert Stoppelaer to London where he painted portraits in oil, black lead, crayons, and miniatures in water-colour and enamel; was also a well known mezzotint engraver. Studied under John Brooks of the Battersea enamel factory. Painted a full-length portrait of Frederick, Prince of Wales, in 1736, which attracted attention and brought the artist many patrons. Had an introduction to Sir Joshua Reynolds with whom he became friendly. Became interested in the manufacture of porcelain and invented a form of porcelain, for which he and Edward Heylyn took out a patent in 1744. This first formula was evidently not entirely successful, and Frye experimented further until in 1749 he took out another patent on his own. Was manager of the Bow china factory from c. 1744 up to 1759. Later he toured Wales and resumed work as a painter. Exhibited at the Society of Artists 1760–1761. From this time onwards he is said to have worked chiefly as an engraver. Executed a number of engravings of heads almost life size, from his own drawings. Published some of these engravings in 1760 and 1761. W. Pether (q.v.) was his pupil. By his wife, who survived him, he had a son and two daughters. The daughters were said to have assisted their father in painting the china at Bow. The son, according to a notice in the *Hibernian Magazine*, 'turned out an idle, drunken fellow . . .' who died in a barn in a state of intoxication. Thomas Frye died of consumption on 2 April 1762. Frye was a good miniaturist whose works are scarce. He used pure fresh colours and his portraits are softly painted. One signed in gold, parallel to the edge 'Frye 1761' is recorded by Long. I have in my collection a miniature of an unknown man signed 'T.Frye / 1761'. A good oil miniature by Frye, painted in 1737, is in the V. & A. M. A mezzotint self-portrait is reproduced on Pl. XXV of Strickland's *Dictionary of Irish Artists*, where a list of his engravings and numerous sitters may be found. The miniature from my collection was exhibited in Edinburgh 1965.

Fuller. (fl. 1759)
A plumbago miniature on vellum of Francis Lewis, aged 50, signed and dated '1759', was contained in Lot 367 of the Wellesley sale at Sotheby's, June 1920. It was rather stiffly drawn.

*Fuller, Miss Lucia Fairchild. (Mrs. Henry B.) 1872–1924
Born in Boston, 6 December 1872; lived in New York. Exhibited at the R.A. 1910, from c/o Chenil & Co. 183A King's Road, Chelsea. This artist may not have worked in Britain; was possibly the wife of Henry Brown Fuller, an American artist. Was a member of the American Society of Miniature Painters, the Pennsylvania Society of Miniature Painters and the New York Water-Colour Club. Died in 1924.

Fulton, Robert. 1765–1815
Born in Little Britain, Pennsylvania 14 November 1765. Set up as a miniature painter in Philadelphia 1782 and in four years earned sufficient money to establish his mother on a farm free of debt. Came to London 1786 or 1787. Studied oil painting under B. West (q.v.). Worked for a time in Devonshire. Exhibited at the R.A., and Society of Artists 1791–1793. Was residing with Joel Barlow, an author, in Paris in 1794 and painted the first

panorama exhibited there. In 1797 he was experimenting with torpedoes and submarines. In 1803 he launched a steamer on the Seine and later built the S.S. *Clermont*, which left for Albany in 1807. Married in London, 1808, Harriet Livingston. Painted oil portraits and miniatures. Died in New York 23 February 1815. His wife Harriet (q.v.) was also a miniaturist.

Fulton, Mrs. Robert (Miss Harriet Livingston). (fl. 1808)
Née Harriet Livingston, married Robert Fulton (q.v.) in London 1808. A miniature portrait of her by her husband was lent to the Metropolitan Museum, New York in 1927. After her first husband's death in 1815 she married Charles G. Dale.

Furnell, Miss C. (fl. 1843)
Of Norwood. Exhibited at the R.A., 1843. Her exhibits included a portrait of J. Haynes, Esq., and one of Master Behan.

*Furnivall, Mrs. Agnes. (fl. 1902–1903)
Of London. Exhibited at the Society of Miniaturists 1902–1903.

*Fuseli, Fussli or Fuessli, Henry, R.A. (Jean Henry). 1741–1825
Born in Zurich in 1741. Schidlof suggests that this well-known artist painted miniatures, but I have been unable to verify this statement. He died in 1825. A self-portrait in pencil, $10\frac{1}{2} \times 8\frac{1}{2}$ in., is in the N.P.G.

Futvoye, Peter. (fl. 1830)
Of Bath. Was living in 1830 at Spa Villa, Bathwick Hill, Bath. An artist of this name taught japanning and painting in imitation of marble, etc., at Bath from 1809 or earlier.

G

G. (fl. 1656–1660)
A good miniature of c. 1656–1660, signed with a whitish cursive initial 'G' on the background, and representing a man in armour is in the V. & A. M. Long noted that the artist's name might possibly have been Gage, about whom I can find no information. The miniature was in the collection of an old Scottish family. The face of the sitter is modelled with red brush strokes; there are red lines under the upper eyelids and red touches at the nostrils; some of the brush strokes on the nose and those modelling the contours of the cheeks are rather long. The background is dark.

*G., B. (fl. 1837). See also **B., G.**
A miniature of an unknown man signed 'G.B.' and dated '1837' was sold at Christie's 15 October 1963.

*G., B.M. (fl. c. 1825)
A miniature of a girl of about seventeen years of age, painted c. 1825, and signed 'B.M.G.', is in the collection of R. Bayne Powell Esq. The miniature is painted with a grey wash, the cheeks and lips being heightened with red, the general effect being rather charming.

*G., F.M.D. See **Garth**

*G., H. (fl. 1757)
A miniature of Sir (?) Heathcote, signed and dated '1757' was seen by Mr. A. J. B. Kiddell.

G., I. See also **Greenhill, John**

Two rectangular miniatures representing Charles II and Catherine of Braganza, formerly in the Propert and Pierpont Morgan collections, were said to be signed in gold 'I.G.'. Dr. G.C. Williamson attributed them to John Greenhill (q.v.).

G., J. or I. (fl. 1759). See **Green, J.**

A miniature of a child signed with cursive initials 'J.G.' or 'I.G.' and supposedly dated '1759' is reproduced in the Albert Jaffé catalogue, Pl. 47. It is ascribed to J. Green.

G., S. (fl. 1806)

A miniature of the actress Mrs. Mountain (1786?–1841) signed 'S. G.' and dated 1806 is at the N.P.G.

*G., Syb. (fl. 1910)

A miniature portrait on ivory of Edward VII in uniform, in my collection is signed 'Syb.G/10.' (1910).

*Gabain, Miss Ethel. (fl. 1911–1912)

Of Bushey, Herts. and London. Exhibited at the R.A., 1911 and 1912. Executed miniatures and landscapes in black and white. Possibly identical with Ethel Leontine Gabain, recorded by Benezit.

*Gabrielli, William. (fl. 1901–1904)

Of London. Exhibited at the R.A. 1901 and 1904, from 895 Fulham Road, Fulham, and from Palewell Park, East Sheen.

*Gadelet. (fl. c. 1830)

An artist of this name was working at 18 High Street, Marylebone, London, c. 1830. A miniature by him was seen by Mr. A. J. B. Kiddell who noted that it was of poor quality.

*Gaglier, D. (fl. 1839)

Schidlof records seeing two miniatures by the above artist in a private collection in London. One of a lady signed (in black capitals) 'Gaglier F/1839' and the other of a man, signed (in gold capitals) 'D. Gaglier'. The artist may have worked in England as his style showed the combined influence of both the English and Continental schools. The flesh parts are painted with blue-green shadows. He mixed a lot of gum with his paints and executed his backgrounds in either long, distinct cross brush-strokes or gouache.

Gahagan. (fl. early 19th century)

Of Bath. Miniature painter, modeller and lithographer. Was working at Bath in the early part of the 19th century. Perhaps identical with the Mr. Gahagan who was awarded a premium by the Society of Arts in 1777.

*Gaiffe, Mrs. Alice P. (fl. 1907)

Of Paris. Exhibited at the R.A. 1907, from 16 Avenue de la Grande Armée, Paris.

*Gaillard, Mme. (fl. 1833). See also **Chaceré de Beaurepaire, Mme.**

Exhibited at the Paris Salon 1833 and may be identical with the artist Mme. Chaceré de Beaurepaire (q.v.).

*Galer, Miss Ethel C. H. (fl. 1907–1911)

Of London. Exhibited at the R.A. 1907–1911, from 110 Croxted Road, Dulwich. Her sitter in 1907 was Mrs. Balfour Neill.

*Gallaher, Miss Mabel. (fl. 1909–1913)

Exhibited at the R.A. 1909–1913, from Brightside,

Christchurch Park, Sutton. Her sitters were H. A. Summers Esq. and Mrs. Marson Elms.

Galland, J. R. (fl. 1818)

Of London. Exhibited at the R.A., 1818. May have worked for a time in Scotland. One exhibit was of a 'young lady of Edinburgh'; another, a self-portrait. The Berlin exhibition of 1906 contained two miniatures on ivory signed 'J. Galland', and dating from the early part of the 19th century. Graves erroneously records his name as Gallaud.

Gallandat de Rovray, Fanny. (fl. 1848)

Of London. Exhibited at the R.A., 1848, a 'Head of Louis XV', from 25 South Molton Street, Grosvenor Square. Long gives the name as Galland(at) but in the R.A. catalogues it is spelt Gallandat.

Gallaway, Alexander. (fl. c. 1794–1812?)

A Scottish artist about whom little is known. Advertised in the *Glasgow Courier*, 31 May 1794 and 3 June 1794: 'Drawing Academy. / Gallaway and Williams acquaint their friends and the public, that they / have removed their Drawing Academy to 2d. story of Horn's Court, / Argyll-street, which will open on Monday the 2d. of June./

Miniature Painting
By Mr Gallaway, and
Views of Any Particular Place,
Taken from Nature,
By Mr Williams.
Specimens to be seen at the Academy.'

Gallaway was living at Smith's Land, Trongate, Glasgow, and in 1811–1812 he was at 6 James's Square, Edinburgh. He exhibited at the Society of Artists, Edinburgh, 1808, where he is known to have been working up to 1812. His signature may be found on the front with cursive or Roman initials and he also often signed in full on the reverse followed by a date. His miniatures are well painted, and some of them are modelled with a minute soft stippling. His works are scarce. A good miniature of a lady signed with initials and dated '1804' was Lot No. 96 sold at Christie's 13 December 1966; it was illustrated. Examples of his work are at the V. & A. M. and the Ward Usher Museum, Lincoln. A characteristic of his work is his method of drawing a pillar in the background. A miniature of Richard Brinsley Sheridan, signed on front 'A.G./ 1796' is in the E. Holzscheiter Collection (Meilen), Zurich. Two unsigned miniatures by him of James Donaldson, and his daughter Jane, are in the collection of Colonel N. D. Leslie, O.B.E.

Gambel. (fl. 1773). See also **Groth, A.**

Said to have been a pupil of C. F. Zincke (q.v.). Exhibited two enamel copies of the Annunciation, after Guido Reni, at the Free Society of Artists in 1773. Until recently, miniatures in enamel signed G. have been attributed to either Gardelle (q.v.) or Gambel, and one called Flora Macdonald, from the Seymour collection, and another of William Henry, Duke of Gloucester, in my collection, were both assigned to Gambel. On 2 May 1966 three enamels by A. Groth (q.v.) were sold at Sotheby's; one of Thomas Edwards Freeman, was signed 'A.Groth pinxt. 1753', one of a lady, was signed 'G.' on the front, and the third painted in a similar manner was unsigned. The one of the Duke of Gloucester, although of an even finer quality, is certainly by the same hand, and that of Flora Macdonald may well be by Groth also.

Gamble, Miss Louisa. (fl. 1842)

Of London. Exhibited at the R.A. 1842, from 7 Camden Street, Camden Town.

*Gamlen, Miss Madeline F. (fl. 1907–1912)

Exhibited at the R.A. 1907–1912, from New Place, Welwyn, Herts. Exhibited a self-portrait in 1907.

*Gard, H. (fl. 1790)

A miniature of a lady signed in gold 'H.Gard/ 1790' was seen by Long.

Gardelle, Théodore. 1722–1761. See also **Groth, A.**

Born in Geneva 30 November 1722. Came of a family of goldsmiths and jewellers. Was apprenticed as an engraver. Ran away to Paris when only 16; returned home but went to study in Paris 1744–1750. Returned to Geneva for a time but his immoral conduct detracted from any success he might have had. Knew Voltaire. Was in Paris 1756 and travelled from there to Brussels and London, where he arrived c. 1759. Practised as a miniature and portrait painter. Murdered his landlady, Mrs. King, cut her up and burnt her; attempted suicide in prison. Was executed, 4 April 1761 and hung in chains on Hounslow Heath. An engraving of Gardelle on the way to his execution is at the B.M. The house in which Gardelle murdered his landlady was occupied from 1763–1778 by Edward Fisher, a mezzotint engraver. According to Vertue, some of Gardelle's miniatures were executed in oil. The miniature of Flora Macdonald, signed 'G' mentioned by Long, was probably by Groth (q.v.).

Gardie, Mrs. (fl. 1828)

Exhibited at the R.A., 1828. Probably the wife of A. N. Gardie (q.v.). Her address was not noted. She was possibly identical with the Mme. Gardie of Paris who exhibited at the Salon in 1831–1837 and painted miniatures on ivory and porcelain.

Gardie, A. N. (fl. 1828)

Of London. Exhibited at the R.A. 1828, from 48 Frith Street, Soho Square. Probably the husband of Mrs. Gardie (q.v.) who exhibited in the same year; she is thought to be identical with Mme. Gardie of Paris.

*Gardiner, William Nelson. 1766–1814

Born in Dublin, 11 June 1766, the son of John Gardiner 'crier and factotum' to William Scott, Justice of the King's Bench, and his wife, Margaret Nelson, a pastry cook in Henry Street. Entered the Dublin Society schools in 1781 and studied there for three years, obtaining a silver medal. Went to London and endeavoured to support himself by painting portraits and assisting a Mr. Jones in making profile shade likenesses. Is chiefly known as an engraver but he also executed silhouettes, painted scenery and was an actor. Some of his works may have been miniatures. Exhibited subject pictures and drawings at the R.A., 1787–1793. Became eccentric after the death of his wife and child and committed suicide on 8 May 1814 at his house in Pall Mall. The N.P.G. has a small water-colour portrait by him of Philip, 1st Earl of Hardwicke, after W. Hoare.

Gardner, Daniel. 1750–1805

Born in 1750. Entered the R.A. Schools, 17 March 1770. Obtained a silver medal, 1773. A notable pastellist who is thought to have painted miniatures, but no signed ones have so far come to light. One of Francis Powell, Esq. signed 'D.G.' and attributed to him was sold in the Hand collection at Sotheby's, 25 November 1952. Gardner died in 1805.

Gare, G. (fl. 1802–1818)

Of London. Exhibited at the R.A., 1802–1818.

He had an address at 14 Fountain's Court, Strand.

*Garford, Miss Nina B. (fl. 1906–1909)

Exhibited at the R.A. 1906 and 1909, from Rosemount, Exmouth, Devon. Her sitters included Miss Ethel A. Garford.

Garis, Madame. 17th century

May possibly have worked in England. Sanderson in his *Graphice*, 1658, p. 20, mentions sundry contemporary English miniature painters and says: ' . . . pick me out one equall to Madam Garis, a Brabanne; Judgement and Art mixed together in her rare pieces of Limnings, since they came into England.'

*Garman, Miss Mabel. (fl. 1900)

Exhibited at the R.A. 1900, from Great Barr, Birmingham.

*Garner, Miss Dorothy. (fl. 1903–1905)

Of London and Bushey, Herts. Exhibited at the Society of Miniaturists, 1903–1905.

*Garnett, Miss Catherine Grace. See Godwin, Mrs.

*Garnett, Miss Frances. (fl. 1904–1914)

Of Jersey. Exhibited at the R.A., 1904–1914.

Garrard, George, A.R.A. 1760–1826

Born 31 May 1760. Notable painter and modeller of animals, not usually considered a miniaturist, but exhibited two portraits of horses in miniature at the R.A., in 1788. Died, 8 October 1826.

*Garrick, Thomas. (fl. *c.* 1820)

I have in my collection an attractive miniature of a young lady, *c.* 1820, which according to tradition was painted by the above artist. The miniature is painted on porcelain against a plain buff background; the draughtsmanship is good, and the face well modelled and painted in soft colours, the features being shaded with pale grey cross-strokes. I have been unable to trace any artist of this name, but the quality of the miniature places the artist high among the rank of those who painted on porcelain.

Garth. (fl. 1725)

An enamel portrait of Sir Edward Walpole, signed 'F.M.D.G.' and dated '1725', said to be by Garth, was in the H. G. Bohn Collection; this was sold at Christie's in March 1885.

Gaskell or Gaskel, J. (fl. 1774–1778)

Of London. Exhibited at the Society of Artists, 1774 and at the R.A., 1776–1778. His name is sometimes spelt Gaskel.

*Gatliffe. (fl. 1796)

Advertised in the *Bristol Journal*, 17 December 1796, as a miniature and profile painter of 29 Queen Street, Bristol. He charged from 2 to 10 guineas.

Gauci, G. (fl. 1810–1823)

Of London. Exhibited at the R.A. and S.B.A., etc., 1810–1823. Some of his works were miniatures. May have been a son of M. Gauci (q.v.).

Gauci, M. (fl. 1810–1846)

Exhibited at the Associated Artists in Water-Colours, 1812. Worked chiefly as a portrait-lithographer. His sons, P. and W. Gauci were working with him at 10A Charles Street, Goodge Street, London. G. Gauci (q.v.) may have been another son. Lithographed portraits by him are at the B.M. A miniature by him of the Duchess of

Angoulême, painted on ivory and signed 'M.Gauci, 1810' is in the Ward Usher Collection, Lincoln. A miniature of the artist's family signed on the reverse 'by M Gauci No 5 Thayer Street, Manchester Square' is mentioned by Schidlof. I have seen a reasonably well painted miniature signed by this artist.

Gay, B. (fl. 1807–1811)

Of London. Exhibited at the R.A., 1807 and 1811. Long records seeing a rather poor miniature of a lady, signed 'Gay / 181' which may have been by the above artist and was French in manner. It has been suggested that he was identical with P. Gay. A miniature by this latter artist was exhibited in Berlin in 1912. His work is recorded by Schidlof who says that he worked in France at the end of the 18th century.

Gayleard, Miss Sophia. (fl. 1839–1846)

Of London. Exhibited at the R.A., 1839–1846. She exhibited from 56 Beaumont Street, Devonshire Place, except for the last year when the number is given as 36; this may have been a misprint.

*Gayler, Mrs. Ellen A. (fl. 1903–1906)

Exhibited at the R.A. 1903 and 1906, from 71 Carlton Hill, St. John's Wood. Her sitters included Helena, daughter of Dr. and Lady Agnes Frank.

Gaywood, Richard. (fl. *c.* 1650–1680)

Worked *c.* 1650–1680. Pupil of Hollar (q.v.); engraver, etcher and draughtsman of portraits etc. May possibly have executed plumbago portraits. The B.M. has an Indian ink portrait ($4\frac{1}{2}$ in. $\times 2\frac{3}{4}$ in.) by him of John Browne.

Gear, J. W. (fl. 1821–1852)

Of London. Son of J. Gear, sen., Marine Painter to H.R.H. the Duke of Sussex. Exhibited at the R.A., S.B.A., etc., 1821–1852. Painted miniatures and theatrical portraits and at least one water-colour on porcelain. Some engravings after J. W. Gear are at the B.M. He and his father both exhibited at the R.A., from the same address, 29 Wellesley Street, Euston Square, in 1821. Some of his miniatures were placed in brooches and bracelets.

*Geddes, Miss Margaret Sarah. See Carpenter, Mrs. William

*Gee, Miss Lucy. (fl. 1897)

Exhibited at the R.A. 1897, from Hardwick Cottage, Woburn Sands, Bletchley.

*Geer, Ignatius de. See Du Geer, Ignatius

*Genibrett, Miss Annie. (fl. 1909–1911)

Of London. Exhibited at the R.A. 1909 and 1911, from 30 St. Mark's Road, North Kensington.

Gent, Mrs. (Miss S. S. Daniell). (fl. 1825–1845)

Of London. Née S. S. Daniell. Probably the daughter of William Daniell, R.A., from whose address, 14 Russell Place, she exhibited. Exhibited at the R.A., B.I., etc., 1825–1831 under her maiden name from the above address, and from 1832 as Mrs. Gent from various London addresses, including the family one again in 1833. Painted portraits, fancy subjects and miniatures. Her sitters included Miss R. Daniell, Mrs. Daniell, Mrs. William Wood, Miss Bincks, the celebrated pianist, and Lady Denman, painted in 1836; an engraving after this portrait is at the B.M.

*George, Miss Esther. (fl. 1902)

Exhibited at the R.A. 1902, from Dentney Vicarage, nr. Swaffham, Norfolk.

*George, Miss Jessie L. (fl. 1910)

Of London. Exhibited at the R.A. 1910, from 41 Asmuns Place, Hendon.

George, T. (fl. 1826). See also **George, Thomas**

Possibly identical with Thomas George (q.v.). A miniature on ivory of Richard Bird (1802–1842) of Calcutta, signed on the reverse 'Painted by T. George / London Octr 1826' is in the V. & A. M.

George, Thomas. 1790?–1840? See also **George, T.**

Thought to have been born at Fishguard *c.* 1790. Possibly identical with T. George (q.v.) of London, whose miniature on ivory of Richard Bird (1802–1842) of Calcutta, signed on the reverse 'Painted by T. George / London Octr 1826' is in the V. & A. M. Was living at Haverfordwest, 1821–1824. Exhibited at the R.A. and B.I., 1829–1838. Painted portraits, miniatures and subject pictures. Appears to have signed on the reverse in full followed by a date, and also with hesitant cursive initials. Died in Madeira *c.* 1840. The B.M. have some lithographed portraits after George. Examples of his work are in the National Museum of Wales.

Gerbier, Sir Balthasar. 1592–1667

Born in Middelburg, 23 February 1592, son of Anthony Gerbier, by his wife Radigonde Blavet, Protestant refugees from France. May have been a pupil of Hendrik Goltzius. Gerbier was an adventurer, painter, architect, musician, author, courtier and diplomat. He was married and had three sons, George, James and Charles, and five daughters, Elizabeth, Susan, Mary, Katherine and Deborah. Went to Rome where he made copies of paintings after Raphael in crayon. These are referred to by Edward Norgate (q.v.) in his *Miniatura*. After the death of his father he accompanied one of his brothers to Gascony, where he acquired a knowledge of drawing, architecture, fortifications and armaments, which knowledge brought him to the notice of Prince Maurice of Orange, in whose service he was in 1615. Practised miniature painting in England. Became a retainer of the Duke of Buckingham and acted as his private architect and keeper of York House. Is said to have accompanied Buckingham and Charles I to Spain in 1623; however, letters to the Duke of Buckingham from the Duchess and from Gerbier between 26 March 1623 and 8 February 1624, show that Gerbier did not go to Spain at that time, but that Vertue, who stated this, had misread the MS. Gerbier met Rubens in Paris in 1625 and again in January 1627. Entered the King's service, 3 December 1628 after Buckingham's assassination, and was knighted in the same year. Rubens stayed at his house in London in 1629. Was sent by Charles I as envoy to Brussels in 1631 and sailed with his wife and family on 17 June. Gerbier occupied a position of special trust, a position which he betrayed in November 1633 by giving information to the Infanta Isabella for the sum of twenty thousand crowns. Thereafter his political career suffered a decline. He was superseded at Brussels, and having incurred many debts abroad had difficulty in financing the return of his family to England. In 1652 he opened an Academy at his house in Bethnal Green, London, where he lectured on many subjects. Many of his lectures and pamphlets were published. In 1652 he left England once more and went to Holland. In the same year he sailed from Texel with his wife and family and a number of colonists to carry out a mining scheme in Guiana. They touched at Cayenne where a mutiny broke out among his followers. They killed his daughter Katherine and wounded another. He returned to Amsterdam for a time, but after the restoration decided to return to England. Failing to regain his position at Court he returned to architecture. Supplied the designs for Lord Craven's house at Hampstead Marshall, in Berkshire. He died at Hampstead Marshall, in 1667, whilst supervising the building of Lord Craven's house, and was buried in the chancel of the church. The house was subsequently burnt down. Gerbier drew miniatures in pen and ink, crayons, and painted on vellum. Works by him are scarce. One of outstanding merit is of George Villiers, 1st Duke of Buckingham, K.G. (1592–1628) painted on vellum, $5 \times 3\frac{1}{2}$ in. signed and dated 'Gerbier 1618' and inscribed 'Fidei Coticula Crux'. This fine equestrian portrait, owned by the Duke of Northumberland, is one of the few known examples of this artist's work. It was exhibited in Edinburgh, 1965. The details are superbly painted and the horse trappings almost gem-like. A pen and ink miniature of Prince Charles (afterwards Charles I) signed 'Gerbier fec 1616' in small Roman script, is in the V. & A. M. A miniature by Gerbier of Prince Maurice of Orange and Nassau is in the collection of H.M. the Queen of the Netherlands. Captain William Wynde, an architect, is said to have been a pupil of Gerbier. A triple portrait by W. Dobson (q.v.) of Dobson, Sir C. Cotterell and Gerbier, is in the collection of the Duke of Northumberland. The B.M. has minutely finished pen and ink portraits by Gerbier and the Pepysian Library at Magdalene College, Cambridge, contains drawings by Gerbier.

Gerhard. (Matthias Christoph?). (fl. c. 1795)

Long records seeing a miniature of c. 1795 painted in the style of Johns (q.v.), on the back of which was a printed card of 'Gerhard, miniature and profile painter, 7. Frankfort St: Plymouth.' This was probably by Matthias Christoph Gerhard who was working in Strasburg c. 1756–1792. In the latter year he advertised a course of drawing and painting in Strasburg.

*Gething, Miss May. (fl. 1906–1911)

Of London. Exhibited at the R.A., 1906–1911. Her sitters included the Rev. S. R. Fraser-Frizell.

*Ghee, Mr. (fl. 1795)

A Mr. Ghee advertised in the *Artists Birmingham Gazette*, 14 December 1795. 'Miniature Painter / 3. Bull St. Birmingham. / 3 Guineas on delivery.'

Gheeraedts, Marc. 1561/2–1635

Born in Brugge in 1561/2. Although this celebrated portrait painter has been said to have painted miniatures, no proof of this has so far come to light. He died in London, 19 January 1635.

Giachosa, Fernando. (fl. 1836–1849)

Exhibited at Berlin in 1836 and at the R.A., 1842–1849. In 1849 his address was 7 Queen's Road, St. John's Wood, and the exhibit was a 'Portrait of a Bavarian girl in her national costume', not a miniature. O'Brien illustrates a miniature of one of the sons of Emperor Nicholas of Russia which he stated was signed on the front 'Ferdinando Giachosa 1836' and inscribed on the reverse 'A Russian Imperial Prince, painted by Ferdinando Joachim G. R. A. Giachosa. After the large picture of Professor Krueger – Emperor Nicholas on horseback, surrounded by all his sons and staff 1834'.

Gibbs, Miss. (fl. 1845)

Of London. Exhibited at the R.A. 1845, from 36 Haymarket; her sitter was Mr. John Stow.

*Gibbs, Percy W. (fl. 1900–1914)

Of London and East Molesey, Surrey. Exhibited at the R.A., 1900–1914. Painted miniatures and portraits and subjects in oil.

*Gibson, Miss Bessie. (fl. 1905–1914)

Of Edinburgh and Paris. Said to have been born in Australia. Exhibited at the R.A., 1905–1914. Her sitters included W. Gibson, Esq., and Mrs. McConnell of Queensland.

Gibson, D. (Dirck?). (fl. 1656–1658)

The existence of a seventeenth-century miniaturist who signed D. Gibson in full or with a monogram D.G. has been established, but so far nothing of importance is known about him, or his relationship, if any, to the three other artists of that name, R. Gibson (q.v.), E. Gibson (q.v.) and W. Gibson (q.v.). His style is very similar to that of R. Gibson, making identification difficult. Signed works by D. Gibson are dated 1656, 1657 and 1658. Richard and Anna Gibson had nine children of whom one, a son Dirck, is recorded as a sculptor in the Hague c. 1690–1712. It is possible that he may have painted miniatures at an earlier date and be identical with the above artist. A signed miniature of Lady Catherine Dormer (died 1659) is in the V. & A. M. A miniature of an unknown man in armour, attributed to Gibson, from my collection, and one of the Hon. Peregrine Bertie (died 1700) from the collection of T. Cottrell-Dormer, Esq., were exhibited in Edinburgh in 1965.

Gibson, David. (fl. 1788–1797)

Of London and Edinburgh. Exhibited at the R.A., 1790–1795. Executed miniatures and engravings. Described as 'painter of the High Kirk parish, Edinburgh' when he married Miss Anne Roebuck, daughter of Dr. John Roebuck, at Bo'ness on 17 July 1788. In the *Manchester Chronicle*, 23 April 1796 and the *Manchester Mercury*, 16 May 1797, advertisements appeared stating that 'Mr Gibson, miniature painter of London, advertises short stays in Manchester'. I have seen a miniature by Gibson in a family collection owned by Mrs. Lang of Edinburgh; it is of a man in a brown coat, signed on the left, 'D.Gibson / 1793' in cursive writing. The miniature is on ivory and is painted slightly in the manner of C. Robertson (q.v.). It was executed with a soft technique, and was pleasing in its effect. (Pl. 124: nos. 334, 335.)

Gibson, E. S. (fl. 1843)

A miniature on card signed 'E.S.Gibson '43' (1843) was seen by Long who noted that the treatment was weak and woolly.

Gibson, Edward. 1668–1701

Was born in 1668. A relative of William Gibson (q.v.) and perhaps a brother of Richard Gibson (q.v.). Painted in oil and drew in pastel, may have painted miniatures. Lived in Catherine Street, Strand, London. Died in 1701 at the age of 33 and was buried in Richmond, Surrey. His self-portrait in crayon is in the N.P .G., and is signed and dated '1690'. It was given to the Gallery in 1920 by Francis Wellesley. The Wellesley collection was sold at Sotheby's 28 June 1920 and this portrait was No. 382 and was reproduced in the catalogue.

*Gibson, Miss Mary Josephine. (fl. 1885–1908)

Of London. Exhibited at the R.A., S.M., etc., 1885–1908, from 36 Pembroke Road, Kensington and from 77 Blenheim Crescent, Ladbroke Grove. Schidlof records her as Mrs. Gibson, but the R.A., and S.M. catalogues specify that she was Miss Gibson. She exhibited a considerable number of miniatures of well-known persons, including the Earl and Countess of Bathhurst, Lady Portal, Col. Sir John Williams Wallington, K.C.B., and Lady Wallington. A miniature of Mrs. Agnes White, wife of J. Douglas White, by M. Josephine Gibson, was Lot 146 at Christie's 13 November 1962.

Gibson, Richard. 1615–1690

Born in 1615, perhaps in Cumberland. Called 'The Dwarf'. Became a page to a lady in Mortlake and having shown an aptitude for art, was instructed by F. Cleyn (q.v.) then director of the tapestry works. Later studied Lely's work, and came under his influence. Was noticed at Court and appointed a page to Charles I, attracted the attention of Queen Henrietta Maria, and a bride was found for him of his own height — 3 feet 10 inches. Waller wrote a poem on the occasion of their marriage (published 1640). His wife's name was Anna Shepherd, by whom he had nine children, the five who lived being of normal size — Susan Penelope (later Mrs. Rosse) (q.v.), John and Johan Gibson, who was an officer in the Netherland Army and Dirck Gibson (q.v.?) a master sculptor in the Hague, and Rose Anna (wife of Marinus van Vrijbergen). Lely painted the portrait of Gibson and his wife. Several portraits of Cromwell by R. Gibson are said to have existed, but their present whereabouts are unknown. He was patronised by the Earl of Pembroke; spent a lot of time in Holland from 1677, where he taught Princess Mary of Orange. On 4 March 1679 he hired a house on the east side of Boekhorstraat at the Hague for 290 florins per annum, having previously resided with J. Nieulant, a silversmith. He was in the Hague 24 September 1681 and may have remained there until 1688. He died in London 23 July 1690 and was buried in Covent Garden Church, having probably returned to England after the accession of William III and Mary in 1688. His daughter Anna had become involved in matrimonial difficulties and in 1681 Richard Gibson brought a case before the Court to defend her rights. Details of this episode are given by Graham Reynolds in *English Portrait Miniatures*, p. 79. A self-portrait in chalk is at the B.M. A miniature of a lady, signed on the reverse 'R. Gibson Fecit / 1673' is in the Uffizi Gallery, Florence. There is also an example of his work at the V. & A. M. An interesting unfinished portrait of his wife was Lot 74 at Sotheby's 6 March 1967. The miniature, which was executed in plumbago and grey wash, realised £240. A miniature copy of Titian's 'Marquis del Gusto with his Mistress' by Gibson dated '1640' is in the collection of the Duke of Portland. Two other miniature copies after this painting exist — one by Peter Oliver (q.v.) dated '1629' and the other by David Des Granges (q.v.) dated '1639'.

In the *Burlington Magazine* (CXXIII, 1981) John Murdoch and V.J. Murrell published a convincing article setting out the reasons for thinking that the monogrammist 'DG' was not an artist called D. Gibson, but was in fact Richard Gibson the dwarf (sometimes called Dick), who used the letter D to signify 'dwarf' or 'Dick'. The question of the identity of the Gibsons has puzzled scholars for years and now it seems plausible to accept the findings by these two authors, that D. Gibson and R. Gibson were the same person, although why he changed his signature from D.G. to R.G. remains a mystery. According to Van der Doort Gibson was known early in his career as Dick or Dwarf and he may have used those initials then, only later adopting R.G. He is known to have copied a number of pictures by Lely, Van Dyck and earlier artists such as Titian. Lely painted a famous double portrait of Gibson and his wife Anne, which is in the Kimbell Art Museum, Fort Worth, Texas.

Gibson, Susan Penelope. See Rosse, Mrs. Susan Penelope

Gibson, William. *c.* 1644–1702/3

Was born *c.* 1644. Nephew of R. Gibson (q.v.) the Dwarf. Was a pupil of Gibson's and of Lely. Said to have been an eminent limner and to have painted portraits of well-known persons. Purchased part of Lely's collection after his death; also imported pictures from the continent. Was employed by Henry Cavendish, Earl of Ogle, son of the 2nd Duke of Newcastle. Is stated to have died in 1702 aged 58, and to have been buried at Richmond, Surrey. May have been identical with the 'William Gibson, gent', who lived in the parish of St. Giles-in-the-Fields, and was buried at Richmond, Surrey, 11 December 1703. The *Daily Courant*, 13 March 1704, had the following announcement – 'Sale of drawings & prints of Mr. William Gibson, Limner, lately deceased, at the lowermost Great House, in the Arched Row, over against the end of Portugal Row, in Lincoln's Inn, Fields.'

*Gilbert, Henry. (fl. 1820)

The S.N.P.G. has three miniatures on paper signed on the front 'Henry Gilbert. Edinburgh. 1820'.

Giles, James. d. 1780. See also **Barber and Giles**

Well known for his painting on china and enamel. Barber and Giles (q.v.) exhibited enamel miniatures at the Society of Artists in 1762. In 1763 Mortimer's *Universal Directory*, described James Giles as 'China and Enamel Painter, Berwick-Street, Soho'. Further information about him is recorded by W. B. Honey in *English Pottery and Porcelain*, where he is mentioned as James Giles, of Cockspur Street, an 'Independent decorator'. He may have painted some of the china at Bow, and certainly was an outside decorator of Worcester porcelain. In 1768 he advertised as 'China and Enamel Painter' and 'Proprietor of the Worcester Porcelaine Warehouse . . .' This was disclaimed by the factory, but it seems certain that Giles was responsible for certain specimens of printed Worcester ware painted over in enamel colours. He had a workshop in Kentish Town. F. Brayshaw Gilhespy records his death as in 1780.

Giles, R. H. (fl. 1825–1871)

Of Gravesend (1826–1835), Plymouth (1849–1854) and London. Exhibited at the R.A., 1826–1871. Was Headmaster of St. George's Church of England Secondary School, Meadow Road, Gravesend 1825–1830. His R.A. exhibit for 1871 was of Jeannie, daughter of James Dunlop, Esq., of Tolcross (Edinburgh).

Gillberg, Jacob Axel. 1769–1845

Born in Stockholm 1769, son of an engraver, Jacob Gillberg. Was a pupil of Cornelius Hoyer (q.v.) and of the Academy of Stockholm of which he became a member in 1796, and later a professor. Was appointed a Director for life in 1840. From 1788–1797 Gillberg travelled, studying in Denmark, the Low Countries, France and England, where he was influenced by the English style of painting. The Nationalmuseum, Stockholm, has examples of his work. He died at Stockholm 1845.

*Gillespie, J. H. or I. H. (fl. *c.* 1820–1838)

Of London and New York. Executed silhouettes and profile miniatures. Charged 4 Dollars per portrait. After working in London, Edinburgh, and Liverpool, *c.* 1820, Gillespie was in Halifax (Nova Scotia) in 1829, Baltimore 1837 and Philadelphia 1838, having also been in New York.

*Gillet, John. (fl. 1886–1892)

Of London. Exhibited at the R.A., 1886–1892. His sitters included his daughter Elise and 'the late Sir Jamsetjee Jeejeeboy, Bart.'

Gillies, Miss Margaret. 1803–1887

Born in Throgmorton Street, London 7 August 1803, second daughter of William Gillies, a Scottish merchant. Was educated by an uncle, Adam Gillies, who was a judge in Edinburgh. She knew Sir Walter Scott and other notable persons. Returned to London and was a pupil of F. Cruickshank (q.v.), and later in Paris under Ary Scheffer. Exhibited at the R.A., B.I., O.W.C.S. (Associate member 1852) etc., 1832–1887. Best known for her miniatures, but also painted portraits in oil and genre subjects. Had a distinguished clientele which included Dickens, Leigh Hunt, Macready and Wordsworth. Miss Gillies painted Wordsworth at her own 'earnest request' in 1839 at Rydal Mount, Ambleside. She remained a month with the family with whom she became very friendly and painted several miniatures of Wordsworth, his wife Mary, and their daughter Dora. This last miniature is at Dove Cottage, and others by her of Wordsworth and his wife and one of Miss Isabella Fenwick, are in the Wordsworth family collection. The large double miniature of Wordsworth and his wife is one of two replicas, the original having been destroyed by fire. She had a sister, Mary, who was an authoress. Margaret Gillies died at Warren, Crockham Hill, Kent, 20 July 1887. She tended to idealise her sitters, but her miniatures show character and the one of Miss Fenwick is particularly charming. She used a lot of gum with her paint. A miniature by her of Leigh Hunt is at the N.P.G. Some of her works were engraved.

Gillray, James. 1757–1815

Was born in 1757. A famous caricaturist and illustrator. Not usually considered a miniaturist but the N.P.G. has a miniature on ivory which is supposed to be a self-portrait. This may have been a copy from a larger portrait. Died 1 June 1815.

Gimber, Stephen Henry. 1806/10–1862

Born in England *c.* 1806 (according to Groce and Wallace); other authorities give the date as *c.* 1810. Went to New York *c.* 1829; exhibited at the National Academy 1836–1842. He and his wife Louisa (also English) settled in New York City *c.* 1829 where Gimber worked for a time with Archibald L. Dick. Moved to Philadelphia in 1842 and worked as an engraver and lithographer until his death in 1862. The B.M. has an engraved portrait of Baron Tenterden after S. H. Gimber.

Girardy, J. de. (fl. 1784)

Exhibited flower pieces at the R.A. 1784, from 10 Great Pultney Street, London. Long noted that he saw a rather weak miniature of a man, signed 'J de G.' It was painted in the manner of Andrew Plimer (q.v.).

*Glardon, C. See also **Glardon, Charles Louis François**

An oval enamel miniature by the above artist, depicting autumn, with infant bacchanals, fruit etc., was sold at Christie's 25 October 1960. The artist was possibly identical with Charles Louis François Glardon (q.v.).

*Glardon or **Glardon-Leubel, Charles Louis François.** 1825–1887. See also **Glardon, C.**

Born in Geneva, 6 April 1825. Painted enamel portraits. Pupil of his brother, Jacques Aimé Glardon. Exhibited at the R.A. 1872–1876, from Geneva and London, including portraits of Miss Margaret Sandbach (enamel) and Miss Sophia Sandbach. Died in Geneva 1887. Possibly identical with C. Glardon (q.v.). Was a good artist, painted from life as well as copying the works of old masters. Some of his enamels have a slightly cold colouring. Examples of his work are in the Musée Rath, Geneva, including a portrait of his mother as well as one of his wife and of François Diday. Schidlof records an enamel in a private collection in London which is signed 'C. L. Glardon / fecit. 1853 / Geneve.'

*Glew, Edward Lees. 1817–1870

Born in Dublin 3 March 1817, son of Thomas Faulkner Glew and his wife Susanne Purcell. Was educated at Trinity College but left without taking a degree. Became a portrait painter and in 1849 exhibited six portraits at the R.H.A., one of which was said to have been a miniature. Went to England and settled in Walsall. Published a *History of Walsall* in 1852 and started a newspaper in Birmingham. Went to America and practised as a painter in New York, Philadelphia and Trenton. Died at Newark, New Jersey, on 9 October 1870.

Godbold, Samuel Barry or **Berry.** (fl. 1842–1875)

Of London. Exhibited at the R.A., B.I., and S.B.A., etc., 1842–1875. His sitters included Lieut. Col. Hanmer and Dr. Harding, Bishop of Bombay. He painted landscapes, mainly of Ireland, portraits and miniatures.

Goddard, James. b. 1756

Was born in 1756. Of London. Entered the R.A. Schools, 18 December 1771 aged '15. 23 Jan last'. Exhibited at the Society of Artists and Free Society of Artists 1771–1783. Painted portraits in oil and crayons, and miniatures. May have painted figure subjects and flowers in enamel on watch cases and étuis.

Goddard, John. (fl. 1811–1842)

Of London. Exhibited at the R.A., 1811–1842. Painted flower pieces and miniature portraits. Tended to use a yellowish colour with light green shadows and painted with vertical crossed brush strokes. Long noted a miniature inscribed 'I. Goddard' on the edge and 'J.Goddard, 1812' on the reverse. He did not consider it of very high quality. A number of his sitters were naval officers or members of the theatrical profession.

Goddard, Thomas. (fl. 1779–1792)

Of London. Exhibited at the R.A., 1779–1788. Advertised in the *Winchester Journal*, 24 September 1792.

*Godelet. See **Godlet, F.**

*Godfrey, Miss L. M. (Ellen). See **Watson, Lizzie May (Mrs. W. P.)**

Godlet, F. (fl. 1826)

Was working from 18 High Street, Marylebone in 1826. A miniature of *c.* 1810 was inscribed in a rather spidery hand on the reverse 'Godelet / No 15 / Henrietta Street / Manchester / Square'. The artist may have been identical with Godlet.

*Godman, Mrs. J. Harrison. (fl. 1907)

Of London. Exhibited at the R.A. 1907, from 44 Hosack Road, Upper Tooting.

Godwin, Mrs. Catherine Grace (Miss Catherine Garnett). 1798–1845

Born in Glasgow 25 December 1798, daughter of Thomas Garnett (1766–1802) the celebrated physician, after whose death in 1802 she was an orphan and was brought up by a Miss Worboys at Barbon, near Kirkby Lonsdale. Married Thomas Godwin formerly of the East India Company in 1824. Exhibited at the R.A., etc., 1829–1832. Her exhibits at the R.A. were as an Hon. Exhibitor. Painted miniatures and wrote poetry, which won praise from Wordsworth. An engraving of a self-portrait is prefixed to her poems. Died in May 1845.

Godwin, E. (fl. 1801–1816)
Of London. Exhibited at the R.A., 1801–1816. Lived at 13 Cleveland Street, Fitzroy Square, etc. Painted landscapes and miniatures.

*Gonore, or Gonord, Le Sieur. (fl. 1792)
Advertised in *The Times*, 4 May 1792, as 'Late of the Royal Palace at Paris. 60 Haymarket. Profile Portraits in miniature or camé, painted on ivory for rings, pins, &c; neatly executed for 1 guinea. For ½ guineas if taken at his rooms. Now lives at Mr. Wallis's 60 Haymarket.' Schidlof mentions a François Gonord who died *c.* 1820, probably in Paris, and who may have been a relation.

*Goodacre, Miss Grace (Mrs. A. Grant). (fl. 1908–1914)
Of London. Exhibited at the R.A. 1908–1914, from Colinette Road, Putney and from Littlecote, Northwood. Her sitters included Edith and Mabel, daughters of L. C. B. Goodacre, Esq.

*Goodchild, Miss Florence A. (fl. 1907–1910)
Of London. Exhibited at the R.A. 1907–1910, from Elmwood Lodge, Long Lane, Finchley. One of her exhibits was a miniature of Forbes Robertson, the actor, as Julius•Caesar. She also painted a miniature of Joan, daughter of Francis Black, Esq.

*Goodman, Mrs. Kathleen. (fl. 1910)
Exhibited at the Society of Miniaturists 1910, from The White House, Marsham, Norwich.

*Goodman, Miss Maude. (Mrs. Scanes). (fl. 1860–1900)
Of London. Exhibited at the R.A., N.W.C.S., etc., 1874–1900. Painted subject pictures in oil and water-colour and miniatures. A miniature of the Rt. Rev. J. C. Ryle, Bishop of Liverpool, is in the Walker Art Gallery, Liverpool, and is signed on the front 'Maude Goodman'. Her exhibit in 1892 was of Miss Olive Goodman, possibly her sister. According to Duveen's handwritten notes in my R.A. catalogues her paintings realised good prices; in 1886 her picture 'Une Chanson de fleurs' was sold for £115.

Goodman, T. (fl. 1784–1812)
Of London. Exhibited at the R.A. etc., 1784–1812. Schidlof gives his initial as I, but I have found no justification for this.

*Goodwin, Miss Edytha M. (fl. 1907–1912)
Daughter of Albert Goodwin who painted landscapes. Exhibited at the R.A. and S.M. 1907–1912, from Ellerslie Lane, Bexhill. Her sitters included the Rt. Rev. Dr. C. J. Ridgeway, Bishop of Chichester, Mrs. Norman Elliott and Miss Christabel Goodwin.

*Goodwin, Miss Helen M. (fl. 1907–1910)
Of Paris. Exhibited at the R.A. 1907 and 1910, from addresses in Paris.

*Gordon, Miss Isobel. (fl. 1908–1912)
Of Alassio, Italy, and London. Exhibited at the R.A. 1908–1912, from Molino-di-Sopra, Alassio and Rossetti Mansions, Chelsea.

*Gordon, Sir John Watson. See Watson Gordon, Sir John and Watson, John

*Gorham, Miss Edith. (fl. 1907)
Exhibited at the R.A. 1907, from Merrymount,

Bushey, Herts. Her sitter was the Rev. Canon Carner, D.D.

*Goshawk, Miss Louis G. (fl. 1898)
Of London. Exhibited at the R.A. 1898, from 18 Carmalt Gardens, Putney.

Gosse, Thomas. (fl. 1804–1830)
Of London. Working in Exeter January 1804 and at Skinner Street, Poole, in 1830. Was the grandfather of Sir Edmund Gosse, poet and critic.

*Gosse, William. (fl. 1830–1840)
A miniature of Philip Henry Gosse, F.R.S. (1810–1888) who was a marine zoologist, was painted in 1839 by his brother Wm. Gosse, and is at the N.P.G. Exhibited at the R.A. 1839, from 10 Alfred Place, Bedford Square. The exhibit was of Thomas Bell, Esq., F.R.S., Professor of Zoology at King's College, London. He may have been identical with the Gosse (no initial given) who exhibited a portrait at the R.A., in 1814. (Pl. 130: no. 344.)

*Gosset, Isaac, F.S.A. (the elder). 1713–1799
Born in London 2 May 1713. Noted for portrait waxes. Exhibited at the Society of Artists 1760–1775, and at the Free Society of Artists 1778. A miniature by this artist is known to have existed and was noted by the S.N.P.G. Died in London 28 November 1799.

*Gottschalk, Miss Blanche. (fl. 1890–1910)
Of London. Exhibited at the R.A. etc. 1890–1910, from various London addresses.

*Gould, Miss Florence E. (fl. 1897–1901)
Of London and Hull. Exhibited at the R.A., 1897–1901. One of her exhibits was a miniature portrait of Neville Gordon Gould.

Goupy, Bernard
Mentioned by Redgrave, but there is no evidence that any such artist existed.

Goupy, Joseph. 1680?–1768? or before 1782
The above artist is said by some authorities to have been born at Nevers, but the late Mr. C. R. Grundy in his article in the *Walpole Society*, Vol. IX, pp. 77–87, contended that Joseph Goupy was probably born in England *c.* 1680. He was a nephew of Louis Goupy (q.v.). Is known to have been studying at Kneller's Academy in London in 1711. Became a fashionable drawing master. Said to have assisted P. Tillemans with scene painting 1720–1725. Painted small figure subjects, drew landscapes, executed miniatures in body colours, made some etchings after his own work and that of other artists and copied Italian paintings. Taught the Prince of Wales who employed him at Kew and Cliveden House. The Prince is said to have made him his cabinet painter in 1736 and to have sent him to Paris in 1749. Goupy was also drawing master to George III who is said to have granted him a small pension on his accession. Was an associate of Dahl, Rysbrack, Wootton and Dr. Brook Taylor. Became involved in an action brought against him in 1738 by Charles Hedges, brother of John Hedges, with whom Goupy had been friends for some years. Charles alleged that Goupy had failed to repay money which he had borrowed from John Hedges; this was refuted by Goupy but owing to the absence of documents, the outcome of the case is not known. Quarrelled with Handel whom he caricatured. Was a member of the Society of Artists in 1765 in which year he exhibited there. His name remained on the list of Non-Exhibitors drawn up by the Secretary for the years 1766, 1767 and 1768. His collection was sold by auction in March 1765. The date of his death in London is uncertain and

may have been as early as 1766 and not later than 1782. Walpole in his *Anecdotes* describes him as 'another fine painter in water-colours but in a different style from Lens. The latter stippled the faces and finished highly; Goupy imitated the boldness of strokes in oil.' Later he says, after mentioning Louis Goupy, 'His nephew Joseph, and Bernard Lens were two of our best miniature-painters, and their works worthy of any cabinet.' This last statement has been erroneously quoted as of Louis. A painting of a group by Gavin Hamilton, 'An Artists' Club' 1735, contains a portrait of Goupy, reproduced in *Walpole Society*, Vol. VI, plate XVI. Examples of his work are in the B.M., and the N.P.G. has an interesting miniature by Goupy of Dr. Brook Taylor. This is full of detail and well executed.

Goupy, Louis. d. 1747
Born in France before 1700, uncle of Joseph Goupy (q.v.) and said to have been a nephew of Bernard Lens III (q.v.). Was a pupil at Kneller's Academy in London, 1711. In 1720 studied under L. Chéron (q.v.). Painted miniatures, portraits in oil, worked in fresco and crayons and taught miniature painting. Accompanied Lord Burlington to Italy. His self-portrait was engraved by G. White (q.v.). Long quotes Walpole as saying that he was one of our best miniature painters and 'worthy of any cabinet' but this was in fact said about his nephew Joseph, and Bernard Lens. Died in London, 1747.

*Gowan, Miss Mary. (fl. 1908–1914)
Of London. Exhibited at the R.A. 1908–1914, from addresses in Streatham Common.

*Grace, Alfred Fitzwalter, R.B.A. d. 1903
Of London. Exhibited at the R.A., B.I., N.W.C.S., etc., 1865–1893. Painted landscapes and miniatures. Died in London 12 November 1903.

Graglia, Alessandro. (fl. 1777–1779). See also **Graglia, Andrea** and **Grallia, A. C.**
Of London. Exhibited at the R.A., 1777–1779. Probably related to Andrea Graglia (q.v.) whose address he shared in 1777. He moved later to 9 Carlisle Street, Soho Square. Painted miniatures and portraits in oil. Possibly identical with A. C. Grallia (q.v.).

Graglia, Andrea. (fl. 1777–1796). See also **Grallia, A. C.** and **Graglia, Alessandro**
Of London. Exhibited at the R.A., 1777–1791. Probably related to Alessandro Graglia (q.v.) with whom he was living in 1777 at 5 Bridges Street, Covent Garden. A. C. Grallia (q.v.) exhibited from the above artist's address and may have been identical with, or related to, Alessandro Graglia. A miniature of Lady Seton, signed and dated '1796', on ivory, was Lot 396 in the Wellesley Sale at Sotheby's in 1920.

*Graham, Miss Frances J. (fl. 1908–1914)
Exhibited at the R.A. 1908–1914, from Carnethick, Fowey, Cornwall.

*Graham, I. or J. (fl. 1737)
A miniature on enamel by the above artist is in the Rijksmuseum, Amsterdam. It is inscribed on the reverse, 'J. Hage / I. Graham / F. 1737'. I have not been able to discover any further information about this artist.

*Graham, Mrs. Lilias Jane. (fl. 1883–1898)
Of London and Bath. Exhibited at the R.A. etc., 1883–1898, from 40 Woodstock Road, Bedford

Park (1885) and 19 Brock Street, Bath (1898). The miniatures were of Beatrix Graham and Jean Graham.

Grallia, A. C. (fl. 1792). See also **Graglia, Andrea** and **Graglia, Alessandro**

Of London. Exhibited at the R.A. 1792, from the address used by Andrea Graglia (q.v.) in 1791. Possibly identical with either Andrea or Alessandro Graglia, or related to them. His address in 1792 was 34 Great Titchfield Street, Cavendish Square.

Granges, David des. See **Des Granges**

*Grant, C. (fl. 1837). See also **Grant, Charles**

A miniature of an unknown man, seated on a chair, half-length, is inscribed on the reverse 'Painted by C^r Grant Jan 17th 1837', and is in the collection of R. Bayne Powell, Esq. The sitter is painted against a pale blue background, the features are well painted. A large water-colour portrait of a man and a lady is recorded by Schidlof. It was signed 'C. Grant'. The artist may have been identical with Charles Grant (q.v.).

*Grant, Charles. (fl. 1825–1839). See also **Grant, C.**

Exhibited at the R.A. 1825–1839, from Castle Street, Leicester Square and Mornington Place, Hampstead Road. Painted portraits many of which may have been miniatures. His sitters included W. Lund, Esq. Was possibly identical with C. Grant (q.v.).

*Grant, Sir Francis, P.R.A., R.S.A. 1803–1878

Born in 1803, 4th son of Francis Grant, Laird of Kilgraston, Perthshire. Was a fashionable portrait painter and executed equestrian figures and studies. Is not known as a miniaturist, but a miniature of the 6th Duke of Atholl, and said to be by the above artist was illustrated in *The Connoisseur* in October 1930. He died in Melton Mowbray 5 October 1878.

*Grant, J. (fl. 1809)

Of Bath. Executed tinted pencil portraits, faces, etc., in the manner of Edridge (q.v.). Signed 'J. Grant, Bath' followed by a date. I have seen a portrait in pencil with the face tinted in water-colour signed 'J.Grant, Bath / 1809' on the reverse and with a cursive 'JG' on the front.

*Granville, Miss Evelyn. (fl. 1883)

Of London. Exhibited at the R.A., etc., 1883. Duveen recorded that the price of the exhibit was £7. 7. 0.

*Granville, Miss Mary. See **Delany, Mrs.**

Gratia, Charles Louis. 1815–1911

Born in Rambervillers (Lorraine) 25 November 1815. Was a pupil of H. Decaisne. Was in England 1848–1857. Exhibited at the R.A., etc., 1851–1864. Returned to France and died at Mont Lignon, August 1911. Was best known for his pastel portraits but is thought to have also painted miniatures. His exhibits at the R.A. were catalogued as by L. Gratia, with whom he is presumably identical.

Gratia, L. See **Gratia, Charles Louis**

Gratise, S. (fl. 1791–1795). See also **Gratitien, S.**

The above artist was probably identical with Sebastian Gratitien (q.v.) who exhibited from the Society of Artists in 1791 from 132 Pall Mall, from which addres$_{\vartriangle}$ Gratise exhibited at the R.A., in 1792 and 1793. Exhibited at the R.A., 1791–1795. No address is recorded for 1791 but in 1795 he was at 10 St. Alban's Street, Pall Mall. Long noted having seen two miniatures signed on the edge 'Gratise

pinxit londini mai 1795' and 'Gratise pinxit anno domin 1795 mai 5. 10 st Albans St., Pall Mall.' The work shows the influence of Cosway (q.v.). Schidlof records a miniature in a private collection signed 'gratise pinxit 1792'.

Gratitien, Sebastian. (fl. 1785?–1791). See also **Gratise, S.**

The above artist was probably identical with S. Gratise (q.v.). Gratitien exhibited at the R.A. in 1790, from 55 Great Windmill Street, when he is styled as Painter to the Elector of Cologne, and at the Society of Artists 1791 from Mr. Sebastian Gratise, 132 Pall Mall. His exhibits in 1790 included a miniature of the Elector of Cologne. According to Long, Gratitien was working as early as 1785.

Grattan, George. 1787–1819

Born in Dublin 1787; entered the Dubin Society Schools and was awarded medals in 1797 and succeeding years. Was awarded gratuities in 1800 and 1801. Painted miniatures while still a student but there is no record of his having painted any later in his career. He painted portraits, landscapes, historical subjects and domestic scenes. In 1802 he won a prize for a model in clay. Exhibited in Dublin 1801–1813. Was in London *c.* 1807. Returned to Dublin, 1813. Exhibited at the R.A., and B.I., 1812. Due to failing health he moved to Cullenswood, where he died, 18 June 1819, and was buried on 21 June in the old churchyard at Glasnevin. An exhibition of his works was held in Dublin after his death.

Graves, The Hon. Henry Richard. 1818–1882

Born 9 October 1818, son of Thomas North, 2nd Baron Graves. Exhibited at the R.A., 1846–1881. Married Henrietta Wellesley 1843. Painted portraits in oil and miniature. Had a distinguished clientele. A miniature in oil of Miss Evelyn Pennefather Hankey, 1852, by the above artist was lent to the exhibition at the South Kensington Museum, 1865. He died on 28 April 1882.

Gray. (fl. 1819) See also **Grey** or **Gray, J.W.**

Of Bath. Was living in St. James's Street, Bath from 1819. An exhibition held at the Victoria Art Gallery, Bath 1903 records the spelling of the name as Grey (q.v.).

*Gray, Catherine Esther, née Geddes. (fl. *c.* 1841)

Painted small portraits in water-colour on card *c.* 1841. They lacked quality and Long thought the painting weak.

*Gray, Miss Ethel. (fl. 1902)

Exhibited at the R.A. 1902, from 19 Beaumont Street, Oxford.

Gray, George. (fl. 1854–1873)

Of London. Exhibited at the R.A., etc., 1854–1873. Was an enamellist. Many of his works were after those of other artists.

*Gray, Henry (I). (fl. 1790?). See also **Gray, Henry (II)**

A miniature of a lady inscribed on the reverse 'Duchess of York, 1790, Henry Gray' is in the collection of Mrs. Walter Scott. The artist may have been identical with Henry Gray (II) (q.v.) and the miniature painted from an earlier portrait.

Gray, Henry (II). (fl. 1823–1898). See also **Gray Henri (I)**

Of London. Exhibited landscapes and miniatures at the R.A. and B.I., 1849–1897. Was a good draughtsman and used pure, fresh colours to which he added a lot of gum. A portrait of the Prince of Wales, on ivory, signed on the reverse 'Painted by H. Gray / 1871' is in a private collection in Paris.

Gray, John Westcott. 1786–1878

Of London. Exhibited at the R.A. 1828, from 14 Old Bond Street, and not 1878 as recorded by Long and Schidlof.

*Gray, Miss Monica F. (fl. 1900–1905)

Of London. Exhibited at the R.A., 1900 and 1905. Painted miniatures and landscapes in oil.

*Grebner, W. (Willem?). (fl. 1817)

A miniature of a lady, signed 'W.Grebner fecit 1817' was formerly in the Hand collection. This may have been by Willem Grebner, who was born in Vreeland 7 December 1784, died in Amsterdam 28 January 1866. He was a Dutch painter, lithographer and engraver. It is not known if he ever worked in Britain.

Green, Benjamin Richard. 1807/8–1876

Born in London, 1807/8; son of James Green (q.v.) and Mary Green (q.v.). Entered the R.A. schools, 15 December 1826 aged 19. Was awarded premiums at the Society of Arts in 1824–1827. Exhibited at the R.A., N.W.C.S., S.B.A., etc., 1832–1876. In 1834 became a member of the N.W.C.S. Was working at Inverness in 1840. Painted portraits and miniatures. Published works on perspective; taught and lectured on the subject. Was Secretary of the Artists' Annuity Fund. Died in London 5 October 1876.

*Green, Miss E. Margaret (Mrs. F. Curtis). (fl. 1900–1903)

Of London and Redhill, Surrey. Exhibited at the R.A. 1900–1903, from Rossetti House Studios, Chelsea and from 43 London Road, Redhill. She exhibited a miniature of Mrs. Frederic Green in 1901.

*Green, J. See also **G., J.** or **I.**

A miniature of a child signed with cursive initials 'J.G.' or 'I.G.' and stated to be dated 1759 is reproduced in *Miniaturen-Katalog*, Albert Jaffé, where it is ascribed to J. Green.

Green, James. 1771/2–1834

Born in Leytonstone, Essex 13 March 1771/2. Entered the R.A. Schools, 18 February 1791 aged 19. Exhibited at the R.A., B.I., S.B.A., etc., 1793–1834. His exhibits included portraits of Bartolozzi and Benjamin West (q.v.). Was a member of a sketching club *c.* 1800 together with Shelley (q.v.), J. C. Nattes, W. H. Pyne, etc. Married 13 February 1805, Mary Byrne (Mrs. James Green (q.v.)). Was a member of the Associated Artists, 1808–1810 and their first treasurer. He was the father of B. R. Green (q.v.). Painted miniatures, oil portraits, landscapes and figure subjects. Many of his works were engraved. He died in Bath, 27 March 1834. Portraits in oil by James Green are at the N.P.G. and Salford Museum. Letters by him relating to the Associated Artists are in the V. & A. M. Library.

Green, Mrs. James (Miss Mary Byrne). 1776–1845

Born 1776, née Mary Byrne, second daughter of William Byrne, the engraver. Said to have been a pupil of 'Arland'? probably L. A. Arlaud (q.v.). Worked in London. Exhibited at the R.A., B.I., S.B.A. etc., 1795–1845. Made studies after Reynolds and Gainsborough. Married James Green (q.v.) 1805. Was a member of the Associated Artists in Water-Colours from 26 November 1807–1810. Retired from the profession after her husband's death in 1834 but continued to exhibit. Some of her works were engraved. She is represented in a drawing at the B.M. by A. E. Chalon (q.v.) showing students at the B.I. 1807. She was a good artist who painted with freedom and charm and placed her sitters well. She died 22 October 1845 and was buried at Kensal Green. The V. & A. M. has MS letters by her relating to the Associated Artists. A charming rectangular miniature of an unknown lady against a landscape background, is in the collection of Major R. M. O. de la Hey and was exhibited in Edinburgh, 1965. A large miniature by her of Queen Adelaide, signed 'M^y Green' is at Windsor. A miniature by her of Joseph Farington, R.A., after Lawrence was Lot 158 at Knight, Frank and Rutley's 14 December 1911.

Green, Miss Letitia Jane. (fl. 1824–1828)
Of London. Probably related to B. R. Green (q.v.) whose address, 27 Argyll Street, she shared. Awarded a silver palette in 1824 by the Society of Arts and other awards in 1825, 1826, and a gold Isis medal 1828, for an original miniature portrait.

Green, Mrs. Mary. See Green, Mrs. James

Green, Rupert. c. 1768–1804
Was born c. 1768. Son of Valentine Green (1739–1813) the engraver. Wrote a tragedy before he was nine years old. Was taught engraving. Won a premium at the Society of Arts in 1781. Was in partnership with his father c. 1785–1798; made little advance in art and 'his father proposed to establish him as a Merchant for the publication of Prints.' He married Susannah Slade, spinster, of St. Georges, Southwark at St. Mary-le-bone, 26 June 1790. She was reputed to have a fortune of some £40,000 but her father lost his money and as she was a vain and extravagant person, the family were soon in financial difficulties. They were obliged to live near Chelsea, where he and his wife and six children were chiefly supported by charity. Rupert Green's health finally gave way and he died on 16 November 1804 and was buried at Hampstead. A portrait drawing of Master Rupert Green, by John Downman (q.v.) executed in 1778 may have been of him. A miniature of a lady, on ivory, signed on the reverse 'Mr. Rupert Green, 15 Millman's Row, Chelsea' was reproduced by Hand in *Signed Miniatures*. There was a lot of stippling on the face and the background was grey, yellow and brown, reminiscent of some of the work of S. Shelley (q.v.). A miniature of a child, signed on the reverse, 'Mr R. Green / Miniature Painter / 15. / Millmans Row / Chelsea' was sold at Christie's on 19 December 1967. The miniature was not of any great merit.

Green, William, junior. (fl. 1752)
A good plumbago miniature of an unknown lady by the above artist, signed and dated 'Gul. Green Junr delin. 1752' was Lot 39 at Sotheby's, 14 April 1969.

*Greene, Georgiana M. K. (Mrs. E.). (fl. 1909)
Exhibited at the R.A. 1909, from Cappagh Lodge, Monaghan, Ireland.

Greener, Miss Mary Ann. (fl. 1845–1853)
Of Greenwich and London. Exhibited at the R.A. and S.B.A., etc., 1845–1853.

Greenhead, Miss. (fl. 1795–1800)
Of London. Exhibited at the R.A., 1795–1800. Her early contributions were as an Hon. Exhibitor.

Greenhill, John. 1649–1676. See G., I.
Was born in Salisbury 1649. Said to have executed miniatures, but known chiefly as a portrait painter and engraver. When the Pierpont Morgan Collection was sold at Christie's, 24 June 1935, Lot No. 95, a portrait of Charles II and Lot No. 96, of

Queen Catherine of Braganza (married Charles II in 1662) were signed 'I.G.' and 'J.G.' and catalogued as by Greenhill. Both miniatures were in gouache. The Wellesley collection contained a pair of miniatures of an unknown gentleman and his wife, executed in Indian ink on paper, which were ascribed to J. Greenhill. Died in London, 1676.

Greenlees, William
A miniature of James Maidment (1795?–1879) is at the S.N.P.G. It is not very well painted.

Greenwood, John, F.S.A. 1727–1792
Born 7 December 1727 in Boston, U.S.A., son of Samuel Greenwood, a merchant. Studied under Thomas Johnston. Was living in Surinam, 1752–1758. Went to Holland where he became an art dealer. Came to England c. 1763. Exhibited at the Society of Artists, 1764–1776. Painted portraits, landscapes, marine subjects, executed mezzotint engravings and was an auctioneer. Died in Margate, 16 September 1792. According to Fielding his portrait was engraved by Pether (q.v.).

*Greenwood, Miss Minnie L. (fl. 1907–1909)
Exhibited at the R.A. 1907 and 1909, from 1 Friar's Terrace, York. Her exhibits included 'General' Booth, probably William Booth, 1829–1912, founder of the Salvation Army.

Greese, John Alexander. See Gresse

Gregg, Thomas Henry. b. 1801
Of London and Cambridge. Entered the R.A. Schools, 31 October 1821 aged 20 years. Exhibited at the R.A., S.B.A., and B.I., etc., 1824–1872. Painted miniatures, portraits and genre subjects. A directory of 1834 gives his address as 14 Rufford's Buildings, Islington.

*Gregory. (fl. c. 1790)
Known only by an oil miniature (on card?) c. 1790 inscribed 'Gregory / min^t Painter / 74 Newgate Street.' This miniature was noted by Long.

Gregory, A. (fl. 1821)
A well painted miniature of an officer signed and dated 'A. Gregory / 1821' is in a private collection.

*Gregory, Edward John, R.A., P.R.I. 1850–1909
Born in Southampton, 1850, where he worked under von Herkomer. Went to London, 1870 and became a pupil at the South Kensington Museum. Became a member of the R.I., 1872 of which he later became President. Exhibited at the R.A., N.W.C.S., R.I., S.M., etc., 1870–1908. Painted portraits, miniatures, landscapes and executed engravings. Was elected R.A., 1898. Died in Marlow, 1909.

*Gregory, Miss Elsie. (fl. 1901–1910)
Of London. Exhibited at the R.A. 1901–1910, from addresses in Swiss Cottage and Hampstead. Painted miniatures and subjects in water-colour.

*Gregson, Miss Isabelle B. (fl. 1903–1910)
Of London. Exhibited at the R.A., 1903–1910.

Gresse, Grease or Greese, John Alexander. 1741–1794
Born in London, 1741, son of a Genevese, after whom Gresse Street is named. According to Schidlof he was called Jack Grease. Was a pupil of G. Scotin and T. Major, engravers, as well as having instruction from F. Zuccarelli, and he also worked for J. B. Cipriani. Won several premiums at the Society of Arts, 1755–1762. Had further study at the Duke of Richmond's Gallery and the St. Martin's Lane Academy. Exhibited at the Society of Artists, 1766–1768 and at the Free Society of Artists, 1763–

1764. Became a member of the Society of Artists in 1776. Had a fashionable practice as a drawing master and taught the daughters of George III. Painted miniatures, water-colour landscapes and executed some etchings. Was a collector and inherited property from his father. Died, 19 February 1794, and was buried at St. Anne's, Soho.

Grevedon, Pierre Louis (called Henri). 1776–1860
Born in Paris, 17 October 1776. Became a pupil of Regnault. Obtained an honorable mention at a competition in Rome in 1803. Exhibited at the Paris Salon, 1804. Went to Russia till 1812 and became a member of the Academy of St. Petersburg. Travelled to Stockholm; went to London c. 1814 in which year he exhibited a self-portrait in the drawing section of the R.A., as well as two mythological subjects. He returned to Paris in 1816. Painted portraits, mythological subjects and miniatures, but is best known as a lithographer. Exhibited again at the Paris Salon, 1824–1829. He obtained various medals and in 1832 was awarded the Légion d'honneur. Died in Paris, 1 June 1860. His miniatures were well drawn and his brushwork had the effect of 'pointillistique'. His treatment of the hair was good and the clothes were finely drawn. The backgrounds to his miniatures were almost always a uniform colour in gouache. He signed Henry Grevedon, Henri Grevedon and H. Grevedon. At least one miniature known to me is signed and dated 'henry Grevedon, 1818' in cursive lettering.

*Grew, J. (fl. 1788–1790)
Said to have been a miniaturist. Exhibited at the R.A. 1788–1790, from 20 Bartholomew Close. All his exhibits were taken from intaglios.

Grey. (fl. c. 1845). See Gray
May have been identical with the Gray (q.v.) who was working at Bath, 1819. Painted water-colour heads in miniature c. 1845, some of which were seen by Long, who considered them weak.

*Grey or Gray, Catherine. (fl. c. 1841)
This artist is recorded by Long as working in c. 1841 and may be identical with or related to the Grey (q.v.) (no initial given).

*Grey, Mrs. Edith F. (fl. 1890–1911)
Exhibited at the R.A., N.W.C.S., S.M. 1890–1911, from Newcastle-on-Tyne. Executed miniatures, subjects and landscapes in water-colour and flowers and birds in oil.

Grieg, Mrs. M. A. (fl. 1852)
Of London. Exhibited at the R.A. 1852, from 156 Sloane Street, Belgrave Square. The R.A. catalogues give the spelling of her name as Grieg, both in the index and the catalogue, not Greig as in Long and Schidlof.

*Griesbach, Miss Julia A. (fl. 1882–1883)
Of London. Exhibited at the R.A., 1882–1883.

Griffin, William. b. 1752
Of London, born in 1752. Entered the R.A. Schools, 8 April 1772 aged '21 next August'. Exhibited at the R.A. and Society of Artists, 1772–1776. Was in Birmingham, 18 May 1778. Painted portraits and miniatures, some of which were executed in crayons and chalks.

*Griffith, Miss Hilda M. (fl. 1910–1914)
Of London. Exhibited at the R.A. 1910–1914, from addresses in North London.

*Griffith, Moses. 1747–1819

Born in Caernarvonshire, 25 March 1747, not 6 April 1749 as given by Pennant. Of humble parentage, Griffith received such education as he had from the Free School of Bottwnog, and was self-taught in art. It has been said that he studied at the Society of Arts, but according to a note on a sheet of his portraits this was not so. In *Walker's Monthly*, for the months of August and September 1938 and January 1939, there is a full description of Griffith's life and art and his connection with Thomas Pennant (1726–1798), a traveller and naturalist for whom he executed architectural drawings, scenery and sketches on a miniature scale. After T. Pennant died, he continued to work at a later date for Davis Pennant, son of his earlier patron. Painted a number of miniatures on card. Many of these from the Thomas Pennant and Earl of Denbigh Collections were sold at Sotheby's, 26 March 1962; they were of local celebrities and were attractive and well painted. Griffith died on 11 November 1819. T. Pennant, Captain F. Grose and Griffith toured many parts of Britain providing Griffith with many different subjects executed in water-colour and Indian ink. A miniature of a lady by the above artist is at the V. & A. M.

Griffiths, J. (fl. 1818–1821)

Of London. Exhibited at the R.A., 1818–1821.

*Griffiths, Miss Mary E. (fl. 1893–1898)

Of London. Exhibited at the R.A., etc., 1893–1898.

Griffiths, Thomas. *c.* 1777–1852

Was born in Liverpool *c.* 1777. Started his career in Liverpool as a painter and plumber. Entered the R.A. Schools 19 December 1815. Returned to Liverpool where he painted miniatures; had a successful practice and was well off. Bought property and was a dealer and picture restorer. Was Secretary of the Liverpool Academy in 1822. From 1824–1828 he lived at 57 St. Anne Street, Liverpool. He died in Liverpool in 1852 and had a daughter who survived him. An example of his work is at the Walker Art Gallery, Liverpool.

*Grimaldi, Miss Argenta Louisa. b. 1884

Born 1884, second daughter of Wyndford Beaufort and Louisa K. Grimaldi, née Soames. Was descended from the same family as William Grimaldi (q.v.) whose ancestors were of the noble family of Grimaldi of Genoa, and of the Merovingian Kings of France and Princes of Monaco. The artist's sister was Claudia Henriette Grimaldi (born 1882). Exhibited at the R.A. 1908–1909, from Hathewolden, Porchester Road, Bournemouth, Hants.

*Grimaldi, Miss Louisa Frances (Mrs. John Edmeads). 1785–1873

Born in Maidstone, Kent, 15 April 1785; daughter of William Grimaldi (q.v.) and his wife Frances, née Willis. Painted miniatures. Married, 13 September 1809 at St. George's, Hanover Square, the Rev. John Edmeads, vicar of Preshute, Wilts. (died May 1849). His widow died without issue, 23 June 1873.

Grimaldi, William. 1751–1830

Born in Shoreditch, 26 August 1751, eighth Marquess Grimaldi. Was a descendant of the noble family of Grimaldi of Genoa and of the Merovingian Kings of France and Princes of Monaco. William was the son of Alexander Grimaldi, seventh Marquess (1714–1800), and his second wife Esther Barton (died 1774). Studied under T. Worlidge (q.v.) who may have been his uncle, and

who married Arabella Grimaldi (see Worlidge). Was in Paris 1777–1783. Was friendly with John Wesley and his wife. In 1783, at Maidstone in Kent, he married Frances, daughter of Robert Willis Esq., of Kent. She was the sister of Mary Willis (wife of Sir John Stirling) with whom she was co-heiress to her father's estate. There were four children of the marriage, viz: William (1786–1835), Henry (1792–1806), Louisa Frances (q.v.) (1785–1873) and Stacey, ninth Marquess (1790–1863). Worked in London and the provinces. Was in Chester, 6 September 1774. Exhibited at the Free Society of Artists, 1768–1770, the Society of Artists, 1772 and the R.A., 1786–1830. Was miniature painter to the Duke and Duchess of York (1791), George III and George IV (1824). Made copies of works by Reynolds, Hoppner, Beechey and others. Painted miniatures in water-colour and enamel. He was living at 2 Albemarle Street, London in 1807 and at 16 Upper Ebury Street, Chelsea, when he died on 27 May 1830. A number of his works, including a self-portrait, were sold by the family in 1960. His work is often similar to that of continental artists; it is a little uneven in quality but I have seen miniatures by Grimaldi of outstanding merit, which would place him much higher in the list of the best artists of the period than has hitherto been the case. Characteristics of his work may be found by examining the shading on the face and nostrils; the lower outline of the lids is usually picked out in a rather bright red. Opaque white may be seen in the hair, particularly on portraits of men. The signature is usually placed near the edge of the ivory, 'Grimaldi' without initials and written horizontally, 'W. Grimaldi A.R.' in italics with the letters sometimes shaded. A.R. is supposed to indicate Académie Royale, of which he was not in fact a member. Other signatures include his name and address followed by inscriptions relating to his appointment to members of the Royal Family. Examples of his work may be seen at the V. & A. M., the London Museum, the Wallace Collection and the B.M., etc. Some of his works were engraved. Three fine miniatures by him were exhibited in Edinburgh in 1965, viz: Admiral Lord Rodney, after Reynolds; Mme Anna Storace; and John Ord.

Grimani, F. (fl. 1808–1831)

Of London. Exhibited at the R.A., 1808–1831. The exhibit in 1815 was a miniature portrait of his wife. He lived at 35 Westmoreland Place, City Road.

*Grimshaw, Miss Emma. (fl. 1903)

Of Port Rush, Co. Antrim, Ireland. Exhibited at the Society of Miniaturists, 1903.

Grisée, Louis Joseph. b. 1822. d. after 1867

Born 23 February 1822 at St. Cyr-l'École. Was a pupil of Paul Delaroche and became a student at The École des Beaux-Arts, Paris, 19 September 1842. Exhibited at the Salon, 1844–1867. Painted pictures in oil, portraits, genre subjects and enamel paintings, some of which were copies after Hall, Dumont, etc. According to Nachemsohn in *Signed Enamel Miniatures*, p. 37, Grisée worked in London and died after 1867.

Groombridge or **Groomrich, William.** 1748–1811

Born in Goudhurst or Tonbridge, Kent, 1748, where he was living in 1773; also worked in London, Bromley and Canterbury. Exhibited miniatures, portraits and landscapes at the Free Society of Artists and the Society of Artists 1773–1776 and exhibited landscapes only at the R.A., 1777–1790.

According to the *London Gazette*, 10 October 1778, 'William Groombridge, Limner, formerly of St. Anne's, Soho, lately of Paris. Insolvent Debtor. Went abroad to escape his creditors and returned to take advantage of Insolvent Debtor's Act, going to Prison and then petitioning for release'. His name has been spelt Groomrich in error. Was in Philadelphia *c.* 1794. His wife, Mrs. Catherine Groombridge (also an artist), conducted a school for girls in Philadelphia *c.* 1794–1804, when the family moved to Baltimore and she started another school there. Groombridge exhibited at the Society of Artists in Philadelphia and posthumously at the Maryland Historical Society. He died in Baltimore, 24 May 1811. His wife died in Jamaica on 20 November 1837.

Groomrich, W. 1748–1811. See **Groombridge, William**

*Groots. (fl. 1754)

Was advertising from Cleveland Court, in St. James's Palace, in the *Daily Advertiser*, 21 June 1754.

*Grossing, Mr. (fl. 1679)

According to information at Woburn Abbey, under an entry for 1679, 'Paid Mr Grossing for his Lordship's picture in little £5.' This refers to William, 5th Earl of Bedford.

*Grosvenor, The Hon. Mrs. Norman. (Caroline). (fl. 1889–1893)

Of London. Exhibited at the R.A. etc., 1889–1893.

Groth, A. (fl. *c.* 1739–1753). See also **Gambel** and **Gardelle, Théodore**

Said to have been a German artist who painted miniatures in water-colour and enamel, and according to Walpole 'made no great proficience'. Confusion has arisen over this artist due to the fact that scanty information has been available about him and all miniatures signed G have in the past been attributed to either Gambel (q.v.) or Gardelle (q.v.). The situation was clarified when three enamel miniatures by him were taken to Sotheby's where they were sold, 2 May 1966. They were apparently of one family. One of Thomas Edwards Freeman, was signed and dated on the reverse, 'A. Groth pinxt. 1753'. Another, possibly his sister, signed on the front of the enamel 'G', and the third of a young man, Walter Edwards Freeman (unsigned). Groth was apparently working in England *c.* 1739–1753 and must not be confused with Johann Jakob Groth, a painter at the Ludwigsberg Porcelain factory. Schidlof noted a miniature in enamel on gold of William Augustus, Duke of Cumberland, son of George II, signed 'A Groth Fecit 1744'. An enamel miniature in my collection of William Henry, Duke of Gloucester, signed 'G.' on the front, was attributed to Gambel, but it is almost certainly by Groth; it is very like the Freeman family but is more brilliant and the detail of the costume more meticulously painted. Characteristics appear to be the strong delineation of the eyebrows, shadows down the nose, a thinly drawn mouth with emphasised top lip, greenish yellow stippling on the face and touches of opaque white on the lace work. The colours are bright and fresh. No miniatures on ivory are at present known.

Groth, Johann Jakob. See **Groth, A.**

Groves, Mrs. J. (fl. 1814–1818)

Of London. Exhibited at the R.A., 1814–1818. Was a student at the B.I. in 1817. Painted portraits, fruit and flowers and made a miniature copy of

Dobson's self-portrait. She has previously been recorded as exhibiting at the R.A. up to 1820, but there is no evidence in the R.A. catalogues that she was an exhibitor in either of the last two years. Graves records that she exhibited at the O.W.C.S.

*Grubbe, Mrs. Marie Ellen. See Lucas, Miss Marie Ellen Segmont

Grundy, John. 1780–1843

Born 2 June 1780 at Bolton-le-Moors, Lancs, son of James Grundy. Married Elizabeth Leeming in 1805 by whom he had four sons and a daughter. May have served in the Bolton Volunteer Infantry. Was an amateur painter and cotton-mill owner. His family became connected with various forms of art for several generations. Died 24 October 1843 and was buried at the New Jerusalem Church, Bolton Street, Manchester. F. Gordon Roe, who supplied Basil Long with numerous items of interest over miniaturists, was a relation of Grundy's and an example of his work is in the family.

Gubbins, Miss Henrietta. (fl. 1843–1849)

Of Leamington. Exhibited at the R.A., 1843–1849. A lithographed portrait of Colonel Adams (died c. 1855) by P. Gauci after Gubbins, is at the B.M.

*Guest, D. (fl. 1804). See also **Guest, T., junior**

A miniature of an unknown lady, signed in scratched writing on the front 'D.Guest pinx / 1804' is in the collection of R. Bayne Powell, Esq. Possibly identical with the Thomas Douglas Guest who entered the R.A. Schools, 23 December 1801, aged 21 years, who may have been identical with, or related to, T. Guest, jun. (q.v.).

Guest, Henry

Probably identical with the Henry Guest who won a premium at the Society of Arts in 1826. A miniature of Sir G. Maclean, executed on paper by Guest was loaned to the exhibition at the South Kensington Museum, 1865.

Guest, T., junior. (fl. 1801). See also **Guest, D.**

Of London. Probably the son of Thomas Guest recorded in the Council Minutes of the R.A. Schools, 31 March 1777 and possibly the Thomas Douglas Guest who entered the R.A. Schools 23 December 1801 aged 21 years, and who obtained a gold medal in 1805. T. Guest, jun., exhibited miniatures at the R.A. 1801, from 76 St. James's Street.

*Guillemard, Miss Mary F. (fl. 1882–1883)

Of Cambridge. Exhibited at the R.A. etc., 1882–1883.

Guise, Miss Priscilla. See Wright, Mrs. John

*Gulland, Miss Elizabeth. (fl. 1886–1910)

Of Bushey, Herts, and said to have lived in Edinburgh. Exhibited at the R.A. etc., 1886–1910. Painted subject pictures in oil and water-colour and executed engravings. Copied the works of Sir Henry Raeburn, R.A., George Romney, R.A., Thomas Gainsborough, R.A. and George Richmond, R.A. Executed some miniatures – her sitter in 1907 being Miss Jessie Gulland, possibly her sister.

Gullick, Thomas John. (fl. 1851–1884)

Of London. Exhibited at the R.A., B.I. and S.B.A., 1851–1880. Painted miniatures some of which were for brooches and bracelets. Published a recipe for glass-painting in 1884. An engraved portrait after T. J. Gullick, by J. Timbs, is at the B.M.

*Gunn, Miss. 18th century

A miniature by the above artist, about whom nothing is at present known, is in the collection of the Duke of Northumberland. It is of Captain the Hon. Francis Hay Drummond. On the reverse of the miniature there is an inscription, part of which is indecipherable, stating that the sitter served in the Peninsular War where he never received a wound, and that he was drowned in the river Earn in October 1810. The end of the inscription reads as follows: 'This sketch was drawn by Mip Gunn'. This artist may have been an amateur. The eyelashes and eyebrows were distinctly drawn and the sitter painted against a yellow/gold background.

Gunter, Marcus. (fl. 1725)

Was working in London as an enamellist and goldsmith in 1725. An enamel copy of a painting by Teniers, 'L'Operateur' and formerly in the David Weill collection, was signed on the reverse 'Marcus Gunter oreficus fe 1725'. He sometimes signed M. Gunter. He executed a number of enamels of Roman Emperors which were formerly in the Nachemsohn Collection.

*Gush, Frederick. (fl. 1852)

I have seen a miniature of a man, signed on the reverse 'Fred Gush, 1852'. It is well painted and the colouring is pleasing. (Pl. 135: no. 359.)

*Gush, H. (fl. 1832)

I have seen a miniature, signed and dated 'H Gush, 1832'. It was reasonably well painted.

Gush, Miss R. (fl. 1857–1879)

Of London and Malden. Exhibited at the R.A., 1857–1879. Probably the daughter of William Gush (q.v.) from whose address, 15 Stratford Place, she exhibited. From 1867 she exhibited from The Grange, Old Malden. A large number of her portraits were of members of the family.

Gush, William. (fl. 1832–1835)

Lived at 1 Old Jewry. Won several awards at the Society of Arts, 1832–1835 for an anatomical drawing, a miniature portrait and a portrait in oils. A number of portraits of Methodist ministers by Gush were engraved in the *Methodist Magazine*. Some engravings of his portraits are at the B.M. This artist, recorded by Long, is presumably identical with the William Gush who exhibited at the R.A. and B.I., 1833–1874, from 15 Stratford Place, from which address Miss R. Gush (q.v.), presumably his daughter, also exhibited for some years. He painted figures, portraits and miniatures.

Gwatkins, Mrs. Robert Lovell. See Palmer, Miss Mary

Née Theophila Palmer ('Offy' to Sir Joshua Reynolds, her uncle). Daughter of John Palmer of Torrington and sister of Miss Mary Palmer (q.v.). Long, Schidlof and others have confused the two sisters; it was in fact Miss Mary Palmer, later wife of the 5th Earl of Inchquin (created 1st Marquess of Thomond in 1800) who was the miniaturist and not Mrs. Gwatkins.

Gwynn, William. (fl. 1807–1817)

Of London. Exhibited at the R.A., 1807–1817. F. Gordon Roe saw a miniature by this artist signed 'Painted by / Willᵐ Gwynn / 22 Bolsover St, Oxford Str / 1811'. The draughtsmanship was weak. The B.M. has an engraved portrait of C. S. Wittell after Gwynn.

H

H. (fl. c. 1755–c. 1779)

In the sale at Christie's 1 May 1928, Lot 134 was a small miniature of Gertrude, Duchess of Bedford, signed with a Roman 'H' and a date partly hidden by the frame c. 1755. Long records having seen another example c. 1779, and noted that the work was good. A miniature of Mrs. Dorothy Manton, née Stephenson, signed 'H' is in the collection of E. G. Paine of New York.

*H., A.K. 18th-century

An 18th century miniature of an unknown lady, signed 'A.K.H.06' (1806) was Lot 31 at Christie's, 19 July 1960.

*H., C. 18th century

Lot 40 at Christie's, 15 October 1963 contained two miniatures signed with initials 'CH' one of which was of an officer in a dark uniform, silver epaulettes and red collar.

H., C.S. See also S., H.C.

A miniature lent to the exhibition at the South Kensington Museum, 1865, was stated to be signed 'C.S.H.' and to be of a 'Nobleman of the St. John family'. A miniature of a man signed 'H.C.S.' was sold at Christie's on 15 October, 1963.

*H., G. (fl. 1757)

A miniature of Sir(?) Heathcote, signed 'G.H.' and dated '1757' was seen by Mr. A. J. B. Kiddell.

H., I. (fl. 1775–1799)

A good miniature of a man signed 'IH / 1778' (Roman caps.) painted with a bluish shading on the face and a stippled background, is at the V. & A. M. Long saw another signed with cursive initials 'IH / 1775' and one with a cursive monogram dated '1791'. An enamel miniature signed 'IH / 1775' was also seen by Long and is now at the V. & A. M. A miniature of a lady, with a scratched cursive signature 'IH / 1799' in which the face was stippled has also been noted. Lot 81, at Sotheby's 19 December 1960, was a miniature of a lady, signed and dated 'IH.1777'.

*H., J. (fl. 1807–1815)

Miniatures signed 'J.H.' and dated '1807' and '1815' were seen by Long, who considered them competently painted. A double miniature of a mother and child, both portraits signed 'J.H.', was Lot 44 at Sotheby's, 25 July 1966.

H., L. (fl. 1525). See also **Horenbout**

According to the catalogue of the H.G. Bohn Collection, which was sold at Christie's, March 1885, Lot 218 was a full-length portrait of Elizabeth Strafford, wife of Thomas Howard, Duke of Norfolk. It was 7½ × 5 in. and signed and dated 'L.H.' (in gold) '1525'. This miniature may possibly have been by Horenbout (q.v.).

*H., L.T. See also Hope, Lancelot

A pair of miniatures, signed with initials 'L.T.H.', one of which was said to be a self-portrait of the artist, were sold at Sotheby's on 30 November 1964. It was suggested that these might have been the work of Lancelot Hope (q.v.).

*H., N. 19th century

A miniature of an unknown sitter signed in

monogram 'NH' was seen by Long in 1933, who stated that it was not the work of N. Hone (q.v.).

H., T.K. (fl. 1786). See also **Hauck, F. L.**

Two miniatures were lent to the exhibition at the South Kensington Museum 1865, one a portrait of a little girl holding a pear, and the other of a boy holding a whip – both were signed 'T.K.H. 1786'. According to Long, these were by Hauck (q.v.), the signature not having been correctly deciphered.

Haag, Carl, R.W.S. 1820–1915

Born in Erlangen, Germany, 20 April 1820. Studied at the School of Fine Arts, Nuremberg under A. Reindel, and later at Munich 1844–1846. Went to Brussels and in 1847 to England after visiting Rome. Exhibited at the National Academy, New York, in 1848 and at the R.A. etc., from 1849–1888. Became a member of the O.W.C.S., 1850 and obtained the patronage of Queen Victoria. Travelled on the Continent etc. Died at Oberwesel, Germany, 24 January 1915. A self-portrait of the artist is at the B.M. He is best known for his pictures in water-colour.

*Hacker, Lilian (Mrs. A.). (fl. 1909–1912)

Of London and Glynde, Sussex. Exhibited at the R.A., 1909–1912. Was the wife of Arthur Hacker, R.A. (1858–1919), painter of subject pictures, London scenes and portraits.

*Haddan, Miss Isabel. (fl. 1907–1909)

Of Hove, Sussex. Exhibited at the Society of Miniaturists, 1907–1909.

*Hadden, Miss Nellie. (fl. 1885–1904)

Of Sunningdale, Berks. Exhibited at N.W.C.S., S.M. etc., from 1885–1904.

Hadfield, Maria Louisa Cecilia. See Cosway, Mrs.

Hähnisch, Anton. 1817–1897

Born in Vienna, 28 October 1817. Was a pupil at the Academy at Vienna and lived there until 1847 when he went to Berlin and afterwards travelled to many places including Frankfurt, Paris, London (1850–1862), Edinburgh, back to Berlin 1869. Was at Rome 1872–1873 and from there went to Karlsruhe. Exhibited at Vienna 1836–1847, and at the R.A., 1851–1869. Painted miniatures on ivory, porcelain-glass, pastel portraits, portraits in water-colour, and also executed lithographs; some examples of these latter portraits are at the B.M. He died at Karlsruhe in 1897. He had a distinguished clientele, which included H.R.H. Prince Frederick of Prussia, H.R.H. the Princess Royal of Prussia and Lady Mary Victoria Hamilton.

*Haig. (fl. 1765)

Known only by a family miniature of Lady Rhonddas, signed 'Haig', and by a miniature, recorded by J. J. Foster, of Anthony Blake of Melo Park, Co. Galway, dated '1765' and signed 'Haig'; this was sold at Sotheby's, 12 May 1921. May possibly have been an Irish artist.

*Haig, Miss E. Cotton. (fl. 1891–1897)

Of 11 Ramsay Garden, Edinburgh. Exhibited at the R.A., 1891–1897. Painted pictures in oil, and miniatures. Her exhibits included miniatures of Miss Cecilia Worsley Haig, and Colonel Fell.

*Haines, Miss Katherine Sybil. (fl. 1907–1921)

Of Weymouth, Cheltenham and Guernsey. Exhibited at the R.A., 1907–1921, and at the Paris Salon.

Haines, William. 1778–1848

Born at Bedhampton, Hants, 21 June 1778; moved to Chichester, and was educated at Midhurst Grammar School. Studied engraving under Thew at Northaw, Herts. In 1800 went to Cape Town where he executed drawings of natives. Visited Philadelphia, returned to England in 1805. Worked in London and Chichester. Exhibited at the R.A., B.I., S.B.A., and O.W.C.S., 1808–1840. Painted small portraits in oil and water-colour, miniatures, and executed engravings. Many of his patrons were naval officers. A miniature of an officer signed 'W. Haines Pinx / 29 Orchard St / Portman Sq / July 1831' was seen at the V. & A. M.; it was well painted. Haines inherited some property and retired to live at East Brixton, where he died on 24 July 1848. A miniature of Admiral Blackwood, after Hoppner, in the Bernard Falk Collection was carefully painted and had some stippling in the shading of the face. One of H.R.H. Frederick Augustus, Duke of York, by him, was engraved by Thomson, and published by G. B. Whittaker, February 1827. A miniature of a lady, signed and dated 'June, 1816' is in the collection of E. G. Paine of New York.

Hale, Miss Marianne A. See Havell, Mrs. George

Hales, Miss. (fl. 1815)

Exhibited at the R.A. 1815, as an Hon. Exhibitor. The portrait was of Mrs. Dennison. The artist may have been identical with Miss Marianne Hale (q.v. under Havell, Mrs. George).

*Haley, Miss Margaret (Mrs. H. F. W. Reynolds) (fl. 1906–1914)

Of Manchester, Liverpool and Liscard, Cheshire. Exhibited at the R.A., 1906–1914. Her exhibit in 1914 was a self-portrait.

Halkett, C. 19th century

A miniature portrait of Samuel Halkett (1814–1871), Librarian, painted in water-colour on ivory, $3\frac{1}{2} \times 2\frac{7}{8}$ in. by C. Halkett is at the S.N.P.G. It is not of any great merit.

*Hall, Anthony. 16th century

Son of Anthony Hall. Recommended by his father to Lord Burghley (died 1598) as a *Poursuivant* (an office he did not obtain). He was educated at Emmanuel College, Cambridge. Showed aptitude for Heraldry and showed 'a pretie skill in counterfeiting pictures after the lyfe or otherwise'. It is not certain that Hall painted miniatures, but the above information was recorded by C. F. Bell.

*Hall, The Misses Ethel and Margaret. (fl. 1895). See also **Hall, Miss Margaret**

Exhibited at the R.A. 1895, from 11 Gloucester Walk, Kensington in the joint names of Ethel and Margaret Hall. Margaret may have been identical with the Miss Margaret Hall (q.v.) who exhibited in 1899.

*Hall, Henry Bryan, senior. 1808–1884

Born in London, 11 March (or according to Groce & Wallace, May), 1808. Studied engraving under B. Smith, Henry Meyer (q.v.) and Ryall, in London. Executed etchings as well as painting portraits and miniatures in oil and crayon. Was employed by Ryall to execute the portrait work on the plate of the painting of the Coronation of Queen Victoria, after Hayter (q.v.). Went to New York City in 1850 and established himself in a successful engraving and publishing business in which he was joined after 1860 by his sons Henry Bryan Hall, jun., Charles Bryan Hall and Alfred Bryan Hall, all of whom were pupils of their father. H. B. Hall, sen., exhibited at the National Academy,

1862–1875. He died at his home in Morrisania (N.Y.) on 25 April 1884. Was possibly identical with the H. B. Hall who exhibited drawings at Suffolk Street in 1840.

Hall, John. 1739–1797

Born at Wivenhoe, near Colchester, 21 December 1739. Was a celebrated engraver, who worked for a time as an enamel painter at Battersea, where he may conceivably have painted a few enamel portraits. Died in London, 7 April 1797.

*Hall, Miss Lilian. (fl. 1908–1919)

Of London. Exhibited at the R.A. 1908–1919, from various addresses in London. Her sitters included H.R.H. Princess Patricia of Connaught.

*Hall, Miss Margaret. (fl. 1899). See also **Hall, The Misses Ethel and Margaret**

Exhibited at the R.A. 1899, from 52 Palace Garden Terrace, Kensington; possibly identical with Miss M. Hall (q.v.) who exhibited jointly with Miss Ethel Hall (presumably her sister) in 1895.

*Hallam, Miss Lesa. (fl. 1901–1914)

Of London. Exhibited at the R.A. and S.M., 1901–1914.

Halle, Mr. and Mrs. (fl. c. 1845)

Had addresses at 100 and 51 Fleet Street, London. A rather inferior, badly drawn miniature of c. 1845 was seen by Long. The face was painted in a buff colouring and the engraved card had the address altered in MS.

Hallen, Maria. (fl. 1829)

Of London. Exhibited an enamel painting of St. Cecilia at the R.A. in 1829, from 17 Nelson Square.

*Halls, Robert. (fl. 1898–1909)

Of London and Birkenhead. Exhibited at the R.A., 1898–1909. His sitters included Pope Pius IX, and Madame Sarah Bernhardt.

Halpin, John Edmund. b. 1764

An Irish artist born in Dublin 1764, son and pupil of Patrick Halpin (fl. 1755–1787) an engraver, and his wife Eleanor. Was a pupil of F. R. West and J. J. Barralet at the Dublin Society Schools, and exhibited copies of their drawings in 1780 at the Society of Artists in William Street, Dublin. Was later sent to London to study art. Had ambitions of becoming an actor, and was advised by Macklin to do so, but his father objected and he returned to Dublin and obtained a successful practice as a miniaturist. He acted in Dublin in 1790 but finding that he did not improve his position he returned to painting miniatures and settled in London. W. Ridley engraved a portrait of his miniature of William Macredy for the *Parson's Minor Theatre*, 1794. A portrait of Halpin in character was engraved in the *Hibernian Magazine*, March 1790.

Halton, E. W. See Hatton, E. W.

This artist is listed by Graves and Long as having exhibited at the R.A. in 1848 but the R.A. catalogues give no such artist. There has obviously been some confusion and the portrait of Thomas M. Hugh, Esq., ascribed to Halton in error was, in fact, painted by E. W. Hatton of 12 Lansdowne Terrace, Caledonian Road.

Hamburger, Johann Conrad. 1809–c. 1870

Born in Frankfurt-am-Main, 3 March 1809; studied at the Städelsches Institute there. Worked in London, 1830–1836. Exhibited at the R.A., 1830–1834. Was appointed Portrait Painter in Water-Colours to William IV in 1834. Went to Amsterdam in 1836 and exhibited there up to 1861. Died in Amsterdam *c.* 1870 (1871 according to Benezit). Hamburger worked in many different ways and was influenced by the English, French and Viennese Schools. Many of his miniatures were large and painted on several pieces of ivory joined together. A number of his works are in the collection of H.M. the Queen of the Netherlands; one of Maurice, Prince of Holland, is signed on the reverse 'C. Hamburger, fec. Amsterdam July 1850' and on the front 'C.H.'. A miniature of a lady, signed and dated '1833' is in the collection of E. G. Paine of New York.

*Hamer, B. (fl. 1799)
A miniature by this artist was seen by Mr. A. J. B. Kiddell. It was signed on the reverse 'B. Hamer / drawn 21st March / 1799 age 23 yrs / 9 months / 9 days.' The draughtsmanship was weak.

Hamilton, Gustavus. *c.* 1739–1775
Born in Ireland *c.* 1739, son of the Rev. Gustavus Hamilton, Vicar of Errigal in the Diocese of Clogher, and Rector of Gallon in the county of Meath, and his wife Jane Cathcart, whom he had married when serving as a curate in Enniskillen, 1721–2. The artist was one of the youngest of several children. His family claimed descent from the family of Hamilton of Priestfield, Midlothian. Hamilton was a pupil of R. West at the drawing school at George's Lane, and was an apprentice of Samuel Dixon in Dublin, where with J. Reily (q.v.) and D. O'Keeffe (q.v.) he was employed to colour prints of birds and flowers produced by Dixon. Hamilton became a miniaturist and obtained a fashionable clientele. A self-portrait in crayon is illustrated on Pl. XXIX in Strickland's *Dictionary of Irish Artists*. He exhibited in Dublin from 1765–1773 from Parliament Street, 1 Dame Street, and, shortly before his death, Cork Hill. He died on 16 December 1775 aged 36 and was buried at St. Werburgh's. Hamilton's miniatures are usually small in size and probably intended for lockets or bracelets; they are signed in different ways, i.e. Ham, G.Ham., G.Ham^{tn}, G.H., Gus Hamilton, etc., often followed by a date. His miniatures vary in quality, some being a little stiff. Often the face is shaded with a blue tinge. A good miniature by him of an unknown lady, signed 'Ham^n / 1764' is in the National Gallery, Dublin.

Hamilton, Henry Thomas. (fl. 1812–1813)
Of London. Possibly the Henry Hamilton who entered the R.A. Schools, 26 February 1811. Exhibited at the R.A. 1812–1813, from 80 Pall Mall, the exhibits being 'An apostle' and a miniature of a lady.

*Hamilton, Innes. (fl. 1902–1914)
Of London. Exhibited at the R.A. 1902–1914, from 4 Scarsdale Studios, Kensington. His sitters included Mrs. Alfred Campbell and Toby, son of Lord Hylton.

Hamilton, M. (fl. 1839). See also **Hamilton, Mrs. Mary F.**
Exhibited at the R.A. 1839, portraits of the daughter of C. Nockells, Esq., and the Hon. Frederick Pepys, fifth son of the Lord High Chancellor. Schidlof records a miniature of a lady, painted on ivory, signed 'M.Hamilton' which was sold in Vienna, September 1921. The artist may have been identical with Mrs. Mary F. Hamilton (q.v.).

Hamilton, Miss Maria (Mrs. Thomas Bell later **Lady (Maria) Bell).** d. 1825
Of London. Probably identical with Maria Hamilton, sister and pupil of William Hamilton, R.A. (q.v.), and a pupil of Sir Joshua Reynolds. Exhibited a mythological subject at the B.I. 1807, from 82 Strand, and, as Mrs. Bell (afterwards Lady Bell) in 1809 from 47 Dean Street, Soho. Exhibited at the R.A., and B.I., 1809–1816, and as Lady Bell, 1819–1824. Her husband, Thomas Bell of Sheffield (afterwards Sir Thomas Bell) became Sheriff of London. Painted portraits, copied portraits by other artists, was a modeller and executed a few miniatures. Died 9 March 1825.

Hamilton, Mrs. Mary F. (fl. 1807–1849). See also **Hamilton, M.**
Of London. Probably the sister-in-law of Miss Maria Hamilton (q.v.), as she exhibited from the same address (i.e. 82 Strand). Thought to have been the wife of William Hamilton, R.A. (q.v.). Worked in London and Brighton. She exhibited a miniature copy after Titian at the B.I. in 1807 and miniature portraits at the R.A. 1825–1849. Two of her exhibits were on marble. Possibly this artist was identical with M. Hamilton (q.v.).

*Hamilton, Mrs. Olivia. (fl. 1900–1905)
Of Bromley, Kent. Exhibited at the Society of Miniaturists, 1900–1905.

*Hamilton, T. (fl. 1767)
Two miniatures were lent to the exhibition at the South Kensington Museum 1865, representing Mrs. Dobson, signed 'T.Ham^n 1767', and Mrs. McCausland, signed 'T.Ham^n 1767'. The artist may have been identical with or related to Gustavus Hamilton (q.v.), or John Hamilton (fl. 1767–1785) of Dublin, a draughtsman and etcher.

Hamilton, William, R.A. 1751–1801
Was born in 1751. Painted portrait and figure subjects in oil and water-colours and may have executed miniatures. A miniature of Miss Clara Anna Clutterbuck of Bath, dated '1758' is attributed to Hamilton although Long considered it to be more like the work of H. Hone (q.v.). This portrait is at the Ward Usher Museum, Lincoln, and was formerly in the Lumsden Propert Collection. Possibly the husband of Mrs. Mary F. Hamilton (q.v.). Died 1801.

Hamlet, T. 1779–1815.
Was born in 1779. Worked in Bath and Weymouth. Is best known as a silhouettist, but also executed miniatures. A profile miniature on ivory of a small boy was in the collection of the late Mr. Ernest Hart. On the reverse of the portrait was an old inscription stating that it had been painted in May 1815 by Hamlet of 2 Bond Street, Bath. It was not of any great merit. Hamlet described himself as 'Profile Painter to Her Majesty, and the Royal Family'. The *Bath Chronicle* records Hamlet's death as taking place on '9th Nov. 1815 aged 36. Profile painter of 2 Old Bond St. Bath'. The V. & A. M. has a silhouette by Hamlet.

*Hamlet, William. (fl. 1785)
Possibly the father of T. Hamlet (q.v.). Advertised in the *Birmingham Gazette*, 26 September 1785 and in the *Oxford Journal*, 18 June 1785, 'From abroad'. He advertised his charges as '2/6 shaded and coloured 5/- and Full length 10/6'.

*Hamley, Miss Barbara. (fl. 1881–1901)
Of London. Exhibited at the R.A., N.W.C.S., S.M., etc., 1881–1901.

Hamlin, N. (fl. 1777–1793)
Of Bath. Practised 1777–1793 in Bath and lived

at Saville Row. His name was included in an exhibition of works by Bath Artists held at the Victoria Art Gallery, Bath, in 1903.

Hamlyn, Augusta. (fl. 1779–1830)
The above artist was probably identical with the Augusta Hamlyn, of Plymouth, who was awarded a silver palette by the Society of Arts in 1824, for a chalk drawing. The suggestion that she was the artist who exhibited a still-life at the R.A. in 1819 must have been a mistake, as the entry was recorded as Jane T. Hamlyn, both in the index and the catalogue. According to notes made by Long, A. Hamlyn had addresses at Bond Street, Bath; 2 Quiet Street, Bath; and 18 Clare Street, Bristol from 1779–1792, and at Belle Place and King Street, Plymouth, from 1819–1830. Jane T. Hamlyn, to whom she was undoubtedly related, exhibited from Belle Place, Plymouth, in 1819.

Hammond, Mrs. (fl. 1810–1826)
Of London and Greenwich (1822). Exhibited at the R.A., 1810–1826. Her exhibits included theatrical portraits.

Hancock, Robert. (fl. 1830–1833)
Was working in Bristol from 1830–1833 and had addresses at 12 St. John Street and 2 Wine Street, Bristol. Possibly the son of Robert Hancock (1730–1817), the engraver, also of Bristol, who executed small crayon portraits *c.* 1796. Engraved portraits after R. Hancock of Coleridge, Lamb, Wordsworth, etc., are in the B.M.

Handasyde, Charles. (fl. 1760–1776)
Worked in London, Cambridge and Tunbridge Wells. Exhibited at the Society of Artists and Free Society of Artists 1760–1764, and at the R.A., 1776. Was awarded a premium by the Society of Arts, 1765 for an historical painting, and another in 1768 (both paintings were on enamel). Executed some mezzotint portraits of himself and drew likenesses in Indian ink and black lead. Long noted an advertisement dated 1 October 1751 which stated that he had 'Returned from Tunbridge Wells and now lodges at Mr. Brooksby's, Milliner, in Pall Mall; where he continues to draw likenesses in India ink on vellum at 1 guinea apiece and in black lead at ½ a guinea. One hour's sitting only required'.

*Handler, Miss Blanche. (fl. 1906–1914)
Of London and Croydon. Exhibited at the R.A., 1906 and 1914.

*Handley, John. (fl. *c.* 1825)
Long noted having seen a small three-quarter length portrait in oil, on millboard, *c.* 1825; on the back of this was a label 'John Handley / portrait & / miniature painter / 5 Redmans Row / Mile End / London / From 3 guineas & upwards'. The painting was quite good.

*Hands, Miss Lizzie. (fl. 1907–1908)
Of London. Exhibited at the R.A. 1907 and 1908, from 57 Portsdown Road, Maida Vale. Exhibited miniatures and subjects in water-colour.

*Hankey, Mrs. W. Lee, R.M.S. née Mabel Emily Hobson. d. 5 January 1943
Of London. Exhibited at the R.A. 1889-1897, under her maiden name, and 1898-1914 under her married name, Mabel Hankey. Married W. Lee Hankey (born 1869) also an artist *c.* 1897. Undoubtedly related to Cecil J. Hobson (q.v.) as both exhibited from 28 Lilyville Road, Fulham in 1896. Her sitters included Lady Elizabeth Bowes-Lyon (later Queen Elizabeth, wife of H.M. King George VI), Lady Elphinstone, the Master of Lindsay and the Hon. Margaret Lindsay, children of Lord Balcarres.

*Hannam, Miss Florence. (fl. 1890–1898)

Of London. Exhibited at the R.A., etc. 1890–1898, from 42 Blenheim Terrace, Abbey Road. Painted historical subjects and miniatures.

Hanneman. See Hunneman, Christopher William

Hanwell, W. (fl. 1809)

Of 31 New North Street, Red Lion Square, London. Exhibited a self-portrait at the R.A. in 1809.

*Harbutt. (fl. *c*. 1820)

A miniature of Henry Harrison, signed by the above artist and painted *c*. 1820 is in the collection of E. G. Paine of New York. The artist has not been previously recorded. He may have been related to Mrs. B. Harbutt (q.v.) or W. Harbutt of London, who exhibited landscapes at the S.B.A. in 1783.

*Harbutt, Mrs. B. Cambridge (Elizabeth). (fl. 1883–1895)

Of Bath. Exhibited at the R.A., etc., 1883–1895, including portraits of Noel Cambridge Harbutt, Owen Cambridge Harbutt, and Isaac Pitman, Esq., inventor of phonography. She exhibited from Paragon Art Studios, 15 Bladud Buildings, Bath.

*Harcourt, Mrs. G. (Mary L.). (fl. 1900–1914)

Of Bushey, Herts. and Arbroath. Exhibited at the R.A., 1900–1914. Painted miniatures and subjects in water-colour.

Harden, Silvester. See Harding, Sylvester

Hardie, R. (fl. 1810–1829)

Exhibited at the R.A. etc., from London addresses, 1810–1829.

Harding, Chester. 1792–1866

Born in Conway, Massachusetts, 1 September 1792. Was self-taught in art, and worked as a pedlar, soldier, innkeeper and sign painter. Succeeded in becoming a fashionable portrait painter. Worked at St. Louis, Philadelphia, Washington and Boston. Came to London 1823 and obtained the patronage of the Dukes of Sussex and Hamilton. According to Brydall's *Art in Scotland*, he worked in Scotland painting portraits and miniatures. Brydall also stated that Harding and P. Paillou (q.v.) were the most extensively employed artists of the period. Harding returned to Boston in 1826 and remained there until his death. There is an engraved portrait of the Duke of Sussex after Harding at the B.M. According to the *Dictionary of Artists in America* (1964 edition) by Groce and Wallace, he returned on a visit to England and Scotland in 1846. He died in Boston, 1 April 1866.

Harding, Edward J. 1804–1870

An Irish artist. Born in Cork, 1 March 1804. Painted portraits in oil, Indian ink, and water-colour besides being a successful miniaturist. Examples of his work were in an exhibition held in Cork in 1852, including portraits in water-colour and a miniature of Lady Deane and her children. Harding died on 19 August 1870. A miniature by him of a lady is reproduced by Schidlof, Pl. 264.

*Harding, Emily J. (Mrs. E. W. Andrews). (fl. 1877–1898)

Of London. Exhibited at the R.A., 1877 and 1897–1898. Wife of Edward W. Andrews (q.v.).

Harding, Frederick. (fl. 1814–1857)

Of London and Totnes (1857). The Society of

Arts awarded him premiums in 1814 and 1815. Exhibited at the R.A. and S.B.A., 1825–1857. Pigot's *London and Provincial Directory*, 1834, gives two London miniaturists of this name, who may have been identical; one at 8 Upper Berkeley Street, the other at 3 Shorter's Court, Bank. He signed F.H., F Harding, Fred^k Harding and Fred^c Harding, sometimes followed by a date. His works are not of any great merit; he used a rather red flesh colour and brown shadows. Long records seeing a miniature of William IV by him.

Harding, George Perfect, F.S.A. *c*. 1780–1853

A son of Sylvester Harding (q.v.). Exhibited at the R.A. and S.B.A., 1802–1840. Worked chiefly in London and visited country houses where he made water-colour copies of oil portraits, some of which were engraved in historical publications. Many of these were painted on a small scale. Harding was a Fellow of the Society of Antiquaries, 1839–1847. He married late in life and had a large family which he had difficulty in supporting and was obliged to sell his accumulated works. He exhibited a self-portrait at the R.A., in 1813; this was probably the one which was engraved by J. Brown, a copy of which is in the B.M. He died at Hercules Buildings, Lambeth, 23 December 1853. I have seen a number of miniatures by Harding, including a fine one of George IV when Prince of Wales. He frequently signed in full 'G.P.Harding, f'. Several of his portraits were engraved. Examples of his work are in the B.M. and N.P.G.; and the National Museum of Wales, Cardiff, contains a good miniature copy of a portrait of an Earl of Pembroke. A miniature in water-colour on paper of Sir Kenelm Digby, after P. Oliver (q.v.) signed on the front 'G.P. Harding del' is in my collection.

*Harding, Miss Gertrude C. (fl. 1903–1904)

Of London and Torquay. Exhibited at the R.A., 1903 and 1904.

Harding, H. J. (fl. 1823–1825)

Of London. Exhibited at the R.A., and S.B.A., 1823–1825. Executed miniatures in water-colour on paper and ivory as well as copying portraits in pencil. He signed H. Harding followed by a date, sometimes the signature in pencil. His work, although superficially skilful, lacked quality.

*Harding, James Duffield, junior. 1798–1863

Born in Deptford, 1798. Exhibited at the R.A., 1811–1818. Best known for landscapes and engravings, but also painted in oil and water-colour. Schidlof included him as a miniaturist, but I have not so far found confirmation of this statement. He died at Barnes, 4 December 1863.

Harding, John. (fl. 1826)

Of London. Working in 1826 from 6 Argyle Street, Oxford Street, London.

Harding, Sylvester. 1751–1809

Born in Newcastle-under-Lyme, 5 August 1751. His date of birth has always been recorded as 25 July 1745 but he is presumably the artist of this name who entered the R.A. Schools on 25 November 1776 when his age was noted as '25 5th Aug last'. Was sent to London when only ten years of age to learn a trade which he disliked. Ran away when he was fourteen and joined some strolling players with whom he toured until 1775 when he went to London and took up miniature painting. Exhibited at the Free Society of Artists in 1776 and 1782, at the R.A., 1777–1802 and at the Society for Promoting Painting and Design in Liverpool, 1787. His name has been erroneously recorded as Silvester Harden. He painted miniatures, figure subjects,

copied old family portraits in miniature, executed engravings and published *Biographical Mirror*, and the *Memoirs of Count de Grammont*, besides illustrating *The Economy of Human Life*. He died in Pall Mall, 12 August 1809. Copies of portraits by him in water-colour are in the B.M. A portrait of James Wilder (landscape and figure painter) by Harding is in the N.G. Dublin.

Harding, Thomas

A miniature on ivory of Mrs. Siddons, signed 'T.H.' was lent to the exhibition at South Kensington Museum, 1865 when it was catalogued as by Thomas Harding, about whom nothing is known. This may have been an error. It was possibly the work of T. Hazelhurst (q.v.) or T. Hargreaves (q.v.).

*Hardman, Mrs. Emma L. (fl. 1888–1906)

Exhibited at the R.A., N.W.C.S., etc. 1888–1906, from Eastcot, Northaw, Herts., and Potter's Bar. Executed miniatures and subjects in oil. Was probably related to Mrs. Minnie Hardman (q.v.). Was the wife of Thomas Hardman, also an artist.

*Hardman, Mrs. Minnie J. or I. (fl. 1900–1903)

Exhibited at the R.A. and S.M. 1900–1903, from Northaw, Herts. Painted miniatures and flowers in oil. Probably related to Mrs. Emma Hardman (q.v.).

Hardy, Charles (fl. 1802–1817)

Of London. Exhibited at the R.A., 1806–1810. I have seen a good miniature signed on the reverse 'C.Hardy Pinxit / 92 Norton St, Portland Pl (or St)'. It had a brownish shading. In 1817 Hardy was working at Clapton. His sitters in 1807 included Mr. J. Hardy.

*Hardy, Dorofield. (fl. 1882–1899)

Of London. Exhibited at the R.A., etc., 1882–1899, from 48 Tavistock Crescent, Westbourne Park. Painted genre subjects and miniatures, including one of H. W. Hoskyns, Esq.

*Hardy, Miss Florence. (fl. 1896–1897)

Of London. Exhibited at the R.A., 1896–1897. In 1896 her address was c/o Mr. Dudley Hardy (also an artist), Oakhurst, Ravenscourt Square, and in 1897 she exhibited from 82 Portsdown Road, Maida Vale, from which address Thomas B. Hardy, to whom she was probably related, exhibited a water-colour in the same year.

*Hardy, J. (fl. 1809–1810). See also **Hardy, James** and **Hardy, Jonathan**

The above artist exhibited miniatures at the R.A. 1809–1810, from 118 Bunhill Road, Finsbury Square and 15 New Bridge Street. His exhibits included a self-portrait and a miniature of Master I. Cragg. He may have been identical with or related to either James Hardy (q.v.), or Jonathan Hardy (q.v.). The miniature of a man, noted by Schidlof, signed on the reverse 'J.Hardy July 21 1809' may be by the above artist.

Hardy, James. (fl. 1832). See also **Hardy, J.** and **Hardy, Jonathan**

Was working in Brighton in 1832 and living at 163 Royal Colonnade. Painted portraits and miniatures. A mezzotint portrait of the Rev. J. Sortain of Brighton after Hardy is at the B.M. Schidlof notes a miniature of a man signed on the reverse: 'J.Hardy July 21 1809'. This portrait may have been the work of either J. Hardy (q.v.) or Jonathan Hardy (q.v.).

*Hardy, Jonathan. (fl. 1813). See also Hardy, J. and Hardy, James

I have in my collection a rectangular miniature of a gentleman, on ivory signed on the reverse of the frame 'Mr Joseph Hardy of Lisbon / Painted in London Oct 13th 1813 by / Jona^n Hardy'. The miniature is well painted; the face is shaded with a bluish tinge. He may have been identical with or related to J. Hardy (q.v.).

*Hardy, Miss Muriel. (fl. 1906–1914)

Of Newbury, Berks., and Ringmer, Sussex. Exhibited at the R.A., 1906–1914. Painted miniatures and landscapes in water-colour. Her sitters included Miss Winifred Hardy and Mr. and Mrs. J. Herbert Laurence.

*Hardy, Miss Nina. (fl. 1890–1919)

Of London and Windsor. Exhibited at the R.A., etc., 1890–1919. Executed miniatures and studies in oil.

*Hargreaves, Francis. (fl. 1810–1854)

Of Liverpool; son of Thomas Hargreaves (q.v.) who undoubtedly taught him art. Little is known about this artist whose miniatures are scarce. I have seen two examples of his work in Liverpool. One is in the City of Liverpool Museum and is of Henry Threlfall Wilson, inscribed on the reverse 'Francis Hargreaves pinxit / 1846 / Liverpool'. The painting is slightly hesitant and although well modelled is not of the same quality as that of his father. The other example is in the Walker Art Gallery, Liverpool, and is a portrait of John Gibson, R.A., after a portrait painted in 1839 by Penry Williams. It is executed in pencil and water-colour on paper, rectangular, $9 \times 7\frac{1}{4}$ in. According to an old note pasted on the reverse of the original frame, this was a 'Copy by Francis Hargreaves, 1845, Liverpool'. In 1930 Long was shown four family miniatures by the above artist. They were signed and dated as follows: '𝒯 Hargreaves / April 1810', 'Hargreaves Pinxt / Liverpool 1812', '𝒯 Hargreaves / pinxit Liverpool 1821' and '𝒯 Hargreaves pinx^t / 1830'. The Walker Art Gallery, Liverpool also has in its collection a miniature of a young girl dressed in white attributed to Thomas Hargreaves; it is inscribed on the reverse in pencil '𝒯 Hargreaves (cursive) / Pinxt / 1843'. Having had the opportunity to examine his work, it is more than likely that this latter miniature is by Francis Hargreaves. As in the case of the portrait of H. T. Wilson, the painting shows the same tentative treatment. Having compared the signature of Thomas Hargreaves with that of his son, it is evident that whereas Francis Hargreaves wrote the initial of his Christian name with a flourish on the tail, his father's normal practice was to inscribe the initial T with a straight downstroke. A miniature of a lady is recorded by Schidlof as being signed on the reverse 'Francis Hargreaves / Pinxit / 1845 / Liverpool'.

Hargreaves, George. 1797–1870

Was born in 1797. Son of Thomas Hargreaves (q.v.). Exhibited at the R.A. 1818 and 1820, from Princes Street, Soho and 15 Gt. Russell Street, Bloomsbury. The exhibits included a self-portrait in 1818. Exhibited at the S.B.A., 1824–1834. Was an associate in 1822 and a member, 1823–1831 of the Liverpool Academy. His address in 1828 was Bold Place, Liverpool. Hargreaves died in 1870. He signed Geo.Hargreaves, followed by a date, on the reverse of his miniatures which were not of great merit, and only slightly resembled the work of his father. The self-portrait already referred to was probably the one sold at Sotheby's, 3 December 1925. The B.M. has two engraved portraits after

Hargreaves. A miniature of Mrs. Richard Yates, inscribed on the reverse '1st wife of / Richard Vaughan Yates / Copy by / Geo. Hargreaves' is in a collection of family miniatures owned by Lieut. Colonel C. H. F. Thompson. The portrait is painted slightly in the manner of the work of T. Hargreaves (q.v.), the flesh colours being a pinkish orange, the painting smooth, without any stippling, the hair neatly painted in distinct curls. The background is a greyish brown and the effect rather amateurish.

Hargreaves, James. (fl. 1820)

Probably a son of Thomas Hargreaves (q.v.). The Ward Usher Museum, Lincoln, has a miniature copy of Phillip's portrait of Byron which is said to be by James Hargreaves, 1820.

*Hargreaves, T. (fl. 1829–1843)

Of Woolwich. Presumably related to, or the son of, Thomas Hargreaves (q.v.). Exhibited at the R.A., etc., 1829–1843. In 1829 his address was given as the Royal Military Barracks, Woolwich, and the exhibit was a portrait of an officer. From this information it is most likely that he was serving in the Army.

Hargreaves, Thomas. 1774–1846/7

Born in Liverpool, 16 March 1774 (not 1775 as recorded by Long); the son of a woollen-draper. Took up miniature painting at an early age. Entered the R.A. Schools, 29 March 1790 aged 16. From March 1793 Hargreaves was an articled assistant to Sir Thomas Lawrence (q.v.) by whom he was employed for some years. Worked for a time in oils, but owing to ill-health returned to Liverpool c. 1795. Exhibited intermittently at the R.A., S.B.A., L.A., 1798–1835 and was a member of the Liverpool Academy from 1810–1835; and in 1824 was one of the original members of the S.B.A. Worked chiefly in Liverpool but also exhibited from London. His wife's maiden name was Quaile, by whom he had several sons including Francis and George Hargreaves (q.v.). James Hargreaves (q.v.), T. Hargreaves (q.v.) and W. Hargreaves (q.v.) are also thought to have been his children. A miniature of his wife and a self-portrait were among other examples of his work sold at Sotheby's, 3 December 1925. He died in Liverpool, 23 December 1846 (5 January 1847 according to Dibden). Hargreaves was a good artist and his work shows the influence of Lawrence. The majority of his miniatures are rectangular but he also used an oval format. He painted in oil and water-colour and used both ivory and paper as a base. His signatures included T. Hargreaves, Thos Hargreaves pt., followed by a date on the reverse and occasionally T.H. (cursive capitals) on the front, also followed by a date. He used a pink flesh colouring which is very effective and painted with a fine brush stroke. Like many other artists he made pencil sketches for his miniatures. Of these 785 are in the Local History Department of the City of Liverpool Library, about 50 of which are identified. Many of these drawings are excellent, the draughtsmanship is strong and the character of his sitters admirably portrayed. Examples of his work are in the V. & A. M., and the Walker Art Gallery, Liverpool, which contains his self-portrait. The B.M. has engraved portraits after Hargreaves. Several family miniatures by him are in the collection of Lieut. Colonel C. H. F. Thompson. These include the owner's grandmother, Mrs. Samuel Henry Thompson, painted at the time of her wedding in 1837. This miniature is most attractive and delicately painted. The sitter is placed against a pale bluish grey background and is wearing a white dress edged with pearls with a pink rose at her bosom.

Hargreaves, W. (fl. 1813)

Of Liverpool. Probably related to, or another son of, Thomas Hargreaves (q.v.). Exhibited at the R.A. 1813, a miniature of Miss Sarah Smith of Drury Lane.

*Harland, Miss Mary. b. 1863

Born in Yorkshire, 8 October 1863. Travelled in Europe. Established herself in Santa Monica, California. Worked in London and Paris. Exhibited at the R.A., 1903 and 1905.

*Harley, Mrs. See Rowney, Miss Lilian

*Harley, Lady Elizabeth, Marchioness of Carmarthen. 1686–1713

Born 1686. Amateur painter; daughter of Robert Harley, Earl of Oxford. Goulding in his catalogue of the Welbeck Abbey Miniatures (Walpole Society, Vol. IV) catalogues a pen and ink drawing on paper by this artist of Sir Francis Walsingham (d. 1590) after the engraving on p. 82 of Holland's Herwologia, 1620. There was formerly in the collection a pen and ink drawing by her of a column in St. Peter's, Rome which induced Prior to write the following verse:

When future Ages shall with Wonder view
These glorious lines, which Harley's daughter drew,
They shall confess that Britain Could not raise
A fairer Column to the Father's Praise.

She died in 1713.

*Harlow, George Henry. 1787–1819

Born in London, 10 June 1787. Was a pupil of Sir Thomas Lawrence. Exhibited at the R.A. and B.I., 1804–1818. Painted subjects, portraits in oil, chalk, and water-colour, and is recorded as a miniaturist by Schidlof, but I have been unable to confirm this fact. He did execute some small portraits in pencil, several of which are in the N.P.G., together with other examples of his work. His sitters included W. H. West Betty, the boy actor.

*Harman, Miss Geraldine. (fl. 1880–1906)

Of London. Exhibited at the R.A., N.W.C.S., etc. 1880–1906, from 40 St. Julian's Road, Kilburn. Undoubtedly related to Harriette Harman (q.v.) who exhibited from the same address from 1881–1898. An example of the above artist's work is in the Museum in Bristol.

*Harman, Miss Harriette. (fl. 1881–1898)

Of London. Exhibited at the R.A., etc., 1881–1898. Undoubtedly related to Geraldine Harman (q.v.) who exhibited from the same address, 40 St. Julian's Road, Kilburn, 1880–1906.

Harper, Thomas. (fl. 1817–1843)

Of London and Brighton (1821). Exhibited at the R.A. 1817–1843, from addresses in London and Brighton. His exhibits included portraits of actors and actresses in character, and miniatures including some of children. In 1840 he exhibited a portrait of Mrs. Harper. Long noted an example of a rectangular miniature with a scratched signature 'Harper / 1825'. He considered the work of no great merit. This artist must not be confused with the T. Harper who exhibited landscapes at the R.A. in 1840 from 84 Pratt Street, Camden Town. A miniature of a lady, a member of the Lockhart family, signed and dated 'T. Harper 1823' is in the V. & A. M.

*Harraden, Richard. 1756–1838

Born in London 1756, his father was a physician and the family came from Flintshire, the name being originally spelt Hawarden. Spent some time in Paris; left on the taking of the Bastille and returned to England. Worked in London as an artist. In 1798 moved to Cambridge and lived at Trumpington. Published views of Cambridge, etc., and is noted by Long as having painted profiles and miniatures. In conjunction with his son R. B. Harraden he published *Cantabrigia Depicta*. Died 2 June 1838. Long noted seeing a miniature painted at Cambridge, 5 July 1802.

*Harrand, Miss Lucie. (fl. 1903–1905)
Of London. Exhibited at the Society of Miniaturists, 1903–1905.

*Harrington, Mrs. (fl. 1775–*c*. 1787)
Of Birmingham. Mrs. J. Collins (q.v.) was her pupil and assistant. Advertised in the *Oxford Journal* 1 July 1775, 'The lady who takes miniature profiles, in the Broad Street (Oxford)'. Letters patent were granted to her on the above date.

*Harriott, Mrs. See Dietz, Miss Diana

Harris, Miss. (fl. 1834)
Of London. Was awarded the silver Isis medal by the Society of Arts in 1834 for a miniature copy of a portrait. Her address was 26 Lamb's Conduit Street.

Harris, John, senior. d. 1834
Of London. Painter, engraver and miniaturist. Exhibited at the R.A., 1797–1814. Father of John Harris, jun. (q.v.). In 1797 he exhibited paintings of insects in the miniature section of the R.A., from Amelia Street, Walworth. A miniature of Henrietta Howard, Countess of Suffolk (1681–1767) by J. Harris, after an earlier portrait attributed to M. Dahl, is in the N.P.G., and may be by the above artist. Died in 1834. Engraved portraits after J. Harris are in the B.M.

*Harris, John, junior. *c*. 1792–1873
Of London. Son of John Harris, sen. (q.v.). Entered the R.A. Schools, 10 January 1812 aged 20. Exhibited at the R.A., B.I., etc., 1822–1852. Painted miniatures, genre pictures and portraits. Died 28 December 1873. Benezit records the above artist as an engraver.

*Harris, Miss Kate. d. *c*. 1908
Of Richmond, Surrey. Exhibited at the Society of Miniaturists, 1905–1908.

*Harris, Miss Lilian E.A. (fl. 1904–1911)
Of London. Exhibited at the R.A. 1904 and 1911, from 26 Russell Square. Painted miniatures and still life in oil.

*Harris, Miss Sarah Eliza. (fl. 1910)
Of Rochester, Kent. Exhibited at the Society of Miniaturists, 1910.

*Harris, Thomas. (fl. 1775)
The *Bristol Directory* of 1775 gives a Thomas Harris, Limner, 8 Cannon Street, Bristol. A Mr. Harris of Bath married on 7 October 1773, and may have been identical with this artist.

Harris, W.
A good rectangular miniature of Thomas Moore (1779–1852) was catalogued as by this artist when it was sold at Christie's, 11 May 1926.

*Harrison, Miss Annie Jane. (fl. 1888–1914)
Of Newcastle and London. Exhibited at the R.A., 1888–1914. Painted miniatures and studies in oil.

Her sitters included Lady Muriel Willoughby and Lady Evelyn Guinness.

*Harrison, Miss Dorothy E. (fl. 1910)
Of Windsor. Exhibited at the Society of Miniaturists, 1910.

*Harrison, Gerald E. (fl. 1890–1908)
Of London, Brighton and East Grinstead. Exhibited at the R.A., etc., 1890–1908. Executed miniatures, portraits and fancy subjects in oil.

Harrison, J. (fl. 1784–1793)
Of London. Possibly the John Harrison who entered the R.A. Schools, 30 September 1777 aged '17, 12 December 1776'. Exhibited at the R.A., 1784–1793. Did not exhibit in 1783 as recorded by Schidlof. Executed drawings and miniatures.

Harrison, J. (fl. 1846–1865)
Worked in York 1846, 1848, 1850 and 1851 and later in London. Exhibited at the R.A., 1846–1865. In 1846 he was at 5 Gilly-gate, York; in 1848 at 7 Museum Street, York; in 1850 at York and 5 Grafton Street and in 1851 at York and 51 Coleshill Street, Eaton Square. He lived thereafter at various addresses in the Eaton Square district. Harrison exhibited portraits and studies (1846–1850) and miniatures (1851–1865). He had a distinguished clientele which included Lady Seymour, the Marchioness of Ormonde, Lady Burghesh, Lady Cosmo Russell, Lady Elizabeth Russell, Lady Troubridge, Master C. Scrope of Danby Hall, Yorks., and members of the Gaussen family of Brookman Park, Herts. Many of his miniatures were of children. Undoubtedly related to the John Harrison who exhibited mythological paintings, etc., at the B.I., 1808–1852 and from whose address 3 Grafton Street East, Fitzroy Square, and York, the above artist exhibited. May also have been related to or identical with the J. Harrison who exhibited portraits at the R.A., 1801–1834 and undoubtedly related to J. B. Harrison who shared his address, 28 Elizabeth Street, in 1865. There are some engraved portraits at the B.M., after J. Harrison, but it is uncertain which artist executed the originals. The dates given above do not conform to those given in Graves' *Dictionary of Artists*, but have been checked from original sources.

*Harrison, J. (fl. 1856)
Exhibited at the R.A. 1856, from 2 Mount Etna, Mile End Road. The exhibit was of Miss Sperling.

*Harrison, Miss Violet E. (fl. 1904–1908)
Of London. Exhibited at the R.A. 1904–1908, from Alexandra House, Kensington and the Lyceum Club, 128 Piccadilly.

*Harrisson, Miss Sarah C. (fl. 1899–1900)
Of London and Dublin. Exhibited at the R.A. 1899–1900, from c/o H. Chisholm, 30 Cheyne Road, Chelsea. Her sitters included Mrs. Everard Milman.

*Harston, Mrs. Georgina. (fl. 1901)
Of London. Exhibited at the R.A. 1901, from 87 Prince of Wales Mansions, Battersea Park.

Hart, Samuel. (fl. *c*. 1785–1820)
Of Plymouth. A Jewish artist who began his career as a jeweller in Plymouth but later became apprenticed to Abraham Daniel (q.v.) of Bath in 1779 to study miniature painting and engraving. Was friendly with Northcote who assisted him with the study of drawing. Executed mezzotint engravings and engravings on wood. Married twice; his son S. A. Hart (q.v.) followed his profession. In

1806 he attended Abraham Daniel on his death bed and took down his will. Visited London in about 1820. Was not very successful in business. Although it is assumed that he probably painted miniatures as a pupil of Daniel none are at present known to be by him.

Hart, Solomon Alexander, R.A. 1806–1881
Born in Plymouth, April 1806, son of Samuel Hart (q.v.) by whom he was brought to London in 1820. Became a pupil of S. Warren, an engraver; entered the R.A. Schools, 15 August 1823 aged 17¼. Painted miniature portraits and miniature copies of old masters and in 1825 executed a dozen miniatures of Edmund Kean for pins and snuff boxes. Exhibited at the R.A., B.I., N.W.C.S., etc., 1826–1881; was awarded a premium by the Society of Arts in 1826. Elected A.R.A., 1835 and R.A., 1840. Became noted as a painter of historical subjects in oil and drew book illustrations. Died at Fitzroy Square, London, 11 June 1881.

*Hart-Dyke, Mrs. R. C. (Millicent). (fl. 1905–1909)
Exhibited at the R.A. 1905–1909, from Dacre Lodge, New Barnet, Herts. In 1905 exhibited miniatures of her sons Ashley and Wyndham.

Hartley, Mary. (fl. 1786)
Thought by Long to have been an amateur artist. A miniature copy of 'St Peter' by Titian, painted in 1786, was seen by Long who considered the drawing to be poor.

*Hartog, Miss May. (fl. 1899)
Of London. Exhibited at the R.A. 1899, from 48 Tavistock Crescent, Westbourne Park, from which address Dorofield Hardy (q.v.) also exhibited in the same year.

*Harvand, Miss Lucy. (fl. 1902)
Of London. Exhibited at the R.A. 1902, from 11 Alwyne Square, Canonbury Park.

*Harvey, George, A.N.A. 1800/1–1878
Born in Tottenham *c*. 1800/1. Went to America at the age of 20 and spent several years in Ohio, Michigan and Upper Canada before establishing himself as an artist. Settled in Brooklyn (N.Y.) by 1828 in which year he was elected Associate of the National Academy. Moved to Boston in the following year, where he painted numerous miniatures. Returned to England soon after this to study art, and returned to America *c*. 1833. Built a house near Hastings-on-the-Hudson, close to Washington Irving's home which Harvey helped to design. Commenced a notable series of 'atmospheric views' of American scenery, which he executed in water-colour. Intended to have forty of them engraved and published by subscription but in spite of many trips to and from England and America the project failed for lack of support. Only four of the views were published; the collection was preserved intact until 1840 and nearly half of them are now owned by the New York Historical Society. Little information is available about the latter part of Harvey's life. He apparently made his home in England, but continued to make painting trips to North America, including Florida and Bermuda, until about two years before his death which took place in England in 1878. George Harvey, a landscape and portrait painter was his nephew and pupil. A miniature of a young girl in a white dress painted on ivory, signed 'G.Harvey' and painted *c*. 1840 is in the Metropolitan Museum, New York. Schidlof records a miniature of a young lady which is signed on the reverse 'Geo Harvey. A.N.A. / Done in Boston U.S.'

Harvey, Miss Jane. 19th century

Said by Dr. G. C. Williamson to have been a younger daughter of John Harvey, surgeon, of Sunderland and to have been a miniaturist of some repute in the north of England. Taught in the school of her sister Margaret Harvey (a poetess) at Bishop's Wearmouth. Worked in the manner of A. Plimer (q.v.); taught Andrew Morton (1802–1845) the portrait painter. A miniature catalogued as by her was in the collection of Lord Hothfield.

Harvie, J. S. (fl. 1804–1811)

Of Edinburgh. Exhibited at the R.A., 1811, a miniature portrait of the Rt. Hon. the Earl of Buchan. The S.N.P.G. has a miniature by Harvie of Francis, 1st Marquis of Hastings, 1804.

Hasfield

Of Bath(?). Worked in the manner of S. T. Roche (q.v.). A miniature ascribed to Hasfield was seen by Long.

*Haskins, R. (fl. 1735–1745)

A plumbago miniature *c.* 1735–1745 signed by the above artist was in the collection of Mrs. Young of Antrim, Ireland. It was seen by Mr. A. J. B. Kiddell who considered the work good. The artist named Maskins, recorded by Long, is identical with Haskins. A plumbago miniature signed 'R.Haskins Fecit, 1736' is in the V. & A. M.

Haslem, John. 1808–1884

Born in Carrington, Cheshire in February 1808 where he received his early education; was then sent to an uncle in Derby and at the age of 14 entered the Derby china works and studied under George Hancock. Practised drawing in his spare time and painted portraits, flowers, etc. Executed miniatures on enamel and porcelain and painted in water-colour. Copied the works of old masters in miniature, but also painted portraits from life. Was a pupil of E. T. Parris in 1835 when he came to London. Exhibited at the R.A. and S.B.A., 1836–1876. Was patronised by Queen Victoria, the Prince Consort, the Duchess of Gloucester, the Duke of Sussex and other members of the Royal family. Was awarded a silver medal by the Society of Arts in 1843. Published a history of *The Old Derby China Factory*. He died in Derby in 1884. Some of his enamels are in the style of Petitot senior (q.v.). A miniature on porcelain of John Milton (1608–1674), signed and dated on the reverse 'John Milton, painted by John Haslem, 1837' is in my collection and was exhibited at Edinburgh in 1965. A miniature by Haslem of Mrs. Wilson is reproduced by F. Brayshaw Gilhespy, pl. III in *Derby Porcelain*, and one of Prince Albert, from the Derby Art Gallery, is reproduced pl. 182 in *British Portrait Miniatures*, Foskett 1963. Haslem loaned three miniatures to the exhibition at the South Kensington Museum 1865 – his self-portrait (enamelled from life 1852), Mrs. James Brotherton (enamelled from life 1855) and Lady Henrietta Fermor (enamelled after a picture by R. Thorburn, A.R.A. (q.v.) 1850). He exhibited some of his works at the 1851 exhibition. An enamel portrait of Wellington by Haslem signed and dated 1852 is in the Ashmolean Museum, Oxford.

Hassel or **Haessel, Werner.** (fl. 1674–1707)

Worked in London and Germany. Became a pupil of Kneller who painted his portrait which was engraved by P. Schenck. Hassel painted miniatures in water-colour, enamel and oil portraits etc.; some of his works were engraved. George Lambert, the landscape painter was one of his pupils. Said to

have signed W.H., W.Hassel, and Werner Hassel, all followed by a date. Hassel was a good artist whose works are scarce. Has sometimes been erroneously called William Hassel. Vertue records seeing a miniature by him of a Scotsman signed 'W.H. 1685'. The Bayrisches Nationalmuseum, Munich, has an enamel battle-piece signed 'Werner Hassel 1674 Decembris.' A miniature of a lady, signed and dated 'WH 1687' on parchment is in the V. & A. M.

Hastings, E. (Edward?)

Long records seeing a miniature portrait of Robert Lucius West (q.v.) (an Irish artist), which was signed 'E.Hastings' and dated '1824'? The work was reminiscent of that of J. Comerford (q.v.) without being as good. The artist may have come from Dublin and been a pupil of Comerford's. He may have been identical with Edward Hastings of London, a portrait painter who exhibited at the R.A., B.I. and S.B.A., 1804–1827. His exhibits included portraits (some of which may have been miniatures), views, drawings, etc. Edward Hastings had a distinguished clientele which included actors and actresses. Some of his works were engraved. A portrait of Shute Barrington by this latter artist is at Balliol College, Oxford. His addresses included 8 and 9 Alfred Place, Bedford Square, from which addresses W. A. Hastings (q.v.) and Capt. Thomas Hastings, to whom he was probably related, also exhibited.

Hastings, William A. (fl. 1829–1834)

Of London. Undoubtedly related to Edward Hastings (q.v.) and Capt. Thomas Hastings, painter, all of whom exhibited from 8 and 9 Alfred Place, Bedford Square, London. Schidlof mentions a portrait of a small boy, painted on card and signed 'W.A.Hastings.' Exhibited at the S.B.A., 1829–1831. Was working at 8 Alfred Place in 1834.

Hatfield, W. (fl. 1780)

An artist whose work is known only by a large oval enamel portrait of Dr. Johnson, after Reynolds; it is signed and dated '1780' and is at the Ashmolean Museum, Oxford. The stippling on the face is very definite and the dots so distinct that in places they could be counted.

Hatton, E. W. (fl. 1845–1859 or 1882). See also **Halton, E. W.**

Of London. Exhibited at the R.A. 1845–1859, and was presumably identical with the E. W. Hatton who exhibited a portrait of Mary Theresa Hatton in 1882. Has been confused with E. W. Halton (q.v.) whose name is given by Graves and Long as exhibiting at the R.A., in 1848. I have been unable to find any evidence of Halton's existence and it is probable that E. W. Hatton's portrait of Thomas M. Hugh, Esq., exhibited from 12 Lansdowne Terrace, Caledonian Road, was erroneously recorded as the work of Halton. In 1845 E. W. Hatton exhibited a miniature of Hugh Ross, Esq. (possibly Hugh Ross (q.v.)) and in 1847 he exhibited a self-portrait and one of Mr. William John Hatton.

Hauck, F. K. See **Hauck, F. L.**

Hauck, Friedrich Ludwig. 1718–1801. See also **H., T.K.**

Born in Homburg, 10 August 1718; probably the son and pupil of Jacob Hauck, a painter. Travelled in Germany and England. Long records seeing two 'quaint and stiff miniatures' in an English family collection which were apparently signed 'F K Hauck / p / 1786'. The Museums at Groningen and

Nuremburg each have two oil portraits by him; one of those at Nuremburg is by 'F.L.Hauck und Sohn, 1787'. The son is unknown and the miniature seen by Long signed 'F.K.Hauck' could have been by him, or the second initial was misread. Hauck died in Offenbach on 4 October 1801.

Haugh, George. (fl. 1777–1818)

Worked at Doncaster and (1778) London. Exhibited at the R.A. and B.I., 1777–1818. Painted landscapes and portraits and was evidently also a miniaturist as the V. & A. M. has a portrait of a man painted on ivory and signed on the reverse 'G. Haugh Portr. Painter Doncaster'. This miniature is either a self-portrait, or by the above artist.

*Haughton, Matthew. 1768–1821

Was born in 1768. Son of Moses Haughton, sen. Best known as an engraver in Liverpool. Did some work for *The Life of Lorenzo de Medici*, by William Roscoe, 1795. Haughton executed a miniature for Roscoe, which the latter sent to Horace Walpole in 1796 (*Walpole Correspondence*, edited by Lavis and Bennett, Vol. 15, pp. 280–281, 1952). The miniature is now in the Roscoe family collection. Died at West Bromwich, 24 March 1821.

Haughton, Moses, senior. 1734–1804

Born in Wednesbury, Staffordshire 1734. Was trained in the art of enamelling and worked at a Birmingham factory. Exhibited at the R.A., 1788–1804. Lived for a time in London; painted still-life etc., in water-colour and executed enamels and miniatures on ivory. Exhibited a self-portrait at the R.A. in 1800. Died at Ashted, nr. Birmingham, 23 December 1804. His son Matthew Haughton (q.v.) was an engraver and painted at least one miniature. His nephew Moses Haughton, jun. (q.v.) was also a miniaturist.

Haughton, Moses, junior. 1772/4–1848

Nephew of Moses Haughton, sen. (q.v.). Born in Wednesbury, Staffordshire 1772/4; later went to London and studied under Stubbs (q.v.). Entered the R.A. Schools 12 October 1795 aged 21. Exhibited at the R.A., and B.I., 1808–1848. Was evidently a successful miniaturist and also painted scriptural and rural subjects in oil, besides executing some engravings. Was friendly with Fuseli and according to Farington in his *Diary* of 27 February 1804, he resided in Fuseli's house at Berners Street and paid him 100 guineas a year. 'He paints miniatures at from 5 to 8 guineas a head'. Died in 1848. A miniature by Haughton of John Smith, picture dealer, and a drawing by him after a portrait by Fuseli, are at the B.M. Examples of his work are at the Walker Art Gallery, Liverpool, including two miniatures of William Roscoe, one of which is inscribed on the reverse 'William / Roscoe / the Historian / Painted By / Moses / Haughton / His Friend / 1790'. This is an early work of the artist; the face has a yellowish-brown shading and the hair is painted with vertical cross-strokes. The whole effect is rather reddish. The second portrait of Roscoe is a large rectangular miniature on ivory. The face is well modelled and the hand very well drawn. It was painted in 1811. Also in this collection is a rectangular miniature of Mrs. Thomas Roscoe; an outstanding point of this attractive portrait is the manner in which the artist has painted the sitter's eyes a brilliant blue/violet; the curls of her hair are very loosely painted.

Haürn, Mrs. (fl. 1775)

Of London. Exhibited at the Society of Artists in 1775.

*Havell, Mrs. Christabelle. (fl. 1902–1904)

Of London. Exhibited at the R.A. 1902 and 1904,

559

ffrom 7 Dilke Street, Tite Street, Chelsea. Her sitters included Ruth, daughter of Sir Henry Burton Buckley. Painted miniatures and portraits in water-colour.

*Havell, Edmund, junior. b. 1819
Was born in Reading, 1819. Worked in Reading (1835–1844) and London. Exhibited at the R.A., 1835–1895. Was undoubtedly the son of Edmund Havell who painted landscapes, and whose address he shared. Painted oil portraits, miniatures and possibly landscapes and figure subjects. His sitters included Major Ormsby Gore, Charles Kingsley and Mrs. Charles Kingsley.

Havell, Mrs. George (Miss Marianne Hale). (fl. 1822–1828)
Née Marianne A. Hale. Exhibited from London addresses under her maiden name at the R.A., 1822–1825 and under her married name, 1826–1828. Her husband, George Havell, whom she married c. 1825, also exhibited at the R.A. Schidlof mentions a portrait of a lady, on ivory, signed on the reverse 'Painted by Marianne Hale June 18th 1823, London.'

*Havergal, Mrs. E. (fl. 1909)
Exhibited at the R.A. 1909, from Brent Eleigh Rectory, Lavenham, Suffolk.

*Havers, Mrs. C. See Buckingham, Miss Ethel

Haverty, Joseph Patrick, R.H.A. 1794–1864
Born in Galway 1794. Became an artist and exhibited a portrait from Galway in 1814 at the Hibernian Society of Artists. In the following year he exhibited from Dublin but evidently returned to Galway and also worked in Limerick and London. Exhibited at the R.H.A., 1826–1861, of which he became an Associate in 1824/5 and was a member 1829–1837 in which latter year he resigned his membership whilst he continued to exhibit. Exhibited at the R.A., B.I., etc., 1835–1858. Painted portraits, figure subjects and miniatures, besides being a lithographer. By his wife Maria, whom he married in 1816 (died 1852) he had numerous children of whom his second son Thomas Haverty (born c. 1825) was also an artist. He died after a long illness at 44 Rathmines Road, Dublin 27 July 1864. A miniature by him of Richard Lalor Sheil is in the N.G., Dublin. A list of many of his works is given by Strickland.

*Haviland, Francis O.A. (Frank). d. c. 1912
Of London. Exhibited at the R.A. 1894–1910, mainly from Addison Studios, Blythe Road, Kensington. Painted miniatures, portraits and studies in water-colour. Two of his pictures were exhibited posthumously in 1912.

Havill, Frederick. d. 1884?
Was living in 1840 at 51 High Street, Exeter. Possibly identical with or related to the Frederick Havill of Cheltenham who exhibited portraits at the R.A., 1849–1874. A portrait of David Livingstone, by this latter artist, who died in 1884, is in the N.P.G.

Haward, Francis, A.R.A. 1759–1797
Born 19 April 1759. Entered the R.A. Schools, 25 March 1776 aged '17. 19th next April'. Exhibited at the R.A., 1783–1797. Best known for his en-gravings of portraits; exhibited a miniature in 1783 in which year he became an Associate Engraver of the R.A., and was engraver to the Prince of Wales. Thought to have died in Marsh Street, Lambeth 1797.

*Hawker, Miss Ethel B. (fl. 1910–1913)
Of Wimbledon and New Malden, Surrey. Ex-hibited at the R.A., 1910–1913. Executed religious subjects.

Hawkins, Henry. b. c. 1796
Was born c. 1796. Entered the R.A. Schools 31 October 1821 aged 25. Exhibited at the R.A., B.I. and S.B.A., 1822–1880. Painted portraits, land-scapes and genre subjects and possibly a few minia-tures. A miniature of J. Hadley, Esq., painted on ivory, was catalogued as by Hawkins when it was loaned to the exhibition at the South Kensington Museum, 1865.

Hawkins, Mrs. W. (Louisa). (fl. 1839–1868)
Of London. Exhibited at the R.A., etc., 1839–1868. Schidlof records a signed miniature by this artist 'Painted by Louisa Hawkins 1839, 2. Cam-bridge St'. He considered her a skilful artist and noted that several of her works were engraved.

*Hawksett, Samuel. 1776–1851
Of Belfast. Born 1776. Practised in Belfast where he was principal portrait painter of the time. Ex-hibited at the R.H.A. 1826–1834, and was a member and treasurer of the Association of Artists in Bel-fast. A miniature of the Rev. William Bruce, D.D., by him, was engraved in 1827 by Adcock. Died in 1851.

*Hawley. (fl. 1800)
Of London. Long noted an artist of this name who advertised in the *Morning Herald*, 16 July 1800 and gave the address as 9 Strand.

Hay, Miss J. (fl. 1797–1812)
Of London. Exhibited at the R.A. and B.I., 1797–1812. Her exhibits included miniatures and figures.

Hay, John. (fl. 1768–1783)
Of London. Was a pupil of Cosway (q.v.). Exhibited at the Society of Artists, the Free Society of Artists and at the R.A., 1768–1783. Painted portraits and miniatures, executed drawings in blacklead and in 1783 'An Inside of an Alehouse at an Election Time'. Some of his work was executed in oil, and some engravings after his portraits are at the B.M. I have seen a miniature of a lady by this artist signed 'JH' (monogram) '17 . .' the last figures being indecipherable. It had grey shading, rather woolly hair treatment and the initials were scratched in.

*Hay, Mary. (fl. 1797)
This artist is recorded by Schidlof who states that she worked in England in the latter part of the eighteenth century and specialised in executing miniatures on enamel. An allegorical subject on enamel, which was sold in Paris in 1928, was signed 'Mary Hay, 1797'.

Hay, W. (fl. 1776–1797)
Worked in London, Plymouth (1787) and Bath (1790). Advertised in the *Bath Chronicle* 29 January 1789. Exhibited at the R.A., 1776–1797. Painted portraits, landscapes and miniatures. Some of his work was engraved. The B.M. has two examples. Long saw a miniature of an officer c. 1792 signed in cursive script 'W Hay', the 'a' and 'y' being curiously conjoined. The general effect of the miniature was pleasing; the complexion was slightly brick-red.

Hayes, Edward, R.H.A. 1797–1864
An Irish artist born in Co. Tipperary 1797. Studied at the Dublin Society's School under J. S. Alpenny. Worked at Clonmel (c. 1820), Waterford (1824) and Kilkenny. Exhibited at the R.H.A., from 1830, became an Associate in 1856 and a member in 1861. Settled in Dublin in 1831. Died at 4 Salem Place, Dublin 21 May 1864 and was buried at Glasnevin. Painted portraits, still-life and land-scapes in oil, besides executing miniatures and pencil and water-colour portraits. Examples of his work are at the N.G., Dublin. Two portraits by Hayes are in the family collection of Mme Stuart Steven-son of Edinburgh – they both represent her great-grandfather, the Hon. Matthew Fortescue; they are executed in water-colour and are signed 'Edw, Hayes, Dublin' and 'Edwᵈ Hayes'. One portrait is a profile of the head executed in the manner of a design for a medal or relief. It is painted mainly in sepia, with grey shading in the hair. It is set in a circular design as for a medal and on the inner edge of the circle over the head is inscribed 'Matt Fortescue' in block letters. The other portrait is unfinished, pencil and wash, mainly sepia, showing the sitter seated with a King Charles spaniel beside him. The draughtsmanship of both portraits is excellent.

Hayes, J.W. (fl. 1841)
A miniature of an unknown man, signed on the reverse 'J.W. Hayes / Pinxit Augᵗ 16 1841 / 1. Frith St. Soho Square / London.', was seen by me in 1978. He was in the manner of the Scottish School of miniaturists.

Hayls, John. 1600?–1679
Born in England c. 1600. A pupil of Miereveldt and imitator and copyist of Van Dyck. Was a rival of Lely. Painted portraits in oil and water-colour, and, according to Vertue (B.M. Add. MSS. 23069 p. 24b) painted miniatures. After Samuel Cooper (q.v.) tried painting in oil, Hayls is reputed to have told Cooper that he would turn to limning if he (Cooper) painted in oil and for this reason Cooper kept to limning. Hayls was in Rome in 1651 and London, 1658. He painted portraits of Flatman (q.v.) and Hoskins (q.v.). No miniatures by him are known to exist. He died in Bloomsbury, London in 1679 and was buried in St. Martin's Church. A pen-and-ink and wash drawing of a lady, by Hayls is at the B.M., and an oil portrait of Pepys is at the N.P.G.

*Hayman, F. (fl. 1730–1748)
A miniature portrait by F. Hayman on paper dated '1730' of Prince Charles Edward was seen in 1960 and another miniature of the Prince dated '1748' was in a private collection, which has since been dispersed. The artist may have been identical with Francis Hayman (1708–1776), portrait painter.

Haynes. (fl. 1811)
A young man of this name applied to the Court of Directors of the East India Company in 1811 for permission to go to India as a portrait and minia-ture painter. This is referred to in *Farington's Diary* for 26 June 1811.

*Hayter, Lady. 18th century
Wife of Sir George Hayter (q.v.). Said by Long to have been a miniaturist.

Hayter, Miss Anne. (fl. 1814–1830)
Of London. Daughter of Charles Hayter (q.v.) and sister of Sir George Hayter (q.v.) and of John Hayter (q.v.) whose address, 13 Foley Place, she

shared in 1829. Was awarded premiums by the Society of Arts in 1814 and 1815. Exhibited at the R.A., O.W.C.S., etc., 1814–1830. Painted the background of a miniature by Sir George Hayter in 1818.

Hayter, Charles. 1761–1835

Was born at Twickenham, 24 February 1761; his mother's maiden name being Elizabeth Holmes. Entered the R.A. Schools 30 January 1786 aged '24. 24th last Feb'. Worked in London and Winchester (1832). Exhibited at the R.A., etc., 1786–1832. Married in 1788 at St. George's, Hanover Square, Martha Stevenson (1762–1805), daughter of Thomas and Mary Stevenson. Three of his children, Sir George Hayter (q.v.), Miss Anne Hayter (q.v.) and John Hayter (q.v.) were artists. Was Professor of Perspective to Princess Charlotte. Executed portraits in crayon and pencil and painted miniatures. Was the author of *An Introduction to Perspective*, 1813 and *A New Practical Treatise on Three Primative Colours*, 1828. Died in London, 1 December 1835. He signed Chaˢ Hayter and C. Hayter, often followed by a date and address. His drawings are usually signed on the back, but some of his miniatures are signed on the front. An album of some 440 pencil portraits by Hayter, many of them named, are in the V. & A. M. His addresses included No. 279 Opposite Norfolk Street, Strand; 27 Henrietta Street, Covent Garden and 16 Buckingham Street, Portland Place. Hayter often placed a sketch of the sitter beneath the ivory when beginning a miniature. Examples of his miniatures are in the V. & A. M., including a group of a lady and two children, signed on the front 'C Hayter 1800' and on the reverse 'C.Hayter / London / 1800'; another example is of a boy holding a copy of the group already referred to. A pencil portrait in miniature of an unknown gentleman, in profile, and signed on the front 'C Hayter' is in my collection. Some engraved portraits after C. Hayter are in the B.M.

Hayter, Sir George, K.S.L. 1792–1871

Was born in London 17 December 1792, son of Charles Hayter (q.v.) and his wife Martha Stevenson. Entered the R.A. Schools, 21 January 1808 aged 15. In the same year became a midshipman in the Navy, but returned in 1809 to an artistic career. Exhibited at the R.A., B.I., etc., 1809–1859. Worked in Southampton in 1811 and in 1812 became a member of the Assoc. Artists in Water-Colours. In 1815 the B.I., awarded him a premium of £200; went to Italy in the same year and remained there for three years; returned again in 1826. Settled in England in 1831. Painted miniatures, oil portraits and historical subjects. Held the appointment of miniature painter and portrait painter to Princess Charlotte and Prince Leopold of Saxe-Coburg and in 1837 portrait and history painter to Queen Victoria. Was knighted in 1842. Was a member of the Academies of Rome, Bologna, Florence, Parma and Venice. He was a Knight of St. Luke's Academy, Rome. Had a distinguished clientele. Henry Collen (q.v.) was his pupil. His wife, Lady Hayter (q.v.), is said to have been a miniaturist. He died at 238 Marylebone Road, London on 18 January 1871. Hayter was a good artist and an accurate draughtsman. His signature appears to have been G.H. followed by a date. The B.M. has numerous portrait drawings by Hayter, and engraved portraits by him. Drawings and portraits in oil are in the N.P.G. Miniatures by Hayter are in the V. & A. M., as well as a pencil portrait of him as a baby and another of him as a young man by his father, C. Hayter. His sister, Miss A. Hayter (q.v.) painted the background of a miniature by Hayter of 'Charlotte Stanley; a Gypsey'. It was inscribed on the reverse 'This

picture . . . was painted by G. Hayter for N. Ogle, Esqʳ his 81st picture 1811 Southampton and the background was painted to it by Miss A. Hayter 1818'. Works by Hayter were exhibited at the South Kensington Museum 1865.

*Hayter, John. 1800–1895

Was born in London 1800, son of Charles Hayter (q.v.) and his wife Martha. Exhibited at the R.A., B.I., O.W.C.S., etc., 1815–1879. Entered the R.A. Schools, 24 November 1815 aged 15. Painted portraits and subject pictures. He was a prolific artist who had a distinguished clientele. Some of his exhibits at the R.A. were in the Drawing and Miniature section. A portrait of Lady Georgiana Frances Spencer and John Poyntz, Viscount Althorp, executed in crayons and dated 'May 1838' was exhibited at the South Kensington Museum, 1865. Among his exhibits at the R.A. was a portrait entitled 'The Cricketer; Master E. Landseer' painted when the artist was 15, and portraits of 'Julian, Laura and Charley, Children of the artist'. Died in 1895. A large portrait by Hayter of Sir Benjamin Hallowell Carew is in the N.P.G.

*Hayward, Gerald Sinclair. 1845-1926

Of London. Exhibited at the R.A., 1879–1883. His sitters included the Misses Gautier, Mrs. Halhed, and Mrs. G. S. Hayward. His address was Holly-Village, Highgate.

Haywood, Miss J. M. (fl. 1852–1854)

Of London. Exhibited at the R.A. and B.I., 1852–1854.

*Haywood, Miss Lily. (fl. 1903–1906)

Of London. Exhibited at the R.A. and S.M. 1903–1906, from 8 Cottesmore Gardens, Kensington. Her sitters included Mrs. Barber.

*Hazlehurst, Joseph B. (fl. 1817–1818)

Exhibited portraits at the R.A., 1817. These were probably miniatures. A pair of miniatures signed in full and dated 'J.B. Hazlehurst, No 21 Grey Walk, Lambeth / A.D. 1818' were sold in 1958. They were signed with Roman caps 'J.B.H.' on the front. The backgrounds were hatched, the features shaded with a blue tint, and eyelids outlined. No stippling was used. His sitters included the Rev. S. Bennett, Chaplain of the Penitentiary, Millbank, and Mr. J. Egling. His address in 1817 was 11 Brownlow Street, Long Acre.

Hazlehurst, Thomas. *c.* 1740–*c.* 1821

Was born in Liverpool *c.* 1740 where he practised as a miniaturist, 1760–1818. Exhibited at the Society for Promoting Painting and Design in Liverpool, 1787 and at the Liverpool Academy, 1810–1812. His address in 1793 was 9 Rodney Street, Liverpool. He shared the same initials as Hargreaves (q.v.) but the signatures differed. Hazlehurst usually signed his miniatures on the front T.H. in neat Roman caps, whereas Hargreaves used cursive initials. Hazlehurst's early work was reminiscent of that of C. Robertson (q.v.) but his later work was slightly in the manner of J. Barry (q.v.). He sometimes used a blue shading on the face and occasionally his painting has a rather tight and slightly hard appearance, the hair being executed with numerous curves combined with parallel straight lines. A miniature of an unknown officer in my collection is well painted and has good colouring; it is signed 'T.H.' Examples of his work are in the V. & A. M. The local History Department of the City of Liverpool Libraries contains a collection of 387 paintings of Lancashire flora by Thomas Hazlehurst.

Hazlitt, John. 1767–1837

Born 1767. Son of a Unitarian minister (died 1820) and his wife, née Grace Loftus (1746–1847) of Peterborough, and brother of William Hazlitt (q.v.). His place of birth is uncertain; Redgrave gives Wem, Salop, and others Marshfield, Gloucestershire. Lived at Maidstone and at Brandon near Cork, and in 1783 was taken to New York and travelled with his father in the U.S. In *c.* 1785 was painting miniatures at Salem and conducted an art school at Boston, 1785. Worked for a time at Hingham, Massachusetts. Returned to London in 1787. His wife was Mary Pearce of Portsea. Became known to Sir Joshua Reynolds and copied some of his works. Exhibited at the R.A. and B.I., 1788–1819. Exhibited a self-portrait at the R.A., in 1803. Among his sitters were Edridge (q.v.), Coleridge, Dr. Jenner and Miss Lamb. Painted miniatures, figures and oil portraits. When living in Great Russell Street in 1804 he charged 7 guineas for a miniature. In 1832 he moved to Stockport where he remained until his death on 16 May 1837. The Bentlif Art Gallery, Maidstone, has several oil portraits by Hazlitt of his family, a pencil self-portrait, and miniatures including those of himself, his wife and daughter, Harriet. The B.M. has some engravings after his work. He died in Stockport, 16 May 1837.

Hazlitt, William. 1778–1830

Born 10 April 1778, son of a Unitarian minister and brother of John Hazlitt (q.v.). He and his brother were taken to America in 1783. Returned to England, 1786 or 1787; lived at Wem; studied at a Unitarian College at Hackney. Was a pupil of his brother. Met Coleridge and became attracted to reading and writing. Was in Paris, 1802–1803 where he copied pictures. Exhibited at the R.A., 1802 and 1805. Married Miss Stoddart in 1808 and by 1812 was settled in London where he devoted his time to journalism and literature. Married for the second time in 1824. Died in lodgings in Frith Street, London, 18 September 1830. Painted oil portraits and miniatures. The N.P.G. has an oil portrait of Charles Lamb, by W. Hazlitt, and the B.M. has a few engravings after his portraits.

Heape, M. See Heape, Miss M.

Heape, Miss M. (fl. 1821–1823)

Probably identical with M. Heape who in 1822 was at 56 New Street, Birmingham. Won a premium at the Society of Arts in 1822 and exhibited at the R.A., 1821–1823. Worked in London and Birmingham. An engraved portrait of Miss Hallande, after M. Heape is at the B.M.

Heaphy, Miss Elizabeth. See Murray, Mrs. Henry John

Heaphy, Miss Mary Ann. See Musgrave, Mrs. W.

Heaphy, Thomas. 1775–1835

Was born in London, 29 December 1775, son of J. G. Heaphy and father of Thomas Frank Heaphy, Mary Ann Heaphy (q.v.) and Elizabeth Heaphy (q.v.). His mother was French. Served his apprenticeship to a dyer and was subsequently articled to R. M. Meadows, an engraver. Was a pupil of John Boyne who kept a drawing school and a friend of James Holmes (q.v.). Married early in life. Exhibited at the R.A., B.I., O.W.C.S., N.W.C.S., S.B.A., 1797–1834. Coloured prints, painted portraits, genre subjects, miniatures and portraits in water-colour. Became portrait painter to the Prince of Wales in 1803 and an Associate of the O.W.C.S., in 1807 but resigned in 1812. In the same year he went to the Peninsula and followed the army, painting portraits of the British officers, including a portrait of the Duke of Wellington with his General Staff which was much admired. Was the first President of the S.B.A., in 1824. Was in Italy, 1831 and copied the works of old masters. Became one of the first members of the N.W.C.S. Is known to have developed land in the St. John's Wood district, London. Died at 8 St. John's Wood Road, London, 23 October 1835. Miniatures by Heaphy are scarce; he is best known for his small water-colour portraits which often depict the sitter full length, and genre subjects. A miniature of an unknown man, signed 'T. Heaphy 1815' is in the V. & A. M.; the shading on the portrait is predominantly brown. A miniature of a lady signed in red 'T.H: 1803' with the artist's name and address on the reverse is also in the V. & A. M. Examples of his work are also in the N.P.G. The B.M. has engraved portraits after Heaphy. In a monograph by W. T. Whitley, 1933, it is stated that he charged 12 to 15 guineas for oil portraits, 12 to 40 guineas for water-colours and 10 to 50 guineas for miniatures. His charge for teaching was 1 guinea per hour and 2 guineas for three hours.

*Heard, W. M. (William). b. c. 1777
Entered the R.A. Schools, 9 March 1805 aged 28, when he was listed as a miniature painter. According to the Council minutes he was called William.

*Heath, Dudley. (fl. 1892–1913)
Of London. Exhibited at the R.A., etc., 1892–1913. Painted miniatures and subjects and portraits in oil and water-colour. Author of *Miniatures* published by the *Connoisseur*, 1905.

Heath, Henry Charles. 1829–1898
Born 1829. Son of Charles Heath, the engraver. Educated at King's College, London, where he gained prizes and distinctions and trained as an engineer. Took up miniature painting as a profession after his father's death in 1848. Was helped by Henry Corbould. Became a student at the R.A. Schools. Assisted Thorburn (q.v.) but soon had a connection of his own. Exhibited at the R.A. and S.B.A., etc., 1851–1898. Gave up miniature painting for photography for some years, but took up the former again in 1872. Was appointed miniature painter to Queen Victoria in c. 1890 and in 1894 became an original member of the Society of Miniature Painters (now The Royal Society of Miniature Painters, Sculptors & Gravers). Heath died in 1898. His eldest son, Sir Frank Heath (1863–1946) made a name for himself as an educationalist and a head of a Government department. Lionel Heath (q.v.) exhibited from the same address as the above artist, 12 Pall Mall East, 1897–1898.

*Heath, Lionel. (fl. 1892–1911)
Was probably the son of Henry Charles Heath (q.v.). Exhibited at the R.A. 1892–1911, from addresses in London. His sitters included the Countess of Warwick, Lady Gertrude Foljambe, the Rt. Hon. F. J. Savile Foljambe, Mrs. Lionel Heath (presumably his wife) and Raymond, son of Dr. Frank Heath. His wife, M. Forsyth Heath (q.v.) was also a miniaturist and exhibited from their address, 40 Norland Square, Holland Park.

*Heath, Mrs. Lionel. See **Heath, Mrs. M. Forsyth**

*Heath, Mrs. M. Forsyth (Mrs. Lionel Heath). (fl. 1908–1909)
Of London. Exhibited at the R.A. 1908–1909, from 40 Norland Square, Holland Park, from which

address her husband Lionel Heath (q.v.) also exhibited.

*Heath, Miss Margaret A. (fl. 1886–1914)
Of London. Exhibited at the R.A., N.W.C.S., etc. 1886–1914, from various London addresses. In 1896 she exhibited a miniature of Abraham Thomas. This miniature was at one time in the O'Brien collection and signed on the reverse 'Margaret A. Heath 1896'; from the costume it would appear to have been copied from a portrait of c. 1810, or the sitter was in fancy dress. She also painted subjects in oil and water-colour. In 1914 she exhibited a miniature of Henry Heath (q.v.) to whom she was probably related.

*Heath, R. C. (fl. 1862). See also **Heath, Henry C.**
Of London. Exhibited at the R.A. 1862, from 283 Regent Street. The exhibit, which was a portrait of Mrs. Ferguson of Raith, Kirkcaldy, may have been a miniature. He may have been identical with or related to Henry Charles Heath (q.v.).

*Heaton, Mrs. Sermonda Henniker. See **Henniker Heaton, Mrs. Jack**

Heidemanns, H. P. (fl. 1845–1864)
Born in Amsterdam. Worked in London and exhibited at the R.A. 1845–1864, and in 1848 at the Academy of Berlin.

*Heigel, Franz Napoleon. 1813–1888
Born in Paris, 15 May 1813, son of J. Heigel, a miniaturist, of Paris and Munich. Heigel was taught by his father and after attending the Academy at Munich returned to Paris where he became a pupil of J. Guérin. Travelled in France, Belgium and Italy, 1838–1846. Settled in Munich and was appointed painter to King Louis I and Louis II of Bavaria. Taught members of the Royal Court. Painted miniatures and portraits in water-colour. Heigel was an excellent draughtsman and his miniatures are of a high quality. He may have visited Britain. He exhibited at Suffolk Street, etc., in 1866 from Munich. I have seen a miniature of a lady painted in water-colour on paper signed 'F.N. Heigel, 1847'. A fine miniature of Henry Everard, signed horizontally 'F.N. Heigel / 1847' is in the collection of Mme H. Stuart Stevenson of Edinburgh. He represents a member of her family. Heigel died in Munich, 22 June 1888.

*Heigel, Miss Henriette. (fl. c. 1840)
Probably the sister of Franz Napoleon Heigel (1813–1888) (q.v.) and daughter of Josef Heigel (1780–1838). The family worked in Paris and Munich. Schidlof refers to a miniature on ivory c. 1840 signed 'H.Heigel'; this is undoubtedly by the same artist who may have visited Britain. A miniature of a gentleman by this artist was sold at Christie's, 15 October 1963.

Heighway, R. (fl. 1787–1793)
Exhibited at the R.A., etc., 1787–1793. Painted rustic subjects, and miniatures, some of which were painted on the reverse of glass and which, although crude, were quite effective. He worked in London, Lichfield and Shrewsbury. An oil painting attributed to Heighway is in the V. & A. M. A portrait of a girl painted on glass by 'Highaway' was exhibited at the South Kensington Museum, 1865.

Heins, D. d. c. 1756
Born in Germany. Was working as a portrait painter at Norwich and Cambridge c. 1725–1756. Executed mezzotint engravings and painted a small oil miniature of Cowper's mother (died 1737) and a

portrait of Nelson's mother in 1743. His wife Abigail proved his will, 30 August 1756. Their son, John Theodore Heins (q.v.) followed his father's profession. Information about the father and son appears to have been confused and the *D.N.B.* gives both their names as John Theodore. The Society of Artists and the Free Society of Artists recorded by Graves give a D. Heins as exhibiting, 1767–1770 but his date of death makes this impossible. Bryan's *Dictionary of Painters* gives the father's name as D. Heins but the dates of death differ. The B.M. has some engraved portraits after D. Heins.

Heins, John Theodore. 1732–1771
Born in Norwich 1732, son of D. Heins (q.v.). Was apprenticed to a snuff manufacturer in Norwich. Took up painting and was taught by his father. Worked in Norwich and London. Exhibited at the Free Society and the Society of Artists, 1767–1770. Graves gives the name as D. Heins in error. Painted oil portraits, miniatures; etched portraits; engraved in mezzotint and drew and engraved views. Died in Chelsea of a decline, 11 May 1771. An engraved portrait after Heins is at the B.M. Information regarding the lives of J. T. Heins and his father seems confused and both the *D.N.B.* and Bryan's *Dictionary of Painters* give different versions. The *Evening Post*, 11 May 1771 gives J. T. Heins's obituary.

*Hellier, Mrs. Gertrude S. (fl. 1907–1908)
Exhibited at the R.A. 1907–1908, from Thornedene, Holmesdale Road, Bromley, Kent.

*Helps, Mrs. E. B. (fl. 1903)
Of Folkestone, Kent. Exhibited at the Society of Miniaturists, 1903.

Heming, Mrs. Matilda (I) (Miss Matilda Lowry). (fl. 1804–1821). See also **Heming, Mrs. Matilda (II)**
Née Matilda Lowry, born before 1796, daughter of the engraver Wilson Lowry. Obtained a gold medal from the Society of Arts in 1804 for a landscape. Exhibited at the R.A. 1808–1809, under her maiden name from 57 Tichfield Street, Portland Place, and under her married name from the same address, 1820–1821. Painted landscapes and portraits, some of which may have been miniatures. Was possibly identical with the Mrs. Matilda Heming (II) (q.v.) who exhibited at the R.A. in 1847, 1848 and 1855 from 45 Robert Street, Hampstead Road. The exhibits were in the Drawing and Miniature section. A small portrait in watercolour of Wilson Lowry, and attributed to his daughter, Matilda Heming, is in the N.P.G.

*Heming, Mrs. Matilda (II) (fl. 1847–1855). See also **Heming, Mrs. Matilda (I)**
Of 45 Robert Street, Hampstead Road, London. Exhibited at the R.A., 1847–1855. Was possibly identical with Mrs. Matilda Heming, (I) (q.v.). The above artist's exhibits were all in the Drawing and Miniature section. Her sitters included Miss Ellen Winifred Johns and Miss Eda Fortescue.

*Hemming, Miss Edith. (fl. 1904–1910)
Of London and Dollar, Scotland. Exhibited at the R.A., 1904 and 1910. Her sitters included George W. Hemming, Esq., K.C. and Joan, daughter of Capt. Norman Hemming, R.N.

*Hemming, J. (fl. 1838)
Schidlof records this artist as working in England c. 1838 and notes a miniature of Frances Jessica, daughter of the 1st Marquess of Normanby, painted as a child, on ivory, signed on the right 'JH'

(monogram) and on the reverse 'by J. Hemming / 1838'.

Hénard, Charles. 1757 – d. after 1808

Of London and Paris. Born at Bourg-en-Bresse, 1757. Was a pupil of Taraval. Exhibited at the R.A., 1785–1800 and at the Paris Salon, 1791–1808. His miniatures are of a high quality, the eyes of his sitters being rather dark, the eyebrows strongly marked and the mouth indicated in bright red. He used a yellowish colouring when painting the eyelids and shadows on the face. A scraper is often used in the hair; the backgrounds are usually brownish-blue gouache, or landscapes. His usual signature appears to have been 'Henard' sometimes followed by a date. His exhibit in 1800 was of Madame Rose Didelot, in the character of Calypso, in the ballet of Telemachus; it was not a miniature. Long records the initial of the above artist as M in error. Said to have died after 1808.

Henault (Hainault?). (fl. 1797–1799)

Worked in London. Exhibited at the R.A. in 1797 and 1799 from 20 and 23 Haymarket. In 1799 he is recorded in the index but not in the catalogue. Painted genre subjects and miniatures. Schidlof identifies him as the artist named Hainault who was a member of the Academy of St. Luc and exhibited there in 1752, and worked in Paris during the second half of the 18th century.

*Henderson, J. (fl. 1782–1783)

Of London. Exhibited at the Society of Artists and the Free Society of Artists, 1782 and 1783. His exhibits were a portrait and 'Portraits in ivory'. His address was 7 Little St. Martin's Lane.

Henderson, P. (fl. 1799–1829)

Of London. Exhibited at the R.A. and B.I., 1799–1829. Painted flower subjects and portraits.

*Henderson, Robert. 1826–1904

Born in Dumfries, Scotland, 1826. Exhibited at the R.A., 1883–1895. In this latter year his address was c/o Dickinson & Foster, 114 New Bond Street. His sitters included the Duke of Rutland, K.G. Died 19 October 1904.

*Heneage, The Hon. Adela M. (fl. 1905)

Exhibited at the Society of Miniaturists in 1905 from Hainton Hall, Lincoln.

*Henn, Miss Marion R. (fl. 1898–1907)

Of London, North Wales and Westcliff-on-Sea. Exhibited at the R.A. and S.M., 1898–1907.

*Hennet. (fl. c. 1780)

I have seen a miniature of an unknown man, 18th century, signed 'Hennet / p'. It was well painted and had a cloud background with greyish shading. It may have been the one sold at Sotheby's, 19 December 1960, lot 86. The Art Institute of Chicago has a miniature of a man c. 1780 painted on ivory and signed in the same manner.

*Henniker Heaton, Mrs. Jack or **Mrs. Sermonda.** (fl. 1903–1908)

Of London. Exhibited at the Society of Miniaturists (of which she was an Hon. Member), 1903–1908. Her address in 1903 was c/o Dr. G. C. Williamson, The Mount, Guildford, who was the author of numerous books on miniatures.

Henning, Mrs. See Heming, Mrs. Matilda (II)

Graves gives this artist as exhibiting in 1854 but it would appear to be a mis-spelling for Mrs. Heming (II) (q.v.), who exhibited from the same address.

Henri, Pierre. (fl. c. 1790–1812)

Born in Paris. Studied in London; Long suggests at the R.A. Schools, but his name does not appear in the list of this period. Went to America c. 1790–1812 and practised at Richmond and Philadelphia as well as Charleston, where he advertised in the *City Gazette*, 1791–1792 that he would 'undertake to re-do all portraits not having a pleasing resemblance to the sitter'.

Henshaw, Miss Emily. (fl. 1839)

Exhibited at the R.A., 1839.

*Henwood, T. (fl. 1832)

A rectangular miniature signed 'T. Henwood, 1832' was seen by Long in 1924.

*Hepburn Edmunds, Miss Nellie M.H., V.P.R.M.S. See Edmunds, Miss Nellie M.H.

*Herapath, Miss Hilda W. (fl. 1908–1910)

Of London. Exhibited at the R.A. 1908 and 1910, from Addison Road, Kensington.

*Herbert, Charles. (fl. 1766)

A miniature signed and dated '1766' was sold at Sotheby's, 18 February 1963.

Herbst, Miss. (fl. 1801). See also **Herbst, G.**

Exhibited a miniature at the R.A. 1801, as an Hon. exhibitor. Was possibly identical with G. Herbst (q.v.) who exhibited at the R.A. in 1800.

Herbst, G. (fl. 1800). See also **Herbst, Miss**

Exhibited portraits at the R.A., in 1800 and may possibly have been identical with Miss Herbst (q.v.).

Herman or **Hermann.** (fl. c. 1820–1840)

Worked from c. 1820–1840. A signed miniature of Mr. F. A. Molesworth painted in 1839 was exhibited at the South Kensington Museum in 1865. This artist has been identified as Carl Hermann who was working in Vienna before 1839, but Schidlof considers this improbable. R W. Herman of 24 Green Street, Grosvenor Square exhibited a landscape at the B.I. in 1847.

Hertocks or **Hertochs, A.** (fl. 1626–1672)

A Dutch portrait engraver who worked in England, 1626–1672. A miniature portrait signed 'AH' and painted on parchment, said to represent Mrs. Cromwell (died 1653), mother of the Protector, was lent to the South Kensington Museum, 1865. Another miniature unsigned but in the same technique is in the Ernst Holzscheiter Collection, Meilen.

Hervé. (fl. c. 1809)

This artist had an address in the Abbey Churchyard, Bath c. 1809. Was undoubtedly related to or identical with one of the other artists of this name.

*Hervé, A. (Alfred?). (fl. 1841–1843)

Of London. Exhibited at the R.A. 1841–1843, from 145 Strand. His sitters were Thomas Wilkins, Esq., head of East India Company Service, and Mr. J. D. Wilkinson. Was probably related to the other artists of this name.

Hervé, C. (Charles?). (fl. 1806 or 1811–1816)

Of London. Exhibited at the R.A., 1806 or 1811–1816. Was a brother of F. Hervé (q.v.) and Peter Hervé (q.v.) etc. Long gives his dates of exhibiting at the R.A., as from 1803 but in that year no initial is recorded and no address is given; it is therefore a matter of conjecture which of the family was responsible for the portrait. In 1806 a C. Hervey is recorded in the R.A. catalogues as exhibiting from 308 Oxford Street a miniature of Mrs. Bland; the

exhibit may have been by the above artist or P. Hervé (q.v.) who was living at this address from 1807–1808. His address in 1816 was 12 Cheapside from where Francis Hervé exhibited for many years.

*Hervé, C., junior. (fl. 1828). See also **Hervé, C. S.**

Exhibited at the R.A. 1828, from 128 Strand, the sitter being M. D'Esperieux. Undoubtedly related to the other artists of this name. Graves and Long give the entry in 1828 to C. S. Hervé (q.v.) but the catalogue identifies the artist as C. Hervé, junior, and there is every possibility that he was an hitherto unrecorded member of the family.

Hervé, Mrs. C. (Margaret). (fl. 1783–1800)

Of London. Exhibited at the Society of Artists, 1783 and at the R.A. 1800, from 20 Warren Street, Fitzroy Square. Graves has erroneously recorded that she exhibited until 1816.

Hervé, C. S. (fl. 1835–1858). See also **Hervé, C., junior**

Of London. Undoubtedly related to the other artists of this name. Exhibited at the R.A., etc., 1835–1858. His addresses included 248 Regent Street, Oxford Street and 392 Strand. He was presumably identical with the C. S. Hervé who exhibited a portrait of Mr. Joseph Tussaud at the S.B.A., in 1835 from 138 Regent Street. Charles Hervé (q.v.) (born c. 1834) was probably his son. C. S. Hervé had a distinguished clientele including Major General Sir Joseph O'Halloran, K.C.B., Lady H. Smythe, General Count Michaelowitz, Madame H. de la Monniene (possibly a mis-spelling of de la Monnière, a family name) and in 1852 a miniature of his daughter. Long and Graves give his dates of exhibiting as from 1828 but the catalogues for that year identify the artist as C. Hervé, junior (q.v.) who may have been a hitherto unrecorded member of the family.

Hervé, Charles. b. c. 1834/5

Was born c. 1834/5. Long records this artist as having lent two of his miniatures to the V. & A. M. These were still on loan in 1929. Hervé also lent a miniature of Monsieur Tussaud, which may have been the portrait painted by C. S. Hervé (q.v.) who may have been his father.

Hervé, Francis or **de la Monnière Hervé, F.** (fl. 1818–1831/40?)

Of London. Undoubtedly related to several other artists of this name. Was probably a brother of C. Hervé (q.v.) and P. Hervé (q.v.) and possibly the father of Rosa de la Monnière Hervé as both of them exhibited from 206 Oxford Street in 1837 in which year he is described as F. de la Monnière Hervé. Exhibited at the R.A. 1818–1831, and was probably the Hervé (no initial given) who exhibited, 1832–1840 from 12 Cheapside, from which address F. Hervé exhibited for many years. His sitters included Mr. P. Hervé, Mrs. F. Hervé, Hector Campbell, Miss Love of Covent Garden Theatre and Edward Orde, Esq.

Hervé, Henry. (fl. 1801–c. 1817)

Of London. Exhibited at the R.A., 1813–1816. Undoubtedly related to C. Hervé (q.v.) and F. Hervé (q.v.) whose address he shared. Was in Great Russell Street in 1817 and later at 12 Cheapside. He advertised that he had taken upwards of 12,000 likenesses by Hawkins' Patent Machine; and that he cut paper silhouettes at 2s. 6d. each and charged from one guinea upwards for miniatures. May have been identical with the H. Hervé who exhibited at the R.A. in 1843, from 21 Paradise

Place, Stockwell, from which address C. S. Hervé (q.v.) exhibited in 1835.

Hervé, Mrs. Margaret. See Hervé, Mrs. C.

Hervé, Peter. *c.* 1775–1827

Was born *c.* 1775 (according to Strickland). Worked in London. Probably a brother of C. Hervé (q.v.) and F. Hervé (q.v.). Exhibited at the R.A. 1802–1820, from various London addresses including 308 Oxford Street and 45 Great Russell Street. Founded in 1812 the National Benevolent Institution where a miniature profile portrait of him is preserved. Suffered from ill health at an early age. He died on 6 June 1827. The *Calcutta Journal*, 28 June 1820, p. 685, records details of Hervé's charitable efforts and his difficulties in accomplishing them; an appeal is made for subscribers towards a book by Hervé on France. His sitters included Mrs. Liston (the actress), Dr. Jenner, 'Mr Bennet, the artist', Mrs. C. Hervé, etc.

Hervé, Rosa de la Monnière. (fl. 1837)

Exhibited at the R.A. in 1837 from 206 Oxford Street, the same address as Francis Hervé (q.v.) who was probably her father. The exhibit was a portrait of Madame Victor Hugo.

Hervier, A. (Auguste?). 19th century. See also **Hervier, Marie Antoine**

An artist about whom little is known. May be identical with Marie Antoine Hervier (q.v.) but must not be confused with Augustin Jean Hervieu(e) who exhibited at the R.A. 1824–1858, and painted portraits, historical pictures etc., but not, so far as I know, any miniatures. In 1819 Hervier (no initial given) exhibited at the R.A., from 2 Cirencester Place, 'Portrait of the artist in his study' and in 1827 A. Hervier exhibited 'Nymphs and Cupids' from 5 Union Place, New Road, Regent's Park. In the same year A. Hervieu, Member of the Academy of Fine Arts at Lille exhibited from 78 Newman Street, (not miniatures). This established the fact that there were two artists and that their work had previously been confused. M. Fielding gives both artists and only records Auguste Hervier as a miniaturist. He evidently worked in America from *c.* 1827–1858. It was A. Hervieu who knew Mrs. Trollope and not Hervier as recorded by Long.

*Hervier, Marie Antoine. (fl. 1810–1817). See also **Hervier, Auguste**

Possibly identical with Auguste Hervier. Father of Adolphe Hervier. Was a pupil of David and Aubrey. Exhibited at the Paris Salon, 1810–1817, including a self-portrait and the portrait of his wife. Lived at 7 Quai des Fleurs, Paris and was for a time in England.

*Hesday, W. J. L. (fl. 1824)

Long saw a miniature of Capt. Aitchison painted by this artist at Calcutta in 1824.

Heseltine, Charles. (fl. 1822)

Working in 1822 at Grotto Street, Hull. The Council Minutes of the R.A. Schools give a William Heseltine, for 21 June 1800, but he does not appear in the Register. He was probably the William Heseltine who exhibited portraits at the R.A., 1799–1805 and may have been related to the above artist.

*Heseltine, T. or F. (fl. 1797–1798)

Possibly a pupil of Scouler (q.v.). Long saw five miniatures by the above artist signed and dated 1797–1798. One was signed 'T. Heseltine 1798', another was a copy of 'Diana' after Scouler. Was possibly related to one of the artists of this name

recorded by Benezit.

*Hetherington, W. Scott. (fl. 1905–1912)

Of London. Exhibited at the R.A., 1905 and 1912.

Heuhan or **Heughan, J.** (fl. 1806–1813)

Of Glasgow. Exhibited at the R.A., 1810–1813. A miniature of a man in my collection is signed with a scraper close to the edge of the frame on the front 'J. Heuhan P 1806'. It is quite well painted, shaded with stippling on the grey brown background, the flesh part being shaded with a brownish yellow on the side away from the light, and a pink tint on the other; a sense of humour can be discerned on the sitter's face. The above artist's name is erroneously recorded as Heuham by Schidlof.

Hewett, G. (fl. 1823–1825)

Of London. Exhibited at the R.A., etc., 1823–1825. The exhibit in 1823 was of Master Hewett.

*Hewett, J. (fl. 1795)

A miniature painter and drawing master of Cock Lane, Bath and, from 17 December 1795, of 10 Bridge Street, Bath.

*Hewitt, Miss Beatrice M. (fl. 1884–1901)

Exhibited at the R.A., and N.W.C.S. 1884–1901, from Fontenroy Road, Balham and 4 Addison Studios, Blythe Road, Kensington. Her sitters included the Duchess of Newcastle and Mary, Countess of Mar and Kellie.

*Hewitt, Miss Ena (Mrs. Harold Adams). (fl. 1900–1902)

Of London. Exhibited at the Society of Miniaturists 1900–1902.

*Hewlett, Miss Florence. (fl. 1908–1912)

Exhibited at the R.A. 1908–1912, from addresses in Richmond, Surrey. Her sitters included the Rev. Lionel Walsh.

Hewson, Stephen. (fl. 1775–1805)

Of London and Birmingham (1790). Exhibited at the Free Society of Artists and the Society of Artists, 1775–1791 and at the R.A., 1781–1805. He has previously been recorded as exhibiting at the R.A. from 1777, but I have been unable to find any evidence for this and the R.A. catalogues do not list him before 1781. He exhibited miniatures (one in oil), portraits, figure subjects, still life and landscapes. Had addresses at Frith Street, Soho and at Mr. Leserver's 107 High Street, Birmingham (21 June 1790); may have visited Cheltenham *c.* 1797. An engraving of R. Penrose after Hewson is at the B.M.

*Heydermann, William (Willie). (fl. 1886–1913)

Of London. Exhibited at the R.A. 1886–1913, from various London addresses. Painted miniatures and executed engravings. His sitters included H.R.H. Prince George of Greece.

Hibbert, Miss. (fl. 1836–1840)

Of London. Exhibited at the R.A. and S.B.A., 1836–1840. Long suggests that she might have been the daughter of George Hibbert (1757–1837), merchant, collector and alderman of London. Her sitters included the Rt. Hon. Sir John Cowan, Bart., Lord Mayor of London, the Rt. Hon. Lord Barham, the Rt. Hon. Samuel Wilson, Lord Mayor of London and in 1840, the Lady Mayoress.

*Hibbert, J. (fl. 1807)

A miniature signed and dated '1807' was sold at Sotheby's and seen at the V. & A. M. The artist may have been related to Miss Hibbert (q.v.).

*Higgins, Miss Elsie. (fl. 1899)

Exhibited at the R.A. 1899, from Red House, Rye, Sussex.

Higginson, Mrs. Alexander. See Isaacs, Miss Martha

Higgs, R. See Higs, R.

*Higham, Miss Beatrice A. (fl. 1898–1900)

Exhibited at the R.A. 1898 and 1900, from Stratton House, Burnt Ash Road, Lee, Kent.

Higham, J. W. (fl. 1821–1835)

Worked at Norwich (1821–1822) and London. Exhibited at the R.A. and S.B.A., 1821–1835. Painted enamel miniatures, most of which were copied from oil paintings. Worked slightly in the manner of H. Bone (q.v.). Usually signed in full on the reverse 'J. W. Higham'. He executed a portrait of H. Fuseli after Moses Haughton (q.v.). Painted a large enamel copy of a self-portrait of Sir Joshua Reynolds.

Higs, or Higgs, R. (fl. 1786–1796)

Of London. Exhibited at the R.A., 1786–1796. Most of his portraits were on enamel. His address was 99 Gray's Inn Lane.

*Hill, Mrs. Diana. See Dietz, Miss Diana

Hill, J. (fl. 1775–1791)

Of London. Exhibited at the Society of Artists, 1775 and at the R.A., 1777–1791.

*Hill, Mrs. Kate E. (fl. 1897)

Exhibited at the R.A. 1897, from 29 Skell Bank, Ripon, Yorks.

*Hill, Miss Lucie M. (fl. 1903–1904)

Exhibited at the R.A. 1903 and 1904, from 12 Kensington, Bath, Somerset.

Hill, Thomas, junior. (fl. 1779)

A miniature on ivory of William Edwards by Thomas Hill, junior, 1779, is at the National Museum of Wales, Cardiff.

Hilliard, Laurence. 1581/2–1647/8

Born in London, 1581/2; the fourth of eight children born to Nicholas Hilliard (q.v.) and his wife Alice, née Brandon. Was baptised at St. Vedas, Foster Lane, on 5 March 1582. Probably began his apprenticeship under his father *c.* 1597. Finished his training as a goldsmith by 7 June 1605 when he received the freedom of the Goldsmiths' Company. Was well educated and besides being trained as a goldsmith and limner could speak Spanish. Worked for James I and Queen Anne of Denmark, and inherited his father's appointment as limner to James I. The patent was drawn up on 13 October 1608, giving him the office of 'his Majesty's limner in reversion'. He duly held this office, which carried with it an annuity of £40, on his father's death in 1619. He is known to have leased a tenement in Gutter Lane from *c.* 1612. When returning to his house in Fleet Street on 18 June 1622 he was attacked and wounded by four 'turbulent' people and as a result of this, lost the use of one of the fingers of his right hand and was unable to 'worke so exactly in the said arte as formerly he was used and accustomed to doe'. His name occurs regularly in the list of James I's payments. Miss Auerbach in her book *Nicholas Hilliard*, 1961, gives much fresh information about father and son and includes a transcript of Laurence's will which was signed on 21 February 1640. The will was proved and probate granted to his son Thomas on 8 March 1647/8, as Jane Hilliard, his wife, who was his executrix did not want to enter it. From this it would appear that Laurence died much later than has hitherto been supposed, and that the approximate date of his death was at the end of 1647 or early in 1648. He and his wife Jane had four children, Brandon, Thomas, Charles and a daughter, Lawrence. He seems to have been particularly fond of his daughter and at the end of his will, after making bequests to his family and leaving 'my most Loving wiff Jane Hillyard' his sole executrix, he ends 'Lastly I charge by all loue and kyndness that hath ever bin betwixt vs that shee shewth more loue and kyndness to myne and her Daughter Lawrence whom eu' I pray God to Bless'. The original of this will is at Somerset House. The daughter is recorded in later documents as Lawrence Rich. Hilliard painted many of the stock replicas of miniatures of James I and his Queen, and their family. Only a few signed miniatures by him have survived; these bear a Roman monogram: LH or HL. He does not seem to have attempted anything very ambitious in composition; those of his works which are known being confined to the bust only, without any attempt to portray hands. Some of his miniatures have a blue or cerise curtain background and are reminiscent of the work of his father without being comparable in quality or inspiration. The general treatment and inscriptions are similar but lack the brilliance so apparent in the works by Nicholas Hilliard. Among the outstanding miniatures by Laurence are the following – a lady wearing a wide-brimmed hat, in the V. & A. M., an unknown man of 1640, in the Fitzwilliam Museum, Cambridge, and two fine miniatures of men in the collection of Earl Beauchamp. These represent an unknown man signed 'LH' and inscribed 'Ano Dni 1636. Ætatis Svæ 37', and another signed 'LH' and inscribed 'Ano Dni 1638. Ætatis Svæ 31'. These last two miniatures were among those exhibited in Edinburgh in 1965. I have in my collection two miniatures attributed to Laurence Hilliard. One is of an unknown lady with a ladybird painted on her ruff, and formerly in the Buckingham collection at Stowe, and the other of an unknown man painted against a brilliant blue background, wearing an embroidered black doublet with a lace ruff and inscribed in gold on the background: 'Ano Dni. 1621 Ætatis suæ 74'. This miniature was once in the Morgan Williams collection when it was attributed to P. Oliver (q.v.) and reproduced in *The Connoisseur*, May 1910. It is contained in a green translucent enamel locket of the period, with groups of fruit and festoons of drapery showing through the enamel. This miniature is mentioned by Long, *British Miniaturists*, p. 210, as being 'another miniature in the Hilliard manner'. For further information on Nicholas and Laurence Hilliard and their families see *Nicholas Hilliard*, by E. Auerbach, 1961.

Hilliard, Nicholas. 1547–1619

Born in Exeter, 1547; son of Richard Hilliard (1519?–1594) an Exeter goldsmith, and his wife Laurence, née Wall, daughter of John Wall also of Exeter, and London, to whom Richard was apprenticed. Nicholas Hilliard served his apprenticeship as a goldsmith and jeweller under Robert Brandon, not under his grandfather John Wall as has always been supposed. Evidence for this is to be found in the Minutes of the Goldsmiths' Company, that on Friday 13 November 1562, the Court of the Goldsmiths' Company in London received 5s. from Robert Brandon 'for the presentment of Thomas Sammon and Nicholas Helyard, his apprentices'. Prior to this Nicholas is said to have studied the work of Holbein (q.v.), and had already tried his hand at miniature painting. Three minia-

tures exist of *c.* 1560 by him; two self-portraits and one of Edward Seymour, Duke of Somerset (possibly after Holbein). After serving seven years' apprenticeship, Hilliard became a freeman of the Goldsmiths' Company, on 29 July 1569, and took his oath. He is known to have had a number of apprentices, including John Cobbold, 1570, Gualter Reynolds, William Smyth, 1573, William Franke, 1573, John Pickerynge, 1574/5, Rowland Lockey (q.v.) 1581, his son L. Hilliard (q.v.) and I. Oliver (q.v.). Hilliard and a brother John, about whom little is known, but who became a freeman of the Goldsmiths' Company, 5 September 1569, were working together in London *c.* 1571. The date on which Hilliard was appointed Limner and Goldsmith to Queen Elizabeth is unknown, but it is possible that it was shortly after he ended his apprenticeship, as his superb rectangular miniature of the Queen, *c.* 1569 in the collection of the Duke of Portland, is his most youthful portrait of her and depicts Her Majesty dressed in robes of State, crowned, and holding the orb and sceptre. In the centre of the cross surmounting the orb is a small diamond. His earliest known dated portrait of her is that of 1572, in the N.P.G., London. On 15 July 1576 Hilliard married as his first wife, Alice the beautiful daughter of Robert Brandon, at St. Vedas, Foster Lane. His self-portrait painted in 1577 and that of Alice painted in 1578, both in the V. & A. M., show them to have been an exceptionally good-looking couple. In the autumn of 1576 they went to Paris and remained there for about two years. Sir Amyas Poulet, English Ambassador in Paris, writing on 8 December 1576 to John Peter, auditor of the Exchequer, requested financial support, because of the expense involved through 'dyuers Gentlemen recommended unto me by the Queenes Matie as Master Doctor Cesar, Mr. Throgmorton and Mr. Helyer . . .'. The Hilliards were still in Paris in February 1578 but Alice evidently returned to England before her husband, probably before the birth of their first son Daniel (baptised 16 May 1578). Several more children were born to them and were baptised as follows:— Elizabeth (4 October 1579), Francis (24 December 1580), Laurence, who followed his father's profession (5 March 1582), Lettice (25 May 1583), Penelope (31 October 1586), and Robert (30 March 1588). On 27 December 1584, a stillborn child of Nicholas Hilliard was buried. Whilst in France, Hilliard worked for the Duc d'Alençon and is thought to be the Nicholas Belliart, an English artist, mentioned in that nobleman's accounts as receiving a salary in *c.* 1577. Hilliard met some interesting people in France, including Jacques Gautier, the painter, Pierre Ronsard, the poet, Blaise de Vigenère, an eminent author and critic who was a great admirer of Hilliard, and probably Francis Bacon, who was in France, 1576–1579. Hilliard was back in England before 30 April 1579, when an indenture was made between him and Robert Brandon, who lent him money. After his return Hilliard together with Cornelius Devosse and Arnold or Arthur van Brounckhurst (q.v.), became involved in a speculation in gold mining in Scotland, details of which are recorded in *The Discoverie and Historie of the Gold Mynes in Scotland*, 1619. Hilliard apparently procured a patent to work the Crawford Moor Mines for nineteen years. The project was a financial failure, for although gold was found, the Earl of Morton, Regent for Scotland, would not allow it to leave the country. In 1581 the apprentice book of the Goldsmiths' Company contains evidence that Rowland Lockey . . . 'haue put myself prentice to Nicholas Hilliard for the terme of 8 yiers . . .'. The Hilliards lived in a house called 'Maydenhead' in Gutter Lane for 35 years; the house belonged to the Goldsmiths'

Company and the lease reverted to Hilliard on the death of its previous occupant, Nicholas Johnson, in *c.* 1578. In 1584 Hilliard was mentioned in a patent drafted in favour of George Gower, Serjeant Painter to the Queen, as being her painter for making 'purtraicts pictures or proporcons of our body and person in small compass in lymnynge only . . .'. In the same year he was commissioned to make the Queen's second Great Seal and was rewarded 'for good service' by being given lease of lands in Huntingdonshire, Lincolnshire, Yorkshire and Denbighshire, as well as the lease for 21 years of Poyne Manor, Stanmore, Middlesex. In 1594 he inherited from his father land in St. Pancras, Exeter, and the patronage of the church of St. Pancras in that city. In spite of these potential assets and influential friends such as Lord Burghley, the Earl of Leicester, Sir Robert Cecil (to whom he seems to have had special access), Sir Philip Sidney and Sir Christopher Hatton, Hilliard never resolved his financial difficulties. In 1591 the Queen rewarded him with a sum of £400 'for his good and faithful service'. In the same year Robert Brandon died and his will made no provision for Nicholas or his children. Such money as he left to Alice was to be administered by the Goldsmiths' Company; from this it is apparent that his father-in-law had lost all confidence in Nicholas and his improvident ways. Between 1598 and 1600 Hilliard petitioned the Goldsmiths' Company several times for his lease of the house in Gutter Lane to be renewed. His case was deferred each time. As Hilliard had expended some £200 on repairs to the house he was anxious to retain it. Finally through the intervention of the Queen, via the Lords of the Privy Council, a letter signed, among others, by Sir Robert Cecil, was sent to the Company requesting that Hilliard should be allowed to have the property. This request was granted on consideration of a fine of £30 (which he had difficulty in paying) and an annual rent of £3. The Goldsmiths' Company asked that in consideration of this favour Hilliard should 'make and bestowe on the Companie a faire picture in greate of her Matie to remayne in the Howse for an ornam't'. This is thought to refer to a large painting of the Queen rather than a miniature. In 1613 Hilliard's house was leased to his son Laurence for 21 years, his father having presumably moved earlier. From *c.* 1591 Hilliard was evidently working on a third Great Seal which was never completed, but for which allowances were paid up to 1609. On 17 August 1599 he was granted an annuity of £40 a year through the good offices of Sir Robert Cecil, and Hilliard wrote that the annuity would be a 'good stay and comfort to him when living with his friends in the country, at the house rent and the table free'. In *c.* 1600 Hilliard wrote his *Treatise concerning the Arte of Limning*, commissioned by Richard Haydocke, a copy of which is preserved in the library of Edinburgh University. In 1601, still in financial difficulties, Hilliard approached Sir Robert Cecil to obtain permission to 'depart the Realm for a year or two', to recoup his finances. There is no evidence that permission was granted. Only a year before Hilliard had been granted the lease of land in Lancashire. In *c.* 1601 Hilliard painted Sir Robert Cecil's portrait and asked Sir Robert to take Laurence Hilliard into his service. This request was repeated five years later after Laurence had had more experience. James I on his accession continued Queen Elizabeth's patronage and Hilliard painted a number of miniatures of the Royal Family. The date of Alice Hilliard's death is unknown, but she evidently pre-deceased her husband and there is reason for thinking that Hilliard may have married a second time although there is no proof of this. According to an entry in the Parish Register of St. Mary at

Hill, London, a 'Nicholas Hilliard married Susan Gysard' on 3 August 1608. In 1617 James I granted his 'well beloved Servant Nicholas Hilliard, gentleman, our principal Drawer for small Purtraits and Imbosser of our Medallions of Gold' a monopoly for twelve years to make, engrave, and imprint Royal portraits, with the sole right to dispose of these pictures. We know of only one engraving which he authorised to be done; this was a print of Queen Elizabeth, engraved by Francis Delaram. In the same year Hilliard was imprisoned in Ludgate for a debt due to William Pereman, a yeoman usher of the Chamber. He made his will on 24 December 1618. In it, he gave 20s to the poor of the Parish of St. Martin-in-the-Fields 'where I now dwell'; household goods to the value of £10 to my 'trustie Servannte Elizabeth Deacon my Attendant in this my sickness'; and a proportion of the arrears of his pension to his sister, Anne Avery, wife of Thomas Avery, his attorney. The residue he left to his son Laurence, whom he made his sole executor. No mention being made of a wife, it is presumed that one or both of them had pre-deceased him. He died aged 72 and was buried in St. Martin-in-the-Fields, 7 January 1619. Hilliard's method of painting is fully described in his 'Treatise' which contains advice on all the essential points to be observed in painting miniatures. He condemned the use of green or black to model the face, and explains how he painted the Queen in an 'open alley of a goodly garden, where no tree was neere nor anye shadowe at-all'. This absence of shading on the features, is one of the great differences between the work of Hilliard and that of Oliver. He painted on parchment stuck onto card (often playing cards), using opaque pigments, the colours being mixed with gum arabic. Hilliard usually painted his sitters placed three-quarters left, showing an indentation of the profile at the level of the eye. The eyes were drawn perfectly round and the eyelids with a bold curve. Unfortunately his carmines have in most cases faded, leaving the features rather mask-like. He gave great attention to detail and mastered the intricate details of lace to perfection. He often inscribed his miniatures in gold against his usual blue background, giving the sitter's age and the date of the portrait, i.e. 'Ano Dni . . . Ætatis Suæ . . .' In keeping with the popular practice in Flemish and German portraiture, he often added a symbol, or riddling motto, or placed small flowers against the corsage or doublet. His sense of poetry and delicate painting of the finery of this extravagant era ensured his success with the Elizabethans. This is illustrated in his miniature of an 'unknown man against a background of flames', and the 'unknown youth leaning against a tree among roses', etc. In his more developed style he paints the sitter's hair with more breadth and freedom, with dark curls set over a light ground. His early works were mostly circular with an occasional rectangular one; later he used an oval shape, which he favoured. He was not at his best when drawing hands and legs. Only a few of his miniatures are signed. Both self-portraits are circular and signed almost identically; that in the collection of the Duke of Portland is inscribed ' +OPERA QVEDAM IPSVS NICHOLAIS HELIARD IN ÆTATIS SVÆ 13' and signed with a monogram 'NH 1550'. The second 5 of the date has been added in different gold over the inscription which was originally 6. The second version in the collection of the Duke of Buccleuch bears a similar inscription which has probably also been altered and rewritten. The portrait of Edward Seymour, Duke of Somerset, also in the Buccleuch collection (circular) is dated '1560' and signed 'NH' (monogram). These three portraits show the influence of earlier artists such as Holbein. It is Hilliard's portrait of the young Queen Elizabeth of

c. 1569, in Robes of State, which reveals his goldsmith's training. This is particularly noticeable in his method of painting the jewels, with slightly raised blobs of paint. His style began to mature between 1571 and 1576, and his earliest known dated portrait of the Queen (1572) illustrates this second phase perfectly. The inscription: 'Anð Dni 1572. Ætatis Suæ 38' follows the shape of the upper border of the miniature which is slightly oval. On either side of the Queen's head he inscribed E and R in capital letters, each surmounted by a crown, against a blue background. His best and most prolific period spanned the years between 1572 and 1600. He executed some fine rectangular miniatures, painted against either landscapes or interiors of rooms, such as those of George Clifford, 3rd Earl of Cumberland (*c.* 1590) in the National Maritime Museum, Greenwich; Robert Dudley, Earl of Leicester (*c.* 1586); and Sir Anthony Mildmay (*c.* 1595) in the Cleveland Museum of Art, Ohio. The exhibition held at the V. & A. M., in 1947 to commemorate the 400th anniversary of Hilliard's birth did much to clarify the problem of distinguishing his miniatures from those of I. Oliver when a large number of miniatures by both artists were exhibited. Hilliard was said to have been a good crayon draughtsman and may have painted some oil portraits. Examples of his work may be seen at the V. & A. M., the N.P.G., London, the Fitzwilliam Museum, Cambridge, the National Maritime Museum, Greenwich, the Metropolitan Museum of Art, New York, the Cleveland Museum of Art, Ohio, the Nationalmuseum, Stockholm and the Nelson Gallery-Atkins Museum, Kansas City, etc. Many are in private collections such as those of H.M. the Queen, the Duke of Portland, the Duke of Buccleuch, Earl Beauchamp, the Earl of Radnor, the Duke of Rutland and many more. Van Der Doort's catalogue of the collection of Charles I, edited by Oliver Miller (*Walpole Society*, Vol. XXXVIII) gives details of 13 miniatures by Hilliard then owned by the King. Eight miniatures by him were exhibited in Edinburgh, 1965. For further information see the Exhibition Catalogue *Nicholas Hilliard and Isaac Oliver* (V. & A. M., Handbook) by Graham Reynolds, 1947, and *Nicholas Hilliard* by Erna Auerbach, 1961.

*Hills, J. (fl. 1777)
Advertised in the *Daily Advertiser*, 28 March 1777. Painted on glass and executed miniatures in water-colour and enamel.

*Hilson, Miss Jessie M. (fl. 1900–1910)
Of Jersey, C.I. Exhibited at the Society of Miniaturists, 1900–1910.

*Hinchley, Mrs. Edith M. or **Mrs. T. E. W.** or **Mrs. J. W. (Miss Edith M. Mason).** (fl. 1902–1914)
Née Edith M. Mason. Of London. Exhibited at the R.A. 1902–1914, from 55 Redcliffe Gardens, London. Married *c.* 1907 after which time she exhibited under her married name. Was a member of the Royal Society of Miniature Painters and the Royal Cambrian Academy. A miniature of Miss Joyce Lucy is in my collection, signed on the front 'EMH' and on the reverse 'Miss Joyce Lucy / of Callart / by Edith M. / Hinchley'. The portrait is painted in water-colour on paper. Her sitters also included Ratana, daughter of Khan Chner Norrarat, and Mrs. Frederick Manningham Buller.

Hincks, William. (fl. 1773–1797)
An Irish artist, born in Waterford. Was appren-

ticed to a blacksmith and taught himself art. Was working in Dublin in 1773. Exhibited there 1773–1780, at the R.A., 1781–1797 and at the Free Society of Artists, 1782. Painted oil portraits and miniatures; executed a set of drawings of the progress of linen manufacture which he engraved. Made an engraving of his portrait of William Shipley, and others. Long records seeing Hincks' miniature of William Shipley which he considered to be good.

*Hinton, G. (fl. 1841)
Exhibited at the R.A. 1841, from 22 Percival Street, Clerkenwell, an enamel of Tancred and Clorinda, after A. Kauffman (q.v.).

*Hird, Mrs. Linda H. (fl. 1910)
Of London. Exhibited at the Society of Miniaturists, 1910.

Hirst, John. (fl. *c.* 1819–1820)
Worked *c.* 1819–1820 at 1 Thomas Street, Belfast.

Hitchcock, J. (fl. 1790–1793)
Of London. Exhibited at the R.A., 1790–1793. Painted landscapes, miniatures and portraits.

Hoadley, Peter. 18th century
Son of Benjamin Hoadley (1676–1761) Bishop of Winchester and his wife Sarah Curtis (died 1743) who was a pupil of Mary Beale (q.v.). Said by Dr. G. C. Williamson to have been a miniature painter and to have died young, near Hoorn. A miniature painted on vellum, of William III and Queen Mary, signed in gold 'P.H.' is possibly by Hoadley, painted after an earlier portrait. The portrait has the appearance of having been painted by an amateur, although the costume is well executed. It is in the Mauritshuis, The Hague.

*Hoadley, Mrs. Sarah. See Curtis, Miss Sarah

*Hob, Mr. (fl. *c.* 1810)
Long records a miniature signed 'Mr Hob / portrait p / No 20 Smalle Brist.' *c.* 1810. It was painted with a soft effect.

Hobday, William Armfield. 1771–1831
Born in Birmingham 1771, son of a wealthy manufacturer. Entered the R.A. Schools, 19 November 1790 aged 18. Exhibited at the R.A. and B.I., 1794–1830. Worked in London, Bath and Bristol, where he settled in 1802/4. Returned to London *c.* 1817. Painted miniatures, water-colour portraits, large oil portrait groups, some subject pictures and speculated in a panorama. Had a fashionable clientele. He was married, and was friendly with Chinnery (q.v.) whom he met at Bristol. Lived extravagantly, and went bankrupt in 1829. Opened 'Hobday's Gallery of Modern Art' in Pall Mall. Some of his pictures were engraved. A miniature self-portrait of Hobday on paper, 1793, signed 'W. Hobday pinxt' is at the V. & A. M. Died 17 February 1831. Miniatures by Hobday of Mr. and Mrs. Bacon were loaned to the exhibition at the South Kensington Museum, 1865.

*Hobson, Cecil J. (fl. 1896–1914)
Of London. Exhibited at the R.A., 1896–1914. Undoubtedly related to Miss Mabel E. Hobson (q.v.) whose address he shared in 1896. Exhibited from 28 Lilyville Road, Fulham, 1896–1897 and 18 Dancer Road, Fulham, 1898–1900. Also exhibited from other London addresses. His sitters included Mrs. Hayes Fisher, Mrs. Wilfred Grantham, Mrs. Hazelton Curtis and the children of Mrs. Wilfred Grantham.

*Hobson, Miss Mabel E. See Hankey, Mrs. W. Lee

*Hockey, Miss Sarah. (fl. 1906–1913)
Of London. Exhibited at the R.A. 1906–1913, from various London addresses. Painted miniatures and flowers in oil.

Hodge. (fl. 1765–1775)
Of London. Exhibited at the Society of Artists and Free Society of Artists, 1765–1775.

Hodges, John William. (fl. 1842)
Working at Cowley Road, Oxford in 1842.

Hodges, William, R.A. 1744–1797
This well-known landscape painter exhibited at the R.A., B.I., etc., 1766–1794; he is recorded by Graves (S.A.) as having exhibited a miniature at the Free Society of Artists in 1768 but as it is down to 'Mr. Hodges' this could be a mistake and the artist referred to may have been Hodge (q.v.).

*Hodgson, Mr. (fl. 1774)
Of Tavistock Street, Covent Garden. Advertised in the Morning Post, 8 December 1774 as charging one to two guineas for miniatures, 4 profiles for 2s. 6d., in carved gilt frames 3s. 6d.

*Hoffay, A. A. 18th century
A miniature of an officer in a blue coat, signed in full vertically on the front 'A.A.Hoffay' was sold at Sotheby's, 25 July 1966. There was blue shading on the face and it was painted with long brush strokes.

Hogarth, William. 1697–1764
This well-known painter is not usually regarded as a miniaturist, but J. J. Foster reproduced, on Pl. XXX of his British Miniature Painters, 1898, a miniature portrait of Handel attributed to Hogarth, and mentions a miniature of Sir R. Walpole, which was also ascribed to him. A miniature of an unknown girl at a looking glass, ascribed to Hogarth, from the collection of Earl Beauchamp was exhibited in Edinburgh, 1965. The V. & A. M. has an oil sketch also said to be by him.

*Hogg, Mrs. Edith Browning. (fl. 1905–1914)
Of Blackburn and Dewsbury. Exhibited at the R.A., 1905–1914. Her sitters included the Right Rev. Bishop Thornton, D.D., Vicar of Blackburn.

*Hogge, Miss Muriel R. (fl. 1905–1912)
Of London and Newbury, Berks. Exhibited at the R.A., 1905 and 1912.

Hoit, Albert Gallatin. 1809–1856
Born in Sandwich, New Hampshire, 13 December 1809; graduated at Dartmouth College, U.S.A. Painted principally oil portraits, but also executed miniatures, including a self-portrait on ivory in 1838. Was in Europe, 1842–1844 and may have worked in Britain. Returned to the U.S.A. and worked in Boston until his death, 18 December 1856.

Holbein, Hans, the younger. 1497/8–1543
Born in Augsburg; son of Hans Holbein the Elder, by whom he was almost certainly taught to paint. In 1514 he and his brother Ambrose went to Basle where he remained until 1526, designing title-pages and book illustrations, besides painting frescoes and pictures. Became a citizen of Basle, 1520. Formed a friendship with Erasmus who gave him letters of introduction to Sir Thomas More when Holbein set off for England in 1526. Holbein went by way of Antwerp and, on arrival in England, was entertained by Sir Thomas More at his house in Chelsea. Was introduced to Henry VIII and his Court. Returned to Basle in 1528 where he had left

his wife and family. His wife was reputed to be the widow of a master tanner and, according to Vertue, had a 'froward temper'. By 1531 Holbein was back in England where he soon obtained many patrons. Said to have been taught limning by Lucas Horenbout (q.v.) and to have begun to paint miniatures at this period. He is always considered the 'Father of the art'. He was a versatile artist and besides the activities already mentioned also executed designs for architecture and jewellery. His name does not appear in the Crown accounts before 1536 and it is not known at what precise date he entered the King's service. In 1539 Holbein was sent to Holland to paint Anne of Cleves. This historic portrait is now in the Louvre. The superb miniature (still contained in its turned ivory box) which is a replica of the upper part of the portrait, is in the V. & A. M. together with the miniature of Mrs. Pemberton. These are two of his masterpieces. Of his family life we know little. His large portrait of his wife and two children, said to have been painted before 1529, portrays them with unhappy expressions. Henry VIII was impressed with Holbein's genius and gave him accommodation in the Palace, a salary of 200 florins as well as payment for any pictures he painted, and provided him with a workshop in Whitehall Palace. A fine set of portrait drawings is in the collection of H.M. the Queen at Windsor, and from these some of his paintings have been identified. He was undoubtedly one of the greatest artists of all times, and has been widely copied both in large and small portraits as well as in miniature; this has made attributions difficult. Of all the miniatures said to be by Holbein, only sixteen are at present accepted as authentic. They include: Mrs. Pemberton and Anne of Cleves (both in the V. & A M.), Lady Audley, Henry Brandon and Charles Brandon (in the collection of H.M. the Queen), Thomas Wriothesley (in the Metropolitan Museum, New York). A young man (in the collection of H.M. the Queen of the Netherlands), A Man aged 24 in 1543 (Stadt Museum, Danzig), two miniatures said to represent Queen Catherine Howard (one in the collection of H.M. the Queen, the other in the collection of the Duke of Buccleuch), a Man with initials H. M. aged 27 (National Museum, Munich), and Lord Abergavenny (collection of the Duke of Buccleuch). The question as to whether either or both of the self-portraits (one in the Wallace Collection and the other in the Buccleuch Collection) are by Holbein is still a matter of dispute. The late Carl Winter in an article in the Burlington Magazine, November 1943 says 'As for the portraits of Holbein, dated 1543, the common preference for the Wallace version (the other being in the collection of the Duke of Buccleuch) is founded upon real superiority. It is far from impossible that it is by Holbein himself . . . On the other hand, the assumption cannot be excluded that, together with several similar versions, the Wallace miniature may be, as Ganz maintains, a very early memorial portrait painted by another hand'. Holbein had already painted small round oil portraits before leaving Holland which may have been the forerunners of his miniatures. These latter were painted against blue backgrounds on thin parchment or card; they are round, but not always true circles; the one of Thomas Wriothesley having been cut to an oval form at a later date; the backgrounds are relieved by clear inscriptions in letters of pure gold, giving the date and sometimes the age of the sitter. Little shading is used and the whole painting is in perfect harmony, the hair and features being neatly painted in clear outline, one's eye being directed to the face of the sitter. He painted with opaque colours, which were probably mixed with gum. His 'so-called' self-portraits are both inscribed and dated 'HH / AᵒN 1543 ETATGIS SUÆ 45'. Holbein made his will 7

October 1543 and was buried 29 November 1543 at St. Andrew, Undershaft, London. For further information see Holbein, by P. Ganz, 1956 edition, English Portrait Miniatures by G. Reynolds, 1952, and Artists of the Tudor Court, 1983.

Holder, Miss Louisa Jane. (fl. 1830–1843)
Was awarded premiums from the Society of Arts in 1830 and 1832. Exhibited at the R.A., 1843. A miniature of a man c. 1840 had on the reverse a printed card describing the artist as 'miniature painter and teacher of drawing' and giving her address as 13 Pultney Street, Golden Square. Schidlof says that the miniature catalogued in the C. J. Wawra sale at Vienna 1913, and signed 'Holder p. 1844' was by J. M. Holder (1796–1861), a German artist who did not work in Britain.

*Holland, Miss Ada R. (Mrs. Sachs). (fl. 1888–1908)
Of London. Exhibited at the R.A., N.W.C.S., etc. 1888–1908, from Rossetti Studios, Chelsea. Painted miniatures, portraits and subjects in oil. Her sitters included Edwin Sachs, Esq., possibly her husband.

*Holland, Miss Esme. (fl. 1909–1910)
Of London. Exhibited at the Society of Miniaturists, 1909–1910.

*Holland, Sir Nathaniel Dance. See Dance, Nathaniel, R.A.

Holland, Peter. b. 1757 – c. 1812
Born in 1757. Entered the R.A. Schools, 8 October 1779 aged '22 yrs 1st March last'. May have been a pupil of Samuel Finney (q.v.) from whose address he exhibited at the R.A., in 1781 and 1782. Holland was still living in London in 1784 but had moved to Liverpool by 1787 and exhibited at the Society for Promoting Painting and Design in Liverpool. Painted landscapes and portraits as well as miniatures and exhibited at the R.A. in 1793 from Liverpool. Became the first Vice-President of the Liverpool Academy in 1810 and exhibited there in 1812 in which year he ceased to be a member.

Holland, William Langford. (fl. 1774–1787)
Was a pupil of the Dublin Society Drawing Schools where he won prizes in 1774 and 1776 obtaining a medal in 1779. He exhibited three crayon drawings at the Society of Artists, William Street, Dublin in 1777. Holland worked for some time at 12 Suffolk Street, Dublin, painting miniatures in profile and water-colour portraits on glass backed with white satin, for which he charged 7s. In 1786 he advertised his charge as being from one to five guineas per portrait. Some of his silhouettes have his trade label on the back. In 1787 he was working in Kilkenny as a 'Miniature painter in profile à la Marlborough'.

Hollar, Wenceslaus. 1607–1677
Born at Prague on 13 July 1607, the son of a court official. He studied engraving at Frankfurt c. 1627–1629 under a topographical engraver by the name of M. Merian. In 1629 Hollar went to Strasbourg where he remained until 1632, when he went to Cologne. He became known to Thomas Howard, 2nd Earl of Arundel, with whom he travelled and in 1636 came with him to London. Hollar was captured by Parliamentarians at the siege of Basing House, but later escaped and by 1644 was living in Antwerp. By 1652 he was back in London, but travelling evidently appealed to him and in 1668 he accompanied an expedition to Tangier. He is best known for his etchings and engravings which included landscapes and portraits, one of his best

567

.known works being the illustration of Thoroton's *Antiquities of Nottinghamshire* published in 1677. The only known miniature by Hollar is that of Margaret Roper, daughter of Sir Thomas More, probably copied from a portrait by Holbein; this is in the collection of H.M. the Queen at Windsor.

*Hollingdale, Richard. (fl. 1850–1899)

Of London and Strood, Kent. Exhibited at the R.A., B.I., etc., 1850–1899. Painted subject pictures and miniatures. His sitters included Miss Violet Dewey and Marshall Dewey, Esq.

Hollins, John, A.R.A. 1798–1855

Born in Birmingham, 1 June 1798, son of a glass painter. Exhibited at the R.A. and B.I., etc., 1819–1855. Went to London in 1822 and to Italy 1825, returning in 1827. Painted portraits in oil, subjects from the poets, etc., water-colour landscapes and miniatures. Was elected A.R.A., 1842. Died unmarried, in Berners Street, London, 7 March 1855.

*Hollis, Miss Julia. (fl. 1906–1911)

Of London. Exhibited at the R.A. 1906–1911, from 16 Frognal Mansions, Hampstead.

*Hollway, Miss Janet. (fl. 1887–1897)

Of London. Exhibited at the R.A. and N.W.C.S., 1887–1897.

*Holman, Miss Agnes Gladys. (fl. 1910)

Of Manchester and London. Exhibited at the Society of Miniaturists, 1910.

*Holme, Miss Dora. (fl. 1899–1905)

Exhibited at the R.A. 1899–1905, from Red House, Bexley Heath, Kent and from Upton Grey House, Winchfield, Hants. Her sitters included the Viscountess Hayashi.

Holmes, James. 1777–1860

Son of a dealer in precious stones of Clerkwell. According to Schidlof, Holmes was born at Burslem, Staffordshire. Showed early aptitude for art and when young was apprenticed to R. M. Meadows, an engraver. Learnt French from a refugee. Entered the R.A. Schools, 19 March 1796 aged 19½. Exhibited at the R.A., B.I., O.W.C.S., N.W.C.S., etc., from 1798–1849. Was a member of the O.W.C.S., from 1813–1821 having joined the Associated Artists in Water-Colours, 1809. In 1824 he was one of the founder members of the Society of British Artists, becoming its President in 1829. Numbered among his friends, T. Heaphy (q.v.), W. Westall, R. Westall, as well as Beau Brummell (q.v.). Taught drawing at Worcester and London; painted water-colour figure subjects, miniatures, pictures in oil, and was also an engraver and lithographer. Knew Byron whom he painted, and was asked to join him in Italy to paint his daughter. Was musical and was patronised by George IV whose portrait he painted and who often invited him to the Court to play music and sing. Was financially successful but was ruined by being security for a firm which failed in 1846. His wife died in 1853 and he spent some of his remaining years in Shropshire. Died in London, 24 February 1860. Holmes used a lot of gum with his paints; his miniatures are well drawn and expressive. His signature varied, and was J.H. followed by a date, J. Holmes, or Jˢ Holmes Pt, also dated. Occasionally the miniatures were signed and dated with an address on the reverse. James Holmes, jun. (q.v.) was presumably his son. A miniature of Byron signed 'J.H. 1816', said to have been painted on 12 April 1816, was loaned to the exhibition at the South Kensington Museum, 1865. The B.M. has engraved portraits after Holmes, and the N.P.G. has an oil portrait by him.

Holmes, James, junior. (fl. 1836–1859)

Of London. Presumably a son of James Holmes (q.v.). Exhibited at the R.A., B.I., and S.B.A., 1836–1859. Painted figure subjects etc., and miniatures, including one of Miss E. E. Kendrick (q.v.). Long noted a miniature signed on the reverse 'J. Holmes Jun / Pinxit 1846'; it was well painted. The highlights were obtained by the use of a scraper and opaque white; rather laboured stippled brown shading was used on the face.

*Holroyd, John Newman. (fl. 1903–1905)

Of Newport, Isle of Wight. Exhibited at the Society of Miniaturists, 1903–1905.

*Holt, Miss Margaret. (fl. 1902)

Of London. Exhibited at the Society of Miniaturists, 1902.

*Home, Robert. 1752–1834

Born in Hull, 6 August 1752, third, but eldest surviving child of a family of eight children born to Robert Boyne Home, an army surgeon, and his wife Mary, née Hutchinson, whose father Colonel Hutchinson was Governor of St. Helena. Determined to avoid becoming a doctor, as his parents wished, Home ran away when he was about twelve years old and became a stowaway on board a whaler which was bound for Newfoundland. Was put off when the ship reached Newfoundland about eighteen months later, due to illness. In December 1767 Robert Home returned to his family who were living in London. He developed an aptitude for drawing and assisted his brother-in-law, Dr. John Hunter, with anatomical diagrams. Came under the influence of Angelica Kauffman (q.v.) who gave him some instruction and encouraged him to continue with art. Settled in London for a time. Exhibited portraits and mythological subjects at the R.A., 1770–1813. In 1773 he visited Paris and Florence en route to Rome where he remained studying until 1778. Returned to London where he hoped to establish himself as a portrait painter, but after two years left for Dublin under the patronage of Lord Lifford, Chancellor of Ireland. Exhibited at the Artists' Exhibition in Dublin in 1780. On 8 September 1783 married Susanna, the eldest daughter of Solomon Delane. Met John O'Keeffe, the landscape painter. Was commissioned by Trinity College to paint a series of eight portraits for the new theatre. The arrival of Gilbert Stuart in Dublin seriously affected Home's practice and this, coupled with his wife's ill health, made him decide to return to London in 1789. In the following year his wife died of consumption leaving him with four sons and a daughter. According to family information, he left England in 1790 for India, without having obtained the East India Company's permission. He arrived in Madras in January 1791. Home obtained the address of John Smart (q.v.) who was living in Madras. Smart painted a miniature of Home, which is signed and dated '1791.1'. Met William Hickey who employed him to make a copy of a portrait by Romney; accompanied the troops in Lord Cornwallis's campaign, 1792, and made numerous sketches of the country which were engraved and published in London in 1794 under the title *Selected Views in Mysore*. Went to Calcutta in 1795 where he met and married an old friend of the family, Miss Anna Alicia Patterson. The ceremony took place on 17 September 1795 at the home of his lifelong friend James Colvin who had married in 1786, his wife's sister Maria Margaret Patterson. In 1814 he went to Lucknow to take up his appoint-

ment as Portrait Painter to the Nawab of Oudh. After the death of his second wife on 17 August 1817, his daughter Anne Walker, whose husband John Walker had died after a fall from a horse soon after the birth of their daughter Jean, left England accompanied by Jean, to look after her father. In 1828 when about 75 years of age, Home resigned his appointment at Lucknow and the family moved to Cawnpore. Anne Walker died in 1829 after a period of ill health, to the great grief of her father. Of his sons, Robert, John and Richard all obtained commissions in the East India Company. In spite of the fact that Home had the full use of only one arm, due to damage to the elbow joint, after an attack of measles, his work was not impaired by this disability. Although he is best known as a portrait and subject painter he certainly executed miniatures. Evidence that he was still painting miniatures in India is to be found in his family papers, where his 'fine Miniature cabinet, a beautiful piece of furniture' is described. It is still in the possession of the family. A miniature of Sir Edward Paget, by him, is in the N.P.G. This is at present the only known example of his work in miniature. Home had a distinguished clientele, including Lord Cornwallis, the Marquess of Hastings, the Duke of Wellington, Sir Eyre Coote, and many more. One of his best known pictures is 'The Delivery of Tippoo Sahib's two sons as hostages to Lord Cornwallis' painted in Madras in 1797. He continued to paint up to the end of his life, and died on 12 September 1834. He was buried with his daughter in the cemetery in Cawnpore. Many of his works were engraved. A general account of his life and work, together with a list of many of his portraits, is to be found in Strickland's *Dictionary of Irish Artists*, pp. 500–508. Further information is in the *Walpole Society*, Vol. XIX, pp. 42–49. I am indebted to his great-great-grandson, Mr. E. P. John Westby, for allowing me access to an unpublished biography of Home by Ella B. Day, his great-granddaughter.

Hone, Horace, A.R.A. 1754/6–1825

Born in Frith Street, London; second son of N. Hone (q.v.) by whom he was taught art. Entered the R.A. Schools, 19 October 1770 when his age was noted as '17 Feb 11th next' making his date of birth 1754, not 1756 as previously recorded. Exhibited at the R.A., 1772–1822 and was elected A.R.A. in 1779. Went to Ireland in 1782 and had a successful practice in Dublin, living in Dorset Street. Became miniature painter to the Prince of Wales in 1795. His practice declined after the Union of England and Ireland, and he returned to England and settled in London in 1804. Worked in Bath in the same year. Was friendly with Farington who mentions him in his Diary. Hone suffered from mental ill health from as early as 1807. He was married and had a daughter Sophia Matilda who died unmarried. Hone died at 20 Dover Street, London on 24 May 1825 and was buried in the grounds of St. George's Chapel, Bayswater Road. He was a good artist who painted in water-colour and enamel besides executing engravings. He had a distinguished clientele which included Mrs. Siddons, the 4th Duke of Rutland, Lord Albemarle, the 1st Earl of Charlement, the Duchess of Buckingham and Lord Edward FitzGerald, etc. Hone's style of painting varies a great deal; it is usually elegant and his miniatures of ladies are attractive and well posed. He painted the eyelashes distinctly, and frequently used a good deal of stippling to model and shade the face. The eyes of his sitters are often rather dark. One of his finest and largest enamels is that of Mrs. Elizabeth Prentice, wife of Thomas Prentice of Dublin. It is fully inscribed on the reverse and signed and dated '1807'. It is in the collection of E. G. Paine of New York. His usual signature is HH in monogram, three sloping lines crossed by a horizontal one, this is often followed by a date. A self-portrait is in the N.P.G., and another is in the N.G., Dublin. I know of two identical miniatures of Mrs. Siddons, both signed and dated '1784'; one is in the N.G., Dublin and the other was sold at Sotheby's, 19 June 1967 for £650. Examples of his work are in the V. & A. M. and the Fitzwilliam Museum, Cambridge. The B.M. has engraved portraits after Hone. Two good miniatures by him were exhibited in Edinburgh in 1965; George Saville, jun., signed and dated 'HH 1782' from the collection of Earl Beauchamp, and one of Edward Gibbon signed and dated 'HH 1785' from the collection of J. B. Robertson.

Hone, John Camillus. 1759–1836

Was born in 1759. A younger son of N. Hone (q.v.) and a pupil of his father. Exhibited at the Free Society of Artists and the R.A., 1775–1780. Worked in India from c. 1780–1790 and was teaching drawing in Calcutta in April 1785. He returned home c. 1790 and settled in Dublin, where he was given the appointment of 'Engraver of Dies' in the Stamp Office, by the Lord Lieutenant, the Earl of Westmorland. In 1809 he exhibited three oil portraits at an exhibition in Hawkins Street, but did not exhibit again elsewhere. In October 1807 he married his cousin, Abigail, daughter of Joseph Hone of York Street and widow of the Rev. John Conolly of York Street. Hone painted miniatures and oil portraits. He died at his house in Summerhill, Dublin, on 23 May 1836 and was survived by his widow who was said to have been 103 when she died, 4 February 1855. An oil portrait of him at the age of nine, by his father, is in the N.G., Dublin. It was engraved by W. Baillie in 1771.

Hone, Nathaniel, R.A. 1718–1784

Was born in Dublin on 24 April 1718, the third son of Nathaniel Hone of Wood Quay, a merchant, and his wife Rebeckah, daughter of Samuel Brindley. Hone came to England as a young man and practised as an itinerant portrait painter. He married in February 1742 at York Minster, Mary Earle, about whom there appears to have been some mystery. The lady was in receipt of an annuity from an unknown member of the nobility upon whom she had some claim. She was presumably either the Lord's illegitimate daughter or, according to *The Diary of Sylas Neville*, edited by B. Cozens-Hardy 'some Lord's cast-off mistress', whom Hone is said to have married for £200 a year. She died in 1769 and Hone later married a second time and his widow survived him. Hone settled in London for a time. In 1750 he went to study in Rome and in 1752 became a member of the Academy at Florence. It was about this time that he became acquainted with Sir Joshua Reynolds, who was also in Italy, and it has been suggested that a feud sprang up between the two men which later culminated in a dispute between Hone and the Royal Academy. He returned to England in 1752 and lived in Henrietta Street, Covent Garden. He went to Dublin on 24 July 1752 and visited Paris on 3 August 1753 in which year he was living in Frith Street, London. Exhibited at the Society of Artists, 1760–1768 and was one of its earliest members. In 1769 Hone became a founder member of the R.A., and exhibited there, 1769–1784. In 1775 he sent his picture 'The Conjurer' to the R.A., where it was taken to be a satirical caricature of Angelica Kauffmann (q.v.) and Sir Joshua Reynolds. The picture was refused by the Council of the Academy. Hone later arranged

exhibitions of his own work in St. Martin's Lane, where this controversial painting was exhibited. Said to have been extravagant on pleasure and personal adornment. J. T. Smith, in his *Life of Nollekens*, describes Hone as a 'tall upright, large man, with a broad-brimmed hat and a lapelled coat buttoned up to his neck'. He painted oil portraits, and miniatures on ivory and in enamel, besides executing some etchings and mezzotints. A number of self-portraits are listed by Strickland, together with lists of other portraits by Hone. He died at 44 Rathbone Place, London, on 14 August 1784 and was buried in Hendon Churchyard. The death of his widow at Hendon was announced in the *Dublin Chronicle*, 15 February 1791. Hone had ten children, including John Camillus Hone (q.v.) and Horace Hone (q.v.), Nathaniel, a Captain in the Wiltshire Militia, Samuel and Apelles, who died young, Lydia, died 1773 aged 15, Amelia, married Ambrose Rigg, Mary, married Dr. Metcalfe, and Sophia and Floreth, who died young. A large collection of Hone's prints and drawings was sold by auction in February 1785. John Plott (q.v.) was a pupil and assistant of Hone. His earliest known miniature is in a private collection and is signed in full 'N. Hone' and dated 1747. His miniatures are usually small and well painted, many of them being set into bracelets. He generally signed with a simple monogram NH, in which the last stroke of the N forms the first stroke of the H; most of his miniatures are dated, his latest known ones being 1770, after which he appears to have given up miniature painting. Hone painted the lace on his sitters' costume with opaque white, occasionally he shaded the faces of his male sitters with soft diagonal hatching. He charged an average of ten guineas for a miniature. Works by him are frequently seen in the sale rooms and in private collections. Examples of his work are in the V. & A. M., the N.P.G. (who have a self-portrait on enamel), the B.M. the Fitzwilliam Museum, Cambridge, the Ashmolean Museum, Oxford, the N.G., Dublin (an oil self-portrait) and many other collections. Examples of his miniatures were exhibited in Edinburgh in 1965 and at the South Kensington Museum, 1865.

Honthorst, Gerard van. 1590–1656

Born in Utrecht, 4 November 1590. Was a pupil of A. Bloemaert. Worked for some years in Rome and was in England from 5 April 1628 – 8 December 1628, during which time he painted portraits of Charles I and his Queen. Famous as a painter of portraits and figure subjects. Not known as a miniaturist with the exception of an oil miniature on copper which was catalogued as by him when it was sold in Berlin in November 1909. Died in Utrecht, 27 April 1656.

Hood, Isaac. See Whood

Hook, Mrs. Eliza. (fl. 1773–1786)

Of London. Exhibited at the Society of Artists, 1773–1775 and at the R.A., 1777–1786. The exhibits included a portrait of a lady in the character of Flora, and miniatures in rings.

*Hooper, Miss Irene. (fl. 1908–1911)

Of London. Exhibited at the R.A. 1908–1911, from 15 Shepherd Street, Mayfair.

*Hoorne, Mrs. (fl. 1776)

Exhibited five miniatures at the Society of Artists from Mr. Picot's, 16 Strand, in 1776.

*Hope, E. (fl. 1868)

Of London. Said by Graves to have exhibited a miniature in 1868.

Hope, Lancelot. (fl. 1815–1822)

Worked in Liverpool c. 1822. Two miniatures seen by Long had a printed trade card on the back which read 'LANCELOT HOPE / Portrait and Miniature Painter, / Respectfully informs the inhabitants of Liverpool and (the) / vicinity . . .' The advertisement goes on to say that Hope would attend parties at private houses without any extra charge, 'Liverpool, 29th July 1822'. Long did not consider the miniatures to be of any great merit. Five miniatures of the Bainbridge family, painted by Hope in 1815, were sold at Sotheby's, 6 November 1967. One of Henry Bainbridge is in the collection of R. Bayne Powell, Esq. It is inscribed on the reverse 'Henry Bainbridge / 1815 by Hope'. The modelling is good and the work expressive. The brushwork is rather loose.

*Hopkins, Miss Beatrice. (fl. 1909)

Exhibited at the R.A. 1909, from Dornie, Westward-Ho, North Devon. The exhibit was of Miss Dorothy Hopkins.

Hopkins, J. (fl. 1791–1809)

Of London and Dublin (1800). Exhibited at the R.A. 1791–1809, and in Dublin, 1800. Returned to London in 1802. Painted portraits, landscapes etc., in oil and water-colour. According to a MS seen by Long his widow died in May 1835 in distressed circumstances; Constable took an interest in her. Several engraved portraits after Hopkins are at the B.M.

Hopkins, Thomas. d. 1794

Painted enamels and executed engravings. Schidlof and Benezit note that he was a pupil of H. Bone (q.v.). Died in London, 4 August 1794.

*Hopley, Edward William John. (fl. 1844–1869)

Of London. Exhibited at the R.A., B.I., etc., 1844–1869. Painted allegorical subjects and portraits. In 1860 he exhibited a miniature entitled 'Sappho' at the R.A.

Horenbolt. See Horenbout

Horenbout, Horenbolt or Hornebolte, Gerard. d. c. 1540

Son of Willem Horenbolt, of Ghent, whose family had been established as artists there for some generations. Gerard was admitted to full membership of the Guild of St. Luke at Ghent in 1487. Was made court painter to Margaret of Austria, Regent of the Netherlands, in 1515. He was best known for his miniatures in Books of Hours and other illuminated manuscripts, and was responsible for sixteen illuminations in the Sforza Book of Hours (for which he received payment in 1521) and for works in other books of this kind. He also painted altar-pieces, portraits and executed designs for vestments, tapestries and stained-glass windows. Horenbout married Margarethe de Vandere (or Swanders) (died 26 January 1529), by whom he had Susanna and Lucas Horenbout (q.v.). Met Albrecht Dürer in May 1521 when he and his daughter Susanna were in Antwerp; Dürer purchased a miniature from Susanna and considered it to be a remarkable achievement for a girl of 18. The family came to England c. 1522, but Gerard's name does not appear in the Royal household accounts of Henry VIII before October 1528 and occurs up to 1531, after which time it is believed he returned to Ghent, where he died c. 1540. For further information see *Gerard and Lucas Horenbout in England*, by Hugh Paget, in the *Burlington Magazine*, November 1959, pp. 396–402.

Horenbout, Horenbolt or Hornebolte, Lucas. c. 1490/5 – 1544

Son of Gerard Horenbout of Ghent (q.v.) and

brother of Susanna Horenbout (q.v.). Was employed by Henry VIII from 1525 until his death. His name is first recorded in the Royal household accounts together with that of his father in October 1528. He is alleged to have taught Holbein (q.v.) the art of miniature painting; it is now generally accepted that the earliest known miniatures painted in England are probably the work of this artist. Three miniatures of Henry VIII, two in the collection of H.M. the Queen, and the other at the Fitzwilliam Museum, Cambridge, are now considered to be the work of Horenbout. Mr. Hugh Paget gives much valuable information about the family in an article published in the *Burlington Magazine*, 1959. A miniature of Lady Jane Seymour, third wife of Henry VIII painted in her 25th year and formerly attributed to Holbein, was sold for 3,800 guineas at Christie's on 25 July 1967, when it was re-attributed to Horenbout by Graham Reynolds. One of the miniatures of Henry VIII from the Royal collection was exhibited in Edinburgh in 1965; it is inscribed 'H.R.VIII AN° ETATIS XXXV°' executed on vellum, 1¾ in. diameter and showing the King wearing a beard; the other version, in the Royal collection, and the one at the Fitzwilliam Museum show him without a beard. In 1978 and 1983 a small collection of miniatures was assembled at the Victoria and Albert Museum for inspection, and on the basis of style and technique a number were attributed with some confidence to Hornebolte.

Horenbout, Horenbolt or Hornebolte, Susanna. 1503–1545

Daughter of Gerard Horenbout of Ghent (q.v.) and sister of Lucas Horenbout (q.v.). Came with her parents to England during the reign of Henry VIII c. 1522. Was taught limning by her father and is said to have practised the art in England where she settled, and later married an Englishman. Her work was admired by Dürer. Her husband's name is given as either John Parker, or Worsley, a sculptor who may have been a second husband. She is said to have been rich and well thought of when she died in Worcester in 1545.

Hornblower, Joshua. (fl. 1793–1795)

Was working at Bath Street, Birmingham in 1793 and 1795.

Hornsby, W. (fl. 1821)

Of London. Exhibited at the R.A. 1821, from 1 Lancaster Street, Burton Crescent.

*Horrak, John or T. (fl. 1862)

Exhibited at the R.A. 1862, from 14 Pall Mall, portraits of Mr. John Scott and Mr. Dominic Colnaghi. Was possibly identical with T. Horrak who exhibited at the R.A., 1858 (no address given). The exhibits were studies and sketches, some of which were in the drawing and miniature section.

*Horrell, Mrs. Nora. (fl. 1910–1914)

Of Worthing. Exhibited at the R.A., 1910 and 1914.

*Horsford, Miss Olive. (fl. 1907–1914)

Of London. Exhibited at the R.A. and S.M. 1907–1914, from addresses in South Hampstead. One of her exhibits was of Mrs. S. L. Horsford.

Horsley, T. J. (Thomas?). b. 1755?

Of London. Exhibited at the R.A., 1820–1833. Possibly identical with Thomas Horsley who entered the R.A. Schools 8 April 1778 aged '24 Nov. 2 next'; the entry in the Council Minutes gives the name as J. Horsley. A miniature of Miss C. Byrne, signed on the reverse 'T. J Horsley pinx t/

Jany 1829' was sold at Sotheby's in 1966. It was reminiscent of the work of F. Buck (q.v.) but less florid. A self-portrait of the artist is in the N.G., Sydney. His work is slightly reminiscent of that of W. J. Newton (q.v.).

*Horsley, Colonel Walter Charles, C.B. d. 1934

Long recorded that the above artist, who was an officer in the Artists Rifles, exhibited a watercolour portrait in 1875.

*Horwitz, Emmanuel (Henry?). (fl. 1901–1914)

Of London. Exhibited at the R.A. 1901–1914, from 45 Roland Gardens. Exhibited miniatures, portraits, and subjects in oil and water-colour. Undoubtedly related to Helena Horwitz (q.v.) as both artists exhibited from the above address in 1911 and also related to Louise Horwitz (q.v.). Was probably identical with Emmanuel Henry Horwitz (died after 1934) who exhibited at the N.W.C.S., etc., from 1886–1890.

*Horwitz, Miss Helena. (fl. 1889–1913)

Of London. Exhibited at the R.A., 1889–1913. Undoubtedly related to Miss Louise B. Horwitz (q.v.) and Emmanuel Horwitz (q.v.) who exhibited from the same address in 1911. Painted miniatures, subjects and portraits in water-colour.

*Horwitz, Miss Louise B. (fl. 1892–1914)

Of London. Exhibited at the R.A., 1892–1914. Undoubtedly related to Miss Helena Horwitz (q.v.) whose address, 13 Grazebrook Road, Clissold Park, she shared.

*Hosein, Nazeer. (fl. 1901)

Of Delhi and London. Exhibited at the Society of Miniaturists, 1901.

Hoskins, John, d. 1664/5

No information is available about the above artist's date of birth or parentage. His earliest known miniatures date from c. 1620 suggesting that he must have been born before the end of the 16th century. The approximate date of c. 1595 is a possibility, allowing time for his apprenticeship and practice in oil painting before he started painting miniatures. It is known that he had a son named John, who may have painted miniatures, or assisted his father with his work. For many years attempts were made to distinguish between the work of the two men on grounds of style, but this proved too difficult and although they may both have been artists, without any corroborative evidence it is impossible to distinguish between them. For the present therefore, all works attributed to Hoskins are taken to refer to John Hoskins, sen. John Hoskins, jun., is named in his father's will, and W. Sanderson, in his treatise *Graphice* published in 1658 says 'For Miniature or Limning, in watercolours, Hoskins, and his son, the next modern since the Hilliards, father and son'. Vertue also assumed that there was an elder and a younger Hoskins, and early collections often contain lists of portraits attributed to one or other of these men. Hoskins' sister was Barbara Cooper and Alexander Cooper (q.v.) and Samuel Cooper (q.v.) were her sons. According to tradition these boys were 'bred up under the care of Mr. Hoskins'. In the appendix to De Piles' *The Art of Painting*, published in 1706, Hoskins is referred to as 'a very eminent limner in the reign of King Charles I, whom he drew with his Queen, and most of his court. He was bred a face-painter in oil but afterwards taking to miniature he far exceeded what he did before. He died in Covent Garden about 40 years ago.' The earliest miniatures signed I.H. are datable by costume to the years

between 1620–1625. The Duke of Portland has an invoice stating that on 16 July 1626 John Holles, 1st Earl of Clare, paid £14 'to Hoskins ye picture drawer for 2 pictures in little'. He was known to Constantine Huygens, the famous Dutch poet and statesman, and mentioned by John Aubrey with reference to Bishop Overall's wife 'the greatest beautie of her time in England. That it was so I have attested from the famous limner Mr. Hoskins...' Hoskins was a friend of Cornelius Johnson (q.v.) to whom he gave a miniature of George Villiers, Duke of Buckingham. This was sold at Sotheby's in 1925 in the Weardale collection. It was inscribed on the reverse 'Hoskins drawn by himself & by him given to Old Johnson, yᵉ painter of whose son I bought it at Utrecht, 1700 F.St.J.' The date and reason for Alexander Cooper and his brother Samuel being taken into the care of their uncle is not known. By c. 1631 Alexander had gone to Holland but Samuel was still with Hoskins up to 1634/5 when Sir Theodore Turquet de Mayerne records visiting him. He described Hoskins method of painting and how he kept his colours in small turned ivory dishes to prevent them from drying up (B.M. — MS Sloane 2052, folios 29, 77, 149 verso). The possibility that Hoskins went to France is suggested by the fact that a miniature by 'old Hoskins' of 'The French King' was Lot 55 at the sale of Richard Graham's collection, 6 March 1711/12. Charles I appointed Hoskins his limner on 20 April 1640 and granted him a life annuity of £200 'providing that he work not for any other without his Majesty's licence'. How often this permission was obtained we do not know, but as he only received one instalment of £50 it is not surprising that he had to depend on a wider circle of sitters for his livelihood. In 1660 he petitioned for payment 'out of some delinquent's estate', of £4,150 arrears of the £200 a year pension, from which he had received no benefit since 1640. The date on which S. Cooper left his uncle is not known. Hoskins is reputed to have become jealous of his nephew's success, and according to De Piles 'finding that the court were better pleas'd with his nephew's performances than with his, he took him in partner with him; but still seeing Mr Cooper's pictures were more relished, he was pleas'd to dismiss the partnership'. From 1644–1645 Hoskins began to sign his works I.H. in separate bold letters, and as Cooper was well established by this time, and signing his miniatures in a similar way, the older man may have changed his style in order to compete with Cooper. J. J. Foster in *Samuel Cooper and The English Miniature Painters of the XVII Century*, pp. 7–8, gives a summary of Hoskins' will, which he made on 30 December 1662 in the Parish of St. Paul's, Covent Garden, when he was 'weak in body but of good and perfect memory.' He appointed his wife Sarah sole executrix, and bequeathed £20 to his son John (who was married and had a daughter called Mary) 'to purchase a ring or to be expended as otherwise he should think fit'. According to Foster, on 15 February 1664 a memorandum was appended 'relating to the will of John Hoskins the elder, limner of Bedford Street' confirming the disposition of his property to his wife, to which John Parker and Wyatt and Eliza Maddox (who made her mark) signed on oath. Hoskins senior died in Bedford Street on 22 February 1664/5 and was buried in St. Paul's, Covent Garden. He was a great artist and bridged the gap between Hilliard (q.v.) and his followers and the rise to fame of Samuel Cooper. Hoskins succeeded in adapting the style of miniature painting to conform to new ideas introduced by Van Dyck. He painted the eyes in the manner of Hilliard showing the pupils clear with light reflected in them. He used subdued colouring and the whole effect of his portraits is simple and dignified. His miniatures painted before 1632 were usually on a blue or brown background, occasionally a red curtain or landscape was introduced. After he came under Van Dyck's influence, he ceased to use the soft yellowish colours which merged so perfectly with the others used in his early work, and his portraits painted after 1644 were executed with a freer and more vigorous brushstroke and a *pointilliste* dotting of a greenish colour more frequently used on the continent. Like his predecessors he painted on parchment stuck on to card, and used mainly the oval upright format, varying it with occasional rectangular ones, as in the case of the superb miniature of Charles I, signed and dated '1632'. This is in the collection of Earl Beauchamp. A smaller rectangular miniature formerly in the de la Hey collection and now in the collection of H.M. the Queen, represents Queen Henrietta Maria wearing a dress designed for her by Inigo Jones, for a Masque 'Tempe Restor'd' in which the Queen appeared as 'Divine Beauty'. This is a problem miniature; it is recorded by Van Der Doort in the catalogue of the collection of Charles I as by Hoskins, but is signed 'SC' in pencil on the reverse. It might have been the combined work of both Cooper and Hoskins, or the signature added at a later date. This miniature was sold at Sotheby's on 27 May 1968 when it realised the then world record price of £7,500. Hoskins' earliest signatures were IH in monogram, the cross-bar of the H being traversed by an I; other signatures are an H with a dot above the first vertical line, and I.H.; the punctuation varies, a semi-colon often being placed after the initials. Many of his miniatures are signed in gold, others in brown or red. Besides painting miniatures, Hoskins also executed some subject pictures after old masters; one of Mercury, Venus and Cupid, after Correggio, is in the Burghley House collection. He also copied the works of Van Dyck. Many of his miniatures are dated. Examples of his work are in the V. & A. M.; the Ashmolean Museum, Oxford; The Wallace Collection, London; and the Rijksmuseum, Amsterdam. Others are in private collections including those of H.M. the Queen, the Duke of Buccleuch, the Duke of Portland, the Duke of Devonshire, the Marquess of Bristol, the Duke of Northumberland, etc. Details of many of these are given by Long, *British Miniaturists*, pp. 224–226.

Hounsom, George. (fl. 1796–1806)

Of London. Exhibited at the R.A., 1796–1806. Long saw a portrait by Hounsom of Nelson which was not of very high quality. Some of his portraits were engraved, and two are at the B.M. Schidlof considered Hounsom a clever artist and possibly a pupil of G. Engleheart (q.v.). A miniature of a lady, signed and dated on the reverse 'G. Hounsom / pinxit / 1804' was sold at Sotheby's in 1966; it was of poor quality. Another of a man, on the reverse of which was a label 'George Hounsom / Miniature Painter / No 31 / GERRARD STREET / SOHO', was sold at Sotheby's in 1967. He appears to have had a distinguished clientele which included the Earl and Countess of Banbury (1798), H.R.H. the Duke of Kent (1804), and 'the Late Viscount Lord Nelson' (1806). The dates given above are the years that the portraits were exhibited at the R.A.

*Houston, Miss Margaret M. (fl. 1904)

Exhibited at the R.A. 1904, from The College, Coleraine, Co. Derry, Ireland.

Houston, Richard. *c.* 1721–1775

Born in Dublin *c.* 1721, possibly the son of Richard Houston, baker, whose widow had assistance from the Dublin Corporation in 1731 at the rate of £4 per annum, to help to maintain a large family.

Houston was apprenticed to John Brooks, an engraver, and learnt to execute mezzotints. Went to London *c.* 1750 and established himself near Charing Cross. Made mezzotints after Reynolds etc., and painted a few miniatures including one of Penelope Pitt, which he engraved in 1761. The promise of a successful career was spoilt by his indolence and dissipated habits; he was obliged to give up his own business and work for Sayer, the publisher. He became heavily in his debt, and Sayer had him arrested and confined to Fleet Street Prison, where Sayer kept him well employed. He was out of prison *c.* 1774 when he then worked for Carrington Bowles. He died in Hatton Street, 4 August 1775.

*Hovenden, Miss Ethel L. (fl. 1899)

Of London. Exhibited at the R.A. 1899, from Glenlea, Thurlow Park Road, W. Dulwich. Her exhibit was of Madeline, daughter of F. Hovenden, Esq.

Howard, Miss Annie. d. *c.* 1915

Of London. Exhibited at the R.A., S.B.A. and S.M., 1859–1903. Her sitters included Lady Victoria Cavendish-Bentinck (daughter of William Arthur, 6th Duke of Portland, K.G.). This miniature is in the Portland Collection and is signed 'A. Howard 1893'; the gold setting being engraved with the name and date '28 December 1893'. Died in London *c.* 1915.

*Howard, Miss Beatrice. (fl. 1900)

Of London. Exhibited at the R.A. 1900, from 38 Lincoln's Inn Fields.

*Howard, Miss Charlotte E. (Mrs. Charlotte Lugard). (fl. 1885–1894). See also Lugard, Mrs. Nell

Exhibited at the R.A. and N.W.C.S., 1885–1893 under her maiden name; married E. J. Lugard *c.* 1894 and exhibited at the R.A. in that year as Mrs. Charlotte Lugard from 68 Croydon Road, Beckenham, Kent. Her sitters included the Rev. Charles Broadley Howard, the Rev. Charles Parish, Miss Irene Shimield, The Countess of Hopetoun, the Hon. C. W. Thesiger, Rev. F. G. Lugard, M.A., and Capt. F. J. D. Lugard, D.S.O. (later Baron Lugard 1858–1945), her brother-in-law. A miniature of this latter sitter was donated by the artist's husband Major E. J. Lugard, D.S.O., to the N.P.G. The above artist was presumably identical with or related to Mrs. Nell Lugard (q.v.).

Howard, Miss Sarah T. (fl. 1840–1851)

Of London. Undoubtedly related to Frank Howard, portrait and figure painter, and Henry Howard, R.A., all of whom exhibited from 5 Newman Street. Miss Howard exhibited at the R.A. from this address 1840–1847 and from 34 Fitzroy Square, 1849–1851. Her sitters included the Earl and Countess of Wicklow, the Ladies Katherine and Maria Howard, and Alexander M. Harris, Esq., of the Madras Army.

*Howarth, Mrs. Linda I. (fl. 1910)

Of Blackpool. Exhibited at the Society of Miniaturists, 1910.

*Howell, Miss Ada M. (fl. 1898–1914)

Of Eastbourne. Exhibited at the R.A., 1898–1914.

*Howell, Catherine. (fl. 1707)

A fine copy of the miniature by I. Oliver (q.v.) of 'The Brothers Browne' at Burghley House, is in the collection of Earl Spencer at Althorp. It is painted in oil on copper and signed and dated, 'Catherine Howell, pinxt / 1707', 9¼ × 10¼ in. The miniature is well painted and is a faithful copy of the original.

Howell, Sophia H. M. (fl. 1781–1788)

Of London. Exhibited at the R.A. 1781–1788, as an Honorary Exhibitor. Her exhibits included a self-portrait in 1787. Opinions differ as to her ability; Long records seeing a miniature of a man, signed on the reverse in a fine hand 'Sophia Howell / 1785, which he did not regard as very skilful although it was not unattractive. Schidlof considered her work to be reminiscent of that of H. Hone (q.v.) and to be of a high quality.

Howes, John. (fl. 1770–1793). See also Howse, I.

Of London. Entered the R.A. Schools, 28 June 1770 obtaining a silver medal in 1772. Exhibited at the R.A., 1772–1793. Painted miniatures, enamels, figure subjects and oil landscapes with figures.

*Howgego, Miss Eva C. (fl. 1909)

Exhibited at the R.A. 1909, from 80 Grange Park Road, Leyton, E. London.

Howse, I. (fl. 1768). See also Howes, John

A miniature in the Whitehead sale was catalogued by Christie's as by I. Howse, 1768. It may have been an error and this artist may be identical with J. Howes (q.v.).

*Höyer, Cornelius. 1741–1804

Born in Hammermøllen near Kronborg in February 1741. One of the first students at the Academy of Copenhagen and one of the greatest Danish miniaturists. Worked in Italy, Paris, Dresden, Stockholm, Berlin, St. Petersburg and largely in Copenhagen where he became successively an Associate and Member of the Academy and later Painter to the King. Was evidently working in England in 1795 as he advertised in *The Sun* in April 1795 from 3 Little Tichfield Street, Portland Street, as painter to the King of Denmark. Was influenced by J. B. Massé and E. J. Alphen. A number of his works are recorded by Schidlof. He died in Copenhagen, 2 June 1804.

Hoyoll, Philip. b. 1816

Born in Breslau 1816. Studied under W. von Schadow at the Düsseldorf Academy, 1834–1839, and later settled in Breslau. Was working in London from 1864. Exhibited in Berlin 1836–1846 and at the R.A. and B.I., etc., 1864–1875. Painted miniatures, portraits and genre subjects. He lent one of his miniatures, of Miss Lydia Thompson, to the exhibition at the South Kensington Museum in 1865.

*Hubbard, W. (fl. 1809–1867)

Of London and Crayford, Kent. Exhibited at the B.I., etc., 1867. Painted flower scenes, small full-length figure groups, landscapes, interiors (on paper) and miniatures. His colours were rather vivid. O'Brien mentions a pair of miniatures signed and dated 'W. Hubbard 1832'.

Huckelbridge, Miss M. (fl. 1837–1852)

Of London. Exhibited at the R.A., 1837–1852. A good artist who was influenced by the work of Ross (q.v.) and A. Robertson (q.v.). Used fresh colours and painted with assurance.

Hudson. See Hudson, W. H.

*Hudson, Mrs. (fl. 1774–1796)

Of Bath (1774), Birmingham (1779 and 1795) and Coventry (1796). Daughter of Henry Chilcot, goldsmith and jeweller of Green Street, Bath, from which address she advertised in the *Bath Chronicle*, 8 December 1774. On 27 September 1779 she advertised in the *Birmingham Gazette* from 28 New Hall Street, Birmingham, saying that she would execute 'likenesses in hair, rings, lockets, & bracelets'. On 21 December she advertised in the same journal 'By Mrs Hudson, from late Secard's Pall Mall, Likenesses, miniatures. Profiles from 5ˢ 6d –

10ˢ 6d each. Modelling in wax.' According to the *Coventry Mercury*, 4 April 1796, she was working in that city. She may have been identical with the Mrs. Hudson who exhibited a landscape at the Free Society of Artists in 1764 from Pall Mall.

Hudson, Frederick Henry. *c.* 1820 – 1868
Was the son of W. Hudson (q.v.) as they exhibited at the R.A., from the same address in London in 1843; the exhibit was a self-portrait and the address 9 Percy Street, Bedford Square. Hudson exhibited at the R.A., 1843 – 1855. His initials were not F. M. as stated by Schidlof.

*Hudson, W. H. (fl. 1806–1823). See also **Hudson, William J. L.**
A miniature of an officer signed 'Hudson, 1806, Calcutta' was sold at Sotheby's, 3 February 1927 and a miniature of J. Milne, Esq., signed on the reverse 'W.H. Hudson, Calcutta Aug. 1823' was sold at Christie's, 7 November 1961; this was probably by the same artist who is listed by Long without any initials. Was possibly related to W. J. L. Hudson (q.v.).

Hudson, William C. 1782 – 1850
Of Croydon (1803–1807) and London. Exhibited at the R.A., S.B.A. and N.W.C.S., 1803–1846. Painted flowers and miniature portraits. Signed vertically in white (on the front) W. Hudson followed by a date, and on the reverse of one, 'Painted by / Mr W. Hudson 77 Cheapside / November 9th 1822'. In 1829 Hudson was working at 7 Ludgate Street and Schidlof records a miniature of an officer signed on the reverse 'Painted by Wᵐ Hudson / 71 New Bond St. / 1833'. Was possibly the father of F. H. Hudson (q.v.).

*Hudson, William J. L. 1779–1834. See also **Hudson, W. H.**
Born in October 1779. Possibly a relation of W. H. Hudson (q.v.). Hudson obtained permission, 18 February 1808, from the Court of Directors to go to India as a 'free mariner' on 21 July 1809. He married a Miss Eliza Philbrow, by whom he had at least six children. Lived for a time in Bengal. Early entries in the E.I.R. describe him as a miniature painter but from 1823–1826 he is called a painter and 'scene painter' and from 1827 his occupation is given as a portrait painter. He died in Calcutta on 6 July 1834 aged '54 years, 8 months, and 19 days'. A miniature of General James Patrick MacDougall, signed and dated 'July, 1827, Calcutta' is in the collection of E. G. Paine, of New York.

Hüet-Villiers, Jean François Marie. 1772–1813
Born in Paris, 14 January 1772, second son of J. B. Hüet, a well-known painter who instructed him in art. Used the name of Hüet-Villiers and Villiers-Hüet, having taken the name Villiers from Villiers-sur-Orge where his father owned land. Enlisted in 1792 and took up painting on leaving the army. Exhibited at the Paris Salon, 1799–1812. Came to England and exhibited at the R.A., B.I., etc., 1803–1813, including a self-portrait at the R.A., in 1803. Became a member of the Associated Artists in Water-Colour on 29 July 1807. Was appointed miniature painter to the Duke and Duchess of York in 1805 and was also painter to the King of France. Painted miniatures on ivory, alabaster and marble; executed chalk portraits, made drawings of Westminster Abbey and published etchings of cattle and trees as well as painting mythological and fancy subjects, some of which were engraved. He also painted in oil and water-colour. He died at 96 Great Marlborough Street, 28 July 1813 and was buried in St. Pancras Old Churchyard. **He was a good artist whose works are usually in the manner of the French school.**

Examples of his miniatures are in the V. & A. M., and date from 1806–1807; they are all signed Hüet-Villiers followed by a date. Volumes containing drawings by him are at Westminster Abbey. His usual signature was Hüet-Villiers, followed by a date, Villiers-Hüet or Villiers H; occasionally he signed in monogram VH. Other examples of his work are in the Ashmolean Museum, Oxford, and the Musée Condé, Chantilly, as well as in private collections including that of H.M. the Queen.

Huey, A. (fl. 1814–1818)
Of London. Exhibited at the R.A., 1814–1818. A miniature by Huey of William Henry West Betty (1791–1874) the child actor, was in the Jeffrey Whitehead Collection and was exhibited at the Burlington Fine Arts Club, London in 1889. A miniature of a gentleman signed on the reverse and dated 'April 1816' from '15 Howard Street, Strand' was Lot 23 at Christie's on 23 May 1967. It was well painted, the face being shaded with blue and the work executed with a *pointilliste* technique. The artist had expressed the sitter's character well. Huey exhibited a miniature of Rear Admiral W. Bligh (of the *Bounty*) at the R.A., in 1814.

Hugel, E. (fl. 1818–1826)
Of London. Exhibited a miniature of Napoleon's mother at the R.A., in 1818. Long saw a miniature of Napoleon signed and dated 'E.H. 1826' which was by the above artist.

Hughes, Miss. (fl. 1838)
Probably the daughter of G. Hughes (q.v.) from whose address, 99 St. John's Road, Islington, she exhibited at the R.A., in 1838.

*Hughes, Miss Alice. (fl. 1890–1899)
Of Newport. Exhibited at the R.A., etc., 1890–1899 from Widcombe, near Newport, Isle of Wight.

Hughes, George. (fl. 1813–1858)
Of London. Exhibited from various London addresses at the R.A., B.I., etc., 1813–1858. Lived from 1825 for many years at 99 St. John's Road, Islington. Hughes painted portraits (including one of Miss Ellen Tree), landscapes and miniatures. Miss Hughes (q.v.) who exhibited from his address in 1838 may have been his daughter. A pair of rectangular miniatures of a man and wife with a curtain background signed and dated 'Feb 8th, 1842' and inscribed on the reverse 'painted at 99 St. Jno Hunt Road, London' were sold at Sotheby's 9 February 1961.

*Hughes, Miss Gwen. (fl. 1903–1914)
Exhibited at the R.A. and S.M. 1903–1914, from 126 Queen's Road, Richmond, Surrey.

*Hughes, Miss Lily, Jones-. (fl. 1896–1910)
Of Herts., and North Wales. Exhibited at the R.A., 1896–1910. Her exhibit in 1910 was 'the artist's mother'.

*Hughes, Mrs. Rose Edith. (fl. 1910)
Of Dunbartonshire. Exhibited at the Society of Miniaturists, 1910.

Hughes, W. (William?). (fl. 1828–1829)
Of London. Exhibited at the R.A., 1828–1829. Possibly the William Hughes who entered the R.A. Schools, 22 April 1829 aged 23.

*Huhn, Miss Mathilde. (fl. 1907–1913)
Of London. Exhibited at the R.A. 1907 and 1913, from addresses in Chelsea. Her sitter in 1913 was 'The Lord Farnham'.

*Hulbert, Fanny. (fl. 1841)
A miniature of a small girl, signed on the reverse 'Fanny Hulbert, 1841' is illustrated, on Pl. 25, fig. 2, by O'Brien.

Hull, Thomas H. (fl. 1775–1827)
Of London. Exhibited at the R.A., 1775–1827. On 17 April 1780 the *Northampton Mercury* mentions Thomas Hull, 'miniature painter in Mark Lane, London' and the *Morning Chronicle*, 13 November 1795, records that he had moved from 31 Ely Place to 23 Northumberland Street. Hull evidently also worked in Leeds in 1796, when the *Leeds Intelligence*, 13 June 1796 notes his arrival in Leeds from Northumberland Street, London. According to the *Harleian MSS*, one Thomas Hull married Frideswide Wells at St. Mary-le-Bone on 8 June 1795. This may possibly have been the artist. Hull painted good miniatures some of which were engraved. He usually signed 'Hull' followed by a date. Often there is a blue shading on the chin of his male portraits, and Long records that he painted with a 'sort of broken effect round the eyes' which may be seen under a lens. Examples of his work are in the V. & A. M. The B.M. has some engravings after his work.

*Hulston, Miss Winifred. (fl. 1904–1908)
Of London and Natal. Exhibited at the Society of Miniaturists, 1904–1908.

*Humble, Mrs. d. 1724. See also **Humble, Catharine**
Daughter of Willem de Keyser (q.v.) of Antwerp. Painted small oil portraits and miniatures. Married a Mr. Humble who made her give up art. Was possibly identical with Catharine Humble (q.v.). She died in England in 1724.

Humble, Catharine. (fl. *c.* 1710–1720). See also **Humble, Mrs.**
Three large oil miniatures *c.* 1710 were seen by Long; one was illegibly signed 'H . . . / pinxit' on the front and on the back was scratched the signature 'Catharin Humble (?) pinxit' I have seen two good miniatures by this artist, one of Lady Elizabeth Beddingfield, daughter of the 2nd Earl of Burlington, signed on the reverse 'Catherine Humble' and dated '1720'; the other was of a man, possibly a relation, signed in the same hand 'A.D. / 1717'. Both portraits were oil on copper. The above artist may possibly have been the daughter of Willem de Keyser (q.v.) who is known to have been a miniaturist and to have married a Mr. Humble.

*Humphreys, Robert. (fl. 1832)
A miniature of a man by the above artist signed and dated on the reverse '1832 Dublin' was seen by Mr. A. J. B. Kiddell in 1966. It was heavily shaded with green.

Humphry, Ozias, R.A. 1742–1810
Born in Honiton, Devon, 8 September 1742, son of George Humphry, a peruke-maker and mercer, and his wife, Elizabeth. Was educated at the local Grammar School; showed aptitude for drawing and was sent to London in 1757, when on the advice of Reynolds he studied at the St. Martin's Lane School and the Duke of Richmond's Gallery. Returned to Honiton in 1758 just before the death of his father on 19 February 1759. Not wishing to assist his mother with the family lace business, he continued his interest in portrait painting and in 1760 was apprenticed to Samuel Collins (q.v.) at Bath; on Collins' removal to Dublin to avoid his creditors, Humphry succeeded to his practice. In 1762 Humphry was given rooms at the house of Mr. Thomas Linley, the musician, and during his time in Bath became acquainted with Gainsborough.

Went to London in 1763 with a further introduction to Sir Joshua Reynolds, who after seeing his work, persuaded him to leave Bath and settle in London. This he did in 1764. Exhibited at the Society of Artists, 1765–1771, becoming a member in 1773. Was employed by the King. In 1773 Ozias Humphry and George Romney departed for Italy, staying at Knowle Park the home of the Duke of Dorset, en route to the coast. This tour, undertaken because of a severe fall that Humphry had had from his horse in 1772, enabled him to visit among other places, Rome, Florence, Venice and Naples. Returned to London in 1777 and was elected A.R.A. in 1779, R.A. in 1791 and served as a member of the Hanging Committee in 1793. Exhibited at the R.A., 1779–1797. Humphry left for India on 25 January 1785, reaching Calcutta early in August. He worked in Calcutta, Moorshedabad, Benares, Lucknow, etc., painting portraits of Europeans and natives. The Indian climate did not agree with him and after difficulties over payment which led him to sue the Governor, General Sir John Macpherson, without success for fees due to him for portraits of affluent natives, he returned to England in 1787. Humphry painted miniatures, some of which are on paper, executed small portraits in water-colour in the manner of Downman (q.v.), and portraits in oil and crayon. Many of his miniatures were copies of oil paintings commissioned by the Duke of Dorset, who was one of his best patrons. By 1792 his sight was failing and he was obliged to give up miniature painting for crayon portraiture and became portrait painter in crayons to the King. The last portraits he drew were those of the Prince and Princess of Orange, which were his last exhibits at the R.A., in 1797. His sight totally failed him and he passed the remainder of his life in seclusion. His character was said to have been somewhat spoiled by conceit and a quick temper. Although he was practically engaged to Miss Mary Boydell before her departure for India, this attachment was broken off and Humphry remained unmarried. By a young woman called Dolly or Delly Wickers, he had a son, who was called William Upcott (1779–1845), a family name. This boy later became a celebrated collector and kept in close touch with Humphry whom he referred to as his 'godfather'. Humphry died on 9 March 1810 at 39 Thornhaugh Street, Bedford Square, London, in lodgings kept by the widow of Henry Spicer (q.v.), and was buried at St. James', Hampstead Road. He bequeathed many of his finest works to William Upcott, many of whose collection of books, manuscripts, prints and drawings etc., sold in 1846, were purchased by the British Museum and the Bodleian Library, Oxford. Among Humphry's pupils were William Singleton (q.v.), Richard Collins (q.v.) who was living with him in 1780, Thomas Day (q.v.) and H. Spicer. H. Bone (q.v.) copied works by Humphry on enamel. Some of his portraits were engraved. He was a good miniaturist and an excellent draughtsman; his portraits are not always signed. His usual signature was OH in monogram, the H being set within the O. Sometimes he signed on the reverse O:H: / 1770 or O: Humphry pt. Humphry was undoubtedly one of the best miniaturists of the eighteenth century. His portraits are usually elegant, and his style, which altered slightly and became broader and more fully developed by c. 1780, is usually distinguishable once it has been examined. The early portraits, particularly those of women, have a rather limpid, clearcut appearance, without showing the individual brush-strokes on the face; sometimes the eyebrows are made up of a number of fine, almost parallel lines. The eyes sometimes have a slightly sleepy look. Six fine miniatures by Humphry were exhibited in Edinburgh in 1965, including

those of Queen Charlotte and Charlotte Augusta, Princess Royal, from the collection of H.M. the Queen, and an interesting one of Sahib Zada, inscribed on the reverse 'Sahib Zada, Eldest Son / and Presumptive / Heir to Asoph / Ub Dowlah Nabob / Vizier of Oude / Ozias Humphry / R.A. Pinxt / 1786', from the collection of E. G. Paine of New York. The V. & A. M., and the N.P.G., have examples of his work and the B.M. has six of his drawing books. Miniatures by him can also be found in many private collections. Many of his letters are at the R.A. Oil paintings by him are at the Walker Art Gallery, Liverpool, who also have a portrait of George Stubbs by Humphry executed in pastel and gouache on paper. This was shown in an exhibition of 'Early English Drawings and Watercolours' held in the Walker Art Gallery in 1968. For further information see the *D.N.B.*, *Ozias Humphry*, *R.A.*, by Dr. G. C. Williamson and the *Walpole Society*, Vol. XIX.

Hunneman or **Hanneman, Christopher William.** 1755–1793

Born in May 1755. Entered the R.A. Schools, 6 December 1773 when his age was noted as '18 last May'. The Council Minutes give the spelling of his name as Hannemann. He was awarded a silver medal in 1776. Exhibited at the R.A., 1776–1793. Had a good practice in London. Painted miniatures and portraits in oil and crayon. He died 21 November 1793.

Hunt, Robert. c. 1775 – c. 1848/50

Born in Philadelphia, son of Isaac Hunt and Mary Shewell. Of London. Exhibited at the R.A., 1802–1818, his address in 1817 and 1818 being Stoke Newington. Painted miniatures, portraits, historical subjects, shells and flowers. In 1806 he exhibited a miniature of his two sons, and in 1808 a miniature of Mr. J. Hunt. Possibly identical with the Robert Hunt who was premiated by the Society of Arts, 1789–1790. Has also been identified with an artist of the same name who exhibited at the R.A. in 1832 from Elizabeth Street, Islington, and again in 1842 (no address given). This exhibit was a landscape. Schidlof gives his name as Richard who, he says, won prizes at the Society of Artists, but I have been unable to trace this information. A miniature of an unknown man signed 'R. Hunt 1806' is recorded by Schidlof.

Hunt, T. (fl. 1803)

Exhibited at the R.A. 1803, several miniatures of his family (one of which may have been a self-portrait); a miniature of Mrs. Smith, formerly Miss Dixon of the Theatre Royal, and M. Talma, the French actor.

Hunt, William Henry. 1790–1864

Born in London, 28 March 1790. Entered the R.A. Schools, 21 January 1808. Famous watercolour painter of genre subjects, fruit, flowers, landscapes, etc. Of his few known miniatures a portrait of J. Abernethy, after Lawrence, belongs to the Royal College of Surgeons. Died in London, 10 February 1864.

***Hunter, Miss Ada.** (fl. 1886–1898)

Of London. Exhibited at the R.A., 1886–1898. Her last address was 130 Finsborough Road, Earl's Court, London.

***Hunter, J. P.** (fl. 1824)

A small miniature signed and dated 'Aug.1824' by this artist was seen by Long. He did not consider it of any great merit. The artist was probably iden-

tical with the J. P. Hunter recorded by Graves as exhibiting at Suffolk Street in 1827.

Hunter, Matthew. (fl. 1780–1829)

Of Dublin. Entered the Dublin Society's schools in 1779 and won awards in 1780, 1781 and 1783. Had a practice in Dublin and executed portraits in miniature and crayon. His charge was two guineas for each portrait. He was still working in 1829.

Hunter, T. (fl. c. 1787)

Working in Armagh c. 1787 and probably identical with the 'Master Thomas Hunter' who exhibited a number of chalk drawings at the Society of Artists in William Street, Dublin 1775 and 1777. Painted miniatures and executed crayon portraits.

Huntley, Miss Georgina or **Georgiana.** (fl. 1818–1825)

Of Buckingham Place, Fitzroy Square, London. Won a silver medal at the Society of Arts in 1820 for a miniature of the Duke of Gordon and a silver palette in 1821 for a group of portraits in watercolour. Was presumably identical with the Miss Georgiana Huntley who exhibited at the R.A. 1818–1825, from 25 Buckingham Place, Fitzroy Square; 16 Newman Street and 10 New Road, Fitzroy Square. Her exhibits were genre subjects and portraits, some of which may have been miniatures.

Huquier or **Hequier, James (Jacques) Gabriel.** 1725–1805

Born in Paris 1725, son and pupil of Gabriel Huquier, a painter and engraver. Married 30 November 1758 Anne-Louise Chéreau, the daughter of the engraver Jacques Chéreau, by whom he had two children, Anne Genevieve (20 November 1759) and Jacques Gabriel (14 October 1760). Came to London c. 1771; was in Shrewsbury, 9 November 1776, Cambridge 1783, and lived for a time at 18 Great Charles Street, Birmingham. Was a member of the Academy in Paris. Exhibited at the R.A., and Society of Artists, 1771–1786, including a self-portrait in crayons, in 1771. Painted miniatures, portraits in pencil and crayon, besides executing etchings and engravings and publishing and dealing in prints. Died in Shrewsbury, 7 June 1805. The B.M. has some engravings after him, and a pencil portrait of him by J. Greenwood.

***Hurry, Agnes.** (fl. 1901–1914)

Exhibited at the R.A. 1901–1914, from various London addresses. Painted miniatures and a design for a locket.

Hurter, Charles Ralph (or Rudolph). b. 1768

Son of J. H. Hurter (q.v.) probably born in Berne in 1768 where his father lived, 1768–1770, and was living with him in London. Was working as early as 1780. Entered the R.A. Schools, 29 March 1781 'age 13 25th March Inst.'. In 1782 he was awarded a silver medallion by the Society of Arts for drawings and portraits. Accompanied his father to Karlsruhe in 1786. Exhibited at the R.A., from London addresses, 1787–1789 and was working up to 1791. Many of his works were enamel miniatures which were well executed; he also painted large portraits and exhibited one at the R.A., in 1787. Long records seeing a fairly good enamel portrait of a lady signed on the reverse 'C. Hurter pint / 1789'. A number of enamels by Hurter were in the collection of the Countess of Dartrey, including portraits of Queen Charlotte, Cromwell, and large ones of Charles I and Henrietta Maria.

Hurter, Johann Heinrich. 1734–1799

Born in Schaffhausen, 9 September 1734. Was working in Berne 1768–1770. Was advised by Liotard (q.v.) to go to Versailles but did not meet with much success and went from there to the Hague, where in 1772 he became a member of the Painters' Guild. Settled in London *c.* 1777 supposedly on the advice of Lord Dartrey whose family have a number of miniatures by him. Exhibited at the R.A. 1779–1781, and was appointed a court painter. Between 1785 and 1787 he travelled to Schaffhausen, Karlsruhe, the Hague and Paris after which he returned to London where he founded a factory for mathematical and other instruments. Hurter later divided his time between Germany and London. Received a large commission from the Empress Catherine of Russia in 1787. He painted miniatures on enamel, many of which were copied from old masters, and also executed pastel portraits. Was given the rank of 'Freiherr'. He died at Düsseldorf, 2 September 1799. He used a variety of signatures. His work is often soft in effect, but his colouring is good. I have seen some fine enamel copies after Van Dyck of Charles I and Henrietta Maria, one pair being signed on the front in full as well as on the reverse. Examples of his work are mainly in private collections. Three miniatures by him were exhibited in Edinburgh in 1965. They represented Georgiana Spencer, Duchess of Devonshire, signed and dated on the reverse 'J. Hurter pinxit 1780'; William Cavendish, 5th Duke of Devonshire, also signed and dated on the reverse, 'J. Hurter pinx 1782' (both from the collection of Earl Beauchamp) and George III, signed and dated on the reverse 'J.H. Hurter p: 1781' from the author's collection. The Liverpool Museum has an enamel miniature of Thomas, Lord Dartrey, said to be signed on the reverse 'Hurter Fec. 1784'. An enamel portrait of Frederick the Great, painted by Hurter in 1768 is at the Hohenzollernmuseum, Berlin.

Hussey, Giles. 1710–1788

Born at Marnhull, Dorset, 10 September 1710. Is best known as a portrait painter. Studied under Richardson and later in Italy etc. A miniature of Prince Charles Edward, attributed to Hussey is in the collection of the Duke of Northumberland, and a profile portrait also of Prince Charles Edward, executed in Indian ink, was lent to the exhibition at the South Kensington Museum in 1865 by Lord Arundel of Wardour.

Hutchinson, George. (fl. 1885–1887)

Of London. Exhibited at the R.A., 1885–1887. Painted miniatures and subject pictures in oil.

*Hutchinson, Miss Gertrude K. (fl. 1904–1907)

Of London. Exhibited at the R.A. 1904–1907, from 105 Belgrave Road, London. Her sitters included the Baroness Christian de Linden and 'The Lady Eva Forbes'.

Hutchinson, J. or Joseph

Long records the date of death of the above artist as 1810 but after careful research it would appear that the biographical information has been confused. In the present state of our knowledge this is now thought to relate to Joseph Hutchisson (q.v.) (1747–1830). I have been unable to trace any J. Hutchinson of Bath who died in 1810.

Hutchinson, Joseph. See **Hutchisson, Joseph**

*Hutchison, junior. See **Hutchisson** or **Hutchison, William Henry**

Hutchisson, Hutchison or **Hutchinson, Joseph.** 1747–1830

Born in Dublin 1747, son of a currier in Nicholas Street, who failed in his business. Entered the Dublin Society schools in 1764 and was apprenticed to G. Carncross, an heraldic painter. Went to London *c.* 1790 and practised as a portrait and animal painter in crayons and oil, and later as a miniaturist. According to information kindly supplied to me by the City of Bath Municipal Libraries he was identical with the J. Hutchinson (q.v.) recorded by Long who worked in Bath. The name was spelt variably Hutchison, Hutchisson or Hutchinson, the latter spelling also being given by Strickland. Hutchisson exhibited at the R.A. 1792–1819, from various London addresses. He may have been related to the Joseph Hutchison who entered the R.A. Schools, 20 March 1795 aged 34. He is said to have resided in Bath from *c.* 1795 until his death in 1830. His known addresses in Bath are as follows: 1799–1804, 1 Westgate Buildings (and 18 Northgate Street in 1804); 1805–1817, 24 Union Passage; 1818, Green Street; 1819–1821, 2 Burton Street; 1822–1827, 9 Bath Street; 1828, St. Michael's Place; 1829–1830, 4 St. James' Parade. His sitters included musicians and members of the medical profession; the Rev. William Jay; Mme. Storace; Mrs. Dickens and Dr. Somers. During the visit of the Duke and Duchess of York to Bath in 1801 he was given a sitting by the Duchess. Exhibited in Bath, 1795–1809. His wife was probably the Mrs. Hutchison 'wife of Mr Hutchison, portrait painter' whose death was recorded in Bath on 8 July 1802. The *Bath Chronicle* for 28 August 1817 records the marriage of Margaretta, daughter of Mr. Hutchison, portrait painter of Burton Street (probably the above artist) to Mr. Thomas Phillips, jun., jeweller of Union Passage. He took up lithography under the influence of Thomas Barker who had sponsored the art when it was introduced to the city by Thomas Redmond in 1813. The *Bath Chronicle* of 2 September 1830 records his death at his lodgings 'No. 4 St. James' Parade after a lingering illness, Mr. Joseph Hutchison aged 83, upwards of 40 years an eminent portrait painter in this city (Sept. 1 1830)'. Several portraits by him are in City collections in Bath, including William Clark, J.P., Mayor of Bath 1821, and Princess Frederica, Duchess of York and Albany (both in the Guildhall), Venanzio Rauzzini (1747–1810), musician, Director of Concerts at Bath, and Joseph Barratt, bookseller (both in the Pump Room). A miniature of Rauzzini, which was engraved by R. Hancock and published in 1800 is also in the Pump Room. The Nottingham Museum has two portraits painted in water-colour which are attributed to the above artist. The exhibition, 'Four Centuries of Portrait Miniatures' from the Heckett Collection, Pennsylvania, held in the Carnegie Institute in 1954, contained a miniature of an unknown man, signed and dated 'I.H. / 1798' (block capitals) which was attributed to Joseph Hutchison

*Hutchisson or **Hutchison, William Henry.** (fl. 1818–1825)

Of Bath. According to information recorded by a former curator of the City of Bath Municipal Libraries and Victoria Art Gallery, the above artist was the son of Joseph Hutchison (q.v.) (1747–1830). W. H. Hutchison is identified with the Hutchison, jun. (no initial given) who is listed in the Bath Directories from 1818–1824. In 1818 he is recorded as a figure and portrait painter of Green Street, where his father was also living. In 1824 his address was 45 Pulteney Street. It is not certain that W. H. Hutchisson painted miniatures, but a self-portrait in pencil and water-colour, $8\frac{3}{4} \times 7$ in. signed 'Hutchisson junr' and dated 'Bath 1820' is in the Victoria Art Gallery, Bath.

I

I., G. (fl. *c.* 1622)

A miniature of Francis Holles *c.* 1622 and signed 'G I' with four dots round the initials, is in the collection of the Duke of Portland. A miniature of William, Duke of Hamilton stated to be on card and to be signed 'G.I.' was lent to the exhibition at the South Kensington Museum 1865. The artist has not yet been identified.

*I., H. See **H., I.**

I., P. (fl. 1623). See also **P., I.**, and **Palmer, Sir James**

A miniature of a man dated '1623' and signed with a 'P' which looked like a monogram 'IP' or 'PI' was in the collection of Mr. W. V. Paterson.

*I., S. (fl. 1791)

Long saw a miniature signed 'S.I. / 1781'. It may have been the work of Samuel Ireland, the engraver.

Imhoff, Carl Christoph Adam, Freiherr von. d. *c.* 1800

Born in Nuremberg. Served in the English army. Thought to be identical with the artist spelt Imoff who was working in London in 1768 when a miniature of the Queen painted from life was exhibited by him at the Society of Artists. Went with his wife, née Anna Maria Apollonia Chapuset, or Chapusset or Chapusettin, to India in 1769; was in Calcutta 1770. Produced etched portraits in caricature *c.* 1771–1777. He divorced his wife *c.* 1775, who married Warren Hastings, 8 August 1777. Imhoff then married Louisa von Schardt. He had two children by his first wife, General Sir Charles Imhoff (died 1853) and Julius Imhoff (died 1799) and several by his second wife including Amalie von Helwig, the poetess (born 1776). The B.M. has two engraved portraits by him of his first wife. He was a skilful artist who worked in the manner of Liotard (q.v.). 'Mr Immoff' sat to George Engleheart (q.v.) in 1782 and 1786; he may have been the above artist. Julius Imhoff was in the Bengal Civil Service in 1790, and died in Calcutta on 23 September 1799 having had three sons by an Indian consort.

Imoff. See **Imhoff, Carl Christoph Adam, Freiherr von**

*Inchbald, Joseph. d. 1779

Painted miniatures. Referred to in *Tragedy Queens of the Georgian Era* by J. Frye, p. 181. His wife's name was Elizabeth and he was friendly with Siddons, Kemble, etc. Died 6 June 1779.

*Inchiquin, the Countess of. See **Palmer, Miss Mary** (later **Marchioness of Thomond**)

Ingham, Charles Cromwell. 1796–1863

Born in Dublin in 1796. Entered the Dublin Society Schools in 1809 where he obtained prizes in 1810 and 1811. Was a pupil of William Cuming for four years. Exhibited from Cuming's house, 14 Clare Street, in 1815, 'Portrait of a lady' and 'Death of Cleopatra'. For the latter picture the Irish Institution awarded him a premium of £32.2s.6d. Ingham exhibited again in 1816 and in the same year went to New York where he settled. He painted portraits, miniatures, and subject pictures. Was one of the original members of the National Academy of Design founded in 1826, and was its Vice-President for many years. Exhibited at the R.H.A., in 1829 and 1842 from New York. Ingham died in New York on 10 December 1863.

*Ingham-Brooke, Mrs. C. (fl. 1900)

Of Drogheda. Exhibited at the Society of Miniaturists, 1900.

*Ingle, Miss Leura. (fl. 1907–1909)

Of London. Exhibited at the R.A. 1907 and 1909, from 25 Kensington Gate. Undoubtedly related to Mabel Ingle (q.v.) who exhibited from the same address in 1906. In the catalogue entry for her exhibit of Margaret, daughter of Col. H. C. B. Gray, 1907, her Christian name is given as Laura, but in all other cases it is spelt Leura.

*Ingle, Miss Mabel. (fl. 1906)

Of London. Exhibited at the R.A. 1906, from 25 Kensington Gate. Undoubtedly related to Leura Ingle (q.v.) who exhibited from the same address in the following year.

Inglis or **Langlois, Esther.** c. 1571–1624/5

A Frenchwoman, possibly of Scottish extraction. Born in France c. 1571, from whence her father, Nicholas Langlois, a Huguenot, and her mother Marie Prisott fled with their children after the massacre of 24 August 1572. They settled in Edinburgh and Esther's parents taught French there between 1578–1585. In about 1596 she married Bartholomew Kello, who became 'Curé de Willingale-Spayne' near Chelmsford in 1607. Earlier than this they had moved to London and Esther retained her maiden name. A MS book, said to have been offered to Henry, Prince of Wales in 1609, was inscribed 'A Book of the Armes of England doone by me Esther Inglis, Januar the first, 1609'. It contains a skilfully limned portrait of Esther Inglis, dressed in black with a wide spread ruff round her neck and a jaunty little high peaked hat set over her yellow hair. There is an oil portrait on panel of her, dated '1595' by an unknown artist at the S.N.P.G. The B.M. has MSS by her, two of which contain self-portraits. The Bodleian Library, Oxford, contains 'Les Proverbes de Solomon' beautifully written in French c. 1624 in which the headings and endings of the chapters and the margins are decorated with pen and ink drawings by her, and in addition the arms of the Earl of Essex to whom the volume is dedicated.

*Inglis, Miss Margaret. (fl. 1906)

Of London. Exhibited at the R.A. 1906, from 5 Wentworth Mansions, Hampstead.

Inman, Henry. 1801–1846

Born in Utica, New York State, 28 October 1801, son of English parents who settled in New York in 1812. In 1814 he became a pupil and assistant of John Wesley Jarvis with whom he worked for seven years, often accompanying him to towns in the south and in 1822 to Boston. He married a Miss O'Brien, and they remained in New York about twelve years. Inman had his own studio in partnership with his pupil Thomas S. Cummings. Was a founder member and first Vice-President of the National Academy in 1826. Went to Philadelphia c. 1831; was partner in a firm of lithographers (Inman and Childs) until 1835. Was in New York in 1838 and London 1843–1845 after which he returned to New York where he remained until his death, 17 January 1846. Worked as a portrait painter, miniaturist, lithographer, and executed landscapes. Was a good artist who drew well and expressed character. Suffered from failing health from c. 1840. Wordsworth and Macaulay sat to him. Was in financial difficulties when he died on 17 January 1846 soon after his return to New York. In order to raise funds for the support of his family an exhibition of his works was held in New York City in the year of his death.

*Inman, Miss Mabel D. (fl. 1906)

Of London. Exhibited at the R.A. 1906, from 69 Warwick Road, London. Her sitter was Mrs. H. T. Inman.

Inskipp, James. 1790–1868

Was born in 1790. Was employed by the Commissariat Department but retired on a pension. Exhibited at the R.A., B.I. and S.B.A., 1816–1864. Had a practice in Walworth in 1817 as a miniature painter, but later painted principally portraits in oil and water-colour and genre subjects. In 1838 published *Studies of Heads from Nature*. Lived in Godalming Surrey for twenty-five years until his death 15 March 1868.

Ireland, Miss Jane. (fl. 1792–1793)

Daughter of Samuel Ireland, engraver and collector. Exhibited at the R.A. 1792–1793, from 8 Norfolk Street, Strand. Painted miniatures, etched and painted small water-colour portraits, one of which, of Charles Lloyd, is at the B.M.

*Irvine, Miss R. (fl. 1908)

Of London. Exhibited at the R.A. 1908, from 101 Lansdowne Road, Holland Park.

*Isaac, Miss Nellie. (fl. 1904)

Of London. Exhibited at the R.A. 1904, from 20 Dennington Park Road, West Hampstead.

Isaacs, Miss Martha (Mrs. Higginson). (fl. 1771–1782)

A Jewess; described as a pupil of Mr. Burgess (probably Thomas Burgess who kept an art school in Maiden Lane). Exhibited at the Free Society of Artists 1771–1774, when she was living with her father, and later at other London addresses. Painted miniatures, still-life, figure subjects and crayon portraits. Was possibly related to the Miss Isaacs of Irish origin who accompanied William Hickey and others to the coronation of George III in Westminster Abbey. Arrived in Bengal in 1778, reference being made to the fact in Hickey's *Memoirs*, Vol. II, p. 157, 'During the period that Mr. Cleveland and I lived together (i.e. January–April 1778), a young Jewess of the name of Isaacs arrived in Calcutta to exercise the profession of miniature painting.' Cleveland had known Miss Isaacs' family in England and asked Hickey to sit to her. She later married on 5 July 1779 Alexander Higginson of the Board of Trade, having earlier renounced her Jewish faith and been baptised into membership of the Church of England, receiving the name of Martha. She presumably accompanied her husband back to England in 1782, when she retired.

*Isabey, Jean Baptiste. 1767–1855

Born in Nancy, 11 April 1767, son of a merchant. This outstanding French miniaturist who was taught art by Girardet, Claudot and David, became very popular at the French Court and had apartments in Versailles. Had a distinguished clientele; controlled the ceremonies of Napoleon's coronation; had the patronage of Louis XVIII and Charles X. Held various appointments including that of Royal draughtsman and painter and was an Officer of the Légion d'honneur. Married twice, firstly in 1791 Jeanne Laurice de Salienne, by whom he had three children, and in 1829, shortly after the death of his first wife, Mlle. Marie-Rose Maistre, by whom he had two children. Was apparently in London c. 1815–1820, after which time he returned to Paris. In 1837 Louis Philippe appointed him Assistant Keeper of the Royal Museums and gave him apartments at Versailles. Was granted a pension by Napoleon III. Was a prolific artist and one whose

works have been frequently copied. Many miniatures supposedly signed by him are either fakes or by one of his pupils. He painted miniatures on vellum and ivory and a number of portraits in water-colour on card. Executed drawings and a few enamels besides a few portraits in oil. He was a good draughtsman and one of the greatest miniaturists of the 18th century. Until c. 1800 he favoured a dark background, executed in gouache, or occasionally landscapes; after this time he introduced light sky backgrounds and in the case of his portraits of ladies, depicted them with draped gauze veils over their heads and round the face; often flowers were placed on the veiling. He signed Isabey, or I. Isabey, often followed by a date and written in vertical letters of the same height; a similar signature, but somewhat larger, and in pencil, may be found on his drawings and water-colours. He died in Paris, 18 April 1855. Examples of his work may be found in the Wallace Collection, Manchester Square, London; the Ward Usher Collection, Lincoln; the National Library of Vienna; the Louvre, and many private collections. A self-portrait (one of several) is in the Wallace Collection.

J

J., J. See **Jennings, J.** and **Jukes, J.**

*J., J.M.B. See **B., J.J.M.**

*J., R. (fl. 1765). See **R., J.** and **R., I.**

A miniature of a lady, signed and dated 'J.R. 1765' is in the collection of E. G. Paine of New York.

*J., T. See **T., J.**

*Jackson, Cyril H. (fl. 1903)

Exhibited at the R.A. 1903, from 16a Chaucer Road, Forest Gate, Essex.

Jackson, G. (fl. 1810)

A miniature portrait on ivory of a gentleman, signed 'Jackson' and dated '1810' is in the N.G., Dublin where it is attributed to the above artist.

Jackson, J., junior (Joseph?). d. 1850

Was in Oxford (1816–1823), Cheltenham (1824) and London. Exhibited at the R.A., 1816–1835. Probably identical with Joseph Jackson, a portrait and miniature painter and restorer who settled in Charleston, South Carolina from 1834–1850. When he arrived in Charleston he was referred to as 'formerly of Oxford (England)'. He stopped in New York City en route and was listed in the City Directory for 1833, and exhibited as J. Jackson at the National Academy. He died in June 1850 and his wife and son, Henry, carried on his restoring business.

Jackson, John, R.A. 1778–1831

Born in Lastingham, Yorks., 31 May 1778, son of a tailor to whom he was apprenticed. Said to have received instruction in art from the local schoolmaster and to have painted miniatures at York in 1797. Was patronised by Sir George Beaumont and went to London in 1804. Entered the R.A. Schools,

9 March 1805, aged 27. Exhibited at the R.A., and B.I., 1804–1830; was elected A.R.A., in 1815 and R.A., in 1817. Painted miniatures and became an eminent painter of oil portraits, and painted some portraits in water-colour. He died at St. John's Wood, London, 1 June 1831. A self-portrait in oil is at the V. & A. M. and examples of his work are at the B.M., the National Gallery, the N.P.G., and the N.G. Dublin, etc.

*Jackson, Joseph. See **Jackson, J., junior**

*Jackson, Mrs. Mary E. (fl. 1904–1907)
Of London. Exhibited at the Society of Miniaturists 1904–1907.

*Jackson, Miss Mildred. (fl. 1902)
Of London. Exhibited at the R.A. 1902, from 43 Longridge Road, Earl's Court. Her sitters included Grace, daughter of John Houlton Jackson, Esq.

*Jackson, Mrs. Morton (Diana). (fl. 1901–1910)
Exhibited at the R.A. and S.M., 1901–1910, from The Thicket, Addlestone, Surrey. Her sitters included Ursula, daughter of W. Page Phillips, Esq., and Myrtle, daughter of M. S. Jackson, Esq. She also executed portrait studies.

Jackson, Samuel. 1794–1869
Born in Wine Street, Bristol, 31 December 1794, son of a merchant. Started on a business career but became a pupil of F. Danby, A.R.A., in Bristol, and painted landscapes. Exhibited at the B.I., O.W.C.S., etc. Was an Associate of the O.W.C.S., 1823–1848. Visited Egypt and the West Indies. Only known as a miniaturist by two rather weak miniatures described as portraits of Princess Charlotte of Wales and Lady Georgiana Dover, at the Glynn Vivian Art Gallery, Swansea. They are signed 'S.H.J.', and attributed to Jackson. He died in Clifton, Bristol, in December 1869.

Jackson, William. (fl. 1774–1787)
Of Liverpool. Exhibited at the Liverpool Society of Artists 1774, and at the Society for Promoting Painting and Design in Liverpool, 1784 and 1787. Painted portraits, landscapes, marine subjects and a few miniatures.

*Jacob, Jacob. 1774/6–1853
The above artist was born in or near Falmouth in 1774 or 1776. An article by Florence Abrahams in the *Jewish Chronicle*, 18 March 1960, provides the name of this artist who has been hitherto unrecorded. A pair of miniatures representing Jacob Jacob and his wife Sarah Kate (née Simons) (1776–1846) were purchased in an antique shop in Philadelphia in *c.* 1960 and subsequently brought to London. They are now in the possession of Mr. Alex Jacob, the artist's great-great-grandson. Jacob and Sarah were first cousins, both being grandchildren of a man who was called Zender Falmouth, one of the first Jews to settle in Falmouth. The artist and his wife spent their entire lives in or near Falmouth. Mr. Alex Jacob has given me Jacob's date of birth as 1774, but according to an inscription on paper placed behind the miniatures, that of the artist read 'Painted by me in 1820 in my 44th year—I. Jacob' and that on the reverse of his wife's miniature 'My wife Sarah, aged 40—J. Jacob'.

Jagger, Charles. *c.* 1770–1827
Was born *c.* 1770. Worked almost exclusively in Bath. Had addresses in Green Street (1809), Milsom Street (1811–1821 etc.). May have been

a pupil of T. Hargreaves (q.v.) in Liverpool. Died in Bath 1827. Was a good artist who drew with accuracy and the faces of his sitters are usually finely executed. He used both hatching and stippling in the backgrounds and often used a horizontal brush stroke which gave the effect of a honeycomb. He signed with a scratched or written signature which was often placed along the edge of the miniature, e.g. Jagger pinxt, or Jagger. The B.M. has some engravings after Jagger and the Holburne Museum, Bath, has a good rectangular miniature of Sir Thomas William Holburne. Two miniatures of Baduley Townsend Rogers, formerly ascribed to him, in the V. & A. M., are now thought to be the work of C. Ford (q.v.). Scovell (q.v.) is said to have succeeded to his practice

Jakush, M. See **Takush, M.**

*James, Miss Alice. (fl 1887–1897)
Of Bath. Exhibited at the R.A., 1887–1897. Duveen records that her exhibit in 1887 sold for 4 guineas, and that other miniatures by her sold for 10 guineas.

*James, E. (fl. 1831)
An enamel miniature of William IV in uniform, signed on the reverse 'E. James/Jany 1831' is in the N.G., Dublin. The colouring is rather bright with pink flesh tints.

James, Miss G. (fl. 1826–1828)
Of Canterbury. Exhibited at the S.B.A., 1826–1828.

Jameson. (fl. *c.* 1794)
According to M. Clouzot the above artist was painting miniatures on enamel in Dublin *c.* 1794.

Jamesone, George. 1587–1644
Born in Aberdeen, 8 February 1587, son of a master mason. Studied in Antwerp 'under Rubens alongside of Vandyck'. Returned to Aberdeen in 1620 and married Isabel Tosh or Toche 1624. Soon became well known and moved to Edinburgh 1633. Painted portraits, miniatures and probably historical subjects and landscapes, including a group of himself with his wife and daughter Mary. Was patronised by the Earl of Mar and Sir Colin Campbell of Glenorchy. He died in 1644, and was buried in Greyfriars Churchyard, Edinburgh. He left considerable legacies.

Jansen, Janssen, Janssens, Cornelius. See **Johnson, Jonson, Jansen or Janssens, Cornelius, the Elder**

Janvry, H. de. (fl. 1793–1800)
A Frenchman, working in England *c.* 1793. Exhibited at the R.A. 1798–1800, from London addresses. May have worked in America. Painted miniatures *en grisaille* on a dark background, many in profile, besides miniatures in water-colour and enamel, and also engraved stones. His signature was H.J. (the J passing through the cross bar of the H), H.J., and H. de Janvry. Sometimes he added a date. Examples of his work may be seen at the V. & A. M. and the N.P.G., London. A profile portrait of Mrs. Fitzherbert (wife of George IV) signed in monogram and dated '1796' is at the V. & A. M.

Jaques or **Jacques, Miss Julia.** (fl. 1826–1836)
Of London. Exhibited at the R.A., N.W.C.S., etc. 1826–1836, not 1870 as recorded by Long and Schidlof.

Jarvis, John Wesley. 1780–1839/40.
Born in South Shields 1780, nephew of the famous

John Wesley in whose charge he was left by his father, who emigrated to America *c.* 1785. Was taken to Philadelphia in 1795. From 1796–1801 Jarvis was apprenticed to the engraver Edward Savage (q.v.). After his apprenticeship ended he moved to New York City and from 1802–1810, worked in partnership with Joseph Wood, painting portraits and miniatures. He moved to Baltimore in 1810, but returned to N.Y.C., in 1813, where he painted a series of full-length portraits of heroes of the War of 1812, for the New York City Hall. Henry Inman (q.v.) became his apprentice in 1814 and John Quidor also studied under him for a short time. From 1820 onwards he spent his winters in the South – New Orleans, Richmond and Washington. Became paralysed in 1834 and spent his remaining years in N.Y.C. where he died on 12 January 1840 (according to Groce & Wallace) or 14 January 1839 (according to Long). Jarvis was a good artist and his portraits are well drawn. The Metropolitan Museum, New York, has a portrait of a man, signed 'Jarvis 1809'. He is said to have been a wit and a raconteur.

*Jay, Miss Cecil. (Mrs. G. Hitchcock). (fl. 1903–1906)
Of Bushey, Herts., Oswestry and Paris. Exhibited at the R.A. 1903–1906, from various addresses. Painted miniatures and subjects in oil. Also executed drawings. Wife of George Hitchcock of Paris and Holland. Was a member of the R.M.S., London.

Jean, Philip. 1755–1802
Born at St. Ouen, Jersey, 1755. Served in the Navy under Rodney as a youth, and later devoted himself to painting. Married as his first wife, Anne Noel (died 1787) by whom he had a son, Roger Jean (q.v.), and secondly, Marie de Ste Croix, by whom he had three daughters. Exhibited at the R.A., 1787–1802. Painted miniatures and portraits in oil; was patronised by the Royal Family and painted full-length portraits of George III and Queen Charlotte as well as miniatures of the Duke and Duchess of Gloucester and their family. Died, 12 September 1802 at Hempstead, Kent, leaving a widow and four children. His style varied a great deal and he seems to have imitated a number of miniaturists including Cosway, Shelley and Meyer (q.v.) etc. His usual signature is P. Jean and P. Jean pinxit, followed by a date. One of his finest miniatures is that of Dominic Serres; this is at the N.P.G., and is dated '1788'. It was exhibited at the South Kensington Museum in 1865. The B.M. has engravings after Jean. A miniature of the artist's second wife with three of her children and her stepson Roger, is owned by the Société Jersiaise. His self-portrait was exhibited at the B.F.A.C., 1889. A fine miniature of Paul Sandby, signed and dated 'P. Jean 1787' was lent by Mrs. Blofeld to the exhibition in Edinburgh, 1965. It depicted the sitter holding his drawing book, with a view of Windsor Castle in the background. Two other miniatures by him of Miss Tyers and Master Tyers, both signed and dated '1787' were lent to the same exhibition by Mr. and Mrs. J. Starr of Kansas City. A miniature of Marechal De Turenne (1611–1675), after an earlier portrait, is in the collection of the Duke of Northumberland and is signed 'P. Jean pinxt 1785/6'. Examples of his work are in the V. & A. M., and numerous private collections. A miniature of Anne Noel, by P. Jean was sold at Sotheby's, 9 June, 1969.

Jean, Roger. *c.* 1783–1828
Born at St. Helier, Jersey *c.* 1783; son of P. Jean

(q.v.), by his first wife Anne Noel (died 1787). Exhibited at the R.A., 1801–1803, from London addresses. His exhibits included portraits of Mrs. Jean, Miss Brown, Mrs. Green and Mr. Bone. Settled in Norwich in 1813 where he lived until his death on 9 December 1828. A miniature of an unknown man, signed by this artist, was Lot 11 at Sotheby's, 18 February 1963, and another, also of an unknown man, signed on the front 'R.Jean / 1801' was Lot 35 at Christie's on 19 December 1967. Schidlof records seeing a miniature of a man with the artist's trade card on the reverse: 'Mr R. Jean, Miniature Painter, Brewer Street, Golden Square'. It was quite good quality though a little hard. Long noted a rather stiff looking miniature of an officer signed with cursive capitals 'RI' and dated '1808' which he attributed to Jean. The one sold at Christie's was quite well modelled, and expressive. An engraved portrait of T. L. Bellamy, after R. Jean, is in the B.M. A miniature by P. Jean of Roger with his stepmother Marie de Ste Croix, and his three stepsisters is owned by the Société Jersiaise.

*Jeffcock, Robert S. (fl. 1904–1905)
Of Harpenden, Herts. Exhibited at the Society of Miniaturists, 1904–1905.

Jeffray, W. (fl. 1788–1789)
Of London. Exhibited at the R.A. 1788–1789, including a portrait on vellum.

*Jemmett, Miss M. K. (fl. 1904–1910)
Of Feltham, Middlesex. Exhibited at the Society of Miniaturists, 1904–1910.

*Jenkins, Miss Elsie M. (fl. 1909)
Of London. Exhibited at the R.A. 1909, from 111 Highbury Quadrant.

Jenkins, M. (fl. 1830). See also **Brewer, Mrs. Mary**
Of London. Exhibited at the R.A. 1830, from 6 Red Lion Square, a portrait of Miss Jane Jenkins. The above artist was possibly identical with Mrs. Mary Brewer (q.v.).

*Jenner, G. (fl. 1810)
A miniature signed by this artist and dated '1810' was seen by Mr. A. J. B. Kiddell.

*Jennings, F. Nevill. (fl. 1903–1905)
Of London. Exhibited at the R.A. and S.M., 1903–1905, from Fair Lawn, Honor Oak Road, Forest Hill.

Jennings, James, F.S.A. (fl. 1763–1793). See also **Jukes, J.**
Of London. Exhibited at the Society of Artists, 1763–1783. Elected F.S.A. in 1771 and was a Director in 1780. Exhibited at the R.A., 1793. All miniatures signed J.J. have now been ascribed to Jennings or Jukes (q.v.), many of them, although small, are of a high quality. One of the best examples I have seen is of an unknown lady of the Hunter Blair family which is in my collection; it is signed 'JJ / 1774'. Lot 94 at Christie's, 13 December 1966 was a miniature of a gentleman, signed 'J J' (block letters); it was catalogued as by J. Jukes (q.v.) and was certainly quite different from the works attributed to Jennings.

*Jennings, Miss Mary. (fl. 1885–1889)
Of Brighton. Exhibited at the R.A., 1885–1889.

Jenour, Charles. (fl. 1825–1850)
Of London. Exhibited at the R.A., 1825–1832. A miniature of Mrs. Bullock-Andrews and five

children c. 1834 was seen by Long who considered the effect rather stiff. According to Long he was supposed to have been working up to 1850.

*Jervas or **Jarvis, Charles.** 1675?–1739
Born c. 1675 probably in Dublin; son of John Jervas of Clonliske and his wife Elizabeth, née Baldwin. He had four brothers and two sisters. Went to London as a young man and became a pupil and assistant of Sir Godfrey Kneller, with whom he remained for about a year. Jervas is best known as a portrait painter, but executed a number of small portraits including one of Thomas Murphy, drawn in pencil on vellum, and inscribed on the reverse 'Thomas Murphy / natus Clonmeliae / in Hibernia 1698 done in Jamaica 1733'. This portrait is in the N.G., Dublin and was at one time in the F. Wellesley collection, sold at Sotheby's in 1920. Jervas had the patronage of Norris, Keeper of the King's pictures and was permitted to copy works at Hampton Court, where he made small copies of the cartoons of Raphael. Had a fashionable clientele, and held office as Principal Painter to George I and George II. Studied for a time in Rome. Married a wealthy widow, and lived in Hampstead in a house which he filled with many works of art and where he entertained leading celebrities of the day, including Pope, Swift, Addison, Lady Mary Wortley Montagu, etc. Jervas made a translation of *Don Quixote*, which was not published until 1742, after his death. In 1738 his health broke down and he revisited Italy. On his return he went to live in his brother-in-law's house in Cleveland Court, where he died on 2 November 1739. He was survived by his widow Penelope, who proved his will, 3 December 1739. His large collection of art was sold after his death. The first part was sold in 1740 and the remainder in April 1747, after his widow's death. Lists of many of his works are given by Strickland in his *Dictionary of Irish Artists* pp. 545–552. Many of his works were engraved.

Jessop or **Jessup, Miss Anne Phyllis.** See **Beechey, Lady**

*Jetts, Mr. (fl. 1747)
A Mr. Jetts, limner, advertised in the *Daily Advertiser*, 5 March 1747 as of Paradise Row, Chelsea.

*Jevons, Mrs. Louisa E. (fl. 1893–1901)
Exhibited at the R.A. 1893–1901, from Hatfield Hall, Durham. Her sitters included Mrs. Fitzhugh Whitehouse and Principal Jevons, R.A.

*Jewesbury, Miss Lilian M. (fl. 1909–1910)
Of London. Exhibited at the Society of Miniaturists, 1909–1910.

*Jobling, Mrs. Isa. (fl. 1903–1910)
Of Whitley Bay, Northumberland. Exhibited at the Society of Miniaturists, 1903–1910.

Jocelyn, Miss Caroline Mary. See **Ffoulkes, Mrs. John Powell**

Jocelyn or **Jocelin, Nathaniel.** 1796–1881
Born 31 January 1796 in New Haven, Connecticut; son of Simeon Jocelin, a clock-maker and engraver. Was apprenticed to a clock-maker but in c. 1813 studied engraving under George Munger. Executed engravings, portraits and miniatures. Published at least one print under the name of Jocelin & Munger. Was associated with the Hartford Graphic & Bank Note Engraving Co. In 1818 he and his brother, S. S. Jocelyn, went into partnership and collaborated until 1843. Was in Savannah,

1820–1822 and on his return to New Haven established himself as a portrait painter. He exhibited at the National Academy, New York, 1826 and became an Academician in 1846. Visited England and France in 1829. Had a studio in New York City, 1843–1847. His studio was burnt in 1849 and he afterwards gave up painting and took up bank note engraving and was a founder of the National Bank Note Co., from which he retired in 1864. Died in New Haven, 13 January 1881.

Johns. (fl. 1791–1816)
Worked in England towards the end of the eighteenth century and the early part of the nineteenth century. It has been suggested that he was a Dutchman, but there is no evidence to support this theory. The quality of Johns' work varies, at best the modelling is good and the colouring pleasing. He sometimes used a bluish shading on the flesh parts, drew the eyelashes and eyebrows in great detail, and often placed his sitters against a dark background. He worked in London, Leeds, Halifax, Scarborough, York, and, before 1795, was in Brussels. Evidence for this is to be found in various numbers of the *Leeds Intelligence* – (3 August 1795) 'Mr Johns, miniature painter to the late Court of Brussels . . . is returned from York . . . Staying in Leeds for a fortnight.' (12 October 1795) 'Mr Johns returns from Scarborough to Leeds.' (15 February 1796) 'Mr. Johns having stayed 5 months in Leeds is to stay 2 or 3 weeks in Halifax before returning to London.' His miniatures are scarce. One called 'The Flower Girl' signed on the front 'Johns', formerly in the collection of Major R.M.O. de la Hey, was sold at Sotheby's on 27 May 1968 for £380. It was exhibited at Edinburgh in 1965 and is a most attractive miniature, painted in clear bright colours. A miniature of a child catalogued as probably by W. S. Lethbridge (q.v.) was Lot 92 at Christie's, 25 June 1968; it was in fact signed 'Johns' close to the frame. This and the one of the 'Flower Girl' both have a suggestion of a smile on the sitter's faces. A portrait in water-colour of Leopold II, Emperor of Austria, signed and dated '1791', is in the Albertina, Vienna and a miniature of James Smithson, painted by Johns at Aachen, 11 May 1816, is in the National Gallery, Washington. Other examples of his work are in the V. & A. M., and the Kaiser Friedrich Museum, Berlin.

*Johns, Edwin Thomas. (fl. 1905–1908)
Exhibited at the R.A. 1905–1908, from addresses in Ipswich. Painted miniatures and subjects in water-colour.

*Johnson. See **Johnson, V.**

*Johnson, Miss A. (fl. 1845). See also **Johnson, Miss M. H.**
Exhibited at the R.A. 1845, from 89 Strand 'Helen, daughter of J. B. Johnson, Esq.' (possibly a miniature). Possibly sister of or identical with Miss M. H. Johnson (q.v.) who also exhibited from this address.

*Johnson, Miss Bertha J. (fl. 1906–1914)
Of London. Exhibited at the R.A. 1906–1914, from The Homestead, Hornsey Lane.

Johnson, Jonson, Jansen or **Janssens, Cornelius, the Elder.** 1593–1661/2
Baptised in London, 14 October 1593. His name has been spelt in various ways, the modern use being Johnson. His family came from Cologne but later settled in Antwerp and from there came to

England. Contemporary with and known to J. Hoskins (q.v.). Married 16 July 1622 Elizabeth Beke or Beck. In 1643 he left for Holland. On 10 October of that year it is recorded in the Journals of the House of Commons that 'Cornelius Johnson, Picture Drawer, shall have Mr Speaker's Warrant to pass beyond the seas with Mr Emanuel Passe and George Hawkins and to carry with him such pictures and colours, bedding, household stuff, pewter and brass as belonged to himself.' During his stay in England he lived in Blackfriars, London. He is best known for his large oil portraits, but also executed miniatures in oil and water-colour. Miniatures by him are scarce, one of Sir Nicholas Crisp was sold with the Sotheby heirlooms in 1955. The Duke of Devonshire has one of a man in a falling ruff, exhibited in Edinburgh in 1965. Another, in the collection of the Duke of Portland, is painted in oil on copper and signed on the reverse 'C. Johnson, fecit 1639'. I know of none by him in water-colour. He signed C.J. in monogram, and charged five broad pieces for a head. He copied many large paintings in miniature. His son Cornelius followed his father's profession. He is said to have been ruined by the extravagance of his second wife and to have died a poor man in 1661 or 1662, probably in Utrecht or Amsterdam. A large self-portrait in oil is at the N.P.G. A fine pair of oil miniatures of Mr. and Mrs. Peter Vandeput by Johnson were Lot 75 at Sotheby's, 6 March 1967, when they realised £790. The sitters were married in England and the portraits were probably painted before the artist went to Holland in 1643.

Johnson or **Jonson, Cornelius, the Younger.** b. after 1622

Born after 1622, son of Cornelius Johnson (q.v.). Accompanied his father to Holland, 1643. In 1664 was living with his mother in Utrecht. Was proposing to come to England in 1675. Said to have married for the second time in 1681. Was practising as a miniature painter in Utrecht in 1698 and was still alive in 1700. Painted oil portraits and miniatures of which there are few known examples at present.

*Johnson, Cyrus. b. 1848

Born 1 January 1848. Worked in London. Exhibited at the R.A., N.W.C.S., etc., 1871–1917. Was a member of the Royal Institute of Painters in Water-Colours and of the New Water-Colour Society. Painted genre subjects, landscapes, portraits and miniatures.

*Johnson, Miss Edith. (fl. 1894)

Of London. Exhibited at the R.A. 1894, from 28 Queens Road, Norland Square, Notting Hill.

*Johnson, Mrs. Esther Borough. (fl. 1886–1913)

Of London and Richmond. Exhibited at the R.A., etc., 1886–1913. Executed subject pictures in oil and water-colour, studies of heads and miniatures.

Johnson, Miss M. H. (fl. 1843–1848). See also **Johnson, Miss A.**

Of London. Possibly a daughter of Thomas Burgeland Johnson (died 1840), writer on field sports, whose portrait she exhibited in 1843. Exhibited at the R.A., B.I. and S.B.A., 1843–1848 and in 1845 was awarded the silver Isis medal by the Society of Arts for a miniature of a lady. Painted miniatures, portraits, figure subjects, etc. Exhibited from 89 Strand, from which address Miss A. Johnson (q.v.) also exhibited in 1845. The two were possibly related or identical. Miss M. H. Johnson

may possibly have been identical with the Miss Helen Mary Johnson who exhibited at the B.I., 1865–1867.

*Johnson, Miss Marie. (fl. 1902–1914)

Of London. Exhibited at the R.A. 1902–1914, from various London addresses. Her sitters included Mrs. Percy Collins and Miss Gertie Sumnel.

*Johnson, Miss Nelly. (fl. 1903–1904)

Of London. Exhibited at the Society of Miniaturists, 1903–1904.

Johnson, Robert. 1770–1796

Born in Shotley, Northumberland, 1770, son of a joiner and carpenter. Studied under Bewick, the engraver, in Newcastle. Painted portraits in water-colour and miniatures on ivory. Made water-colour sketches from nature and designs which were used by Bewick in *Water Birds and Fables*. Was employed to copy portraits at Taymouth Castle. He died as a result of catching a severe cold, at Kenmore, Perthshire, 26 October 1796 and was buried at Ovingham. Schidlof mentions having seen two miniatures by him he thought well painted: one of Nathan Theodore Fielding (q.v.) and the other supposedly of James Heath Millington (q.v.) (the latter artist's dates make this impossible). The colouring was pink with light green shadows. The V. & A. M. has a miniature of a lady by him.

Johnson, V. (fl. 1802–1803)

Of Nottingham. Exhibited at the R.A., 1802–1803. Possibly the artist who is noted in the *Leeds Intelligence*, 18 June 1804 'Johnson miniature painter from London is in Leeds', and again, 18 October 1808 ' . . . Short stay in Sheffield'. Exhibited a self-portrait at the R.A., in 1802.

Johnston, Mrs. David (Miss Mary Ann Wheeler). (fl. 1834–1859)

Née Mary Ann Wheeler; daughter of T. Wheeler (q.v.) from whose address, 55 Regent's Quadrant, she exhibited at the R.A. in 1834, under her maiden name. Married David Johnston c. 1836 in which year she is recorded in the R.A. catalogues as Mrs. D. Johnston, late Miss M. A. Wheeler. She continued to exhibit at the R.A. until 1843, from High Street, Peckham, and, according to Long, exhibited elsewhere until 1859.

*Johnstone, Mrs. (I). (fl. 1835–1859). See also **Johnstone, Mrs. (II).**

Of London. Exhibited at the R.A. 1835–1859, from various London addresses including 4 Clarendon Place, Vassall Road, North Brixton. She was an Honorary Exhibitor in 1835. Was presumably the Mrs. Johnstone (II) (q.v.) who exhibited a miniature at the Society of Female Artists in 1858.

Johnstone, Mrs. (II). (fl. 1858). See also **Johnstone, Mrs. (I)**

Of London. Exhibited at the Society of Female Artists in 1858. Was possibly identical with Mrs. Johnstone (I) (q.v.).

Johnstone, William Borthwick, R.S.A. 1804–1868

Born in Edinburgh, 21 July 1804, son of a lawyer. Studied law in Edinburgh but later devoted himself to painting. Exhibited at the Royal Scottish Academy, 1836–1838, and was its treasurer for many years; became an Associate of the R.S.A., 1840, and R.S.A., 1848. Studied at the Trustees Academy, 1840–1842 in which year he went to Italy. Returned to Scotland in 1844. Had lessons in miniature painting from R. Thorburn (q.v.) in London. Painted landscapes, historical subjects and

miniatures; wrote on art and was a collector. Married a daughter of J. C. Brown, A.R.S.A. Died at 3 Gloucester Place, Edinburgh, 5 June 1868. A portrait of W. B. Johnstone by J. Phillip, R.A., dated 1861, was presented to the National Gallery of Scotland by his wife in 1868 together with one, also by Phillip, of Mrs. W. B. Johnstone.

Jones. (fl. 1782–1783). See **Jones, B.** and **Jones, R.**

Worked at Bath (c. 1782), Manchester (29 July 1783) and London. Painted miniatures in profile, taught painting on silk and glass in imitation of needlework etc., for which he charged one guinea. Advertised, September 1782 'new-invented Optical Instruments, for copying drawing, painting natural flowers, insects etc.' Executed likenesses in crayon at 15s. each, gilt frame included; charged two guineas for likenesses on paper and 5s. for miniature profiles on glass. May have been identical with either B. Jones (q.v.) or R. Jones (q.v.).

*Jones, Miss Agnes A. (fl. 1908–1912)

Of Canonbury, London. Exhibited at the R.A., 1908 and 1912. Her sitters included Trevor, son of Arthur Tooth, Esq. Possibly the Agnes Jones who exhibited a landscape at Suffolk Street in 1893.

Jones, B. (fl. 1774). See **Jones**

Of London. Pupil of Thomas Pether (q.v.). Exhibited at the Free Society of Artists, 1774. Executed drawings in chalk, black-lead, and painted miniatures. Possibly identical with the Jones (q.v.) who worked at Bath, Manchester and London.

*Jones, Charles Stansfield. (fl. 1909)

Of London. Exhibited at the Society of Miniaturists, 1909.

Jones, Miss Charlotte. 1768–1847

Was born in 1768. Daughter of Thomas Jones of Cley, Norfolk. Studied under Cosway (q.v.). Worked in London and Manchester (25 March 1788); was at Bath (6 December 1792) where she had an address at Grove Street. She exhibited at the R.A., 1801–1823; one of her exhibits in 1807 was an enamel of the 'late Rt. Hon. Charles James Fox.' Became miniature painter to H.R.H. Princess Charlotte of Wales, c. 1808. Painted miniatures on ivory and enamel and profile portraits in crayon; charged 25 to 30 guineas. Received a bequest from Mrs. Cosway (q.v.) 1838. Became partially blind and died in Upper Gloucester Place, London, 21 September 1847. Her works lack assurance and are not of great merit. Some of her miniatures are at Windsor Castle. A self-portrait and a portrait of George IV when Prince Regent, are at the Holburne Museum, Bath.

*Jones, Mrs. D. Brynmor (Florence). See Brynmor-Jones, Mrs. D.

*Jones, Miss E. Nora. (fl. 1890–1901)

Of London. Exhibited at the R.A., S.M., etc., 1890–1901. *The Bazaar* on 24 January 1898 noted that she was exhibiting at that time.

Jones, Edward. c. 1775–1862

Was born c. 1775. Studied at the Dublin Society Schools. Exhibited at Dublin 1800–1821. He succeeded in obtaining a considerable practice. Executed portrait drawings and miniatures, some of which were engraved for the *Methodist Magazine*. Was secretary of the Hibernian Society of Artists. Lived for many years in Chatham Street, Dublin. Retired in 1827 and died at his daughter's home, 16 Charlemont Mall, on 17 February 1862. Was probably the Edward Jones who exhibited shipping scenes (one of Ireland) at the B.I., in 1839–1840.

Jones, Miss Eliza. (fl. 1815–1852)

Of London. Probably identical with Miss Eliza L. Jones who won a premium at the Society of Arts in 1807. Exhibited at the B.I., R.A., and O.W.C.S., 1815–1852. Her sitters included Queen Victoria, Sir F. Chantrey, Sir C. Napier, Lady Caroline Lamb and H. Edridge (q.v.). Painted religious subjects, figure subjects, etc. and miniatures, some of which were on enamel. Some of her miniatures were after Cosway (q.v.). The *Annals of the Fine Arts*, Vol. I, p. 428, records an Eliza Jones, miniaturist, as living at 74 Great Portland Street, London.

*Jones, Miss Elizabeth Emma. See Soyer, Madame Emma E.

Jones, G. (fl. 1832)

Of London. Exhibited a portrait of Napoleon at the R.A. 1832, from 38 Leicester Square.

*Jones, G. Kingston. (fl. 1906–1907)

Of London. Exhibited at the Society of Miniaturists 1906–1907.

*Jones, Miss Jessie H. (fl. 1901)

Exhibited at the R.A. 1901, from Ireton Lodge, Wolverhampton.

Jones, John. (fl. *c.* 1745)

A plumbago portrait of George, Lord Grenville *c.* 1745 and catalogued as by this artist was lent to the exhibition of miniatures in Manchester 1926.

Jones, John Hammond. (fl. 1822–1833)

Of London. Exhibited at the R.A., 1828–1833. Was awarded a silver Isis from the Society of Arts in 1833, for his fluid to be used as a vehicle for colours in miniature painting. Full details are to be found in the *Transactions of the Society of Arts*, Vol. L. p. 30. The solution, which consisted of borax in distilled water, in every quart of which was ¼ oz gum Tragacanth which had to be dissolved, was then used to cover the ivory or porcelain, two to three layers being necessary, each being allowed to dry before the next was applied; then the colours were laid on, each one mixed with a few drops of the liquid. This process was supposed to render whatever colour it was united with so firm and hard that, when dry, tints could be laid on as easily as they could on paper. A miniature of an unknown lady, in my collection, is signed 'J. Hammond Jones' at the bottom right hand corner. The lady is depicted looking pensive as she writes a letter. The draughtsmanship is good and the painting smooth with soft colours. The V. & A. M. has a small water-colour portrait by J. H. Jones of J. G. Barratt, aged 3. The miniature is signed and dated '1822'. Two miniatures by J. H. Jones were lent by Mrs. Jones to the exhibition at the South Kensington Museum, 1865.

*Jones, Miss M. (fl. 1859)

Exhibited at the R.A., 1859, in the Drawing and Miniature Section and may possibly have been identical with Miss Matilda Jones (q.v.).

*Jones, Miss Mabel Bugett (Mrs. Puleston). (fl. 1898–1909)

Of London. Exhibited at the R.A., 1898–1909.

*Jones, Mrs. Marion Clayton. See Clayton Jones, Mrs. Marion Alexandra

Jones, Miss Matilda. (fl. 1825–1843). See also **Jones, Miss M.**

Of London. Exhibited at the R.A., 1825–1843. Was awarded several medals by the Society of Arts in 1826–1828 for miniatures. Was possibly identical with the Miss M. Jones (q.v.) who exhibited at the R.A. in 1859, in the Drawing and Miniature Section.

Jones, R. (Robert ?). (fl. 1780–1812 ?). See also **Jones**

Exhibited a miniature of 'An old man's head' at the R.A., in 1780 as an Hon. Exhibitor. Was possibly the Robert Jones who entered the R.A. Schools, 30 December 1797 aged 27, and probably identical with the R. Jones who exhibited at the R.A., 1798–1812, including architectural subjects, figures and miniatures. In 1798 he exhibited a miniature of the porter of the Royal Academy. The B.M. has an engraved portrait of W. Holland after R. Jones. He was also possibly identical with the Jones (q.v.) who worked in Bath, Manchester and London.

Jones, R. P. (fl. 1776–1786)

Of the Custom House, London. Exhibited at the Society of Artists and the R.A., 1776–1786, including a miniature for a ring. Painted miniatures and executed drawings from cameos.

*Jones, Robert. See Jones, R.

Jones, Mrs. S. (fl. 1797–1812). See also **Jones, Miss Sophia**

Of London. Exhibited at the R.A., etc., 1797–1812. Painted portraits, figure subjects and miniatures. May have been identical with or related to Miss Sophia Jones (q.v.), as they both exhibited from 23 Clarges Street, Piccadilly. In 1807 Mrs. S. Jones exhibited portraits of Miss Jones and Miss J. H. Jones.

Jones, Miss Sophia. (fl. 1789–1800). See also **Jones, Mrs. S.**

Of London. Exhibited at the R.A., 1789–1800. May have been identical with or related to Mrs. S. Jones (q.v.) as both artists exhibited from 23 Clarges Street, Piccadilly.

Jonson, Cornelius, the Elder. See Johnson, Cornelius, the Elder

Jonson, Cornelius, the Younger. See Johnson, Cornelius, the Younger

Jonvaux. (fl. 1831–1835)

Exhibited at the R.A. 1831, and at the Paris Salon 1835. As no address is given the artist may not have lived in England.

Jopling, Joseph Middleton. 1831–1884

Born in London 1831. Son of a clerk in the Horse Guards and held a similar appointment. Was self-taught. Exhibited at the R.A., N.W.C.S., S.B.A. etc., 1848–1884; was a member of the (Royal) Institute of Painters in Water Colours, 1859–1876. Was an active volunteer and won the Queen's prize for shooting in 1861. Was director of the fine art section of the exhibition at Philadelphia. Died in Chelsea, December 1884. Best known for landscapes, but lent a portrait on ivory of Miss Florence Ashton to the exhibition at the South Kensington Museum, 1865.

Joseph, Caroline (fl. *c.* 1800–1820)

Worked in England *c.* 1800–1820. A water-colour portrait by her 3½ x 3 in. after a miniature of the Rev. T. Beresford is at the B.M.

Joseph, George Francis, A.R.A. 1764–1846

Born, possibly in Dublin, 25 November 1764.

Entered the R.A. Schools, 3 December 1784, aged 20. Exhibited at the R.A. and B.I., 1788–1846. Was a cousin of Samuel Joseph, the sculptor. Worked in London and Cambridge. Won a gold medal at the R.A., 1792, and was awarded premiums by the B.I., 1811 and 1812. Elected A.R.A. in 1813. Painted oil portraits, subject pictures and miniatures, some of which were in oil on copper. He used a lot of gum with his paint. He died at Cambridge in 1846 and was buried in St. Michael's Churchyard. The B.M. has a portrait in water-colour of Charles Lamb, by Joseph and some engravings after him. A miniature of G. Field, signed on the reverse and dated '1807', was in the Melvill A. Jamieson Collection, London. A portrait of him by Varley is in the V. & A. M.

*Josling, H. Stanley. (fl. 1905–1906)

Of London. Exhibited at the R.A. 1905 and 1906, from 27 Shaftesbury Avenue.

Judlin, Alexis. b. 1746

Born according to Schidlof at Thann (Alsace) in 1746. Entered the R.A. Schools, 22 October 1773, aged 27. Exhibited at the R.A. 1773–1776, and at the Paris Salon 1791 and 1793. He obtained a pension from the King (George III). Said to have worked in several courts in Europe. Painted portraits in oil and miniatures. His work shows a combination of both British and Continental techniques; he painted the costume of his sitters in gouache and the backgrounds in water-colour. Signed Judlin, A. Judlin, and Judlin f., followed by a date. A miniature of the Chevalier d'Eon, 1776, by Judlin is at the V. & A. M. Schidlof records works by this artist in collections on the Continent. A charming miniature of a young lady reading a letter is in the collection of the Duke of Northumberland. It is signed on the letter 'A Londen (or Conden)/judlin 1772'. The sitter is wearing a white dress and has an upswept hair-style ornamented with pearls from which falls a small gauze veil. A lilac curtain is draped behind her head.

Jukes, John. 1772–1851. See also **Jennings, J.**

Born, 6 January 1772. Presumably related to or the son of Andrew Jukes of the Bombay Medical Service, an amateur landscape painter. Said by his family to have been apprenticed to Sir Joshua Reynolds. Entered the R.A. Schools, 14 October 1791, when his age was recorded as 19. Exhibited at the R.A., from London addresses, 1791–1799. His address from 1792–1794 was 120 Strand and 1795–1799, 3 Tavistock Row, Covent Garden. His sitters included Miss Green, Mr. A. Jukes (probably Andrew Jukes), Mr. J. Jukes (possibly a self-portrait), Mrs. Moseley, and in 1799 Mr. Jukes of Bombay; this may have been a second miniature of A. Jukes. John Jukes sailed to Bombay in August 1812 in the *Caroline* which reached its destination on 10 April 1813. Long saw two rectangular miniatures of a lady and gentleman, executed in Bombay in 1816. Jukes was apparently in India over twelve years before returning to England. He left Bombay in the *Cambridge*, 11 August 1824, in which year notice was given in the *Bombay Courier* on 24 July 1824, of the impending sale of his furniture etc., preparatory to his departure for England; in the same journal on 14 August there is an account of a farewell dinner given to him by the Bombay Billiard Club and mention is made of his having been in Bombay for over twelve years and that 'almost every person belonging to this Presidency had some token of his talents connected with the dearest objects of their affection.' Much of this information was given by Sir William Foster, *Walpole Society*, Vol. XIX, p. 56, who refers to two miniatures, one of James Henry Crawford (Bombay) and his wife, both painted in 1816. Jukes died on 21 October 1851. His family were in possession of a large number of miniatures painted in oil and water-colour which were seen by Long in 1932. The fact that Jukes and J. Jennings (q.v.) share the same initials makes identification difficult. Those I have seen which were undoubtedly by Jukes have been signed J. J. on the front in thicker and bolder block lettering than that used by Jennings who signed in thin cursive initials, similar to those used by Smart (q.v.). The style of Jukes' painting differs from that of Jennings and is bolder and the portrait more thickly painted. Some of Jukes' portraits were painted against a dark curtain; the treatment of the hair is rather wiry. A miniature of a gentleman, signed 'JJ' (block letters) was Lot 94 at Christie's, 13 December 1966. It was quite well painted. Occasionally his miniatures are signed on the reverse, e.g. 'Painted by J. Jukes/Aug. 1804'. The B.M. has an engraved portrait of H. Gibbon after J. Jukes.

K

K. (fl. 1762). See also **Kay, John**

A miniature on ivory said to represent Sir R. Abercrombie and signed 'K/1762' in cursive initials was seen by Long. The initals had a flourish at the top which might have been intended for a monogram IK or JK.

*K., T. (fl. 1804)

A miniature of General Sir Frederick Adam, G.C.B. (1784–1853), Governor of Madras, painted in water-colour and signed 'T.K., pinx 1804' was seen at the S.N.P.G., and was in the collection of Capt. C. K. Adam.

Karlsteen or **Carlsteen, Arvid.** 1647–1718

Born at Geelskogen, Sweden, 16 March 1647. Became a medallist in Avesta, and later in Stockholm. Went to Paris in 1668 where he remained for some time, then went to London where he was a pupil of J. Roettier, a medallist. Studied miniature painting and engraving. Was summoned to Stockholm on the occasion of the coronation of Charles XI, and became medallist to the King and executed numerous orders for foreign courts. Travelled abroad. Was knighted in 1692; was a keen art collector. He died at Stockholm, 8 May 1718. His collection, which contained a number of miniatures, was split up by a lottery held on 24 May 1718. Miniatures by this artist are rare; the Nationalmuseum, Stockholm has one of Charles XI by Karlsteen.

*Karuth, Miss Ethel. (fl. 1901–1910)

Of London. Exhibited at the R.A. and S.M. 1901–1910, from. various London addresses. Her sitters included Mme. Sara Bernhardt in 'L'Aiglon'.

Kauffmann, Maria Anna Angelica Catharina, R.A. 1741–1807

Born in Switzerland, 30 October 1741. This famous artist and painter of portraits and historical subjects came to England in 1766. It is alleged that she painted miniatures but this fact has never been established. She died in Rome, 5 November 1807.

*Kay, Miss Harriet M. (fl. 1902)

Of Edinburgh. Exhibited at the R.A. 1902, from 2 Great Stuart Street. Her exhibits included a miniature of Mrs. A. C. Kay.

Kay, John. 1742–1826. See also **K.**

Born near Dalkeith, Scotland, in April 1742, son of a stonemason who died when the boy was eight years old. He was taken care of for five years by his mother's relations in Leith, where he was not at all happy. Kay was then apprenticed for six years to a Dalkeith barber, after which time he set up on his own in Edinburgh, and painted miniatures in his spare time, besides sketching horses, dogs, shipping, etc. In 1782 he received an annuity of £20 and devoted his time to painting miniatures and etching portraits and caricatures; some of these latter got him into trouble. He exhibited at the Edinburgh Association of Artists, 1811–1816 and at the Institute for the Encouragement of the Fine Arts in 1822. Married firstly Lily Stevens, by whom he had ten children, and secondly in 1785, Margaret Scott. Was financially embarrassed and had assistance from a Mr. Nesbet who had taken an interest in him and whose heir settled an annuity of £20 on Kay. Kay died above Gillespie's shop, Geddes Entry, 227 High Street, Edinburgh on 21 February 1826 and was buried in the Greyfriars' Churchyard. His usual signature on his etchings is I. Kay or IK. Long records seeing a miniature signed 'I.K./1810' in which the draughtsmanship was not very good. His *Series of Original Portraits and Caricature Etchings* was issued 1837–8 and reprinted 1877. It contained biographical matter. An oil self-portrait is in the S.N.P.G. A miniature of William Low, an Edinburgh portrait painter, catalogued as by Kay was loaned to the exhibition at the South Kensington Museum, 1865.

Kay, William. (fl. 1795)

Son of John Kay (q.v.) of Edinburgh. A miniature portrait of Lord Byron as a boy of seven years of age, signed and dated '1795' by the above artist and executed in water-colour on paper, was in the F. Wellesley collection sold at Sotheby's in 1920. It was illustrated in the catalogue of the sale f.p. 133. The portrait is of little artistic merit and is not well drawn. According to the *D.N.B.*, Kay etched several portraits.

Kean, Michael. 1761–1823

Born in Dublin in 1761. Entered the Dublin Society Schools in 1771 where he won a silver medal. Was a pupil of E. Smith. Practised for a few years in Dublin, painting miniatures and crayon portraits. Went to London and entered the R.A. Schools, 29 October 1784 aged '23 16 last Oct'. Exhibited at the R.A., 1786–1790. In 1795 William Duesbury, junior took him into partnership at the Derby china factory. Duesbury died in 1796 and Kean married his widow in 1798 and remained in virtual possession of the china factory until 1811. After selling the Derby factory in 1811 Kean returned to London. He is said to have been hot tempered and was for many years separated from his wife. He died in November 1823. Kean was Captain of the 6th Company of the Old Derby Volunteers. His son became a Captain in the Navy. Six miniatures by him were loaned to the exhibition at the South Kensington Museum, 1865, including a portrait of Lunardi, the aeronaut. The V. & A. M. has a miniature of an unknown man by Kean.

Keeffe, Daniel. See **O'Keeffe, Daniel**

*Keeling, R. Lee. (fl. 1905)

Exhibited at the R.A. 1905, from c/o Messrs. H. Graves & Co., Pall Mall, S.W.1.

Keen, W. (fl. 1804)

Of London. Exhibited at the R.A., 1804, a portrait of Mr. Simpson.

Keenan, John. (fl. 1780–1819)

Of Dublin. Pupil and assistant to Robert Home (q.v.) the portrait painter. Went to London c. 1790 and was at Bath (1792), Exeter (1794–1799), Taunton (1798), London (1801), Windsor (1803–1812 and 1815), Newbury (1808–1809). Exhibited at the R.A. and B.I., 1791–1815. Was appointed portrait painter to Queen Charlotte in 1809 and was patronised by the Royal Family. Painted miniatures, oil portraits and groups of children. Returned to Ireland c. 1817 and lived in White Lane, Dublin. Some of his portraits were engraved. His wife and he both taught drawing and she was probably the Mrs. Keenan who had addresses at Windsor, Newbury, Manchester and Preston, and who painted landscapes. He exhibited a miniature of Robert Southey, in Ireland, 1817. Nothing is known about him after 1819. The B.M. has engraved portraits after Keenan.

Keenan, Miss L. (fl. 1834–1835)

Of London. Exhibited at the R.A., etc., 1834–1835. Said to have painted a miniature of Queen Charlotte. Her sitters also included Trehawke Kekewich, Esq., Lord Rolle, and Lady Yarde Buller.

*Keighly, Miss Mabel. (fl. 1907)

Exhibited at the R.A. 1907, from 7 Skardon Place, Plymouth.

Keiser, Willem de. See **Keyser, Willem de**

*Kelham, Robert. (fl. 1776)

Advertised as a miniature painter in the *Chelmsford Chronicle*, 7 February 1776.

*Kellar, James. 1750–1810

Born in London 1750. Visited France and Italy and discovered he had a talent for painting. Did not practise seriously until after 1783. Studied art in St. Petersburg from 1785–1788. Was in Frankfurt in 1789 after which time he settled in Riga where he died in 1810. Schidlof suggests that his miniatures showed the influence of Füger.

*Keller, Mrs. Evelyn. (fl. 1892–1913)

Of Walton-on-Thames. Exhibited at the R.A., 1892–1913. Her sitters included Josceline, daughter of L. E. Keller, Esq.

*Keller, Miss Fanny H. M. (fl. 1883–1892)

Of London. Exhibited at the R.A., 1883–1892. Her exhibit in 1885 was of Esther, daughter of J. J. Duveen, Esq.

*Kellow, Miss Kate. (fl. 1893)

Of London. Exhibited at the R.A., 1893.

Kelson, d. 1778

The *Freeman's Journal* for 20 January 1778 announced the death in Dame Street, Dublin of 'Kelson, miniature painter'. Nothing else is known about this artist.

Keman, Georges Antoine. 1765–1830

Born at Schlettstadt, 7 August 1765. Went to Paris in 1784 and became a pupil of Jean-Michel and Jean Pierre Diebolt. Returned to Schlettstadt in 1789 and the following year went to Strasburg. He returned to Paris where he painted members of the aristocracy and actors, before going to London in 1792. Exhibited at the R.A., 1793–1807. Painted miniatures and paintings in oil. Entered the R.A. Schools, 22 March 1793 aged 27. Became miniature painter to the Duke of Cumberland from 1805. Settled at Bristol in 1796 and married Miss Hanna Smith in 1797. Returned to London 1807 and c. 1816 visited France, Italy and Switzerland before returning to Schlettstadt where he remained until his death. Whilst in England he painted some religious subjects, copied some pictures for Sir Thomas Stokes, and worked in numerous country houses. Major R. M. O. de la Hey has a large oval miniature by Keman and there is another miniature at the V. & A. M. by him. The B.M. has engraved portraits after Keman.

*Kempe, Miss Cicely. (fl. 1906)
Of London. Exhibited at the R.A. 1906, from 14 Montagu Place.

*Kempthorne, Miss Helen Mary. (fl. 1905–1913)
Of London. Exhibited at the R.A. and S.M. 1905–1913, from 15 Briardale Gardens, Hampstead.

*Kemp-Welch, Miss Edith M. (fl. 1898–1914)
Exhibited at the R.A. 1898–1914, from Kingsley, Bushey, Herts. Executed miniatures, subjects in oil, water-colours and drawings. A number of miniatures by this artist were sold at Sotheby's, 12 December 1966. Undoubtedly related to Miss Lucy E. Kemp-Welch who exhibited a large oil painting at the R.A., in 1898 from Kingsley, Bushey. Her sitters included W. W. Shackleton, Esq., M.D., the Hon. Edith Gibbs, Miss E. Buckland Kemp-Welch, and Martin Kemp-Welch.

*Kendall, Miss Ethel M. L. (fl. 1904–1914)
Of Beckenham and London. Exhibited at the R.A., 1904–1914.

Kendrick, Miss Emma Eleonora. c. 1788–1871
Born, c. 1788. Daughter of the sculptor Joseph Kendrick. Was awarded several prizes by the Society of Arts, 1810–1817. Exhibited at the R.A., S.B.A., O.W.C.S. and N.W.C.S., 1811–1840. Became miniature painter to Princess Elizabeth of Hesse-Homburg, and to William IV in 1831. Painted miniatures, genre subjects in water-colour and published *Conversations on the Art of Miniature Painting* in 1830. She died, 6 April 1871. The quality of her work varied a great deal and her drawing was not always accurate. She signed in full, e.g., Emma Eleanora Kendrick / Pinxit 1828 / Duchess St. / Portland Place. The V. & A. M. has a miniature by her of Lady Caroline Lamb. Long records seeing two miniatures by her which showed the influence of Sir Thomas Lawrence (q.v.).

*Kennedy, J. (fl. 1823–1825)
Exhibited at the R.A. 1823, from 198 Regent Street, London. A miniature of T. Edwards, painted on card and signed on the front 'J. Kennedy' and on the reverse 'T. Edwards, August 19th 1825. Born the 24th of January 1805. Left England for Jamaica on Sunday the 11th November 1827— 5 ft 10½ ins. high', was in the O'Brien Collection; it was not of any great merit. Possibly the same artist whose portrait in oil is at Magdalen College, Oxford, and signed on the reverse 'J. Kennedy of Oxford 1850'. Schidlof refers to a miniature of a young lady painted on ivory and signed 'J. Kennedy'.

Kenwell, Miss Anna Maria. See Charretie, Mrs. John

*Kenyon, Miss Gertrude. (fl. 1903–1909)
Of London. Exhibited at the R.A., and S.M., 1903–1909. Her sitters included Mrs. F. Wardale and Miss Winnie Wardale.

Kerr, Lady Louisa. (fl. 1830)
A miniature on ivory 'Portrait of a Lady in the Character of the Muse, Polyhymnia' 1830, by Lady Louisa Kerr was lent to the exhibition at South Kensington Museum in 1865. The artist may have been Harriett Louisa, daughter of the 6th Marquess of Lothian who married Sir John Stuart Forbes, Bt., 13 June 1834 and who died, 24 April 1884. Two silhouette portraits by Lady Louisa Kerr are recorded in the catalogue of portraits belonging to the 4th Earl of Liverpool in 1905.

Kerrich, Rev. Thomas. 1748–1828
Born, 4 February 1748, son of a clergyman. Educated at Magdalene College, Cambridge. After taking orders he travelled on the Continent for some years after 1771. Received a medal from the Antwerp Academy in 1776. Painted portraits in oil, drew highly finished portraits in pencil and chalk, some of which were engraved; etched plates of monuments and was one of the earliest lithographers. Became Librarian to Cambridge University in 1797. Died at his home in Free School Lane, Cambridge, 10 May 1828. Bequeathed MSS to the B.M., who have engraved portraits after him, and a chalk portrait of the Rev. W. Cole. Lot 494 in the catalogue of the F. Wellesley sale at Sotheby's, June 1920 was a small pencil drawing of William Pitt, by Kerrich. According to the catalogue this was drawn in 1776 when Pitt was a student at Cambridge; he and Kerrich were close friends.

Kerry, Dryden. (fl. 1822)
Of Birmingham. Working in 1822 at Little Charles Street. Painted 'fancy miniatures'.

Kershaw, T. (fl. 1803)
Of London. Exhibited at the R.A., 1803.

*Kersterman, Mrs. Frances W. (fl. 1797)
Née Frances W. Bingham. According to a note made by the late Basil Long, the above artist painted miniatures in 1797. She signed her works along the edge and copied the works of Wood (q.v.) and Plimer (q.v.).

Ketterlin, Louis. 1770?–1799?
No exact biographical information regarding this artist is at present available. According to Thieme-Becker he was born in London in 1770; Williamson describes him as a Frenchman who resided in Rathbone Place, London, and who died there in 1799. He was possibly related to J. J. Ketterlin (d. 1813), a Swiss miniaturist who worked at Basle. A miniature of J. L. Buffon, signed 'Ketterlin' is reproduced on Pl. LXIV of Williamson's *History of Portrait Miniatures*. A miniature of Lord Winterton, signed 'Ketterlin 1765' is in the V. & A. M. If this miniature is by the above artist then his date of birth must have been considerably earlier than the date given by Thieme-Becker.

Kettle, Miss Clara E. F. d. after 1865
Of Weymouth and London (1847–1848). Exhibited at the R.A., S.B.A., etc., 1845–1856. Lent some miniatures, including a self-portrait, to the exhibition at the South Kensington Museum 1865.

Keymer, Matthew or R. (fl. 1795–1805)
Worked in Norwich and at Yarmouth c. 1795–1805 or later. Painted portraits and miniatures, including a miniature from life of Nelson, painted at 'The Wrestlers', Yarmouth. This portrait was presented by the artist to a club called the 'Society of Friends'. A profile miniature on card of T. J. Irwine, K.B., is in the V. & A. M., on the reverse of which is the remains of the artist's trade card, where he advertised that he painted portraits and

miniatures, for which his charge was 'miniatures, from £2. 2.' and oil portraits from £1.'11. 6d. A printer and publisher of this name flourished in Yarmouth up to 1813, and may have been related. A mezzotint signed M. R. Keymer was sold at Sotheby's, 4 March 1931.

Keyser or Keiser, Willem de. c. 1647–1692
Born at Antwerp c. 1647; was trained as a jeweller but also painted miniatures (some in enamel), oil portraits and religious subjects. Came to England in 1687 and was at first quite successful but after the 1688 revolution his practice deteriorated. He sought the philosopher's stone. Died in London, 1692. His daughter who died in England in 1724 painted small oil portraits. An enamel portrait of James II believed to be by him is in the collection of the Duke of Buccleuch.

Kilburn or Kilbrunn, Lawrence. 1720–1775
Was born in 1720. Worked in London before 1754 when he went to New York and advertised in the local press both as a painter and dealer in paints, window-glass, etc. Painted portraits and miniatures. Married Judith Eyrand of New York in 1761. Died, 28 June 1775. His name has been spelt Kilbrunn.

*Kindnik, Mrs. Eleanor. 18th century
Of 6 Upper Marylebone Street, Fitzroy Square, London. An 18th-century miniature by this artist was seen by Mr. A. J. B. Kiddell.

*King, Miss Agnes Gardner. (fl. 1882–1907)
Of London. Exhibited at the R.A., N.W.C.S., etc., 1882–1896. A family group of Lord Kelvin, James Thomson and Mrs. Elizabeth King, by the above artist is in the N.P.G. It is executed in pencil and signed and dated 'Agnes G. King, 1907'.

King, Daniel. d. c. 1664
Son of William King, a Chester baker. Was apprenticed, 3 September 1630, to Randle Holme, a painter of Chester with whom he remained for ten years. Went to London, where he probably knew Hollar (q.v.). It is not certain that this artist painted miniatures but he published topographical books with etched illustrations executed by himself. King wrote *Miniatura or the Art of Limning* which was probably assembled from various sources. Said to have been robbed by his wife and to have died heartbroken near York House, Strand, London, c. 1664.

*King, Mrs. Emilie. (fl. 1908–1914)
Exhibited at the R.A. 1908–1914, from Holywell, St. Ives, Huntingdonshire.

King, Emily. (fl. 1848–1849)
Of London. Exhibited at the R.A. 1848–1849, from 39 Foley Place, Portland Square. Her exhibits were a sketch from nature and a portrait of Miss Fores.

*King, Mrs. Preston. (fl. 1903)
Of Gay Street, Bath. Exhibited at the Society of Miniaturists, 1903. Her sitters included the Rt. Rev. George Lanchester King, Anglican Bishop of Madagascar.

Kingsbury, Henry. See Kinsbury, Henry

Kinsbury, Henry. (fl. 1776)
Of Westminster. Exhibited at the Society of Artists, 1776. The exhibits were a miniature and a mezzotint and the artist was probably identical with Henry Kingsbury, a draughtsman and mezzotint engraver who was working c. 1750–1780.

Kipling, Miss Mary. (fl. 1841–1848)
Of London. Exhibited at the R.A., 1843–1848.
Schidlof refers to having seen a miniature on ivory
of Mrs. Alfred Kipling, signed on the reverse 'by
Mary Kipling / 1841'. She appears to have been an
artist of only average ability. Her address was 8
Pleasant Row, Lower Road, Islington.

Kirby, Miss U. (fl. 1855–1857)
Of London. Exhibited at the R.A. 1855–1857,
from 12 Blandford Square.

Kirchhoffer, Henry, R. H. A. c. 1781–1860
Thought to have been born in Dublin c. 1781;
descended from a Swiss surgeon. Son of Francis
Kirchhoffer and his wife Sarah, née Brooke.
Entered the Dublin Society Schools, 1797. Exhibited
at Dublin in 1801. Went to live at Cork where he
remained for several years, returning to Dublin in
1816 when he settled at 4 Russell Place. Whilst at
Cork he exhibited at the first Munster exhibition in
1815. Exhibited at Dublin, 1817, 1819 and 1821,
and at the R.H.A., 1826–1835, being an original
Associate and Member of the Society and its
secretary c. 1830. Painted landscapes, portraits,
miniatures and figure subjects. Went to London
in 1835 and later lived at Brighton. Exhibited at the
R.A., 1837–1843. Died at 71 St. John's Wood
Terrace, London, 20 March 1860. A water-colour
portrait of Charles Robertson (q.v.) by Kirchhoffer
is in the N.G., Dublin. He signed H Kirkhoffer,
and in monogram HK as well as HKirchhoffer and
Kirchoffer. A miniature of a child, signed and dated
'Cork, 1809' and one of Benjamin Bagwell, signed
and dated 'Cork 1805' are in the collection of E. G.
Paine of New York.

*Kirk, Mrs. Alexander, née Constance Mortimore,
see **Mortimore.**
Of Kent. Exhibited at the R.A. 1905–1914, from
Heathfield Cottage, Keston and from Brook
Cottage, Tunbridge Wells. Painted Blanche and
Alice, daughters of the Rev. John Hudson, Lady
McRobert and Mrs. Foster Mortimore.

Kirk, Thomas. 1765/6–1797
Was born in 1765 or 1766. Entered the R.A.
Schools, 10 February 1784 aged 18, '17th last Oct.'
Was a pupil of Cosway (q.v.). Awarded a premium
by the Society of Arts in 1785. Exhibited at the R.A.,
1785–1796. Painted historical, mythological and
biblical subjects, drew book illustrations besides
executing some miniatures and engravings. He died
of consumption, 18 November 1797, and was buried
at St. Pancras Church. According to Redgrave he
was good at painting portraits of children.

Kirkley, Miss Caroline. (fl. 1796–1797)
Of London. Sister of Miss S. Kirkley (q.v.) with
whom she shared a house. Exhibited at the R.A.,
1796–1797. Miniature painter and engraver. Her
address was 9 Howland Street. A Miss Kirkley
exhibited at the R.A. in 1793 from 1 Howland
Street, and was probably related to or identical with
the above artist or her sister.

Kirkley, Miss S. (fl. 1796–1797)
Of London. Sister of Miss C. Kirkley (q.v.) with
whom she shared a house. A Miss Kirkley exhibited
at the R.A., 1793, and Miss S. Kirkley exhibited
there, 1796–1797, from 9 Howland Street.

Kirkpatrick, Richard. (fl. 1812–1817)
Of London. Exhibited at the R.A. and B.I., 1812–
1817. Painted portraits and exhibited a frame of
six 'lead drawings; portraits'.

*Kirkwood, Miss Elizabeth H. (fl. 1910)
Of Edinburgh. Exhibited two miniatures on

enamel at the R.A. 1910, from The Studio, 68
Thistle Street.

Kirwan, William Bourke. b. c. 1814
Born at Dublin c. 1814, son of Patrick Kirwan, a
picture dealer. Was a pupil of Richard Downes
Bowyer, a portrait painter. Exhibited at the R.H.A.,
1836–1846. Worked for Henry Gonne, the engraver
and for Hodges of Grafton Street. Exhibited miniatures and domestic subjects in water-colour, besides
working as an anatomical draughtsman for surgeons
and as a picture dealer. On 8 and 9 December 1852
he was tried for the murder of his wife, Sarah Maria
Louisa, née Crowe. He was found guilty and condemned to death; the sentence was later commuted
to transportation for life. He was released a few
years later and is said to have died in America.
Before his wife's death he had been living with a
Maria Theresa Kenny, by whom he had eight
children. The B.M. has a drawing by him.

Kitchen, H. (fl. 1802)
Of London. Exhibited at the R.A. 1802, from 8
Addle Street, Aldermanbury. The exhibits were
Portrait of a Turk; A gentleman; Miss Engram;
The Miser; The Abbé Tardy; and Portrait of a lady.

Kitchingman, John. c. 1741–1781
Was born c. 1741. Pupil of William Shipley (q.v.);
entered the R.A. Schools, 4 April 1769. Won a
silver medal in 1769 and premiums at the Society
of Arts 1762–1770 and exhibited at the Free Society
of Artists 1766–1769 and at the R.A., 1770–1781.
Painted portraits, genre, marine and landscape
subjects, and miniatures in oil and water-colour.
Married young, but was separated from his wife;
led an intemperate life; died during an amputation,
28 December 1781. An example of his work is at
the V. & A. M.; it is signed 'J.K. / 1766'.

Kneller, Sir Godfrey. 1646–1723
No miniatures are at present known to be by
Kneller but the *London Gazette*, 27 May 1689
contained an advertisement 'Lost about 5 or 6
weeks since out of a pocket Almanack, a man's
picture in little upon a plate, fresh complexion, in
his own hair and great whiskers etc. Whoever shall
bring it to Mr. Godfrey Kneller at his house, in the
Great Piazza, Covent Gdn., shall have a guinea
reward.' This may well have been painted by him.
Several miniatures attributed to him were lent to
the exhibition at the South Kensington Museum,
1865 including one catalogued as 'Sir Godfrey
Kneller, Knt.; the Painter, when young. Painted by
himself'.

Kneller, John Zachary. 1644–1702
Born at Lübeck, 6 October 1644; brother of Sir
Godfrey Kneller (q.v.) with whom he came to
England after travelling in Italy. Painted architectural decorations, still-life pieces and executed
miniature copies in oil and water-colour of portraits
by his brother. He died in Covent Garden, London
in 1702 and was buried in the church there. His
work is not of outstanding merit. He signed I.Z.K.
A miniature called James II, signed 'I.Z.K.' and
another of John Thurloe, after Hoskins (q.v.) are
in the collection of Earl Beauchamp. The V. & A.
M. has oil miniatures on copper of William III and
the Duchess of Manchester.

Kneller, W. 1754?–1823
Was born c. 1754. Of Fareham, Hants. Exhibited
at the R.A., 1819. According to a note by Long he
was buried on 2 October 1823 aged 69.

*Knight, Miss Adah. (fl. 1893–1926)
Of Gloucester, Boscombe, Hants. and Bournemouth. Exhibited at the R.A., 1893–1926. Her
sitters included the Rt. Rev. the Lord Bishop of
Gloucester.

*Knight, Miss Bertha W. (fl. 1906–1910)
Of Exeter, London and Bletchley, Bucks.
Exhibited at the Society of Miniaturists 1906–1910.

Knight, Charles. b. 1771?
Of London. Exhibited at the R.A. 1793, 1796
and 1816. Possibly identical with the Charles
Knight who entered the R.A. Schools, 27 March
1788, 'age 17 April 8. 1788'. May have been
identical with the Charles Knight, miniaturist, who
worked in Philadelphia, 1803–1817, after which
time he is said to have returned to England. Long
suggests that he may have been identical with
Charles Knight, the London engraver (1743–1827?).

Knight, John Baverstock. 1785–1859
Born, 3 May 1785 at Langton Rectory, nr.
Blandford, Dorset; son of a militia Captain, who
sent him to be educated at Child Okeford. Worked
as a land surveyor, but took up painting and was
an accomplished artist. Lived at Piddlehinton,
Dorset. Exhibited at the R.A. in 1819, from Dorset,
and was possibly identical with the J. Knight, jun.
who exhibited in 1818 from Great Suffolk
Street. Painted portraits in oil, water-colour
landscapes, and executed crayon drawings, miniatures etc. Died near Broadway, Dorset, 14 May
1859.

Knight, Miss Julia. (fl. 1834)
Of 14 Portman Street, London. Was awarded a
silver medal for a copy of a miniature by the
Society of Arts in 1834.

Knight, Miss Mary Ann. 1776–1851
Born, 7 September 1776 in London; daughter of
John Knight, a merchant, and his wife, née Wood-
cock. Was a pupil of Andrew Plimer (q.v.) who
married her sister Joanna Louisa Knight. Exhibited
at the R.A., and O.W.C.S., 1803–1836. Had a considerable clientele. Died 1851. A sketch book of
hers, containing numerous first sketches of interesting persons was sold at Christie's on 9 February
1960, together with several other of her works. She
occasionally painted in oil. Her self-portrait in
miniature, and that of Montagu Bertie, Lord
Norreys (later Earl of Abingdon) were exhibited at
South Kensington in 1865. She worked in the
manner of A. Plimer. Dr. G. C. Williamson in his
life of *Andrew and Nathaniel Plimer*, gives details of
her work and a list of her sitters. According to her
note books, she painted 696 miniatures between
1802–1835, for which she obtained a price of two
to forty guineas. The National Gallery of Scotland
has a portrait of R. Owen of Lanark, painted by
her.

*Knight, William Milner. (fl. 1900–1901)
Exhibited at the Society of Miniaturists 1900–
1901, from Bushwood, Leytonstone, Essex.

Knipe, Miss Eliza. (fl. 1784–1787)
Of Liverpool, where she taught drawing.
Exhibited at the Society for Promoting Painting
and Design, in Liverpool in 1784 and 1787, including
a miniature.

Knogwell. (fl. 1703)
An enamel portrait of a man in green coat and
white cravat, signed 'Knogwell, 1703' was sold at
the Jaffé sale at Cologne, 27–29 March 1905.

Knowles, Leonora C. E. (fl. 1844)

Of London. Exhibited at the R.A. 1844, from 162 Aldersgate Street. The miniature was of Cornélie, daughter of M. Scheffer of Paris.

*Knownlie, Richard. (fl. *c.* 1676)

The above artist's name is recorded as a limner in the Parish Register of St. Michan's, Ireland in 1676. No further information is available.

*Knox, James. d. 1681

An artist of this name said to have painted miniatures died, 23 March 1681 'of the Parish of St. Mary, Aldermary'. This fact is recorded in the *Harleian Society* Vol. V. 1880.

Kortright, Mrs. H. S. (Primrose M). (fl. 1909–1911)

Exhibited at the R.A. 1909 and 1911, from Grenville Lodge, Bexhill-on-Sea. Her sitters included Freda, daughter of the artist. She was the wife of H. S. Kortright who also exhibited at the R.A.

*Kraftmeier, Miss Martha. (fl. 1899)

Of London. Exhibited at the R.A. 1899, from 23 Tanza Road, Hampstead.

Krüger or **Krueger, Johann Wilhelm Georg.** b. 1728 d. after 1788

Born in London, 1728. Worked in Paris and Berlin. Exhibited at the Academy of St. Luc in Paris, 1774. Settled in Berlin *c.* 1781 and died there in or after 1788. Was an enamellist who painted allegorical subjects.

*Kuhm, Miss Cissie. (fl. 1910)

Of London. Exhibited at the R.A. 1910, from c/o C. H. West, 117 Finchley Road, N.W.

*Küssner, Miss Amalia (Mrs. Amalia Coudert). 1876–1933

Born in 1876 at Terre-Haute, Indiana. Studied in America. Came to England in 1896 when she exhibited at the R.A. All her exhibits were under her maiden name. Had a distinguished clientele which included King Edward VII, Cecil Rhodes, Lady Alington, and the Czar and Czarina of Russia. Her husband was Mr. Charles du Pont Coudert of Windlesham Hall, Windlesham, Surrey. An article appeared in the *Evening Standard* on 21 March 1933 recording a claim filed in the King's Bench and heard on that day. The artist's husband described how a car in which he and his wife were touring Italy, left the road and plunged into a river; they were rescued but his wife later died. Part of the claim was for personal effects and miniatures. Mr. Coudert alleged that the driver of their hired car fell asleep but the defence said that a tyre on the car had burst.

L

*L. (fl. 1525)

A miniature of Sir John Boling Hatton, and his mother, the heiress of Holdenby, Northampton, signed 'L. 1525' was lent to the exhibition at the South Kensington Museum, 1865, when it was catalogued as by Lucas de Herre. The artist's dates of 1534–1584 make this impossible, unless the date on the portrait was misread.

L., C. (fl. *c.* 1785–*c.* 1787). See also **Pope, Mrs. A.**

Long saw a miniature of a lady *c.* 1787 signed 'CL' and one of a member of a Welsh family *c.* 1785. A miniature of an officer signed 'CL / fct' is in the de la Hey collection. A fairly good miniature signed CL was sold at 20 Cadogan Place, 2 January 1929. These works may have been by Miss C. M. Leigh, later Mrs. A. Pope (q.v.)

L., H. (fl. *c.* 1620). See **Hilliard, Laurence**

The above monogram is one found on miniatures by L. Hilliard (q.v.). Long refers to a miniature of a lady *c.* 1620 signed in monogram 'HL'. This was formerly at the B.M., and was transferred to the V. & A. M. in 1942. It may possibly be the work of L. Hilliard.

L., I. (fl. *c.* 1649)

Long saw a miniature of a lady dressed as a widow *c.* 1649, signed 'IL'. It was not of any great merit.

*L., J.C. (fl. 1670–1674)

A miniature by the above artist *c.* 1670 is in the V. & A. M. He translated Gerhard of Brugge's *Limning*, published by Robert Pricke in 1674, edited by W. Gore, whose portrait by P. Cross (q.v.) is in the V. & A. M.

*L., L. (fl. 1790). See also **M., E.**

I have seen a well painted miniature of William Seddon, Esq. (1757–1808) of Acres Barn, nr. Manchester, signed and dated 'L.L./ 90' (i.e. 1790). The sitter was a lawyer, and the miniature belonged to a descendant who also owned a replica, signed 'E.M. / 92' (1792). They were both competently painted and were slightly in the manner of T. Day (q.v.), with a fresh colouring on the face, opaque white on the hair, and a fair amount on the waistcoat and cravat. A pale blue sky background reveals the translucency of the ivory.

L., M. (fl. *c.* 1795). See also **Lowe, Mauritius** and **Lucan, Countess of**

A miniature of a young girl, signed 'M L / fecit' painted *c.* 1795 was formerly in the de la Hey collection and was Lot 102 at Sotheby's, 27 May 1968, when it was suggested that it might have been the work of Mauritius Lowe (q.v.), but as this artist died in 1793 this is unlikely. Stylistically it has no affinity to the works of Lowe which are in the V. & A. M. and the artist may have been the Countess of Lucan (q.v.). The miniature is attractive and well drawn.

*Lack, Miss Zara. (fl. 1905)

Exhibited at the R.A. 1905, from Brooklyn, Surbiton Hill Park, Surbiton.

Lacon, G. See **Lacon, J.**

Lacon, J. (fl. *c.* 1740–1760)

Worked in Bath in the middle of the 18th century. Painted miniatures and water-colour portraits. Many of his miniatures were small and reminiscent of the work of N. Hone (q.v.). He owned a puppet show in Bath, which was very popular at this time. Was probably identical with G. Lacon. Mr. F. Gordon Roe found a record of Lacon having painted a miniature copy of one of Rembrandt's self-portraits in 1753; he gave the initial as G but this was probably a mistake for J. Two miniatures by J. Lacon were in the Wellesley collection sold in 1920; one was of an unknown man, signed and dated '1760', and the other of Miss Sarah Verney, signed and dated 'J. Lacon / 1756'; this last miniature is now in the V. & A. M.

*L'Admiral, John. 1699–1773

Born at Amsterdam, 10 January 1699. Chiefly known as an engraver; came with his brother Jacob to London where they took part in the experiments of Le Blond (q.v.), for colour printing. According to Houttuyn's biography published in 1774, is reputed to have painted miniatures. He died on 2 June 1773 in Amsterdam.

Laffert, Carl Friedrich. 1783–1825

Born in Berlin, 1783. Executed miniatures on porcelain and on enamel, and painted a few religious pictures in oil. Exhibited at Berlin, 1802–1816; worked at the Berlin porcelain factory. Went to London and exhibited at the R.A., 1809–1813. Returned to Germany in 1815 and settled in Berlin from 1817 to the end of his life. Died 26 August 1825.

Laidlaw, Robert. (fl. 1740)

Long recorded that a Robert Laidlaw 'late of Cheltenham and 7 Conduit St, off Bond St', was painting miniatures and profiles in 1740.

*Laidman, Miss Edith A. (fl. 1904–1914)

Of London; Bushey, Herts., and Milford, Surrey. Exhibited at the R.A., 1904–1914. Her sitters included the Rev. R. Nattrass. Undoubtedly related to Ida F. Laidman (q.v.) who exhibited from the same addresses in Bushey and Milford.

*Laidman, Miss Ida F. (fl. 1905–1913)

Of Bushey, Herts., and Milford, Surrey. Exhibited at the R.A., 1905–1913. Undoubtedly related to Edith Laidman (q.v.) who exhibited from the same addresses.

Lainé, Francis. 1721–1810

Born in Berlin, 1721. Son of a French Huguenot refugee in Berlin. Was taught enamelling by Chodowiecki, who married his sister. Went to London when he was 20. Went to India where he was employed as an engineer by the East India Company. Met Tippoo Sahib and Haider Ali. Returned to France in 1759; became a member of the Academy of St. Luc in 1773; exhibited there, 1773 and 1774; exhibited at the Society of Artists, 1776, 1777 and 1790 and at the R.A. 1786–1789, from London addresses. Lived chiefly in Paris and had property at Villiers-le-Bel, Pontoise. Knew many important artists in France, including Hall, Fragonard and Greuze. His wife was the daughter of a Swiss bishop. Painted miniature portraits, fancy subjects in miniature, including some for snuff boxes and buttons etc. Worked both on ivory and enamel, and executed some of his miniatures *en grisaille*. Is supposed to have invented a method of doing genre subjects in hair. He seldom signed; when he did his signature was F. Lainé. He died in Passy, Paris in 1810. Examples of his work are in the Louvre.

*Laing, Miss Georgina. (fl. 1901–1910)

Exhibited at the R.A. and S.M. 1901–1910, from 8 The Temple, Dale Street, Liverpool.

Lair. (fl. 1776)

Of London. Exhibited at the R.A., 1776 a miniature of the 'Holy Family'. Schidlof suggests that he may have been identical with F. L'Aine, of Berlin and Paris, but I have found no evidence for this assumption. Several artists named Lair are recorded by Benezit.

Laird, Miss Alice H. (fl. 1840–1865)

Of London and (1858) Glasgow. Exhibited at the R.A., 1846–1865. Was a member of the Society of Lady Artists.

*Lake, Mabel H. (Mrs. C. P. Blatchley). (fl. 1907–1909)

Of Sutton, Surrey and London. Exhibited at the R.A., 1907 and 1909. Her sitters included Hilda W. Lake.

Lamb, Lady Caroline. 1785–1828

Born 13 November 1785; daughter of the 3rd Earl of Bessborough. Spent six years in Italy as a child. Married the Hon. William Lamb (Lord Melbourne), 3 June 1805. Became infatuated with Byron. Wrote novels. An engraving of a miniature by her of Byron was illustrated in the *Connoisseur*, XXX, 1911, p. 259. Died in London, 26 January 1828.

Lamborn, Peter Spendelowe. 1722–1774

Born in Cambridge 1722; son of a watchmaker. Studied engraving in London under Basire. Practised at Cambridge. Exhibited at the Society of Artists 1764–1774, and was a member in 1765. Painted miniatures, etched portraits, drew architectural and other antiquities. Engraved plates for Bentham's *Ely Cathedral*. Married Mary Wale, 6 January 1762, by whom he had four children. Died at Cambridge, 5 November 1774. An etched portrait of H. Homer after P. S. Lamborn, is at the B.M.

*Lamming, H. (fl. 1898)

Of London. Exhibited at the R.A. 1898, from 33 Kenilworth Road, Ealing.

Lamont, or La Monte, Miss Elish. *c.* 1800–1870

Born in Belfast *c.* 1800. Was self-taught; worked as a miniaturist in Belfast where she obtained the patronage of many titled persons. Exhibited at the R.H.A., 1842–1857. Worked in Dublin, 1857–1859. Settled in England towards the end of her life and became a friend of Dickens and Ruskin. She and her sister Frances wrote and illustrated *Christmas Rhymes*, 1846. Died in Rochester, 1870.

*Lancaster, Mrs. Vera. (fl. 1910)

Of London. Exhibited at the R.A. 1910, from 14 Ladbroke Terrace.

*Lance, George. 1802–1864

Of London. Was born *c.* 1802. Was presumably identical with the George Lance who entered the R.A. Schools, 15 January 1820, aged 17. Exhibited at the R.A., B.I., N.W.C.S., etc., 1824–1864. Painted portraits and subject pictures, chiefly of fruit and flowers. A 'Bouquet of Flowers', executed on a stone slab, painted in water-colour on a green background, circular, 2¾ in. diameter was Lot 377 in the Pierpont Morgan sale, 24 June 1935, when it was catalogued as by the above artist. His self-portrait in pencil 8¼ × 6¼ in. is in the N.P.G.

*Landseer, Sir Edwin Henry. 1802–1873

Long noted that this well-known artist may have painted a few miniatures, but I have been unable to confirm this suggestion.

*Landseer, Miss Jessica. 1810–1880

Born in London 1810. Daughter of the engraver John Landseer, and sister of the famous animal painter Sir Edwin Landseer (q.v.). Exhibited at the R.A., 1816–1866. Painted miniatures, landscapes and executed engravings. Died in Folkestone, 29 August 1880. A miniature by her is in the V. & A. M., and is inscribed in faded ink on card at the back: 'From / a sketch of / Mrs. Bradshaw / by E. Landseer R.A. / Jessie Landseer. / 1844.'

Lane, Miss Anna Louisa. (fl. 1769–1782)

Of London. Exhibited at the Society of Artists, 1769–1776 (Hon. Exhib.) and at the R.A., 1778–1782. Undoubtedly related to William Lane (q.v.) from whose address 130, Pall Mall, she exhibited. Painted oil portraits, miniatures, some of which were in oil on ivory, and executed portrait drawings.

Lane, Richard James, A. E. 1800–1872

Was born in 1800. An engraver. May not have painted miniatures, but lent pencil portraits by himself, two of which were signed with initials, to the exhibition at the South Kensington Museum in 1865. Numerous engraved portraits after him are at the B.M. Died, 21 November 1872.

Lane, Theodore. 1798/1800–1828

Born in Isleworth in 1798 or 1800; son of a drawing-master from Worcester. Was a pupil of J. Barrow. Painted water-colour portraits and miniatures but is best known as a humorous artist; etched sporting prints and social subjects, and executed book illustrations. Exhibited at the R.A., B.I. and S.B.A., 1816–1830. Said to have been killed on 21 May 1828 at New Horse Bazaar, Gray's Inn Road, London, by falling through a skylight. He left a widow and two children. An oil painting by him is at the Tate Gallery and the B.M. has drawings by him.

Lane, William. *c.* 1746–1819

Was born *c.* 1746. Of London. Exhibited at the R.A. and B.I., 1798–1815. Engraved gems and painted portraits and miniatures; drew in crayons. A portrait of Susan Skinner, wife of the 3rd Lord Gage, signed and dated '1804', and executed in pencil and red chalk, is in the collection of Viscount Gage. Lane died in Hammersmith on 4 January 1819. The B.M. has engraved portraits after him. He may have executed some engravings after Cosway (q.v.) and Reynolds. A pencil drawing on paper of Mrs. Abington, signed on the right 'W. Lane Sc.' and on the left 'Rd Cosway del' is in the N.G., Dublin.

Langdon, Isaac. (fl. 1830). See also **Langdon, T.**

Was living at 37 Milsom Street, Bath, in 1830. Either related to or identical with T. Langdon (q.v.) who lived at the same address.

Langdon, T. (Thomas?). (fl. 1785–1802). See also **Langdon, Isaac**

Of London. Exhibited at the R.A. 1785–1802, from various London addresses. His sitters included the son of an African Prince; Captain Tichart; Captain Hope; Mrs. and Miss Beckingham, and Mrs. Langdon. Was probably identical with the miniaturist T. Langdon who had addresses in Bath, 1809–1822, including 37 Milsom Street (1819–1822) where I. Langdon (q.v.) was living in 1830. The wife of T. Langdon of Bath taught painting on glass, velvet etc., and modelling in wax. A Thomas Langdon, engraver, who may have been related to or identical with one or other of these artists entered the R.A. Schools, 10 March 1783 aged '14, 6th last Feby'. The B.M. has engraved portraits after T. Langdon. Four miniatures representing members of the Burgoyne family, by T. Langdon, were sold at Christie's on 9 July 1968; these included two particularly charming miniatures of the Misses Burgoyne as children.

Langlois, Camille, junior. (fl. 1835–1847)

Son of Claude Bernard Camille Langlois (q.v.), of Sens. Worked in London. Exhibited at the R.A., 1835–1847 and obtained a prize from the Society of Arts in 1836 for an original miniature. Executed studies from life, subject pictures, portraits and miniatures.

Langlois, Claude Bernard Camille. 1786–*c.* 1860

Born in Sens, 24 October 1786; son of the portrait painter Claude Louis Langlois of Sezanne (1757–1845). Exhibited at the R.A. from London addresses 1831–1849, not 1841 as stated by Long. Died in Brighton *c.* 1860. Examples of his work are in the V. & A. M. Painted portraits and miniatures. His exhibits included a portrait of his father, and one of Rajah Rammohun Roy's son. Was the father of Camille Langlois, junior (q.v.).

Lanmann, Mrs. H. (fl. 1836)

Of London. Exhibited at the R.A. 1836, from 18 Alfred Place, Bedford Square.

Lansdell, Elizabeth. (fl. 1847)

Of Burwash, Sussex. Exhibited at the R.A., 1847. The portrait was of the Earl of Ashburnham.

Laporte, Miss Mary Ann. b. *c.* 1795

Born *c.* 1795. Daughter of John Laporte the water-colour painter. Worked in London. Exhibited at the R.A., 1813–1818. Was a member of the N.W.C.S., 1835–1846. Painted portraits and fancy subjects.

*Largillière, Nicholas de. 1656–1746

Baptised in Paris, 10 October 1656. One of the great historical and portrait painters of France. Not usually thought of as a miniaturist, but a miniature painted in oil on copper was seen by Mr. A. J. B. Kiddell, who thought it correctly attributed. Largillière died in Paris on 20 March 1746.

*Larkin, Miss. (fl. 1827). See also **Larkin, T.** and **Larkin, Miss J.**

Exhibited at the R.A., 1827. Probably identical with or related to Miss J. Larkin (q.v.) and T. Larkin (q.v.).

Larkin, Miss J. (fl. 1828–1832). See also **Larkin, T.** and **Larkin, Miss**

Of London. Exhibited at the R.A. 1828–1832, and probably identical with or related to T. Larkin (q.v.) who exhibited at the R.A., 1825, and Miss Larkin (q.v.) who exhibited in 1827.

*Larkin, T. (fl. 1825). See also **Larkin, Miss J.** and **Larkin, Miss**

Exhibited at the R.A., 1825. Possibly identical with or related to Miss J. Larkin (q.v.) and Miss Larkin (q.v.).

*Larkinge or Larkin, William. (fl. *c.* 1610–1620)

Lady Anne Clifford in her diary of January 1619 noted that 'The 16th came my Lord of Arundel, and his Lady. The same day I sent my cozin Hall of Gretford, a letter and my picture with it, which Larkinge drew at Knowle, this summer'. This is supposed to refer to a miniature. A series of full-length portraits from Redlynch are his masterpieces, painted *c.* 1614; exhibited at the Tate Gallery 1970.

Larkins, W. (fl. 1853–1856)

Of London. Exhibited at the R.A., 1853–1856. His exhibit in 1853 was a self-portrait.

*Laroon or Lauron, Marcellus. 1648/9?–1701/2

Born in the Hague, probably in 1648 or 1649; second son of a Frenchman, Marcel Lauron. *An Essay Towards an English School of Painting*, appended to R. de Piles, *The Art of Painting*, 2nd edition, 1744, p. 396, states that he was born in 1653, and that he died aged about 52; his son gives his age at death as 53. He is known to have died on 11 March 1701/2. Said to have accompanied his father to England and to have lived in and around Yorkshire for some years. The date on which Laroon arrived in this country is uncertain, nor is there any documentary evidence regarding his time in Yorkshire, but he was in London by 1674, when, on 15 July of that year, he appeared at the Painter-Stainers' Company, 'and paid his Quarteridge And promised to bring his proofe peece'. At about this time, he married Elizabeth Keene, daughter of Jeremiah Keene, a builder, of Little Sutton near Chiswick, who held positions of responsibility in the area. Of the children born to Laroon and his wife, John was born on a date unknown, Marcellus on 2 April 1679, Elizabeth, christened 1682, James christened, March 1683/4, Elizabeth, christened March 1688/9 and Charles, christened August 1690. Of these Marcellus Laroon, jun. (1679–1772) followed his father's profession as an artist. Robert Raines in *Marcellus Laroon*, 1967, gives an account of the work of father and son, and gives the spelling of the father's name as Lauron. In 1680, Laroon senior moved into a house on the West side of Bow Street where he lived for the rest of his life. He was employed by Sir Godfrey Kneller to paint the draperies for his portraits. Taught his sons art, and gave them a good education in French, general subjects, fencing, dancing and music. Laroon possessed great talent, and painted historical subjects, portraits and miniatures as well as executing engravings and drawings. His earliest known portrait is that of Charles II painted for the Mathematical School of Christ's Hospital. De Piles says of him, 'He painted well, both in great and little, and was an exact draftsman; but he was chiefly famous for drapery, wherein he exceeded most of his contemporaries'. Miniatures by him are scarce, one of the Duke of Monmouth, after a portrait by Lawrence Cross(e) (q.v.) in the collection of the Duke of Portland, painted in 1683, was sold at Christie's, 9 February 1960, when it was catalogued as of an unknown man. It is signed in monogram, 'ML'. His wife must have died before 1701, in which year he made his will where she was not mentioned. He left furniture and furnishings to his 'kinswoman', Mrs. Elizabeth Burgess, who probably looked after him, and the rest of his property to be divided between his children with specific bequests. His three sons received all his limnings, drawings, pictures and paintings, divided equally between them. A large number of these, if not all, were sold in 1725. Laroon died of consumption in Richmond, Surrey, early in 1702, where he was buried. His son, John, was left as sole executor. A number of works by Laroon are reproduced in *Marcellus Laroon* by Robert Raines, 1967 including those of *The Cryes of the City of London*.

*Lassam, Miss Susie. (fl. 1908–1914)
Of London. Exhibited at the R.A. and S.M., 1908–1914, from Rose Cottage, Dulwich Village, S.W. Her sitters included Lady Teazle.

*Latchford, Miss Alice. (fl. 1895)
Of London. Exhibited at the R.A. 1895, from 50 Pen-y-wern Road, London.

Laurence. c. 1685–1774
Of London. A newspaper cutting dated in MS., March 1774, says, 'Yesterday morning died aged 89, Mr. Laurence, Enameller, in Cold Bath Fields, Clerkenwell'.

Laurence or **Lawrence, Samuel.** 1812–1884
Born in Guildford, 1812. Exhibited at the S.B.A., 1834, and at the R.A., 1836–1882. This well-known portrait painter executed portraits of contemporary celebrities, in oil and crayon. Travelled in Italy and America. His name is spelt alternately Laurence and Lawrence in the R.A. catalogues. He died at his house, 6 Wells St., Oxford Street, London, 28 February 1884. A number of his exhibits were in the

Drawing and Miniature section at the R.A., and may have been small portraits or drawings of miniature size. The only recorded miniature by him is that of Jane Carlyle, painted in oil; this is in the N.P.G.

*Law, Mrs. Mary I. (fl. 1905)
Of Pretoria, South Africa. Exhibited at the R.A. 1905, from Eaton Hall Hotel, Pretoria. Her sitters included Miss Fielden.

*Lawless, Mrs. Florence Piercy. (fl. 1907–1913)
Of London and Devon. Exhibited at the R.A. and S.M., 1907–1913.

Lawranson or **Lawrenson, Thomas. F.S.A.** (fl. 1733–1786)
Said to have been an Irishman. Practised in London; was working as a portrait painter, 1733–1786. Became a Fellow of the Society of Artists, 1771 and exhibited there, 1762–1777. Painted oil and crayon portraits, landscapes and oil miniatures. The N.P.G. has oil portraits by T. Lawranson and the B.M. has two engraved portraits after him. His son, William Lawranson, was a portrait painter and mezzotint engraver.

Lawrence, George. c. 1758–1802
Of Dublin. One of three brothers all of whom were artists. John and Robert Lawrence (q.v.) also worked in Ireland. George became a pupil at the Dublin Society schools in 1771 and worked under F. R. West and J. Mannin. As the pupils were usually taken at about twelve years of age, his date of birth was probably c. 1758. He exhibited at the Dublin Society of Artists, 1774 and in other exhibitions up to 1802, in which year he died. Lawrence executed drawings and portraits in crayon as well as portraits in oil and miniatures. An account of his work was published in the *Connoisseur* Vol. XCVII, pp. 206–209, by Edward McGuire, who illustrated a number of pastel portraits by him and one portrait in oils. The size of his portraits were usually 9 × 7 in. oval, and larger ones were only executed on commission. His miniatures were well painted and drawn. A miniature of a gentleman wearing a blue coat, is in the National Museum of Ireland, and is signed and dated '1793'; he also painted a miniature of Sir Denis Pack, signed 'G. Lawrence, No 35 Frederick Street, Dec 11th, 1788'. Printed labels, found on the reverse of portraits in pastel of the Barnewell Family read—'Likenesses Engaged; / In CRAYONS, and in MINIATURE / At one Guinea Each; The same size of the CRAYONS, in OIL / At one Guinea and a Half / BY LAWRENCE, / No 15, Exchange Street.' He later charged two guineas each according to a label in his own writing on the reverse of a pastel portrait, which gave his address at that time as 34 Grafton Street (c. 1781). He signed his works G. Lawrence followed by a date, or G.L. followed by a date.

Lawrence, John. (fl. 1771–1793)
Of Dublin; brother of George Lawrence (q.v.) and Robert Lawrence (q.v.). Entered the R.A. Schools, 5 December 1771 and from 1784–1786 was practising at 34 Grafton Street and from 1786–1793 at 35 Frederick Street.

Lawrence, Robert. (fl. 1794–1820)
Of Dublin; brother of George and John Lawrence (q.v.). Practised as a miniaturist at 35 South Frederick Street, Dublin, 1794–1820.

Lawrence, S. (fl. 1809)
Nothing is known about this artist, who is listed by Long as a miniaturist, except that he exhibited at the Edinburgh Incorporated Society of Artists in 1809. There was only one exhibit and this was a

water-colour painting of a shell. I have been unable to confirm the fact that he painted miniatures.

Lawrence, Sir Thomas, P.R.A. 1769–1830
Born in Bristol, 13 April 1769; the fourteenth of the sixteen children of Thomas Lawrence, a Supervisor of Excise, and of Lucy Read, his wife. Lawrence's father was something of a spendthrift, and gave up his job in order to go into the business of innkeeping. He became landlord of 'The White Lion' at Bristol, which proved a failure, and in 1773 moved to Devizes to 'The Black Bear', a coaching inn of some repute. At the early age of five, Thomas showed an aptitude for drawing and recitation, and by 1779 had gained a reputation as an infant prodigy. An interesting example of Lawrence's portraits of this period is in the collection of the Misses Baumgartner. It is a profile portrait in pencil representing one of their ancestors, and has an inscription on the back of the frame—'C. P. Esqre / AE^t. 67. / Drawn by Lawrence. / Nov 22nd 1777 AE^t. 8. / The above written by me shortly after / the date when the likeness of Charles / Pepys, of Impington, was taken at the / Bear Inn, Devizes. / Sir Thomas Lawrence, President / of the Royal Academy / Died on this day, / January 7th 1830. / Saml Knight'. Long mentions eight miniatures of the Weld family executed on vellum by Lawrence at the age of eleven, at Lulworth Castle. Such of these early portraits as are known by this famous portrait painter are signed in a copper plate hand on the margin, e.g. Aet^t 11 Thomas Lawrence Fecit; T. Lawrence, Fecit, and T. L. (cursive) fe, etc. Among those who acted as assistants to Lawrence were T. Hargreaves (q.v.) and G. R. Ward (q.v.). W. M. Bennett (q.v.) was one of his pupils. The only miniature at present accepted as authentic is the self-portrait which was painted by the artist for Miss Croft, and now in the collection of Mrs. O. G. S. Croft, Croft Castle. One of the 3rd Marquess of Londonderry, in the collection of the present Marquess, has been attributed to Lawrence but Dr. K. Garlick considers it to be by another hand. A miniature of Mary, Lady Templetown and her son Henry, later 2nd Viscount Templetown, after the large painting by Lawrence in the National Gallery of Art, Washington (Mellon Collection), was sold at Christie's on 25 June 1968. Lawrence became one of the leading portrait painters of the day, being appointed principal portrait painter in ordinary to the King, 1792, elected R.A., 1794, knighted 1815 and elected P.R.A., 1820. He died suddenly on 7 January 1830 and was buried on 20 January with great honours in St. Paul's Cathedral. For further information see standard works of reference including *Sir Thomas Lawrence*, by Kenneth Garlick, 1954 and the *Walpole Society*, Vol. XXXIX. *A Catalogue of the Paintings, Drawings and Pastels of Sir Thomas Lawrence*, by Kenneth Garlick, 1964.

Lawson, Miss M. Stace. (fl. 1832)
Of Turnham Green. Won a silver medal from the Society of Arts in 1832 for a miniature copy of a portrait.

Layton, Thomas. (fl. 1826)
Was working in 1826 at 11 Bridge Street, Lambeth.

Lea, John. (fl. 1823–1826)
Of London. Exhibited at the R.A. 1823, a portrait of the Rev. J. Angel James of Birmingham. Was working at 6 Great Charlotte Street, Blackfriars Road, London, 1823–1826.

Leader, G. (fl. 1792–1804)
Of London. Exhibited at the R.A., 1792–1804. Most of his exhibits were wax portraits, but in 1804

he exhibited a portrait of a lady, on ivory.

Leakey, James. 1775–1865

Born in Exeter, 20 September 1775; son of a wool-stapler of Bradford-on-Avon, Wilts. supposedly of Irish descent. Exhibited at the R.A., 1821–1846. Worked in London and Exeter; painted oil portraits, landscapes, subject pictures and miniatures. He married Miss Eliza Hubbard Woolmer in 1815, by whom he had eleven or twelve children. Whilst in London he knew Constable, Lawrence (q.v.), Wilkie, etc. Lawrence once introduced him as 'The English Wouvermans'. Leakey is mentioned by Farington, whose miniature in oil he painted in 1810, after three sittings. Farington also records that Bishop Fisher had shown him an oil portrait by Leakey in 1810 and adds that Leakey 'has met with much success in the west of England & now paints landscapes'. In 1809 he was commissioned to paint two fancy pictures for Sir Thomas Baring, at 500 guineas each. He was too busy to execute the commission but painted portraits of the Baring family. As a result of these large orders he renounced a project of emigrating to Canada. He is said to have 'given up the brush for the pulpit'. He was living in 1811 next door to John Raphael Smith (q.v.) and is mentioned by Mrs. Frankau in *John Raphael Smith*, 1902, pp. 34, 35, who says that Smith was known as 'Old Vice' and Leakey as 'Young Virtue'. He died in Exeter, 16 February 1865, aged 90. The *Exeter Gazette* published an article on him, 16 February 1865, in which they said 'Leakey's high character as a citizen earned him general esteem and respect.... For upwards of 60 years he had been known as a humble & devoted servant of God his Saviour.' Leakey's miniatures are well drawn and usually painted in oil on ivory. The fact that he did not, as far as is known, sign his work means that they often pass unrecognised. Passmore (q.v.) painted oil miniatures in the manner of Leakey. One of his daughters, Caroline Woolmer Leakey, was a religious writer. A miniature by him of Sophia Westlake Arundel is in the V. & A. M. An oil portrait of S. Cousins is in the N.P.G., and an engraving after one of his works is in the B.M. A miniature of a lady in a white dress seated against a landscape background is in the collection of Major R. M. O. de la Hey.

*Lear, Charles Hutton. 1818–1903

Born in 1818; the son of prosperous parents. Entered the drawing school of Henry Sass in *c.* 1830 and the Royal Academy schools in 1839, where he studied for the next seven or eight years. Exhibited at the R.A., B.I., etc., 1842–1852. Executed portraits, heads and subject pictures. Is recorded here because of a set of 27 pencil heads, now in the N.P.G., which Lear sketched surreptitiously in the life school of the R.A. These depict many well-known artists of the day and were done to amuse his father and were accompanied by verbal descriptions of the sitters. The sketches were executed from *c.* 1845–1846 and give a vivid impression of such artists as W. Mulready, D. Maclise, W. Etty and J. M. W. Turner, etc., in unguarded moments when they were engrossed with their work. The sketches were executed in black chalk on tinted paper with touches of chinese white. Lear's last known drawings are of Lord Brougham dated '1857' and a sketch of J. M. W. Turner, which was probably done from memory. After this the artist is said to have 'fallen into ill-health' and given up his profession except as a pastime. He died on 12 September 1903, leaving an estate of over £160,000. An article on this artist illustrating some of the portraits was written by Richard Ormond and published in *Country Life*, 9 February, 1967, pp. 288–289.

*Leared, Mrs. L. (fl. 1904)

Exhibited at the R.A. 1904, from 12 St. Augustine's Road, Birmingham. Her sitter was Ernest Colles.

Le Blond, Jacob Christoph. 1667–1741

Born in Frankfurt, 21 May 1667; studied in Zurich and Paris, and later in Rome under C. Maratti. Settled in Amsterdam *c.* 1700 as a miniaturist. Had to give up painting miniatures *c.* 1720 through eye trouble. Came to England where he tried to develop his invention of printing in four colours, without success; a tapestry factory was also a failure. He went to Paris in 1732 where he established a new firm and obtained a licence from Louis XV. Henrietta Wolters was his pupil in Holland. He died in poverty in Paris, 16 May 1741.

Le Blond, Robert. (fl. 1817–1822)

Worked at Cambridge, Rugby etc. in the 19th century. Left a diary in which he states that he painted 872 miniatures for an aggregate of £793 between 1817 and 1822.

*Lebour, A. (fl. 1853–1869)

Of London. Exhibited at the R.A., B.I., etc., 1853–1869. Executed figure paintings and possibly some miniatures. In 1863 the exhibit at the R.A. was a portrait of Mlle. Fanny Jarvis Rubini.

Leckie, Miss Mary Mulready. See Stone, Mrs.

Leclerc or Le Clerc, David. 1679/80–1738

Born in Berne, 1679/80; son of the medallist Gabriel Le Clerc of Rouen. Was a pupil of Joseph Werner (q.v.) in Berne, and in 1698 went to Frankfurt where he obtained a bursary from the Landgrave Karl v. Hessen-Cassel which enabled him to travel to Paris and London; he worked for the Prince for 31 years. He was in London, 1715–1717. Painted portraits, landscapes and flowers in oil and miniatures on parchment and on enamel. A large miniature on parchment of the Landgrave Karl v. Hessen-Cassel signed 'D. le Clerc pinx. 1714' is in the Landesmuseum, Cassel. Died in Franfurt-on-Main, 1738.

Leclerc or Le Clerc, Jakob Friedrich. b. 1717

Said to have been born in London, 1717; son and pupil of David Leclerc (q.v.). Was taken by his father to Frankfurt when less than a year old. Worked there as a miniaturist and enamellist till 1768; then at the Court of the Duke of Deux-ponts, and later in Vienna, where he remained until his death. He was one of the best German miniaturists of his time. His draughtsmanship was good and his portraits full of expression. He died in Vienna.

Lecocq, Miss. (fl. 1772–1773)

Of Richmond. Exhibited at the Free Society of Artists, 1772–1773 as Hon. Exhibitor.

Le Croy. (fl. 1663–1671)

Known only by a reference in George Vertue's MS. No. 23,072, p. 29, at the B.M.... 'sold Mr. Le Croy a Serpentine Stone aggat muller for lymning.' and 'Sold to Mr. Croy, a purphery grinding stone & muller for limning.'

*Ledger, Miss Mildred M. (fl. 1901–1914)

Of London. Exhibited at the R.A. 1901–1914, from 20 Park Hill Road, Hampstead. Painted miniatures and subjects in water-colour. Amongst her sitters were Mrs. H. F. Glanville and Mrs. Henry Ledger.

*Lee, Frederick W. (fl. 1894–1896)

Of London. Exhibited at the R.A. 1894 and 1896, from Campden Hill and Holland Park Road.

*Lee, Herbert. (fl. 1906)

Exhibited at the R.A. 1906, from Hogarth House, St. Luke's Road, Maidenhead, Berks.

Lee, Joseph. 1780–1859

Born, 16 January 1780; second son of John Lee of Islington, Middlesex, and his wife Rachel (née Oldroyd). Began an unsuccessful business career and turned to art. Believed to be self-taught when he was about 30 years of age, and to have studied the work of Zincke (q.v.) upon whose work he modelled his own. Painted enamel miniatures some of which were from life, but the majority from the works of other artists – Van der Helst, Romney, Petitot (q.v.), Boit (q.v.), etc. Exhibited at the R.A., 1809–1853, and the S.B.A. 1824, from various London addresses, including 21 Seymour Place. His wife Ann, by whom he had eight children, died in 1827. Received appointments as Enamel Painter to H.R.H. the Princess Charlotte of Wales and to H.R.H. the Duke of Sussex, but does not appear to have been financially successful and was latterly in receipt of an allowance from his nephew Charles Lee (1804–1880), an architect. Joseph Lee, whose height was 5ft. 8 in., used to carry an enamel of Napoleon I in his pocket as a show piece. He died, 26 December 1859, at 13 Victoria Place, Gravesend. An enamel of Frederick, Duke of York, by him, is in the Wallace Collection, London. A miniature, said to be a portrait of his mother, in my collection, is signed 'JO. Lee'. His work is well executed and the colouring pleasing. Other examples of his work are at the V. & A. M., the Wallace Collection, and in private collections, including that of H.M. the Queen. A miniature of Prince Leopold of Saxe Coburg, signed in full on the reverse, is in the N.G., Dublin.

*Lee, Miss May B. (fl. 1905–1914)

Of London. Exhibited at the R.A. 1905–1914, from 58 Moring Road, Tooting Bec. Exhibited a self-portrait in 1906 and one of J. Bridges Lee, Esq.

*Lee, Mrs. R. (fl. 1828–1843)

Née Anne Maria Turner; daughter of Charles Turner, A.R.A., the engraver and his wife Ann Maria Blake. Painted flower pictures. Exhibited at the R.A., 1843. Her only known miniature, of Mrs. Mary Savery, painted *c.* 1828, was in the O'Brien collection and was purchased from the artist's family. It is recorded by O'Brien, *Miniatures in the 18th & 19th Centuries*, p. 95, Pl. 63, Fig. I. The portrait is attractive and is painted on ivory.

*Leeds, Miss Mary. (fl. 1909–1912)

Exhibited at the R.A. 1909 and 1912, from addresses in Haslemere, Surrey. Her sitters included Sir Charles Strickland, Bt.

Leeming, J. (fl. 1817). See also **Leeming, T.**

Working in 1817 at Park Street, Grosvenor Square. Probably identical with T. Leeming (q.v.) who had the same address.

Leeming, T. (fl. 1811–1822). See also **Leeming, J.**

Of London. Probably identical with J. Leeming (q.v.). Was in Oxford in 1814. Exhibited at the R.A., 1811–1822. Married a Miss Link of Hereford. The B.M. has two engraved portraits after T. Leeming.

*Lees, Miss Louie C. (fl. 1903–1904)

Of London. Exhibited at the R.A. 1903 and 1904, from 40 Pembroke Road, Kensington. Her sitters included Miss Marjory Dennistoun, Mrs. Andrew Carew and Miss Emily Alington.

*Leeson, Miss Olive. (fl. 1907–1911)

Of London. Exhibited at the R.A. 1907–1911, from Collingham House, Cromwell Road.

*Lefebure, Thomas. 1636–1720

Was born in 1636. A miniature of Johann Friderich Obrecht, aged one, from the collection of Mrs. Hugh Myers, was sold at Sotheby's, 1 November 1965. It was signed and dated on the reverse 'Thomas Lefebure, 1678'. He was probably related to other artists of this name who worked in France. It is not known if he worked in England and he is unrecorded by Benezit. Schidlof states that he was born in Brussels and that he died in Durlach, 27 September 1720.

*Lefebvre or **Lefevre, Rolland,** called **'de Venise'.** *c.* 1608–1677

Said to have been born in Bagneux *c.* 1608. Became a member of the Academy of St. Luke in Rome, 1636; was an associate of the Royal Academy of Paris, 1662 and a member in 1665, besides being a member of St. Luc of Paris. Said to have been in England in 1638 and to have returned in *c.* 1676 shortly before his death in London in 1677. Painted historical pictures, portraits in oil and miniatures, some of which were engraved. A miniature of Cromwell by Lefebvre is in the Sheffield Museum. According to Benezit this artist was a protégé of Prince Rupert, in London, having previously worked for a time in Venice.

Lefevre or **Le Fébure, Claude.** 1632–1675

Born at Fontainbleau, 17 September 1632. Was influenced by the work of Le Sueur and Lebrun. Painted oil portraits, flowers and historical subjects; etched some portraits and is said to have painted miniatures. Worked in Paris and for some years in England. Became a professor at the Académie Royale. Died in Paris, 25 April 1675. The Duke of Buccleuch has a large circular three-quarter length portrait of Louis XIV, 13¼ inches in diameter, ascribed to him.

*Legard, Joseph. (fl. 1772)

Miniature painter and music master, noted in the *Manchester Directory*, 1772 as of 'Hanging Bridge, Manchester.'

*Legrand, Miss Louise. (fl. 1891)

Of Plymouth. Exhibited at the R.A., 1891.

*Le Hardy, F. (fl. 1793). See also **Le Hardy, Thomas**

It seems probable that there were two artists, Thomas Le Hardy (q.v.) and the above artist, both miniaturists and who were probably related. In 1793 F. Le Hardy exhibited a miniature portrait of a boy at the R.A. from 9 Henrietta Street, Covent Garden. The initial in the catalogue entry is given as J, which is presumably a misprint. The late Sidney Hand had in his collection a miniature of a naval officer, signed on card on the reverse 'Mr. F. Le Hardy, Miniature Painter'. Miniatures signed 'Le Hardy' (no initial given) are at the V. & A. M.

Le Hardy, Thomas. (fl. 1794–1802). See also **Le Hardy, F.**

Information regarding the above two artists, who were probably related, is rather confusing. It has always been held that T. and F. Hardy or Le Hardy were possibly identical, but it seems more than likely that there were three artists; Thomas Le Hardy, who exhibited at the R.A. 1794–1802, from 24 Bedford Street, Covent Garden, Weymouth and Bath; F. Le Hardy (q.v.) who exhibited at the R.A., in 1793 from 9 Henrietta Street, Covent Garden, both miniaturists, and Thomas Hardy, a portrait painter who was living at 4 Great Marlborough Street from 1788–1794. In 1790 an F. Hardy exhibited at the Society of Artists. The exhibits have always in the past been attributed to Thomas Le Hardy, but in my opinion the F was a misprint and they were probably the work of Thomas Hardy, the portrait painter, who exhibited at the R.A., from the same address in that year. The fact that Le Hardy's style varied considerably may be accounted for if there are, as I suggest, two miniaturists. A miniature formerly in the O'Brien collection is signed and dated 'T. Le Hardy / 1792' – the features are well modelled and the painting good. His sitters included the Prince of Bouillon and Mrs. Goodenough. In 1794 he exhibited a self-portrait. Miniatures signed 'Le Hardy' (no initial given) are at the V. & A. M. Neither Thomas Le Hardy nor F. Le Hardy is recorded as exhibiting at the R.A., in 1807 as stated by Long and Schidlof.

Leigh, Miss Clara Maria. See Pope, Mrs. Alexander

*Leigh, Miss Dora B. (fl. 1902–1903)

Of Paris. Exhibited at the R.A. 1902 and 1903, from Boulevard Raspail, Paris. Painted miniatures and subjects in oil.

*Leinque, Madame Bertha. (fl. 1901)

Of London. Exhibited at the R.A. 1901, from 34 Oakley Street, Chelsea.

Leith, Miss J. W. (fl. 1828)

Of London. Living in 1828 at 32 Kenton Street, Brunswick Square, when she received a silver palette for a copy of a miniature portrait, from the Society of Arts.

Le June, Elizabeth. (fl. 1844)

Exhibited at the R.A. in 1844, from 51 Warren Street, Fitzroy Square, from which address Henry Le June, A.R.A. also exhibited; she was possibly his sister. According to the *D.N.B.* she was also a musician and gave it up for photography. She worked nearly all her life in Naples.

Lely, Sir Peter. 1618–1680

This famous artist is reputed to have painted a few oil miniatures, but it is not certain that this is a fact. A plumbago miniature of Mrs. Christopher Wren was attributed to Lely, but is probably by D. Loggan (q.v.). An oil miniature of Charles II said to be signed with the painter's monogram was shown at a meeting of the Archeological Institute, 5 May 1865, and one of the Earl of Dalkeith, also signed with his initials was shown at the same Society in 1860. Long recorded that Lely was said to have painted three oil miniatures of Charles I.

*Le Maire, Barthelemy. (fl. 1670)

A miniature of Queen Anne, painted in oil on copper, is in the collection of the City of Liverpool Museum. It is attributed to the above artist on the basis of an inscription engraved on the brass frame into which the miniature is set. The front of the frame is inscribed at the top 'Le Maire Fecit' and a crown and sceptre and two hearts inscribed 'Two in One – For Ever'; below are the Royal Arms and 'Semper Eadem'. On the reverse of the frame, part of the inscription reads: 'A Medall upon the / apy / Union of Great Brittain to / the Immortall Glory of Her / Most Excellent Maiesties Queen / Anne July the 3 Anno Dᵐ 1708 / in the 7th year of Her Maieties / Reigne / Made By / Barthelemy Le Maire His Most / Excellent Maiestys King Charles / the 2ᵈˢ of blessed Memori / Ingraver in Ordinary / Sworn at Whithall the 25th / of Iune 1670 in the 22ᵈ of / His Maiesties Reigne / Made by the said Le Maire / in the 63 year of / his age.' I have not so far, been able to trace Le Maire, either as an engraver or a miniaturist.

Lemoine, Madame. (fl. 1816)

Exhibited at the R.A., 1816. Schidlof identifies this artist as probably identical with Mme. Sainte Edmee Lemoine, née Blot, who was a pupil of Augustin (q.v.), and who worked as a miniaturist in Paris, where she exhibited at the Salon under her maiden name, 1810–1812, and as Mme. Lemoine, 1814–1824. One of her exhibits at the R.A. was a miniature of 'Mr. Lemoine'.

*Lendrum, Miss Florence (fl. 1900)

Exhibited at the R.A. 1900, from Sunny Bank, Egerton, Huddersfield, Yorkshire.

Lens, Andrew Benjamin. b. *c.* 1713. d. after 1779

Second son of Bernard Lens III (q.v.) by whom he was probably taught to paint. His date of birth was probably *c.* 1713, as a miniature of him as a boy of about ten years of age, in the V. & A. M., was painted by his father in 1723. A self-portrait executed in 1742 which was formerly in the collection of Dr. G. C. Williamson, was said to have been painted when the artist was 29. He exhibited at the Free Society and Society of Artists, 1764–1779. Painted portraits, miniatures, mythological subjects etc., and executed engravings. He must not be confused with Andries Lens (1739–1822) who was a director of the Antwerp Academy until 1781. According to a note in the *Evening Post*, 31 October 1738, he was then living c/o Mr. MacCulloch's, Broad Street, Golden Square. He worked in the manner of his father, although not all his miniatures are of equal quality. His usual signature is a cursive monogram ABL. A large collection of miniatures by himself and his father was sold in 1777 by 'Mess. LANGFORD, At their House in the Great Piazza, Covent Garden'. An example of his work is in the V. & A. M., and the B.M. has drawings by him after portraits by other artists. A profile miniature called Mary Queen of Scots, probably after one by his father, after a miniature in the collection of the then Duke of Hamilton, signed 'by A. B. Lens' on the reverse, was sold at Christie's, 15 October 1963. An attractive miniature of an unknown lady in a crimson dress, signed on the front in monogram 'ABL', formerly in the de la Hey collection, is now in my collection. A miniature of his mother, Mrs. B. Lens, possibly after the miniature by Bernard Lens, signed in monogram 'ABL' is in the Ward Usher Museum, Lincoln. A profile miniature of A. Pope is in the collection of the Duke of Buccleuch.

Lens, Bernard (I). *c.* 1631–1708

Born *c.* 1631. Enamel painter; father of B. Lens II (q.v.) and grandfather of Bernard Lens III. Died, 5 January 1708 aged 77 and was buried in St. Bride's Church, Fleet Street, London.

Lens, Bernard (II). 1659–1725

Son of Bernard Lens I. Born in London, 1659. Was a draughtsman, etcher, mezzotint engraver and drawing master. He and J. Sturt had a drawing school in London. Was a master at Christ's Hospital (not B. Lens III as stated by Long). He is hardly known as a miniature painter, but the V. & A. M. has a finished portrait of R. Newcourt, in

Indian ink, by him. The B.M. has topographical drawings by him. The fact that there were three artists all of the same name may have led to some confusion. He is thought to have sometimes signed 'Barnard Lens'. His son Bernard Lens III (q.v.) was one of the best miniaturists of his period. His brother Edward (q.v.) was also a master at Christ's Hospital and succeeded him c. 1725. He died, 28 April 1725.

Lens, Bernard (III). 1682–1740

Born in London, 1682, son of Bernard Lens II (q.v.). No doubt had some training in art from his father; studied at the Academy of Painting in Great Queen Street, Westminster. Became one of the principal miniature painters of the day. Was miniature painter to George I and George II. Taught drawing at Eton; also taught Edward Harley, afterwards 2nd Earl of Oxford, the Princesses Mary and Louisa, the Duchess of Portland, Horace Walpole, etc. Worked in London, Bristol (1714), Bath (1727) as well as at country houses including Welbeck. When Robert Harley enquired about the best man to teach his son he was told in a letter 'I have sent for Mr. Lens a very able and the best master we have in London, a sober, diligent man and very careful'. This almost certainly refers to the above artist as he is known to have been responsible for a number of miniatures still at Welbeck, and for making a particular type of pearwood frame which has come to be called a 'Lens frame', and which he made for many of the miniatures in the Duke of Portland's collection. He married Catherine Woods on 30 November 1706 at Gray's Inn Chapel, by whom he had three sons, Benjamin, who became a clerk in the exchequer office, A. B. Lens (q.v.) and P. P. Lens (q.v.) both miniaturists. Lens copied a number of oil paintings by Kneller, Rubens, Van Dyck, etc., and miniatures by Cooper (q.v.) Hilliard (q.v.), Petitot (q.v.) etc. He was working from c. 1700 and Vertue records seeing drawings by him dated 1703 and 1704. The earliest known miniature by him is of the Rev. Dr. Harris of Rochester, inscribed 'B. Lens ad vivum pinxt 1707'. He made several copies of a portrait of Mary, Queen of Scots (see under L. Crosse), one of which is in my collection and signed in monogram 'BL' on the front and inscribed and signed in full and dated '1720' on the reverse. This portrait was also copied by A. B. Lens and C. da Costa (q.v.). He painted miniatures on vellum and was the first British artist to paint on ivory, a method adopted earlier by Rosalba Carriera (q.v.) an Italian artist; also executed archaeological drawings, sketches and published in 1735, *The Granadier's Exercise* and a *New and Complete Drawing Book*. The B.M.'s copy of this is dated 1750 and the Guildhall one, 1751. It is possible that this work may have been by his father. He painted several self-portraits, one of which is in the collection of the Duke of Portland, signed and dated 'BL. 1718'; another is at the Ashmolean Museum, Oxford, signed and dated '1724' and a third is at the N.P.G. He painted a miniature of his wife, in 1733, at the age of 52 and this is now in a private collection in America. Lens was one of the last miniaturists to make copies of classical, mythological and religious oil paintings, some of which were quite large. Although he introduced the use of ivory as a base on which to paint, he still painted in the old way in gouache, only using transparent water-colour on the face and any exposed parts of the flesh. The real advantage that the luminosity of ivory had over vellum was not fully realised until later in the century. His works often show the influence of Kneller, particularly in the shape of the face and the flesh colouring. He favoured a greenish brown shading, which was not suited to ivory. The costume of his sitters was

usually painted to perfection although some of his work is of uneven quality. He usually signed BL in monogram, often in gold, followed by a date, or inscribed in full on the reverse, or both. He used a variety of shapes for his miniatures, oval, rectangular and circular. Examples of his work may be found at the V. & A. M., the B.M., N.P.G. and many other museums as well as in almost all large private collections. His portrait of his wife was exhibited in Edinburgh, 1965 together with seven other miniatures by him.

*Lens, Edward. (fl. 1725–1749/50)

Brother of Bernard Lens II (q.v.). Was a master at Christ's Hospital June, 1725–1749/50. Succeeded Bernard Lens II and may have painted miniatures. After his death a John Lens applied for the job at Christ's Hospital but it was given to Alex Cozens.

*Lens, John. (fl. 1752–1753)

Was undoubtedly related to the other artists of this name. Evidence for his existence is to be found in various advertisements published in the *Daily Advertiser*, which read as follows: *The Daily Advertiser*, 2 October 1753. 'Lens, John. *Miniature Painter*, Price 2s. a new drawing book of 12 Landscapes designed by John Lens, engraved by J. Cousse.' The same paper, for 14 September 1752, published a further advertisement: 'J. Lens, Drawing & Painting in Miniature accurately taught by J. Lens at Mr. Dickenson's Print Seller, the Corner of Belle Sauvage Inn, Ludgate Hill.' And the same advertisement appeared again on 25 October 1752 with the address 'Nag's Head Court, Snow Hill'. On 25 May 1964 a miniature of a John Lens, Naval Gunner, aged twenty four years, painted by Bernard Lens III (q.v.) was sold at Sotheby's. It was inscribed on the reverse 'John Lens. AEtatis 24 gunner / Bernard Lens AEtatis 26 fecit / March ye 24 1708'. The artist and sitter were probably brothers and John Lens was more than likely the one who became an artist and was identical with the one referred to in the advertisements.

Lens, Peter Paul. 1714?–1750?

Son of Bernard Lens III (q.v.). His dates can only be judged by an inscription on the back of a miniature stating that he was 15 in 1729, pointing to his date of birth as c. 1714, and an inscription on a miniature at Belvoir Castle 'Peter Lens pinxit, 1750'. No miniatures dated after this are so far recorded. He painted portraits and miniatures, some of his portraits being in oil. Was a leading member of the Club in Ireland called 'The Blasters'; and professed himself a votary of the devil. After the Irish House of Lords took the matter up, Lens fled to England. He was apprenticed to his father 23 July 1729. His work resembles that of his father, but is not as good. His miniatures are usually small in size, and he often painted his sitters full face, the head occupying a large portion of the ivory. Lens signed PL in cursive monogram in front, P. Lens, also in front, or P. P. Lens pinxᵗ on the reverse. These signatures are sometimes followed by a date. Examples of his work may be seen at the V. & A. M. A miniature of an unknown man is in my collection, signed on the front in gold monogram 'P.L.' A number of his works are in private collections, including that of the Duke of Portland. The Duke of Northumberland has three signed miniatures by P. Lens, and one unsigned; these have a distinct stippling on the background, grey shading all over the face and a large amount of opaque white used in the hair. The one in this collection, of Hugh Percy, 1st Duke of Northumberland, is not by Lens as stated by Foster in his Catalogue of the

Northumberland Collection, but is probably by J. Meyer (q.v.).

*Lens, Thomas. (fl. 1765)

The above artist is recorded in the *Public Advertiser*, 7 August 1765. 'At Richmond, Miniature Paintings in the neatest Manner at 1 gn. & a half bracelets, and 1guin. Rings, by Thomas Lens'. He was probably related to the other artists of this name.

*Leonard, Mr. (fl. 1826)

The above artist was living in the High Street, Cheltenham in 1826. He was a miniature painter and taught drawing.

*Lepec, M. C. (Charles). (fl. 1871)

Exhibited at the R.A., in 1871 in the Miniatures and Enamels Section. His address was 12 Rue de Pré aux Clercs, Paris.

Lequeutre, A. (fl. 1831–1836)

Exhibited at the R.A. 1831–1836, from 30 Upper Berkeley Street, London. Schidlof suggests that he may have been identical with J. H. Lequeutre (1793–1877), but as the Academy catalogues consistently give his initial as 'A' this seems unlikely.

Le Roy or Leroy, Louis. (fl. 1779–1797)

A miniature of a girl after Peters, signed 'L. Le Roy / 1779' in white, was seen by Long. The miniature belonged to a Huguenot family and may have been painted by a French artist working in England. A French miniature signed 'L.L.R.' and dated '1797' was sold at Christie's, 23 February 1923. This artist may have been identical with the Le Roy noted by Schidlof, who worked in France and perhaps in Russia, 1772–1781.

*Le Royde, Miss Meta. (fl. 1901–1902)

Of London. Exhibited at the Society of Miniaturists, 1901–1902.

*Le Sage, Miss Clara. (fl. 1909)

Of London. Exhibited at the R.A. 1909, from 21 Holland Street, Kensington.

Leschallas, J. (fl. 1791–1823)

Of London. Exhibited at the R.A. and B.I., etc., 1791–1823; painted portraits, genre pictures and miniatures, some of which were copies of oil paintings.

Leslie, Charles Robert, R.A. 1794–1859

Born in Clerkenwell, London, 1794. Entered the R.A. Schools, 23 March 1813 aged 19. Exhibited at the R.A., and B.I., 1813–1859. Painted figure subjects, and is only known as a miniaturist by an oil portrait of the Princess Royal, 1841, which is circular and is 3½ in. diameter. This is at the V. & A. M. He died in St. John's Wood, London, 5 May 1859.

*Leslie, Peter. b. 1877

Born in London, 1877. Son and pupil of George Dunlop Leslie, an artist. Worked in Wallingford, Berks.; Lindfield, Surrey and Bushey, Herts. Exhibited at the R.A., 1899–1918. Painted genre subjects, portraits in oil, water-colour and at least one miniature. The sitter was Mrs. Jack Leslie, presumably a relation.

Lesseuf, A. (fl. 1832)

Of London. Exhibited at the R.A., 1832.

L'Estrange. (fl. 1832–1834)

An English portrait painter and miniaturist who worked at Halifax, Nova Scotia, 1832–1834.

*Le Sueur, Miss Clara M. (fl. 1909)

Of London. Exhibited at the R.A. 1909, from 7 Forburg Road, Stamford Hill. Her sitter was Captain G. Le Sueur.

Lethbridge, Walter Stephens. 1771/2–1831?

Born at Charlton, Devon, baptised there, 13 October 1772; son of a farmer. Apprenticed to a house painter; later assisted a travelling artist. Went to London and is said to have been a pupil of the R.A. Schools, but the fact that his name does not appear in the register, nor in the minutes, suggests that this was a mistake. Exhibited at the R.A. and S.B.A., 1801–1829; his exhibits included theatrical portraits and those of himself and his wife. He worked in London and Canterbury (1805). The *Kentish Gazette*, 27 August 1805 has the following notice – 'Likenesses painted in miniature. Mr. Lethbridge is just arrived in Canterbury. Price 3 guineas & upwards.' In 1831 he retired to Stonehouse, Plymouth, where he is said to have died in 1831. Some of his portraits were engraved. He usually signed in full on the reverse, followed by an address, e.g. 'W. S. Lethbridge / Pinxit / 391 Strand / London.' One of his characteristics was to paint the background with soft strokes which ended in a blob of pigment; the hair was painted with a broad wash, often scratched, and opaque white was used to depict lace painted over a grey ground. The V. & A. M. and the N.P.G. have examples of his work, and the B.M. has engraved portraits after him. A large oblong miniature of the artist and his wife was exhibited at the R.A. 1818, and sold at Sotheby's in 1925, and again on 26 March 1962.

Leventhorp, Miss M. (fl. 1796)

Exhibited at the R.A. 1796, as Hon. Exhibitor.

L'Evêque or L'Evesque, Henri. 1769–1832

Born at Geneva, 27 December 1769. Trained as an engraver. Accompanied De Saussure up Mont Blanc and published engravings of the expedition. Established a studio in Geneva for teaching enamel painting with the assistance of his brothers Jean Michel (q.v.) and Jean Abraham. Worked in Spain and Portugal; was in England 1812–1823 and exhibited at the R.A., etc. 1812–1819. In 1815 he became enamel painter to H.R.H. Princess Charlotte of Wales. The Society of Arts awarded him a silver medal in 1819 for an enamel painting of figures. Painted landscapes, enamel portraits from life, and enamel copies of old masters, as well as water-colour views. Returned to Geneva in 1823 and later went to Rome where he remained until his death, 25 April 1832. He was a good artist and his works are lively and full of expression. An oil painting said to be by him is at the Bentlif Art Gallery, Maidstone.

L'Evêque, Jean Michel. b. 1772

Born in Geneva, 30 December 1772; brother and associate of H. L'Evêque (q.v.) and not identical with him as suggested by Long. Worked in Geneva and later established himself in Paris where he worked until his death. Painted enamels and executed engravings. Exhibited enamels and views of Portugal at the Association of Artists in Water-Colours in 1812, when his name is recorded as J. L'Evêque.

*Levy, Miss Ada H. (fl. 1908–1914)

Of London. Exhibited at the R.A. 1908–1914, from 29 Cumberland Terrace, Regent's Park.

*Levy, Miss Mabel M. (fl. 1896–1898)

Of London. Exhibited at the R.A. 1896–1898, from various addresses in London.

Lewis (I). (fl. *c.* 1760). See **Lewis, Charles**

A miniature of an unknown man, *c.* 1760 was part of Lot 2 at Christie's, 20 June 1913. It was signed 'Lewis pinxt', and was not of a very high quality. The artist may have been identical with C. Lewis (q.v.). The *Newcastle Journal*, 1 September 1764, records a 'Mr. Lewis, portrait and miniature painter' as visiting Newcastle-on-Tyne and lodging in Rosemary Lane. It is impossible to be sure which of the artists named Lewis this referred to.

*Lewis (II). (fl. late 18th century)

Strickland records an artist of this name who practised in Limerick as a limner in the latter part of the eighteenth century. Nothing is known about him except that his widow died in Limerick in October 1792. He may possibly have been related to John Lewis, a portrait and scene painter who was working in Ireland, 1750–1757.

Lewis, Miss. (fl. 1802–1803)

Exhibited at the R.A. 1802–1803, as an Hon. Exhibitor. One of her exhibits was entitled 'Three sisters, Misses Lewis'.

Lewis, Mrs. (fl. 1783)

Exhibited at the Society of Artists in 1783. Executed miniatures, crayon landscapes and needle-work fruit pieces (Hon. Exhib.).

*Lewis, Charles. (fl. 1762). See **Lewis. (I).**

A miniature of an unknown lady, signed and dated by the above artist '1762' was sold at Sotheby's in March 1964. The artist was possibly identical with Lewis (I) (no initial given) (q.v.).

Lewis, E. (fl. 1847–1855)

Of High Street, Tunbridge Wells. Exhibited at the R.A., 1847–1855.

*Lewis, Miss Grace R. (fl. 1900)

Of London. Exhibited at the R.A. 1900, from 46 Brixton Hill. Her sitters included the Rev. C. B. Lewis and Miss Hartwell.

Lewis, J. (fl. 1744)

Said to have worked in England. Is known only by two enamel miniatures representing Sir Francis and Lady Fanny Fust. The portrait of Sir Francis is signed and dated '1744' and that of the lady, signed on the reverse 'The Lady Fanny / Fust, / wife of / Sir Frank Fust B^t / J. Lewis fecit'. On the front left is a coat of arms and below 'F.F. 1744'. The miniature of Sir Francis is in the Louvre and is not of any outstanding merit.

Lewis, J. (James?). (fl. 1801–1808)

Of London. Possibly the James Lewis who entered the R.A. Schools, 14 December 1798, aged 22. Exhibited at the R.A. and B.I., 1801–1808. Painted portraits, miniatures and subject pictures. Graves (*B.I.*) records this artist as exhibiting a landscape in 1812 at the B.I., from 21 King's Road, Chelsea, but this may possibly be the work of one of the other artists of this name. *Billinge's Liverpool Advertiser*, 15 September 1800, records that a Mr. Lewis 'from the Royal Academy, has left London for a short time and is now in Liverpool'; he may have been identical with the above artist. His exhibits included Mrs. and Miss Essex; portrait of Miss Knight, 'taken after her demise', and Mrs. Montolieu. In 1806 he exhibited a miniature portrait of Master Ackerman, which is presumably the miniature now in the collection of E. G. Paine of New York. This shows the boy holding artist's equipment and is signed on the reverse 'Portrait of Master Akerman / J Lewis / 101 Strand' – the artist's address from 1805–1808. The general effect is good.

*Lewis, John Hardwick. 1840–1927

Born in Hyderabad (India) 1840; pupil of his father Frederick Christian Lewis, jun. and of T. Couture in Paris. From 1875–1885 he worked in California, Dinan, London and Switzerland. Painted miniatures, views, and genre subjects in water-colour. Died in 1927 at Veytaux, near Chillon.

*Lewis, Miss Mabel Terry. (fl. 1897–1899)

Of London. Exhibited at the R.A., and the Society of Miniaturists, 1897–1899. She is recorded as exhibiting at the latter Society in *The Times*, 10 May 1897.

*Lewis, Miss Mary. (fl. 1895–1900)

Of London. Exhibited at the R.A. 1895–1900, from various London addresses.

*Lewis, Mrs. Tyrrell. (fl. 1897)

The Times of 25 October 1897 records that the above artist exhibited a miniature of 'The Countess of Annesley and child' at the Society of Miniaturists.

Lewis, William. (fl. 1804)

Exhibited a miniature self-portrait at the R.A., 1804. Worked in London. Has been identified with the landscape painter William Lewis, who exhibited at the R.A., 1804–1838, but there is no proof of this.

*Ley, Margaret (Mrs. Sewell). (fl. 1906–1913)

Of Surbiton, Bushey Heath and Harrow-Weald. Exhibited at the R.A., 1906–1913. Her sitters included Miss Rosamund Ley, Miss Dorothy Walker and Miss McLeod. Exhibited under her married name from 1911.

*Liberty, Miss Amelia. (fl. 1854–1856)

Of London. Exhibited at the R.A., 1854–1856. Her exhibits included a portrait of Master Henry Kemble, grandson of Charles Kemble, Esq. which was in the Drawing and Miniature Section.

Light, T. (Thomas?). (fl. 1806–1808)

Of London. Exhibited at the R.A., 1806–1808. Possibly Thomas Light who entered the R.A. Schools, 15 January 1807 aged 19. Probably the son of Edward Light (1747–1832), a professor of music and inventor of musical instruments, whose miniature he exhibited in 1807. He also exhibited a miniature of Mr. R. Light (stated to be a Professor of Music); this may have been another member of the family, or a misprint for E. Light. In 1807 he exhibited a self-portrait.

*Lightfoot, M. (fl. *c.* 1785–*c.* 1786)

Worked in Edinburgh, Leeds and Glasgow. 'Likenesses in miniature profile will be taken here (Edinb) in a few weeks, from Glasgow.' This advertisement was published in the *Caledonian Mercury*, 18 September 1786. Assisted Miers (q.v.) prior to 1785.

Lilburne, Mrs. T. (fl. 1825)

Exhibited at the R.A. 1825, as Hon. Exhibitor.

Lilly, Henry. *c.* 1589–1638

Of St. Botolph's, Aldersgate; born *c.* 1589, second son of John Lilly of London, a joiner. The family came from Bromsgrove, Worcestershire. Lilly became a Painter-Stainer, (apprenticed 1605), and established himself in Little Britain; committed to Marshalsea for meddling in the funeral of a Mr. Williamson without instructions from Norroy, King of Arms. In 1634 he was appointed Rose Rouge and Rouge Dragon in January 1638. Died, 29 (or 19?) of August 1638 and was buried in Farnham Church, Essex. Was a skilful illuminator and limner and was a herald and genealogist of some note. Some of his illuminations included small portraits. Executed pedigrees for the families of Howard, Digby, Newdegate and Sandys. For further information see *The College of Arms*, London, 1963.

Lily, Peter. (fl. 1800)

A miniature on ivory of a naval officer, catalogued as by Peter Lily, and stated to be signed and dated on the reverse as having been painted in September 1800, was lent to the exhibition at the South Kensington Museum in 1865. Probably identical with the miniaturist of this name who advertised in 1800 as from 50 New Bond Street, London.

Lincell, C. See Linsell, Charles

*Lindley, Miss Maud. (fl. 1907–1914)

Of London. Exhibited at the R.A. 1907 and 1914, from 134 Blackheath Hill, Greenwich and from 14 Steele's Road, Hampstead.

*Lindsay, Miss Gertrude. (fl. 1906)

Exhibited at the R.A. 1906, from Barby Road, Rugby.

*Lindsey, S. Arthur. (fl. 1902–1914)

Exhibited at the R.A. 1902–1914, from Limners-land, Southbourne, Herts. His sitters included Mrs. A. G. Boileau Lang; Mrs. F. M. St. Leger Harrison and Mr. and Mrs. W. H. Longbottom.

*Lingwood, Mrs. Mildred. (fl. 1907)

Of London. Exhibited at the R.A. 1907, from 9 Rusthall Avenue, Bedford Park.

Linley, J. (fl. 1786–1793)

Of London. Exhibited at the R.A., 1786–1793. Painted portraits and made enamel copies of Shakespearean subjects. Schidlof says he painted on porcelain but I have found no proof of this. He exhibited from 7 Great Warner Street, Cold Bath-fields.

Linnell, John. 1792–1882

Born in Bloomsbury, London 1792; son of a carver and gilder. Entered the R.A. Schools, 28 November 1805 and was awarded medals in 1807 and 1810. Studied under John Varley and under James Holmes (q.v.). Exhibited at the R.A., B.I. and O.W.C.S., 1807–1881 and was a member of the O.W.C.S., 1812–1820. Painted miniatures at the outset of his career; also painted portraits, landscapes and executed engravings. Was influenced by William Blake. The majority of his miniatures date from 1805–1827. He painted in a rather casual style and had a curious method of stippling, not easy to describe. Died at Redhill, 20 January 1882 and was buried at Reigate. A miniature by Linnell of George Rennie (1791–1866) is at the N.P.G. The V. & A. M. has a miniature of Mrs. Augusta Harvey, signed in front 'I LINNELL. F. 1827'; it has an architectural and landscape background. The N.P.G. has a self-portrait and other portraits by Linnell (not miniatures). A miniature of Mrs. Rennie as a girl, was sold at Sotheby's in 1963. It was signed and dated '1828', and a receipt in the case gave the artist's address as 6 Cirencester Place, Great Titchfield Street. A miniature by him of Princess Sophia is at Windsor. Portraits of the artist's children dated '1824' and one of Mrs. Linnell dated '1820' were lent by the artist to the exhibition at South Kensington Museum in 1865.

Linsell, Cornelius (fl. 1800–1832)

Of London, Burton (nr. Lichfield) 1808, and Oxford (1824–1830). Exhibited at the R.A., 1800–1830. Schidlof mentions a miniature of a young man

wearing a dark blue coat, in front of a red curtain, painted on ivory and signed in gold 'C.L. / 1832' and on the reverse 'Painted by / C^s Linsell / Oxford. 1832'. He considered him an artist of only average ability.

*Linton, Sir James Dromogle. 1840–1916

Born in London, 26 December 1840. Became a pupil of J. M. Leigh; was a member of the Royal Institute of Painters in Water-Colours from 1867 and later became President. In 1885 he was knighted by Queen Victoria. Painted in oil and water-colour; was a lithographer and a miniaturist. Died in London, 3 October 1916.

*Lintott, Harry Chamen. (fl. 1900–1912)

Of London. Exhibited at the R.A. and S.M. 1900–1912, from various London addresses. His sitters included General Sir George White, V.C., G.C.B.

Liotard, Jean Etienne. 1702–1789

Born in Geneva, 22 December 1702; son of Antoine Liotard, a French Protestant jeweller in Montelimar, and twin brother of Michel Liotard, the engraver. Studied in Geneva under Daniel Gardelle, and from 1725 under J. B. Masse, in Paris. Travelled extensively, visited Italy in 1736 with the Marquis de Puysieux. In 1736 was working in Rome and Naples. Whilst in Florence he met Sir William Ponsonby (afterwards Lord Bessborough) with whom he travelled to Constantinople where he remained for five years, living in Turkish fashion. Went to Vienna in 1743 and was in Venice, 1745, Darmstadt, 1746, Lyons and Geneva, 1747. From 1748–1753 was working in Paris, where he became painter to the King and a member of the Academy of St. Luc, where he exhibited 1751–1753. Visited England several times between 1753 and 1774. Married at the Hague in 1756, Mlle. Fragues, daughter of a French merchant living in Amsterdam. Was back in Paris in 1757 and settled in Geneva in 1758. Exhibited at the R.A., 1773–1774. The Emperor Joseph II invited him to return to Vienna in 1777 and he lived in the Hofburg. Painted miniatures on ivory and enamel; executed portraits in pastel and oil, besides being an accomplished crayon draughtsman. Was one of the best miniaturists of his period. The Musée d'Art et d'Histoire, Geneva, has a whole room devoted to his works. He signed a number of ways – Stef. Liotard fecit 1731; Liotard 1782; par J. Liotard / 1758; J. E. Liotard / Lion 1746, etc. Died at Geneva, 12 June 1789. The majority of his works are on the continent, or in private collections. The V. & A. M. has a chalk drawing by him. The E. Holzscheiter collection, Meilen, contains three examples of his work including a charming miniature on ivory of Lady Mary Wortley Montagu in Turkish dress. It is softly painted with the translucency of the ivory clearly visible against a gouache background. An enamel miniature on gold of George III as a young man, is in the collection of H.M. the Queen of the Netherlands and is signed on the reverse 'Peint par liotard, 1754'. A number of his works are in the Rijksmuseum, Amsterdam, including a large enamel portrait of the Empress Maria Theresa, $24\frac{1}{2} \times 20$ inches, signed and dated 'peinte par Liotard de Genève, a Lion, 1747'. The Hofbibliothek, Vienna, contains the artist's self-portrait on enamel.

Lisle, Madame de (Fortunée). (fl. 1832)

Exhibited at the B.I. in 1832, from 137 New Bond Street, London. Painted figure subjects. The N.P.G. has a miniature of Dionysius Lardner painted in oil on wood by Miss Edith Fortunée Tita De Lisle

(q.v.). Both Long and Schidlof attribute this in error to the above artist and state that her Christian name was Fortunée. Graves in his Dictionary of the B.I. styles her Madame De Lisle, without giving her a Christian name. Miss E. F. T. De Lisle may have been her daughter. In view of the confusion over the work of these two artists, Madame De Lisle may not have been a miniaturist.

*Lister, Miss Margaret M. (fl. 1905)

Of London. Exhibited at the R.A. 1905, from 38 Pembridge Villas, Bayswater.

*Lister, Miss May. (fl. 1898–1899)

Of London. Exhibited at the R.A. 1898–1899, from addresses in London.

Littleford. (fl. 1762–1763)

Exhibited at the Society of Artists, 1762–1763.

*Littler, Miss Emily. (fl. 1902–1911)

Exhibited at the R.A. 1902–1911, from Jocelyns, Sawbridgeworth, Herts. In 1904 exhibited a portrait of 'Miss Littler', possibly a self-portrait.

Livesay or Livesey, Richard. 1750?–c. 1823

Possibly the Richard Livesay who entered the R.A. Schools, 21 March 1774 'age 23 Dec 1773'. Was a pupil of Benjamin West (q.v.). Worked in London, Windsor, Eton, Winchester, etc., and visited Ireland. Exhibited at the R.A., 1776–1821. Lodged c. 1781 with Hogarth's widow. Taught drawing to George III's family and from 1796 was drawing master at the Royal Naval College, Portsmouth. Painted oil portraits, domestic subjects, miniatures (some in oil) and was also an engraver. The B.M. has some engravings after his work. Died at Southsea c. 1823. The N.P.G. and Eton College have oil portraits by this artist.

Livingston, Harriet. See Fulton, Mrs. Robert

*Llewellyn, Marion (Mrs. W.). (fl. 1896–1913)

Of London. Née Marion Meates. Exhibited at the R.A. 1896–1913, from Campden Hill. Was the wife of William Llewellyn, painter, who also exhibited at the R.A.

*Lloyd, Ernest H. D., V.P.S.M. (fl. 1895–1910)

Of London. Exhibited at the R.A. and S.M. 1895–1910, from various London addresses. His exhibits included a miniature of 'the late Bishop Smythies', Mrs. J. Smart and Mrs. Martin Colnaghi.

*Lloyd, Miss Ethel A. (fl. 1898–1899)

Of London and the Isle of Wight. Exhibited at the R.A., 1898 and 1899.

*Lloyd, Mrs. Hugh, R.A. See Moser, Miss Mary, R.A.

*Lloyd, Miss Olwen M. (fl. 1910)

Of Cheadle Hulme, Cheshire. Exhibited at the Society of Miniaturists, 1910.

*Lloyd, Miss Winifred E. (fl. 1897)

Of London. Exhibited at the R.A. 1897, from 10 Sheffield Gardens, Campden Hill.

*Lock, Miss Beatrice. (fl. 1906)

Of London. Exhibited at the R.A. 1906, from 4 St. James's Terrace, Regent's Park. Exhibited a portrait of her mother, and one of B. Fossett Lock, Esq.

Lock, Frederick. (fl. 1840–1846)

Of London. Exhibited at the R.A., 1843–1846. Possibly identical with Frederick William Lock (q.v.). An engraving published in 1840 of Queen

Victoria and the Prince Consort, after F. Lock, is at the B.M.

*Lock, Frederick William. (fl. 1845–1871)

Of London. Possibly identical with F. Lock (q.v.). Said by Graves to have exhibited at the R.A., etc. 1845–1871. In 1861 the R.A. catalogues record F. W. Lock in the index, and W. F. Lock in the catalogue entry. The exhibit was in the miniature section and represented Sir James Outram. He did not exhibit at the R.A. again until 1871 when the entry was 'Tommy Fair', not a miniature.

Lock, Samuel Robert. (fl. 1849–1854)

Worked in Brighton (1849) and London. Exhibited at the R.A., etc., 1849–1854.

Locke. (fl. c. 1850)

Henry Turner Munns (1832–1898) is reputed to have had some lessons c. 1850 from a travelling miniature painter named Locke. This artist may have been identical with F. Lock or S. R. Lock (q.v.).

Lockey, Rowland. (fl. c. 1581–c. 1616)

Probably born c. 1566/9, depending on whether his age was twelve or fifteen when he became apprenticed to N. Hilliard (q.v.). An entry in the *Apprentice Books of the Goldsmiths' Company*, provides the information that 'I Rowland Lockey son of Lenard Lockey of thi paresh of St. Brids in Flitstrete crasbomaker haue put myself prentice to Nicholas Hilliard for the terme of 8 yiers biginning at the fest of St. Meghel in anno ani 1581

              by me Rouland Lockey'.

This would mean that he probably ended his apprenticeship in 1589 and he would normally have been made a freeman of the Company soon after; he was certainly one by 1600 when his brother Nicholas became his apprentice for a term of 8 years. Rowland Lockey's name and that of Hilliard are found in the account book of Elizabeth, Countess of Shrewsbury, for the years 1591–1597, and Lockey evidently painted a number of pictures for Sir William Cavendish, second husband of Bess of Hardwick, and payments were made to him between the years, 1608–1613. He painted miniatures, portraits in oil and 'perspectives' and was said to have been a good draughtsman. From his will, made on 15 February, 1615/16, when he was living in the Parish of St. Dunstan's in the West, we learn that his wife's name was Martha, whom he made his executrix and left all but certain legacies to her. He left 20s to his apprentice John Langton and all his 'Italian Printes and all my plasters ...' to his brother Nicholas, who was also left the lease of the house in which his father lived in Fleet Street. Few miniatures can at present be ascribed to Lockey, and it is possible that some of his works are among those ascribed to Hilliard. The group of Sir Thomas More and his family c. 1600 (based on a painting by Holbein), formerly in the Sotheby Heirlooms, sold at Sotheby's, 11 October 1955, is attributed to him and may have been the original from which the oil group in the N.P.G. was taken. Evidence for Lockey having painted these portrait-groups is to be found in the notes of William Burton the antiquary (1575–1645) who records that 'Nicholas Hilliard ... left ... another expert scholler, Mr. Rowland Lockey ... who was both skilful in limning and in oil-works and perspectives; at whose house I once saw a neat piece in oil containing in one table the picture of Sir John More ... and of Sir Thomas More, lord chancellor, his son, and his wife; and of all the lineal heirs male descended from them; together with each man's wife, until that present year living.' The quality of the miniature is very fine and as the composition is slightly different from that of the oil painting, may well have been

the original. Other portraits which resemble Lockey's style and may be by him are 'An unknown Lady with a Dog' in the National Gallery of Victoria, Melbourne; an 'Unknown Man' in the collection of H.M. the Queen; and one of a lady called 'Lady Hay' formerly in the Sotheby Heirlooms. Attribution is difficult as Lockey undoubtedly copied from earlier pictures. For further information see *Nicholas Hilliard* by E. Auerbach, pp. 254–262.

Lodder, W. P. J. (fl. 1783–1804)

Was a pupil of J. J. de Loutherbourg; worked in London and possibly in Liverpool. Exhibited at the Free Society of Artists in 1783 and at the R.A., 1801–1804. His sitters included Prince William of Gloucester, Sir William and Lady Stirling, de Loutherbourg, etc. Long records seeing two miniatures by him of Henry de Quincey, and his brother, one signed 'W. Lodder/1797' on the reverse, both probably painted in Liverpool; and one from another collection signed 'W. J. P. Lodder/August 1801/Jermyn St.' The draughtsmanship was a little weak and the miniatures painted with a soft touch. The modelling of the features suggested the influence of J. Meyer (q.v.). Lodder painted portraits, miniatures and landscapes. The B.M. has engraved portraits of Sir E. Coote and the 1st Viscount Hill, after W. Lodder.

Loder. (fl. c. 1810–1814). See also **Loder, R.**

Was working in Dublin c. 1810 and 'taking likenesses' in Cork in 1814 for one pound. Painted miniatures, flowers, landscapes, and taught painting on velvet. May have been identical with R. Loder (q.v.).

Loder, R. (fl. 1801). See also **Loder**

Of London. Exhibited at the R.A., 1801. Probably identical with the artist Loder (q.v.) who was working in Dublin (1810) and Cork (1814).

Loehr, Charles Louis. 1745/6–1778

Born in Geneva, 1 January 1746, according to Long, or 1745 (Schidlof). Studied in Geneva and Paris. Painted miniatures in water-colour and enamel. Was in London for a time but returned to Switzerland in 1776. Died in Vevey 7 June 1778.

Loggan, David. 1635–1692

Born in Danzig, of Scottish descent, 1635. Became a pupil of the engraver W. Hondius and later studied under Crispin van de Pass, in Amsterdam, where he remained for seven years. He later came to London where he was influenced by W. Hollar (q.v.). In 1662 he was employed by the King's Printers to engrave the title page of the Book of Common Prayer, produced in that year. Said to have visited Paris with Le Davis. Returned to London and on 15 June 1663 married Anna Jordan, of Kencote, Oxfordshire, at the church of St. Sepulchre, London. During the plague he left London and by 1665 was settled at Nuffield, near Oxford. He knew Anthony Wood, who records some of their meetings at the Mermaid Tavern, in Oxford. By 1669 he was living in a house in Oxford, when he was appointed Public Sculptor to the University, with a stipend of 20 shillings per annum. Loggan matriculated in 1672 and in 1675 became a naturalised Englishman. From 1676 he had a permanent address in London. In 1690 he was made engraver to Cambridge University. Loggan is best known for his engraved works on Oxford and Cambridge, *Oxonia Illustrata* (1675) and *Cantabrigia Illustrata* (c. 1676–1690), his numerous engraved portraits and his fine plumbago portraits on vellum. He is known to have drawn a portrait on satin. The names of two of his sons have been

traced; John (born c. 1672) who became a clergyman and Justinian (died 1718) who served in the Grenadier Guards, and who was survived by his widow and three children. Loggan had several pupils, including Edward Le Davis, Robert Shepherd, Robert White (q.v.) and Michael Vanderguicht. He numbered among his friends, Sir Thomas Isham, 3rd Bart. He died in the late summer of 1692 and was buried in the church of St. Martin-in-the-Fields on 1 August. Loggan's plumbago portraits are among the finest of their kind; they are carefully drawn and expressive; not infrequently there is a buff or yellowish tinge on the face. His usual signatures are DL: DL del (followed by a date), either in cursive or Roman initials, or D. Loggan. Accounts of Loggan's life and work are in the *D.N.B.*, the *Walpole Society* Vol. XIV, pp. 55–64, A. Clark's *The Life and Times of Anthony Wood*, 1891–1900, and *Samuel Cooper*, by J. J. Foster, pp. 75–77. Examples of his work are in the V. & A. M., the B.M., the N.P.G., the Ashmolean Museum, Oxford, etc. A miniature of the first wife of Sir Christopher Wren, formerly ascribed to Sir Peter Lely, now attributed to Loggan is in my collection. It is executed in pencil and wash, the face being tinted; this, and one of Bibye Lake, as a child, signed and dated 'D.L. 1675' from the collection of Mrs. Bloefeld, were exhibited in Edinburgh in 1965.

Loggan, J. (fl. 1790)

Of London. Exhibited at the R.A., 1790. Painted portraits, mythological subjects, etc., and probably miniatures.

Long, W. P. (fl. 1785–1800)

Exhibited an enamel portrait of a Russian, at the R.A., in 1800. An enamel by him of c. 1790 was formerly in the collection of Mr. Nachemsohn. One of a man, in the N.G., Dublin, is signed on the front 'WPL/1785' and is painted in the manner of N. Hone (q.v.). The colouring is bright.

*Longe, Mrs. Blanche Adeline Douglas. (fl. 1900–1901)

Of Hounslow and Norwich. Exhibited at the Society of Miniaturists 1900–1901. Wife of Lt. Col. Douglas Longe.

Lonsdale, James. 1777–1839

Born in Lancaster, 16 May 1777. Pupil of Romney; entered the R.A. Schools, 23 October 1801, aged 24. Not usually regarded as a miniaturist, but the N.P.G. has a miniature self-portrait by him, as well as oil portraits. Long saw a miniature on ivory in 1932 with a scratched signature 'Lonsdale. 1801' (vertically). Died in Berners Street, London, 17 January 1839.

Lord, John (I). (fl. 1834–1855). See also **Lord, John (II)**

Of London, Liverpool (1841) and Silsoe (1852–1855). Exhibited at the R.A., B.I., etc., 1834–1855. Possibly related to the artist of the same name who worked in Dublin etc.

Lord, John (II). c. 1835–1872. See also **Lord, John (I)**

Probably born in Dublin c. 1835. Studied at the Royal Dublin Society schools where he obtained prizes in 1851 and 1852. Went to England and in 1857 was employed at the Newcastle School of Art until 1863. Worked for a time in Liverpool. Exhibited two enamels at the Dublin exhibition in

1861. Died whilst on a visit to Dublin, 11 March 1872. Was possibly related to the artist John Lord (I) (q.v.).

Losa, G. C. Rumpf. See Rumpf Losa, G. C.

*Loul, H. B. (fl. 1830)
Worked in England c. 1830. Schidlof records a miniature by the above artist which was signed 'H.B. Loul 1830'. He considered the work to be reminiscent of that of A. Robertson (q.v.) but rather softer. Some of his miniatures were large in size.

Loup, Miss. (fl. 1797)
Exhibited at the R.A. 1797, as Hon. Exhibitor.

Loutherbourg, Annibal Christian Henry. b. c. 1765
Baptised in Paris, 1765; son of P. J. de Loutherbourg. Was a pupil of A. Vestier (q.v.) and a student at the École des Beaux Arts in Paris. Was in London before 1792 and exhibited at the R.A. in 1793, when he described himself as miniature painter to the King of Prussia. Writing on 28 February 1792 from Berlin, Daniel Chodwiecki mentioned that the miniature painter Loutherbourg from London was there and was winning applause at Court which he did not quite deserve. He added that he was an amiable man.

Lovatt, William. (fl. c. 1824–1828)
Was working as a miniaturist at 57 Upper Islington, Liverpool c. 1824–1828.

Love, (John?). 18th century
Worked at No. 12 Haymarket where he advertised in an undated newspaper:—
MEDALLIONS OF LOYALTY
A Striking LIKENESS of HIS MAJESTY in Miniature, circumscribed with curious pencil work, under glass on a principle entirely new; One Guinea and a Half each. Sold by
LOVE, NO 12 Haymarket
Perfumer to His Royal Highness the Prince of Wales; Where those beautiful Powders, so much admired at the Drawing-Room, St. James's on Thursday last, are only to be had.
A John Love entered the R.A. schools, 15 October 1772 aged '20. 10th Inst.' and may have been identical with the above artist.

Love, Horace Beevor. 1800–1838
Born in Norwich, 1800 where he lived. Exhibited in Norwich and at the S.B.A., 1833 and 1836. Painted portraits and miniatures and executed portrait drawings. The Norfolk families of Beevor and Love were united by marriage, hence the name. Died in 1838 and was survived by his widow. Examples of his work are at the V. & A. M., the Norwich Castle Museum, the N.P.G. and engravings after Love are at the B.M.

Lovegrove. (fl. 1770)
Of Great Marlow. Exhibited at the Free Society of Artists, 1770.

Lovell, Patience. See Wright, Mrs. Patience

Lover, Samuel, R.H.A. 1797–1868
Born in Dublin, 24 February 1797, son of S. Lover, a lottery-office keeper and money changer, in whose office he worked from the age of 13 to 17 years. Had an aptitude for music and drawing, but his father's disapproval of any pursuit which was

not money-making led to quarrels, which ended by Samuel leaving his father and taking up art. He supported himself from 1814 by teaching drawing, whilst studying at the same time. He exhibited in Dublin in 1817 and 1819 and again in 1823. His early works were landscapes and marine subjects but with the encouragement of J. Comerford (q.v.) with whom he had become friendly, he attempted miniatures. He exhibited at the R.H.A., 1826–1835 becoming an Associate in 1828 and a Member in 1829. Resigned as a Member of the R.H.A., 15 March 1836 and was made an Hon. Member. Exhibited at the R.A., 1832–1862. Came to London in 1834. His exhibits at the R.A. included a miniature of Paganini. Was in America, 1846–1848. Besides painting, he was a composer, author and book illustrator and etched some of his own works. Some of his portraits were engraved. When the advent of photography lessened the demand for miniatures he began to interpret his own songs and tales, and started 'Irish Evenings', a monologue entertainment of songs, recitations and stories. He married twice, firstly in 1827, a daughter of John Berrel, a Dublin architect. She died in 1847 and he then married in 1852 a Miss Wandby. His miniatures vary in quality and slightly resemble the work of W. C. Ross (q.v.) and S. J. Rochard (q.v.). His colours tend to be rather pink and are mixed with a lot of gum. For the last four years of his life he lived in retirement in Jersey, where he died on 6 July 1868. He was buried in Kensal Green Cemetery on 15 July 1868. The N.G., Dublin has a self-portrait signed on the reverse 'Sam. Lover/R.H.A.', and one of him by J. Harwood, painted in oil and dated '1856'. A miniature of an unknown man, signed horizontally in yellow 'S. Lover R.H.A.' is also in the N.G., Dublin. A self-portrait executed in plumbago on card, and at one time in the Wellesley collection was sold at Christie's, 2 April 1968. This portrait is well drawn and expressive.

Low, William. (fl. c. 1840–1850)
Worked in Dublin c. 1840–1850 and at Belfast. Painted miniatures and executed silhouettes.

*Lowe, Miss Annie E. (fl. 1904–1910)
Of London. Exhibited at the R.A. 1904–1910, from various addresses in North London.

Lowe, Miss E. Linnie. (fl. 1905)
Exhibited at the R.A. 1905, from The Municipal School of Art, Margaret Street, Birmingham. The exhibit was a self-portrait.

*Lowe, J. (fl. c. 1756)
A sepia drawing of Mary, Queen of Scots, signed by this artist and dated 175– (the last figure being indecipherable) c. 1756 was seen by Mr. A. J. B. Kiddell in 1923. It may have been by a relative of J. M. S. Lowe of Berlin (1756–1831).

Lowe, Mauritius. 1746–1793. See also L., M.
Was born in 1746; said to have been the natural son of the Earl of Sunderland, who made him an allowance. Exhibited at the Society of Artists, 1766–1769. Entered the R.A. Schools, 9 August 1769; was awarded a gold medal for an historical subject. Studied under G. B. Cipriani, R.A. Was sent by the Academy to Rome in 1771 and was recalled in 1772. Exhibited at the R.A., 1770–1786 (not miniatures). Painted historical subjects and miniatures. Married a servant girl by whom he had a number of children. Was befriended by Dr. Johnson. Died in poor lodgings in Westminster, 1 September 1793. Two miniatures by him are in the V. & A. M.; both are signed 'MLowe/1766'. They are slightly in the manner of Peter Paul Lens (q.v.).

Lowe, T. (fl. 1838–1845)
Of London. Exhibited at the R.A., 1845. Long records seeing a miniature on porcelain signed 'Painted by T. Lowe/1838'. The miniature was 9 inches high.

Lowry, Miss Matilda. See Heming, Mrs. Matilda (I)

Lubersac, P. F. de (or T.F.). (fl. 1795–c. 1800)
Of London. Exhibited at the R.A., 1795–1798. May possibly have been a Frenchman. In 1795 he exhibited a miniature of a French Admiral. Is said to have worked in Hamburg, c. 1800. There seems to be some confusion about this artist's initials, which are recorded in the R.A. catalogues as P.F. and in two instances T.F. The B.M. has an engraved portrait of W. H. Jervis after T. F. de Lubersac.

Lucan, The Countess of (Lady Margaret Bingham). d. 1814. See also L., M.
Née Margaret Smyth; daughter and co-heir of James Smyth. Married in 1760 Sir Charles Bingham, Bart. (1735–1799), who was created (1776) Baron Lucan of Castlebar, Co. Mayo, and in 1795, Earl of Lucan. Said to have begun painting miniatures c. 1771. There are frequent allusions to her in Walpole's letters and in the memoirs of Mrs. Delany. Some of her works were taken from life, others were copies of works by Isaac Oliver (q.v.), Peter Oliver (q.v.), Hoskins (q.v.), Cooper (q.v.) and Reynolds etc. Was in Paris for a time where she made some miniature copies. She died on 27 February 1814 and was survived by five children, one of whom, Lavinia, married the 2nd Earl Spencer in 1781. Her work is not of outstanding merit. A miniature of Miss Sarah Sophia Banks, sister of Sir Joseph Banks, botanist, was Lot 387 in the Pierpont Morgan sale, 24 June 1935. She painted miniatures, flowers and birds. Her usual signature seems to have been a monogram MB, ML, or MBL. She illustrated an edition of Shakespeare's historical plays, with decorations of portraits, tombs, heraldic devices, flowers, birds, etc. This work in five volumes is preserved at Althorp. A miniature of the Duke of Lauderdale is in the collection of H.M. the Queen of the Netherlands. It is signed on the reverse 'Duke of Lauderdale/after S. Cooper/by/Lady Bingham/1774', and is quite well painted. A miniature on ivory, 1774, by Lady Bingham, was loaned to the exhibition at the South Kensington Museum, 1865 by Lord Cremorne. A miniature of a young girl, formerly in the de la Hey collection and signed 'M.L./fecit' painted c. 1795, is possibly by her. A miniature of Captain Cook, after the portrait by Dance, and once in the collection of Sir Joseph Banks, is in my collection. It is inscribed on the reverse 'In ye poss of/Sir Josh Banks' and signed 'MB' monogram. A collection of fourteen miniatures by her are at Althorp, including a copy of 'The Laughing Girl' after Reynolds. Several of the miniatures by her have the name of the sitter inscribed in gold on a small black panel at the base of the portrait.

*Lucas, Albert Durer. b. 1828
Born in Salisbury 1828; the son of Richard Cockle Lucas (1800–1883), a well-known sculptor and engraver. A. D. Lucas exhibited at the B.I., etc., 1859–1878. He painted flowers and subject pictures and is known as a miniaturist by two miniatures of flowers that were sold at Christie's on 28 May 1968. They were both signed and dated 'A. D. Lucas, 1876'. Both these works were attractive and meticulously executed; the colours were good.

*Lucas, Miss Marie Ellen Segmont (Mrs. M. E. Grubbe). d. 1951

Daughter of John Seymour Lucas, A.R.A., F.S.A. (1849–1923), of New Place, West Hampstead, London, and of the Priory, Blythburgh, Suffolk. Exhibited at the R.A. 1910 and 1914, from London and Southwold, Suffolk. Married Captain Laurence Carrington Grubbe, by whom she had issue. Her exhibits included a miniature of her husband. She also painted Mrs. Sydney William Lee (1851–1916) whose husband had studied under J. Seymour Lucas. Died at Blythburgh, Suffolk, 4 November 1951.

*Lucas, Mrs. Marie Ellen Seymour. d. 1921

Née Cornelissen. Of London, Exhibited at the R.A. 1901–1913, from New Place, Woodchurch Road, West Hampstead. Wife of John Seymour Lucas, an historical and genre painter, and mother of Miss M. E. Lucas (q.v.). Executed genre subjects in oil, portraits and miniatures.

*Lucas, Miss Mary Lancaster. (fl. 1891–1910)

Of London. Exhibited at the R.A. 1891–1910, from various London addresses. Painted miniatures and subjects in oil. Exhibited at the Salon of the Society of French Artists, in Paris, 1910.

*Lugard, Mrs. Charlotte E. See Howard, Miss Charlotte E.

*Lugard, Mrs. Nell. (fl. 1906–1907). See also **Howard, Miss Charlotte E.**

Of Haslemere, Surrey. Exhibited at the Society of Miniaturists 1906–1907. Was presumably identical with or related to Mrs. Charlotte E. Lugard, née Howard (q.v.). Her sitters included a number of members of the Lugard family, including General the Rt. Hon. Sir Edward Lugard, G.C.B. and Sir Frederick Lugard, K.C.M.G., C.B., D.S.O. (later Lord Lugard).

*Luke, Miss Flora. (fl. 1910)

Of London. Exhibited at the R.A. 1910, from 25 York Place, Baker Street.

*Luker, Miss Louise or **Louisa H. (Mrs. Burrell).** (fl. 1901–1912)

Of Bushey, Herts., and London. Exhibited at the R.A., 1901–1912. She is recorded as Mrs. Burrell from 1908. Her sitters included Miss Joan Proctor, Mrs. Comerford Bradley, Master Noel Cazalet and Mrs. S. Thursby Pelham.

*Lumsden, Miss Alice C. (fl. 1906)

Of Shanklin, Isle of Wight. Exhibited at the Society of Miniaturists 1906.

Lupton, Thomas. (fl. 1811–1820)

Of London. Exhibited at the R.A., 1811–1820. His address in 1811 was 6 St. James's Place, Clerkenwell. The above artist is recorded by Long as a miniaturist; he may have been related to or identical with Thomas Goff Lupton (1791–1873), the engraver.

*Lush, Harry. (fl. 1906)

Exhibited at the R.A. 1906, from 4 Hopwood Terrace, Church Road, Teddington.

Luttrell or **Lutterell, Edward.** 1650?–1723?

The date and place of Luttrell's birth are still unknown, although it is traditionally held that he may have been born in Dublin c. 1650. Went to London as a young man and studied law at New Inn. Became attracted to art and was a pupil of Edmund Ashfield (q.v.). Drew crayon portraits and engraved portraits in mezzotint. Invented a method of using crayons on copper plates. Some of his

portraits are small enough to be classed as miniatures. He may have executed plumbago portraits. The date of his death is not known but in 1723, Vertue in a list of the 'Names of living painters of note in London and their pictures by whom painted' included 'Mr. Lutterel, painter in crayons, by himself, several, one head as big as the life'. He signed EL in cursive initials with flourishes, and E. Lutterell fe, followed by a date. Examples of his work are in the N.G., Dublin, the N.P.G., London, the B.M., and the Bodleian Library, Oxford.

*Luxmoore, Miss Myra E. d. c. 1920

Of London. Exhibited at the R.A. and S.M., etc., 1887–1918. Painted portraits and subject pictures in oil, drawings and miniatures. She exhibited a self-portrait in oil in 1893. Died c. 1920.

*Lynch, Daniel. (fl. 1827–1841)

Exhibited at the R.A., N.W.C.S., etc., 1827–1833. Painted figure subjects and a few miniatures. Long saw a miniature signed 'D. Lynch' c, 1830, and another one signed and dated '1841'. Possibly a relation of J. H. Lynch (died 1868) of Dublin, a portrait painter and lithographer.

*Lynde, Raymond. (fl. 1899).

Of London. Exhibited at the R.A. 1899, from 10 Porchester Gardens.

*Lyndhurst. See Burrard, Lady

Lyon, J. (fl. 1803–1806)

Of London and Liverpool. Exhibited at the R.A., 1803–1806, in which latter year his address was 7 Nassau Street, Soho. The Liverpool Museum contains a miniature by the above artist representing Mrs. Lenham. The sitter is seated in a church beside a tomb holding a child, and looking up at a white marble bust of a man, set over a memorial tablet. On the reverse of the frame is the name of the sitter and an inscription 'Mr. J. Lyon, Painter, etc., 182 Brownlow Hill'. Gore's *Liverpool Directory* records a George Lyon, painter, of 2 Back Russell Street with a shop at 60 Brownlow Hill; Joseph Lyon, painter, of 2 Rupert Street and George Lyon & Son who had various addresses in Brownlow Hill. The miniature, although not of outstanding merit, is slightly reminiscent of the work of Richard Crosse (q.v.).

Lyon, Miss L. (fl. 1828)

Of 22 Nassau Street, Cavendish Square; was awarded a silver medal from the Society of Arts in 1828 for a copy of a portrait. May have been related to J. Lyon (q.v.) who was living at 7 Nassau Street, Soho in 1806.

*Lyster, Lady Charlotte. See Cooper, Lady Ashley

M

*M., A.

A miniature of a gentleman, signed 'AM', oval 2½ in., was sold as Lot 89 at Christie's, 15 October 1963.

M., D. (fl. c. 1659–1676). See also **Myers, David**

The above miniaturist was working in England c. 1659–1676. He signed with a monogram DM. At least sixteen miniatures by him are known, dating from 1659–1676. His work is unpretentious, and has

a naive charm, without succeeding in reaching any great heights. His drawing is weak, and when he attempted full-length portraiture as in the case of the miniature of a man said to be Henry Fitzroy, Duke of Grafton (in the collection of the Duke of Buccleuch) seated with his arm round a spaniel, the result is almost ludicrous. It is possible that the above artist was David Myers (q.v.) as there is a recorded inscription on an old box giving this name, and Long noted a miniature inscribed 'To Earl Clarendon' signed DM (monogram) in gold, and inscribed in old ink 'Purchased 3 Sept 1803. Edw Hyde Ld Clarendon 1608 d 1674' etc. 'Painted by David Myers'. Long noted that the card had a prepared surface. This is the rectangular miniature of the Earl of Clarendon, now in the collection of R. Bayne-Powell, Esq. Other miniatures by him are those of William Hevingham, signed and dated '1659', Sir William Bastard, signed and dated '(16)66'; Mary, Lady Leigh, signed 'D.M.' and dated '1670'; Thomas, Lord Leigh of Stoneleigh, signed; and Henry Terne, in armour, not signed. Some of his works have been wrongly attributed to Dixon (q.v.) the monogram having been misread.

*M., E. (fl. 1792). See **L., L.**

A miniature of William Seddon, Esq. (died 1808 aged 51) of Acres Barn, Lancs., is signed 'E.M./92' (1792). It is well painted and is a miniature of high quality; the draughtsmanship is good, and the colouring fresh and clear. A second miniature identically painted, of the same sitter, is signed 'L.L'. Both these miniatures are in a family collection in Edinburgh and it is impossible to discover which, if either, is the original or if they are both after another portrait.

*M., H. (fl. 1680)

Lot 149 at Sotheby's, 3 December 1930, was an oil miniature c. 1680, signed in yellow or gold 'HM'.

M., H. (fl. 1762–1771)

A small miniature of a man signed 'HM' (in monogram) '1771' was sold at Christie's, 1 May 1928. It was highly finished with stippling on the background and a minute stippling on the face. A miniature of an unknown lady signed 'HM' (monogram) '/1762' was seen by me at Sotheby's in 1968. It was strongly stippled on the background and reminiscent of the work of the Lens family (q.v.).

*M., J. (fl. 1820)

A miniature of a gentleman signed on the reverse 'J.M. 1820', oval 3⅝ in. was sold at Christie's, 13 November 1962.

*M., J.H. See Millington, James Heath

M., M. (fl. 1828)

A miniature of an officer signed 'M.M.' and dated '1828' was seen by Long in the collection of Lord Monson.

*M., R. (fl. 1768)

A pair of miniatures of children signed 'R.M.' and dated '1768' were seen by Mr. A. J. B. Kiddell. They were dotted round the eyes in a way not usually seen.

*M., T. (fl. c. 1710)

A miniature of a judge c. 1710, and signed '$\frac{T}{M}$' was in the O'Brien collection.

*Maas, Miss Edith. (fl. 1890–1909)

Of London. Exhibited at the R.A., 1890–1909. Her sitters included C. E. Gudgeon, Esq., Vice-Consul of Liberia.

Mabbett, Richard. b. 1760

Of London. Exhibited at the R.A., 1780–1781. Probably the artist of this name who entered the R.A. Schools, 25 March 1779 (age 19, 2 March 1779). Long saw two examples of his work which he did not consider very good; they were almost in monochrome. He signed R^d M/pinx^t/1781, and RM/1780. His address was '24 Viller's St., Strand'. A miniature of a lady signed 'RM/1780', is in the V. & A. M., and is attributed to him.

Macarthur. (fl. c. 1851)

Of Bell's School, Inverness. Worked c. 1851. Painted miniatures on ivory, and portraits in oil and crayon.

*Macbeth, Robert Walker, R.A. 1848–1910

Born in Glasgow, 30 September 1848. Second son of Norman Macbeth, R.S.A. Was educated in Edinburgh and Friedrichsdorf, Germany. Returned to Britain and studied at the R.S.A. Schools. Went to London, 1871 where, with his friends, E. J. Gregory and (Sir) Hubert von Herkomer, he joined the staff of the newly founded *Graphic Newspaper*. Studied at the R.A. Schools. Exhibited at the R.A., O.W.C.S., N.W.C.S., etc., 1870–1909. Was elected A.R.A., 1883 and R.A., 1903. He was made an Associate of the Royal Society of Painters in Water-Colour (O.W.C.S.) in 1871 and a Member in 1901; also exhibited in Paris where he was awarded medals for his work. He was chiefly known for his paintings in water-colour, oil paintings and etchings, but in 1905 and 1906 exhibited miniatures at the R.A. Was an original member of the Society of Painter-Etchers. Married in 1887, Lydia, eldest daughter of General Bates of the Bombay Native Cavalry, by whom he had a daughter. During the latter part of his life lived chiefly at Washford, nr. Dunster. Died at Golders Green, 1 November 1910. His wife survived him.

McBride, Archibald. b. c. 1798

Born c. 1798 in County Monaghan. Worked as a miniaturist in Dublin (1841), Belfast (1852) and the north of Ireland.

*McBryde, Miss Nellie. (fl. 1901)

Of London. Exhibited at the R.A., 1901, from St. Andrew's House, Mortimer Street.

McCall, Mac Call or McCall, William. b. 1786?

Of London. Born 1786? William McCall entered the R.A. Schools, 3 September 1818, aged 22, and was probably identical with this artist. Exhibited at the R.A., B.I., etc., 1818–1837. Painted portraits, miniatures, etc.

MacCarthy, J. (fl. 1838). See also **MacCarthy, John Silvester**

Long records seeing a miniature of Queen Victoria, painted in rather a loose manner and inscribed on the reverse 'July 30. 1838/J Maccarthy principal painter/in Miniature to his Royal/Highness the Duke of Kent'. It was painted slightly in the manner of Mrs. Mee (q.v.). The artist was possibly identical with J. S. MacCarthy (q.v.).

*MacCarthy, John Silvester. 18th century. See also **MacCarthy, J.**

An oval eighteenth-century miniature by this artist was seen by Long, it was signed along the edge, 'I. Silvester Maccarthy '97' and had a flourishing inscription on the reverse giving his full name. Possibly related to or identical with J. MacCarthy (q.v.). The miniature referred to is now in the V. & A. M.

*McCausland, Miss Elizabeth. (fl. 1806–1807)

Among the Edgeworth family portraits is a miniature of Miss Charlotte Edgeworth (1783–1807), second daughter of R. L. Edgeworth, by his third wife, Elizabeth Sneyd (Maria Edgeworth's half sister). The miniature is inscribed on the reverse by a later hand 'Charlotte Edgeworth, 1807 by Eliz McCausland'. According to family correspondence Miss McCausland painted three versions of this portrait in the late autumn of 1806. She was evidently well known to the Edgeworth family, who talk of 'being glad that she had the divertissement of the season in Dublin'.

*McClatchie, Miss Florence. (fl. 1900)

Of London. Exhibited at the R.A. 1900, from 28 Edith Road, West Kensington. Her exhibit in that year was 'portrait of a gentleman'.

MacClise or **McLise, Daniel, R.A.** See **Maclise, Daniel, R.A.**

Macco, Alexander. 1767–1849

Born in Creglingen, 29 March 1767. Said to have been a pupil of an engraver named Arzberger. Went to Mannheim, in 1781–1784, where he studied at the Academy under Verschaffelt. Was awarded a gold medal. Had financial assistance from the Court of Anspach. Went to Rome in 1784–1797, returned to Germany, and worked for a time in Austria and Bohemia. Was in Berlin in 1800, and from then until 1807 he was in Prague, Vienna, Frankfurt, Mannheim and Paris. From 1807–1816, he was chiefly in Vienna, and 1817–1819 worked in Frankfurt, Hamburg, etc. Came to England in 1825 for two years, after which he returned to Germany, living first at Weimar, and in 1829 in Dresden. Macco finally settled in Bamberg, where he died, 24 June 1849. He painted portraits in oil, historical subjects, was a lithographer and etcher, and executed miniatures. Characteristics of his work are the fine and somewhat dry execution, the hair being painted in hard curls, much of the miniature is in gouache the background being executed in long darker crossed brush-strokes. A number of his miniatures are in the possession of descendants of the artist near Munich.

McCormick or **Mac Cormick.** 19th century

A miniature of a naval officer signed 'McC' (?), and which was somewhat reminiscent of the work of Andrew Robertson (q.v.) was sold at Puttick and Simpson's, 11 November 1921. It was catalogued as by McCormick. Schidlof refers to an artist called Mac Cormick as working in England c. 1830.

*McCracken, Miss M. (fl. 1908)

Of London. Exhibited at the Society of Miniaturists, 1908.

*Macdonald, Miss Ionë. (fl. 1904–1905)

Of London. Exhibited at the R.A., 1904 and 1905, from addresses in Chelsea.

*McDonald, Miss Madeline M. (fl. 1900)

Of London. Exhibited at the R.A. 1900, from 30 Ledbury Road, Bayswater.

*McDowall, Miss Jessie. (fl. 1905)

Of Sketty, Glamorganshire. Exhibited at the Society of Miniaturists, 1905.

Macgavin, J. (fl. 1797–1820). See also **Macgavin, W.**

Of London, Coventry (1806), Bath (1819) and Bristol (1820). Exhibited at the R.A., 1797–1820. An advertisement in *The Manchester Mercury*, 20 August 1816, reads 'Macgavin, Mr. Miniatures. Specimens may be seen at Mr. Edmonds, at 10 Brown St., Manchester. Price 2 Guineas & upwards.' This may be either J. Macgavin or W. Macgavin (q.v.), to whom the above artist was probably related.

Macgavin, W. (fl. 1793–1807). See also **Macgavin, J.**

Of London. Exhibited at the R.A., 1793–1807. Was undoubtedly related to J. Macgavin (q.v.); they both exhibited from addresses in Great Marlborough Street. In 1793 W. Macgavin exhibited a self-portrait at the R.A. Either he or J. Macgavin was the artist who was at Mr. Edmonds, 10 Brown Street, Manchester, 20 August 1816.

*McGowan, William J. (fl. 1902–1907)

Of London. Exhibited at the R.A., 1902 and 1907.

*M'Hwraith, (Andrew?). (fl. 1715)

A Mr. (Andrew?) M'Hwraith, limner, married Anne Mossman, 13 July 1715. This is recorded in *The Scottish Record Society* 1701–1750, by H. Paton, 1908.

Macintosh. (fl. 1768–1769)

Of Kensington, London. Exhibited at the Society of Artists, 1768–1769.

McKenzie, Alexander. b. 1750

Born 1750. Worked in London. Entered the R.A. Schools, 19 October 1770, when his age was noted as being '21 1st Jany 1771'. Exhibited at the Free Society and R.A., 1777–1799. Was noted for his portraits in wax, but may have painted some miniatures.

Mackenzie, Mrs. Isabella. (fl. 1843–1846)

Of London. Exhibited at the R.A., 1843 and 1846. Painted fruit and miniatures.

Mackenzie, Miss Jane. (fl. 1852–1858)

Of London. Probably a daughter of Mrs. I. Mackenzie (q.v.) from whose address she exhibited. Exhibited at the R.A., 1852–1858; also at the Society of Female Artists in 1857.

McKenzie, William. (fl. 1820–1828)

Possibly the William MacKenzie who entered the R.A. Schools, 21 June 1781, aged '16 Aug. 7. 1781'. Was working at 3 Castle Street, Edinburgh in 1820. A miniature called Lord Seaforth, signed and dated '1828', was seen at the S.N.P.G. (The Earldom was extinct in 1815, so this must have been taken from an earlier portrait.)

Mackie, J. B. (fl. 1838–1839)

Of Deptford. Exhibited at the R.A., 1838–1839. His sitter in 1839 was Edward Downing, Esq.

Mackie, W. B. (fl. 1830–1831)

Of London. Exhibited at the R.A., 1830–1831.

*Mackinlay, Miss Georgia A. E. (fl. 1898–1910)

Of London. Exhibited at the R.A., 1898–1910, from various London addresses.

Mackintosh, E. (fl. 1890)

A miniature of a young lady signed by the above artist was sold at Sotheby's Belgravia 12 October 1978.

Mackreth, Miss Harriet F. S. (fl. 1828–1842)

Of London and Newcastle-on-Tyne. Exhibited at the R.A. and S.B.A., 1828–1842, and the Northern

Academy of Arts, Newcastle-on-Tyne in 1828, in which year an R. Mackreth also exhibited there. I have seen a miniature by the above artist signed on the reverse 'Harriet Mackreth/High Swinburne Place/Newcastle-on-Tyne/1834/Portrait of/Mip Ginger/London'. The miniature was well painted and there was blue shading on the face.

*Mackubin, Miss Florence. (fl. 1901)

Exhibited at the R.A. 1901, from 301 Charles Street, North Baltimore, Maryland, U.S.A. Her sitter was Miss Mary E. Wilkins.

*McLaren, Miss Charlotte G. (fl. 1900–1907)

Of Glasgow and Edinburgh. Exhibited at the R.A. 1900–1907, from Bath Street, Glasgow and Queen Street, Edinburgh. Her sitters included Miss Kathleen Cameron, and Mrs. and Miss Burnet.

*Maclear, Arthur. (fl. 1900–1903)

Exhibited at the R.A. and S.M., 1900–1903, from 19 Forest Hill Road, Bedford.

Macleay, Kenneth, R.S.A. 1802–1878

Born in Oban, 4 July 1802; son of Dr. Kenneth Macleay. Went to Edinburgh at the age of 18; entered the Trustee's Academy, 26 February 1822. Soon obtained recognition as a miniaturist. Was one of the founder members of the Scottish Academy in 1826; resigned; was re-elected an Associate, and R.S.A., 1829. Exhibited at the Institute for the Encouragement of the Fine Arts in Scotland, 1822–1829; at the R.S.A., 1828–1879, his last exhibit being posthumous; and the R.A., 1865. Died in Edinburgh, 3 November 1878. Macleay married a daughter of Sir A Campbell of Aldenglass. He executed drawings and portraits for Queen Victoria; painted miniatures on ivory and paper. He painted with a soft touch rather in the manner of Thorburn (q.v.). I have seen several miniatures by him; they were all well painted. He used a sepia shading on the face and often delineated the features with a reddish colour. I have seen one on ivory where he used a blue shading on the face. He frequently signed in full on the reverse Painted by/Kenneth Macleay/ Edinburgh followed by a date. Examples of his work are at the N.P.G., and at the S.N.P.G., Edinburgh. Others are in private collections, including that of Mrs. Seton Dickson, Ayrshire. A miniature of a young man, possibly a self-portrait is in my collection. It is signed on the reverse, 'Painted by / Kenneth Macleay / Edin- Febr. 1829'.

*Macleod, Mrs. Anne Eliza. (fl. 1830)

Long noted seeing a miniature painted, 26 August 1830 by this artist of her daughter Mary Lowther Macleod, aged eleven. It was a good miniature and well painted.

Macleod, D. (fl. 1793–1802)

Of London. Possibly a Scottish artist as his only exhibit at the R.A., 1793, from 23 Strand, represented a Highlander. He was working in Edinburgh in 1802. Long did not consider his work very good; he thought it coarse and weakly drawn.

Maclise, MacClise or **McLise, Daniel, R.A.** c. 1806–1870

Born in Cork, c. 1806. Studied at the Cork Academy, 1822. Entered the R.A. Schools, 21 April 1828, aged 20. Was awarded silver and gold medals, 1828–1831. Exhibited at the R.A., B.I., etc., 1829–1870. Was elected R.A., in 1840. Painted principally historical subjects and portraits in oil, but also painted portraits in water-colour, miniatures on ivory and executed some lithographs. Died in Chelsea, 25 April 1870. A miniature of two boys (pencil tinted) signed, 'D. McLise 1828', was sold at Sotheby's, 13 July 1927. The Pierpont Morgan sale,

24 June 1935, contained two miniatures catalogued as by him; they represented James Henry Leigh Hunt, essayist and poet, and William Makepeace Thackeray, both from the Leigh Hunt family collection. He painted with a long parallel brush stroke, the flesh tints being yellowish with reddish brown shadows. He expressed the character of his sitters in a remarkable way. Schidlof records a miniature, signed on the reverse, 'Daniel McClise/Decr 1828/London'. A full account of his work is given by Strickland. Several small portraits in water-colour by him were exhibited at the R.A., 'British Portraits', Winter Exhibition 1956–57. A number of works by Maclise are in the N.P.G.

McMor(e)land, Patrick John. 1741– d. after 1809

Born in Scotland in 1741. Worked in Scotland, Manchester 1774–1777, London 1777, Liverpool c. 1781, and returned to Manchester in 1793. Exhibited at the Society of Artists, 1774–1775, at the R.A., 1776–1782, and in Liverpool, 1784–1787. Lectured on art and taught at Manchester in 1809. Painted miniatures on ivory and enamel miniatures for rings, 'stained' portrait sketches, tinted drawings of landscapes, Italian views and seascapes. His work varied; at best it was of a high quality, and I have seen miniatures by him which are very attractive. He signed P.M. or P.M.^c. Examples of his work are in the V. & A. M., and the B.M. has an engraved portrait of Elizabeth Raffald after McMoreland. A miniature of an unknown lady, signed on the front 'P.Mc./1799', is in the collection of R. Bayne-Powell, Esq. A miniature of an unknown man signed 'P.Mc 1803' is in the S.N.P.G.

*McNalty, Miss Kathleen. (fl. 1903)

Of London. Exhibited at the R.A. 1903, from 19 Lansdowne Road, Blackheath.

*Maconechy, Miss Sophie M. H. (fl. 1905–1907)

Of London. Exhibited at the Society of Miniaturists, 1905–1907.

*Macpherson, Giuseppe. b. 1726. See also **Macpherson, James** or **Joseph**

Born in Florence, 19 March 1726, presumably of Scottish extraction. Little is known about this artist, who was probably identical with James Macpherson (q.v.). The Connoisseur, November 1959 contains an interesting article by John Fleming, pp. 166, 167, about his work and training. Macpherson is said to have been a pupil of Pompeo Batoni, and to have worked in Florence and Milan. If he is identical with James Macpherson, he was in Paris and London (1754). Giuseppe Macpherson executed many life-size portrait groups, painted in oil and commissioned by various 'gran personaggi Inglesi'. He also painted miniatures, many of which were on enamel, and was a skilled copyist. He is described as having a special talent for painting on enamel, and as being 'almost the only painter in Europe who possesses this art to perfection, as may be seen in the many works in this medium produced by his hand'. This was written in 1776, when Macpherson was living in Florence. One of his patrons was George, 3rd Earl Cowper (1738–1789) a leading connoisseur of the day who settled in Florence c. 1760. In 1767, Earl Cowper loaned a group of sixty miniature copies by Macpherson of the Uffizi self-portraits to an exhibition organised by the Florentine Academy at SS. Annunziata. These were probably part of the collection which he presented to George III on 20 January 1773. They form part of the Royal Collection at Windsor. The second half of the collection which Cowper presented to the King, was brought over by him when he returned from Florence in May 1786, and presum-

ably added to the others in that year. Macpherson had a distinguished clientele which included some of the crowned heads and dignitaries of Europe, and other notable persons. In 1778 he was prevailed upon to present his self-portrait, painted in miniature on goatskin, to the Grand Duke of Tuscany for inclusion among those by famous painters in the Grand Duke's collection. Giuseppe Pelli, the Director of the Grand Ducal Gallery, recommended its acceptance, and said that 'it would do honour to Florence to enrich the collection with a work which shows that we still have some men of true merit'. For this Macpherson was awarded a gold medal on 31 May 1778. The original self-portrait is in the Uffizi Gallery, Florence, and a replica of it on canvas, also executed by Macpherson, is in the Duke of Wellington's collection. This latter portrait was exhibited at the R.A., in 1960. It is not known when Macpherson died. For further reference see James Macpherson (q.v.).

*Macpherson, J. See **Macpherson, James** and **Macpherson, Giuseppe**

Macpherson, James or **Joseph.** b. 1726? See also **Macpherson, Giuseppe**

The artist James Macpherson is recorded by Long and others as having worked in London, Paris, Florence and Milan. He was probably identical with Giuseppe Macpherson (q.v.). C. F. Bell noted in his copy of British Miniaturists (now at the V. & A. M.) that James Macpherson was the artist mentioned in Giuseppe Baretti by L. Collinson Morley, 1909, pp. 83, 90. Writing in a letter dated 15 April 1754, Baretti (an Italian poet and lexicographer 1716–1789) mentions a portrait 'which I have had done in enamel by a young gentleman called Macpherson, a Florentine by birth but of Scotch extraction, who was in Italy three or four years ago'. Bell notes that 'this was apparently Baretti's own portrait'. In another letter of 8 August of the same year, Baretti again mentions Macpherson as being 'then in London' (i.e., 1754). If, as seems likely, the two artists were identical, he was born in Florence, 19 March 1726. An enamel miniature of an unknown lady, formerly in the Nachemsohn Collection and now in the N.G., Dublin, is signed 'Macpherson 1741', and catalogued as by J. Macpherson. Long noted that his work was reminiscent of the manner of Alan Ramsay's oil portraits. A collection of miniatures painted by Giuseppe Macpherson is at Windsor Castle. According to Clouzot, Macpherson is known to have signed Mâcson. A miniature of General Paoli, painted in Florence by James Macpherson, is in the collection of the Marquess of Exeter.

*Macpherson, Joseph. See also **Macpherson, James** and **Macpherson, Giuseppe**

Schidlof states that, according to Zani, Macpherson's christian name was Joseph, and that he was born in 1726. The names may have been confused, but the date of birth accords with that given for Giuseppe Macpherson (q.v.) who was probably identical with James (or Joseph) Macpherson (q.v.).

Macpherson, M. (Mary?). (fl. 1828–1834)

Of London. Exhibited at the R.A. and N.W.C.S., 1828–1834. A miniature of a man, signed on the reverse, 'by M. Macpherson, Aremcester Place, Fitzroy Square', was sold in Vienna, 31 March–3 April 1925. The artist's address in 1828 was 84 Newman Street. Foster records the name of the above artist as Mary.

Mâcson. See **Macpherson, James**

*Madden, Edward. (fl. 1861)

The above artist about whom nothing is known is recorded as having exhibited a miniature at Florence, 1861. He may have been related to George Madden (q.v.).

Madden, George. 18th century

Became a pupil at the Dublin Society Schools. Was patronised when young by the 4th Earl of Bristol, Bishop of Derry (1730–1803) who took him to Italy. He returned to Dublin, but after marrying a rich widow took up residence in Belfast, and retired from his profession.

*Madeley, Miss Lucy. (fl. 1905–1914)

Of London. Exhibited at the R.A., 1905–1914. Painted miniatures and landscapes in oil.

*Madge, Miss J. Annie. (fl. 1898–1905)

Of Swansea and Liverpool. Exhibited at the R.A., 1898–1905.

Maguire, James Robert, A.R.H.A. (fl. 1809–c. 1850)

Of Dublin. Living in College Green in 1809. Exhibited 1809–1849 at the R.H.A., etc. Painted miniatures, oil portraits and views. Was an Associate of the R.H.A., 1826–1830. Some of his works were engraved. Schidlof records a James Robert Magnire, about whom he gives the same information as that recorded for the above artist; this is obviously an error and the two artists identical.

*Maguire, Sidney Calton. (fl. 1880–1882)

Of London. Exhibited at the R.A., etc., 1880–1882. Was undoubtedly related to T. H. Maguire (q.v.), Miss H. J. Maguire and Miss A. A. Maguire, all of whom exhibited from 6 Bloomfield Crescent, Westbourne Terrace. His sitters included The Rt. Hon. W. E. Gladstone, M.P. All his known works are on enamel.

*Maguire, Thomas Herbert. 1821–1895

Born in London 1821. Exhibited at the R.A., B.I., etc., 1846–1887. From 1848–1855 he lived at 98 Gt. Russell Street and from 1856–1863 at 29 Wimpole Street. His address from 1864–1876 was 6 Bloomfield Crescent, Westbourne Terrace, from where Miss A. A. Maguire, Miss H. J. Maguire, both artists and S. C. Maguire (q.v.) also exhibited, and were probably his children. Thomas Maguire painted portraits in oil and crayons, figure subjects and miniatures and executed lithographs. In 1856 he is recorded as being 'Lithographer to the Queen'. He died in April 1895. Some of his exhibits were engravings after miniatures by Thorburn (q.v.) and others, and after portraits by T. Watts and F. Winterhalter. Some of his miniatures were on enamel, including those of Sir Frederick Leighton, P.R.A. and Mrs. Ashton.

Mainwaring, Miss Mary. (fl. 1822–1824)

Of London. Exhibited at the R.A., 1822–1824. Was an Hon. Exhibitor in 1822, and in 1824 lived at 'Chichester-rents, Chancery-lane'. One of her miniatures was of 'Mr. Broadhurst, of the Theatre Royal English Opera House'.

*Mair, Miss Maud (Mrs. Frank Eastman). (fl. 1902–1914)

Of London. Exhibited at the R.A. 1902–1914, from various London addresses. Wife of Frank S. Eastman (q.v.). Her sitters included Lady Gore, Mrs. Herbert Fisher, The Earl of Lisburne, Major General J. H. Bedford, Constance, daughter of the Bishop of Swansea and 'the late Mrs. H. T. Eastman'. She exhibited under her married name from 1906.

*Maitland, The Viscountess Gwendolen Lucy, later **Countess of Lauderdale.** (fl. 1890–1928)

Née Vaughan Williams, daughter of Judge R. Vaughan Williams of Flintshire, and wife of Frederick Colin, Viscount Maitland (b. 1868), later 14th Earl of Lauderdale. Exhibited at the R.A. and S.M. 1900–1906, from 14 Lower Sloane Street. Her sitters included The Hon. Mrs. White Ridley, H.R.H. Princess Alice of Albany, H.R.H. Princess Mary of Wales and the Hon. Ian Maitland. Exhibited a self-portrait in 1902.

Malbone, Edward Greene. 1777–1807

Born in Newport, Rhode Island, U.S.A., August 1777. One of the greatest American miniaturists. Was instructed by a scene painter and by Samuel King, a miniaturist. Copied engravings. Went to Providence at the age of 17 and had a successful practice as a miniaturist. Went to Boston, 1796, New York, 1797 and Philadelphia, 1798. Lived in the country during an epidemic of yellow fever. Visited several towns, was in Charleston in 1800. Met Fraser and Allston (q.v.) with whom he came to England in May 1801. Said to have studied at the R.A. Schools, but the records do not give his name. Malbone returned to America in December 1801. Worked in various towns; visited Jamaica for health reasons, but finding it did not suit him, he returned to America and died suddenly in Savannah, 7 May 1807. Painted oil and pastel portraits as well as miniatures. Signed Malbone and E.G.M. One miniature sold at Sotheby's, 16 June 1927, was signed in fine writing on the background, 'E. Malbone'. Examples of his work are at the Metropolitan Museum, New York and the Pennsylvania Academy of Fine Art, etc. His style is slightly reminiscent of that of Andrew Robertson (q.v.). Many of his works are rather pale in colour. A miniature said to be a self-portrait, signed 'E.G.M. 1797', but now identified as John L. Sullivan, is reproduced as the frontispiece by Wehle. 157 miniatures by him are listed in *Early American Portrait Painters in Miniature*, by Theodore Bolton, New York, 1921.

Malden, Lady Sarah (later **Countess of Essex**). *c.* 1761–1838

Born *c.* 1761; daughter of Henry Bazett of St. Helena. Married firstly Edward Stephenson and secondly, on 6 June 1786, Viscount Malden who was created 5th Earl of Essex in 1799. Painted miniatures, many of which were copies of pictures, and executed enamels. Was at Bath in 1788. Before 1799 she signed SM, afterwards S Ex or S Essex. Died in Hill Street, Berkeley Square, London, 16 January 1838, after a long separation from her husband. Some of her miniatures are good, others are amateurish. A miniature of the Duchesse de la Vallière, 1788 by the above artist was Lot 13 at Sotheby's, 29 January 1962. It came from the collection of the Earl of Essex. An enamel miniature of Lord Coventry, signed and dated '1813', and one of Algernon Percy, Earl of Northumberland, after Van Dyck, were sold at Sotheby's on 12 December 1966. A miniature of the Duchess of Queensberry, signed on the reverse 'Duchs. Queensbury/SE Pinx/1(8)08' is in the N.G., Dublin, which also contains a portrait by this artist after Titian.

*Mallam, Miss Beatrix. (fl. 1900–1904)

Of London. Exhibited at the Society of Miniaturists, 1900–1904.

Malmqvist, Alexander Magnus. 1796–1853

Born in Schonen, Sweden, 1796. Studied in Lund, 1815. Exhibited in Sweden from 1818; was awarded prizes in 1819 and 1821. Studied miniature painting in France (1822) and then in England.

Painted historical subjects and portraits as well as miniatures. Became insane and was sent back to Sweden in 1830. Retained the ability to paint well in spite of his mental condition. Died in hospital in Malmö, 1853. His self-portrait is at the National-museum, Stockholm.

*Malready, W. (fl. 1784)

A miniature signed 'W. Malready 1784' was noted by Long as having been exhibited in 1905.

*Maltby, Mrs. E. See Worsfold, Emily M.

Mandy, James Cleverley. b. *c.* 1792

Was born *c.* 1792 in London. Entered the R.A. Schools, 19 February 1812, aged 20. Exhibited at the R.A. and O.W.C.S., 1811–1833. Painted landscapes, portraits and miniatures.

Manini, 'Chevalier' Gaetano. *c.* 1730–*c.* 1780/90

Born in Milan, 1730? Said to have been a pupil of the Academy of Bologna under D. Creti. Came to England *c.* 1750. Exhibited at the Society of Artists and the Free Society of Artists, 1761–1772. Worked for some years in Ireland after which time he returned to London. Painted historical and allegorical subjects, portraits and miniatures. Worked in crayon, oil and enamel. His colouring was inclined to be gaudy. He died between 1780 and 1790. The V. & A. M. has an enamel of Francis of Lorraine signed on the reverse, 'G.M.F./1754'. Two other enamels by this artist are at the Ashmolean Museum, Oxford.

*Manley, C. M. (fl. 1831)

A miniature copy of an Italian 16th-century picture of the Virgin and Child, signed 'C.M. Manley/April 1831' was seen by Long who recorded that it was carefully painted but that the draughtsmanship was poor.

*Mann, Miss Dora. (fl. 1898–1907)

Exhibited at the R.A. and S.M., 1898–1907, from addresses in Weybridge, Surbiton Hill, Surrey, Walton-on-Thames and London. Her exhibit in 1898 was a self-portrait. A miniature of Miss Winstanley Brown as a child, signed on the front, 'D. Mann. 97' (1897), is in my collection. It was given to me by the sitter who still practises as a miniaturist in Edinburgh.

Manners, John. (fl. 1826)

An English artist, living in 1826 at 115 Fleet Street, London. His work was not of outstanding merit, and his draughtsmanship not very accurate. His colours lack freshness; the background is painted in oblique brush strokes. Schidlof refers to a miniature in a collection in Paris signed, 'Painted by J. Manners, 90 Strand opposite Southampton'.

Manners, W. H., junior. (fl. *c.* 1827–1830)

Of London. Exhibited at the R.A. 1830. A miniature *c.* 1827/8 signed 'W. H. Manners, jun. 286 High Holborn, 3 doors from Gt. Turnstile' was noted by the V. & A. M. The above artist may have been related to J. Manners (q.v.).

Mannin, Mrs. Mary A. (Miss M. Millington). *c.* 1800–1864

Born *c.* 1800 née Mary A. Millington; possibly a sister of J. H. Millington (q.v.). Probably a pupil of Sir W. C. Ross (q.v.), whose style she copied. Exhibited at the R.A. 1829–1832, under her maiden name from 92 Strand, London, and 1833–1857 as Mrs. Mannin. Married *c.* 1832. Died in Brighton, October 1864. Was a clever miniaturist, who was said to have excelled at painting children. Many of her works are on card. She modelled the face with some long red strokes on the nose and cheeks and painted the hair in a mass. A miniature of an unknown lady signed 'Mannin 59' (1859), is in the collection of R. Bayne-Powell, Esq.

*Manning, Miss Lilian. (fl. 1901–1903)

Of London. Exhibited at the R.A., 1901 and 1903, from 27 Perryn Road, East Acton.

Mansell, Major. (fl. 1802)

Exhibited at the R.A., 1802 (Hon. Exhibitor).

*Mansell, Miss Marianne. (fl. 1876–1896)

Of London. Exhibited at the R.A., etc. 1876–1896. Painted subject pictures in oil and miniatures. Her sitters included Miss J. Hyde-Parker and George White, Esq.

Mansion, André Léon Larue, called. 1785–c. 1834

Born at Nancy, 29 November 1785; son of Jacques Larue, *called* Mansion, a painter and miniaturist who is said to have taught Isabey (q.v.). Pupil of his father and of Isabey. Married Mlle. Marie Bryan, also a miniaturist. Worked in Paris; exhibited at the Paris Salon, 1808, 1819, 1822 and 1834. Visited London several times and exhibited at the R.A. in 1829 and 1831. Painted miniatures usually of large dimensions on ivory, card and on enamel, besides executing some pictures in oil (two of which are in the Museum at Nancy); they are a family scene, and a still-life of birds. Mansion also painted on porcelain and worked for a time at the Sèvres factory. Died in Paris c. 1834. He made drawings of officers of various British regiments which were engraved. Was the author of *Lettres sur la Miniature, 1822* which was followed by an English edition. Examples of his work may be seen at the Wallace Collection, London, and the Nottingham Art Museum, the Louvre, etc. He was influenced by Isabey but never attained such excellence.

Manzini, Camille. (fl. 1834–1842)

A French miniaturist; worked in Paris and lived at 44 Rue Poissoniere. Exhibited at the Paris Salon, 1834–1838. Moved to London; exhibited at the R.A., 1842, including a portrait of the Bishop of London (Charles James Blomfield, Bishop of London 1828–1856). A miniature by him, signed and dated 'C. Manzini, 1841' of Thomas Grenville, is at the N.P.G.

*Marchant, Nathaniel, R.A., F.S.A. 1738–1816

Born in Sussex, 1738; a pupil of E. Burch (q.v.). Best known as an engraver and medallist. Exhibited at the R.A., B.I., etc., 1781–1811. Visited Rome c. 1773. In 1766 was a Member of the Society of Artists. Held appointments as engraver to the Royal Mint, and gem engraver to the King. Associate of the R.A., 1791, and R.A., 1809. Was a member of the Academies at Stockholm and Copenhagen. Published a catalogue of 100 impressions from gems, engraved by himself. Mr. A. J. B. Kiddell saw three miniatures of historical scenes painted by Marchant. Died in 1816.

Marcuard, C. (fl. 1810–1819)

Of London. Exhibited at the R.A., 1810–1819.

Mareschal, P. (fl. 1850)

Of London. Exhibited at the R.A., 1850, a 'Holy Family' and a 'Portrait of Rembrandt'. Possibly Mlle. Pauline Meréchal of Paris. Pupil of Ducluzeau, who painted copies of old masters on ivory and porcelain. Exhibited at the Paris Salon, 1848–1863.

*Margetson, Mrs. Ellen M. (fl. 1908–1911)

Of London. Exhibited at the R.A. and S.M., 1908–1911, from 18 Albert Hall Mansions.

*Marke, Mr. (fl. 1795)

The *Bristol Journal*, 7 February 1795, noted 'Miniature Painting. Mr. Marke has returned from Southampton to his painting apartment, 14 Queen Street, Bristol.'

*Marks, Miss Anne. (fl. 1893–1907)

Of London. Exhibited at the R.A., 1893–1907. Painted pictures in oil and miniatures.

*Marquand, Miss Emily R. (fl. 1903–1904)

Of Willesden. Exhibited at the R.A., 1903 and 1904.

*Marsh, Miss Eva. (fl. 1905)

Exhibited at the R.A. 1905, from Astolat, Salisbury Road, Worthing, Sussex.

Marsh, Mary Ann. (fl. 1828)

Working in 1828 at 8 Congreve Street, Birmingham.

Marsh, R. (Robert?). (fl. 1791)

Of Hoxton. Exhibited at the Society of Artists, 1791. Possibly the Robert Marsh who entered the R.A. Schools 23 November 1781, aged '19. Feb 15. last'.

Marshal, Alexander. (fl. 1660–1690)

Worked as a painter and miniaturist in England. Painted portraits after Van Dyck, etc., and flowers on parchment. Long records seeing a miniature of the Countess of Dysart resembling one by Hoskins (q.v.) at Ham House, but said to be reversed, signed 'Alex(?) Marshal'. The M had a flourish at the top and the h and l were tall, leaning over to the right. C. F. Bell in a note says that his was not reversed but was a different version with completely different landscape background. It is one of a pair of what are believed to be memorial portraits.

Marshall, Thomas. 1788–1874

Of London. Exhibited at the R.A. 1828. A recently discovered pair of miniatures by him, in the collection of Mrs. M. Platt, have provided his christian name and dates. His self-portrait is signed and dated 1829; that of his wife Elizabeth Jane signed and dated 1826. His dates are inscribed on the reverse of his miniature. His address in 1828 was 53 South Audley Street, Grosvenor Square.

*Marshall, Miss Winifred. (fl. 1898–1914)

Of London. Exhibited at the R.A. 1898–1914, from Red Brick House, Campden Hill Road and from 9 Kensington High Street. Her exhibits included a picture of Sarah Bernhardt in *La Dame aux Camelias*. Another of her sitters was Lady Rowena Paterson.

Marston. See Aldous, W.

Said to have exhibited at the R.A., 1825. This is a mistake; the exhibit was of a Mr. Marston, catalogue No. 718, and the artist W. Aldous (q.v.).

Martin, Elias, A.R.A. 1739–1818

Was born in Stockholm, 8 March 1739. Entered the R.A. Schools, 3 November 1769. Son of a cabinet-maker whose trade he learnt. Studied in Paris, 1766. Came to England, 1769. Exhibited at the Society of Artists, the Free Society and R.A., 1768–1790; was elected A.R.A., 1770. Married Augusta Lee, 1773. Lived in Bath, 1778–1791. Long records that he was living at 37 Fish Hill, London, 11 April 1796. Became painter to the King of Sweden. Painted portraits in oil and water-colour, landscapes and is said to have executed a few miniatures. Died in Stockholm, 25 January 1818.

*Martin, Miss Merian. (fl. 1902–1908)

Of West Kensington, London. Exhibited at the R.A., 1902–1908.

*Martin, Richard. (fl. c. 1815)

Working c. 1815. A miniature by him signed 'Rd. Martin' on the reverse with the address New Road, Knightsbridge, London, was seen at Sotheby's. It was not of outstanding quality. It had a spongy blue background, with touches of yellow, and yellow shading under the sitter's chin.

*Martin, Miss Rosa P. (fl. 1899–1901)

Exhibited at the R.A. 1899, from St. Cuthbert's, Castle-Bar-Park, Ealing.

*Martindale, Miss Blanche E. (fl. 1904)

Of London. Exhibited at the R.A. 1904, from 61 Westmorland Road, Bayswater.

Mary, Princess of Hesse. 1723–1772

Born, 22 February 1723; 4th daughter of George II, by Queen Caroline of Anspach. Married in 1740, Frederick, Prince of Hesse-Cassel, son and heir of William VIII of Hesse-Cassel. Left her husband on his conversion to Roman Catholicism in 1754 and lived at Rumpenheim. On the death of her father-in-law she administered Hanau, as Regent. A circular miniature on ivory of Louisa, Queen of Denmark, in the character of 'Spring' was, according to an inscription on the back, painted by Princess Mary for her mother, Queen Caroline. It was not of any great merit, and was painted in the manner of B. Lens (q.v.). It was probably painted c. 1750. She died at Hanau, 14 January 1772.

Maskall, Miss. (fl. 1808–1813)

Of London. Undoubtedly related to Miss Mary Maskall, a portrait painter and Miss E. Maskall, a landscape painter, all of whom exhibited from Mitre Court, Milk Street in 1808 and 1812. Miss Maskall exhibited at the R.A., 1808–1813, and may possibly have exhibited in 1807. The R.A. catalogues for that year record Miss Mary Maskall in the index, and Miss Maskall in the catalogue. The exhibit was a profile miniature. Miss Maskall exhibited a profile miniature of her brother in 1808. A. Maskall published a lithographed portrait of Mrs. Sherwood by, and after, M. Maskall.

*Maskall, Miss Mary. See Maskall, Miss

Maskins. See Haskins, R.

*Mason, Miss Edith M. See Hinchley, Mrs. Edith M. (Mrs. T. E. W. or J. W.)

*Mason, Miss Ethel M. (fl. 1906–1910)

Of Buxton, Derbyshire. Exhibited at the Society of Miniaturists, 1906–1910.

*Mason, Mrs. Evelyn. (fl. 1884–1905)

Exhibited at the R.A. etc., 1884–1905, from London and Farnham, Surrey. Painted pictures in oil and miniatures.

*Mason, Miss Josephine. (fl. 1902)

Of London. Exhibited at the R.A. 1902, from 169 Ebury Street, London.

*Mason, Miss Mary M. (fl. 1904)

Of London. Exhibited at the R.A. 1904, from 12 Mayfield Avenue, Chiswick.

*Massey, Mrs. Gertrude. (fl. 1898–1911)

Of London. Exhibited at the R.A. and S.M., 1898–1911, from various London addresses including 75 Newman Street from which address her husband exhibited a water-colour at the R.A., in 1913. Executed miniatures and portraits in oil.

Her exhibits included miniatures of H.R.H. Princess Mary of Wales and T.R.H. Prince Edward and Prince Albert of Wales. H.H. Princess Toussonn was also one of her sitters. A miniature of a lady, *c.* 1907, oval on ivory signed 'Gertrude Massey' on the front, is in the collection of Miss E. Clifford-Smith.

*Mather, Miss Elizabeth N. (fl. 1904)
Exhibited at the R.A. 1904, from 27 Forest Drive, West Leytonstone, London.

*Mather, George Marshall. (fl. 1832–1833)
The above artist is hitherto unrecorded and is known only by three miniatures which were sold at Christie's on· 28 May 1968. One of an unknown gentleman seated, against a curtain background, holding an open book in his hand is signed on the front 'Mather 1832' and on the reverse 'Painted by/ George Marshal Mather/72 Princes St./Edin^r/July 1832'. The other two miniatures are of unknown ladies, one of which is signed on the reverse 'Painted by/George Marshall Mather/72 Princes St./Edin^r/ 1833'. As he worked in Edinburgh, it is possible that this artist was Scottish.

*Mathews, Miss Janet D. (fl. 1910)
Exhibited at the R.A. 1910, from Ellel Hall, Lancaster.

Matthew, Sir Tobie. 1577–1655
Born in Salisbury, 3 October 1577; son of Tobias Matthew, (1546–1628), Dean of Christ Church, Oxford, 1576, who later became Archbishop of York. Educated at Oxford. Entered Parliament, 1601. Travelled abroad. Became a Roman Catholic. Knew Norgate (q.v.) and Bacon. Published translations, said to have executed limnings, was a wit and a linguist. Died at Ghent, 13 October 1655.

*Matthews, Miss Edith E. (fl. 1901–1910)
Of Highbury Park and Moseley, Birmingham. Exhibited at the R.A., 1901 and 1910.

Matthews, Henry. d. 1830
Worked in London. Exhibited at the R.A., 1798–1808.Was in the service of the East India Company, 1801–1827. In the London offices of the company there are two water-colours by this artist. Some of his exhibits were groups. Died in January 1830.

Matthews, T. (fl. 1813)
Exhibited at the R.A. 1813, as Hon. Exhibitor.

Maucourt, Charles. 1718? or 1728–1768
There seems to be some confusion over the dates and place of birth of this artist. Long gives the country of his birth as Germany, Benezit states that he was born in Paris, 1728 and Schidlof gives his year of birth as 1718. He worked in Strelitz (1752), Schwerin, Paris and London (1761–1767). Exhibited at the Society of Artists, of which he was a member, 1761–1767. Died in London in January 1768, leaving a destitute child. Painted oil portraits, miniatures and executed engravings. Long recorded seeing a miniature *c.* 1740, signed 'C.M.' in gold, which may have been by him. Schidlof notes a miniature signed 'MANCOURT', the date being indecipherable. It was skilfully painted in gouache on ivory and was reminiscent of the work of A. Vestier (q.v.). The flesh parts were pink with blue shadows.

*Maul, Miss Berta. (fl. 1901–1903)
Exhibited at the R.A. 1901 and 1903, from 6 Oxford Place, London Road, Cheltenham and Glingarth, Donro Road, Cheltenham. Painted miniatures and subjects in water-colour.

Mauris, Jacques. (fl. 1774–1786)
A Swiss enamellist. Worked for a time in London. Exhibited at the R.A., 1774–1775. In 1786 he was in Rochefort. The Louvre contains his self-portrait on enamel, signed 'Jacques Mauris fecit par lui d'apres lui', and a portrait of his wife signed 'Mc Mauris, âgée de 22 ans fecit par J. Mauris 1774. Epoux'. His work was of a high quality.

Mauritz, C. (fl. 1781)
Of Kennington Common. Exhibited at the R.A., 1781.

*Maw, Miss Cecilia. (fl. 1903–1911)
Of London and Bushey, Hertfordshire. Exhibited at the R.A., 1903–1911.

May, A. (fl. 1813)
Of London. Exhibited at the R.A. 1813, from Leadenhall Street.

*May, Arthur Dampier. (fl. 1872–1907)
Of London. Exhibited at the R.A., N.W.C.S., S.M., etc., 1872–1907. Executed oil portraits, subject pictures and miniatures.

*May, Mrs. C. Kiltgard. (fl. 1907)
Of Billericay, Essex. Exhibited at the Society of Miniaturists, 1907.

*Mayer, Miss Florence K. (fl. 1907)
Of London. Exhibited at the R.A. 1907, from Belgrano, Strawberry Vale, Twickenham.

Mayking, Peter. (fl. 1828)
Working in 1828 at 36 St. Peter's Square, Leeds.

Mayor, Christophe Élysée. 1837–1914
Born in Geneva, 2 January 1837. Studied enamelling under C. Glardon and G. Lamunière. Worked in Paris, and with W. C. Bell (q.v.) in London. In 1873 became a Professor at the École des Beaux-Arts in Paris. Died in Paris, 12 April 1914.

*Mead, Miss M. Grace. (fl. 1906–1913)
Of London. Exhibited at the R.A. 1906–1913, from 2 Russell Road, Kensington.

*Meade, Miss Hope. (fl. 1904–1909)
Of Dulwich Common, London. Exhibited at the R.A. 1904–1909, from The Woodlands, Dulwich Common. One of her sitters was Mrs. L. T. Meade.

Meadows, J. (fl. 1812–1845)
Of London. Exhibited at the R.A., B.I., etc., 1812–1845.

*Meadows, Joseph Kenny. 1790–1874
Born in Cardiganshire, 1 November 1790; son of a naval officer. Exhibited at the R.A. and Suffolk Street, 1830–1838, and was possibly identical with the K. Meadows who exhibited at the R.A. in 1845 and 1853, both exhibits being in the Drawing and Miniature section. J. K. Meadows executed genre subjects and illustrations, as well as portraits, one of which, of Mrs. Buckstone, may have been a miniature. He received a pension from the Government from 1864. An example of his work is in the V. & A. M. He died in August 1874.

Meadows, Robert Mitchell. b. 1763? d. before 1812
Entered the R.A. Schools, 7 January 1784, aged '20. 26 last Novr'. Known as an engraver, and may possibly have painted miniatures. T. Heaphy (q.v.), J. Holmes (q.v.) and R. Woodman (q.v.) were his pupils.

Meadows, W. (fl. 1830–1832)
Of London. Exhibited at the R.A., 1830–1832.

His address was 19 North Street, Lambeth. His sitters included Mr. Drinkwater Meadows of the Theatre Royal, Covent Garden.

Meakin, Miss M. L. (fl. 1843–1862)
Of London and Newbury (1862). Exhibited at the R.A., 1843–1862. Painted miniatures before 1845 but later devoted herself to painting flowers and fruit.

Mee, Miss. See **Robertson, Mrs.**

Mee, Mrs. Joseph (Miss Anne Foldsone). *c.* 1770/5–1851
Née Anne Foldsone; daughter of an artist John Foldsone, a copyist of pictures, living in 1770 in Little Castle Street, Oxford Market, London, who died while young. Anne was educated at a French lady's school in London. Had artistic gifts as a musician, poetess and painter. Was a protégée and pupil of Romney. Said to have supported her mother and eight brothers and sisters at an early age. She obtained the patronage of George IV (when Prince of Wales) and was working at Windsor Castle in 1790 and 1791. By 1804 she was asking as much as 40 guineas for a miniature. Sometime before 1804 she married Joseph Mee, of Mount Anna, Armagh (died 1849) by whom she had six children before she was 33. One daughter, Anna Elizabeth, married Yuyr Burges, by whom she had a son, Henry Cust Burges, who was painted by his grandmother when about 20 years of age. Mrs. Mee painted all the Burges family. Anna Elizabeth lived to be 92. Another daughter, Mrs. Robertson (q.v.) also painted miniatures. Joseph Mee was possessed of a fairly large estate in Armagh and left a handsome property and houses, etc. Family tradition has it that he was proud of his wife's hair and that after a violent quarrel she cut it close to her head just to spite him! He was a barrister, who was said to have been jealous of his wife and would not let men sit to her. She exhibited at the R.A. and B.I., 1804–1837. Was in Brighton in 1834. She died 28 May 1851 when, according to her obituary in the *Gentleman's Magazine*, she was 76, making her date of birth 1775. Mrs. Mee was influenced by Cosway (q.v.) but her work is uneven and not always well drawn. Often the eyes are rather large, and in her early work the colour scheme is simple. The face is usually painted with a mixture of stippling and hatching. Some of her miniatures are large. Engravings were made after her works. The Wallace Collection has a miniature by her, and a number of her works are in the collection of H.M. the Queen. Two miniatures by her were exhibited in Edinburgh in 1965, one of Mrs. Andrew Stuart (of which there are two versions) one from the collection of Madame Stuart Stevenson, and the other from my collection, of Miss Mary Brisbane, sister of Sir Thomas Brisbane. This latter miniature is of outstanding quality. A self-portrait of the artist and three other family miniatures thought to represent her husband and two sons are at the V. & A. M.

Meens. See **Meyer, Jeremiah**
Lady Charlotte Finch, in her diary, 18 January 1764, refers to 'Prince Frederick' having sat for his picture to 'Mr Meens'. Long thought this referred to Jeremiah Meyer (q.v.).

*Mehain, J. 18th century
Possibly an Irish artist. A miniature of George William Molyneux, in the style of S. Cotes (q.v.) was signed, 'pt by J Mehain'.

*Meihé, Miss Winifrede A. (fl. 1900)
Of London. Exhibited at the R.A. 1900, from Limatburg, Ambleside Drive, Streatham.

Mejanel, P. (fl. 1834)

Of London. Exhibited at the R.A. 1834, from 15 Percy Street, Bedford Square.

*Melhuish, Miss Gertrude. (fl. 1905–1913)

Of Cricklewood, London. Exhibited at the R.A. 1905–1913, from 43 Blenheim Gardens, Cricklewood.

Melle, Francesco. (fl. 1773–1775)

Worked in Portugal and London. Exhibited at the Free Society of Artists and the Society of Artists, 1773–1775. Painted allegorical and historical subjects, miniatures and frescoes. Was Painter in Fresco to the King of Portugal.

Melville, Alexander. (fl. 1846–1878)

Worked in London. Exhibited at the R.A., B.I. and S.B.A., 1846–1878. His wife Eliza Anne Smallbone was also an artist. The Melville A. Jamieson collection contained a miniature on ivory of a man signed on the reverse 'Painted by Alex: Melville. 1858'. He painted portraits and allegorical subjects in oil, besides this one known example in miniature.

*Melville, William. (fl. 1815–1851?)

Painted figure subjects and portraits as well as miniatures, some of which were in oil. He went to India in 1815 and was in business in Calcutta, 1826–1834. The firm of Fergusson & Co., of which he was a partner, failed in 1832, and left him stranded. He painted portraits in various parts of India, the last trace of him being at Simla, 1843. Long saw a highly finished miniature of Sir Harry Smith (founder of Ladysmith), and his wife, both full of character. One was signed, 'W. Melville/Pinxet 1842.' on the front, the other was signed in white on the reverse, 'W. Melville/Pinxet/1842'. He was possibly identical with the artist who exhibited at the B.I., in 1851.

*Mendelssohn, Mrs. Florence. (fl. 1910)

Of London. Exhibited at the Society of Miniaturists, 1910.

*Mengs, Ismael. 1688–1764

Born in Copenhagen, 1688. Was a pupil of B. Coiffre, and, according to Benezit studied under an English painter named Cooper. Worked in Dresden, Leipzig and Italy. Painted portraits in oil, miniatures on parchment, and on enamel. A miniature of an artist holding a miniature, painted on vellum, oval $3\frac{3}{8}$ in. high, in a turned wood frame, was attributed to this artist when it was sold at Christie's on 15 October 1963. Examples of his work are in the Louvre. His self-portrait and a miniature of an unknown lady are reproduced by Schidlof, *The Miniature in Europe*, Vol. 4.

*Merbitz, Mlle. Marguerite P. de. See **De Merbitz, Mlle. Marguerite, P.**

*Mercer, Andrew. 1775–1842

Born in Selkirk, Scotland, 1775. Was destined for the ministry, and in 1790 studied at Edinburgh University, but gave up thoughts of ordination and worked in Edinburgh as a miniaturist and author; wrote poetry for magazines. Settled in Dunfermline; drew patterns for damask manufacturers there and wrote books on the town. Was financially unsuccessful, and died in poverty in Dunfermline, 11 June 1842.

Mercier, Mrs. Dorothy. (fl. 1761)

Widow of Philip Mercier (1689–1760), portrait painter. Exhibited four miniatures and two flower pieces at the Society of Artists, 1761, in which year she was appointed by the Society 'to look after the miniatures, etc.'. On 25 July of the same year she was granted £10.10s. from the Society's charity.

Merendez, Luis. (fl. 1766–1800)

Little is known about this artist who is said by E. Lemberger to have flourished, 1766–1800, and to have worked in Madrid and London.

*Merrick, Miss Marianne A. (fl. 1902–1911)

Of London. Exhibited at the R.A. 1902–1911, from 5 Carlisle Street, Edgware Road.

*Merrylees, Miss A. M. See **Merrylees, Miss Annie R.**

*Merrylees, Miss Annie R. (Mrs. A. M. Arnold). (fl. 1894–1914)

Of London. Exhibited at the R.A, 1894–1914. Up to 1898 she exhibited under her maiden name but evidently married *c.* 1899 as in 1900 she is entered as A. R. Merrylees (Mrs.). Her husband was Reginald Edward Arnold, R.B.A., a silversmith of Hatton Garden, Bedford Gardens and later of Hampstead, where he died aged 84 on 10 February 1938 at 'The Cottage', and was survived by his wife. In 1902 the above artist is recorded in the R.A. catalogues as Mrs. A. Merrylees Arnold and was probably identical with the Annie R. Arnold (q.v.) who exhibited at the R.A., 1901 and 1914. Her sitters included the Lady Helen Vincent, A. Cameron Corbett, Esq., Mrs. Cameron Corbett, the Hon. Thomas Erskine, younger son of the Earl of Mar and Kellie, the Hon. Francis Erskine, Lady Evelyn Cavendish, etc.

Merves, Augustus. *c.* 1755–1818

Practised miniature painting in England in the early part of the 19th century. Died suddenly in Shoreditch in 1818. His son, then aged 33, claimed to be the Dauphin of France.

*Messer, Miss Mabel B. (fl. 1910)

Of London. Exhibited at the R.A. 1910, from The Limes, Rye Hill Park, Peckham Rye. The exhibit was a miniature of her father.

*Metcalf, Eliab. 1785–1834

Born 5 February 1785 at Franklin (Mass.). Painted miniatures and silhouettes. Worked in Halifax, Nova Scotia, 1810. Long noted this artist as perhaps having worked in England, but I have found no evidence of this. He travelled for his health and worked in New York, New Orleans, Cuba, Halifax, Nova Scotia, etc. Died in New York, 15 January 1834.

*Methven, Miss Florence C. (fl. 1902–1906)

Of London. Exhibited at the R.A. and S.M., 1902–1906.

*Meyer, Mrs. Cornelia. (fl. 1894)

Of Parkside, Hampton Wick. Exhibited a miniature of Miss Olga Meyer at the R.A., 1894. I have seen an attractive miniature of a lady by the above artist after Andrew Robertson (q.v.), on the reverse of which is a pencilled inscription 'F or T Ross'. The miniature is in the collection of J. Robertson, a descendant of the artist, and was left by Robertson's daughter Emily to Charles Robertson, son of his first wife. The sitter may be A. Robertson's mother, who was a Ross. The miniature was loosely painted.

*Meyer, E. (fl. 1819)

A circular miniature of a girl by E. Meyer, signed and dated '1819' was Lot no. 19 at Sotheby's, 5 June 1967. Nothing appears to have been recorded about this artist, who may have been related to one of the numerous Continental artists of this name recorded by Benezit.

Meyer, Henry Hoppner. 1782/3–1847

Born in England, 1782/3; a nephew of John Hoppner. Pupil of F. Bartolozzi. Exhibited at the R.A., B.I., S.B.A., 1821–1833; was one of the founders of the S.B.A. in 1828, and its President in 1828. Went to America, 1830. Painted portraits in oil, watercolour and miniature; executed engravings. Painted President Jackson in 1833. Exhibited at the Artists' Fund Society in Philadelphia (1835–37 and 1840) and at the Pennsylvania Academy (1847). Died in London, 28 May 1847.

Meyer, Jeremiah, R.A. 1735–1789

Born in Tübigen, Germany, 18 January 1735; came of an artistic family, his father being portrait painter to the Duke of Würtemberg. Was brought to England by his father when fourteen years of age (*c.* 1749). Studied at the St. Martin's Lane Academy, and at a cost of £200, plus £200 for materials. Became a pupil of Zincke (q.v.), who was then practically in retirement, and remained with him from 1757–1758. Exhibited at the Society of Artists, 1760–1767. Was awarded in 1761 a gold medal by the Society of Arts for a profile of George III, from memory. Was naturalised in 1762. Was appointed miniature painter to the Queen, and painter in enamel to the King in 1764. Became a founder member of the R.A., and exhibited miniatures, enamels and water-colours there, 1769–1783. Meyer also painted portraits in oil. Married in 1763, Barbara Marsden (born 1743) who shared his love of art and was an accomplished artist, winning premiums at the Society of Arts, 1755–1758. Was a lover of music. Their daughter, Mary, whom Reynolds painted as 'Hebe' (exhibited, 1772), ran away from home whilst young, and was taken back to her mother by 'Mr. Engleheart', presumably George Engleheart (q.v.). Another daughter, Frances Isabella (1784–1815) married Colonel John Haverfield in 1815, and may have been the Miss Meyer mentioned by J. Farington in his diary, 22 March 1809. They had two sons, George Charles (1767–1793), who held a post in the East India Company and blew his brains out in Calcutta, 12 February 1793; and William (b. *c.* 1778), whose miniature by his father was loaned to the exhibition at the South Kensington Museum in 1865. According to a Latin inscription on the reverse, it was painted when the boy was ten years of age, and was signed 'J. Meyer, R.A. 1788'. The owner was Mr. William Meyer, possibly a grandson of the artist. Meyer was a friend of William Hayley, the poet (who mentioned him in his poems), and Romney, who painted the Meyer family. According to an advertisement in *Adam's Weekly Courant*, Meyer was visiting Chester and staying in Northgate Street, 2 June 1772. In 1787, Meyer accompanied Romney to Windsor. He lived for many years in Covent Garden, and occupied successively two houses, one of which had been previously occupied by Zincke and J. Deacon (q.v.). Meyer retired to Kew, where he died, 20 January 1789, having contracted a fever whilst assisting at a contested election. He was buried at Kew. His pupils included Richard Collins (q.v.) and Diana Dietz (q.v.). Meyer was undoubtedly one of the best eighteenth-century miniaturists, and one who has been better appreciated as time has gone on. His signature which is rare, is a cursive monogram JM. His early work was slightly reminiscent of the manner of Lens (q.v.) and G. Spencer (q.v.), but he soon developed a characteristic style of his own; this is apparent from *c.* 1770. The draughtsmanship of the mouth and nose is slightly angular, the eyes being rather sunk under the eyelids, and often placed close together, the lips tending to protrude slightly and the hair being drawn in very distinct lines. The cravats and edging of the ladies' costume are usually touched up with opaque white. His method of hatching on the face became more and more pronounced. As in the case of some other miniaturists, his carmines have sometimes faded. Meyer imparted an elegance to his miniatures which the late Carl Winter likened to the porcelain of Meissen and Nymphenburg. H.M. the Queen possesses some outstanding examples of his work; others are in the V. & A. M., the B. M., the Ashmolean Museum, Oxford, etc. This latter museum has a number of his miniatures, some unfinished, which were presented by a descendant of the artist. Five miniatures by him were exhibited in Edinburgh in 1965, including those of Queen Charlotte, from the collection of H.M. the Queen, and Mrs. Damer, from the collection of E. G. Paine of New York. Both these portraits are of outstanding merit. Three fine examples of Meyer's work were sold at Sotheby's, 12 December 1966. They represented Mrs. Thomas Hayley, Thomas Alphonso Hayley as a child, and Mrs. William Hayley. Mr. William Meyer loaned several miniatures by Meyer to the exhibition at the South Kensington Museum, 1865, including some enamels, one of which represented General Lawrence, and another, William Hayley; this latter portrait was signed 'J.M.', and engraved on the reverse of the frame, 'Meyer pinxt 1774'.

*Meyerheim, Robert. (fl. 1875–1914)

Of Horsham, Sussex. Exhibited at the R.A., N.W.C.S., etc., 1875–1914. Painted landscapes in water-colour, oil paintings and in 1910 exhibited a miniature of 'Rhododendrons'.

Meytens, Martin van der. 1695–1770

Born in Stockholm, 24 July 1695; son and pupil of Martin van Meytens, the elder, a Dutch painter, descended from Daniel Mytens. Went to Holland in 1712, and in 1714 came to London to study the work of Van Dyck and others. Studied enamelling under C. Boit (q.v.) in Paris, 1717. Painted portraits of Louis XV, the Duc d'Orleans and Peter the Great, who invited him to enter his service. Worked in Dresden, Vienna (1721) and Venice (1723). Spent some time in Rome, Naples, Florence, Turin, Genoa and, after returning to Venice, he settled in Vienna in 1726 where he became Court painter to the Emperor. Went to Stockholm in 1730 to see his parents, but returned to Vienna after sixteen months. Became favourite painter of the Empress Marie Therese, who appointed him director of the Academy in 1759. He painted miniatures in water-colour and enamel and oil portraits, and his works are scarce. He died in Vienna, 23 March 1770. A miniature of Carl V of Sweden, signed on the reverse 'MB Meytens/Pinx' is in the N.G., Dublin. The signature is cursive and the work reminiscent of that of Boit.

*Michael, Frederick Howard. (fl. 1892–1914)

Of London. Exhibited at the R.A., etc. 1892–1914, from various London addresses. Painted miniatures, subjects in oil and landscapes in water-colour.

*Middleton, Miss Etta. (fl. 1909–1911)

Of Hoby, Leicestershire, St. Albans and Dunstable. Exhibited at the R.A. and S.M., 1909–1911.

*Miers, J. (fl. 1760–1810)

Of 111 Strand, London. Profile painter and jeweller, best known for his silhouettes, but may have painted a few miniatures. Worked in Manchester, Newcastle, etc.

Milbourne (John?). 18th century

A miniaturist; a member of a club of artistic friends, among whom were Edridge (q.v.), Pack (q.v.), William Alexander, Michael Bryan, etc. Possibly the John Milbourn who accompanied John Russell, R.A. (q.v.) to Guildford, prior to 1768. Premiums were awarded by the Society of Arts to John Milbourn, 1763, John Milbourn, 1764 and John Milbourn, junior, 1765. John Milbourn exhibited crayon portraits at the R.A., 1772–1774. *The Gentleman's Magazine*, 29 October 1795, records that Frederick, 2nd son of John Milbourn, who was drawing master at New Road, Marylebone, died in his 16th year of lockjaw caused by an accident with a pistol. An English artist, called John Milburn, and his wife were living in New York City in 1850, and may have been related to the above miniaturist.

*Mileham, Miss Mary Livock (Mrs. C. Crickmer). (fl. 1899–1906)

Of Sydenham, Letchworth and London. Exhibited at the R.A. and S.M., 1899–1906.

Miles, Master. (fl. 1766)

Exhibited a miniature of a horse at the Free Society of Artists in 1766, when a schoolboy at the Rev. Mr. Barclay's, Tottenham High Cross.

*Miles, Arthur. (fl. 1851–1880)

Of London. Exhibited at the R.A., B.I., etc., 1851–1880. Executed figure subjects, portraits in chalk and other portraits, some of which may have been miniatures. Was probably related to L. C. Miles who exhibited from the same address, 31 Francis Street, Bedford Square, in 1860. A portrait in chalk of T. F. Robson, by the above artist, is in the N.P.G.

*Miles, Miss C. Isadore. (fl. 1904)

Of Lee, London. Exhibited at the R.A. 1904, from Enmore, Burnt Ash Hill, Lee.

Miles, Edward. 1752–1828

Born at Yarmouth, Norfolk, 14 October 1752. Became an errand boy to a surgeon who encouraged him in drawing. Went to London in 1771. Entered the R.A. Schools, 20 January 1772, 'age 19 Oct 14 last'. Copied pictures by Reynolds in miniature; Beechey painted his portrait. Exhibited at the R.A., 1775–1797. Worked in Norwich (1779 and 1782), Russia (1797–c. 1806), Philadelphia (1807–1828). In 1792 he was appointed miniature painter to the Duchess of York, and later to Queen Charlotte. Whilst in St. Petersburg he became Court painter to the Czar. He settled in Philadelphia where he died, 7 March 1828. Was friendly with Sir Thomas Lawrence (q.v.). James Reid Lambdin, an American miniaturist, was his pupil. His work is often not recognised and is sometimes attributed to Cosway (q.v.) and others. His miniatures are inclined to be pale, and frequently have a yellowish colouring. The eyes, mouth and nose are neatly painted and the lips clearly defined. Many of his works are in America. He painted portraits and taught drawing. His works are not signed which makes attribution difficult. During the latter part of his life he hardly painted any portraits but confined himself to teaching drawing at the Academy in Philadelphia, of which he had been a founder member. Examples of his work are at Windsor Castle, the V. & A. M., and in the collection of Major R. M. O. de la Hey. Two miniatures by Miles were exhibited in Edinburgh in 1965.

Miles, G. H. (fl. 1824–1840)

Of London. Exhibited at the R.A., etc., 1824–1829. Two water-colours by him, dated 1833 and 1840, are at the B.M.

Milford, H. (fl. 1808–1811)

Exhibited at the R.A., 1808–1811 (Hon. Exhibitor). In 1811 the miniature exhibited was of Mr. H. Milford, and may have been a self-portrait. In this year the index gives the name as H. Milford, and the catalogue entry states that it was by J. Milford; this may have been a printer's error.

*Millar, Miss. (fl. 1791)

Painted portraits in miniature. 'Removed from 7–16 North East Entry of St. James's Square, Edinburgh. Continues to paint portraits in miniature. Jan 10. 1791.' This information was noted by Long.

Millar, G. (fl. 1830)

Of Bath. Miniature painter and drawing master. Living at 4 Walks, Bath in 1830.

*Millar, James. c. 1735–1805

Born about 1735. A miniature of James Skey by the above artist is in the V. & A. M. The painting is rather coarse, the face being executed in distinct cross strokes, but the expression well drawn. Died in 1805.

*Millard, Miss Elsie M. (Mrs. O'Keefe). (fl. 1898–1908)

Of London and 12 Charleville Road, Rathmines, Dublin. Exhibited at the R.A., 1898–1908. Her exhibits in 1905 were of J. G. O'Keefe, possibly her husband, and Z. Mennell, Esq. She exhibited under her maiden name, 1898–1899, and under her married name from 1905. She exhibited miniatures of Miss Evelyn Millard, possibly her sister, in theatrical roles.

*Miller, Harrison. (fl. 1910)

Of London. Exhibited at the R.A. 1910, from 8 Park Road, Clarence Gate.

Miller, J. d. 1764

Worked in London. Supposedly famous for his work. A miniature bust portrait on ivory of an unknown man is at the V. & A. M. It is signed 'Miller 1729' in gold; the face is painted in transparent colour, with a soft stippling, shaded with red; the background is brown and the hair painted with circular touches of gouache. Died in Southampton Street, Bloomsbury, 8 January 1764.

*Miller, Miss Jessie J. A. I. (fl. 1882–1888)

Of London. Exhibited at the R.A., 1882–1888.

Millet, F. (fl. 1838). See also **Millet, J.**

Exhibited at the R.A., 1838. Possibly identical with J. Millett (q.v.). Schidlof records a French miniaturist Frédéric Millet, d. 1859, who may have exhibited, although so far as is known he did not come to England.

Millett, H. (fl. 1809–1817)

Of Bath (1809), London (1810–1817). Had an address at the Abbey Churchyard, Bath; was in York, 1812. Exhibited at the R.A., 1809–1817. A miniature painted in York, 1812, of Eliza Sarah Beaumont was seen by Long. Schidlof mentions a miniature of a young lady formerly in the Jeffrey Whitehead Collection, and attributed to Millett which he considers to be the work of T. Hargreaves (q.v.). A miniature sold in Vienna, September 1921, of Mrs. Bridgeworth, was signed on the reverse, 'Mrs Bridgeworth by H. Millett, 157 New Bond Street'.

Millett, J. (fl. 1837). See also **Millet, F.**

Exhibited at the R.A., 1837. Possibly identical with F. Millet (q.v.).

Millington, Henry. *c.* 1735–1764

Born *c.* 1735 according to Schidlof. Of London, Bath (1757) and Bristol (1756). Exhibited at the Free Society of Artists, 1761–1764. Charged 3½ guineas per miniature at Bath, where he had an address c/o Thomas Roger's, watchmaker in the Churchyard, Bath, 21 March 1757. Was at the Hotwells, Bristol, 22 November 1756. He painted miniatures and portraits in water-colour. His death is recorded in *The Gazette* on 17 September 1764 as of Leicester Square. The B.M. has an engraved portrait after Millington.

Millington, James Heath. 1799–1872

Born in Cork, 1799. Spent his early years in England, returned to Ireland in 1821 and had rooms at 22 Patrick Street, Cork, where he set up as a miniaturist; moved to Dublin in the same year, where he exhibited an oil portrait. Entered the R.A. Schools, 1 April 1826. Won several prizes there including a silver medal. Exhibited at the R.A., B.I. and S.B.A., 1831–1870. Was for a short time curator of the school of painting at the R.A. Millington lent several of his works to the exhibition at South Kensington in 1865. He died of a heart disease at 3 Chepstow Place, Bayswater, 11 August 1872. His signatures varied, e.g., J. H. Millington 1836, painted in white vertically on the background, and J.H.M. followed by a date (scratched). May have been influenced by W. Etty, a fellow pupil at the R.A. Schools. Some of his work is in the manner of A. E. Chalon (q.v.). Examples of his work are at the V. & A. M. An attractive miniature of the Lady Anne Hudson (d. 1826), daughter of the 1st Marquess Townshend, was sold at Christie's, 18 February 1969. It was signed and dated, 'J.H. Millington, 1818'.

Millington, Miss Mary. See **Mannin, Mrs.**

*Mills, Mrs. Ernestine. (fl. 1900)

Of London. Exhibited at the R.A. 1900, from 21 St. Mary Abbott's Terrace.

*Milner, Miss Jessie. (fl. 1897–1914)

Of London. Exhibited at the R.A. 1897–1914, from Lawn House, Atkins Road, Clapham Park. Painted miniatures and landscapes in water-colour. Her sitters included Rita, daughter of G. W. Milner, Esq. and Mrs. Alfred von Berg.

Miltenberg, J. Jacob. (fl. 1776–1790)

Possibly descended from a family of Swiss craftsmen of the same name. Worked in London. Exhibited at the R.A., 1776 and 1786. The exhibits were an enamel of 'The Judgement of Paris' and a miniature painting of 'Cupid and a Nymph'. An enamel miniature of a theologian was formerly in the David Weill Collection, Paris. It is signed on the reverse, 'J.J. Miltenberg pinxit 1790'. The sitter is wearing a black robe over a white shirt; under his right arm he holds a bible; the background is green/grey. Schidlof erroneously records the artist's initials as 'J.F.'. The miniature is reproduced in *Miniatures and Enamels, Les Beaux-Arts,* 1957, No. 324.

*Milton, Miss. (fl. 1783)

Worked in Bristol. *The Bristol Journal,* 12 April 1783, states that she painted miniatures for 1 to 3 guineas.

Milton, J. (fl. 1826–1836)

Of London. Exhibited at the R.A., 1826 and 1836.

Milward, John. (fl. *c.* 1696–1700)

Pupil of C. Boit (q.v.), *c.* 1696–1700. Some letters by him are in the possession of the Duke of Portland at Welbeck Abbey. These are referred to by

R. W. Goulding, *Welbeck Abbey Miniatures, Walpole Society,* Vol. IV, p. 18.

Mintorn, Miss. (fl. 1828–1829)

Lived at Woodfield Cottage, Bristol, and Redland, nr. Bristol. Was awarded a large silver medal by the Society of Arts in 1828, for an original miniature portrait, and a further award in 1829.

*Mischef, Mrs. Pansy. (fl. 1910)

Of London. Exhibited at the R.A. 1910, from 51 Queen's Gate.

Mitchell, Miss. (fl. 1810–1812)

Of London. Daughter of J. T. Mitchell (q.v.), from whose address, 52 Upper John Street, Fitzroy Square, she exhibited at the R.A., 1810–1811; in 1812 her address was Pomona Cottage, Queen's Elm. One of her exhibits was a portrait of her mother.

*Mitchell, Miss E. Grace (Mrs. P. Henry). (fl. 1902–1904)

Of London and Knapp Hill, Surrey. Exhibited at the R.A. 1902 and 1904, from Pembroke Square, Kensington and from Beaufort Cottage, Knapp Hill. Her sitter in 1904 was Lord Macnaghten.

Mitchell, J. T. (fl. 1798–1830)

Worked in London and America. Exhibited at the R.A., B.I., S.B.A., etc., 1798–1830. Assisted in forming an artists' volunteer corps in 1803. Said to have gone to America and to have worked for a time in Baltimore. Painted miniatures in water-colour and enamel, some of the latter were after Van Dyck. His signatures varied, e.g. ITM (scratched), ITM (cursive), I. T. Mitchell, followed by a date (separate letters) and Mitchell, followed by a date. His miniatures are executed in a fine *pointilliste* touch with soft outlines. Sometimes he painted lines under the eyes in the manner of Smart (q.v.). Occasionally his work is reminiscent of J. Barry (q.v.). He is said to have worked with J. Trewinnard at 40 Strand, London and to have charged 3 to 5 guineas for his miniatures. A miniature with a printed label on the reverse was seen by Mr. A. J. B. Kiddell. A good miniature of a man signed along the edge, 'I.T. Mitchell, 1803' is in the collection of Major R. M. O. de la Hey. Examples of his work may be seen at the V. & A. M.

*Mitchell, Mrs. Mary. (fl. 1889–1894)

Of Bickley, Kent and London. Exhibited at the R.A., 1889–1894. Her sitters included Mrs. T. Willes Chitty and Mrs. H. B. Mitchell, probably a relation.

*Mitchell, Mary Brice (Mrs. Fitzgerald?). (fl. 1823)

According to Long's notes this artist painted a miniature of Napoleon in 1823, after Isabey (q.v.).

*Mitchell, W. (fl. *c.* 1830–1837)

Worked in England, *c.* 1830. Painted miniatures and portraits in oil. Schidlof records a miniature in a private collection of a young officer painted on ivory, signed on the reverse, 'W. Mitchell/Miniature &/Portrait Painter/May 1837'. The signature was in yellow.

Moeller. See **Möller, A.**

*Mogford, Thomas. (fl. 1827–1850)

According to information at the V. & A. M. this artist worked in England, 1827–1850. He may have been identical with the Thomas Mogford who

exhibited landscapes at the R.A. and B.I., 1838–1866.

*Moir, John. (fl. *c.* 1800–1830)

Of Edinburgh, *c.* 1800. Painted miniatures on ivory and portraits in oil, from Wardrop Close, Lawnmarket, Edinburgh. A miniature signed and dated on the reverse, '9 Gardener's Cresc, Edinburgh, 1828', and another, '1830' were seen by Long.

Moira, Edward (Eduardo) Lobo. 1817–1887

Born at Villa Nova de Foscôa in October 1817. Came to London and became an actuary at the Portuguese Embassy. Took up miniature painting and acquired a very distinguished clientele, which included many royal persons. Among these were Louis Napoleon Bonaparte, when President of the French Republic, and H.R.H. the Prince of Wales. In 1877 he painted the Princess Beatrice for H.M. the Queen (Victoria). He exhibited at the R.A. and N.W.C.S., 1848–1887. Most of his life after his arrival in England seems to have been spent in London; but from 1878–1885 he was in Chislehurst, Kent. Returned to London, 1886. Died 1887, probably at 9 Colville Terrace, Bayswater, London on 2 January. Three miniatures by Moira, including that of H.R.H. Princess Alice, were lent to the exhibition at South Kensington Museum, 1865, when his address was given as Lower Seymour Street, Portman Square. A number of his miniatures are in the collection of H.M. the Queen, including those of Prince Albert and Queen Victoria. A miniature of the Prince Imperial, son of the Empress Eugenie and Napoleon III is in the collection of E. Bayne Powell, Esq. The sitter is wearing the uniform of a Woolwich cadet. It is signed in orange paint on the front, 'E. Moira ft. 1872'.

*Moira, Gerald Edward (Lobo). (fl. 1891–1897)

Born in London; son of Edward Moira (q.v.). Pupil of J. W. Waterhouse. Exhibited at the R.A., etc., 1891–1897. Painted miniatures, large portraits in oil and frescoes.

Mole, John Henry, V.P.R.I. 1814–1886

Born in Alnwick, 1814; was self-taught in art. Employed by a solicitor in Newcastle-on-Tyne, whom he left *c.* 1835 to practise miniature painting; also painted landscapes. Worked in Newcastle until 1847. then in London. Exhibited at the R.A., N.W.C.S., B.I., S.B.A., etc. 1845–1886. Was an associate of the N.W.C.S. 1847 (later R.I.), a member, 1848, and Vice-President, 1884. After 1847 painted chiefly landscapes. Died at 7 Guildford Place, London, 13 December 1886, and was buried at Brompton. His miniatures were well painted with a pleasant colouring, and strong bluish half tints; he used pronounced stippling. A miniature of a young lady in a low cut dress, painted on ivory, is signed on the reverse, 'J.H. Mole Pinxt May 1855'. This was seen by Schidlof in a private collection. A water-colour sketch of an unknown lady, executed on paper, 11½ in. × 9 in., is in the collection of D. R. Perriam, of Carlisle. On the reverse of the painting is an inscription, 'A member of the Earl of Ravensworth's family/ by J. H. Mole'. As the lady is wearing a coronet she may have been the Countess of Ravensworth. The painting is slightly in the manner of Sir W. J. Newton (q.v.).

*Molineux, Miss Muriel N. (fl. 1906–1914)

Exhibited at the R.A. 1906–1914, from Hessle, East Yorkshire.

*Möller, Moeller, Millar or Millear, Andreas. 1684–1758 or 1762

Born in Copenhagen, 30 November 1684. Worked in England, 1728–1731; and re-visited in 1734. Painted portraits in oil and miniatures. Worked in Germany, and was painter to the Court of Hessen-Cassel from 1717. Was in Vienna, 1724 and 1737; became painter to the Danish Court in 1740. Died in Berlin in 1758 or 1762. His name has been spelt in various ways. His work was good and the heads of his sitters expressive; his way of painting the clothes was rather stiff. Examples of his work are at the Landesmuseum, Cassel, and The Frederiksborg, Copenhagen.

Möller, Johannes Heinrich Ludwig. 1814–1885

Born at Lübeck, Germany, 1814. Worked in Copenhagen, Paris, Stockholm (1848), Lübeck and St. Petersburg. Exhibited at the Paris Salon, 1843–1847. Exhibited at the R.A., 1851–1873. In 1851 he is described as 'Moller, the Chevalier J; Member of the Danish Royal Academy of Fine Arts'. Came to London, c. 1865, in which year he lent two miniatures by himself to the exhibition at the South Kensington Museum; they were of H.M. Christian VIII of Denmark, dated '1846' and H.M. the Emperor Alexander II of Russia, dated 1860. His address at that time was 8 Shaftesbury Villas, Hornsea Rise. Whilst in London he painted for Messrs. Dickinson of New Bond Street. Died in London, 31 October 1885. Miniatures by him of George, Duke of Cambridge and Princess Augusta of Cambridge, both after Stuart, are at Windsor Castle.

Monies or **Monier, A. H.** (fl. 1797–1809)

Exhibited at the R.A. 1797–1809, from various London addresses, including 29 Henrietta Street and 32 Oakley Street, Lambeth. May have been identical with Alexander Monies who was awarded a premium at the Society of Arts in 1776. His sitters included Miss Lambton and Master G. Russell, son of Lord W. Russell.

Monk, E. V. H. (fl. 1829)

Of London. Exhibited 'Sporting nymphs' at the R.A., 1829.

Monk, M. C. (fl. 1780)

Exhibited at the R.A., 1780. The artist's name is omitted in the index. The exhibit was a miniature of a gentleman.

*Montagu, Miss Ella. (fl. 1905)

Of London. Exhibited at the R.A. 1905, from Alexandra House, Kensington.

Montague. (fl. 1803–1806). See also **Montague, J.**

Of London. Exhibited at the R.A., 1806. Perhaps identical with J. Montague (q.v.). His address in 1803 was Borough Road, Southwark; was possibly related to H. Montague (q.v.), who exhibited a miniature of T. Nichols, Esq., in the same year, from '2 Saint George, Southwark'.

*Montague, H. (fl. 1803)

Of London. Exhibited at the R.A. 1803, from '2 Saint George', Southwark. Possibly related to Montague (no initial given) (q.v.), who exhibited from Southwark in the same year.

Montague, J. (fl. 1797). See also **Montague**

Of London. Exhibited at the R.A., 1797. Possibly identical with the Montague (q.v.) who exhibited in 1806 from Southwark. His exhibits included a miniature of 'One of the sitting magistrates at Bow Street, taken from memory'.

Montgomery, Robert, M.A. 1807–1855

Born, 1807; wrote religious poems. B.A., Lincoln College, Oxford, 1833; M.A., 1838. Curate of Whittington, 1835; Incumbent of St. Jude's, Glasgow, 1836; Minister of Percy Chapel, St. Pancras, London, 1843. Died in 1855. A miniature self-portrait, c. 1827, painted on card, is at the Holburne Museum, Bath; the background is bluish, and the face shaded in brown, in the manner of a work by W. J. Thomson (q.v.) in the V. & A. M. R. Smith (q.v.) exhibited a miniature portrait of Montgomery at the R.A., 1854.

*Moody, Miss Fanny (Mrs. Gilbert King). b. 1861

Born 10 May 1861. Worked in London. Was a pupil of J. T. Nettleship. Executed miniatures of dogs, and subjects in oil. Exhibited at the R.A., etc., 1885–1914.

Moore. (fl. 1775)

A newspaper cutting of November 1775 in the V. & A. M. Library states that a young man, a limner of the name of Moore, who had been employed in executing some pieces at Lord Fingal's, at Wolverhampton, jumped into one of the fish-ponds to bathe, and stuck in the mud and was drowned. It is not certain that in this instance the term 'limner' means miniature painter.

Moore, J. (fl. 1824–1837)

Of Sheffield (1827) and London. Exhibited at the R.A., 1827–1837. A John Moore entered the R.A. Schools, 18 November 1823, aged 20. Schidlof mentions a miniature exhibited at South Carolina, 1936, of Mrs. David Lamb, junior, née Mary Henderson (1794–1833), signed on the reverse, 'J. Moore Pinxit 20 Mason Str. Liverpool, 1824'.

Moore, J. W. (fl. 1834)

Exhibited at the R.A. 1834, two portraits which may have been miniatures. His address was 8 Broad Street, Bloomsbury, Holborn. In 1832 J. W. Moore is recorded in the index of the R.A. catalogues as exhibiting from 4 Brecnock Place, Camden Town. The catalogue entries however give nos. 783 and 794 to J. M. Moore (q.v.), and no. 828 to J. W. Moore.

Moore, James. (fl. c. 1789)

Son of a sculptor named Mohr, came to England from Württemberg, or Hanover, to escape military service. Long records seeing a miniature by this artist of a man, c. 1789. It was executed with rather fine strokes and was well painted, but the draughtsmanship was weak.

*Moore, Mrs. Jennie. (fl. 1910–1914)

Of Birmingham and London. Exhibited at the R.A., 1910 and 1914. Executed a portrait miniature on enamel and a study in water-colour.

Moore, J. Marchmont. (fl. 1832?–1835)

Of London. Exhibited at the R.A., N.W.C.S., etc., 1832?–1835. In 1832, three exhibits are given in the R.A. index to J. W. Moore (q.v.), but the catalogue entries record No. 828 as by J. W. Moore, and Nos. 783 and 794 by J. M. Moore.

*Moore, Miss Leslie. (fl. 1903)

Exhibited at the R.A. 1903, from The Cottage, Falconer Road, Bushey, Herts.

*Moore, William. 1790–1851

Born in Birmingham, 1790. Settled in York from 1827. Painted portraits in oil, pastels and water-colour. Died in 1851. His sons Henry, Albert and Edwin, all inherited their father's talent, and became artists.

Mor, More, or **Moro, Sir Antonio.** 1512/19–1575/7

Born in Utrecht, 1512/19. Pupil of Jan Scoreel; a member of the Antwerp guild in 1547. Worked for Charles V. Visited Portugal, Rome, 1550–1551, and Madrid, 1552. Came to England, 1553; painted portraits of Queen Mary and other persons. Thought to have returned to Utrecht, 1555–1557. Accompanied Philip II to Spain in 1559; returned to Utrecht, 1560. Went to Brussels, 1567, then to Antwerp, 1568, where he died in 1575, or 1577. This outstanding Dutch portrait painter is thought to have painted some oil miniatures. A good circular oil miniature of 'Bloody Mary' is in the collection of the Duke of Buccleuch, and thought to be by Mor. One of William Paulet, Marquess of Winchester, in the collection of R. Bayne Powell, Esq., is also attributed to him.

Moreau, John. (fl. 1809–1838)

Possibly identical with John Marraud, who entered the Dublin Society's Schools in 1799, and who in that and the following year, won medals for drawing. In 1800 was given £10. 10s. by the Society 'to buy colours and canvas and to encourage his genius'. John Moreau was living in Dorset Street, Dublin in 1809 when he exhibited landscapes. Was in London, 1810 and 1811; exhibited at the R.A. in those years. Returned to Dublin, 1812; exhibited there, 1812–1814, and again in 1816. In 1838, he exhibited miniatures at the R.H.A. from 26 Lower Ormond Quay. Painted landscapes, miniatures and small chalk portraits. The B.M. has a litho-graphed portrait of J. Stiles, after J. Moreau.

*Morgan, Miss Edith F. (fl. 1905–1912)

Of London and Paris. Exhibited at the R.A., 1905–1912. Probably the artist mentioned by Benezit as having been born in Cambridge, and having exhibited at the Salon, 1908.

*Morgan, Edwin E. (fl. 1908–1914)

Of London. Exhibited at the R.A. 1908–1914, from Temple Studio, 2 Breams Buildings, Chancery Lane. His sitters included Miss Maud Morgan and Charles Marks, Esq.

*Morgan, Miss Ethel M. (fl. 1900–1914)

Of London. Exhibited at the R.A., 1900–1914. Painted miniatures and executed drawings.

Morgan, James H. (fl. c. 1824)

Worked c. 1824 at 2 Brunswick Street, Liverpool.

*Morgan, Miss Olga. (fl. 1897–1907)

Of London. Exhibited at the R.A. 1897–1907, from various London addresses.

*Morgan, Miss Olive F. (fl. 1906)

Of London. Exhibited at the R.A. 1906, from 25 Lower Belgrave Street, Eaton Square.

Morinière, F. de la. (fl. 1850)

Worked in London. Exhibited at the R.A. 1850, from 12 Piccadilly. His name is given as de la Morinière, F. in the index and F. de la Morinière in the catalogue.

Morland, George. 1763–1804

Born in London, 26 June 1763; son of Henry Robert Morland (q.v.). Famous painter of genre subjects, animals, etc. Painted miniatures before 1786. Exhibited at the Free Society, Society of Artists and R.A., 1773–1804. Mentioned as a miniaturist in *The Manchester Mercury*, 27 March 1773 and in *The Manchester Journal*, 27 March 1773, as 'Miniature painter from Chester and now at Mr. Jonathan Smith's on East Side of St. Ann's Sq.'. Two miniatures existed on the lids of snuff-boxes representing a landscape painted on ivory and an interior of a stable on copper. In 1939 Schidlof saw a box which contained a miniature of a land-scape, signed 'G. Morland'. He died in London, 29 October 1804.

*Morland, Henry Robert. *c.* 1731–1797

Father of George Morland (q.v.). Painted portraits, genre subjects and executed engravings. Said by Thieme and Becker to have painted miniatures. Exhibited at the Society of Artists, Free Society of Artists and R.A., 1760–1792. Painted a portrait of George III. Died in London, 30 November 1797.

Morland, Thomas. d. 1747 or 1748

A miniature signed 'Tho Morland, pinxit 1729' is mentioned by J. J. Foster, and Long saw a miniature on card of Henry Claud Monewick of Dover, dated '1842'. A sale of his prints, drawings and books is recorded in *The Daily Advertiser*, 26 January 1748.

Morrant, F. (fl. *c.* 1799)

A miniature of an unknown man wearing the 'Windsor Uniform', signed 'F. Morrant / pinxt', is in a private collection. The artist used a lot of gum with his paints and the portrait was well painted.

Morris, Miss Charlotte B. (fl. 1828–1867)

Of London. Probably the daughter of Mrs. T. Best Morris (q.v.). Exhibited at the R.A. 1855–1867. A miniature signed 'Charlotte Morris 1828', and thought to be by this artist, was shown to the V. & A. M., in 1954. It had rather pink colouring.

*Morris, Miss Edith E. (fl. 1903–1911)

Of South Croydon and Plymouth. Exhibited at the R.A., 1903–1911.

Morris, James. (fl. 1813–1816)

Of London. Exhibited at the R.A., 1813–1816. His address in 1813 was 27 Great Pulteney Street and in 1814–1816, 31 Mount Street, Grosvenor Square. Long recorded seeing a miniature inscribed on the reverse, 'Mary Bond Brough', by Morris, from '26 Mary-le-Bone, (Brough?) Jewellers'.

*Morris, Miss M. G. (fl. 1907–1910)

Of London. Exhibited at the R.A., 1907–1910. Her sitters included Barbara, daughter of Major General F. E. A. Chamier, and Mrs. Sydney Wells.

Morris, Mrs. T. Best (Miss Charlotte Sharpe). d. 1849

Née Charlotte Sharpe, one of four daughters of William Sharpe, an engraver of Birmingham, who brought his family to London, *c.* 1816. Exhibited at the R.A., 1817–1841. Married Captain Best Morris in 1821, but continued painting in order to support her family. Probably the mother of Miss C. B. Morris (q.v.) and sister of Mrs. Seyffarth (q.v.) and of Elizabeth Sharpe (q.v.). Exhibited under her married name from 1821–1841. Died in 1849.

*Morse, Samuel Finley Breese. 1791–1872

Born in Charlestown (Mass.), 27 April 1791; son of Jedidiah Morse; decided to devote himself to painting and in 1811 came to London, where he studied under Benjamin West (q.v.). Painted portraits, miniatures and historical subjects. Exhibited at the R.A. and B.I., 1813–1815. Returned to America in 1815 and worked in New England, Charleston and South Carolina. Settled in New York City in 1823; was one of the founders of the National Academy of Design and its first President. From 1829–1833 he travelled in Europe. Returned to New York and gave most of his time to the perfecting of the electric telegraph. Became embittered by disputes and intrigues over the history and administration of the telegraph. Died in New York City, 2 April 1872.

*Morten, Miss Jessie. (fl. 1903–1905)

Of London. Exhibited at the R.A., 1903 and 1905.

Mortimer, John Hamilton, A.R.A., F.S.A. 1741–1779

Born in Eastbourne, 1741. Exhibited at the R.A., the Free Society and Society of Artists, 1762–1779. Well known painter of portraits and historical subjects; not known as a miniaturist, but Long records seeing a small miniature of a lady, *c.* 1769, signed with a monogram which slightly resembled that of Mortimer's, which had an extra loop at the top on the right.

*Mortimore, Miss Constance. (fl. 1899) See **Kirk, Mrs. Alexander**

Of London. Exhibited at the R.A. 1899, from 78 Eccleston Square. Her sitter was Miss Betty Helen Paine.

Mortimore, Henry. (fl. 1793)

Working in Bradninch, Devon in 1793.

*Morton, Mrs. Ellen. (fl. 1894)

Exhibited at the R.A. 1894, from 8 Tower Street, York.

Morton, Miss Maria. (fl. 1837–1851)

Of London. Exhibited at the R.A., 1839 and 1851. A miniature of a girl, signed on the reverse, 'Maria Morton / Nov^{br} 30th 1837', was sold at Sotheby's in 1967. It had a rather purple shading.

Moseley, Mrs. Henry (Miss Maria A. Chalon). *c.* 1800–1867

Née Maria A. Chalon; born in London *c.* 1800. Daughter of Henry Barnard Chalon, the animal painter, whose wife was the sister of James Ward, R.A. Was taught art by her father and friends and had an aptitude for music. Was premiated by the Society of Arts in 1813 and 1818. Worked in London. Exhibited at the R.A. 1819–1840, under her maiden name, and 1841–1866 under her married name. She also exhibited at the B.I., in 1863. Her marriage to Henry Moseley, a portrait painter, took place *c.* 1841. Her sitters included H. B. Chalon, James Ward and Tenniel. Became 'portrait paintress' to the Duke of York *c.* 1823. Painted miniatures in oil and water-colour. Died in 1867. Her work was of a very high quality, and had some affinity to that of Sir W. C. Ross (q.v.). A miniature of William Mellish of Hodstock Priory, Nottinghamshire, is signed on the reverse 'Maria Chalon pinxit, 1832'. It is a fine miniature; the features are painted with brush strokes rather than stippling, the shading round the head and mouth is grey and a scraper has been used in the hair. A fair amount of gum is apparent on the jacket and background. An unsigned miniature of Lady Mary Osborne (died 1862) in my collection has a mauvish background, the features are well painted and executed with soft colouring. The miniature was exhibited in Edinburgh in 1965.

Moser, George Michael, R.A. 1704/6–1783

Born in Schaffhausen, 17 January 1706 (1704 according to Long). Son of a metal worker. Studied in Geneva; came to England when he was young. Was employed to chase brass-work for furniture; was also a medallist and enameller; his chief work being the decoration of boxes, watch-cases and seals. Taught George III drawing before his accession; worked for George II; engraved George III's first Great Seal. Was manager of the St. Martin's Lane Academy (so called from *c.* 1736); was an original member of the Society of Artists where he exhibited, 1760–1767. Was first keeper and also an original member of the R.A., where he exhibited, 1769–1770. Was friendly with Goldsmith and Dr. Johnson. Moser is said to have executed some miniatures on ivory. His daughter, Mary Moser, R.A. (q.v.) was also an artist and a founder member of the R.A. His nephew, Joseph Moser (q.v.) was one of his pupils. Died at Somerset House,

24 January 1783 and was buried at St. Paul's, Covent Garden. A miniature of an unknown lady, signed 'G.M. Moser / F' is no. 272 of the David Weill Collection in the Louvre. *The History of the Royal Academy*, by Sidney Hutchison, 1968, contains numerous references to G. M. Moser.

Moser, Joseph. 1748–1819

Born in Greek Street, Soho, London, June 1748. Son of a Swiss artist, Hans Jacob Moser, who was a brother of G. M. Moser (q.v.), from whom Joseph had lessons in art. Painted portraits and other subjects on enamel. Exhibited at the R.A., 1774–1787. Painted heads on enamel for jewellery decoration. After his marriage he retired to the country; wrote in the *European Magazine*, etc. Became a magistrate. Died at Romney Terrace, Westminster, 22 May 1819. An enamel miniature of an unknown man, signed 'İM / 1767', is in the collection of R. Bayne Powell, Esq. The flesh colouring is rather pink.

Moser, Miss Mary, R.A. (Mrs. Hugh Lloyd, R.A.). 1744–1819

Born in London, 27 October 1744; daughter of George Michael Moser, R.A. (q.v.). Was awarded premiums by the Society of Arts for her drawings in 1758 and 1759. Was a founder member of the R.A., in 1768. Exhibited at the Society of Artists and R.A., 1760–1792, under her maiden name; married Captain Hugh Lloyd *c.* 1793; exhibited at the R.A., 1797–1802, under her married name. Painted flowers in gouache and oil and may have executed some on enamel; in 1792 she exhibited a landscape. Was employed by Queen Charlotte to paint a room at Frogmore for which she is said to have been paid over £900. Died in London, 2 May 1819. An example of her work is at the V. & A. M. and at the B.M.

Mosnier, Jean Laurent. 1743/4–1808

Born in Paris, 1743/4. Was a pupil at the Académie de St. Luc, of which he became a master in 1766, and in 1776 he painted Marie Antoinette from life. Became a celebrated artist and was in great demand. In 1786 he became an Agréé, and in 1788 a member of the Académie Royale. Exhibited at the Paris Salon, 1787 and 1789 and at the R.A., 1791–1796, including a portrait of Rodney. Was one of the first French artists to emigrate to England on the outbreak of the Revolution, and appears to have lived in London. Mosnier went to Russia *c.* 1796 where he became official painter to Alexander I. He became a member of the St. Petersburg Academy in 1802 and was a professor there; painted several portraits of the Empress. He painted portraits in oil as well as miniature, which he specialised in from 1778–1788. He died suddenly at St. Petersburg, 10 April 1808. His work was good and his technique original; he painted with broad bold strokes, using gouache and painting the hair in uniform masses. The draperies are well painted; he used a lot of opaque white. Some of his works were engraved. Engravings after Mosnier are in the B.M., as well as a portrait of him by O. Humphry (q.v.). Examples of his work are in the Louvre.

Mossman, David. 1825–1901/6

Born in Islington in 1825. Worked as a miniaturist and portrait painter in Newcastle (1853–1857) and London. Exhibited at the R.A., N.W.C.S., etc., 1853–1888. Some of his works were exhibited at South Kensington in 1865 when his address was given as 74 Westbourne Park Villas. Two miniatures were lent by the artist and represented Miss J. Mossman, painted in 1857, and Charles Lawson, Esq., late Lord Provost of Edinburgh painted in 1864. The other exhibits represented Philip John Canning Howard and the three daughters of Mr.

P. H. Howard, painted in 1858; both of these miniatures were lent by Mr. P. H. Howard. David Mossman died in 1901 or 1906. A portrait by him, of Richard Grainger, the architect, is at the Laing Art Gallery, Newcastle.

*Mothersole, Miss Jessie. (fl. 1901–1914)

Of London. Exhibited at the R.A., 1901–1914. Executed miniatures and painted subjects in water-colour.

*Mott, Miss Alice M. (fl. 1877–1908)

Exhibited at the R.A. etc., 1877–1908, from Walton-on-Thames, Surrey and London. Amongst the miniatures she exhibited was one of 'La Comtesse Leon Muiszech'. A miniature of an unknown gentleman by the above artist is illustrated on Pl. XXXV of *Miniatures*, by Dudley Heath.

*Muckle, Mrs. Mary J. (fl. 1909–1914)

Exhibited at the R.A. 1909–1914, from Redmond, Kings Langley, Herts., and from 7 Netherton Grove, Fulham Road, London.

*Muir, Miss Ada M. (fl. 1902–1912)

Of London. Exhibited at the R.A. 1902–1912, from 56 Kyverdale Road, Stamford Hill.

*Mullen, or **Mulleu, M.** (fl. 1803)

I have seen a miniature on ivory signed on the reverse, 'M Mullen (or Mulleu) 30th April 1803'. It was of average ability.

Müller, William James. 1812–1845

Born in Bristol, 1812; died there on 8 September 1845. This famous painter of landscapes and figures in oil and water-colour is not known as a miniaturist but for a miniature self-portrait at the N.P.G.

Mulready, William, R.A. 1786–1863

Born at Ennis, Ireland, 1 April 1786; was brought to England as a child. Entered the R.A. Schools, 23 October 1800, aged 14. He exhibited at the R.A., B.I., etc., 1804–1862. Noted as a painter of genre subjects. According to Strickland, in his early days he 'tried his hand at everything from a miniature to a panorama'. The N.P.G. has an oil miniature of John Varley, his father-in-law, by Mulready. He died in his house in Linden Grove, Bayswater on 7 July 1863 and was buried in Kensal Green cemetery, where a monument to his memory was erected by his friends.

Mulrenin, Bernard, R.H.A. 1803–1868

An Irish artist, born of humble origin in Co. Sligo, 1803. Showed aptitude for drawing as a child and received encouragement from some of the local personages. Practised as a miniaturist. Went to Dublin in 1825. Exhibited at the R.H.A., 1826–1866; became an Associate in 1837, and a Member, 1860. Exhibited at the R.A., 1851. Was miniature painter to the Lord Lieutenant of Ireland, the Earl of Clarendon, 1848. Painted portraits in oil, small portraits on marble (these were painted upon a faint photographic base), and miniatures on large square pieces of ivory. Strickland considered his work lacked power and vitality, and to have been executed with over much stippling. Some of his drawings were in Indian ink, and he also executed a few lithographs, and copied some pictures. He died on 22 March 1868, at 23 Great Brunswick St., Dublin, where he had resided since 1837. Examples of his work are at the N.P.G. and N.G., Dublin.

Mulvany, George Francis, R.H.A. 1809–1869

Born in Dublin, 1809; the second son of Thomas James Mulvany, R.H.A. (q.v.). His father was Keeper of the R.H.A. from its foundation until his death, so that as a boy, Mulvany had a unique opportunity to study art, and when young showed aptitude for painting. Studied in Dublin and Italy. Exhibited in Dublin, 1827–1869. Became an Associate of the Dublin Academy, 1830, and a full member in 1835. Succeeded his father in 1845 as Keeper of the R.H.A. Was untiring in his efforts to found the National Gallery of Ireland, which was opened in 1864, and of which he had become a Director in 1862. Exhibited at the R.A., 1836 and 1839. Was a prolific painter and produced a large number of portraits and subject pictures, and a small number of miniatures. He painted in oil and crayon. Died after a short illness at his house in Herbert Place, Dublin, 6 February 1869, and was buried on 10 February at Mount Jerome. The members of the R.H.A. attended his funeral as a body to pay their respect. Strickland lists a number of his works, *Dictionary of Irish Artists*, pp. 152–155, including a miniature by him of Christopher Moore, the sculptor, exhibited at the R.H.A. in 1845.

Mulvany, Thomas James, R.H.A. 1779–1845

Born in Dublin, 1779. Studied under F. R. West in the Dublin Society Schools, where he showed promise as a figure draughtsman. Painted miniatures at the outset of his career, exhibited eight in Dublin in 1802; subsequently devoted himself to figure composition and landscapes. Exhibited in Dublin, 1810–1844. Was an original member of the R.H.A., and was appointed its first Keeper, retaining this office until his death, when he was succeeded by his son, G. F. Mulvany (q.v.). Some of his works were lithographed. He had three sons, John Skipton Mulvany, R.H.A., architect, G. F. Mulvany and William Thomas, an engineer. Taught art, was a brilliant conversationalist, and was much in demand socially. Wrote some articles on Irish artists, and edited the life of James Gandon. Died of paralysis after three days' illness at Dirker Lodge, Cross Avenue, Booterstown, 27 February 1845, and was buried at Mount Jerome.

*Munier-Romilly, Mme. Amélie. 1788–1875. See also **Romilly, Mme. d'Ausse**

Born in Geneva, 1788. Was a pupil of Firmin Massot. Painted portraits in oil, and water-colour, subject pictures as well as miniatures. Was probably identical with Mme. d'Ausse Romilly (q.v.). The N.P.G. has a pencil drawing by the above artist of Lady Jane Franklin.

*Munn, James. (fl. 1764–1774)

Exhibited at the Society of Artists and the Free Society, 1764–1774, from Mr. Munn, St. Martin's Lane; and Mr. James Munn, Brompton; and Stanhope St., Clare Market. His exhibits included landscapes, portraits, flowers, etc.; some of these may have been miniatures. A head on vellum was executed in black lead.

Munns, Henry Turner. 1832–1898

Born in Northampton, 1832. Worked in a shoe factory. Was a pupil of a travelling miniature painter named Locke (q.v.). Became a notable portrait painter in Birmingham, and may have painted some miniatures. Died 1898.

*Murdoch, Miss Alice M. (fl. 1906)

Of London. Exhibited at the R.A. 1906, from 187 Goldhurst Terrace. One of her exhibits was a portrait of her mother.

*Mure, Elizabeth. (fl. *c.* 1830). See also **Mure, Mary**

A miniature by the above artist of Catherine Mure, *c.* 1830 was seen by Mr. A. J. B. Kiddell. She may have been identical with or related to Mary Mure (q.v.).

Mure, Mary. 18th or 19th century. See also **Mure, Elizabeth**

Miniatures by the above artist are in the collection of the Duke of Northumberland, and one of Elizabeth, wife of the 1st Marquess of Exeter is in the Burghley House Collection. The pair of miniatures at Alnwick are rectangular, and represent Peter Burrell, Esq., of Beckenham, Kent and his wife, Mrs. Burrell, mother of Isabella, Countess of Beverley. There is an oval copy of the latter portrait by an unknown artist also in the Northumberland collection, which is erroneously called the original in the catalogue compiled by the late J. J. Foster. The miniature of Mr. Burrell is signed in white horizontally, 'M. Mure' in cursive writing. It is slightly in the manner of B. Lens (q.v.), with distinct dotting all over the pale grey background; the face is shaded with yellow / orange flesh colours, deep orange delineation under the eyelids, nostrils and mouth.

Murphy Denis Brownell. d. 1842

Born in Dublin. Was a pupil at the Dublin Society Schools, where he was awarded a prize in 1763. Practised as a miniaturist in Dublin at 36 Golden Lane. Exhibited at the Dublin Society of Artists in 1765 and 1768. Murphy evidently left Ireland for a time and in April 1792, advertised his return from London having 'improved himself by studying'. He obtained little recognition in Dublin and in 1798 took his family to England. He worked in Lancaster, Whitehaven, Newcastle and also in Scotland, but finally settled in London in 1803. He appears to have found success as a miniaturist and had several sitters of distinction. Exhibited at the R.A. and B.I., 1800–1827. Painted portraits and miniatures, some of which were copies of large paintings which he executed on enamel. In 1810 Murphy was appointed Painter in Ordinary to Princess Charlotte, and was commanded to copy Lely's 'Windsor Beauties'. His daughter, born in Dublin, 1794, became Mrs. Anne Jameson, authoress. Murphy died in London, March 1842. Besides copying the works of other artists, he certainly executed some original portraits, many in miniature. His sitters included John Crome, landscape painter, now in the N.P.G., and Wordsworth. This latter miniature is in the N.G., Dublin, and is inscribed in a later hand on the reverse, 'W. Wordsworth / by / Murphy / '. It was formerly in the collection of the Countess of Mayo. He also painted Stephen Kemble, presumably the son of Roger Kemble, and brother of John Kemble.

Murphy, J. (John?). (fl. 1817)

The above artist was working in 1817 in Lower Brook St., Grosvenor Sq., London. He may have been identical with John Murphy, a mezzotint engraver who was born in Ireland *c.* 1748, and died in London after 1820.

*Murray, A. 18th century

Long saw four miniatures by this artist, mid-eighteenth century, and noted that they may have been copies of other portraits.

*Murray, Christina

A miniature of Mary Queen of Scots, after Zucchero, is in the collection of the Countess of Seafield, and said to be by this artist.

Murray, Mrs. Henry John (Miss Elizabeth Heaphy).
c. 1815–1882

Née Elizabeth Heaphy, born in London *c.* 1815; daughter of Thomas Heaphy (q.v.) and sister of Mary Ann Heaphy (q.v.). Exhibited at the R.A., N.W.C.S., etc., 1834–1882. Accompanied her father to Italy in 1831. Married in *c.* 1845, Henry John Murray, British Consul in Gibraltar. Exhibited from Tangier in 1847; travelled in the Mediterranean, Morocco and America. Was in Philadelphia, 1856–1861 and Boston in 1868. Exhibited at the Pennsylvanian Academy. Was a member of the New Water-Colour Society in 1861. Exhibited under her maiden name, 1834–1843, and under her married name, 1846 until her death in San Remo on 8 December 1882.

Murray, R. (Robert?). (fl. 1763–1770)

Of London. Presumably identical with the artist called Murray (no initial given), who exhibited at the Society of Artists and the Free Society of Artists, 1763–1770, and who was in Fetter Lane in 1763. In 1765 he exhibited a self-portrait in oil. He may have been identical with Robert Murray, who was a pupil of Benjamin West (q.v.) in Dublin and was awarded a prize in 1748. *The Dublin Courant*, 5–8 November 1748, stated that he was 'brother of Miss Martha Murray, who at the age of 11, was remarkable for her excellence in engraving'.

Murton, T. (or J.) H. (Thomas?). (fl. 1802)

A miniature of Lady Charlotte Finch, after an earlier portrait, is signed on the front in pencil, 'T [or J] H Murton' and inscribed on the reverse 'T [or J] H Murton, London, 1802' and the name of the sitter. It must be after another portrait as Lady C. Finch died in 1796. A miniature signed, 'Thos. H. Murton' and dated 'Aug. 12th 1804', was sold at Sotheby's, 18 February 1963, and was probably by the above artist.

Musgrave, Mrs. W. (Miss Mary Ann Heaphy). (fl. 1821–1847)

Née Mary Ann Heaphy; daughter of Thomas Heaphy (q.v.) and sister of Elizabeth Heaphy (q.v.). Exhibited at the R.A., etc., 1821–1847. Worked in London until *c.* 1837 and in Edinburgh, 1841–1847. Married W. Musgrave, the portrait painter in 1832/ 1833, after which latter date she exhibited under her married name. She was a good miniaturist who worked in the manner of Sir W. J. Newton (q.v.). Her address in 1847 was 32 Royal Circus, Edinburgh. Schidlof mentions a miniature by her signed on the reverse, 'Painted by Mrs. Musgrave in 1838'. An attractive miniature of an unknown lady, inscribed on the reverse (in a later hand), 'drawn by Mrs. Musgrave / 22 Newman St.', was sold at Christie's on 17 December 1968.

*Muspratt, Miss Aimée. (fl. 1902–1906)

Of Norfolk, Hampshire and Paris. Exhibited at the R.A. 1902–1906.

Muss, Charles. 1779–1824

Born in Newcastle-on-Tyne, 1779; son of Boniface Musso, an Italian drawing master, who taught John Martin, the painter. Was employed at Collins' glass-works in London, where Martin also worked, and who for a time shared his house. Exhibited at the R.A., 1800–1823. Said to have joined an artists' volunteer corps in 1803. Became bankrupt *c.* 1809. He and Martin were then employed by another glass and china business. Muss worked for George III and painted a large enamel of the 'Holy Family' after Parmigiano, which he sold to George IV for 1,500 guineas, it measured 20½ in. × 15¼ in. Was enamel painter to William IV. Cleaned the famous

portrait of Richard II in Westminster Abbey. Made a stained-glass window of the 'Descent from the Cross' after Rubens, which was placed in St. Bride's, Fleet Street. Etched and published illustrations to Gay's fables. Was a member of the Artists Fund. Died, 14 June 1824, leaving his widow and children in reduced circumstances; they were assisted by Martin. His pupils included Nixon, Hoadley, Buckler and Jones. Examples of his work may be seen at the V. & A. M. and N.P.G. Much of his work was good. A miniature of an unknown lady, probably painted after Smart (q.v.), and signed 'Paint by C. Muss 1818' was formerly in the David Weill Collection and was exhibited at Garrard's, 5–17 June 1961. A miniature by Muss of Charles James Fox, set in a box, was sold at Christie's, 27 February 1968. Examples of his work are in the collection of the Duke of Northumberland.

Mussard, or Mussaro, Andreas. (fl. 1724–1765)

Mussard came from Geneva and painted miniatures on ivory and on enamel. A miniature of a man by him, signed and dated, '1751' is at the Holburne Museum, Bath, where he was working, 24 October 1765. *The Daily Advertiser*, 9 September 1751, had the following notice: 'Musard Andreas. Limner in enamel & miniature, famous for likenesses & attitude, also for History Pieces, is arrived in London, & lodges at Mr Tricketts, Stationers, in Black Fryars, Broadway. He was a disciple of the famous Rosalba in Venice. Price 10 guineas for enamel, 5 guineas in miniature or water-colours, and 2 guineas Dray-colours and crayons.' Long refers to a miniature which he thought was British, signed on the reverse, '3 guineas / Andreas Mussaro pinxit / 1755'. This must have been the work of Mussard. The V. & A. M. has a miniature signed and dated, 'Andreas / Mussard / Pinxit. 1724'.

Mussard, Jean Antoine. b. 1707

Born in Geneva, 1707. Probably the son of Jean V. Mussard, also of Geneva. Exhibited at the Society of Artists, 1763–1768, from London addresses. Painted miniatures, chiefly on enamel. Was a talented artist who used pure pleasant colours, and succeeded in producing forceful portraits which were well drawn; he used brown-red deep shadows, and blue-grey half tints for his shading. Examples of his work are at the Louvre. He signed J. A. Mussard pinxit and Johannes-Antonius Mussard Genevensis pinxit en 9bre 1723, etc. A miniature of a girl with fruit, signed on the reverse, 'Jean Mussard / fecit 1727', is in the N.G., Dublin.

Myddleton or Middleton, J. (fl. 1803)

Exhibited at the R.A., 1803. Was possibly the John Middleton who won a premium at the Society of Arts in 1794.

*Myers, David. 17th century. See also **M., D.**

An inscription on an old box gives this name, and Long records a miniature inscribed, 'Painted by David Myers'; the card had a prepared surface. This artist may well be the one who signed D.M. (q.v.), fl. *c.* 1663–1676.

*Myers, Miss Hannah. (fl. 1893–1913)

Of London. Exhibited at the R.A. 1893–1913, from various London addresses. Executed miniatures, subjects and portraits in oil and drawings.

Myles. (fl. *c.* 1770)

A miniature of the Rev. Charles Tyrrell, *c.* 1770, inscribed on the reverse, 'By Myles of Bath', was at The Rookery, Rougham, Suffolk, in 1905.

N

N., A. (fl. 1809–1816). See also **Nelson, A.**

An artist with the initials 'A.N.', exhibited a landscape at the R.A., in 1809, and a miniature in 1813. A miniature on ivory of Lord Adam Gordon, said to have been signed, 'A.N.ᵗd. 1816', was loaned by the Duke of Richmond to the exhibition at the South Kensington Museum, 1865. The above artist may possibly have been identical with A. Nelson (q.v.).

N., H. (fl. 1759–1769)

Painted miniatures on ivory and signed HN, sometimes followed by a date. The initials tend to sprawl, and are cursive. The artist used a certain amount of opaque white on the draperies, and stippling on the background. Some of the works are in the manner of S. Cotes (q.v.), and P. Carwardine (q.v.). Two miniatures, signed 'H.N.', were lent by Sir Charles Rouse Boughton to the exhibition at the South Kensington Museum, 1865, both dated 1759. The same exhibition contained a miniature of a child, signed and dated, 'H.N. 1759', and one of William Ffinch, Esq., signed and dated, 'H.N. 1769'. A miniature of a young boy, signed 'H.N.' and dated '1760', wearing a blue coat and Van Dyck collar, was sold at Sotheby's, 25 July 1966. By family tradition, this miniature is of Sir Clowdisley Shovell (1650–1707). A miniature of a young man wearing a grey coat and a blue vestock, signed 'HN' and dated '1756', is at the V. & A. M.

*N., I. (fl. *c.* 1750)

Four miniatures of children, painted *c.* 1750, and signed 'I.N. fecit', were seen by Mr. R. Hutchison, Keeper of the S.N.P.G., who had them photographed. They were at Crathes, Aberdeenshire, and were among the contents of part of the house which was burnt in 1966. They may have represented the children of the 6th Bart., Sir Thomas Burnett of Leys (d. 1783?).

*N., N.R. (fl. 1774)

A miniature of the Duchess of Ancaster is signed and dated, 'N.R.N. pinxit 1774'.

N., P.

Sir Philip de Malpas Grey Egerton, Bt., lent three oval miniatures mounted in a gold box to the exhibition at the South Kensington Museum, 1865. The miniatures were of Mary, daughter of Sir Hoskins Egles Styles, wife of Philip Egerton of Tatton, and her two sons. The centre miniature was signed, 'P.N.'.

*N., S. See **S., N.**

N., W. (fl. 1771)

A plumbago portrait of Cromwell, signed 'W.N.' and dated '1771', is mentioned in the 14th Annual Vol. of the *Walpole Society*, 1926, p. 80. Long saw a miniature of a lady signed on the reverse, 'Joanna Baillie / W.N.'.

Nailor or Naylor, Miss. (fl. 1819)

Exhibited at the R.A., 1819 (Hon. Exhibitor). According to the catalogue of the Duke of Northumberland's collection, compiled by J. J. Foster, the collection contained a miniature of the 3rd Duke of Northumberland by 'Miss Naylor', who was possibly identical to the above artist. I was unable to trace this miniature when I examined the miniatures at Alnwick.

Naish. See also **Naish, William** and **Naish, John**

A miniature of the late 18th, or early 19th century, of a man, was sold in the Jeffery Whitehead Collection at Christie's, August 1915. At the back was a trade card of 'Mr Naish, miniature painter; late a student of the R.A.'; he was then in Bristol and was seeking patrons. This may have been either J. Naish (q.v.) or W. Naish (q.v.).

Naish, John. b. 1771. See also **Naish** and **Naish, William**

Of London. Entered the R.A. Schools, 18 February 1791, aged 20. Exhibited at the R.A., 1790–1795.

Naish, William. c. 1767–1800. See also **Naish** and **Naish, John**

Born in Axbridge, Somerset c. 1767. Entered the R.A. Schools, 28 November 1788, aged 21. Worked in London; had a large practice which included many of the theatrical profession. Exhibited at the R.A., 1786–1800. Was for a time in Bristol. He is said to have died at his house in Leicester Sq. late in 1800. A miniature by him of H. W. Wymann, was signed and dated on the reverse, 'Naish, 97 / H. W. Wymann. 27 College Green, Bristol'. I have in my collection a miniature of a man in a black coat, signed on the reverse 'Naish' in rather sloping writing. A bluish shading is evident round the mouth and chin, the eyelids drawn with firm, distinct lines; the hair shows the strands painted separately, some being painted in deepish blue. The V. & A. M. has an example of his work. The B.M. has engraved portraits after Naish.

Nash, Edward (G?). 1778–1821

Born in 1778; sixth of eleven children born to Thomas Nash (1743–1809) and his wife, née Mary Woodbridge. T. Nash was a wealthy merchant of Coventry. The family had been 'Kentish men' for 400 years and T. Nash left £96,000 and property in Kent and London. E. Nash exhibited from London addresses at the R.A., 1800–1820. Said to have been a pupil or assistant of S. Shelley (q.v.). Left Portsmouth for India in the 'Hercules', 9 January 1801, arriving in Bombay in May 1801. Said to have made money in India. Returned to England in the 'Dover Castle', February 1810, and landed at Deal, 6 July 1810. According to his relatives he was a hunchback and suffered from illness. Lived from 1811–1818 at 6 George Street, Hanover Square, where Shelley, with whom he was friendly, lived until his death in 1808. Worked for a time in the Lake District. Knew Coleridge, Southey and Wordsworth, etc. A miniature signed 'E. Nash, Camberwell, Surrey, Jan 1797', was seen at the V. & A. M. He is also said to have signed E. G. Nash pint Bombay, November 1801, and E. Nash pinxit. His work is reminiscent of that of Shelley and often has a yellow tinge and slightly brown shading. He sometimes exaggerated the size of the eyes and as he did not always sign his miniatures, many of them are probably unattributed. In his will, dated 31 March 1817, he left his property to his mother; £1,000 each to his eldest brother, Thomas (a hop-grower), and younger brother, Richard; casts and figures to his friend, Wm. Haines; wines, liqueurs and £20 to Miss Shelley for a ring. The rest to be divided between his brothers and sisters, except for his drawings and miniatures, which were left to his brother, William Woodbridge Nash, whose wife was Elizabeth Waring. He died unmarried in London, 3 January 1821. Examples of his work are at the V. & A. M. and the B.M.

Nash, Miss Elizabeth F. or M. (fl. 1830–1836)

Of Cambridge (1830) and London. Exhibited at the R.A., 1830–1836. The R.A. catalogues for 1830 record her as Elizabeth M. Nash, but Long gives her second initial as F.

*Nathan, Mrs. Estelle. (fl. 1898)

Of London. Exhibited at the R.A. 1898, from 37 Barkstone Gardens.

Naylor, Miss. See Nailor, Miss

Neal(e), Miss. (fl. 1797–1800)

Of London. Exhibited at the R.A., 1797–1800. There seems to have been some confusion over the identity of the above artist. Long states that exhibit no. 984, in the R.A. catalogue for 1797, records the name as Miss Neate; this is, in fact, a mistake. The name is Miss Neale and the exhibit a miniature of a gentleman, but her name is not recorded in the index. In 1798 Miss Neale exhibited two miniatures of officers from 10 Great Queen Street, Westminster, from which address she exhibited again in 1800. In this latter year the name is spelt Neal.

*Neatby, William J. (fl. 1906–1914)

Of London. Exhibited at the R.A. 1906–1914, from 56 Glebe Place, Chelsea and from 4 Wentworth Studios, Manresa Road. Painted miniatures and subjects in water-colour.

Neate, Miss. See Neal(e), Miss

*Nelson, A. (fl. 1766–1790). See also **N., A.**

Of London. Exhibited at the R.A., Society of Artists, etc., 1766–1790. Worked in the West Indies c. 1790. Painted landscapes and, according to Long's notes, miniatures. He may have been identical with the artist who signed A.N. (q.v.).

Nelson, Horatio. (fl. 1834–1849)

An Irish artist; entered the Dublin Society Schools in 1834. Was established as a miniaturist at No. 16 College Green, in 1836. Exhibited at the R.H.A., up to 1845. Painted portraits in oil, miniatures and was the first to introduce the daguerreotype process into Dublin. *Saunders' Newsletter*, July 1844, mentions his invention, and in the following year calls attention to his 'coloured daguerreotypes'. Some woodcut views after his drawings appeared in the *Dublin Penny Journal*. He is said to have died in 1849.

*Netscher, Casper or **Gaspard.** 1639–1684

Born in Heidelberg in 1639. Said to have executed oil miniatures in England. Benezit states that his miniatures were most interesting, and that he visited England during the reign of Charles II. He died in the Hague, 15 January 1684. J. J. Foster, in *Miniature Painters, British and Foreign*, mentions several works by him and states that he was patronised by James, Duke of York. A miniature of Queen Mary II, painted in oil on board, is mentioned by Foster. Two miniatures representing William III and Queen Mary, painted in oil on copper, are in the collection of the Duke of Portland; they are both well painted. According to R. W. Goulding, miniatures by him are rare. His son, Constantijn Netscher, 1669–1722, painted members of the Portland family, and Henrietta Churchill, later Duchess of Marlborough. Constantijn did not come to England although he was urged to do so.

Nevin, D. M. (fl. 1783)

Of London. Exhibited at the Free Society of Artists, 1783.

Newberry, W. M. (fl. 1836–c. 1905)

Of London. Exhibited at the R.A., etc., 1836–1845. Graves (*R.A.*) gives No. 758 as his 1840 entry; this No. is in fact missing in the printed catalogues, and Graves must have taken it from an annotated copy. A miniature of Mrs. Brunton, painted on ivory, signed on the front, 'W. M. Newberry', c. 1905, is in the collection of R. Bayne Powell, Esq. The portrait is strongly painted with a good sense of colour, the modelling is also good. A scraper has been used in the hair.

Newcombe, George W. 1799–1845

Born in England, 22 September 1799; worked in London. Exhibited at the R.A., etc., 1825–1828. Painted miniatures and oil portraits. Went to New York, 1829, where he settled. Became an Associate of the National Academy, 1832. Died in New York, 10 February 1845.

Newell, Edward John. 1771–1798

Born at Downpatrick, Ireland, 29 June 1771. Of Scottish parents. Left home at 17 and spent a year at sea; was apprenticed to a painter and glazier. Worked for two years as a glass-stainer in Dublin and Limerick. Settled in Belfast in 1796 and took up miniature painting without any previous training. Joined the United Irishmen, whom he betrayed to the Government, giving much false information. Fled to England, and in 1798 returned to Belfast to complete arrangements to emigrate to America. On the eve of his departure in June of that year he was secretly assassinated. He wrote an autobiography containing a reproduction of a self-portrait taken from a sketch.

Newell, Jabez. b. c. 1797

Of White Cross Street, London. Was awarded a silver medal by the Society of Arts in 1813 and a premium in 1815 as Master Jabez Newell. Entered the R.A. Schools, 24 November 1815, aged 18. Possibly identical with J. Newell who exhibited a portrait of Mr. W. Newell at the R.A., in 1817, from 32 White Cross Street, Cripplegate, from which address Miss S. Newell (q.v.) also exhibited from 1819.

Newell, Miss S. (fl. 1819–1838)

Of London. Exhibited at the R.A. and S.B.A., 1819–1838. Her work is not of any great merit. Schidlof mentions having seen a miniature by her, painted on ivory, and signed on the reverse, 'Miss Newell del / March 1821'. Undoubtedly related to J. Newell who exhibited at the R.A. from the same address, 32 White Cross Street, Cripplegate in 1817.

Newey, John. 19th century

An early 19th-century miniature copy of a Titian, inscribed on the reverse, 'John Newey / Whittall Street / Birmingham', was seen by Long. The Newey family were manufacturers, and the artist may have been one of the family, or an amateur miniaturist. The work was quite skilfully executed.

*Newman, Mrs. Adelaide C. (fl. 1900–1907)

Of London. Exhibited at the R.A. 1900–1907, from 2 Woburn Square, and from Dene, Hatch End, Middlesex.

Newman, T. H. (fl. 1841)

Of London. Exhibited at the R.A. 1841, from 25 Granville Street, Somer's Town. The exhibit was 'Portrait of an artist', and may have been a self-portrait.

*Newman, Thomas. (fl. c. 1698)

The above artist is recorded by Strickland, who noted that his name occurs as a limner in the Parish Registers of St. Michan in 1698.

Newman, Thomas. (fl. 1813–1818)

Was a pupil at the Dublin Society Schools, and

was awarded a prize in 1813 and 1815. Exhibited in Dublin, 1815 and 1817. Painted portraits, landscapes and miniatures. Had addresses in Bride Street, and Great Ship Street, Dublin. Was still living there in 1818.

*Newmarch, Miss Ethel M. (fl. 1903–1914)
Exhibited at the R.A. 1903–1914, from Howden Lodge, Clarendon Road, Southsea.

*Newton, Miss Gertrude A. (fl. 1906–1911)
Of London. Exhibited at the R.A. 1906–1911, from 49 Ravenscourt Gardens, Ravenscourt Park.

Newton, John. d. 1635
A limner of Cambridge. Died 1635. His widow, née Anne Hales, married Joseph Jackson, a minister of Woodensborough, Kent. His son, Samuel Newton (1628–1718), was a notary public, Alderman and later Mayor of Cambridge in 1671.

Newton, John. (fl. 1824)
Was working in 1824 at 82 Dame Street, Dublin. He may have been identical with or related to John Orr Newton (fl. 1835–1843), a painter of subject pictures and domestic scenes, who exhibited at the R.H.A.

Newton, Richard. 1777–1798
Was born in 1777. Worked as a miniaturist in London. Was a caricaturist and an engraver. Etched 'Blue Devils', 1795. Lived at 13 Brydges Street, Covent Garden, where he died, 9 December 1798. Drawings and caricatures by him are in the B.M.

Newton, Sir William John. 1785–1869
Born in London, 1785; son of James Newton, engraver, and nephew of William Newton, architect. Trained as an engraver, but took up miniature painting. Entered the R.A. Schools, 15 January 1807, aged 22. May have been a member of an artists' volunteer corps, 1803. Exhibited at the R.A. and B.I., 1808–1863. Became very popular and had a distinguished clientele which included many royal and titled persons, Members of Parliament and fellow artists. Married Anne Faulder in 1822, by whom he had a son, H. R. Newton, an architect. Was appointed miniature painter to William IV and Queen Adelaide in 1833, and painter to Queen Victoria; was knighted in 1837, the year of her accession. His two largest works, 27 in. × 37 in., were executed on large pieces of ivory joined together, a method for which he was said to have been responsible, and which proved to be unsatisfactory, owing to the effect that changes of temperature have on ivory. The works portrayed were, 'The Marriage of Queen Victoria' and 'The Christening of the Prince of Wales'. He died in London on 22 January 1869, at 6 Cambridge Terrace, Hyde Park. Newton's work was good and he must rank among the best British miniaturists of his period. At his best he equals Sir W. C. Ross (q.v.) and A. Robertson (q.v.), and he is not inferior to them as has been suggested in the past. He was a good draughtsman, and painted the faces with a fresh natural colour, and yellowish shadows. Two particularly fine examples of his work were exhibited at Edinburgh in 1965. They were from a private collection and represented Viscount and Viscountess Cardwell, and were both signed on the reverse; the latter's portrait being inscribed, 'Mrs Cardwell / Sir W. J. Newton / Piniat / miniature Painter in / Ordinary to Her Majesty / & the Queen Dowager / 6 Argyle St / 1838'. This was a typical signature. He occasionally signed on the front W. I. N. (Roman capitals) followed by a date, and Wᵐ J Newton / pinxᵗ / 6. Duke Street / St James's / 1812. He painted

portraits in water-colour and chalk on paper, and miniatures on ivory. A collection of his miniatures is at the Glynn Vivian Art Gallery, Swansea. Examples of his work are at the V. & A. M., the B.M., and the N.G., Dublin, as well as in a number of private collections including that of H.M. the Queen.

*Nichols, Miss Catherine Maud, R.P.E. 1847–1923
Was born in Norwich in 1847. Exhibited at the R.A., N.W.C.S., S.M., etc., 1877–1910. Executed portraits, landscapes, etchings and miniatures. Was elected a member of the Royal Society of Painter Etchers and Engravers. Died in Norwich, 30 January 1923. Examples of her work are at the Museum of Norwich.

Nichols or **Nicholls, Miss Mary Ann.** (fl. 1838–1851)
Of London. Was awarded a premium by the Society of Arts in 1838. Exhibited at the R.A., S.B.A., etc., 1839–1850. Painted flowers, miniatures and imitated cameos in the style of De Gault. Signed M.A. Nichols, followed by a date. Some of her miniatures were *en grisaille* in profile. A miniature (cameo profile) of a man signed, 'M.A. Nichols 1851', is in the collection of Commander E. Culme-Seymour.

*Nicholson, Hugh. (fl. 1893–1896)
Of London. Exhibited at the R.A., 1893–1896. His exhibit in 1893 was of his mother. His other sitters included Lord Ronald Gower, Mrs. James Kendall, Mrs. Charles Holland, The Lady de Tabley, Mrs. Carlisle and her sister, Mrs. W. G. Pirrie.

Nicholson, William, R.S.A. 1781–1844
Born in Ovingham-on-Tyne, 25 December 1781; second son of a schoolmaster, who became master of the grammar school at Newcastle-on-Tyne. Was self-taught in art. Early in his life he went to Hull where he painted miniatures of officers. Returned to Newcastle. In 1814 Nicholson settled in Edinburgh where he resided for the rest of his life. Exhibited at the R.A., and O.W.C.S., 1808–1822; the Edinburgh Exhibition Society, 1814–1816; and at the Institute for the Encouragement of the Fine Arts in Scotland, 1821–1825. Was one of the founders and first secretary (1826–1829) of the (Royal) Scottish Academy; exhibited there, 1827–1844. Painted portraits in oil and water-colour, landscapes, miniatures and executed etchings, some of which were published and represented many notable persons such as Robert Burns, George Thomson, Professor Playfair, Bishop Cameron, Sir Walter Scott, etc. Married in 1821, Maria Lamb of Edinburgh, by whom he had at least two sons and two daughters who survived him. He is not thought to have exhibited any miniatures after 1827. According to Brydall, his miniatures 'are delicate and refined'. His later oil portraits show the influence of Raeburn. His large self-portrait in oil is in the S.N.P.G. Nicholson died in Edinburgh, 16 August 1844.

*Nicholson, Miss Winifred U. (fl. 1906–1909)
Exhibited at the R.A. 1906–1909, from Willowgrove, Marple, Cheshire. Her sitters included Mrs. Graham Bruce.

Nihell, Miss A. See **Nihill**

Nihill or **Nihell, Miss A.** (fl. 1825–1829)
Exhibited at the R.A. 1825 and 1829, as an Hon. Exhibitor. In 1825 the name was spelt Nihill, and in 1829, Nihell.

*Nimmo, John Jules. b. c. 1830
Born in Paris c. 1830. Was a pupil of Meuret. Painted miniatures and copied the works of Old Masters. Worked in Paris and exhibited at the Salon, 1853–1881. Was in Edinburgh in 1856. The Hanover Exhibition, 1918, contained two miniatures by him, one of which was a portrait of an old man painted on ivory and signed on the reverse, 'J. Nimmo. 4 Young Street, Edinburgh 1856'. The E. Holzscheiter Collection, Meilen, contains a miniature of Serge de Morny as a child, signed vertically, 'Nimmo 1864'.

Nitson, J. E.
A miniature by the above artist, of Queen Charlotte, was sold in 1805.

Nixon, James, A.R.A. c. 1741–1812
Born c. 1741. Of London and Edinburgh. Entered the R.A. Schools, 17 March 1769. Was a member of the Society of Artists; exhibited with them, 1765–1771, and at the R.A., and B.I., 1772–1807. Became A.R.A., 1778 (diploma dated 2 November 1778). Painted portraits in oil and water-colour, historical subjects, miniatures and, according to an undated MS in my possession, executed book illustrations. Miniatures were his chief interest, and many of his subjects were actresses in character. Nixon was appointed limner to the Prince Regent, and, in 1792, miniature painter to the Duchess of York. He was living in Edinburgh on 9 June 1797 at 9 St. Andrew's Square. The author of the MS states that Nixon was greatly influenced by Sir Joshua Reynolds, and refers to some correspondence in which Nixon speaks of the 'way in which the overpowering excellence of Reynolds' work' fills his mind. He was very attached to the Royal Academy, and 'never tired of speaking about it, and declaiming that to it, he owed all his success in life'. His sitters included Joseph Farington, whom he painted in 1765 and in 1770, the Duchess of Rutland, and the Duchess of Devonshire. Nixon was not financially very successful, and was ultimately obliged to receive a pension from the R.A. Augustus Toussaint (q.v.) was his pupil. According to the author of the MS already mentioned, Nixon spent most of his time in Devonshire. He died in Tiverton, 9 May 1812. Most of his miniatures are painted in fairly strong bright colours to which a lot of gum has been added. The faces of his sitters are shaded with slightly irregular soft cross-strokes; the hair being painted broadly without much detail. Many of his portraits have a dark background of apparently thick foliage. He did not always sign his work, and when he did, it is not easy to detect. Sometimes he signed with a small N, partly concealed in the background, or with a larger cursive N, which is more easily apparent. His works, which are fairly scarce, are often of a high quality and are slightly reminiscent of the work of Reynolds. His miniatures of ladies often depict them holding a bird. He was a good artist and one worthy of greater recognition than has hitherto been the case. Examples of his work may be found at the V. & A. M. The B.M. has engraved portraits after Nixon. The City of Liverpool Museum contains a miniature of Miss Gunning signed, 'N', by the above artist.

*Noar, Miss Eva. (fl. 1907–1914)
Exhibited at the R.A. 1907–1914, from Studio, Eccles, Manchester.

*Noble, Miss Florence K. (fl. 1904–1905)
Of London. Exhibited at the R.A. 1904 and 1905, from addresses in Chelsea.

*Nodder, F. P. (fl. 1773–1778). See also **Nodder, Frederick P.**

Of London. Exhibited at the Society of Artists and the Free Society, 1773–1778, including a miniature, 'Head of Socrates'. Made portraits, etc., in human hair and painted in oil on satin. May possibly have been identical with or related to Frederick P. Nodder (q.v.) who, according to the *D.N.B.*, is identified as the F. P. Nodder who exhibited paintings of flowers at the R.A., 1786–1788. The R.A. catalogues do not give a full christian name, and it is possible that the information has been confused, and that the *D.N.B.* is mistaken in suggesting that Frederick P. Nodder was the father of the above artist.

Nodder, Frederick P. d. *c.* 1800. See also **Nodder, F.P.**

There appears to be some confusion regarding the identity of the above artists. F. P. Nodder (q.v.) is recorded as exhibiting at the Society of Artists and the Free Society, 1773–1778, including a miniature, 'The Head of Socrates'. He was probably identical with the F. P. Nodder who exhibited flower paintings at the R.A., 1786–1788. Neither the Society of Artists, the Free Society nor the R.A. catalogues record a full Christian name, but the *D.N.B.* records as Frederick, and suggests that the artist who painted flowers and was 'botanical painter to Her Majesty', was the son of the F. P. Nodder who exhibited in 1773. Frederick P. Nodder etched illustrations for botanical works. He died *c.* 1800.

*Nogués, Jules. b. 1809. See also **Nogués, T.**

Born in Auch, France, 12 May 1809. Self-taught. Painted portraits in water-colour, pastels and crayons. Exhibited at the Paris Salon, 1835–1844. Was possibly the J. Nogués who exhibited at the R.A., in 1843, his sitters being Miss A. Harling, Mrs. A. Ward, Mr. John Eyre and Mrs. Temsson. The address was given as 23 Cockspur Street. He was probably related to T. Nogués (q.v.). The N.P.G. has a small portrait in water-colour of Frederick Nash (1782–1856), also an artist, signed by J. Nogués, and painted in 1839.

Nogués, T. (fl. 1840). See also **Nogués, Jules**

Of London. Exhibited at the R.A. in 1840, from 125 Regent Street. Long and Graves record him as exhibiting at the R.A. in 1843, but the catalogue for this year gives the exhibits to J. Nogués, probably Jules Nogués (q.v.) to whom T. Nogués was possibly related. His sitters included Miss Fanny Elsler.

Noireterre or **Noireserre, Mlle. Marie Thérèse de.** (fl. 1785–1803)

Pupil of Mme. Labille-Guiard. Exhibited at the Salon de la Correspondance and at the Paris Salon, 1785–1803. Worked in Paris and London, where she became a member of the Society of Arts. Some of her works were engraved. Examples of her art are at the Louvre and in several private collections in France. Her self-portrait and that of her father, and other members of the family, were sold in Paris, 21–22 May 1931. Benezit gives the alternative spelling as Noireserre or Noiresterres.

Norgate, Edward. *c.* 1581–1650

Baptised, 1581; son of Dr. Robert Norgate, Master of Corpus Christi College, Cambridge. Norgate is chiefly associated with the art of illuminating and known for his treatise, *Miniatura or the Art of Limning*, edited by Martin Hardie and published in 1919 from the MS in the Bodleian Library, Oxford. It is now known that he painted miniatures, and three or four authentic portraits by him exist. The first to be identified was of his first wife, Judith,

née Lanyer, whom he married in 1613. This miniature is in the V. & A. M., and is inscribed and signed on the reverse, 'Juditha Norgate. 1617. æt; 25. Non obijt sed abijt. Pudicitæ, Pietatis, et Venustatis rarissimum decus. Suauissimæ Conjugi Ed: Norgate', which may be translated, '. . . She has not died: she has departed. Rarest ornament of Modesty, Affection and Beauty. To his most sweet wife, Ed: Norgate.' Norgate remarried in 1619. He was employed in London as an heraldic draughtsman, and illuminated the letters on Royal Patents. He had many friends among the leading painters of the day, including Van Dyck and Sir Balthasar Gerbier (q.v.), and held various positions at the Courts of James I and Charles I, including that of tuner and 'Keeper of His Majesties Organs' and other instruments (1611). Taught the sons of the Earl of Arundel heraldic painting; the Earl also sent him to Italy to buy pictures. Became Blue Mantle Pursuivant in 1616, Windsor Herald, 1633 and Clerk of the Signet, 1638. Was employed to take letters to Paris, Venice and Ireland from 1612 onwards, and received payment for writing and limning royal letters to foreign sovereigns. On 10 March 1630, Norgate was granted the monopoly to write, limn and prepare letters to be sent to princes overseas. In 1639 he went with Charles I to Scotland and in the same year was sent to the Low Countries to purchase pictures for Queen Henrietta Maria. Was frequently consulted as an art connoisseur. Norgate died at the Heralds' College, London and was buried at St. Benets', Paul's Wharf on 23 December 1650. He was an able follower of Hilliard and Oliver (q.v.) and it is regrettable that so few of his miniatures are known. His portrait of his wife, at the V. & A. M., is a charming example of his work. An unsigned replica of this which has just been cleaned and is in a fine state, together with two miniatures thought to represent John Harrison, junior (painted *c.* 1620) and his wife, Mary, née Bucueham (painted 1630, aged 20), and a Coat of Arms of John Harrison, junior, dated 1622, attributed to Norgate, all belong to Miss Lawson Tancred, a descendant, who also possesses an oil portrait of Mary Harrison dated '1630'. John Harrison was interested in Heraldry, and may have been related to, or friendly with, Norgate which would account for a second miniature of Judith Norgate being in the Harrison family. These miniatures are both attractive and meticulously painted in the Hilliard/Oliver tradition. The hair is painted in distinct and fairly thick strands, the doublet and dress of the sitters and the lace, are well painted. The Coat of Arms may well have been at one time on the reverse of the miniature of John Harrison.

*Norriss, Miss Bess. (fl. 1908–1932)

Of London. Exhibited at the R.A. and R.S.M. 1908–1932, from various London addresses.

*North, F. D. (fl. *c.* 1795–1800)

A miniature of a man, *c.* 1795–1800, is in the V. & A. M., and is signed, 'F.D. North'.

*North, Mrs. S. W. (Jane A.). (fl. 1873–1891)

Of London. Exhibited at the R.A., 1873–1891. Her sitters included Mrs. Edwin Goad, Miss Florence Goad and H. Stewart, Esq.

Northcote, William. (fl. *c.* 1824)

Was working in Sligo *c.* 1824. Nothing further is known about him.

Norton, James. (fl. 1787)

Working in Dublin, 1787. Mentioned in *Faulkner's Journal*, 14 June 1787, as a miniature painter at 11 Crampton Court.

Notz, J. (Johannes). 1802–1862

Born in Oberstrass, nr. Zurich, 14 September 1802. Was a pupil of Pfenninger, and studied at the Academy of Munich. Worked in Munich, Aarau, Basle, Alsace, Paris and London (1827–1842). Exhibited at the R.A. 1831–1840, from various London addresses; was for some years in Margaret Street, Cavendish Square. Visited Rome between 1842 and 1847, after which time he settled in Zurich where he died. Was a draughtsman, lithographer and miniaturist, as well as executing portraits in water-colour. Some of his miniatures are in lead and silver point, and others in water-colour. One in my collection executed in silver point on paper, is signed on the front 'J. Notz, 1828'; and inscribed on the reverse 'Mrs Hopkinson mother of Mrs Jane Seymour (1768–1850)'. The features are well drawn and expressive. There is a lot of cross hatching on the face and the pencil is heavily used to shade the dress.

*Nowlan, Miss Carlotta. (fl. 1885–1911)

Exhibited at the R.A. etc., 1885–1911, from The Elms, Cheam, Surrey. The majority of her exhibits were of flowers.

Nowlan, Frank. *c.* 1835–1919

Born in Co. Dublin, *c.* 1835. Came to London in 1857; studied at Leigh's School and the Langham School of Art. Exhibited at the R.A., etc., 1866–1918. Painted in oil, water-colour and enamel; executed and restored miniatures. Was patronised by the Royal Family. Invented unforgeable cheques. Died 1 May 1919 in London. Examples of his work are at the V. & A. M.

Nunes, (A.J.?). (fl. 1778?–1797)

Exhibited at the R.A., 1778?–1797. Painted portraits in oil, and miniatures. The exhibit in 1778 was by A. J. Nunes, and was a portrait of a gentleman by candle-light. Graves identifies this artist with the Nunes who exhibited in 1797.

Nursey, Perry, senior. d. *c.* 1839

An enthusiastic lover of art and an amateur painter. Exhibited at the R.A. 1799–1801, from London addresses. Moved to Little Bealings, nr. Woodbridge, Suffolk. Was a friend of Sir D. Wilkie, R.A. Claude Lorraine Nursey (died 1873), an artist, was his son. P. Nursey died *c.* 1839, 'after a very chequered existence'. An oval plumbago miniature of a Dr. Clarke, signed 'P Nursey pinx^t', is at the V. & A. M. It recalls the manner of Foster (q.v.), but the costume is drawn with a softer touch.

*Nutt, Miss Elizabeth S. (fl. 1909)

Exhibited at the R.A. 1909, from 10 Bannerdale Road, Sheffield.

*Nye, Miss Elsie L. (fl. 1898–1911)

Exhibited at the R.A. 1898–1911, from Camperdown, Wallington, Surrey.

*Nye, Miss Maud. (fl. 1900)

Of London. Exhibited at the R.A. 1900, from 16 Colville Terrace, Kensington Park.

O

*O., C.R. (fl. *c.* 1800). See also **C., R.O.**
Lady Liddell had a miniature *c.* 1800, signed '$c^R{}_o$'.

Oakley, Miss Louisa. (fl. 1850)
Of London. Exhibited at the R.A. 1850, from 80 Somerset Street, Portman Square.

*Oakley, Octavius.** 1800–1867
Born in April 1800. Worked as an artist in Leamington, Derby and London. Painted portraits in water-colour and miniatures. Exhibited at the R.A., O.W.C.S., etc., 1826–1867. Long noted seeing an oval miniature on ivory of J. Jewell, M.A., F.R.S., said to have been painted by Oakley and presented to a Miss Flint. He thought the drawing accurate. Died in London, 1 March 1867.

*O'Brien, Miss Marjorie.** (fl. 1908–1909)
Exhibited at the R.A. 1908 and 1909, from Caritas, Bushey, Herts. Her sitters included Lady Burrell.

*O'Connor, C.** 18th century
An 18th-century miniature of an unknown lady by this artist, signed on the reverse, was seen by me in Edinburgh in 1963. It was quite well painted.

*O'Connor, Miss Evelyn B.** (fl. 1907)
Exhibited at the R.A. 1907, from 4 Clarence Parade, Southsea.

O'Connor, James Arthur. 1792–1841
Born in Dublin in 1792; son of William O'Connor an engraver and print-seller. James was self-taught except for a few lessons from William Sadler (q.v.). Exhibited in Dublin, 1809–1821, and at the R.A., B.I., etc., 1822–1840, as well as at the R.H.A., 1836–1840. Best known as a landscape painter, frequently introduced small figures in red coats or dresses into his pictures. His self-portrait in miniature, 4½ in. × 3½ in., executed in oil, is reproduced by Strickland, *Dictionary of Irish Artists*, Pl. LVII. Visited Brussels in 1826, Paris in 1832, and accompanied by his wife went to Chalons, Saarbrucken and on to Frankfurt in 1833. Returned to London. He suffered from weak eyesight and in 1839 his health began to fail and he was unable to work; he became poor and died in humble lodgings at 6 Marlborough Street, Brompton, London on 7 January 1841, leaving his widow unprovided for. A subscription headed with twenty guineas from the Prince Consort was started for her benefit. A number of paintings by him are in the N.G., Dublin.

O'Connor, Joseph. (fl. 1788). See also **Connor, Joseph**
Worked as a miniaturist at 88 Fleet Street (Dublin?), 1788. Possibly identical with Joseph Connor (q.v.) of Cork.

*Oddie, Miss Maude G.** (fl. 1897–1904)
Of Watford, Herts. Exhibited at the R.A., 1897 and 1904.

Ogg, C. H. (fl. 1842–1843)
Of Putney. Exhibited at the R.A. and S.B.A., 1842–1843.

Ogier, P. (Peter?). (fl. 1793–1800)
Of London. Possibly the Peter Ogier who entered the R.A. Schools, 22 October 1789, aged 20. Exhibited at the R.A., 1793–1800. Was in Bath at 'Mr. Lintern's Music Shop, Abbey Churchyard', where he advertised that he painted miniatures at 3 guineas each, 1 January 1795, and again on 12 March 1795, that he charged 5 guineas.

Ogle
The above artist is mentioned in the *Proceedings of the Bath Natural History and Antiquarian Field Club*, VIII, 1897, p. 215.

O'Keeffe or **Keeffe, Daniel.** 1740–1787
Born in Dublin, 1740; studied at the Dublin Society Schools. His father was a native of King's County, and his mother an O'Connor from Wexford. Won several prizes, and was for a time employed by Samuel Dixon to colour prints of birds and flowers. In 1762 he was established as a miniaturist in Temple Bar; later went to London and exhibited at the Free Society of Artists in 1769 and 1783, and the R.A., 1771–1786. Was known as Daniel Keeffe until 1775 when he added the 'O' to his name. His brother John describes him as 'tall and thin, very fair and delicately florid, blue eyes his hair light'. He was in Bath *c.* 1776, and is said to have left Salisbury in a hurry, July 1777, due to debt. He died of consumption at his lodgings in Brompton, 22 June 1787. A miniature on ivory of Bridget Tuite, wife of Thomas Bradshaw, stated to be signed 'D.K. 1763', was lent to the exhibition at the South Kensington Museum in 1865. (Pl. 248:

*O'Keefe, Mrs. Elsie. See **Millard, Miss Elsie M.**

*O'Keefe, Manus Massey.** 1834–1868
Born in Cork, 1834. Originally a saddler, later an attorney's clerk; noted for his drawings which he executed in the manner of the early Irish illuminators. He died in distressed circumstances in the Mercy Hospital, Cork, 3 May 1868.

*Oldfield, Mrs. Millicent.** (fl. 1904–1906)
Of Preston and Bristol. Exhibited at the R.A., 1904 and 1906.

Oldham, John. 1779–1840
Born in Dublin, 1779; apprenticed to an engraver. Took up painting, and exhibited in Dublin, 1801 and 1802. Painted miniatures and oil portraits. Invented machines, and was employed as an engraver. Took profile miniatures with a machine he invented, 'at 11/4½ each'. Was employed by the Bank of England. Died in Montague Street, Bloomsbury, London, 14 February 1840. For further information see Strickland, *Dictionary of Irish Artists*, pp. 193–195.

Oliver, Archer James, A.R.A. 1774–1842
Was born in 1774. Entered the R.A. Schools, 13 August 1790, aged 16. Exhibited at the R.A. and B.I., 1791–1841, including portraits of W. Wood (q.v.) and G. Chinnery (q.v.). Became A.R.A. in 1807. Was for a short time curator of the painting school of the R.A. Was a fashionable painter of portraits, still life, domestic subjects and miniatures. Was supported during the latter part of his life to a great extent by the R.A. He died in 1842. A portrait of him by J. Varley is in the V. & A. M. A miniature of Mrs. Baumer, painted in 1805, catalogued as by the above artist, was loaned to the exhibition at the South Kensington Museum, 1865, by Mrs. Barwise.

Oliver, Isaac. d. 1617
Born in Rouen; son of Huguenot parents, Pierre Ollivier and his wife, whose maiden name was Typhan or Tyffen. The family fled to England with the boy in 1568, to escape religious persecution, and according to information published by the Huguenot Society, Isaac Oliver lived with his parents in 'Mr Harrison's house' in 'Fletlane' (Fleet Street). The date of Isaac Oliver's birth is still unknown; Vertue places it at 1556, but later authorities have suggested that it might have been as late as *c.* 1565. This latter date allows for the fact that his apprenticeship probably started when he was 13 or 14 years old, and that he served under N. Hilliard (q.v.), for about the usual seven years, bringing the period of his independent works up to *c.* 1580. Unfortunately no indenture has survived to give us the date on which he became Hilliard's apprentice, nor does his name, or that of his father, appear in the Minutes of the Goldsmiths' Company. Evidence that he was Hilliard's pupil is to be found in Richard Haydocke's *Tracts* when he says that 'Mr Isaac Oliver' was Hilliard's 'scholar for limning' and mirrored his master's 'true and liveley Image'. The fact that his early works so closely resemble those by Hilliard adds confirmation to the statement. The 1706 translation of de Piles' *Art of Painting* gives the information that Oliver was 'a very famous limner . . . eminent both for history and faces, many pieces of which were in the possession of the late Duke of Norfolk; some of them being admirable copies after Parmeggiano &c. He received some light in that art from Frederico Zucchero . . . He was likewise a very good painter in little'. He remained proud of his French nationality throughout his life and only became an English subject in 1606. He never seems to have mastered the English language, if one may judge from his often curious inscriptions. On the basis of a Dutch inscription on a miniature in the collection of H.M. the Queen of the Netherlands, it has always been held that Oliver visited Holland in 1588 but this is now in doubt as the sitter is known to be Colonel Dierderik Sonoy (1529–1597), who visited England in 1588 where the miniature was probably painted and was wearing civilian dress. It is inscribed on the front 'Sonder erch Verhouwe Æ Suæ 59 Ao. Dm 1588. Isacˢ. Oliverˢ. f.'. From an inscription on the reverse of a miniature of Sir Arundell Talbot, we know that he was in Venice in 1596. He evidently married three times, his first wife, said to have been called Elizabeth, died in 1599, and was buried on 6 September at St. Peter's, Cornhill, aged 28. She bore him a son, Peter Oliver (q.v.), who followed his father's profession. In February 1602, Isaac married as his second wife, Sarah Gheeraerts, daughter of Susanna de Critz and Marcus Gheeraerts, the elder, at the Dutch Church of Austin Friars. There is no record of her death, but his third and last wife Elizabeth Harding (Hardinge or Harden), by whom he had a son Jacques, baptised 8 January 1609, was his executrix and survived him. The couple were married at Isleworth on 23 or 29 July 1606. The church was burned at a later date and the remains of the register are now almost illegible. It was after this marriage that Isaac secured the right of denization. His circle of friends included Cornelius Johnson (q.v.) whose sister married Nicasius Russell, a goldsmith. Oliver was godfather to one of their sons in 1616, and in 1618 Oliver's widow acted as godmother to another son of this marriage. His other friends included John de Critz the elder, and Robert Peake. His merit as an artist was acknowledged even in his own lifetime; Henry Peacham (q.v.), in *The Gentleman's Exercise*, says, 'nor must I be ingratefully unmindful of mine owne Countriemen, who have beene, and are able to equall the best, if occasion served, as old Mr Hilliard, Mr Isaac Oliver inferiour to none in Christendom for the countenance in small'. Although an unfinished miniature of Queen Elizabeth exists, of *c.* 1600,

which is a realistic representation of Her Majesty, no payments by the Crown are recorded during her reign. Payments to Oliver start during the reign of James I, although Hilliard remained the King's limner and was succeeded by his son Laurence (q.v.). So great was the demand for limnings, that each member of the Royal Family could choose his own artist, and Isaac was attached in 1604 to Queen Anne's household, and was appointed 'her Ma^tes painter for the Art of Lymning' for a fee of £40. Oliver was also a member of Prince Henry's household, and attended his funeral on 7 December 1612. He received payment for three portraits of Prince Henry in 1608/9, and in 1610/12 further payments are recorded, which suggest that some of his works were large paintings. This would accord with Vertue's conviction that Oliver painted oil portraits. A large-scale equestrian portrait of Henry, Prince of Wales, oil on canvas c. 1610 is now attributed to Oliver (No. 180, *The Elizabethan Image*, 1970). His usual fee for a miniature appears to have been £5. 10s. to £10, according to size; the relevant entry is as follows. 'Mr Isacke for three Pictures £32 one great Picture £34 three other Pictures £30, one greate and two little pictures £40'. From this it would appear that he received about £30 for a large painting. Oliver's name occurs in various Exchequer books kept to record money paid out for Prince Henry, for portraits he painted of him and for which he received £5. 10s. each. In 1612/13 money was owing to him for a portrait miniature of Princess Elizabeth, and in 1617 he was paid for four pictures drawn for Prince Charles. After his death his widow received £40 for three pictures he had made for the Prince. Oliver died at his house in Blackfriars, London in 1617 and was buried at St. Anne's Church, Blackfriars, 2 October 1617. In his will, made on 4 June 1617, and proved on 30 October 1617, Oliver bequeathed to his wife a third of his effects and the lease of his house in Blackfriars 'except all my drawings already finished and unfinished and lymning pictures, be they historyes, storyes, or any thing of lymning whatsoever of my owne hande worke as yet unfinished; all which I give and bequeathe to my eldest sonne Peter, yf he shall live and exercise that arte or science which he and I nowe doe. . . .' In the event of Peter's death, they were left to any of his sons who should follow his profession. The other two parts of his effects were to be sold and equally divided between his sons and daughters. He also willed, that his 'sayed sonne Peter shall have the first proffer of the sale of my pictures that shal be soulde and fyve shillings in the pound cheaper then any will give for them'. Until 1596 Oliver painted in the manner of Hilliard but showing Flemish influence. He painted with a crisp precise brush stroke with little variation of colour, and achieved the shadows by the use of dark greys and black, a method condemned by Hilliard who favoured the flat manner more akin to that of the illuminator. The backgrounds were usually blue-white. His earliest known miniature was thought to be that of an 'Unknown Man aged 59 in 1588', in the collection of H.M. the Queen of the Netherlands; but Miss Auerbach in *Nicholas Hilliard*, illustrates a portrait of an 'Unknown Girl' aged 20 in 1587, which was discovered in a drawer at Drumlanrig Castle. It is signed, 'I.O.' in monogram, in gold on a blue ground. After his visit to Italy in 1596, Oliver was obviously influenced by Italian painting; his treatment was softer and he used more varied colours. His last phase is characterised by a freer and more ambitious style, in which he incorporated landscapes and interiors of rooms, etc., as in the one of Richard Sackville, 3rd Earl of Dorset, signed 'Isaac Olliuierus fecit 1616', in the V. & A. M. Oliver succeeded in modelling the features with a

roundness unlike his predecessors, and placed his sitters against a background of pinkish-grey and reddish-pink. His drawing of hands, although slightly theatrical in pose, was better than Hilliard's; a characteristic is the way he placed them in front of the bosom. His most usual signature is I.O. in monogram, formed like a Greek Ph, surrounded with four dots. Occasionally he signed in full, and added an inscription in either Latin or French, as in the case of one in the V. & A. M. of Sir Arundell Talbot, signed on the reverse, 'adi. 13. Magio. 1596. In Venetia. Fecit m. Isacq oliuiero Francese Φ v. 14. da L 8'. One of Oliver's most important and ambitious works is that of 'The Three Brothers Browne' and their servant. This large rectangular miniature is in the collection of the Marquess of Exeter at Burghley House. It depicts the brothers, Anthony, John and William Browne, grandsons of the first Viscount Montacute, and their servant, standing in a room against panelling, on which Oliver has inscribed on the centre panel 'Figuræ conformis affectus' and on the left hand panel, 'Ano. Dom. 1598.' The miniature is signed 'I.O.' (monogram) on the carving of the panelling, and the age of each of the subjects is inscribed on the background. A fine copy of this miniature, by Catherine Howell (q.v.), executed in oil on copper and signed and dated 'Catherine Howell, pinxt / 1707', is in the collection of Earl Spencer at Althorp. The miniature of Richard Sackville in the V. & A. M., and one of an 'Unknown Young Man' (at one time said to be Sir Philip Sidney), in the collection of H.M. the Queen, are also among his finest rectangular works, and typify all the grandeur and opulence of the period. One of his most remarkable portraits in pencil and crayon is a 'Head of a boy', which was for many years mistakenly thought to represent Henry Frederick, Prince of Wales. This is in the collection of the Duke of Buccleuch, and was executed c. 1590. Of his subject pieces the most notable that have survived are those of 'The Prodigal Son', once in the collection of Charles I, and now in the collection of the Duke of Portland, and 'The Head of Christ', in the V. & A. M. The preliminary drawing for the large limning of the 'Entombment of Christ', which contained twenty-six figures, and which Peter Oliver completed after his father's death, is in the B.M. A full description of the miniature is recorded in Van Der Doort's catalogue of the collection of Charles I, edited by Oliver Miller, *Walpole Society*, Vol. XXXVII, p. 103. The same catalogue contains details of thirteen limnings by I. Oliver. Apart from executing these historical pieces, he painted many presentation portraits of the Royal Family. One of his finest miniatures is a circular portrait of a lady, said to be Frances Howard, Countess of Essex and Somerset, signed 'IO' (monogram); so exquisitely is it painted that one feels one can see the wind blowing her gossamer veil. It is in the collection of the Earl of Derby, and is at present on loan to the Manchester Art Gallery. This, together with the superb miniature of Edward Herbert, 1st Baron Cherbury, from the collection of the Earl of Powis, was loaned to the exhibition in Edinburgh, 1965. This exhibition also contained thirteen other miniatures by Oliver, including the artist's self-portrait, from the collection of H.M. the Queen, and a portrait of his wife from the collection of the Duke of Portland. The catalogue and monograph, compiled by Graham Reynolds, for the Hilliard Exhibition, held at the V. & A. M., in 1947, clarified many points regarding the work of these two artists, and gave details of eighty-five works by Oliver. According to tradition he painted oil portraits, but none are at present known to be authentic. He was working without any loss of skill until the end of his life and was certainly one of the greatest miniaturists of the

British school. For further information see *Nicholas Hilliard*, by E. Auerbach, pp. 232–254.

Oliver, John. 1616–1701

Born 1616. Glass painter and mason. Probably one of the three commissioners for rebuilding London after the Fire. Possibly identical with John Oliver who engraved mezzotint portraits and etched views after Hollar (q.v.). William Faithorne (q.v.) drew his portrait. A miniature of c. 1670 described as of the Earl of Essex by John Oliver is at the Louvre. It is painted in water-colour and the face has a brownish grey shading, suggesting a French influence. He died in 1701.

Oliver, Peter. c. 1594–1647

Born c. 1594. Eldest son of Isaac Oliver (q.v.) by his first wife, Elizabeth (d. 1599). Was a pupil of his father, and assisted him in his work. Little is known about his private life; nor do we know if he married more than once. By his will dated 12 December 1647 and proved 15 December 1648, he appointed his wife Anne sole heir and executrix to his estate and to their house at Isleworth. Oliver was evidently a sick man at the time and the will was signed only with his mark. Oliver did not, as far as is known, have any children. His father in a will made in 1616, the year before his death, left Peter 'All my drawings already finished and unfinished and lymning pictures, be they historyes, storyes or anything of lymning whatsoever of my owne hande worke as yet unfinished . . . yf he shall live and exercise that arte or science which he and I nowe doe'. Peter Oliver was responsible for making a number of replicas of miniatures of Prince Henry and Prince Charles; many of these were executed during his father's lifetime. He completed at least one of his father's religious history pieces, 'The Entombment of Christ'. Full details of this are given in Van Der Doort's catalogue of the collection of Charles I, edited by Oliver Miller, *Walpole Society*, Vol. XXXVII, p. 103. Van Der Doort noted that it was dated 1616 and says, 'Which piece was begun by the old Oliver and since by yor Ma^ts appointment finished by his sonn Peter Oliver'. The preliminary drawing for this picture is in the B.M., but the original has been lost. Many other miniatures by Peter Oliver, after Titian, Correggio, Holbein (q.v.), etc., are listed in Van Der Doort's catalogue; 14 in all as against 13 of Isaac Oliver's. One of these paintings, 'The Holy Family' after Correggio, was discovered in a country sale and later sold in London at Christie's, 15 December 1964, for 820 guineas. It was signed and dated, '1630'. The fact that Peter and his father worked so closely together has made attribution difficult, particularly of portraits painted c. 1610–1617. The majority of his original portraits were painted c. 1620, and his dated limned copies occur up to 1639. His self-portrait drawn in black lead on vellum, signed 'PO' (monogram) and inscribed 'se ipse fe', and a portrait of his wife, also drawn in black lead, signed 'P. Oliver, his wife', are in the collection of the Earl of Derby, and according to Vertue were taken from a leaf of his pocket-book. Another self-portrait is in the collection of H.M. the Queen. Peter Oliver died in 1647 and was buried at St. Anne's, Blackfriars, 22 December 1647. Vertue records that after the restoration of Charles II, the King was anxious to obtain some of the replicas of miniatures formerly in the collection of Charles I. He visited Oliver's widow and chose many of these miniatures, for which he granted her a pension of £300 a year for life. On hearing that some of these paintings had been given to the King's mistresses, she remarked that had she known the King would have given them to 'such whores, bastards or strumpets, the King should never have had them'. This got back to the King and apparently her pension was never paid again. Oliver painted, like his contemporaries, on vellum or parchment, stuck on to card, the shapes being oval, rectangular and even heart-shaped. The backgrounds vary from blue-grey, violet and brown, to those where a reddish brown curtain is placed to the rear of the sitter. His usual signature is PO, conjoined, and often surrounded with dots, and P. Oliuier / Fe, etc. His technique resembled that of his father, but some of his modelling is broader and freer. Norgate (q.v.) records that Oliver tried some of Sir Nathaniel Bacon's pink, which he thought so successful that he 'used none other to his dyeing day'. A number of his limnings are in the collection of H.M. the Queen. Examples of his work may be seen in the V. & A. M., including 'The Flight into Egypt' and 'The Rape of Lucrece', both after Titian. Other examples are in the B.M., which has small pen and sepia studies by him. The Rijks-museum, Amsterdam has several miniatures by Oliver, and many are in private collections, such as those of the Duke of Portland, the Duke of Buccleuch and Earl Beauchamp. Major R.M.O. de la Hey has a portrait of Charles II as a young man signed 'PO' (monogram), similar to one in the collection of H.M. the Queen. One of his finest works is the dyptych of Sir Kenelm and Lady Digby, after Van Dyck, dated '1632', and is at Sherborne Castle. A superb limning of 'Venus and Adonis', after Titian, signed and dated, '1631' is in the collection of the Marquess of Exeter. Seven miniatures by P. Oliver were exhibited in Edinburgh, 1965.

*Oliver, Mrs. Rachel. 19th century
Née Rachel Hutchinson. Possibly an amateur artist. I have seen a miniature painted in oil on ivory stuck onto card, and inscribed on the reverse, 'My father William Hutchinson / died in 1816 / .... by Rachel Oliver / née Hutchinson'. Part of the inscription is indecipherable. Pencilled underneath in another hand are the words, 'William Hutchinson father of Rev Hutchinson'.

O'Neal, Jeffrey Hamet, F.S.A. (fl. 1763–1772)
A native of Ireland. Went to London where he painted miniatures, landscapes and small conversation pieces. Was employed by a print-seller called Smith in Cheapside, to design 'Japan pieces'. Exhibited at the Society of Artists of which he was a fellow, 1763–1772. O'Neal worked for the porcelain factory at Worcester, and is mentioned by W. B. Honey, *English Pottery and Porcelain*, p. 187, as painting 'incorrect but very charming figure, animal and landscape subjects'. Some of his paintings on porcelain are signed with his initials.

Opie, John, R.A. 1761–1807
Celebrated portrait painter, said to have painted miniatures, but this fact has not been established. The miniatures mentioned by Jane Beetham (q.v.) of T. de W. Morgan and his wife are now thought to be by J. Barry (q.v.).

*Orchard, Miss Gertrude. (fl. 1897–1905)
Of London and Eastbourne. Exhibited at the R.A. and S.M., 1897–1905.

*Orde, Alice (Mrs. J.). (fl. 1895–1899)
Exhibited at the R.A. 1895–1899, from addresses in London, Woking and Tongham, Surrey.

Orme, Daniel. 1766–1832?
Born in Manchester, 25 August 1766; son of a merchant. Entered the R.A. Schools, 7 March 1785 aged '18 25th last Aug.'. Worked in London. Exhibited at the R.A., 1797–1801, including portraits

of his brother, William Orme, the painter, and Lord Nelson. Painted miniatures, oil portraits; engraved in stipple, etc. Was engraver to George III. Returned to Manchester in October 1814, where he continued to practise as a miniaturist, etc. Taught oil painting, drawing and etching. Died in Buxton after 1832. A water-colour by Orme is at the V. & A. M. A miniature portrait of Lady Nelson, painted in 1798, is in the National Maritime Museum. A self-portrait of the artist was Lot 22 at Sotheby's, 24 July 1967. The miniature was signed in pencil on the reverse; the inscription having been traced over in pen at a later date reads: 'D. Orme / ætat 55 / Aug 25 / 1821'. A miniature of Viscount Duncan, signed on the reverse, 'Lord Viscount / Duncan / Drawn by Mr Orme / Holles Street / London 1797', is in the collection of H.M. the Queen of the Netherlands. The miniature is loosely painted, the colouring strong. It was engraved by Orme in 1797, a copy of which was presented to Admiral de Winter.

*Orphoot, Miss M. J. C. (fl. 1907–1908)
Of North Berwick, Scotland. Exhibited at the Society of Miniaturists, 1907–1908.

Orr, J. N. J. (fl. 1843)
Of Chelsea. Exhibited at the R.A. 1843, from 12 Barossa Place, Trafalgar Square, Queen's-elms. The exhibits were a portrait of a lady, and 'the water lily'. No initial was given in the R.A. catalogues.

Osborn or **Osborne, C.** (fl. 1822–1825). See also **Osborn, R.**
Of Norwich. Exhibited at the R.A., etc., 1822–1825. It has been suggested that he may have been identical with R. Osborn (q.v.), but as both artists exhibited at the R.A., in 1822, R. Osborn from 30 Tavistock Place, London and C. Osborn from Norwich, from which place he consistently exhibited, this suggestion seems unlikely.

Osborn or **Osborne, R.** (fl. 1818–1822). See also **Osborn, C.**
Of London. Exhibited architectural drawings at the R.A., 1818–1822, and was probably identical with the Osborne, jun., who exhibited an architectural drawing at the R.A., 1793. In 1821, the R.A. catalogue no. 642 is stated to be by R. Osborn, and was a miniature of a lady. The address given was 30 Tavistock Place, from which address R. Osborn had exhibited in the previous year. Long also gives the name of C. Osborne (q.v.) and suggests that the two artists may have been identical, but this seems unlikely as in 1822 both of them exhibited at the R.A., from different addresses.

Ott, A. (fl. 1790)
Exhibited at the R.A. 1790, from a London address. Said to have been miniature painter to the Duke of Orleans. Schidlof mentions two other artists of this name, F. Ott and J. Ott, both of whom worked on the Continent.

*Overton, J. (fl. 1822). See **Overton, T.**
Schidlof mentions seeing a miniature of Mrs. Franklin, signed and dated 'J Overton P. 1822', which was well drawn and painted in pleasant colours. This may have been by T. Overton (q.v.).

Overton, Thomas. (fl. 1818–1838). See **Overton, J.**
Of London. Exhibited at the R.A. and N.W.C.S., etc., 1818–1838. Painted portraits of naval and military officers. May have been identical with J. Overton (q.v.) referred to by Schidlof. His address in 1838 was 50 George Street, Portman Square.

*Owen, Miss Alice H. (fl. 1910)
Of London. Exhibited at the R.A. 1910, from 206 Castellain Mansions, Maida Vale.

P

*P., B.
A miniature signed 'B.P. fecit' was noted by Mr. A. J. B. Kiddell.

P., C. (fl. 1795)
A miniature of a man signed, 'CP/1795' was Lot 71 at the sale at Christie's, 12 July 1927. The painting of the background was reminiscent of the work of Shelley (q.v.), but the face was shaded in blue. The work was not of any outstanding merit.

P., G. 18th century
Two miniatures by the above artist are in the collection of Earl Spencer. One is of Lady Sunderland wearing a yellow dress and pink wrap, and is signed on a grey background on the spectator's left, with cursive initials 'GP'; the other is a portrait of a child in a pink dress (after an unsigned miniature also at Althorp) and is signed 'GP' in Roman capitals. The work is reminiscent of that of B. Lens (q.v.).

P., I. (fl. 1623). See also **I., P.**
Long recorded a miniature of a man dated '1623' and signed with a 'P' in the form of a monogram, which looks like 'IP' or 'PI'.

P., I. (fl. 1790)
A miniature signed 'I.P. 1790', was sold at Sotheby's, 1 May 1958.

P., N.A. (fl. c. 1800–1803)
A miniature of a man in a blue coat c. 1800–1803, with a minute trellis background in grey, signed in white, 'N.A.P.', was seen by Long. It showed French influence; there were many distinct dark lines in the hair. It was of average ability. Another miniature of a boy, similarly signed, was in the E. Salaman collection.

*P., P. (fl. c. 1678)
A miniature of a man, aged 19 in 1678, painted in oil on parchment was sold at Sotheby's, 21 February 1966. Two other miniatures signed 'P.P.' were exhibited at the Exhibition of Miniatures in Oils, at The Fine Art Society, 1928.

P., S. (fl. 1756)
A miniature of a lady c. 1756, painted in the manner of P. P. Lens (q.v.) and G. Spencer (q.v.) and signed 'SP' in irregular Roman capitals, was recorded by Long.

P., S. (fl. 1792–1800). See also **Polack, Solomon**
Lot 361 at the Hawkins Sale at Christie's, 30 March 1928, was a small miniature c. 1798–1800. The colouring on the face was hot and the features rather cramped; it was signed 'S.P.' in Roman capitals and may have been by Solomon Polack (q.v.). Long also noted seeing a miniature signed in a similar way, c. 1792.

P., W. (fl. 1674–1676). See also **Powlet, W.**
Miniatures signed 'WP / 1676' and 'WP', both in cursive script, the former of Charles II and the latter of an unknown man, formerly called James II,

are in the Jones Collection at the V. & A. M. They are large rectangular miniatures and similar in style to other miniatures by this unidentified artist. The Rijksmuseum, Amsterdam has a 'Madonna Praying' probably after Guido Reni and dated '(16)74', and a portrait of an old woman after Rembrandt, both signed with a cursive monogram 'WP'. The Duke of Buccleuch has a miniature said to represent 'Moll' Davis signed with a monogram 'WP' (not cursive). Most of these miniatures have a brownish shading on the flesh parts. It has been suggested that these miniatures are the work of W. Plowman, but Mr. Oliver Millar, during research in the Royal Archives, has discovered the existence of a limner called William Powlet (q.v.), who may possibly be the artist concerned.

P., W. (fl. c. 1789)

A good miniature of a lady c. 1789 signed 'W.P.' in white, was seen by Long. The hair was greenish in colour. A miniature on enamel of George Washington (1732–1799) signed 'WP', is in the collection of the Duke of Buccleuch. This latter miniature which was exhibited in Edinburgh in 1965, was probably inspired by the original painting by Gilbert Stuart.

Pack, Faithful Christopher. 1759–1840

Born in Norwich, 1759; son of a Quaker merchant whose family may have been connected with the Packs of Prestwold, Leicestershire. Started in his father's business, but showed artistic talent and having gained a local reputation, went to London in 1781, where he received encouragement from J. H. Mortimer. Studied for about a year under Reynolds, some of whose paintings he copied. Worked in Liverpool, 1783–1787; exhibited at the Society for Promoting Painting and Design there in 1784, and at the R.A. and B.I., 1786–1840. In 1787 he returned to London and joined a club of artistic friends among whom were Thomas Herne, Edridge (q.v.), Milbourne (q.v.), Marchi, Michael Bryan, etc. Went to Ireland in c. 1789; practised in Dublin and perhaps at Cork. Met Gilbert Stuart in Dublin in 1789, when attending an artists' dinner on St. Luke's Day. Exhibited in Dublin, 1790–1821. In c. 1795 Pack returned to England; was in Ipswich in September 1795, and spent some years in Bath, where he taught drawing and painting, and had an address at 19 Green Park Street, Bath. In 1802 he returned to Dublin where he lectured on drawing and painting. In 1807 he applied to the Dublin Society for a grant. He was President of the Society of Artists in 1812, and Vice-President of the R.H.S., in 1814. His offer to lecture in the theatre of the Dublin Society was declined in 1820. On 21 March 1821 a sale of his pictures including a number of his own works was held at his residence, 33 Dawson Street, after which he returned once more to London where he remained until his death. He painted portraits in oil and pastel, landscapes in oil and water-colour, and executed a few miniatures. Latterly he also practised as a chiropodist. He exhibited a self-portrait at the R.A., in 1786. His wife died in August 1840, and he died at 20 Sandwich Street, Gray's Inn Lane on 25/26 October 1840, aged 81.

Paert. (fl. c. 1807–1811)

A miniature of a man, probably painted in England c. 1807–1811 and signed 'Paert', was seen by Long. It was of no great merit.

*Page, Miss Sarah. (fl. 1892–1914)

Exhibited at the R.A. 1892–1914, from addresses in Neuilly-sur-Seine, France, and London.

*Paget, Mrs. Henrietta. (fl. 1905–1907)

Of London. Exhibited at the R.A. 1905–1907, from 76 Park Hill Road, Hampstead. Her sitters included Mrs. Hugh Fairfax Cholmeley and her son, Francis.

Paillou, Peter, senior. (fl. 1744–1780/84)

There were undoubtedly two artists of this name, probably father and son. Recent research on the part of Miss A. Lysaght, has revealed the fact that the above artist was noted for his paintings of birds and animals, and that he worked for Thomas Pennant (1726–1798) at Downing, Flintshire, and for Taylor White (1701–1772) of Wallingwells, Nottinghamshire. It is at present impossible to be certain that Paillou senior ever painted miniatures, and it seems more than likely that all miniatures signed 'P. Paillou' are the work of P. Paillou junior (q.v.), who was born c. 1757. Paillou senior exhibited at the Free Society of Artists in 1763 from Hassels Row, Tottenham Court Road, and was probably the artist who exhibited a 'Horned Owl (from Peru) in Feathers' at the Society of Artists in 1778. Paillou would have no doubt learned the art of 'feather painting' from a famous feather book produced in 1618 by Dionisio Minaggio of Milan, a copy of which was in Taylor White's collection. Works by several artists of animals and birds from the Pennant collection were acquired by the McGill University Library, Montreal c. 1926, including some of the earliest known paintings by Paillou. They are dated 1744 and represent a Bird of Paradise and an Owl. In c. 1760–1761 Paillou began to work for Pennant who in his Literary Life of 1793; wrote 'About 1761 I began my British Zoology, which when completed, consisted of CXXXII plates on imperial paper. . . . The painter was Mr. Peter Pallou (sic) an excellent artist, but too fond of giving gaudy colours to his subjects. He painted, for my hall at Downing, several pictures of birds and animals, attended by suitable landscapes . . . all have their merit, but occasion me to lament his conviviality, which affected his circumstances and abridged his days'. Paillou senior was still working for Pennant in c. 1780, and executed the frontispiece to Arctic Zoology, 1784–1787. His date of death must have been between 1780–1784, in which latter year the above work was published.

Paillou, Peter, junior. c. 1757. d. after 1831

Born c. 1757. Of London, and Scotland (c. 1820). Presumably the son of Peter Paillou senior (q.v.), who painted pictures of birds. Entered the R.A. Schools, 27 February 1784, aged '27, 1 Decr.', making his year of birth c. 1757. It must have been his father who exhibited at the Free Society of Artists in 1763, as he would have been only 6 years old at the time. Either artist could have exhibited at the Society of Artists in 1778 from Paradise Row, Islington, 'A Horned Owl (from Peru) in Feathers', although it seems likely that this was the work of Paillou senior. It was P. Paillou junior who exhibited at the R.A., 1786–1800. His addresses were 9 White Lion Row (1786–1787), 66 Harley Street (1788–1793), and 1 Charlotte Street, Portland Place (1794–1800). He was working in Glasgow in 1820 from 2 Queen Street. A characteristic of the above artist's work appears to be the way he painted his sitters against a sunset background; this is totally different from the few miniatures also signed P. Paillou, which are painted with a rather green colouring. Some have book-case or foliage backgrounds, as in the case of the fine portrait of William Rowley, M.D. (1742–1806), who practised as a 'man-midwife'. It is signed and dated 'P. Paillou, 1789' and is at the V. & A. M. Paillou drew a composite portrait of Mary Queen of Scots for the

historian Chalmers, which was engraved. This was probably the miniature exhibited at the R.A., in 1793. I have seen many miniatures by Paillou, all of which have been well modelled; the flesh colours are usually smoothly painted and not stippled. Three miniatures by Paillou were loaned to the exhibition in Edinburgh in 1965, including the one of William Rowley, M.D. from the V. & A. M.; Adam Crookes of Leven, signed and dated 'P. Paillou 1805' from the National Galleries of Scotland; and an unknown man, signed and dated 'P. Paillou 1805' from my collection. A miniature signed and dated '1831' by Paillou was sold at Sotheby's in 1962. Examples of his work are also in many private collections and in the Nationalmuseum, Stockholm. Schidlof mentions a miniature of a young lady signed 'Paillou'. A mezzotint of Robert Scott of Glasgow, by Paillou, was published in 1818, a print of which is in the B.M.

*Pairman, John. 19th century

A miniature of the Rev. John Brown (1754–1832) of Whitburn, by this artist is in the Scottish National Portrait Gallery. There is an orange/red shading on the face.

*Palmer, Mrs. Eleanor, A.R.M.S. (fl. 1905–1914)

Exhibited at the R.A. and S.M., 1905–1914, from Groley Place, Altrincham, Cheshire. Her sitters included the Duchess of Westminster and the artist's daughter.

*Palmer, Mrs. Emmeline A. (fl. 1900–1911)

Exhibited at the R.A. 1900–1911, from addresses in Watford and Bushey, Herts.

Palmer, Sir James. 1584–1657

Was born in 1584. Third son of Sir Thomas Palmer of Wingham, Kent and his wife née Margaret Pooley. Collector and amateur artist, Palmer was a close friend of Charles I and gave him constant help in forming the Royal Collection. Was Gentleman of the Bedchamber to James I in 1622 and subsequently Gentleman Usher of the Privy Chamber to Charles I, and in 1645 was made Chancellor of the Order of the Garter. Was also one of the Governors of the Royal Tapestry Works at Mortlake. He is recorded as a limner in Van Der Doort's catalogue of Charles I's collection; the miniature was 'Tarquin and Lucretia' which according to catalogue entry no. 69, was 'Don by Sr James Paumer after Titian, given to yor Maty'; unfortunately this miniature has disappeared. In 1949 Mr. Graham Reynolds published in The Burlington Magazine, Vol. 91, some fresh evidence to support the presumption that Palmer was a miniaturist and gives details of five miniatures of a hitherto unrecognised hand and signed 'P', an inscription which had previously been supposed to be an unsuccessful attempt to forge the signature of I. Oliver (q.v.). It is now established that miniatures signed in this way are by the same hand, and in all probability are by Sir James Palmer. The known examples are as follows: (1) James I wearing the ribbon of the Garter, background of red curtain, signed at left and dated (1) 623 above the signature; this was Lot 61 at Sotheby's, 1 May 1958 (formerly in the collection of W. V. Paterson, Esq.). (2) An unknown man signed on the right and dated across the background at the left '1623', the property of Lord Glenconner. (3) A man said to be Sir Robert Carr, Earl of Somerset, signed at the right, and dated at left '1619', against a background of red curtains, in the Fitzwilliam Museum, Cambridge. Lieut. Col. P. D. S. Palmer of Dorney Court, has a frame containing miniatures of five members of the family, including one of Elizabeth,

Lady Garrard, wife of Sir William Garrard (Palmer's mother-in-law); this is dated '1614' across the right-hand background, and is clearly by the same hand as the ones mentioned earlier. One of Martha, Lady Palmer (died 1617), daughter and heiress of Sir William Garrard, and wife of Sir James Palmer, although not signed, is considered by Reynolds to be another work by this artist and, unless strong evidence in favour of another artist is forthcoming, they are for the present ascribed to Palmer. He died in 1657. Palmer's son, Roger, was the husband of the notorious Countess of Castlemaine. A miniature of George Villiers, Duke of Buckingham signed in monogram and dated '1627' was Lot 79 at Sotheby's, 1 March 1965; the monogram on this miniature is an O traversed by an I and encircled by four dots: ·ϕ·

Palmer, Miss Mary (later **Marchioness of Thomond**). d. 1820

Eldest daughter of John Palmer of Torrington and his wife Mary, sister of Sir Joshua Reynolds, P.R.A. Mary kept house for her uncle who left her his fortune on his death. Her youngest sister, Theophila (Offy), was his favourite niece, and stayed with him on and off, until her marriage to Robert Lovell Gwatkin in 1781. Long and Schidlof have confused the two sisters, and thought they were one and the same. Mary was the amateur painter who copied many of Reynolds' portraits, and painted miniatures. After the death of Sir Joshua Reynolds in 1792, she married the 5th Earl of Inchiquin on 21 July in the same year, and her husband was created 1st Marquess of Thomond in 1800. He died, 10 February 1808 and Mary died at Baylis, Bucks., on 7 September 1820. A miniature by her of Reynolds' self-portrait, painted c. 1790 is illustrated by O'Brien, Pl. 41, Fig. 3. An attractive portrait of Mary Palmer by Reynolds, painted in 1785, is reproduced, Pl. XIIb, in *Sir Joshua Reynolds*, by Derek Hudson, 1958.

*Palmer, Miss Maude C. (fl. 1903–1914)

Exhibited at the R.A. 1903–1914, from addresses in Gorey, Jersey and Bexhill-on-Sea. Executed miniatures and subjects in oil.

Palmer, William. 1763–1790

Born in Limerick, 18 November 1763; son of a linen draper. Entered the Dublin Society Schools where he obtained a medal in 1781. Came to London and entered the R.A. Schools, 10 October 1783, aged 19. Was awarded premiums by the Society of Arts in 1784 and 1785. Exhibited at the R.A., 1784–1788. He returned to Limerick c. 1788 where he practised as a portrait painter in oil and crayon and executed miniatures. Some of his works were engraved. He wrote some poems, few of which were published. Suffered from consumption and died in Bruff, 26 July 1790.

Pane, J. (fl. 1797)

Exhibited at the R.A., 1797. The exhibit was 'portrait of an artist'.

*Pannell, Miss Lillie. (fl. 1909–1914)

Of London. Exhibited at the R.A. 1909–1914, from Tooting Common.

*Parberry, Mrs. c. 1724–1746

Was born c. 1724; daughter of Ishmael Parberry of Salisbury Court (died 1746). Recorded by Vertue, *Walpole Society*, Vol. XXII, p. 120, 'Dec 174¾ . . . A young woman who makes great progress in the Art of limning and water-col painting. She is the daughter of Mr Parberry, chaser in gold and works, an ingenious artist', and on p. 134, 'Mr Ishmael Parberry of Salisbury Court, deceased in Sept 1746

and also his daughter who was a curious limner, died about a fortnight before him . . . his daughter's works, drawings & some limnings that showed she had a genius for art but taken away in her prime, being about 22 years of age'.

Pardon, James. (fl. 1811–1829)

Of London, Canterbury (1814–1825) and Yoxford, Suffolk (1828–1829). Exhibited at the R.A., etc., 1811–1829. Painted landscapes and miniatures. Schidlof says he also worked in Oxford, but this appears to be an error for Yoxford. His sitters included Sir Charles Blois, Bart., and J. Bird, Esq., author.

Parez, Lewis. (fl. 1821–1831)

Of London. Exhibited at the R.A., etc. 1821–1831, from 14 Finsbury Place. His sitters included J. H. Wiffen, author of *Julia Alpinula*, and J. Drake, Esq.

*Parguez, Mlle. Marguerite. (fl. 1908)

Of London. Exhibited at the Society of Miniaturists, 1908.

*Paris, Miss Louisa Catherine. (fl. 1833)

I have seen a miniature by the above artist, signed on the reverse 'Miss Flipwell / by / Louisa Catherine Paris / from Mrs Green's / April . 1833'. The artist appears to be hitherto unrecorded, and I have been unable to find out any further information. She was possibly a pupil of Mrs. James Green (q.v.).

*Park, Charles R. (fl. 1897)

Exhibited at the R.A. 1897, from Haverstock Hill, London.

*Park, J. Chalmers. (fl. 1909–1910)

Of Leeds. Exhibited at the Society of Miniaturists, 1909–1910.

Park, Miss R. (fl. 1834)

Of Greenwich. Exhibited at the R.A., 1834.

Parker, (John?). (fl. c. 1765)

A miniature of a man c. 1765 inscribed on the reverse 'Parker' is at the V. & A. M. If this name is the signature it may be by John Parker who painted portraits and figure subjects, and who lived in Rome for some years. He was awarded premiums by the Society of Arts, 1762–1763 having returned to England c. 1762. He died in Paddington c. 1765.

*Parker, Miss Elizabeth R. (fl. 1907)

Exhibited at the R.A. 1907, from 79 West Regent Street, Glasgow.

*Parker, Miss Ethel N. (I). (fl. 1802–1807)

Schidlof records the above artist as working in London as a miniaturist from 1802–1807. I have not been able to verify this statement, and in view of the fact that a Miss Ethel N. Parker (II) (q.v.) exhibited at the R.A., 1902–1905, it is possible that the two artists were identical and Schidlof's dates printed in error.

*Parker, Miss Ethel N. (II). (fl. 1902–1905)

Of London. Exhibited at the R.A. 1902–1905, from 10 Jubilee Place, Chelsea.

*Parker, Mrs. Neta. (fl. 1910)

Exhibited at the R.A. 1910, from Netherton, Torquay.

*Parker, Mrs. Susanna. See Horenbout, Miss Susanna

Parkhill, Mary. (fl. c. 1810)

Worked c. 1810; may have been an amateur artist.

*Parkinson, Mrs. Florence. (fl. 1893–1914)

Of London. Exhibited at the R.A. 1893–1914, from various London addresses. Executed miniatures and statuettes in bronze.

Parnall or **Parnell, J.** or **G.** 19th century. See also **Parnell, Miss G.**

The R.A. catalogues for 1845 give J. Parnall in the index and G. Parnell in the catalogue entry. The exhibit was of his mother. Miss G. Parnell (q.v.) exhibited a portrait of Gervas Parnell, Esq., in 1846, who may possibly be the artist referred to in 1845.

Parnell, Miss G. (fl. 1846–1857). See also **Parnall, J.**

Worked in London and Hastings (1852). Exhibited at the R.A. and S.B.A., 1846–1857, including a portrait of Gervas Parnell, Esq., in 1846, who may have been her father, or a relative.

*Parr, Miss Agnes R. (fl. 1885–1910)

Of London and Gravesend, Greenhithe and Wallington. Exhibited at the R.A., N.W.C.S. and S.M., 1885–1910.

*Parris, Edmund Thomas. 1793–1873

Born 3 June 1793 in the Parish of St. Mary-le-bone, London; son of Edward and Grace Parris. Showed an early aptitude for art, and was placed with Messrs. Ray & Montague, the jewellers, to learn enamel painting and metal chasing. Studied mechanics in his leisure time which subsequently proved useful to him. Said to have entered the R.A. schools in 1816, but the list of entrants, published in Vol. XXXVIII of the *Walpole Society*, does not record his name. Exhibited at the R.A., B.I., etc., 1816–1874 (the last exhibit being posthumous). Is best known as a fashionable portrait painter, and for historical subjects, panoramas, designs for windows, screens, etc. According to a note by Long, he painted some miniatures. Parris invented an ingenious device for gaining access to the cupola in St. Paul's Cathedral when Sir James Thornhill's paintings were restored, and for which he obtained the commission. His sitters included Queen Victoria and Queen Adelaide, who appointed him her historical painter in 1832. He prepared a model for a piece of tapestry, forty feet long, for the Paris Exhibition of 1867. Parris had a drawing school for a time at his house in Grafton Street. He invented a medium which produced a dull fresco-like surface, which is known as 'Parris's Medium'. His father-in-law was John Field (probably the silhouettist). He died at 24 Francis Street, Bedford Square, on 27 November 1873.

*Parrott, Charles M. (fl. 1906–1909)

Exhibited at the R.A. 1906–1909, from addresses in Wolverhampton and Dulwich.

Parrott, G. (fl. 1844)

Of London. Exhibited at the R.A. 1844, from 7 Bennet Street, St. James's. The exhibit was of his youngest sister. Miss G. Parnell (q.v.) exhibited from the same address in 1846.

Parry, H. (David Henry?). (fl. 1826)

Working in 1826 at 23 Newman Street, London. May have been David Henry Parry (1793–1826), a Manchester portrait painter, who died in London in 1826. David Henry Parry was the second son of Joseph Parry (1744–1826), a Liverpool artist who moved to Manchester, where his second son was born, 7 June 1793. He was taught art by his father and encouraged by success, moved to London in May 1826. He had already obtained several commissions when he died suddenly on 15 September 1826. Married Elizabeth Smallwood, who with their three sons, survived him. Brother of James Parry (q.v.).

Parry, J. (Joseph?). (fl. 1802–1803)

Of London. Exhibited at the R.A., 1802–1803. Identified by Graves as the gem engraver who exhibited at the R.A., 1830–1841, but may possibly have been identical with Joseph Parry (1744–1826) who worked in Manchester from 1790, and was a member of the Liverpool Academy, 1810–1812; no miniatures by him are known. Father of David Henry Parry (q.v. under H. Parry) and James Parry (q.v.).

Parry, James. 1805?–c. 1871

Schidlof records his date of birth as 1805? Of Manchester; son of Joseph Parry (1744–1826) and brother of D. H. Parry. Worked in Manchester. Exhibited at the Royal Manchester Institution, 1827–1856. Painted landscapes, portraits, figure subjects and miniatures, as well as executing engravings, many from his own works, including plates in Corry's *History of Lancashire, 1825, View of Manchester from Strawberry Hill*, etc. He also engraved works by his brother and other artists. Lived at 12 Mulberry Street, Manchester in 1828 and subsequently at 5 Grove Street, Gartside, Manchester. A self-portrait in oil is in the Museum at Salford. He died c. 1871.

Pars, William, A.R.A. 1742–1782

Son of a chaser. Born in London, 28 February 1742. Studied at the Duke of Richmond's Gallery and the St. Martin's Lane School. Entered the R.A. schools, 5 December 1769. Exhibited at the Society of Artists and the Free Society of Artists, 1760–1764, and at the R.A., 1769–1776. Was a member of the Society of Artists in 1763. In 1764 he was awarded a medal by the Society of Arts. Accompanied Dr. Chandler and Mr. Revett to Greece, 1764–1766. Later went with Lord Palmerston to the Continent; visited Italy, Switzerland and the Tyrol. In 1775 he was given a pension of £60 from the Dilettanti Society to study art in Rome; he left for Rome in October of that year, accompanied by Mrs. Smart (first wife of John Smart (q.v.)), who eloped with him, and ultimately died in Rome. Pars lost all his possessions between Calais and Paris. He is best known for his topographical drawings of Irish and continental scenes and oil portraits, but painted miniatures during the early part of his career. He died in Rome in 1782. Some of his works were engraved by P. Sandby, W. Woollett and W. Byrne.

Parsey, Arthur. (fl. 1829–1837)

Of London. Exhibited at the R.A., 1829–1837. Was a 'Professor of Miniature Painting and Perspective' in the Burlington Arcade. In 1831, published *The Art of Miniature Painting on Ivory*, in which he claims to have been the first artist to advocate the use of the scraper, and explains the method. Schidlof mentions a miniature of a lady signed 'Parsey'.

*Parsons, John W. b. 1859

Born July 1859. Exhibited at the R.A. 1894–1906, from addresses in Netherbury and Pulborough. Studied in Edinburgh and Paris. Was a member of the R.S.B.A.

*Parsons-Norman, Miss J. Pattie. (fl. 1900)

Of Thorpe, Norwich. Exhibited at the Society of Miniaturists, 1900.

Partridge, Miss Charlotte. (fl. 1847–1853)

Of London; sister of Miss Ellen Partridge (q.v.) with whom she lived. Exhibited at the R.A., 1847–1853. Some of her portraits may have been larger than miniatures. All her exhibits were from 2 York Place, Portman Square.

Partridge, Miss Ellen. (fl. 1844–1893)

Of London; sister of Miss Charlotte Partridge (q.v.) with whom she lived. Exhibited at the R.A., B.I., etc., 1844–1893. Belonged to the Society of Lady Artists.

*Pasquier, junior. (fl. 1810–1835)

Probably the son of Pierre Pasquier (q.v.). Worked in France, 1810–1835. His work is often confused with that of the older artist. May have been the artist of this name who exhibited at the Salon, 1822–1833 (no christian name given). A miniature by him, formerly in my collection, of an officer, was signed 'Pasquier' along the edge of the ivory. It is not certain that he worked in England.

Pasquier, Pierre. 1731–1806

Born in Villefranche, Rhône in 1731. Became an agréé of the Académie Royale, 1768 and a member in 1769. Visited England, 1771–1772; exhibited enamels at the R.A., 1772; and at the Paris Salon, 1769–1783. His address in Paris was 45 Rue St. André. Painted miniatures on enamel and on ivory, and was said to have also painted portraits in oil and pastel. Had lodgings in the Louvre in 1774. Was in Flanders and Holland, 1780–1781. Died in Paris, 14 November 1806. Pasquier was an excellent artist who painted with strong colours and a large *pointilliste* technique. An example of his work is at the V. & A. M. An enamel of Louis XVI and his family was at the Winter Palace in Petrograd.

Passmore. (fl. 1810–1817)

Painted oil miniatures in the manner of Leakey (q.v.) and copied pictures. Went to London, copied paintings at the B.I., in the autumn of 1810. Farington in his Diary of 29 May 1817 records a visit from the Rev. Goyer Patch of Exeter, who spoke of Passmore, who, he said, had turned out 'unprincipled & profligate. Forty pounds was subscribed for Him when He came to London where He now is. Bone has noticed Him, & He is reported to be employed in copying pictures'. A Richard Passmore of Gutter Lane married on 22 October 1777, and may have been related to him.

Pastorini, F. E. (fl. 1812–1833). See also Pastorini, T. E.

Of London. Exhibited at the R.A., and O.W.C.S., 1812–1833. Was a relative of Benedetto Pastorini (born 1746), an Italian artist who came to England. This artist is possibly identical with T. E. Pastorini (q.v.).

Pastorini, Joseph. c. 1775–1839

Born c. 1775. Worked in London. Entered the R.A. Schools, 1 April 1795, aged 20. Exhibited at the R.A., 1812–1834. Was a relative of Benedetto Pastorini and F. E. Pastorini (q.v.), Italian artists who came to England. Painted in water-colour on paper or card as well as on ivory. A miniature on card of Mr. T. B. Vacher, signed on the reverse 'Painted by J^h Pastorini / No 41 Rathbone Place / Novr 22, 1827', is at the V. & A. M. Some of his work was coarse, but his profile miniatures painted in water-colour, partly sketched in pencil, are delicately executed. Long mentions a miniature which recalled the work of J. Barry (q.v.). He died in London, 3 August 1839. A miniature of William Frederick, Duke of Gloucester, signed 'Pastorini', is at Windsor Castle.

Pastorini, T. E. See also Pastorini, F. E.

The R.A. catalogues for 1817 give exhibit no. 805 as being by T. E. Pastorini, both in the index and catalogue entry. This may have been a mistake for F. E. Pastorini (q.v.). The exhibits were of Miss Davis, Miss A. Tomkins and J. Cornell, Esq. The address given was 50 Great Titchfield Street, from which address F. E. Pastorini exhibited. *The Annals of the Fine Arts*, Vol. I and II, also record T. E. Pastorini from the same address.

Pastorini, W. V., junior. (fl. 1825–1826)

Of London. Exhibited at the R.A. 1825–1826, from 21 Greek Street, Soho Square. Was undoubtedly related to the other artists of this name.

*Paterson, Miss J. J. (fl. 1910)

Exhibited at the R.A. 1910, from Bradstones, West Derby, Liverpool.

Paterson, Patrick. (fl. 1825)

Working in 1825 at Cruden's Court, Broad Street, Aberdeen.

Paton, David. (fl. 1660–1695)

Was one of the few Scottish miniature painters of the seventeenth century. He was a good draughtsman who, as far as is known, practised only in Scotland. Paton painted several portraits in oil, but is best known for his highly finished miniatures in plumbago, some of which were copied from pictures. He accompanied the Hon. William Tollemache, youngest son of the Duchess of Lauderdale, on the Grand Tour. MSS relating to this are at Ham House. Some of his miniatures were engraved, a well known one being that of Sir James Dalrymple, which was engraved by a fellow artist, R. White (q.v.). A fine example of his work is that of Viscount Dundee, which is at the S.N.P.G., and a rectangular miniature of Charles II, also plumbago, inscribed 'D. Paton fecit 1669 ~ / S. Couper invent 1665'. A receipt has been preserved at Oxenfoord Castle, Midlothian in which 'David Paton, limner, of Edinburgh, acknowledges having received from David McGill, Professor of Philosophy, in the name of Robert, Viscount Oxford, £186.8s. as interest on £780 Scots money from 20 May, 1690 to 20 May, 1695 as payment for a miniature portrait of the Prince of Wales set in silver and for two silver frames for other pictures.'. The document is dated 5 June 1695. Examples of his work are at Ham House, and in private collections. A miniature said to be of Richard Maitland, 4th Earl of Lauderdale, signed on the reverse, 'D. Paton fe.Romæ / 1674', is in the V. & A. M.

Patten, Miss. (fl. 1826–1836)

Of London. Exhibited at the R.A., 1826–1836. She exhibited consistently from 12 Goulden Terrace, Islington, except for 1836, when her address was 19 Richard Street, Islington.

Patten, C. (fl. 1825–1827)

Of London. Exhibited at the R.A., 1825–1827. Probably the son of W. Patten, senior (q.v.). Had the same address as George Patten (q.v.), W. Patten and W. Patten, junior (q.v.), i.e. 34 Ludgate Hill.

Patten, E. (fl. 1794–1817)

Of London. Exhibited at the R.A., 1794–1808. Was working in 1817 at 135 Strand.

Patten, George, A.R.A. 1801–1865

Born 29 June 1801; son and pupil of W. Patten (q.v.). Entered the R.A. Schools, 9 August 1816, and in the same year was awarded a silver palette by the Society of Arts. Exhibited at the R.A. and B.I., 1819–1864. Practised as a miniaturist up to 1830, after which date he also painted life-size oil portraits and some subject pictures. Was elected A.R.A., in 1837, and in the same year went to Italy. Was in Germany in 1840 where he painted a portrait of Prince Albert who appointed him his Portrait Painter in Ordinary. Lived for some time at Ross,

Herefordshire, but evidently moved nearer London and died at Hill House, Winchmore Hill, 11 March 1865. He was undoubtedly related to G. B. Patten, who exhibited at the B.I. in 1836 from his address, 59 Berners Street. The V. & A. M. has two miniatures by him and a miniature by Patten of W. Martin, as well as an oil portrait of William Hone, are at the N.P.G.

Patten, William. (fl. 1791–1817)
Of London; father of George Patten (q.v.), C. Patten (q.v.) and W. Patten, junior (q.v.). Exhibited at the R.A., 1791–1806. Was working up to 1817 and possibly died c. 1826, not on 22 August 1843, as previously recorded. This date probably related to W. Patten, junior, who is consistently styled 'Jun' in the indexes of the R.A. catalogues up to, and including, 1826. The family address for many years was 34 Ludgate Hill.

Patten, William, junior. d. 1843?
Of London; son of W. Patten (q.v.), and brother of G. Patten (q.v.) and C. Patten (q.v.), who all shared the same address, 34 Ludgate Hill, for some years. From 1830 onwards, W. Patten, junior, lived at 23 Howland Street, Fitzroy Square. Said to have studied at the R.A. Schools, but his name is not recorded in the list of entrants published in Vol. XXXVIII of the *Walpole Society*. Exhibited at the R.A., and B.I., 1810–1844. Attended the funeral of Sir Thomas Lawrence (q.v.) in 1830. Was probably the W. Patten who died on 22 August 1843, as in 1844 'the late W. Patten' is recorded in the R.A. index and catalogue, and in the same year W. Patten, junior, is recorded in the B.I. as 'the late'. Painted miniatures, large portraits and subject pictures. He exhibited a self-portrait at the R.A. in 1811. His sitters included the Earl of Huntingdon, Sir Edward Banks and the Rev. Robert Morrison, D.D., F.R.S., M.R.A.S. W. V. Patten (q.v.) was presumably his son as both exhibited from 23 Howland Street.

Patten, William Vandyke. (fl. 1844–1871)
Of London; probably a son of W. Patten, junior (q.v.) from whose address he exhibited at the R.A., etc., 1844–1871. Some of his miniatures were imitations of cameos in the style of De Gault. Long saw a miniature copy in water-colour, of a portrait by Van Dyck, signed in red 'W.V. Patten del 1854'.

*Patterson, Miss Ida M. F. (fl. 1900–1908)
Of London. Exhibited at the Society of Miniaturists, 1900–1908.

*Patterson, Miss Kate M. (fl. 1894–1905)
Exhibited at the R.A. and S.M., 1894–1905 from 8 Holland Place Chambers, Church Street, Kensington. Painted miniatures and flowers in oil.

*Pattinson, Miss Annie. (fl. 1899–1905)
Of London. Exhibited at the R.A. 1899–1905, from 49 Buckland Crescent, Hampstead. She exhibited a self-portrait in 1904.

*Pattison, Miss E. (fl. 1914). See also **Pattison, Mrs. Eunice**
Exhibited at the R.A., 1914, from Gumley Rectory, Market Harborough. Possibly identical with Mrs. Eunice Pattison (q.v.) who exhibited at the R.A., 1900–1903. Her sitter in 1914 was Ursula, daughter of Lady Churchill.

*Pattison, Mrs. Eunice. (fl. 1900–1903). See **Pattison, Miss E.**
Of Billesdon, Leicester and Market Harborough. Exhibited at the R.A., 1900–1903. Possibly identical with Miss E. Pattison (q.v.) who exhibited at the R.A. 1914, from Market Harborough.

*Patton, Miss K. (fl. 1900)
Of 24 Hatch Street, Dublin. Exhibited at the Society of Miniaturists, 1900.

*Pauncefote, Miss Clara. (fl. 1897–1901)
Of Folkstone and London. Exhibited at the R.A., R.M.S., and S.M., 1897–1901.

Paye, C. W. (fl. 1806–1808)
Of London. Exhibited at the R.A., 1806–1808. Probably the son of R. M. Paye (q.v.) and brother of Miss E. A. Paye (q.v.).

Paye, Miss Eliza Ann(e). See **Briane, Mrs. Elizabeth Ann(e)** and **Braine, Mrs.**

Paye, Richard Morton. c. 1750–1821?
Said to have been born in Botley, Kent c. 1750. Was employed in London as a chaser. Took up art. Exhibited at the R.A. 1773–1802, and at the Society of Artists and the Free Society of Artists, 1783–1791; also at the Society for Promoting Painting and Design in Liverpool, 1787. Painted miniatures, oil portraits, candle-light subjects, portraits, genre subjects, etc., also executed wax models (and possibly wax portraits), and engravings. Was for a time patronised by Dr. Wolcot ('Peter Pindar'). Many of his portraits and pictures were engraved. A picture by him has been mistaken for a Velasquez and another for a work by Wright of Derby. He married a Miss Hayward. His right hand became paralysed after an attack of rheumatic fever, and he was obliged to paint with his left. Said to have died in 1821. His son, R. M. Paye, junior, was an engraver, and he was probably the father of C. W. Paye (q.v.) and Miss E. A. Paye (q.v.). Due to the fact that Paye rarely signed, his works are little known; he used bright colours and drew well. The V. & A. M. contains a miniature which is described as 'a girl holding a hen', signed on the reverse, 'R. M. Paye fecit'. This is presumably the miniature which was formerly in the Wellesley collection, sold at Sotheby's in June 1920, and which was called 'a girl with her favourite turkey'. This is an attractive miniature, and depicts the sitter holding a young white turkey against her breast. She wears a blue dress with a light yellow shawl round her head and shoulders. According to the Wellesley catalogue this was exhibited at the R.A., in 1789, but the entry (111) for that year, 'the favourite turkey', was not in the miniature section.

Payne, John. (fl. 1798)
Wrote a treatise entitled *The Art of Miniature Painting* and also wrote on oil painting, etc. Was living at 2 Castle Street, Holborn, London in 1798 in which year the second edition of his treatise was published. This can be seen in the V. & A. M. library.

Peacham, Henry, M.A. c. 1576–c. 1641
Born in South Mimms, nr. St. Albans c. 1576; son of a clergyman. Studied at Trinity College, Cambridge. Taught at a school at Wymondham, Norfolk. In 1606 published *Graphice*, or *The Art of Drawing with the Pen and Limning in Water Colours*; later editions were called *The Gentleman's Exercise*. In 1622 he published *The Compleat Gentleman*. I have a 1634 edition of the two books bound together. He was for a time tutor to the sons of Lord Arundel. From 1613–1614 he toured on the Continent. Settled in Hoxton, London, 1615. Was the author of several other works. Was skilled at music, painting and engraving, and took likenesses, some of which may have been miniatures. A miniature of Prince Henry on horseback, in armour, is published in the preface to a treatise entitled *Le*

Pourtraiet de Monseigneur le Prince. He remained a bachelor and is said to have died poor in c. 1641.

Peake, Miss Emma. (fl. 1855–1858)
Of London. Exhibited at the R.A., etc., 1855–1858. From 1855–1856 her address was 4 Trafalgar Square, Brompton, and 1857–1858, 2 Chelsea Villas, Fulham Road.

Peake, Sir Robert. c. 1592–1667
Born c. 1592. Son of Robert Peake, James I's Serjeant-Painter who taught Faithorne (q.v.). Studied engraving under John Payne (1607–1647); became a miniature painter, engraver and printseller. Fought on the Royalist side during the Civil War; was knighted in 1645. Taken prisoner, as were Faithorne and Hollar (q.v.), at the siege of Basing House, 1645. Was subsequently exiled, but returned to England at, or after, the Restoration. He died in 1667 and was buried in St. Sepulchre's Church, London.

Peale, Charles. (fl. 1768)
Of London. Exhibited portraits and miniatures at the Society of Artists in 1768 from 'Mr Peale, Silver St, Golden Square'. Was perhaps related to, or identical with, Charles Willson Peale (q.v.).

Peale, Charles Willson. 1741–1827
An American artist; born in St. Paul's Parish, Queen Anne's County, Maryland, 15 April 1741. Apprenticed to a saddler at Annapolis, then was a clock-maker and goldsmith. Took up painting when about twenty-two years old. Had his first instruction from John Hesselius in return for a new saddle. Was brought up to believe himself heir to an English estate, but this proved an illusion. Studied painting in Boston c. 1765 where he visited J. S. Copley (q.v.) and was influenced by his style of painting. Was in London, 1767–1769 and studied under Benjamin West (q.v.). Was taught miniature painting, mezzotint engraving, modelling and painted portraits in oil. He returned to America in 1769 and worked in Philadelphia, New York, Maryland and Virginia. Settled in Philadelphia, 1776. Served as an infantry officer during the War of Independence. Painted several portraits of Washington and other officers. Bought a house in Philadelphia in 1780. Married three times. In 1762 he married his first wife, Rachel Brewer (died 1790). In 1791 he married Elizabeth de Peyster of New York. His third wife, whom he married in 1805, was Hannah Moore of Pennsylvania. Painted many notable persons including John Wesley. Helped to found the Pennsylvania Academy of Fine Arts. He did not, as far as is known, ever sign his miniatures and gave up miniature painting in 1786, according to a painted handbill of 19 October of that year, but continued to paint large portraits for some years after. A full account of his work was published in 1952: Vol. 42, Part I of *The Transactions of the American Philosophical Society*, by Charles Coleman Sellars. A large number of miniatures are illustrated in this work.

Peale, Rembrandt. 1778–1860
Born in Bucks County, Pennsylvania, 22 February 1778; son and pupil of C. W. Peale (q.v.). Painted a portrait from life of George Washington in 1795. Travelled with his brother Raphael for several years; came to London in 1801 and studied under Benjamin West (q.v.), 1802–1803. Exhibited at the R.A., 1803 and again in 1833. Returned to America in c. 1804, and was in Philadelphia where he painted numerous portraits for the 'Peale Museum'. Made trips to Paris in 1807 and 1809. From 1812–1813 he was in Baltimore, and founded

the Baltimore Gas Company. Was in Philadelphia, Boston and New York, 1822–1828. Travelled to Europe, visiting Paris, Naples, Rome and London. Was back in New York in September 1830, but returned to England again in 1832–1833, after which time he settled in New York and succeeded Trumbull (q.v.) as President of the American Academy. Became a member of the National Academy. In *c.* 1843 he moved back to Philadelphia where he remained until his death on 3 October 1860. Painted historical subjects, portraits and miniatures as well as publishing books on art. Married Harriet Cany in November 1840, who was also an artist. Rosalba Carriera Peale (1799–1874) was his daughter. She was also an artist and copied paintings.

*Pearce, Mrs. Marie G. (fl. 1825–1830)
The above artist painted a miniature on ivory of a Naval Officer *c.* 1825–1830 which was inscribed on the reverse 'Painted in oils by Mrs Marie G. Pearce / Miniature artist / Tavistock'.

Pearce, William. (fl. 1798–1799)
Of London. Exhibited at the R.A., 1798–1799. Possibly the William Pearce who entered the R.A. Schools, 31 December 1792 aged 28 years, and perhaps identical with an artist of this name who painted a rural genre picture in the manner of Wheatley.

Pearson Miss. (fl. 1824–1826)
Exhibited at the R.A., etc., 1824–1826 (Hon. Exhibitor). The exhibit in 1824 was a portrait of her sister.

*Pearson, Miss Eleanor M. (or W.). (fl. 1899)
Exhibited at the R.A. 1899, from Greyside, Muswell Hill, London.

*Pease, C. W. (fl. 1844). See **Pease, William**
Worked in Providence (Rhode Island), 1844. Possibly identical with W. Pease (q.v.) listed by Long.

*Pease, George. (fl. 1794)
A miniature of a man formerly in the Hand Collection, was signed and dated '1794' by this artist.

Pease, William. (fl. 1823–1832). See also **Pease, C. W.**
Of Woolwich. Exhibited at the R.A., etc., 1823–1832. Perhaps identical with C. W. Pease (q.v.).

Peat, Miss M. (fl. 1795–1797)
Worked in London. Sister of T. Peat (q.v.). Exhibited at the R.A., 1795–1797. Miss Peat and her brother exhibited at the R.A., from the same address, 184 Oxford Street in 1796.

Peat, Thomas. (fl. 1791–1831). See also **Peate, J.**
Brother of Miss M. Peat (q.v.) who exhibited from the same address in 1796. Worked in London, Bath (1819–1822), Leamington (1828) and Bristol (1830–1831). Exhibited at the R.A., 1791–1805. Painted miniatures in water-colour and enamel, and is thought to have painted portraits in oil, and to have imitated Reynolds. An old cutting of *c.* 1791 gives his address as No. 290 Holborn, Near Great Turnstile, and a poem is quoted which says . . .
In striking likenesses, those talents rare,
With the ingenious Peat few can compare;
Examples of his work are at the V. & A. M., and the London Museum. An enamel portrait of Mrs. Cussans, née Holburne, is at the Holburne Museum, Bath. The B.M., has an engraved portrait of W. Bradley after Peat. The Cognacq-Jay Museum, Paris, has a miniature on enamel of a child with a

dog, signed 'Peat', and an enamel portrait of Georgiana, Duchess of Devonshire, also signed 'Peat', is at the Louvre. The R.A. catalogues, 1792, record portraits by T. Peat, some of which were not miniatures. A miniature of an unknown woman inscribed on the reverse 'Painted by T. Peat', is in the collection of Mrs. Walter Scott.

Peate, J. See **Peat, T.**
The R.A. catalogue for 1792 records a J. Peate as exhibiting 'Five portraits, enamel', but the exhibits are given to T. Peat (q.v.) in the index. The address was given as 290 High Holborn, which was the address of T. Peat with whom he was probably identical.

*Peel, Miss J. (fl. 1867)
Of London. Exhibited at the R.A., 1867.

*Pegler, Charles William. d. *c.* 1832
Of London. Exhibited at the R.A., etc., 1823–1833. Painted portraits and miniatures. His sitters included the sons of the Rt. Hon. the Master of the Rolls (1823), the Rev. Dr. Willis, John Abernethy, Esq., the Bishop of Jamaica, Lord Dundas and Miss Rivière. These were all large portraits. Evidence that he painted miniatures is to be found in the *D.N.B.*, Vol. XLVIII, p. 335, where it is stated that 'A miniature of him (William Rivière (q.v.)), when a young man, by C. W. Pegler is in the possession of his son, Mr. Briton Rivière, R.A.'. The R.A. catalogues and index for 1832 record him as 'the late C. W. Pegler'.

*Pegram, Frederick. b. 1870
Born 19 December 1870. Exhibited at the R.A., etc. 1889–1904, from 32 Cheyne Row, Chelsea and from The Grove, Singleton, Chichester. Executed miniatures, illustrations and drawings. His sitters included Mrs. Fred Pegram, presumably his wife.

Pegsworth, J. (fl. 1781)
Exhibited at the R.A. 1781, from 6 Throgmorton Street, London. The exhibit was a portrait of a gentleman, not a miniature, but the artist has been described as a miniaturist.

Pelham, Henry. 1749–1806
Born 14 February 1749 in Boston, U.S.A.; son of Peter Pelham, a mezzotint-engraver and his second wife, Mary Singleton, widow of Richard Copley, and mother of J. S. Copley (q.v.). Trained as a civil engineer; may have studied under Copley. Left America *c.* 1777 and exhibited at the R.A., 1777–1778, when his address was 'at Mr. Copley's, Leicester Fields'. Went to Ireland, 1778 or 1779, and was agent to Lord Lansdowne. Exhibited at Dublin, 1780. Married Miss Butler, daughter of William Butler of Castlecrine, and had no issue. Pelham was a portrait and miniature painter, engraver and map-maker. Drew illustrations for Grose's *Antiquities of Ireland*. Was accidentally drowned in the Kenmare River, 20 September 1806. A miniature by him of Stephen Hooper, 1773, is at the Metropolitan Museum, New York. He was a good artist who drew well. The hair of his sitters is stippled and the background painted with a close oblique brush stroke.

Pelham, James (I). d. *c.* 1850
Father of James Pelham (II) (q.v.), recorded by H. C. Marillier in the *Liverpool School of Painters*, 1904, p. 189, as 'A miniature painter of some skill whose work is now seldom seen'. No works by the above artist are at present known, and according to a note in the Walker Art Gallery, he was not considered to be 'equal to his son in ability'.

Pelham, James (II). 1800–1874
Born in London, 16 September 1800; son of J. Pelham (I) (q.v.), with whom he has often been confused. Began his career as a portrait painter in London; also worked in Edinburgh, Norwich, Lincoln, Newcastle, York, Carlisle, Cheltenham, Bath and Bristol. Exhibited at the R.A., 1832–1837 and at the S.B.A., L.A., etc., up to 1868. His addresses included 15 King's Mead Terrace, Bath (1832), 8 Buckingham Place, Fitzroy Square (1836), and 21 Elizabeth Terrace, Islington (1837). His sitters included the Viscount and Viscountess Weymouth, the Rev. W. Dampier, T. Vaughan, Esq., W. H. Carter, M.D., and T. Colbeck, Esq. Painted portraits in oil and water-colour, miniatures and, towards the latter part of his career, subject pictures. He married in 1838 and is said to have moved to Liverpool soon after. He became an Associate of the Liverpool Academy in 1848, and was elected a member within a short time. Was Secretary of the L.A., 1854–1860/7. He took a prominent part in directing the Liverpool Academy Schools. Pelham had nine children of whom eight survived; of these, James Pelham (III) (1840–1906) and Emily became artists, and James succeeded his father as Secretary of the L.A., in 1867. The advent of photography lessened the patronage for miniature painting, and as was the case with many other artists, Pelham was obliged to turn to other forms of art. Died in Liverpool, 17 April 1874, and was survived by his widow and children. The Walker Art Gallery, Liverpool have two miniatures by Pelham, one of John Robertson (1820–1879), a Liverpool portrait painter. This miniature is painted on ivory; the painting is rather loose, with pinkish flesh colouring, shaded with blues and greens, a scraper being used on the hair and beard. The face of the sitter is very expressive. The other portrait is of an unknown man, profile on paper, well drawn, the eyebrows highly arched as in the manner of J. Barry (q.v.).

*Pender, Lady Denison. (fl. 1908–1910)
Of London. Exhibited at the Society of Miniaturists, 1908–1910.

*Penley, A. (fl. 1836). See also **Penley, Aaron Edwin**
A miniature of Mrs. Dyson, by A. Penley, signed and dated '1836' was sold at Christie's on 27 June 1961. The above artist may have been identical with A. E. Penley (q.v.).

Penley, Aaron Edwin. 1807–1870. See also **Penley, A.**
Was born in 1807. Practised as a miniaturist in Manchester, 1834–1835, and Cheltenham. Exhibited at the R.A., B.I., S.B.A., N.W.C.S., etc., 1835–1869. Was Water-Colour Painter in Ordinary to William IV. Was a member of the N.W.C.S., 1838–1856 and an associate from 1859. Taught drawing at Addiscombe Military College and at Woolwich. Wrote works on water-colour painting. Is best known as a drawing master and landscape painter. Died at 5 Eliot Hill, Lewisham, 15 January 1870. A miniature of Mrs. Dyson, signed and dated 'A. Penley, 1836', was sold at Christie's, 27 June 1961 and was probably by this artist.

Penley, William Henry Sauley. (fl. 1830)
Working in 1830 at 70 Queen Street, Portsea, Hampshire. Was a drawing master and miniature painter.

*Pennington, Miss Elsie L. (fl. 1909–1911)
Exhibited at the R.A. 1909 and 1911, from Rowledge, Farnham, Surrey.

*Pennoyer, Mrs. C. Ellen. (fl. 1893–1894)
Of London. Exhibited at the R.A. 1893 and 1894, from 42 Clovelly Mansions, Grays Inn Road.

Penny, C. (fl. 1814–1825)

Of London. Exhibited at the R.A., 1814–1825. The B.M. has engraved portraits by and after C. Penny. In 1814 he exhibited, as an Hon. Exhibitor, a portrait of his brother.

*Penny, Miss Gwenneth I. (fl. 1909–1913)

Of London. Exhibited at the R.A. 1909–1913, from 3 Park Hill, Ealing West. Her sitters included Capt. G. A. Jamieson (16th Cavalry), H.S. Maydell, Esq. (30th Lancers) and Vice-Admiral Stokes-Rees, C.B.

Penny, J. S. (fl. 1793–1813)

Of London. Exhibited at the R.A., 1793–1813. Was an amateur artist who painted flowers and miniatures. Some of his entries at the R.A. were as an Hon. Exhibitor, including 'a portrait of his child', in 1813. Was possibly identical with, or related to, the J. Penny who exhibited subject pictures at the R.A., in 1788.

*Penstone, Ed. (Edward?). (fl.1906)

Exhibited at the R.A. 1906, from 1 Stamford Hill, London.

*Pépin, Mlle. Clémentine Antoinette. 19th century

Born in Orsay. Pupil of Cordier, Brandon and Mme. Cheron. Exhibited at the Paris Salon, 1866–1878. It is not certain that the above artist worked in Britain, but two miniatures by her after Reginald Easton (1807–1893) (q.v.), are in the collection of H.M. the Queen. They represent Prince Albert and Princess Victoria Louise of Schleswig-Holstein. Mlle. Pépin also painted miniatures from life, and after old masters.

Pepys, Mrs. Samuel. 1640–1669

A French girl, née Elizabeth St. Michel, born, 23 October 1640. Wife of Samuel Pepys, the diarist, whom she married in 1665. According to an entry in Pepys diary, 7 May 1665, 'Yesterday begun my wife to learn to limn of one Browne (Alexander Browne (q.v.)), which Mr. Hill helps her to, and by her beginning, upon some eyes, I think she will [do] very fine things, and I shall take great delight in it.' There are several other entries in Pepys diary which refer to her paintings. Mrs. Pepys had apparently asked her husband to give her a string of pearls, and on 22 August 1665, he recorded in his diary, 'I promising to give her one of £60 in two years at furthest, and less if she pleases me in her painting.' She died 10 November 1669 and was buried at St. Olave's, Hart Street.

*Perceval, The Hon. John. 1711–1770

Was born in Westminster, 24 February 1711; eldest son of John Perceval, 1st Earl of Egmont, and his wife, Catherine. Sat in the Irish House of Commons, 1731–1748; became M.P., Westminster, 1741. Was a keen politician. Succeeded his father as 2nd Earl of Egmont, 1748. Created Baron Lovel and Holland of Enmore in 1762. First Lord of the Admiralty, 1763–1766. Was an amateur artist and painted miniatures. Evidence for this is to be found in the Historical MSS and Commission MSS of the Earl of Egmont, Vol. I, p. 100. His father, writing on 5 August 1730, says, 'This day my son's picture in miniature done by himself came home, set in gold, and is admired for its neatness and likeness.' He died at Pall Mall on 4 December 1770 and was buried at Charlton, Kent on 11th of the same month.

*Percy, Mr. (fl. 1783–1784)

Modeller in stained wax at Chelmsford, 3 September 1784 and advertised that he executed miniatures for bracelets and necklaces. On 6 May 1783 he was in Chester.

Percy, The Hon. Algernon. 1779–1833

Born 19 August 1779; second son of Algernon, 2nd Baron Lovaine, 1st Earl of Beverley, and his wife, Isabella Susannah, née Burrell. Became Minister Plenipotentiary to Swiss cantons. Painted miniatures and was probably a pupil of Bouvier (q.v.) whose miniature of his mother, Isabella, Countess of Beverley, he copied. This miniature which is a faithful replica of the original, together with a self-portrait, signed 'A. ·:· Percy 1805' and dated on the opposite side of the miniature, 'Janv 30', are in the collection of the Duke of Northumberland. The works closely resemble those of Bouvier, and are well painted. The draughtsmanship is good and in the case of the self-portrait, painted against a grey / brown gouache background, flesh colours are strong, and the shading round the eyes rather blue. The artist died unmarried, in 1833.

Percy, E. (fl. 1806)

A miniature of Hugh, Earl Percy, afterwards 3rd Duke of Northumberland, K.G. (1785–1847), signed 'E. Percy 1806' in cursive writing, is in the collection of the Duke of Northumberland. Long suggested that the artist was possibly either Elizabeth (died 10 January 1820), or Emily (died 20 June 1844), both daughters of the 2nd Duke of Northumberland. The miniature is well painted against a gouache background. The artist may possibly have been identical with The Hon. Algernon Percy (q.v.).

*Perkins, Charles P. (fl. 1874–1887)

Of London and Brighton. Exhibited at the R.A., 1874–1887. He exhibited a miniature of Mrs. Perkins in 1878, and in the same year, an enamel of an 'old painting'.

Perlotto, Tito. 1788–1858

An Italian artist, born in Lonigo, 1788. Worked in London, 1816–1824, and again after 1848. Exhibited at the S.B.A. 1854. Said to have died in Westminster, 6 October 1858.

Perrache, Jean Théodore. b. 1744. d. after 1789

Born in Geneva, 3 May 1744. Became a partner in 1777 with P. F. Marcinhès. Took part in 1782 in the Geneva revolution, was appointed a Burgess of the city, but this was cancelled by the succeeding regime, and he left in 1783 and came to London. Exhibited at the R.A., 1784–1785. Painted portraits on enamel. D. I. Troll (1748–1812) was his pupil. Said to have been associated with D. B. Murphy (q.v.). He painted the features with a very fine brush stroke, and emphasised the eyebrows and the eyes. His signature varies—'Perrache, Lond' or 'Perrache fecit' may be found on the front, and occasionally he signed in full on the reverse, with the name of the sitter. An enamel miniature of a girl by Perrache is in the collection of Earl Beauchamp.

*Perrins, John W. Ross. (fl. 1884–1893)

Of London. Exhibited at the R.A., N.W.C.S., etc., 1884–1893. Executed paintings in oil, miniatures, studies and flower pictures.

*Peter, A.

A miniature of a young girl, catalogued as by A. Peter, oval 3⅞ in., was sold at Christie's, 15 October 1963. This may have been by Amelie von Peter, recorded by Schidlof as working in Munich and Vienna c. 1835. Thought to have been an amateur painter.

Peters, Miss. (fl. 1780)

Exhibited at the R.A., 1780 (Hon. Exhibitor).

Peterson, Otto Fredrik. c. 1673–1729

Born in Stockholm, 1673 (or 1672, according to Th. B.); son of a goldsmith, Otto Petersson, and his pupil. Studied under Martin Hannibal. Came to London: was a pupil and later an assistant of Charles Boit (q.v.). Works by this artist are rare. He used pleasant colours and drew well. He appears to have signed F. Peterson, pinxit. He died in Marshalsea Prison in 1729, where he was imprisoned for debt. An enamel by Peterson of 'Venus and Cupid', after Luca Giordano, is in the collection of the Duke of Devonshire.

Pether, Abraham, F.S.A. 1756–1812

Born in Chichester, 1756; pupil of George Smith. Became a member of the Society of Artists; exhibited there and at the Free Society of Artists, R.A. and B.I., 1773–1811. Painted chiefly landscapes and moonlight scenes, but exhibited at least two miniatures, one of which was in oil. Was an ingenious mechanic and a good musician. He died in Southampton, 13 April 1812, leaving a widow and nine children destitute.

Pether, Thomas. (fl. 1772–1782)

Of London and Norwich (1778–1782). Made wax portraits, drew heads in chalk and painted miniatures. Exhibited at the Free Society of Artists, 1772–1782. B. Jones (q.v.) was his pupil. Schidlof gives his name as Abraham, but this must be a mistake. He was probably identical with the Rev. Thomas Peter who is recorded in the R.A. catalogue, 1782, as exhibiting 'portrait of a lady, model', as an Hon. Member.

Pether, William, F.S.A. 1738 ?–1821

Born in Carlisle, 1731 (according to Schidlof and Benezit) or c. 1738; cousin of Abraham Pether (q.v.). Studied under Thomas Frye (q.v.). Received premiums from the Society of Arts in 1756, 1760 and 1767. Exhibited at the Free Society and Society of Artists, 1761–1780; was a member of the latter, and in 1776 one of its directors. Exhibited at the R.A., 1781–1794. Worked for some time in London and in Richmond, Surrey (1777), Nottingham (1780) and settled in Bristol c. 1804, where he worked as a drawing master and picture cleaner. He died in Montague Street, Bristol, 19 July 1821 and was buried at Horfield Churchyard on 25 July 1821. His pupils included E. Dayes (q.v.) and H. Edridge (q.v.). A miniature by him is in the collection of the Duke of Portland; it is of Lord Richard Cavendish (1752–1781), painted on ivory, and signed 'W. Pether, 1770'. There is light brown stippling on the background. He exhibited a self-portrait at the Society of Artists, 1777 with the name reversed (Don Mailliw Rehtep). A miniature of a man, attributed to Pether is at the V. & A. M.

Peticolas or **Petticolas, Edward F.** 1793–c. 1853

Born in Philadelphia in 1793; son and pupil of Philip A. Peticolas. Studied under T. Sully (q.v.). According to Groce and Wallace, visited Europe and was in England, France and Italy, 1815–1819. In 1826, and again from 1830–1833, was in Europe; Long states that he was in England in 1826. Is known to have practised as a miniaturist in Richmond, Virginia. He married in Virginia c. 1820, Jane Pitfield Braddick, by whom he had a son, Arthur Edward Peticolas, who followed his father's profession, but later turned to medicine. Died c. 1853. A miniature of E. Etting, signed 'E. F. Petticolas, 1799', is in the Pennsylvania Academy of Fine Arts.

Petitot, Jean, senior. 1607–1691

Born in Geneva, 12 July 1607; fourth son of a

French sculptor. Was apprenticed in 1626 to his uncle, Jean Royaume, a jeweller. Left Geneva *c.* 1633 and probably settled in Paris. Petitot is said to have had his early instruction in enamelling from Pierre Bordier (q.v.) whose cousin, Jacques Bordier (q.v.), became his lifelong friend and collaborator. Petitot may have been a pupil of Jean and Henri Toutin of Blois. Between 1633 and *c.* 1637, Petitot and J. Bordier came to England, where Petitot was employed by Charles I, and had encouragement from Sir Theodore Turquet de Mayerne and Van Dyck. The King gave him an apartment in Whitehall, and according to some authorities, knighted him. Charles I possessed a boxwood carving of Lucretia by Petitot. He obtained so many commissions that Bordier is supposed to have painted the hair, and often the backgrounds and clothes on many of his enamels, whilst Petitot executed the faces. It is more than probable that he had other assistants of whom we have no knowledge. Some of his finest works were produced *c.* 1640 and he was still in England in 1643. Long quotes a letter of 18 May 1650, p. 470, Vol. I of *Memoirs of the Verney Family*, 1904 in which Lady Herbert refers to a miniature of Princess Sophia, which she did not accept as it was not well done: 'the truthe was it was donne by his companion' (i.e. Bordier) 'who does now most of his work'. Lady Herbert also mentions the increase in price for his enamels. The exact date and year that Petitot and Bordier returned to France is not known for certain, but they were there by *c.* 1645-1646. In 1651 he married Marguerite Cuper at Charenton, whose sister Madelaine married Bordier. Petitot was well patronised by Louis XIV and the French Court and was given a pension and a residence at the Louvre. In 1686, after the Revocation of the Edict of Nantes, being a zealous protestant, he was imprisoned for heresy. Eventually, weakened by illness, he recanted, and after his release fled to Switzerland, and settled in Geneva where he continued to practise his art. Petitot was later received back into the Huguenot Communion. He was patronised by John Sobieski, King of Poland, and many other notable persons. On 1 April 1691, whilst working on a portrait of his wife, he was seized by an attack of paralysis from which he died only two days later, on 3 April. During his lifetime he wrote a journal, and *Prayers and Meditations* for various occasions. This MS contained drawings by him, and two portraits in Indian ink. This work and an account of his life were published by E. Stroehlin at Geneva, 1905. He had seventeen children of whom his eldest son, Jean Petitot junior (q.v.) followed his profession. According to Vertue (B.M. Add. MSS 23,072, p. 64), a younger son lived and died in England (being a Major in the British Army); he possessed several enamels by Petitot, and was probably the father of Major General William Petitot who died at Northallerton, 26 July 1764, aged 60. The supposition is that William was the grandson of Petitot. Some of Petitot's enamels are painted after portraits in oil by other artists, such as Van Dyck, Nanteuil, Mignard and Lebrun. The best of his works are very beautiful and painted in harmonious colours, the features being expressively drawn. A stippling touch can often be distinguished on the face, when examined under a lens. The majority of his works are small, two exceptions being the Countess of Southampton, signed and dated '1643' in the collection of the Duke of Devonshire, and the superb enamel of Mary, Duchess of Richmond and Lennox (1622–1685), after Van Dyck, octagonal, signed and dated on the reverse 'J. Petitot fec 1643'. This enamel, once in the Pierpont Morgan Collection, and now in the Nationalmuseum, Stockholm, was lent to the Edinburgh exhibition in 1965 and illustrated in the catalogue. Petitot is known to have

executed a few miniatures in water-colour on parchment. These were probably sketches for portraits on enamel. The Duke of Portland, who has a large collection of this artist's work, has one of a man, on parchment, signed 'P.72' (1672), and a self-portrait on enamel; the monogram 'JP' is on the pale blue enamel back. Typical signatures are J.P. f 1639, J. Petitot, 1640, J. Petitot fe 1640 and J. Petitot fec 1638, besides P.72, already mentioned. Several artists of later periods copied his works, including J. Haslem (q.v.) and J. Lee (q.v.). Enamels by him, or in his manner, are numerous; owing to the number of assistants and followers, it is difficult to be certain in many cases of definite authenticity. Miniatures by him are in many private collections including those of the Duke of Northumberland, who has a miniature on vellum of Charles I and Henrietta Maria dated '1636', the Duke of Buccleuch, the Duke of Devonshire, etc. Other important examples are in the V. & A. M., the N.P.G., The Ward Usher Museum, Lincoln, The Louvre, The Rijksmuseum, Amsterdam, the Musée Condé, Chantilly, The Nationalmuseum, Munich and the Nationalmuseum, Stockholm. For further information see 'Jean Petitot and Jacques Bordier at the English Court', by R. W. Lightbrown, *The Connoisseur*, June 1968, pp. 82–91.

Petitot, Jean, the younger. 1653–1702

Born in Blois, 2 January 1653; eldest of seventeen children born to Jean Petitot (q.v.) and his wife, née Marguerite Cuper. Sent by his father to England to have some instruction in limning from Samuel Cooper (q.v.). This must have been before 1672, the year in which Cooper died. Petitot did not like the method of his instruction and is said to have returned to France 'without much improvement'. In 1677 however, he was back in England and apprenticed to a miniaturist in London. He worked for Charles II until 1682. Petitot returned to Paris and in 1683 married at Charenton, his cousin, Madeleine Bordier (born in Paris, 8 May 1658, died in Geneva, 11 January 1736), she being the daughter of his father's friend and brother-in-law, Jacques Bordier (q.v.). On the death of Bordier, Petitot succeeded him as representative of the Republic of Geneva in Paris. Petitot returned to England *c.* 1696, but evidently returned to France and died in Paris, 25 October 1702, and was buried in his own garden, 27 October 1702, after refusing to become a Catholic. His widow died in Geneva, 1736. One of his sons or a nephew, is said to have become a Major General in the British Army. Vertue records that he painted in water-colour and enamel; no examples in water-colour are at present known. He worked in the style of his father but did not always succeed in attaining such a high quality. He used a rather pink flesh colouring on the faces of his portraits on enamel, and painted the costume with great care. The hair of his sitters is painted with a fine and distinct brush stroke. His self-portrait, in a yellow costume embroidered with flowers, enamelled on gold, is signed on the reverse 'Jean Petitot fait par lui-même l'an 1676 décembre âgé de 23 ans'. This was exhibited at the Albertina, Vienna in 1924, and sold in Vienna in May 1930. A miniature of Anne, later Countess of Exeter, in the Burghley House Collection, is attributed to him and was exhibited in Edinburgh in 1965. An oil portrait by him is in the Musée d'Art et Histoire, Geneva. He also painted numerous miniatures on parchment. Two miniatures attributed to him are in the National Collection of Fine Arts, Smithsonian Institution. They represent Henri Jules, Duc d'Albret and Louis de Bourbon, Prince de Condé.

Petrie, James. d. 1819

Born in Dublin of Scottish parents, his father

being a native of Aberdeen, and his mother of Edinburgh. Studied in the Dublin Society Schools; practised at No. 82 Dame Street where he had a jeweller's business and dealt in coins and antique objects. Painted landscapes, portraits in oil, published some engravings, drew illustrations for magazines. Exhibited in Dublin, 1801–1815. Was arrested during the Rebellion on suspicion of being connected with United Irishmen. Was in the Provost Prison; appears to have owed his release to Major Sandys, whose portraits he painted. By his first wife, Elizabeth, daughter of Sacheverell Simpson of Edinburgh, who died 18 April 1793, he had a son, George Petrie, P.R.H.A. His second wife, Wilhelmina Bate, whom he married, 20 July 1808, survived him and carried on the jewellery business for some years after his death in 1819. She died, 12 November 1862. Examples of his work are at the N.G., Dublin, including a miniature of Lord Edward Fitzgerald, inscribed on the reverse 'Painted from life'; water-colour on paper.

*Pettafor, Miss Mabel M. (fl. 1903–1909)

Exhibited at the R.A. 1903–1909, from 32 Park Road, Southborough, Tunbridge Wells.

*Peyton, Emily M. (Mrs. J. W.). (fl. 1905–1910)

Of London. Exhibited at the R.A., 1905 and 1910. In the former year, exhibited a miniature of H.R.H. Princess Louise of Battenberg.

Phelps, Miss Eliza H. (fl. 1778–1780)

Of London. Exhibited at the R.A., 1778 (Hon. Exhibitor), and 1780 from 5 Downing Street.

*Phillip, John, R.A., H.R.S.A. 1817–1867. See also **Phillips, J.**

Two miniatures, formerly in the O'Brien Collection, and illustrated in *Miniatures in the 18th and 19th Centuries*, Pl. 67 and 78, were attributed to the above artist who was a well known Scottish subject and portrait painter. The miniatures which were signed 'J. Phillips', were in all probability not by him, but by the miniaturist J. Phillips (q.v.).

*Phillips or Philips, Lady Agatha.

Long recorded the above artist as a miniaturist, but did not record her dates, and I have been unable to trace her name.

Phillips, George Henry. (fl. 1819–1827)

Of London. Exhibited at the R.A., B.I., O.W.C.S., etc., 1819–1825. Possibly the George Phillips who entered the R.A. Schools, 15 January 1807 aged 16 years. Painted some landscapes and miniatures.

*Phillips, J. (fl. *c.* 1838–1840). See also **Phillip, John, R.A.**

Two miniatures signed 'J. Phillips', were formerly in the O'Brien Collection when they were attributed to J. Phillip, R.A., a well known subject and portrait painter. Phillip is not known to have painted miniatures, and stylistically it seems most improbable that they are by him. A pair of miniatures of a lady and gentleman, painted *c.* 1840, and signed 'J. Phillips' are in the collection of E. G. Paine of New York. The miniatures in the O'Brien Collection were signed 'J. Phillips Pinxit', painted *c.* 1838, and 'J. Phillips. 1840 pinxt'.

*Phillips, R. (fl. 1702)

A miniature in plumbago, signed and dated 'R. Phillips 1702', is in the collection of E. G. Paine, of New York.

*Phillips, Miss Sara C. (fl. 1908–1911)
Exhibited at the R.A. 1908 and 1911, from Middlegate, Northwood, Middlesex. Her sitters included the late Dr. C. D. F. Phillips.

Phillips, Mrs. T. (fl. 1819–1821)
Worked in Bath, 1819–1821 when her address was 20 Union Passage, Bath.

Phillips, Thomas, R.A. 1770–1845
Entered the R.A. Schools, 18 February 1791 aged 20. This well-known portrait painter is not usually regarded as a miniaturist, but his exhibits at the R.A. 1792–1846, are said to have included a miniature in 1797. The original R.A. catalogues for that year do not show any such entry under the miniature section, but do list a portrait, No. 545, in the Antique Academy section.

*Phillpotts, Miss Maud S. (fl. 1899–1900)
Exhibited at the R.A. 1899 and 1900, from Schoolhouse, Bedford.

*Phipps. (G.W.?). (fl. 1829)
Painted miniatures on ivory for 10 dollars each at Halifax, Nova Scotia, 1829. May have worked in England. Possibly identical with an artist named G. W. Phipps, a native of Massachusetts, who was living in New Haven, Connecticut in 1850, aged 45.

Picken, Miss Eleanor E. (fl. 1842)
Of London. Exhibited at the R.A., etc., 1842.

Pickersgill, Miss M. A. (fl. 1832–1838)
Of London. Daughter of H. W. Pickersgill, R.A. Exhibited at the R.A. etc., 1832–1838, from her father's address, 18 Soho Square.

*Picket, Miss Mary S. (fl. 1898–1909)
Exhibited at the R.A. 1898–1909, from addresses in London and Guildford.

Picot. (fl. 1783?–1807)
A miniature of a man c. 1807 signed 'Picot' in cursive French script was seen by Long. It is not certain that this artist worked in England. May possibly have been a son of François Picot (q.v.) and a pupil of Duplessis. Has been identified as the artist of this name who was working at the Hague in 1783. He is said to have painted rather large miniatures.

Picot, François. b. 1698. d. after 1762
Born in Geneva, 12 April 1698; nephew of the jeweller, Isaac Picot. Studied miniature and enamel painting under Jean Cuchet, 1707, and in Paris, Italy and Germany. Opened a drawing school in Geneva c. 1730. Exhibited work by his pupils in 1736. Was imprisoned for sedition; an attempt to release him led to a fight, 21 August 1737. Was in Amsterdam, 1760–1762. Evidently came to England, and considered a portrait of the Queen of England one of his best works. Boasted of having painted an enamel, the circumference of which was five feet. A miniature of an unknown man in armour, signed and dated, 'Picot / pinx / 1724', was sold at Sotheby's 20 January 1969.

Pierce, Sarah. (fl. 1785–1790)
Of London. Exhibited at the R.A., 1785–1790.

Pierce, Mrs. W. (Miss Anne Beaumont). (fl. 1820–1836)
Of London. Née Anne Beaumont. Exhibited at the R.A., B.I. and S.B.A., 1820–1836. Married c. 1832. Painted miniatures and domestic subjects. The exhibits after 1832 were under her married name.

Pigott, Miss Annabella. (fl. 1797–1802)
Exhibited at the R.A. 1802, three miniatures from memory.

*Piggott, Miss Mary H. C. (fl. 1907–1909)
Exhibited at the R.A. 1907 and 1909, from Hartsholme, Seaford, Sussex. Her sitters included Mrs. Thomas Piggott.

Pike, J. (fl. 1749)
J. J. Foster records an example of this artist's work as being in the collection of Earl Cathcart and dated '1749'.

*Pilkington, Miss Maude E. (Mrs. H. Price). (fl. 1893–1914)
Of London. Exhibited at the R.A. 1893–1914, from addresses in London. Her sitters included Lady Stenning. Exhibited in her maiden name until 1914.

Pilsbury, E. (fl. 1810)
Exhibited at the R.A., 1810 (Hon. Exhibitor).

Pine, Simon. d. 1772
Son of John Pine, engraver; brother of Robert Edge Pine (1742–1790). Worked in Dublin c. 1762–c. 1770, living in Hog Hill, Dublin, 1765–1767. Said to have practised in Connaught. Was in Bath (1770–1772) and London. Exhibited at the Society of Artists, 1765–1771, and at the R.A., 1772. Knew Gainsborough at Bath c. 1767 according to W. T. Whitley, so may have come to England earlier than was supposed. Died in Bath, 1772.

*Pitcairn, Miss Constance. (fl. 1881–1904)
Of Haslemere, Surrey. Exhibited at the R.A., S.M., etc., 1881–1904. Her sitters included Queen Alexandra, Edward VII and Miss Maude Pitcairn.

Pitman, Miss Sarah Bennard. (fl. 1839–1841)
Of London. Exhibited at the R.A., 1839–1841. Her exhibit in 1841 was a 'Portrait of her sister'.

*Pitt, Elizabeth. 17th century
Possibly an amateur artist. A miniature executed in plumbago, inscribed on the reverse, 'Sir Wadham Wyndham, Judge of the Court of Common Pleas, in the Reighn of King Charles ye 2nd. Drawn by Eliz: Pitt', was seen at Sotheby's. The sitter's dates were 1610–1668.

*Pitt, Miss Ethel. (fl. 1909).
Exhibited at the R.A. 1909, from the Studio, 107 Whiteladies Road, Bristol.

Pitt, Mrs. W. (fl. 1848–1851)
Of London. Exhibited at the R.A. 1848–1851, from 5 Bath Terrace, Camberwell New Road.

*Pitts, Miss Mary. (fl. 1895–1914)
Of London. Exhibited at the R.A. 1895–1914, from various London addresses including 21 Baker Street from which address Miss K. A. Smith (q.v.) also exhibited in 1896.

Pizzetta, U. (fl. 1813)
Of London. Exhibited at the R.A. 1813, from 98 Swallow Street.

Place, George. d. 1805
Son of a Dublin linen draper. Entered the Dublin Society Schools in December 1775, where he studied under F. R. West; practised for a time in Dublin, then went to London where, in 1791, he was living at 37 Southampton Street. Exhibited at the R.A. 1791–1797 from various London addresses. On 31 December 1792, Place was entered on the R.A. School list but not admitted. Worked for a time in York. Obtained permission on 22 February 1797 to

go to Bengal as a miniaturist, but did not go at once, and fresh permission was granted, 28 February 1798, and he was allowed to take his wife with him. Seems to have established himself in Lucknow. Said to have received between five and six thousand pounds from the Nawab, and to have painted pictures of the Nawab and his court. It is probable that most of Place's paintings executed in Lucknow perished during the Mutiny, including his best known work depicting an incident at the battle of Laswari (1803), when Lord Lake's horse having been killed, his son dismounted and gave him his own charger. This was engraved by R. Cooper after Place's death in Lucknow, 11 August 1805. He painted in oil as well as in miniature. He tended to shade the faces of his sitters with a good deal of blue; the eyelids are often modelled with long brush strokes. Few of his miniatures are signed. Examples of his work are at the V. & A. M., including a portrait of Alexander, 4th Duke of Gordon, and one of an unknown officer. This last miniature was exhibited in Edinburgh in 1965. The B.M. has an engraved portrait of W. Cramer after Place.

Plant, W. d. c. 1850
Of London. Was awarded a gold Isis medal by the Society of Arts in 1818 for an enamel painting. Was then living in Fetter Lane. Exhibited at the R.A. and O.W.C.S., 1819–1828. Executed enamel copies of oil paintings. John Haslem, in The Old Derby China Factory, gives information about Plant, whom he says was brought up as a china painter and was frequently employed by the china enamellers in London. During the latter part of his life he painted portraits and small enamels of a decorative character for jewellery, and was employed by Messrs. Rundall and Bridges of London, to paint a number of enamel miniatures which had been commissioned by Queen Victoria. He was a highly nervous man, and this condition increased as time went on, and eventually prevented him from working. Haslem thought his work good, but 'feeble in colour'. Towards the end of his career he was very slow and took weeks or months to complete an order. He died c. 1850.

Playford, (George?). d. 1780
Worked in London. Said to have made clever copies of miniatures after Cosway (q.v.). Died in Lamb's Conduit Street, 24 October 1780.

Plees, Rev. William Gordon, M.A. 1781–1849
Born 1781; son of William Plees and his wife, Janet (née Gordon). Was admitted to Blundell's school, Tiverton in 1791. Ordained Deacon, 1809, Priest, 1810. M.A., St. John's College, Cambridge. Served his title at St. Brelade, Jersey. Temporary Chaplain to the troops at Elizabeth Castle, Jersey. Vicar of Cressing, Essex, 1814–1819; admitted Sizar as 10 year man, Cambridge, 1818; Vicar of Ashbocking, Suffolk, 1833–1849. Married at St. Mary's, Putney, Surrey, 16 May 1805, Elizabeth Ann Bunyon, by whom he had twelve children, of whom Maria (1828–1901), married, 1 September 1859, at Ipswich, Robert Roe (q.v.) of Cambridge. Their younger son, Fred Roe, R.I., R.B.C. (1864–1947), was the father of F. Gordon Roe, F.S.A., who supplied Long with many items of information; and to whom Long left his own copy of British Miniaturists, to which I was allowed access. Plees was an amateur portrait painter who also painted miniatures. He died 19 August 1849, and was buried in the chancel of Ashbocking Church.

Plimer, Andrew. 1763–1837
Born in Wellington, Shropshire where he was baptised, 29 December 1763; son of a clockmaker,

Nathaniel Plimer, and his wife, Eliza; his father and uncle being partners in a clockmaking business in the town. He and his brother, Nathaniel (q.v.), were apprenticed to the trade, but neither of them liked it, and they are said to have run away and joined some gypsies with whom they toured for two years. They arrived in London in 1781, and Andrew obtained employment as a manservant to Richard Cosway (q.v.), who is said to have realised his artistic ability and allowed him to take lessons. Plimer left Cosway in 1785 and set up on his own. He had a practice in 32 Great Maddox Street, Hanover Square, for a year, after which time he went to 3 Golden Square, which was considered a fashionable part of London. He exhibited at the R.A. etc., 1786–1830, and was probably the artist who exhibited three large pictures at the B.I., in 1819. The catalogue for that year records the name as J. Plimer and the index, A. Plimer. The exhibits were: (1) A Winter Scene, (2) Telemachus landing in the island of Calypso, (3) The finding of Moses. Unless these were the work of an artist about whom we have no knowledge, this is the only occasion on which Plimer is known to have executed this type of painting. He is probably the 'Mr Plimer' recorded as having been in Cambridge, 16 November 1793 and 1 November 1794. In 1796 he moved to 8 Golden Square. On 21 February 1801 he married at Wicken, Northamptonshire, Joanna Louisa Knight (1774–1861), by whom he had five children, four daughters and a son who died young. The eldest daughter, Louisa, married John Scott, M.D. of Edinburgh. She was the only one to survive her parents, and it was at her house in Hawick that Mrs. Plimer died in 1861. The family toured through Devon and Cornwall in 1801, and in c. 1815 Plimer was working in Exeter. After about three years, the family returned to London and lived in Upper York Street, Montagu Square. In c. 1820 Andrew toured the West of England and finally arrived in Scotland where he is said to have been successful in obtaining patrons. In 1835 he and his family settled in Brighton, where he died on 29 January 1837 at Western Cottage, Western Road, Brighton and was buried at Hove. He left a considerable amount of property. Plimer was capable, at his best, of producing well executed and charming miniatures, but not all his works are of equal merit. His draughtsmanship is not always good, but his grouping where several persons are included in the picture is effective. His portraits of men are often better than those of women, which one feels are not always true likenesses, but were idealised; thin cross-hatching on the background, to the left and right of the sitter, elongated necks in the case of ladies' portraits, long noses and the treatment of the eyes, are all characteristics of Plimer's work, together with thin cross-strokes of shading on the hair. His works fall into two phases, the earlier examples up to c. 1789 being attractive and more natural than those executed later. They are often signed A.P. followed by a date as in the case of one of Thomas Ireland, which was lent by Earl Beauchamp to the Edinburgh exhibition 1965, signed and dated 'A.P. 1787', inscribed on the reverse 'Thomas Ireland. Painted by Andrew Plimer pupil of Cosway 1787'. In the second phase he did not sign his work. It was marked by a sameness of appearance, both in features and costume. His palette was restricted and the flesh colours inclined to fade. The size of his ivories increased from comparatively small ones to those measuring up to 3½ in. He painted on vellum, paper and card, and executed portraits in oil as well as miniatures. He was a prolific artist and examples of his work are to be found in most collections, including those of the V. & A. M., the Fitzwilliam Museum, Cambridge, the Ashmolean Museum, Oxford, etc.

Several miniatures by Plimer were exhibited in Edinburgh in 1965, including two representing the children of Major General Charles Morgan lent by Lord Methuen. These are particularly charming. A number of miniatures of the Plimer family, including portraits of Andrew's wife and children, were sold at Sotheby's, 27 January 1964. For further information regarding this artist, see *Andrew and Nathaniel Plimer*, by Dr. G. C. Williamson.

Plimer, Nathaniel. 1757–1822

Born in Wellington, Shropshire in 1757; elder son of Nathaniel and Eliza Plimer, and brother of Andrew Plimer (q.v.). Left home with his brother and joined some gypsies, with whom they wandered about the country for over two years, during which time they adapted themselves to the life, made their own brushes and assisted in decorating the caravans, and making scenery. Arrived in London in 1781. Nathaniel obtained a position as a servant to H. Bone (q.v.), the enameller. After a short time he left and joined his brother as a pupil of Richard Cosway (q.v.). He exhibited at the R.A., 1787–1815 and at the Society of Artists, 1790–1791 from 31 Maddox Street. Little is known about him except that he is believed to have remained in London all his life and to have died there in 1822. He married and had four children: Georgina, Mary, Louisa and Adela. This last daughter married Andrew Geddes, a native of Edinburgh, a well-known portrait painter. A portrait by Geddes of Andrew Plimer is in the N.G., Edinburgh. As in the case of Andrew, only his works painted before 1789 are signed and dated N.P. in small Roman capitals. Although his miniatures do not possess the brilliance and dash of those executed by his brother, many of them are good, and are softer and more realistic. He used more stippling in the shading, and the eyelashes are often to be found dotted in on the lower lid. The general treatment is slightly more woolly. His works are not always easily identified and are not met with as frequently as those of his contemporaries. Two examples of his work were shown at Edinburgh in 1965; one of an unknown man, signed and dated 'NP 1787' from the collection of Major R. M. O. de la Hey, and the other of The Prince of Wales (later George IV) from my own collection. Examples of his work are also in the V. & A. M., the Fitzwilliam Museum, Cambridge and the Cleveland Museum of Art, Ohio (Ed. B. Green Collection). For further information regarding this artist see *Andrew and Nathaniel Plimer*, by Dr. G. C. Williamson.

Plott, John, F.S.A. 1732–1803

Born in Winchester, 1732; became clerk to an attorney and accountant. Went to London, 1756, studied under Richard Wilson, R.A., and N. Hone (q.v.) whose assistant he became. Exhibited at the Society of Artists, 1764–1776, was a director, 1774; he also exhibited at the R.A., 1772–1803. Painted miniatures on ivory and enamel and executed some oil portraits. Moved to Winchester where he was elected a member of the City Corporation. Began a book on land snails. Many of his miniatures are of a very high quality, and his work deserves more recognition than has hitherto been the case. A miniature of Miss Anne Locke, painted on ivory, signed 'JP', and inscribed on the reverse 'By J. Plott, Pinxt 1778', is a fine example and painted in the manner of R. Crosse (q.v.); it was exhibited in Edinburgh in 1965 and illustrated in the catalogue. The B.M. has engraved portraits after Plott. A miniature of Mrs. Lydia Butt, the artist's aunt, painted in 1776, is in the V. & A. M. Two miniatures by Plott were lent to the exhibition at the South Kensington Museum, 1865; one was of a young

gentleman, painted on ivory and dated '1802'. The other was an enamel of Charles I after Van Dyck, from the collection of Earl Spencer; this is signed on the reverse, 'K. Charles I / after Vandyke J.P. (monogram) pinxt.'

Plowman, Elise. (fl. 1843)
Of London. Exhibited at the R.A., 1843.

Plowman, Frederick Prussia. 1760–1820
Born in Dublin, 1760; entered the Dublin Society Schools, 1773; won prizes in 1776 and 1779, including 'six heads after Rosalba'. Was influenced by Reynolds. Probably the Frederick Plowman who entered the R.A. Schools, 6 October 1780 aged '21 next Nov'. Painted miniatures, crayon and oil portraits and religious subjects. He was working in Limerick in 1808. Died at Marino, Co. Down, 1820.

*Plowman, W. See **Powlet, William** and **P., W.**

Poate, R. 19th century
A miniature of a man c. 1830–1835, stated to be by R. Poate, was lent to the Christchurch Mansion Museum in Ipswich in 1927. A Portsmouth artist of that name exhibited at the B.I., etc., 1845–1869, and painted figure subjects.

*Pocock, Miss Julia. (fl. 1871–1903)
Of London. Daughter of Lexden L. Pocock, and sister of Miss H. J. Pocock and Miss Lilian J. Pocock (q.v.), all of whom were artists. Exhibited at the R.A., etc., 1871–1903. Executed subjects in water-colour, miniatures and portrait medallions.

*Pocock, Miss Lilian J. (fl. 1908–1928)
Of London. Daughter of Lexden L. Pocock, and sister of Miss H. J. Pocock and Miss Julia Pocock (q.v.), all of whom were artists. Exhibited at the R.A., 1908–1928. Painted miniatures (mostly religious subjects) and subjects in water-colour.

*Pocock, Miss Margaret. (fl. 1883)
Of London. Exhibited at the R.A., 1883.

Polack, Joel Samuel. (fl. 1823)
Son of Solomon Polack (q.v.) from whose address he exhibited at the R.A., 1823.

Polack, Solomon. 1757–1839
Born in the Hague, 1757. Worked in England and Dublin probably before 1790. Exhibited at the R.A., and S.B.A., 1790–1835. Lived at 130 and 158 Strand. Designed and etched plates for a Hebrew Bible. By his will he left his property to his wife, Sarah. He died 30 August 1839 at 8 Park Terrace, Kings Road, Chelsea. Administration was granted in 1839 to his widow and to his son, Joel Samuel Polack (q.v.). The V. & A. M. has two miniatures by him, and one by his son. A miniature, from the collection of Mr. Alfred Rubens, by Polack, is illustrated in the *Jewish Historical Society*, Vol. XVIII, showing his trade label. His work is not of outstanding merit. *The Artist's Birmingham Gazette*, 21 August 1786, contains an advertisement stating that 'S. Polack Artist of Wormwood Street, London, visits Birmingham. Miniatures.' This may have related to Solomon Polack.

*Poland, J. (fl. 1785–1787)
A miniature painter of this name from Vienna worked in Norfolk, 5 May 1787, Coventry, 28 June 1786 and Manchester, 8 October 1785. Possibly the son of Josef Poland (1692–1740), an historical painter who died in Vienna.

Pole, Thomas, M.D. 1753–1829

Born in Philadelphia, 1753; son of John Pole, a native of Wiveliscombe; became a Quaker. Lived from 1802 in Bristol, where he had an extensive medical practice. Started the Adult School Movement in Bristol. Was an amateur painter, principally of landscape and architectural subjects; executed silhouettes and small miniatures in Indian ink and sepia, some of which were signed, 'T. Pole, M.D. Delin. aetat.71.Bristol, 1st month, 1825'. Died in Bristol, 1829.

*Pollard, Miss Mary Alice. (fl. 1904–1906)

Of Great Malvern, Worcestershire. Exhibited at the Society of Miniaturists, 1904–1906.

*Pollard, Miss Renira. (fl. 1887–1901)

Of London and Norwich. Exhibited at the R.A., N.W.C.S., S.M., etc., 1887–1901. Painted miniatures and flowers.

*Pollen, Miss Anne. (fl. 1814)

Niece of Mrs. S. P. Cockerell. Executed small water-colour portraits on paper, some of which were seen by Long and signed 'Anno, 1814'.

*Pond, Arthur. c. 1705–1758

Born in London c. 1705. Worked in Rome in 1726. Became a member of the Royal Society in London in 1752. Was a portrait painter and engraver, and according to Schidlof also painted miniatures. Died in Rome, 9 September 1758.

Ponthon, A. (fl. 1798). See also **Ponthon, N. A.**

Exhibited at the R.A. 1798, from 43 Fetter Lane, Holborn, 'A portrait of Mr Stregling'. May be identical with N. A. Ponthon (q.v.) who exhibited at the R.A. 1799–1800, from 55 Mount Street, Grosvenor Square and 6 Yeates Court, Carey Street. A miniature signed 'A. Ponthon Miniature Painter / No 6 Yeates Court, Carey St' was seen by Long, so it is possible that there were two artists of this name.

Ponthon, N. A. (fl. 1799–1800). See also **Ponthon, A.**

Possibly identical with, or related to, A. Ponthon (q.v.). Exhibited at the R.A. 1799–1800, from 55 Mount Street, Grosvenor Square. The exhibits in 1799 are not under the numbers given in the index (1065 and 1066), but the catalogue does give No. 694—Ponthon (no initial and no address), 'portrait, a miniature'. N. A. Ponthon exhibited in 1799, No. 1077 and 1078, 'A model of Lord Nelson' and a 'Portrait of Mr. Blines', both in the Model Academy. In 1800 N. A. Ponthon exhibited a miniature of Mr. Ward from 6 Yeates Court, Carey Street, the same address that Long noted on a miniature signed 'A. Ponthon', who exhibited in 1798 from 43 Fetter Lane, Holborn. The V. & A. M. has a miniature by him with his printed trade card on the reverse. His work may have been influenced by G. Engleheart (q.v.).

Ponty, Charles. (fl. 1716)

Worked in Worcester and Hanley in 1716. Advertised in *The Worcester Postman*, No. 365, 1716, that 'Mr Charles Ponty, Limner, gives constant attendance at his summer house in *Sansomefields*, Worcester, every *Thursday*, *Friday*, and *Saturday*, and at his house at *Robertsend-street*, in Hanley, every *Monday*, *Tuesday*, and *Wednesday*, to draw pictures by the life, in great or little, and other curiosities in *Painting*, viz. large historical pictures for halls, stair-cases. . . . He also mends and copies any picture very justly, and paints any sort of dials with proper ornaments. . . .' He painted an altar piece for Great Malvern Church.

Pool(e), Charles. (fl. *c.* 1820–1825)

Worked in Belfast *c.* 1820–1825. In *c.* 1820 his address was Donegall Square, East Belfast. Painted miniatures and oil portraits. Strickland records the spelling of his name as Pool.

Poole, R. (fl. 1809?–1820)

Was working in Belfast *c.* 1820. A miniaturist of this name was working in Newry, in *c.* 1809. Possibly related to C. Pool(e) (q.v.).

Pope, Alexander. 1763–1835

Born in Cork in 1763; son of T. Pope (q.v.). Entered the Dublin Society Schools, 1776; was a pupil of H. D. Hamilton, the pastellist. Exhibited in Dublin, 1777 and 1780 and at the R.A., 1785–1821. Became an actor and appeared at Covent Garden in 1785, as well as at Drury Lane, the Haymarket and in Dublin. Painted miniatures, crayon portraits and a few in oil. He was married three times; first in August 1785, in Dublin to Elizabeth Young, an actress (died March 1797), who was buried in Westminster Abbey. She left her house in Half Moon Street, Piccadilly to her husband, from where he exhibited from 1787. He married secondly on 24 January 1798, Maria Anne Campion (Mrs. Spencer), a young and pretty widow, also an actress and native of the County of Waterford, who died in 1803, aged 26, and was also buried in Westminster Abbey. His third wife, whom he married on 25 June 1807, was Clara Maria Wheatley (q.v.), daughter of Jared Leigh. She was an amateur painter and widow of Francis Wheatley (q.v.). Pope died in his house in Store Street, Bedford Square, 22 March 1835 and his widow died in the same house on 24 December 1838 (or 1839—*The Gentleman's Magazine*). A list of some of his portraits is given by Strickland and includes some miniatures. He had a distinguished clientele including Mrs. Siddons, Miss Siddons, the Duke of Leeds, Mrs. Pope (presumably his second wife, exhibited 1799), W. Moneyhill, Esq., R. Walpole, Esq., Mrs. Reynolds and Mr. C. Kemble. He also painted a large portrait of Michael Bryan, Esq., the first compiler of *Bryan's Dictionary of Painters and Engravers*. In my copy of this work, a previous owner has inserted a coloured print of an attractive portrait by Pope of an unknown lady, *c.* 1820 which was illustrated in *The Connoisseur* (no date given). Examples of his work are at the B.M., and the Royal Dublin Society; the Garrick Club has a miniature by him of Mrs. Billington. Some of his works were engraved.

Pope, Mrs. Alexander (Mrs. Wheatley). 1750?–1838

Née Clara Maria Leigh, daughter of Jared Leigh, an amateur artist. Married Francis Wheatley, R.A. (q.v.), who was unfaithful to her. Exhibited at the R.A., 1796–1838 (up to 1807 as Mrs. Wheatley). Painted miniatures, portraits, domestic subjects, flowers, etc. Became a widow in 1801. Married Alexander Pope (q.v.), 25 June 1807 as his third wife. Survived her husband and died at their home, 29 Store Street, London, 24 December 1838 (1839 according to *The Gentleman's Magazine*). Mrs. Beechey exhibited a portrait of her at the R.A. in 1799. Two portraits of her by A. Pope were engraved.

*Pope, Miss Annie. (fl. 1906)

Of London. Exhibited at the R.A. 1906, from The Ingle, Cedar Grove.

Pope, Somerville Stevens. See **Pope-Stevens, Somerville**

Pope, Thomas. d. 1775?

Son of Stevens Pope of Cabragh, and brother of Justin Pope-Stevens senior. Worked in Ireland about the middle of the 18th century. Father of A.

Pope (q.v.), Somerville Pope-Stevens (q.v.), Justin Pope-Stevens jun., and Thomas Pope-Stevens, all of whom were artists. Pope was self-taught in art; practised as a miniature painter and copied old masters. Was living in 1771 and was probably the Thomas Pope whose death was announced in *Exshaw's Magazine* as taking place on 26 September 1775.

Pope-Stevens, Somerville. d. *c.* 1818

Son of Thomas Pope (q.v.) and elder brother of Alexander Pope (q.v.). Was a pupil in the Dublin Society Schools, 1764 and later studied under Thomas Roberts, landscape painter. In 1766, whilst living in Stephen Street, he exhibited at the Dublin Society of Artists as 'Somerville Pope'. Was awarded a premium in 1770. Exhibited up to 1772 under the latter name, but on the death of his uncle, J. Pope-Stevens (died 1771), he came into property at Cabragh, near Dublin and took the additional name of Stevens. Exhibited as 'Somerville Pope-Stevens' in 1772. He exhibited in 1800, 1809 and 1812. In 1783 he was High Sheriff for the County of Dublin. Painted landscapes, fruit pieces and many copies after Vernet; said by Schidlof to have painted miniatures. Died *c.* 1818.

*Porter, Miss Ethel. (fl. 1899–1914)

Of London. Exhibited at the R.A. 1899–1914, from various London addresses. Executed portraits in oil and watercolour and miniatures. The entries for this artist are confusing as her name is given variously as Miss Ethel Porter, E. Porter-Bailey and Mrs. Ethel Porter-Bailey. In 1899 she exhibited from 30 Tite Street, from which address Miss Maud Porter also exhibited. Her sitters included Mrs. Bruce Ingram, Miss Frances Perkin and Mrs. Emerson Armstrong.

*Porter, W. (fl. 1788–1802)

Of London. Exhibited at the R.A., 1788 and 1799–1802. Among the exhibits in 1788 were crayon portraits which may have been miniatures. Schidlof notes him as a miniaturist, but I have not, so far, found any evidence for this, as all his other entries appear to have been portraits and none were in the miniature section.

Possé.

Long records seeing a rather crude miniature portrait of Mrs. Sliman with a printed label at the back stating that it was by 'Possé, pupil of Cosway'.

Pot, Heindrick Gerritsz. *c.* 1585–1657

Born in Haarlem *c.* 1585. Painted historical and genre pictures and portraits some of which may have been small enough to be classed as miniatures, and were painted in oil. Was in London, 1631–1633 during which time he painted portraits of the Royal Family. His work was influenced by Frans Hals. He died in Amsterdam in October 1657. A portrait by him of Charles I of England is in the Louvre.

*Poultney, R. Curzon. (fl. 1894–1896)

Of London. Exhibited at the R.A. 1894–1896, from various London addresses. His sitters included the Marchioness of Ormonde, the Countess of Yarborough and the Lady Beatrice Butler.

*Powell. (fl. 1790)

A miniature signed 'Powell' and dated '1790' was seen by Long; it was of poor quality.

*Powell, Miss Ælfrida. (fl. 1901–1905)

Of London. Exhibited at the R.A. and S.M., 1901–1905 from 43 Sutherland Avenue. Her sitters included Adeline, daughter of the late Sir John

Blois, Bt. In 1901 she exhibited a miniature called 'Looking glass portrait', possibly a self-portrait.

*Powell, Miss Dorothy V. (fl. 1909–1911)

Exhibited at the R.A. 1909–1911, from 40 Lebanon Park, Twickenham and from Studio, 15 Hill Rise, Richmond, Surrey.

Powell, F. (fl. 1814). See also **Powell, John**

Of London. Exhibited an enamel copy on china at the B.I. 1814, from 53 Great Marylebone Street. The subject, 'Girls playing with a Kitten', was after Wright of Derby; its dimensions were 12 in. × 10 in. He was probably identical with J. Powell (q.v.) who exhibited the same subject at the R.A. in 1813, from the same address.

Powell or **Powel, John.** (fl. 1809–1830). See also **Powell, F.**

Of Worcester and London. The above artist has been wrongly identified as Joseph Powell, the landscape painter. John Powell was employed at the Chamberlain Works at Worcester in 1808 and exhibited paintings on enamel on porcelain at the R.A. and B.I. 1809–1830, from various London addresses. His exhibits were copies of paintings by old masters, figure subjects and flowers. His addresses included 27 Thayer Street (1808–1811), 53 Great Marylebone Street and 4 Duke Street, Manchester Square. Information regarding this artist is given by Geoffrey A. Godden, F.R.S.A., in his *Encyclopaedia of British Pottery and Porcelain Marks*, p. 508, 1964. He is described as a 'China painter and seller', of 91 Wimpole Street and 19 Wimpole Street. Signed examples of his china are recorded by Godden, one being a painted mark on a Swansea porcelain cup, 'Powell, / 91 Wimpole St.' and a very rare painted mark on a pair of vases,

> 'J. Powell,
> China enameller to their
> R. & I. Highnesses the
> Princess Charlotte,
> Prince Leopold and
> Gloucester
> 19 Wimpole Street.'

In a directory of 1818, Powell is listed as 'China Painter to his S.H. Prince Leopold & the Princess Sophia of Gloucester'. He was probably identical with the F. Powell who exhibited an enamel copy on china at the B.I. in 1814 from 53 Great Marylebone Street, as the exhibit 'Girls playing with a Kitten', after Wright of Derby, was exhibited by J. Powell at the R.A. in 1813.

Powell, John. (fl. 1778–1785)

Of London. Possibly the John Powell who entered the R.A. Schools, 3 November 1769. Pupil and assistant of Sir Joshua Reynolds; made small copies of the latter's pictures. Exhibited at the R.A., 1778–1785. May have painted miniatures.

*Powell, Joseph Rubens. (fl. 1835–1871)

Of London. Exhibited at the R.A., B.I., etc., 1835–1871. Executed subject pictures, landscapes and in 1835 and 1836 exhibited portraits of gentlemen, at the R.A., which may have been miniatures.

*Powell, W.B. (fl. 1837–1845)

Worked in Devonport or Plymouth. Long records seeing two miniatures by this artist, one signed 'W.B. Powell Pinxit / July 12th 1845' and the other 'W.B. Powell Pinxit / June 16th 1845'. They were rather crudely painted.

*Power, Miss Molly. (fl. 1904–1913)

Exhibited at the R.A. and S.M. 1904–1913, from Glenbrooke, Greenhithe, Kent and Holly Lodge, East Molesey, Surrey.

Powle, George. (fl. 1764–1770)

Of London. Exhibited at the Free Society of Artists and the Society of Artists, 1764–1770. Pupil of Worlidge (q.v.) in whose manner he worked. Lived for a time in Hereford and Worcester. Was associated with the engraver, Valentine Green. Made drawings of Hereford which were engraved. An etched portrait by Powle, published in 1771, is at the B.M.

*Powlet, W. 17th century. See also **P., W.**

The name of William Powlet, limner, has been discovered in the Royal Archives, and he may be the unidentified artist who painted miniatures which are signed W.P. A small miniature of Prince James Francis Edward Stuart, signed 'W.P.' is in the collection of Major R. M. O. de la Hey. One of an unknown man signed 'WP' in monogram, and another of Charles II signed and dated 'WP / 1676' are in the V. & A. M.

*Pownall, Miss Ellen Louise. (fl. 1888–1890)

Of London. Exhibited at the R.A., 1888–1890. Possibly identical with, or related to, the Miss Pownall (no initial given) who exhibited a subject in water-colour at the R.A. in 1874.

Poyntz, Lady Ann. (fl. 1696)

Christie's catalogue, 8 December 1913, Lot 114, was 'A miniature of Sir Nicholas Poyntz, turned to his right, wearing black doublet and jewelled cap with plume, by Lady Ann Poyntz—signed and dated 1696'. The portrait showed a man in 16th-century costume. Anne, second daughter of Charles Howard, 1st Earl of Carlisle, married, 2 August 1670, Sir Richard Graham, Bart., afterwards 1st Viscount Poyntz. The miniature may have been by her, or possibly a daughter.

*Praga, Alfred, P.S.M. 1867–1949

Born in Liverpool, 1867. Was sent to Paris to become a doctor, but his leaning towards art led him to neglect his studies, and he spent much of his time in the Louvre. Went to Antwerp to study art and later spent some time at Heatherley's School of Art. Experimented with painting a miniature, which was seen by Dr. Lumsden Propert who persuaded him to take up miniature painting seriously. Exhibited at the R.A., N.W.C.S., and S.M., 1887 onwards. Was one of the Founder Members of the Society of Miniaturists of which he was President. His sitters included H.R.H. Princess Henry of Battenberg, the Viscountess Althorp, the Rt. Hon. Lord Alveston, Lord Chief Justice of England, etc. His wife was an authoress, by whom he had one son. He lived for many years at The Grey House, Campden Hill. An article in *Hearth and Home*, 7 April 1904, gave an account of his work. He conducted 'The Praga School of Miniature and Portrait Painting' where he gave instruction in miniature painting, portrait painting and art generally, in oil, water-colour, etc. Died 25 February 1949.

*Pratt, Edward D. (fl. 1908–1911)

Of London and Leeds. Exhibited at the R.A., 1908 and 1911.

Pratt, Matthew. 1734–1805

Born in Philadelphia, 23 September 1734; son of a goldsmith. Was apprenticed to J. Claypoole, his uncle, who was a portrait painter. In 1757 he went to Jamaica for six months. Married Elizabeth Moore, 1760. Went to London in 1764 with Benjamin West's fiancée; studied under West. Spent

two and a half years in London, then went to Bristol for eighteen months. Returned to America, 1768 and worked in Philadelphia. Visited England and Ireland in 1770 and in the same year, returned to Philadelphia. Died in Philadelphia, 9 January 1805. Examples of his work are reproduced by Wehle in *American Miniaturists*, p. 99.

Prendergast, Edward. d. 1812

Born in Co. Kerry. An Irish miniaturist. Died in High Street, Galway in March 1812.

*Prentice, Miss Marie. (fl. 1908–1910)

Exhibited at the R.A. and S.M., 1908–1910, from 319 Sauchiehall Street, Glasgow and Airdrie.

Preston, E. (fl. 1824–1843)

Of London. Exhibited at the R.A., N.W.C.S., etc., 1824–1843.

Preston, John. (fl. 1830)

Was working in 1830 in Painswick, Gloucestershire.

Preston, Thomas. (fl. 1764–1773)

Of London. Exhibited at the Free Society of Artists, 1764 and 1773. Painted miniatures and executed drawings in Indian ink. Long saw a miniature of Mr. J. Bowman in the Hon. Frederic Wallop's collection; it was c. 1769, softly painted and signed boldly 'Preston', in grey and buff on the front. The background was stippled. The signature was horizontal and the letters separate.

Prewett or **Prewitt, William.** (fl. 1735–1750?)

Born in Suffolk according to Benezit. Was a pupil of Zincke (q.v.) and one of the best enamellists of the British school. Miniatures by him are scarce. Two signed works by him are in the V. & A. M.; one is of Mr. and Mrs. John Knight and Mr. Newsham, after Vanderbank, signed and dated on the front, 'W. Prewett / pinx 1735'. The other is of Mr. Newsham, signed and dated on the reverse, 'W. Prewett pinx 1736'. A good miniature of Horace Walpole, signed and dated 'W. Prewett pinx 1735' is in the collection of the Duke of Buccleuch (see also the *Walpole Society*, Vol. XLII, pp. 8–9, pl. 4a), and one of Charles, Lord Binning (1692–1732), is in the collection of the Earl of Haddington. A miniature of an unknown man, signed on the reverse 'W. Prewett / pinxt', is in the E. Holzscheiter Collection, Meilen, Zurich. Not all his miniatures are signed, and many may pass unrecognised. A miniature of an unknown man, signed on the reverse 'W. Prewett', is in the N.G., Dublin. It is softly painted as in water-colour.

*Price, Miss Isabella. (fl. 1885–1886)

Of London. Exhibited at the Grosvenor Gallery, 1885–1886.

Prieur, Paul. b. c. 1620. d. after 1683

Born in Geneva, c. 1620; only son of a Parisian jeweller, whose wife's maiden name was de Mahis. After his father's death, he lived with his mother in Geneva (1632–1638) where he was apprenticed to J. Planchant, a jeweller, in 1635. Went to Paris c. 1640. Worked in Spain, England and Denmark where he worked as painter on enamel to the Court, 1660–1681. Was in London, 1682 and 1683. Prieur painted many enamel miniatures for Frederick III and Christian V, including portraits of their families. Between 1671 and 1680, Royal orders amounted to 25,000 crowns. He was a good artist, but one whose work varied, some of it being rather hard. He emphasised the outlines of the nose, eyes and mouth, and painted the faces with a pronounced stippling. His works are frequently signed and dated on the reverse, i.e., Prieur a / Londre / 1682 (or 3), this being the latest date yet known of any of his works. Examples of his miniatures are at the V. & A. M., and a large collection is at Rosenborg Castle, Copenhagen, including one of Frederick III, after van Mander, inscribed on the reverse 'Paulus Prieur Fecit / Anno 1663', and fourteen small replicas, as well as a fine circular enamel of Christian V as a child, and his brothers and sisters, after an earlier painting, signed 'Prieur 1671'.

*Pringle, Miss Mary. (fl. 1897–1901)

Of London. Exhibited at the R.A. 1897 and 1901, from 4 Cedar Studios, Glebe Place, Chelsea.

*Pritchett, Miss Dora C. (fl. 1903–1909)

Of London and Horley, Surrey. Exhibited at the R.A., 1903 and 1909.

*Procter or **Proctor, Miss Irene.** (fl. 1902–1905)

Exhibited at the R.A. 1902–1905, from Twickenham Park, London and 3 Winton Avenue, Westcliffe-on-Sea. Her exhibits included Master Samuel and James Procter, L. Procter, Esq., and Mrs. J. G. Buchannon.

Provis, Ann(a) Jemima. (fl. 1787)

Of London. Exhibited at the R.A., 1787. Said to have had 'the receipt for colouring used by the great Venetian masters', which had been brought from Italy by her grandfather, and which she made known to some English artists.

*Prowett, W. (fl. c. 1785)

A miniature portrait of Mrs. Inchbald, the dramatic actress (1753–1821), painted c. 1785, is illustrated by O'Brien, Pl. 23, and attributed to the above artist.

Pugh, Edward. c. 1760–1813

Born c. 1760. Worked in London and Chester (1800). Exhibited at the R.A. and B.I., 1793–1808. Joined an Artists' Volunteer Corps in 1803. Made drawings for *Modern London*, 1805 and *Cambria Depicta*, 1816. May have been the Mr. Pugh, who was in Manchester, 23 September 1797. Said to have taken up oil painting late in life. Died in Ruthin, June 1813. A miniature of a man signed 'Pugh' on the reverse, with a London address and dated '1803', was exhibited at the Leicester Galleries in August 1926. An engraved portrait after E. Pugh of T. Edwards is at the B.M. The V. & A. M. has a miniature by him signed and dated on the reverse, 'Painted by / Pugh on 28th / April 1803'.

Pugh, T. (fl. 1803)

A miniature of a man signed with a scratched cursive signature, 'T. Pugh 1803' was in the collection of Mr. Joseph Tisserand.

*Pughe, Miss Buddig A. b. 1867

Born in Aberdovey, 17 December 1867. Studied in London and Paris. Worked in Liverpool. Exhibited at the R.A., etc., 1886–1888. Her sitters included Miss Bolton and Lyne Stevens, Esq.

Pulham, F. (fl. c. 1810)

A miniature of c. 1810 of James Neild, signed 'F. Pulham', is at Windsor Castle. It is not of very good quality.

Pulham, Mrs. James Brook. See **Violet, Miss Maria**

Puntita, Madame. (fl. 1859)

Of London. Exhibited at the R.A. 1859, from 8 Montague Street, Portman Square.

Purcell, Edward. (fl. 1812–1831)

Exhibited at the Dublin Society of Artists, 1812–1815 whilst living at Rehoboth Place, Circular Road. Practised for a short time in Waterford. Was in England for some years, returning to Dublin in 1831. Advertised in *Saunders' Newsletter*: 'Edward Purcell, professor of drawing from London, proposes giving instruction at 73. Augier Street. Has taught many of the best families in England'. There is no more information about him after this date. A miniature by him of J. J. McGregor was engraved by S. Freeman, for Vol. III of Will's *Lives of Illustrious Irishmen*.

Purcell, John. (fl. 1830–1833)

Was living at 4 Granby Place, Bristol, 1830–1833.

Pyatt, William. (fl. 1813)

Long saw a miniature of a man in a blue coat, signed neatly in ink on the reverse, 'Painted by Wm Pyatt / March 11th 1813'. It was rather coarsely painted and showed French influence in arrangement and in its uniformly opaque grey background.

*Pyke-Nott, Miss Evelyn C. E. See **Shaw, Mrs. Evelyn Byam**

*Pyke-Nott, Miss Isabel Codrington (Mrs. P. G. Konody). 1874–1943

Born in 1874, daughter of John Nott Pyke-Nott of Bydown House, North Devon, and sister of Evelyn Pyke-Nott (q.v.), and of John, James and George Pyke-Nott. Was awarded a scholarship to the Academy School of Art when only 15 years of age. Was a versatile artist and painted miniatures, large oil paintings, portraits and subjects in watercolour. Exhibited at the R.A., 1894–1929, as well as holding 'one man shows' in London and Paris. She married as her first husband P. G. Konody, who was for many years an art critic on the *Observer*, by whom she had two daughters; and secondly Gustave Mayer of Colnaghi's. Her miniatures, which formed only a small part of her work, were painted during the early years of her first marriage, and were exhibited under her maiden name. She gave up painting for many years, and c. 1918 resumed her painting under her two christian names, Isabel Codrington. Her work met with great success and examples of her paintings are in galleries in England, Australia and Canada. A miniature by her of Constance Collier, an actress, is in the possession of her daughter Mrs. Pauline Jell, to whom I am indebted for the information regarding her life. One of her most notable works was that of a gypsy woman, 'Zillah Gee Hawker'; this was exhibited at the 'Artistes Francais' in 1928 and at the R.A. in 1929, when it was reproduced on the cover of the illustrated catalogue for that year.

Pym, B. (fl. 1793–1811)

Worked in London. Exhibited at the R.A., 1793–1805. Was a miniaturist and engraver. Francis James Jackson, diplomatist, sat to him on 5 March 1811. This information is contained in a letter to Jackson's mother.

*Pyne, Miss Annie. (fl. 1910)

Of London. Exhibited at the R.A. 1910, from 27 Cathcart Hill, Dartmouth Park Hill.

*Pyne, Miss Eva E. (Mrs. A. Warden). (fl. 1894–1913)

Of London. Exhibited at the R.A. 1894–1913, from various London addresses. Possibly related to Miss Annie Pyne (q.v.) from whose address she exhibited in 1911. Her sitters included her grandmother and Mary Olive Elliott, eldest daughter of George Elliott, Esq.

Pyne, William Henry. 1769–1843

Born in London, 1769. Well-known water-colour painter of landscapes, etc. and writer on art. Exhibited at the R.A., and O.W.C.S., 1790–1815, and is believed to have executed a few miniatures. Died at Paddington, 29 May 1843. I am informed by Mr. A. J. B. Kiddell that the above artist wrote under the name of Ephraim Hardcastle.

Q

*Q., A. (fl. 1793)

A miniature of an unknown lady, signed and dated 'A.Q. / 1793' on the front of the portrait was sold at Christie's on 17 December 1968. The miniature, though quite attractive, is loosely painted. (Pl. 281: no. 699.)

Quelen, De. (fl. 1802)

Worked in London. Exhibited at the R.A., 1802. Judging from the names of the sitters, this artist was probably French.

*Quinnell, Cecil Watson. 1868–1932

Born in Meerut, India, 31 May 1868. Worked in London. Exhibited at the R.A. 1897 and 1899, from 7 Flanders Road, Bedford Park. Died in London, 15 September 1932. Painted portraits and miniatures.

*Quistgaard, J. W. von R. (fl. 1909)

Of Paris. Exhibited at the R.A. 1909, from 49 Rue des Belles Feuilles, Paris. His sitter was Dr. G. C. Williamson, author of many books on miniature painting and art. The above artist may have been identical with Johan Valdemar Quistgaard (or Rhehling-Quistgaard) of Denmark (born 9 February 1877).

R

R., A.

A fine enamel signed 'AR' of Lord Rodney, after a painting by Reynolds, was lent to the V. & A. M., in 1927. It was probably late 18th century. A miniature signed 'A.V.R.' was seen by Long.

*R., A.E. (fl. 1807)

Exhibited at the R.A., 1807, catalogue No. 803, 'Portrait of a school-boy'. This unknown artist was an Hon. Exhibitor.

*R., A.V. See **R., A.**

R., I. (fl. 1751–1774). See also **Reubert, J.**

A number of miniatures signed I.R. and dated between the years 1751–1774 are known to exist. Long recorded seeing one signed 'Jean Reubert, 1761' which he thought might be by the same artist, and another signed 'J.R. 1751'. He also saw two large and well painted miniatures of a clergyman and his wife, signed 'I.R. / 1762', and a bracelet miniature of a lady signed 'I.R. / 1759' is in the V. & A. M. I have seen a miniature signed with cursive initials 'I.R. / 1761' and another of a Staff Officer signed 'I.R. / 1774' was sold at Christie's,

15 October 1963. A miniature in my collection of Bishop Palliser (1646–1727), later Archbishop of Cashel, signed 'I.R. / 1759', was one of three family portraits all by the same artist. As Archbishop Palliser died in 1727, the miniature of him must have been painted from an earlier portrait.

R., J. or T. (fl. 1765). See also **J., R.** and **Redmond, T.**

A miniature lent by Sir T. W. Holburne, Bart. to the exhibition at the South Kensington Museum in 1865, stated to be signed 'J.R.', may have been by T. Redmond (q.v.). It represented a gentleman in 'old Windsor uniform', and was painted on ivory. A miniature of an unknown lady, signed and dated 'J.R. 1765' is in the collection of E. G. Paine of New York.

R., M. 18th century. See **R., N.**

Long records seeing a miniature of a man and one of a lady, c. 1760, signed 'MR' in Roman monogram, painted in the manner of N. Hone (q.v.). A portrait of a lady c. 1755 was part of Lot 116 at Christie's, 25 April 1928; the shading on the face was yellow.

*R., N. (fl. 1772). See also **R., M.**

A miniature of an unknown man, executed on paper in pencil and wash, and signed with a cursive monogram 'NR' or 'MR' / '1772', is in the collection of R. Bayne Powell, Esq. The work is good and the character of the sitter well expressed.

R., P. (fl. c. 1790)

A small well painted miniature of a gentleman in the Windsor uniform, c. 1790, and signed with scratched initials 'PR' in Roman capitals on the background was seen by Long.

R., T. (fl. 1802)

A miniature of a man wearing a green coat and white cravat, signed 'TR / 1802' (cursive initials), was seen by Long. It had a greenish tone, and was in the manner of Comerford (q.v.) and T. C. Thompson (q.v.).

R., V. (fl. c. 1660)

A miniature c. 1660 signed 'V.R.' was in the collection of the late Mr. Sidney Hand.

Raeburn, Sir Henry, R.A. 1756–1823

Born in Stockbridge, Edinburgh, 4 March 1756. This famous Scottish portrait painter is known to have painted miniatures early in his career, but probably ceased to do so c. 1780. He was removed from school when he was about fifteen, and apprenticed to Mr. Gililand, a jeweller, and goldsmith. He began to paint miniatures in water-colour of his friends. These received attention and he was sent to David Martin's studio to see his work, and decided to become an artist. He later turned to painting oil portraits. David Deuchar, the seal engraver, gave him some instruction and commissioned the miniature of himself, now in the S.N.P.G. It is inscribed on an old label, probably written by Deuchar's son, on the reverse: 'David Deuchar, Esq; of Morningside, by Sir Henry Raeburn, being the second portrait done by him during the time he was an apprentice with Mr. Gilland, Jeweller, Parliament Square, Edinburgh'; and in a later hand, 'Painted about 1773'. Another authentic miniature by Raeburn is in the collection of Earl Spencer. It represents George John, 2nd Earl Spencer (1758–1834), painted in Rome c. 1785 after a portrait by Gavin Hamilton. References to this miniature are contained in two letters among the Spencer family papers. He died in Edinburgh, 8 July 1823.

Raimbach, Abraham. 1776–1843

Born in Cecil Court, St. Martin's Lane, London, 16 February 1776; son of a Swiss and his English wife, née Martha Butler. Pupil of J. Hall, engraver. Entered the R.A. Schools, 12 August 1797 and was awarded a silver medal there in 1799. Exhibited at the R.A., 1797–1805. In 1802 spent two months in Paris. Joined an Artists' Volunteer Corps in 1803. Became a member of the Society of Engravers in 1804. Married in 1805. Was awarded a gold palette by the Society of Arts in 1806. Painted miniatures and executed numerous engravings after Wilkie and others. Went to live in Greenwich, 1831 where he remained until his death on 17 January 1843, and was buried beside his parents in Hendon. A portrait of him by Sir D. Wilkie is at the N.P.G. A miniature of Frederick Raimbach, by A. Raimbach, painted in 1800, is at the V. & A. M. Of his children, David Wilkie Raimbach (q.v.) and Miss Emma Harriet Raimbach (q.v.), were also miniaturists. His *Memoirs and Recollections* were privately printed in the year of his death, 1843. They were edited by his son, Michael Thomson Scott Raimbach, who, on his death in 1887, bequeathed the portrait of his father by Wilkie to the N.P.G.

*Raimbach, David L. (fl. 1887–1912)

Of London and Birmingham. Exhibited at the N.W.C.S., 1887 and at the R.A. and S.M., 1903–1912 from 42 Fortune Gate Road, Harlesden and from 56 Lissenden Mansions, Highgate. Was probably related to several other artists of this name. Executed studies of heads, miniatures and a scene from Dickens.

Raimbach, David Wilkie. 1820–1895

Born 16 April 1820; youngest son of Abraham Raimbach (q.v.); godson of Sir David Wilkie. Brother of Miss Emma Harriet Raimbach (q.v.). Worked in London, Belfast (1850–1852), Limerick (1854–1855) and Birmingham (1868). Exhibited at the R.A., B.I., etc., 1843–1868. Painted portraits, seascapes and miniatures. Was for twenty years headmaster of the Birmingham School of Art, and until shortly before his death, an examiner for the Science and Art Department. Died 20 February 1895 in Birmingham. A miniature of Mr. P. Rannus by him is at the V. & A. M.

Raimbach, Miss Emma Harriet. 1810–c. 1882

Born 6 July 1810; eldest surviving daughter of Abraham Raimbach (q.v.). Was awarded a silver medal by the Society of Arts in 1826 when living at 10 Warren Street, Fitzroy Square. Subsequently resided in Greenwich. Exhibited at the R.A., etc., 1835–1855. Painted water-colour portraits and miniatures, as well as pencil landscapes. Entered the Convent of the Good Shepherd, Hammersmith c. 1847; later went to a convent in Caën where she was known as 'Sister Mary of St. Arsène'. Died in Caën c. 1882. A miniature of Master E. H. Raimbach, signed 'EHR / 1833', is at the V. & A. M., and Long saw a good and highly finished water-colour portrait by her. A tablet on the wall of St. Mary's Parish Church, Hendon records the death of her father, A. Raimbach (q.v.), and a sister, Juliet Harriet (1806–1816).

*Raimbach, Louis. (fl. 1882–1883)

Of London. Exhibited at the R.A. 1882–1883, from 125 Finborough Road, South Kensington.

*Raine, H. Keyworth. (fl. 1897)

Of London. Exhibited at the R.A. 1897, from Studio, 20 Newman Street.

Raines, William. (fl. 1830)

Was living in 1830 at 17 York Street, Bath. Mentioned in the proceedings of the *Bath Natural History and Antiquarian Field Club*, VIII, 1897, p. 214.

*Ram, Miss Jane Adye. (fl. 1892–1910)

Of London. Exhibited at the R.A., etc., 1892–1910, from Eccleston Studios, 49 Hugh Street, Eccleston Square. Executed oil paintings and miniatures.

Ramage, John. c. 1748–1802

A native of Dublin, born c. 1748; entered the Dublin Society Schools in 1763. Does not appear to have worked in Dublin, but after marrying early in life, Elizabeth, daughter of Henry Liddell, a London merchant, went to America. In 1775 he had established himself in Boston as an artist and goldsmith, and in the same year became a second Lieutenant in the Royal Irish Volunteers, a Regiment formed by the Irishmen of the city; he fought on the English side in the War of Independence. In 1780 he had a studio in New York, No. 25 William Street, where in October 1789, Washington sat to him for a miniature. This is recorded in Washington's diary, who noted under 3 October 1789, 'Sat for Mr Ramage near two hours to-day, who was drawing a miniature picture of me for Mrs. Washington'. It represented Washington in full uniform, without a hat, and was set in a chased gold frame made by the artist. Ramage married twice. His first wife died in 1784, and he then married Catherine, daughter of John Collins of New York in 1787. Left New York for Montreal after becoming involved in debts. Some of his household goods were sold up by a Sheriff in 1794. He died in Montreal, 24 October 1802. Ramage painted miniatures and portraits in crayon and pastel. A number of his works are in the U.S.A., including a miniature of Gilbert Budd, dated on the reverse, 'Jan 19th 1791', in the collection of E. G. Paine of New York.

*Ramsden, Richard H. (fl. 1883–1884)

Of London. Exhibited at the R.A., 1883–1884. His sitters included Miss Florence Cholmondely Tyas and Miss Gertrude Williamson.

*Randal, Charles. (fl. 1892)

Of London. Exhibited at the R.A., 1892. Painted miniatures and landscapes in water-colour.

*Randon, D. (fl. c. 1705). See also **Rawdon, D.**

A miniature of Susannah and the Elders, by the above artist, signed and dated '1705', executed on parchment, was Lot 63 at Christie's 22 April, 1969. The artist may possibly be identical with D. Rawdon (q.v.).

*Rappard, Miss Josine. (fl. 1886–1894)

Of Wandsworth. Exhibited at the R.A., N.W.C.S., etc. 1886–1894, from 28 Gorst Road, Wandsworth Common.

Rauw. (fl. 1820). See **Rouw, H.** and **Rouw, Peter**

According to the sale catalogue at Sotheby's, 16 June 1927, Lot 136 was a miniature of an officer of the 60th Regiment, inscribed on the reverse, 'Jany. 19th, 1820. Painted by Rauw, Painter & Sculptor.' The painting was rather hard and stiff. This may have been by either H. Rouw (q.v.) or Peter Rouw (q.v.).

Raven, J. See **Raven, S.**

Raven, Samuel. c. 1775–1847

Born c. 1775. Worked in Birmingham. Was living at 28 Bartholomew Street, 1828–1829. J. Raven is recorded at the same address, 1822–1823; the J may be a misprint. S. Raven died in Birmingham, 10 December 1847. He painted the lids of papier-mâché snuff-boxes and miniatures. The N.P.G. has a miniature of John Emery by Raven, and the V. & A. M. has a circular papier-mâché box with a portrait of George IV, after Lawrence, signed 'S. Raven' on the lid. Said to have been patronised by the Duke of Kent, H.R.H. the Duke of Sussex and Prince Leopold of Saxe-Coburg.

Rawdon, D. (fl. 1705). See also **Randon, D.**

Long records seeing a copy on ivory ($\frac{1}{16}$ in. thick), of a picture by Titian or Giorgione, signed 'D. Rawdon Fecit 1705'. He noted that it was one of the earliest miniatures on ivory which he had seen. Lot 121 on the 18th day of the Strawberry Hill sale in 1842, was catalogued as 'A miniature painting after Raphael, by D. Rawdon, 1763'. The date may have been wrongly deciphered.

Rayment, F. See **Raymont, F.**

Raymond, Francis. (fl. 1778)

Of Upper Tooting. Exhibited at the Free Society of Artists, 1778.

Raymont or Rayment, F. (fl. 1829)

Exhibited at the R.A., 1829. The name is spelt Raymont in the index and Rayment in the catalogue. The exhibit was a portrait of Mrs. Longley.

*Rayne, Miss Dorothy. (fl. 1909–1914)

Exhibited at the R.A. 1909–1914, from Pond House, Teddington. Was undoubtedly the sister of Miss Lilian M. Rayne (q.v.).

*Rayne, Miss Lilian M. (fl. 1909–1914)

Of Teddington. Exhibited at the R.A., 1909–1914. Undoubtedly the sister of Miss Dorothy Rayne (q.v.), who exhibited from the same address, and a portrait of whom she exhibited in 1911.

Read, Miss. (fl. 1799–1800)

Of Silsoe, Beds. Exhibited at the R.A., 1799–1800.

Read, Miss Catherine. 1723–1778

Born in 1723 of a well-to-do Scottish family; studied in France and Italy; established herself in London as a portrait painter in oil and pastel, and also painted miniatures. Exhibited at the R.A., the Society of Artists and the Free Society of Artists, 1760–1779 from St. James's Place, London and Jermyn Street. She painted a number of portraits of children, including her niece, Helena Beatson (later Lady Oakeley), who later joined her in India. Sir William Foster, in *British Artists in India*, *Walpole Society*, Vol. XIX, pp. 63–65, gives some details of their stay in that country. On 25 January 1777 they obtained permission to go to Fort St. George, having been to Bombay; she painted the family of the Nawab of the Carnatic in 1777. She was urged to go to Calcutta, but appears to have decided against it on grounds of health. In a letter quoted by Dodswell, *Nabobs of Madras*, pp. 171, 198, it says, 'The old lady is vastly liked by everybody, and has been visited by the young Nabob (of Arcot). I hear she is going to draw his picture; if this should be her fortune it will be a great thing for her.' After her niece married Charles Oakeley, 21 October 1777, she is said to have looked down upon her 'shabby old aunt'. She became in bad health and in early October 1778, accompanied by her brother (a surgeon), she went to Negapatam to take a passage for the Cape of Good Hope; she died on 13 December 1778 before reaching her destination. She is said to have made her will on 29 June 1777, giving directions that she should be buried in Madras. Three of her paintings are illustrated in *Women Painters of the World*, edited by W. Shaw Sparrow, 1905. Many of her works were engraved including one of the celebrated Gunning sisters.

Read, Frederic. 1800 – 1875

Had a Portuguese mother and spent some years in Lisbon as a boy. Attended a school in Red Lion Square, Holborn 1810 – 1812. By his wife Mary née Ransome (d.1831) he had one child, Frederick Titus (q.v.). Worked in London, Bath (1829) and Cheltenham (1832 – 1843). Exhibited at the R.A. and S.B.A. 1817 – 1852. His address in 1829 was 12 Caroline Buildings, Widcombe, Bath. In c. 1850 he moved to Hampton Wick in Middlesex, where he died in 1875 and where he was buried. A collection of ten miniatures by this artist, representing Henry VIII and his six Queens, Elizabeth I, Mary Queen of Scots and Edward VI (after Holbein), was sold at Sotheby's, 12 April 1960. He used a minute stippling on the faces of his sitters. His signature is usually F. Read fᵗ (scratched), or in full on the reverse with a date and address. His work is slightly reminiscent of that of Ross (q.v.). The Victoria Art Gallery, Bath, has five miniatures by him including portraits of himself and his wife. There is also one by him at the V. & A. M.

Read, F., junior. (fl. 1855-1857) See **Read, Frederick Titus**

Of London. Exhibited at the R.A. 1855-1857, including a portrait of George Baxter, noted for 'Baxter Prints', and 'the artist's eldest son'. His address was 2 Alfred Place, Bedford Square.

Read, Frederick Titus. 1824 – 1904

Born 5 May 1824, only child of Frederic Read (q.v.) and Mary Read, named after his godfather Titus West who left him his house 2 Alfred Place, Tottenham Court Road. Identical with F. Read junior (q.v.). Worked as a miniature painter, teacher and restorer. Copied works by Cosway and according to Lumsden Propert '. . .a copy by you is no joke'. Painted historical miniatures and is known to have executed copies of Henry VIII and his wives, after Holbein. A miniature of an unknown lady was lent by Mr. D. Coutts Marjoribanks, M.P. to the exhibition at the South Kensington Museum in 1865, when it was catalogued as by F.T. Read. He died in 1904 and was buried in the churchyard at Hampton Wick.

Read, J. C. (fl. 1841–1849)

Was awarded a premium by the Society of Arts in 1841. Exhibited at the R.A., 1847–1849. Worked in Hammersmith.

Read, Mrs. John. See **Beetham, Miss Jane**

Read, Miss Katherine. See **Read, Miss Catherine**

Read, William. (fl. 1778–1796)

Of London. Exhibited at the R.A., 1778 and 1781, and 'a portrait of an artist' at the Society of Artists in 1778, from various London addresses. Was working in Bath, 22 January 1789. Probably identical with the artist of the same name who exhibited 'Subjects from Henry the Fourth' at the R.A., 1808. Two miniatures by him are illustrated in O'Brien; one is of Richard John and Jane Tibbets, inscribed on the reverse 'Jane Tibbets 4 years 4 months old, Richard John Tibbets, 2 years 4 months old / Barton Seagrave—W. Read.pinxit.1796'; the other of a man standing by a column, a church and steeple in the background, is signed on the front 'WRead 1786', the two first letters being joined. Long records seeing a somewhat mediocre miniature signed 'Reid / 1782' which may have been by him. The B.M. has an engraved portrait of H. Worthington after W. Read.

*Reading, Miss Beatrice. (fl. 1902–1903)

Of London. Exhibited at the R.A. 1902 and 1903, from 142 Abbey Road, West Hampstead.

Record, W. S. (fl. 1826)

Long recorded seeing a small water-colour portrait of a lady, painted on card by the above artist in April 1826. It was not of any outstanding merit, although it did show a certain degree of technical skill, and expressed something of the sitter's character.

Redmond, Thomas. c. 1745–1785

Born c. 1745 or earlier; son of a clergyman at Brecon (not an incumbent, as no Vicar of that name is recorded at that time). Was apprenticed to a house painter at Bristol. Went to London and studied at the St. Martin's Lane Academy. Exhibited at the Society and Free Society of Artists, 1762–1771 and at the R.A., 1775–1783. Exhibited from Brecon, 1767 and, from 1769 onwards, from Bath. From 1782–4 he lived in Church Street, Bath. Died in Bath, 1785 and was survived by three sons. Painted pictures and small crayon portraits. Signed TR in cursive capitals (sometimes in a light colour on a dark spot of the background); these signatures have been read as JR. Redmond sometimes used a yellowish brown shading on the face, the features being drawn with long brush strokes. Occasionally he used stippling. Long records having heard of a miniature by him dated '1758'. Some of his work is reminiscent of N. Hone (q.v.). The V. & A. M. has a miniature of a clergyman by Redmond, signed 'TR'. The sitter may have been a member of a family named Fenton.

*Ree, Rd. (Richard?)

This artist is recorded by Long with no further information.

*Reed, Miss Annie L. (fl. 1888)

Of Gipsy Hill. Exhibited at the R.A., 1888. Her sitters included Sidney Colvin, Esq.

*Reed, Hilda (Mrs. B.). (fl. 1895–1899)

Of Hexham, Northumberland. Exhibited at the R.A., 1895 and 1899.

*Reed, Miss M. (fl. 1895)

Of London. Exhibited a miniature of Col. C. Reed, C.B., at the R.A. 1895, from 293 Oxford Street, was possibly identical with Miss Mary E. Reed (q.v.).

*Reed, Miss Mary E. (fl. 1897)

Exhibited at the R.A. 1897, from 24 Welbeck Street, Cavendish Square. Was possibly identical with Miss M. Reed (q.v.).

Reekes, Richard. (fl. 1810)

Exhibited at the R.A. 1810, from a London address when he described himself as 'Miniature Painter to H.R.H. the Princess of Wales'.

*Reeves, Miss Edith M. (Mrs. B. A.). (fl. 1896–1898)

Of London. Exhibited at the R.A., 1896–1898. Painted portrait miniatures and miniatures of dogs.

Reid, Alexander. 1747–1823

Born in Kircudbrightshire, 1747. Exhibited at the Society of Artists, 1770. Was in Paris before the Revolution. Worked in Dumfries. Painted oil portraits, landscapes and miniatures. Burns sat to him in January 1796. The S.N.P.G., Edinburgh has a miniature on ivory of Burns which is believed to be the portrait which Burns stated in a letter, 29 January 1796, that he was giving sittings for. Reid succeeded to a family estate in Kirkeenan, near

Dalbeattie, in 1804, where he settled. He died unmarried in 1823.

*Reid, Miss Isabella E. (fl. 1897–1906)
Exhibited at the R.A. and S.M., 1897–1906, from 37 Albyn Place, Aberdeen. Her sitters included Professor Reid, F.R.C.S.

*Reid or Reed, Miss Marion. (fl. 1909–1911)
Of London. Exhibited at the R.A. 1909–1911, from 112 Goldhurst Terrace, N.W.

*Reilly, Charles A. (fl. 1906)
Of London. Exhibited at the R.A. 1906, from 49 Chesilton Road, Fulham.

*Reilly, Mrs. Nell P. (fl. 1904)
Exhibited at the R.A. 1904, from Moss Lane, Pinner, Middlesex.

*Reilly, U. 18th century
The above artist, who is hitherto unrecorded, is known only by a miniature of an unknown officer, which was sold at Sotheby's on 22 April 1968. The miniature is signed on the front 'U. Reilly'; the sitter is wearing a red jacket, with a blue collar, gold epaulettes; the background is shaded with cross hatching and the general effect is slightly amateurish. (Pl. 286: no. 714.)

*Reily, Francis. (fl. 1903)
Exhibited at the R.A. 1903, from 68 Forest Road, Southport. The exhibit was a portrait of the artist's mother.

*Reily, James. d. 1780 or 1788
Educated at the Blue-Coat School, Oxmantown, Ireland, 1745–1748; was apprenticed to Samuel Dixon, for whom he coloured prints. Being poor, but having aptitude for drawing, was placed by the Dublin Society at Robert West's drawing school. After completing his apprenticeship he set up his own practice as a miniaturist in Capel Street, moving later to a house in Grafton Street where he resided up to his death. Married in 1760, Jane Blackley of County Meath. He exhibited at the Dublin Society of Artists, 1765–1779. Painted portraits and is said to have attempted without success to paint historical pictures, and also executed miniatures. His miniatures are well drawn and expressive. He signed J. Reily followed by a date, and Reily followed by a date. Examples of his work are at the N.G., Dublin and at the V. & A.M. (Pl. 286: no. 715.)

Reinagle, Miss. (fl. 1791–1807)
Presumably one of the daughters of Ramsay Richard Reinagle, R.A. Painted portraits and miniatures. Exhibited at the R.A., 1791–1807.

Reinagle, Miss Maria Anna Theresa. See Schetky, Mrs. J. G. C.

Reinagle, Philip, R.A. 1749–1833
Born in 1749. Entered the R.A. Schools, 28 February 1769; studied under Allan Ramsay. Exhibited at the R.A. and B.I., 1773–1832. Elected A.R.A., 1787 and R.A., 1812. Was a skillful copyist of old Dutch pictures. Painted portraits, animals, hunting scenes and landscapes; is only known as a miniaturist by a miniature in oil on ivory of Mrs. Elizabeth Spilsbury, which he painted c. 1800 and which was lent to the exhibition at the South Kensington Museum in 1865. Died in Chelsea, 27 November 1833. (Pl. 287: no. 716)

Reisen, Charles Christian. 1680–1725. See **Christian, Jacobus**
Was a seal engraver in London. There is no evidence that he ever painted miniatures, but Goulding notes a miniature at Welbeck Abbey of the Duchess of Lennox and Richmond, inscribed in ink on the reverse 'Mʳ Christian Pictor'. This may be by Reisen or Jacobus Christian (q.v.).

*Rémandas, Mme. Lily. (fl. 1889–1895)
Of London. Exhibited at the R.A., 1889–1895.

Renshaw, Ellen. (fl. 1840–1842)
Of Clapton. Exhibited at the R.A., 1840–1842.

Renton, John. (fl. 1799–1839)
Of London. Exhibited at the R.A., 1799–1839. Painted landscapes, portraits, etc., and some miniatures, one of which was exhibited at the R.A., in 1799 (No. 711). A portrait in oil on panel by him was lent by Mr. Wm. Tite, M.P., to the miniature exhibition at the South Kensington Museum in 1865. He imitated the style of several other artists in his drawings.

*Renton, John D. (fl. 1907–1912)
Exhibited at the R.A. 1907–1912, from Clare House, Tiverton, Devon.

*Reubert, Jean. (fl. 1761). See also **R., I.**
A miniature signed 'J. Reubert' and dated '1761' was seen by Long. The artist may have been the one who signed 'I.R.', and whose works appear in the sale rooms from time to time. For more information see under **R., I.**

Reurie. 17th century
Mentioned by Sanderson in his *Graphice*, 1658 who says, 'Reurie for most Paintings, usually in little'. From the context it would appear that he painted in oil.

*Reuss, Miss Lilly. (fl. 1890)
Of Manchester. Exhibited at the R.A., 1890, a miniature of Arthur Poole, Esq., as 'Sergeant Buzfuz'.

Reyland. See Ryland

*Reynolds, Miss C. Jean (Jeannie). (fl. 1909–1911)
See also **Reynolds, Miss Caroline J.**
Exhibited at the R.A., and S.M. 1909–1911, from Ellesmere, 242 Kew Road, Kew Gardens and Sunbury-on-Thames. Probably identical with Miss Caroline J. Reynolds (q.v.) who exhibited at the R.A., 1898.

*Reynolds, Miss Caroline J. (fl. 1898). See also **Reynolds, Miss C. Jean**
Exhibited at the R.A. 1898, from Langham, Alton, Hants. Was probably identical with Miss C. Reynolds (q.v.) who exhibited at the R.A. Her sitters included Mrs. Forster Reynolds.

Reynolds, E. (fl. 1822)
Of London. Exhibited at the R.A. 1822, from 1 Beaufort Buildings, Strand.

Reynolds, Miss Elizabeth. See Walker, Mrs. William

Reynolds, Miss Fanny. (fl. 1828–1830)
Of London; daughter of S. W. Reynolds, the engraver, and sister of Miss Elizabeth Reynolds, later Mrs. William Walker (q.v.), with whom she lived at one time. Exhibited at the R.A., 1828–1830.

Reynolds, Miss Frances. 1729–1807
Born in Plympton, 10 May 1729 (Redgrave), or 6 June 1729 (*D.N.B.*). Sister of Sir Joshua Reynolds for whom she kept house in London. She painted miniature copies of pictures by her brother as well as some original oil portraits. Wrote an *Essay on Taste*, and some verse. Knew Dr. Johnson, the Duke of Marlborough and Goldsmith. After Reynolds' death she moved to a large house in Queen Square, Westminster where she exhibited her own works. Her self-portrait, on ivory, was among those lent to the exhibition at the South Kensington Museum in 1865. She died at her house, 1 November 1807. According to Redgrave, her work was of no outstanding merit, and Dr. Johnson, who sat to her, described the portrait as 'Johnson's grimly ghost'.

Reynolds, Sir Joshua, P.R.A. 1723–1792
The only reason for thinking that this great portrait painter ever painted miniatures is recorded by Long and is an account, which he autographed against Lord Granby, 27 January 1762, for painting three portraits of his lordship and a miniature of Lady Granby, amounting in all to £117. 4s. (Maggs Bros. Catalogue, No. 488, 1927, p. 204). Many miniaturists had his permission to copy his paintings. The exhibition at the South Kensington Museum, 1865 contained three portraits attributed to Reynolds; Lord George Augustus Cavendish (died 1794), a sketch on paper, a profile portrait of Mrs. Edmund Burke, pencil on paper, and a miniature on ivory of the Rt. Hon. Edmund Burke when a young man. The *Evening Standard*, 22 July 1927, p. 6, col. 3, referring to Lord Portarlington's heirlooms said, 'I trust the Mrs. FitzHenry miniature by Sir Joshua Reynolds, a great rarity, which forms part of the collection, will not leave the country; but as it has been valued by an expert at £12,000, there is a probability that it will.'

*Reynolds, Miss Marian W. (fl. 1901–1905)
Of London, Exhibited at the Society of Miniaturists, 1901–1905.

*Reynolds, Reginald F. (fl. 1902)
Of London. Exhibited at the R.A. 1902, from 86 Castelnau, Barnes.

*Rhodes, W. P. (fl. 1871–1878)
Of London and Llandudno. Exhibited at the R.A., etc., 1871–1878. The exhibit in 1871 was 'Head after Van Dyck', enamelled on porcelain, and his address, 9 Shawfield Street, King's Road, Chelsea. In 1876 he exhibited what was probably a subject picture from 32 Madoc Street, Llandudno, N. Wales.

Rhone, Sexton. d. 1783
Nothing is known about this artist who is recorded by Strickland as having worked as a miniaturist in Ireland. He died at Killaloe on 20 May 1783.

*Rice, Lieut. Henry, R.N. b. 1788
Was born in 1788. A miniature self-portrait; one of Princess Charlotte, daughter of George IV, and another of Princess Amelia, daughter of George III, after a miniature by A. Robertson (q.v.) are all reproduced by O'Brien, Pl. 53 and 54. His self-portrait is inscribed on the reverse, 'Painted by Henry Rice. Lt. R.N. of himself, April 1833, aged 45'. The portrait of Princess Amelia is inscribed on the reverse, 'Painted by Lt. Henry Rice, RN'. The miniature of Princess Charlotte, which is probably after a miniature by Jeremiah Steele (q.v.), is similarly signed on the reverse.

*Richards, Miss Anna. (fl. 1898–1899)
Of London. Exhibited at the R.A., 1898 and 1899. Probably related to W. T. Richards who exhibited large oil paintings from the same address, 21 Pembridge Road, Notting Hill Gate.

Richards, J. (fl. 1762–1783)

Of London. Exhibited at the Society of Artists and the Free Society of Artists, 1762–1783. His exhibits were principally landscapes, but included two miniatures. The *D.N.B.* identifies him with John Inigo Richards, R.A. (died 1810), but Long considered this unlikely.

Richards, Letitia. (fl. 1828)

Painted in miniature and on velvet. In 1828 was living at Brownlow Hill, Liverpool.

Richards, M. (fl. 1774)

Of Birmingham. Exhibited at the Liverpool Society of Artists, 1774. The exhibit was 'Rural Conversation' on enamel.

*Richardson, Miss Ada E. (fl. 1902–1914)

Of London. Exhibited at the R.A. 1902–1914, from addresses in North London. Her sitters included Miss Katie Richardson.

*Richardson, Miss Amy. 19th century

The following miniatures after Sir W. C. Ross (q.v.) were catalogued for sale at Sotheby's, 12 December 1966, but were withdrawn by the family before the sale took place. They were of The Rev. Joseph Gibbs, The Rev. John Lloyd Crawley and Mary Crawley, and were by the above artist.

*Richardson, Jonathan, junior. 1694–1771

Only son of Jonathan Richardson, portrait painter, with whom he lived. Assisted his father. Amateur portrait painter. A portrait of a man signed by him was Lot 27 at Sotheby's, 18 February 1963. He died in Queen Sq., Bloomsbury, 6 June 1771, aged 77, and was buried in the churchyard of St. George-the-Martyr. A supposed self-portrait of the artist when a boy, probably after a portrait executed by Jonathan Richardson senior, is in the V. & A. M. It is pencil on vellum and signed on the reverse 'R / 5 May 1735'.

Richardson, Joseph. (fl. *c.* 1825–1828)

Worked in Manchester *c.* 1825–1828 at 104 London Rd.

Richardson, P. (Pitt) H. (fl. 1739)

A miniature, said to represent Lady Mary Wortley Montagu, by the above artist, signed and dated '1739', is in the collection of E. G. Paine of New York. (Pl. 287: no. 717.)

Richardson, Mrs. Samuel or **Richardson, Mrs. T. M.** See Schetky, Miss Caroline

Richmond, George, R.A. 1809–1896

Born in Brompton, 28 March 1809; younger son of T. Richmond (q.v.). Entered the R.A. Schools, 23 December 1824. Exhibited at the R.A., B.I., etc., 1825–1880. Was in early life, a friend of Blake, E. Calvert and S. Palmer. Went to France in 1828 for some months. Eloped with Julia Tatham whom he married at Gretna Green in 1831, and by whom he had fifteen children. Painted miniatures and portraits in oil and water-colour. Went with his wife and Samuel Palmer to Italy in 1837–1839. After his return to England, devoted himself principally to crayon portraits. Was a prolific artist and painted many of the principal personages of the day. Was a good musician, and one of the earliest cigarette smokers in England. Became A.R.A., in 1857, and R.A., in 1866. Practised sculpture towards the end of his life. Was the father of Sir W. B. Richmond, R.A. Died at 20 York Street, Portman Square, London, 19 March 1896 and was buried at Highgate. Some miniatures by him were lent to the exhibition at the South Ken-

sington Museum in 1865. Examples of his work are at the V. & A. M., and N.P.G.

Richmond, Thomas. 1771–1837

Born in Kew, 28 March 1771, younger son of Thomas Richmond (1740–1794) and his wife, Ann Bone, who was a cousin of George Engleheart (q.v.). His father's family came from Yorkshire and Thomas Richmond senior was 'groom of the stables' to the Duke of Gloucester, and later proprietor of the 'Coach and Horses' in Kew. Was a pupil of his cousin, George Engleheart, and also studied at the St. Martin's Lane Academy. Worked in London and Portsmouth. Exhibited at the R.A., 1795–1829. He married Anne Oram (died 1859) some time before 1802. He painted her miniature in 1808. His sons, Thomas jun., and George Richmond (q.v.), both followed their father's profession. Was employed by the Royal family to copy miniatures by Cosway (q.v.) and Engleheart. Richmond made copies of portraits by Reynolds and executed numerous miniatures on ivory and paper, and large oval portraits in water-colour. His work shows the influence of G. Engleheart. He died in London, 15 November 1837, and was buried in Paddington Churchyard. Many of his sitters were Naval and Military officers. By no means all his works are signed. Those on paper are frequently painted with the heads in colour and the rest in pencil; some portraits are full or half-length. His signature is a cursive R followed by a date, and from *c.* 1800 he sometimes added his address, 42 Half Moon Street. He was a good artist and drew with strength and vitality; his water-colour portraits on paper are very attractive. Many of his unsigned miniatures may be ascribed to Engleheart. I have seen a set of eight profile miniatures on paper, of the family of the Duke of Buccleuch, all painted in 1796. Two miniatures by Richmond were exhibited in Edinburgh in 1965, including one of an unknown man from my collection which is of exceptionally fine quality and brilliant colouring.

Richmond, Thomas, junior. 1802–1874

Born 16 September 1802; elder son of Thomas Richmond senior (q.v.) and brother of George Richmond (q.v.). Entered the R.A. Schools, 25 November 1820 aged 18. Exhibited at the R.A. and S.B.A., 1822–1860. Was awarded a silver Isis medal by the Society of Arts in 1823. Worked in Sheffield and London. Accompanied Miss Tatham to Gretna Green to marry George Richmond in 1831. Visited Rome in 1840 where he met Ruskin. Bought an estate in Windermere where he lived until his death, 13 November 1874. Was buried in Brompton, London. Painted miniatures and portraits in oil and water-colour.

Richter, Christian. 1678–1732

Born in Stockholm, 1678; son of Hans Davidson Richter, assessor to the Goldsmiths' Corporation, and his wife Brita B. Selling. Was apprenticed as a goldsmith, 1695–1698. Studied metal engraving under Arvid Karlsteen. After visiting Berlin and Dresden he came to London in 1702 where he knew the Swedish painters Hysing and Dahl, as well as Boit (q.v.). He modelled a wax portrait of Augustus II; became a leading miniaturist, painted in oil and is said to have executed miniatures on enamel. Much of his work was copying in miniature, paintings by Lely, Kneller, Dahl and Cooper (q.v.); these are faithful replicas, but he had his own style and, therefore, earned his place as a first rate miniaturist. The reason for his painting being mainly confined to copying was said to have been due to an unpleasant illness, which had disfigured his face. His brother David, and a cousin David, were also miniaturists. Died in Brewer Street, Golden

Square, and was buried, 18 November 1732, in St. James's, Piccadilly. He used a minute stippling on the face combined with a number of nearly perpendicular small brush strokes which, with a lens, can be seen even on the eyeballs. He favoured a reddish grey shading and painted on a thin parchment previously prepared. He normally signed on the reverse of the card with a cursive C.R. in pencil with a date below it. Occasionally the surname is written in full and only very rarely is the signature on the front. Long records a miniature of a man, sold at Sotheby's, 3 February 1927, signed on the reverse 'CRichter pint / 1732 / London'. Examples of his work are at the V. & A. M., N.P.G., and the Wallace Collection, London, who have a copy by him of Cromwell after Cooper, of which another identical version is in my own collection. Five miniatures by him were exhibited in Edinburgh, 1965, including that of Sir James Thornhill, inscribed and dated on the reverse 'Sir James Thornhill, Richter Pinxit London 1718'; John Churchill, 1st Duke of Marlborough, signed and dated on the reverse, '1714'; Matthew Prior; and a fine rectangular miniature of Mrs. Elizabeth Eliot, née Craggs, inscribed and dated on the reverse, 'Richter, 1726. London'. Other examples of his work are in the collections of Earl Beauchamp and the Duke of Portland, who has a particularly charming miniature of Lady M. Harley, after Dahl. Miniatures by him were loaned to the South Kensington Museum exhibition, 1865.

Richter, Miss Henrietta S. (fl. 1842–1849)

Of London. Exhibited at the R.A., 1842–1849. In 1842 and 1844, she was an Hon. Exhibitor. Undoubtedly related to H. J. Richter (q.v.), as both exhibited from 86 Lisson Grove for some years.

Richter, Henry James. 1772–1857

Born in London, 18 March 1772; son of a German artist. Probably the Henry Richter who entered the R.A. Schools, 19 November 1790 aged 18. Undoubtedly related to Miss H. S. Richter (q.v.) who shared the same address, 86 Lisson Grove, for some years. Studied under Cruickshank, the anatomist, and T. Stothard. Painted landscapes, portraits and figure subjects, and presumably also executed miniatures as it is recorded that J. Sartain (q.v.) had instruction from him on miniature painting, and some of his exhibits at the R.A. were in the Drawing and Miniature section. Was also an engraver. Exhibited at the R.A., B.I., O.W.C.S., etc., 1788–1856; was a member of the O.W.C.S., 1813. The B.I. purchased a picture of a religious subject by him in 1812 for £525. He wrote on metaphysics. Died at 101 Lisson Grove, London, 8 April 1857.

*Richter, Jean Louis. 1766–1841

Born in Geneva, 20 August 1766. Painted miniatures on ivory and on enamel. Was a pupil of Philippe and David Roux, and in 1828 was associated with Julien Troll. He painted chiefly genre subjects and landscapes on enamel for boxes. I have found no evidence that he came to England, but the N.G., Dublin has a miniature on enamel of Charles James Fox, which is attributed to him, and an oblong enamel view of a palace, signed on the front 'Richter à Genève'. Died in Geneva, 21 July 1841.

*Rickaby, Charles. (fl. 1769)

A letter from the Rev. Dr. John Sharp to David Garrick, from Corpus Christi College, Cambridge, 26 May 1769, says, 'We have just set our seal to an instrument finely illuminated by Mr Charles Rickaby, to be delivered to the Danish Ministers and sent to Copenhagen. . . . It is drawn on vellum with various emblematic paintings in water colours, of the Arts and Sciences'. This information occurs in the *Private Correspondence of David Garrick*, 1931, Vol. I, p. 349.

Rickards, Samuel, F.S.A. *c.* 1735–1823

Was born *c.* 1735. Worked in London. Exhibited at the Society of Artists (Director, 1776) and the Free Society of Artists, 1768–1776, and at the R.A., 1776–1777. Exhibited a miniature of Thomas Pennant in 1775. A miniature of a lady with a bird by him, *c.* 1772, with a landscape background, mostly in opaque colour, is at the V. & A. M. He spent the last years of his life in Alfreton, Derbyshire, where he died, 12 March 1823 aged 88, and was buried in the churchyard where his gravestone exists. A miniature, said to be by him, of General Barker, is in the collection of E. G. Paine of New York.

Rickerby, Miss Eliza Greenup. (fl. 1835–1844)

Of Chelsea. Was awarded premiums by the Society of Arts in 1835, 1838 and 1842. Exhibited at the R.A., 1840–1844. Executed drawings and miniatures. A miniature of a young girl, signed and dated 'Eliza Rickerby, 1842', was reproduced by Sidney Hand, *Signed Miniatures*. In 1844 she was an Hon. Exhibitor at the R.A.

*Ricketts, Miss Amy. (fl. 1889–1890)

Of Bath. Exhibited at the R.A., 1889–1890. Duveen recorded that she was asking 10 gns. for her portrait of Miss Agnes Huntingdon in 1890.

*Rigaud, Stephen François Dutilh. 1777–1861

Born in London, 1777; son of the painter John Francis Rigaud. Entered the R.A. Schools, 27 March 1792, aged 14. Obtained a silver medal in 1794 and a gold one in 1801. Became a Founder member of the Royal Society of Painters in Water Colours (O.W.C.S.), 1804/5, and exhibited there, and at the R.A. and B.I., 1797–1852. Painted portraits in oil and water-colour and historical subjects. Schidlof lists him as a miniaturist, but I do not know of any miniatures by him. He died in London, 1861. Some water-colours by him are in the V. & A. M.

*Rinzi, Ernest. 1836–1909

Was born in 1836. Of London. Exhibited at the R.A., 1886–1899, including portraits of 'the late Marchioness of Abergavenny', 'the late Lord Randolph Churchill', and other notable persons. In 1894 he painted James Stirling Stuart (born 1891) and Rae Stirling Stuart (born 1890). The former miniature is now in the collection of Mme H. Stuart Stevenson, the sitter's sister, and is signed 'E. Rinzi', in block letters on the front. There is a slight suggestion of a photographic base, but it is well painted and expressive. Died in June 1909, according to Schidlof, or 12 July 1909 according to Benezit. An attractive miniature of a child, 'Iris', *c.* 1895, signed 'E. Rinzi', is in the collection of Miss Alison Warner.

Rippingale, Alexander. (fl. 1830–1831). See also Rippingille, Alexander

The above artist is recorded by Long as living at 8 Lower Crescent, Bristol in 1830 and 1831. He may be identical with Alexander Rippingille (q.v.), the subject and portrait painter. Long noted seeing a miniature by Rippingale, *c.* 1825, which he considered pleasing.

Rippingille, Alexander. (fl. 1824–1835). See also Rippingale, Alexander

Subject and portrait painter. Possibly identical with Alexander Rippingale (q.v.). Lived at Clifton,

Bristol. Exhibited at the R.A. and S.B.A., 1824–1835. His only exhibit at the R.A. was in 1834, when his address was given as 91 Dean Street, Soho Square. The B.M. has engraved portraits after A. Rippingille.

*Rippingille, or Rippingale, Edward Villiers. 1798–1859

Born in Kings Lynn, 1798; son of a farmer. Was self-taught in art. Exhibited at the R.A., B.I., etc., 1813–1857. Painted figure subjects and rural scenes. Worked in London and Bristol. May have painted miniatures as one signed 'E.V. Rippingale / 1818' is in the collection of Major R. M. O. de la Hey. Was probably identical with the Rippingille (no christian name given) recorded by Long. Said to have been in Bury St. Edmunds in 1810. Visited Italy and France and for some years painted Italian scenes and subjects. Was an author and lecturer in art; spoke in several large towns in the provinces and at the R.I., London. According to Redgrave, he died suddenly at the railway station, Swan Village, Staffordshire, 22 April 1859.

*Rischgitz, Miss Alice. (fl. 1880–1898)

Of London. Exhibited at the R.A., etc., 1880–1898. Her address in 1898 was Cambridge Lodge Studios, Linden Gardens, Bayswater.

Rising, John. b. 1753?

Of London. Probably the one who entered the R.A. Schools, 31 December 1778 aged '25 last June'. Exhibited at the Society of Artists, R.A., and B.I., 1785–1815. Painted in oil and is said to have executed enamels. Long saw a good enamel miniature of J. Dewar, stated to be by Rising, and another on ivory, a copy of the same original, also attributed to him.

Rising, William Henry. (fl. 1818–1823)

Drawing master and miniaturist. Exhibited at the R.A. 1818, from 85 Great Portland Street. Was living in 1823 in Long Brook Street, Exeter.

*Risso, Signor. (fl. 1778)

An Italian artist; worked in Newcastle-on-Tyne in 1778.

Rivers, Charles. (fl. 1791–1804)

Of London. Was awarded a premium by the Society of Arts in 1791. Exhibited at the R.A., 1799–1804.

*Rivett-Carnac, Eva Mary Bernard (Mrs. C. G.). (fl. 1880–1912)

Née Orr. Of 10 Redcliffe Gardens (1905) and Swefling Rectory, Saxmundham, Suffolk. Exhibited at the R.A., 1905–1912. Was probably the wife of the Rev. C. G. Rivett-Carnac, whose daughter Eileen's miniature was exhibited at the R.A. in 1914, by Miss Aimée M. Davies (q.v.). Her sitters included Miss Marie Lohr. The N.P.G. has a miniature of Edward Fitzgerald (1809–1883), post-humously painted by Mrs. Rivett-Carnac.

Rivière, Daniel Valentine. *c.* 1776 or 1780?–1854

Of Huguenot descent. Said to have been born in 1780. An artist Daniel Rivière entered the R.A. schools, 5 November 1796, when his age was given as 19 or 20. If the two were identical this would make his date of birth *c.* 1776. He was entered as an engraver and obtained a silver medal in 1800. D. V. Rivière became a gold medallist of the Royal Academy, and a well-known drawing master. Exhibited at the R.A., 1823–1840, from 8 Cirencester Place. He married, in 1800, Henrietta Thunder, by whom he had eleven children; among them were H. P. Rivière, A.R.W.S. (q.v.), W.

Rivière (q.v.), R. Rivière, the bookbinder, and Miss F. Rivière (q.v.). He painted in oil and miniature. Died 1854.

Rivière, Miss F. (fl. 1828–1854)

Daughter of D. V. Rivière (q.v.) and sister of H. P. Rivière (q.v.) and W. Rivière (q.v.). All of them exhibited from 8 Cirencester Place in certain years. Miss F. Rivière exhibited at the R.A., 1832–1834, not in 1831 as stated by Graves and Long. She was awarded a premium by the Society of Arts in 1828. A miniature of a lady, 6¼ in., signed on the reverse with the address 'Cirencester Pl. Fitzroy Sq. Dec. 1854', and a sketch of the artist in pencil, were sold at Sotheby's, 26 March 1962.

*Rivière, Henry Parsons, A.R.W.S. 1811–1888

Born 16 August 1811; son of D. V. Rivière (q.v.) and brother of Miss F. Rivière (q.v.) and of W. Rivière (q.v.). Entered the R.A. Schools, 14 June 1830 aged 19. Exhibited at the R.A., B.I., O.W.C.S., N.W.C.S. etc., 1832–1888. Painted figure subjects in water-colour and in 1839 and 1840, exhibited two portraits in the drawing and miniature section which may have been miniatures. In 1834 he became a member of the N.W.C.S. and in 1852 was elected an Associate of the O.W.C.S. Exhibited from 8 Cirencester Place, 1835–1836, from London Street, 1839–1840, and from 14 Foley Place in 1849. Went to Rome in 1865 and remained in Italy until 1884 when he apparently returned to London. Died in St. John's Wood, 9 May 1888.

*Rivière, William. 1806–1876

Born in London, 22 October 1806; son of D. V. Rivière (q.v.) and brother of Miss F. Rivière (q.v.) and of H. P. Rivière (q.v.). Entered the R.A. Schools, 23 December 1824, aged 18. Exhibited at the R.A., B.I., etc., 1826–1860. Painted portraits, domestic subjects and landscapes in oil and water-colour. May have painted miniatures as in 1839 he exhibited a portrait of the Rev. Henry Stebbing, in the drawing and miniature section at the R.A. He was drawing master at Cheltenham College, 1849–1859, and later moved to Oxford. Died suddenly at 36 Beaumont Street, Oxford, 21 August 1876. A miniature of him as a young man by C. W. Pegler (q.v.) was formerly in the possession of his son, Briton Rivière, R.A.

*Roberts, Miss Dorothy F. (fl. 1910–1914)

Of London. Exhibited at the R.A. 1910–1914, from 10 Portsdown Road, Maida Vale and from 15 Lincoln Street.

*Roberts, Ellis William. 1860–1930

Born 27 October 1860 in Staffordshire. Worked in London. Exhibited at the R.A., etc., 1886–1893. Painted miniatures and portraits in oil. Had a distinguished clientele, including The Dowager Marchioness of Ormonde, the Lady Ruby Elliot, the Lady Eileen Elliot, the Countess of Powis, the Countess of Mar and Kellie and Ivy, daughter of Lady Algernon Gordon-Lennox, later the Duchess of Portland. Died in London, 1930.

Roberts, James. b. 1754?

Son of a landscape engraver of the same name. Possibly the James Roberts who entered the R.A. Schools, 14 March 1771 aged '18 May 7th next'. Was awarded a premium by the Society of Arts, 1766. Exhibited at the R.A., 1773–1799. He was portrait painter to the Duke of Clarence, 1795. Painted small whole length portraits, including some of actors; painted miniatures and published in 1809 *Introductory Lessons. . . . Water Colours.* Worked principally in London, but lived in Oxford *c.* 1784–1795. The B.M. has drawings on vellum by him which he made for Bell's *British Theatre*. The Garrick Club has portraits by him.

Roberts, John (I). (fl. 1774–1815). See also Roberts, John (III)

Of London. Exhibited at the Society of Artists, 1774–1776, and at the R.A., 1777–1815. Possibly identical with the John Roberts (III) (q.v.) who worked in Manchester *c.* 1825. The Duke of Northumberland has a miniature of Lady Charlotte Campbell, daughter of John, 5th Duke of Argyll, which was catalogued by J. J. Foster as by John Roberts. The miniature is signed 'Roberts' in cursive letters; it is strongly delineated; the painting is rather coarse. Other miniatures attributed to one of the artists of this name were loaned to the exhibition at the South Kensington Museum in 1865. According to the catalogue notes on the artist whose works were exhibited, this John Roberts was born *c.* 1752, and died *c.* 1834. All the exhibits were on ivory, and represented Mr. W. H. de Merle (as a boy) *c.* 1800, Miss de Merle, afterwards Mrs. Tyrrell, and Sir George Beaumont, Bt.

Roberts, John (II). *c.* 1768–1803

Born in Scotland, 1768? Executed miniatures, crayon portraits, mezzotints and stipple engravings. Went to New York, 1793. Gave up art to experiment in steam navigation. Was a musician and a drunkard. Died in New York, 1803.

Roberts, John (III). See also Roberts, John (I)

Working *c.* 1825 at 19 Irwell Street, Manchester. Possibly identical with the John Roberts (I) (q.v.) who exhibited at the R.A., 1777–1815.

*Roberts, Miss Katherine M. (fl. 1900–1913)

Of Liverpool, Shrewsbury and London. Exhibited at the R.A., 1900–1913. Executed miniatures, portraits and subjects in oil. Her sitters included Thomas Roberts, Esq.

*Roberts, Miss Violet M. (fl. 1904)

Exhibited at the R.A. 1904, from Claremont, St. Helier, Jersey.

Robertson, Miss. (fl. 1843)

Exhibited at the R.A. 1843, from 36 Harley Street, the same address as Mrs. James Robertson (q.v.), and was probably her daughter.

Robertson, Mrs. 19th century

Said to have been the daughter of Mrs. Mee (q.v.). Long records seeing a well painted miniature of a lady *c.* 1840, which according to the inscription on the frame was painted by 'Robertson daughter of Mrs. Mee'.

Robertson, Alexander. 1772–1841

Born in Aberdeen, 13 May 1772; son of William Robertson, an architect, and his wife, née Ross; brother of Archibald and Andrew Robertson (q.v.). The father was not, as has always been asserted, a cabinet-maker, but did delicate woodwork as a hobby and to supplement his income. Alexander studied under Shelley (q.v.) in London. He painted miniatures and water-colour landscapes. He and Archibald went to New York, Alexander in 1792, and Archibald in 1791. The brothers collaborated in running a drawing academy there. Alexander married Mary, daughter of Bishop Provoost. He was said to have been talented and amiable; he had a large family, but was not very well-off. Besides assisting at the Columbian Academy of Painting, he exhibited at the American Academy from 1817, and was its Secretary from 1817–1825, becoming Keeper, 1820–1835. Died in New York in 1841.

Robertson, Andrew, M.A. 1777–1845

Born in Aberdeen, 14 October 1777; son of William Robertson, architect, and his wife, née Ross. His father was not, as has been supposed, a cabinet-maker, but did delicate woodwork as a hobby and to supplement his income. Andrew was one of three brothers, of whom Archibald and Alexander (q.v.) were also miniaturists. Began his artistic career at the age of 14. Studied under Nasmyth and Raeburn; was musical, and at the age of 16 was Director of concerts in Aberdeen. Taught drawing, miniature painting and portraiture, etc. In 1794 he took his M.A., at Aberdeen. In 1801 he went to London. I am informed by his descendant, J. B. Robertson, Esq., that he did not make the journey on foot as has previously been stated, but went by sea. He was noticed by Benjamin West (q.v.) whose portrait in miniature by him was exhibited in Edinburgh in 1965. He entered the R.A. Schools, 23 October 1801. Exhibited at the R.A., B.I., O.W.C.S., etc., 1802–1842. Was an officer in the volunteer corps during the threat of Napoleonic invasion. Was in Aberdeen in 1803 and 1808. He had a distinguished clientele and was appointed miniature painter to the Duke of Sussex in 1805. He visited Paris in 1814. In 1808 and 1809 he was a member of the Associated Artists in Water-Colours where, in 1808, he exhibited portraits of five princesses. His pupils included F. Cruickshank (q.v.) and a relation of his mother, Sir W. C. Ross (q.v.), who was, for a time, his assistant. Robertson married twice; by his first wife (Jenny?), he had two sons, Charles and Edward (q.v.) also a miniaturist, and a daughter Mary. By his second wife (probably the one described as a daughter of Samuel Boxill of Barbados) he had a son, Samuel and a daughter, Emily, who edited the *Letters and Papers of Andrew Robertson*, 1895. Robertson died at Hampstead, 6 December 1845. His price for a miniature in 1792 was 10/6; by 1807 it was 12 guineas for a small one. He was a first rate miniaturist and a good draughtsman. His miniatures are often reminiscent of the work of Raeburn. He sketched in the features in brown monochrome, and when painting, placed his table so that the light slanted over his left shoulder, his sitter being in front of him, rather to the right. His usual signature was AR in monogram. Two self-portraits from the family collection were exhibited in Edinburgh in 1965, a small one painted in 1811, and the other painted in 1838 when he is wearing glasses. In the same exhibition were other portraits of note by him; a large miniature of 'Jenny' (his first wife, according to family tradition), signed 'A.R.' (monogram followed by a symbol); one of the portraits of Princess Amelia (of which he executed several replicas), signed and dated '1811', from the collection of H.M. the Queen; John Trumbull, President of the New York Academy of Fine Arts (painted 1815); Sir Thomas Lawrence, P.R.A.; and two miniatures of George IV as Prince Regent. Another miniature of interest was lent by H.M. the Queen; it was of Sir Francis Legatt Chantry, with a bust of George IV, signed in monogram and dated '1831'. A miniature of the 6th Duke of Roxburghe, signed 'AR.1837', is in my collection. It is a fine example of the large rectangular miniatures of this period. Robertson exhibited this, and one of the Duchess of Roxburghe, at the R.A., in 1837. Examples of his work are at the V. & A. M., N.P.G., the Ashmolean Museum, Oxford, etc. For fresh information about the Robertson family, I am indebted to J. B. Robertson, Esq., a descendant of the artist.

Robertson, Andrew. d. *c.* 1881

There was evidently a second miniaturist of this name, as some of the pictures sold at Christie's, 18 June 1881, included works dated '1846' and '1850'

(after the famous A. Robertson's (q.v.) death). They were described as 'the Property of Andrew Robertson Esq, Miniature Painter Deceased'.

Robertson, Archibald. 1765–1835

Born 8 May 1765 at Monymusk, near Aberdeen; son of William Robertson, an architect, and his wife, née Ross. Brother of Alexander and Andrew Robertson (q.v.). Was a friend of Raeburn in Edinburgh, where he first worked. Went to London in 1786; was a pupil of Shirreff (q.v.) and of an artist named Peacock. Said by Long to have studied at the R.A. Schools, but he is not recorded in the list published in the *Walpole Society*, Vol. XXXVIII. He went to New York in 1791; the Earl of Buchan asked him to deliver a box made of part of the oak tree that sheltered William Wallace. Robertson took the opportunity of visiting Philadelphia, and painted a miniature of Washington on a slab of marble, which is now owned by the New York Historical Society. He settled in New York and established the Columbian Academy with his brother Alexander, who joined him in 1792. Painted miniatures in oil and water-colour and drew in crayon. Wrote a treatise on miniature painting and executed 'devices in hair work for lockets'. Married Eliza Abramse of New York by whom he had a large family. Died in New York, 6 December 1835. His self-portrait, and one of his wife by him, are illustrated in Wehle, Pl. IV and XII. He signed AR in monogram and as his work is scarce in Britain, some may have been attributed to his brother. A miniature of an unknown officer was lent by the present descendant, J. B. Robertson, Esq., to the exhibition in Edinburgh in 1965. It is signed AR (monogram) P; the initials are slightly cursive. Examples of his work are in the Smithsonian Institution, Washington, the Metropolitan Museum, New York, and the Philadelphia Museum of Art. His wife was also a talented artist. I have seen his paint box which is in the Rosenbach Museum, Philadelphia. An oil portrait of George Washington (1732–1799), by Robertson is at Sulgrave Manor, Northampton. It was commissioned by David Stewart, 11th Earl of Buchan (1742–1829), and presented to Sulgrave Manor by the 15th Earl of Buchan in 1951.

Robertson, Charles. *c.* 1760–1821

Of Dublin; born *c.* 1760; said to have been the son of a jeweller in Dublin, perhaps the Alexander Robertson who died at Ormond Quay in July 1768. Charles began by executing designs in hair, and when only about nine years of age, exhibited some of this work at the Dublin Society of Artists in 1768 and 1769, his address being Essex Street where he lived with his elder brother, Walter Robertson (q.v.). In 1772, 1773 and 1774, 'Master Charles Robertson' exhibited likenesses in hair, and in 1775 he exhibited miniatures for the first time. He took his own studio in 69 South Great George Street, Dublin, moving in 1783 to 11 Clarendon Street. Was in London, 1785–1792, and again in 1806. Exhibited at the R.A., 1790–1810, and in Dublin up to 1821. Besides executing designs in hair and miniatures, he painted small portraits in water-colour and flower pieces. Was Secretary of the Hibernian Society of Artists, and its Vice President in 1814, and one of the Committee of Artists who struggled for a charter of incorporation. His miniatures are of a high quality; they are delicately painted with soft modelling. Often the shading on the face is grey or blue. The fact that he did not sign his portraits makes identification difficult, and they frequently pass unrecognised. He married Christina, daughter of Thomas Jaffray, by whom he had at least five children, Charles, Thomas, Christiana, Maria and Clementina (q.v.). A miniature by their father of Charles, Thomas and Christiana was lent to the exhibition in Edinburgh, 1965, by Major R. M. O. de la Hey. He died in his house, Holles Street, Dublin, 10 November 1821, aged 62. A small full-length portrait by H. Kirchhoffer (q.v.), is in the N.G., Dublin, who also have his painting desk and examples of his work, including a miniature of his daughter Maria, and one of his brother Walter Robertson (q.v.). I have seen several fine examples of his work in private collections. The V. & A. M. and the Fitzwilliam Museum, Cambridge, have miniatures by him.

*Robertson, Charles. 1794–1858
This artist is recorded by the V. & A.M., as being born 29 September 1794. Died 1858.

Robertson, Charles John. b. 1779?
Of London, Gainsborough (1811–1812), Chiswick (1825–1827) and Isleworth (1830). Exhibited at the R.A. and O.W.C.S., 1798–1830. Probably the C. J. Robertson who entered the R.A. Schools, 21 October 1797 aged 18. In 1829 was an Hon. member of a sketching society of which A. E. Chalon (q.v.), J. J. Chalon, H. Bone (q.v.), etc. were members. He has been referred to as an Irishman, but he may have been confused with Charles Robertson (q.v.). Long records an important miniature by him of Lady Nelthorpe, which he exhibited at the R.A., in 1814, on ivory, approx. $7\frac{3}{4} \times 5\frac{3}{4}$ in., signed on the reverse, 'C. J. Robertson. pinxit / Apr:1813'. It was well painted and reminiscent of Andrew Robertson (q.v.). The colours were harmonious and the portrait well drawn. The shading on the face was brown and grey, and the short soft strokes with which the face was painted were almost indistinguishable. A miniature of an unknown lady, signed on the reverse, 'C.J. Robertson / pinxit / 1820', is in the collection of R. Bayne Powell, Esq.

Robertson, Mrs. Christina. See Robertson, Mrs. James

Robertson, Miss Clementina. See Siree, Mrs. John

Robertson, Edward. b. 1809
Son of Andrew Robertson (q.v.) by his first wife. Presumed to have been born in London, 1809. Entered the R.A. Schools, 6 December 1827 when his age was noted as 18 years. Exhibited at the R.A., 1830–1837. Was in Dublin c. 1831–1832, and exhibited at the R.H.A., 1826. A miniature by him of his brother, Captain Charles Robertson (1808–1889), belonging to the Robertson family, was lent to the exhibition in Edinburgh in 1965. It was inscribed and dated on the reverse, 'Portrait of / Captain Chas Robertson / Painted by / Mr Edward Robertson / Glasgow / 1837'. Whether the artist was working in Glasgow at this time, or visiting his relations, is not known. Captain Robertson was present at the signing of the Maori Treaty at Russell, March 1840, and conveyed the document to Governor Phillip in Sydney. Cape Robertson, New Zealand, is named after him. Miniatures by this artist are scarce. According to the Robertson family, he died in Dublin. Was living at 27 Dame Street, Dublin in 1831 and 34 Gerrard Street, Soho in 1832.

*Robertson, G. 19th century
An early nineteenth-century miniature with a scratched signature by this artist was seen by A. J. B. Kiddell.

*Robertson, Henry Robert, R.P.E. 1839–1921
Born in Windsor, 1839. Exhibited at the R.A., B.I., N.W.C.S., etc. 1861–1907, from Steele's Studios, Haverstock Hill. In 1909 he is said to have exhibited in Liverpool. Was a member of the Royal

Society of Painter-Etchers and of the Royal Society of Miniature Painters. Was a prolific and versatile artist, executing miniatures, landscapes in oil and water-colour, etchings and possibly engravings and drawings. His sitters included Cardinal Newman, Master Donald S. Robertson and Mrs. H. R. Robertson, presumably the artist's wife. Died in London, 6 June 1921.

Robertson, Mrs. James (Miss Christina Sanders). (fl. 1822–1849)
Née Christina Sanders, niece of George Sanders (q.v.). Married in or before 1823, James Robertson, a painter. Exhibited at the R.A., B.I., S.B.A., etc., 1823–1849; and at the R.S.A., 1829–1839, of which she was made an Honorary Member in 1829. Went to St. Petersburg and painted portraits of the Czar and Czarina in 1843. Was made a member of the Imperial Academy in St. Petersburg. Was back in England in 1844. Painted oil portraits and miniatures. She signed C.R. followed by a date, and C.R. pinxit, in either cursive or block letters. She was a good artist who painted with clear bright colours. Her draughtsmanship was good, particularly when drawing hands; many of her miniatures are large. The Museum of Decorative Arts in Paris has a large oval miniature by her dated '1848'. I have seen several miniatures by her in London sales, which have passed unrecognised. Three miniatures by her are in the collection of the Duke of Northumberland; they include a miniature of the 3rd Duke of Northumberland, in coronation robes, signed on the front, 'C.R. 1825', and one of Charlotte, 3rd Duchess of Northumberland; both miniatures were exhibited at the R.A., in 1825. The miniature of the Duchess has blue shading on the face, and the jewellery is highlighted with opaque white.

*Robertson, Mrs. Jane K. (Mrs. C. K.). (fl. 1899–1906). See also **Robertson, Mrs. K.**
Of London. Exhibited at the R.A., 1899–1906. She exhibited a miniature of the Earl of Hopetoun, Lord Chamberlain, in 1899. May have been identical with Mrs. Kay Robertson (q.v.). Was presumably the wife of C. Kay Robertson who exhibited at the R.A., from the same address, 28 Tite Street, Chelsea.

*Robertson, Miss Janet S. (fl. 1903–1914)
Of Primrose Hill, London. Exhibited at the R.A. 1903–1914, from 9 Elsworthy Terrace, Primrose Hill. Painted miniatures and subjects in water-colour. Her sitters included Lady Hawley and Arthur, eldest son of Sir Hubert Llewellyn Smith, K.C.B., Miss Agnes Robertson, Mrs. Donald Robertson and Mrs. Martindale.

Robertson, Joan. (fl. 1817)
A miniature of two children picking flowers in a wood and fully inscribed, signed and dated '1817' on the reverse is in a private collection. The frame bears a further inscription identifying the children as Elizabeth and Sarah Mary, daughter of The Hon. Henry Cavendish. The painting is excellent and large in size. $7\frac{1}{4} \times 4\frac{3}{4}$ in.

*Robertson, Mrs. Kay. (fl. 1898). See also **Robertson, Mrs. J. K.**
Exhibited at the R.A. 1898, from The Nest, Carshalton, Surrey. Was possibly identical with Mrs. J. K. Robertson (q.v.).

*Robertson, Miss Margaret Forbes. (fl. 1892–1893)
Of London. Exhibited at the R.A., etc., 1892–1893, from 22 Bedford Square, from which address Eric Forbes-Robertson also exhibited.

Robertson, Walter. d. 1801
Probably the son of a Dublin jeweller (possibly Alexander Robertson, died 1768); elder brother of Charles Robertson (q.v.). Entered the Dublin Society Schools, 21 November 1765. Established himself as a miniaturist in Essex Street c. 1768, moving later to Great George Street and other addresses. Executed designs and likenesses in hair; exhibited in Dublin, 1769–1777. He married twice, first in September 1771, Margaret Bentley of Stephen Street, Dublin, and secondly, in 1781, Eleanor Robertson, who survived him. He went to London c. 1784 and was practising there for a few years. On returning to Dublin he became bankrupt in 1792 and his property, which consisted of a number of houses, was sold by auction. He had met Gilbert Stuart in London and in 1793 accompanied him to America. Was known as 'Irish Robertson' to distinguish him from the two Scottish miniaturists, Archibald and Alexander Robertson (q.v.). Painted a portrait of Washington which was engraved. The original miniature was lost in the great fire at Baltimore in 1904. He also painted Mrs. Washington and other distinguished persons. Robertson copied some of G. Stuart's portraits in miniature. He left America in 1795 for India and died in Futtehpore in 1801, not 1802 as stated by Long. He was a good draughtsman and skilful at modelling heads; typical indications of his work are elegance, starched frills, powdered hair, backgrounds painted with a fine cross-hatching, and the facial contours modelled by means of long fine brush strokes shaded with blue, particularly in the sockets of the eyes. The Smithsonian Institution, Washington has some good examples of his work; one of these is his miniature of Captain Joseph Anthony which is strong and vigorous; the sitter is almost smiling giving the impression of a good likeness. A miniature of him by his brother Charles is in the N.G., Dublin and was seen by me in 1967. It has unfortunately been in a strong light and the colours have faded. Brief details about his stay in India are to be found in the *Walpole Society*, Vol. XIX, p. 66.

*Robertson, Miss Winifred J. (fl. 1907)
Of London. Exhibited at the R.A. 1907, from 11 Thurlow Road, Hampstead.

*Robins, Joseph. d. c. 1848
Was employed by Mr. Wilks, the non-conformist divine, to paint for the *Evening Magazine*. Painted miniatures, and later turned to landscapes. Died in extreme poverty c. 1848.

*Robins, T., junior. (fl. 1773)
Worked in Bath; son of Thomas Robins (q.v.). The *Bath Chronicle*, 11 February 1773, contained the following advertisement: 'Robins T., of Merchant Court, Bath. Continues to teach the art of drawing and painting of flowers, birds, insects and landscapes as his late father did'. It is not certain that Robins junior painted miniatures.

*Robins, Thomas, senior. d. before 1773
Worked in Bath, 18 November 1754. Was a painter and engraver and taught drawing. Long records that he died before 1773.

Robins, William. 18th century
A mezzotint engraver working in the first half of the 18th century. A plumbago portrait of Colley Cibber, signed 'W. Robins / Delin 1713 (?)', is in the collection of H.M. the Queen.

Robinson. (fl. c. 1750)
A miniature of a young boy in a blue dress and red wrap of c. 1750, was seen by Long and was inscribed on the reverse in an old hand, 'Robinson /

Nov 16. 54 / IVL:'. The name may not refer to the artist.

Robinson. 18th century

A miniature on ivory of Mrs. Phillips, afterwards Mrs. Pocock (1790), was lent to the exhibition at the South Kensington Museum in 1865 and catalogued as by 'Robinson'.

*Robinson, A. Marjorie. (fl. c. 1910)

A miniature of an unknown lady c. 1910 is in the N.G., Dublin. It is quite well painted and attractive.

*Robinson, D. G. 18th century

A miniature of an unknown gentleman, seated on a terrace, and signed 'D.G. Robinson', 18th century, was part of Lot no. 1 at Christie's, 13 February 1962.

*Robinson, Miss Dorothy A. F. (fl. 1905)

Exhibited at the R.A. 1905, from 28 Alexandra Road, Southport. Her sitter was Mrs. Eardly-Wilmot.

Robinson, John. 1774?–c. 1829

An English miniaturist who went to Philadelphia in 1817. Possibly the John Robinson who entered the R.A. Schools, 11 November 1797, aged 23. This would make his date of birth c. 1774. T. Bolton lists twelve portraits by him. He died in Philadelphia c. 1829. The South Carolina Exhibition, 1936, contained a portrait of Mrs. R. D. Hurtel, on ivory, signed 'J.R.'. He exhibited at the Pennsylvania Academy, 1816–1824. Portraits by him of Benjamin West (q.v.) and an English lady were exhibited by him in February 1818.

Robinson, Joseph. b. 1768? d. after 1816

Of London and Tunbridge Wells (1813). Possibly the J. Robinson who entered the R.A. Schools, 13 August 1790, aged 21. Exhibited at the Society of Artists, 1790–1791 and at the R.A., 1798–1816. His sitters included the Rev. Rowland Hill, the Rev. W. Jay of Bath, Dr. Jenner and W. R. Biggs, R.A.

*Robinson, Miss Mildred. (fl. 1899–1901)

Of Hampton Wick and Kingston-on-Thames. Exhibited at the R.A. and S.M., 1899–1901.

Robinson, R. (fl. 1797–1802)

Of London. Exhibited at the R.A., 1797 and 1802; his exhibit in the latter year was a portrait of Lord Nelson.

*Robinson, Thomas. d. 1810

Born on the shores of Lake Windermere, Westmorland. Showed artistic talent at an early age; was a pupil of Romney c. 1785. Was invited to go to Ireland; practised as a portrait painter in Dublin; was in Laurencetown, 1793 and Belfast, 1801; returned to Dublin in 1808. Exhibited at the Dublin Society of Artists (of which he became President), 1809 and 1810. Painted portraits and historical scenes. Long records seeing a miniature by him signed 'T.R. / 1802', which was painted in the manner of Comerford (q.v.). He died at his house, 7 Jervis Street, on 27 July 1810, and was survived by his wife, Ruth (née Buck), by whom he had a son Thomas Romney Robinson (born 1793), an astronomer and mathematician.

*Robinson, W. S. d. c. 1905

Born in Leeming near Northallerton. Was self-taught. Painted water-colours and oil, and executed landscapes. Worked for a time in Sheffield. Knew Montgomery the poet. Married and had one child who died young. I saw a pair of large miniatures on paper of two officers in uniform in 1962, one of which was signed 'W.S. Robinson 1848'. The drawing was good, and the colouring artistic. He died in Fullwood, Scarborough c. 1905 when he was over 80 years old.

Robson's, Thomas. (fl. 1768)

A plumbago miniature of James Earle, signed and dated 'Thomas Robson's Feb. 15. 1768', was seen by me in 1977.

Roch, S. T. See **Roch(e), S. T.**

Roch(e), Sampson Towgood. 1759–1847

Born in Youghal, 1759; son of Luke Roch and grandson of James Roch of Glyn Castle, near Carrick-on-Suir. Was born deaf and dumb. Showed aptitude for art, and was sent to Dublin to study the works of painters who were then practising in Dublin. Began to paint likenesses. He was first noted as an artist in 1784, when practising as a miniaturist at 152 Capel Street; he is thought to have been working in England earlier. He spelt his name with and without an e. Roche was evidently away from Dublin from 1786–1788, when he advertised in the *Dublin Evening Post* from his old address in Capel Street, saying that he had 'returned to Dublin'. The *Dublin Chronicle*, 7 June 1788, records that 'Sampson Roche, of the City of Cork, married at Youghal, Miss Roch, only daughter of James Roch, of Odel Lodge, Co. Waterford'. He lived in Grafton Street, 1789–1792, and in that year moved to Bath where he had a flourishing practice. He was patronised by the Royal Family, and painted the Princess Amelia. Said to have been offered a knighthood, but declined on account of his infirmity. Exhibited at the R.A. 1817, from 11 Pierpont Street, Bath. He retired from his profession and returned to live with his relations at Woodbine Hill, Co. Waterford, where he died in February 1847, and was buried on 20 February in the family burying place at Ardmore, Co. Waterford. His self-portrait in miniature and one in oil are mentioned by Strickland as being at Woodbine Hill in 1913. He was a good artist, but rather too often gave his sitters an incipient smile or smirk. Characteristics to note are the shading under the eyes, and definite outlines to nostrils, lips, etc. He sometimes painted the dress with opaque colours. He signed his miniatures Roch and Roche (more often the former) with and without initials, and followed by a date, e.g. Roch / 1789, and S. Roch / 1796, or Roche / 1786. Examples of his work are in the V. & A. M., the Holburne Museum, Bath and the N.G., Dublin.

Rochard, François Théodore. 1798–1858

Born in France, 1798; son of René Rochard and his wife, née Talon, and younger brother of S. J. Rochard (q.v.). Studied in Paris and joined his brother in London c. 1820. Exhibited at the R.A., S.B.A. and N.W.C.S., etc., 1820–1855, becoming a member of the latter society in 1835. Was awarded a silver medal by the Society of Arts in 1823 for a water-colour copy of a portrait, and another for an oil copy of an historical subject. Painted miniatures, portraits and genre subjects. Obtained a fashionable clientele and was patronised by royalty. Married c. 1850, and retired upon his savings, and lived in Notting Hill, where he died in 1858. Mrs. F. Dixon (q.v.) was his pupil. Many of his miniatures were painted for bracelets and consequently are small, but larger ones are known. The V. & A. M. has a rectangular miniature of Miss Blood, signed on the reverse 'Peint par F^{cis} Rochard / 19 Howland Street / Fitzroy Sq^{re} / July 1833', and some sketches of ladies' heads, which are by one of the brothers. F. T. Rochard's work very closely resembles that of his brother; he usually signed F. Rochard, F.R. or F. R^d. A fair amount of gum is apparent in his painting.

Rochard, Simon Jacques. 1788–1872

Born in Paris, 28 December 1788; son of René Rochard and his wife, née Talon. Drew crayon portraits when still a child in order to support his widowed mother and twelve children. Studied engraving under Ransonnette senior and Desnoyers, and miniature painting under Mlle. Bonnieu, L. F. Aubry, and said to have also studied under Isabey (q.v.) and J. F. L. Mérimée. Entered the Académie des Beaux-Arts, Paris, 16 November 1813. Copied miniatures for Augustin (q.v.). In 1815 he went to Brussels to escape conscription. Sketched Wellington, 13 June 1815; the Duke of Richmond also sat to him in Brussels. Rochard went to Spa in November 1815, and arrived in London, 1816 with introductions from the Duke of Richmond and Lady Caroline Lamb. Became popular and had a distinguished clientele; painted Princess Charlotte, the Duke of Devonshire, etc. Exhibited at the R.A., B.I., S.B.A., and N.W.C.S., 1816–1845. Painted chiefly miniatures, but executed engravings and painted pictures in oil. His work was influenced by that of Reynolds and Lawrence. He knew Wilkie and Delacroix. His wife, née Henriette Petitjean, remained abroad; their daughter was married to an English officer. He became wealthy and collected old masters. In 1846 he settled in Brussels and exhibited at the Brussels Salon, 1848–1869, and at the Paris Salon, 1852, and the Paris exhibition, 1867. He married, as his second wife, at the age of 80, Henriette Pilton, by whom he had a son. Was nearly ruined by the failure of Moore's Bank, and died a few days later, 13 June 1872, at 23 Rue des Douze Apôtres, Brussels. He was an excellent miniaturist, who used pure fresh colours, and painted with a broad brush stroke; the flesh colours on the face are pink, shaded by yellow-brown shadows; he used a lot of gum with his paints, and a scraper to obtain lines in the hair. Examples of his work may be seen at the V. & A. M. and the Ashmolean Museum, Oxford, as well as at the Louvre. He signed Rochard often followed by a date, frequently scratched on the edge of the miniature; the miniature of Sir John Rennie, at the V. & A. M., is signed 'Rochard Febry 1831'. The B.M. has engraved portraits after S. J. Rochard.

*Rocher. 18th century

A miniature on enamel of James Fitzjames, Duke of Berwick, K.G. (1670–1734), by Rocher is in the collection of Earl Beauchamp. The sitter was the natural son of James, Duke of York, later James II, and Arabella Churchill. He is depicted by the artist wearing armour and the ribbon of the Garter. The miniature is well painted and colourful. As the Duke of Berwick spent much of his life on the Continent, this miniature may have been painted there and not in England.

*Rocher, Miss Ida. d. c. 1906

Of Higham, near Rochester. Exhibited at the Society of Miniaturists, 1905–1906. Died c. 1906.

*Rode, Godfried Hendrik. b. 1752. d. after 1793

Born in the Hague, 1752; pupil of J. J. Schalch and of J. H. Hurter (q.v.). Executed miniatures on enamel and ivory. Became in 1782 a member of the Brotherhood of the Hague, and in 1783 was awarded a large silver medal. Long recorded seeing an enamel of George IV as a young man, 6 × 5 in., inscribed on the reverse 'G.H. Rode, pinx London / November 1781'. Long also recorded another miniature signed 'G.H. Rode px / 1784 / An St'. Schidlof mentions other examples of his work.

Roe, Robert. 1793–1880

Born 1793; eldest son of Joseph Roe of Ipswich, and Jemima (née Coe). Said to have been born in Suffolk and to have studied miniature painting under 'Wageman', probably T. C. Wageman (q.v.). Was an engraver and print-seller at Cambridge, where he spent most of his life, living firstly in Trumpington Street, and for many years at 14 King's Parade. Said to have taught miniature painting at one guinea a lesson. Became acquainted with Edward Fitzgerald and W. M. Thackeray, whom he is said to have given his first instruction in etching. Was one of the founders of the Printsellers Association, and attended the inaugural meeting in London, 5 February 1847. Designed eagles for gate piers on Backs Road of St. John's College, Cambridge. Married as his first wife in 1821, Mary Elizabeth Edleston (died 1856); and secondly in 1859, Maria Plees, daughter of the Rev. W. Gordon Plees (q.v.), and having issue by both. Fred Roe, R.I., R.B.C. (1864–1947), was his youngest son by the second marriage. Thieme and Becker and Schidlof confuse Robert Roe with his eldest son of the first marriage, Robert Henry Roe (1822–1905). Mr. Fred Roe was the father of F. Gordon Roe, whose annotations have been most valuable both to the late Basil Long and to the present author. Robert Roe died 31 July 1880, and was buried in Cambridge.

Roffe, Alfred Thomas. b. c. 1803

Of London; born c. 1803. Entered the R.A. Schools, 29 November 1822 aged 19. Was awarded a premium by the Society of Arts when a boy in 1813 and 1814. Exhibited at the R.A., etc., 1822–1829.

*Roger, Mr. or William? (fl. 1841)

A rectangular miniature of a young girl by the above artist is in the collection of E. G. Paine of New York. It is signed 'Mr Roger' or 'WM Roger', and inscribed on the reverse in another hand, 'Catherine Hardy / aged 14 years / Painted by / (either) Mr Roger or Wm Roger / Aberdeen / 1841'.

*Rogers, Edward J. (fl. 1904)

Of London. Exhibited at the R.A. 1904, from 8 Denning Road, Hampstead.

*Rogers, Miss Ethel B. (fl. 1896)

Exhibited at the R.A. 1896, from Anglesea House, Paignton, Devon.

*Rogers, Miss Evelyn E. (fl. 1889–1894)

Of Kingston and Teignmouth (1894). Exhibited at the R.A. and N.W.C.S., etc., 1889–1894.

Rogers, Miss Jane M. (fl. 1849–1861)

Exhibited at the B.I., 1849–1857 and according to Graves, in other exhibitions up to 1861. The exhibit in 1857 was an enamel on porcelain after Raphael, when her address was 3 Upper Fitzroy Place, Kentish Town. She also painted subject pictures.

*Rogers, John. (fl. 1748)

The above artist is recorded as having married, on 4 June 1748, at All Hallows, Staining, 'Gentleman, Painter, in Miniature'. (Stepney Register.)

Röhl or **Roehl, Maria Christina.** 1801–1875

Born in Skönstavik, near Stockholm, 27 July 1801, where her parents were in business. Was a pupil of Hamrén and Prof. Forssell. Travelled for purposes of study, 1849–1856, visiting Paris, London, Liverpool, etc. Noted for her crayon and pastel portraits, but also painted miniatures on ivory. Died 30 June 1875. Benezit spells her name Roehl.

Rola. (fl. 1843)

Exhibited at the R.A. 1843, from 23 Coleshill Street, Eaton Square, London.

*Rolleston, Lady Eliza. (fl. 1907–1913)

Of London. Exhibited at the R.A. 1907 and 1913, from 54 Curzon St. Her sitters included the Duchess of Rutland and Lady Diana Manners and The Lord Bishop of Peterborough.

*Romilly, Madame D'Ausse. 1788–1875. See also **Munier-Romilly, Mme. Amélie.**

Exhibited at the R.A. 1828–1837, from a London address. Possibly identical with Mme Amélie Munier-Romilly, née Romilly (q.v.), who was born in Geneva, 1788 and died there in 1875; she was a pupil of Firmin Massot. Painted portraits in oil and water-colour, and miniatures. Lived in Paris, 1812–1825, and was in London, 1836. The Musée d'Art et d'Histoire, Geneva, has examples of her work. Her sitters included Lady Louisa Fitzmaurice. The R.A. catalogue of 1837 gives the name as Madame Munier-Romilly, and her address as 2 Chester Terrace, Regent's Park.

Romney, George, F.S.A. 1734–1802

Long mentions an alleged self-portrait of Romney which was exhibited at Manchester in 1926. J. J. Foster mentions a self-portrait (possibly the one already referred to) from the Propert collection, exhibited in 1889, and three drawings in pencil and ink and a small miniature on ivory of Lady Emily McLeod (the study for her portrait), all from the Wellesley collection. A small self-portrait in pencil is in the N.P.G.

Romney, John. c. 1786–1863

Born c. 1786. Worked in London and in the North of England. Was awarded a premium by the Society of Arts in 1806. Entered the R.A. Schools, 21 January 1808, aged 22. Was best known as an engraver, but exhibited miniatures at the R.A., 1807–1813. Died in Chester, 1 February 1863.

*Ronan or **Ronayne, Patrick.** (fl. early 19th century)

Born in Carrick-on-Suir where he lived for most of his life. Practised portrait painting and painted religious pictures. Long noted seeing a miniature inscribed on the reverse, 'Painted / from the life / by P. RONAN / Carrick-on-Suir /'. He is said to have left Carrick c. 1804 and to have lived in Cork where he died.

Rondi, Enrico. (fl. 1850–1873)

Born in Biella, Piedmont. Exhibited in Turin, 1850–1851, and in Florence, 1861. Was in London and exhibited at the R.A., 1853–1873.

*Room, Henry. 1802–1850

Born in 1802; worked in Birmingham and London. Exhibited at the R.A., B.I., etc., 1826–1848. Painted portraits, subject pictures, historical subjects and miniatures. Whilst in Birmingham, Room acquired a notable reputation as an artist. Said to have gone to London in 1830, although he exhibited at the R.A., in 1826 from 4 Goulden Terrace, Pentonville; his address in 1829 was Cherry Street, Birmingham, after which time he exhibited for many years from 17 Old Bond Street. His sitters included the Rev. Charles Room and Thomas Clarkson Esq., M.A. (1760–1846), Anti-Slavery agitator. This was painted for the Central Negro Emancipation Committee, the year in which the sitter was admitted to the Freedom of the City of London. I have seen, in a private collection, an attractive miniature of an unknown lady by this artist, signed on the front, up the right side, 'H. Room', with the artist's visiting card stuck on to the reverse of the frame which reads, 'Mr Henry Room / Portrait & Miniature Painter / Old Bond Street'. The miniature is well modelled, is a good character study and elegant. The work is slightly reminiscent of that of Sir W. C. Ross (q.v.). Room died in London, 27 August 1850. Examples of his work are in Birmingham, the N.P.G., and the S.N.P.G., Edinburgh, who have a large portrait by him of Thomas Campbell (1777–1844), poet and critic.

Roos, William. 1808–1878

Born in Amlwch, Anglesea, 1808. Painted portraits and historical subjects, as well as executing miniatures and engravings. Died in Amlwich, 4 July 1878. A miniature by him of his mother dated on the reverse '1804', is in the National Museum of Wales, Cardiff.

Rooukin or **Roonkin, J.** b. 1761?

Of London; b. 1761? Possibly identical with John Roonkin who entered the R.A. Schools, 11 October 1782, aged '21 last 7. Jan'. This latter artist was listed then as an engraver. The R.A. catalogue 1785, records J. Rooukin in the catalogue and J. Roukin (in the index), from 1 Greenfield Street, Mile End. The exhibits were a miniature, 'Portrait of an artist', and two items in the drawing section. In 1792, J. Rooukin of 5 Swan Street, Minories, exhibited a miniature at the R.A. A miniature signed and dated 'Feb^r 20. 1794', was in the collection of the late Sidney Hand. Schidlof records seeing a miniature of Samuel Cooper of Farnborough, signed on the reverse, 'I. Rooukin pinxit / Feby 20. 1794'. He employed an unusual technique and painted the whole miniature with parallel brush strokes fairly well spaced, and inclined from upper right to lower left. The flesh colour is rather yellow, and the clothes painted in gouache. A fair amount of gum is used to paint the shadows and folds.

Rose, Mrs. Susan Penelope. See **Rosse, Mrs. Susan Penelope**

Rosenberg, Charles (Carl) Christian. 1745–1844

Born 21 November 1745 in Germany. Known as Rosenberg of Bath. Came to England at the age of 14 as page to Queen Charlotte; was King's Messenger to George III and William IV. Described himself in the *Bath Chronicle*, 11 October 1787, and on subsequent dates, as 'from Vienna'. Married Elizabeth Woolley at Bath Abbey, 4 February 1790. In 1793 and 1795 he was in North Parade, Bath, and was in Leeds in 1798. Said to have also worked in Cheltenham and Ramsgate. Painted principally silhouettes and miniatures. Died 13 November 1844 and was buried in Brompton Cemetery; was survived by his widow who died, 30 June 1853. Many of his descendants have been artists, including his son, Thomas Elliott Rosenberg (q.v.). Rosenberg was 'His Majesty's Profile Painter'. Some of his silhouettes are at the V. & A.M.

*Rosenberg, Miss Ethel Jenner. (fl. 1883–1901)

Of London. Daughter of the artist, George Frederick Rosenberg of Bath. Exhibited at the R.A., and S.M., 1883–1901. Executed miniatures and drawings. Was a prolific artist. Her sitters included Edith, daughter of Col. Stanley Clarke, Miss Madeleine Stanley, the late Col. Sir Edward

Fitzgerald Campbell, Bart., Mrs. Edward Campbell, the Rev. Aubrey Moore, the Hon. Bridget Astley, daughter of Lord Hastings, Miss Augusta Spottis-woode, the Lady Lilford and Sir Alexander Nisbet, M.D., R.N. A miniature of Lady Scourfield by the above artist is in my collection; it is signed on the front in monogram 'EJR' (the J being longer than the other letters), and dated under the monogram '98' (1898). A label on the reverse of the locket is inscribed 'Lady Scourfield, painted by Ethel J. Rosenberg (Miss) New Bond St.'.

*Rosenberg, Thomas Elliott. 1790–1835

Born 19 November 1790; son of C. C. Rosenberg (q.v.). Worked in Bath from 1803 up to his death and lived at 14 The Grove, 6 New King Street (1819–1822) and 7 Walcot Terrace or Parade, Bath (1830). Painted miniatures, landscapes and silhouettes; taught drawing and perspective. The Victoria Art Gallery in Bath has a miniature and several landscapes by him. Died 17 June 1835.

*Rosenberg, William George Home. (fl. 1871–1884)

Of London. Exhibited at the R.A., etc., 1871–1884 from 22 Newman Street, Oxford Street, and 5 Northumberland Street, Charing Cross.

*Ross, Mrs. E. C. 19th century

Worked as a medallist, portrait painter and miniaturist. Was a pupil of Signor Casella. Her daughter, Miss E. M. Ross (q.v.), also painted miniatures.

*Ross, Miss Eleanor M. (fl. 1900–1907)

Of North Berwick, Edinburgh and London. Exhibited at the Society of Miniaturists, 1900–1907. Mrs. E. C. Ross (q.v.) was her mother.

Ross, Hugh. 1800–1873

Was born in 1800; son of William Ross (q.v.) and his wife, née Maria Smith, and brother of Sir William Ross (q.v.) and Miss Magdalena Ross (q.v.). Exhibited at the R.A., 1814–1845. The Society of Arts awarded him prizes in 1815, 1816 and 1820. A portrait of him by E. W. Hatton was exhibited at the R.A., in 1845. A miniature of Sir W. C. Ross by him is at the N.P.G. He painted miniatures and portraits in water-colour. Died in 1873.

Ross, Miss Janet (Mrs. Janet Barrow). (fl. 1816–1828)

Was awarded a premium by the Society of Arts in 1816. Exhibited at the R.A. 1817–1828, from the same addresses as a portrait painter named W. Ross junior. Was probably the Miss Ross who was a student at the B.I. in 1817, when she painted miniature copies after Reynolds. *The Tabley House Papers* (*Walpole Society*, Vol. XXXVIII) record an unreceipted bill, 8 March 1809, for '£21 for three copies of a miniature, made out to Lady Leicester' by Janet Ross. She was an aunt of Charles Dickens and said to have been the original of 'Miss La Creevy' in Dickens' *Nicholas Nickleby*. A miniature portrait of Dickens, painted by her in 1830, was exhibited at the Grolier Club, New York, 23 January 1913–8 March 1913. Thought to have been the wife of Edward Barrow, journalist (d. 29 October 1798). The V. & A. M. has a miniature by her of Mrs. Balguy, née Emma Broadbent, signed on the reverse 'Painted by J. Ross-Decb' 1827', and one of Frederick Dickens (1820–1868), brother of Charles Dickens.

Ross, Miss Magdalena (Mrs. Edwin Dalton). 1801–1874

Born 1801; daughter of William Ross (q.v.) and his wife, Maria, née Smith. Sister of Sir W. C. Ross (q.v.) and of Hugh Ross (q.v.). Exhibited at the R.A., etc., 1820–1856. May have been the Miss M. Ross who won awards from the Society of Arts in 1823 and 1826. Married Edwin Dalton (q.v.) in 1841 or 1842; exhibited under her married name in 1842. In 1850 she was miniature painter to the Queen. A miniature portrait of her by Sir W. C. Ross is in the V. & A. M. She died in 1874. A miniature of King Leopold I of the Belgians and one of Louise, Queen of the Belgians (the latter after Sir W. C. Ross), both painted in 1840, are in the collection of H.M. the Queen. Many of her portraits were of children. She exhibited a miniature of her mother, Mrs. Maria Ross (q.v.) in 1835. Was said to have been a favourite of Delacroix, with whom she painted, and to have exhibited at the Paris Salon.

Ross, Mrs. Maria. See **Smith, Miss Maria**

Ross, Miss Maria. (fl. 1833)

Daughter of Hugh Ross (q.v.). Exhibited at the R.A., 1833. The Miss M. Ross who won medals from the Society of Arts in 1823 and 1826 may have been either this artist or Miss Magdalena Ross (q.v.).

Ross, W. S. (fl. 1817)

Working in 1817 at Macclesfield Street, Soho, London. Possibly the W. Ross who entered the R.A. Schools, 25 November 1815, aged 17, and who was awarded silver medals in 1817 and 1821.

Ross, William. d. after 1842

Son of a gardener to the Duke of Marlborough, whose family came from Ross-shire. Exhibited at the R.A., 1809–1825. Married Maria Smith (q.v.), sister of Anker Smith, A.R.A. (q.v.). Their children, Sir W. C. Ross (q.v.), Hugh Ross (q.v.) and Miss Magdalena Ross (Mrs. E. Dalton) (q.v.) were all miniaturists. Mrs. Ross died in 1836; William Ross must have died after 1842, for the V. & A. M. has a chalk portrait of him of that date by Sir W. C. Ross. A fine miniature of him, also by Sir W. C. Ross, was lent to the exhibition in Edinburgh, 1965, by R. L. Bayne-Powell, Esq.

Ross, Mrs. William. See **Smith, Miss Maria**

Ross, Sir William Charles, R.A. 1794/5–1860

Born in London, 3 June 1794/5; son and pupil of W. Ross (q.v.) and brother of Hugh Ross (q.v.) and Miss Magdalena Ross (q.v.). Showed artistic ability at an early age; won prizes at the Society of Arts, 1807–1817, for drawings, historical paintings and in 1816 for an original portrait of the Duke of Norfolk, besides executing miniatures. Exhibited at the R.A., 1809–1859. In 1814 he became, for a time, an assistant of Andrew Robertson (q.v.) to whom he was related on his mother's side. Ross had many distinguished sitters including Queen Victoria, the Prince Consort, their children and other members of the Royal Family. He worked for a time at the Portuguese Court. Became A.R.A. in 1838, and R.A. in 1842 and was knighted in the same year. In 1843 he won a premium of £100 in the Westminster Hall competition. Was a prolific worker and painted over 2,200 miniatures. He suffered a paralytic stroke in 1857 and died unmarried, 20 January 1860, and was buried in Highgate. Ross was undoubtedly one of the greatest miniaturists of his period, and was said to have been an extremely amiable and benevolent man. He was a fine draughtsman and skilful in his use of colours and arrangement of his subjects. Many of his miniatures are fairly large, but as in the case of the one in the collection of H.M. the Queen, of Prince Ernest and Prince Edward of Leiningen, playing with a macaw and Queen Victoria's dog, they are gracefully composed and painted with ease and assurance. He arranged his painting table so that the light came down aslant, from over his left shoulder. Besides all the portraits he painted of the English Court and members of the aristocracy, he was in great demand abroad and painted Louis Philippe, King of France, Prince Louis Napoleon, the King and Queen of the Belgians, the Empress Eugenie and many more. He often signed his works in full on the reverse, e.g. Painted by Sir W.C. Ross R.A. / Miniature painter to the Queen / 1841, W.C. Ross, or W. Ross. A miniature of Napoleon III by Ross, formerly in the Hand collection, is 17¾ in. × 13½ in. This was painted on a single piece of ivory. An exhibition of some 220 of his works was held in London the year of his death; the complete list of these was published by J. J. Foster in *Miniature Painters British and Foreign*, Vol. 1. A number of artists made excellent copies of miniatures by Ross, including Faija, Heath, Meuret, E. Moira and E. Taylor (q.v.). A large number of his miniatures are in the collection of H.M. the Queen, and other examples are in the V. & A. M., the N.P.G., the B.M., the Wallace Collection, the Nottingham Art Gallery, etc. Others are in private collections including those of the Duke of Northumberland.

Rosse (or Rose), Mrs. Susan Penelope (Miss Gibson). c. 1652–1700

Born c. 1652; daughter of Richard Gibson (q.v.) and his wife, Anna née Shepherd, who had nine children of whom Susan and four others survived and, in spite of the fact that their parents were both dwarfs, grew to be of normal size. Susan followed her father's profession and was his pupil; she studied and frequently copied miniatures by S. Cooper (q.v.), one of the most notable being her full scale copy of Cooper's sketch of the Duke of Monmouth as a boy, of which the original is in the collection of H.M. the Queen. Mrs. Rosse's copy is in the collection of the Duke of Buccleuch. She also painted portraits from life. A pocket-book containing fourteen unframed and sometimes un-finished miniatures, including some of the artist's family, and two self-portraits, is at the V. & A. M. These were for many years regarded as the work of Samuel Cooper, but an inspection of the inscrip-tions on the reverse led to their identification. She married a jeweller named Michael Rose or Rosse (born 1650, died after 1735). Vertue obtained much of his information from her husband who showed him portraits of the Gibson family. She died in Covent Garden in 1700, aged 48, and was buried in the church there. Some of her most attractive miniatures are those executed on a very small scale, i.e. about an inch high, as in the case of two in my collection of Louise Renée de Keroualle, Duchess of Portsmouth, and Barbara Villiers, Countess of Castlemaine, later Duchess of Cleveland. These and one of Gilbert Burnet, Bishop of Salisbury, 3¼ in. × 2⅝ in., were exhibited in Edinburgh, 1965. A characteristic of her work is the way she gives her sitters a slightly pouting lower lip, on which the highlight is often dark. Many of her miniatures are unsigned, all the signed ones being those painted after her marriage. The signature is either SPR or SR, occasionally the letters are sloping. She appears to have copied Cooper's method of painting a thin layer of white on the vellum before commencing the portrait. In 1682 she painted a half-length portrait of an ambassador from Morocco whilst he was sitting to Kneller. The present whereabouts of this is unknown. Apart from the examples of her work in the V. & A. M., there are some in private collections such as those of H.M. the Queen, the Duke of Portland and the Duke of Buccleuch.

*Roth, Mr. (fl. 1766)

The Oxford Journal, 29 November 1766, states that 'Mr Roth Portrait painter is just arrived in Oxford, who paints miniatures and pictures for bracelets'. A Mr. Roth was in Clare Street, Bristol, 10 March 1781, but this may have been one of the other artists of this name.

*Roth, George (senior?). 18th century

Presumably the father of George Roth junior (q.v.). George Roth is probably the artist who was employed by Allan Ramsay in 1767 and 1768 to assist in painting draperies. He was probably the same artist sought by Lawrence (q.v.), when he applied to Reynolds in 1790 for the address of 'one Roth a journeyman, painting draperies'. Reynolds paid 'Roth the drapery-painter, only twenty guineas for copying one of these portraits. . . .' (Royal portraits). The fact that there were several artists named Roth makes identification difficult; it is not certain that the above artist painted miniatures; he was presumably the G. Roth senior who exhibited fish at the R.A. 1811–1815, from 58 Dean Street, Soho.

Roth, George, junior. (fl. 1771–*c.* 1793). See also **Roth, William, junior**

Of London and Bath (1776); undoubtedly related to G. Roth senior (q.v.), T. Roth (q.v.) and W. Roth junior (q.v.). Exhibited from 5 Great Queen Street, at the Society of Artists, 1771–1776, including five small portraits in oil and other portraits; F.S.A., in 1771, and exhibited at the Free Society of Artists from Great Queen Street (no number given) in 1775. G. Roth senior (q.v.) who was presumably his father, exhibited at the R.A., 1811–1815, from 58 Dean Street, Soho. The exhibits which were catalogued under Roth (no initial) in 1813, were probably by G. Roth junior or W. Roth junior, as they were miniatures. Long records seeing a miniature in oil on canvas *c.* 1793 'Sketch of likeness Painted in profile by / G. Roth, at no 9 / London Lane, Norwich / Price five shillings, sitting one hour.'

Roth, Thomas. (fl. 1803–1828)

Worked in London, and was undoubtedly related to G. Roth senior (q.v.), G. Roth junior (q.v.), and W. Roth junior (q.v.). Exhibited at the R.A. and B.I., etc., 1803–1828. Painted portraits in oil and water-colour and miniatures on ivory and enamel, many of which were copies after old masters. His work varies in quality, some of it is equal to that of the best enamellists. A pair of enamel miniatures of Charles I and Henrietta Maria, after Van Dyck, signed on the front, were for sale in London in 1966. They were brilliantly executed with strong clear colours, and were slightly reminiscent of the work of Hurter (q.v.). His signature is usually T. Roth / London, T. Roth pinx / London (followed by a date), and Roth. Sometimes, as in the case of the miniatures of Charles I and his Queen, he signed on the front, and at other times on the reverse. Long records seeing a small oil portrait on panel inscribed 'TRoth pinx. 80 Dean St, Soho Apr. 1818'. It has been suggested that his work on ivory is reminiscent of that of J. C. D. Engleheart (q.v.). The background is executed in almost parallel and vertical brush strokes. Examples of his work are in the V. & A. M., including one of General Sir Ralph Abercromby, after Hoppner, signed on the reverse, 'T. Roth pinx / London June 1810'. An enamel portrait of Cromwell after Cooper (q.v.), signed on the reverse, 'TRoth June / London', preceeded by a monogram 'CC', is in my collection. It is not as well executed as others I have seen. An enamel miniature of Henry VIII by Roth is in the collection of Earl Beauchamp.

Roth, William, junior. b. 1754? See also **Roth, G., junior**

Undoubtedly related to G. Roth senior (q.v.), G. Roth junior (q.v.), and T. Roth (q.v.). Of London and Reading (1769). Probably the William Roth who entered the R.A. Schools, 18 December 1771, aged '17. 15th last'. Exhibited at the Society of Artists, 1768 when he is entered as 'Mr Roth, Junr, / at Mr Roth's, / Great Queen Street'; in 1769 his address is 'Mr Roth Junr / at Mr Hosiers, Wax chandler, / Frith Street'; in 1770 he is given as 'Mr Will Roth Junr / at Reading'. From 1773–1777 he exhibited from his father's house, 52 Great Queen Street, and in 1775 he exhibited at the Free Society of Artists from the same address. He painted miniatures and portrait and figure subjects in oil. G. Roth exhibited from 51 Great Queen Street, and from 67 New Compton Street, from which address T. Roth exhibited for some years. A miniature of an unknown officer, signed 'W. Roth' is in the collection of E. G. Paine of New York.

Rothwell, Thomas. *c.* 1742–1807

Of Liverpool. An enamel painter and engraver. Working in 1761. Died in Birmingham, 16 January 1807 when his age was alleged to have been 65.

*Rought, J. (fl. 1752)

The above artist was painting in Oxford, 6 February 1752, according to the *Daily Advertiser*.

Rouquet, Jean or **André.** 1701–1758

Born in Geneva, 1701; son of French Protestants who fled to Switzerland. Came to London *c.* 1723 (if one accepts his own statement that he had spent thirty years in England when he left for France in 1753). Another tradition that he came to England in the reign of George II would advance the year of his arrival to *c.* 1727. Vertue records that in 1739 Rouquet was the best of Zincke's (q.v.) imitators, and that he charged 10 guineas a head. He is said to have been friendly with Hogarth, Garrick and Foote, and several of the wits of the day. Exhibited at the Paris Salon, 1753–1757, and published *L'État des Arts en Angleterre* in 1755. He joined the Académie Royale in 1753. Painted the portraits of Louis XV and Mme. de Pompadour, and was given a studio in the Louvre. He went mad and died at Charenton, 28 December 1758. Rouquet was a good artist and his enamels are attractive. Miniatures by him are scarce, and, as they are not always signed, may often pass unrecognised or catalogued as 'style of Zincke'. Occasionally he signed his works on the front with a cursive R or JR (monogram). He painted the costume of his sitters with care and delicacy; his work was marked by a grace and prettiness that is only apparent in certain miniatures painted by Zincke. Characteristics of his work are small, slightly protruding eyes and the appearance of moisture on the lower lip of his sitters. His portrait of William Pitt, Earl of Chatham, in the V. & A. M. is a typical signed example of his work. A miniature of an unknown man *c.* 1750, signed on the front 'R' (cursive), is in the N.G., Dublin, who also have a miniature of an unknown girl similarly signed. Three miniatures by Rouquet were exhibited in Edinburgh in 1965: Letitia, Countess of Exeter, signed 'JR' (monogram) from the Burghley House Collection, and Captain William Fermor, R.N. (1723–1744) and Lady Musgrave, both from the collection of Earl Beauchamp.

Rouse, George. (fl. 1755)

Advertised in 1755 that he drew 'Gentlemen and Ladies' Pictures in Indian Ink, in a small oval, at Half a Guinea each, with Frame and Glass, at the Bridge Ward Coffee-House, under the Piazza on London Bridge'. It is not known if these were miniatures or silhouettes.

*Rouse or **Rowse, James.** 1802–1888

Born in 1802. Was apprentice at the Derby China Factory where he was noted for his paintings of flowers and figure subjects, and also painted miniatures on porcelain and in oil. Left Derby before 1830, went to the Potteries and worked at Coalport. Worked in Birmingham. Painted small enamels for jewellery. Returned to Derby by 1875 and was employed by Hancock at the China Factory. Died in 1888. Examples of his work are in the Derby Art Gallery, including his self-portrait in miniature on porcelain.

*Roussel, Theodore, R.B.A. (fl. 1886–1908)

Of London. Exhibited at the R.A., S.M., etc., 1886–1908.

*Roust, H. (fl. 1819)

A miniature of a gentleman, signed and dated '1819', was Lot 42 at Christie's, 19 July 1960. This may have been by Jean Henri Roust (born 1795) of Paris, who worked as a miniaturist there, exhibiting at the Paris Salon, 1824–1833. He became official painter to the Duchess of Berry. Painted from life as well as copies after old masters; painted insects. He is noted by Schidlof, who says that his miniatures are carefully painted and like those on porcelain.

Rouw, H. b. 1775?

Of London. Possibly the brother of Peter Rouw junior (q.v.) the wax modeller, who exhibited at the R.A., 1795–1840. H. Rouw exhibited at the R.A., 1796–1821. Was also a wax modeller, but exhibited a miniature in 1803. Was presumably the H. Rouw who entered the R.A. Schools, 10 October 1794, aged 19, when he was noted as a painter.

*Rouw, Peter, junior. *c.* 1771–1852

A wax modeller, born *c.* 1771, son of Peter Rouw senior (d. 1807). Exhibited at the R.A. and O.W.C.S., 1795–1840. Some of the exhibits in 1803 are given as portraits, and were probably miniatures, as those in wax were specified. He died at Pentonville, 9 December 1852.

Rovray, Fanny Galland(at) de. See **Gallandat de Rovray**

Rowand, William. See **Rowland, William**

Rowe, Susan. (fl. 1853)

Of 1 High Street, Tunbridge Wells. Exhibited at the R.A., 1853.

*Rowland, Miss Edith. (fl. 1902)

Exhibited at the R.A. 1902, from Eversleigh, Derby Road, Woodford, Essex.

Rowland, or Rowand, William. (fl. 1777)

Of Glasgow; worked *c.* 1777 in New York; advertised in a New York paper, 6 December 1777, as 'lately from Glasgow'. Painted portraits in oil, miniatures and taught drawing. According to Schidlof and Fielding, the above artist's name was Rowland, but Long and Groce and Wallace give the spelling as Rowand.

Rowlandson, Thomas. 1757–1827

Born 1757; entered the R.A. Schools, 6 November 1772, aged 15, '14 July last'. He exhibited at the R.A., and Society of Artists, 1775–1787. Rowlandson, famous for his draughtsmanship and caricatures, is not usually regarded as a miniaturist, but two of his portraits exhibited at the R.A., in 1781 were catalogued as miniatures. No. 334 was a 'portrait of a lady in fancy dress', and No. 339 was a 'portrait of a gentleman'. Died in 1827.

*Rowlatt, Miss. (fl. 1845)

This artist is recorded by O'Brien in *Miniatures in the 18th & 19th Centuries* as working in the middle of the 19th century. Pl. 49, Fig. 1, is a reproduction of a miniature by her painted on card, and inscribed on the reverse, 'Hannah Jeed painted by Miss Rowlatt, April 21st 1845'.

*Rowley, Miss A. M. (fl. 1872)

Of London. Exhibited at the R.A. 1872, from 33 Cadogan Place.

*Rowney, Miss Lilian (Mrs. Harley). (fl. 1899–1914)

Of London. Exhibited at the R.A. and S.M., 1899–1914 from various addresses in South Hampstead. Executed miniatures and subjects in water-colour. In 1899 she is recorded in the index of the R.A. catalogue as Rowney, L. (Mrs) and her exhibit was a miniature of Darent, son of Percy Harley, Esq. She is recorded as Mrs. Harley from 1904.

*Rowse or **Rouse, Miss Neta.** (fl. 1900)

Of Teignmouth, Devon. Exhibited at the R.A., 1900.

*Roxburgh, Mrs. Ethel G. (fl. 1909)

Exhibited at the R.A. 1909, from The Serpentine, Grassendale, Liverpool.

Rubidge, Joseph William R. (fl. 1823–1824)

Exhibited at the P.A., etc., 1823–1824. An extract from the *Sunday Times*, 30 December 1934, gives the following information from a letter written after Napoleon's death: 'A Mr Rubidge has taken a very happy likeness of Napoleon after death. He intends taking it home, and engraving it. It was taken on the 2nd day after death.' Long recorded this artist, and Schidlof supplies the christian names, but no details.

*Ruby, Miss Honorine. (fl. 1903)

Of Winchester, Hants. Exhibited at the Society of Miniaturists, 1903.

*Ruffle, Miss Emma M. (fl. 1908–1910)

Of London. Exhibited at the Society of Miniaturists, 1908–1910.

Rumpf, C. (fl. 1780). See also **Rumpf Losa, G. C.**

The above artist who was presumably identical with, or related to, G. C. Rumpf Losa (q.v.), is recorded in the R.A. catalogue for 1780 (not in the index), as exhibiting a miniature of an unknown man. The artist was probably related to others of this name who worked in Germany.

Rumpf Losa, G. C. (fl. 1775–1781). See also **Rumpf, C.**

Of London. Exhibited at the R.A. and Society of Artists, 1775–1781, from 44 Piccadilly and 98 Cornhill. In 1775 G. C. Rumpf exhibited a subject picture at the Society of Artists and in the same year G. Rumpf exhibited a model in wax at the R.A.; both entries were from 98 Cornhill. In 1781 G. C. Rumpf Losa is recorded as exhibiting a miniature of an unknown lady at the R.A. In 1780 C. Rumpf is recorded in the R.A. catalogue (not in the index), as exhibiting a miniature of an unknown man. He was presumably identical with, or related to, the above artist.

*Runciman, A. 19th century

Long records seeing two miniatures by the above artist representing Jane Wharton (1778–1821), daughter of Thomas Wharton and Lady Sophia Duff, and one of Mary Wharton (1781–1869), sister of Jane, both signed 'AR' in monogram, from the collection of Sir Christopher Chancellor.

I have not been able to trace this artist, and it seems unlikely that it was Alexander Runciman (1736–1785), the notable Scottish artist.

*Runciman, Miss Kate. (fl. 1903)

Of London. Exhibited at the R.A. 1903, from 105 Bridge Road, Battersea.

Ruse. 17th century

This artist is mentioned in a letter of 6 December 1653, quoted in *Memoirs of the Verney Family*, 1904, by F. P. Verney and M. M. Verney, Vol. I, p. 473: 'Carey is very desirous of your picture but is troubled to heare that sitting is a posture you like not, hee that drew plans, lives in the new street by Cursitor ally a Dutch man, his name is Ruse, my brother paid him 3*l*., as I take it for frame and case and all.' This appears to refer to a miniature.

Russel or **Russell (Thomas ?).** (fl. 1779)

Of London. Exhibited a miniature and a portrait at the Free Society of Artists in 1779. Details of his exhibits are given under John Russell, R.A. (q.v.) by Graves, but his name is spelt Russel, and the address given as 'at Mr. Hagarty's, 1 Queen St., Golden Sq.', not Mortimer St., Cavendish Sq., which was the address recorded for John Russell in the R.A. catalogues for 1779. He was possibly identical with Thomas Russell who entered the R.A. schools, 7 December 1770, aged '22, 21st Nov'; the Council Minutes give the name as Russel.

Russell, Gilbert

Wrote *The Art of Miniature Painting in oil and on ivory*, one edition of which appeared in 1855; styled himself R.A., but was not a member of the Royal Academy. It is not known if he painted miniatures.

Russell, John, R.A. 1745–1806

Born in Guildford, 29 March 1745; son of a bookseller. Was a pupil of Francis Cotes, R.A. (q.v.); entered the R.A. Schools, 17 March 1770 and obtained a silver medal in that year. Exhibited at the Society of Artists, the Free Society of Artists, R.A. and B.I., 1768–1806. Elected A.R.A. 1772 and R.A., 1788; was portrait painter to George III and the Prince of Wales. Known chiefly for his portraits in crayon and oil, but painted a few miniatures. He died in Hull, 20 April 1806. Many of his portraits were engraved. Several of his miniatures are mentioned by Dr. G. C. Williamson in his *John Russell, R.A.*, 1894. A large miniature by him of George IV, when Prince Regent, is in the Elizabeth White McCarthay Collection at the Philadelphia Museum of Art, U.S.A. It is sketched in water-colour with broad sweeping strokes, on ivory, and is said to be the sketch for the portrait in pastel by Russell. His diaries are in the V. & A. M.

*Ruthven, Mrs. M. E. (fl. 1903–1905)

Of London and Maidenhead, Berks. Exhibited at the Society of Miniaturists, 1903–1905.

*Rutley, Miss Maude. (fl. 1895–1898)

Of London. Exhibited at the R.A. 1895–1898, from 44 Adelaide Road, and 43 Chapter Road, Willesden Green.

*Ryde, Miss Florence. (fl. 1894)

Exhibited at the R.A. 1894, from 9 Upper Winchester Road, Catford.

*Ryder, Miss Harriet E. (fl. 1897–1904)

Of Lee, London. Exhibited at the R.A. 1897–1904, from addresses in Lee. Her sitters included His Honour Stephen Galty, Chief Justice of Gibraltar, Bertha and Grace, daughters of Hyla Elkington, Esq., and Thomas Lockwood, Esq.

Ryland or **Reyland, Joseph.** (fl. 1769–1778)

Of Westminster (The Salopian Coffee House, Charing Cross, 1769), Norwich (8 June 1771), and 25 Bennett Street, Westminster (1776 and 1778). Exhibited two miniatures at the Society of Artists, 1775 and he or another artist of that name, exhibited a wax portrait at the R.A., 1787. Painted miniatures for bracelets, rings or snuff boxes for one guinea each. Prepared colours for painting, and taught ladies to paint silks 'that shall never alter from being in the rain, by chemical preparation'. Long saw two miniatures by this artist of *c.* 1775 and 1786, which were of considerable merit. Some of his work was etched, and examples are at the B.M. *The London Gazette*, 30 June 1778, records J. Ryland of Bennett St., as an 'Insolvent debtor'. The advertisement for 1769, records the spelling of his name as Reyland.

Rymsdyk or **Rymsdyck, Andrew van.** 1753/4 – *c.* 1789

Son of Jan van Rymsdyk (q.v.) whose pupil and assistant he became. Worked in London from 1767 and may have been the artist of this name who is referred to in a number of press notices as working in Bristol, Norwich and Chester (see J. van Rymsdyk). Andrew exhibited at the Society of Artists in 1769 from Charles Street, St. James's, and in 1776 from 89 East Queen Anne Street, Cavendish Square. He exhibited at the R.A., 1775 and 1778. This latter exhibit was from 'Mr Frewin's, Porter Street, Soho' (no initial was given). He painted portraits in oil, still life, and miniatures on enamel and on paper, besides executing drawings in chalk. He was sometimes called Rymsdyk junior. I have seen several miniatures on paper by the above artist, all of which were attractive and well drawn. He often signed A.v. Rymsdyk followed by a date. A typical characteristic of his work is the way he places his sitters slightly to the right of the picture, his signature frequently being at the top of the oval. Examples of his work are in the V. & A. M., and the N.G., Dublin. An attractive miniature of an unknown lady, signed and dated, 'Drawn by / Andrew Rymsdyk, 1781', is in the collection of Miss D. M. Kleinfeldt.

*Rymsdyk, Jan van. (fl. 1758–1778)

A Dutch artist, who worked for some time in Bristol, and visited Chester? (1783). His son, A. van Rymsdyk (q.v.), was his pupil and assistant. He painted portraits, miniatures and chalk drawings, some of which were engraved. He made drawings of natural history subjects, herbs, fossils, etc., and anatomy, and was a drawing instructor. A number of press notices relate to him, and it is not clear if any of them refer to his son. Long says that he was living in 1778, and the date of his death is not recorded. The *General Evening Post*, 22 July 1755, says 'Thirty one tables of Anatomy, engraved by GRIGNION, after Riemsdyk'. In 1758 and 1759 he was living in All Saints Lane, Bristol. Felix Farley's *Bristol Journal*, 16 December 1758, states that he was painting portraits in All Saint's Lane 'at 4 guineas each', and in January 1759, 'J. V. Riemsdyk' of the same address painted 'portraits at 4 guineas, half length and whole length in proportion'. *The Daily Advertiser*, 20 September 1775, has an advertisement from Charles Street, St. James's Square, for 'Engravers who understand to imitate chalk drawings'. *The Norfolk Chronicle*, 13 October 1781, states that 'Mr Rymsdyk, miniature painter, Member of the Royal Academy, London has arrived in Norwich'. This and the advertisement on 22 July 1783 in *Adam's Weekly Courant*, which advertises that a 'van Rymsdyk, miniature painter and Member of the Royal Academy, London, visits Chester. He draws accurate likenesses &c, 1 guinea each', may have related to his son, A. van Rymsdyk (q.v.).

S

S. 16th century. See also Shute, John and Stre(e)tes, Gwillim

A miniature of Edward VI, painted on vellum, and signed 'S', is in the collection of Earl Beauchamp. It may possibly be by either John Shute (q.v.) or Gwillim Stre(e)tes (q.v.). It was exhibited in Edinburgh in 1965, and is illustrated in the catalogue.

S. (fl. c. 1760)

An enamel miniature of a lady c. 1760, signed 'S', is in the collection of Major R. M. O. de la Hey; the signature is not the usual one by Gervase Spencer (q.v.).

S. (fl. 1775). See also Singleton, W.

A miniature of Mr. Thomas Gibson, signed 'S / 75' (1775), painted in the manner of O. Humphry (q.v.), is in the V. & A. M. It may be by William Singleton (q.v.), or Henry Spicer (q.v.).

*S. See Σ.

S. (fl. c. 1820)

Long records seeing a large rectangular miniature c. 1820, of Mary, daughter of William Hamilton Nisbet, and wife of Thomas, 7th Earl of Elgin, signed 'S'; it was slightly in the manner of Mansion (q.v.).

S., F. See Smiadecki, F.

S., G. (fl. 1801)

A miniature of a lady in a white dress, signed 'GS / 1801', is in the collection of Major R. M. O. de la Hey.

*S., H.C.

A miniature of an unknown man, wearing a brown coat, yellow waistcoat and black cravat, signed 'H.C.S.', 8 inches high, was part of Lot 25 sold at Christie's, 15 October 1963.

S., I. See Saunders, Joseph

S., N. 18th century. See also Salway, N.

An early 18th century miniature of an unknown gentleman in a 'crimson velvet dress', painted on ivory and signed 'N.S.', was loaned to the Exhibition at the South Kensington Museum in 1865. This was from the collection of Lady Dorothy Nevill, and may have been the work of N. Salway (q.v.).

S., S. 18th century. See also Stanley, Mrs. Sarah and Shrubsole, S.

A miniature of Queen Anne, probably after Kneller, painted early 18th century, signed in gold 'S:S:', is in the Ward Usher Museum, Lincoln. It is not very well painted. This may have been the work of Sarah Stanley (q.v.) or S. Shrubsole (q.v.).

S., S. (fl. 1771). See also Shrubsole, S. and Smith, Miss Sophia

Long records seeing a miniature signed in white 'SS (monogram) / 71' (i.e. 1771), painted in the

manner of Scouler (q.v.). I have seen a miniature after an earlier painting, also signed in white 'S.S.' and inscribed on the reverse 'The Holy Family / copy by / S. Shrubsole'. Miniatures signed S.S. are frequently attributed to Miss Sophia Smith (q.v.). A miniature of an unknown lady, signed minutely 'S.S.80' (i.e. 1780), was seen by Long. The hair was painted in a mass with a few lines; the face shaded with a grey stippling. The background was painted with a fine soft perpendicular stroke.

S., W. (fl. 1807)

A miniature of a lady in a white dress signed 'W.S. (Roman capitals) 1807', is at the V. & A. M. The painting suggests that the artist was influenced by G. Engleheart (q.v.).

Sacco, Guiseppe. 1805–1889

Born in Palermo, 24 April 1805; brother of Francesco Sacco. Painted miniatures with great success; was painter to the Court of Naples, and later to Louis Philippe in Paris. In 1833 his address was 10 Rue du Helder. He exhibited at the Paris Salon in that year, and again in 1848, including his self-portrait. Came to London and exhibited intermittently at the R.A., 1852–1857. Had a distinguished clientele. In 1865 he loaned miniatures of H.M. the late King of Naples and of H.M. the Empress Dowager of Russia to the exhibition at the South Kensington Museum, when his address was given as 41 University Street. He is reputed never to have used a lens. His fiancée died, and he remained single. After retiring he lived in straitened circumstances in Cardiff, where he died, 14 February 1889, at the house of a friend named Strina. His draughtsmanship was accurate, and many of his works were very good. Instead of stippling, he obtained his results with strokes of the brush. He painted a small miniature of Queen Victoria, on which he highlighted the sheen on the hair with a little gold. His backgrounds were usually 'skies' or a bluish tint. Sacco was one of the artists who executed 'eye miniatures'; Long records seeing one where the eyelashes were each painted separately, and the reflection in the eye was well done. He painted an imaginative miniature of the 'End of the World', crowded with small figures; a small picture-gallery interior (approx. the size of a farthing); and a life-size 'Head of Christ' which was considered his masterpiece. The ivory for it cost £300. According to Long, it was exhibited at the R.A. in 1852, and subsequently at 5/- per head for admission. He was offered £3,000 for this painting which he refused. I have been unable to trace this work among the exhibits for that year, but Sacco did exhibit a miniature of 'the Holy Virgin with the pear', R.A. catalogue no. 870. Sacco executed pencil sketches of his sitters, some of which were slightly tinted. Long records seeing a book of these in a private collection and a miniature signed 'Sacco f^t 1852'.

*Sachs, Mrs. Jessie W. (fl. 1900–1906)

Of London. Exhibited at the R.A. in 1900 and 1906, from 32 Whiteheads Grove, Chelsea. Her sitters included Phyllis Sachs and Lawrence Tessier Sachs.

Sadler, Thomas. (fl. 1670–1700)

Second son of John Sadler (1615–1674), a Master in Chancery, and his wife, Jane Trenchard, whom he married in 1645. Sadler was educated at Lincoln's Inn and intended to take up a legal career, but as a result of a friendship with Lely, whose pupil he became, he turned to art. According to Walpole, who obtained information from the artist's grandson, Robert Seymour Sadler, he 'painted at first in miniature for his amusement, and portraits towards the end of his life, having by unavoidable misfortunes been reduced to follow that profession.

There remain in his family a small moonlight, part of a landscape on copper, and a miniature of the Duke of Monmouth, by whom and by Lord Russel he was trusted in affairs of great moment'. Sadler painted during the reign of Charles II and up to the time of William III. He executed a portrait of Bunyan in 1685 which was engraved in mezzotint. A miniature of John Bunyan, painted in oil and ascribed to Thomas Sadler, was loaned by Mr. David Laing, to the exhibition at the South Kensington Museum in 1865. His son, Thomas Sadler junior, was deputy clerk of the Pells, and was also an artist.

Sadler, William H(?). (fl. 1768–1788)

Born in England; son of a musician. Taken by his father to Dublin as a boy and placed in the Dublin Society Schools in 1765; was awarded a premium in 1768. Practised in Dublin as a miniaturist and painted portraits in oil and crayon, historical and still life subjects, wall decorations, and executed mezzotint engravings. Obtained the patronage of the La Touche family. Exhibited at the Dublin Society of Artists in 1777 from South Great George Street, and in 1780 from 13 Great Ship Street. Was living in 4 East Park Street, in 1784. Died in Dublin c. 1788.

*St. Aubin. See St. Aubin, Augustin de

*St. Aubin, Augustin de. 1736–1807. See also St. Aubin, J. de

Born in Paris, 3 June 1736; was an engraver and illustrator who worked in France and may have come to England. The Wellesley sale at Sotheby's in 1920 contained six small portraits by this artist executed in pencil on paper or vellum, one being heightened with colour. They represented Cardinal Flechier and five unknown sitters in profile; their sizes varied from 3 in. to 10 in. A miniature in the Edgeworth family of the Abbé Henry Essex, Edgeworth de Firmont (who attended Louis XVI on the scaffold), may be by this artist. A print of an oval version of this portrait is reproduced in C. S. Edgeworth's life of the Abbé. The print is inscribed 'De St Aubyn pinxit', and at the bottom of the page is 'publ De St Aubyn, 61 Berners St. 1800', from which address St. Aubin (no initial) was exhibiting, 1801–1802, at the R.A. The Abbé was only in England in 1796. The artist died in Paris, 9 November 1807.

St. Aubin, J. See St. Aubin, J. de and St. Aubin, Augustin de

*St. Aubin, J. de. (fl. 1796). See also St. Aubin, Augustin de and De St. Aubin

The above artist exhibited at the R.A. in 1796, from which address St. Aubin (no initial) was recorded only in the catalogue entry. He was possibly identical with De St. Aubin (q.v.) who exhibited at the R.A. in 1795, from 47 Berwick Street, Soho, and related to, or identical with, Augustin de St. Aubin (q.v.) who exhibited from 61 Berners Street in 1801–1802. Long records a J. St. Aubin and states that he exhibited at the R.A. from 1795–1802, but in this he must have been mistaken.

*St. Clair Scott, Mrs. A. E. See Scott, Mrs. A. E. St. Clair

Sage, Jas. W. (fl. 1863)

Lot 29 at Christie's, 5 March 1974 was a portrait of an unknown man by the above artist, signed on the reverse 'Painted by Jas. W. Sage / London April. 1863.'

Salaman, Miss Kate. (fl. 1834–1856)

Of London. Exhibited at the R.A., B.I. and

S.B.A., 1834–1856. Miss Augusta Cole, afterwards Mrs. Samwell (q.v.), exhibited a portrait of her at the R.A., in 1842. She was a relative of Ernest Salaman who had a collection of miniatures. A miniature of A. Abraham, Esq., signed and dated on the reverse '1852', by the above artist, was Lot 4 at Sotheby's, 10 April 1962, and another of Phineas Abraham, Esq., signed on the reverse and dated '1853', was Lot 19 at Christie's on 19 November 1968.

*Salisbury, O. (fl. 1806)

The above artist appears to have been hitherto unrecorded. Two miniatures by him are in the collection of Mr. Michael Kimber. They represent members of his family, Mr. Joseph Barrington, later Sir Joseph Barrington, and his wife Lady Barrington. These portraits were seen by me in 1967. The miniature of Joseph Barrington is signed on the front '1806 / O. Salisbury' (in cursive writing), and on the reverse is an inscription, 'Mr. Joseph Barrington / Aged Forty years / 1st April 1806'. The sitter is wearing a black coat, white cravat and waistcoat and is painted against a stormy-cloud background. A fair amount of gum is used with the paint, blue shading over and below the eyes, the eyebrows and nose being delineated in brown and the nostrils clearly defined. The hair is painted with fairly thick brush strokes. The portrait of Lady Barrington, née Mary Bagot, daughter of Daniel Bagot, is also painted against a stormy background and in a similar manner to that of her husband. As the sitters came from Limerick, the artist may possibly have been Irish, and the painting is slightly reminiscent of the work of A. Buck (q.v.).

Salkeld, Mr. (fl. 1780–1789)

Worked in London, Manchester and Reading, 1780–1789. Painted miniatures on ivory for lockets, bracelets and rings, for two to three guineas each. An old newspaper cutting, 1788, states 'STRIKING LIKENESSES taken by Mr SALKELD, ... Ladies and Gentlemen may be taken at their own houses in town, on giving him notice by letter, post paid, at his house, No 3 Surrey side of Westminster-bridge.' *The Manchester Mercury*, 14 November 1780, advertises that he is at 'Mr Lord's Spring Gardens, Market St. Manchester', and according to a note by Long, he was in Reading, 29 June 1789.

Salway, N. (fl. 1720–1760). See also **S., N.**

A miniature of the Earl of Godolphin in the costume of c. 1720 and stated to be signed 'N.S.', was lent to the B.F.A. exhibition, 1889. It was possibly by this artist. According to Benezit he was working up to c. 1760.

Sambat, Jean Baptiste. c. 1760–1827

Born in Lyon c. 1760. Worked for Mirabeau whose portrait he painted several times; accompanied him to Germany and England c. 1784. Returned to Paris, 14 July 1790. Exhibited there, 1790 (or according to Schidlof, 1793) to 1794. Kept a diary from the day he got to Paris, noted political facts, miniatures he painted and prices obtained. Was imprisoned during the revolution and made money by painting fellow prisoners. He painted Fabre d'Églantine, and the Minister of Police, Fouché, with whom he became friends. His daughter, Agiathis, also an artist, was obliged to earn sufficient money to provide for the whole family. Examples of his work are in the Louvre and the Museum at Bordeaux; a good miniature signed 'Sambat 1791', on ivory, of a lady holding a dog, is in the Wallace Collection, London. He died in Paris, 29 February 1827.

Sampson, J. (fl. 1840–1842 ?). See also **Sansom, J.**

Of London. Exhibited at the R.A., 1840–1842? The exhibit in 1840 was from the same address as T. Sampson (q.v.), 2 Percy Street, Bedford Square. In 1841 he exhibited a portrait (not a miniature) of an Essex Rector. Was presumably identical with the J. Sansom recorded as exhibiting a miniature at the R.A. in 1842 from Eaton Street, Grosvenor Place.

Sampson, Thomas. (fl. 1838–1856)

Of London. Exhibited at the R.A. and B.I., etc., 1838–1856; probably related to J. Sampson with whom he shared an address in 1841. Painted figure subjects and landscapes, and executed miniatures.

Samuel, Richard. (fl. 1768–1785)

Of London. Exhibited at the Society of Arts, 1768 and 1775. Won two gold medals at the Society of Arts for historical drawings, and in 1773 a premium for an improvement in laying mezzotint grounds. Exhibited at the R.A., 1772–1785. Published a pamphlet *On the Utility of Drawing and Painting*, 1786. Painted portraits in oil and miniatures. The N.P.G. has an oil portrait by him, and the B.M. has an engraving of a portrait of Miss Gibbons after Samuel, published 1780.

Samwell, Mrs. (Miss Augusta Cole). (fl. 1831–1869)

Née Augusta Cole; of London. Exhibited at the R.A., and S.B.A., 1831–1869. Undoubtedly related to Miss Ellen Cole, Miss Emily Cole and Miss Mary Ann Cole, who all shared the same address for a time. Married in c. 1864, and thereafter exhibited under her married name. Her exhibits included a portrait of Miss Samwell (possibly her daughter), Lord Fitzroy and Mr. and Mrs. Fitzroy. Painted miniatures for rings and bracelets.

Sanders, Miss Christina. See Robertson, Mrs. James

Sanders, George. 1774–1846

Born in Kinghorn, Fife, 1774; educated in Edinburgh; served his apprenticeship to Smeaton, a coach-painter. Worked in Edinburgh as a miniaturist, drawing master and book illustrator. Went to London c. 1805 and was well patronised, obtaining 30 guineas for an average size miniature and up to 70 guineas for a large one. Painted a miniature of Byron in 1807, and an oil portrait in 1809; his other sitters included the Princess Charlotte. In 1811 Farington records that he had given up miniature painting for oil portraits and 'gets 250 guineas for a whole-length. He was accustomed to work hard, and is said to have risen at 4 a.m. and gone to bed at 8 p.m.'. Sanders paid frequent visits to the Continent where he painted water-colour copies of the works of old masters. Exhibited portraits at the R.A., 1834 from 15 Edward Street, Portman Square. He suffered with ophthalmia. Died at Allsop Terrace, New Road, London, 20 or 26 March 1846. A small full-length portrait of him was painted by Andrew Geddes and is in the N.G., Edinburgh, who also have two miniatures by him. One is of an unknown lady, and the other of Oswald Hunter, M.D., F.R.C.P. This latter miniature is well painted and shows the influence of Raeburn. The face is painted with a brick red colour shaded with grey. Several miniatures by him were lent to the exhibition at the South Kensington Museum, 1865, including those of the Marquess of Blandford (1818), the Marchioness of Blandford (1819), David Pennant, Esq. (1823) and Lady Caroline Susan Pennant (1823). A miniature by him of Lady Shelley is reproduced in *The Diary of Frances*, *Lady Shelley*, 1912. Some of his works were engraved. He has been confused with G. L. Saunders (q.v.).

*Sanders, John, senior. (fl. 1771–1774)

Exhibited at the R.A. 1771–1774, from Great Ormond Street. Painted portraits and perspective views, and is not recorded as a miniaturist. He has been confused with John Sanders junior (q.v.) undoubtedly his son. The fact that there were four artists who exhibited at the R.A. under the name of J. Sanders or Saunders during this period, has led to errors of identification. The artists concerned were as follows: John Sanders senior (the above), John Sanders junior, Joseph Sanders (q.v.) and J. Sanders (architect). In 1775 the R.A. catalogues specify that John Sanders junior was the artist exhibiting, and the above artist's name does not occur again. An examination of the dates of exhibition, addresses and subject matter clarifies the position with regard to the other two artists, all of whom occur under Sanders or Saunders. The *D.N.B.* record John Sanders senior as a pastel painter of merit who practised in Norwich, Stourbridge, etc., and suggest the possibility that he was the father of John Sanders junior.

Sanders, John, junior. 1750–1825

Born in London, 1750; son of John Sanders senior (q.v.). Probably the John Sanders who entered the R.A. Schools, 21 August 1769 and was awarded a silver medal in 1770. Exhibited at the R.A. 1775–1788, from Great Ormond Street (1775–77 and 1782), Norwich (1778–81), Great Queen Street (1783–87), and Great Russell Street (1788). During his residence in Norwich he married a Miss Arnold in c. 1780, by whom he had five daughters and a son, John Arnold Sanders (q.v.). He moved to Bath in 1790 and was probably the J. Sanders who advertised in the *Bath Chronicle*, 1 November 1792, from 9 Lansdowne Place, Bath as 'Teaches Painting, Drawing, Miniatures painted (bracelets etc.)'. His other addresses in Bath were: Northumberland Buildings (1795), Green Park Place (1809), and Green Park Buildings (1811). His exhibits at the R.A. included portraits, figures, stained drawings, crayon portraits, drawings and views of Norwich Cathedral, but no miniatures. According to the *D.N.B.*, a portrait at Longford Castle, of Judith, Countess of Radnor, painted in 1821, is a good example of his work. Madame d'Arblay, in her *Journal*, mentions him as painting a portrait of Princess Charlotte of Wales. He died in 1825 at Clifton. As with the other artists of this name, the spelling occurs as Sanders and Saunders, thus causing confusion in identification. Careful examination of dates of exhibition, addresses and subject matter has clarified the position to some extent. A pair of miniatures of Sir Bedford Hinton Wilson, K.C.B., and Lady Wilson, by J. Sanders, signed and dated '1790', were Lot 24 at Christie's, 21 November 1967.

*Sanders or Saunders, John Arnold. b. c. 1801

Born in Bath c. 1801; only son of John Sanders junior (q.v.), and his wife, née Arnold (of Norwich). According to the *D.N.B.* his parents were married in Norwich c. 1780, and had six children, the above artist and five sisters. His parents had moved to Bath in 1790. He exhibited at the R.A. and B.I., 1810–1814, all his exhibits being landscapes, and I have not so far found any evidence to support Schidlof's statement that he was a miniaturist. He painted in oil and water-colour and was a popular drawing master. His addresses included 3 New King Street, Bath (1810), 23 Beaumont Street, Portland Place (1812–1813), and 8 Foley Street (1814). According to information in the *D.N.B.*, he emigrated to Canada in 1832. Schidlof gives the spelling of his name as Saunders, but the R.A. catalogues spell it consistently as Sanders, although others of the family use the alternative spelling.

Sanders, Joseph. See **Saunders, Joseph**

Sanderson. (fl. 1770)

Exhibited a miniature at the Society of Artists, 1770 as an Hon. Exhibitor.

Sanderson, Sir William. c. 1586–1676

Born c. 1586. Was secretary to the Earl of Holland and Chancellor to the University of Cambridge. Was a Royalist and 'employed in many negotiations of good consequence both at home and abroad'. Knighted by Charles II. Married the daughter of Sir Edward Tyrrell, Bart. He and his wife were given a pension of £200 a year by Charles II in 1671. Wrote historical works and *Graphice: the Use of the Pen and Pencil*, 1658. It is assumed that he painted miniatures, as a portrait of him was reproduced in the latter work which contained poems to him. *Graphice* is largely a plagiarism, but it contains useful information about contemporary artists, etc. Died 15 July 1676 and was buried in Westminster Abbey.

Sands, Anthony. c. 1806–1883

Son of a Norwich shoemaker, born c. 1806. Was a dyer, but later became a drawing-master and painted portraits in oil, subject pictures and miniatures. Worked in Norwich. Married Mary Ann Negus by whom he had Anthony Frederick Augustus Sand(y)s (1829–1904), also a painter, who seems to have added a y to the name. A small portrait of A. Sands, by his son, is in the N.P.G. It was painted in 1848. Sands died in Norwich in 1883. His daughter, Miss Emma Sand(y)s (1834–1877), was also an artist.

*Sandwell, Augustus. 18th century

Long recorded seeing a miniature in the manner of Abraham Daniel (q.v.) with a modern inscription on the reverse stating that it was by 'Augustus Sandwell, a pupil of Cosway'.

*Sandys, Miss Winifred. (fl. 1910–1913)

Of London. Exhibited at the R.A. 1910–1913, from 5 Hogarth Road, Earls Court and from 10 Aubrey Road, Campden Hill. Her sitters included Miss Gertrude Sandys.

*Sansom, J. (fl. 1842). See also **Sampson, J.**

Exhibited at the R.A. in 1842, from Eaton Street, Grosvenor Place. The exhibit was a miniature and the artist may have been identical with J. Sampson (q.v.).

*Sansom, Miss Nellie. (fl. 1894–1900)

Of London. Exhibited at the R.A. 1894–1900, from addresses in West Kensington. Executed miniatures and fancy subjects in water-colour.

*Santagnello, Agrese. (fl. c. 1845)

Long saw a miniature c. 1845 signed 'AS.' of 29 Nutford Place, Edgware Road which was by this artist.

*Sare, Mrs. See **Farhall, Miss Hilda M.**

Sargeant. 19th century. See also **Sargent, Frederick**

Charles James Turrell (q.v.) (1846–1932), is said to have been the pupil of a miniaturist by the name of Sargeant. He may have been identical with F. Sargent (q.v.).

Sargent, Frederick. d. 1899

Of London. Exhibited at the R.A., 1854–1874. Long records seeing a large oval miniature of Queen Victoria by him, signed 'FS'; according to the in-

scription on the reverse, the Queen gave him three sittings for it. The work showed Cosway's influence. Sargent also painted on porcelain; an example dated '1886' was seen at the V. & A. M. He died 14 April 1899. Portraits by him are in the N.P.G., and the B.M. has a lithographed portrait of Queen Victoria after F. Sargent, and two etched portraits.

Sargent, Mrs. W. K. (fl. 1855)

Of London. Exhibited at the R.A. 1855, from 11 Camden Cottages, Camden New Town.

Sarjent, Miss Emily. (fl. 1845–1864)

Of London. Exhibited at the R.A., etc., 1845–1864. Some of her miniatures were executed for brooches.

Sarney. (fl. 1766–1767)

Of Stanhope Street, London. Exhibited a flower piece and a miniature at the Free Society of Artists, 1766 and 1767.

Sartain, John. 1808–1897

Born in London, 24 October 1808. Was a pupil of Henry J. Richter (q.v.). Went to America in 1830 and settled there. Worked chiefly as an engraver but also painted miniatures. Became the owner of *Cambell Foreign Semi-Monthly Magazine* in 1843, and from 1841–1848 worked for *Graham's Magazine*; was one of the owners of the *Union Magazine*, 1849–1852. Drew sketches for the statues of La Fayette and Washington in Philadelphia, and designs for bank notes. He was very active in the art life of Philadelphia, serving as an officer of the Pennsylvania Academy, the Artists' Fund Society and the Philadelphia School of Design for Women; besides being in charge of the Centennial Exposition in 1876. Married the daughter of a London engraver to whom he was apprenticed (probably H. Richter), by whom he had eight children, four of whom became engravers or painters. He died in Philadelphia, 25 October 1897, shortly after finishing his autobiography which was published two years later.

Satchwell, Robert William. (fl. 1793–1818)

Only son of William Satchwell (1732–1811) by his third wife, Charlotte, daughter of the Rev. Robert Willis, whom he married 15 October 1768. Satchwell worked in London. Exhibited at the R.A., 1793–1818. His sitters included Dr. Monro, J. Varley, George Barret and S. Prout. Worked for a time in Cassel. Painted miniatures, portraits in water-colour, sometimes after oil paintings, designed frontispieces, etc. Drew illustrations in Indian ink for *Crotchet Lodge* (not published), and executed miniatures for Lodge's *Portraits*. Several of his works were engraved. He, or another artist of the same name, painted miniatures after Reynolds. Miniatures by him are scarce. A miniature at the V. & A. M. by him, shows red hatching and green stippling on the face. Other examples of his work, including a miniature of Captain Boys and one of the artist's father, are also at the V. & A. M. Schidlof mentions seeing miniatures by him which were equal in quality to the work of Ross (q.v.) and Newton (q.v.). He worked from 18 Broad Street, Golden Square and signed his miniatures in full on the reverse.

Satchy. (fl. 1758–1762)

A miniature of Miss Perkins of Deedham, Suffolk, executed in either pencil or Indian ink on vellum, signed and dated '1758' on the reverse, was Lot 699 in the Wellesley sale at Sotheby's, 1 July 1920; it was slightly in the manner of Ferguson (q.v.). Mr. E. G. Paine of New York has a miniature of a young man by this artist, signed and dated on the reverse 'Satchy, Delin 1762'.

*Saunders, Mrs. or Miss. (fl. 1826)

The above artist (no christian name given), is noted in Griffiths' *New Historical Description of Cheltenham*, 1826, p. 80: '(Mrs?) Saunders. Exhibition of Cabinet pictures in Harding's style from the old masters, is in Winchcombe Street. This lady teaches drawing and takes likenesses, in a manner peculiar to herself, on ivory, or on imitation ivory. Drawings lent to copy'.

*Saunders, G. N. 18th century

I saw a miniature on ivory of a lady in a shawl, signed 'G. N. Saunders / 34 Berners St / Oxford St.'. It was 18th century, rectangular and was well painted.

Saunders, George Lethbridge. 1807–1863

Born 1807. Has been confused with George Sanders (q.v.) (1774–1846). G. L. Saunders exhibited at the R.A. and S.B.A., 1829–1853, with a gap from 1839–1851, which was probably when he was in America and painting at Richmond, Virginia, etc. Exhibited in America, 1840–1841. He evidently returned to England c. 1851 and died in Bristol, 25 August 1863. His miniatures are well painted, his draughtsmanship is good and he used pure colours mixed with gum, and painted with a broad brush stroke. His signature is usually G. L. Saunders, scratched parallel with the edge of the miniature. His flesh tints tend to be rather yellow with strong blue half-tints and red-brown shadows. Examples of his work are at the V. & A. M. Miniatures of Caroline Sargent and Thomas Bartow by Saunders are illustrated by Wehle, Pl. XXXIII. A miniature of Matthew Gregory Lewis (1775–1818) is in the N.P.G. The B.M. has several engraved portraits after Saunders.

*Saunders, H. L. (fl. 1870)

Of London. Exhibited at the R.A. 1870, from 57 Queen's Crescent, Haverstock Hill. His exhibits were portraits of Mrs. William Kershaw and 'Maud'. Graves in his *Dictionary of Artists* records the initials as J.K., but I can find no evidence for this.

Saunders, Miss Hebe. See **Barnard, Mrs. Philip Augustus**

*Saunders, John, junior. See **Sanders, John, junior**

*Saunders, John Arnold. See **Sanders, John Arnold**

Saunders, Joseph. (fl. 1772–1811)

Of London. Exhibited at the Free Society of Artists and Society of Artists, 1772–1776, at the R.A., 1778–1807, and at the B.I. in 1808. Painted miniatures and executed engravings. His son, Robert Saunders (q.v.), was also a miniaturist. He signed J. Saunders or IS. A miniature of Sir John Clavering, signed 'IS', and another of a young lady in a white dress, signed in the same way, are at the V. & A. M. Schidlof notes a miniature of Catherine Helm, playing the piano, signed in monogram and on the reverse 'Joseph Saun .... / Great Maddox .... / Hanover Sq^{re}'. A Joseph Sanders is entered in the list of those at the R.A. schools, 8 April 1775 with the remark 'to be discharged'. J. Saunders of 19 King Street, Soho exhibited (1822) 'Sophonisba', and (1824) 'Shepherd and Shepherdess', both in the Antique Academy, and possibly miniatures; these may have been by the above artist. He is not, as is suggested by the *D.N.B.*, identical with John Sanders senior (q.v.). A miniature of an unknown lady, signed on the front in Roman capitals, 'IS', is in the City of Liverpool Museum. This is an attractive miniature and is reminiscent of the work of Cosway and Plimer (q.v.).

The hair is loosely painted in separate strands, the artist has used fresh brilliant colours, and pink flesh tints. A fair amount of gum is mixed with the paint. A miniature of Miss Sarah Morgan (later Mrs. Thomas Mabray), signed on the reverse 'J. Saunders / 1811', is in the collection of E. G. Paine of New York.

Saunders, Robert. b. 1774
Born 1774; son of Joseph Saunders (q.v.). Entered the R.A. Schools, 22 March 1793, aged 19. Exhibited at the R.A., 1790–1828. Painted miniatures. His addresses included 33 Great Maddox Street, Hanover Square (1790), where he styled himself as R. Saunders junior; 51 Rathbone Place (1800–1804) and 13 Great Titchfield Street, Cavendish Square (1811–1819). The exhibits of 1828, which included a miniature of the Rev. Dr. Owen, are listed without an address. The V. & A. M. has a well-painted miniature of a man inscribed on the reverse 'By / Mr. R. Saunders / January 1810'. The B.M. has an engraved portrait of Elizabeth Plunkett after R. Saunders.

Savage, Edward. 1761–1817
Born in Princetown, America, 26 November 1761; trained as a goldsmith, later took up painting miniatures and engraving. Painted a portrait of Washington c. 1789. Came to London, 1791; studied under West. Returned to America; was in Boston, and in c. 1794 established himself in Philadelphia; married in the same year. In 1800 he settled in New York; moved to Boston again c. 1812. Died in Princetown (Mass.), 6 June 1817. He possessed an important collection of art which formed the basis of the Museum of Boston, having been purchased by E. A. Greenwood.

Savill. (fl. 1661–1662)
Evidence for the existence of this artist is to be found in Samuel Pepys's diary. Both Pepys and his wife sat to Savill, a painter in Cheapside, London, in 1661–1662; the portraits cost £6; Savill delivered them on 22 February 1661/2 and varnished them at Pepys's house on 11 June 1662. Pepys also sat to Savill for a 'portrait in little'; this cost £3 and is thought to have been an oil miniature. On 3 May 1662, Pepys records 'Thence, at the goldsmith's, took my picture in little which is now done, home with me, and pleases me exceedingly, and my wife'. This miniature may have been the one loaned to the exhibition of oil miniatures held at the Fine Art Society, New Bond Street, London, June 1928. The miniatures from this exhibition are now in the Rosenbach Museum, Philadelphia, the catalogue of which records a miniature by 'Saville', said to be of John Dryden (1631–1700).

Saword, Mrs. (fl. 1808–1811)
Of Blackheath. Exhibited at the B.I., 1808 and at the R.A., 1811. Her exhibit at the B.I. was a miniature of Shakespeare.

*Sawyer, Miss Amy. (fl. 1887–1908)
Exhibited at the R.A. etc., 1887–1908, from Croydon and Russell House, Ditchling, Sussex. Painted miniatures and portraits and subjects in oil and water-colour.

Saywell. (fl. c. 1810)
Of Derby. Long saw a small self-portrait of him in oil c. 1810 from which it may be assumed that some of his works were small enough to be ranked as miniatures. I have been unable to trace any further information regarding this artist.

Scadden, Robert. (fl. c. 1760–1770)
An oil miniature of B. Giles, aged 28, which was exhibited at the Free Art Society, New Bond Street, London in June 1928, as by this artist, is now in the Rosenbach Museum, Philadelphia. It is a good miniature, oil on copper, c. 1760–70, 3 in. × 2⅝ in., and is engraved on the reverse with the artist's name. The B.M. has an engraved portrait of Dorothy Jeffery, after R. Scadden.

*Scafe, Mr. (fl. 1854)
The above artist is mentioned by John Haslem in *The Old Derby China Factory*, published 1875, p. 115. Under the entry relating to W. Cordon, he says, 'After a time, patronage falling off, probably from failing powers, about 1854 Cordon got employment in the Staffordshire Potteries, where he was shortly afterwards found by Mr. Scafe, a miniature painter and photographer, of Baker Street, Portman Square, who had advertised in the local papers for someone who could assist him in combining enamelling with photography. This led to Cordon entering into an engagement with Scafe, which, however, did not result in anything advantageous to either party.'

Scanlan, Robert Richard. b. c. 1801
Of Plymouth and London. Born c. 1801. Entered the R.A. Schools, 30 December 1822, aged 21. Exhibited at the R.A. and B.I., etc., 1832–1876. Painted miniatures and figure subjects. Many of his drawings and miniatures were exhibited at the 13th exhibition of pictures at the Plymouth Athenæum in 1833, when a small portrait of an Indian nurse was noted as 'really exquisite'.

*Scannell, Miss Edith M. S. (fl. 1870–1903)
Of London. Exhibited at the R.A. and S.M., etc., 1870–1903, latterly from 41 Egerton Terrace. Executed miniatures and painted fruit pieces in oil.

Schalcken, Godfried. 1643–1706
Born in Made, Holland, 1643; came to London in 1692, where he remained for some years. Returned to Holland in 1698. Painted candle-light genre pieces and portraits in oil, some of which were miniature size. An oil miniature of a lady inscribed 'GS', was catalogued as by him when it was exhibited at the Fine Art Society, New Bond Street, London in June 1928. This miniature is now in the Rosenbach Museum in Philadelphia. Died in The Hague, 13 November 1706.

Scharf, Georg, senior. 1788–1860
Born in Mainburg nr. Munich, 1788; son of a tradesman; studied in Munich, Paris and Antwerp. Was attached to the British Army in the Waterloo campaign. Came to London in 1816. Exhibited at the R.A., 1817–1850. Painted miniatures, taught drawing and was a successful lithographer and illustrator; painted figure subjects and water-colour drawings. Was the father of Sir George Scharf, Director of the N.P.G. Is not remembered as a miniaturist, but Long records one of a lady stated to be signed 'Scharf 1808', and catalogued as by him. In 1833 Scharf became a member of the N.W.C.S. Died in London at 29 Great George Street, 11 November 1860. Said to have been influenced by the British school of miniaturists.

*Schell, Anton. (fl. 1894)
Exhibited at the R.A. 1894, from 6 Albert Road, Brighton. Possibly related to Miss Lily Schell, also of Brighton, who exhibited at the R.A.

Schetky, Miss Caroline (Mrs. Samuel or T. M. Richardson). 1790–1852
Born in Edinburgh, 3 March 1790; daughter of John George Christoph Schetky, a musician, and his wife, née Reinagle (q.v.), and younger sister of J. C. Schetky, marine painter. Went to America c. 1818 and lived with another brother, George Schetky, in Philadelphia. According to Long and Fielding, she married a T. M. Richardson, but Groce and Wallace give her husband's name as Samuel Richardson, of Boston, whom they say she married in 1825. Exhibited at the Pennsylvania Academy, 1818–1826, and later at the Athenæum, Boston. She was organist at the Brattle Street Church for some years. Died 14 March 1852. Her mother was also an artist and an accomplished musician. Caroline Schetky painted miniatures, portraits, landscapes and still life.

Schetky, Mrs. John George Christoff or **Christoph.** d. 1795
Née Maria Anna Theresa Reinagle. Born in Edinburgh; eldest daughter of Joseph Reinagle, a Hungarian composer, of Edinburgh, and his wife Anne Laurie, and sister of R. R. Reinagle, R.A. Married in Edinburgh, January 1774, John George Christoff Schetky, a Hungarian musician, by whom she had eleven children. Her sons, J. C. Schetky and J. A. Schetky, were artists. One of her daughters wrote of her mother that 'she was a highly accomplished artist in both painting and music, having a splendid voice'. Died in Edinburgh, 1795. Her daughter, Caroline Schetky (q.v.), was a miniaturist.

*Schick, P. (fl. 1853–1854)
Exhibited at the R.A. 1853–1854, from 11 Robertson Street, Hastings. His sitters included G. A. Martin, Esq., M.D., and his children and Mrs. Albert Hambrough. His address in 1854 was Union House, Ryde, Isle of Wight.

*Schipper, George. (fl. c. 1810)
Of Holland. Lived in London c. 1810 and was an artist and miniature painter, and had a shop called 'The Three Beggars'.

*Schmid, or **Schmidt.** (fl. 1842)
Exhibited at the R.A. 1842, from 15 Maddox Street, Regent Street, 'Portrait of Dr. Granville' (possibly a miniature). The artist is described as 'Painter to the King of Prussia'. The name is spelt Schmid in the index, and Schmidt in the catalogue (no initial given), possibly identical with the Schmidt of Berlin who exhibited a large oil portrait of H.R.H. the Duke of Sussex at the R.A., in 1843, and with C. Schmid who exhibited large oil portraits at the R.A., 1846–1857 from 8 Harley Street, Cavendish Square, 17 Bentinck Street, Manchester Square, and Aix-la-Chapelle, including a portrait of H.R.H. the Prince of Prussia.

*Schmid, L. (fl. 1834)
Exhibited a portrait of 'F. Nadorp, a distinguished German artist at Rome' (possibly a miniature), at the R.A. 1834, from 11 Park Place, Regent's Park. Perhaps Louis (Ludwig) Schmidt who in 1835 exhibited an oil painting at the B.I., (not a miniature), from 1 Caroline Place, Regent's Park.

*Schmidt, C. (fl. 1871). See also **Schmitt, Guido** and **Schmidt, S.**
Of 34 Acacia Road, Regent's Park. Possibly identical with S. Schmidt (q.v.). Exhibited at the R.A. 1871, two enamels; 'the Last moments of Count Egmont', after Gallait, and 'Titian's Flora', after Titian. The former enamel sold for 50 guineas and the latter for 40 guineas. The R.A. index for 1871 lists this artist as G. Schmidt, but in the catalogue both exhibits are given to C. Schmidt; this was probably a printer's error, which led Long to assume that they were by Guido Schmitt (q.v.),

who at no time exhibited miniatures at the R.A., and was never at this address.

*Schmidt, S. (fl. 1872). See also **Schmidt, C.**

Exhibited at the R.A. 1872, from 144 Albany Street, Regent's Park, 'The execution of Lord Strafford, after Delaroche' (enamel). The index lists this artist as S. Schmitt, and the catalogue entry gives S. Schmidt. Possibly identical with C. Schmidt (q.v.) who painted similar subjects in enamel in 1871.

Schmitt or **Schmidt, Guido.** (fl. 1846–1884). See also **Schmidt, C.**

The above artist together with E. Schmid, C. Schmid and C. Schmitt, etc., are listed by Long as exhibiting portraits, figures and enamels at the R.A., 1846–1884. Guido Schmitt exhibited only oil portraits, figure subjects and engravings at the R.A., and B.I., etc., 1859–1884. There is no doubt that the enamel copies referred to by Long were not by this artist since at the time when these were exhibited (1871–1872), he was residing at 291 Regent Street, whereas the miniatures were exhibited by C. Schmidt (q.v.) (1871) of 34 Acacia Road, Regent's Park, and by S. Schmidt (q.v.) (1872) of 144 Albany Street, Regent's Park. The E. Schmid referred to is probably E. Allan Schmidt who exhibited at the R.A., 1868–1877. These exhibits were three large oil paintings, not miniatures.

Schönberg, C. L. (fl. 1825)

Was working in 1825 at 51 Marischal Street, Aberdeen.

*Schröder, Miss Enid. (fl. 1904–1908)

Of London. Exhibited at the R.A. 1904 and 1908, from 56 Queen's Crescent, Haverstock Hill.

Schröder, Georg Engelhard. 1684–1750

Born in Stockholm, 30 May 1684; seventh child of V. E. Schröder and his wife, Lucia Lindemeijer, half-sister of O. F. Peterson (q.v.). Came of a family of German goldsmiths; was apprenticed to David von Krafft. Became a miniaturist and painted portraits and historical subjects. Was in Venice in 1713 and subsequently in Paris. Came to London and studied at Vanderbank's Academy in St. Martin's Lane. Went to Sweden in 1724 where he became Court painter. Died 17 May 1750.

Schwanfelder, Charles Henry. 1773/4–1837

Born in Leeds, 11 January 1773/4; son of a house decorator and painter of tea-trays, snuff-boxes, etc. Was trained to this trade, but took up art. Exhibited at the R.A., B.I., etc., 1809–1826. Painted portraits, animals, birds, etc. Lived in Leeds, but was a frequent visitor to London. He was appointed animal painter to H.R.H. the Prince Regent, later George IV. Died in London, 9 July 1837, and was buried in Leeds. Miniatures by him are scarce. A miniature catalogued as by him of William Ward was shown at the Old Leeds Exhibition in 1926. An oil self-portrait of Schwanfelder, from the collection of the Leeds Corporation, was reproduced in the catalogue of the exhibition, f.p. 240.

Sciptius or **Seiptius, George Christian.** 1744–1795

Born in Dresden in 1744. Painted in the porcelain factory of Louis Fournier in Copenhagen, 1764–1766. Came to London and exhibited a portrait of a gentleman, and two flower pieces on enamel, at the Society of Artists, 1768, from 'The Rev Mr Degullion's, Bentinck Street'. Exhibited flower pieces, portraits, etc., on enamel at the R.A., 1778–1780. Some of his exhibits were enamelled imitations of cameos. The R.A. catalogue of 1780 records the spelling of his name as Seiptius. Evidently returned to Copenhagen where on 27 July

1785 he made an application to the Royal Porcelain Factory for employment which was refused. Died in Copenhagen, 26 June 1795. Miniatures of Queen Juliana Marie of Denmark and King Christian VII, signed and dated 1783, are in the National Museum of Frederiksborg.

Scotney, Francis. (fl. 1811–1833)

Of London. Exhibited at the R.A., B.I., and O.W.C.S., 1811–1833, and at the S.B.A., 1824. Painted miniatures on ivory and enamel, landscapes in oil and architectural drawings; was also a goldsmith. Long noted a miniature signed on the reverse 'F. Scotney / Silversmith, Jeweller & Cutler / no. 3 & 4 Duke St. West Smithfield . . . .'.

Scott, Miss. (fl. 1802–1804)

Of London. Exhibited at the R.A., 1802–1804, including a self-portrait, in 1803. Her address was 2 Lambeth Road.

Scott, A. (fl. 1807–1808)

Of London. Exhibited at the R.A. 1807–1808, from 29 Mortimer Street, Cavendish Square. In 1807 no initial was given, either in the index or the catalogue entry.

*Scott, Mrs. A. E. St. Clair. (fl. 1900–1905)

Of London. Exhibited at the Society of Miniaturists, 1900–1905. Was possibly related to Stanley St. Clair Scott (q.v.).

Scott, B. F. (fl. 1790–1792)

Of London. Exhibited at the Society of Artists 1790–1791, from 18 Broad Court, Bow Street, Covent Garden, and at the R.A., 1792.

Scott, Miss Emily. (fl. 1840–1855)

Of London and Brighton. Exhibited at the R.A., etc., 1840–1855. Painted portraits in water-colour. Schidlof mentions one sold in Vienna in 1919 signed 'Em Scott'. Said to have exhibited from 1836, but I have been unable to find her in the R.A. catalogue before 1840, from which date she exhibited from 23 Cannon Place, Brighton, and Maddox Street, Hanover Square.

Scott, Miss Emily Anne. See **Seymour, Mrs. C. A.**

Scott, F. (fl. 1822)

Of London. Exhibited at the R.A. 1822, from 41 Rathbone Place. The exhibit was a portrait of J. Tilley, Esq.

Scott, F. J. (fl. 1849–1867)

Of Chatham. Exhibited a self-portrait at the R.A., 1849. A miniature by him of Alexander Campbell of Inverness, signed and dated '1867', was sold at Christie's, 13 November 1962.

*Scott, Miss J. Mary (Mrs. H. W. Finch). (fl. 1903–1913). See also **Scott, Miss Janet M.**

Of London. Exhibited at the R.A., 1903–1913, from various London addresses. Possibly identical with Miss Janet M. Scott (q.v.).

Scott, James. b. 1802?

Of London. Exhibited at the R.A., B.I., etc., 1821–1844. Possibly the artist who entered the R.A. Schools, 1 April 1826, aged 24. He worked in the style of Samuel Lover (q.v.), but was not an artist of any great merit. Schidlof notes that he used a yellowish colouring for the flesh parts and a large amount of gum with his paints.

*Scott, Miss Janet M. (fl. 1898). See also **Scott, Miss J. Mary.**

Exhibited at the R.A. 1898, from 12 Homefield Road, Wimbledon. Possibly identical with Miss J. Mary Scott (q.v.), later Mrs. H. W. Finch. A miniature signed 'J.M.S.' and on the reverse, 'J. M. Scott / 99' (1899), is in my collection.

*Scott, Stanley St. Clair. (fl. 1903–1904)

Was a member of the Society of Miniaturists, 1903–1904. Was possibly related to Mrs. A. E. St. Clair Scott (q.v.).

*Scott, Thomas D. (fl. 1889–1894)

Of London. Exhibited at the R.A., 1889–1894, including a portrait of Mr. Alexander Scott.

*Scott, Mrs. W. W. (fl. 1844)

Of Sussex Cottage, Park Village East, Regent's Park. Exhibited at the R.A., 1844. Presumably the wife of William Wallace Scott (q.v.), mother of Miss E. A. Scott, later Mrs. C. A. Seymour (q.v.), and related to W. Scott, a portrait painter, all of whom exhibited from the same address.

Scott, William Wallace, 1820–1905

Born 1 August 1920. Worked in London. Probably the husband of Mrs. W. W. Scott (q.v.), and father of Miss E. A. Scott, later Mrs. Seymour (q.v.), and undoubtedly related to W. Scott, a portrait painter, all of whom exhibited from the family address, 11 Sussex Cottage, Park Village East, Regent's Park. Exhibited at the R.A., B.I., etc., 1841–1859. Exhibited a miniature of Miss Scott in 1846 and a portrait of T. Webster, R.A. According to Fielding, he went to America and had a studio in New York City for many years. Died in New York, 6 October 1905. Scott painted subject pictures as well as miniatures.

*Scott-Smith, Miss Jessie. (fl. 1883–1898)

Of Balham. Exhibited at the R.A. and N.W.C.S., 1883–1898.

Scouler, James. c. 1740–1812

Born in Edinburgh 10 January 1740; son of James Scouler, a native of Edinburgh, who was an organ builder and music shop proprietor. Studied at the Duke of Richmond's Gallery and the St. Martin's Lane Academy. The Society of Arts awarded him a premium for a drawing in 1755. Exhibited at the Society of Artists, 1761–1768. Scouler exhibited at the Free Society of Artists, in 1767 only, whereas Long states that he exhibited at this Society, 1769–1776. Exhibited at the R.A., 1780–1787. Lived in Great Newport Street up to c. 1776, and at 47 Great Russell Street from c. 1780 until his death. Painted miniatures and crayon portraits, and, according to Clouzot, p. 181, he painted on enamel. May have visited India between 1776 and 1780, although there is no conclusive evidence for this. Mr. Danton Guerault saw a miniature painted in the manner of Scouler and signed in front 'J.S.' and the words 'at sea'. On the back was an inscription stating that it was painted by J.S. on his way to India in 1779(?), the last figure being indistinct. (John Smart, who shared the same initials did not go to India until 1785.) Scouler had some money invested in the East India Company and a miniature of his brother Robert, signed and dated 'J. Scouler 1768', is inscribed on the reverse 'Robert Scouler / Ensign in India / Brother to James Scouler / Portrait Painter / 1768'. This miniature, from the collection of the Hon. Kenneth R. Thomson, was lent to the exhibition in Edinburgh in 1965, and is illustrated in the catalogue. Scouler died in London, 22 February 1812, leaving an estate of £7,500. Most of Scouler's miniatures are small, but there are some exceptions and some of his works are as large as $5\frac{1}{2}$ in. Many of his early miniatures show a marked resemblance to the work of Smart (q.v.) and it is more than probable that some of them have been wrongly attributed as some were signed J.S., the initials being very similar, and the draughtsmanship and painting not unlike Smart's. According to Williamson, the Hothfield collection contained a self-portrait of Scouler, signed and dated '1763', and a miniature of his brother, Alexander Scouler, signed and dated 'J. Scouler 1771'. I have an early example of his work representing a man in a plum coloured coat signed in white on the front 'J. Scouler / 1764', against a blue stippled background, the face is shaded in a bluish tone and the coat painted in gouache, with a fair amount of gum mixed with the paint. His later works are usually signed with his surname in full, parallel to the edge of the miniature, or J. Scouler Pinxt, followed by a date. He sometimes scratched his signature along the edge. The V. & A. M. has a certificate of the probate of his will and several miniatures by Scouler, including one of 'Diana' signed and dated 'Scouler / 1773', $3\frac{7}{8} \times 3$ in. An exceptionally fine miniature of a lady (possibly an actress), signed and dated '1778', was Lot 44 at Sotheby's, 29 October 1962, and was sold for £360. This example of his work places him among the ranks of the great miniaturists. The Glasgow Art Gallery has a large miniature of 'Flora' (a lady holding a bouquet), signed along the edge 'J. Scouler 1772'. A number of his miniatures are in private collections. A pair of an unknown man and an unknown lady, from the collection of Mr. & Mrs. J. W. Starr of Kansas City, and one of Lady Banks, from the collection of Earl Beauchamp, were exhibited in Edinburgh in 1965. A miniature of David Garrick (1717-1779) and his wife, signed and dated, 'J. Scouler 1768' was lent by the V. & A. M. to the Bicentenary Exhibition of the Royal Academy, 1968.

Scovell or Scovill, James. (fl. 1815-1840)
Of Bath, 1815-1840; son of an umbrella manufacturer of Wade's Passage, Bath. Was self-taught and is said to have succeeded to C. Jagger's practice (q.v.). In c. 1839 his address was Paragon Buildings, Bath. Schidlof mentions a miniature of a lady wearing a white dress, red shawl and blue bonnet, painted on card, and signed 'J. Scovell 1821', which was sold in Brussels, 18-19 December 1934. He did not consider the work of any great merit.

Seabrook, Miss Sarah Sophia. (fl. 1822-1824)
Of London. Was awarded a premium by the Society of Arts in 1822. Exhibited at the R.A. 1824, from 78 Hatton Garden. The exhibits were a self-portrait and a miniature of Miss Beveridge.

Seager, (Edward?). c. 1809-1886
Was born c. 1809. A miniaturist and silhouettist who worked in London, where he taught drawing. Went to the U.S.A., and Canada. Was working in Halifax, N.S., in 1840. Died 1886. Was possibly the Edward Seager who lived in Boston, 1845-1850, and whose wife was a miniaturist. According to Groce and Wallace, the two above artists are identical. Seager taught John Rogers, a sculptor. Exhibited at the Athenæum, 1847-1848.

Seager, Mrs. (Sarah?). (fl. 1827)
Exhibited a portrait at the R.A., 1827. Possibly identical with the wife of Edward Seager (q.v.) who was working as a miniaturist in New York in 1845. Mrs. Sarah Seager exhibited at the National Academy. A Miss Seager, presumably her daughter, lived with her in New York City, and was also an artist.

Seaman or Seeman, Abraham. (fl. 1724-1731)
May have been a relative of Isaac and Enoch Seaman (q.v.), and identical with, or related to, Noah Seaman (q.v.). The only reason for suggesting that Abraham and Noah Seaman might be identical, is the fact that an enamel miniature of an

unknown man, in the collection of H.M. the Queen of the Netherlands, is signed on the reverse with a cursive 'N.S.', and on the reverse 'Abraham Seaman / pinx 1724'. It is conceivable that this portrait was painted by N. Seaman and represents Abraham Seaman. Long mentions an enamel signed 'A:S: pinx:1725-', and Schidlof notes one of a man signed on the reverse 'A. Seaman 1731'. A miniature signed 'A:S:' (cursive), and dated '1725', was sold in 1933. Those works I have seen by Abraham have strong delineation round the nose and eyebrows.

*Seaman, Seeman or Zeeman, Enoch. 1694-1744
Was born in 1694; son of a portrait painter from Danzig who brought him to London when young; brother of Isaac Seaman (q.v.). Long recorded that the above artist was working in Britain c. 1743, and that he painted portraits, some of which may have been miniatures. Died in London, 1744. A miniature catalogued as of 'B. Zeeman the younger by his father', painted in oil, was exhibited at the South Kensington Museum, 1865. The name is recorded as B. Zeeman in the catalogue and E. Zeeman in the index. The portrait may have been by the above artist.

Seaman or Seeman, Isaac. d. 1751
A portrait painter who worked in London; brother of Enoch Seaman (q.v.) (1694-1744), a painter, and son of a Danzig portrait painter. Long records seeing a miniature copy on vellum of the head of Alexander Pope, after Kneller, c. 1730. This was authenticated by an 18th century inscription on the reverse. The face was softly stippled and the shading on the face, red. The background was brown. Seaman advertised from 'Air St., Piccadilly', 20 April 1745. He had a son, Paul, who was an artist. Died in London, 4 April 1751.

Seaman, Noah. (fl. 1724-1741)
Little is known about this artist who may have been a brother of Enoch Seaman (q.v) and of Isaac Seaman (q.v.), and identical with, or related to, Abraham Seaman (q.v.). A miniature of an unknown man on enamel, in the collection of H.M. the Queen of the Netherlands, is signed on the front with a cursive 'N.S.', and on the reverse 'Abraham Seaman / pinx 1724'. The same collection contains an enamel of an unknown man which is signed on the reverse in yellow 'Noah Seaman / pinx 1728'. It is painted in a different technique from that signed Abraham Seaman, with tighter painting, more stippling and better draughtsmanship. A miniature of a lady, signed and dated '1724', was sold in 1874, and an enamel portrait of George Frederic Handel, signed 'N.S. fecit 1741', is in the Louvre. Another example of his work, of an unknown man, is in the N.G., Dublin; it is strongly painted. Seaman was a good artist, and some of his work is reminiscent of that of Zincke (q.v.). A miniature of an unknown man, signed on the reverse 'Noah Seaman / pinx', is in the V. & A. M.

Seaton or Seton, John Thomas. d. after 1806
Son of a gem engraver (probably Christopher Seaton who exhibited at the Society of Artists, 1760-1766). Studied as a boy under F. Hayman, and at the St. Martin's Lane Academy. Exhibited at the Society of Artists, of which he was a member, 1761-1777, and at the R.A., 1774. Was in Bath (1766), at Mrs. Sledges, Henrietta Street, London (1769), and Edinburgh (1772-1774). In 1775 he decided to go to India and on 22 November 'Mr John Seaton' was given permission to 'go to Bengal to practise the profession of a portrait

painter'. He probably reached India in August 1776, and lived in Calcutta for about nine years, during which time he painted many portraits, including those of Col. Allan Macpherson and his wife and brother; Sir Eyre Coote; etc. He returned to England in the autumn of 1785. O. Humphry (q.v.) records the fact that he had 'just returned to England after an easy time in Bengal and with twelve thousand pounds in his pocket'. This may have been only rumour. He is best known for his portraits in oil, and small full lengths in landscapes, but in 1762 he exhibited a miniature at the Society of Artists. Said to have been living in Edinburgh in 1806. Two large portraits in oil by him are in the S.N.P.G.

*Seed, T. (fl. 1834)
Long noted seeing a miniature of a youth, signed 'T. Seed Pinx. 1834'. Possibly related to T. S. Seed of Southampton, recorded by Benezit as working 1795-1820.

*Seeley, Miss Ellen. (fl. 1880-1888)
Of Richmond and Littlehampton, Sussex (1888). Exhibited at the R.A., 1880-1888. One of her miniatures was on porcelain. Her sitters included Lilian and Muriel, the children of the Rev. Henry Seeley.

Seeman. See Seaman, Abraham, Enoch, Isaac and Noah

*Segar, Francis. (fl. c. 1590-1613). See also **Segar, Sir William**
Son of Francis Segar and his wife Anne, née Sherard; brother of Sir William Segar (q.v.). The work of the two brothers is so far indistinguishable. Both artists are mentioned by Francis Meres in his *Wit's Commonwealth*, 1598, which contained lists of the leading painters in England: 'William and Francis Segar bretheren'. David Piper, in his article (no. 2) on *The Lumley Inventory, Burlington Magazine*, Vol. 99, 1957, notes that Francis is first mentioned in the inventory in 1590 (not in the capacity of a painter) and that there are several records of him as a servant, or 'Councillor', to Maurice, Landgrave of Hesse. There is no record of him after 1613. He may possibly have painted some miniatures.

*Segar, Sir William. d. 1633. See also **Segar, Francis**
Son of Francis Segar and his wife Anne, née Sherard. The brothers William and Francis Segar (q.v.) were contemporaries of N. Hilliard (q.v.); little is known about them, and until more information is available, it is impossible to be certain which of the two men is responsible for works signed Segar. William has been identified as Sir William Segar who held important positions at Court. He was Somerset Herald, 1588/9, Garter King of Arms, 1603 and was knighted in 1616. He may well have been the more important artist, and is said to have been trained as a scrivener, and, through the patronage of Sir Thomas Heneage, was admitted into the College of Arms. He was the author of several heraldic treatise, including *Honor Military and Civil*, 1602. The Household Accounts of Sir Thomas Egerton, Lord Keeper of the Great Seal, record payments to him as follows: 'paid Mr. Segar alias Somersett the hearold for her Maties picture' for which he was paid £9. 10s. How much of Segar's work was based on paintings by other artists is not known. He died at Richmond, 13 (?10) December 1633 and was buried in the chancel of Richmond Church. He married first, Helen or Eleanor, daughter of Sir (?) Somers of Kent, Knight; and secondly, Mary, daughter of Robert Browne of Evington, Herefordshire. Sir William

was the father of several children, including Thomas Segar (died 1670), Bluemantle Pursuivant; Penelope Segar, wife of Nicholas Charles (died 1613), Lancaster Herald; and was the great-grandfather of Simon Segar (fl. 1656–1712). A miniature of Dean Colet on the Statute Book of St. Paul's School, 1585/6 (based on the lost memorial bust in Old St. Paul's), in the Mercers' Hall, is set within an illuminated title page, and painted on a blue background with the sitter's face more modelled than those painted by Hilliard. This is thought to be by one of the Segars. David Piper has published his research on the Segars in the *Burlington Magazine*, Vol. 99, 1957. Several large portraits in oil, such as one of Robert Devereux, 2nd Earl of Essex, 1590, in the National Gallery, Dublin, have plausibly been attributed to one or both of the Segars. Miss Auerbach provides the information that, although he was made Garter Principal King in 1603/4, Sir William Segar was only definitely appointed in 1606/7, and had to procure a new patent. Payments for heraldic work are recorded to him between 1604 and 1609. The London Survey of *The College of Arms, 1963*, pp. 48–49, records details of his various appointments and works on heraldry. For other works see the *D.N.B.* An important illuminated manuscript of the arms and badges of the Kings of England, dedicated to James I, 1604, is at the B.M., and is probably by this artist.

Séguier, Mrs. John. See Stewart, Miss Margaret

Seiptius or Seipsius. See Sciptius, George Christian

*Selby, Miss E. Margaret. (fl. 1903–1909)
Of London. Exhibited at the R.A., 1903–1909. One of her exhibits was a portrait of Mrs. Selby.

*Sellers, Mrs. Kate R. (fl. 1907–1909)
Of London. Exhibited at the R.A. 1907 and 1909, from 8 Muswell Road, Muswell Hill.

*Selous, Miss Dorothea M. (fl. 1908–1909)
Of London and Hove, Sussex. Exhibited at the R.A., 1908 and 1909.

Selous, G. See Slous, Gideon or George

*Selwyn, M. L. d. 1820
A rectangular miniature by this artist is reproduced in O'Brien, p. 140, fig. I. It is of a small girl with a dog in her arms, signed on the reverse 'A. Barnard, painted by M. L. Selwyn'. Long noted that this artist painted after Greuze, and that he or she died in 1820.

Serre, I. A. or J. A. (fl. 1784)
Long records an enamel portrait of Lady Anne Farmer by I. A. Serre, 1754, possibly the same miniature which was lent by Lord Cremore to the exhibition at the South Kensington Museum, 1865. This was probably Jean Adam Serre of Geneva, 1704–1788, who is recorded by Schidlof. He painted miniatures on ivory and enamel. Was pupil, friend and companion of Liotard (q.v.) whom he helped with his works. Was the first person to extract a brown colour for enamels from platinum and invented the recording barometer. Published several works on harmony. A miniature on ivory of Marie Therese, Empress of Austria, signed on the reverse 'Marie Therese / Imperatrice Reine / peinte a Vienne / d'apres Nature en / 1746 / par I. Adam Serre', is in the Museum in Geneva. It is not certain that this artist ever worked in Britain, but Long records that 'Serre', no initial given, who painted miniatures and enamels, lodged, 21 April 1755 at 'Two Chairmen', Marylebone Street, Piccadilly.

*Seth, Miss Florence. (fl. 1908–1914)
Of London. Exhibited at the R.A., 1908–1914.

Severn, Joseph. 1793–1879
Born in Hoxton, 7 December 1793; son of a musician. Was apprenticed to an engraver. Entered the R.A. Schools, 24 November 1815, aged 22 and obtained a Gold Medal in 1819. Became a friend of Keats, the poet, *c.* 1816. Won a prize at the R.A., for an historical painting in 1818. Exhibited at the R.A. and B.I., etc., 1817–1868. Severn accompanied Keats to Italy in 1820 and painted his portrait. In 1828 he married Elizabeth, daughter of Archibald Montgomerie, Lord Montgomerie. In 1860 he became British Consul in Rome. Severn died in Rome, 3 August 1879. Is little known as a miniaturist and painted chiefly portraits and genre subjects in oil and water-colour. A miniature of Keats by him is in the N.P.G. Schidlof gives his name as Severs in error, and his mention of a miniature of Keats at the Newport Gallery is, in fact, the one mentioned above at the N.P.G.

*Sewbridge, Julia
A miniature of Miss M. A. Biggs, after A. Plimer (q.v.), by the above artist, was Lot no. 57 at Christie's, 13 November 1962. It was not of a very high quality.

*Sexton, Mr. (fl. 1787)
A Mr. Sexton, limner, married Miss Hutchinson, by special licence, 10 May 1787 (*Gentleman's Magazine*, LVII).

Seyffarth or Seyfarth, Miss Agnes E. (fl.1850–1859)
Of London. Daughter of Mrs. Woldemar Seyffarth (q.v.). Miss Seyffarth exhibited at the R.A., etc., 1850–1859. Executed miniatures and historical paintings.

Seyffarth or Seyfarth, Mrs. Woldemar (Miss Louisa Sharpe). 1798–1843
Née Louisa Sharpe. Born 1798; third daughter of William Sharpe, a Birmingham engraver, who brought her to London *c.* 1816. Took up miniature painting. Exhibited at the R.A. and O.W.C.S., 1817–1842. Was elected a member of the O.W.C.S. in 1829, and did not exhibit at the R.A. after this date. Gave up miniature painting, and painted costume subjects and domestic and sentimental scenes, illustrated poems, many of which were engraved in the *Keepsake* and other annuals. In 1834 she married Professor Woldemar Seyffarth of Dresden, by whom she had Agnes E. Seyffarth (q.v.). Charlotte Sharpe, later Mrs. T. B. Morris (q.v.), Eliza Sharpe (q.v.) and Mary Anne Sharpe were her sisters. She died in Dresden, 28 January 1843.

Seymour, Mrs. C. A. (Miss Emily Anne Scott). (fl. 1844–1880)
Of London and Manchester. Née Emily Anne Scott; probably the daughter of William Wallace Scott (q.v.) and of Mrs. W. W. Scott (q.v.), and related to Walter Scott, a portrait painter, all of whom exhibited from the same address, Sussex Cottage, Park Village East, Regent's Park. Exhibited at the R.A., under her maiden name, 1844–1855. Mrs. Seymour was living in Liverpool *c.* 1870 or 1880. In 1844 she exhibited a miniature of William Scott, Esq. She loaned a self-portrait to the exhibition at the South Kensington Museum, 1865.

Seymour, Colonel John. (fl. *c.* 1710)
An amateur miniaturist; working *c.* 1710. A small self-portrait by him executed in Indian ink and shaded with Indian ink is in the B.M.

Seymour, Robert. *c.* 1800–1836
Born in London *c.* 1800; son of a Somersetshire gentleman who had become a cabinet-maker; was apprenticed to a pattern-drawer in Spitalfields. Subsequently took up painting. Exhibited at the R.A., 1822. Painted figure subjects, portraits in oil and some miniatures. Designed book illustrations and executed etchings. Knew Joseph Severn (q.v.). Married Jane Holmes in 1827. Shot himself, 20 April 1836.

Shakespear, J. (fl. 1807)
Exhibited at the R.A. 1807, as an Hon. Exhibitor. It has been suggested that he might have been John Shakespear (1774–1858), the Orientalist, who, in 1807, was a professor at the Royal Military College, Marlow, but there is not, so far, any evidence to support this theory.

*Sharp, Miss. 17th century
Long saw a good miniature of James Sharp (1613–1679), Archbishop of St. Andrews. It was after a portrait by Lely, and was executed in Indian ink in the style of Paton (q.v.). The miniature was said to be by his daughter. Archbishop Sharp, by his wife Helen, daughter of Moncrieff of Randerston, had two sons and five daughters.

Sharpe, Miss Charlotte. See Morris, Mrs. T. Best

Sharpe, Miss Eliza. 1796–1874
Born in Birmingham, August 1796; one of four daughters of William Sharpe, a Birmingham engraver, who brought them to London *c.* 1816. Exhibited at the R.A., 1817–1867, and was a member of the O.W.C.S., 1829–1872. Began as a miniaturist, but subsequently painted costume and sentimental subjects, some of which were engraved in the *Annuals*. Towards the end of her life, she copied pictures and the Raphael Cartoons at the South Kensington Museum. Was a sister of Miss Mary Anne Sharpe (q.v.), Mrs. W. Seyffarth (q.v.) and of Mrs. T. B. Morris (q.v.). She lent a miniature of Mrs. George Bishop, painted on ivory, to the exhibition at the South Kensington Museum, 1865. She died at Burnham, Maidenhead, 11 June 1874.

*Sharpe, J. F. (fl. 1826–1838)
Of London, 1826–1831, and Southampton, 1832–1838. Exhibited at the R.A., etc., 1826–1838. Painted portraits and miniatures. Had an address in West Hackney for some years. Exhibited a miniature of Miss S. M. Sharpe in 1830, and a self-portrait in 1835. A miniature of Mrs. S. Stephens, signed on the reverse by this artist, was seen by Mr. A. J. B. Kiddell, and Schidlof records a miniature of a young lady surrounded by clouds, signed on the reverse, 'J. F. Sharpe / Southampton / Pinx^t 1835'. He noted that it was reminiscent of the style of Chalon (q.v.), but not as good.

Sharpe, Miss Louisa. See Seyffarth, Mrs. Woldemar

Sharpe, Miss Mary Anne. 1802–1867
Born in Birmingham, August 1802; one of the four daughters of William Sharpe, a Birmingham engraver, and sister of Mrs. W. Seyffarth (q.v.), Mrs. T. B. Morris (q.v.) and Miss Eliza Sharpe (q.v.), all of whom came to London with their father *c.* 1816. Exhibited at the R.A., etc., 1819–1863. In 1865 she lent a miniature of a little girl to the exhibition at the South Kensington Museum. Died in 1867.

*Sharples, James, senior. 1750/2–1811
Born in Lancashire, 1750/2. Painted portraits in pastel, and some miniatures. Exhibited at the R.A., 1779–1785. Married as his third wife Ellen Wallace

(q.v.); was the father of Rolinda Sharples (q.v.) and James Sharples (died 1839), pastellist, and of Felix and George Sharples, who were the children of earlier marriages. He has been identified with 'Mr Sharples of Duke St. Liverpool' who exhibited there in 1774 at the first exhibition of the Liverpool Society of Artists; the exhibits included a portrait and two small oval portraits, possibly miniatures. Sharples took his third wife Ellen, James, and his two elder children, George and Felix, to America in c. 1794/6. Mr. and Mrs. Sharples returned to Britain c. 1801, but went back to America in 1809, accompanied by Rolinda. He died in New York, 26 February 1811. Examples of his work are in the Bristol Art Gallery, the Metropolitan Museum, New York, the Boston Museum, and the Independence Hall in Philadelphia.

Sharples or **Sharpless, Mrs. James (Ellen).** 1769–1849

Born in Birmingham or Bath, 4 March 1769, née Ellen Wallace. She was a pupil in Bath of James Sharples (1750/2–1811) (q.v.), a pastellist, whom she married as his third wife in 1787. Most of her work was confined to miniature copies of old masters and numerous copies (chiefly pastels, 5 × 4 in.) of portraits by her husband. She was said to be too nervous to paint many originals. According to Groce and Wallace, she was an expert needlewoman. A Mrs. Sharpless exhibited at the Society of Artists in 1783 from 45 Gerrard Street, Soho (the address of James Sharples) when she was described as 'Embroideress to Her Majesty'; the exhibitor may have been James Sharples' first or second wife, and not Mrs. Ellen Sharples. Mr. and Mrs. Sharples, accompanied by their family, went to America c. 1794–6, having been captured en route and imprisoned by the French. The family returned to England c. 1801 to look after property in Bath which belonged to Mrs. Sharples. Felix and James jun. returned to America in 1806. She exhibited at the R.A. 1807, from 82 Hatton Gardens, London, including a portrait of Washington. In 1809 she and her husband returned to America where he died in New York, 26 February 1811. Leaving her step-son Felix in America, Mrs. Sharples returned to Britain with her son James and her daughter Rolinda, and took up residence in Clifton, Bristol, where she died, 14 March 1849, having survived her children. She left £3,465 for founding the Bristol Fine Art Academy, now the Royal West of England Academy, to which she had already given £2,000. Examples of her work are in the Bristol Art Gallery as well as a number of small pastels by her husband. A miniature portrait of her at the Bristol Academy shows that in her youth she was a beautiful woman. The N.P.G. has examples of her work.

Sharples, Miss Rolinda. 1793/4–1838

Daughter of James Sharples (q.v.) and his third wife Ellen Sharples (q.v.). There are conflicting accounts as to where and when Rolinda Sharples was born; she was either born in England c. 1793 or in New York c. 1794. She accompanied her family to England in 1801, and resided with them in Bath until 1809, when she and her parents returned to America. After their father's death in 1811, Rolinda and James returned to Britain with their mother, with whom they lived in Clifton, Bristol. Rolinda exhibited at the R.A. and S.B.A. 1820–1836, and became a member of the latter. She was a good artist, and painted miniatures, portraits in oil and genre subjects. She died of cancer on 10 February 1838 in Bristol. A self-portrait and other works, including a portrait by her of her mother, are in the Bristol Art Gallery. In the same collection is a large oil painting depicting 'The Trial of Col. Brereton, after the Bristol Riots 1831'.

Examples of her work were reproduced by Arnold Wilson in 'Rolinda Sharples and her Family', *Country Life*, 4 January 1968.

*Shaw, Miss E. Sylvia. (fl. 1903–1912)

Of Highgate, London. Exhibited at the R.A., 1903–1912. Executed miniatures and studies in oil and water-colour.

*Shaw, Mrs. Evelyn Caroline Eunice Byam (Miss Evelyn Pyke-Nott). 1870–1960

Born 3 May 1870; daughter of John Nott Pyke-Nott of Bydown House, N. Devon. Studied painting at the St. John's Wood School of Art, and later at the R.A. Schools. Exhibited at the R.A., 1894–1899 under her maiden name, and 1900–1914 as Mrs. Byam Shaw. Married in 1899, John Byam Lister Shaw (1872–1919), the well-known painter and illustrator, by whom she had four sons and two girls (one of whom died in infancy). Her sister, Isabel Pyke-Nott (q.v.), exhibited from the same address, 4 St. Edmunds Terrace, Regent's Park. Mrs. Byam Shaw executed oil paintings and miniatures. She gave up oil painting about the time of her marriage, and due to failing eyesight, had to give up miniature painting c. 1914. Died 16 January 1960. Her sitters included Jimmie, son of J. M. Pike-Nott, George Byam Shaw, Major General C. F. Gregorie, Mrs. R. J. Spencer Phillips, and members of her family. Of her surviving children, a daughter is the wife of Rear Admiral A. F. Pugsley, Glen Byam Shaw is Director of Production to the Sadlers Wells Company, and James Byam Shaw, the well-known art dealer, to whom I am indebted for this information, has just retired after 25 years with Colnaghi's, and is a Trustee of the Paul Mellon Foundation for British Art. A large oil painting by her is in St. Paul's Church, Knightsbridge, and several of her miniatures, including a self-portrait, are in the possession of the family.

Sheldrake, J. (fl. 1780)

Exhibited at the R.A. 1780, 'Maria from Sterne' which was catalogued as a miniature.

Sheldrake, Timothy, M.D. (fl. 1740–1770)

Born in Norwich; came of an old Norfolk family. Published works on scientific and botanical subjects, 1756 and 1759. Is not known as a miniaturist, but the F. Wellesley Collection, sold at Sotheby's in 1920, contained a miniature on ivory of David Garrick, painted in 1745, and a plumbago miniature of Alexander Pope, the poet, signed; both catalogued as by Sheldrake. A miniature also said to be of Garrick, by Sheldrake, and painted in 1749, is reproduced in *L'Exposition de la Miniature à Bruxelles en 1912*, Pl. XX.

Shelley, Samuel. 1750/56–1808

Was a native of London, born in Whitechapel, 1750/56. Was said to be largely self-taught. Entered the R.A. Schools, 21 March 1774 aged '17 last March', thus making his date of birth 1756, six years later than had hitherto been supposed. Was awarded a premium by the Society of Arts, 1770. Exhibited at the Society of Artists, 1773 and 1775, and at the R.A., 1774–1804, as well as at the B.I. and O.W.C.S., of which he was an original member. In c. 1800–1804 he was a member of a sketching club whose other members included J. Ward, J. Green, J. C. Nattes, R. Hills and W. H. Pyne. Shelley painted miniatures, water-colour figure subjects, oil paintings; drew book illustrations and engraved some of his own works; others were engraved by Bartolozzi, J. R. Smith, etc. He had addresses in Soho, Henrietta Street, Covent Garden

and finally No. 6 George Street, Hanover Square where he remained until his death on 22 November 1808. E. Nash (q.v.) and Alexander Robertson (q.v.) were his pupils. He was an artist of considerable ability whose miniatures are easily distinguishable once his style and technique have been examined. Characteristics of his work are a yellowish green flesh tint (this is sometimes used on the background as well), a slightly enlarged pupil of the eye, and the use of rather more gum than that used by other artists. This gives his miniatures the appearance of oil paintings. His draughtsmanship was good, and his miniatures of ladies and children, charming. He was particularly fond of painting portrait groups, and not infrequently used larger and longer ivories than those used by many artists, and placed the oval on its side in order to accommodate the group more artistically. His signatures vary. Occasionally it is S.S. on the front, but more frequently he signed Sam Shelley on the reverse, followed by his address; often he did not sign at all. He was a prolific artist, not all of his works being of equal merit. He sometimes copied the works of Reynolds. Long lists most of his addresses in *British Miniaturists*, p. 397. His effects were sold on 22 March 1809, including a collection of 'old masters' and a number of his miniatures, ivories, etc. A catalogue of the sale is at the V. & A. M., who have examples of his work. The B.M. has some of his drawings. An oval family group, once in the Pierpont Morgan collection, is illustrated in Foskett's *British Portrait Miniatures*, f.p. 132. The R.A. Diploma Gallery contains a letter and drawings by Shelley. The Fitzwilliam Museum, Cambridge, the City of Liverpool Museum and the Ward Usher Museum, Lincoln, have miniatures by him. A colourful miniature of an officer is in the collection of Col. G. Warland, and several fine miniatures by Shelley are in the collection of Major R. M. O. de la Hey, two of which were loaned to the exhibition in Edinburgh, 1965. A number of miniatures by Shelley were loaned to the exhibition at the South Kensington Museum, 1865, including seven family miniatures from the collection of the Duke of Marlborough. A good miniature of a Cadet officer is in the Holzscheiter collection, Meilen.

*Shelton, Miss Esther M. (fl. 1901–1914)

Of Hornsey, Enfield and London. Exhibited at the R.A., 1901–1914. Executed miniatures and drawings. Her exhibit in 1901 was a self-portrait.

*Shenton, Miss Annie F. (fl. 1904–1906)

Of London. Exhibited at the R.A. 1904 and 1906, from 54 Greyhound Mansions.

Shephard, Robert (fl. 1793–1795). See also **Shepherd, Robert**

Working in 1793–1795 at Lombard Street, Birmingham. Presumably identical with Robert Shepherd (q.v.).

Shepherd, Robert. (fl. 1822). See also **Shephard, Robert**

Was working in Great Brook Street, Birmingham in 1822. Painted fancy miniatures and was probably identical with Robert Shephard (q.v.).

Shepherd or **Sheppard, Miss Sarah (Mrs. S. Cotes).** d. 1814

The above artist was an amateur painter who is thought to have painted miniatures. She was the wife of Samuel Cotes (q.v.). Died in 1814.

Sheppard, G. (fl. 1797–1802)

Of London. Exhibited at the R.A., 1797–1802. All his exhibits were in the miniature section.

Sheppard, Miss Sarah. See Shepherd, Miss Sarah

Sheppard, William. 17th century

The name of this portrait painter and limner occurs in the *Calendar of State Papers, Domestic, 1651–1652*, 1877, p. 50, under the date 5 December 1651, where it states that 'William Sheppard, an English limner, travelling in Italy to perfect his art, from thence went lately to Constantinople, upon the *John Baptist*, a Dutch ship, which being cast away near Samos, he, with two other Englishmen, were taken up by the Captain Bassa, and carried to Rhodes, where they are kept in restraint; his wife here having solicited us (the Levant Company) on his behalf, we desire you (Sir Thomas Bendish, Ambassador at Constantinople) to use what means you have for procuring his release at his own charge, which will be a work of much charity.'. William Sheppard returned to London and lived near the Royal Exchange after the Restoration, and is said to have retired to Yorkshire at a later date. He taught Francis Barlow (q.v.) and painted a portrait (not a miniature) of Thomas Killigrew, the poet, at Venice in 1650. No miniatures by him are at present known. Benezit records his dates as *c.* 1602–*c.* 1660, and states that he died in Italy.

Sherborne. (fl. 1776)

Of London. Exhibited at the Society of Artists in 1776 from Mr. Read's, Vauxhall. Possibly identical with C. Sharborne (1716–*c.* 1787), an engraver.

Sheridan, James. *c.* 1734–1840

Of Dublin. A miniaturist who died in the Corn Market, Dublin in December 1840, aged 106. The announcement of his death in the *Dublin Evening Post*, stated that he had subsisted on charity for several years before his death.

Sheriff or **Sherriff, Charles.** See Shirreff, Charles

Sherlock, William, F.S.A. b. *c.* 1738. d. after 1806

Born in Dublin *c.* 1738 or earlier; son of a fencing master who was said to have been identical with 'Sherlock, the prize fighter'. W. Sherlock studied at the St. Martin's Lane Academy and in 1759 obtained a premium for figure drawing and another for engraving in 1760, both from the Society of Arts. Sherlock studied in Paris under Le Bas the engraver. He exhibited at the Society of Artists, 1764–1780, being appointed a Director in 1773, and at the R.A., 1796–1806. He engraved a series of portraits for Smollett's *History of England*. Painted portraits in oil and water-colour, including small whole-lengths and miniatures. Was also a picture dealer and copyist. His son, William P. Sherlock (q.v.), was a successful artist in water-colour and also painted miniatures. The son is not recorded by Long or Schidlof and it is possible that the works of the two artists may have been confused. W. Sherlock senior exhibited a miniature of Miss A. Sherlock, possibly his daughter, at the R.A., in 1803, and one of 'Miss Sherlock' in 1805, from 43 Broad Street, Golden Square. A self-portrait of the artist is in the collection of K. Guichard, Esq., and is inscribed on the reverse 'Portrait of / Wm. Sherlock Sen. / 180(5) / by Wm. Sherlock Sen. / 43 Broad St / Golden Square', from which address he and W. P. Sherlock both exhibited in 1806. The miniature is exceptionally well painted and is executed in a stronger and firmer style than many of the artist's works. It shows a continental influence and the background is shaded with cross-hatching. Examples of his work are at the V. & A. M. including a portrait of Sir John Andrew Stevenson, the composer, signed 'Shirlock / 1805'.

*Sherlock, William P. b. 1775?

Of London; son of William Sherlock (q.v.) and probably identical with the Wm. Sherlock who entered the R.A. Schools on 31 December 1794, aged 19. Exhibited at the R.A., 1801–1810. Both he and his father exhibited at the R.A., from 43 Broad Street, Golden Square, in 1806. W. P. Sherlock was a successful imitator in water-colour of the works of Richard Wilson. Executed landscapes, architectural illustrations for Dickenson's *Antiquities of Nottinghamshire*, 1801–1806, and published etchings after Girtin, Prout and Cox, besides paintings portraits and miniatures. Exhibited a miniature of a lady at the R.A., in 1803, in which year his father exhibited a miniature of Miss A. Sherlock, probably the artist's sister.

Sherratt, C. (Charles?). b. 1770?

Of 130 The Strand. Exhibited a portrait of a lady in the miniature section at the R.A., 1792. Possibly identical with Charles Sherratt who entered the R.A. Schools, 31 December 1786, aged 16, '1st March last'. May have been related to E. Sherratt (q.v.).

Sherratt, E. (fl. 1787)

Of 10 Castle Street, Strand. Exhibited a self-portrait at the R.A. in 1787, under the miniature section. Was possibly related to C. Sherratt (q.v.).

*Shervill, Alfred H. (fl. 1898–1902)

Of London. Exhibited at the R.A., 1898–1902.

*Sherwin, John Keyse. 1751–1790

Born in London in May 1751. Entered the R.A. Schools, 7 December 1770, aged '19 last May'. Was awarded a silver medal in 1771 and a gold medal in 1772. Exhibited at the R.A. and Society of Artists, 1774–1784. Executed engravings, landscapes, drawings in chalk and crayon, oil paintings and portraits, at least one of which was a miniature in pencil of David Garrick (1717–1779). This latter portrait is in the N.P.G., and is signed on the front 'D. Garrick / J. K. Sherwin Del^t / from ye life'. Died 20 September 1790

Sherwin, M. S.

Long records seeing two rather inferior enamels of religious subjects, both signed on the reverse 'M. S. Sherwin'; one was signed 'Sherwin' on the front.

Shiercliffe, Edward. (fl. *c.* 1765–1786)

Worked in Bristol and Bath *c.* 1765–1786. Painted enamel miniatures. In 1775 he was living at 11 St. Augustine's Back, Bristol, and was probably the son of Edward Shiercliffe, bookseller, of the same address. Said to have been alive in 1786. His work is reminiscent of that of Gervase Spencer (q.v.). An enamel miniature of a lady, signed on the reverse 'Edward Shiercliffe Bristol 1765', is at the V. & A. M. This enamel was exhibited in Edinburgh in 1965 and illustrated in the catalogue.

Shipp, Miss Susan. (fl. 1822–1830)

Of Bath. Miniature painter and drawing teacher. In 1822 her address was 7 Chapel Row, Bath, and in 1830 she was at 10 Norfolk Buildings, Bath.

*Shipwright, Miss Emily A. (fl. 1893–1904)

Of London. Exhibited at the R.A. 1893–1904, from 27 Charlotte Street, Portland Place. Painted miniatures and still life.

Shirreff, Charles. b. *c.* 1750

Born in Scotland, possibly in Edinburgh, *c.* 1750.

His father's name was Alexander, not Charles, as recorded by Long. He entered the R.A. Schools, 9 August 1769, when his age was not recorded, and won a silver medal there in 1772. Shirreff exhibited at the Free Society of Artists, 1770–1773, and at the R.A., S.B.A. and B.I., 1771–1831. His name has been spelt variously; Sherrif, Sheriff and Shirreff. He was deaf and dumb. Sir W. Foster records in *British Artists in India, Walpole Society*, Vol. XIX, pp. 67–69, that when he petitioned the East India Company in August 1778, to be allowed to go to India, he stated that he had lost his speech and hearing when about four years old, but was able to make himself understood by means of signs. He stated that he went to London in 1768 and asked that in view of his infirmity, his father and sister Mary should be allowed to accompany him to India. This request was granted on 16 September 1778, but for some reason the project was abandoned. His father is said to have lost money in 1772 after the failure of Fordyce's Bank, and Shirreff is said to have had to help to support the family. He had been educated in Edinburgh by Thomas Braidwood (1715–1806). Shirreff took a keen interest in the stage and executed many portraits of actors and actresses, including Mrs. Siddons, who said that he was 'more successful in her portraits than any miniature painter she had sat to'. He was working in Bath, 1791–1795, and is said to have worked in Brighton, Deptford and Cambridge. In 1795 he renewed his application to go to India, and was given permission to go to Bengal as a miniature painter, 30 December 1795. He took his passage on the *Lord Hawkesbury*, which reached Madras, 9 January 1797, and the Hugli on the 28 February. There is reason to think that he remained in Madras for some time as miniatures of Robert Sherson, Madras Civil Service, and Miss Catherine Taylor (later Mrs. Robert Sherson), were painted by him at Madras in 1797. These miniatures are in the V. & A. M. *The New Oriental Register* for Madras shows him to have been residing there in 1800. He also worked in Calcutta where he was living in 1804. In 1807 he announced his intention of returning to England and that his 'Finger Alphabet' was nearly completed, and would be sent to subscribers as soon as possible. He left India on 25 January 1809 in the *Sir William Bensley* and landed at Gravesend, 16 July 1809. He appears to have lived for a time in London and exhibited portraits from various London addresses, including a self-portrait, Dr. Kay of St. Helena and the late Nawab of the Carnatic. He is said to have retired to Bath, and to have died there, but so far his date of death has not been traced. Characteristics of his work are the method of criss-cross hatching used both in modelling the features and shading the background. His miniatures tend to be plain and unflattering, but are neatly executed. He signed C. Shirreff pinx^t, followed by a date and often the address, on the reverse. Engravings of his portraits are at the B.M. A miniature signed and dated 'C. Shirreff pinx / Cawnpore / July / 1806' was sold at Sotheby's in January 1963. A miniature of Renira van Tryll Gerooskerken, wife of Capt. John Albert Bentinck, R.N., is in the collection of the Duke of Portland.

Shirving, Archibald. See Skirving, Archibald

*Shores, Mrs. Alice M. (fl. 1905)

Exhibited at the R.A. 1905, from The Nook, Claygate, Esher.

*Shortt, Mrs. G. H. (fl. 1909–1910)

Exhibited at the Society of Miniaturists 1909–1910, from Southwick Rectory, Sunderland.

*Shrubsole, S. 18th century. See also **S., S.**

A miniature of the Holy Family, after an earlier painting, signed on the front 'S.S.' in white cursive initials, and inscribed on the reverse 'Holy Family / copy by / S. Shrubsole', is in the Wordsworth family collection. It is painted on card; the colouring is pleasant and the work appears to be 18th century.

*Shurick, Mr. d. *c.* 1744

The Daily Advertiser, 9 February 1744, announces the 'Sale of the collection of pictures and miniatures of the late ingenious Mr. Shurick. Painter in enamel deceased.'.

Shute, John. (fl. 1550–1570?)

Born in Cullompton, Devon. Practised book-illuminations, painted portraits and probably miniatures. In 1550 was sent by the Duke of Northumberland to Italy, where he studied architecture. Published a book on the subject in 1563. Lack of authentic works has made identification uncertain. A miniature of Edward VI, signed 'S', in gold, from Earl Beauchamp's collection, is thought to be by either J. Shute or G. Str(e)tes (q.v.). A portrait of a lady, said to be the Infanta of Portugal (1521–1578), signed 'I.S.' and ascribed to John Shute, was Lot 230 in the Pierpont Morgan sale, 24 June 1935. The miniature of Edward VI was exhibited in Edinburgh in 1965 and illustrated in the catalogue. The date of his death is uncertain; some authorities give it as 25 September 1563, others suggest that he flourished until *c.* 1570.

Sillett, Sellett or **Selleth, James.** 1764–1840

Born in Norwich, 1764; son of James Sillett of Eye, Suffolk. Began his career in Norwich as a heraldic painter. Went to London and is said to have studied at the R.A. schools, 1787–1790. His name, however, does not appear in the list of entrants of the R.A. schools, published in the *Walpole Society,* Vol. XXXVIII. Became a good miniaturist and painted fruit, flowers and game, both in oil and water-colour. Exhibited at the R.A., etc., 1796–1837. Painted theatrical scenery at Drury Lane and Covent Garden. Went to Kings Lynn *c.* 1804 and while there made the illustrations for Richard's *History of Lynn,* published 1812. Moved to Norwich in 1810 where he resided for the rest of his life. Was President of the Norwich Society of Artists in 1815. Published in 1826, *A Grammar of Flower Painting,* and in 1828, a set of 59 views of public edifices in Norwich. Died at Norwich, 6 May 1840. Married in 1801, Ann Banyard of East Dereham, through whom he inherited some property. His daughter Emma was a well-known flower painter.

Silverthorne, J. (fl. 1849)

Exhibited at the R.A., 1849.

*Silvester, Miss Jessie M. (fl. 1903–1905)

Of London. Exhibited at the R.A. 1903–1905, from addresses in Upper Clapton. Executed miniatures and subjects in water-colour.

Simcock, T. (fl. 1779–1791)

Of London. Exhibited enamels at the R.A., 1779–1782, and a miniature on opal at the Society of Artists in 1791, when his address was 1 Alphabet Court, Stanhope Street, Clare Market.

*Simmons or **Simmonds, Mrs.** or **Miss.** (fl. 1779)

Of Bristol. Taught painting and drawing and according to a note by Long 'took likenesses in miniature at 1 guinea each', on 3 July 1779.

*Simmons, W. St. Clair. (fl. 1878–1898)

Of London. Exhibited at the N.W.C.S., etc., 1878–1898. Lived for many years at 57 Bedford Gardens, Kensington. Executed oil paintings, subjects and landscapes in water-colour, and miniatures. His sitters included Henry, son of the Rev. Richard Fitzherbert; and Lady Maud Rolleston.

*Simon, Miss Eva. (fl. 1892–1908)

Of London. Exhibited at the S.M., etc., 1892–1908.

Simon, J. P. (fl. 1785). See also **Simon, P.**

Of London. Exhibited at the R.A. 1785, from 6 Meard Street, Dean Street, Soho; possibly John Peter Simon, an engraver, who entered the R.A. Schools, 31 December 1778, aged '14 Aug. 1st last', and perhaps identical with P. Simon (q.v.).

Simon, P. (fl. 1786). See also **Simon, J. P.**

Of London. Exhibited at the R.A. 1786, from 107 Wardour Street, Soho. Was perhaps identical with J. P. Simon (q.v.).

Simpson, Miss Agnes. (fl. 1827–1848)

Of London. Exhibited at the R.A., etc., 1827–1848. Undoubtedly related to J. Simpson (1782–1847), portrait painter, P. Simpson, C. Simpson, G. Simpson senior (q.v.) and G. Simpson junior (q.v.), all of whom exhibited for many years from 10 Carlisle Street. All the exhibits at the R.A. up to 1845 are catalogued as by Miss Simpson (no christian name given); those for 1847 and 1848 are given to Agnes Simpson, without the style of Miss. In 1847 her address was 7 Gloucester Road, Bayswater, and in 1848, 28 Somerset Street, Portman Square. It is conceivable that there were two artists. In 1844 Miss Simpson exhibited a miniature of Geo. Simpson, Esq., F.R.C.S., and one of J. Marchant, Esq.

*Simpson, Miss Annie L. (fl. 1896)

Exhibited at the R.A. 1896, from 52 Prescott Street, Halifax.

*Simpson, Miss Caroline Bridgeman. (fl. 1831)

I have seen a good miniature by the above artist, signed on the reverse 'Portrait of / Mrs. Bridgeman / Simpson / 1831'. The portrait was painted with fresh colours, slightly in the manner of Ross (q.v.), and was certainly reminiscent of the Scottish school of painters. This miniature was Lot 42 at Christie's, 5 November 1968, when it realised £170.

Simpson, G., senior. (fl. 1799–1826)

Of London. Exhibited at the R.A., 1799–1826. An engraved portrait of R. Patch, after G. Simpson, published, 1806, is in the B.M. In 1799 G. Simpson exhibited 'a Portrait of a lady' (not in the index); in 1807 he exhibited as an Hon. Exhibitor, 'A View near Finchley'; in 1812 and 1813 he exhibited miniatures from 10 Carlisle Street, Soho, and in 1826, landscapes from 18 Buckingham Place, New Road. Possibly the father of G. Simpson junior (q.v.), and undoubtedly related to several other artists of this name who all exhibited from the family address, 10 Carlisle Street, Soho in various years. A miniature of Miss Mary Hume, niece of David Hume, by George Simpson, signed and dated '1799', formerly in the Wellesley collection, was said to have been the miniature exhibited at the R.A. in 1799. It was exhibited in Glasgow in 1911, and in Brussels in 1912. It is reproduced on Pl. XIX of the Brussels catalogue.

Simpson, G., junior. (fl. 1807–1821)

Exhibited at the R.A., 1807 and 1821. In 1807 the entry was a miniature portrait of Mr. Mason.

He was an Hon. Exhibitor. In the same year G. Simpson senior (q.v.), also an Hon. Exhibitor, entered 'A View near Finchley'. G. Simpson junior was probably the son of G. Simpson senior whose address, 10 Carlisle Street, he shared.

Simpson, J. or T. (fl. 1786)

A miniature signed on the reverse 'J. (or T) Simpson / Jan^ry 8. 1786' is at the V. & A. M. It is not of any great merit.

Simpson, John. b. 1811. d. after 1871

According to G. Godden, *British Pottery & Porcelain,* p. 33, Simpson was born in 1811. Little is known about him, but he was presumably related to W. P. Simpson (q.v.), who shared his addresses in various years. Simpson worked at the Minton Porcelain Works from 1837–1847, and was noted for painting figure subjects. In 1847 he moved to London where he became a successful enamel painter and miniaturist. Exhibited at the R.A., 1847–1871, not from 1831 as stated by Long and other sources. Painted enamel portraits, some of which were on porcelain, from life, from photographs and after the works of other artists such as Lawrence (q.v.), Moira (q.v.), Ross (q.v.) and Winterhalter, etc. He exhibited from 8 Garway Road, 1847–1851; 7 Denbigh Terrace, Westbourne Grove, 1852–1857; 3 Royal Hill, Queen's Road, Bayswater, 1858–1865 and 6 Queen's Road, Bayswater, 1869–1871. His exhibits included portraits of Her Grace the Duchess of Sutherland, Mr. and Mrs. Webster (after Thomas Webster, R.A.), Miss M. E. Clapham and the Rev. H. Grattan Guiness, 'enamelled on porcelain from a photograph'. He signed his work either John Simpson, or Simpson, on the reverse of his portraits followed by a date. A miniature of Queen Victoria, after Winterhalter, painted on porcelain, signed on the reverse and dated '1845', was Lot 240 at Christie's, 28 June 1966, when it realised £125. It was an attractive work, well painted and colourful. A good miniature of an unknown man on porcelain, signed on the reverse 'John Simpson 1843 / after Jean', was sold at Sotheby's in 1962. The V. & A. M. has a number of family miniatures by him including a self-portrait, one of his wife, and a third of Ellen Simpson, painted in 1863.

*Simpson, Mrs. Maria C. E. (or Marie). See **Burt, Miss M. C. E.**

Simpson, Miss Mary. (fl 1849–1858)

Of London. Exhibited at the R.A., 1849–1858. Her addresses were 6 Bedford Street, Bedford Square and 9 Gower Street, Bedford Square. Her sitters included Henry Duesbury, Esq.

*Simpson, Matthew. (fl. 1625–1649)

Worked in England, and taught the children of Charles I between the years of 1625 and 1649. Is supposed to have painted portraits and miniatures. He later went to Sweden. Benezit records that he signed his works M. S.

Simpson, T. Penkhule. (fl. 1847)

The above artist exhibited a large enamel painting of flowers at the B.I. in 1847. The address given was 'Near Newcastle-under-Lyme'.

*Simpson, Thomas. b. *c.* 1782.

Born *c.* 1782 Thomas Simpson, miniaturist, is recorded as entering the R.A. Schools, 3 December 1801, aged 19. Nothing more is known about him and he has not been previously recorded.

*Simpson, W. Graham. (fl. 1878–1889)

Of London. Exhibited at the R.A., etc., 1878–1889. His sitters included the Hon. Lady Smythe.

Simpson, William Page. (fl. 1859–1877)

Of London, and Stoke-on-Trent (1877). Painted enamels on copper and porcelain. Exhibited at the R.A., etc., 1859–1877. Was probably related to John Simpson (q.v.), from whose address, 3 Royal Hill, Queen's Road, Bayswater, he exhibited.

Sims, William. (fl. 1821–1867)

Of London. Exhibited at the R.A. and B.I., etc., 1821–1867. Painted portraits, landscapes and miniatures.

*Simson, Mrs. S. (fl. 1900). See also **Spicer-Simson, Mrs. Margaret**

Exhibited at the R.A., 1900, from 37 Rue Boileau, Auteuil, Paris. Her sitters included F. I. Simson, Esq., and the Hon. Mrs. Duff Tollemache. The above artist may have been identical with Mrs. Margaret Spicer-Simson (q.v.).

*Singleton, Mr. d. 1815

The death is recorded in the *Bury and Norwich Post* of 'Mr. Singleton, of Bury St. Edmunds, formerly a miniature painter in London, died on June 2, 1815'.

*Singleton, Henry. 1766–1839

Of London; born 19 October 1766; brother of Miss S. M. Singleton (q.v.) and of Miss Maria Singleton (q.v.), and husband of Mrs. H. Singleton (q.v.) who appears to have left him before 1815. William and Joseph Singleton (q.v.) were his uncles. Exhibited at the R.A. and B.I., etc., 1784–1839. Best known as a portrait and historical painter in oil, but his exhibits included a few miniatures. The family shared the same addresses for many years. Died in London, 15 September 1839.

Singleton, Mrs. Henry. (fl. 1807–1822?)

Wife of Henry Singleton (q.v.) (1766–1839), whom she appears to have left before 1815. (The *D.N.B.* says that he died unmarried.) She exhibited at the R.A. and B.I., 1807–1822? The exhibit in 1822 may have been executed by Miss M. Singleton (q.v.), as it was a large oil portrait, and the address given was 3 Mortimer Street, the one from which Miss M. Singleton exhibited, 1815–1820; not 4 Haymarket, which was Mrs. Singleton's last address in 1811, and from which her husband and other members of the family exhibited. An enamel portrait of Mrs. Singleton by Henry Bone, R.A. (q.v.), is in the Nottingham Art Museum.

Singleton, Joseph. b. c. 1751

Born c. 1751; brother of William Singleton (q.v.) and uncle of Henry Singleton (q.v.). J. Singleton worked in London. Entered the R.A. Schools, 7 December 1770, aged 19. Exhibited at the R.A., 1773–1788? Painted miniatures and, according to Schidlof, executed copies and genre pictures in oil, but I can find no evidence for this statement. The R.A. catalogues only list miniatures. In 1784 the entries in the index appear to have been confused; no. 308 (a miniature) is given to both W. and H. Singleton in the index, but given to J. in the catalogue. In 1788 no. 400 (a portrait of a lady) is given to H. Singleton in the index, but listed in the catalogue as by J. Singleton. This latter artist had addresses in King Street, Covent Garden and Bedford Street.

*Singleton, Miss Maria M. (fl. 1808–1822?). See also **Singleton, Miss S. M.**

Sister of Henry Singleton (q.v.), painter, and of Sarah Macklarinan Singleton (q.v.). Exhibited at the R.A., 1808–1822? Painted portraits. In 1788 the index of the R.A. catalogues gives no. 63 to Miss S. M. Singleton, but the catalogue lists it as by Maria M. Singleton. In 1819 she was living at 3 Mortimer Street, Cavendish Square and her exhibit no. 927, 'a portrait of a lady', was probably a miniature. In 1822 a Mrs. Singleton is given as exhibiting from the above address, a portrait of Mr. Ab Salame, His Majesty's Oriental Interpreter. This was probably a mistake for Miss M. Singleton.

Singleton, Miss Sarah Macklarinan. (fl. 1787–1806)

Of London; sister of the painter Henry Singleton (q.v.) and of Maria Singleton (q.v.). Exhibited at the R.A., 1787–1806. In 1787 her address was Banger Court, Shoe Lane; in 1788 it was 3 Great Tower Street, and from 1789–1794 she shared the same address as H. Singleton, 22 Norton Street, nr. Portland Chapel. Exhibit no. 63 in 1788 is given to her in the index, but listed as by Maria M. Singleton in the catalogue. From 1795 she was at 4 Haymarket.

Singleton, William. d. 1793. See also **S**.

Brother of Joseph Singleton (q.v.) and uncle of Henry Singleton (q.v.) and of Miss S. M. Singleton (q.v.). Lived for a time at the same address as both the above. Was a pupil of O. Humphry (q.v.). Worked in London. Exhibited at the Society of Artists, 1770–1790, and at the R.A., 1779–1790. Painted portraits, sketches and fancy heads, as well as miniatures and enamels. Died in 1793. A miniature portrait of Thomas Gibson, on ivory, signed 'S / 75' (1775), is at the V. & A. M., and shows the influence of Humphry. Schidlof records an enamel miniature of a lady in a red dress, signed 'S / 74' (1774), as being by the same artist. Lot 14 at Sotheby's, 6 March 1961, was an enamel miniature of a lady, signed and dated '1774'.

Siree, Mrs. John (Miss Clementina Robertson). 1795–c. 1853/8

Née Clementina Robertson. Born in Dublin, 1795; daughter and pupil of Charles Robertson (q.v.). Exhibited in Dublin under her maiden name, 1812–1830 and up to 1832 as Mrs. Siree. She married John Siree, a medical student, in 1830. He never qualified and died of fever in Fleet Street in 1835, aged 35. Mrs. Siree practised her profession for many years after his death and also taught music, languages and drawing. In 1853 she was living at No. 3 Westland Row, Dublin, and is thought, by Strickland, to have died in, or soon after, that year; other authorities give 1858. She must not be confused with her sister Christina nor with Mrs. Christina Robertson (q.v.) who was also an artist. The N.G., Dublin, has a miniature by her of her husband and two miniatures by her on paper. She worked slightly in the manner of Charles Robertson. Her signature is usually to be found on the reverse.

Sisson, Richard. d. 1767

Came of a well-known Dublin family who were engaged in the linen trade, and had a factory at Lucan. Educated at Shackleton's school in Ballitore, Co. Kilkenny where he made a lasting friendship with Edmund Burke. Was apprenticed to F. Bindon, a portrait painter. Studied in France and Italy and lived for some months with Burke in Paris. Returned to Dublin and practised as a portrait painter in oil, pastel and miniature; also worked in London. Exhibited in Dublin, 1765–1767. Married in 1763 a Miss Smith of Ann Street, Dublin. He painted a miniature of Burke and executed a mezzotint of W. Pitt the elder. Died in his house in William Street, Dublin, in April 1767, leaving his widow in straitened circumstances. She opened a school and Edmund Burke afterwards provided for her son.

*Sissons, Miss Hilda H. (fl. 1902–1903)

Of North Ferriby, Yorkshire. Exhibited at the Society of Miniaturists, 1903; was a member of the Society in 1902.

*Sivanfelder, John James. (fl. 1773)

Long noted that this artist 'Limner from Berlin, at Lower Head Row, Leeds', was painting miniatures in Leeds, 23 March 1773.

Skaife, T. or J. (fl. 1840–1852)

Of London, Liverpool (1847) and Blackheath (1851–1852). Exhibited at the R.A., 1846–1852. Painted a portrait of Lady Bulwer Lytton in Geneva which was exhibited at the R.A. in 1848. A miniature, catalogued as by J. Skaife, signed and dated '1840', was Lot 67 at Sotheby's, 17 July 1962. It may have been by the above artist.

Skelton, Miss Catherine. (fl. 1823)

Exhibited at the R.A., 1823, a portrait of Miss Skelton, possibly a self-portrait.

Skinner, John. b. 1753

Was born in 1753; entered the R.A. Schools, 20 January 1772, aged '18 last Aug.' Was awarded premiums at the Society of Arts in 1772 and 1773. Was in London (1776) and Rochester (1787). Exhibited at the R.A., 1776 and 1787. A miniature of a man, painted on ivory, and signed on the front vertically 'I. Skinner / Nov. 1774', is in the V. & A. M. It has a greenish hue.

Skirving, Archibald. 1749–1819

Born in Athelstaneford, nr. Haddington, Scotland in 1749; son of a song-writer and farmer, Adam Skirving. Exhibited at the R.A., from a London address, in 1778. Started life as an excise officer. Turned to miniature painting; went to Rome, 1786–1794; was captured by the French on his return journey and imprisoned for a year. Was back in Edinburgh in 1796. His imprisonment caused him to suffer from a serious eye condition (unocular elipopia), which necessitated his giving up miniature painting. He took up large-scale portrait painting in pastel and oil, and taught painting privately. The statement that he met Burns is not true, although he painted his portrait. In a letter in the collection of one of his descendants, he mentions that he never met Burns. He died at Inveresk in 1819 and was buried at Athelstaneford. Examples of his work are in the N.G., Edinburgh and the S.N.P.G. A miniature of a man said to be by him and signed, in monogram, 'AS' and dated '1798', is in the collection of E. G. Paine of New York.

Skurry, Miss E. (fl. 1800)

Of Walworth. Exhibited at the R.A. 1800, from 5 Baker's Row, Walworth.

*Slade, Sydney. (fl. 1908–1914)

Exhibited at the R.A. 1908–1914, from Westcliff, Seaton, Devon.

Slater, Miss Henrietta Vane. 1815–1866

Was born in 1815; daughter of John Slater (1786–1835) (q.v.). Worked as a miniaturist. Was a niece of Joseph Slater junior (q.v.). Died in 1866.

Slater, Isaac Wane. 1784/5–1836. See also **Slater, J.W.**

Born in Kensal Green, 1784/5; second son of Joseph Slater senior (1750–1805) (q.v.), and his wife Anne Wane, and brother of Joseph Slater junior (q.v.) and John Slater (q.v.). Exhibited at the R.A., 1821–1836 from 70 Newman Street (1821), 70

Berners Street (1833) and 17 Newman Street (1834 and 1836). Married Anne Holdsworth. It has been suggested that I.W. Slater was identical with J. W Slater (q.v.) from whose address he exhibited in 1821, but this cannot be certain as the R.A. catalogues and indexes give his initials consistently as J. W. for 1806–1836, with the exception of the four years 1821, 1833, 1834 and 1836. I.W. Slater died in London on 17 April 1836 and was buried at Kensal Green. Long records seeing a miniature of a man signed in black along the edge in cursive script 'I. W Slater'; the work showed the influence of Cosway (q.v.). A miniature of an unknown lady, signed on the front 'I. W Slater', was sold at Sotheby's, 22 April 1968. It was well painted. A miniature of the Hon. Mrs. Augustus Phipps, signed 'I. (or J) W. Slater', is in the V. & A. M., which also has one of Mrs. Luke Freeman, née Tilleard, signed and dated '1805'.

Slater, J. W. (fl. 1806–1831). See also **Slater, I. W.**

It has been suggested that the above artist is identical with I. W. Slater (q.v.) due to the similarity of the initials, but the R.A. catalogues for the years 1806–1831, with the exception of 1821, 1833, 1834 and 1836, are consistent in the use of the initials J. W., and it seems possible that there were, in fact, two artists. In 1821, I. W. Slater (q.v.) exhibited from 70 Newman Street, the same address as J. W. Slater exhibited from in 1820–1828, although these artists never exhibited together. J. W. Slater painted miniatures, chiefly members of the theatrical profession and the Marquis of Graham, son of the Duke of Montrose. He exhibited from a number of London addresses, and if he was a separate artist, was undoubtedly related to the other artists of this name. A miniature of a man signed and dated on the reverse, 'J. W. Slater, 1818', was sold at Sotheby's in July 1966. It was well painted with rather a reddish complexion.

Slater, John. 1786–1835

Born in 1786; third son of Joseph Slater (1750–1805) (q.v.), and brother of I. W. Slater (q.v.) and of Joseph Slater junior (q.v.). Exhibited at the R.A., under the name of J. Slater junior, 1808 and 1811; in 1810 two J. Slaters exhibited from 17 Charlotte Street, one of whom was presumably the above. He is probably identical with the J. Slater who exhibited from 8 Upper Cumming Street, Pentonville in 1818, and later worked at Hall Place, St. John's Wood. Married a cousin, Elizabeth Slater, in 1808, by whom he had two sons and six daughters, among whom were Adela, Carissima, Matilda and Henrietta (q.v.), who were painted by either I. W. Slater or J. W. Slater (q.v.) in c. 1827. He painted miniatures, portraits, flowers and studies of heads. Died 1835.

*Slater, Joseph. 1750–1805

Born in 1750; son of John Slater of Bromley, Middlesex (1666–1721). Entered the R.A. Schools, 18 December 1771 aged '21 next July'. May have been the J. W. Slater recorded by Strickland as being in Dublin in 1770. Exhibited at the Free Society of Artists in 1772 from Mr. Moore's, Poland Street, and at the R.A., 1773, 1774 and 1786 from 2 Park Court, Knightsbridge; and in 1787 from Upper Mall, Hammersmith. Married on 4 June 1776, at St. James's Westminster, Anne, daughter of Isaac Wane or Vane, by whom he had four sons and three daughters, of whom Joseph junior, Isaac Wane and John (q.v.) became miniaturists. He moved latterly to the Cottage, Hounslow, where he died in 1805. Executed crayon portraits, sketches and miniatures. The fact that several of the family had the same initials has led to some confusion over these artists, and it is not at present possible to identify their work.

Slater, Joseph, junior. c. 1779–1837

Son of Joseph Slater (1750–1805) (q.v.) and his wife, Anne. Exhibited at the R.A., 1805–1833 (except for the years 1822–1828 and 1830), from 47 Greek Street (1805), 17 Charlotte Street (1806–1810), 17 Newman Street (1811–1814) and 70 Newman Street (1815–1833). Married Catherine, daughter of the Rev. James Bean, Librarian of the B.M., by whom he had a son (1809–1854). Painted large oil portraits and sketches some of which may have been miniatures. His sitters included politicians and members of the theatrical profession. He executed two portraits of William Wilberforce and one of the Rt. Hon. the Speaker of the House of Commons, as well as one of his children in 1817, and exhibited a self-portrait (a sketch) in 1808. Said to have often painted on stone. Died 25 February 1837 and was buried in Hove.

Slater, Josiah. b. c. 1780

This artist is recorded by Long who states that he worked in London and was in Bath in 1814, in which year he painted a portrait of his wife. This and two drawings, said to be by him, are in the B.M.; one of two children executed in 1807, signed 'J. S.' and the other 'J. Slater'. Long records seeing a miniature by him signed on the reverse. May have been confused with one or other of the J. Slaters who were artists, one of whom was limner to Grillon's club.

*Slaughter, Stephen. (fl. 1732)

Earl Beauchamp has an oil miniature of Patrick Ross in a long white wig, wearing a blue coat with gold buttons, a yellow waistcoat and a lace neckerchief, painted in oil on copper against a dark background and inscribed on the reverse, 'Patrick Ross by Stephen Slaughter at Paris 1732'. Long records the above details under R. Slaughter, probably in error. The above miniature may have been by the Stephen Slaughter, died 1765, who worked in Ireland and London, and is best known as a portrait painter. Details of his work are recorded by Strickland, pp. 359–361.

*Sledge, S. 18th century

I have seen a miniature profile on paper, pencil and wash, of a man in 17th-century fancy dress against a dark shaded background. A label on the reverse stated that it was by the above artist: 'Miniature Profiles / accurately taken / By S. Sledge / Henrietta St. / Covent Garden'. It was quite well executed.

*Slee, Miss Mary. (fl. 1909)

Exhibited at the R.A. 1909, from 54 Lowther Street, Carlisle.

*Slinger, Miss Edith C. (fl. 1903)

Exhibited at the R.A. 1903, from 22 Church Road, Urmston, nr. Manchester.

*Slocock, Miss Mabel I. (fl. 1898–1902)

Of London. Exhibited at the R.A. and S.M., 1898–1902.

*Sloper, Harold C. W. (fl. 1900)

Of London. Exhibited a portrait of Oliver Cromwell, after Sir Peter Lely, at the R.A., 1900. His address was 14 Rectory Grove, Clapham.

Slous or **Selous, Gideon** or **George.** (fl. 1791–1839)

Of Deptford (1791) and London. Came of a Huguenot family which settled in Jersey. Exhibited at the R.A., B.I., etc., 1791–1839. The family name was changed to Selous c. 1837. Both the R.A. and B.I. give his name as George. His son Henry Courtney Selous (b. 1796) was a portrait painter. G. Slous painted figure subjects and landscapes as well as miniatures. Visited Italy and Switzerland.

A miniature of a man painted on ivory, signed 'G. Slous Pinx / 1804', is in the V. & A. M. It is well painted and shows character. Schidlof does not record the signature accurately. Schidlof mentions a portrait of a young lady on ivory, signed on the left 'G. Slous / 1802', and on the reverse 'G. Slous / 54 Great Marlborough Street', which he said was of a very good quality and painted with pleasant colours. In 1799 Slous exhibited a self-portrait and a miniature of Mrs. Slous at the R.A.

*Smail, Mrs. J. Isdale. (fl. 1901)

Of Hayes, Kent. Exhibited at the Society of Miniaturists, 1901.

*Small, Alexander G. (fl. 1900–1914)

Of London. Exhibited at the R.A., 1900–1914. Executed miniatures, portraits and subjects in oil. His sitters included Mrs. Alexander Small, presumably his wife.

*Small, Florence (Mrs. Deric Hardy). (fl. 1900–1911)

Of London. Exhibited at the R.A., 1900–1911. Executed miniatures and subjects in oil.

*Smallfield, Miss Beatrice C. (fl. 1895–1913)

Of London. Exhibited at the R.A., 1895–1913.

*Smart. (fl. c. 1820)

Working in London c. 1820. Painted rather mediocre portraits in water-colour, signed with a pen 'Smart 5, Marchmont St., Brunswick Sq.'.

*Smart, Miss Dorothy A., R.S.M. b. 1879

Born in Tresco, Scilly Isles, 19 August 1879. Exhibited at the R.A. 1909, from 4 Bridgeland Street, Bideford, Devon. Her sitter was Lady Wilson. Miss Smart was a member of the R.S.M.

Smart, J. (fl. 1786–1813)

Of Ipswich. Not to be confused with John Smart (q.v.). Was in Ipswich (1786–1787 and 1791), Norwich (1788, etc.) and London. Exhibited portraits, landscapes and miniatures at the R.A., 1786–1813, including a self-portrait in miniature in 1798. He had a drawing school in Ipswich in 1791. Long records seeing miniatures bearing a curious monogram which was either SP or JS, which may have been by him. A miniature of an unknown man, signed with a monogram such as the one described by Long, which appears to me to be 'JS' in cursive letters and dated '1813', is in the collection of R. Bayne Powell, Esq. The details of the face are expressive and the waistcoat meticulously painted; but the artist appears to have concealed his inability to draw hands by tucking the man's hand under his waistcoat.

*Smart, James. 1701–1739

Born 7 March 1701; eldest son of John Smart of Ripon, Yorks. Information about this little-known miniaturist is to be found in the *Yorkshire Illustrated*, April 1949, p. 26. Miss Mary Fitzwilliam saw miniatures by this artist which attracted her attention and caused her to search for information. She found an article written in an old newspaper of 1839 which gave details about his life and parentage. So far as is known he only painted portraits of children, and according to the article, was 'Europe's first children's miniaturist'. He seems to have worked almost entirely in Yorkshire, and to have commenced painting when he was eighteen years of age. His first two miniatures were of his two brothers, William aged seven, and Henry aged nine. These were at one time in the possession of a Mr.

Joseph Bentley of Bradford. Some of his miniatures had his label on the reverse, and two seen by Miss Fitzwilliam were known to have been painted in 1731. His only known portraits, of a boy and girl, in the possession of Mr. K. W. Sanderson of Leeds, are painted in oil on copper. An entry in an old diary seen by Miss Fitzwilliam describes the artist as of 'genteel appearance', and added that the pictures gave 'eminent satisfaction'. Miss Fitzwilliam intended publishing a book on this artist, but died before it was completed, and I have been unable to trace the manuscript.

Smart, John. 1742/3–1811

This artist is alleged to have been born near Norwich, Norfolk. Early authors give his year of birth as 1740 or May 1741, and although there is still no knowledge of his place of birth or parentage, it seems likely that he was born c. 1742/3. *The Gentleman's Magazine*, June 1811 records that Smart, at his death on 1 May, was in his 70th year; and Cansick's *Monumental Inscriptions* records that he was aged 69 at death. Nothing is known about his education or early life. In 1755 the Society of Arts held its first competition and it provided the first evidence of Smart's existence. He and Richard Cosway (q.v.) entered the section offering premiums for children under 14 years of age. According to Robert Dossie, in *Memoirs of Agriculture*, Smart was then under the age of 12. He was awarded 2nd prize and Cosway 1st prize. Smart's awards at the Society of Arts were as follows:

1755 2nd Prize for a 'Nude male figure of a River God'.
1756 1st Prize 'A figure startled by a rising serpent'.
1757 1st Prize 'Portrait in chalk of William Shipley'.
1758 1st Prize 'A dancing Faun' (class for under 18 years of age).

These drawings with the exception of that of William Shipley (the whereabouts of which is unknown), are in the Library of the Royal Society of Arts. On 23 September 1755 Smart became apprenticed to William Shipley at his school in St. Martin's Lane. Exhibited at the Society of Artists, 1762–1783, and at the R.A., 1797–1811. Elected F.S.A., 1765, Director, 1772, Vice-President, 1777 and President, 1778. Smart took a leading part in the affairs of the Society of Artists (which later became incorporated). In 1777 a medal bearing Smart's portrait was struck; I know of at least two made in silver, one in silver alloy and others in bronze. In the R.A. lists for 1784 there are two entries which for many years were attributed to Smart, but, as these were not miniatures, and the address was 39 Davies Street, not 68 Berners Street (which was Smart's address from 1765), it is now generally accepted that they were probably by another artist of this name (of whom there were several). Smart's earliest known miniature (formerly in the Wellesley Collection) was dated '1760', and judging by the modelling and draughtsmanship, he may well have painted some earlier. By his first wife, whom he married c. 1760, and whose maiden name is unknown, he had three children; John (born 1762?, died young), Anna Maria (1766–1813) and Sophia (1770–1793). Their mother eloped with the artist William Pars, A.R.A. (q.v.) who took her to Rome where she died of consumption, 6 June 1778. John Smart junior (1776–1809) (q.v.), who followed his father's profession, was not, as has always been supposed, the son of his first marriage, but the natural son borne to him by Sarah Midgeley, by whom he also had a daughter Sarah (1781–1833). Evidence for this has been found in the Guardianship Proceedings of the Court of Chancery for 1790 where there are references to arrangements relating to the care, maintenance and education of these children, as well as adequate provision for their

mother. Nothing is known about Sarah Midgeley after this date. Smart obtained permission from the Court of Directors of the East India Company, on 28 July 1784, to go to India and practise his profession, and to take with him his daughter Anna Maria. He and his daughter left for India 19 April 1785 on board the *Dutton* and arrived at Madras on 6 September 1785, where he took up residence in North Street, Fort St. George. In 1786 Anna Maria married Robert Woolf of the Madras Civil Service by whom she had nine children. Sophia Smart was then granted permission to go to India and join her father; she married Lieut. John Dighton (afterwards Lieut. Gen.) in 1790 and did not survive the birth of a son, John in 1793. For ten very successful years Smart was patronised by personnel of the East India Company, government officials and Indian Princes, including Muhammad Ali, the Nawab of Arcot, and his family. The Nawab failed to pay Smart all the money due to him and 4,114 pagodas were still owing to him when he left the country. By May 1804 this debt had still not been settled and interest at 6% was claimed from September 1795. Ozias Humphry (q.v.) was very perturbed to hear of Smart's intention to go to India, as he feared the competition might seriously affect him. In point of fact these fears were groundless as, apart from short visits to Bombay and Bengal, Smart spent almost the whole of his time in Madras. He left Madras on 27 April 1795 on the *Melville Castle*, and arrived at St. Helena on 15 August. There he joined his daughter, Anna Maria Woolf, and her family who accompanied him for the rest of the voyage, leaving St. Helena on 5 September and arriving at Portsmouth on 19 November. Smart took up residence at 20 Grafton Street, London for which he had paid the rates since 1790 and where, in all probability, John Smart junior and Sarah had been living. In c. 1799 he married, as his second wife, Edith (Vere?). No record of this marriage has been found and the only authority to give the name is Dr. G. C. Williamson. The christian name of Edith was provided by an inscription on the back of a silhouette of c. 1800, said to be of Smart and engraved on the reverse:　　　　Edith

　　　　　　from her husband
　　　　　　John Smarte
　　　　　　Russell Place
　　　　　　Fitzroy Square

(No. 2 Russell Place, Fitzroy Square, being the house to which Smart had moved at about this time). The profile does not bear a close resemblance to the artist and may have been of another member of the family. Smart married at St. Mary-le-bone Church on 14 February 1805 Mary Morton (1783–1851) as his third wife by whom he had a son, John James (1805–1870). Smart was then described as a widower. Mary Morton was described by Farington as a 'well disposed woman & Has brought Him to habits of regularity in attending Divine Service'. Prior to this marriage, both John junior and Sarah, had been living with their father. In a letter to the East India Company, 28 May 1808, Smart asked for permission for John junior to go to India as a miniaturist giving his address as Russell Place, and stating that he had taught him the art of miniature painting. On 27 May of the same year, Smart had an indenture drawn up on behalf of his daughter Sarah, on whom he settled a considerable sum of money, and who moved to Charlotte Street not far away. John Smart junior arrived in Madras on 11 February 1809 and died on 1st or 2nd of June the same year. On 28 April 1811 John Smart senior made his will in which he made ample provision for his wife and the care and education of John James. He died on 1 May 1811, after an illness of only nine days, and was buried in St. James's Burial Ground, Hampstead Road, St. Pancras. The inscription

placed upon his monument read: 'In Memory of / John Smart Esqre / of Russell Place Fitzroy Sq / Who departed this life / May 1st 1811 aged / 69 years / Deeply lamented by his family and numerous friends'. This was followed by an epitaph almost identical to that written by William Hayley for Jeremiah Meyer (q.v.). The obituary in *The Gentleman's Magazine*, Vol. LXXXI, Part 1, p. 599 is as follows: 'In his 70th year, after an illness of only nine days, John Smart Esq., of Russell Place, Fitzroy Square, miniature painter. To most philanthropic and hospitable principles, he added great eminence as an artist . . . .'. Smart was undoubtedly one of the greatest miniaturists of the eighteenth century. His apparently effortless portrayal of his sitters without any resort to elaborate backgrounds or draperies, and the delightful simplicity of the portraits, single him out at once as a great artist. His accuracy of draughtsmanship is apparent right from his earliest drawings as a boy of eleven, and his prize drawing of a nude male figure posing as a river god shows a very accurate knowledge of anatomy for a boy of his years. The fact that from the outset he made a practice of signing and dating his miniatures has been invaluable to students of miniature painting. His normal signature was J.S. in cursive initials on the front of the miniature. The punctuation varies, but the date is almost invariably placed on the line under the initials; occasionally he signed J. Smart in full, J. Smart delin, and John Smart pinxit. Those miniatures painted in India had an 'I' under the date, as in the case of Major Richard Gomonde in the collection of K. Guichard, Esq., signed and dated 'JS / 1790 / I'. He made a habit of executing small pencil drawings on paper, often lightly coloured, which were probably in most cases preliminary drawings for his miniatures, a practice used by other artists including George Engleheart (q.v.). Some of these sketches are signed on the reverse, with an occasional note added about the sitter, or signed round the extreme edge of the portrait. His miniatures are painted both on paper and on ivory, and up to c. 1775 were small in size, about 1½ in. After c. 1775 Smart used an ivory of 2 in. and from c. 1790 increased this to 3 in. Unlike most artists, there was not any great change of style or technique in any of his three phases. He used a brilliant palette and his colours have retained their brightness in a remarkable way; one rarely, if ever, sees them faded. One unmistakeable characteristic of Smart's work is the way he painted the lines and even crow's feet round the eyes, and drew the eyelashes in minute detail, each lash separate; this is particularly apparent where the portrait is in profile. From c. 1760–1766 the face is shaded with a slight bluish tinge and the draughtsmanship is not as perfect as in those painted later when he had abandoned the use of a blue shading and used a brick-red which is typical of his work. His portraits of children are delightful; an outstanding example is that of his grandson, Master Robert Woolf, now in the Huntingdon Art Gallery, San Marino, California. This miniature is painted in watercolour on paper and is fully inscribed on the reverse, and signed and dated, 'J. Smart / London, July 16th, 1796'. His portrayal of women is both attractive and decorative; their expressions are serene and the details meticulously drawn. With older people he was perhaps not quite so successful, but his miniatures of men, many of whom were in uniform, are brilliantly painted and full of character. His backgrounds are usually restrained and drab, often brown or greenish-brown, greenish-grey and creamy white. His pencil and water-colour sketches sometimes have a light landscape or seascape background. Smart's rarely seen enamel miniatures are almost identical in appearance with those executed in water-colour. He also executed some fine paintings of fish. Examples of his work may be seen in the V. & A. M., the B.M., the Wallace Collection, London, the Ashmolean Museum, Oxford, the Fitzwilliam Museum, Cambridge, as well as in many private collections, including those of Lord Wharton and Mrs. Burton-Jones, and a number of museums abroad. In 1965 Mr. & Mrs. J. W. Starr presented 51 miniatures, representing one for every year of his work from 1760–1810, to the William Rockhill Nelson Gallery & Mary Atkins Museum in Kansas City, and here it is possible to examine his painting throughout the whole of his working life. Twenty-five of his miniatures were exhibited in Edinburgh in 1965, including one of his nine self-portraits, the best of which is at the V. & A. M. For further information see *John Smart, the Man and His Miniatures*, by D. Foskett, 1964. This contains a list of his known sitters (not exhaustive) and details of his works sold at Christie's in 1937 from the collections of three of Smart's great-grandchildren.

Smart, John, junior. 1776–1809

Born in 1776; the natural son of John Smart (q.v.) and Sarah Midgeley, and not, as has frequently been stated, the offspring of his father's first marriage—also named John, who died in infancy. Evidence for this attachment and the existence of John Smart junior (as he was always referred to) and his sister Sarah (1781–1853), is to be found in the Guardianship Proceedings of the Court of Chancery for 1790, when Smart senior made arrangements for the care, maintenance and education of these infants, and adequate provision for their mother. A document to this effect was signed on 26 March 1785 when Thomas Parkinson and Philip Paumier were appointed guardians of the children, and a trust formed for their benefit and that of their mother. Being dissatisfied with the way this trust was being carried out, Smart later executed a Deed Poll at Fort St. George on 14 October 1788, appointing Edmund Monk of Fleet Street, a jeweller, and Robert Bowyer (q.v.) jointly, to be his attorneys and to supervise the children's education. Before Smart senior left for India, he had arranged that certain leasehold property in Water Lane, Fleet Street, should be kept for the use of Sarah Midgeley and the children. Apart from this scanty information, nothing is known about John Smart junior's early life. He must have been about 8 years old when his father left for India in 1785, and his sister Sarah about four years old. Whilst it is possible that Smart junior studied under Daniel Dodd (q.v.), he could not have been the Master Smart who exhibited as Dodd's pupil at the Free Society of Artists in 1770 nor the one who exhibited at the Society of Artists in 1775 and 1776. John Smart junior exhibited at the R.A., 1800–1808. He did not, as has always been stated, go to India with his father who returned to England in 1795. I have not so far been able to discover by whom he was taught art, but evidence of his having been a pupil of his father is contained in a letter from Smart senior to the Hon. Court of Directors of the East India Company, 28 May 1808, from 2 Russell Place, where the family appear to have lived after Smart senior returned to London. The letter asks for permission for John junior to go to India in the following terms: 'Having been pleased formerly to allow me to go to India to follow my profession of a miniature painter, I respectfully solicit the same indulgence for my son John Smart who has been taught by me and has obtained a proficiency in the same line that will do honour to me and credit to himself . . .'. It is possible that in his father's absence Smart junior was taught by Cosway (q.v.), and that Dr. G. C. Williamson's reference to 'Honest John' and 'Good Little John' might have been about the

boy, but there is no conclusive evidence for this assumption. Proof that John junior was living with his father in Russell Place up to his departure for India in the *Asia*, 1808, was found in the entries in Messrs. Coutts's ledgers, where sums of money were recorded as having been paid to him by his father between 1804 and 1807. On 17 August 1808, his father paid the sum of £210 to Captain Tremenheere for his passage to India. This was the last recorded payment on the young man's account. Before his departure, John made his will which was signed at 2 Russell Place, and witnessed by John Stevens. In it he bequeathed all his property to his sister Sarah, whom he appointed sole executrix. No mention is made of his mother who, in all probability, had died some years before. He arrived in Madras on 11 February 1809 and, soon after his arrival, opened an account at Harrington's Bank. Although he had obtained permission to go to India as a miniaturist, the *Calcutta Monthly Journal* for 12 February 1809, gives John Smart junior's name at the head of a list of nine cadets who had travelled on the *Asia*, and only recently I purchased an unrecorded profile self-portrait on ivory of John junior, wearing cadet uniform, signed and dated 'J.S.J. / 1808'. Among his effects sold after his death, were such articles as a red coat with epaulet, sword with belt, pistol, etc. His time in Madras was of short duration for only four months after his arrival he died. No information has so far been discovered as to the cause of his death, and nothing is known about his life in Madras. The entry in the Register of Burials at St. Mary's Church, Fort St. George gives the date of death as '1st June 1809', but *The Madras Courier* of 7 June records it as on 2 June. His will was proved by his sister Sarah on 14 February 1810, and letters of administration were granted to Gilbert Ricketts, Esq., Registrar of the Madras Probate Court, 10 July 1809, to deal with his estate. Sarah later gave a power of attorney to John Dighton, husband of Sophia her half-sister (died 1793), to act as her agent and receive the money on her behalf. As an artist, John Smart junior's work was not comparable to that of his father, and, in spite of the fact that there was a close resemblance, it lacks the draughtsmanship and quality so unmistakeable in the older man's work. His composition was not as good, and sometimes the sitter is placed rather to the bottom of the picture with a large space above the head. The majority of Smart junior's portraits were on paper or card, although he also used ivory. A self-portrait in black lead was exhibited at the R.A. in 1808 and is probably the one now in the collection of E. G. Paine of New York; it is signed and dated '1800'. He signed in a manner very like his father: J.S.J (junior), J, Smart Jun. or J. Smart Junior, in cursive lettering; most of his portraits are dated. His sitters included the Hon. Edward P. Lygon, the Hon. Mrs. Walpole, Miss Binney, Horatio Townsend, Esq., His Serene Highness the Prince of Condé, Miss Green, Miss M. A. Green and Miss F. Green, Mr. Boyd, Mr. Dodgson, Robert Woolf junior (his cousin), and a fine portrait of Captain (later Admiral) Robert Williams, signed and dated 'John Smart Junior / 1801'. This has a seascape background and was formerly in the Wellesley Collection. He also executed an interesting set of ten pencil drawings after Holbein, after the well-known portraits in the collection of H.M. the Queen. They are dated '1798' and must have been taken from the originals as several of these were not engraved before 1812. Although they have a look of Smart's modelling about them, they are good strong drawings. They represent Anne of Cleves, Lady Barkley, Lady Butts, Lady Hobbs, Lady Parker, H. Howard, the Earl of Surrey, Sir John Godslave, Judge Moore,

John Poines and Phil Melanchton. For further information see *John Smart, the Man and His Miniatures*, Foskett, 1964. A miniature of Capt. Robert Woolfe junior, signed and dated, 'J.S.J. 1805', from the collection of E. G. Paine of New York, was exhibited in Edinburgh in 1965.

Smart, Samuel Paul. b. 1755?

Of London. Probably the Samuel Smart who entered the R.A. Schools, 11 June 1771 aged '17. 12th Dec next'. Exhibited at the R.A. 1774–1787, and at the Society of Artists, 1777–1778. His address was given in 1777 as Mr. Samuel Smart, Bethnal Green and in 1778, 'at Mr Boujonnar's, 15 Finch Lane, Cornhill'. The only work at present known by this artist is in my collection, and is of a man in a red coat, painted on ivory, and inscribed on the reverse in a later hand as by Samuel Paul Smart. It has a brick red complexion slightly in the manner of John Smart (q.v.), but without the quality of his painting. It is, however, a pleasing miniature. S. P. Smart painted portraits as well as miniatures.

Smeeton, G. or J. (fl. 1832–1856)

Of Kibworth, Leicestershire and 4 Charles Street, Middlesex Hospital. Exhibited at the R.A. and B.I., etc., 1832–1856. The R.A. catalogues for 1832 record J. Smeeton as exhibiting a portrait of Mr. Cartwright, and that of 1833 records G. Smeeton of the same address as exhibiting a portrait of E. Bradley. J. Smeeton exhibited 'Repose' at the B.I., from 41 Parade, Leamington in 1856.

*Smiadecki or Smiadecky, Franciszek. mid-17th century

Little is known about this artist who is thought to have been Polish or Russian, and to have been taught in Sweden by either Alexander or Samuel Cooper (q.v.). Schidlof says that he was a serf of the Orloff family and that he went to Sweden when young. He painted miniatures in oil and on vellum. All those at present known date from the middle of the 17th century. His signature is F S, sometimes in monogram. One in the Duke of Buccleuch's collection, 'called' Andrew Marvell, in oil on copper, signed 'FS' (monogram), and one of an unknown man on vellum were exhibited in Edinburgh in 1965. In a sale at Christie's, 9 March 1959, there were two miniatures, both signed in monogram, one of a boy dated '1664'. The Nationalmuseum, Stockholm has a miniature of a man in oil, signed 'F.S.'. An unsigned miniature of a man by this artist is in the collection of Earl Beauchamp. A superb miniature of an unknown man signed FS (monogram) was Lot 129 at Sotheby's, 24 February 1969 when it realised £1,000. The quality of this portrait is so outstanding that it places Smiadecki among the first rank of those who practised miniature painting in Britain. The features are superbly modelled, the eyes strongly delineated and the lace edged linen collar painted to perfection. Several miniatures by this artist were in the collection of Major R. M. O. de la Hey.

Smibert, John. 1688–1751

Born in the Grassmarket, Edinburgh, 24 March 1688; son of a dyer; was apprenticed to a house-painter and subsequently worked for a coach-painter in London, and copied pictures. Studied at an Academy opened 18 October 1711 in Great Queen Street, London, and not at Sir James Thornhill's Academy, as has always been supposed. Was in Italy, 1717–1720. Returned to London and in 1728 went to America; settled in Boston in 1729 where he married a wealthy lady. Said to have painted a few miniatures, but I have not been able to confirm this statement. Henry Wilder Foote, in

John Smibert, p. 213, published 1950, states that the miniature said to represent George Calvert, 1st Lord Baltimore (but more probably depicting his son), exhibited in Washington in 1925 and attributed to Smibert, was definitely not by him, and that he 'is not known to have painted any miniatures'. He died in Boston, 2 April 1751.

*Smirke, Miss Dorothy. (fl. 1901–1913)
Of Teddington and Richmond, Surrey. Exhibited at the R.A., 1901–1913. Painted miniatures and still life in water-colour.

Smith. See also **Smith, Charles**
A miniature painter named Smith is mentioned by O. Humphry (q.v.) as having been in India for five years (*c.* 1780), and having 'cleared £20,000' during his stay. See *Ozias Humphry* by Dr. G. C. Williamson, p. 117. Was undoubtedly identical with Charles Smith (q.v.).

Smith, Miss. (fl. 1822)
Of 16 Weston Street, Somers Town, London. Was awarded a silver medal in 1822 by the Society of Arts for an original miniature, and another for a copy of a miniature.

Smith, Miss (Sophia?). (fl. 1799–1804)
Of London; daughter of John Raphael Smith (q.v.) and a sister of Miss Emma Smith and of John Rubens Smith (q.v.), both artists. Miss Smith (no initial) exhibited at the R.A. 1799–1804, from her father's addresses, St. George's Row, Hyde Park and 31 King Street, Covent Garden. Long and Graves etc., record her christian name as Sophia, but I have been unable to confirm this statement. Her exhibits included landscapes, portraits and, in 1800, portraits of 'Miss Nicholson, Mrs. Knight and others', which may have been miniatures. I have been informed by the Royal Academy that, in spite of careful research, they have been unable to find any record of the above artist's name being Sophia. She must not be confused with Miss Sophia Smith (q.v.) of Bath who worked from *c.* 1760–1767.

*Smith, Miss A. (fl. 1804). See also **Smith, Alice**
Exhibited a self-portrait at the R.A., 1804. Possibly identical with Alice Smith (q.v.).

Smith, Alice. (fl. *c.* 1805). See also **Smith, Miss A.**
Possibly of Bolton. Recorded by Long as having painted, *c.* 1805, a fairly good miniature of Elizabeth Darbishire of Bolton, afterwards Mrs. Ashworth Clegg. Possibly the sister of Sophia Darbishire (q.v.). She may have been identical with Miss A. Smith (q.v.) who exhibited a self-portrait at the R.A., in 1804.

Smith, Anker, A.R.A. 1759–1819
Born in Cheapside, London in 1759; son of a silk merchant. Educated at the Merchant Taylors' School; articled to a solicitor and later became a pupil of the engraver James Taylor with whom he worked until 1782. Was a noted engraver and also executed some miniatures. Exhibited at the R.A., etc., 1794–1818. Long states that he did not exhibit miniatures after 1798, but he did, in fact, exhibit them up to 1814. Was elected A.R.A. in 1797. Married Charlotte Susannah Snape (born 1770), niece of Faunteroy Bowyer, by whom he had Fred William Smith, Herbert Luther Smith (q.v.) and Edwin Dalton Smith (q.v.). Few miniatures are at present known to exist by the above artist; two are in my collection, a self-portrait inscribed on the reverse, 'Anker Smith / Painted / by himself', and that of his wife signed on the front close to the edge (scratched), 'A. Smith pinxt 91' (1791), inscribed on the reverse, 'Mrs. Anker Smith', and on paper backing the miniature, 'Charlotte Susannah Snape / Niece to Faunteroy Bowyer / Born 1770 / Married 1790 Anker Smith / died . . .'. Long gives the date of

the marriage as 1 November 1791. Smith was the brother of Mrs. Maria Ross (q.v.), wife of William Ross (q.v.). Besides painting miniatures, Anker Smith executed engravings and pastel portraits. He died in London, 23 June 1819. The miniatures I have seen show him to have been a competent artist; his technique is slightly reminiscent of the work of Bogle (q.v.), softly painted, the upper lips strongly delineated. The miniature of Mrs. Smith has a fair amount of gum with the paint, the eyebrows, eyelashes and curls clearly defined. The backgrounds of both miniatures are a grey-brown colour. A miniature of a clergyman, signed horizontally up the left side of the portrait, 'A. Smith Pinx 1810', was sold at Christie's, 25 July 1967.

*Smith, Mrs. Anne. See **Smith, Mrs. S. Catterson**

*Smith, Bell (F. M.?). 19th century
Long records seeing a miniature of Mme. de Toulon which was signed in white along the edge 'Bell Smith'. Schidlof also records a miniature by this artist which was sold in Vienna in November 1921. It was painted on ivory and signed 'Bell Smith'. The artist was possibly identical with F. M. Bell Smith who exhibited at the B.I. 1852–1865, from various London addresses. In 1846 B. Smith of 96 Great Portland Street exhibited a miniature of a lady and a portrait of Mrs. Bell Smith at the R.A.

Smith, Bryce. (fl. 1843–1861)
Of London. Exhibited at the R.A. and S.B.A., 1843–1861.

Smith, C. (Charles?). 18th century. See also **Smith, Charles**
A miniature of Sir Joshua Reynolds, painted on ivory, and said to have been signed 'C. Smith' on the sitter's right arm, was in the H. G. Bohn Collection sold at Christie's, March 1885. The artist was probably identical with Charles Smith (q.v.), who was in India, and Smith (q.v.).

Smith, Mrs. C. H. b. *c.* 1810. d. after 1875
Of London. Exhibited at the R.A., 1836–1875. Possibly the wife of Charles Harriot Smith (1792–1864), sculptor and architect.

*Smith, Charles. *c.* 1750–1824. See also **Smith, C. (Charles?)**
Born in the Orkneys; entered the R.A. Schools, 25 October 1771, aged '21 last Sept.', thus making his year of birth 1750, not 1748/9 as previously recorded. Established himself in London as a portrait painter, but lost patrons because of his violent political opinions. Exhibited at the Society of Artists in 1776 from Mr. Mortimer's, 23 Rathbone Place. A full account is given of his life by Sir William Foster, *Walpole Society*, Vol. XIX, pp. 72 & 73. He left Spithead for India, 12 March 1783, reaching Madras in July, and the Hugli on 13 September. Smith's movements for the following two years remain a mystery, but he must have spent some time in Madras, as Humphry (q.v.) records that he charged 75 pagodas for a bracelet size miniature whilst in Madras, and proportionately for larger ones. In June 1785 he was in Calcutta and obtained letters of introduction to the Nawab of Oudh from John Macpherson (Governor General). Some months later he was seen by Humphry in Benares. From there he went to Lucknow (February 1786). The Nawab and Humphry sat to him simultaneously. He was in Benares in 1787 when he wrote to Humphry in connection with a claim on the Nawab. He was back in London by 1789 when he exhibited at the R.A., from Newport Street, Leicester Fields, and continued to exhibit at the R.A., from London and Edinburgh up to 1823, and at the B.I., 1817 and 1822. Smith produced a musical

entertainment entitled 'A Day in Rome' at Covent Garden, October 1798; this was not successful and, in 1802, he published another work called 'A Trip to Bengal'. He executed two self-portraits, both of which were engraved by S. W. Reynolds. He was living in Scotland in 1823 and on 19 December 1824 he died in Leith aged 75 years.

*Smith, Mrs. Clarendon
A miniature of Lady Gibbs, after Cosway (q.v.), and a miniature of Sir Vicary Gibbs by Mrs. Clarendon Smith, also after Cosway, were Lot 15 at Sotheby's, 12 December 1966.

Smith, Miss Clifford. (fl. 1839–1854)
Of London. Exhibited at the R.A., 1839–1854.

*Smith, Miss Constance I. or J. (fl. 1890–1893)
Of Bath. Exhibited at the R.A., 1890–1893. In each of the two years she exhibited her name is given as Miss C. J. Smith in the R.A. index, and Constance I. Smith in the catalogue entries. Her address was Weston Lodge, Weston Road, near Bath.

Smith, D. (fl. 1799)
A miniature of Johanna Coppinger née Goold was painted by the above artist in 1799. According to an inscription on the reverse it was cleaned and restored by W. Andrews on 27 January, 1891.

*Smith-Dorrien, Mrs. Mary L. H. (fl. 1898)
Exhibited a miniature of the Lady Evelyn Eyre at the R.A. 1898, from The Elms, Chalfont St. Peter, Bucks.

Smith, Miss E. D. (fl. 1838)
Exhibited at the R.A., 1838 (no address given).

Smith, Edwin Dalton. b. 1800. d. after 1866
Born in London, 23 October 1800; son and pupil of Anker Smith (q.v.); was probably a pupil of J. Burgess (q.v.). Exhibited at the R.A., S.B.A. and N.W.C.S., 1816–1866. Early in his career painted flowers and fruit, later painted miniatures. Signed E. D. Smith in cursive script, Edwin D. Smith Pinxit followed by a date, and sometimes in full on the reverse giving an address and a date. His work is reminiscent of Shelley (q.v.) and Egley (q.v.). A miniature of Earl Nelson, signed on the reverse in full from 7 Hereford Street, Mayfair, and dated '1846', and on the front 'E.D.S.', was seen by Mr. A. J. B. Kiddell.

Smith, Miss Eliza. See **Aders, Mrs. E.**

*Smith, Miss Elizabeth. (fl. 1799)
Lot 65 at Christie's, 9 November 1965, was a miniature of a lady signed on the reverse and dated '1799', by Elizabeth Smith. The artist was possibly identical with Miss Eliza Smith, later Mrs. E. Aders (q.v.).

Smith, Miss Emma. b. 1783
Of London; daughter of J. R. Smith (q.v.). Born 17 September 1783. Exhibited at the R.A., and Associated Artists in Water Colours, 1799–1808. In 1803 the Society of Arts awarded her their greater silver medal for a drawing of Achilles and Thetis. Painted miniatures, figure subjects and views. Possibly the Miss Emma Smith who was awarded a silver medal for a drawing after Veronese (1789–1890). The B.M. has engraved portraits after Emma Smith.

Smith, G. b. 1763?
Of London. Exhibited at the Society of Artists 1790, from Wapping. Exhibited at the R.A., 1791–1805. Painted miniatures and portraits, some of which were in crayon. May have been the George Smith who entered the R.A. Schools, 7 February 1794 aged 31.

*Smith, George G. (fl. 1894)
Of London. Exhibited at the R.A. 1894, from 38 Springfield Road, St. John's Wood.

*Smith, Gilbert. 19th century

The above artist worked during the latter part of the nineteenth century. He was a very able miniaturist and executed a number of clever copies of the works of John Smart (q.v.).

Smith, H. (fl. 1839)

Of London. Exhibited at the R.A., 1839. The exhibit was a portrait of two children.

Smith, Hannah. (fl. 1830)

Was working in Bath in 1830 at 22 Kingstone Buildings.

*Smith, Mrs. Hannah E. (fl. 1888–1911)

Of London. Exhibited at the R.A., 1888–1911.

*Smith, Herbert Luther. 1811–1870

Born in London, 1811; son of Anker Smith (q.v.). Entered the R.A. Schools, 15 December 1826 aged 16. Was awarded a silver medal in 1828 and 1830. Exhibited at the R.A. and B.I., etc., 1830–1854. Painted portraits, historical subjects and miniatures. Executed numerous copies for Queen Victoria. Died in London, 13 March 1870. Schidlof mentions a miniature of a judge on card, signed 'Herbert Smith 1852'; this was sold in Vienna in November 1934.

Smith, Isabella. (fl. *c.* 1825–1828). See also **Smith, Miss J.**

Worked *c.* 1825–1828 successively at 40 Rusholme Road, Manchester and 52 Rusholme Lane, Manchester. Schidlof suggests that she may be identical with Miss J. Smith (q.v.), but this seems unlikely as the R.A. gives the latter artist's initial consistently as J.

Smith, Miss J. (fl. 1802–1809). See also **Smith, I.**

Of London. Exhibited at the R.A., 1802–1809. Schidlof suggests that she may be identical with Isabella Smith (q.v.), but this seems to me unlikely as her initials are consistently given as J. in the R.A. catalogues. Her address for some years was 34 York Buildings, New Road. Her sitters included Mrs. Smith, Mr. Smith, the Countess of Kingston, Viscount Kingsborough, Mrs. Williamson, Sir J. Daljiel and Sir W. Busk, Lady Busk and H. Busk, Esq.

*Smith, J. B. (fl. 1830–1841). See also **Smith, James Bennett H.**

Of London. Exhibited at the R.A., 1830–1841. Painted flowers from nature, portraits and miniatures. His address from 1835–1841 was 2 Coventry Street, Leicester Square. His sitters included W. Nightingale, Esq., W. A. Smith, Esq., Alfred Hervé, Esq. (possibly A. Hervé (q.v.)), Master Herbert Clifford Smith and Mrs. Thomas Alexander. The above artist was possibly identical with, or related to, James Bennett H. Smith (q.v.) who exhibited at the R.A. and B.I., 1842–1847, in which latter year he is described as 'the late'. J. B. H. Smith painted portraits, miniatures and subject pictures from 7 Cleveland Street, Fitzroy Square.

Smith, J. C. (fl. 1838–1840)

Of London. Exhibited at the R.A., 1838–1840. In 1840 his exhibit was of Mrs. Chappell Smith.

Smith, James. (fl. 1773–1789)

Of London. Exhibited at the Society of Artists, 1773 and the Free Society of Artists 1776, from addresses in Covent Garden. Exhibited at the R.A., 1779–1789. Painted miniatures and portraits in crayon.

*Smith, James Bennett H. d. 1847? See also **Smith, J. B.**

Of London. Exhibited at the R.A. and B.I., 1842–

1847. Painted portraits, miniatures and subject pictures. His address was 7 Cleveland Street, Fitzroy Square. He may have been identical with, or related to, J. B. Smith (q.v.). In 1847 both the R.A. catalogues and the B.I. record him as 'the late'.

*Smith, Miss Jane B. (fl. 1909)

Of London. Exhibited at the R.A. 1909, from 14 Rylett Crescent, Shepherds Bush.

Smith, Joachim, F.S.A. (fl. 1760–1813)

Of London. Exhibited at the Society of Artists, the Free Society of Artists and the R.A., 1760–1813 (not 1814 as recorded by Graves). Primarily a modeller of wax portraits, and although the Society of Artists lists in 1777 'Miniature portraits in composition, which will not suffer by Time or Fire', these were, in all probability, made of a composition and not paintings. The B.M. has an engraved portrait of Elizabeth Carter after J. Smith.

Smith, John Raphael. 1752–1812

Born in Derby, 1752; younger son of Thomas Smith, a landscape painter of that town. Apprenticed to a linen draper in Derby and later served in a shop in London. Took up miniature painting in his spare time and exhibited at the Society of Artists, 1773–1790, at the Free Society of Artists, 1782, and at the R.A., 1779. Was a famous engraver and draughtsman; drew crayon portraits, etc., and miniatures and frescoes. His brother was Thomas Correggio Smith (q.v.). John Rubens Smith (q.v.), Miss Emma Smith (q.v.) and Miss (Sophia?) Smith (q.v.) were his children. He died in Doncaster, 2 March 1812 and was buried there. His self-portrait is in the N.P.G., London.

Smith, John Rubens. 1775–1849

Born 23 January 1775 in London; son of John Raphael Smith and entered the R.A. Schools, 11 November 1797, aged 22. Painted portraits in water-colour, miniatures, topographical paintings, executed engravings and lithographs, taught drawing. Exhibited at the R.A., 1796–1811. Emigrated to America by April 1809. Established himself in Boston. Moved to Brooklyn (N.Y.) *c.* 1814 where he set up a drawing academy. In *c.* 1830 he had a similar academy in Philadelphia. Published several books on drawing. Lived latterly in New York City where he died, 21 August 1849. His son, John Rowson Smith (1810–1864), was a well-known scenic and panoramic artist. Examples of his work are in the Brooklyn Museum.

*Smith, Joshua. (fl. 1903–1910)

Of London. Exhibited at the Society of Miniaturists, 1903–1910.

*Smith, Miss Kate A. (fl. 1895–1897)

Of London. Exhibited at the R.A. 1895–1897, from Chelsea and 21 Baker Street from which address Miss Mary Pitts (q.v.) also exhibited in 1897. Was possibly identical with Miss Kate Alice Smith who exhibited a flower painting at Suffolk Street in 1879.

*Smith, Mrs. Lucy Bentley. (fl. 1879–1906)

Of Devonport and London. Exhibited at the R.A. and N.W.C.S., etc., 1879–1906, latterly from 14 Rylett Crescent, Shepherds Bush. Undoubtedly related to Jane B. Smith (q.v.) who exhibited from the same address in 1909. According to Graves, Schidlof and Benezit, the above artist is recorded as Miss Lucy Smith, later Mrs. Bentley, but this must be an error, for the R.A. catalogues record her under her married name of Mrs. Lucy Bentley Smith from her earliest entry of 1879.

Smith, Miss M. (fl. 1824)

Of 16 Bucklersbury, London. In 1824 the Society of Arts awarded her a silver Isis medal for a miniature. Was possibly identical with either Miss Mathilda Smith (q.v.) or Miss Martha Smith of 17 Norfolk Street, Strand, who was awarded a silver palette in 1825 for a chalk drawing of a head.

Smith, Miss M. A. (fl. 1804–1810)

Of London. Exhibited at the R.A., 1804–1810. Long suggests that she may have been identical with Miss Smith who exhibited at the R.A., 1815 (no address), or Miss Smith who exhibited at the R.A. 1816–1817, from the address of J. T. Mitchell (q.v.) of 40 Strand.

*Smith, Miss Margaret. (fl. 1906–1914)

Exhibited at the R.A. 1906–1914, from Wood Stanway and Didbrook, Winchcombe, Gloucestershire.

*Smith, Miss Margaret E. (fl. 1909–1914)

Exhibited at the R.A. 1909 and 1914, from 27 St. Saviour Gate, York. In 1909 she exhibited a miniature of H.R.H. Princess Mary of Wales.

*Smith, Miss Maria (Mrs. W. Ross). 1766–1836

Born in 1766; daughter of a city merchant and sister of Anker Smith (q.v.). Wife of William Ross (q.v.) and mother of Sir W. C. Ross (q.v.), Hugh Ross (q.v.) and Miss Magdalena Ross (q.v.). Exhibited at the R.A., Society of Artists and B.I., 1791–1814. Died in London, 20 March 1836.

Smith, Miss Mathilda. (fl. 1823–1824)

Of London. Exhibited at the R.A., 1823–1824. Was awarded in 1823 a large silver palette for a water-colour portrait (a copy). May have been identical with Miss M. Smith (q.v.).

Smith, Nathaniel. b. *c.* 1740/1

Of London. Studied at Shipley's academy and the St. Martin's Lane Academy and was a pupil of Roubiliac in 1755. Obtained prizes at the Society of Arts, 1761–1767. In 1762 he assisted J. Wilton, and later became assistant to Nollekens. Exhibited at the Free Society of Artists and the Society of Artists, 1761–1773, and at the R.A., 1772–1773. Was best known as a sculptor but also painted miniatures. The V. & A. M. has a bust by him and an enamel plaque of a stag hunt, 1760. His son, John Thomas Smith, was also an artist.

*Smith, Miss P. or Mrs. P. (fl. *c.* 1830)

A miniature of *c.* 1830 by this artist is at the Garrick Club, London.

Smith, Richard (Parsons?). (fl. 1837–1855)

Of London. Long records seeing a miniature by Richard (Parsons?) Smith dated 'May 1834', which was probably by this artist. Exhibited at the R.A., 1837–1855, including a portrait of the poet Montgomery. In 1838 was awarded a silver Isis medal by the Society of Arts for a miniature. In 1855 he exhibited a portrait of Lieut. General Sir William Napier.

Smith, Captain Robert. 19th century

The above artist lent the following miniatures, painted by himself, on ivory, to the exhibition at the South Kensington Museum in 1865: Mobarruk Nissan, Begum Princess of Delhi, painted 1832, Nusser ud deen Hyder, King of Oude, 1832, and 'Portrait of an Indian Nautch Girl'. Possibly identical with Lieut. Robert Smith of Queen's Buildings, Brompton who was awarded a silver medal by the Society of Arts in 1816 for a view of Palermo, and with Captain Robert Smith (1792–1882), an amateur artist, of Dirleton, Haddington, Scotland, born 14 September 1792, in Dublin. Served in the 44th Regiment. Executed portraits, landscapes and pencil drawings. Was the father of Robert Henry Soden Smith (1822–1890), Keeper of the Art Library at South Kensington. Capt. Smith died at his house in Frankfort Avenue, Rathgar, 26 November 1882.

*Smith, Miss Ruby. (fl. 1899)

Exhibited at the R.A. 1899, from 78 Eastgate St., Winchester, Hants.

*Smith, Mrs. S. Catterson (Miss Anne Wyke). d. 1886

Née Anne Wyke; daughter of Robert Titus Wyke, an artist of Wexford, and his wife née Hatchel. Exhibited at the R.H.A. Married Stephen Catterson Smith senior (1806–1872), to whom she had six sons and four daughters, of whom Stephen and Robert became artists. According to Schidlof, she worked in London for a time. Died 8 December 1886.

Smith, Miss Sophia. (fl. 1760–1767). See also **S., S.**

Of Bath. Schidlof gives her date of birth as c. 1740, but I have been unable to verify this. Exhibited at the Society of Artists, 1766–1767, as an Hon. Exhibitor. Painted miniatures, flowers and insects. Miniatures signed and dated by the above artist have been recorded between 1760 and 1767. The earliest known example was of an unknown lady, signed and dated '1760', which was sold at Christie's in October 1963. Long records seeing a miniature portrait in the manner of G. Spencer (q.v.), signed 'SS / 176–', which may have been by this artist. I have seen a number of miniatures signed SS, often followed by a date, which have been attributed to the above artist. These could have been the work of S. Shrubsole (q.v.). The above artist was not identical with the Miss (Sophia?) Smith (q.v.) recorded by other authorities, and there is not, so far, any evidence that the two artists were related, or that the later Miss Smith was called Sophia. Sophia Smith could not have been the daughter of J. R. Smith (q.v.) who was born in 1752. A miniature of Frances, Countess of Northampton, wife of George, 6th Earl of Northampton (died 1758), signed 'S.S.', and attributed to Sophia Smith, was sold at Christie's on 28 May 1968. A miniature of an unknown lady, signed and dated '1761', is in the V. & A. M.

Smith, Thomas. (fl. 1773–1788). See also **Smith, Thomas Correggio**

Of London. Exhibited at the Society of Artists, 1773–1774, and at the R.A., 1783–1788. Possibly identical with Thomas Correggio Smith (q.v.).

Smith, Thomas Correggio. (fl. 1767–1769). See also **Smith, Thomas**

Eldest son of Thomas Smith of Derby, landscape painter; brother of J. R. Smith (q.v.) and possibly identical with Thomas Smith (q.v.). Pupil of his father. Exhibited at the Society of Artists, 1767–1769, and perhaps at the R.A., 1783–1788. Was living near St. Michael's Church, Derby, March 1768. He was not financially successful and his work was mediocre. He died in Uttoxeter 'somewhat beyond middle age'.

*Smith, Thomas Reynolds. 1839–1910

Born in Newcastle-on-Tyne in 1839. Noted by Schidlof and Benezit as a miniaturist and sculptor of ivory. Died in 1910.

*Smith, Miss Vera C. (fl. 1907–1914)

Exhibited at the R.A. 1907–1914, from Ashleigh, Dudley, Worcestershire. Her sitters included Mr. and Mrs. T. Woodall Smith and Madame Ivanoff.

Smith, W. A. See **Smith, William**

Smith, William (W. A.?). b. 1754?

Of London. Possibly the William Smith who entered the R.A. Schools, 30 November 1772, aged '19 Dec 29th next'. Exhibited at the R.A. 1774, and possibly identical with an artist of the same name who exhibited a portrait of Major Drummond at the R.A. in 1802 from 250 Holborn, and with an artist who signed W. A. Smith. The Duke of Richmond lent several miniatures to the exhibition at the South Kensington Museum in 1865, among which were several signed in the following ways: a portrait of a gentleman, signed 'W.A.S. 1787'; a portrait of Alexander, 4th Duke of Gordon, signed 'W.A. Smith'; and another of the same Duke, on vellum, signed 'W. Smith delin^t, 1782'; three of the Countess of Westmorland, one on ivory, signed 'W. Smith pinx^t 1787', another on vellum, signed 'W.A. Smith 1792', and a third on vellum, signed 'W.A. Smith 1793'. The signatures were both cursive and in capitals, and were painted with a green shading. One in the Dyson Perrins Collection, of a man, signed 'WA / S', c. 1790, is painted with blue and red shading on the face, and has very red lips, and may have been by this artist.

Smithson. (fl. 1794–1830)

Exhibited at the S.B.A., in 1830. Possibly identical with the artist of this name recorded by Long. A miniature in the collection of the V. & A. M. is inscribed on the reverse, 'Smithson / Barbados / 1795', and signed 'S' on the front. A miniature in the same style, of a lady, signed 'Smithson' (with a long S) in front, and dated '1795', was in the Sidney Hand Collection. Long also noted seeing a copy by Smithson of a miniature painted by John Smart (q.v.) in 1771; the copy was signed in front, 'Smithson / 1794'. By reason of the attempt to copy another artist's work, this differed from the style of the others mentioned above, which were painted with a minute touch and some hatching low down on the background. There is some scratching in the hair.

Smitz, Gaspar. d. 1707

Born in Flanders; called 'Magdalen Smith'. Came to England after the Restoration. Studied in Rome and later settled in Ireland. Was noted for his miniature portraits in oil, but best known for his Magdalenes, one of which is signed and dated '1662', and is in the Painters' Hall, London. He also painted flower pieces and obtained high prices for his work. In his picture of 'The Magdalene' he often introduced a large thistle plant in the foreground. In Dublin he became a member of the Corporation of Cutlers and Painter-Stayners, and in 1681 the Guild of St. Luke. He was extravagant. Said to have died in distressed circumstances in Dublin in 1707, but the Guild of St. Luke does not record his name after 1688. One of his 'Magdalenes' was engraved in mezzotint by John Smith.

Smybert, John. See **Smibert, John**

Smyth, Miss Margaret. See **Lucan, The Countess of**

Snagg, Thomas. 1746–1812

Born in London, 28 February 1746, where his father Richard Snagg and his grandfather, Henry Snagg, owned a successful business as upholsterers. Thomas was apprenticed to his father but, on the death of the latter in 1760, and of his grandfather in

1763, he succeeded, while still a minor, to their property which included a residential estate called Holbrook, near Chislehurst, Kent. In 1764, when only 19, he suddenly decided to go on the stage, and for this purpose adopted the name of Wilks and, as Snagg-Wilks, acted in Manchester, etc. and later at Drury Lane with Garrick. In c. 1770 he went to Ireland and acted in Dublin. On 1 June 1773 he married Elizabeth, daughter of Benjamin Garstin of Dublin, after a romantic elopement, which was aided and abetted by his friend Henry Tresham, the artist. His wife died in 1774 after the birth of a son, Thomas, and he disposed of Broomfield, the estate which he had purchased, and returned to England. Was in Edinburgh, 11 December 1782. On 16 March 1783 he married at St. George's, Hanover Square, Sarah Lilley, and in the same year sold the family estate at Chislehurst and went abroad. He travelled through Europe and lived for a few years at St. Petersburg where he painted the portrait of the Empress Catherine. He left Russia in 1793 and, while passing through France en route for England, was arrested with his wife and children, together with a number of other English subjects, and was detained at Arras by the order of Robespierre. After the fall of Robespierre he was released and, early in 1794, returned to London. His painting of the interior of the prison showing portraits of his fellow prisoners, was engraved and published in 1802 by P. Mazell. He dissipated most of his inheritance by extravagance and improvident living and, in 1800, returned to the stage. After the death of his second wife he returned to Dublin and, in 1804, exhibited three miniatures and four landscapes in oil from 172 Great Britain Street. On 19 February 1805 he married as his third wife, at St. Mary's Church, Mrs. Eliza Robinson, née Dobson (a widow), who died 1825. He died in Dublin, on 1 February 1812 and was buried in the churchyard of St. Paul's, Dublin. By his will he left his wife his painting of Killiney Bay and two frames of miniatures containing the head of the Empress Catherine II and those of Van Dyck and Rubens. To his son Thomas, by his first marriage, he left 'all the paintings of my own that I may leave, whether in oil or miniature, and all designs and drawings'. His wife defeated this bequest by selling, a week before his death (22 January 1812), all his drawings, miniatures, etc. His great-grandson, Sir Thomas Snagge, owned his self-portrait in miniature and two miniatures of his daughters painted in the prison at Arras. A miniature of an officer, signed 'Snagg 1783', was seen at Sotheby's.

Snellgrove, T. (fl. 1800–1827)

Of London. Exhibited at the R.A., 1800–1827. Painted portraits and miniatures.

Snelling, Matthew. (1621–1678)

Baptised at King's Lynn, 14 October 1621. Son of Thomas Snelling and Margaret née Clark, who married as her second husband Ambrose Blagge on 21 July 1625. Matthew married on 3 December 1663 at St. Dunstan's-in-the-West, Elizabeth, daughter of Peter Maplesden, by whom he had two children, Peter and Isabella. Matthew had a long connection with the family of Mary Beale. He was evidently well known to the important artists of the day, including Samuel Cooper (q.v.) who is recorded as having painted his portrait in chalk in 1644, the size being 8 × 6 in. This miniature, the present whereabouts of which is unknown, was sold at 'Mr. Rose's sale in 1723', when it was remarked by Vertue that it was 'finely drawn ... the hands & drapery meanly done'. Mr. Rose, or Rosse, was, in fact, the husband of Susan Penelope Rosse (q.v.). Snelling worked as a portrait and miniature painter in London from c. 1647–c. 1670. He also knew

Charles and Mary Beale (q.v.) who had a wide circle of friends. According to C. Beale's diary, on '4th March 167½ Mʳ Matthew Snelling offered me for my Venus & Cupid of Rottenhamer — 30 guineas. I refused it and woud have 40 guineas. I reckon it worth 50'. Snelling also supplied Beale with colours on more than one occasion, two of which are recorded by Beale on the dates of 13 September 1654 and 7 July 1658. Snelling worked slightly in the manner of Hoskins (q.v.), but did not succeed in attaining anything like his merit. He was said by Vertue to have been 'a gentleman and seldom painted unless for Ladies with whom he was a mighty favorite & a gallant'; also that he 'contrivd or furthered the match between the Duke of Norfolk and his second lady, who was the mother of George and Frederic Howard'. Snelling's miniatures were not, as has been stated, all of ladies; some were after the works of other artists such as Van Dyck. His works vary in style and technique; those I have seen are good. His signatures are usually M:S:Fe, either in cursive or block letters, and followed by a date. Three examples of his work were exhibited in Edinburgh in 1965. One was of Henrietta Maria (1609–1669), Queen of Charles I, from the collection of the Duke of Northumberland. It depicts the Queen as St. Catherine and is signed and dated, 'M:S / :fe / 1649'. This miniature (possibly after Van Dyck), is unlike his other works and gives the impression of a chinese glass painting when looked at from a distance, while the eyes of the sitter are almond shaped, like those of an oriental. The other two exhibits were from the collection of Earl Beauchamp and represented Frances Cranfield, Countess of Dorset (died c. 1687), on vellum, signed and dated on the reverse, 'M.S. / August / 1654', and her husband, Richard Sackville, 5th Earl of Dorset (1622–1667), signed and dated on the reverse, 'MS / fec / June / 1655'. This latter miniature was illustrated in the catalogue of the exhibition. A miniature of Charles I by Snelling, after Van Dyck, signed 'M:S: / Fe: / 1647', is in the collection of Denys Bower, Chiddingstone Castle. The miniature is drawn with fine brush strokes on paper prepared with a thin coating of plaster. A life-size oil portrait of Baldwin Harvey by Snelling is at the Royal College of Physicians.

*Sneyd, Miss Eleanor F. (fl. 1892–1893)
Of 55 Portland Place, London. Exhibited at the R.A., 1892–1893.

*Solomon, Miss Rebecca. (fl. 1851–1910)
Of London. Exhibited at the R.A. and B.I., etc., 1851–1910. Painted miniatures, landscapes in water-colour and figure subjects. Undoubtedly related to, and possibly the sister of, Abraham and Simeon Solomon, all of whom shared the same addresses at varying times. A portrait of A. Solomon, Esq. by the above artist was exhibited at the R.A., in 1852. Duveen noted, in his set of the R.A. catalogues, that her pictures were selling for as much as £300.

Somer, Paul van. 1576–1621
Dr. G. C. Williamson, in his catalogue of Lord Hothfield's miniatures, lists a portrait of Sir Henry Spelman, painted on a playing card of the three of hearts, said to be inscribed on the reverse as by van Somer. This may have been by the younger Paul van Somer (1649–1694?), who is recorded as having painted small portraits in London.

*Soper, Harold C. W. (fl. 1900). See also **Soper, William**
Of London. Exhibited a miniature of Oliver Cromwell, after Sir Peter Lely, at the R.A. in 1900. Possibly identical with William Soper (q.v.).

*Soper, William. (fl. 1882–1903). See also **Soper, Harold C. W.**
Of London. Exhibited at the R.A., 1882–1903. Painted enamel miniatures including one of Miss Laubach and another of 'Jones Esq', after Grimaldi (q.v.). May have been identical with Harold C. W. Soper (q.v.).

Soret, Nicolas. 1759–1830
Born in Geneva, 28 January 1759. Was apprenticed to a clockmaker, but took to miniature painting in water-colour and enamel. Came to England in 1782 and later went to Ireland, returning to Geneva c. 1784; visited St. Petersburg and revisited the city again after his marriage in 1792. Worked for Catherine II of Russia. Painted portraits in imitation of cameos. Returned to Switzerland in 1799. Died 30 November 1830. Clouzot mentions a self-portrait on enamel and one of Mme. L. Soret, probably his mother. Schidlof records several works by Soret who was apparently a good artist. He signed N. Soret, Soret and Soret px, etc., often followed by a date. A pair of enamel miniatures of Mr. Meade Hobson and his wife, Mary, by Nicolas Soret, signed and dated '1784', were Lot 41 at Christie's, 7 November 1967.

*Soutten, Miss Dora. (fl. 1905–1907)
Of London. Exhibited at the R.A., 1905 and 1907.

Soutterant, F. A. de. (fl. 1797)
Of London. Exhibited at the R.A. 1797, from 10 George Street, Portland Place. The Louvre contains an enamel miniature of a 'young girl laughing' signed 'Souhaitrond', which might conceivably be by the above artist. Benezit suggests that the two artists are identical.

Souville, (Alexander?). (fl. 1713)
The Duke of Portland has, in his collection, a miniature copy of a portrait of Matthew Prior, signed on the reverse 'Souuille F.C. 1713', and a miniature by the same hand of Queen Elizabeth after a portrait by Marc Gheeraerts, No. 122 in the Welbeck Collection of pictures. This latter miniature is set into the lid of a tortoiseshell box which was given to Edward, Lord Harley by Matthew Prior who had purchased it in Paris. Writing to Lord Harley, 13 March 1721–2, Adrian Drift (Prior's secretary), says: 'The picture was done from the Original of Queen Elizabeth (now in Your Lordship's possession) by Mr Suville.' The artist may have been Alexander Souville, a French artist who was working in England in 1685.

Sowerby, James. 1758?–1822
Of London; born 1758? Exhibited at the Society of Artists, 1774–1783, from Mr. Wright's, Pimlico and Bolt & Tun Passage, Fleet Street, and at the R.A., 1779–1790. Was probably the artist of this name who entered the R.A. Schools, 31 December 1777 aged '19. 22 last March'. Schidlof gives his date of birth as c. 1750, on what grounds I do not know. Sowerby painted miniatures, portraits and landscapes as well as fish, flowers and fruit. Long recorded that he went to Paris for a time and took his daughters with him. According to family information, he was painted by one of the Heaphys (q.v.). Sowerby died at his home, Mead Place, Lambeth, in 1822, not, as recorded by Schidlof and Benezit, in Paris in 1803.

*Soyer, Madame Emma E. (Miss Elizabeth Emma Jones). 1813–1842
Née Elizabeth Emma Jones. Born in London, 1813. Said to have been an infant prodigy. Pupil of Simoneau who married her widowed mother in 1820. Miss Jones worked in London, Canterbury and Shrewsbury. Painted genre subjects, portraits and, according to Schidlof, miniatures. Exhibited at the R.A. and B.I., the Paris Salon, etc., 1823–1843, her last exhibit at the B.I., in 1843, being posthumous. Schidlof and Benezit record her name as Elizabeth Emma Soyer and she must not be confused with the Miss Eliza Jones (q.v.) who was also exhibiting at this time. Miss E. E. Jones exhibited under her maiden name until 1837; on 12 April of that year she married Alexis Benoit Soyer (1809–1858), the well known chef-de-cuisine of the Reform Club, etc. From 1833–1837 she exhibited from addresses in Fitzroy Square, and after her marriage, from 26 Charing Cross. She died in childbirth, 29/30 August 1842, in London and was buried at Kensal Green Cemetery on 8 September where her husband erected a 'sumptuous' monument in memory of her. She was a frequent exhibitor in Paris where her reputation stood higher than in her native country.

*Spaight, Mrs. Gustava. (fl. 1910)
Exhibited at the R.A. 1910, from 6 Harcourt Road, Boscombe, Hants.

Spalding, G. (fl. 1821–1832)
Of London. Exhibited at the R.A., 1821–1832.

Spanburg. See Spornberg, W.

*Spark, Miss Adelaide. (fl. 1906–1914)
Of London. Exhibited at the R.A. 1906–1914, from 8 Wolverton Gardens, Ealing Common. Her sitters included Miss Mabel Spark and Miss Ethel Spark.

*Sparks, Herbert B. (fl. 1893)
Of London. Exhibited at the R.A., 1893.

Sparrow, Ann. (fl. 1837)
A fairly good oval miniature of Sir James Mackintosh, painted in 1837 by Ann Sparrow, after F. W. Wilkin (q.v.), is at the Ashmolean Museum, Oxford.

*Speaight, Mrs. Alice L. See Cundy, Miss Alice Langford

*Spencelayh, Charles. b. 1865
Born in Rochester, 26 October 1865. Worked in Chatham and New Brompton, Kent. Exhibited at the R.A., etc. 1887–1899. Painted miniatures, figure subjects and portraits. Was still alive in 1948.

Spencer, Gervase. d. 1763
Spencer's date of birth is not at present known and c. 1715 has been suggested. He started life as a gentleman's servant but, finding that he could copy a miniature successfully, took up painting and became a fashionable miniaturist. Dated works by him occur from 1740 in which year Vertue, who saw his work, recorded that he had been a footman to 'Dr W'. Long noted that he was in Great Marlborough Street on 28 May 1751, an address he later exhibited from. Exhibited at the Society of Artists, 1761–1762 when his address was given as 28 Suffolk Street. Painted miniatures on ivory and enamel, some of which were on gold. Spencer also executed a self-portrait in Indian ink (now in the B.M.), and some etchings including a self-portrait. It is not known by whom he was taught art and, whilst it is possible that he taught himself to paint in water-colour, it would seem likely that he had some training in the art of enamelling. Graham Reynolds suggests that he may have had some tuition from Rouquet (q.v.). Died in Great Marl-

653

borough Street, 30 October 1763, and was survived by his daughter who married a Mr. Lloyd, after whose death all Spencer's remaining works and painting materials were sold in London in December 1797. Spencer's portrait was painted by Reynolds. One of his pupils was Henry Spicer (q.v.). His work varied a great deal and he was probably at his best when he was painting ladies; the majority of his miniatures are small, but a few are known that are as large as 3 in. Spencer had the ability to vary his style to suit the medium in which he was working; his enamels have a softness about them and his miniatures in water-colour are clearly defined and meticulous. Although he excelled at painting a pretty girl, I have seen many portraits of young men which are equally good, whereas his portrayal of older men is often slovenly. His signatures vary, the most common being G.S. in either red, black or gold (the punctuation varies). Other signatures are G.S.f. and G. Spencer; occasionally he signed on the reverse, e.g. Spencer / Pinxit / 1747. In his earlier works the signatures are usually cursive, but on the later ones they are often in irregular Roman capitals. An enamel signed 'S' on the front and 'G. Spencer 1755' on the reverse was sold at Sotheby's in 1962. Spencer was a prolific artist and is represented in almost every good collection. Most of his works that one sees date between 1745 and 1761. A self-portrait in water-colour is in the collection of Major R. M. O. de la Hey. Examples of his work may be seen at the V. & A. M., the Ashmolean Museum, Oxford and the Ward Usher Museum, Lincoln which contains a good miniature said to represent Lady Mary Wortley Montagu in oriental dress. A number of his miniatures were in the Nachemsohn collection and the Duke of Northumberland has an attractive miniature said to represent Mary, daughter of Sir Berkeley Lucy, signed 'G.S.1748'. Earl Beauchamp also has some miniatures by him and the Earl of Powis has two very small portraits set in rings.

*Spencer Edwards, Miss R. See Edwards, Miss R. Spencer

Spicer, Henry, F.S.A. 1743–1804
Born in Reepham, Norfolk, 1743. Was a pupil of G. Spencer (q.v.). Exhibited at the Society of Artists, 1765–1783; was the secretary in 1773. Exhibited at the R.A., 1774–1804. Was elected F.S.A., 1770. Exhibited from various London addresses. He went to Dublin, c. 1776 where he painted portraits of prominent people. Was back in London by 1782. On 2 November 1789, he was appointed Painter in Enamel to H.R.H. the Prince of Wales whose portrait he painted, and the Royal Warrant is in the possession of his descendants, as is an unsigned painting of him attributed to Sir Joshua Reynolds. He had a distinguished clientele which included the Duke of Northumberland, Earl Moira, Sir Joshua Reynolds, Charlotte Augusta, Princess of Wales, Lord Nelson, etc. Some of his works were engraved. He was patronised by the Earl of Dartrey whose family retained a few enamels by him. Among his friends were several artists: G. Stubbs (q.v.), J. H. Mortimer, William Hamilton and Ozias Humphry (q.v.), whose portrait and that of his brother, the Rev. W. Humphry, he painted. He had two daughters who followed his profession, Miss J. Spicer (q.v.) and Miss M. A. Spicer (q.v.). Spicer was ill for some time before his death, which took place at 7 Great Newport Street, London, 8 June 1804. He died a poor man. Ozias Humphry lodged until his death in 1810 with Spicer's widow at 39 Lower Thornhaugh Street. Spicer was a good artist but did not equal Spencer. His painting is smooth and the brush strokes on the face are well blended, the colouring, fairly bright. He usually signed in front with a cursive S, or HS followed by a date, and occasionally signed H. Spicer pinxt followed by a date. A miniature of Edmund Burke, on enamel after a crayon portrait by O. Humphry, was lent to the exhibition at the South Kensington Museum in 1865. An enamel representing Capt. J. Jarvis, Earl St. Vincent, by Spicer is at the Holburne Museum, Bath. A fine enamel miniature by Spicer, of Marie Antoinette, is owned by Miss Betty Constable Maxwell and her sister, Mrs. Chalmers Davidson, and has an interesting historical and family history. It was presented to Lady Stourton (then Catherine Weld), by the Queen of France when her husband, Charles X (1757–1831) was living in exile at Lulworth Castle. Lady Stourton gave the miniature to Bishop Vaughan (1814–1902) who in turn presented it to the Hon. Mrs. Constable Maxwell on her marriage in April 1890. The miniature is signed on the front 'S / 89' (i.e. 1789). There is an inscription on the paper stuck on the back of the frame which reads 'Marie Antoinette / late Queen / of France / N8 / died 16 October 1793 / Painted by Mr. Spicer'. A rare early miniature by Spicer executed on ivory of an unknown lady, signed and dated 'HS / 1767' in cursive writing, is in the collection of W. A. Twiston Davies.

Spicer, Miss J. (fl. 1801–1802)
Daughter of H. Spicer (q.v.). Exhibited at the R.A. 1801 and 1802, from her father's address. Painted enamel miniatures including one after O. Humphry (q.v.). Sister of Miss M. A. Spicer (q.v.). A miniature by J. Scouler (q.v.), thought to represent Miss J. Spicer, is in the N.G., Dublin.

Spicer, Miss M. A. (fl. 1799–1803)
Daughter of H. Spicer (q.v.) and sister of Miss J. Spicer (q.v.). Exhibited at the R.A. 1799–1803, from her father's address. Painted landscapes and enamel miniatures. Long records seeing a good enamel portrait of a Mr. Ralph Addison inscribed on the reverse 'Ma (?) Spicer pinxt / 1801'.

*Spicer-Simson, Mrs. Margaret. b. 1874. See also Simson, Mrs. S.
Née Schmidt. Born in Washington, U.S.A., 6 March 1874. Exhibited at the R.A. 1901, from 1 Gayton Crescent, Hampstead. Wife of Theodore Spicer-Simson, an American artist. The above artist may have been identical with Mrs. S. Simson (q.v.).

*Spiller, Miss Jessie R. (fl. 1905–1913)
Of London. Exhibited at the R.A. 1905–1913, from 2 Lindfield Gardens, Hampstead. Her sitters included Mrs. Herbert Spiller.

Spilsbury, Jonathan. b. c. 1737
Born c. 1737. Entered the R.A. Schools, 25 March 1776 aged 39. Practised as an engraver of mezzotints from 1759. Was awarded premiums by the Society of Arts in 1761 and 1763. Exhibited at the R.A. and B.I., 1776–1807. Painted miniatures, oil portraits and Scriptural subjects. Said to have been a pupil of Worlidge (q.v.). Miss Mary Spilsbury, later Mrs. John Taylor, was presumably his daughter, and exhibited from the same address, 10 St. George's Row, Hyde Park.

*Spooner, Mrs. M. D. See Davison, Miss Minnie Dibden

*Spornberg, Jacob. (fl. 1800–1828)
This artist was noted by Long as being resident in Bath, 1800–1828, and not to be confused with W. Spornberg (q.v.), to whom he was probably related. Recorded as the 'Inventor of the Etruscan Profile'. Miniatures by him are at the Art Gallery, Bath. He may have been the artist who was responsible for the engraved views of Bath, published in 1803.

Spornberg, W. (fl. 1773–1793)
Worked in Bath c. 1773–1793. Probably related to J. Spornberg (q.v.), and possibly of Swedish origin. W. Spornberg is usually classified as a silhouettist who painted profile portraits in red and black on concave glass. May have painted miniatures. Resided at 2 Lillyput Alley and 5 Lower Church Street, Bath. Examples of this artist's work, on glass, are in the V. & A. M.

*Sprague, Miss Edith. (fl. 1883–1899)
Of London. Exhibited at the R.A. etc., 1883-1899, from Bingham Studios, Bingham Place, Nottingham Street. Painted miniatures and large portraits in oil.

*Sprinck, Mrs. Emilie M. (fl. 1908)
Of London. Exhibited at the R.A. 1908, from 19 Friern Park, North Finchley.

Spry, William. (fl. 1832–1847)
Of London. Exhibited at the R.A., B.I., N.W.C.S. and S.B.A., etc., 1832–1847, including, in 1847, a miniature group of flowers in oil. Painted flowers in oil and water-colour.

Spurgeon, Miss. (fl. 1803–1804)
Of Lowestoft. Was awarded a silver medal by the Society of Arts in 1803–1804 for copies of two miniature paintings.

Stagg, Richard Morrell. See Staigg, Richard Morrell

*Stagg, Miss Vivien D. (fl. 1905)
Of London. Exhibited at the R.A. 1905, from 4 Briar Road, Cricklewood.

Staigg or Stagg, Richard Morrell. 1817–1881
Born in Leeds 7 September 1817; worked for an architect; went to America in 1831 and settled in Newport, Rhode Island, where he received encouragement from W. Allston (q.v.). Painted miniatures on ivory, many of which were on a large scale and later executed portraits in oil, genre subjects and landscapes. Worked for some time in Boston. Was elected a member of the National Academy of Design in New York in 1861. Was in Paris, 1867–1869. A number of his miniatures are listed by Bolton, and some by Schidlof, including several of the Thurston family. He signed Rich. M. Staigg and R.M. Staigg, followed by a date. His work is reminiscent of that of Newton (q.v.). He died in Newport, Rhode Island, 11 October 1881. Wehle illustrates a pair of miniatures of John I. Linzee and Mrs. John I. Linzee by him, on Pl. XLVIII.

*Stamp, Miss Winifred. (fl. 1901)
Of London. Exhibited at the R.A. 1901, from 29 High Street, Hampstead.

Stanesby, Alexander. c. 1832–1916
Of London. The son of John Stanesby (q.v.). Won premiums when still a boy from the Society of Arts, 1845 and 1847. Exhibited at the R.A. and S.B.A., 1848–1854, including portraits of the artists George Lance and W.P. Frith.

Stanesby, John. 1786–1864
Exhibited at the R.A. 1821–1854. Father of Alexander and Joshua (qq.v.).

*Stanesby, Joshua. *c.* 1829–1917

Son of John Stanesby (q.v.) and brother of Alexander (q.v.). Worked in London. Painted interiors, portraits and genre subjects, and at least one miniature; the exhibition in South Carolina, 1936, contained a miniature on ivory, painted after a portrait in oil, of John Henderson (1762–1803), signed on the reverse 'J. Stanesby senʳ Pinxt. 8. Robert Terrace, Chelsea Feb 28th 1848'.

*Staniforth, Ann E. (fl. 1834)

A miniature copy of the Duke of Nassau (1628–1695), after C. Johnson (q.v.), and signed 'Portrait of the Prince of the House of Nassau from the original by Cornelius Jansen, Ann E Staniforth, London, January 1834', is illustrated by O'Brien, Pl. 69, fig. 1. A miniature portrait of Bernadotte, King of Sweden, by E. Staniforth, after Way, was shown at the Burlington Fine Arts Club Exhibition, 1889, and may have been by the above artist. A miniature of an unknown lady of the Court of Charles I, by the above artist after C. Johnson (q.v.), was sold at Christie's, 7 November 1967.

*Stanley, Mrs. Sarah. *c.* 1697–1764. See also **S., S.**

Elder daughter of Sir Hans (1660–1753) and Lady Elizabeth Sloane; b. *c.* 1697. Married in 1719, George Stanley (who committed suicide, 31 January 1733–4) by whom she had a son, Hans Stanley (1720?–1780), and a daughter, Elizabeth (died 1738, aged 18 years), and for whom she erected a monument by Rysbrach in the chancel of Holy Rood Church, Southampton. Sarah Stanley died, 19 April 1764. The V. & A. M. has six copies of paintings by old masters by the above artist, signed and dated between 1732 and 1738. They are signed variously; S (or Sarah) Stanley, or Stanley Fecit, followed by a date. The technique and colours, especially the blues, are very typical of the work of Lens (q.v.).

Stannard, Joseph. 1797–1830

Born in Norwich, 13 September 1797. Apprenticed to Robert Ladbrooke of Norwich. Studied the work of Dutch masters in Holland, 1821–1822. Exhibited in Norwich, 1816–1830, and at the B.I., etc., 1819–1829. Painted marine and river subjects, portraits, miniatures and executed etchings. His wife Anna was also an artist and exhibited at the R.A. and B.I., etc. Stannard died in Norwich, 7 December 1830. Some miniatures by him, painted on card, a few of which are unfinished, are in the Yarmouth Museum.

*Stansfield, Miss Ellen L. (fl. 1900–1910)

Exhibited at the R.A. and S.M., 1900–1910, from 63 de Parys Avenue, Bedford. Her sitters included H.M. Queen Alexandra and 'H.M. the late King of Denmark'.

*Stanton. (fl. 1805)

A miniature of 'Lady Ann Lenox', signed 'Stanton' was sold in 1805.

*Stark. (fl. 1790)

A miniature of a man in a blue coat, signed 'Stark / 1790', was seen by me in London in 1963. The artist had mixed a lot of gum with his paints and the work was not of any great merit.

Staveley, William. (fl. 1785–1805)

Came of a very old Yorkshire family who dated back to Saxon times. Was a member of a younger branch who had been yeomen for some generations. His father was a frame maker whose trade name was 'W. & J. Staveley, frame-makers, gilders etc, Stonegate York'. Exhibited at the R.A., and in Liverpool, 1785–1805. Long recorded seeing a small oil portrait on panel, bearing the family trade label. A miniature by him, dated '1787', was in the Strawberry Hill sale, 1842. His son, Lieut. Gen. William Staveley (1784–1854), inherited a talent for drawing and, as an officer in the Royal Staffs. Corps, did most of Wellington's reconnaissance work in the Peninsular War.

*Stavely, Miss Amy D. (fl. 1909)

Of London. Exhibited at the R.A. 1909, from 49 Gordon Mansions.

*Stead, Miss Ella M. (fl. 1895)

Exhibited at the R.A. 1895, from Red Barn, Formby, Lancs.

Steel(e), Jeremiah. b. *c.* 1780. d. after 1826

Worked in Nottingham (1801), Bath (1804), Liverpool (1808) and London. Said to have been a pupil of A. Robertson (q.v.). Exhibited at the R.A. and B.I., 1801–1826. Became a member of the Liverpool Academy, 1810, its Vice-President, 1812–1814 and President in 1814. A portrait of Steel, by T. Hargreaves (q.v.), was exhibited at the R.A., in 1808. He was an artist of average ability. He painted the face with minute strokes, and executed the background with fine sloping strokes and used a yellowish-pink colouring, mixed with blue. He appears to have signed on the reverse, J. Steel, followed by a date, or Steel, J. A large miniature of John Wynne, dated '1820', is in the V. & A. M. A miniature of Princess Charlotte by Steel, after G. Dawe, is at Windsor Castle. A miniature, signed 'Steel, Norwich', and possibly by the above artist, was sold in the Hand Collection, 1952. It was painted with blue-mauve tints, the face was rather red and the whole effect photographic.

*Steele, Madame Louise. (fl. 1875–1877)

Of London. Exhibited at the R.A., 1875–1877. Her sitters included J. Steele, Esq., and Mrs. J. Steele. All but one of her miniatures were enamelled on gold. Her address was 101 Clarendon Road, Notting Hill.

*Steer, Henry Reynolds, R. I., R.M.S. 1858–1928

Born in London, 1858. Studied at Heatherley's. Exhibited at the R.A., R.I., N.W.C.S. and S.M., etc., 1880–1901. Elected R.I. 1894, and R.M.S., 1896. Lived in Leicester. Painted subject pictures in oil, domestic subjects and miniatures. Died in Leicester, 1928. An example of his work is in the Walker Art Gallery, Liverpool. The miniature is signed on the front, 'H.R. Steer / 1912', and the sitter's name 'Dorothy Day', is written in a circle of leaves, also on the front. The artist used a pink flesh colouring which was shaded with orange and blue-grey; the modelling of the face is good.

*Stein, Miss Lillie. (fl. 1900–1910)

Of London and Beckenham, Kent. Exhibited at the R.A. and S.M., 1900–1910.

*Steiner. 17th century

A limner of this name is recorded by Vertue, *Walpole Society*, Vol. XVIII, p. 156: 'Steiner a limner, did paint in limning, very well in the manner of Warner architect drew very curious born in Switzerland . . . he was at Vienna when Siege was in 1683. he was Standing on the Walls to take a View of the Camp. was wounded in the knee & always went lameish afterwards. he livd in England & dy'd at Mortlack'.

*Steinthall, Mrs. Emeline P. (fl. 1890–1905)

Of Ilkley, Yorks. Exhibited at the R.A., 1890–1905. Executed busts and miniatures.

*Stenning, Miss A. Maud. (fl. 1905–1914)

Of Beckenham. Exhibited at the R.A. and S.M., 1905–1914. Her sitters included General Sir George Marshall, K.C.B.

*Stephen, Miss Eleanor. (fl. 1906)

Of London. Exhibited at the R.A. 1906, from 62 Queen's Gate.

Stephens, A. b. 1790?

Of London. Exhibited at the R.A., 1812–1839. His address for many years was 124 Newgate Street, London. Was undoubtedly related to W. Stephens (q.v.) who exhibited from the same address. Schidlof records his date of birth as 1790.

Stephens, L. (fl. 1824–1829)

Of London. Exhibited at the R.A., 1824–1829.

Stephens, W. (fl. 1795–1840)

Probably a son of A. Stephens (q.v.) from whose address he exhibited at the R.A., in 1840. Long records that he was in Leeds, 25 May 1795 and charged 1 to 2 guineas for a miniature.

Stephenson, Mrs. See **Malden, Lady Sarah**

*Sterry, Miss Eleanor S. (fl. 1897–1910)

Exhibited at the R.A. and S.M., 1897–1910, from 3 Bedford Place, South Croydon and 14 Friends Road, Croydon.

Stevens, Alfred. 1817–1875

Was born in Blandford, 1817; baptised in 1818. Famous sculptor and painter, known as a miniaturist only by two miniatures on ivory of Alfred Pegler, noted by Long in a private collection. From the photographs of these portraits, the artist appears to have worked in the manner of Sir W. C. Ross (q.v.). Died 1 May 1875.

Stevens, T. (fl. 1831–1844)

Of London. Exhibited at the R.A., 1831–1844. He exhibited his self-portrait at the R.A., in 1834.

Stevenson, J. H. (fl. 1776–1833)

Of London. Exhibited at the Society of Artists and the Free Society of Artists, 1776–1791, and at the R.A., 1792–1833. Had addresses at 9 Crown Court, Duke Street, Westminster and 19 Pitfield Street, Hoxton. Painted genre pictures, architectural drawings and miniatures. Schidlof notes a miniature on ivory of Benjamin Treacher, signed on the reverse 'Painted by J.H. Stevenson 13 Artillery Court / Chiswell St. / Finsbury Square / 1803'. His work is reminiscent of that of Comerford (q.v.). A portrait by him of the Rev. W. B. Collyer, painted in 1806, was engraved by G. Picart.

Stevenson, Miss R. (fl. 1801–1802)

Of London. Exhibited at the R.A., 1801–1802.

Stevenson, W. (fl. 1848)

Of London. Exhibited at the R.A., 1848. His portraits of Chief Justice Kendal Bushe (1767–1843) and General Sir James C. Chatterton, were engraved. His address in 1848 was 32 Upper Norton Street, Portland Place, when he exhibited miniatures of the children of Captain T. T. Talbot, R.N.

Stevenson, William. (fl. 1777–1782)

Of London. Exhibited at the R.A., 1777–1778. In 1782 he had a drawing academy at 100 Pottergate Street, Norwich. Painted miniatures. Long records a miniature signed 'WS', *c.* 1780, which was perhaps by him.

Steward, A. See **Stewart, Alexander**

*Stewart, Alexander. (fl. 1807–1817)

Of London. Practising in 1817 at 30 Bishopsgate Street, London. Long recorded that many of his miniatures were circular. A miniature of a man painted on ivory and signed on the reverse, 'Painted by / Alexʳ Stewart / London / 1807', in cursive writing, is in the V. & A. M. Miniatures of an officer and his wife, signed and dated '1807', are in the collection of E. G. Paine of New York. Was probably identical with the A. Steward recorded by Long.

Stewart, Anthony. 1773–1846

Born in Crieff, Perthshire, 1773. Studied under Alexander Nasmyth in Edinburgh and executed landscapes, sketches and drawings of Scottish scenery. Later devoted himself to miniature painting. Practised first in Scotland and later in London. According to an entry in *The Scottish Record Society*, 1922, he married in 'St. Andrew's Parish, Edinburgh 5 July 1793, Janet Weir of Tron Parish, daughter of Alexander Weir, the painter'. Stewart exhibited at the R.A., 1807–1820. Painted miniatures of Princess Charlotte and Princess (afterwards Queen) Victoria. In June 1794 he was introduced to Joseph Farington by Caleb·Whiteford at the Shakespeare Gallery in London. Stewart died in Stockwell, London, in December 1846 and was buried at Norwood. His daughters, Miss Grace Campbell Stewart (q.v.) and Miss Margaret Stewart (q.v.), were also miniaturists and were taught by their father. He appears to have excelled in painting portraits of children who are usually shown full face, and executed in light clear colours. His miniatures vary in quality and those of adults are not always as well drawn as those of children. Examples of his work are in the collection of H.M. the Queen, and others are in the V. & A. M., and the National Galleries of Scotland. One from this last gallery, of Major Edward Fanshawe, R.E., painted in 1824, was exhibited in Edinburgh in 1965.

Stewart, Miss Grace Campbell. d. 1863

Daughter and pupil of Anthony Stewart (q.v.), and sister of Miss Margaret Stewart (q.v.). Exhibited at the R.A., 1843–1856. Worked in London and said to have been a good miniaturist. Died 1863.

Stewart, Henry. (fl. 1826)

Exhibited at the R.A. 1826, and was presumably identical with the artist of this name who was working at 52 Rusholme Lane, Manchester in 1828. Schidlof says he was a mediocre artist.

Stewart, Hope. (fl. 1845)

A miniature on card of Sir W. Hamilton, Bart., dated '1845', was loaned to the exhibition at the South Kensington Museum in 1865. The sitter was Professor of Logic at the University of Edinburgh, and the portrait lent by Mr. Hope Stewart, presumably the artist. This artist was probably identical with Hope J. Stewart who exhibited at the B.I., 1860–1864, and at other galleries, 1859–1865. This latter artist painted subject pictures and figures.

Stewart, J. 19th century. See also **Stewart, James, R.S.A.**

A small miniature of Thomas Sheridan (1719–1788), father of Richard Brinsley Sheridan, and attributed to J. Stewart, is in the V. & A. M. A pair of miniatures of a man and a woman were sold at

Sotheby's on 17 October 1966; on the reverse of one miniature was an artist's label stating that 'Mr J. Stewart' was a portrait painter of 26 Princes Square, St. George's East. The companion miniature had on the reverse a letter from a Mrs. Reid, enquiring about a miniature and a miniature frame. The artist may possibly have been identical with James Stewart, R.S.A. (q.v.), and the portrait of Thomas Sheridan executed from an earlier work. The artist's work is reminiscent of that of Shelley (q.v.).

*Stewart, James, R.S.A. 1791–1863. See also **Stewart, J.**

Born in Edinburgh, 1791. Studied under Robert Scott and at the Trustees Academy. Exhibited at the R.A. and R.S.A., 1821–1859, and at the B.I., up to 1861. Painted portraits, genre subjects, landscapes and was an engraver. Worked in Edinburgh and London. In 1833 he emigrated to Algoa Bay, Cape Colony and became a sheep farmer. When, in 1834, an insurrection broke out, his farm was destroyed, and the family fled to Somerset (Cape Colony). He was obliged to take up art again. Taught, and painted portraits in order to earn sufficient money to purchase another farm. He died in Cape Colony in 1863. I have seen three small portraits in pencil and wash; one was signed 'Stewart, 1834' and the other two, 'J. Stewart 1837'. These portraits appeared to resemble the works of the above artist who was probably identical with the J. Stewart (q.v.) noted by Long. The draughtsmanship was good and the style was that of an engraver.

*Stewart, Miss Katharine or **Katherine.** (fl. 1887–1911)

Of London. Exhibited at the R.A., etc. 1887–1911, from addresses in Hampstead and Earls Court.

Stewart, Miss Margaret (Mrs. John Séguier). 19th century

Elder daughter and pupil of Anthony Stewart (q.v.), and sister of Miss G. C. Stewart (q.v.). Married John Séguier (1785–1856). Said to have been a good miniaturist. Her husband was also an artist and succeeded his brother William, as superintendent of the B.I. Their son, F. P. Séguier, was the author of *A Dictionary of Painters*, London, 1870.

*Stewart, Mrs. Mary. (fl. 1888–1907)

Of London. Exhibited at the R.A., 1888–1907. Her sitters included several members of her family including Charles Stewart, Esq., Mrs. Charles Stewart, Marjorie and Kathleen, daughters of C. E. Stewart, Esq. and Ph. Jennings, Esq.

*Stock, Henry J., R.I. (fl. 1874–1909)

Of London. Exhibited at the R.A., N.W.C.S. and S.M., etc., 1874–1909. Painted figure subjects and miniatures.

*Stocks, Lumb, R.A. 1812–1892

Born in Lightcliffe, 20 November 1812. Chiefly known as a draughtsman and engraver. Pupil of C. W. Cope and C. Rolls. Said to have painted a few miniatures at the outset of his career. Exhibited at the R.A., etc., 1832–1892. Became an A.R.A., 1853 and R.A., 1871. Died in London, 28 April 1892.

*Stoddard, Miss Edith. (fl. 1903–1908)

Of London. Exhibited at the R.A. 1903–1908, from 20 Scarsdale Villas, Kensington. Exhibited miniatures and drawings. Probably related to Florence Enid Stoddard (q.v.) who exhibited from the same address.

*Stoddard, Miss Florence Enid. (fl. 1904–1914)

Of London. Exhibited at the R.A. 1904–1914, from various London addresses. Probably related to Edith Stoddard (q.v.) from whose address she exhibited, 1904–1908.

Stoker, Bartholomew. 1763–1788

Was born in 1763; son of W. Stoker of Ballyroad, Ireland. While studying under F. R. West in the Dublin Society Schools, he worked as an upholsterer with William Macready of Bride Street. Executed portraits in crayon and miniatures with some success. Several of his portraits were engraved. He died in Suffolk Street, Dublin, 12 June 1788, aged 25, and was buried in the churchyard at Maryborough, where his parents were interred. His sitters included Richard, Earl of Donoughmore, Robert Jephson, the Duchess of Rutland, the Earl of Mornington, the La Touche family and Henry Flood. This latter portrait was copied in pencil by J. Comerford (q.v.) from which Heath's engraving in Barrington's *Historic Memoirs* was taken.

*Stone, Miss Ada. (fl. 1903–1914)

Of London. Exhibited at the R.A. 1903–1914, from various London addresses. Possibly identical with Ada Stone who exhibited still life at Suffolk Street, etc., 1879–1888.

Stone, Mrs. (Miss Mary Mulready Leckie). (fl. 1840–1846)

Née Mary Mulready Leckie. Worked in London. Exhibited at the R.A., 1840–1846. Married *c.* 1844. Her sitters included Miss Elizabeth Jonas of the Royal Academy of Music, James F. Wulff, Esq., and Frank, son of J. Balsir Chatterton, Esq. Most of her entries were as an Honorary Exhibitor.

*Stooke, James. (fl. 1800)

Of Bristol. Long recorded the name of this artist who may not have painted miniatures, but who painted on convex glass filled with white wax. Examples of his work are in the Bristol Art Gallery. He was apprenticed to 'Francis Freeman Philips a portrait painter of Bristol in 1800, for 7 years. During which time the said James Stooke must not frequent Taverns, nor play at Dice, nor contract Matrimony'. After this time he was to have the sum of four shillings and sixpence given to him towards purchasing his freedom of the City of Bristol. Most of his silhouettes were of his family and, according to Long, not outstanding work. A characteristic is a small sprig or group of dots placed on muslin caps, fichus, etc.

Stordy, John. d. 1799

Born in Ireland; brother of Charles Stordy, landscape painter. Worked as a watchmaker in Capel Street and was awarded four pounds, eleven shillings, by the Dublin Society for making enamelled plates for watches. Exhibited in William Street, Dublin, 1769–1770, from Grafton Street, where he was working as a watchmaker and miniaturist. Came to London *c.* 1771 and exhibited at the R.A., 1786–1788. Did not succeed in obtaining a successful practice, and died in poverty in obscure lodgings in Kensington Gravel Pits in 1799. He was perhaps identical with the artist called Story, mentioned by Pasquin as travelling in England and practising in Carlisle, Northumberland and Wales *c.* 1773. I have seen a miniature signed on the reverse 'J Stordy / 49 Mortimer St, / London'. He is also known to have been in York in 1773. A miniature of a lady, signed 'Stordy Pxt / 1787', is in the Castle Museum, Nottingham; it is reminiscent of a weak painting by H. Hone (q.v.), the base of the nose has a red outline, the shading on the face bluish, and the sitter painted against a sky background.

Story. See **Stordy, J.**

Stothard, Robert Thomas, F.S.A. (fl. 1821–1865)
Of London; possibly the son of Thomas Stothard, R.A. Exhibited at the R.A. and B.I., 1821–1857. He lent a miniature of Miss A. M. Birkbeck, which he painted in 1830, to the exhibition at the South Kensington Museum in 1865. A lithographed portrait of T. Stothard, by R. T. Stothard, is in the B.M. Executed miniatures and paintings in oil.

*Strachan, A. W. (fl. 1910)
Of London. Exhibited at the Society of Miniaturists, 1910.

Strange, Sir Robert. 1721–1792
Born in Pomona of an old family from Kirkwall, Orkneys, 14 July 1721. His family trace back to John Strange of Balcaskie in the 14th century. Educated in Kirkwall up to the age of fourteen, after which time, the death of his father compelled him to earn a living. He wanted to go to sea, but was persuaded to join an attorney in Kirkwall, and later joined his brother, a lawyer, in Edinburgh. Was apprenticed to Richard Cooper, an artist at whose house he lived. Visited his mother in the Orkneys, but returned to work with Cooper c. 1741. Fell in love with Miss Lumisden, sister of the secretary to Prince Charles Edward. She stipulated that, if they were to become engaged he should fight for Prince Charles, which he did. They were married in 1747 and in 1748, accompanied the Chevalier to Rouen. They remained in Rouen for about a year, during which time Strange studied under Descamps. Gave up his intention of becoming a miniaturist and went to Paris where he studied under Le Bas in 1749. Returned to London in October 1750 and took up engraving. Was joined by his wife and family. Visited Paris several times and spent four years in Italy where he copied the work of old masters in chalk and water-colours. Elected a member of the Academy of St. Luke in Rome, 1763. Was a member of the Society of Artists and exhibited, 1760–1775; F.S.A., 1772. Was a good engraver and painted a limited number of miniatures. Some of these were lent to the exhibition at the South Kensington Museum, 1865, including two of Prince James Francis Edward Stuart (one in oil and one in ivory); four of Prince Charles Edward (one being sepia on paper, another on ivory, a third, Indian ink on paper; for the fourth no medium is given). The following miniatures by him were also lent: the Countess of Albany, Princess Louisa of Stohlberg; Sir Thomas Strange, 2nd son of the artist; Cardinal York, Henry Benedict; Col. R. M. Strange (born 1760), 3rd son of the artist; Charles I (a copy); William Lumisden, Esq. (father-in-law of the artist); George III and Mr. James Strange. A miniature of Lord George Murray, signed 'R. Strange del', is in the collection of Mr. Donald Nicholas. Greuze, Romney and Raeburn painted portraits of Strange. He was knighted in 1787 and died at 52 Great Queen Street, Lincoln's Inn Fields, London, 5 July 1792. Long considered that Strange's work was influenced by that of French artists.

*Stratten, Miss Lucy A. (fl. 1890–1905)
Of Hessle, East Yorks. and London. Exhibited at the R.A., 1890–1905. Her sitters included the Viscount and Viscountess Mountgarret and Miss Kathleen Molineux. She exhibited a self-portrait in 1901.

Stre(e)tes, Gwillim. (fl. 1546–1556)
A portrait painter of Netherlandish origin who worked in Britain c. 1546–1556. Was Court painter to Edward VI and Queen Mary. Painted portraits of the Earl of Surrey, Edward VI, etc. May have painted miniatures. A miniature of Edward VI, signed 'S' in gold, painted on a blue background on vellum, in the collection of the Earl of Beauchamp, is thought to be either by the above artist or Shute (q.v.). It was exhibited in Edinburgh in 1965 and illustrated in the catalogue.

*Strellett, Ephraim. (fl. 1906–1911)
Of London. Exhibited at the R.A. and S.M., 1906–1911. Examples of this artist's work are reproduced in *Miniatures in the 18th & 19th Centuries* by O'Brien, including three miniatures of the Hon. Mrs. Donough O'Brien.

Stribling, John. (fl. 1823)
Of Reading. Worked in 1823 at Crown Corner, Reading. Taught drawing.

Stroëhling, Ströhling, Stroely or **Ströling, Peter Edward.** b. 1768. d. after 1826
Born in Dusseldorf in 1768 (according to Schidlof). Long records that he was a Russian, educated at the Czar's expense. Studied in Italy c. 1792, after working in Paris and different parts of Germany; was in Vienna in 1796, and in the same year went to St. Petersburg, where he stayed for five years. Was in London, 1803–1807, and again, 1819–1826. Exhibited at the R.A. and B.I., etc., 1803–1826. Painted portraits and figure subjects, oil portraits and miniatures, and executed full length portrait drawings in the manner of Cosway (q.v.). Had a distinguished clientele. A portrait of Queen Louise of Prussia by him is in the Hohenzollern Museum, Berlin, and other examples of his work are in the National Library, Vienna, various Russian museums and private collections. Long records a miniature of a lady, signed along the edge, 'P Stroehling–1792'. The N.P.G., Edinburgh, has a light pencil sketch of Sir Walter Scott by him. Several miniatures by him were lent to the exhibition at the South Kensington Museum, 1865, most of which were on ivory; they represented, among others, the Princess Elizabeth, Marie Antoinette, Louis XVIII, the Dauphin of France, a lady in Turkish dress, and a portrait of her two children. His work varies rather and is not all of equal merit. He used a blue-grey shading on the features, fine lines in the hair and often opaque white on the dress; the backgrounds are usually in gouache, frequently grey, with fine brush strokes of white painted almost horizontally. Said to have died in London c. 1826. He often signed Stroehling (according to Long) and Stroley (according to Schidlof). It is possible that Schidlof has confused two different artists, as the South Kensington Museum catalogue gives the spelling as Stroehling. A Peter Edward Stroehling married Louisa Sheldon at St. Mary-le-Bone, 5 November 1812, and was probably identical with this artist.

*Stroud, Miss Maud (Mrs. W. Wheelwright). (fl. 1895–1912)
Of London, Roehampton and Ditchling, Sussex. Exhibited at the R.A., 1895–1912. Painted miniatures, portraits and subjects in oil. Her married name, Mrs. W. Wheelwright, is recorded in the index of the R.A. catalogues, 1898. She exhibited under her married name from 1903 onwards.

Strutt, William Thomas. 1777–1850
Born 7 March 1777; younger son of Joseph Strutt, author, artist and antiquary. Had a position in the Bank of England. Exhibited at the R.A., 1795–1822. Painted flowers, animals, landscapes and miniatures. Worked in London from various addresses. O'Brien illustrates a miniature of a lady, c. 1826, signed on the front, 'Strutt, Exeter'. The B.M. has an engraved portrait of the Rev. J. Campbell after him. Strutt died in Writtle, Essex, 22 February 1850. He had several sons who survived him.

Stuart, Gilbert Charles. 1755–1828
Born 3 December 1755 at Narrangansett, Rhode Island, U.S.A. Son of a Scottish snuff grinder of Perth and his wife Elizabeth, daughter of John Anthony, a farmer of Newport, Rhode Island. The additional name of Charles was evidently added after his baptism when only George is recorded. Was a pupil of Cosmo Alexander with whom he went to Scotland in 1772. Studied for a short time at Glasgow University and, in 1773, worked his passage back to America. Returned to England in 1775; studied under Benjamin West. Exhibited at the R.A., 1777–1785. Was in Dublin, 1789, where he obtained a large practice and had a distinguished clientele. Was always deeply in debt, and was in a debtors' prison in 1790. Returned to America in 1793 and worked in various parts of the country. Stuart is best known for his large portraits, but painted a few miniatures, some of which may have been after works by Benjamin Trott or Walter Robertson (q.v.). Two miniatures by him were in the Guelph Exhibition in 1891 and represented Princess Charlotte of Wales. He painted three life portraits of Washington. A full-scale work on Gilbert Stuart was published by Lawrence Park in 1926. It contained details of two miniatures by him; one of John Henderson, painted in oil, $3\frac{7}{8} \times 3$ in., inscribed on the reverse, in his handwriting, 'John Henderson / born in Goldsmith Str / London, March 8, 1747 / died Nov 25, 1785 / buried in / Westm Abbey / Gilb^t Stuart, pinx' (formerly in the Wellesley Collection); and General Henry Knox (1750–1806), an unfinished miniature, the present whereabouts of which is unknown. It was painted by Stuart as an object lesson for Miss Sarah Goodrich (1788–1853), an American miniaturist, who painted a miniature of Stuart, reproduced by Park, p. 281, No. 469. He died in Boston, 9/10 July 1828 and was buried in the Old Cemetery at Newport, Rhode Island. His wife Charlotte, née Coates, who survived him, died 1 September 1847, aged 77 years. She and their fourteen children were buried in the family grave and a monument was erected by friends in 1892. His daughter Jane (died 1888) was also an artist and assisted her father latterly with his work. A number of his works were engraved. Details of his life and sitters are recorded by Strickland in his *Dictionary of Irish Artists*.

Stubble, Henry. (fl. 1770–1792)
Of London. Awarded a premium by the Society of Arts in 1770. Exhibited at the R.A., 1785–1791, and is known to have been working up to 1792. Said to have assisted William Wood (q.v.). Long recorded a set of five miniatures and duplicates of three which were sold at Sotheby's, 1 May 1930, and included portraits of Lady Middleton (afterwards Lady Barham), Commissioner Wallis, Mrs. Wallis and Miss Betty Wallis. They were up to 5 in. high and not very well drawn. A large oval miniature on paper of Philip Rashleigh, by Stubble, signed and dated on the reverse 'H.J. Stubble / Little Carrington Street / Mayfair London 1786', is in the V. & A. M. A miniature by him of William Smith (1728–1793), belongs to the New York Historical Society. No. 1 in the catalogue of the Joseph Collection, is a portrait of Cosway (q.v.), said to have been on ivory and inscribed on the reverse 'Richard Cosway Esq, R.A. The first of painters and my particular friend. Drawn in London by Stubble, 1792; belonging to Maria Cologan'; $3 \times 4\frac{1}{4}$ in. It is in the style of Cosway.

Stubbs, George, A.R.A. 1724–1806

Born in Liverpool, 24 August 1724; son of a currier and leather-dresser. Pupil of Hamlet Winstanley (q.v.), a Warrington artist. Moved to Wigan after a quarrel with Winstanley in *c.* 1744; practised as a portrait painter in Leeds and later in York where he studied anatomy; then worked in Hull and in 1754 went to Italy. Returned to Liverpool for a time, but left again *c.* 1756 and lived for four years on a farm in Lincolnshire. In 1760 went to London. Exhibited at the Society of Artists, 1761–1774, holding various offices including that of President, and Director. Exhibited at the R.A. and B.I., 1775–1806; became A.R.A., 1780, and was elected R.A., but declined the honour. He is best known for his portraits and paintings of animals, and executed engravings. No miniatures by him are at present known, but on the advice of Richard Cosway (q.v.), he experimented in enamel painting in 1771, and studied chemistry for two years. He found new colours, and painted some of the largest enamels ever executed in England. His large oval enamel, $34\frac{1}{2} \times 25\frac{1}{4}$ in., of Warren Hastings on horseback, is in the Victoria Memorial Hall, Calcutta. He published works on anatomy. He died 10 July 1806 and was buried in Marylebone Church. A portrait of Stubbs by G. Dance is in the R.A. (diploma gallery). A self-portrait of Stubbs, painted in enamel on a Wedgwood plaque, $26\frac{1}{2} \times 20\frac{1}{4}$ in., was sold at Sotheby's for £8,000 on 12 July 1967. The portrait is signed and dated '1781'. Information regarding Stubbs is given in *Early Art in Liverpool* by J. Mayer, 1876, pp. 93–130.

Stump, Samuel John. 1778–1863

Born, probably in America, in 1778. Studied at the R.A. Schools, 3 October 1796, aged 18. Worked in London and Brighton (August 1809). Exhibited at the R.A., Associated Artists, B.I., O.W.C.S. and S.B.A., 1802–1849. Painted miniatures, water-colour portraits, landscapes (including Italian and Swiss views), a few oil portraits, and executed engravings. Many of his sitters were members of the theatrical profession. Was a member of the Sketching Society to which J. J. Chalon (q.v.) and others belonged, and an old list of members of the Society calls him 'The American Stump'. He was a prolific artist and many of his miniatures are rather dull, but I have seen some examples which are well painted and attractive, including one in my collection of Mrs. Honey, the actress, portrayed as a 'Fortune Teller'. He signed S.J. Stump Pinxit / No. 7 Cork Street / Burlington Gardens / 1816, Stump / Miniature Painter / 8 / Leicester Square, and occasionally Stump, scratched on the front of the miniature. He occasionally used a small octagonal engraved label which reads 'Stump / Miniature Painter / Leicester Square'. A miniature of an unknown man signed 'Stump Pinxt', is in the collection of the Earl of Haddington, and was exhibited in Edinburgh in 1965. A pair of miniatures of members of the Wordsworth family were seen by me in 1967; they are good examples of his work. The portrait of the man is signed 'Stump / pinx' in the same buff coloured paint as the background; the signature being indecipherable, except under a strong lens. For a full list of his addresses, see Long's *British Miniaturists*, p. 425. Examples of his work are in the V. & A. M., the Ashmolean Museum, Oxford, the Glynn Vivian Art Gallery, Swansea and the Guildhall Art Gallery, London which contains, among others, his self-portrait in miniature and those of Edmund Kean, Maria Foote, Countess of Harrington, etc.

Sturry, Agnes. 19th century

A miniature on ivory of a young woman signed 'Agnes Sturry' is in a private collection and is of good quality.

*Sturry, J.

A miniature by this artist is inscribed on the reverse, 'at Mrs Guthrie's, East Haddon Hall, Northampton'. It was seen by Mr. A. J. B. Kiddell.

*Sturt, Mrs. Florence M. (fl. 1897)

Exhibited at the R.A. 1897, from Trehenne, Bushey, Herts.

*Style, Miss Amy. (fl. 1904–1914)

Of London and Richmond. Exhibited at the R.A., 1904–1914. Her sitters included a Miss M. L. Style.

*Sugars, Miss Fanny. (fl. 1903)

Exhibited at the R.A. 1903, from Blacklow Brow, Huyton, Liverpool.

Sullivan, Luke. 1705–1771

Born in Co. Louth, 1705; was brought to England at an early age when his father became groom to the Duke of Beaufort who assisted Sullivan to obtain instruction in engraving, probably from Le Bas. Graham Reynolds suggests that the date given of his birth may be an error, and that he may have been born twenty years later, in view of the fact that his earliest known miniature is signed and dated '1750', although he had been executing engravings from 1746. He assisted Hogarth and engraved his 'March to Finchley'. Exhibited at the Society of Artists, of which he was a member, 1764–1770, from different London addresses. He painted water-colour landscapes, architectural views, miniatures, and executed etchings. Was a member of a club of amateur artists and others which met in Leicester Square. Long records a notice from *The Public Advertiser* (no date given), which says 'Among the several miniature painters, no one has so distinguished himself as Mr. Sullivan'. Women had a fascination for Sullivan and his chief practice is said to have been among the girls of the town, and he resided almost entirely at taverns and brothels. Died at the White Bear Tavern, April 1771. J. T. Smith, in his *Life of Nollekens*, says he was a handsome, lively fellow and that he lodged at the 'White Bear', Piccadilly, and frequented the 'Feathers' in Leicester Fields; was much attached to the good things of this world and died in a miserable state of disease and poverty. In J. T. Smith's *A Book for a Rainy Day*, he gives a further account of him regarding his work, when he says, 'Sullivan ... was, in my humble opinion, the most extraordinary of all miniature painters. I have seen three or four of his productions, one of which was so particularly fine, that I could almost say I have it on my retina at this moment. It was a portrait of a most lovely woman as to features, flesh and blood ...'. Miniatures by him occur in the sale rooms from time to time and are usually rather attractive and date between 1750–1770. He had a strong sense of colour harmony and his style of prettiness is reminiscent of the French school of Hall and Fragonard. He signed his miniatures on the front with a monogram, LS, the S clinging to the stalk of the L which hangs below it. Examples of his work are at the V. & A. M., including one of an unknown lady, signed and dated '1760', illustrated by Reynolds, *E.P.M.*, Pl. XVI. Other examples are in private collections and the B.M. has drawings by him, and an engraved portrait of J. Battishill after him. Two miniatures by Sullivan were lent to the exhibition in Edinburgh, 1965. One of an unknown lady, signed and dated '1767', from the collection of Mrs. Blofeld, was illustrated in the catalogue, Pl. 44. An attractive miniature of an unknown lady signed 'LS' (in monogram) and dated '1760', is in the collection of Major R.M.O. de la Hey.

Sully, Lawrence. 1769–1803/4

Born in Kilkenny, 28 December 1769; elder brother of Thomas Sully (q.v.). Went to America, 1792; worked in Charleston, Richmond (Virginia), and Norfolk (Virginia); married Sarah Annis of Annapolis. He died in Richmond, 1803/4, and his widow married his brother, T. Sully, *c.* 1804. Miniatures by Sully are in the Metropolitan Museum, New York. A miniature of a lady by him is illustrated by Wehle, Pl. XXXII.

Sully, Thomas. 1783–1872

Born in Horncastle, Lincs. 19 June 1783; youngest son of Matthew and Sarah Chester Sully, English actors who took him to Charleston, South Carolina in 1792. Educated at Charleston College, he then entered an insurance office. Neglecting his work, he was sent to study art under a French miniaturist, Belzons (an uncle by marriage). After disagreements between the two, Sully left for Norfolk, Virginia where he joined his brother, Lawrence Sully (q.v.), also a miniature painter. Sully took up this form of art and, by 1801, was painting professionally. In 1804 he went to Richmond and from there to Petersburg and North Carolina, where he married the widow of his brother Lawrence. Lived in Richmond until 1806 when he went to New York and, in 1807, to Boston where he met Gilbert Stuart (q.v.) who gave him every assistance; returned to New York; visited Philadelphia and London (1808–1810). Knew B. West (q.v.) and Sir T. Lawrence (q.v.). Returned to Philadelphia in the spring of 1810 where he settled until his death, although he visited other cities from time to time. Exhibited at the R.A. and B.I., from Philadelphia, and London, 1820–1840. Painted a full-length portrait of Queen Victoria in London between 1837 and 1838. Is better known for his portraits in oil than his miniatures. The majority of his works are probably in America. The Wallace Collection has an oil portrait of Queen Victoria by him, and the N.P.G. has one of Mary Anne Paton. Two miniatures by him are illustrated by Wehle, Pl. XXXI and Pl. XXXII (the artist's wife). He died in Philadelphia, 5 November 1872. A biography of T. Sully, by E. Biddle and M. Fielding, was published in 1921. He painted portraits in water-colour and oil, genre subjects and miniatures. Said to have had nine children, six of whom survived infancy, and all became either amateur or professional artists. His step-daughter, Mary Chester Sully, married John Neagle, the portrait painter.

Summers, S. N. (I). (fl. 1764). See also **Summers, S. N. (II)**.

The above artist exhibited a small full-length portrait of a boy at the Free Society of Artists in 1764. He was probably related to S. N. Summers (II) (q.v.). His address in 1764 was Portland Street.

Summers, S. N. (II). b. 1774? See also **Summers, S. N. (I)**.

Of Chelmsford. Exhibited at the R.A., 1795–1806. Was probably the artist of this name who entered the R.A. Schools, 18 October 1793 aged 19. In 1795 he exhibited a miniature of 'an old man's head'. Long records seeing a miniature of a boy of ten years old by Summers, painted in Chelmsford in 1802. The artist of the same name, who exhibited a small full-length portrait of a boy, at the Free Society of Artists in 1764, was possibly his father.

*Sunderland, Miss Olive. (fl. 1905–1910)

Exhibited at the Society of Miniaturists 1905–1910, from Eggington Vicarage, Leighton Buzzard, Bedfordshire.

Supple, Charles. (fl. *c.* 1815)

Long records seeing a miniature of a lady *c.* 1815,

inscribed on the reverse, 'Charles Supple to be framed'. He thought it was probably the work of a provincial artist.

Surrey, J. (fl. 1852–1858)
Of London. Exhibited at the R.A., 1852–1858. The last exhibit was of Mr. W. J. Surrey.

*Sutcliffe, Miss Heather. (fl. 1896)
Exhibited at the R.A. 1896, from Ewe Cote Hall, Whitby, Yorks.

Sutton, J. (Joseph?). b. 1763?
Of Cockermouth, Cumberland. Possibly the Jos Sutton who entered the R.A. Schools, 16 July 1796 aged 33. Exhibited at the R.A., 1798–1801, including at least one miniature. Th. B. state that he was an engraver and that he worked up to 1824. He exhibited a portrait, and a miniature, at the R.A. in 1798 of 'a young lady in the society of Quakers'.

Sutton, S. H. 19th century
An enamellist who worked in the 19th century. Painted dogs' heads. A head of a bloodhound on enamel, signed on the reverse, 'S.H. Sutton', was in the collection of Comm. Melvill A. Jamieson.

*Swainson, William. (fl. 1884–1888)
Of London. Exhibited at the R.A. and N.W.C.S., 1884–1888.

*Swanwick, Harold, A.R.C.A. 1866–1929
Of Cheshire. Born 1866. Exhibited at the R.A., R.I. and N.W.C.S., etc., 1889–1913. Was an Associate of The Royal Cambrian Academy and a member of the Royal Institute. Executed miniatures and studies in oil and water-colour. Was probably the father of Kate Swanwick (q.v.) who exhibited from the same address in 1908. His sitters included Mrs. Harold Swanwick, presumably his wife. Died 13 April 1929.

*Swanwick, Miss Kate. (fl. 1906–1908)
Exhibited at the R.A. and S.M., 1906–1908, from Clive, Middlewich, Cheshire. Was probably the daughter of Harold Swanwick (q.v.) from whose address she exhibited.

*Swayne, Miss Winifred. (fl. 1905–1914)
Of Hereford. Exhibited at the R.A., 1905–1914. Her sitters included Mrs. R. A. Swayne and the Rev. W. P. Vincent.

*Swifte, Miss Beatrice Mary. (fl. 1902–1905)
Of Dover, Kent. Was a member of the Society of Miniaturists in 1902 and exhibited, 1903–1905.

*Sykes. d. c. 1733
The above artist is recorded by Redgrave as a portrait painter and collector; Benezit states that he was a miniaturist. He died in Lincoln's Inn Fields c. 1733. He was in his day an eminent painter. His collection of pictures was sold in June 1733.

Sykes. (fl. 1769–1809)
The above artist is recorded in a letter as having been living in York in 1809. Forty years before he is said to have painted pleasing portraits in miniature and oil, and small 'conversations, composed with much elegance and fancy'. Possibly related to, or identical with, G. Sykes (q.v.) who also painted 'conversation pieces'.

*Sykes, Mr. d. 1771
The death of a Mr. Sykes, portrait painter at Yarmouth, is recorded in *The Gazetteer*, 13 August 1771. He may have been identical with one of the other artists of this name.

Sykes, Mrs. (fl. 1840–1859)
Of London. Exhibited at the R.A., 1840–1859.

Sykes, Francis. (fl. 1746?–1765)
Owing to lack of detailed information regarding the artists named Sykes, of whom there were several, it is difficult to be certain which of them were responsible for the various exhibits at the Society of Artists, 1761–1774. Francis Sykes, a portrait painter in enamel and miniature, was living on the south side of Leicester Square in 1763. He may have been identical with the Frans Sykes who registered his will in The Hague, 27 August 1743, and who was a miniaturist. Long records a miniature signed 'Fraˢ Sykes / Pinxt. 1746'. A good enamel portrait of Princess Elizabeth Caroline (1741–1759), signed 'F. Sykes Pinxt. 1759', is reproduced on Pl. 86 of G. Biermann's *Die Miniaturensammlung . . . des Grossherzogs . . . von Hessen. The Public Advertiser*, 1769, states that 'Monday last being His Majesty's Birthday, the Queen presented the King with the Portraits of their Royal Highnesses the Princess of Wales, and the Bishop of Osnaburg, in a Ring, painted from the Life, in Enamel, by that ingenious Artist, Mr Sykes, and curiously set with Brilliants; with which His Majesty was highly pleased, and met with universal Approbation'. A portrait painter named F. Sykes, F.S.A., exhibited a whole-length portrait of a clergyman at the Society of Artists in 1776 from York, and may have been related to one or other of the artists of this name.

Sykes, George. (fl. 1761?–1773)
The above artist is said to have exhibited at the Society of Artists, 1761–1773. It has been suggested that the exhibit in 1761, which was a miniature on enamel, was perhaps the work of F. Sykes (q.v.), but as the information regarding the different artists named Sykes appears to have been confused, it is impossible to be certain which one painted it. Graves (*S.A.*) gives the name as George Sykes in 1770 and, in 1774, 'A portrait on board drawn with a hot poker', is listed as by 'Mr Sykes Junr, at Mr Warner's Music Shop, Glass Street, Piccadilly'. He may have been identical with the Sykes (q.v.), no initial, who was in York in 1809. George Sykes is said to have painted in oil and executed miniatures, some of which may have been enamels and conversation pieces. An English artist named Sykes bought miniatures by Petitot (q.v.) at a Paris sale in 1752, and was imprisoned in the Bastille in 1755. M. Clouzot records this information under G. Sykes, and other authorities give it under Francis Sykes (q.v.). A miniature on ivory of a lady, signed 'G. Sykes / 1770' in black, is in the V. & A. M. The background is stippled; opaque white is visible on the pearls and lace, and opaque light brown strokes on the hair. An enamel at Woburn Abbey is said to be the work of G. Sykes.

*Sykes, Miss Marianne. (fl. 1876–1891)
Of London. Exhibited at the R.A., etc., 1876–1891. Her sitters included Algernon, son of Albert Dibley, Esq., Charles Pigott, son of Sir Eustace F. Piers, Bart., Mr. & Mrs. Henry Nash, Elizabeth, Countess of Devon and the Earl of Abingdon.

Symonds, E. (fl. 1836)
Of Dover. Exhibited at the R.A., 1836.

T

*T. (fl. c. 1700)
An enamel miniature of an unknown man c. 1700, signed 'T' on the reverse, is in the National Gallery of Ireland. The miniature is well painted; the background is stippled and the hair painted loosely.

T., C. (fl. 1897). See also **C., T.**
A miniature of a lady signed 'C.T.' and dated '1897', was sold at Christies', 10 April 1962, 3⅜ in. diameter.

T., I. (fl. c. 1772)
Long records seeing a miniature of the Plees family c. 1772, signed 'I.T.'. A miniature of a man in a blue coat, white waistcoat and side whiskers, signed 'I.T.', was sold at Christie's, 15 October 1963. I am informed by Mr. F. Gordon Roe that the miniature c. 1772, seen by Long, was of Mrs. Michael Maynard.

T., J. (fl. 1786)
An amateur who exhibited at the R.A., 1786. I saw a miniature of a lady in a mob cap, 18th century, signed 'T.J' in cursive initials, which may have been by the above artist.

T., O.
A miniature signed in monogram 'OT' is reproduced by Jaffé in *Miniaturen-Sammlung* (Albert Jaffé, Hamburg 1905),

Tacchetti, Camillo (Padre). 1703–c. 1772
Born in Verona, 1703. Was a monk at the St. Leonardo Monastery in Verona. Pupil of F. Ramelli. Worked as a miniaturist in Rome (1748, according to Lemberger), 1760, according to Schidlof. Was in London and exhibited as Padre Tacchetti at the Free Society of Artists, 1768; no address was given.

*Tait, Mrs. Nevin
A pair of miniatures of the Rev. and Mrs. Charles Crawley, by the above artist, were Lot 17 at Sotheby's, 12 December 1966.

Takush, M. (fl. 1833–1837). See also **Tekusch, Miss M.**
Of London. Exhibited at the R.A. 1834 and 1837. Painted enamel portraits from life and copied the works of other artists including Hilton. Was probably identical with Miss M. Tekusch (q.v.) and with 'M. Jakush' of London who exhibited at the R.A. in 1836, an enamel copy of a picture after Moses Haughton senior (q.v.). A pair of fine enamel miniatures of Samuel and Elizabeth Takush, the artist's parents, both signed and dated '1833' were sold at Sotheby's 24 February 1969.

Talbot, Hugh. b. 1799. d. after 1847
Born in Belfast, 1799. Was living in Dublin in 1841 when at the age of 22 he began to exhibit at the R.H.A., 1821–1847. Painted views, domestic subjects and a few miniatures. Nothing else is known about him.

*Talfourd, Field W. 1815–1874
Born in Reading, 1815. Worked in London. Exhibited at the R.A. and B.I., 1845–1874. Painted

large oil portraits, chalk drawings and may have executed some miniatures. Died in London in 1874. Chalk drawings by him of Robert Browning and Elizabeth Barrett Browning are in the N.P.G.

Tallent, J. (fl. 1797)

Of London. Exhibited a portrait of the Duke of York at the R.A., 1797.

*Tankerville, The Earl of. 1852–1931

Born 30 March 1852; George Montagu Bennet, second son of the 6th Earl of Tankerville. Succeeded his father as 7th Earl in 1899. Married 23 October 1895, Leonora Sophie, daughter of J. G. van Marter of New York City, by whom he had two sons and two daughters. Exhibited at the R.A. in 1900 from Chillingham Castle, Belford, Northumberland. His sitters included the Countess of Tankerville, the Countess of Charneville and Lord Ossulston (born 1897), the present Earl.

*Tanner, Miss Lois. (fl. 1910–1914)

Of London. Exhibited at the R.A. 1910 and 1914, from 29 Pelham Place, South Kensington.

Tannock, James. 1784–1863

Born in Kilmarnock, 1784; son of a shoemaker, into which trade he was apprenticed. Became a house painter; took up portrait painting and gained notice. Was a pupil of Alexander Nasmyth; practised in Glasgow and Greenock (1806–1809), where he painted portraits in oil and miniatures. Returned to Glasgow, but *c.* 1810 went to London. Entered the R.A. Schools, 26 February 1811 aged 27. Exhibited at the R.A. and S.B.A., 1813–1841. His young brother, William Tannock, was also an artist. Died in London, 6 May 1863. The S.N.P.G., Edinburgh has three oil portraits by him. An example of his work is at the V. & A. M.

*Tarver, Miss Henrietta M. (fl. 1899–1914)

Exhibited at the R.A. 1899–1914, from The Bungalow, Old Bushey, Herts. Her sitters included Mrs. Henry Tarver, Miss Josephine Tarver, Mrs. Arthur Francis and Miss Blanche Waldron.

Tatham, Frederick. 1805–1878

Worked in London and Winchester (1840–1841). Was awarded a premium by the Society of Arts, 1824. Exhibited at the R.A., 1825–1854, and at the B.I., 1828 and 1829. Painted miniatures and water-colour portraits and was a sculptor. His work is reminiscent of that of A.E. Chalon (q.v.). The B.M. has some drawings and water-colours by him.

Taulin, G. (fl. 1637)

An enamel miniature of Lady Digby, catalogued as by 'G. Taulin, 1637', in an enamelled case with a Latin motto, supported by two goddesses, was Lot 55 on the 11th day of the Strawberry Hill sale in 1842.

Tavistock, Anna Maria, Marchioness of (later **Duchess of Bedford**). 1783–1857

Born 1783, neé Lady Anna Maria Stanhope, daughter of Charles, 3rd Earl of Harrington. Married 8 August 1808, Francis, Marquess of Tavistock, afterwards 7th Duke of Bedford. A miniature portrait by her of William Russell, afterwards 8th Duke of Bedford, signed 'Anna Maria', was catalogued as by her in G. Scharf's *Third Portion of a Catalogue of Pictures . . . Duke of Bedford*, 1878. She died 3 July 1857. She was said to have been an artist of some ability. A miniature of an unknown lady, signed under a coronet in monogram, 'AMT / 1820', is in the N.G., Dublin. It may be a self-portrait of the artist.

Tayler, Charles Foot. (fl. 1818–1853)

In 1818 was awarded a silver Isis medal for an original miniature by the Society of Arts. Exhibited at the R.A., 1820–1853. From 1820–1821 he lived in the Isle of Wight; later settled in Bath where he had several different addresses from 1822–1845 and onwards. He seems to have had a distinguished clientele and painted a number of the theatrical profession. Long refers to a miniature of a little girl holding a doll, signed 'C.F. Tayler 1810', or '1819', and obviously an early work. An attractive miniature of a lady, inscribed on the reverse, 'Painted by Chas. F. Tayler / 8 Oxford Row, Bath 1833', was lent to the exhibition in Edinburgh in 1965 by Major R. M. O. de la Hey. He was a good artist who used a pale pink flesh colour shaded with a slightly greenish tinge; his portraits are often well drawn and expressive. He frequently painted his miniatures against stylised landscape backgrounds. The B.M. has two engraved portraits of actresses after his work. A good rectangular miniature of a man signed 'C.F. Tayler / 1822', is in the V. & A. M. Four exceptionally fine miniatures by the above artist were sold at Christie's, 2 April 1968; they represented Sir Henry Franks Frederick Johnson, 3rd Baronet of Bath and other members of the Johnson family.

Tayler, E. (fl. 1802–1830). See also Taylor, E.

Of 25 Leadenhall Street, London. Exhibited at the R.A., 1802–1830. Was a goldsmith, jeweller and miniaturist. Long records seeing a miniature with his engraved card at the back; the miniature had bright vermilion touches at the nostrils, lips and corners of the eyes. His name was sometimes spelt Taylor. Probably identical with E. Taylor (q.v.).

Tayler or Taylor, Edward, R.S.M. 1828–1906

Born in Orbe, Switzerland, 1828; son of an English father and Swiss mother; he was nephew of Frederick Tayler, and his pupil. Exhibited at the R.A. and S.M., etc., 1849–1905 from London addresses; also worked in Nottingham. Was a founder member of the Royal Society of Miniature Painters and its Treasurer. Was patronised by members of the Royal family including H.R.H. Princess Beatrice, Prince Ludwig of Hesse and the Princess Alice. Died in London, 13/14 February 1906. Harry Tayler (q.v.) was his son. He signed E.T. often in monogram; the E preceded the T and the bar of the T did not project to the right. A miniature of a lady, stippled with a yellowish colouring, is in the Nottingham Art Museum. A miniature of H.R.H. Princess Beatrice by him, signed and dated '1864', is at Windsor Castle.

*Tayler, Harry. (fl. 1882–1883)

Of London. Son of Edward Tayler (q.v.). Exhibited at the R.A. 1882–1883, from 26 Haymarket. He exhibited a miniature of Mrs. H. Tayler, presumably his wife. Painted miniatures and portraits.

*Tayler, Mrs. May. (fl. 1905–1907)

Of London. Exhibited at the R.A. and S.M., 1905–1907. Her sitters included H.R.H. Princess Christian of Schleswig-Holstein, H.R.H. Princess Ena of Battenburg and H.R.H. Princess Victoria of Schleswig-Holstein.

Taylor, Alexander. d. 1804

Of London. Exhibited at the Society of Artists, 1774–1778, and at the R.A., 1776–1796. Was probably the Alexander Taylor who entered the R.A. Schools, 4 December 1775 (no age given), and identical with the Alexander Taylor mentioned by

Sir W. Foster, *Walpole Society*, Vol. XIX, p. 74. Went to India in 1797 and, according to a manuscript list of inhabitants of Calcutta in 1804, he was a Scotsman who had obtained permission to remain there from the Governor-General in Council. He advertised in 1802 as from No. 69 Cossitollah Street, and announced that he continued to paint portraits in oil and miniature. *The Calcutta Gazette*, 12 April 1804, announced his death on 'the 4th instant', *c.* 1796. May have been the artist referred to by Farington as being in Rome in 1790. A miniature of Don Manuel de Godoy, favourite of Queen Marie Louise of Spain, by Taylor (possibly Alexander Taylor), *c.* 1796, was mounted in the name-board of a piano, according to W. Dale's *Tschudi, the Harpsichord Maker*, 1913.

*Taylor, Alfred Henry. d. 1868

Of London. Exhibited at the R.A., B.I. and N.W.C.S., etc., 1832–1867. Was a member of the N.W.C.S. Long records that he painted miniatures on card. Painted subject and figure paintings. Died 1868.

Taylor, Anne. (fl. *c.* 1830). See Taylor, Mrs. W.

An important miniature on ivory, signed 'Anne Taylor', *c.* 1830, was sold at Sotheby's, 28 November 1928. The artist may be identical with Mrs. W. Taylor (q.v.). Mr. A. J. B. Kiddell thought the artist was probably from Edinburgh.

*Taylor, Mrs. B. V. Walden. (fl. 1910–1914)

Exhibited at the R.A. 1910 and 1914, from 74 Park Road, Green Lane, Ilford.

Taylor, E. See also Tayler, E.

Long records that E. Taylor exhibited at the R.A. in 1825, from Fulham; but this appears to be a mistake as the entries for that year are given in the index to E. Tayler (q.v.) of 25 Leadenhall Street, but two of these exhibits are catalogued as by E. Taylor. The artists were presumably identical.

Taylor, Isaac, F.S.A. 1730–1807

Born in Worcester, 13 December 1730; son of a brass founder. Practised painting and engraving as a youth. Settled in London in 1752 and became a well-known engraver. Exhibited at the Society of Artists, 1765–1780; his exhibit in 1770 was 'A fancy head; a miniature, a first attempt'. He married in 1754, Sarah H. Jefferys by whom he had a son, Isaac (1759–1829), whose son, also named Isaac Taylor junior (q.v.), was a miniaturist. Taylor died in Edmonton, 17 October 1807.

Taylor, Isaac, junior. 1787–1865

Born in Lavenham, Suffolk, 17 August 1787; son of Isaac Taylor (1759–1829), engraver and author, and grandson of Isaac Taylor, F.S.A. (q.v.). Lived as a youth in Colchester and Ongar. Trained as a draughtsman and engraver and painted miniatures, including one of his sister, Jane, and a self-portrait in 1817. Executed silhouettes and anatomical drawings; became an author on philosophical subjects, etc. Settled in a large farmhouse in Stanford Rivers, Essex in 1825. Married in the same year, on 17 August, Elizabeth Medland, second daughter of James Medland of Newington, by whom he had nine children. Invented sundry mechanical devices. Died in Stanford Rivers, 28 June 1865. A crayon portrait of him by J. Gilbert, 1862, is in the N.P.G.

Taylor, John. 1739–1838

Born in Bishopgate Street, London in 1739; son of a customs officer. Was called 'Old Taylor'. Pupil of F. Hayman; studied at the St. Martin's Lane

Academy. Exhibited at the Society of Artists and the Free Society, 1764–1777, and at the R.A. and B.I., etc., 1780–1838. Was elected F.S.A., 1772 and Director, 1775. Executed miniatures, some of which were on enamel, minutely finished black-lead portraits, oil portraits (some small) and chalk drawings. Was in Oxford, 1767–c. 1771, Bristol, 3 June 1775 and Manchester, 1777. Charged from 5–15 guineas for paintings according to size. Took up teaching. Invested his earnings in annuities which expired in 1840. Died in Cirencester Place, 21 November 1839, in his 99th year. Not to be confused with a contemporary, John Taylor (1735–1806), a marine and landscape painter. Six pencil portraits by Taylor were in the Francis Wellesley Collection, sold at Sotheby's, 1920. They included a head of the Duke of Wellington, set into a box made from the tree under which Wellington stood at Waterloo, Mrs. Harcourt (profile), Miss Hervey of Ickworth, George Lewis Scott, LL.D., and the Rev. B. N. Turner. A good miniature of a man said to be a Provost of an Oxford College, probably a Bishop, signed 'John Taylor / 1774', is in the collection of E. G. Paine of New York.

Taylor, M. (fl. 1798)

Was working in Exeter, January 1798 and Plymouth, February 1798. Charged two to five guineas for a miniature.

*Taylor, Miss P. (fl. 1900–1901). See also **Taylor, Miss Pattie**

Of London. Exhibited at the Society of Miniaturists, 1900–1901 and was probably identical with Miss Pattie Taylor (q.v.) who exhibited at the Grafton Gallery, 1897.

*Taylor, Miss Pattie. (fl. 1897). See also **Taylor, Miss P.**

The above artist is recorded in *The Morning Post*, 22 June 1897, as exhibiting miniatures at the Grafton Gallery. Possibly identical with Miss P. Taylor (q.v.).

*Taylor, R. (fl. 1817)

Long recorded seeing a miniature of Amelia Nisbet, signed 'R. Taylor. Pinxit. Aug. 1817'.

*Taylor, S. (fl. 1838–1849). See also **Taylor, Stephen**

Of London. Exhibited at the R.A., 1838 and 1849. The exhibits were in the Drawing and Miniature section. He was possibly identical with, or related to, Stephen Taylor (q.v.).

Taylor, Stephen. (fl. 1806–1812). See also **Taylor, S.**

Of London and Andover (1806–1807). Long records seeing several miniatures by the above artist, including one signed 'Painted by / Stepn Taylor / at Andover / Dec 5 1806', another signed 'Stepn Taylor / Andover / 1807', and a miniature of a man, signed 'S. Taylor', c. 1812. He is said by Long to have painted an oil interior of a room. A portrait on ivory of Harriet, Marchioness of Donegal, painted c. 1845 and catalogued as by 'Taylor', was loaned to the exhibition at the South Kensington Museum, 1865, and may have been by the above artist. Was possibly identical with, or related to, the S. Taylor (q.v.) who exhibited in the Drawing and Miniature section at the R.A., in 1838 and 1849. This artist must not be confused with the Stephen Taylor who painted animals and game.

Taylor, Mrs. W. (fl. 1822). See also **Taylor, Anne**

Exhibited at the R.A., 1822. May have been identical with Anne Taylor (q.v.). A large miniature by Anne Taylor, c. 1830, was Lot 136 at Sotheby's 28 November 1928.

*Teape, James S. (fl. 1897–1914)

Of London. Exhibited at the R.A., 1897–1914. In 1907 exhibited a miniature of the Bishop of London and, in the following year, one of Professor A. Steinheil.

*Teed. (fl. 1788)

Mr. A. J. B. Kiddell saw a miniature signed 'Teed, 1788, London'.

Teerlinc, Levina. d. 1576

Née Levina Benninck; second daughter of Simon Benninck (1483?–1561), a Flemish miniaturist. Married George Teerlinc of Blankenberg. Settled in London, 1545. Held the post of Court Painter for a salary of £40 or £44 a year, paid quarterly. A handful of miniatures has been attributed to her, including 'The Elizabethan Maundy' in the collection of Countess Beauchamp. It is possible that she may have had some contact with Nicholas Hilliard (q.v.), as she was still at court when he began his career. The miniatures of the two children aged 4 and 5, in 1590, in the V. & A. M., formerly ascribed to her, have been established as the work of Isaac Oliver (q.v.); and of two attributed to her in the Pierpont Morgan Collection, one was the work of N. Hilliard, and the other too late in period to have been by her. She painted on card. A miniature called Elizabeth of Bohemia in the E. Holzscheiter Collection, Meilen, has been attributed to Levina Teerlinc. It is probably by Isaac Oliver; the costume is c. 1610, making it too late to be by her, as she died in 1576. Miniatures attributed to Levina were exhibited at the V. & A. M. in 1983. For reference see the Catalogue *Artists of The Tudor Court*, pp.52, 53.

Teesdale, Miss Emma. (fl. 1851)

Exhibited at the R.A., 1851. The exhibit was of Frank Teesdale, Esq.

Tekusch, Miss Margaret. (fl. 1845–1888). See also **Takush, M.**

Of London. Exhibited at the R.A. and S.B.A., 1845–1888. Was a member of the Society of Lady Artists. A miniature on ivory of Mrs. Venturi, catalogued as by Miss Tekusch, was lent to the exhibition at the South Kensington Museum, 1865. She was possibly identical with M. Takush (q.v.). The B.M. has a lithograph portrait in colours of Countess Waldegrave after a drawing by M. Tekusch.

*Temple, Miss Vera. (fl. 1902–1910)

Of London. Exhibited at the Society of Miniaturists, 1903–1910. Was a member of the Society in 1902. Her exhibits included miniatures of members of the Royal family, including T.R.H. Princess Mary and the Princes Edward Albert, Henry and George, the Queen of Spain and 'General, Baden Powell', later Sir Robert Baden Powell.

Terborch or **Terburg, Gerard.** c. 1617?–1681

Born in Zwolle c. 1617? Was in London in 1635 (the period of his stay is unknown); was in Rome by 1640. Famous painter of genre pictures and small oil portraits, some of which were miniature size. Died in Deventer, 8 December 1681.

*Terry, Miss Edith Blanche. (fl. 1900–1910)

Of London, Bath and Oxford. Exhibited at the Society of Miniaturists, 1900–1910.

*Tetley, Miss Ivy L. D. (fl. 1904–1910)

Of London. Exhibited at the R.A. and S.M. 1904–1910, from Woodville Priory, Honor Oak Rise.

Tetley, William Birchall. (fl. 1774)

Born in London. Went to New York where he advertised in 1774 as a painter of 'portraits in oil, or in miniature'; taught painting.

Tetlow. (fl. 1767–1775)

Exhibited at the Society of Artists, 1767–1770, as an Hon. Exhibitor, and at the R.A., 1775, also as an Hon. Exhibitor, the entry at the R.A. being 'Medusa and Cleopatra, after an antique gem'. Painted miniatures and at least one portrait.

Thach(e), Nathaniel. b. 1617?

Baptised at Barrow, Suffolk, 4 July 1617; son of Richard Thache, chandler, of St. Martin-in-the-Fields, London, and his wife, née Priscilla Cradock, daughter of Richard Cradock, rector of Barrow, and grandfather of Mary Beale (q.v.). In the will of Mary Beale's father, dated 2 April 1644, he is mentioned as 'Nathl Thach, late of London, picture drawer'. Until recently the only recorded work by this artist was a fine miniature of a lady who has been described as Henrietta, Duchess of Orleans, or Anne of Gonzaga. This miniature, from the collection of Major R. M. O. de la Hey, was loaned to the exhibition in Edinburgh, 1965. It is in brilliant condition, painted on vellum, and signed 'N. Thach 1649'. The lady, who may well be one of the Palatines, is depicted wearing a head-dress of feathers. I have seen other miniatures by this artist who undoubtedly deserves a higher place among the ranks of his contemporaries than has hitherto been supposed. A miniature of Maurice, 4th son of Frederick V, Elector Palatine, signed 'NThach', is in the collection of H.M. the Queen; it is in a fine state of preservation. A portrait of Charles II as a young man, signed on the front 'NThach / F / 165-', the last figure being indecipherable, is in the Mauritshuis at the Hague. This latter portrait is a fine example of the artist's work; there is blue shading on the face, slightly reminiscent of the work of P. Cross (q.v.). A miniature catalogued as an unknown lady, but now known to be Princess Sophia of the Palatine, Electress of Hanover and mother of George I, after a portrait by Honthorst, was sold at Sotheby's, 29 March 1965. It was signed and dated '1651'. It seems possible that Thach worked at least for a time on the Continent. His name has been erroneously given as Thaeb, Thack and Thatch.

*Thacker, Mrs. Arthur. See **Way, Miss Frances Elizabeth**

*Thacker, Miss Winifred H. (fl. 1895–1896)

Of Rottingdean, Sussex. Exhibited at the R.A., 1895 and 1896.

*Thatcher, Mrs. (later Mrs. Smith). (fl. c. 1820)

I have seen a miniature of a lady c. 1820, inscribed on the reverse 'Mrs Thatcher, aft [afterwards] Mrs Smith'. It was not of any particular merit. The artist may have been related to C. F. Thatcher (q.v.).

*Thatcher, C. F. (fl. 1816–1846)

Of London. Exhibited at the R.A. and B.I., etc., 1816–1846; from 1816 his address was Cottage House, Paddington Green. He moved to Manor House in 1833 and 2 Park Place in 1836. He painted landscapes, sculptural subjects and miniatures. A miniature of a young lady, signed on the reverse 'Painted by C. F. Thatcher, 1827', is illustrated in O'Brien, Pl. 65, Fig. 1. Thatcher's draughtsmanship was not first class and his colourings tend to be rather cold.

*Theweneti, Edward. 1806–1889

Born 1806; brother of Lorenzo Theweneti (q.v.) and of Michael Theweneti (q.v.) with whom he shared various houses in Bath and a studio at 14 Bond Street. Painted portraits, landscapes and miniatures, and was described in 1850 as 'a fortification and drawing master'. From 1860 Edward and his brothers were photographers. He and his brother Lorenzo were described latterly as 'Gentlemen'. Died at 29 Henrietta Street, Bath, 13 January 1889. His wife was described in the *Bath Directory*, c. 1868, as 'a professor of pianoforte and engraving'. The death of a Harriet Theweneti, possibly a relative, is recorded in the *Bath Chronicle*, 16 July 1921. The date of death is given as 11 January and her age as 90. This may have been the Miss H. Theweneti who lent family portraits to the exhibition in Bath in 1903.

Theweneti, Lorenzo. c. 1797–1878

Born probably in Italy, c. 1797. Exhibited at the R.A., 1824–1831; one of three brothers, Edward and Michael (q.v.) also being artists. According to Long's notes, all three brothers were described as drawing masters, portrait and miniature painters and landscape painters. From 1860 they were photographers and portrait painters and, latterly, in the case of Edward and Lorenzo, described as 'Gentlemen'; Lorenzo was working in Cheltenham (1824), London (1826–1827) and Bath from 1829 onwards. Living at 2 Charles Street (1829), 28 Milsom Street (1833) and in 1837 the three brothers lived at 7 Macaulay Buildings, Bath with a studio at 14 Bond Street, London. From 1841–1849 they lived at 2 Henrietta Street, Bath and moved, in 1850, to 29 Henrietta Street where Lorenzo died in 1878. His obituary notice in the *Bath Chronicle*, 4 April 1878, gives his age as 89, and states that he probably painted more portraits than any other artist in the neighbourhood. He was a Roman Catholic and a man of deep piety. The press notice of his death gives his age as 81. An exhibition of the 'Works of Old Bath Artists', held in 1903, contained a number of his portraits, including a self-portrait in oil, and miniatures of Bishop Baines, John Theweneti junior and an oil portrait of his brother Michael (q.v.). A miniature of a gentleman (possibly Italian), is illustrated by O'Brien. The sitter is holding a letter on which the artist painted a red seal which is inscribed 'L Theweneti June 17. 1828'. The miniature is well painted and the colouring pleasing. His miniatures are carefully finished and worthy of attention. Some of his works were engraved. Examples of his work are in the V. & A. M. and at the N.P.G.

Theweneti, Michael. 19th century

According to notes left by Long, the above artist was a brother of Lorenzo Theweneti (q.v.) and of Edward Theweneti (q.v.). All three brothers shared the same addresses at times. In 1837 their address was 7 Macaulay Buildings, and their studio, 14 Bond Street, London; from 1841–1849 they were at 2 Henrietta Street, Bath and from 1850 at 29 Henrietta Street. All of them were described as drawing masters, portrait and miniature painters, and landscape painters. From 1860 they were described as photographers and artists. A portrait of the artist by his brother Lorenzo was exhibited in Bath in 1903. A miniature of the artist's mother, signed 'M. Theweneti' is at the V. & A. M.

Thick(e), W. (fl. 1787–1814)

Of London. Exhibited at the R.A., 1787–1814. Was probably the father of Miss C. Thicke (q.v.) and Miss E. Thicke (q.v.), all of whom exhibited from the same address, 17 Duke Street, Portland Place. Was presumably identical with the 'Mr Thick'

who was in Leeds, 26 October 1795, when the family address was given in *The Leeds Intelligence*. A miniature of an unknown lady, in the collection of E. G. Paine of New York, has a trade card on the reverse which states that Thick worked in Wakefield and Hull.

Thicke, Miss Charlotte. (fl. 1802–1846)

Probably the daughter of W. Thick(e) (q.v.) from whose address she and Miss Eliza Thicke (q.v.), undoubtedly her sister, exhibited. Charlotte exhibited at the R.A., etc., 1802–1846. Long records seeing a frame containing nine miniatures (a family) which, according to the inscription on the reverse, were by Miss Thickie (sic) of the same address (17 Duke Street, Portland Place), April 1803; they were mostly in profile and executed in pencil and wash, or colour, on card. Although naive, they were attractive, and obviously early works by the artist.

Thicke, Miss Eliza. (fl. 1801–1836)

Of 17 Duke Street, Portland Place, London. Probably the daughter of W. Thick(e) (q.v.) and sister of Miss Charlotte Thicke (q.v.). Exhibited at the R.A., 1801–1836. Schidlof records a miniature of a child, on ivory, signed on the reverse 'Elizth Thicke 17 Duke Street, Portland Place July 13. 1803'.

*Thiede, Edwin Adolf. (fl. 1882–1889)

Of London. Exhibited at the R.A., 1882–1889. Executed portraits in oil and miniatures.

*Thielche. 18th century. See Thielke, H.D.

In the Diary of Lady Charlotte Bury (1775–1861), mention is made of a woman of the bed-chamber to Queen Charlotte, and groom of the bed-chamber to George III, having a son who painted miniatures. This artist may have been identical with H. D. Thielke (q.v.).

*Thielke or **Thielcke, Henry D.** b. 1789? See also **Thielche**

Worked in England. Undoubtedly the artist who entered the R.A. Schools on 4 January 1806, aged 17, and obtained a silver medal in 1807. Exhibited at the R.A. and B.I., 1805–1816; painted historical subjects, portraits, miniatures and executed engravings. Possibly identical with Thielche (q.v.). A miniature of H.R.H. Princess Charlotte Augusta of Wales (1796–1817), signed and dated '1818', by H. D. Thielcke, was lent to the exhibition at the South Kensington Museum, 1865, by H.R.H. the Duke of Cambridge. This must have either been taken from an earlier portrait or finished after the Princess's death. His address from 1805–1813 was Queen's House and from 1814–1816, 21 King Street, Covent Garden. His sitters included 'Rev. Mr. Kuper, Chaplain to his Majesty', exhibited in 1807.

Thirtle, John. c. 1777–1839

Was baptised in Norwich, 22 June 1777; son of a shoemaker. After practising as a miniature painter, he set himself up in Norwich as a frame-maker, carver and gilder. Exhibited at the R.A., 1808. Was a member of the Norwich Society of Artists and exhibited with them from 1805. Married J. S. Cotman's sister-in-law. Painted water-colour landscapes and full length and small water-colour portraits in the manner of Cosway (q.v.). He died at Norwich, 30 September 1839 and was buried at Thorpe Hamlet. A miniature, formerly in the Ernest Salaman Collection, was signed with a scratched signature, 'J. Thirtle'. The shading of the face was grey with touches of bright red in the corners of the eye, under the ear, etc. He also signed J.T. Examples of his work are in the V. & A. M. and the Norwich Castle Museum.

Tholson, W. (fl. 1810)

Of London. Exhibited at the R.A. 1810, from 84 Margaret Street, Cavendish Square.

Thomas. (fl. 1770)

Exhibited 'A miniature of Socrates' at the Society of Artists, 1770. No initial or address was given.

*Thomas, Miss Eleanor L. (fl. 1906–1914)

Exhibited at the R.A. 1906–1914, from addresses in London, Bushey and Radlett, Herts. Executed miniatures and portraits in oil.

*Thomas, Miss Rose E. (fl. 1900–1906)

Of London. Exhibited at the Society of Miniaturists, 1900–1906.

*Thomas, Mrs. Sybil. (fl. 1897)

Of London. Exhibited at the R.A. 1897, from 122 Ashley Gardens.

Thomasen. 18th century. See also **Thomasen, I.**

A miniature of Charles I, set into a brooch, executed in pen and ink, c. 1704? was lent to the exhibition at the South Kensington Museum, 1865, by Sir Philip de Malpas Grey Egerton. In the resumé of artists in the catalogue, he is described as 'Master of a Grammar School in Cheshire, at the beginning of the 18th c, and noted as a calligrapher'. He may have been related to, or identical with, I. Thomasen (q.v.) of Dublin and London; if so the suggested date of the miniature was probably an error.

*Thomasen, I. (fl. c. 1780–1792). See also **Thomasen**

The above artist executed profile miniatures in the style of Miers (q.v.). Worked for ten years in London, Cheshire, Lancashire and Staffordshire. Went to Dublin in 1790, but left again in 1792, after advertising the fact in *The Dublin Chronicle*. May have been identical with, or related to, the Thomasen (q.v.) whose pen and ink miniature of Charles I was loaned to the exhibition at the South Kensington Museum, 1865. This latter portrait was said to have been painted c. 1704, but the date may have been misjudged.

*Thomason, J. (fl. 1785–1793)

Assisted Miers (q.v.) in Leeds; painted miniatures and silhouettes; advertised in *The Leicester and Nottingham Journal*, 9 June 1787. Settled in Dublin, 1790–c. 1793.

*Thompson, Mrs. Edith H. (fl. 1903–1904)

Exhibited at the Society of Miniaturists, 1903–1904, from Binstead Vicarage, Alton, Hants.

*Thompson, Mrs. Heather. (fl. 1903–1906)

Exhibited at the R.A. 1903–1906, from addresses in St. Buryan, Cornwall and Limnerslease, Guildford. Painted miniatures and flower pieces in oil.

*Thompson, Miss Isa. (fl. 1900)

Exhibited at the R.A. 1900, from 29 Victoria Avenue, Whitley Bay.

Thompson, N. (fl. 1809–1813)

Of London and Edinburgh (1813). Exhibited at the R.A., 1809. Mr. A. J. B. Kiddell saw a miniature of Miss Thompson of Duddington, dated '1813'. The artist's sitters included Sir J. Carr, Miss Douglas and Miss Mortimer.

Thompson, Thomas. b. 1762?

Of London. Exhibited at the R.A. and B.I., 1793–1810. Possibly the artist of this name who entered the R.A. Schools, 6 October 1780, aged '18. 14 last July', and was awarded a silver medal in 1788. Painted sea pieces, etc., and miniatures. He did not exhibit any miniatures after 1796, and as there was more than one artist of this name, it is possible that there may have been some confusion regarding identification.

Thompson, Thomas Clement, R.H.A. 1778/80–1857
Born in Belfast, ?1778 or 1780. Entered the Dublin Society Schools in 1796. Practised as a miniature painter in Belfast and Dublin. Exhibited in Dublin, 1801–1854, including the R.H.A. of which he was one of the original members; resigned in 1856 and was made an Hon. member. Went to London in 1817 and c. 1848 was in Cheltenham where he settled. Exhibited at the R.A. and B.I., etc., 1816–1857. His miniatures are painted in the manner of Comerford (q.v.). He abandoned miniature painting before 1809 and painted portraits in oil. Some of his works were engraved. He died of chronic bronchitis at 18 Cambray Place, Cheltenham, 11 February 1857, aged 79 years (according to Strickland). A self-portrait is in the N.G. of Ireland. Long recorded seeing miniatures by him signed T.T., followed by a date, and a miniature of a man in the V. & A. M. is signed on the background, 'T. Thompson / 1802'; all the letters of the signature are separate and the S a long one.

Thompson, Thomas H. (fl. 1783)
Exhibited at the Free Society of Artists, 1783, no address given. Executed fancy subjects on enamel and chalk drawings.

Thompson, W. J. See **Thomson, William John**

Thomson, E. (fl. 1801)
Of London. Exhibited at the R.A. 1801, from 18 Rathbone Place.

Thomson, Miss E. C. (fl. c. 1840–1845)
Of Edinburgh. Three miniatures by the above artist are in the family collection of Major M. Sandys. One is signed on the reverse 'Miss E. C. Thomson / Artist / 25 George St. /Edinbʳ'.

*Thomson, Miss E. Gertrude, R.M.S. d. c. 1932
Of London. Exhibited at the Society of Miniaturists, 1908–1910. Died c. 1932.

Thomson, E. W. 1770–1847
Born 1770. Of Paris (c. 1824–1830) and London. Began as an engraver and then took up miniature painting. Exhibited at the R.A., 1832–1839, including a portrait of W. J. Newton, Esq. (1832), probably the miniaturist. Some of his work shows the influence of Isabey (q.v.) and of A. E. Chalon (q.v.). Died in Lincoln, 27 December 1847. He used a yellowish flesh colouring, with greyish brown shadows, and painted with oblique crossed brush strokes; occasionally he used touches of pencil in the white parts of the clothes. His signature was E. W. Thomson pinxᵗ / rue du fg Sᵗ Honore, or E. W. Thomson followed by a date and address. Schidlof noted a miniature self-portrait which was sold in Vienna, 1924, signed on the reverse 'E. W. Thomson Pinxit aged 36. 1806 Glasgow'. An attractive miniature on card of the Princess von Lieven, signed and dated '1817' is in the E. Holzscheiter Collection, Meilen. It was formerly in the Pierpont Morgan Collection.

Thomson, H. (fl. 1818)
Exhibited at the R.A. 1818, as an Hon. Exhibitor. Not identical with Henry Thomson, R.A., 1773–1843.

Thomson, William John, R.S.A. 1771/3–1845
Born in Savannah, Georgia, U.S.A., 1771/3. Possibly the W. J. Thomson who entered the R.A.

Schools, 21 January 1808, aged 35. Son of a Government official who lost his post during the rebellion and who retired to England on a small pension, bringing his son with him. Thomson had to earn a living at an early age and painted miniatures and portraits in London. Possibly the W. J. Thomson who exhibited a 'Principal front of a stable' at the R.A., in 1795. Exhibited at the R.A., B.I., Associated Artists, O.W.C.S. and S.B.A., 1796–1843. Became a member of the Associated Artists, 29 July 1807 to 1809. In 1808 was considered with a view to his election to the R.A. His family lived in Edinburgh and, in 1797, his marriage is recorded in 'Tron Parish, md. 12.5.1797 at Edinburgh, Miss Helen Colhoun of Tron Parish, dau. of Captain James Colhoun of the Army' (*Scottish Records*, Grant, 1922). Returned to Edinburgh to the family home in 1812. Exhibited at the Edinburgh Association of Artists, 1810–1813, the Edinburgh Exhibition Society, 1814, 1815, the Institute for the Encouragement of the Fine Arts in Scotland, 1821–1830, and the R.S.A., 1830–1843; became a member of the latter in 1829. Painted portrait miniatures, portraits, landscapes and genre subjects. Was offered a knighthood which he declined. His address in 1820 was 20 Dundas Street, Edinburgh. He died in Northumberland Street, Edinburgh, 24 March 1845. He was a good artist whose work is reminiscent of that of Stump (q.v.). He used greenish tints in shading and sometimes a deep brown-red, and executed the backgrounds and clothes in cross hatching. The V. & A. M. has a portrait of Catherine, Lady Blantyre, on ivory, signed on the reverse 'Painted by W:J:Thomson / Decʳ 1812 / Edinburgh'; also other miniatures signed with cursive initials in front and inscribed with the artist's name, address and date on the reverse. The Kunstgewerbe Museum, Dresden has a miniature of a lady, on ivory, and signed on the reverse 'William:J:Thomson / Nov. 1815, Edinburgh'. A miniature of Dorothea Hay Mackenzie (died 1820), first wife of Sir David Hunter Blair, 3rd baronet, and of Ann Elizabeth Norris (died 1858), daughter of J. Norris, and wife of Major General Thomas Hunter Blair, are in the collection of Sir James Hunter Blair, and a miniature of Sir George Clerk, 6th Bart., painted 1805, is in the collection of Sir John Clerk of Penicuik.

*Thomson. Miss Winifred Hope. (fl. 1890–1914)
Of London. Exhibited at the R.A. 1890–1914, from 57 Onslow Square and from 59 Pont Street. Her sitters included the Duke of Rutland and his two daughters, the Lady Victoria and the Lady Elizabeth Manners, and Doris and Olivia, daughters of L. Vernon Harcourt, Esq.

*Thopas, Johannes or **Johan.** c. 1630–c. 1700
Born in Assendelften (?) c. 1630. Painter and draughtsman who specialised in small portraits which he executed very finely in pencil and Indian ink. May have visited England. The sale at Sotheby's, 18 February 1963, contained, as Lot 29, two plumbago miniatures by him of the Rev. John Kinderley in clerical robes, and another of Charles II, signed and dated '1660'. In 1668 he was a member of the Brotherhood of Haarlem where he was still living in 1681, and where he is said to have died in c. 1700. A miniature of a man in a black doublet with a white lace collar, seated on a chair, with a curtain and pillar in the background, was formerly in the Wellesley Collection. It is executed in black chalk, heightened with white, on vellum, and is signed across the pillar, 'J. Thopas fecit'. The pair to this portrait, of the gentleman's wife, was also in the Wellesley Collection, and was sold as Lot

780–81 at the sale of this collection at Sotheby's in June 1920.

Thorburn, Robert, A.R.A., H.R.S.A. 1818–1885
Born in Dumfries, 10 March 1818; son of a tradesman. Educated at the High School there. Showed an early aptitude for drawing. When only fifteen studied under Sir W. Allan (q.v.) at the drawing academy of the Royal Institute of Scotland in Edinburgh, and was awarded two first prizes there. Went to London c. 1836 and studied at the R.A. Schools. In order to support himself and his family, and to obtain early recognition, he took up miniature painting. Exhibited at the R.A., etc., 1837–1884, principally from London addresses, and at the R.S.A., 1835–1856. Was elected A.R.A., 1848; became an Hon. member of the R.S.A., 1857. Won a gold medal in Paris in 1855. Worked for some time in Edinburgh and lived latterly in Kelso and, in 1884, in Tunbridge Wells. He died in Tunbridge Wells, 3 November 1885. Painted miniatures, crayon drawings, oil portraits, landscapes, etc. W. B. Johnstone (q.v.) was his pupil and H. C. Heath (q.v.), his assistant. Many of his works are very large; some are full length. Some good examples of his miniatures are in the collection of H.M. the Queen at Windsor Castle, including one of Queen Victoria, $6\frac{5}{8} \times 5\frac{5}{8}$ in., signed on the reverse. This was exhibited in Edinburgh in 1965, together with one of Lady Munro (unfinished), from the National Gallery of Scotland. A list of miniatures painted by Thorburn was published by Foster, *M.P.B.F.*, Vol. I, pp. 96, 97. His son Archibald (died 9 October 1935) was well known for his painting of birds.

Thornhill, Sir James. 1675–1734
Born in Melcombe Regis, 1675. Celebrated painter of portraits, figure subjects and ceilings, etc.; is not usually thought of as a miniaturist, but a portrait of a gentleman, catalogued as by him, was lent to the exhibition at the South Kensington Museum, 1865, and stated to be in oil on copper. This or another miniature attributed to Thornhill is mentioned in *The Archaeological Journal*, Vol. XV, 1858, p. 279. A miniature of him by C. Richter (q.v.), on vellum, inscribed and dated on the reverse, 'Sir James Thornhill, Richter Pinxit London 1718', was lent by Mrs. Blofeld to the exhibition in Edinburgh in 1965. Died nr. Weymouth, 13 May 1734.

*Thornton-Clarke, Miss Emmeline. See **Clarke, Miss Emmeline Thornton**

*Thorp, Miss A. Constance. (fl. 1893?–1898)
Of London. Exhibited at the R.A. 1897 and 1898, from 4 Brunswick Square. Probably identical with Miss Adelaide C. Thorpe who exhibited a portrait of Miss Ethel Davis in the Etchings, Drawings and Engravings section of the R.A., in 1893.

*Thorp, Miss Florence. (fl. 1904)
Of London. Exhibited at the R.A. 1904, from 64 Gloucester Place, Portman Square.

*Thorp, Miss Theresa. (fl. 1906–1909)
Exhibited at the R.A. 1906 and 1909, from addresses in Preston, Lancs. and London.

*Thring, Miss F. (fl. 1903–1911)
Exhibited at the R.A. 1903–1911, from Cambridge Road, Teddington.

Thwaites, W. (fl. 1819)
Of London. Exhibited at the R.A., 1819.

*Thynne, The Rt. Hon. Lady John. (fl. c. 1815)
A rather good miniature of c. 1815 by this artist was seen by Long.

Tidey, Alfred. 1808–1892

Born in Worthing, 20 April 1808; son of J. Tidey who kept a private school; brother of Henry Tidey (q.v.), water-colour painter. Went to London and soon worked up a practice. Exhibited at the R.A. and B.I., etc., 1831–1877. Entered the R.A. Schools in 1834. Had a distinguished clientele, including Royalty; painted portraits of the Empress Frederick, Crown Princess of Germany; Arnold of Rugby, Miss Ellen Tree, etc. In 1855 he married Miss Justina Campbell, by whom he had three sons. He resided principally in London, but also worked in Jersey, Twickenham and Germany, and travelled frequently on the Continent. Was a member of the Dudley Gallery Art Society. Received help and encouragement from John Constable, R.A. Died at Glenelg, Springfield Park, Acton, 2 April 1892. He was a good artist and his portraits are well drawn and pleasing. Examples of his work are in the V. & A. M., where a MS list of his works may be seen, the N.P.G. and in private collections including that of H.M. the Queen.

Tidey, Henry F. 1813–1872

Born in Worthing, 7 January 1813; brother of Alfred Tidey (q.v.) and son of J. Tidey. Henry Tidey exhibited at the R.A., B.I. and N.W.C.S., etc., 1839–1872. Painted portraits in water-colour and subject pictures, and may have painted miniatures, as many of his exhibits were in the Drawing and Miniature section of the R.A. His sitters included 'the children of Alfred Tidey Esq'. This portrait was exhibited from 30 Percy Street in 1861; he lived at this address for many years. Died in London, 21 July 1872.

Tiffin, Walter Francis. (fl. 1844–1867)

Of London and Salisbury; probably related to the painters Henry Tiffin and James Benjamin Tiffin, with whom he shared an address, 434 West Strand. Exhibited at the R.A., 1844 (under the name of W. T. Francis, his mother's maiden name), and from 1845–1867, at the R.A., B.I. and S.B.A. under his own name. Painted landscapes, still-life and miniatures, some of which were painted for brooches.

Tillotson, J. (fl. 1821–1856)

Of London. Exhibited at the R.A., 1821–1856. Mrs. Mary Tillotson (q.v.), who was probably his wife, exhibited from the same address.

Tillotson, Mrs. Mary. (fl. 1839–1844)

Exhibited at the R.A. 1839–1844, from the same address as J. Tillotson (q.v.), and was probably his wife.

Tilstone, J. R. (fl. 1827–1829)

Of London. Exhibited portraits, probably miniatures, at the R.A. 1827 and 1829, from 17 Norfolk Street.

*Tilt, E. P. (fl. 1868)

Of Epsom. Son of F.A. Tilt (q.v.), lived at Lovelands, Walton Heath, Epsom. Exhibited at the R.A., 1868. The entry was entitled 'Ada', and may have been a miniature.

*Tilt, F. A. (fl. 1866–1868)

Of London and Epsom. Father of E.P. Tilt (q.v.) with whom he shared an address. Exhibited at the R.A., 1866–1868. Had a distinguished clientele which included H.M. Queen Victoria whose portrait he painted in 1867, 'by Command; the original miniature for which the enamel was prepared for Mr. Peabody'; T.R.H. the Prince and Princess of Wales; Prince Albert and Prince George (also by command); the Earl and Countess Danvers; the Duke and Duchess de Frias; the Marquess of Anglesea, etc.

Many of his miniatures were stated to be on enamel, the others were on ivory. A portrait of Sir William Erle by him is at the N.P.G., London.

*Tod, Richard. (fl. 1910)

Of Edinburgh. Exhibited at the R.A. 1910, from 26 Frederick Street, Edinburgh.

Todd, Harriett. (fl. *c.* 1799)

Long records seeing a miniature copy by this artist of a supposed portrait of Mary Queen of Scots of *c.* 1799, as well as two pencil copies by her from engravings of the Bartolozzi school. May have been an amateur artist, but if so had attained a fair degree of proficiency.

Todderick, Miss. (fl. 1762–1774)

Of London. Exhibited at the Society of Artists and the Free Society of Artists, 1762–1774. She exhibited a miniature of Queen Charlotte at the Free Society in 1763. Her address at that time was Holles Street, Cavendish Square, although in the catalogue of the Free Society she gave her address as The Star & Garter Warehouse, Tavistock Street, Covent Garden. From 1770–1774 she exhibited at the Society of Artists from 65 Berners Street.

Tomalin, Miss Mary Jane. (fl. 1838–1859)

Of London. Exhibited at the R.A., 1838–1859.

*Tomasich, y Haro, Antonio. 1820–1890

A Spanish miniaturist born in Almeria, 1820. Studied in Paris; worked in Spain, Mexico, Havana and London. Executed portraits of numerous members of the Spanish Court. A miniature of the Rev. Charles Crawley by him, after Sir W. C. Ross (q.v.), and one of William Gibbs, signed and dated '1872', were catalogued for sale at Sotheby's, 12 December 1966. Died in Madrid, 25 November 1890. He was a good artist; his miniatures are expressive and painted with a broad brush stroke. The backgrounds are usually painted in gouache. Seven miniatures by Tomasich are reproduced in *La Miniatura Retrato en España* by Mariano Tomás, 1953, including one of William Gladstone.

Tomkins, Miss M. (fl. 1817–1825)

Of London. Was awarded a premium by the Society of Arts in 1817. Exhibited at the R.A., 1824–1825.

*Tomkins, Miss M. Flora. (fl. 1906–1914)

Exhibited at the R.A. and S.M., 1906–1914, from addresses in Cheltenham and the Isle of Wight.

Tomlinson, George Dodgson. 1809–1884

Born in Nottingham, 26 October 1809. Worked as a miniaturist in Huddersfield. Exhibited at the R.A., 1848, 1851 and 1872. Died in Huddersfield, 15 September 1884.

Tomlinson, J. (fl. 1765/70–1853)

Of London. Exhibited at the R.A., etc., 1824–1853. Long records a miniature of a lady stated to be signed 'I. Tomlinson 1824', which was possibly by this artist.

Tonelli, Signora Anna. *c.* 1763–1846

Née Anna Nistri; born in Florence *c.* 1763; daughter of a miniaturist. Exhibited at the R.A., 1794–1797. Taught drawing to the children of the second Lord Clive with whose family she lived in London and India. Married a violinist. Painted miniatures, water-colour portraits, pastel copies, etc. Died in Florence, 22 July 1846. Schidlof records a miniature on ivory, signed on the reverse 'Anna Tonelli / face in Firence / 1816'. Pastel portraits by her are in the collection of the Earl of Powis and the B.M. has engraved portraits of J. Courtenay junior and the Duchess of Northumberland, after her work.

Tonkin, John. See Torkin

Toomer, Joseph. (fl. 1780–1781)

The above artist is known to have painted two large tinted miniatures on paper of a lady and gentleman in March 1781. E. G. Paine of New York has a miniature of a lady, signed and dated 'Joseph Toomer / Dec. 18 1780', by the above artist.

*Tooth, Miss Susan K. (fl. 1894–1897)

Of London and Colchester. Exhibited at the R.A., 1894–1897.

Toplis, Charles H. (fl. 1840–1872?)

Of London. Exhibited at the R.A., etc., 1840–1847, from various London addresses. Painted portraits, some of which may have been miniatures. His exhibits included a portrait of James Toplis (not a miniature), and a 'Study of an East Indian'. Was possibly identical with C. H. Toplis who exhibited a portrait of Dr. Selle (not a miniature), at the R.A., in 1872 from Petersham, Surrey.

Torkin or Tonkin, John. (fl. 1830)

Was working in 1830 in Chapel Street, Penzance.

Torond, Francis. 1761?–1812

A Frenchman born 1761? Worked in Bath and in London from 1784. Is best known for his silhouettes and groups of full-length figures; also painted religious pictures and miniatures. *The Daily Advertiser,* 11 January 1776, contained the following advertisement: 'Drawing, Painting, Etching & Engraving, Taught at his Academy, 18 Well St., Oxford St.'. Died 12 June 1812.

*Touche, D. (fl. 1843)

A miniature of a young girl, signed and dated '1843', by this artist, was sold at Christie's, 15 October 1963. Schidlof records a Mlle Touche who painted on porcelain from life, and copied well-known pictures. She lived in Versailles and exhibited at the Paris Salon, 1833 and 1834. She may have been identical with the above artist.

Toussaint, Augustus. *c.* 1750–*c.* 1790–1800

Born *c.* 1750; son of a jeweller in Denmark Street, Soho, London. Was apprenticed to Nixon (q.v.). Won premiums at the Society of Arts, 1766 and 1768. Exhibited at the R.A., 1775–1788. Practised miniature painting on ivory and enamel. He is reputed to have been friendly with J. Smart (q.v.), and to have devoted much of his time to designing elaborate frames for miniatures, including some for Smart and, in particular, the one which contained the miniature of Smart's son John who died in infancy. Toussaint inherited property from his father and retired to Lymington where he died *c.* 1790–1800; he was buried in the churchyard there.

*Towgood, Miss Mary Y. (fl. 1895–1899)

Of London. Exhibited at the R.A., 1895–1899. Painted miniatures and landscapes in water-colour.

Townley, Charles. 1746–*c.* 1800

Born in London, 1746; son of the Rev. J. Townley, headmaster of the Merchant Taylors' School. Studied in Rome and Florence. Exhibited at the Society of Artists and the Free Society of Artists, 1778–1783, and at the R.A., 1779–1795. Painted portraits in oil, and miniatures; executed portraits in pastel, chalk and black-lead, and was an engraver; some of his works were after other artists including Cosway (q.v.). Had various London addresses. Said to have gone to Berlin *c.* 1776, but to have returned to London before his second visit to Berlin in 1789, when he executed numerous portraits, and was appointed engraver to the King of Prussia. Was in Hamburg, 1789 or 1790 and from there returned to England. Died c. 1800.

*Townsend, Mrs. Louisa. (fl. 1896–1909)
Exhibited at the R.A. 1896 and 1909, from addresses in North Devon and London.

Townshend, The Hon. Emily. 19th century
Long records seeing a good miniature representing Diana c. 1830–1845 which, according to the inscription on the reverse, was copied by the above artist from a picture by Guido; in the same collection there was a miniature portrait of a youth in a cadet's uniform, signed on the reverse, 'ET(?) / 1827'; the initials were cursive.

*Traies, William. 1789–1872
Born in Crediton, Devon, 1789. Exhibited at the R.A. 1817, 1822 and 1845, from London and Exeter. Painted landscapes and miniatures. Long records seeing a miniature on paper of Miss Downman, painted by him, which was exhibited in 1932. He drew the illustrations for a work on natural history by Dr. Neal, in Exeter, 23 April 1872.

Trail, Miss Ann Agnes (Sister Agnes Xavier). (fl. 1823–1833)
Of London. Exhibited at the R.A. and S.B.A., 1823–1833, including portraits of several persons with Scottish names. Was, according to Schidlof, a member of a religious order of St. Margaret (presumably London). He records a miniature on ivory of a young lady with her two children, signed 'Ann A. Trail 1824', and considered that her work was reminiscent of that of J. C. D. Engleheart (q.v.). Her sitters included the Rev. Dr. Chalmers, the Cardinal Prince Odescalchi and the Rev. Nerses Sazarien.

Trant, Miss. (fl. 1766)
Exhibited at the Society of Artists 1766, as an Hon. Exhibitor, 'two pictures in miniature'.

*Tremayne, Miss Constance. (fl. 1898)
Exhibited at the R.A. 1898, from Bellefield, Upper Tulse Hill.

Tremlett, John. (fl. 1831–1845)
Of Exeter where he was working in 1831. In 1840 his address was 125 Fore Street, Exeter. Long records seeing a rectangular miniature of c. 1845, signed in front 'JT' (cursive), and on the reverse, in pencil, 'J. Tremlett /– Street / Exeter'; it was not of a very high quality and the painting rather stiff.

*Trevor, Miss Laura. (fl. 1900)
Of London. Exhibited at the Society of Miniaturists, 1900.

*Trew, Miss Vera. (Mrs. H. E. Morriss). (fl. 1909–1910)
Of Seaford, Sussex and London. Exhibited at the Society of Miniaturists, 1909–1910.

*Trewby, Miss Ellen Constance. (fl. 1905–1910)
Exhibited at the R.A. 1905–1910, from Langford Lodge, New Park Road, Brixton Hill. Her sitters included Mrs. Lawrie Trewby.

Trewinard, Miss A. (fl. 1804). See also **Trewinnard, Mrs. A.**
Of London. Possibly identical with Mrs. A. Trewinnard (q.v.), or was her daughter. A Miss A. Trewinard is recorded as exhibiting at the R.A., 1804; her sitter was Miss Elliot.

Trewinnard, Mrs. A. (fl. 1797–1806). See also **Trewinard, Miss A.**
Of London. Exhibited at the R.A., 1797–1806. Possibly identical with, or the mother of Miss A. Trewinard (q.v.), recorded in the R.A. catalogue for 1804. All the other entries are under A. Trewinnard or A. Trevinnard with the exception of 1806, when Mrs. A. Trewinnard is given in the original catalogues. May also have been identical with the Anna Trevingard, recorded by Redgrave, who worked in the second half of the 18th century. Some of Mrs. Trewinnard's work was engraved. A miniature of a lady with a blue cap and white dress, is at the V. & A. M. It is signed in faded ink on the reverse 'No 108 / Mrs. Trewinnard / St Martins Lane'. It has a sky background; the features being shaded with grey. The upper eyelids and between the lips are strongly delineated. Her sitters included Lord Kinnaird.

Triaud, L. E. (fl. 1811–1819)
Of London. Exhibited at the R.A., 1811, 1818 and 1819. The name is variously spelt, L. Triaud, L. E. Triand and L. Triend.

*Tricca, A. 19th century
A pair of miniatures of Allan and Walter Gibbs, as boys, by the above artist were Lot 13 at Sotheby's, 12 December 1966. Possibly identical with Angiolo Tricca (1817–1884) who is recorded by Benezit.

*Trickett, Miss Kate W. (fl. 1907)
Exhibited at the R.A. 1907, from 195 Bristol Road, Edgbaston, Birmingham.

Troby. (fl. 1797)
In the R.A. catalogue, for 1797, No. 957 is catalogued as by Troby, but given to J. Bowring (q.v.) in the index.

Troivaux, Jean Baptiste Désiré. 1788–1860
Born in 1788. Pupil of Aubrey. Painted miniatures and portraits in water-colour. Exhibited at the Paris Salon, 1827–1841. Many of his works are in collections on the Continent. His self-portrait is in the Luxembourg. Long records seeing miniatures by this artist from 1818–1831, signed 'Troivaux'. It is not certain that he ever worked in England. Died in Paris in 1860. The Wallace Collection, London, has a miniature of the King of Rome, signed along the margin 'Troivaux'.

Trossarelli, Gaspare. 1763–1825
Born in 1763. Schidlof records this artist as the son of Francesco Trossarelli and brother of Giovanni Trossarelli (q.v.), with whom he says he studied in Turin, 1778–1789. He is said to have come to London with his brother in 1790, and to have exhibited at the R.A., 1793–1825, the same years that Giovanni exhibited. I can find no evidence that Gaspare exhibited in London. All the exhibits are under J. Trossarelli, i.e. Giovanni (John), except for 1801, when no initial is recorded in the catalogue. Long only records Giovanni Trossarelli and Benezit only records Gaspare and his father. It would appear therefore that there has been some confusion over these artists, and Gaspare may not have been in England. He died in Turin, 11 November 1825.

Trossarelli, Giovanni. See **Trossarelli, J. (John)** and **Trossarelli, Gaspare**

Trossarelli, J. (John) or Giovanni. 18th century
Eldest son of Francesco Trossarelli (1735–1808), a miniaturist of Turin, and brother of Gaspare

Trossarelli (q.v.), with whom he studied at the Academy in Turin. According to Schidlof both brothers came to London in 1790, and both exhibited at the R.A. There seems to have been some confusion over these artists; Benezit records Gaspare Trossarelli as the one who exhibited at the R.A., 1793–1825, and does not record Giovanni. Long records Giovanni (John) as the one who exhibited, and does not record Gaspare. The R.A. catalogues give all the entries to J. Trossarelli, except for 1801, when no initial is given. In 1793 J. Trossarelli exhibited a miniature of H.R.H. Prince William of Gloucester from 14 Charles Street, Grosvenor Square. The name does not occur again before 1801, and there is a further gap until 1811 when J. Trossarelli exhibited from 59 Charlotte Street, Portland Square up to 1825. In 1824 J. Trossarelli exhibited two portraits at the B.I. Long records that Giovanni Trossarelli came to England with a pension from the King of Sardinia where he was Court painter. He taught drawing to the Duchess of Gloucester and painted numerous members of the Royal family, including the Duke of Sussex, the Prince of Hesse-Homburg, and the Duke and Duchess of Gloucester. He also painted the Earl of Pomfret and Viotti (the violinist) in 1818. He painted miniatures, portraits and religious paintings. He was strongly influenced by Cosway (q.v.), and some of his work may occasionally pass as Cosway's. He signed G. Trossarelli pinxit, followed by a date. Examples of his work are at Windsor Castle, and engraved portraits after him are at the B.M. Four miniatures of the Chinnery family by him are reproduced in *The Connoisseur*, XXXI, 1911, pp. 158, 159. (Pl. 373: no. 911.)

*Trotter, Martin. (fl. c. 1828)
Long records seeing miniatures of mythological subjects, on ivory, executed en grisaille c. 1828, by this artist.

*Trowbridge, Miss Lucy P. (fl. 1897)
Exhibited at the R.A. 1897, from 9 Rue Charlet, Paris.

Trumbull, John. 1756–1843
Born in Lebanon, Connecticut, 6 June 1756; son of Jonathan Trumbull, the Governor of Connecticut. Educated at Harvard; fought in the war of Independence, attaining the rank of Colonel, under General Gate in 1776. In 1777 he resigned and went to Boston where he remained until 1779. Sailed for France in 1780. Met Benjamin Franklin who gave him a letter of introduction to Benjamin West, under whom he studied in London. Was imprisoned for treason as a retaliatory measure for the capture and death of Major John André (q.v.) in America, but released through the intercession of Copley (q.v.) and West. Returned to America in June 1781. From 1782–1783 he was contractor for army supplies at New Windsor on the Hudson. Returned to London in 1784, and again studied under West. Exhibited at the R.A. and B.I., etc., 1784–1824. In 1785 he made his first attempt at a composition of a military scene. Visited Paris in 1785, 1786 and 1789, and in the latter year, witnessed the destruction of the Bastille. Was principally in New York, 1789–1794, but visited various cities: Boston and Philadelphia, 1790; Charleston, S.C., Yorktown, Williamsburg, Richmond and Fredericksburg, 1791; Philadelphia, 1792 and Boston, 1793. Returned to London in May 1794 with John Jay, acting as the latter's secretary to the commission for the settlement of claims against Great Britain. Visited Stuttgart, July 1797. Was in London again in 1804 and, after a short stay in New York, was in London, 1808–1816, after which time he spent most of his life in New York, except for 1837–1841,

when he stayed with Dr. Silliman in New Haven whilst writing his biography. Became President of the American Academy of Fine Arts in 1816 and, in 1831, deposited a large collection of his paintings at Yale University, receiving in return an annuity of $1,000. Trumbull died in New York, 10 November 1843. He is best known for his oil portraits and historical subjects, but also painted some oil miniatures on wood, six of which are in the Yale School of Fine Art. A miniature of him by Andrew Robertson (q.v.), on ivory, was painted in 1815 and inscribed by the artist on the reverse, 'John Trumbull / United States Minister in Paris 1797 / President New York Academy of Fine Arts / The Owner of my "Titian" ' (this refers to Robertson's copy of Titian's 'Venus, Mars & Cupid', executed for a Mr. Cox in 1803. The miniature of Trumbull, from the collection of J. B. Robertson, Esq., was exhibited in Edinburgh in 1965. Examples of his work are in the New York Historical Society, and the Metropolitan Museum, New York has a miniature by him.

*Truskett, Miss Irene. (fl. 1793)
Long saw a miniature of a lady, inscribed on the reverse in ink 'Miss Irene Truskett / 1793'. The 'ru' of the name was not clear, and the miniature had, on the face, a spurious signature of O. Humphry's (q.v.) monogram. The miniature was quite well painted.

*Tryon, Miss Diana M. (fl. 1906)
Exhibited at the R.A. 1906, from Elmsloe, Tinwell Road, Stamford, Lincolnshire. Her sitter was General Whichcote.

*Tucker, J. (fl. 1790)
Long records a miniature of a man in a turban, inscribed on the reverse 'J. Tucker / 1790'; it was not of very good quality.

*Tudor, Miss. (fl. 1761–1762)
This artist who apparently worked in Sussex and possibly in Chichester, is recorded in *The Diary of John Barker* by P. C. Yorke, 1931, pp. 147–155:
  5 March 1761 'Miss Tudor commenza mon portrait'
  20 June 1761 'Miss Tudor came Thursday, finished Tom's picture'
  12 February 1762 'Called Miss Tudor, the paintress in miniature—paid her 4 guineas'.

*Tuer, Herbert. d. c. 1680
Born in England. He was the grand-nephew of George Herbert, the poet. Painted portraits in oil and miniatures. Left England in 1650 and went to Holland where, in 1679, he painted in Nimeguen a portrait of Sir Leoline Jenkins (1623–1685), an English diplomat and fellow of Jesus College, Oxford, where the portrait now is. Another portrait of the same sitter by Tuer is in the N.P.G., London. Vertue considered his work to be good. He died in Utrecht? c. 1680.

Turmeau, John (I). b. 1757
Of London; b. 1757. Said to have been the son of Allen Turmeau, an artist of Huguenot descent. Exhibited at the Free Society of Artists as 'Master John Turmeau, aged 15', from Great Earl Street, Seven Dials in 1772. The exhibit was a landscape in human hair. In 1773 a 'Mr Turmeau, junr' exhibited various pictures in hair, and in 1780 'Mr Turmeau' exhibited a miniature portrait of a lady and child from 'corner of Bateman's Buildings, Soho Square'. This artist was a London jeweller who married Eliza Sandry of Cornwall, by whom he had John Turmeau (II) (q.v.).

Turmeau, John (II). 1777–1846
Born in 1777, probably in London; son of John Turmeau (I), a jeweller, and grandson of an artist who was of Huguenot descent. Was educated in Putney and is said to have studied at the R.A. Schools, but the list of entrants, published in the *Walpole Society*, Vol. XXXVIII, does not record his name. Exhibited at the R.A. 1793–1796, from various London addresses. By 1799 was working in Liverpool. Married in 1807, Sarah Wheeler, by whom he had seven or nine children. Exhibited in Liverpool and was one of the founders of the Liverpool Academy in 1810, and was its President, 1812–1814; was Treasurer until 1833 and exhibited there up to 1842. He kept a print shop in Liverpool. Was popular socially; among his friends was John Gibson, R.A. He painted miniatures on ivory and paper and executed portraits in water-colour and oil. His self-portrait is in the Walker Art Gallery, Liverpool and was painted c. 1810–1820. The sitter is wearing glasses and the face shaded with fine cross hatching in brick-red and blue. The modelling of the face is good and he is painted against a grey / brown background. The miniature is inscribed on the reverse in a later hand, 'John Turmeau / painted by himself / presented to the / Liverpool Walker Art Gallery / by the Misses E. & M. Turmeau / after their death'. This self-portrait was probably the one exhibited at the Liverpool Academy in 1822 from 24 Bold Street. It was reproduced, together with a miniature of his daughter, Sarah Susan (1816–1833), by him, in an article by E. R. Dibdin, September 1921, pp. 20–24. He died in Castle Street, Liverpool, 10 September 1846, and was buried at Edge Hill. His eldest son, John Caspar Turmeau (1809–1834), was an architect. A miniature signed 'Turmeau junr / Portrait painter / Sackville St / Piccadilly' on the reverse, and on the front 'I.T. / 1797', was seen by Long who also records seeing some that were reminiscent of the work of Hazelhurst (q.v.), and signed on the reverse 'J. Turmeau / Pinxt / Liverpool / 1799'. A miniature of a Negro youth, signed 'I.T.', was lent by E. G. Paine of New York to the exhibition in Edinburgh in 1965; it is well painted and rather striking. Other examples of his work are in the Ward Usher Museum, Lincoln, and the Walker Art Gallery also contains a set of water-colour profiles of the Roach family; these were exhibited at the Gallery in 1968 in the Exhibition of Early English Drawings and Water Colours. His portrait of Miss Roach is stamped 'Turmeau' under his signature.

Turnbull, Mrs. Walter (Anne Charlotte). See Bartholomew, Mrs. Valentine

Turner, Miss Anne Maria. See Lee, Mrs. R.

Turner, Daniel. (fl. 1782–1801)
Of London; son of John Turner (according to Schidlof). Exhibited miniatures and landscapes at the Free Society of Artists from 'Snow Hill', 1782–1783. The exhibits also included a shipping scene. Exhibited at the R.A., 1796–1801, from 24 Mill-bank Street, Westminster. None of these latter exhibits were miniatures.

Turner, Miss Elizabeth. (fl. 1841)
Of London. Exhibited at the R.A. 1841, from 15 Crown Row, Walworth Road, Surrey.

*Turner, Florence, E. (Mrs. T. C.). (fl. 1905–1909)
Exhibited at the R.A. 1905–1909, from Regent House, Hull.

Turner, J. (fl. 1822)
Of Hampstead. Exhibited at the R.A., 1822.

Turner, James. (fl. 1745–1790–1806?)
An Irishman who, as far as is known, only worked in England from c. 1745. Exhibited at the Society of Artists, 1761–1783, and was a Director in 1773. He exhibited at the Free Society of Artists in 1762 from various London addresses. One of his miniatures was for a ring, and another was of Mrs. Siddons from memory. He was working up to 1790. Some of his works were engraved. According to Pasquin, he invented a colour called the 'patent yellow'. Th. B. says he was alive in 1806.

Turner, Joseph Mallord William, R.A. 1775–1851
Well-known landscape painter. Exhibited at the R.A. and B.I., etc., 1790–1850. Not known as a miniaturist except by a miniature self-portrait, on paper, executed in 1792, which is in the N.P.G. He entered the R.A. Schools, 11 December 1789. Executed landscapes and historical paintings. In the Fowler sale, 6 May 1901, ten works by this artist were sold, including 'the Plains of Waterloo', $3\frac{1}{4} \times 5\frac{1}{4}$ in., which fetched 180 guineas.

Turner, P. (fl. 1781–1785)
Of West Ham, London. Exhibited at the R.A., 1781–1785.

*Turrell, Charles James. 1846–1932
Born in London, 14 January 1846. Said to have studied under a Mr. Sargeant (q.v.). Exhibited at the R.A. and S.M., 1873–1932, from various London addresses, including 27a Old Bond Street, 6 Finchley Road and the Royal Societies Club, St. James's Street. Turrell had a distinguished clientele which included Queen Victoria, Queen Alexandra, Princess Mary, the Queen of Norway and many others. Visited the U.S.A. in 1867 and painted members of many important families there, including those of J. Pierpont Morgan, Vanderbilt and Barber. Married c. 1868. Returned to London c. 1869, but frequently spent his winters in America. Died in White Plains, New York, 13 April 1932. Three works by this artist are in the collection of the Duke of Portland: Winifred, Duchess of Portland, signed 'C.T. 1890', Lady Ottoline Violet Cavendish-Bentinck (sister of William Arthur, 6th Duke of Portland, K.G.), signed 'C.T. 1890', and Lieut. General Arthur Cavendish-Bentinck (1819–1877). This last miniature is not signed, but an inscription on the case gives the sitter's age as 53.

Turrell, E. (fl. 1801)
Long records seeing an oval, enamel, half-length portrait of a man drawn on a white ground in two tones in imitation of a line-engraving and signed neatly on the reverse, 'E. TURRELL / 1801'.

*Turrell, H. C. 20th century
Of Upper Lye Lane, Bricket Wood, Herts. This artist and miniaturist is recorded in *The Evening News*, 13 January 1961, as having left £2,109.

*Turrell, Herbert. (fl. 1898–1911)
Exhibited at the R.A. 1898–1911, from addresses in Chelsea, Chesham and New Barnet. Probably the brother of Charles Turrell (q.v.) from whose address he exhibited in 1900.

Tuvin, John. (fl. 1776–1792)
Of London. Exhibited at the Society of Artists, 1776, and at the R.A., 1778–1792. Tuvin was a reasonably good artist whose work is slightly reminiscent of that of L. Sullivan (q.v.). A miniature said to be of Sir John Fenn, signed 'J. Tuvin', and dated '1776', is in the V. & A. M. A miniature of an unknown lady, signed on the front 'Tuvin pt 1776', is in my collection.

Twining, Miss (Emily?). (fl. 1824–1826)

Of 34 Norfolk Street, Strand; daughter of Richard Twining and his wife, Mary, and sister of Miss Elizabeth Twining (q.v.), whose address she shared. As there were two other sisters, who were not recorded as artists, it is probable that the above artist was Emily. Miss Twining received medals from the Society of Arts, 1824, for a miniature portrait (copy), and an historical subject in water-colour (copy) and, in 1826, for an original miniature portrait.

Twining, Miss Elizabeth. 1805–1889

Was born in 1805; daughter of Richard Twining (1749–1824), Director of the East India Company and head of the famous tea business in the Strand. Lived at 34 Norfolk Street, Strand. In 1824 was awarded a silver palette by the Society of Arts for a miniature portrait (copy), and a large silver medal for a flower composition. Exhibited at the R.A., 1831 and 1835. Her sister, Emily, also an artist, lived at the same address. They had two other sisters. Elizabeth painted book illustrations, pictures of flowers and miniatures; was a philanthropist and writer of religious books, etc. She died in 1889. One of the Miss Twinings was painted by J. Smart (q.v.) in 1801. This miniature is illustrated in *John Smart, the Man and His Miniatures* by Foskett, Pl. XXI, No. 76.

*Twyman, Miss Miriam. (fl. 1891–1892)

Of London. Exhibited at the R.A., 1891–1892.

*Tydes, A. (fl. *c.* 1830)

Two miniatures of children *c.* 1830 by this artist, in a rectangular frame, were Lot 60 at a sale at Sotheby's, 15 June 1933. The signature was scratched 'A. Tydes'. The miniatures were good. Schidlof mentions two miniatures of children by this artist sold in Lucerne in September 1933 which may have been the same portraits.

Tyson, The Rev. Michael. 1740–1780

Born in Stamford, Lincs. 19 November 1740; son of Michael Tyson, Dean of Stamford, and Archdeacon of Huntingdon, by his first wife, Miss Curtis of Woolsthorpe, Lincolnshire. Studied at Corpus Christi College, Cambridge from 1759. Became a member of the Society of Antiquaries in 1768, and of the Royal Society, 1779. Was ordained by Bishop Green in 1770. Tyson was an antiquary, a keen botanist, amateur draughtsman, etcher and miniature painter. He married on 4 July 1778, Margaret Wale of Shelford, Cambs. Became Rector of Lambourne, nr. Ongar, Essex where he died 4 May 1780 from a violent fever, and was buried in the church on 10 May. Tyson could speak Italian, French and Spanish, and his library, which was rich in rare works in these languages, was sold by Leigh and Sotheby in 1781.

U

*Ubsdell, Dan. (fl. 1841–1846)

Exhibited at the R.A. in 1846, from 26 Lombard Street, Portsmouth. His sitter was Lady Pakenham. Was probably related to R. H. C. Ubsdell (q.v.) who was also a miniaturist in Portsmouth. Long noted seeing a miniature which was signed on the front, 'Dan Ubsdell, B.S.A.', and inscribed on the reverse, 'of 26 Lombard St, Portsmouth, Jan 16.

1843'. Two miniatures by him were in the O'Brien collection, one of which was signed and dated '1841'.

*Ubsdell, R.H.C. (fl. *c.* 1809–1849)

Exhibited at the R.A. etc., 1843–1849, from Portsmouth. Executed miniatures and at least one subject drawing. His sitters included Lady Portman and the Earl of Liverpool. He exhibited a self-portrait in 1847. Possibly related to Dan. Ubsdell (q.v.) who also exhibited from Portsmouth. Was probably the R. H. C. Ubsdell who lent four family miniatures to the exhibition at the South Kensington Museum, 1865. They were said to be painted *c.* 1809.

*Underhill, Frederick Thomas. (fl. 1868–1896)

Of London. Exhibited at the R.A. etc., 1868–1896, from 23 Fernshaw Road. His sitters included Andrew W. Levey, Esq.

*Underwood, Miss Annie. b. 1876

Of East Grinstead; born 12 January 1876. Exhibited at the R.A., 1907–1914. Her sitters included Miss de la Hey. Benezit records the artist's name as Ann.

*Underwood, Mrs. C. J. (fl. 1909)

Exhibited at the R.A. 1909, from Boyne Road, Blackheath.

Unwin, R. (fl. 1785–1812)

Of London. Exhibited at the R.A., 1785–1812. Painted enamel portrait miniatures, landscapes and genre subjects. Specialised in enamelling watches and jewellery.

Unwin, Thomas. (fl. 1798–1799)

Of London. Exhibited at the R.A., 1799. Thomas Unwin's name is in the C.M. of the R.A. Schools, 14 December 1798, but not in the register.

*Upjohn, Aaron. d. 1800

The above artist is mentioned by Sir W. Foster in the *Walpole Society*, Vol. XIX, p. 74. Little is known about him, except that he went to India *c.* 1786 as a bassoon player in the band of the *Rodney*. He claimed to be a surveyor and engraver, having been self-taught, but was financially unsuccessful and incurred debts. His name is recorded in the MS lists of residents for 1794 and 1795 as a tradesman 'living at Sealadah', and having been for eight years in Bengal. *The Calcutta Chronicle*, 11 January 1787, contains an advertisement by Upjohn that he 'continues to take likenesses in profile at rs 16 each in gold frames, or rs 12, with a neat border'. These portraits may have been silhouettes or miniatures. In 1788 he announced his intention of returning to Europe and begged all his debtors to pay up by the beginning of November. He evidently changed his mind, and took up printing, and later became a surveyor and engraver. Published in 1794 a map of Calcutta and its environs, engraved by himself from a survey he had taken in the two preceding years. According to one account, he was hiding from his creditors at a friend's house, when he died in 1800, and was buried in Calcutta on 22 June 1800.

Upton, Edward. b. *c.* 1808

Of London. Entered the R.A. Schools, 8 December 1830, aged 22. Was awarded a premium by the Society of Arts in 1831. Exhibited at the R.A. and S.B.A. (of which he was a member), 1838–1874. Was patronised by royal and titled persons, and by W. E. Frost, R.A., and W. P. Frith, R.A. He lent a miniature by himself of Lady

Elizabeth St. Aubyn to the exhibition at the South Kensington Museum, 1865.

*Usher, Miss Elsie F. (fl. 1910–1914)

Born in Worcester. Lived in London where she trained at the Slade School of Art under Professor Brown. Exhibited at the R.A. and at the Liverpool Autumn Exhibition, 1910–1914. According to a letter by her, preserved in the Walker Art Gallery, she painted in a variety of styles, having had little training. The Gallery contains a miniature by her of a young boy called Rex, signed on the front 'E. Usher', and with 'Rex' written horizontally in capital letters. On the reverse of the miniature is a label giving her address as 'The Homestead, Lansdowne, Worcester'.

Utchis(s)on. (fl. 1791)

Of London. Exhibited at the R.A., 1791. His name is spelt variously in the catalogue, Utchison and Utchisson. His address was given as 29 Well Street.

*Uvedale, Samuel. d. *c.* 1866

Of Cork, where he was living in George Street *c.* 1828. Moved to London and taught at South Kensington. Exhibited at the B.I. and S.B.A., 1845–1848. Portraits and flower pieces by him were exhibited at Cork, 1852. Is mentioned in *The Industrial Movement in Ireland*, 1853, p. 332, by J. F. Maguire. Met his death by drowning *c.* 1866. Some of his works were probably miniatures.

Uwins, Thomas, R.A. 1782–1857

Born in Pentonville, London, 24 February 1782; son of Thomas Uwins, a clerk in the Bank of England. T. Uwins, R.A., was trained as an engraver. He entered the R.A. Schools, 31 December 1798, aged 17. Exhibited at the R.A., B.I. and S.B.A., 1804–1857. Was a member of the O.W.C.S.; A.R.A., 1833 and R.A., 1838. Was Librarian of the R.A., 1844, Surveyor of the Royal Pictures, 1845 and Keeper of the National Gallery, 1847. He married in 1851. Is best known for his book illustrations and figure subjects in oil and water-colour. He also executed portraits in water-colour, chalk and miniatures. Travelled to France in 1817; was in Scotland, 1820–1822, and studied in Italy, 1824–1831. He died at Staines, 26 August 1857. Portraits by him, in water-colour and pencil, are in the V. & A. M. and the N.P.G.

V

V. (fl. *c.* 1778)

Lot 95 at Christie's, 28 July 1926, included a miniature of an officer, signed with a cursive V, and Lot 86 at Sotheby's, 9 May 1928, was a miniature of a lady, *c.* 1778, signed 'V'. Long noted that the background and the shading of the face were grey, and the head was too large for the body. (Pl. 376: no. 917.)

*V., B. (fl. *c.* 1890)

A miniature in my collection of an unknown lady, is signed on the front 'VB' in monogram, *c.* 1890. The miniature is well painted and shows character. The features are executed with a fine brush stroke, the draughtsmanship is good and the colouring pleasing.

V., C. 18th century. See also **Vinkeles, Mlle. Cecilia**

Long records seeing two late 18th century circular miniature views of Hale Park, about thirty miles from Bath. They were signed 'C.V.', and may possibly have been the work of a Dutch artist, Cecilia Vinkeles (q.v.), who is said to have painted miniature portraits and other miniatures, and who may conceivably have visited Bath. She was the daughter of the painter Regnier Vinkeles.

Vachot, Mlle. See Foulon, Mme. Lucille

Valck, H. de. See Valk, H. de

Valentine, William. 1798–1849

Born in Whitehaven, England, 1798. Emigrated to Halifax, N.S., where he was a house decorator and drawing master; also painted oil portraits and a few miniatures. Came to London in 1836, but returned to Halifax in 1837. His self-portrait is illustrated by H. Piers in *Artists of Nova Scotia, N.S. Historical Society*, Vol. XVIII, pp. 101 and 165. He died in Halifax, 26 December 1849.

Valk, H. de. (fl. c. 1691–1709)

A Dutch portrait painter who flourished c. 1691, and about whom little is known; he may have worked in England and have been identical with Hendrick de Valck who, in 1693, was a member of the Haarlem guild of painters. The H. G. Bohn Collection (1884 catalogue, p. 254, No. 145; sold at Christie's, March 1885), contained a portrait on copper of Sir Christopher Wren in a blue coat and white cravat, with a powdered wig, signed 'H. de Valk, 1709'. Two portraits by de Valk, representing General Baron Hans Willem van Aylva and his wife, Frouck van Aylva, are in the Rijksmuseum, Amsterdam.

Valsecchi, Cavaliere Pietro Bagatti. 1802–1864

Born in Milan, 13 April 1802. Worked in London and probably in Venice. Exhibited miniatures on enamel at the R.A., 1837, after Signor Palagi of Turin, as well as miniatures of Signor Palagi and Bagatti Valsecchi (possibly a self-portrait), and a Magdalen on enamel after Signor Hayez of Venice. Died in Milan, 27 November 1864.

*Vanacker, Venacker or **van Acker, Johannes Baptista. See Acker, J. B. van**

*Van Assen, Benedictus Antonio. See Assen, Benedictus Antonio van

*Van Der Weyde, Henry. See Weyde, Henry van de

*Van Raalte, Mrs. Charles. (fl. 1902)

Was a member of the Society of Miniaturists in 1902.

Varaker. (fl. 1819)

A miniature of Lady Charlotte Cavendish-Bentinck, later Viscountess Ossington (1806–1889), on ivory, signed 'Varaker', and painted in '1819', is in the collection of the Duke of Portland at Welbeck Abbey. (Pl. 376: no. 919.)

*Varley, Fleetwood. b. 1875. d. after 1935

Long recorded the dates of the above artist and that he executed enamels and landscapes. I have

been unable to discover any further information regarding him, but he was presumably related to a number of other artists of this name recorded in the *D.N.B.*

Vaslet, Lewis. d. 1808

Little is known about this artist who is often called 'Vaslet of Bath'. He may possibly have been of French or Huguenot descent, and related to Lewis Vaslet, master of Fulham School, who was a Frenchman and died 12 June 1731. Vaslet exhibited at the R.A., 1770 and 1771, from London, and 1775 and 1782 from Bath. He was evidently peripatetic and practised in various places including York c. 1770, 1771 and 1778, Oxford, 1780, 1790 and 1796, Bath at intervals from 1775–1808, Ramsgate? 1792 and Norwich, 1793. He painted portraits in crayons and oil, miniatures, landscapes in oil, as well as pictures of game, flowers, fruit and animals. He was at 43 Walcot Street, Bath on 12 July 1787 and had several other addresses in that city. Vaslet is said to have married a lady of means. He died at Bath, November 1808. A miniature said to represent Mrs. Siddons, and, according to an old inscription on the reverse, to have been painted by him, was sold at Sotheby's, 28 July 1935. Some pastels by him are at Merton College, Oxford and the B.M. has some engraved portraits after his work.

Vassar, Miss L. (fl. 1823–1829)

Exhibited a miniature of H. Strachan, Esq., at the R.A. etc., 1823–1829, from 17 Great Marlborough Street. Probably identical with Miss L. C. Vassar (q.v.).

Vassar, Miss L. C. (fl. 1820)

Of Rathbone Place, London. Was awarded, in 1820, a large silver medal for a miniature 'Head of Christ', by the Society of Arts. The artist was possibly identical with Miss L. Vassar (q.v.) of 17 Great Marlborough Street, London who exhibited at the R.A., in 1823.

Vaughan, Edward. 1746 – c. 1814

Of London. Exhibited at the Society of Artists and the Free Society of Artists, 1772–1783, and at the R.A., 1778–1814. His son may have been the Thomas Vaughan who married May Elizabeth Primrose at St. Mary-le-Bone, 21 February 1808, in the presence of Edward Vaughan who was also an artist. T. Vaughan studied in Edinburgh and at the R.A. Schools, 21 June 1800, when his age was noted as '24 11th last Mar.', making his date of birth 1776. A miniature of a gentleman, signed 'EV / 1794', is at the V. & A. M., and is probably by E. Vaughan. Another one, signed 'E.V.' and dated '1793', was lot 63 at Christie's, 29 July 1925.

*Vaughan, Miss Edith M. See Charlton, Mrs. John

Venacker. See Acker, J. B. van

Verelst, Miss Maria. 1680–1744

Born in 1680; daughter of Herman Verelst, a Flemish artist. Her place of birth seems to be uncertain and was either Antwerp (according to Mrs. E. F. Ellet, *Women Artists*) or Vienna (according to Benezit). Was taken to London by her father at the age of three. Said to have been taught by her father and was also a pupil of her uncle, Simon Verelst (q.v.). Painted small and large oil portraits and figure subjects. Was musical and spoke Latin, German and Italian fluently. The Museum at Nuremburg has a portrait by her of a young man. Died in London, 1744. For further information see Mrs. E. F. Ellet, *Women Artists*, 1859.

*Verelst or **Varelst, Simon Peter.** 1644–1721

Baptised at the Hague, 21 September 1644. Painted portraits, flowers and fruit. Came to London during the reign of Charles II and was a successful artist. He is not recorded as a miniaturist, but Long was told of a small oil portrait, signed 'Simon Verelst', which was presumably by him. He taught his niece, Maria Verelst (q.v.), who had accompanied her father, H. Verelst, to England. Died in London, 1721.

Verrio, Antonio. 1634–1707

There is no proof that this famous painter of ceilings was a miniaturist, but a portrait in oil of Queen Anne, said to have been painted in 1703, was lent to the exhibition at the South Kensington Museum in 1865, when it was catalogued as by Verrio.

Vertue, George. 1684–1756

Born in London, 1684, of parents who were 'more honest than opulent'. Engraver and antiquary. Best known for his collection of material for a history of the fine arts in England which was compiled by Horace Walpole after his death, and incorporated in *Anecdotes of Painting*. Was patronised by Edward Harley, 2nd Earl of Oxford, for whom he made drawings, engravings and bookplates, etc. Accompanied the Earl on travels through many parts of England and wrote descriptive accounts which were embellished with pen and ink sketches. Manuscripts by him are in the B.M., and at Welbeck Abbey. Miniatures by him are rare; two are in the collection of the Duke of Portland, including a self-portrait, signed 'G.V.' (monogram), '1729', in a gold case, engraved on the reverse 'Geo: Vertue Lond: f: 1730', and probably given to Lord or Lady Oxford by Vertue; and one of the Hon. Edward Hay (1722–1779), on paper, signed 'G.V.' (monogram), 'f. 1738'. In the same collection is an engraving by him of a portrait of Lady Margaret Harley, afterwards Duchess of Portland, after a marble bust executed in 1723 by J. M. Rysbrack. A miniature by Vertue of Maurice Johnson was engraved by Francis Holl in 1851. A plumbago miniature, said to represent William Shakespeare, 1754, has been attributed to Vertue. He died 24 July 1756 and was buried in the cloisters of Westminster Abbey.

*Vessey, Elizabeth Margaret. 1801 ?–1881

An amateur artist, recorded by Long, who painted miniature copies of pictures and original water-colour portraits.

Vestier, Antoine. 1740–1824

Born in Avallon, 28 April 1740. He is said to have worked for some years in Holland and England. Went to Paris in 1760 and became a pupil of the enamellist, Antoine Révérend, whose daughter, Marie Anne, he married, 30 April 1764. Studied at the Académie Royale of which he became an Associate in 1785 and a full member in 1786. Also studied under J. B. Pierre. Was in London in 1776. Exhibited at the Salon de la Correspondance in 1782, and at the Salon du Louvre, 1785–1806. Painted miniatures in water-colour and enamel and was an outstanding artist who also painted portraits in oil which closely resembled the colouring of his works in miniature. His miniatures have an affinity to the works of P. A. Hall. He died in Paris on 24 December 1824. He signed Vestier, Vestier pinxit 1783, Vestier VIème, Vestier fec. 1783, etc. A number of his works are in the Louvre. The Carnavalet Museum, Paris contains his self-portrait and that of his son, Nicholas.

Vigne, Henry George. 1765–1787

Of London. Probably the Henry Vigne who entered the R.A. Schools, 8 November 1782, aged 17 'Jan 15 last'; and probably the son of a watchmaker, as his address was 'at Mr Vigne's, Watchmaker, 2 Charing Cross'. The family may have been connected with a family of Dublin jewellers of this name. Chinnery (q.v.) married the daughter of a Dublin jeweller named Vigne. H. G. Vigne exhibited at the R.A., 1785 and 1787. His obituary was recorded in *The World*, 24 January 1788.

Villefavard, See **Favard, Ville**

Villiers-Hüet, J.F.M. See **Hüet-Villiers, J.F.M.**

*****Vincent, Miss Alice W.** (fl. 1906)

Of London. Exhibited at the R.A. 1906, from 10 Pembridge Crescent.

*****Vincent, Mrs. Charlotte J.** (fl. 1908)

Exhibited at the R.A. 1908, from Montrose, Heatherley Road, Camberley, Surrey. Her sitters included Doris, daughter of Col. A. C. F. Vincent, C.M.G.

Vinkeles, Mlle. Cecilia. 19th century. See also **V., C.**

Daughter of the painter Reinier Vinkeles and sister of Mlle Elisabeth Vinkeles. May possibly have been the artist whose work was seen by Long, and who signed C.V. (q.v.).

Violet, Miss Maria (Mrs. James Brook Pulham). 1794–1868

Born in London, 1794; daughter of Pierre Violet (q.v.). Lived in London. Exhibited at the R.A., 1808–1811. Was awarded, in 1811–1812, a silver palette for a miniature drawing, a copy, by the Society of Arts. Married James Brook Pulham, a ship's captain in the East India Service (died 13 November 1860, aged 69). Her sister Cecilia married L. Ferrière (q.v.). Maria died 4 November 1868, aged 74, and was buried in St. John's Churchyard, Woodbridge, Suffolk. A drawing of her as a little girl is reproduced in the *Gazette des Beaux Arts*.

Violet, Pierre Noël. 1749–1819

Born in France, 1749. Married Marguerite Becret in, or before, 1771, by whom he had two daughters, Miss Maria Violet (q.v.) and Miss Cecilia Violet (1797–1880), who became the wife of Louis Ferrière (q.v.) in 1815. In 1782 P. N. Violet became a member of the Académie des Arts de Lille. Worked in Paris where he became intimate with a literary group, and exhibited at the Salon de la Correspondance in 1785 and 1787. Published in 1788 a *Traité Élémentaire sur l'Art de Peindre en Miniature*, to which he added a supplement in 1789. Was a member of the revolutionary committee in Paris, but resigned and came to London where he settled. Was befriended by Bartolozzi (q.v.). Exhibited at the R.A., and Society of Artists, etc., 1790–1819. Painted miniatures on paper and on ivory, executed drawings of domestic and fancy subjects and etchings. He had been miniature painter to Louis XVI and his miniatures show the influence of the French school, and are not always of equal merit. He died suddenly at his residence, 1 Charlotte Street, London, 9 December 1819, and was buried at Old St. Pancras Church. He was survived by his wife who died in 1841. He signed in various ways – on the front along the edge P. Violet, and inscribed on the reverse in a florid hand, P. Violet p^t / Londre 1800, Violet 1782 and By P. VIOLET; this latter signature is sometimes seen in capitals on the front. The V. & A. M., has a miniature of a lady, possibly his wife, painted on

card and one of Capt. William Bailey, signed on the reverse, 'P. Violet-p^t / London 1805'. Other examples of his work are in the B.M., the Walker Art Gallery, Liverpool and the Louvre. A circular miniature of an unknown man, signed on the front, 'P. Violet', is in the collection of R. Bayne Powell, Esq.

Vispré, François Xavier (or Saverino). b. *c.* 1730. d. after 1794

Born in Besançon *c.* 1730; younger brother of Victor Vispré (q.v.). Worked in Paris, 1750 and in 1756 published a *Méthode pour devenir peintre en trois heures*. In 1760 he came to London and exhibited at the Society of Artists, 1760–1783. Elected F.S.A., 1771. Went to Dublin, with his brother Victor, in 1776 and exhibited there in 1777. Evidently returned to London by 1780 and exhibited at the R.A., 1788 and 1789. According to a note recorded by Long, he was in Bristol, 29 May 1756, and living in Small Street, and was also in Bristol, 1775. In *c.* 1794 Long records that he was working in Cambridge and charging 3–6 guineas at 'Mr Clarke's, Ironmongers, Bridge St, Cambridge'. The date of his death is not known. He is said to have been a member of the Dublin Society of Antiquaries. Vispré painted miniatures, portraits in crayon and oil, as well as figure subjects, some mezzotints after Liotard (q.v.), and engravings in imitation of drawings; he also executed paintings on glass. Mezzotint portraits of him and of his wife Mary, as well as one of the Chevalier d'Eon, are in the B.M. A miniature of a young girl by him is in the V. & A. M.

Vispré, Victor. (fl. 1763–1780)

Born probably in Besançon; brother of F. X. Vispré (q.v.). Was in London by 1763, having worked for a time in the Hague. Exhibited at the Society of Artists and the Free Society of Artists, 1763–1778, and at the R.A., 1770–1772. Was elected a fellow of the Society of Artists in 1778. In *c.* 1764 he scraped three portraits in mezzotint. Accompanied his brother to Ireland in 1776 and in 1777 exhibited in Dublin, where he remained until 1780. His wife, née Elizabeth Fisher, died in Dublin, 17 March 1780, aged 29, and was buried in the French burial ground in Merrion Row. He and his brother left Ireland in 1780 and, as far as is known, returned to London. The date of his death is not known. He painted fruit pieces in oil on glass, and is said to have painted miniatures.

*****Vivian, Mrs. Comley (Lizzie) (Miss Lizzie Boly-Farquhar).** (fl. 1867–1914)

Of London. Née Lizzie Boly Farquhar. Pupil of her uncle, F. Cruickshank (q.v.). Exhibited at the R.A., 1867–1871, under her maiden name, and from 1886–1914 under her married name. Was the wife of Comley Vivian, a portrait painter who also exhibited at the R.A., 1874–1892; his exhibit in 1877 was of 'Mrs Vivian'. This may have been his wife.

Voyez, John. *c.* 1735–*c.* 1800

The above artist was a Frenchman who worked in England and cut cameos, etc. Was trained as a jeweller and worked in London for Roundell. Worked at the artificial stone manufactory, 1767. Exhibited at the Society of Artists and the Free Society, 1767–1791, from addresses in London and Staffordshire. Worked at the Wedgwood factory, 1768, quarrelled with Wedgwood and was imprisoned in Stafford Gaol, 1769. On his release, worked for Humphrey Palmer. Married as his second wife, in 1770, Sarah Woodhouse, by whom he had a daughter, Sophia Charlotte (born 1774). In 1772 was described as 'a Carver and Manufacturer of Compositions at Cowbridge, near Newcastle,

Staffordshire'. Thought to have modelled for Ralph Wood of Burslem, and to have modelled the 'Fair Hebe Jug', 1788. Two enamel miniatures, in the manner of Zincke (q.v.), and stated to be by this artist, are reproduced in *The Connoisseur*, Vol. IX, 1904, p. 87. A work of *c.* 1766 is described as 'very early', and the costumes of the sitters are earlier still. If these works were by Voyez, they were probably copies. The B.M. has a miniature supposedly by him.

Vully, Miss Louisa Mary. (fl. 1823–1829)

An amateur artist of 59 Stafford Place, Pimlico, London. Was awarded, in 1823, the silver Isis medal from the Society of Arts for drawing a head and, in 1829, a large silver medal for a miniature portrait.

W

W. (fl. 1755–1779). See also **Wooton, John**

Long recorded seeing a miniature of a gentleman, signed 'W.79' (1779), which was not very good, and was painted in grey tones with long brush strokes. A miniature, signed and dated 'W.1755', was Lot 53 at Sotheby's, 9 February 1961. By family tradition this latter miniature was painted by Mr. John Wooton, who does not appear to have been recorded, and may have been an accomplished amateur.

*****W., A.** 19th century

Long records seeing, in 1933, an early 19th century copy of an earlier miniature, signed 'AW' (monogram).

*****W., B.** (fl. *c.* 1767). See also **West, Benjamin**

Long recorded seeing a good miniature of a gentleman, *c.* 1767, signed 'B.W.'. He suggested it might possibly be by Benjamin West (q.v.).

W., D. (fl. 1809)

An artist who signed 'D.W' exhibited at the R.A., in 1809.

W., H.P. 17th century. See also **Wright, H. Pooley**

A miniature of a lady, said to be signed with a monogram, and dated '1646', is reproduced in Williamson's *H.P.M.*, Vol. I, Pl. XXVI, and it has been suggested that this may have been the work of H. Pooley Wright who is supposed to have been a connection of Michael Wright. A miniature of a man in Spanish costume, signed and dated 1645', was seen at the V. & A. M. I also know of a miniature of Princess Mary, daughter of Charles I, signed ' $\begin{smallmatrix} HP \\ W \\ 1646 \end{smallmatrix}$ '; this example is painted in oil.

*****W., J.** or **W., I.** (fl. *c.* 1720–1730)

Long recorded seeing a miniature painted in water-colour of a man in armour *c.* 1720–30, signed in gold with a monogram 'J.W.' or 'I.W.' on a blue background.

W., J.M. See **Wright, John Michael**

*****W., P.** See **Powlet, W.** and **P., W.**

*W., S. (fl. 1761)

I saw, in 1962, a miniature of a young girl with flowing hair and a long curl over one shoulder, signed ' S W '; two others, signed in monogram, are 1761 in the collection of the Countess of Seafield.

*Waddilove, Miss Agnes M. (fl. 1900–1914)

Exhibited at the R.A. and S.M., 1900–1914, from Dormans, Parkstone, Dorset. Her sitters included Eveleen M. Waddilove.

Wade, Robert. (fl. c. 1780–1785)

Worked in Dublin c. 1780–1785. Exhibited there in 1780. He moved in 1780 from Exchequer Street to 61 Great George's Street. Advertised that he took 'likenesses in miniature at a guinea each'. Was living in Parliament Street, 1782–1785 and, afterwards, at 7 Essex Bridge.

Wade, W. R. (fl. 1824–1828)

Of London. Exhibited at the R.A. etc., 1824–1828, from 24 Penton Place, Pentonville.

Wageman, P. (fl. 1816)

The above artist is recorded as a miniaturist in 1816 in the *Annals of the Fine Arts* Vol. I, when his address is given as 214 Strand, from which address he exhibited at the R.A. in the same year. The portraits exhibited were probably miniatures. Was possibly identical with, or related to, T. C. Wageman (q.v.). According to Long, P. Wageman was at 88 Strand in 1817, from which address T. C. Wageman also exhibited.

Wageman, Thomas Charles. 1787–1863. See also **Wageman, P.**

Born in 1787. He may have been identical with, or related to, P. Wageman (q.v.) who is recorded as exhibiting at the R.A. in 1816. T. C. Wageman exhibited at the R.A., B.I. and N.W.C.S., etc., 1817–1857. Was a member of the N.W.C.S., 1831–1832, and was portrait painter to the King of Holland. Painted a few miniatures, but is best known for his portraits in pencil and water-colour, many of which were engraved; also painted pictures of animals and fruit. Many of his sitters were members of the theatrical profession. He died 20 June 1863. Examples of his work are in the V. & A. M., and the B.M. has drawings by him and engraved portraits after his work.

Wagner, Cecilia. (fl. 1814)

Of London. Exhibited at the R.A., 1814, 'a portrait of a young gentleman', from Westmoreland Place.

*Wainwright, Miss Beatrice. (fl. 1909–1913)

Of London. Exhibited at the R.A., 1909 and 1913. Her sitters included Gerald, son of Lord Hugh Grosvener.

Wainwright or **Wainewright, Thomas Francis.** (fl. 1832–1862). See also **Wainwright, W. F.**

Of London. Undoubtedly related to W. F. Wainwright (q.v.) and Mary E. Wainwright, all of whom exhibited from the same addresses in varying years. T. F. Wainwright exhibited at the R.A. and B.I., etc., 1832–1862. According to Long, some of his exhibits may have been miniatures, but having examined the catalogue entries, there is no evidence that this is so; all his exhibits were landscapes or studies from nature. W. F. Wainwright, with whom he must have been confused, was a miniaturist.

*Wainwright, W. F. (fl. 1835–1850). See also **Wainwright, T. F.**

Undoubtedly related to T. F. Wainwright (q.v.) and Mary E. Wainwright, all of whom shared various London addresses. Exhibited at the R.A., 1835–1850. It seems likely that W. F. Wainwright has been confused with T. F. Wainwright who, as far as I can ascertain, never painted miniatures. W. F. Wainwright executed sketches and miniatures. His addresses included 14 Princes Street, Westminster, 74 Albany Street and 24 St. James's Street. His sitters included Viscount Duncannon and the Marquess and Marchioness of Worcester. He exhibited a self-portrait at the R.A. in 1835. A miniature of a lady in a black evening dress, signed 'F.W.', and painted c. 1840, is reproduced by O'Brien, Pl. 80, Fig. 1.

Waite, William. (fl. 1800–1830?)

Of London. Exhibited at the R.A., 1800–1804, and was probably identical with W. Waite of Abingdon who exhibited a portrait of Colonel Wemyss at the R.A. in 1821, and who was still living in Abingdon in 1830. W. Waite published, in 1817, at Abingdon, an engraving of a portrait by himself of G. P. Bidder. Long records seeing some good miniatures by Waite. A miniature of an unknown man, signed 'Waite 1819', is in the V. & A. M. (Pl. 379: no. 926.)

Wale, Samuel, R.A. d. 1786

Of London. Exhibited at the R.A. and Society of Artists, 1760–1778. Was Professor of Perspective to the R.A., of which he was a Founder Member. Best known for his historical paintings in oil and water-colour, and stained drawings, but also executed miniatures. Long records the fact that he was in Cambridge, 6 October 1759, painting miniatures for which he charged 2–4 guineas. At the sale of the Strawberry Hill Collection, Lot 66 is catalogued as 'a beautiful miniature of Anne Boleyn, by Wale, from a portrait by Hoskins'. He died 6 February 1786.

Walker. (fl. 1770)

Of London. Exhibited a miniature at the Free Society of Artists, 1770, from 'Mr Walker, 2 Ludgate Hill'. Possibly identical with James Walker who exhibited pictures at the Society of Artists, 1783 from 49 Upper Marylebone Street, nr. Titchfield Street. The Council Minutes of the R.A. Schools, 11 October 1782, record a Walker (no initial given) who may have been identical with the above artist.

*Walker, Mrs. Benjamin. See Collyer, Miss Kate Winifred

Walker, Mrs. Elizabeth. See Walker, Mrs. William

Walker, George. (fl. 1792–1815)

An amateur artist. Exhibited at the R.A., 1792–1815, as an Honorary Exhibitor. Painted portraits, subject pictures, landscapes and miniatures.

*Walker, Miss Kate I. L. (fl. 1905)

Exhibited at the R.A. 1905, from 39 Rugby Road, Belfast, Ireland.

*Walker, Miss Marcella. (fl. 1872–1912)

Exhibited at the R.A. etc., 1872–1912, from addresses in Mill Hill and Highgate. Executed miniatures and subjects in water-colour.

Walker, Miss Marion. (fl. 1854–1877)

Of London. Exhibited at the R.A., 1854–1877. Was presumably the daughter of Mrs. William Walker (q.v.) from whose address she exhibited.

*Walker, Miss Mary D. (fl. 1907–1914)

Exhibited at the R.A. 1907 and 1914, from 4 Grosvener Terrace, York. Her sitters included The Very Rev. the Dean of York and Dorothy, daughter of the late J. S. Walker, Esq.

Walker, Robert. d. 1658?

This famous English portrait painter cannot as far as is known be ranked as a miniaturist, but an oil portrait of Thomas Wentworth, Earl of Strafford (1593–1641), catalogued as by 'Walker' (no initial given), was lent to the exhibition at the South Kensington Museum, 1865.

Walker, Thomas. (fl. 1810–1822)

Was working in 1822 at Bond Street, Hull. Painted portraits and miniatures, and was the author of a *Treatise upon the Art of Flying by Mechanical Means*, published New Dock Street, Hull, 1810.

*Walker, Miss Wilhelmina. (fl. 1900)

Of London. Exhibited at the R.A. 1900, from 4 Torrington Park, North Finchley. Possibly identical with, or related to, the Miss Wilhelmina Augusta Walker recorded by Graves as exhibiting in London, 1870–1876.

Walker, Mrs. William. 1800–1876

Born in London in 1800. Née Elizabeth Reynolds, second daughter of S. W. Reynolds, the engraver, by whom she was taught painting, and sister of Miss Fanny Reynolds (q.v.). She also had some instruction from T. G. Lupton, Northcote and Clint (q.v.). Exhibited at the R.A. and S.B.A., 1818–1850. She painted miniatures and portraits in oil, as well as executing engravings. Had a distinguished clientele including five Prime Ministers. Was appointed miniature painter to William IV in 1830. Married William Walker (1791–1867), the engraver, in 1829 or 1830, and subsequently assisted him, having engraved in mezzotint herself at an early age. Opie painted her portrait as a child; the B.M. has an engraving of it and one of a self-portrait by her. A miniature by her of her father is in the N.P.G. She died 9 November 1876 and was buried in the Brompton Cemetery. An oil portrait by her of the Earl of Devon is at Christ Church College, Oxford. Miss Marion Walker (q.v.) was undoubtedly her daughter and exhibited from her mother's address. A miniature of her father, Samuel William Reynolds, is at the N.P.G. no. 927.)

*Wallace, Miss Ellen. See Sharples, Mrs. James

Waller, Miss Eliza. (fl. 1828–1842)

Of London and Greenwich (1835–1838). Exhibited at the R.A., etc., 1828–1838. Painted portraits and still life subjects in oil, and miniatures. Schidlof notes a miniature of two young ladies by her signed and dated '1842'.

Waller, William. (fl. 1842)

Working in 1842 at Hill Street, Poole, Dorset.

*Wallis, George, F.S.A. 1811–1891

Born at Wolverhampton in 1811 where he was educated at the Grammar School. Practised as a painter from 1832. Was keenly interested in art education as applied to designs for manufactured goods and for decoration. In 1841 he joined the Government School of Design at Somerset House, and became successively headmaster of the Art Schools of Spitalfields, Manchester and Birmingham. Held important posts in connection with the International Exhibition of 1851 and 1862. Wallis joined the staff of the South Kensington Museum, now the V. & A. M., in 1858, becoming Keeper of its art collection in 1863. He wrote copiously on art subjects. The V. & A. M. has three oil paintings, a water-colour and drawings by Wallis. He is not known as a miniaturist, but I have, in my collection, a small oil portrait by him of his daughter, Esther Mary Wallis, as a baby. It is on wood and has an inscription stuck onto the reverse, 'Esther Mary Wallis / by her Father / George Wallis'. The writing is identical with that in his own catalogue (also in my possession) of the Exhibition of Miniatures held at the South Kensington Museum in 1865. He retired in 1891 and died in the same year.

*Wallis, Henry C. (fl. 1903–1907)
Of Redruth, Cornwall. Exhibited at the R.A., 1903–1907. He was possibly identical with Henry Wallis (1830–1916), whose small portrait on mill-board, of Thomas Love Peacock, is in the N.P.G. The sitter was a novelist, poet and East India Company official.

*Wallis, Miss Rosa. b. 1857
Born in Stretton, Rutland, 5 March 1857. Pupil of the Manchester Academy. Exhibited at the R.A. and N.W.C.S., etc., 1878–1902. Her exhibit in 1902 was a portrait of a lady in fancy dress, executed in enamel on copper.

Walpole, Elizabeth (Miss?). 18th century
An enamel miniature of Nelson, after Hoppner, by the above artist was sold at Sotheby's, 13 June 1913. She was possibly identical with the Miss Walpole who exhibited a portrait at the R.A., 1782. The exhibit, not a miniature, was of her sister Caroline.

*Walpole, Horace. 1717–1797
Born 24 September 1717; fourth son of Sir Robert Walpole, 1st Earl of Orford (1676–1745), statesman. This noted writer and draughtsman, who succeeded as 4th Earl of Orford, studied at Eton and Cambridge, and was a pupil of Bernard Lens (III) (q.v.). Although there is no proof of this, it has been suggested that he may have painted a few miniatures. Travelled in Italy c. 1739–1741. Retired to his estate, Strawberry Hill, Middlesex. Died in London, 2 March 1797. His effects which contained his famous collection of miniatures were sold in April 1842. One of his most famous works is *Anecdotes of Painting in England*, 1762–1771, in which he edited notes collected by George Vertue, and added information regarding many artists.

*Walsh, Mrs. Lucie E. (fl. 1907–1914)
Of Walton-on-Thames. Exhibited at the R.A., 1907–1914.

Walton, Mrs. (fl. 1789)
Exhibited at the R.A. 1789, as an Honorary Exhibitor. The exhibit was a portrait of a young lady in miniature.

*Walton, H. (Henry?). (fl. c. 1790)
A pair of miniatures of ladies, signed 'H. Walton', half-length, 3½ in., were sold at Sotheby's, 18 June 1962. One, executed c. 1790, was skilfully painted. These may have been the work of Henry Walton, F.S.A., who exhibited portraits at the Society of Artists and the R.A. 1771–1779, from London addresses.

*Wanklyn, Miss Edith E. (fl. 1900–1905)
Exhibited at the Society of Miniaturists, 1900–1905, from St. Andrews, Leatherhead.

Wanley, Humfrey. 1671/2–1726
Born in Coventry, 21 March 1671/2; son of Nathaniel Wanley, a divine and compiler; was apprenticed to a draper. Became a celebrated cataloguer of books and MSS. Was Secretary to the S.P.C.K., and Librarian to the 2nd Earl of Oxford. Studied under Boit (q.v.), but had evidently left him before 20 March 1694/5, when Wanley, writing from Coventry, says, 'Everybody here is glad to see me, and gladder that I have left Mr Boit'. One of his fellow pupils was John Milward (q.v.), several of whose letters to Wanley are at Welbeck. No miniatures by Wanley are at present known. He died in Clarges Street, London, 6 July 1726, and was buried in Marylebone Church. Portraits of him are in the Bodleian Library, the N.P.G., the B.M. and the Society of Antiquaries.

*Ward, Mrs. Charlotte Blakeney (Miss Charlotte Blakeney). (fl. 1902–1914)
Née Charlotte Blakeney. Of Chelsea. Exhibited at the R.A., 1902–1914. Executed miniatures and portraits, and subjects in water-colour. Wife of C. D. Ward who also exhibited at the R.A. Her sitters included her father and Mrs. J. M. Duveen.

*Ward, Miss Dorothy P. (fl. 1908–1914)
Of Kent and London. Exhibited at the R.A., 1908–1914. Her sitters included the Earl of Southesk and the Hon. Alexander Carnegie.

Ward, Captain Francis Swain, F.S.A. 1734 or 1750–1794 or 1805.
Of London and India. Born c. 1734 or 1750. Exhibited at the Society of Artists, 1765–1773, and was Secretary to the Society in 1772. Served as an officer in the East India Company. His exhibits were principally Indian and other landscapes, and a few miniatures. Was in India until 1764 when he came to London, but returned to India after 1772, and died in Negapatam in 1794 or 1805. According to Long's notes, Ward's date of birth was 1750 and his death, 1805; Schidlof and Benezit give his date of birth as c. 1734 and his death as 1794.

Ward, George Raphael. 1801?–1878
Son and pupil of James Ward, R.A. (1769–1859). The date of his birth has been given as 1798 and 1797, but his entry to the R.A. Schools, 30 December 1822, gives his age as 21, which would make his date of birth 1801. He was awarded a silver medal by the Society of Arts in 1823. Exhibited at the R.A. and N.W.C.S., etc., 1821–1864. Became an engraver and miniaturist; painted copies in miniature after Sir Thomas Lawrence (q.v.) and other artists. Married Mary Webb (q.v.) c. 1827/8, by whom he had a daughter, Henrietta (1832–1924), who married E. M. Ward, R.A. Ward died in London, 18 December 1878. He signed G. R. Ward on the front and also, on the reverse of the miniature, G. R. Ward, followed by a date and address; George Raphael Ward Pinxt 1828, 7 Newman Street, Oxford Street, etc. His work is not all of equal merit, but at its best it is good; the colours are pleasant with blue-grey shadows. The portraits are painted with minute brush-strokes, cleverly blended and touches of white are often to be seen on the nose, eyelids, lips and pupils. Examples of his work are in the Ernst Holzscheiter Collection, Meilen. A miniature by him of the Duke of Wellington, after Lawrence, was loaned to the South Kensington Exhibition of 1865. A circular miniature of an unknown lady after J. Hoppner, signed 'Ward' on the base of the pillar against which she is leaning, is in the collection of R. Bayne Powell, Esq. It is an attractive miniature and has a continental style of painting.

Ward, Mrs. George Raphael. (fl. 1823–1849)
Née Mary Webb. Exhibited at the R.A. and S.B.A., etc., 1823–1849. Married c. 1828 George Raphael Ward (q.v.), and exhibited under her married name from 1829. Taught miniature painting. May have been taught by her husband before her marriage. A private collection in Paris contains a miniature of a young lady, signed on the reverse 'Portrait of Miss Wiggins / by / Miss Webb / 12 Charles St / Medx Hospital'. A miniature of a lady, after Reynolds, was sold in Lucerne in 1934 and was signed on the reverse 'Mrs G. R. Ward Pinxit, 7 Newman Street'.

*Ward, James. (fl. 1821)
A profile miniature of a gentleman, said to have been signed and dated by James Ward, 1821 (a sketch, 9⅛ in. high), was sold at Christie's, 15 October 1963.

*Warden, Gilbert F. (fl. 1905)
Exhibited at the R.A. 1905, from Birch Grove, Rusholme, Manchester.

*Wardlow, Alexander Hamilton. (fl. 1870–1899)
Of London. Exhibited at the R.A., N.W.C.S., etc., 1870–1899. Undoubtedly related to Miss Annie Wardlow (q.v.) and Miss Mary Alexandra Wardlow (q.v.), all of whom exhibited from the same London addresses – Pembroke Villa, York Road, Acton and 62 Enmore Park, South Norwood. His address in 1898 and 1899 was Branxholm, Woodside, South Norwood.

*Wardlow, Miss Annie. (fl. 1887–1892)
Of London. Exhibited at the R.A. and N.W.C.S., 1887–1892. Undoubtedly related to Alexander Hamilton Wardlow (q.v.) and Miss Mary Alexandra Wardlow (q.v.), all of whom exhibited from the same London addresses – Pembroke Villa, York Road, Acton and 62 Enmore Park, South Norwood. Miss Mary Alexandra Wardlow exhibited a miniature of the above artist in 1889 at the R.A.

*Wardlow, Miss Eleanor Frances. (fl. 1893)
Of London. Exhibited at the N.W.C.S., 1893. Possibly related to the other artists of this name.

*Wardlow, Miss Mary Alexandra. (fl. 1885–1892)
Of London. Exhibited at the R.A. and N.W.C.S., etc., 1885–1892. Undoubtedly related to Alexander Hamilton Wardlow (q.v.) and Miss Annie Wardlow (q.v.), all of whom exhibited from the same London addresses – Pembroke Villa, York Road, Acton and 62 Enmore Park, South Norwood. The above artist exhibited a miniature of Miss Annie Wardlow at the R.A. in 1889.

*Warman, W. (fl. c. 1820–1832)
Of London. Exhibited at the R.A. in 1826, from 1 Parade, Pentonville. This exhibit was of Mrs. W. Warman, probably his wife. Two miniatures by this artist are reproduced by O'Brien (Pl. 94, Figs. 1 and 2); one of a little girl is signed 'W. Warman', c. 1820, and the other, signed 'W. Warman 1832', is of a young lady.

*Warn, Miss Lizzie Baldwin. (fl. 1899–1905)
Exhibited at the R.A. 1899–1905, from addresses in Bushey, Herts. and Derbyshire.

Warner. (fl. 1775–1788)
Of London. Exhibited at the Society of Artists in 1775 and at the Free Society of Artists in 1783, and the R.A., 1788. Painted landscapes and miniatures.

Warwick, Mrs. (fl. 1823)
Exhibited at the R.A. 1823, as an Honorary Exhibitor. The exhibit was a portrait of her brother.

*Washington, Miss Prudence. (fl. 1906)

Of London. Exhibited at the R.A. 1906, from 13 King Street, Baker Street.

Waters, Miss. (fl. 1825)

Of Clapton Square, London. Was awarded a silver Isis Medal by the Society of Arts in 1825 for a miniature portrait, a copy.

Waters, Miss Isabella. (fl. 1829)

An amateur artist of Rippingale Rectory, Falkingham. Was awarded, in 1829, a silver Isis medal from the Society of Arts for an original miniature portrait.

Waters, W. (fl. 1792–1800)

Of London. Probably the son of Edward Waters, an artist. Exhibited at the R.A., 1792–1800. Painted miniatures and views of buildings.

Waters, W. E. R. 1813–1880

Born in 1813. Was painting miniature copies in Paris, August 1830. Presumably identical with W. R. Waters of Dover who exhibited figure subjects at the R.A., B.I. and S.B.A., 1838–1867. Long recorded that he exhibited in Manchester. Had a daughter who married a cousin named Walters. F. Boyd-Waters (1879–1967) (q.v.), his nephew, also painted miniatures. He died in 1880. A well painted miniature copy of an oil painting of Philippe de Champaigne, signed 'WER, Waters Aug. 1830, Paris', was seen by Long; the face and hands were well drawn, the shading reddish; there was slight scratching in the hair.

Watkeys, W. (fl. 1833)

Long records seeing a small oil portrait which was not of any great merit, with 'W. WATKEYS / pinx^t 1833' stencilled on the back of the canvas. Possibly identical with W. Watkeys who exhibited landscapes at the R.A. 1822–1823, from 42 Essex Street, Strand.

Watkins, W. H. (fl. 1843–1849)

Of London. Exhibited at the R.A., 1843–1849.

*Watling, Thomas. (fl. 1801–1803)

A miniaturist about whom little is known. Vol. XIX of the *Walpole Society* contains the information that this artist was listed in the *New East India Kalendar* for 1801, the *New Oriental Register* for 1802 and the East India Records for 1803, as being a miniature painter in Calcutta. No record of his burial has been found, nor does his name occur elsewhere.

*Watson, Harry. (fl. 1901–1914)

Of London. Exhibited at the R.A. 1901–1914, from 18 Kensington Court Place. Executed miniatures and subject paintings in oil and water-colour. One of his water-colours was purchased by the President and Council of the R.A. under the terms of the Chantrey Bequest. His sitters included the Hon. Mrs. Mitford. Was probably the Harry Watson who exhibited landscapes at Suffolk Street in 1893.

Watson, John. 1685–1768

Born in Scotland, possibly Dumfries, 28 July 1685. Settled in Perth Amboy, New Jersey c. 1715. Few works can be ascribed to him with any certainty. Those known are small portrait drawings in pencil and Indian ink; some of these were lent to the exhibition held in the Metropolitan Museum, New York in 1927. He died in New Jersey, 22 August 1768. Watson was noted as a miser and usurer, and as a man of an irascible disposition. His self-

portrait, executed in 1720, on paper, with pencil and a brush dipped in Indian ink, and inscribed on the front 'AET.S.35', is reproduced by Wehle, Pl. 1. He may have been one of the earliest miniaturists working in America. Examples of his work are at the New Jersey Historical Society.

*Watson, John. See **Watson Gordon, Sir John, R.A., P.R.S.A.**

Watson, John. (fl. 1819)

Working in 1819 at 21 Academy Street, Belfast. Possibly identical with the John Watson (q.v.) who exhibited at the R.A., 1848–1852. The O'Brien Collection contained a miniature of a lady holding a letter which bears the signature of the artist: 'J. Watson. Dumfries', painted c. 1840, which was attributed to the above artist, and illustrated by O'Brien, Pl. 51, Fig. 1, who also suggests that the two artists were identical.

Watson, John. (fl. 1848–1852)

Of London. Exhibited at the R.A., 1848–1852. Possibly identical with the John Watson (q.v.) above, who was in Belfast in 1819. His sitters included Master Kelso, eldest son of Captain Kelso of Horkerly Park and Claudius Erskine Goodman, Esq.

*Watson, Miss Josephine M. (fl. 1908)

Of London. Exhibited at the R.A. 1908, from 14 Cantley Avenue, Clapham Common.

*Watson, Lizzie May (Mrs. W. P.) (Godfrey, Miss L. M. (Ellen)). (fl. 1882–1902)

Née Godfrey. Exhibited a self-portrait in oil at the R.A. in 1882, when her name is recorded as Miss L. M. Godfrey in the index, and Ellen in the catalogue entry. Wife of William Peter Godfrey, also an artist. Exhibited a miniature of Cathie, daughter of Lionel K. Pagden, Esq. at the R.A., 1902, from Orchardleigh, Pinner.

*Watson, Miss Rosamund. (fl. 1908)

Of London. Exhibited at the R.A. 1908, from 17 Canonbury Park South.

Watson, William. b. 1810?

Of London. Exhibited at the R.A., etc., 1828–1866. Probably the William Watson who entered the R.A. Schools, 29 December 1829, aged 19. Appears to have had a distinguished clientele. A miniature of Prince Leopold, Duke of Albany, painted in 1854, is in the collection of H.M. the Queen. It is reminiscent of the work of Sir William Ross (q.v.). He also painted members of the family of Lord and Lady Petre and of the Duke of St. Albans. A miniature of a young man, signed and dated 'W. Watson 1833', is reproduced by O'Brien, Pl. 30, Fig. 3.

*Watson, William Stewart. 1800–1870

Born in 1800; son of Captain Andrew Watson, 57th Regiment, and grandson of John Watson of Overmains. Painted a miniature of Miss Ann Scott (1803–1833), second daughter of Sir Walter Scott; the miniature was painted in 1826; and one of Sir Walter Scott in 1825; this latter miniature is referred to in a letter from Scott to Stewart Watson. A copy of a miniature of Scott, aged 5, by Watson, is at Abbotsford, and is signed 'W'. His cousin, John Watson, afterwards Sir John Watson Gordon, P.R.S.A. (q.v.), was also a miniaturist. W. S. Watson died in 1870.

Watson Gordon, Sir John, R.A., P.R.S.A. 1788–1864

Born in Overmains, Berwickshire, 1788; cousin of W. Stewart Watson (q.v.). Studied art at the Trustees' Academy, Edinburgh, in the studio of his uncle George Watson, P.R.S.A., and under Raeburn. Exhibited at the R.A. and B.I., 1814–1864, and at the R.S.A., 1830–1864. From 1814–1825 he exhibited under the name of Watson and, in 1826, he assumed the name of Gordon. Was knighted in 1850 in which year he also became President of the R.S.A., and Her Majesty's Limner for Scotland. Was a well-known Scottish artist and after Raeburn's death, the leading portrait painter in Scotland. Died in Edinburgh in 1864. Said by Long to have painted miniatures and certainly executed small drawings. Long saw a self-portrait in 1924. A small unfinished portrait in pencil on paper of Thomas de Quincey (1785–1859) is at Dove Cottage, Grasmere, Westmorland, which houses the Wordsworth collection. This was possibly the sketch for the large portrait which Watson Gordon painted of de Quincey in 1845, and which is in the N.P.G.

Watts, George Frederick, O.M., R.A. 1817–1904

This famous painter is only known as a miniaturist by a large oval miniature on ivory, c. 1840, of a lady with greenish hair, said to be Mrs. George Vivian of Claverton, and to be by him. It is at the Holburne Museum, Bath.

Watts, J. (fl. 1794–1796)

Of London. Exhibited at the R.A., 1794 and 1796. Executed miniatures on enamel of 'Mr Gibbon' and of the Rev. W. Romaine.

Watts, T. (fl. c. 1765–1770)

A miniature, signed 'TW', of c. 1765–1770, was catalogued as being by T. Watts in Christie's sale, 22 March 1922. It was not very good, and was heavily stippled.

Watts, Walter Henry. 1776 or 1784–1842

Born in the East Indies; son of a Captain in the Navy. May have been identical with the W. H. Watts who is recorded as entering the R.A. Schools, 21 January 1808, when his age was said to be 24. If this assumption is correct, his date of birth was c. 1784, not 1776, as given by Long. Was educated in Cheshire. Worked in London and exhibited at the R.A., B.I., O.W.C.S., and Associated Artists in Water-Colours, 1803–1830; was a member of the last named society in 1808. Was working in Manchester, 14 May 1799 and charged 2–5 guineas for a miniature. He also painted in oil. In 1816 he was appointed miniature painter to Princess Charlotte. Watts became a reporter for *The Morning Post*, 1803, *The Morning Chronicle*, 1813 and *The Representative*, 1826. Rejoined the staff of *The Morning Chronicle*, 1827–1840; wrote in *The Literary Gazette*, and edited *The Annual Biography and Obituary*, 1817–1831. He died in his lodgings in Earl's Court Terrace, Old Brompton, 4 January 1842. He painted profile miniatures on paper with the backgrounds left blank, as in a silhouette portrait.

*Waud, Reginald L. (fl. 1902–1903)

Of London. Exhibited at the R.A. and S.M., 1902–1903. Executed miniatures and large portraits in oil.

*Waugh, Miss Elizabeth J. (fl. 1879–1885)

Of Winchester. Exhibited at the R.A., etc., 1879–1885.

*Way, Miss Frances Elizabeth (Fanny) (Mrs. Arthur Thacker). 1871–1961

Born 28 March 1871 at 20 Lloyd Square,

Clerkenwell; daughter of William Dwyer Way and his wife, Esther, née Langmead. Was educated privately, together with her four sisters. Studied at the Crystal Palace School of Art c. 1886 where, in 1886, she was awarded two silver medals for a painting in oil and a drawing. Spent a year at Lausanne at a school of art run by M. des Molins and her uncle, C. J. Way. Exhibited at the R.A., the Society of Miniaturists, the Royal Society of Miniature Painters, the Royal Institute of Portrait Painters, etc., 1893–1921. Exhibited at the Paris Salon, 1897 and, in the same year, exhibited a self-portrait at the R.A. Was the wife of Arthur Thacker, Esq., and is recorded as Mrs. Arthur Thacker in 1895. Her sitters included the Duke and Duchess of York (later George V and Queen Mary), Mrs. W. Dwyer Way (the artist's mother), Sir Thomas Somer Vine, Mrs. Langtry, Miss Ellaline Terriss, Mrs. Friedberger, Lord Roberts, and her son, G. W. Thacker, Esq., to whom I am indebted for much of this information. Her last portrait was that of her daughter-in-law, Mrs. G. W. Thacker, painted in 1928. Several of her miniatures are still in the possession of the family, and were shown to me in 1964. In a letter to Mrs. Thacker from the Edmonton Urban District Council, dated 2 January 1908, the City Surveyor expressed his satisfaction over some portraits which she had evidently been commissioned to execute from photographs, which was a common practice at this time. All her miniatures seem to have been exhibited under her maiden name of Fanny Way, which was also the signature used on her portraits. The miniatures of the Duke and Duchess of York are in my collection. The colouring is pleasant and the features well painted, but the shading of the backgrounds is rather hesitant.

Way, Johan Vilhelm Carl. 1792–1873

Born in Rute, Gothland, Sweden, 18 June 1792; son of an Englishman employed by the Admiralty. Was brought to London by his father in 1807 and studied drawing. Subsequently became a pupil of Alexandre Latour in Brussels. Returned to London c. 1828. Was a miniaturist and glass painter. In 1821 he became a member of the Academy of Stockholm. Travelled to Copenhagen, London and Paris, 1828–1831. From 1831 he taught the history of art at the Academy of Stockholm. He was a good artist whose works show a strong English influence. He signed Way followed by a date and J. Way. Died in Stockholm, 10 April 1873. The Nationalmuseum, Stockholm has five works by him.

*Wear, Miss Maud M. b. 1873

Born in London, 8 December 1873. Was a pupil at the R.A. Schools. Exhibited at the R.A., 1900–1914, from addresses in London, Bournemouth, Dorset and Kent. Painted miniatures, portraits in oil and subjects in water-colour. Her sitters included Mrs. F. E. Wear.

*Webb, Miss Dora. b. 1888

Born in Stamford, 8 May 1888. Exhibited at the R.A., R.M.S., and in Paris, 1909–1932, from Burton Road, Melton Mowbray. Benezit records her christian names as Mohala Dora. Was a pupil of Alyn Williams (q.v.).

Webb, Miss Mary. See Ward, Mrs. George Raphael

Webber. (fl. 1771). See also **Webber, John, R.A.**

Of London. Exhibited at the Society of Artists, 1771, from Mr. Baker's, King Street, Covent Garden. Possibly identical with John Webber, R.A. (q.v.).

*Webber, A. Huish. (fl. 1898)

Exhibited at the R.A. 1898, from Grove House, Tunbridge Wells. His sitter was Miss Ella M. Webber.

*Webber, Miss Ethel. (fl. 1909)

Exhibited at the R.A. 1909, from Holmwood, Dorking. Her sitters included Alice, daughter of Alex. Webber, Esq.

*Webber, John, R.A. 1750/52–1793

Born in London, 6 October 1750/52; son of a Swiss sculptor. Sent to Berne at the age of 6 and was brought up by a maiden aunt. Studied at an early age with J. L. Aberli, a Swiss artist, who instructed him in both portraiture and landscape painting. Later studied in Paris and, after five years, returned to London and entered the R.A. Schools, 8 April 1775. Exhibited at the R.A., 1776–1792; became R.A., 1791. Was possibly identical with the artist named Webber (q.v.) (no initial given) who exhibited a miniature at the Society of Artists in 1771. In 1776 John Webber exhibited a 'Portrait of an artist' at the R.A.; this was, in fact, a portrait of his brother, Henry, a sculptor. He was best known for his drawings, engravings and aquatints. Was draughtsman to Captain Cook on his third and last voyage. Died in Oxford Street, London on 29 April 1793. A portrait by him of Captain Cook is in the N.P.G.

*Webling, Miss Ethel. (fl. 1880–1903)

Of London. Exhibited at the R.A. and S.M., etc. 1880–1903, from 2 Campden Gardens, Shepherd's Bush.

*Webster, Moses. 1792–1870

Born in Derby, 1792; was apprenticed at the China works there and later worked in Worcester and London. Painted miniatures on porcelain and in water-colours as well as executing flower paintings on porcelain. Exhibited a flower painting at the O.W.C.S. in 1818. Returned to Derby and, in 1827, commenced to teach as a profession, and had many pupils from Derby and Nottingham. Executed views of these counties and painted some landscapes in oil. Towards the end of his life, he was admitted to the Liversage almhouses, Derby, where he died, 20 October 1870.

Webster, Simon. d. after 1820?

Of London. Exhibited at the Society of Artists and the Free Society of Artists, 1762–1780. Was a member of the Society of Artists which, in 1769, voted him money to compensate him for losses in a fire. Executed portraits in oil, crayons, miniatures and landscapes in water-colour. Has been identified as the artist who etched for Ackerman's *Views of Cottages and Farmhouses in England*, 1817–1819.

*Weeks, Mr. (fl. c. 1742)

An attractive miniature, signed on the reverse 'Drawn by Mr. Weeks 174(2?)', the last figure being indecipherable, was seen at the V. & A. M. It was in the manner of the Lens (q.v.) school of painting.

Weigall, Alfred. (fl. 1855–1866)

Of London. Almost certainly the son of Henry Weigall senior, sculptor, from whose address he exhibited, 1855, and from whose family address he exhibited, 1856 and 1858. Exhibited at the R.A., 1855–1866. His addresses were: 38 Wimpole Street (1855–1856), 102 Piccadilly (1858) and 8 Clarendon Road, Victoria Road, Kensington (1859–1866). Painted miniatures. His sitters included: 'Countess Dowager Spencer', Countess Spencer, Earl Spencer, Lady Victoria Spencer and the Hon. Mrs. Best. This latter portrait was lent by the artist to the ex-

hibition at the South Kensington Museum, 1865, which also contained the miniature of Countess Spencer, and one of 'A mother and child'. Miniatures by his brother, Henry Weigall junior (q.v.), were also exhibited at South Kensington. The miniature of Countess Spencer is presumably the one still in the Spencer collection, signed 'A. Weigall 1859'.

Weigall, Miss Emily. (fl. 1853–1860)

Of London. Almost certainly the daughter of Charles Harvey Weigall, and sister of Miss J. Weigall (q.v.), and of A. H. Weigall (painter). Exhibited at the R.A., 1853–1860. Her addresses were: 27 Somerset Street, Portman Square (1853), 13 Michael's Place, Brompton (1854–1860). Her sitters included the Hon. Lena Eden, Lady Amabel Cowper and other members of their respective families. O'Brien reproduces on Pl. 93, Fig. 2, a miniature of a baby, inscribed on the reverse 'Infant son of J. E. E. Weigall Esqre, Emily Weigall Feby, 1859', the year in which it was exhibited at the R.A. She was a good artist and used minute stippling.

Weigall, Henry, junior. 1829–1925

Born 1829, probably in London. Almost certainly the son of Henry Weigall senior, sculptor. Exhibited at the R.A. and B.I., etc., 1846? or 1850–1904. The exhibit, in 1846, is given to H. Weigall in the index, and H. Weigall junior in the catalogue, and may have been by his father, since it was a cameo. Was the brother of A. Weigall (q.v.) who shared his address in some of the earlier years. His addresses were: 27 Somerset Street, Portman Square (1850–1853), 38 Wimpole Street (1854–57), 102 Piccadilly (1858–1866), 35 Bryanston Square (1867–1882), 6 William Street, Lowndes Square (1885–1898), Southwood, Ramsgate (1898–1904). Weigall painted miniatures only during the early part of his career, and most of his works were portraits in oil and subject pictures. He had a distinguished clientele and was patronised by the Royal Family. His sitters included the Duke of Wellington; Alexandra, Princess of Wales; Albert Edward, Prince of Wales; the Archbishop of York (1869 and 1874); Princess Mary Adelaide, Duchess of Teck; Princess Frederica of Hanover; the Viscount Holmsdale, Lady Rose Weigall, etc. He died at Southwood, nr. Ramsgate, 4 January 1925. A miniature by him of the Duke of Wellington is in the collection of H.M. the Queen at Windsor. Two miniatures by him were lent to the exhibition at the South Kensington Museum, 1865.

Weigall, Miss Julia (Mrs. Capes). (fl. 1848–1864)

Of London. Almost certainly the daughter of Charles Harvey Weigall, an artist, from whose address, 13 Michael's Place, Brompton, she exhibited at the R.A., 1848–1852 and 1854–1863; and sister of Miss E. Weigall (q.v.) and A. H. Weigall (artist). In 1853 she exhibited from 27 Somerset Street, Portman Square (the address of H. Weigall senior and H. Weigall junior (q.v.)) and, in 1864, she exhibited from 233 Brompton Road, A. H. Weigall's address. She became Mrs. Capes sometime after 1864. Painted miniatures, landscapes and subject pictures. She had a distinguished clientele including Earl de Grey, Lady Adine Cowper and the Rt. Hon. Lord Auckland, Bishop of Bath and Wells. In 1858 she exhibited a miniature of 'the Artist's Brother' and, in 1859, a miniature of C. H. Weigall.

Weightman. d. 1781

Worked as a miniaturist in London. Died 23 January 1781 in Red Lion Street, Holborn.

Weimes, Mrs. 17th century?

Said by Sanderson in his *Graphice*, 1658, p. 20, to

have painted in oil; apparently she painted miniatures.

*Weir, Miss Edith D. (fl. 1900)
Exhibited at the R.A. 1900, from 58 Trumbull Street, Newhaven, Connecticut, U.S.A.

Weisbrod or **Weissbrod, Friedrich Christoph.** 1739–*c.* 1803
Born in Stuttgart, 13 June 1739. Painted miniatures and enamels. Worked in Ludwigsburg until 1767. In 1773 he became the director of the School of Fine Arts of Ludwigsburg. Was in Mannheim *c.* 1787 and also came to London. A miniature on enamel of an unknown lady, signed on the reverse 'Weisbrod / Pinxt. 1755', is in the N.G., Dublin. This portrait was formerly in the Nachemsohn Collection.

*Weisse, Miss Melanie. (fl. 1900–1902)
Of Southam, Warwickshire. Exhibited at the Society of Miniaturists, 1900–1902.

Weller, Miss Augusta. (fl. 1836–1839)
Of London and Chichester. Exhibited at the R.A. and B.I., etc., 1836–1839. She painted miniatures and subject pictures in oils.

Wellings, William. (fl. 1778–1792)
A silhouettist about whom little is known. A silhouette of two ladies, signed 'Wm Wellings fecit / 1782', is in the V. & A. M. He published an engraved silhouette of George III. Was probably identical with the artist named Welling who exhibited a miniature at the R.A., in 1793; this was a 'portrait of a lady of quality'; he also exhibited a painting of Mr. Kemble and Mrs. Siddons as Cromwell and Queen Catherine. His address was 26 Henrietta Street, Covent Garden. Long recorded that a Mr. Wellings of 26 Henrietta Street, Covent Garden (presumably the above artist) advertised on 1 November 1792 as having worked for 14 years in the same street and that he came from 3 Tavistock Row. He also advertised that he executed 'Miniatures for Lockets, Bracelets, Rings and Fause Montres'. The B.M. has an engraved portrait after Wellings and other examples of his work are in the Colchester Museum.

Wells, Mrs. (fl. 1806)
Of London. Exhibited at the R.A. 1806, from 1 City Terrace, City Road. The exhibits included a self-portrait.

Wells, Henry Tanworth, R.A. 1828–1903
Born in Marylebone, London, 12 December 1828; only son of a merchant of the same names. Educated at Lancing; apprenticed in 1843 as a lithographic draughtsman to Messrs. Dickinson; took up miniature painting. Studied in the evenings at the school of J. M. Leigh and, in 1850, went to Paris where, for six months, he was a pupil of Couture. Was a member of a drawing school which was attended by Rossetti and G. P. Boyce. Had an aristocratic clientele. Exhibited at the R.A. and B.I., etc., 1846–1903; was elected A.R.A. in 1866, and R.A. in 1870. Married Joanna Mary Boyce, sister of G. P. Boyce, at Rome in 1857. Gave up miniature painting *c.* 1861; subsequently executed portraits in oil and crayon. Died at Thorpe Lodge, Campden Hill, Kensington, 16 January 1903, and was buried at Kensal Green. A miniature of Princess Mary, signed and dated '1853', is at Windsor Castle. Oil paintings by him are in the N.P.G., the Tate Gallery, etc. His wife exhibited a painting at the R.A. in 1859–1861, and, in 1862, the entry was 'the late Mrs. H. T. Wells'. Several of his miniatures were exhibited at the South Kensington exhibition of 1865.

*Wensley, William. (fl. 1907)
Of London. Exhibited a self-portrait at the R.A. 1907, from 143 Brecknock Road.

Werner, Joseph. 1637–1710?
Born in Berne in 1637. Pupil of Merian in Frankfort and of Berrettini and others in Rome. Was a celebrated miniaturist who painted portraits and mythological and allegorical subjects. Worked at the French Court; is reputed to have visited Britain, but no evidence has been found to support this theory. He is thought to have died in 1710. A self-portrait on parchment, of the artist is in the V. & A. M. This depicts Werner pointing to a picture executed in pen and ink and placed on an easel. This elaborate and ambitious composition shows a cupid seated on a lion with two other cupids in attendance, standing in front of a large building or temple. On the left-hand side of the miniature, beneath the figure of the artist is a Latin inscription:
'Indomitum fræ nans genius virtute Leonem,
Auspice pictura, ad templum perducit honoris.'
On the opposite side the painting is signed and dated in gold, 'Josephus Wernerus iunior / Roma Aᵒ, 1662'. Several of this artist's works were exhibited in Geneva, 1956, including 'The Judgement of Paris' and 'Jesus and the Samaritan woman at the Well', both from the Musée des Beaux-Arts, Berne.

*West, Miss Amy M. (fl. 1907–1911)
Exhibited at the R.A. 1907 and 1911, from Virginia Cottage, High Street, Bushey, Herts.

West, Benjamin, P.R.A. 1738–1820. See also **W., B.**
Born in Springfield (now Swarthmore), Pennsylvania, 10 October 1738; one of ten children born to John and Sarah West (née Pearson). Was established in Philadelphia as a portrait painter when he was eighteen years old. Went to New York and on 10 July 1760, arrived in Rome where he remained for several years, during which time he was made a member of the academies of Parma, Florence and Bologna. He arrived in London on 20 June 1763. He took lodgings in Bedford Street, Covent Garden, and moved later to Castle Street, settling finally at 14 Newman Street where he rented a studio which he kept for the rest of his life. He sent for his fiancée, Elizabeth Shewell of Philadelphia, to come to London, and married her in 1764. Painted historical subjects, and oil portraits, and is supposed to have painted miniatures. A self-portrait, stated to be by him at the age of eighteen, and given to his sweetheart, is reproduced by Wehle, Pl. II. On the same plate is a miniature of his wife by Matthew Pratt. He taught, and gave encouragement to, many miniaturists including Andrew Robertson (q.v.) who painted his portrait in miniature. This was exhibited in Edinburgh in 1965, and was inscribed on the reverse 'Benjamin West P.R.A. / 1738–1820 / by Andrew Robertson'. He was appointed historical painter to George III in 1772, and elected P.R.A. in 1792, which appointment he held until his death in London on 10 March 1820. His pupils included his two children, Raphael Lamarr and Benjamin jun., Charles Willson Peale (q.v.), John Trumbull and John Singleton Copley (q.v.).

West, Edgar. (fl. 1828)
Worked in 1828 at The Terrace, Lincoln.

West, J. (fl. 1856)
Of London. Exhibited at the R.A. 1856, from 23 Beaumont Street, Portland Place. The portrait was of the Hon. Mrs. Norton.

West, John. (fl. 1795–1830)
Of Bath. Miniaturist and drawing master. In 1795 was in Northumberland Buildings, Bath; had various other Bath addresses, 1801–1830, and was probably the father of Joseph West (born 1797), the landscape painter, who lived with him for many years.

*West, Joseph. b. 1797
Born 1797; son of John West (q.v.), both of Bath. Known as a landscape painter. Exhibited at the B.I., 1824 1834. Is not known as a miniaturist, but a miniature in the collection of the Duke of Alba is signed 'Joseph West', and may have been by the above artist.

West, Robert Lucius, R.H.A. *c.* 1774–1850
Born in Dublin *c.* 1774; son and pupil of F. R. West, a Dublin artist. Won medals in the Dublin Society Schools, 1795 and 1796. Exhibited in Dublin, 1800–1849; was an original member of the R.H.A. Presented the Dublin Society with a portrait of the 'Rt. Hon. John Foster' and was given fifty pounds to go to London and improve his art. He exhibited a 'Subject from Gray's Elegy' at the R.A., in 1808. Was chosen to succeed his father as Master of the Figure School at the Dublin Society Schools in 1809, and retired in 1845 on account of old age. He died on 3 June 1850 and was buried at Mount Jerome. An oil self-portrait in miniature is at the N.G., Dublin.

*West, Miss Sara A. (fl. 1903–1910)
Of Hayes, Kent. Exhibited at the Society of Miniaturists, 1903–1910. Was a member of the Society from 1902.

Westall, Richard, R.A. 1765–1836
Born 2 January 1765 at Hertford? Entered the R.A. Schools, 16 December 1785, aged 20 'Jan 2. 1786'. Exhibited at the R.A., 1784–1836; became A.R.A. 1792, and R.A. in 1794. Is best known for his figure subjects and designs for book illustrations; also painted portraits, some of which may have been miniatures, since the Earl of Derby, Earl Spencer and Mr. D. C. Marjoribanks, M.P., all lent portraits by him to the miniature exhibition at the South Kensington Museum in 1865. One was on paper and some were in water-colour. Held the title of 'Principal Painter to their Royal Highnesses, the Duchess of Kent and the Princess Victoria'. He died 4 December 1836.

*Westerly, Mrs. (fl. *c.* 1831)
Of Scarborough. Painted a miniature *c.* 1831 of 'Mrs Pricilla Hudson'.

*Westhoven, J. (fl. 1855)
Recorded by Schidlof as working in England in the middle of the 19th century. Painted on porcelain. Was perhaps of Dutch descent. Painted with some skill and used pleasant colours. A miniature on porcelain of an unknown lady, signed on the reverse 'J. Westhoven / 1855', is reproduced by Schidlof in *The Miniature in Europe*, Pl. 623.

Westoby, E. b. 1775?
Of London, Halifax (1818) and York (1819). Probably the artist of this name who entered the R.A. Schools, 21 January 1808, aged 23. Painted landscapes and portraits, as well as miniatures. Exhibited at the R.A., 1806–1823.

*Weston, Mr. (fl. 1778)
Advertised as a 'Miniature painter and drawing master from the R.A. London', in Ipswich, 3 October 1778, and in Norwich, 11 July 1778.

Wetherill or **Wetherell.** (fl. 1773–1783). See also **Wetherill, Miss Anne**
Of London and Plymouth. Exhibited at the Society of Artists 1773, from 9 Glanville Street, Rathbone Place, and at the R.A. 1783, from Cursitor Street. Identified by Schidlof as Miss Anne Wetherill, on what grounds I do not know. The R.A. catalogues do not give an initial. A miniature, signed 'Wetherell, Plymouth', and possibly by the above artist, was seen by Mr. A. J. B. Kiddell. Undoubtedly related to Mrs. Wetherill, a portrait painter, who exhibited at the Society of Artists, 1773 from the same address, 9 Glanville Street, and at the Free Society, 1783.

*Wetherill, Miss Anne. (fl. 1780–1781). See also **Wetherill** or **Wetherell**
The details of the above artist, and those of Wetherill (q.v.) (no initial given), and Mrs. Wetherill, a portrait painter, appear to have been confused by Schidlof who gives all the information under Miss Anne Wetherill. Benezit records an Anne Wetherill who exhibited at Lille in 1780 and who may have been identical with the above artist or with Mrs. Wetherill.

*Weyde, Henry van de. (fl. 1875–1880)
Of Norwood. Exhibited at the R.A., 1875–1880. Executed fancy heads, drawings and miniatures.

Wheatley, Francis, R.A. 1747–1801
Born in Wild Court, Covent Garden, London, 1747; son of a master tailor. Studied at Shipleys' drawing school and probably under R. Wilson; was awarded premiums by the Society of Arts, 1762, 1763 and 1769. Entered the R.A. Schools, 13 November 1769, aged 22. Exhibited at the Society of Artists and the R.A., 1765–1801, including his well-known series, 'The Cries of London'. Visited Ireland c. 1767, and again in 1779 with the wife of J. A. Gresse. Returned to London in 1783 or 1784. Was elected A.R.A., 1790, and R.A., 1791. Painted portraits in oil and crayon, historical pictures, water-colour landscapes and figure subjects, and is said to have painted a few miniatures, one of which, 'a portrait of a gentleman', was exhibited at the Society of Artists in 1766. He died from an attack of gout, 28 July 1801. His widow, Mrs. F. Wheatley (Clara Maria) (q.v.), married Alexander Pope (q.v.).

Wheatley, Mrs. Francis. See **Pope, Mrs. Alexander**

*Wheatley, Mrs. John. See **Wolfe, Miss Edith Grace**

*Wheeler, Mrs. Amy E. (fl. 1890–1896)
Of London. Exhibited at the R.A., 1890–1896. Her sitters included Sir Philip Cunliffe Owen, K.C.M., Lady Cunliffe Owen, the Hon. Mrs. Sandilands and Marjorie, daughter of C. Woodbyne Parish, Esq.

*Wheeler, J. or **T.** (fl. 1822). See also **Wheeler, L. J.**
A miniature of a gentleman, signed 'J. Wheeler, 184 Fleet St, London, May 1822', was seen by me at the Art Institute, Chicago. The artist was probably identical with, or related to, the T. Wheeler (q.v.) of the same address recorded by Long, or with the L. J. Wheeler (q.v.) recorded by Schidlof as working in England c. 1830.

*Wheeler, L. J. (fl. c. 1830). See also **Wheeler, J.** or **T.**
The above artist is recorded by Schidlof as working in England c. 1830. A miniature on card of Edward Fitzgerald, signed on the reverse, was sold in Brussels, 6 November 1935. The artist may have been identical with J. Wheeler (q.v.) or T. Wheeler (q.v.).

Wheeler, Miss Mary Ann. See **Johnston, Mrs. David**

*Wheeler, T. or **J.** (fl. 1817–1845). See also **Wheeler, J.** or **T.**
Of London. Born c. 1790, according to Schidlof. Exhibited at the R.A., 1817–1845. Long recorded seeing a miniature of a lady, signed on card on the reverse 'Painted by / T. Wheeler / 184 Fleet Street / London / May – 1819'. The two initials were joined in monogram looking rather like an M. The artist was probably identical with, or related to, the J. Wheeler (q.v.) of the same address who painted the miniature which I saw in Chicago. A miniature of Fanny Tolfrey, signed back and front, 'T. Wheeler Del', and dated '1834', is in the V. & A. M.

*Wheelwright, Mrs. Ethel. (fl. 1908–1909)
Of London. Exhibited at the R.A. 1908 and 1909, from 9 Ravensbourne Gardens, West Ealing.

*Wheelwright, Mrs. Talbot. (fl. 1904)
Exhibited at the R.A. 1904, from 5 Little Ealing Lane, South Ealing. Her sitters included W. M. Wheelwright, Esq.

*Wheelwright, Mrs. W. See **Stroud, Miss Maud**

*Whibley, Alfred T. (fl. 1897–1899)
Exhibited at the R.A. 1897 and 1899, from addresses in Eastbourne and London.

*Whichels, C. John M. (fl. c. 1810)
Painted a miniature of Princess Charlotte c. 1810 which, according to Long, was executed in watercolour on paper. The artist may have been identical with C. John M. Whichelo (died 1865), who exhibited at the R.A., B.I. and O.W.C.S., 1810–1865, and who is best known for his landscapes and marine paintings.

*White, Charles. (fl. 1765–1783)
Of London. Exhibited at the Society of Artists, 1765 (Honorary Exhibitor), and at the Free Society of Artists, 1768–1783. Was an architect, draughtsman, engraver and painted at least one miniature which was exhibited at the Free Society in 1774 from 44 Devonshire Street, Queen's Square, Bloomsbury.

*White, Miss Emilie. (fl. 1902)
Exhibited at the R.A. 1902, from Annaville, Earlswood Road, Strand Town, Belfast.

*White, Mrs. Evelyn. (fl. 1904–1908)
Of London. Exhibited at the R.A. and S.M., 1904–1908, from 5 Stoner Court, Kensington.

*White, Miss Florence. (fl. 1881–1932)
Of London. Exhibited at the R.A. and R.M.S., etc. 1881–1932, from various studios in London. Painted miniatures, portraits and genre subjects in oil. Was a member of the Society of Lady Artists. (Pl. 385: no. 938.)

White, George. c. 1671 or 1684–1732
Born c. 1671 (Redgrave) or c. 1684 (Th. B.); son and pupil of Robert White (q.v.). Executed miniatures in plumbago on vellum, and portraits in oil and crayons. He engraved about sixty portraits after Lely, Kneller, etc. in line and mezzotint. He worked in the manner of his father and signed GW in cursive monogram or, more usually, G. White, with the two first letters forming a monogram. He died at his house in Bloomsbury, 27 May 1732. Examples of his work are in the B.M. A miniature of William Somerville, the poet, signed 'GWhite fec: / 1709', is in the N.P.G.

*White, George. (fl. 1905)
Exhibited at the R.A. 1905, from 82 Park Road, Burslem, Staffs.

White, Joseph. 19th century
Worked in London as a miniaturist in the middle of the 19th century. Said to have painted oil miniatures in imitation of old masters. Probably identical with the artist of this name recorded by Schidlof, who painted a miniature of a young man on ivory, signed on the reverse 'Painted by J. White, London'.

*White, Miss Josephine M. (fl. 1893–1898)
Of London. Exhibited at the R.A., 1893–1898. Painted miniatures and subjects in oil.

White, Mark. (fl. c. 1767)
Studied in the Dublin Society Schools. Said to have started as a merchant in Fleet Street, but being unsuccessful in business, became an artist. Was working as a miniaturist in Cork in 1767.

White, Robert. 1645–1703
Born in London, 1645. Pupil of David Loggan (q.v.). Executed some of the finest plumbago miniatures of the seventeenth century. Was also an engraver, and is known to have engraved about 400 portraits (of which Vertue recorded the names of 275), some being after his own drawings; engraved title pages and landscapes. Travelled extensively in connection with his art; drew buildings for Loggan. Said to have saved a considerable sum of money, but evidently spent it before his death. Lived for a long time in Bloomsbury Market, where he died in November 1703. Three of what are probably his finest works are in the collection of the Duke of Portland; they include his self-portrait which is signed on the front 'R.W. f', and on the reverse 'Robert White, Engraver, Aetat: 33, 1679'. The other two represent James Scott, Duke of Monmouth and Buccleuch, K.G., signed 'R. White delin' on the front, and Charles II, signed on the front 'R. White fecit 1684'. All of these portraits are executed in lead pencil on vellum. Examples of his work are in the B.M., the Ashmolean Museum, Oxford, the V. & A. M., and several private collections. A portrait of the dramatist, Thomas Otway, signed and dated '1680', was exhibited at the South Kensington Museum, 1865. For further information see the *Walpole Society*, Vol. XIV, pp. 64–71, which contains a list of numerous signed, dated or named drawings and engravings by White.

*Whiteside, Miss R. Cordelia. (fl. 1892–1908)
Exhibited at the R.A. and S.M., 1892–1908, from addresses in London, Bromley and the Isle of Man. Her sitters included Lieut. General and Mrs. le Marchant Tupper, Sandalji Effendi of Constantinople and General Sir Robert Biddulph, G.C.B., G.C.M.G.

*Whitfield, George. (fl. c. 1840–1850)
This artist, whose family came from Ashford, Kent, went to Australia where he worked between 1840–1850.

*Whiting, Mrs. Ada. (fl. 1900)
Exhibited at the R.A. 1900, from Cromwell Buildings, Melbourne, Australia. The Museum in Sydney has portraits by her.

*Whitley, Miss Kate Mary, R.I. (fl. 1884–1903)
Of South Wigston, nr. Leicester. Exhibited at the R.A., N.W.C.S. and S.M., etc., 1884–1903. Painted still life and miniatures.

*Whitney, Miss Blanche M. (fl. 1885–1895)
Of London. Exhibited at the R.A. and N.W.C.S.

1885–1895, from 66 South Lambeth Road. Executed miniatures and drawings.

Whittaker, W., junior. (fl. 1827–1828)
Exhibited at the R.A. 1827–1828, from 13 Great Russell Street, Bloomsbury.

Whood or **Hood, Isaac.** *c.* 1689–1752
Recorded by E. Edwards, in his *Anecdotes*, as J. Whood or Hood. Resided in Lincoln's Inn Fields. Had a large practice as a portrait painter in oil, and executed portraits in black-lead on vellum. Was patronised by the Duke of Bedford. Noted for his humour and happy appreciation of passages from *Hudibras*. Was left in reduced circumstances owing to a Chancery suit. Some of his portraits were in profile and a few were engraved. He died in Bloomsbury Square, London, 24 February 1752, aged 63. A portrait in crayons of Dean Swift by Whood is in the Dublin Museum.

Wiche, J. (fl. 1811–1827). See also **Wicke, J.**
Of London. Exhibited at the R.A. and S.B.A., 1811–1827. May have been identical with J. Wicke (q.v.). Two portraits in pencil by this artist are in the B.M.

Wicke, J. (fl. 1817). See also **Wiche, J.**
Practising in 1817 at 225 High Holborn and may have been identical with J. Wiche (q.v.).

*Wicks, Mrs. Adelaide. (fl. 1906–1914)
Exhibited at the R.A. 1906–1914, from addresses in Anerley and Reigate. Her sitters included Donald Taylor Wicks, George Herbert Wicks and John Alexander Gladstone.

Wicksteed, Miss Elizabeth. See Worlidge, Mrs. Thomas

*Widdas, Ernest A. (fl. 1906–1914)
Of London. Exhibited at the R.A., 1906–1914. His sitters included His Worship the Mayor of Royal Leamington Spa and Mrs. Ernest A. Widdas, presumably his wife, and Elizabeth Mary, daughter of P. F. Warner, Esq.

Wiggins, F. (fl. 1790–1791)
Of London. Exhibited at the Society of Artists, 1790–1791, from 80 Bishopsgate Street Within. Painted miniatures.

*Wight, Miss Adelaide. (fl. 1899–1904)
Exhibited at the R.A. 1899–1904, from Avonhead, 152 Anerley Road, Anerley, London and from Redruth, Church Road, Horley, Surrey.

*Wilbee, Miss Christian M. (fl. 1903–1912)
Exhibited at the R.A. 1903–1912, from addresses in London, Harrow-on-the-Hill and Gerrards Cross. Painted miniatures and subjects in oil.

*Wilde, Mrs. Amy. (fl. 1891)
Exhibited at the R.A., 1891. Her address was 57 Grove Street, Liverpool and her sitter, The Lady Henry Fitzgerald.

Wilding, B. (fl. 1762–1769)
Of London. Exhibited at the Society of Artists and the Free Society of Artists, 1762–1769. Long records that he was at the Golden Heart, Sutton Street, Soho, 2 November 1762, when he charged 1 guinea for each portrait. In 1769 he advertised that he was leaving his house in Sutton Street for a house in Great Marylebone Street, opposite Cavendish Square, 'Where he continues to take Likenesses in the strongest Manner for Rings, Bracelets, Snuff Boxes, &c at Two Guineas each . . . . Portraits as large as Life copied in Miniature.'. He

appears to have moved further out of London for, in an old newspaper cutting, he 'hopes that the great Distance he now lives off the City, will be in some Measure compensated for, by his pleasant and airy Situation . . . .'.

Wilkes, Thomas. (fl. 1774)
Of Wednesbury, Staffs. Exhibited a 'Rural Conversation', on enamel, at The Liverpool Society of Artists, 1774.

Wilkie, Sir David, R.A. 1785–1841
Born in Cults, Fife, 18 November 1785; son of a minister. Studied at the Trustees' Academy, Edinburgh, during which time he is said to have painted miniatures. Went to London in 1805 and entered the R.A. Schools, 28 November, aged 21 years. Became a famous painter of genre subjects, etc. Exhibited at the R.A. and B.I., etc., 1806–1842. Elected A.R.A., 1809 and R.A., 1811. Was knighted in 1836. Died at sea near Gibraltar, 1 June 1841. According to J. J. Foster, two small portraits, one of which was of the artist's brother, were exhibited at Burlington House in 1879. In Allan Cunningham's *Life of Wilkie*, mention is made of correspondence in which Wilkie, writing in 1804 to a fellow student, says, 'Send me a piece of ivory the same size as the piece of paper enclosed for painting a miniature on'. I have not been able to trace any miniatures by him, but he did execute a few small-scale drawings.

Wilkin, Charles. 1750 or 1756–1814
Possibly the Charles Wilkin who entered the R.A. Schools, 7 January 1784, aged '28, Nov 4 last'. Was awarded a prize by the Society of Arts in 1771. Exhibited at the R.A., 1783–1808. Worked in London chiefly as a stipple engraver, but also painted miniatures. Father of Francis William (Frank) and Henry T. C. Wilkin (q.v.), and of Louisa and Harriet Wilkin. Hugh Bridport (q.v.) was his pupil. Wilkin died as a result of an accident, 28 May 1814. An oil portrait by him of Sir W. Parsons is at the Oxford Schools.

Wilkin, Francis (Frank) William. *c.* 1791–1842
Was born *c.* 1791; son of Charles Wilkin (q.v.) and brother of Henry T. C. Wilkin (q.v.), Charles, Louisa and Harriet Wilkin. F. W. Wilkin (usually called Frank) entered the R.A. Schools, 2 August 1815, aged 24. Said to have been an 'infant prodigy'; his early works were chiefly in miniature, of which few identified specimens have survived. Exhibited at the R.A. and B.I., 1806–1841. Had early encouragement from Sir Thomas Lawrence (q.v.) and Benjamin West. Executed miniatures and portraits in crayons, sometimes heightened with chalk, and water-colour copies after old masters. Was commissioned by Sir Godfrey Webster, Bart., to paint a picture of the Battle of Hastings to be hung in the Great Hall of Battle Abbey. Wilkin received 2,000 guineas for this picture. He painted a triple portrait in oil of himself, his brother Henry T. C. Wilkin and Benjamin West; this is reproduced in *The Connoisseur*, Vol. 167, No. 673, p. 145. The present whereabouts of this picture is unknown. He had a distinguished clientele and had the patronage of the 1st Marquess of Anglesey; a number of works by Wilkin remain in the Anglesey family collection. He is said to have died of apoplexy on 19 September 1842, when it was stated that he was 51 years of age. He was survived by his widow, Sarah. He made his will on 14 December 1841 at 20 Newman Street, London, where he had been living since *c.* 1837. He left his wife a life interest on his estate which, on her death, was to pass to his brother, Henry, to whom he also left some objects of *vertu* and his 'books, pictures and all things connected with my pro-

fession as an artist'. He left his fishing tackle to his brother, Charles, who was living in Paris. His will was proved on 6 October 1842, and a number of his works were sold at Christie's on 1 April 1843. Francis William Wilkin was said to have been kind-hearted and benevolent. He was a talented artist and a competent draughtsman. According to Sir Gyles Isham, Wilkin nearly always framed his drawings in the same type of 'rich frame' made of gilt, plaster and oak. This fact has greatly assisted in the identification of his portraits. A miniature of Elizabeth Malet, née Palk (died 1827), first wife of Col. Horace Beauchamp Seymour, is in the collection of Earl Spencer at Althorp. The account for this miniature is still in the family. This portrait was copied by Bone (q.v.) in 1828 for which he was paid £38. 15s. A pair of miniatures of Mr. & Mrs. Edward Hughes, catalogued as by Francis William Wilkin and dated '1825', were sold at Sotheby's, 5 June 1967. Other examples of his work are in the collections of H.M. the Queen, Sir Gyles Isham, Bart., Sir Francis Knowles, Bart., the Marquess of Sligo, etc. Long records seeing a softly painted full faced miniature of a child, signed in ink on the reverse 'F. Wilkin / Pinxt. / 1808'. For further information see *The Connoisseur*, March 1968, Vol. 167, No. 673, pp. 144–151.

Wilkin, Henry T. C. *c.* 1801–1852
Son of Charles Wilkin (q.v.), and brother of F. W. Wilkin (q.v.). Worked in London and later in Brighton. Exhibited at the R.A. and S.B.A., 1831–1847. Best known for his crayon portraits, but also painted water-colour copies of pictures by his brother, F. W. Wilkin, and miniatures; lectured on art. Died of heart disease in Brighton, 29 July 1852, leaving his family in reduced circumstances.

*Wilkings, Thomas. (fl. 1793)
The above artist is recorded by Long as having worked in Oxford and Soho in 1793. He charged 4 guineas for a portrait of Mr. Martin of Corpus Christi College.

Wilkins, Mrs. (fl. 1813)
Exhibited at the R.A., 1813.

Wilkins, C. (fl. 1800). See also **Wilkin, Charles**
The R.A. catalogues for 1800 give No. 841, a 'Portrait of Mrs Brown', as by C. Wilkins; no address is given and the miniature may have been by C. Wilkin (q.v.).

Wilkins, J. F. (fl. 1835–1836)
Of London. Exhibited at the R.A., etc., 1835–1836 from 79 High Holborn. His exhibits included a portrait of the Hon. Miss Arundel.

*Wilkins, Miss Mary A. (fl. 1887)
Exhibited at the R.A. 1887, from Cattistock Rectory, Dorchester, Dorset. Her sitters included the Rev. A. D. Wilkins, possibly her father.

Wilkinson, Francis. (fl. 1830–*c.* 1839)
Of Bath. Miniaturist and landscape painter. Was living in 1830 at 2 North Parade, Bath, and *c.* 1839 at 6 Wood Street, Bath.

*Wilkinson, Miss Maude I. (fl. 1899–1914)
Exhibited at the R.A. 1899–1914, from Limnersholme, Falconer Road, Bushey, Herts. Her sitters included Isabel, daughter of Lt. Col. J. E. Baines.

Wilkinson, R. (fl. 1788–1789)
Of London. Exhibited at the R.A., 1788–1789.

Williams. (fl. 1773)
Exhibited at the Society of Artists 1773, from Mr

Christie's, Northumberland Street, Strand, 'A lady in the character of Cleopatra, in miniature'.

Williams. Miss. (fl. 1784)

Exhibited at the R.A., 1784 (Honorary Exhibitor).

***Williams, Mrs.** 19th century

A miniature of Sir Hew Dalrymple-Hamilton, 4th Bart., of North Berwick (1774–1834), is inscribed on the reverse by the 8th Earl of Stair (1771–1857), 'done by my dear sister-in-law Mrs. Williams'. It was probably after a miniature by John Burgess (q.v.).

***Williams, Alyn, P.R.M.S.** 1865–1955

Born at Wrexham, Wales, 29 August 1865. Was a pupil at the Slade School, London, and of J. P. Laurens and Courtois in Paris. Exhibited at the R.A., N.W.C.S., the Royal Society of Miniature Painters (of which he was President), the Paris Salon and in the U.S.A., 1890–1914. Was a very successful miniaturist and had a distinguished clientele. Was noted for his interest in guiding the destinies of the R.M.S.; was Vice-President of the Imperial Art League, and a member of the Philadelphia Society of Miniature Painters. Much of his work is in America. His sitters included Queen Alexandra, His Eminence Cardinal Gibbons, Edward VII, Mrs. Alyn Williams and Sir Gardiner Engleheart, K.C.B., descendant of George Engleheart (q.v.). This last miniature was exhibited in Edinburgh, 1965, and is in the collection of Mrs. F. H. A. Engleheart. Two miniatures by Williams are in the Smithsonian Institution, Washington; they represent Dr. William Henry Holmes (1846–1933), pencil and water-colour on paper, signed 'Alyn Williams P.R.M.S. / 1928', and President William Howard Taft (1857–1930), signed 'Alyn Williams / 1910'. His portraits of Edward VII and Queen Alexandra are in the Guildhall Gallery, London.

Williams, C. (fl. 1825–1826)

Of London. Exhibited at the R.A. 1825–1826, from 26 Aldgate. Painted landscapes and miniatures.

Williams, Mrs. E. See **Williams, Mrs. Walter**

Williams, Edward. 1782–1855

Born in Lambeth, 1782; son of Edward Williams, engraver. Was a pupil of his maternal uncle, James Ward, R.A., and later apprenticed to a carver and gilder. Exhibited at the R.A. and B.I., etc., 1814–1855. Was a successful miniaturist and landscape painter; devoted himself to the latter. Specialised in moonlight subjects. Died in Barnes, 24 June 1855, leaving six sons who were all artists.

***Williams, Mrs. L. Crawshay.** (fl. 1907)

Of Ashstead, Surrey. Exhibited at the R.A., 1907. One of her exhibits was a self-portrait in oil.

Williams, Miss Marianne. (fl. 1836)

Of 11 Charlotte Street. Was awarded a large silver medal by the Society of Arts in 1836 for a miniature.

***Williams, Miss Mary E.** (fl. 1910)

Of Oswestry, Shropshire. Exhibited at the Society of Miniaturists, 1910.

***Williams, Miss Maud.** (fl. 1905–1914)

Of Croydon. Exhibited at the R.A., 1905–1914. Executed miniatures and drawings.

Williams, Penry. c. 1800–1885

Born in Merthyr Tydvil c. 1800; son of a house-painter whom he assisted. Was sent to London by a gentleman whose name is not known. Entered the R.A. Schools, 26 December 1821, aged 19. Won medals at the Society of Arts, 1819–1821. Exhibited at the R.A., B.I., S.B.A. and O.W.C.S., 1822–1869. Was an Associate of the O.W.C.S., 1828–1833. In 1827 he settled in Rome where he remained until his death on 27 July 1885. Williams is best known for his figure subjects in oil and water-colour, and also executed miniatures on paper. A miniature of his father by him is in Cyfarthfa Castle Museum at Merthyr Tydvil. His remaining works were sold at Christie's in 1886. The V. & A. M. and the B.M. have water-colour drawings by him.

***Williams, R. P.** (fl. 1854–1867)

Of London. Exhibited at the R.A., 1854–1867. His sitters included A. L. Boucicault, Esq.

Williams, Samuel. 1788–1852

Born in Colchester of poor parents, 23 February 1788; was apprenticed there to a printer. Taught himself to etch and to engrave on wood; settled in London in 1819 where he became known as a wood engraver. Designed book illustrations, executed pictures in miniature and in oil. Some of his miniatures, painted early in his career, were said to have been excellent. Died on 19 September 1853, leaving four sons, all wood engravers. May have been one of the S. Williams' who exhibited at the R.A. and B.I., 1807–1845.

Williams, Mrs. Walter (E). (fl. 1858)

Of Barnes. Exhibited at the R.A., 1858.

***Williams, William, F.S.A.** (fl. 1763–1793)

Of Manchester (1763), Orchard Street, Oxford Road, London (1766–1769) and Shrewsbury (1780). Exhibited at the Free Society of Artists and the Society of Artists, 1763–1780, and possibly identical with the artist of the same name who exhibited at the R.A. 1770–1792, from Norwich. Painted portraits and landscapes. Advertised in *The Leeds Mercury*, 26 January 1793, as 'Portrait and landscape painter from London, pts small oil portraits at 1 guinea each. North Side, St. Peter's Sq. Leeds.'.

Williamson, John. 1751–1818

Born in Ripon, 1751. Was apprenticed to an ornamental painter in Birmingham, but later took up art and settled in Liverpool, 1783. Exhibited at the Liverpool Academy, 1784 and 1787, and became a member in 1784. Painted portraits in oil, figure subjects, landscapes and miniatures. His address in 1784, was 18 Temple Street, Liverpool, and in 1787, 4 Paul's Square, Liverpool. Was the father of Daniel and Samuel Williamson, both landscape painters. Many notable people in the area sat to him, including William Roscoe; this portrait was the first Roscoe ever sat for. Williamson also painted William Beechey, R.A., H. Fuseli, R.A. and Nathan Litherland. He died on 27 May 1818. Was possibly the J. Williamson who exhibited a portrait at the R.A. 1783, from 1 Ely Place, High Holborn.

***Willink, J.**

A miniature of a lady, signed by this artist, was sold at Christie's, 25 October 1960.

Willis, Miss. (fl. 1839–1843)

Of London. Exhibited at the R.A., 1839 and 1843.

***Willis, Miss Ethel Mary, A.R.M.S.** b. 1874

Born in London, 1874. Studied at the Slade School of Art and was a pupil of Mme. Debillemont-Chardon (q.v.), Paris. Exhibited at the R.A., R.M.S., S.M. and Paris Salon, etc., 1904–1935.

According to an advertisement in the R.I. catalogues, she taught miniature painting, 'the French method of the broadwash, Pencil Drawing, Painting on Vellum, Water Colour &c., with Costume Models. Fees Moderate.'.

***Willis, Miss Iris I.** (fl. 1910)

Of London. Exhibited at the Society of Miniaturists, 1910.

Willis, P. (fl. 1800–1825)

Of London. Exhibited at the R.A. and B.I., 1800–1825. Executed portraits, some in miniature, as well as pictures of birds and flowers.

***Wills or Wells.** (fl. c. 1741)

Nothing is known about this artist apart from a note by Vertue, published in the *Walpole Society*, Vol. XXII, Vertue Bk. III, p. 101: 'Mr Wells made Painter in Miniature to his Majesty its said in the place of Mr Lens (mistaken report in the News papers). Footnote: written Wills corrected to Wells.' As B. Lens (q.v.) died in 1740, Wills was evidently working at this time.

Willson or Wilson, Matthew. 1814–1892

Born in London, 17 July 1814. Went to the United States in 1832 and settled in Philadelphia. Became a pupil of Henry Inman (q.v.). Went to Paris in 1835 and studied under Dubufe. Returned to America and settled in Brooklyn. Exhibited a number of paintings at the National Academy, of which he became an Associate in 1843. Painted miniatures and portraits in oil and pastel. Willson was in New Orleans in the spring of 1845 and, in 1847, went to Baltimore where he remained for at least two years. Later he went to Ohio and was in Boston from 1856–1860, moving to Hartford where he had a studio from 1861–1863. Settled finally in Brooklyn. Spent some time in Washington during the Civil War painting portraits of prominent persons, including one of Lincoln which he painted two weeks before the latter's assassination. Willson died in Brooklyn, 23 February 1892.

***Wilmot, Miss Florence N. F.** (fl. 1901–1906)

Exhibited at the R.A. 1901–1906, from Mickleton Campden, Glos. Her sitters included J. M. Barrie Esq.

***Wilpes.**

A miniature of a lady, on vellum, catalogued as by the above artist, was exhibited at the South Kensington Museum, 1865.

Wilson. (fl. 1779)

Exhibited at the Free Society of Artists, 1779, as an Honorary Exhibitor. Perhaps identical with either Benjamin Wilson (1721–1788) or Joseph Wilson who worked in Dublin and Belfast, 1770–1800.

Wilson, Miss. 19th century

A miniature painting of the Rt. Hon. C. K. Bushe (1767–1843), Lord Chief Justice of Ireland, by Miss Wilson, after an oil painting by Martin Cregan, P.R.H.A. (1788–1870), was lent to the exhibition at the South Kensington Museum, 1865. The catalogue for the exhibition stated that she was an amateur artist.

***Wilson, Miss Beatrice J.** (fl. 1897–1914)

Exhibited at the R.A. 1897–1914, from addresses in Teddington, Woking and St. Leonards-on-Sea.

***Wilson, Miss Grace.** (fl. 1908–1910)

Of London. Exhibited at the Society of Miniaturists, 1908–1910.

Wilson, James. (fl. 1828). See also **Wilson, N. J.**
A portrait and miniature painter; working in 1828 at 2 Suffolk Street, Birmingham. Probably identical with N. J. Wilson (q.v.) who was working in Suffolk Street, Birmingham in 1822.

Wilson, Matthew. See Willson, Matthew

Wilson, N. J. (fl. 1822). See also **Wilson, James**
Was working in 1822 at Suffolk Street, Birmingham and probably identical with J. Wilson (q.v.) who lived in 2 Suffolk Street, Birmingham in 1828.

*Wilson, T. H. (fl. 1846)
Long records seeing a miniature by the above artist which was signed in full with the address '1 Lowther Arcade, Aug. 21. 1846'.

Wilthew, L. (fl. 1781–1785)
Of London. Exhibited at the R.A., 1781–1785. An engraving of a portrait by Wilthew, of the Rev. W. E. Faulkner, published in 1795, is in the B.M.

Wilton, Charles. (fl. 1836–c. 1849)
Of London. Exhibited at the R.A. and S.B.A., 1837–1847. Painted figure subjects and miniatures. Long recorded a miniature of Sir Henry Wellesley, 1st Lord Cowley (1773–1847) (possibly after an oil painting), on the case of which was written 'C. Wilton Art^t / 49 Dorset St / Portman Sq^r'. The date, 1836, was on the back of the miniature. A miniature of a lady, c. 1849, was signed along the front edge 'C. Wilton'; Long did not think it very good. Schidlof considers him a skilful artist, who worked in the manner of Newton (q.v.), but in a drier way, with the use of more bluish colouring.

*Wiltshire, Miss Daisy. (fl. 1906–1909)
Exhibited at the R.A. 1906–1909, from addresses in Bushey and Frome, Somerset. Her sitters included her grandmother.

*Wimpy, Charles. (fl. 1893)
Of London. Exhibited at the R.A., 1893. His sitters included D. M. Hastings, Esq.

Windsor, F. J. (fl. 1839)
Of London. Exhibited at the R.A., 1839.

Wing, Adolphus H. A. (fl. 1848)
Of London. Exhibited at the R.A., 1848, from 40 London Street, Fitzroy Square. The exhibit was a self-portrait (No. 737, not 727 as in the index).

*Wing, C. W. (fl. 1826–1838)
Of London. O'Brien records a miniature by this artist, about whom little is known, dated 1835, and illustrates one of a lady, signed 'C.W. Wing 1838', painted on ivory, Pl. 37, Fig. 3. The artist was living in 1835 at Upper Park Street, London and may have been related to A. H. A. Wing (q.v.). According to Benezit, C. W. Wing engraved 'Views of Brighton' in 1826.

Wingfield, Peter. 1718–1777
Born in Dublin, 1718; son of Richard and Ann Wingfield of Aungier Street, Dublin. Was baptised in St. Peter's on 14 December 1718. He became a watch engraver and goldsmith and resided in Skinner Row up to 1766 when he moved to Mabbot Street. Was made a Freeman of the Guild of Goldsmiths in 1748. Studied enamelling and was awarded a premium by the Dublin Society for two watches of transparent enamel 'not attempted here before'. Took up miniature painting. Exhibited in Dublin in 1765 and 1766. His exhibits included three miniatures, two in water-colour and one on enamel. Went to London in 1767, leaving his wife in Mabbot

Street where she died in 1768. Exhibited at the Society of Artists, 1767, 1768 and 1769, and at the R.A., 1770–1775. Wingfield engraved the ticket for admission to the fireworks in St. Stephen's Green in 1749 for which he was paid £3.5.6d. by the Corporation. He died in 1777.

Wins, M. A. H. (fl. 1843)
Of London. Exhibited at the R.A. 1843, from 30a York Street, Portman Square. The exhibit was a portrait of Mr. G. W. Wins.

Winser, Charles. (fl. 1830–1841)
Of London. Exhibited at the R.A., 1830 and 1841.

*Winstanley, Hamlet. 1698–1756
Born in Warrington, 1698; son of Henry Winstanley, an engraver. Was a pupil of Sir Godfrey Kneller. Was a portrait painter and engraver. Went to Italy and later settled in London. Copied the works of old masters. Is not known as a miniaturist, but Earl Beauchamp has, in his collection, an oil miniature which is said to be a self-portrait. The artist is depicted wearing a black coat trimmed and lined with red, and a black cap. He is holding a palette and brushes. He died in Warrington, 18 May 1756. (Pl. 392: no. 948.)

*Winter, Mrs. Marjorie D. (fl. 1909–1913)
Exhibited at the R.A. 1909–1913, from 70 Swaffield Road, Wandsworth.

*Wise, Miss Constance E. (fl. 1910)
Exhibited at the R.A. 1910, from 3 Downside Crescent, Haverstock, North London.

Witchell, Thomas. b. 1755
Was born in 1755. Entered the R.A. Schools, 31 March 1777, aged '22 last Feby'. Exhibited at the R.A., 1778–1780, from 79 Well's Road, Oxford Road and 57 Titchfield Street, Oxford Street, London.

Withall, Richard Augustus. 1818–1906
Born 5 August 1818; second son of William Withall of 7 Parliament Street, Westminster, solicitor, and Eliza Sarah (née Jefferies). Became a surveyor and was especially successful in connection with railways. Was an amateur miniaturist and painted portraits and fancy landscapes. Said to have been awarded a silver palette by the Society of Arts. Married at St. Mary's Lambeth, 15 October 1850, Letitia, eldest daughter of Latham Osborn junior of Margate, and grand-daughter of Sir Richard Burton of Sacketts Hill House, St. Peter's-in-Thanet. Withall spent his early married life at Binfield Road, Lambeth; later moved to 'Branksome', Lytton Grove, Putney Hill, Surrey where he died, 28 January 1906, and was buried in Putney Vale Cemetery. Related to F. Gordon Roe who has a portrait of Letitia Frances Withall, the artist's eldest daughter, later Mrs. Sydney Williams.

Witheral or Witherell, Samuel Jordon. (fl. 1830)
Was working in 1830 at 10 Whimple Street, Plymouth.

Wivell, Abraham. 1786–1849
Born in Marylebone, London, 9 July 1786; fourth child, and only son, of a tradesman from Launceston, Cornwall who had come to London in 1785. His father died soon after his son's birth, leaving his widow badly off. Learnt shoemaking; was apprenticed to a wig-maker and hairdresser in 1799 for seven years. Set up on his own and, having taken up art, he displayed some of his miniatures in water-colour in the window with the wigs. Married as his

first wife, Mary Davies, 29 October 1809. Knew Nollekens and Northcote who encouraged him in his art. Exhibited at the R.A. in 1822, from 40 Castle Street, East, St. Marylebone and, in 1830, from 5 Edward Street, Hampstead Road. His sitters included R. Burnal, Esq., M.P., and he is known to have painted the portraits of nearly 200 M.P.s for a view of the interior of the House of Commons, which was published by Bowyer and Parkes. Had an aristocratic clientele which included Queen Caroline, George IV and other members of the Royal Family, besides many leading men of the day, and members of the theatrical profession. Married for the second time in 1821. In 1827 he published an *Inquiry into the History of the Shakespeare Portraits*, but the work was a financial failure, and Wivell lost a lot of money. His uncle, A. Wivell, of Camden Town, left him his house, furniture and an annuity of 100 *l*. for life. Invented improved fire-escapes and when the Society for the Protection of Life from Fire was formed in 1836, he was appointed their superintendent with a salary of 100 *l*. He went to live in Birmingham in 1841 and resumed his interest in art. He died in Birmingham, 29 March 1849, and was survived by his second wife and ten children, including his eldest son, Abraham Wivell (q.v.). He executed miniatures in black-lead and in oils, and was known as a portrait draughtsman and experimented in engraving. The B.M. has numerous engraved portraits after Wivell.

Wivell, Abraham, junior. (fl. 1848–1865)
Eldest son of Abraham Wivell (q.v.). Worked in London. Exhibited at the R.A., 1848–1854. Also worked in Birmingham and exhibited at the B.I., from there, 1854–1865. Painted subject pictures and miniatures. His portrait of Sir Rowland Hill was engraved.

*Woakes, Mrs. Maude. (fl. 1905–1907)
Of London. Exhibited at the Society of Miniaturists, 1905–1907.

*Wodehouse, Mrs. E. H. (fl. 1885)
Of Bath. Exhibited at the R.A., 1885.

Wogan, Robert. (fl. 1768–1782)
Of Dublin. Was a jeweller and miniaturist. Executed likenesses in hair from life or pictures and designs for mourning rings, lockets or bracelets. In 1768 he was in Upper Blind Quay and, in 1771, he had moved to Exchange Alley, and from thence to Parliament Street, in 1773. Exhibited at the Dublin Society of Artists, 1768–1775. His name is not recorded after 1782.

Wogan, Thomas. d. 1781
Of Dublin. Probably a son or younger brother of R. Wogan (q.v.). Studied at the Dublin Society Schools which he entered in 1768. Practised as a miniaturist in Dublin. Exhibited at the Dublin Society of Artists, 1772–1775. Was in London from 1776–1778. Exhibited at the R.A., 1776–1778. Returned to Dublin and exhibited there at the Society of Artists in 1780. Lived at the same address as R. Wogan and, after his return from London, at 35 George Street, Dublin. Wogan died in 1781 and was buried on 16 October in St. Andrew's Churchyard.

*Wolfe, Miss Edith Grace, A.R.M.S. (Mrs. John Wheatley). b. 1883
Was born 26 June 1883. Studied at the R.A. Schools, the Slade School of Art and at Caldron's School of Animal Painting. Exhibited at the R.A., 1908–1914, and at the Paris Salon, R.I., R.H.A., and the Liverpool Autumn Exhibition. Married John Wheatley, an artist. Painted subject pictures in oil, miniatures and, according to Benezit, was a

sculptress. The Walker Art Gallery, Liverpool contains a miniature by her, signed on the front 'Edith / Grace / Wolfe'. It represents a lady in costume called 'The Lady Clarissa', and is very loosely painted.

*Wood, Mrs. Annetta T. H. (fl. 1890)
Of Kingston-on-Thames. Exhibited at the R.A., 1890. Her sitters included James Runciman, Esq.

Wood, E. C. (fl. 1830–1831)
Of London. Exhibited at the R.A., etc., 1830–1831. Was an Honorary Exhibitor in 1830 and was at Chalke House, Peckham in 1831.

*Wood, James F. R. d. 1920
Exhibited at the R.A. 1895, from Dale View Road, Stamford Hill. Painted miniatures and large subject pictures in oil. Died July 1920.

*Wood, Miss Marguerite. (fl. 1907)
Exhibited at the R.A. 1907, from 3 Shardcroft Avenue, Herne Hill, S.E. London.

*Wood, Mrs. Rose. 1811–1913. See also **Woods, Mrs.**
Born in Fitzroy Square in March 1811. Was baptised in Old St. Pancras Church and was a niece of Richard Westall, R.A., and, according to Long, may have been the daughter of W. Daniell, R.A. (1769–1837). Was an accomplished painter and did much artistic needlework. Went to America in 1834. Had two husbands, both named George Wood. Lived latterly at The Abbey Cottage, Chertsey, Surrey. In 1834 Mrs. Gent, née Miss S. S. Daniell (q.v.), exhibited a portrait of Miss R. Daniell at the R.A. This may have represented the above artist, who may have been her sister. Mrs. R. Wood died in December 1913 when she left an estate of £1,085. The above artist was possibly identical with Mrs. Woods (q.v.).

Wood, William. 1769–1810
Born in Suffolk in 1769. Entered the R.A. Schools, 16 December 1785, aged '16 19th last Mar.'. Worked in London. Exhibited at the R.A., B.I., etc., 1788?–1808. He was possibly identical with the Wood (no initial given) who exhibited a portrait of a lady (not a miniature) at the R.A. in 1788, from Knightsbridge. He painted portrait and subject miniatures, as well as a few eye-miniatures, water-colour drawings and landscapes; and executed works in crayons and lithographs. Was in Bristol, 1791 and 1803, and Gloucester in 1798. His London addresses included 30 St. James's Place, 1792–1794, 8 Cork Street, 1795–1807 and subsequently he lived in Golden Square. He executed a number of self-portraits, some of which he destroyed as he did not consider them good enough. He noted in his ledgers that in these portraits he wore a blue coat with a red collar, and a straw-coloured waistcoat. In 1792 he exhibited one of these self-portraits at the R.A. He is known to have copied miniatures by Cosway, Engleheart and Smart (q.v.), and portraits after Reynolds. Wood joined an Artists' Volunteer Corps in 1803. He became a founder member of the Associated Artists in Water Colour in 1807, and their President, 1808–1809, and exhibited with them. In 1808 he published *An Essay on National and Sepulchral Monuments*. He was interested in landscape gardening. Dr. G. C. Williamson published a considerable amount of information on this artist, together with a complete list of all his sitters and extracts from his ledgers in *The Miniature Collector*, 1921, pp. 156–173. Wood discovered how to improve the stability of colours on ivory and, like other artists such as Engleheart (q.v.), not infrequently attached a tracing of his portraits to his ledgers for identification purposes, or in case he was required to execute a copy. He died at his house in Golden Square, 15

November 1810 (Redgrave, 2nd Edition, gives 1809). He was a good artist and one worthy of greater recognition than has often been accorded to him. Although Wood's technique is easily recognisable once it has been studied, I know of many cases where his miniatures have not been identified correctly. His portraits have an honesty about them and are well drawn and expressive. A characteristic of his work is the way he painted the backgrounds with short brush strokes, many of which are crossed, and small separate dots of paint. He used a pleasing warm colouring and shaded the features with darkish-brown strokes. His male sitters often have a rubicund complexion. I do not know of any portraits signed on the front; his usual signature is to be found on the reverse as in the case of a miniature of a Cavalry Officer, from the collection of Major R. M. O. de la Hey, signed 'D.J.D.F. by Will: Wood / of Cork Street / Lond / 1807'. This was exhibited in Edinburgh in 1965 together with an attractive miniature of a young lady, reproduced in the catalogue, Pl. 74. The City of Liverpool Museum contains a miniature copy, by Wood, of one of Reynolds' self-portraits; it is signed on the reverse 'Sir J. Reyn / after himself / By Will: Wood'. This miniature is untypical of his work and reminiscent of the work of Shelley (q.v.). Examples of his work are in the V. & A. M., which also has several MS letters by him and his ledgers. Other examples are in the Ward Usher Museum, Lincoln and many private collections including that of H.M. the Queen. A fine portrait of Sandford Peacock, signed on the reverse and dated '1801', is in the Edward B. Greene Collection, Cleveland Museum Ohio. The sitter was living in Devonshire Street and the Ledger No. is 840. Some of his works were exhibited at the South Kensington Museum, 1865 and also in Edinburgh in 1965.

*Woodforde, Samuel, R.A. 1763–1817
Born at Castle Cary, Somerset, 29 March 1763; second son of Heighes Woodforde (1726–1789), of Ansford, and his wife Anne, daughter and heiress of Ralph Dorville. He had a good education and showed an early aptitude for drawing. Became a subject and landscape painter. Entered the R.A. Schools, 8 March 1782, 'age 18, 29th last March'. Studied in Italy until 1791. Exhibited at the R.A., 1784–1815. Was elected A.R.A. in 1800 and R.A. in 1807. Married in 1815 and went to Italy soon after. Died suddenly from a chill at Ferrara on 27 July 1817. Is not known as a miniaturist, but Long recorded that when he was a boy, he executed a miniature portrait of Nancy Woodforde in oil, on the lid of a box, approximately 5 in.

Woodley, C. (Charles?). b. 1801?
Architect and miniature painter. Possibly the Charles Woodley who entered the R.A. Schools, 30 December 1822, aged 21. Was probably taught architecture by James Gandy. Exhibited at the R.A. 1819–1827, from London addresses.

Woodley, G. (fl. 1836–1843)
Of London. Exhibited at the R.A., 1836–1843. Most, if not all, the works of this artist appear to have been sketches.

Woodley, W. (fl. 1821)
Of London. Exhibited at the R.A. 1821, from 12 Wilmot Street, Brunswick Square.

Woodman, Richard. 1784–1859
Born in London, 1 July 1784; son of an engraver of the same name. Studied under R. M. Meadows, stipple engraver. Coloured engravings of W.

Westall's drawings. Was employed by Wedgwood in 1808, but returned to London soon afterwards and, according to Benezit, he went to Italy in the same year. Engraved some large plates. Exhibited at the R.A., B.I. and O.C.W.S., etc., 1820–1854. Died 15 December 1859. C. H. Woodman and R. H. Woodman, both artists, were probably his sons. Long saw signed miniatures on card in Indian ink of the Rev. Thomas Lewis and the Rev. Angell James. He also recorded seeing a water-colour portrait of a child, signed 'R. Woodman Del^t 1827'; he did not consider the work outstanding. Schidlof records seeing a series of works by him in Indian ink which, he says, are well executed. The B.M. has engraved portraits by Woodman and the N.P.G. has a portrait in water-colour of Charlotte Augusta, Princess of Wales.

*Woodruff, Miss Linda. (fl. 1899–1903)
Of London. Exhibited at the R.A. 1899–1903, from 26 Bolton Studios, Redcliffe Road and 16 Chelsea Court. Her sitters included Mrs. B. Haworth Booth and Mrs. A. Byers Fletcher.

Woods, Mrs. (fl. c. 1855). See also **Wood, Mrs. Rose**
Was working c. 1855. She had instruction from a Frenchman, and painted miniature oil landscapes for brooches, etc. Was possibly identical with Mrs. Rose Wood (q.v.).

*Woodward, Miss H. Law. (fl. 1896)
Exhibited at the R.A. 1896, from 9 Poplars Avenue, Willesden Green.

Woodward, J. (fl. 1820–1832)
Of London. Exhibited at the R.A., etc., 1820–1832. Long records seeing two miniatures on card, said to have been painted by this artist in December 1832; one was in profile. The way the features were modelled bore some resemblance to the work of Cosway (q.v.). Woodward may have painted enamels.

*Woodward, Miss Mary. (fl. 1901–1913)
Of London. Exhibited at the R.A. 1901–1913, from Carlyle Studios, 296 Kings Road, Chelsea. Painted miniatures and portraits in water-colour. Her sitters included Martin F. Woodward, Esq. Was possibly identical with the Miss Mary Woodward who exhibited at Suffolk Street in 1893.

Woodward, William. (fl. 1771)
Of London. Exhibited at the R.A. 1771, from 'Mr Penny's Charlotte St.'.

Woolcott, C. b. 1788?
Of London. Possibly identical with the C. Woolcott who entered the R.A. Schools, 21 January 1808, aged 20. C. Woolcott exhibited at the R.A. 1808–1824, from various London addresses including 7 Featherstone Buildings, Holborn and 15 Villiers Street, Strand. He painted portraits, miniatures, seascapes and subject pictures. His sitters included members of the theatrical profession and several clergymen. He exhibited two self-portraits at the R.A.: one in 1808 and another in 1815; this latter portrait was possibly a miniature. The B.M. has an engraved portrait of Sir George Murray by Woolcott which was published in 1819.

*Wooldridge, Mrs. Margaret A. (fl. 1903)
Exhibited at the R.A., 1903, from Belmont, James Street, Stoke-on-Trent.

Woolley, S. (Samuel?). (fl. 1806–1808?)
A miniature of a man, signed in front 'S. WOOLLEY' and dated '1806', was Lot 130 at Christie's, 22 March 1922. It was well drawn and

the colouring pleasant. Long saw a miniature of a man, painted slightly in the manner of Stump (q.v.), signed in front 'S. Woolley' and dated 1808(?). The artist was possibly identical with Samuel Woolley who entered the R.A. Schools, 19 July 1792, aged 19. The latter artist was an architect and was awarded a silver medal in 1792.

*Woolnough, R. C. (fl. 1801–1804)

Long records seeing a miniature, signed on the reverse 'R.C. Woolnough Pinxt / 1801'. I have seen a well painted miniature of an unknown man which was presumably by the same artist. It was sold at Christie's, 19 November 1968, and was signed on the reverse 'Woolnough, Princes Street, Barbi . . .' (the last part of the inscription being indecipherable), and dated '1804'. The face was well modelled and the details of the costume well painted. (Pl. no. 953.)

*Wooton, John. (fl. 1755). See **W.**

A miniature signed and dated 'W. 1755', was Lot 53 at Sotheby's, 9 February 1961. The artist may have been an amateur. The above name was a family attribution.

Worlidge, Thomas. 1700–1766

Born in Peterborough in 1700 of Roman Catholic parents. Was a pupil in London of Alessandro Maria Grimaldi (1659–1732), 6th Marquess, an artist from Genoa, from whose family W. Grimaldi (q.v.) was descended. Worlidge married A. M. Grimaldi's daughter, Arabella (died before 1749). Said to have re-introduced painting on glass in Birmingham. Practised portrait painting in Bath and later settled in London c. 1740. The name of his second wife was Mary. Exhibited at the Free Society of Artists, 1761–1766. Said to have been a pupil of F. Boitard. Painted miniatures and executed portraits in pastel and oil as well as small finished portraits in black-lead and etchings in the style of Rembrandt. A fine miniature by Worlidge of John Milton (1608–1674), after an earlier portrait, is in my collection. This is one of his earliest known works and is signed on the front 'T. Worlidge Fecit. Anno Dom 1737'. He advertised in *The Daily Advertiser*, 4 November 1751, that he had designed a *Book of Heads*. He was living in The Piazza, Covent Garden, 18 February 1752, at Mr. Carne's in St. Martin's Lane, Bath, 24 September 1766 and was at Wicksteed's Toy Shop in the Grove, Bath, 23 September 1754. He married as his third wife, in 1763 the beautiful Elizabeth Wicksteed (q.v.), daughter of the proprietor of the shop. Settled in the same year in Great Queen Street in the house which had been occupied by Kneller and Reynolds. Worlidge is said to have had thirty-two children. He was described as hot-tempered, gluttonous and extravagant. He had a country house near Hammersmith where he died, 23 September 1766, and was buried in Hammersmith Church. His plumbago miniatures are usually good, some are in profile; many are after the works of other artists including I. Oliver (q.v.). His oil portraits are bolder, such as the one of Garrick in the V. & A. M. He may have painted miniatures on ivory, as a self-portrait of the artist in the character of Rembrandt, said to be signed 'T.W.' and catalogued as by Worlidge, was lent to the Exhibition at the South Kensington Museum, 1865. A self-portrait on parchment signed on the front 'TW 176–' (the last figure being indistinct), and on the reverse 'Worlidge by himself', is in the collection of R. Bayne Powell, Esq. His pupils included W. Grimaldi (q.v.) and G. Powle (q.v.). H.M. the Queen has, in her collection, two pencil portraits by him; they represent T. Cibber (1735) and Beau Nash (1736). The B.M. has some pencil portraits by him and the N.P.G. has one of George II.

Worlidge, Mrs. Thomas. (fl. 1763–1767)

Née Elizabeth Wicksteed; daughter of a toyman in Bath. She was said to have been very beautiful. Married (as his third wife) in 1763, Thomas Worlidge (q.v.). Exhibited at the Society of Artists and the Free Society of Artists, 1765–1767. Executed pictures in needlework, portraits and miniatures and worked in crayons. Exhibited a miniature of the Duke of York at the Free Society of Artists in 1767. Continued to sell Worlidge's etchings after his death; married a wine merchant named Ashley who had been a friend of Worlidge. The B.M. has an engraved portrait of her.

*Worrall, Miss Ella. b. 1863

Born in Liverpool, 7 November 1863. Exhibited at the R.A. 1903–1908, from 231 Upper Parliament Street, Liverpool. Was possibly related to J. E. Worrall of Liverpool who exhibited at the R.A., 1862–1868.

*Worsfold, Miss Emily M. (Mrs. E. Maltby). (fl. 1900–1908)

Exhibited at the R.A. 1900–1908, from addresses in Feltham, Middlesex. She is recorded as Mrs. E. Maltby from 1902. Her sitters included Mabel, daughter of W. Worsfold, Esq.

*Worsfold, Miss Maud B. (fl. 1894–1909)

The above artist exhibited at the R.A. etc., 1894-1909, from various London addresses. She painted miniatures and portraits and subjects in watercolour. Her sitters included the Marchioness of Tullibardine, the Rev. G. P. B. Viner and Mrs. H. Alewood King. A very attractive small portrait in pencil and water-colour, on paper, by Miss Worsfold, is in my collection. It represents Lady Viti Paget (died 1918), wife of Rear-Admiral Sir Alfred Wyndham Paget, K.C.M.G., whom she married in 1906. The miniature was painted in July 1908 and is signed in monogram on the front 'MBW'.

*Woulfe, Miss Viola G. (fl. 1895–1914)

Of London. Exhibited at the R.A. and S.M., 1895–1914. Painted miniatures and flower subjects in water-colour.

*Wren, Miss Louisa. (fl. 1882–1908)

Of London. Exhibited at the R.A. and N.W.C.S., etc., 1882–1908. From 1888–1893 her address was 12 Colville Gardens, Bayswater. Her sitters included Mrs. Wilfred Thompson.

Wright, Mrs. See **Wright, Mrs. E. M.**

*Wright, Mrs. E. M. (fl. 1831–1832)

Exhibited at the R.A. 1831 and 1832, from 9 Gower Street North, Bedford Square. No initials are recorded in 1831, but in 1832 the initials are given as E. M. Wright in the catalogue. It has been suggested that the above artist was identical with Miss Sarah Biffin (q.v.), later Mrs. Wright.

*Wright, Miss Edith. (fl. 1905)

Exhibited at the R.A. 1905, from The Willows, Harlesden, London, N.W.

*Wright, Miss Ethel. (Mrs. Barclay). (fl. 1887–1896)

Of London. Exhibited at the Paris Salon, 1887 and at the R.A. 1895–1896, from 6 William Street, Lowndes Square. Painted miniatures, large oil paintings and flower subjects in water-colour.

*Wright, George. (fl. c. 1833)

The *Leeds Directory* records that he painted miniatures in Harrogate c. 1833.

*Wright, H. Pooley. (fl. 1645–1646). See also **W., H.P.**

Long records seeing a rectangular miniature of an unknown man, signed and dated '1645', by the above artist. It was 3⅛ in. and was painted on copper. Another miniature by him dated '1646' is at Ham House.

*Wright, Miss Helen B. (fl. 1903–1914)

Exhibited at the R.A. 1903 and 1914, from Green Bank, Merton Lane, Highgate. Executed miniatures and etchings, drawings and engravings.

Wright, John (Inigo ?). d. 1820

The date of his birth appears to be uncertain. Long and other authorities give it as c. 1760, but Benezit identifies him with Inigo Wright, an engraver, and gives his dates as c. 1745–1820. Wright exhibited at the R.A., 1795–1819. Was intimate with T. Phillips, Hoppner, Lawrence and W. Owen. Married as his first wife, Priscilla Guise, daughter of a musician who was master of the choristers at Westminster. She had previously married a French emigrant who had left her and returned to France. She did not survive the birth of their son, John William Wright (q.v.) in 1802. Wright soon remarried. He committed suicide in 1820. He had several pupils including S. P. Denning (q.v.). Wright was a good artist who painted both oval and rectangular miniatures. Some of his miniatures have a yellowish tinge on the face and the shading on the drapery is slightly mauve. Many of his works were copies of oil paintings, some being after Hoppner, Reynolds, Owen, etc. Col. J. Clark Kennedy has a miniature, c. 1800, of a man in a dark blue coat, signed on the reverse 'J. Wright / Miniature painter / to His Royal Highness / the Duke of Kent / Gerrard St / Soho / no. 28'. I have two examples of his work in my collection; one of a man in a scarlet coat and blue collar, inscribed on the reverse 'by J. Wright 28 Gerrard Street, Soho' (exhibited in Edinburgh in 1965), and one of an elderly man c. 1819. Wright had the following addresses:

  1795–1802 28 Gerrard Street, Soho.
  1803–1804 50 Leicester Square.
  1806–1819 Burlington Gardens.

His miniatures are forceful and some give the impression of oil paintings. He used gouache to paint the linen draperies and the hair, and some of his later works are painted with long hairy strokes on the face. Examples of his work are at the V. & A. M. and the N.P.G. The B.M. has portraits in water-colour and Indian ink, after Hoppner. According to Mr. Douglas Hall, compiler of *The Tabley House Papers*, *Walpole Society*, Vol. XXXVIII, John Wright, whose dates are given c. 1745–1820, sent a bill, on 8 May 1813, to Sir John Leicester for 'a miniature of Lady Leicester (30 gns)'; Drawing of the "Fortune Teller" (Owen); of the "Wood Nymph" (Reynolds); the "Bacchante" (West) (8 gns each). Sir J. L. paid £50 on account.'

Wright, Mrs. John (Miss Priscilla Guise). d. 1802

Née Priscilla Guise, daughter of Mr. Guise, musician and master of choristers at Westminster. She practised as a miniaturist with some success. Married a French emigrant who soon left her and returned to France where he died a few years later. She then married (as his first wife) John Wright (q.v.), by whom she had a son, said to be John William Wright (q.v.). She did not survive the birth and died in 1802.

Wright, John Michael. 1625–1700

Of Scottish descent. Noted 17th-century painter of portraits in oil. A miniature of Sir R. Henley, water-colour on vellum, and signed 'J.M.W.', is in the collection of Earl Beauchamp, and has been attributed to him, but there is no evidence at present that he painted miniatures.

Wright, John William. 1802 or 1805–1848

Born in London, 1802; son of John Wright (q.v.) and his wife (q.v.), née Priscilla Guise. Educated at Loughborough House, Brixton. Was possibly the 'Jno Wm Wright' who entered the R.A. Schools, 4 April 1822, aged 17. If so, either his date of birth was wrongly recorded by previous authors, or he was the son of a later marriage and not of Priscilla Guise, as has always been supposed. Was a pupil of T. Phillips, R.A. Exhibited at the R.A. and O.W.C.S., 1823–1848; became an Associate of the latter Society in 1831, a member in 1841, and secretary in 1844. He painted portraits, domestic subjects and some miniatures, as well as executing book illustrations. He died of influenza in Great Marlborough Street, London, 14 January 1848, leaving his wife and two children in reduced circumstances. Schidlof records that he signed his miniatures 'JWW'. Heath's *Book of Beauty* contains engravings after Wright. His sitters included Ellen Tree, the actress.

*Wright, Miss Lilian F. (fl. 1900–1912)

Of London. Exhibited at the R.A. 1900–1912, and was possibly identical with the artist of this name who exhibited still life at Suffolk Street in 1893. Executed miniatures, flower paintings in oil and drawings.

Wright, Mrs. Patience. 1725–1786

Née Patience Lovell, born in Bordentown, New Jersey in 1725. Married Joseph Wright (died 1769), by whom she had four children: Elizabeth, who became a wax modeller; Joseph (1756–1793), who was a modeller and painter; Phebe, who married John Hoppner, R.A., in 1782; and Sarah. After her husband's death, Mrs. Wright opened a waxworks with her sister, Rachel Wells. In 1772 she came to London and opened another waxworks which was very successful. Her statue of Lord Chatham was placed in Westminster Abbey. During the Revolution Mrs. Wright acted as a spy for the Americans. She died on 23 March 1786. A miniature of General Abercrombie, catalogued as by her, was exhibited at the National Museum, Washington from December 1925 to January 1926.

Wright, Mrs. Priscilla. See **Wright, Mrs. John**

Wright, Robert. (fl. 1840–1847)

Of Dublin. Practised for many years in Dublin and exhibited at the R.H.A. from 1840–1847

Wright, Mrs. Sarah. See **Biffin, Miss Sarah**

Wright, Thomas. 1792–1849

Born in Birmingham, 2 March 1792; taken, when a child, to London and apprenticed to H. Meyer, the engraver. Collaborated for four years with W. T. Fry, also an engraver. Exhibited at the R.A., etc., 1815–1848. Painted portraits in oil, miniatures and executed engravings. Married a sister of George Dawe, the portrait painter. In 1822 went to St. Petersburg; returned to England in 1826. Engraved 'The Beauties of the Court of Charles II'. Returned to St. Petersburg, 1830, to arrange the affairs of George Dawe. Was patronised by the Russian Court and was a member of the Academies of St. Petersburg, Stockholm and Florence. Remained in Russia for 15 years and sometimes signed his name in Russian characters, using Russian spelling. Also signed Tho Wright / 1839 in scratched letters. Died in George Street, Hanover Square, London, 30 March 1849. The B.M. has a small pencil profile portrait of a lady and a boy with a dog, signed 'Thos Wright', with the name 'Rait' in Russian characters and dated '1842'.

Wright, William. (fl. 1819–1841)

Of Bath. Was living at 4 George Street, Bath, 1819–1821, and at 27 Milsom Street, Bath, 1822. Wrote from Windmill House Academy, Stourbridge, 9 July 1841, saying that 'a profile miniature portrait of W. Hardwicke was the first one copied by him'.

Wroughton, Miss Charlotte. (fl. 1821)

Of Bedford Street, Bedford Square. Was awarded a silver medal in 1821 by the Society of Arts for a miniature portrait. She may have been identical with Miss Wroughton of 14 Alfred Place, London who exhibited at the B.I., etc., 1825–1829; the latter exhibits were subject pictures.

*Wyatt, J. (fl. 1873)

Of London. Exhibited at the R.A., 1873. His sitters included J. B. Buckstone, Esq., and the Marchioness of Bute.

*Wyke, Miss Anne. See **Smith, Mrs. S. Catterson**

Wyke, Robert Titus. c. 1790–c. 1870

Born in London c. 1790; son of a Dutch diamond-setter who settled in Dublin. Painted miniatures and executed drawings in water-colour. Was very industrious, but did not achieve much success as an artist, and taught drawing in, and around, Wexford, where he resided in Slaney Street. Married a Miss Hatchell by whom he had a daughter, Anne, who became the wife of S. Catterson Smith, P.R.H.A. Advancing years necessitated his living with his daughter and son-in-law in St. Stephen's Green, where he died c. 1870, aged about 80.

*Wykeham-Martin, Mrs. Julia. (fl. 1906–1909)

Of Bourne End, Bucks. Exhibited at the Society of Miniaturists, 1906–1909.

*Wylde, Miss Tressie or **Thresa.** (fl. 1897–1903)

Exhibited at the R.A. 1897 and 1903, from Alexandra House, Kensington Gore and 19 Palace Gate, London.

*Wynne, E. Kendrick. (fl. 1902)

Of London. Exhibited at the Society of Miniaturists, 1902.

Wyon, Mrs. W. H. (fl. 1831–1846)

Of London. Exhibited at the R.A., 1846. A miniature of a child by her painted on ivory and signed and dated on the reverse, '1831', was sold in Brussels, 6–7 December 1935.

*Wyvill, Mrs. D'Arcy. (fl. 1904–1907)

Of Constable Burton, Finghall, Yorkshire. Exhibited at the Society of Miniaturists, 1904–1907.

*Wyvill, Mrs. Elizabeth. (fl. 1901)

Of Ben Rhyddinge, Leeds. Exhibited at the Society of Miniaturists, 1901.

Y

*Yates, Miss Lilian Delves-. (fl. 1900–1903)

Of London. Exhibited at the Society of Miniaturists, 1900–1903.

*Yates, Mrs. W. E. (fl. 1900–1903). See also **Yeates, Mrs. W. E.**

Of Davenham, Cheshire. Exhibited at the Society of Miniaturists, 1900 and 1903. Was probably identical with Mrs. W. E. Yeates (q.v.).

*Yeates, Mrs. W. E. (fl. 1897). See also **Yates, Mrs. W. E.**

A newspaper article c. 1897 records the above artist as exhibiting in London. The exhibit was a miniature of 'the Princess of Wales with Prince Edward of York in her arms'. The artist was probably identical with Mrs. W. E. Yates (q.v.) of Cheshire.

Yeo, T. P. (fl. c. 1840)

A rather inferior miniature of a lady, c. 1840, signed by this artist, was seen by Long.

*Yewman, E. (fl. 1837)

A miniature, signed 'E. Yewman' and dated '1837', was seen at the V. & A. M. The artist may have been related to Charles Alexander Yewman, a portrait painter of Scottish descent, who worked in Dublin, 1837–1844. The miniature was not of outstanding merit.

Young (I). (fl. 1767–1775). See also **Young (II)**

Of London. Exhibited at the Society of Artists, 1767–1775, and according to Graves, is identical with the artist of this name who exhibited at the Free Society of Artists from Bristol, 1769 and 1783. May also have been identical with the artist of this name who was working in Bath in 1803.

Young (II). (fl. 1771–1803). See also **Young (I)**

The above artist is said to have been a painter of historical subjects and miniatures, and to have been working in Bath in 1803. Long recorded that he was at 'Mr Williams, King Street, Bristol on 27 July 1771'. He may have been identical with Young (I) (q.v.).

*Young, A. D. (fl. 1895)

I have in my collection a miniature of a young lady, signed and dated on the front 'A D Young / 1895'. It is quite well painted with a soft brush stroke, the background being painted with a greenish-blue hatching. The artist was possibly identical with the A. D. Young who exhibited a landscape at Suffolk Street in 1891.

*Young, Mrs. Constance A. (fl. 1902–1903)

Exhibited at the R.A. 1902 and 1903, from Eastleigh, London Road, Norbury.

*Young, Mrs. Francis E. (fl. 1901)

Exhibited at the R.A. 1901, from The Beeches, Burnell Road, Sutton, Surrey.

*Young, J.

A miniature of Jane Shore (died 1527?), after a portrait at Ludlow Castle, was sold at Christie's, 25 October 1960, when it was catalogued as by the above artist.

*Young, Miss Rachel R. B. (fl. 1910)

Exhibited at the R.A. 1910, from 5 Great Western Terrace, Glasgow.

Z

Zeeman, Enoch. See **Seaman** or **Seeman, Enoch**

Zeigler. (fl. 1768). See also **Ziegler, Daniel**

Exhibited at the Free Society of Artists, 1768. Possibly identical with Daniel Ziegler (q.v.).

Ziegler, Miss. (fl. 1844–1863)

Of London; possibly the daughter of H. B. Ziegler, and undoubtedly related to E. Ziegler, all of whom exhibited from the same addresses for many years. She exhibited at the R.A., etc., 1844–1863, and at Leeds Academy, 1853. Painted pictures in oil and miniatures. Her sitters included Lord Auckland, Princess Mary of Cambridge (as a child) and Kootub Minor of Delhi. E. Ziegler exhibited a portrait of Miss Ziegler in 1847.

Ziegler, Daniel. 1716–1806

Born in Mulhouse, France, 18 October 1716. Studied in Lucerne in 1742 and later went to Rome and Paris; was in Dublin, 1763–1764, and lodged in College Green. Painted miniatures, oil portraits and executed copies. Was probably identical with the Zeigler (q.v.) who exhibited at the Free Society of Artists in 1768. Married in London. He and his wife, also a miniaturist, were in Bristol and advertised in the *Bristol Journal*, 10 May 1766. On 28 June 1766, Felix Farley's *Bristol Journal* noted that 'Ziegler and Derecour' were working in Bristol, and that 'Mr Ziegler, limner (lately from Italy) is now come to this City with his wife – he is skilled in port; History and Landscape pt & she in miniatures. The said Mr. Ziegler, Together with Mr. Derecour, will teach also to draw Landscapes, Faces, and every kind of Drawing for work, ornaments, &c at a guinea entrance and half a guinea pr month to attend three times a week. Lodgings at Forster's Coffee House (Bristol)'. Said to have returned to Mulhouse where, according to Schidlof, he died 26 March 1806.

*Ziegler, Mrs. Daniel. (fl. 1766)

Wife of Daniel Ziegler (q.v.). Painted miniatures. Was in Bristol in 1766. The *Bristol Journal*, 10 May 1766, records that 'Madam Ziegler, visits Bristol with her husband, limner'. The same Journal, for 28 June 1766, states that 'Mr Ziegler, limner (lately from Italy) is now come to this City with his wife – he is skilled in port; History & landscape pt & she in miniatures'.

Zincke, Christian Friedrich. 1683/4–1767

Born in Dresden, 1683/4; son of a goldsmith, into which trade he was apprenticed; studied painting in his spare time and had instruction from H. C. Fehling. Came to England in 1706 and studied under C. Boit (q.v.). He soon became known and painted enamel miniatures after oil paintings by Kneller, Lely, etc., and from life. Obtained the patronage of Royalty and had a distinguished clientele. Visited Germany in 1737. He obtained various prices for his enamels; those recorded are £6. 9s. and 15 guineas in 1730, and later 30 guineas. By 1725 his eyesight was giving him trouble, and got worse after his trip to Germany. He lived for years in Tavistock Row, Covent Garden, but moved, in 1746, to South Lambeth. In spite of the fact that failing eyesight prevented him from practising to any great extent, he is known to have taught J. Meyer (q.v.) some-

time after 1748. He was twice married, and by his first wife, said to be very good looking, he had a son Christopher (who was one of the Six Clerks of Chancery from 1768–1789), and a daughter. By his second wife Elizabeth, who survived him, he had a further three or four children. One of his sons, Paul Francis Zincke (q.v.), used to fake portraits of Shakespeare, Milton, etc. (*Literary Gazette*, 1819, p. 459). The *D.N.B.* states that this was a grandson, not a son, of Zincke. He was undoubtedly one of the greatest enamellists of the seventeenth century. By 1752 he had retired from his profession and only painted for his own amusement. He died at South Lambeth, 24 March 1767. His house in Tavistock Row was successively occupied by Deacon (q.v.) and Meyer (q.v.). His pupils included Gambel (q.v.) and W. Prewett (q.v.). J. Rouquet (q.v.) worked somewhat in the same manner. Twenty-five miniatures, of which at least sixteen are signed, are in the collection of the Duke of Portland. These are among his finest works. Having carefully examined this collection, it is clear that the quality of his miniatures is such that it is difficult to distinguish between his work and that of Boit. One of his most attractive enamels is that of Lady Margaret Cavendish Harley and her father, Edward Harley, 2nd Earl of Oxford. It is oblong and executed in superbly fresh colours, signed on the reverse 'C. F. Zincke Fecit 1727', and inscribed with the names of the sitters. This miniature is the subject of a letter from Zincke to the 2nd Earl of Oxford in which he says: '. . . . I have begun it ten times before any Lines pleased me, and really My Lord I find my Eyes scarce Capable of seeing them fine strokes, which I am obliged to use to bring it to Perfection . . . .'. In their article on portraits of Horace Walpole (*Walpole Society*, Vol. XLII, pp. 1–34) C. Kingsley Adams and W. S. Lewis describe and illustrate (their plate 4b) a miniature of Walpole by Zincke, signed and dated 1745; and refer also to a miniature set in a ring (their plate 24b) which they attribute to Zincke or to Bernard Lens. His enamels are not always painted with quite the same smoothness as those of Boit. A red stippling, the dots of which are sometimes blended together, can be observed on the face. One great difference between these two artists' work is that Zincke's enamels almost always have a smooth enamelled back to the miniature; the reverse of Boit's enamels are often rough. Not all Zincke's works are of even merit, but this may have been partly due to his eyesight, and it is thought possible that he employed several assistants who may have painted a large portion of his portraits. This makes identification difficult. He did not always sign his miniatures; known signatures are: C.F.Z. (monogram), C.F. (monogram) Zincke fecit and C. F. Zincke, pinxt, sometimes followed by a date, C. F. Zincke fecit and other variations. The Ward Usher Museum, Lincoln has a miniature of Catherine, Duchess of Buckingham, signed on the front 'FC' (monogram) 'Zincke (or Zinke) fecit / 1724'. Examples of his work are at the V. & A. M., the N.P.G., the Ashmolean Museum, Oxford and numerous private collections. Examples of this artist's work were exhibited in Edinburgh in 1965, including a portrait of Hannah Sophia, Countess of Exeter, lent by the Marquess of Exeter (Burghley House Collection), Mrs. Mitchell, née Burnet, lent by the Earl of Haddington, Margaret Manners, Countess of Salisbury, lent by Earl Beauchamp, and the miniature already referred to of Lady Margaret Harley and her father, Edward Harley. Many of his works were loaned to the exhibition at the South Kensington Museum, 1865. A portrait of Zincke at work, drawn in 1752, by W. Hoare, R.A., who was a friend of his, is at the B.M. He was referred to by his contemporaries as Zink, Zinks and Zincks.

*Zincke, Paul Francis. *c.* 1745–1830

Son or grandson of C. F. Zincke (q.v.) whose works he copied; also faked portraits of Shakespeare, Milton, etc. Schidlof records the above artist as a miniaturist, but I have been unable to verify this statement.

*Zink, George Frederick. (fl. 1882–1914)

Of London. Exhibited at the R.A. and S.M., 1882–1914, from 34 Princess Road, Kilburn Park and 1 Randolph Gardens, Maida Vale. His sitters included the Viscountess Galway, the Countess of Carnarvon and the Dowager Lady Edmonstone. A portrait by him of Queen Wilhelmina of the Netherlands is in the Ashmolean Museum, Oxford.

Zoffany, John, R.A. 1735–1810

It is not certain that this celebrated portrait painter ever executed miniatures. One on ivory, inscribed very boldly in small Roman letters 'Zoffany Pinx^t 1781', is reproduced in *John Zoffany, R.A.*, by Lady Victoria Manners and Dr. G. C. Williamson, f.p. xii. As the coiffure appears to date from *c.* 1788, it is doubtful if Zoffany wrote the inscription, especially as he rarely signed an oil painting. A miniature of the Princess Royal and the Princess Amelia (in oil) was lent to the exhibition at the South Kensington Museum, 1865 when it was catalogued as by Zoffany.

Zucchero or **Zuccaro, Federigo.** 1540?–1609?

This Italian portrait painter is reputed to have painted some miniatures, but none exist than can, with any certainty, be ascribed to him. Several miniatures, attributed to the above artist, were lent to the exhibition at the South Kensington Museum 1865.

Zurich, Johann. *c.* 1685–1735

Born in Dresden, *c.* 1685; son of a Dresden jeweller who taught him this trade and the art of drawing. Took up miniature painting and studied at the Academy in Berlin. Came to England *c.* 1715. Executed miniatures on enamel and ivory. Was overshadowed by Zincke (q.v.). Died in London in December 1735 and was buried near the Lutheran Church in the Savoy, leaving a son of about twelve years of age.

Bibliography

Annals of the Fine Arts, Vol. I, 1817, London.

Antique Collector, London.
April/May, 1965, *John Hoskins, Miniaturist,* Daphne Foskett.

Antiques, U.S.A.
September, 1966, *Miniatures by John Smart,* Daphne Foskett, The Starr Collection in the Nelson Gallery — Atkins Museum, Kansas City.

Archer, Dr. Mildred, *British Drawings in the India Office Library,* 1969, London, 2 vols.

Armstrong, Nancy, *Jewellery, An Historical Survey of British Styles and Jewels,* 1973, London.

Arts Council of Great Britain, Scottish Committee, *British Portrait Miniatures Exhibition Catalogue,* 1965, Edinburgh.

Aubrey, John, *Aubrey's Brief Lives,* edited O. Lawson Dick, 1949, London, reprinted up to 1975.

Auerbach, Erna, *Nicholas Hilliard,* 1961, London.

Bell, C.F. and Poole, Mrs. R. Lane, *English Seventeenth Century Portrait Drawings in Oxford Collections,* The Walpole Society, Vol. XIV, 1926, Oxford.

Bénézit, Emmanuel, *Dictionnaire des Peintres, Sculpteurs, Dessinateurs et Graveurs,* 8 vols., 2nd edition 1960, France; 10 vols., new edition 1976, France.

Bolton, T., *Early American Portrait Painters in Miniature,* 1921, New York.

Boucher, François, *A History of Costume in the West,* 1967, London.

Bourgoing, J. De, *Die Wiener Bildnisminiatur,* 1926, Vienna.
Die Englische Bildnisminiatur, 1927, Vienna.
Die Französische Bildnisminiatur, 1928, Vienna.

Bradford, Ernle, *Four Centuries of European Jewellery,* 1953, London.

Bryan, Michael, *Dictionary of Painters and Engravers,* revised and enlarged by Dr. G.C. Williamson, 1903-5, London.

Brydall, Robert, *History of Art in Scotland,* 1889, Edinburgh and London.

Buckman, Percy and Williamson, Dr. G.C., *The Art of the Miniature Painter,* 1926, London.

Burlington Fine Arts Club Exhibition, 1889, London, two editions, one without plates.

The Burlington Magazine, London.
November, 1943, *Holbein's Miniatures,* Carl Winter.
March, 1947, *A Miniature Self-Portrait by Thomas Flatman,* Graham Reynolds.
May, 1949, *A Newly Identified Miniaturist of the Early Seventeenth Century,* Graham Reynolds.
July, 1957, *The 1590 Lumley Inventory,* David Piper.
November, 1959, *Gerard and Lucas Hornebolt in England,* Hugh Paget.
May, 1978, *Hoskins' and Crosse's: Work in Progress,* John Murdoch.

Caw, James, L., *Scottish Painting Past and Present,* 1908, London.

Christie's catalogues.

Chardon, Mme. G. Debillemont, *La Miniature Sur Ivoire,* 1903, Paris.

Cleveland Museum of Art, *Portrait Miniatures — (The Edward B. Greene Collection),* 1951, Cleveland.

Clouzot, Henri, *Dictionnaire des Miniaturistes sur Émail,* 1924, Paris.

Colding, T.H., *Danish Miniaturists,* 1948, Copenhagen.
Aspects of Miniature Painting, 1953, Copenhagen.

College of Arms, London, The, *16th Monograph of the London Survey Committee,* 1963.

The Connoisseur, London.
September, 1921, *John Turmeau, Miniaturist,* E. Rimbault Dibdin.
March, 1953, *Mrs. Mary Beale,* Elizabeth Walsh.
November, 1959, *Giuseppe Macpherson,* John Fleming.
February and March, 1968, *George Chinnery's Image of Himself,* Richard Ormond.
March, 1968, *Francis William Wilkin,* Sir Gyles Isham, Bt.
July, 1977, *John Thomas Barber Beaumont, Miniaturist and Art Tutor of Henry Alken,* Aubrey Noakes.

Copley, John Singleton, *Exhibition Catalogue,* 1965, U.S.A.

Croft-Murray, Edward and Hulton, Paul, *Catalogue of British Drawings,* British Museum, 1960, London, 2 vols.

Cunnington, C. Willett and Cunnington, Phillis, *Handbook of English Costume in the Sixteenth Century,* London.
Handbook of English Costume in the Seventeenth Century, London.
Handbook of English Costume in the Eighteenth Century, London.
Handbook of English Costume in the Nineteenth Century, London.

Cunnington, Phillis and Mansfield, Alan, *Handbook of English Costume in the 20th Century,* London.

Cunnington, Phillis, *Costume of Household Servants from the Middle Ages,* 1974, London.

de Courtais, Georgine, *Women's Headdress and Hairstyles,* 1973 and 1974, London.

Department of Fine Arts, Carnegie Institute, *Four centuries of Portrait Miniatures, from the Heckett Collection,* 1954, Pennsylvania.

De Piles, Roger, *The Art of Painting,* 2nd edition, 1744, London.

Dibdin, E. Rimbault, *Liverpool Art and Artists in the 18th Century,* The Walpole Society, Vol. VI, 1918, Oxford.

Dictionary of British Artists, 1880-1940, compiled J. Johnson and A. Greutzner, 1976, Suffolk.

Dictionary of National Biography, Oxford.

Ellet, Mrs. E.F., *Women Artists,* 1860, London, 2nd edition.

Evans, Joan, *A History of Jewellery,* 1951, London.

Evelyn, John, *Diary 1625-1706 and Correspondence,* 1871, London.

Farington, Joseph, R.A., *The Farington Diary,* 8 vols., 1922-1928, London.

Fielding, M., *Dictionary of American Painters, Sculptors and Engravers,* 2nd edition with Addendum by James F. Carr, 1965, New York.

Finberg, A.J., *Cornelius Johnson; A Chronological Catalogue,* The Walpole Society, Vol. X, 1922, Oxford.

Fisher, A., *Enamelling on Metal,* 1906, London.

Fisher, Stanley, F.R.S.A., *A Dictionary of Watercolour Painters,* 1972, London.

Foskett, Daphne, *British Portrait Miniatures,* 1963, London.
John Smart, the Man and His Miniatures, 1964, London.
Exhibition Catalogue, British Portrait Miniatures, Edinburgh, 1965.
A Dictionary of British Miniature Painters, 1972, London.
Samuel Cooper, 1974, London.
Samuel Cooper and His Contemporaries, N.P.G. 1974, London.
John Harden of Brathay Hall, 1974, Kendal.

Foster, J.J., *British Miniature Painters and their Works,* 1898, London.
Miniature Painters, British and Foreign, 2 vols., 1903, London and New York.
Chats on Old Miniatures, 1908, London.
Samuel Cooper and the English Miniature Painters of the XVIIth Century, 2 vols., 1914-16, London.
A Catalogue of Miniatures, The Property of His Grace The Duke of Northumberland, privately printed, 1921, London.

Dictionary of Painters of Miniatures, 1926, London.

Foster, Sir William, C.I.E., *British Artists in India,* The Walpole Society, Vol. XIX, 1931, Oxford.

Ganz, Paul, *Holbein,* 1949, London.

Garlick, Dr. Kenneth, *Sir Thomas Lawrence,* 1954, London.
A Catalogue of the Paintings, Drawings and Pastels of Sir Thomas Lawrence, The Walpole Society Vol. XXXIX, 1962-64, Glasgow.

Gibson, W.P., *Miniatures and Illuminations, Wallace Collection Catalogue,* 1935, London.

Gilhespy, F. Brayshaw, F.S.A., *Derby Porcelain,* 1961, London.

Godden, Geoffrey A., F.R.S.A., *Encyclopaedia of British Pottery and Porcelain Marks,* 1964, London.

Goulding, R.W., *The Welbeck Abbey Miniatures,* The Walpole Society, Vol. IV, 1916, Oxford.

Graves, Algernon, A., *Dictionary of Artists,* 1901, London.
The Royal Academy of Arts: Dictionary of Contributors 1769-1904, 8 vols., 1905-6, London.
The Society of Artists of Great Britain, 1760-1791; The Free Society of Artists, 1761-1783, 1907, London.
The British Institution, 1908, London.

Groce, G.C. and Wallace, D.H., *Dictionary of Artists in America,* 2nd edition, 1964, New Haven, U.S.A.

Gwynn, Stephen, *Memorials of an Eighteenth Century Painter, James Northcote,* 1898, London.

Hand, Sidney, *Signed Miniatures,* 1925, London.

Hardie, Martin, *Miniatura, the art of Limning,* edited from Norgate's *Treatise.,* 1919, Oxford.

Harley, Rosamund D., *Artists Pigments, 1600-1835,* 1970, London.

Haslem, John, *The Old Derby China Factory,* 1876, London.

Hayes, Dr. John, *Gainsborough,* 1975, London.

Heath, Dudley, *Miniatures,* 1905, London.

Hilliard, Nicholas, *A Treatise Concerning the Arte of Limning,* with Introduction and Notes by Philip Norman, LL.D., The Walpole Society, Vol. I, 1912, Oxford.

Hinks, Peter, *Nineteenth Century Jewellery,* 1975, London.

Honey, W.B., *English Pottery and Porcelain,* 5th Edition, 1962, London.

Hotson, Dr. Leslie, 'Queen Elizabeth's Master Painter', *The Sunday Times Magazine,* 22nd March, 1970.

Hudson, Derek, *Sir Joshua Reynolds,* 1958, London.

Hudson, Derek and Luckhurst, Kenneth W., *The Royal Society of Arts,* 1954, London.

Hutchison, Sidney C., *The Royal Academy Schools, 1768-1830,* The Walpole Society, Vol. XXXVIII, 1960-62, Glasgow.
The History of the Royal Academy, 1968, London.

Irwin, David and Francina, *Scottish Painters at Home and Abroad,* 1975, London.

Jeffree, Richard and Walsh, Elizabeth, *The Excellent Mrs. Mary Beale,* exhibition catalogue, 1975, London.

Jewish Historical Society of England, Vol. XVIII, 1958, London.

Joseph, Edward, *Catalogue of a Collection of Miniatures,* 1883, privately printed.

Kennedy, H. A., 'Early English Portrait Miniatures in the Collection of the Duke of Buccleuch', *The Studio,* 1917, London, (special number).

Lamb, Sir Walter, R.M., *The Royal Academy,* 1951, London.

Lemberger, Ernst, *Portrait Miniatures of Five Centuries,* London, New York and Toronto.

Les Beaux-Arts, *Miniatures and Enamels from the D. David Weill Collection,* 1957, Paris.

L'Exposition de la Miniature à Bruxelles en 1912, published 1913, Brussels and Paris.

Lister, Raymond, *The British Miniature,* 1951, London.

Long, Basil S., *British Miniaturists,* 1929, London.
Richard Crosse, Miniaturist and Portrait Painter, The Walpole Society, Vol. XVII, 1929, Oxford.

Lugt, F., *Le Portrait-Miniature,* 1917, Amsterdam.

McKay, W.D., *The Scottish School of Painting,* 1906, London and New York.

Mallalieu, H.L., *The Dictionary of British Watercolour Artists,* 1976, Suffolk.

Marillier, H.C., *The Liverpool School of Painters,* 1904.

Mayer, Joseph, *Early Exhibitions of Art in Liverpool,* 1876, Liverpool, privately printed.

Miller, Sir Oliver, *Abraham Van Der Doort's Catalogue of the Collection of Charles I,* The Walpole Society, Vol. XXXVII, 1958-Glasgow.
The Queen's Pictures, 1977, London.

Morgan, J. Pierpont, *Illustrated Sale Catalogue,* Christie's, 1935, London.

Nachemsohn, Jacob, *Signed Enamel Miniatures,* 1926, London.

National Gallery of Scotland Catalogue, 1957, Edinburgh.

National Portrait Gallery Catalogue, 1949 (*Supplement 1948-1953*), 1954, London.
Concise Catalogue, 1856-1969, 1970, London.

Nicholson, Benedict, *Joseph Wright of Derby,* 1968, London.

Norgate, Edward, *Miniatura,* c.1648, edited by Martin Hardie, 1919, Oxford.

O'Brien, The Hon. D., *Miniatures in the 18th & 19th Centuries,* 1951, London.

Ormond, Richard, *Chinnery and His Pupil, Mrs. Browne,* The Walpole Society, Vol. XLIV, 1972-1974, Glasgow.
Early Victorian Portraits, 1973, London.

Peacham, Henry, *The Gentleman's Exercise,* 1st edition, 1607, London.
The Compleat Gentleman, 1st edition, 1622, London.

Pepys, Samuel, *The Diary of,* edited by R.C. Latham and W. Matthews, 1970-1976, London.

Priestley, J.B., *The Prince of Pleasure,* 1969, London.

Propert, J. Lumsden, *A History of Miniature Art,* 1887, London and New York.

Queen's Gallery, The, *Royal Children,* 1963.
Van Dyck, 1968.
George III Collector and Patron, 1974-1975.
The Queen's Pictures, 1977 (Silver Jubilee Exhibition).

Raines, Robert, *Marcellus Laroon,* 1967, London.

Redgrave, Samuel, *A Dictionary of Artists of the English School,* 1878, London.

Reinhardt, Hans, 'Hans Holbein', *Apollo,* December 1976.

Reynolds, Graham, *English Portrait Miniatures,* 1952, London.
Samuel Cooper's Pocket Book, V. & A.M. Publications, 1975, London.

Rijksmuseum Catalogue of Pictures, 1910, Amsterdam.

Robertson, Emily, *Letters and Papers of Andrew Robertson,* 1895, London.

Royal Academy of Arts, London, *Original Catalogues of Exhibitors,* 1769-1912 (author's copy ex Duveen).
17th Century Art in Europe, Winter Exhibition, 1938.
British Portraits, Winter Exhibition, 1956-7.
The Age of Charles II, Winter Exhibition, 1960-61.
Irish Portraits, 1660-1860, Winter Exhibition, 1970.
Royal Society of British Artists (works exhibited at), compiled J. Johnson, 1975, Suffolk.

Sanderson, William, *Graphice,* 1658.

Schidlof, Leo R., *The Miniature in Europe,* 4 vols., 1964, Austria.

Schneeberger, P.-F., *Les Peintres sur émail genevois au XXVIIe et au XXVIIe siècle,* Geneva, 1958.

Scottish National Portrait Gallery Catalogue, 1951, Edinburgh.

Sellars, Charles Coleman, *Portraits and Miniatures by Charles Willson Peale;* Vol. 42 Part I, The Transactions of the American Philosophical Society, 1952, Philadelphia.

Shaw-Sparrow, W., *Women Painters of the World,* 1905, London.

Sotheby's catalogues.

Smith, J.T., *Nollekens and his Times,* 1914, London.

South Kensington Museum, The, *Portrait Miniatures,* Exhibition Catalogue, 1865, London.

Strickland, Walter G., *Dictionary of Irish Artists,* 2 vols., 1913, Dublin and London.

Strœhlin, Ernest, *Jean Petitot et Jacques Bordier; Deux artistes Huguenots du XVII⁰ siècle,* Geneva, 1905.

Strong, Dr. Roy, *Tudor and Jacobean Portraits,* 1969, London.
The English Icon, 1969, London.
Nicholas Hilliard, 1975, London.
The Cult of Elizabeth, 1977, London.
The English Renaissance Miniature, 1983, London.

Tidey, Merle, *The Tideys of Washington, Sussex,* 1973, N. Wales.

Tomás, Mariano, *La Miniatura Retrato en Espana,* 1953, Spain.

Turrell, Charles, *Miniatures by Charles Turrell,* 1912.

Twitchett, John, F.R.S.A. and Bailey, Betty, F.R.S.A., *Royal Crown Derby,* 1976, London.

Usher, J.W. Ward, *An Art Collector's Treasures,* 1916, London.

Vávra, Jaroslav R., *5,000 Years of Glass Making,* 1954, Prague.

Vertue, George, *Note Books,* The Walpole Society, 6 vols., 1930-1955, Oxford and Glasgow.

Victoria and Albert Museum Publications.
Pfungst Collection, 1915.
Wellesley Collection, 1915.
Illustrated Hand List of Miniatures and Silhouettes, 1930.
Nicholas Hilliard and Isaac Oliver, 1947.
Portrait Miniatures, 1948, reprint 1959.
The Orange and the Rose, 1964.
The Care of Miniatures, Publication no. 3, Conservation Dept., 1970.
Artists of The Tudor Court, 1983.

Wallace Collection, *Miniatures and Illuminations Catalogue,* W.P. Gibson, 1935, London.

Walpole, Horace, *Anecdotes of Painting in England,* 1st edition, 1762-71, 5 vols., and subsequent editions, London.

Walpole Society, The, Volumes I-XLV, 1911-1976, Oxford and Glasgow.

Walters, Grant M., *Dictionary of British Artists 1900-1950,* Eastbourne, 1972, 2 vols.

Wark, Robert R., *Early British Drawings in the Huntington Collection,* 1969, California.

Waterhouse, Ellis, *Reynolds,* 1941, London.
Gainsborough, 1958, London.

Wehle, Harry B., *American Miniatures,* 1927, New York.

Wellesley, Francis, *Illustrated Sale Catalogue,* Sotheby's 1920, London.

Whinney, Margaret and Millar, Oliver, *English Art,* 1957, London.

Whitton, Donald C., *The Grays of Salisbury,* 1976, San Francisco.

Williamson, Dr. George C., *Portrait Miniatures,* 1897, London.
Richard Cosway, R.A., 1897, London.
Richard Cosway, R.A., 1905, London.
George Engleheart, 1902, privately printed.
Andrew and Nathaniel Plimer, 1903, London.
The History of Portrait Miniatures, 2 vols., 1904, London.
Miniatures at Belvoir Castle, 1904, privately printed.
Miniatures at Devonshire House, 1905, privately printed.
Miniatures at Castle Howard, 1905, privately printed.
Catalogue of the Collection, the property of J. Pierpont Morgan, 4 vols., 1906-7, privately printed.
John Downman, A.R.A., Connoisseur Extra Number 1907, London.
Portrait Miniatures, Studio Special Edition 1910, London, Paris, New York.
Catalogue of the Duke of Cumberland's Collection, 1914, privately printed.
Catalogue of Lord Hothfield's Collection, 1915, privately printed.
Ozias Humphry, R.A., 1918, London and New York.
The Miniature Collector, 1921, London.
Daniel Gardner, 1921, London and New York.

Williamson, Dr. George C., and Buckman, P., *The Art of the Miniature Painter,* 1926, London.

Winter, Carl, *Elizabethan Miniatures,* 1943, London.

Brown, Lancelot 'Capability', 289, Plate 74A
Brown, Mrs. Maria Bellett, née Roberts, 390, 443, Plates 129A, 129B
Brown, Samuel, 206
Brown, Mrs. Samuel, née Agnes Scouler, 206
Brown, Thomas, 443
Browne, Arthur, 443
Browne, The Hon. John, Plate 8B
Browne, Lady, 128
Browne, Marmaduke, Lieut. Col., 443
Browne, Mrs. Marmaduke, 443
Browne, Nathaniel, 369
Browne, Sir Thomas, 128
Browne, The Hon. William, Plate 8B
Bruce, James, Plate 105A
Bruce, The Hon. Mrs., 473, Plate 144C
Brummell, Mrs., Plate 105F
Brussels, 80, 278, 335, 428
Brussels Salon, 428
Bryan, Mr., Colour Plate 25A
Brydall, Robert, 200, 201
Buccleuch Family, 337
Buccleuch and Queensberry, K.T., The Duke of, 17, 163
Buccleuch and Queensberry, Collection of the Duke of, 44, 47, 58, 86, 91, 103, 108, 109, 111, 128, 134, 154, 155, 175, 178, 200
Buchan, Earl of, 201
Buck, Adam, 231, 233, Colour Plates 19, 21A, Plates 56C, 56D
Buck, Mrs. Adam, 233
Buck, Alfred, 233
Buck, Frederick, 231, 233, Plates 56A, 56F
Buck, Jonathan, 231, 233
Buck, Sidney, 233
Buckingham, Catherine, Duchess of, 171
Buckingham, Lady Katherine Manners, Duchess of, 120, Plates 20H, 33B
Buckingham, George Villiers, 1st Duke of, 80, 86, 87, Plates 13C, 16G, 33C
Bull, Richard, 234, Plate 59C
Bunbury, Master, 364, Plate 104E
Burch, Edward, R.A., 344
Burch, Henry Jacob, 344, Colour Plate 32D, Plates 75C, 83A
Burch, Mrs. Henry Jacob, Junior, 344
Burgess, Joseph, 348
Burgess, Samuel, 348, Plate 96B
Burghley House Collection, 60, 88, 131
Burgoyne Family, 252
Burgoyne, The Misses, 252, Plates 64B, 64C
Burgoyne, Montagu, Plate 64A
Burke, Mrs., 194, Plate 44D
Burley Mill, Kirkcudbrightshire, 223
Burnaby, Lieut. Col. John Dick, 386, Colour Plate 27C
Burney, Fanny (Madam D'Arblay), 203, 204
Burrell Blunt, Lady, Colour Plate 25E
Burroughs, Miss Maria, 368, Plate 105E
Burroughs, William, 368, Plate 105E
Burt, Albin Roberts, 255, Plate 63 I
Burt, Mrs. A.R., 255
Burt, Harry, 255
Burt, Mrs. Harry, 255
Burt, Henry F., 255
Burton, W.K., 353, Colour Plate 21C
Butler, Mr., 190
Butler, Samuel, 95
Butler, Mrs. Violet Victoria, 459, Plates 133A, 133B
Butler, William, 230

Buxton, Miss Jennifer, R.M.S., 463
Byfleet, 310
Byrne, Charles, 234, 241

Cadogan, The Hon. Anne, *called*, Plate 90D
Calais, 147
Calcutta, 193, 209, 283, 329, 374, 389, 393, 394, 443
Calendar of State Papers, 1650-1876, 103
Caley, John Sidey, 367
Callender of Treasury Books, 1672-5, 132
Cambridge, 209, 298
Cambridge, The Dowager Marchioness of, 447
Cambridge University, 136
Campbell, Mr., Plate 44G
Campbell, Sir A., 219
Campbell, Lord George, 219
Campbell, Col. John, 217
Canavari or Canevari, Giovanni Baptista, 463, Plate 135 I
Cannon, Miss Edith Margaret, 463, Plate 137G
Cantabrigia Illustrata, 136
Canterbury, 343
Canton, 389
Capel, Lord, 226
Capel, Arthur, 1st Baron, 85
Caradini, Paolo, 150
Cardwell, Edward Viscount, 427
Cardwell, Viscountess, 427
Carew, The Hon. Susan, 315, Plate 87E
Carew, Capt. The Hon. William, Plate 87F
Carey, Henry, 2nd Earl of Monmouth, 54
Carleton, Sir Dudley (Viscount Dorchester), 29
Carlile or Carlisle, Mrs. Joan, 128, 129, Plate 26A
Carlisle, 275, 282
Carlisle, The Earl of, 282
Carlisle Grammar School, 282
Carlton House, 356, 360
Carlyle, Thomas, 282
Carlyle, Mrs. Thomas, 282
Carnarvon, Charles, 2nd Earl of, 120, 124, Plate 24F
Carnarvon, Elizabeth Capel, Countess of, 124, Plates 23F, 24D
Caroline, The, 190
Caroline, Princess of Wales, 153
Caroline, Queen of George II, 103
Carpenter, William H., 439
Carpenter, Mrs. William H., 439
Carrick, Mr., 282
Carrick-on-Suir, 241, 243
Carrick, Thomas Heathfield, 282, 283, Plates 72A, 72C
Carriera, Rosalba, 22, 147, 148, 162, Plate 36B
Carrington, 413
Carter, Mrs. David, Plate 45D
Carter, Noel N., 353, Plate 102B
Carter, Miss Rose or Rosa, 463, Plate 134F
Carteron, Etienne, 32
Carwardine, John, 190
Carwardine, Mrs. John, 190
Carwardine, Penelope, 190, 194, Plates 40A, 42A, 42B
Cary, Samuel, 291
Cary, Mrs. Samuel, 291
Cashmere, 430
Castlemaine, The Earl of, 82

Castlemaine, Countess of, see Cleveland, Duchess of
Cathcart, Henrietta, Countess of, 416, Plate 119D
Catherine of Braganza, Queen of Charles II, 103, 120, 121, 130, Plate 23D
Catherine II, Empress of Russia, 194, 334
Catt, William, 408
Catt, Mrs. William (Hannah), 408
Cavendish, Elizabeth, 348, Plate 97C
Cavendish, The Hon. Henry, 348
Cavendish, Sarah Mary, 348, Plate 97C
Cavendish, Lord Richard, Plate 101A
Cavendish, Sir William, 66
Cavendish-Bentinck, Lieut. Gen. Arthur, 455
Cavendish Harley, Lady Henrietta, 154
Cavendish, Harley, Lady Margaret, see Portland, Duchess of
Cayenne, 80
Cecil, Sir Robert, 69
Cecil, William, 2nd Earl of Salisbury, 70
Celle, Princess Sophia Dorothea of, wife of George I, 158
Chalon, Alfred Edward, R.A., 239, 316, 337, 420, 421, 422, 426, 430, Colour Plate 23A, Plates 121A, 131A, 131B
Chalon, Henry Barnard, 431
Chalon, John James, R.A., 421
Chalon, Miss Maria A., Mrs. Moseley, 421, 431, 432, Colour Plate 35D, Plates 123A, 123C
Chalon, Professor, 420
Chamberlin, Mrs. Amy Gertrude, 463, Plate 137F
Champion, Richard, 303
champlevé, 25
Charendon, 145, 175
Charles I, 26, 59, 68, 73, 75, 76, 78, 80, 83, 88, 89, 90, 91, 92, 93, 95, 103, 119, 120, 128, 129, 130, 144, 150, 362, 442, Plates 11D, 17, 33E, 129E, Figure 8
Charles II, 76, 83, 84, 91, 100, 104, 114, 117, 120, 127, 128, 130, 141, 144, 146, 158, 200, Plates 15, 19A, 31E
Charles, A., 353
Charles, H.R.H. Prince of Wales, 461, Plate 141E
Charles X of France, 335
Charles X of Sweden, 105
Charles Edward Stuart, Prince, 157, 201, Plate 46C
Charles Gustavus, Prince, 106
Charles Louis, Count Palatine, Plate 20D
Charlotte, Princess, daughter of William IV, 351
Charlotte, H.R.H. Princess of Wales, 212, 255, 411
Charlotte, Queen, wife of George III, 186, 237, 289, 300, 307, 310, 374, 391, 397, 430, Plates 108G, 114E
Charlotte Augusta Matilda, Princess Royal, daughter of George III, 298, 300, 397, 430, Plates 78F, 114G
Chelsea, 68
Cheltenham, 235, 261, 263, 275, 430, 458
Chester, 255, 298, 374
Chester Record Office, 185
Chesterfield, Elizabeth, Countess of, 151, Plate 34D
Chiddingstone Castle, 119
Childe, James Warren, 451, Plate 129C
Chinnery, Sir Brodrick, 388

Geddes, Alexander, 439
Geddes, Mrs. Alexander, 439
Geddes, Alexander James, 439
Geddes, Andrew, A.R.A., 308, 439
Geffrye Museum, London, 111
Geisendorf, Professor P.F., 55
General Steuart, The, 333
Geneva, 49, 144, 145, 146, 147, 152, 173,
    176, 187, 337, 420
Genoa, 183, 298
George I, 117, 157, 158, 169, 195, 298,
    Plate 37
George II, 157, 158, 169, 173, 184, 195, 355,
    Colour Plate 10D
George III, 186, 195, 278, 287, 289, 298, 305,
    306, 307, 310, 374, 375, 391, Plate 44F
George IV, 25, 195, 206, 278, 284, 287, 299,
    305, 315, 355, 356, 360, 364, 373, 401,
    430, Plates 104A, 108D, 124B
George V, 455, 458, Plate 133E
Gerald Norman Gallery, 322
Gerbier, Anthony, 79
Gerbier, Mrs. Anthony, 79
Gerbier, Sir Balthasar, 78, 79, 80, 81, Plates
    13C, 13D
Gerbier, Katherine, 80
Gheeraerts, Marcus, The Elder, 58
Gheeraerts, Mrs. Marcus, 58
Gheeraerts, Marcus, The Younger, 58, 82
Ghent, 44
Gibbon, Edward, *called,* Plate 55A
Gibson, D., 120, 124, 474, Plates 24F, 25D
Gibson, Dirck, 122, 124
Gibson, Edward, 122, 123, 124
Gibson, Elizabeth, 122
Gibson, John, R.A., 274
Gibson, John or Johan, 122
Gibson, Margaret, Wife of Edward, 123
Gibson, Richard (The Dwarf), 121-124, 168,
    Colour Plate 8C, Plates 23B, 23F, 23G,
    24A, 24B, 24C, 24D, 24E, 30B
Gibson, Mrs. Richard, 121, 122, 123, 168,
    Plate 30C
Gibson, Susan Penelope, see Rosse,
    Mrs. Michael
Gibson, Thomas, 192, Plate 43A
Gibson, William, 123
Gifford Scott, Mrs. K., 368
Gilbert, L.H., Collection of, 345
Gilland, Mr., 206
Gillies, Adam, 446
Gillies, Miss Margaret, 218, 446, Plate 130A
Gillies, William, 446
Gilwell, The, 389
Glasgow, 198, 203, 207, 219, 316
Glasgow Art Gallery, The, 295
Glasgow Courier, The, 217
Glenbervie, 218
Gloucester, 384
Gloucester, Maria, Countess Waldgrave,
    Duchess of, 378 Colour Plate 31B
Gloucester, Mary, Duchess of, 307, 413
Gloucester, William, Duke of, 307, 311
Gloucester, William Henry, Duke of, 179,
    442, Colour Plate 13B
Glyn Castle, 241
Glynn, Mr., 140
Glynn Vivian Art Gallery, Swansea, 417, 427,
    437
Godolphin, Francis, 2nd Earl of, 168, Plate 36F
Godolphin, Sidney, 1st Earl of, 149
Goldsmith's Company, The, 49, 50, 58, 69

Goldsmith's Corporation, 154
Golzius, Hendrik, 79
Gomonde, Major Richard, Colour Plate 32C
Gonzaga, Anne of, Princess Palatine, 116, 117,
    Plate 22C
Goodsend, Francis, 298
Goodwood House, 104, 200
Gordon, Lord Adam, Plate 98G
Gordon, Alexander, 4th Duke of, 210
Gordon family, Plate 49F
Gordon, Lord Henry, 425
Gordon, Mrs. Margaret, Plate 51A
Gore, Mr. William, 150, Plate 34A
Gosport, 306
Gothenburg, 147
Goulding, R.W., 133
Goupy, Joseph, 163, Plate 36H
Goupy, Louis, 163
Graeme, Colonel David, 186
Grafton, Henry Fitzroy, Duke of, 127, 128
Graham, Richard, 94
Gravesend, 209
Gray, Alfred, 439, 440, Plate 128E
Gray, Henry, 439, 440, 442, Plates 128A, 128B
Gray, Mrs. Henry, 442
Gray, John Westcott, 439, 440
Gray, Mrs. John Westcott, 439, 440, Plates
    128C, 128D
Gray, Miss Marion, 440
Gray, William John, 439
Great Seal of Ireland, 55
Great Yarmouth, 299
Green, Mrs. James, 354
Green, William, Junior, 192, Plate 38D
Greenwood, Mrs. Ann, Plate 55F
Greer, Marian, Plate 113F
Gregory, A., 354, Plate 98B
Gregory I, Pope, 51
Grier, Mr. and Mrs., Figures 12 and 13
Griffen, Colonel James, Plate 34E
Griffenfeld, Peder Schumacher, Count of,
    147, Plate 32G
Grimaldi, Alessandro Maria, 6th Marquess,
    183
Grimaldi, Alexander, 7th Marquess, 298
Grimaldi, Mrs. Alexander, 298
Grimaldi, Henry, 298
Grimaldi, Louisa Frances, 298
Grimaldi, Stacey, 9th Marquess, 298
Grimaldi, William, Junior, 298, 299
Grimaldi, Mrs. William, 298
Grimaldi, William, 8th Marquess, 298,
    Colour Plates 17A, 23C, 28A, Plates 78B,
    78D, 78G
Groth, Andreas Henry, 178, 179, Colour
    Plates 11B, 13B, Plate 39F, Figure 25
Guards, 1st Foot, 315
Guasto, Marquise del, Plate 24E
Guiana, 80
Guichard, Kenneth, 292
Guidott, Anne Woodruff, Colour Plate 32D
Guildhall Gallery, 458
Guildhall Library, 85
Gwyn, Eleanor (Nell), 127, Plate 25A

Haarlem, 141
Haddington, The Countess of, 460
Haddington, George Baillie-Hamilton, K.T.,
    12th Earl of, 98, 460
Hadfield, Charles, 359
Hadfield, Mrs. Charles, 359
Hadfield, Miss Charlotte, 354, Plate 98A

Hadfield, Miss Maria Catherine Cecilia, see
    Cosway, Mrs. Richard
Hadway, Mrs., née Catherine Gallaway, 217,
    Plate 49H
Hague, The, 89, 104, 105, 116, 117, 122,
    139, 176, 334
Haines, William, 352, 354, Plate 102D
Halifax, 335
Hall, Bernard, 46
Hall, Miss Ethel, 464, Plate 137D
Hall, Joseph, Bishop of Exeter and Norwich,
    87
Hall, Miss Margaret, 464, Plate 137D
Hall, Pierre Adolphe, 189
Haly-Burton, Lady Augusta, 435, Plate 126
Ham House, Richmond, 121, 200
Hamilton, The Duke of, 150
Hamilton, Mrs. E.M., 155, 263, 277, 408,
    431
Hamilton, Emma, 255
Hamilton, Gavin, 206
Hamilton, Gustavus, 192, 228, Colour Plate
    16E, Plates 54B, 54C, 54F
Hamilton, The Rev. Gustavus, 228
Hamilton, Mrs. Gustavus, 228, 229
Hamilton, Hugh Douglas, 231, 234
Hamilton, Sir James, Plate 23A
Hamilton, Sir John, 98
Hamilton, Lady Mary Baillie, Plate 139E
Hamilton, Sir William, 289, Plate 74D
Hamilton, William, The Duke of, Plate 16E
Hamlet, T., 255, Plate 63G
Hampstead Marshall, 80
Hampton Court Palace, 130
Hancock, George, 413
Hancock, R. (Robert?), 258, Plate 66A
Hancock, Robert, engraver, 258
Hand, Mrs., Plate 60B
Hand, The Rev., Plate 60C
Hand, Sidney, Collection of, 302
Hankey, Mrs. William Lee, 464, Plate 138A
Hanmer, Sir Thomas, Figure 17
Hannay, Mrs., 348, Plate 88G
Hanneman, Adrian, 114
Hanover, 157
Hanover, Ernest, King of, Duke of
    Cumberland, 407
Harcourt, Miss Cynthia, Colour Plate 36D,
    Plate 58A
Harden, John, 238, Plate 57D
Harden, Mrs. John, 208, 468
Hardie, Martin, 78
Harding, Frederick, 451, Plate 121B
Harding, George Perfect, F.S.A., 423, 424,
    Plates 122, 127A
Harding, H.J., 354, Plate 98E
Harding, Sylvester, 271, 423
Hardman, John or James, 269
Hardy, Charles, 354, Plate 99G
Hardy, J. (James or Jonathan?), 354
Hardy, Thomas, 260
Hargrave, Lieut. General William, Plate 40G
Hargreaves, Mr., 271
Hargreaves, Francis, 271, 273, 274
Hargreaves, George, 271, 273, Plate 69E
Hargreaves, James, 273
Hargreaves, T., Junior, 273
Hargreaves, Thomas, 246, 271, 273, 274,
    Plates 69D, 69G
Hargreaves, Mrs. Thomas, 273
Hargreaves, W., 273
Harleian Manuscripts, 159

Oliver, Mrs. Isaac, née Sarah Gheeraerts, 2nd wife, 58
Oliver, Mrs. Isaac, Elizabeth, 3rd wife, 58
Oliver, Isaack Peter, 55
Oliver, Mrs. Isaack Peter, 55
Oliver, Jacques, 58
Oliver, Peter, 58, 64, 71, 73-76, 93, 128, 152, 168, Colour Plate 3D, Plates 10, 11C, 11D, 11E, 11F, 11G, 12
Oliver, Mrs. Peter, 73, 75, 76
Olivier, Robert, 55
Ollivier, Pierre, 55, 73
Opie, John, R.A., 305, 310, 444
Orange, Prince Maurice of, 79
Orange, William of, see William III
Orange-Nassau, Wilhelm V, Prince of, 395
Orange-Nassau, Wilhelmine, Princess of, wife of Wilhelm V, 395
Orford, The Countess of, *called*, Plate 113H
Orleans, Henrietta, Duchess of, Colour Plate 7D
Orleans, Phillipe, Duc de Chartres, Prince Regent of France, 153
Ormond, Richard, 443
Ormond Quay, 241
Orpington, Kent, 461
Osborne, Sir Thomas, Plate 27C
Oudh, The Nawab of, 394
Overall, Bishop John, 87
Overall, Mrs. John, 87
Owen, Mary Frances, Lady, 421, Plate 131B
Owen, William, 345
Oxford, 184, 255, 262, 292
Oxford Dictionary, 466
Oxford, Edward Harley, 2nd Earl of, see Harley
Oxford, Henrietta, Countess of, née Cavendish Holles, 149, 159
Oxonia Illustrata, 136

P., A, 354, Plate 103C
Paillou, Peter, Junior, 207, Plates 48A, 48D, 48E, 48F
Paillou, Peter, Senior, 206
Paine, Edward Grosvenor, 193, 194, 204, 226, 275, 349
Paintings on Greek Vases, A. Buck, 233
Palliser, Archbishop of Cashel, 229
Palmer, Sir James, 81, 82, Plate 14C
Palmer, Sir Thomas, 81
Palmer, Lady Thomas, 81
Paoli, General Pasquale de, 361
Paragon Buildings, Bath, 255
Paris, 46, 50, 136, 144, 147, 148, 152, 176, 194, 222, 288, 291, 316, 335, 337, 361, 403, 416, 421, 427, 429, 449
Paris Salon, 175, 335, 422, 428, 449, 455, 458
Park, Catherine, 337, Plate 95B
Park, Frances, 337, Plate 95B
'Park Range', Windermere, 313
Parker, Admiral, 438
Parker, Thomas, 438, Plate 127B
Parmigianino, 59
Parris, E.T., 413
Pars, William, A.R.A., 365
Parsey, Arthur, 354
Passmore, 322
Pastorini, Joseph, 354, Colour Plate 23E, Plate 99F
Patkul, Count, 53
Patna, 283, 330
Paton, David, 200, Plates 46B, 46D

Paton, George, 266
Patten, George, A.R.A., 464, Colour Plate 33B
Pattison, William Ebenezer, Plate 53D
Paul I, Czar of Russia, 300
Payne, John, 136
Peacock, artist, 213
Peacock, Thomas Love, 308, Plate 82E
Peake, Robert, 58, 136
Peake, Sir Robert, 136
Peal, Miss M., 269
Peard, Oliver, 358
Pearse, Master Henry Thornton, 419, Plate 120B
Peat, Thomas, 254, Colour Plate 22B, Plate 60E
Pelham, Miss Emily, 276
Pelham, Henry, 229, 230, Plate 55B
Pelham, Mrs. Henry, 229
Pelham, James, Senior, 275
Pelham, James, Junior, 275, Plate 71D
Pelham, Mrs. James, Junior, 276
Pelham, James, son of James Junior, 276
Pelham, Peter, 229, 290, 291
Pelham, Mrs. Peter, 229, 290
'Pelican Portrait', 54
Pelinck, Mr. E., 58
Pemberton, Mrs. 46, 47
Pembroke College, Cambridge, 78
Pembroke, Countess of, see Clifford, Lady Anne
Pembroke, The Earl of, 122, 123
Penley, Aaron Edwin, 276, Plate 70D
Pennant, Thomas, 206
Penny, Mrs. D., Plate 69D
Pepys, Samuel, 95, 100, 113, 138
Pepys, Mrs. Samuel, 95, 100
Pepys Library, Cambridge, 81
Percy, Lady Charlotte, 337
Percy, Lady Dorothy, 411, Plate 117
Pereman, William, 50
Peter The Great, Tsar of Russia, 148, 158, 465, Colour Plate 13C
Peterborough, 183
Peterson, Frederic, 148
Pether, William, F.S.A., 313, 354, Plate 101A
Petitot, Jean, 26, 144-148, 163, 411, Plates 33B, 33C, 33D, 33E
Petitot, Mrs. Jean, 145
Petitot, Jean, The Younger, 145, 146, Plate 33F
Petty, Sir William, 95
Petworth, 306
Pfungst, Henry, J., The Collection of, 130
Philadelphia Academy, 300
Philadelphia Museum of Art, 214
Philadelphia Society of Miniature Painters, 458
Phillips, Mrs. Pru, Plate 25C
Phillips, Son & Neale, 41
Phillips, Thomas, 345
Phipps, Jessie Percy Butler, 455, Plate 134B
'Phoenix Portrait', 54
Pierpont Morgan, J., The Collection of, 26, 33, 455
Pierpont Morgan J. (Sale 1935), 64
Pierpont Morgan Library, New York, 115
Pigott, Miss Annabella, 354, Plate 98G
Pinchbeck, Christopher, 39
Pindar, Peter (John Wolcot), 361
Pine, S., Plates 40 I, 40J
Piozzi, Hester Lynch, Plate 57E
Pitt, William, The Younger, 176, 247, 250, Plate 61D

Pitti Palace, Florence, 467
Place, George, 239, Colour Plate 24A, Plates 59E, 59F, 59G
Plague, The Great, 114
Planchant, J., 147
Plataganet Stewart, The Rt. Hon. J.A., Plate 68G
Plimer, Adela, 308
Plimer, Andrew, 252, 308, 348, 355, 379-384, 470, Colour Plates 12A, 29C, Plates 110A, 110B, 110C, 110D, 110E, 110F, 110G, 110H, 110 I
Plimer, Mrs. Andrew, 380, 382, 383
Plimer, Andrew, Junior, 380
Plimer, Charlotte, 380
Plimer, Georgina, 308
Plimer, Joanna, 380
Plimer, Louisa, (Mrs. John Scott), 308, 380, 382, 384, Plate 111A
Plimer, Mary, 308
Plimer, Nathaniel, 308, 310, 379, Colour Plates 29D, 30D, Plates 84A, 84B, 84D, 84E
Plimer, Mrs. Nathaniel, Junior, 308
Plimer, Nathaniel, Senior, 308, 379
Plimer, Mrs. Nathaniel, Senior, 308, 379
Plimer, Selina, 380
Plott, John, F.S.A., 306, 354, Plates 75A, 99A
Plymouth, 27, 248, 252, 298, 303, 343
Polack, Solomon, 354, Colour Plate 15F
Pompadour, Mme. de, 175
Pondicherry, 333
Ponsonby, Sir William (later Lord Bessborough), 176
Pooley Wright, H., 143
Pope, Alexander, 97, 166
Pope, Mrs., 97
Portland Family, The Collection of, 17, 26, 39, 54, 76, 83, 86, 97, 103, 111, 122, 130, 133, 140, 141, 144, 149, 153, 154, 155, 159, 160, 167, 168, 173, 181, 364, 455, 459
Portland, Lady Elizabeth Noel, Duchess of, 153
Portland, Henry Bentinck, 1st Duke of, 153
Portland, Jane Martha, Countess of, Plate 33A
Portland, Ivy, Duchess of, 459, Plate 133B
Portland, Margaret, Duchess of, 158
Portland, Lady Margaret Cavendish Harley, Duchess of, 154, 159, 171, Plate 36C
Portland, William Bentinck, 2nd Duke of, 159
Portland, Winifred Anna, Duchess of, 459, Plate 133A
Portman, Henry, 155, Plate 35F
Portsmouth, 311, 351, 367
Portsmouth, Louise de Keroualle, Duchess of, 122, 124
Powell, Francis, 302
Powell, Mrs. Timothy, 329
Powis, The Earl of, 60
Poynter, Miss, 260, Plate 67C
Poyntz-Ricketts, George, 298, Plate 76A
Poyntz-Ricketts, Mrs. 298
Prague, 82
Pré L'Evêque 337
Prentice, Mrs. Elizabeth, Plate 55G
Prentice, Thomas, 231
Prentice, Mrs. Thomas, 231
Preston, Mrs. Boswell, Plate 104B
Preston, Thomas, Colour Plate 15G
Prewett or Prewitt, William, 171, 178, Colour Plate 11D, Plate 39H
Prieur, Paul, 146, 147, Plates 32E, 32G

Royal Institute of Portrait Painters, 455
Royal Military College, Sandhurst, 421
Royal Museum, Stockholm, 149
Royal Pavilion, Brighton, 301, 334, 337,
339, 364, 373, 390, 417
Royal Regiment of Wales, 461
Royal Scottish Academy, 199, 217
Royal Society for the Encouragement of
Arts, Manufacture and Commerce, 200
Royal Society of Miniature Painters,
Sculptors and Gravers, 401, 455, 458,
459, 460, 461
Royal Staffordshire Corps, 329
Royaume, Jean, 144
Ruabon, 298
Rubens, Sir Peter Paul, 79, 114, 163, 190,
334, 407, 468
Rubens, Mrs. Peter Paul, née Hélène Fourment,
334
Runciman, Alexander, 206
Rundle, George, 331, Plate 92G
Rushout, The Hon. Anne, called, Plate 143E
Ruskin, John, 234, 313
Russell, Sir John, 282
Russell, John, R.A., 306
Rutland, Collection of the Duke of, 17
Rutland, Duchess of, 205
Rydal Mount, Ambleside, 446
Rysbrack, John Michael, 195

Sackville, Richard, 3rd Earl of Dorset, 60
Sackville, Richard, 5th Earl of Dorset, 119
Saddlers' Company, 176
St. Albans, 420
St. Brides, 70
St. Cloud, 153
St. George and the Dragon', 119
St. Germain, 116
St. Helena, 251, 267
St. Helier, Jersey, 308
St. James's Palace, 130, 186
St. John's College, Cambridge, 66
St. Lawrence, Isle of Wight, 447
St. Luke, the Guild of, 44
St. Mark's Hospital, London, 442
St. Martin's Lane Academy, 252, 291, 292,
295, 311, 374, 391
St. Neot's, 298
St. Oswald, Lord, 66
St. Ouen, 307
St. Paul's School, London, 323
St. Petersburg, 194, 300, 337
St. Vincent, Admiral John Jervis, Earl of,
Plate 103D
Salamanca, 327
Salisbury, 438, 440, 442
Salisbury, Amelia, Marchioness of, Plate 109C
Saltau, Mrs. William, Plate 107H
Saltonstall, Lady Elizabeth, 120
Saltonstall, Sir Richard, 119, 120
Salway, N., 168, Plate 36F
Sambat, Jean Baptiste, 354, Plate 98D
Sampford Arundel, Sussex, 443
Sancroft, William, Dean of St. Paul's and later
Archbishop of Canterbury, 108
Sandby, Paul, R.A., 269, 287
Sanders, John, Senior, 326
Santa Maria della Grazie, Church of, 363
Santa Maria della Grazie, College of, 363
Sargant, Gertrude, 464
Satchwell, Robert William, 354, Plate 100E
Saunders, Joseph, 326, Plates 81D, 90A

Saunders, Mrs. Joseph, Plate 81E
Saunders, Randle W., Plate 72A
Saunders, Robert, 326, Plates 45D, 83E
Savannah, George, U.S.A., 216
Savery, Mrs., Colour Plate 22B
Saxe-Coburg, H.R.H. Prince Leopold of,
218, 424
Scaife, Mr., 413
Scarborough, 282, 335
'Scarlet, General', called, 460, 461, Plate 139D
Schaffhausen, 334
Scheffer, Ary, 446
Schleswig-Holstein, Prince Christian Victor,
419
Schmid, Ulrich, 45
Schomberg House, Pall Mall, 360
Scollay, Deborah, 291
Scott, Mrs. Gifford, 368
Scott, John, M.D., 382
Scott, Robert, 218
Scott, Sir Walter, 446
Scottish Academy, The Royal, 219, 222, 223
Scottish Arts Council Exhibition, Edinburgh,
1965, 145, 149, 153, 155, 160, 216, 262,
275, 290, 295, 306, 373, 378, 386, 387,
397, 427
Scottish National Portrait Gallery, 206, 208,
269, 337, 443
Scouler or Scouller, Agnes, 295
Scouler or Scouller, James, Senior, 206, 292,
295
Scouler or Scouller, Mrs. James, Senior, 292,
295
Scouler, James, 206, 292, 295, Colour Plate
10F, 12D, Plates 73A, 73E, 73F, 73H
Scouler or Scouller, John, 292, 295
Scouler or Scouller, John, Junior, 295
Scouler or Scouller, Mary, 295
Scouler, Robert, 295
Scourfield, Lady, Plate 134E
Scovell or Scovill, James, 255, Plates 66D,
66E
S., E., 194, Plate 45F
Seafield, Sir James Ogilvy, 1st Earl of, 151,
152, Colour Plate 8E, Plate 34F
Seaman or Seeman, Abraham, 180, Plates
39E, 40G
Seaman, Enoch, 180
Seaman, Isaac, 180, Colour Plate 10D
Seaman, Noah, 180, Colour Plate 10D, 11G
Seamer, James, 35
Seathwaite in Borrowdale, 29
Selby, Sir John, 87, 88
Selous, Henry Courtney, 404
Sentimental Journey, L. Sterne, 231
Serampur, 389
Serres, Dominic, 307
Severn, Joseph, 464, Plate 119A
Sewell, Mrs. Sheila, A.R.M.S., 461, Plate 140G
Seymour, Edward, Duke of Somerset, see
Somerset
Seymour, Lady Jane, 3rd wife of Henry VIII,
44, 46, Plate 4B
Shakespeare, William, 413
Sharpe, Miss Eliza, 445, 464, Colour Plate 33C
Sharpe, Joseph F., 464, Plate 136A
Sharples, Felix, 266
Sharples, George, 266
Sharples, James, Senior, 264, 266
Sharples, Mrs. James, née Ellen Wallace, 3rd
wife, 264, 266, 267, Plate 65C
Sharples, Miss Rolinda, 264, 266, 267

Shelley, Miss, 352
Shelley, Samuel, 214, 300, 301, 307, 314,
351, 352, Colour Plates 17C, 24C and D,
Plates 80A, 80B, 80D, 80E, Figure 19A
Shepherd, Robert, 136
Sherborne Castle, 76, 226
Sheridan, Mrs., 391
Sherlock or Shirlock, William, F.S.A., 291,
292, Plates 74B, 74C
Sherlock, W.P., 292
Shiercliffe, Edward, Senior, 262
Shiercliffe, Edward, 262, Plate 64E
Shipley, William, 200, 358, 365, 375, 391
Shirreff, Alexander, 208, 209, 366
Shirreff or Sheriff, Charles, 208, 210, 213,
Colour Plate 18E, Plates 47G, 47 I
Shirreff, Mary, 209
Sholto-Douglas, Mrs. Phoebe, R.M.S., 461,
Plate 140E
Shoreditch, 298
Shrewsbury, Elizabeth, Countess of, 66
Shute, John, 48
Siddons, Mrs. Sarah, 209, 230, 298, 302,
375, 468
Sidney, Henry, Lord, 226
Signac, Pierre, 147
Sillett, Miss Emma, 280
Sillett, James, Senior, 280
Sillett or Sillet, James, 280, 282, Plates 70B,
70C
Sillett, Mrs. James, 280
Simpson, Christopher, Plate 21G
Simpson, Ellen, 416
Simpson, John, 27, 414, 416, Plate 118B
Simpson, Mrs. John, 416
Simpson, William Page, 414
Singleton, William, 192, Plate 43A
Sir Thomas Lawrence, Kenneth Garlick, 311
Siree, John, 243
Skeffington, Sir William Charles Farrell,
Plate 111C
Skipton Castle, 423
Skirving, Adam, 207
Skirving, Archibald, 207, 208, Colour Plates
20E, 27A, Plates 49A, 49B, 49E
Slade School of Art, 458
Slater, Miss Adela Elizabeth, 325
Slater, Miss Anne, 323
Slater, Miss Carissima Matilda, 323, 325,
Plate 75B
Slater, Miss Henrietta Vane, 325
Slater, Isaac Wane, 323, 325, Plates 89A,
89B, 89C, 89D
Slater, Mrs. Isaac Wane, 323
Slater, John, Junior, 323
Slater, Mrs. John, 325
Slater, John, Senior, 322, 325
Slater, Joseph, Senior, 322
Slater, Mrs. Joseph, Senior, 322
Slater, Joseph, Junior, 323, Plates 75B, 89E
Slater, Mrs. Joseph, Junior, 323
Slater, Joseph, son of Joseph Junior, 323
Slater, Miss Lavinia (Mrs. A. Fennell), 323
Slater, Capt. Michael Atwell, R.N., 323
Slater, Lieut. Col. Mortimer John, 325
Slater, Mrs. Mortimer, John, 325
Slater, Miss Susanah (Mrs. Bean), 323
Sloane, Lady Elizabeth, 195
Sloane, Sir Hans, 195
Slous, Gideon, 354, Plate 100G
Smart, Anna Maria (Mrs. Robert Woolf),
365, 366, 367